The Book of
Saints

St Mary the Blessed Virgin

The Book of
Saints

*A Dictionary of Servants of God
canonized by the Catholic Church*

Compiled by the Benedictine monks of
St Augustine's Abbey, Ramsgate

Sixth edition
Entirely revised and re-set

A & C Black · London

Sixth edition 1989
First published 1921
by A & C Black (Publishers) Limited
35 Bedford Row, London WC1R 4JH

ISBN 0–7136–3006–X

© 1989 A & C Black (Publishers) Limited

A CIP catalogue record for this book
is available from the British Library.

Typeset at The Spartan Press Ltd
Lymington, Hants
Printed and bound in Great Britain by
Courier International Ltd, Tiptree, Essex

Illustrations

(frontispiece) **St Mary the Blessed Virgin**
statue designed by A W N Pugin and carved by G Myers for the Great Exhibition, 1851, and now
in St Augustine's Abbey Church, Ramsgate

St Aaron, July 1
medieval woodcut, British Museum

St Agatha, Feb 5
stained glass window, York Minster, by permission of the Dean and Chapter of York

St Agnes, Jan 21
stained glass window, Parish Church, Martham, Norfolk, photograph by Painton Cowen

St Aidan, Aug 31
statue in Ripon Cathedral, by permission of the Dean and Chapter of Ripon, photograph by Leon
Smallwood

St Alban, June 20
statue in St Alban and St Patrick, Highgate, Birmingham, photograph by Edward Fellows

St Andrew, Nov 30
wood panel at the Parish Church, Ranworth, Norfolk, copyright Courtauld Institute, London

St Anne, July 26
medieval German drawing, British Museum

St Anselm, Apr 21
wood panel in Downside Abbey, Bath

St Antony, Jan 17
medieval German drawing, British Museum

St Antony of Padua, June 13
stained glass in the Victoria and Albert Museum, copyright Royal Commission on the Historical
Monuments of England

St Apollonia, Feb 9
part of the triptych *The Ascension of Saint John the Evangelist* by Giovanni del Ponte, National
Gallery, London

St Augustine of Canterbury, May 27
stained glass window by Edward Burne-Jones, copyright Yale University Press

St Augustine of Hippo, Aug 28
stained glass window, Canterbury Cathedral, copyright Royal Commission on the Historical
Monuments of England

St Barbara, formerly Dec 4
cartoon by Sir Edward Burne-Jones, in the Victoria and Albert Museum, copyright Yale
University Press

St Barnabus, June 11
stained glass window in Lincoln Cathedral, copyright Royal Commission on the Historical
Monuments of England

St Bartholomew, Aug 24
stained glass in Malvern Priory, Worcester, copyright Royal Commission on the Historical
Monuments of England

St Bede, May 25
wood panel in Downside Abbey, Bath

St Dominic de Guzman, Aug 8
part of the Demidoff Altarpiece by Crivelli, National Gallery, London

St Dorothy, formerly Feb 6
detail of the St Bartholomew Altarpiece, by the Master of Saint Bartholomew, National Gallery, London

St Dunstan, May 19
painting formerly in a rood-screen, now in the Church of Great Plumstead, Norfolk

St Eanswithe, Sept 12
painting in the Church of St Mary and St Eanswythe, Folkestone, Kent

St Edith, Sept 16
cartoon by Edward Burne-Jones, in the Birmingham City Art Gallery, copyright Yale University Press

St Edmund, Nov 20
part of the Wilton Diptych, French School *c.* 1395, National Gallery, London

St Edward the Confessor, Oct 13
stained glass in the Church of St Mary, Ross-on-Wye, copyright Royal Commission on Historical Monuments of England

St Elizabeth of Hungary, May 6
medieval woodcut, British Museum

St Erasmus, June 2
medieval woodcut, British Museum

St Ethelreda, June 23
statue in St Ethelreda's Church, London
St Eustace, formerly Sept 20
part of picture by Pisanello, *The Vision of St Eustace,* National Gallery, London

St Fabian, Jan 20
part of wood panel painted by Giovanni di Paolo, National Gallery, London

The Forty Martyrs, formerly March 10
part of the painting, *The Forty Martyrs of Armenia,* by Portormo, Uffizi Gallery, Florence

St Frances of Rome, March 9
engraving by Robetta, British Museum

St Francis of Assisi, Oct 4
part of the altarpiece, *The Virgin and Child with Saints Francis and Sebastian,* by Crivelli, National Gallery, London

St Gabriel, Sept 29
part of the wing of an altarpiece done by the Nuremberg School, York City Art Gallery

St George, Apr 23
part of the painting, *Saint George and the Dragon,* by Uccello, National Gallery, London

St Germanus of Auxerre, July 31
statue in St German's Church, Cardiff

St Giles, Sept 1
statue in St Giles Church, Stoke-on-Trent

St Gregory the Great, Sept 3
medieval German woodcut, British Museum

St Helen, Aug 18
cartoon by Edward Burne-Jones in Birmingham City Art Gallery, copyright Yale University Press

St Hubert, Nov 3
part of the painting, *The Conversion of Saint Hubert,* by the Master of the Life of the Virgin, National Gallery, London

The Holy Innocents, Dec 28
the painting, *The Massacre of the Innocents,* by Giotto, Sacred Convent of St Francis, Assisi

St Isaiah, July 6
a pinnacle from the altarpiece, *The Almighty, the Virgin and Saint John the Baptist,* painted by Giovanni da Milano, National Gallery, London

St Isidore of Seville, Apr 4
part of the painting, *Saint Isidore*, by the Spanish School, National Gallery of Ireland

St James the Less, May 3
statue in Westminster Abbey, by permission of the Dean and Chapter of Westminster

St Jerome, Sept 30
part of the painting, *Saint Jerome in a Landscape*, by Cima, National Gallery, London

St Joan of Arc, May 30
statue in Winchester Cathedral, by permission of the Dean and Chapter of Winchester

St John Houghton, May 4
stained glass in St Ethelreda's Church, London, photograph by Carlos Reyes

St John Fisher, June 22
drawing by Holbein, Royal Library, Windsor, copyright HM The Queen

St John the Baptist, June 24
painting by Hans Memlinc, National Gallery, London

St John, Dec 27
part of the painting, *Saints Matthew, Catherine of Alexandria and John the Evangelist*, by Stephan Lochner, National Gallery, London

St Joseph Patriarch, March 19
painting ascribed to Giovanni Moroni, National Gallery, London

St Jude, Oct 28
stained glass window, Malvern Priory, Worcestershire, copyright Royal Commission on Historical Monuments of England

St Kenelm, July 17
stained glass in the Church of St Peter Mancroft, Norwich, copyright Royal Commission on Historical Monuments of England

St Laurence of Rome, Aug 10
painting by Hans Memlinc, National Gallery, London

St Leonard of Noblac, Nov 6
medieval German woodcut, British Museum

St Longinus, March 15
woodcut by Mantegna, British Museum

St Lucy of Syracuse, Dec 13
part of the Demidoff Altarpiece, by Crivelli, National Gallery, London

St Luke, Oct 18
part of a painting by M J Healy, National Gallery of Ireland

The Magi, Jan 6
tapestry, *The Adoration of the Magi*, by William Morris, in Exeter College, Oxford, photograph by Thomas Photos, Oxford

St Magnus, Apr 16
statue in St Magnus The Martyr Church, London

St Margaret or Marina, formerly July 20
part of a painting by the Circle of the Master of Liesborn, National Gallery, London

St Margaret Clitherow, Oct 21
statue in Margaret Clitherow's House, York, copyright the Royal Commission on Historical Monuments of England

St Mark, Apr 25
cartoon by Edward Burne-Jones, in the Birmingham City Art Gallery, copyright Yale University Press

St Martin of Tours, Nov 11
panel painted by the German School c. 1490, York City Art Gallery

St Mary Magdalen, July 22
stained glass window by William Morris, in All Saints, Langton Green, Kent, copyright Yale University Press

St Simeon Senex, Oct 8
stained glass window, Malvern Priory, Worcestershire, copyright Royal Commission on Historical Monuments of England

St Simon, Feb 18
stained glass window, Parish Church, Orchardleigh, Somerset, photograph by Painton Cowen

St Simon Stock, May 16
statue, Carmelite Friary, Aylesford, Kent

St Stanislaus, Apr 11
part of a panel by the School of Giotto, Sacred Convent of St Francis, Assisi

St Stephen the Deacon, Dec 26
part of the Demidoff Altarpiece, by Crivelli, National Gallery, London

St Teresa of Lisieux, Oct 1
ceramic relief by Kossowski, Carmelite Friary, Aylesford, Kent

St Teresa of Avila, Oct 15
statue, Carmelite Friary, Aylesford, Kent

St Thomas Aquinas, Jan 28
part of the Demidoff Altarpiece, by Crivelli, National Gallery, London

St Thomas More, June 22
part of drawing by Holbein, Royal Library, Windsor, copyright HM The Queen

St Thomas the Apostle, July 3
part of the altarpiece, *The Incredulity of Saint Thomas*, by Cima, National Gallery, London

St Ursula, formerly Oct 21
stained glass, in the Victoria and Albert Museum, copyright Royal Commission on Historical Monuments of England

St Valentine, Feb 14
cartoon by Edward Burne-Jones, in Letchworth Museum and Art Gallery, copyright Yale University Press

St Veronica, July 12
painting, *Saint Veronica with the Sudarium*, by the Circle of the Master of Saint Veronica, National Gallery, London

St Vincent the Deacon, Jan 22
statue in Henry VII Chapel, Westminster Abbey, by permission of the Society of Antiquaries

St Vincent Ferrer, Apr 5
painting, *Scenes from the Life of Saint Vincent Ferrer*, done in the style of Cossa, National Gallery, London

St Vitalis, Nov 4
mosaic, Basilica of St Vitalis, Ravenna

St Wilfrid, Oct 12
cartoon by Ford Madox Brown, copyright Yale University Press

St Winefred, Nov 3
statue in Henry VII Chapel, Westminster Abbey, copyright Royal Commission on Historical Monuments of England

St Wulstan, Jan 19
stained glass window, Malvern Priory, Worcestershire, copyright Royal Commission on Historical Monuments of England

St Zenobius, May 25
part of the painting, *Saint Zenobius revives a Dead Boy*, by Bilivert, National Gallery, London

St Zita, Apr 27
statue, Westminster Abbey, by permission of the Dean and Chapter of Westminster

Preface to the Sixth Edition

Of all the editions of *The Book of Saints* which have been brought out since its first appearance in 1921, this edition is the most radically different from its predecessors. Although the format is largely the same, the changes in the Roman Calendar promulgated in 1969 rendered the 1966 edition almost useless as a work of reference in many ways. Saints whose popularity was very great in the Middle Ages and whose images are consequently familiar to us through their appearance in religious paintings, stained glass windows, sculptures and in the dedications of churches throughout Christendom, such as Catherine of Alexandria and Margaret of Antioch, were removed from the calendar of Saints completely because research had proved that they had never existed. Other saints, such as St Edward the Confessor, were removed from the General Calendar and ascribed only to those particular countries or places where their cult was more immediately relevant; their places in the General Calendar were taken by other saints not only of more appeal, perhaps, to the modern mind but generally representative too of the many different cultures comprising the contemporary Church. The older calendar was too European — indeed, too Italian — in its composition.

When the first edition of *The Book of Saints* came out in 1921 it reflected the great scholarship of the Right Reverend Dom Thomas Bergh (d. 1924), who ruled St Augustine's Abbey, Ramsgate between 1876 and 1906 and was Abbot Visitor of the English Province of the Benedictine (Subiaco) Congregation. He was assisted by two other monks of the Community, and exercized an overall editorial jurisdiction. He was conservative in his outlook and preferred to keep in the book entries which were obviously of legendary rather than historical origin, especially as these were, in his day, hallowed by liturgical use. In this present edition, in the cases such as those of Catherine and Margaret mentioned above, their entries have been kept for several reasons, such as the importance of their legends to Christian art and literature, but in every case the date of their feast-day is labelled 'formerly . . .' and concludes with the statement that their feast-day is now abolished. Thus it is hoped that the book may be useful also to those whose primary interest in the saints is not purely religious but rather in terms of seeking an understanding of Christian art and culture.

Other entries of saints not in the General Calendar of the Roman Catholic Church but probably fictional in part or indeed as a whole have either some remark such as 'said to have been' or 'probably' included in the entry. The discerning reader can easily judge each case according to its merits.

References to the First Eucharistic Prayer, otherwise known as the Roman Canon, may confuse non-Roman Catholics. The Eucharistic liturgy of the Roman Church as revised and promulgated by the Second Vatican Council (1962–5) has several alternative Eucharistic Prayers. The First contains lists of saints recited before and after the words of the Institution of the Eucharist, and these are generally saints honoured in the city of Rome from earliest times. They are therefore familiar to Roman Catholics and a mention is made in each entry of these saints to the fact of their inclusion in that prayer.

Each successive edition of *The Book of Saints* has been an expansion of the previous one, due to the number of people beatified or canonized in the years between the editions. In the Roman Catholic Church the process of canonization is carefully undertaken by the competent authorities who sift, often for years, the evidence for and against the holiness of life of the person in question. Beatification, often viewed as a half-way stage to full canonization, in itself declares the merits and virtues of the subjects to the whole people of God. When a person is finally canonized their Christian life and example are held up before the whole church as a testimony to the living power of God in that individual's life, and as a spur to everyone else, to emulate in their own lives the virtues of the saint. This edition contains an account of those canonized, and many of those beatified, since 1966.

Since the 1960s there has been in the West a far greater appreciation of, and interest in, the Orthodox Churches, not only at the level of ecumenical discussions and visits of Patriarchs and Popes to each other, but also on the level of a vastly increased understanding of the Eastern iconographical tradition among Christians of many denominations. Whilst this reflects in many ways the dis-association of the Church in the West from the mainstream of modern art, it also has helped to underline the spiritual unity of the two ancient divisions of Christendom. Thus icons have become a familiar feature of Roman Catholic and Anglican devotion and are on sale in many repositories and church bookshops. Consequently a great many Eastern saints are now much more familiar to Western Christians than they were formerly. Many of these have been included in this edition, such as St Seraphim of Sarov, whose spiritual writings and holy life have endeared him to many Western Christians.

In a sense this edition is already beginning to go out of date since the process of canonization is continuous and not a few saints have been canonized between the time of writing and of going to press. It is hoped, however, that the present volume is fairly complete. It is impossible, of course, to achieve absolute completeness, not only because God alone knows the number of his saints, but also because of factors such as early confusions by hagiographical writers whereby saints of identical or similar names have become confused: Celtic saints exemplify this phenomenon.

In this edition it has been decided that illustrations should be included, as well as a list of emblems of the saints; moreover, there is a list of patron saints and a short account of the Sibyls of antiquity who often figure along with the saints in early Christian art. It is hoped that both the Christian and the general user of this book will benefit from these additions. In these days of advertisements on hoardings, on television and in magazines, we are all familiar with signs and symbols denoting many differing brands of goods and services. So, too, a large number of saints were made recognizable to our forefathers by these emblems. It is scarcely possible to visit a church or an art gallery and not be confronted by a saint bearing an emblem of some kind. Some emblems are obscure in origin, or have to do with a legend attached to the life of the saint which may not be at all well known today. Some saints share the same emblem, but it must be remembered that in earlier times when bad communications prevailed and many saints were venerated only in particular places, they did not as it were 'clash' with each other. Other emblems such as a palm for martyrdom are shared by whole categories of saints and generally another emblem must be sought as well so as to facilitate identification.

The reader may be helped by the following notes on the general structure of the work.

(1) Names of the saints are printed below in alphabetical order. If there is more than one saint bearing the same name, their order is that of their feast-days throughout the year. Many names have variant spellings: the one chosen here is in each case that held to be the most likely to be the commonest form. In the cases of the names in general

use, for instance Peter, James, Paul, etc., we have in each case inserted a special entry giving its variant forms in modern European languages.

(2) The name is followed by the saint's surname or appellation, if any; for example: James *Kisai*, James *of Tarentaise*, James *the Almsgiver*, and so on.

(3) The liturgical group to which the saint belongs e.g. *Martyr* (M), *Virgin* (V), and so forth. *Confessor* (C) has generally been admitted as understood; it is also a category which no longer appears in the new Roman Calendar. *Monk* or *nun* has also been omitted generally when it is obvious from the entry itself.

(4) The saint's hagiological rank, viz.,
    Saint (St) or *Blessed* (Bl)

(5) The Religious Order, if any, to which the saint belonged.

(6) All saints on the General Calendar of the Roman Church are labelled GC. At the time of writing, the new Roman Martyrology has not been promulgated. All references to the old one have 'former' and 'RM' as part of the entry.

(7) The date of the saint's feast. Many feast-days, except those on the General Calendar, vary from diocese to diocese, or from one religious order to another. Generally speaking, the date given is that most commonly accepted and is usually the date of the saint's death (*dies natalis*) or sometimes the date of the translation of his/her relics.

(8) The year of the saint's death, whether definite e.g. d. 890, or approximate, e.g. *c.* (died *circiter*, or about) 890. Failing this, we give the century, or, if even this is unknown, we place an interrogation mark (?). Whenever possible, especially with more modern saints, we give the year of their birth and death, e.g. 1801–1890.

(9) The text of each entry, giving the chief features of the saint's life. If there is some legendary or uncertain matter, a warning is given, as stated above.

(10) In the case of a few early martyrs whose names in ancient documents occur in the genitive case, it is often not possible to discern, other evidence being absent, the sex of the saint. Thus, the 'Passio S. Zenaidis' might refer to a holy man named Zenaides or to a holy woman called Zenais.

May I conclude by expressing my gratitude to all those members of my monastic community, living and dead, who have helped me with this work. I am of course particularly indebted to the previous editors of *The Book of Saints*, and should like to pay a special tribute to the memory of Father Hugh Capper, editor of the 1966 edition, who died before he could see the present edition in print. I am thankful also to the Rt. Revd. Dom Gilbert Jones, now President of the Subiaco Congregation of Benedictines, and former Abbot of Ramsgate (1972–88), for asking me to undertake this work, and to Abbot Wilfred Rojo, OSB, who has been indefatigable in looking up odd facts and references for me, and to whose research I owe a great deal. I should also like to thank the Very Rev. Dom Laurence O'Keeffe, OSB and Mr Leonard Dewhurst, our librarians, for all their support and patience, and also Dom Edmund Westrop, OSB, for his kind assistance. Nor must Mr Mark Wardil be omitted for a very helpful suggestion.

This book could not have appeared without the expertise and encouragement of Anne Watts of A & C Black who has been endlessly kind and helpful, and of Mr Phil Harris who read the proofs (and my illegible handwriting) with skill and humour despite bouts of severe ill-health. I am grateful to all these folk for their assistance in many ways; any faults or omissions I can only ascribe to myself.

St Augustine's Abbey,   Dom Bede Millard, OSB, BA, MTh.
Ramsgate
All Saints Day 1988

Abbreviations

(i) Chronological

a.	*ante*, i.e., before
c.	*circiter* (or *circa*), i.e., about
d.	died
p.	*post*, i.e., after
q.v.	which see
cent.	century

(ii) Canonical

AC.	Approved Cult
Bl, BB.	Blessed
G.C.	General Calendar of the Roman Catholic Church
PC.	Popular Cult
RM.	Roman Martyrology
St, SS	Saint, saints

(iii) Liturgical

Ab.	Abbot
Abs.	Abbess
Abp.	Archbishop
Bp., Bps.	Bishop, -s
C., Cc.	Confessor, -s
Card.	Cardinal
Comp.	Companions
Dr	Doctor of the Church
H., HH.	Hermit, -s
Mk.	Monk
M., MM.	Martyr, -s
N.	Nun
V., VV.	Virgin, -s
W.	Widow

(iv) Religious Orders

Barn.	Barnabites
Bridg.	Bridgettines
CM.	*Congregationis Missionis* (Vincentians, Paulists)
CP.	*Congregationis Passionis* (Passionist Fathers)
C.SS.R.	*Congregationis Sanctissimi Redemptoris* (Redemptorists)
Orat.	Oratorians
OC.	Order of Carmel (Carmelites)
OCD.	Discalced Carmelites
O. Cart.	Carthusians
OFM.	*Ordinis Fratrum Minorum* (Franciscans)
OFM. Cap.	Capuchins
O. Merc.	Mercedarians
O. Minim.	Minims
OP.	*Ordinis Praedicatorum* (Dominicans)
O. Praem.	Praemonstratensians
OSA.	Augustinians
OSA. Erem.	Augustinian Hermits
OS. Bas	Basilians
OSB.	Benedictines
OSB. Cam.	(Benedictine) Camaldolese
OSB. Cel.	(Benedictine) Celestines
OSB. Cist.	(Benedictine) Cistercians
OSB. Hum.	(Benedictine) Humiliati
OSB. Mont.	Benedictines of Montevergine
OSB. Oliv.	(Benedictine) Olivetans
OSB. Silv.	(Benedictine) Silvestrines
OSB. Vall.	(Benedictine) Vallumbrosans
OSB. Virgil.	(Benedictine) Monte-virginians
OSM.	Order of the Servants of Mary (Servites)
OS. Trin.	Trinitarians
OSU.	Ursulines
SJ.	Jesuits
Tert.	Tertiary

St Aaron, July 1

Aaron (St) Ab.   June 22
d. *p.*552   A Briton who crossed into Armorica (Brittany) and lived as a hermit in the island of Cesambre, now St Malo. Eventually he was joined by a group of disciples and became their abbot. Among the disciples was St Malo, who arrived from Wales about the middle of the 6th cent.

Aaron (St) 1st High Priest   July 1
13th cent B.C?   Great grandson of Levi, son of Jacob, and the first of the Jewish high priests, to which office he was appointed by God Himself. He was the elder brother of Moses, the Hebrew law-giver, with whom he shared the leadership of the people of Israel. Like Moses he never entered the land of promise, but died on Mt Hor, on the borders ·of Edom. What is known of him is to be found in the book of Exodus. In art he is represented with a rod in flower, a censer and a Jewish mitre.

Aaron (St) M.   July 1
See Julius and Aaron.

Aaron (Bl) Abp. OSB.   Oct 9
d. 15 May 1059   He was the first abbot (1040) of the Benedictine monastery of Tyniec in Poland. In 1046 he became the first archbishop of Cracow. According to the Polish legend he had been a monk of Cluny under St Odilo.

Abachum (St) M.   formerly Jan 19
See Marius, Martha, etc.

Abb (St) V. Abs.   Aug 25
Otherwise Ebba, q.v.

Abban (St) Ab.   March 16
5th cent.   An Irish saint, said to be contemporary with St Patrick and nephew of St Ibar. Founder of Kill-Abban abbey in Leinster.

Abban (St) Ab.   Oct 27
6th cent.   Nephew of St Kevin; founder of many monasteries, mostly in S. Ireland. His name is especially connected with that of Magh-Armuidhe, now Adamstown, in Wexford. The lives of this saint, of the foregoing St Abban, and of sundry others of the same name are hopelessly confused.

Abbo (St) Bp.   Sept 19
Otherwise Goeric, q.v.

Abbo (St) Ab. M. OSB.   Nov 13
c 945–1004   Born near Orleans, he took the habit at Fleury (St Benoît-sur-Loire) and was reputed one of the greatest scholars of his age. He was invited by St Oswald of Worcester to take charge of the abbey school of Ramsey in Huntingdonshire, where he stayed for two years (985–7). He was then appointed abbot of Fleury (988), where he introduced the Cluniac observance. He was often called in as mediator between the king of France and the holy see. He was martyred at La Réole in Gascony by monks whom he had set out to reform.

Abbo (St) Bp. OSB.   Dec 3
d. *c* 860   Monk and abbot of the monastery of St Germain at Auxerre. In 857 he was chosen bishop of the same city, but resigned in 859 and died shortly after.

Abbrici (Bl)
See Magdalen Abbrici.

Abdas (St) M.   May 16
Otherwise Audas, q.v.

Abdechalas (St) M.   Apr 21
See Simeon and Comp.

**Abdiesus
(Hebedjesus) (St)** M.   Apr 22
4th cent.   He was one of the vast multitude of Persians, named and unnamed, martyred under King Shapur (Sapor) II. This persecution lasted from A.D. 341 to A.D. 380. Abdiesus is styled a deacon in the pre-1970 RM., and is probably not to be identified with another martyr of the same name who was bishop of Cashcar.

Abdon and Sennen (SS)
MM.   July 30
3rd or 4th cent.   Persian nobles, brought to Rome as captives, who devoted themselves to the service of the imprisoned Christians and to burying the bodies of the martyrs. Some authorities place their martyrdom in the reign of Decius, others in that of Diocletian. They were commemorated on July 30 in the Roman

Calendar in use before 1970. Since then they are celebrated on this day only in local calendars.

Abel (St) Patriarch. Jan 2
The second son of Adam, killed by his brother Cain. He was invoked in the Tridentine litany for the dying, and there is a reference to his sacrifice in the first eucharistic prayer of the Missa Normativa.

Abel, Thomas (Bl) July 30
See Thomas Abel.

Abel (St) Abp. OSB. Aug 5
d. *c* 751 English, or Irish, in origin, he accompanied St Boniface to the Continent. He was chosen archbishop of Reims, his election being ratified by the council of Soissons (744) and by Pope St Zacharias, but he could not take possession of his see, which was occupied by the intruder Milo. He retired to Lobbes, where he became abbot and died.

Abellon (Bl) OP. May 15
See Andrew Abellon.

Abercius (St) Bp. Oct 22
d. *c* 167 Bishop of Hierapolis in Phrygia, in which see he is stated to have succeeded the famous Papias. Imprisoned for his zeal against paganism, he was set free and died in peace at Hierapolis. His epitaph, composed by himself and discovered in 1882, is now in the Lateran Museum. It sheds vivid light on several points of Christian doctrine, e.g., baptism, the eucharist, the Roman primacy. Its authenticity is beyond doubt.

Abibas (Abibo) (St) C. Aug 3
1st cent. Alleged second son of Gamaliel (Acts 5:34, 22:3), at whose feet St Paul had sat. Like his father he became a Christian. He lived till his eightieth year. In 415 his remains were alleged to have been found at Capergamela, near Jerusalem, together with those of SS Stephen, Gamaliel and Nicodemus.

Abibus (St) M. Nov 15
d. 322 A deacon of Edessa in Syria, martyred by burning under the emperor Licinius, and buried with his friends SS Gurias and Samonas.

Abibus (St) M. Dec 9
See Samosata, Martyrs of.

Abilius (St) Bp. Feb 22
d. *c* 98 According to Eusebius, he was third bishop, in succession to SS Mark and Anianus, of Alexandria in Egypt, to which see he was appointed *c* 84.

Ablebert (St) Bp. Jan 15
Otherwise Emebert, q.v.

Abra (St) V. Dec 12
c 342–360 Daughter of St Hilary of Poitiers, born to him before he was made bishop. Following his advice she consecrated herself to God as a nun, but died in her eighteenth year. Her feast is kept at Poitiers.

Abraham (Abraames) (St) Bp. Feb 14
d. *c* 422 A hermit in Syria, who succeeded in converting a village in the Lebanon by borrowing money to pay its taxes. Eventually he became bishop of Harran (Charres) in Mesopotamia. He had a great influence on Theodosius the Younger and his court. He died at Constantinople while on a visit to the emperor.

Abraham (Abraamios) (St) Bp. M. Feb 5
d. *c* 344–348 Bishop of Arbela in Assyria. He was put to death in the village of Telman under Shapur II of Persia.

Abraham (St) C. March 16
d. *c* 366 Surnamed Kidunaia, from the name of his parish at Beth-Kiduna. Flying from a wealthy home and a promising marriage, he lived as a hermit in a desert near Edessa. At the entreaty of his bishop he was ordained and appointed to the town of Beth-Kiduna, which he completely converted to Christianity. His life was written by St Ephrem, who was his personal friend and admirer. The episodes connected with his niece Mary are now considered spurious.

Abraham (St) Ab. June 15
d. *c* 480 Born on the banks of the Euphrates, he journeyed to Egypt, where he fell among thieves, who held him captive five years. He succeeded in escaping and boarded a ship bound for Gaul. He settled near Clermont in Auvergne as a solitary. Eventually he was given charge as abbot of the monastery of St Cyriacus (St Cyrgues) and was ordained. His protection is invoked against fever.

Abraham (St) Patriarch Oct 9
c 1700 B.C. The Father of all believers and progenitor of the Hebrew nation. Born at Ur in Chaldea, Abram, whom God renamed Abraham — the father of many — migrated at God's command to Canaan, the land which God had promised him. Here he lived a pastoral and nomadic life. In his Seed — Christ, the Messiah — all nations have been blessed, in accordance with the covenant which God made with him. He traditionally died at the age of one hundred and seventy-five. Depicted as a bearded old man

offering food to three angels seated beneath the Oak of Mamre (c.f. Gen. 18:1–16), or holding a blanket containing diminutive people symbolising souls.

Abraham (St) H.   Oct 27
d. 367 Surnamed "the Poor" or "the Child". Born at Menuf in Egypt, he became a disciple of St Pachomius. After twenty-three years he retired to a cave, where he spent seventeen years. His cult is widespread among the Copts.

Abraham (St) Abp.   Oct 28
6th cent. Built the monastery of the Abrahamites by the Golden Gate at Constantinople and the monastery of the Byzantines near Jerusalem. Eventually he became archbishop of Ephesus. He was a writer on ecclesiastical subjects.

Abraham (St) Bp.   Dec 6
474–c 558 Born at Emesa in Syria, while still very young he was chosen abbot of a monastery at Kratia in Bithynia. Later he was made bishop of the same place. Twice he secretly fled in search of quiet: the second time finding a refuge in a Palestinian monastery, where he died.

Abrahamite Monks (SS)
MM.   July 8
Between 830 and 840 This group of monks belonged to the monastery founded by St Abraham of Ephesus (q.v., Oct 28) at Constantinople. They were put to death under the emperor Theophilus for their brave defence of the cult of images.

Abran (St)   May 8
See Gibrian.

Abrosimus (St) M.   Apr 22
d. 341 His name is also spelt Abrosima. A Persian priest stoned to death with many of his flock under King Shapur II. The Greeks keep his feast on Nov 10.

Absale (Absalon) (St) M.   March 2
See Lucius, Absalon and Lorgius.

Abudimus (Abudemius)
(St) M.   July 15
4th cent. A native of the island of Tenedos in the Aegean, who was martyred under Diocletian.

Abundantius (St) M.   March 1
See Leo, Donatus, etc.

Abundantius (St) M.   Sept 16
See Abundius, Abundantius, etc.

Abundius (St) M.   Feb 27
See Alexander, Abundius, etc.

Abundius (St) Bp.   Apr 2
d. 469 A Greek priest who became bishop of Como in N. Italy. He was an able theologian and was entrusted by St Leo the Great with a mission to the emperor Theodosius the Younger, which resulted in the calling of the council of Chalcedon (451). St Abundius is represented in art either with a hart or raising a dead child to life.

Abundius (St) C.   Apr 14
d. c 564 Sacrist of St Peter's Rome. St Gregory the Great makes mention of his humble but divinely favoured life. His feast is kept at St Peter's.

Abundius (St) M.   July 11
d. 854 Parish priest of Ananelos, a village in the mountains near Cordoba in Spain. He entertained no thought of martyrdom, but suddenly found himself drawn into the conflict. He valiantly confessed Christ before the tribunal of the Moorish caliph of Cordoba, was beheaded and his body thrown to the dogs.

Abundius (St) M.   Aug 26
See Irenaeus and Abundius.

Abundius, Abundantius,
Marcian and John (SS)
MM.   Sept 16
d. c 303 Their *laus* in the pre-1970 RM. read as follows: "At Rome on the Flaminian Way, the memory of the holy martyrs Abundius, priest, and Abundantius, his deacon, whom the emperor Diocletian ordered to be beheaded ten miles from the city, together with Marcian, a senator, and John, his son, whom Abundius had raised from the dead." Their *Acta*, however, are by no means trustworthy.

Abundius (St) M.   Dec 10
See Carpophorus and Abundius.

Abundius (St) M.   Dec 14
See Justus and Abundius.

Acacius
Note. The following variant spellings of this and all the following entries under the same name should be noted: ACHATIUS, ACHACIUS, ACATHIUS, ACHATHIUS, ACHATES, and even, more rarely, AGATIUS, AGATHIUS.

Acacius (St) Bp.   March 31
d. c 251 Surnamed by the Greeks Agathangelos (the good angel) and the Wonderworker. He was a bishop in Hither Asia, and,

under the Decian persecution, he is said so to have impressed his judges by his defence of Christianity that he was set free. His *Acta* seem to be genuine. He is held in great veneration in the East.

Acacius (St) Bp.   Apr 9
d. *p.*421   Bishop of Amida (Diarbekir) in Mesopotamia, and distinguished for his charity to the Persian prisoners, for whose ransom he melted down and sold the sacred vessels of his church. This won for him the friendship of King Bahram V of Persia, who is said to have forthwith ceased to persecute his Christian subjects.

Acacius (St) M.   Apr 28
See Patrick, Acacius, etc.

Acacius (St) M.   May 8
d. *c* 303   A Cappadocian centurion in the Roman army stationed in Thrace, who was tortured and beheaded at Byzantium under Diocletian. Constantine the Great built a church in his honour. He is the S. Agario venerated at Squillace in Calabria and the San Acato of Avila and Cuenca in Spain.

Acacius (St) M.   formerly June 22
The story of a martyrdom of St Acacius and ten thousand Roman soldiers under his command on Mt Ararat, which had great vogue in the later Middle Ages, is now discarded as pure romance. Cult suppressed in 1969.

Acacius (St) M.   July 28
d. *c* 310   A martyr at Miletus under the emperor Licinius.

Acacius (St) M.   Nov 27
See Hirenarchus, Acacius, etc.

Acca (St) Bp. OSB.   Oct 20
c 660–742   A Northumbrian disciple of St Bosa of York and of St Wilfrid, and a constant companion of the latter in his journeys in England, Italy and Frisia. St Wilfrid appointed him abbot of St Andrew's at Hexham. In 709 Acca succeeded Wilfrid as bishop of the same place. For a time he was exiled from his see. St Bede was his great friend and dedicated several works to him. Acca is described by Bede as "great in the sight of God and man", and he was certainly one of the most learned Anglo-Saxon prelates of his day.

Accursius (St) M. OFM.   Jan 16
See Berardus, Peter, etc.

**Acepsimas (St) and
Comp.** MM.   Apr 22
d. 10 Oct. 376   An octogenarian bishop of

Hnaita in W. Persia, who was racked and flogged to death under Shapur II. The Acts of his martyrdom are quite genuine. With him suffered two priests, Aithala and Joseph. The pre-1970 RM. commemorated many others who suffered about this time in the same persecution. See Persia, Martyrs of.

Acepsimas (St) H.   Nov 3
5th cent.   A hermit who lived for sixty years in a cave near Cyrrhus in Syria in the time of Theodosius I. He died shortly after his ordination.

Acestes (St) M.   July 2
1st cent.   According to the legend he was one of the three soldiers who led St Paul to execution: having been converted by him, they were beheaded after him.

Achacius, or Achatius
(*several*)
See under Acacius.

Achard (St) Ab. OSB.   Sept 15
Otherwise Aichardus, q.v.

Acharius (St) Bp.   Nov 27
d. 640   Monk of Luxeuil under St Eustace. In 621 he was chosen bishop of Noyon-Tournai, and as such fostered the missionary efforts of St Amandus of Maestricht and obtained from King Dagobert I the erection of the see of Térouanne, in which he placed his friend St Omer.

Ache and Acheul (SS)
MM.   May 1
Otherwise Acius and Aceolus, q.v.

Acheric and William (SS)
Mks. OSB.   Nov 3
d. after 860   Hermits, and afterwards monks in a monastery founded by Bidulph, archdeacon of Metz, in the Vosges mountains in the diocese of Strasburg.

Achillas and Amoes (SS)
HH.   Jan 17
4th cent.   Achillas, in Latin Achilleus, is mentioned by Rufinus. He is venerated by the Greeks at the beginning of Lent, together with Amoes. They both lived as solitaries in Egypt and are called in the Greek liturgy "the flowers of the desert".

Achillas (St) Bp.   Nov 7
d. 313   Successor to St Peter the martyr in the see of Alexandria. He ordained the man who afterwards became world-famous as the heresiarch Arius. St Athanasius extols the virtues of St Achillas, who was maligned by the

party of Meletius on account of the purity of his doctrine.

Achilles (St) Bp.   May 15
d. *c* 330   In Latin Achillius. Metropolitan of Larissa in Thessaly. He is supposed to have assisted at the first council of Nicaea. Since 978 his relics have been venerated at Presba (Achilli) in Bulgaria.

Achilleus (St) M.   Apr 23
See Felix, Fortunatus and Achilleus.

Achilleus (St) M.   May 12
See Nereus, Achilleus, etc.

Achilleus Kewanuka(si)
(St) M.   June 3
d. 1886   Before entering the service of King Mwanga of Uganda, he was a clerk. See Charles Lwanga and comps. MM.

Acindynus (St) M.   Apr 20
See Victor, Zoticus, etc.

Acindynus, Pegasius,
Aphthonius, Elpidephorus
and Anempodistus (SS)
MM.   Nov 2
d. 345   Persian Christians, priests and clerics, who suffered for their faith under Shapur II.

Acisclus and Victoria (SS)
MM.   Nov 17
d. 304   Brother and sister, natives of Cordoba in Spain, who suffered martyrdom probably under Diocletian. Their home was turned into a church. They are the principal patron saints of Cordoba and are venerated throughout Spain and S. France.

Acius (Ache) and Aceolus
(Acheul) MM.   May 1
d. *c* 303   The former a deacon, the latter a subdeacon, martyred near Amiens under Diocletian. Their cult is widespread in the diocese of Amiens. Their *Acta*, however, are not trustworthy.

Actinea and Graecina
(SS) VV. MM.   June 16
4th cent.   The former was beheaded at Volterra in Etruria in the persecution of Diocletian. In 1140 her remains, together with those of Graecina, were found in the Camaldolese church of SS Justus and Clement.

Acutius (St) M.   Sept 19
See Januarius and Comp.

Acyllinus (St) M.   July 17
See Scillitan Martyrs.

Ada (St) Abs.   Dec 4
End of 7th cent.   Niece of St Engebert,

bishop of Mans. She was a nun at Soissons and was appointed abbess of Saint-Julien-des-Prés, Mans. Her name has the variants: Adenette, Adna, Adnette, Adrechildis.

Adal-, Aethel-, Al-,
Adre-, Au-, Edil-, Ethel-
Note. All these prefixes to names of Teutonic origin are more or less interchangeable. Thus, Etheldreda, Ediltrudis, Audrey, are one and the same personage. That which appears the more usual manner of spelling a saint's name in English has, as a rule, been followed here.

Adalar (Adalher) (St) M.
OSB.   June 5
d. 755   Monk-priest and companion of St Boniface, with whom he was martyred at Dokkum in Frisia.

Adalard (St) Ab. OSB.   Jan 2
c 751–827   His name is also written Adalhard, Adelhard, Adalardus, Adelardus, Alard. Grandson of Charles Martel, and one of Charlemagne's chief advisers. The ups and downs of his political career belong to general history. He entered the monastery of Corbie in Picardy, of which he became abbot. Driven into exile, he secured the foundation of New Corbie (Corvey) in Saxony. Throughout his career he remained a great abbot.

Adalard (Bl) Mk. OSB.   July 15
d. *c* 824   Surnamed the younger. Monk of Corbie under the abbot St Adalard. Died in his twentieth year.

Adalbald (St) M.   Feb 2
d. 652   Surnamed "D'Ostrevant". Born in Flanders, a son or grandson of St Gertrude of Hamage. He served at the court of Dagobert I and married a Gascon lady named Rictrude, who is also venerated as a saint, as also were their four children, Maurontius, Clotsindis, Eusebia and Adalsindis. Adalbald was slain by some relatives of his wife who disapproved of the match, and was thereafter venerated as a martyr.

Adalbero (Bl) Bp.   Jan 1
d. 1128   A brother of Godfrey Le Barbu, count of Louvain. Successively canon of Metz and bishop of Liège, where he founded the abbey of Saint-Gilles.

Adalbero (Bl) Bp. OSB.   Apr 28
d. 909   He belonged to the family of the counts of Dillingen, and was uncle to St Ulric. Monk (850) and afterwards abbot of Ellwangen, abbot-restorer of Lorsch and bishop of Augsburg (after 887). Chief adviser of Arnulf of Bavaria, tutor to his son Louis and regent of

the empire during the latter's childhood. He was well versed in science and the arts, chiefly as a musician.

Adalbero (St or Bl) Bp. Oct 6
1045–1090 Son of Count Arnold of Lambach. A student at Paris with St Altmann of Passau. Eventually he became bishop of Würzburg and sided with Gregory VII against Henry IV. On this account he was driven from his see (1085) and retired to the Benedictine abbey of Lambach in Austria, to the foundation of which he had largely contributed. It was there that he died. Cult approved in 1883.

Adalbero (Bl) Bp. Dec 15
d. 1005 Of the family of the dukes of Lorraine. Educated at the Benedictine abbey of Gorze, he became bishop of Verdun, but was transferred in the same year (984) to Metz. He was zealous in spreading the Cluniac observance by founding monasteries and churches.

Adalbert (St) Abp. M. OSB. Apr 23
956–997 In Czech, Voitech. Born in Bohemia and educated by St Adalbert of Magdeburg. He was ordained bishop of Prague (983) but, disheartened at the result of his labours, he went to Rome and became a Benedictine at the abbey of SS Boniface and Alexius on the Aventine. Twice he returned to his former mission, and twice he had to abandon it. However, on each occasion he preached instead in Poland, Prussia, Hungary and even Russia, with signal success; hence he is styled the Apostle of the Slavs. He was martyred by the Prussians near Danzig.

Adalbert (St) Abp. OSB. June 20
d. 981 Monk of St Maximin of Trier, he was chosen by the emperor Otto III to evangelize Russia. On their arrival there in 961, all his companions were killed, and he himself escaped with difficulty. He was then appointed abbot of Weissenburg, and in 968 first archbishop of Magdeburg with jurisdiction over the Wends. He did much to encourage learning, especially as abbot of Weissenburg.

Adalbert (St) Mk. June 25
d. c 740 A Northumbrian by birth who became a monk of Rathmelgisi and accompanied St Willibrord as one of his deacons to Friesland. He laboured especially round Egmont, of which abbey he became the patron saint.

Adalbert (Bl) Mk. OSB. Nov 23
d. p. 1045 Monk of Cassoria — Cassauria, Pescara — in the Abruzzi, under his abbot, St Guy. He retired to Mt Caramanico near Chieti, where he founded the abbey of St Nicholas.

Adalgis (Adelgis, Algis)
(St) Priest H. June 2
d. c 686 An Irish monk, disciple of St Fursey. He evangelized the country around Arras and Laon. In the forest of Thiq'erarche in Picardy he founded a small monastery, around which afterwards grew up the village of Saint-Algis.

Adalgis (St) Bp. Oct 7
c 850 Bishop of Novara c 830–c 850. An important churchman under the emperor Lothair. Venerated at Novara, where he is buried in the church of San Gaudenzio.

Adalgott (St) Bp. OSB.
Cist. Oct 3
d. 1165 Professed as a monk under St Bernard at Clairvaux. In 1150 he became abbot of the Black Benedictines at Dissentis and bishop of Chur, where he founded a hospital for the poor and proved himself an excellent pastor.

Adalgott (Bl) Ab. OSB. Oct 26
d. 1031 Monk of Einsiedeln and from 1012 abbot of Dissentis, both of which abbeys are in Switzerland.

Adalsindis (St) Abs. May 3
c 680 Sister of St Waldalenus, abbot-founder of Bèze. She became abbess of a convent near Bèze under the supervision of her brother.

Adalsindis (St) N. OSB. Dec 25
c 715 One of the daughters of SS Adalbald and Rictrudis, who took the veil at Hamay-les-Marchiennes, in the diocese of Arras, under her own sister St Eusebia.

Adam (St) Ab. OSB. May 16
d. p. 1212 Born at Fermo. First hermit, and then monk and abbot, of San Sabino on Mt Vissiano, near Fermo. His relics are enshrined in the cathedral of Fermo, where his feast is kept.

Adam (Bl) Mk. OSB. Cist. Dec 22
d. c 1210 Priest and sacrist in the Cistercian abbey of Loccum in Saxony. Remarkable, like most Cistercian saints, for his devotion to our Lady.

Adam and Eve (SS) Dec 24
First parents of the human race. Adam, according to Genesis, died aged nine hundred and thirty years. Their feast is given different dates in the martyrologies: Jan 18–23, March 24,

April 24, Dec 19, Dec 24. The last date is the most common.

Adamnan (St) Mk. OSB.   Jan 31
d.*c* 680   An Irish pilgrim who became a monk at Coldingham, near Berwick, under the abbess St Ebba. Cult confirmed by Leo XIII in 1898.

Adamnan (St) Ab.   Sept 23
c 625–704   Called also Adam, Aunan, Eunan. An Irish saint who became abbot of Iona (679) and zealously advocated the Roman observance of Easter which, however, his own abbey did not adopt. He is best remembered for his life of St Columba, a most important hagiographical document.

Adauctus (St) M.   Aug 30
See Felix and Adauctus.

**Adauctus and
Callisthene (SS)** M.V.   Oct 4
c 312   These two saints were Ephesians, father and daughter. The former suffered under Maximinus Daza *c* 312. Callisthene escaped martyrdom and devoted herself to works of charity till her death at Ephesus.

Adaucus (Adauctus) (St)
M.   Feb 7
d. 304   An Italian who held the office of finance minister at the imperial court of Diocletian in Phrygia. The emperor sacrificed him on discovering his religion. A large number of Christians were martyred with him, their town, Antandro, being burnt over their heads.

Addai and Mari (SS) Bps.   Aug 5
2nd cent.   They are styled "Our Holy Apostles" alike by Syrians and Persians. Addai was probably a missionary bishop at Edessa in the second century. Of Mari nothing trustworthy is known.

**Aldegrin (Adalgrin,
Aldegrin) (St)** Mk. OSB.   June 4
d. 939   A knight who joined St Odo, the future abbot of Cluny, at Baume, and shortly after embraced the eremitical life near the same abbey.

Adela (St) W.   Feb 24
c 1062–1137   Youngest daughter of William the Conqueror. In 1080 she married Stephen of Blois, played a great part in political affairs, and generously endowed abbeys and churches.

Adela (St) W. OSB.   Sept 8
d. 1071   Wife of Count Baldwin IV of Flan-

ders, who, in her widowhood, received the habit from Pope Alexander II (1067) and retired to the Benedictine convent of Messines, near Ypres, where she died.

Adela (St) W. Abs. OSB.   Dec 24
d. *c* 730   Daughter of Dagobert II, king of the Franks. In her widowhood she founded and became first abbess of Pfalzel (*Palatiolum*) near Trier.

Adelaide (St) Abs. OSB.   Feb 5
d. *c* 1015   Abbess of Bellich (Willich) near Bonn, and of Our Lady of the Capitol at Cologne. Both were Benedictine convents founded by her father.

Adelaide (Aleydis) (St) V.
OSB. Cist.   June 15
d. 1250   A young nun of the Cistercian convent of La Cambre who was visited with many physical afflictions. She became blind, contracted leprosy, and was struck with paralysis. She had to be segregated from her community. She offered up her sufferings for the souls in purgatory and had visions of their being set free through her intercession. Her life was written by a contemporary. Cult confirmed in 1907.

Adelaide (St) W.
Empress.   Dec 16
c 930–999   Daughter of the king of Burgundy, she was married (947) to Lothair II of Italy, on whose death she was treated with great brutality by Berengarius of Ivrea. She was rescued by the emperor Otto the Great, who married her. Again left a widow (973), she was ill-treated by her son and daughter-in-law. In her old age she became the regent of the empire. Throughout her life she received strong support from the abbots of Cluny, with whom she was on terms of close friendship. Before her death she retired to a convent.

Adelbert (*several*)
Otherwise Adalbert, q.v.

**Adelelmus (Fr. Alleaume,
Sp. Lesmes, Elesmes)**
(St) Ab. OSB.   Jan 30
d. *c* 1100   Born at Laudun, Poitou. He became a soldier. On his return from a pilgrimage to Rome he met at Issoire St Robert, founder of Chaise-Dieu, and joined his community. He seems to have been abbot there for a time. In 1079 he was called to Burgos, Old Castile, by Queen Constance of Burgundy, wife of Alphonsus VI of Castile. Adelelmus received from the king a church and a hospital by the gates of Burgos, where the great abbey of St John (now the church of

St Lesmes) was founded with the saint as first abbot.

Adelelmus (Adelhelm) (Bl) Ab. OSB.   Feb 25
d. 1131   A monk of St Blasien in the Black Forest, he was sent to found the monastery of Engelberg in Switzerland, of which he became prior and subsequently abbot.

Adelelmus (St) H.   Apr 27
d. 1152   Born in Flanders, he became a disciple of St Bernard of Thiron, and afterwards founder of the monastery of Etival-en-Charnie.

Adelgott
Otherwise Adalgott, q.v.

Adelheidis (Bl) V. OSB. Cist.   Dec 27
d. 1273   Of the family of Thöningen. She lived as a recluse under the obedience of the Cistercian abbey of Tennenbach.

Adelin, Adelinus
Otherwise Hadelin, q.v.

Adelina (Bl) V. OSB.Cist.   Aug 28
c 1170   Daughter of Bl Guy, brother of St Bernard of Clairvaux. She was educated at Juilly and became a nun, and afterwards abbess, of the Cistercian convent of Poulangy, diocese of Langres.

Adelina (St) V. OSB.   Oct 20
d. 1125   Granddaughter of William the Conqueror and sister of St Vitalis of Savigny. She became abbess of La Blanche at Moriton (les Dames Blanches de Mortain) in Normandy, founded by her brother.

Adelindis (Bl) W. OSB.   Aug 28
d. c 930   In her widowhood she founded and eventually became a nun — and perhaps abbess — of Buchau, on the Federsee in Wurtemburg.

Adeloga (Hadeloga) (St) V. OSB.   Feb 2
d. c 745   A Frankish princess who was the foundress and first abbess of the great Benedictine nunnery of Kitzingen in Franconia.

Adelphus (St) Bp.   Aug 29
5th cent.   The pre-1970 RM. has: "At Metz in France the memory of St Adelphus, bishop and confessor." Nothing more is known about him. His cult at Metz from early times is indisputable.

Adelphus (St) Ab. OSB.   Sept 11
d. c 670   Grandson of St Romaricus, and his successor (653) as abbot of Remiremont. He died at Luxeuil.

Adeltrudis (St) Abs. OSB.   Feb 25
Otherwise Aldetrudis, q.v.

Adeodatus
Saints of this name are better known as Deusdedit or Dieudonné, q.v.

Aderald (St) C.   Oct 20
d. 1004   Archdeacon of Troyes. He led a pilgrimage to Palestine, and on his return "with much booty in the shape of holy relics" he built for their reception the Benedictine abbey of St Sepulchre at Samblières.

Adheritus (Abderitus, Adery) (St) Bp.   Sept 27
d. 2nd cent.   A Greek by birth, successor of St Apollinaris in the see of Ravenna. Since the early Middle Ages his body has been enshrined in the Benedictine basilica of Classe near Ravenna.

Adilia
Otherwise Adela, or Otillia, q.v.

Adjutor (Ayutre) (St) H. OSB.   Apr 30
d. 1131   A Norman knight, lord of Vernon-sur-Seine, who fought in the Crusades and on his return became a monk at Tiron. He afterwards led the life of a recluse at Vernon-sur-Seine, where he died.

Adjutor (St) C.   Sept 1
See Priscus, Castrensis, etc.

Adjutor (St) M.   Dec 18
See Victurus, Victor, etc.

Adjutus (St) M. OFM.   Jan 16
See Berardus, Peter, etc.

Adjutus (St) Ab.   Dec 19
Otherwise Avitus (or Avy), q.v.

Ado (St) Bp. OSB.   Dec 16
799–875   Born in Burgundy and educated under Lupus Servatus at Ferrières, he was professed as a Benedictine at Ferrières, but the abbot of Prüm, near Trier, succeeded in enlisting his services as headmaster of the monastic school at Prüm. After some years the jealousy of certain monks drove him from Prüm, and he travelled to Rome. On his return to France he stayed for a while at Lyons and in 859 was made bishop of Vienne. He proved an altogether admirable bishop. He is best remembered, however, as the compiler of the martyrology which bears his name and of other

minor writings which unfortunately perpetuated some errors of fact.

Adolph (St) Ab. (or Bp.)
OSB.   June 17
See Botulph and Adulph.

Adolphus (St) Bp. OSB.
Cist.   Feb 11
c 1185–1224 Born in Westphalia, of the family of the counts of Tecklenburg, he became a canon of Cologne, but resigned to become a Cistercian at Camp on the Rhine. In 1216 he was nominated bishop of Osnabrück, where he became known as "the almoner of the poor". He died on June 30.

Adolphus Ludigo-Mkasa
(St) M.   June 3
From a tribe of herdsmen. See Charles Lwanga and Comps.

Adolphus and John (SS)
MM.   Sept 27
d. *c* 850 Two brothers, born at Seville of a Moorish father and a Christian mother, who were martyred at Cordoba under Abderrahman II.

Adria (St) M.   Dec 2
See Eusebius, Marcellus, etc.

Adrian
Note. This name is in certain cases also spelt with an initial H.

Adrian (St) Ab. OSB.   Jan 9
d. 710 An African by birth, he became abbot of Nerida, not far from Naples. Pope Vitalian chose him to be archbishop of Canterbury, but he declined the office and recommended instead St Theodore of Tarsus, with whom he came to England as assistant and adviser. He became abbot of SS Peter and Paul, afterwards St Augustine's, Canterbury, where he supervised a flourishing school. He was eminent for his learning as well as his sanctity. His cultus revived in 1091, when his body was discovered.

Adrian (St) M.   March 1
See Hermes and Adrian.

Adrian and Comp. (SS)
MM.   March 4
d. *c* 875 Adrian was a missionary bishop on the isle of May in the Firth of Forth who was martyred by the Danes, together with some fellow missionaries who were monks. The saint's connexion with Hungary seems to be a myth.

Adrian and Eubulus (SS)
MM.   March 5 and 7
d. 308 Both were martyred at Caesarea in

Palestine when they came to visit the Christians there — Adrian on March 5 and Eubulus two days later.

Adrian (St) M.   March 19
d. *c* 668 A disciple of St Landoald. He was murdered by robbers while begging alms for his community near Maestricht, and afterwards locally venerated as a martyr.

Adrian III (St) Pope   July 8
d. 885 He became pope in 884, and almost at once set out to take part in the Diet of Worms, intending to ask for help against the Saracens. He died on his way, near Modena, and was buried at Nonantola. Cult confirmed in 1892.

Adrian Beanus (St) M.
O.Praem.   July 9
See Gorkum (Martyrs of).

Adrian Fortescue (Bl) M.   July 9
1476–1539 Born at Punsbourne in Hertfordshire, he was first cousin to Anne Boleyn. In 1499 he married Anne Stonor. He was a knight of St John and most faithful in the discharge of his duties. He refused the oath of supremacy, and was for this reason beheaded on Tower Hill by order of Henry VIII. Beatified by Leo XIII in 1895.

Adrian (St) M.   Sept 8
d. *c* 304 Adrian, a pagan officer at the imperial court at Nicomedia, befriended the Christian prisoners and was himself cast into prison, where he and his fellow prisoners were tended by his wife, St Natalia, q.v. All the prisoners were martyred on March 4. Natalia survived to transfer her husband's relics to Argyropolis. In later times the relics were translated to Rome. St Adrian is the patron of soldiers and butchers. Nearly all the above is legendary. Cult confined to local calendars since 1969.

Adrian (Bl) M. OP.   Dec 21
13th cent. Adrian, a friar preacher, and twenty-seven companions were put to death by the Muslims in Dalmatia.

Adrio, Victor and Basilla
(SS) MM.   May 17
? Martyrs of Alexandria, whether at the hands of pagans or Arians is not known.

Adulphus
Otherwise Adolphus or Adolph, q.v.

Adventor (St) M.   Nov 20
See Octavius, Solutor and Adventor.

Ae
Note. Names of saints beginning with this

diphthong are frequently spelt with A or E only as the initial letter. Thus for Aelphege we have also Alphege (Alphage) and Elphege.

Aedan
Among many variants of the name the following are the commonest: Aidan, Aedhan, Edan. The Celtic variants are: Maidhoc, Maodhog, Mogue, and in Brittany, Dé. See Aidan.

Aedesius (St) M.   Apr 8
d. *c* 306   His *laus* in the pre-1970 RM. was as follows: "At Alexandria, the memory of St Aedesius, martyr, a brother of blessed Apphian, who, under Maximian Galerius the emperor, openly withstood an impious judge because he handed over to pimps virgins consecrated to God. He was laid hold of by the soldiery, afflicted with the most cruel punishments, and drowned in the sea for the Lord Christ."

Aedh, Aedhan
Note. Holweck lists eighteen more Irish saints of the name of Aedh, and twenty under Aedhan, but the historical data are hopelessly confused.

Aedh MacBricc (St) Bp.   Nov 10
6th cent.   The name is also spelt Aod and Aedsind, and it is latinized as Aidus. He was a disciple of St Illadan at Rathlihen in Offaly, and is said to have founded churches at Rathugh and other places in his native Meath, where he held the office of bishop.

Aegidius
One of the most popular saint's names in the Middle Ages. In Italian: Egidio; in French: Gilles; in Spanish and Portuguese: Gil; in English: Giles, q.v.

Aelgifu (St) W. OSB.   May 18
Otherwise Elgiva, q.v.

Aelphleah, Aelphege (St)
Bp.
Otherwise Elphege, q.v.

Aelred (St) Ab. OSB.Cist.   Jan 12
1109–1167   Born in the north of England, Aelred became master of the household of King David of Scotland. In 1133 he joined the Cistercian community of Rievaulx in Yorkshire. Soon he was made abbot, first of Revesby, then of Rievaulx itself. Austere with himself, he was, we are told, remarkably gentle with his monks, of whom he dismissed not one in seventeen years. His ascetical treatises, especially that *On Spiritual Friendship*, are full of charm.

Aemilian—Aemiliana
—Aemilio—Aemilius
Otherwise Emilian — Emiliana — Emilio — Emilius, q.v.

Aengus (Oengus, Oengoba) (St) Bp.   March 11
d. *c* 830   Known as "the Culdee". He is said to have been first a monk of Clonenagh and then of Tallacht Hill. He is best remembered as the composer of a celebrated metrical hymn to the saints, called Felire (Festilogium, metrical martyrology). Though he was famous in his day, no early account of him is extant and he is not commemorated liturgically in any Irish diocese. From Tallacht Hill he returned to Clonenagh, where he became abbot and bishop.

Aeschilus (St) Bp. M.   June 12
Otherwise Eskill, q.v.

Aethelgifu
Otherwise Ethelgiva or Elgiva, q.v.

Aethelhard (St) Bp.   May 12
Otherwise Ethelhard, q.v.

Aetherius (*several*)
Otherwise Etherius, q.v.

Aetius (St) M.   March 10
See Forty Armenian Martyrs.

Afan (St) Bp.   Nov 16
6th cent.   A Welsh saint of the Cunedda family, supposed by some to have been a bishop. He has given its title to the church of Llanafan, Powys.

Affrosa (St) VM.   Jan 4
Otherwise Dafrosa (or Daphrosa), q.v.

Afra (St) VM.   May 24
? A martyr of Brescia, connected by legend with SS Faustinus and Jovita. The rest of the legend is untrustworthy.

Afra (St) M.   Aug 5
d. *c* 304   A martyr who suffered at Augsburg, probably under Diocletian. She was venerated there from early times, and the great Benedictine abbey of that city was dedicated to her. The story of her being a converted harlot from Cyprus is worthless.

Africa (Martyrs of) (SS)
By Africa here is meant only North Western Africa, or *Africa Latina*. North Eastern Africa goes under the heading Egypt or Ethiopia. The following anonymous groups of martyrs are mentioned in the pre-1970 RM.

Jan 6
d. *c* 210   A number of Christians of either sex burnt at the stake under Septimius Severus.

Feb 11
d. *c* 303   Martyrs known as the "Guardians of the Holy Scriptures". They chose to die rather than to deliver the sacred books to be

burnt. They suffered under Diocletian. St Augustine mentions especially those of Numidia.

Apr 5

d. 459   A large group martyred on Easter Sunday while at the eucharist, under Genseric, the Arian king of the Vandals. The lector, who was at the moment intoning the Alleluia, had his throat pierced by an arrow.

Apr 9

? A group of Christians martyred at Masyla (*Martyres Massylitani*). St Augustine and Prudentius sang their praises.

Oct 16

? Two hundred and twenty Christians were put to death on this day, where, when and how is not known.

Oct 30

? A group of Christians, numbering between one and two hundred, massacred in one of the early persecutions. No other details are available.

Dec 16

d. 482   A great number of women butchered under Hunneric, Arian king of the Vandals.

Africanus (St) M.   Apr 10
See Terence, Africanus, etc.

Africus (St) C.   Nov 16
7th cent.   A saint of Comminges in S. France, celebrated for his zeal for orthodoxy. His shrine was destroyed by the Calvinists, but his cultus still endures. Tradition makes him bishop of that city, but his name is not mentioned in the French Episcopologia.

Agabius (St) Bp.   Aug 4
c 250   An early bishop of Verona. His existence is uncertain.

Agabus (St) C.   Feb 13
1st cent.   A prophet twice mentioned in the Acts of the Apostles (9:28, 21:10–12). A Carmelite legend has led to his being usually represented in art robed in the Carmelite habit and holding the model of a church.

Agamund (St) M. OSB.   Apr 9
See Theodore and Comp.

Aganus (St) Ab. OSB.   Feb 16
c 1050–1100   An abbot of St Gabriel's at Airola in Campania, diocese of St Agatha dei Goti.

Agape (St) M.   Jan 25
See Donatus, Sabinus, and Agape.
Note. The genitive case Agapis in the pre-1970 RM. may designate a saint of either sex.

Agape (St) VM.   Feb 15
c 273   A maiden martyred at Terni, who

belonged to a group of virgins formed by St Valentine into a community. From the sixth to the twelfth century there was a church at Terni dedicated to her.

Agape, Chionia and Irene (SS) VV. MM.   Apr 3
d. 304   Three sisters who it is said were burnt alive with several companions under Diocletian at Salonika. All suffered on April 3 except Irene, who was exposed in a brothel and put to death two days later.

Agape (St) VM.   Aug 1
Otherwise Charity. See Faith, Hope and Charity.

Agape (St) VM.   Dec 28
See Indes, Domna, etc.

Agapitus (St) Bp.   March 16
4th cent.   Bishop of Ravenna.

Agapitus (St) Bp.   March 24
3rd cent.   Bishop of Synnada in Phrygia.

Agapitus (St) M.   Aug 6
See Sixtus II and Comp.

Agapitus (St) M.   Aug 18
d. c 274   A lad of fifteen who bravely confessed Christ and was martyred at Palestrina, near Rome. He is the patron saint of Palestrina, where as early as the fifth century a church was dedicated to him by Pope Felix III (483–492). Cult confined to particular calendars since 1969.

Agapitus (St) M.   Sept 20
See Eustace, Theopistus, etc.

Agapitus I (St) Pope.
                                         Sept 20 (and Apr 22)
d. 536   A Roman by birth and archdeacon of the Roman church, he was elected pope in May 535 and died at Constantinople on April 22, 536. As pope he showed great strength of character in deposing the Monophysite patriarch of Constantinople. His body was taken back to Rome on Sept 20, on which date he was commemorated a second time in the pre-1970 RM. In common with many other Italian saints of the same period he owes his cult to the devotion of St Gregory the Great.

Agapitus (St) M.   Nov 20
See Bassus, Dionysius, etc.

Agapius (St) M.   March 24
See Timolaus, Dionysius, etc.

Agapius (St) M.   Apr 28
See Aphrodisius, Caralippus, etc.

Agapius and Comp. (SS) MM.   Apr 29
c 259   The Spanish saints Agapius and Sec-

undinus, bishops or priests, were banished to Cirta, Numidia, in the persecution under Valerian. There they suffered martyrdom together with Tertulla and Antonia, virgins, and a certain woman with her twin children. The martyr Emilian mentioned by the pre-1970 RM. was not mentioned in the *Acta*.

Agapius (St) M. Aug 19
See Timothy, Thecla and Agapius. St Agapius is also commemorated separately on Nov 20, q.v.

Agapius (St) M. Aug 21
See Bassa, Theogonius, etc.

Agapius (or Agapitus) (St) Bp. Sept 10
d. 447 Bishop of Novara in Piedmont from 417–447. Successor to St Gaudentius, "whose footsteps he followed".

Agapius (St) M. Nov 2
See Carterius, Styriacus, etc.

Agapius (St) M. Nov 20
d. *c* 306 Martyred at Caesarea in Palestine under Diocletian. He was thrice imprisoned for the faith. Again arrested, he was chained to a murderer and taken to the amphitheatre to be thrown to the wild beasts. His companion was pardoned, and liberty was also offered to Agapius if he would renounce Christ. He refused, and a bear was let loose upon him which almost mauled him to death. He was taken back to prison and on the following day weighted with heavy stones and cast into the sea. He is also commemorated on Aug 19.

Agatha (St) VM. GC. Feb 5
d. ? Born either at Catania or Palermo in Sicily, she suffered martyrdom at Catania. According to the *legenda*, she was handed over to a prostitute and her breasts were cut off. St Peter cured her of this mutilation while she was in prison, where she subsequently died. Her cult spread throughout the church. Her name is in the first eucharistic prayer, and in all the martyrologies, Greek and Latin. The miracles by which she has preserved Catania from successive eruptions of Mt Etna are well accredited. She is the patroness of wet-nurses, bell-founders and jewellers. In art she is shown holding a platter in one hand, on which her severed breasts repose, and a knife or shears in the other.

Agatha (St) W. Feb 5
d. 1024 Wife of Paul, count of Carinthia. A model of devotion to her domestic duties and of patience under the brutal ill-treatment of her jealous husband, whom she converted. She is highly venerated in Carinthia.

Agatha Lin (Bl) VM. Feb 18
1817–1858 A Chinese school-teacher, born at Ma-Tchang and beheaded for the faith at Mao-ken on Jan. 28. She was beatified on May 2, 1909.

Agatha (St) V. OSB. Dec 12
d. *c* 790 Nun of Wimborne, disciple of St Lioba, with whom she crossed over to Germany to help St Boniface in his missionary labours.

Agathangelus (St) M. Jan 23
d. *c* 309 Agathangelus was converted and baptized by St Clement, bishop of Ancyra, while the latter was a prisoner in Rome. He followed the bishop to the East, and both were martyred at Ancyra. Their *Acta* are most romantic, but unfortunately spurious.

Agathangelus and Cassian (BB) MM. OFM. Cap. Aug 7
d. 1638 Agathangelus of Vendôme — his baptismal name was Francis Noury — became a Capuchin friar at Vendôme and eventually was sent to Egypt (1633) to work for the reconciliation of the Coptic Christians. There he joined his fellow-Capuchin, Fr Cassian of Nantes. Their mission failed and they passed on into Abyssinia. They were at once reported to King Fasilidas by a German Protestant and stoned to death on entering the country. They were beatified in 1905.

Agathius (St) M. May 8
Otherwise Acacius, q.v.

Agatho (St) Pope. Jan 10
c 577–681 Pope from June 27, 678, to Jan 10, 681. He was a Sicilian of Palermo and probably a monk, whether Benedictine or Basilian is not certain. As pope he convened the sixth oecumenical council held at Constantinople in 680 against the Monothelites. He restored St Wilfrid to the see of York.

Agatho (St) M. Feb 14
See Cyrion, Bassian, etc.

Agatho and Triphina (SS) MM. July 5
d. ? 306 Sicilian martyrs about whom nothing further is known. There is doubt even as to the sex of the latter saint.

Agatho (St) Ab. Oct 21
4th cent. Hermit and abbot in Egypt. Often quoted in the *Lives of the Fathers of the Desert*.

Agatho (St) M. Dec 7
d. 250 This Agatho has been identified with St Besas, whom the pre-1970 RM. mentioned on Feb 27 together with SS Julian and Eunus, q.v.

St Agatha, Feb 5

**Agathoclia (or Agatholica)
(St) VM.**   Sept 17

? The *laus* of the pre-1970 RM. was as
follows: "On the same day the birthday of St
Agathoclia, the handmaid of a certain infidel
woman, who for a long time afflicted her with
stripes and other torments to make her deny
Christ. She was at last taken before the judge
and treated with even greater cruelty, and as
she persisted in the confession of the Faith,
her tongue was cut out and she was cast into
the fire." It is probable that she was a Greek,
but at a later period she was said to have been a
Spaniard, perhaps because she was the patron
saint of Mequinenza in Aragon.

Agathodorus (St) Bp. M.   March 4
See Basil, Eugene, etc.

Agathodorus (St) M.   Apr 13
See Carpus, Papylus, etc.

Agathonica (St) VM.   Apr 13
See Carpus, Papylus, etc.

Agathonica (St) VM.   Aug 10
See Bassa, Paula and Agathonica.

**Agathonicus, Zoticus
and Comp. (SS) MM.**   Aug 22
? 3rd cent. Agathonicus, a patrician, was put
to death in the neighbourhood of Constantinople under Maximian Herculius. Zoticus, a
philosopher of Bithynia, and several of his
disciples were martyred about the same time.
A magnificent basilica was built in their
honour at Byzantium.

Agathopodes (Agathopus) and Theodulus (SS) MM. Apr 4

d. 303 Agathopodes, a deacon, and Theodulus, a young reader of the church of Thessalonica were martyred by drowning under Maximian Herculius for refusing to give up the sacred books.

Agathopodes (Agathopus) (St) C. Apr 25

See Philo and Agathopodes.

Agathopus (St) M. Dec 23

See Theodulus, Saturninus, etc.

Ageranus (Ayran, Ayrman) (St) M. OSB. May 21

d. 888 Ageranus was a monk of Bèze in the Côte d'Or. When the Normans invaded Burgundy (886–889) most of the monks escaped, but Ageranus remained with four other monks — Genesius, Bernard, Sifiard and Rodron — the boy Adalaric and the priest Ansuinus. All were massacred by the invaders.

Agericus (Aguy, Airy) (St) Ab. OSB. Apr 11

d. c 680 A disciple of St Eligius (Eloi) who became abbot of St Martin's at Tours.

Agericus (Aguy, Airy) (St) Bp. Dec 1

c 521–591 Successor of St Desiderius in the see of Verdun (554). He was greatly admired by his contemporaries, SS Gregory of Tours and Venantius Fortunatus. He was buried in his own home, which was turned into a church. Around it was built in 1037 the Benedictine abbey of Saint-Airy.

Aggaeus (St) M. Jan 4

See Hermes, Aggaeus and Caius.

Agia (Aia, Austregildis, Aye) (St) N. OSB. Apr 18

d. c 714 Wife of St Hidulphus of Hainault. Both desiring to become religious, she entered the nunnery of Mons (Castrilocus), while he joined the monks of Lobbes. She is especially venerated by the Beguines of Belgium.

Agia (Aia, Aye) (St) W. Sept 1

6th cent. Mother of St Lupus of Sens.

Agilbert (Aglibert) (St) Bp. OSB. Oct 11

d. c 685 A Frankish monk of Jouarre under the abbot Ado. He studied scripture in France and then crossed over to England and preached in Wessex. He was invited to remain as bishop of the West Saxons, and as such he came in contact with St Wilfrid. The two saints were leaders of the "Roman party" in the synod of Whitby. When King Coinwalch grew impatient of the presence in his realm of a foreign bishop, Agilbert returned to France and was made bishop of Paris in 668. He was buried at Jouarre, where his sarcophagus is still preserved.

Agilberta (Aguilberta, Gilberta) (St) Abs. OSB. Aug 10

d. c 680 Second abbess of Jouarre, elected about the year 660. She was a relative of St Ebrigisil, of St Ado, founder of Jouarre, and of St Agilbert, bishop of Paris.

Agileus (St) M. Oct 15

d. c 300 An African Christian who suffered martyrdom at Carthage. His relics were afterwards translated to Rome. He was held in great veneration in the Latin church, especially in Africa. We have a sermon of St Augustine's in the martyr's honour.

Agilo (Bl) Ab. OSB. Aug 27

d. 957 Monk of St Aper at Toul. He was invited by St Gerard of Brogne to restore monastic discipline at Sithin (Saint-Bertin).

Agilulph (St) M. Abp. OSB. July 9

d. p.720 Monk and abbot of Stavelot-Malmédy and archbishop of Cologne. His martyrdom was the result of the zealous discharge of his ministry, and, it seems, aided by the connivance of Charles Martel.

Agilus (St) Ab. Aug 30

c 580–650 A young Frankish nobleman who became a monk under St Columbanus at Luxeuil. He remained at Luxeuil under the founder's successor, St Eustace, but went with him in 612 to evangelize Bavaria. On his return to France he became abbot of Rebais, near Paris. He is known also as Aile, Ail, Aisle, Ayeul, Ely.

Aglibert (St) M. June 24

See Agoard, Aglibert, and others.

Agnellus of Pisa (Bl) C. OFM. March 13

1194–1235 Born at Pisa, Agnellus was received by St Francis himself among the Friars Minor and sent by him to open a house at Paris. He was later appointed by Francis the first Provincial of the order in England. Agnellus arrived at Dover in 1224 and founded houses at Canterbury and Oxford. He worked also for some time in London. At Oxford he established a school which became famous, and at Oxford he died. Cult confirmed in 1892.

Agnellus (St) Ab. OSB. Dec 14

d. c 596 Hermit and afterwards abbot of San Gaudioso near Naples. He is one of the patron saints of the city and, the pre-1970 RM. added, "was often seen to free the besieged city from its foes by the banner of the cross".

St Agnes, Jan 21

Agnes (St) VM. GC. Jan 21

d. *c* 350? A Roman maiden, aged twelve or thirteen years, who was martyred and buried beside the Via Nomentana, where a basilica in her honour has stood since the time of Constantine the Great. St Ambrose, St Damasus and Prudentius sang her praises. Her name occurs in the first eucharistic prayer, and as a special patroness of chastity she is one of the most popular of saints. Unfortunately the details of her *Acta* are not trustworthy. In art she is usually represented with a lamb and sometimes with a dove with a ring in its beak.

Agnes of Benigamin (Bl)
V. OSA. Disc. Jan 22
Otherwise Inés de Benigamin, q.v.

Agnes of Bohemia (Bl) V.
Poor Clare March 2
1200–1282 Born at Prague, daughter of the king of Bohemia, she was educated by the Cistercian nuns of Trebnitz and twice betrothed. She refused to marry, and, with the help of Pope Gregory IX, became a Poor Clare in a foundation of her own at Prague, to which St Clare sent five nuns from Assisi. Agnes remained here until her death, forty-six years later.

Agnes of Montepulciano
(St) V. OP. Apr 20
1268–1317 Born near Montepulciano in Tuscany, she entered the convent *del Sacco* at the age of nine. At fourteen she was given charge of the temporalities, and at fifteen she was made first abbess of the convent at Procena. After some seventeen years she was asked to return to Montepulciano to take charge of a new house of Dominican nuns. Here she spent the remainder of her life. Canonized by Benedict XIII in 1726. In art she is depicted as a Dominican nun with a lily, lamb and book; or seeing a vision of Our Lady and Her Child.

Agnes of Poitiers (St)
Abs. May 13
d. 588 Chosen by St Radegund to be abbess of the nunnery of Holy Cross at Poitiers, Agnes adopted the rule of St Caesarius, handed to her by the holy bishop himself. She is best known as the friend of the poet St Venantius Fortunatus.

Agnes De (St) M. July 12
d. July 12, 1841 Born of Christian parents at Bai-den in Vietnam, she died in prison for the faith at Namdinh. Canonized in 1988.

Agnes of Venosa (Bl) V.
OSB. Mont. Sept 1
d. *c* 1144 Said to have been one of the dancing girls sent to tempt St William of Vercelli. She repented and joined the Montevergian nuns at Venosa, where she became abbess.

Agnes of Bagno (Bl) V.
OSB. Cam. Sept 4
d. *c* 1105 A Camaldolese nun at Santa Lucia, near Bagno di Romagna in Tuscany. Her cult was confirmed in 1823. Her relics are enshrined in the village church of Pereto.

Agnes Taquea (Bl) M. Sept 10
d. 1626 Wife of Bl Cosmas Taquea. A native Japanese woman beheaded at Nagasaki. She and her husband belong to the group of fifty-one Christians who were martyred on the same day with Bl Charles Spinola, SJ., q.v. Beatified in 1867.

Agnes of Bavaria (Bl) V.   Nov 11
d. 1532 Daughter of Louis IV, duke of
Bavaria, she was educated by the Poor Clares
of St James at Munich, where she died aged
seven.

Agnes of Assisi (St) V.
Abs. Poor Clare   Nov 16
1198–1253 Younger sister of St Clare,
whom she followed, aged sixteen, to the
Benedictine convent of Panso, near Assisi, and
then to San Damiano. She became the first
abbess of Monticelli at Florence, opened
houses at Padua, Venice and Mantua, and
returned to San Damiano, where she died
three months after her sister. Cult confirmed
by Benedict XIV.

Agnes Tsao-Kouy (Bl)
WM.   Nov 24
1826–1856 A young Chinese widow who
served the missionaries as catechist. She was
killed by "cage torture" at Sy-Lin-Hien.
Beatified in 1900.

**Agoard, Aglibert and
others (SS)** MM.   June 24
5th to 7th cent. The pre-1970 RM. has the
legend: "In the neighbourhood of Paris, in the
village of Creteil, the passion of the holy
martyrs Agoard and Aglibert, and numberless
others of both sexes." The Bollandists fix the
date of their martyrdom between the first and
the third centuries, but in all probability it took
place between the fifth and the seventh.

Agobard (St) Bp.   June 6
c 769–840 A native of Spain, he escaped in
his youth from the invading Saracens and
joined the clergy of Lyons in France. He
became archbishop of that city in 813. He
played a prominent part in both the ecclesiastical and the political affairs of his time. But his
greatest work was done as a theologian, chiefly
in the field of liturgy, and he has left many
important writings.

Agofredus (St) Mk. OSB.   June 21
d. 738 Brother of St Leutfrid (Leffroi) and
monk of Holy Cross (La-Croix-Saint-Leuffroi), a Benedictine abbey in the diocese of
Evreux, Normandy.

Agrecius (Agritius) (St)
Bp.   Jan 13
d. c 333 Bishop of Trier and predecessor in
that see of St Maximinus. He took part in the
council of Arles (314). According to his life
composed in the eleventh century, he was
aided by St Helen, wife of Constantine, who
procured for him the garment of our Lord,
known as the Holy Coat of Trier.

Agricola (St) Bp.   Feb 5
d. 420 He is listed as the eleventh bishop of
Tongres in a catalogue of the tenth century
transcribed from the ancient diptychs.

Agricola (St) Bp.   Feb 26
d. c 594 Said to have been bishop of Nevers
between 570 and 594.

Agricola (St) Bp.   March 17
d. 580 In French Arègle or Agrèle. Bishop
of Châlon-sur-Saône. His contemporary St
Gregory of Tours enlarges upon the austerity
of his life.

**Agricola (or Agricolus)
(St)** Bp.   Sept 2
c 630–700 Son of St Magnus, bishop of
Avignon. At the age of sixteen he was professed a monk at Lérins, where he remained
sixteen years. His father called him to Avignon
and made him his coadjutor, and in 660 he
became bishop of the city. He built a church in
Avignon to be served by the monks of Lérins
and also a convent for Benedictine nuns. By
his blessing he put an end to an invasion of
storks. All the above particulars are based on
documents dating only from the fifteenth
century, and only since 1647 has Agricola
been the patron saint of Avignon.

Agricola (St) M.   Nov 4
See Vitalis and Agricola.

Agricola (St) M.   Dec 3
? A martyr in Pannonia, details of whose life
have not come down to us, but whose name
appears in all the ancient registers.

Agricola (St) M.   Dec 16
See Valentine, Concordius, etc.

Agrippina (St) VM.   June 23
d. c 262 A Roman maiden who was mar-
tyred, it is surmised, under Valerian. She is
especially venerated by the Sicilians and by the
Greeks, both claiming to have her relics, the
former at Mineo, the latter at Constantinople.

Agrippinus (St) Bp.   Jan 30
d. c 180 The ninth bishop of Alexandria
after St Mark.

Agrippinus (St) Bp.   June 17
d. 615 Bishop of Como in N. Italy. There
are well-founded doubts about his claim to the
title of saint.

Agrippinus (St) Bp.   July 9
d. 538 Bishop of Autun, who ordained St
Germanus of Paris to the deaconate and the
priesthood.

Agrippinus (Arpinus)
(St) Bp.   Nov 9
2nd or 3rd cent.   Bishop of Naples, where he
has been greatly venerated from time immemorial. His relics are enshrined under the high
altar of the cathedral of Naples with the bodies
of SS Eutychius and Acutius, companions of
St Januarius.

Agritius (St) Bp.   Jan 13
Otherwise Agrecius, q.v.

Aguy
An abbreviated popular form of the names
Agericus and Agritius, q.v.

Aia (St) W.   Sept 1
Otherwise Agia, q.v.

Aibert (Aybert) (St) H.
OSB.   Apr 7
c 1060–1140   Born at Espain, near Tournai,
he became a monk at the abbey of St Crespin,
where for twenty-three years he was provost
and cellarer; then he retired to live as a recluse.
His devotion to the eucharist took the form of
celebrating two daily, one for the living and
one for the dead.

Aichardus (Aicard,
Achard) (St) Ab. OSB.   Sept 15
d. *c* 687   Born at Poitiers, the son of an
officer at the court of Clotaire II. He was
educated at the abbey of St Hilaire at Poitiers
and early in life was professed as a monk of
Ansion in Poitou. Here he spent thirty-nine
years, afterwards becoming abbot of St Benedict's at Quinçay, near Poitiers. Finally he
succeeded St Philibert at Jumièges, where he
ruled close on a thousand monks.

Aichardus (Bl) Mk. OSB.
Cist.   Sept 15
d. *c* 1170   Entered Clairvaux (*c* 1124) and
made his profession in the hands of St Bernard, who sent him to several foundations. On
returning to Clairvaux he was made novice-
master by St Bernard himself.

Aid (St) Ab.   Apr 11
? An Abbot of Achard-Finglas in Co. Carlow,
possibly one and the same with St Aed or
Maedhogh of Clonmore.

Aidan (or Maedoc) (St)
Bp.   Jan 31
d. 626   The first bishop of Ferns in Co.
Wexford, Eire, where he founded and ruled a
monastery as well. In his youth he had become
a monk under St David in Wales and he

St Aidan, Aug 31

returned later in life to live some time with
him. His life contains much legendary matter.

Aidan (Aedan) (St) Bp.   Aug 31
d. 651   A monk of Iona who, at the request
of St Oswald, king of Northumbria, was sent to
evangelize N. England. He fixed his see at
Lindisfarne (Holy Island) where he ruled as
abbot and bishop, his diocese reaching from
the Forth to the Humber. His apostolate,
furthered by numberless miracles, was most
fruitful, as is witnessed by the writings of St
Bede. He died at Bamborough. In art he is
represented sometimes with a stag near him,
suggested by a legend that by his prayer he
once rendered invisible a deer pursued by
huntsmen.

Aidan (St) Bp.   Oct 20
d. 768   An Irish bishop in Mayo.

Aignan (Agnan) (St) Bp. Nov 17
Otherwise Anianus, q.v.

**Aigulphus (Ayoul, Aieul,
Aout, Hou) (St)** Bp. May 22
d. *p.*835 After an excellent education he
chose to live as a recluse. However, about the
year 812 he was against his will placed in the
see of Bourges, which he governed till his
death.

**Aigulphus (Ayou, Ayoul)
(St)** Ab. M. OSB. Sept 3
c 630–676 Born at Blois, at the age of twenty
he entered Fleury, then in its first fervour of
Benedictine observance. He was sent first to
Montecassino to attempt to rescue the relics of
St Benedict, and then (*c* 670) as abbot to
Lérins to introduce the Benedictine rule.
Some malcontents opposed him and caused
him to be taken, with four of his monks, to an
island near Corsica where they were done to
death.

**Ailbe (Albeus, Ailbhe)
(St)** Bp. Sept 12
6th cent. Reputed first bishop of Emly, in
Ireland.

Ailred (St) Ab. OSB. Cist. Jan 12
Otherwise Aelred, q.v.

Aimard (Bl) Ab. OSB. Oct 5
Otherwise Aymard, q.v.

Aimé (Amé) (St) Ab. OSB. Sept 13
Otherwise Amatus, q.v.

Aimo (Aimonius) (St) Mk. Feb 13
d. *c* 790 Founder of the nunnery of St
Victor at Meda in the archdiocese of Milan.

**Aimo (Aymo, Haimo)
(St)** Mk. OSB. Apr 30
d. 1173 Born in the diocese of Rennes,
Aimo joined the community of Savigny in
Normandy. Falsely suspected of leprosy, in
order not to be sent away, he offered to serve
two religious who were actually lepers. Afterwards he was admitted to profession, ordained
priest and appointed to various offices. He had
many severe trials and was favoured with
mystical experiences.

Aimo Taparelli (Bl) C.
OP. Aug 18
1395–1495 A native of Savigliano in Piedmont and a member of the family of the counts
of Lagnasco. He became a Dominican, and
was appointed chaplain to Bl Duke Amadeus
of Savoy and inquisitor general for Lombardy
and Liguria. He died a centenarian. Cult
confirmed in 1856.

Airaldus (Ayraldus) Bp.
O. Cart. Jan 2
d. 1156? Carthusian prior of Portes, in the
diocese of Belley, and, from 1132 to 1156,
bishop of St John of Maurienne in Savoy.

Airy (St) Bp. Dec 1
Otherwise Agericus, q.v.

Aisle (Aileu) (St) Ab. Aug 30
Otherwise Agilus, q.v.

Aithalas (St) M. Apr 22
d. 377 One of the band of Persian martyrs
whose leader was St Acepsimas, q.v.

Aizan and Sazan (SS) MM. Oct 1
d. *c* 400 Two brothers, petty chieftains in
Abyssinia, very zealous in spreading the gospel
in their own country. They were great friends
of St Athanasius.

Ajou (Ajon) (St) Ab. M.
OSB. Sept 3
Otherwise Aigulphus, q.v.

Ajutre (St) H. OSB. Apr 30
Otherwise Adjutor, q.v.

**Alacoque, Margaret
Mary (St)** V. Oct 17
See Margaret Mary Alacoque.

Alacrinus (Bl) Bp. OSB.
Cist. Jan 5
d. 1216 Cistercian prior of Casamari, diocese of Veroli, he was sent as papal legate to
Germany under Popes Innocent III and Honorius III.

Aladius (St) Bp. Oct 1
Otherwise Albaud, q.v.

Alanus (St) Ab. OSB.
Cist. June 28
Otherwise Almus, q.v.

Alanus (Bl) H. OSB. July 18
d. 1311 An Austrian monk who in the ju-
bilee year of 1300 journeyed to Rome and
afterwards joined the Italian community of
Sassovivo. In 1311 he became a recluse.

**Alanus de Rupe (Alain
de la Roche) (Bl)** C. OP. Sept 8
c 1428–1475 A native of Brittany, he
became a Dominican at Dinan, diocese of St
Malo and was stationed at the Dominican
houses of Paris, Lille, Ghent, and Zwoll,
where he died. He is famous for his zeal in
spreading the devotion of the rosary. Cult not
yet officially confirmed.

Alanus and Alorus (SS)
Bps. Oct 26
5th cent. Two bishops of Quimper in Brit-

St Alban, June 20

tany, concerning whom no reliable particulars have come down to us, except the fact of the popular and liturgical cult given to them from early ages.

Alanus (St) Ab. OSB.   Nov 25
7th cent. Abbot-founder of Lavaur in Gascony.

Alaricus (Adalricus, Adalrai) (Bl) H. OSB.   Sept 29
d. 975 Son of Duke Burkhard II of Swabia. Educated, and then a monk, at Einsiedeln in Switzerland. Eventually he became a recluse on the small island of Uffnau, on the lake of Zurich.

Alban Bartholomew Roe (St) M. OSB.   Jan 21
d. 1642 A Suffolk man of Protestant parentage, who was educated at Cambridge and became a Catholic at Douai and a Benedictine under the name of Alban at Dieuleward (now Ampleforth) in 1612. He laboured in the English mission from 1615 to 1642 and was martyred at Tyburn. Canonised in 1970 as one of the Forty Martyrs of England and Wales, q.v.

Alban (St) M.   June 20
3rd or 4th cent. Venerated as the protomartyr of Britain. He was a citizen of Verulam converted by a persecuted priest whom he sheltered in his house. He was executed on Holmhurst Hill, and on this site King Offa

erected the Benedictine abbey of St Alban's, by which name Verulam has since been known. In art he is shown with a very tall cross and a sword; or decapitated, with his head in a holly bush nearby, and his executioner's eyes dropping out.

Alban (St) M.   June 21
d. c 400 A Greek priest of Naxos who, sent into exile by the Arians, preached the gospel in parts of Germany about Mainz. Here he was again attacked by the Arians and put to death. The Benedictine abbey at Mainz, dedicated in his honour, has preserved his memory.

Albaud (Aladius) (St) Bp.   Oct 1
d. c 520 Bishop of Toul. He built the church of St Aper (Epvre), his predecessor in the see, which was at a later period the abbey church of the Benedictine monastery of Saint-Aper.

Alberic (St) Ab. OSB. Cist.   Jan 26
d. 1109 One of the three founders of the Cistercians. He was first a hermit at Collan, near Châtillon-sur-Seine; then he followed St Robert to Molesmes (1075) and was prior there and afterwards accompanied him to Cîteaux (1093) where he was again prior and succeeded St Robert as abbot in 1100.

Alberic Crescitelli (Bl) M.   July 9
1863–1900 Born at Altavilla, Beneventa, he entered the Pontifical Seminary for Foreign Missions at Rome. Ordained in 1887, he went next year to work in the Shensi Province of China. After labouring there twelve years, he was moved to Ningkiang. Captured in the Boxer Rising, he was tortured and beheaded. Beatified 1951.

Alberic (St) H. OSB. Cam.   Aug 29
d. c 1050 A Camaldolese monk who lived as a recluse at Bagno de Romagna in the diocese of Sarsina. His relics are enshrined in the Camaldolese church of S. Anastasio, diocese of Montefeltro.

Alberic (St) Ab. OSB.   Oct 28
d. 779 Abbot of Stavelot-Malmédy. His feast is kept together with that of four other abbots of the same monastery.

Alberic (St) Bp. OSB.   Nov 14
d. 784 (Aug 21) Nephew of St Gregory of Utrecht, he became cathedral prior and, on his uncle's death in 775, bishop of St Martin's at Utrecht. He was a highly educated man, a great friend of Alcuin. His apostolate among the pagan Teutons was exceedingly fruitful.

Alberic (Bl) Mk. OSB.   Dec 24
10th cent. Monk of Gladbach. Others call him Albert, and give him the title of saint.

Albert of Cashel (St) Bp. Jan 8

7th cent. Patron saint of Cashel in Ireland. According to the — rather unreliable — account of his life, he was an Englishman who laboured in Ireland and afterwards evangelized Bavaria, went to Jerusalem and on his return died and was interred at Regensburg.

Albert (St) King Feb 24

Otherwise Ethelbert, q.v.

Albert of Trent (St) Bp. M. March 27

d. 1181 A bishop of Trent who fell a victim in the wars between the emperor Frederick Barbarossa and his vassals.

Albert of Montecorvino
(St) Bp. Apr 5

d. 1127 Of Norman origin, Albert settled with his parents at Montecorvino and became bishop there. In his old age, he lost his sight and was given a coadjutor who treated him with contempt and cruelty. The saint went through this trial with heroic patience.

Albert Thar-Ispan (Bl) May 9

d. 1492 Count of the Cumanian tribes in Hungary, he entered the Pauline order, in which he lived and died renowned for his austerities.

Albert of Bergamo (Bl)
Tert. OP. May 11

d. 1279 Also called "Albert the Farmer". He was a peasant farmer who helped the poor and destitute. For his generosity he was persecuted by his shrewish wife and jealous relatives. He was a native of Ogna near Bergamo, but later lived at Cremona and died there. He was a Dominican tertiary. Cult approved in 1748.

Albert of Bologna (Bl)
Ab. OSB. Vall. May 20

d. 1245 Born at Bologna, a member of the Parisi family. He became a monk at, and eventually abbot of a Vallumbrosan abbey near Bologna, which afterwards was called S. Alberto.

Albert of Csanad (St) Mk. May 28

d. c 1492 Hungarian Pauline monk. He was a Latin poet and orator. He died in the monastery at Bajcs. His body was reputed to remain incorrupt.

Albert (Aribert) of Como
(St) Bp. OSB. June 3

d. c 1092 A hermit at Rho, and afterwards monk and abbot of San Carpofero. He died bishop of Como.

Albert Quadrelli (St) Bp. July 4

d. 1179 Born at Rivolta d'Adda in the dio-

cese of Cremona, he was parish priest of his native town for twenty-five years and in 1168 was chosen bishop of Lodi.

Albert of Genoa (St) C.
OSB. Cist. July 8

d. 1239 Albert, or Lambert, was born at Genoa and was professed as a lay-brother of the Cistercian abbey of Sestri da Ponente, near that city. Eventually he lived as a hermit near the abbey.

Albert of Vallumbrosa
(Bl) Mk. OSB. Vall. Aug 1

d. 1094 A disciple of St John Gualbert, he was cellarer for forty years, and also claustral prior. His cult was approved with that of St Rudolph (q.v.) in 1602.

Albert of Trapani (St) C.
OC. Aug 7

d. 1306 A native of Trapani in Sicily, he entered very young the Carmelite monastery of his native town situated on Mt Trapani. After his ordination, he was stationed at the Carmelite house of Messina, where he devoted himself with marvellous success to the conversion of the Jews. Cult confirmed in 1454.

Albert (St) Ab. OSB. Sept 5

d. 1073 Abbot-founder of Butrio, in the diocese of Tortona.

Albert of Pontida (Bl)
Ab. OSB. Sept 5

d. 1095 (May 1) A soldier of Bergamo, who was severely wounded and vowed, if he were cured, to become a religious. He first went as a pilgrim to Compostella and afterwards founded the Benedictine abbey of Pontida, near Bergamo, dedicated to St James, and placed it under the obedience of St Hugh of Cluny. His relics were enshrined at Santa Maria Maggiore of Bergamo, and in 1928 were brought back to Pontida.

Albert of Jerusalem (St)
Bp. Sept 25

c 1149–1214 An Italian canon regular who became successively prior general of his institute, bishop of Bobbio, bishop of Vercelli, and in 1205, under Pope Innocent III, patriarch of Jerusalem. He is best known as co-founder of the Carmelite Friars, for whom, at the request of St Brocard, he wrote a rule. He was assassinated by an evil-liver whom he had rebuked.

Albert of Sassoferrato
(Bl) C. OSB. Oct 25

d. 1330 (Aug 7) A monk of Santa Croce di Tripozzo before the Camaldolese had taken possession of that house. Cult confirmed in 1837.

Albert the Great (St) Bp.
Dr. OP.   GC. Nov 15
c 1200–1280   A Swabian by descent, Albert was sent to the university of Padua where he joined the Dominicans. Appointed lector of theology, he taught at Cologne and Paris. Here St Thomas Aquinas was his disciple, and Albert was the first to recognize Thomas's genius and to foretell the future work of his pupil. Albert became provincial of his order in Germany and, in 1260, accepted under obedience the see of Regensburg. He resigned two years later and retired to Cologne, where he spent the rest of his life teaching and writing. Albert was the chief pioneer in the application of the Aristotelian system to theology. His printed works fill thirty-eight quarto volumes and deal with all branches of learning. For this reason he is called "the Great" and *"Doctor Universalis"*. He was beatified in 1622 and was equivalently canonized by being declared a Doctor of the Church in 1931.

Albert of Louvain (St)
Bp. M.   Nov 21
c 1166–1192   Born at Mont César in Louvain and chosen bishop of Liège in 1191. His election was opposed by the emperor Henry VI who favoured another candidate. St Albert appealed to Pope Celestine III, who decided in his favour, and Albert was ordained at Reims on Sept 29, 1192, but he was murdered by three German knights only two months afterwards (Nov 24). Cult confirmed in 1613.

Albert of Haigerloch (Bl)
Mk. OSB.   Nov 26
d. 1311   Of the family of the counts of Haigerloch in Hohenzollern. He was a monk of Oberaltaich in Bavaria from 1261 to 1311, where he sanctified himself in the offices of prior and parish priest.

Albert of Sassovivo (Bl)
Ab. OSB.   Dec 10
d. *p*.1102   A son of Count Walter (Gualterio), the benefactor who gave to St Mainardus the site to found the abbey of the Holy Cross at Sassovivo. Bl Albert became a monk there, and eventually third abbot of the monastery.

Albert (St) Bp.   Dec 13
Otherwise Autbert, q.v.

Albert of Gambron (St)
Ab. OSB.   Dec 29
7th cent.   A courtier who became a hermit and afterwards the abbot-founder of the small abbey of Gambron-sur-l'Authion, where the rules of St Benedict and St Columbanus were observed simultaneously.

Alberta (St) VM.   March 11
d. *c* 286   One of the first victims of the persecution under Diocletian. She suffered at Agen in company with St Faith and others of the same city.

Albertinus (St) C. OSB.   Aug 31
d. 1294   A monk of the monastery of the Holy Cross of Fonteavellana — head house of a Benedictine congregation which in 1570 was united with the Camaldolese. He was elected prior general of his congregation and succeeded in making peace between the bishop and the people of Gubbio. Cult confirmed by Pius VI.

Albeus (St) Bp.   Sept 12
Otherwise Ailbe, q.v.

Albina (St) VM.   Dec 16
d. 250   A young Christian maiden who suffered at Caesarea under Decius. The pre-1970 RM. mentioned Formiae, now Mola di Gaeta in the Campagna, as the place of her death, and her relics have certainly from time immemorial been enshrined at Gaeta near Naples. The Greeks maintain that her body was miraculously translated after martyrdom.

Albinus of Brixen (St) Bp.   Feb 5
See St Genuinus.

Albinus (Aubin) (St) Bp.   March 1
d. *c* 554   A native of Vannes. Monk and abbot of Tincillac, between Angers and Saumur, and then bishop of Angers (*c* 529–554). He took a prominent part in the third council of Orleans (538). The abbey of Saint-Aubin at Angers was erected in his memory. Saint-Aubin de Moeslain (Haute Marne) is to this day a popular place of pilgrimage.

Albinus (St) Bp. OSB.   Sept 5
Otherwise Alvitus, q.v.

Albinus (Aubin, Alpin)
(St) Bp.   Sept 15
d. *c* 390   The successor of St Justus in the see of Lyons between 381 and 390. He is said to have built the church of St Stephen and to have chosen it for his cathedral.

Albinus (Albuinus)
(St) Bp. OSB.   Oct 26
d. *p*.760   An Anglo-Saxon monk, whose native name was Witta, but who latinized it as Albinus when setting out as a fellow-worker with St Boniface in the conversion of Germany. In 741 he was ordained bishop of Buraburg in Hesse.

Alburga (St) WN. OSB. Dec 25
d. *c* 800 Sister to King Egbert of Wessex and wife of Wulstan of Wiltshire. She founded Wilton abbey, near Salisbury, whither she retired and took the veil in her widowhood.

**Alcmund (Alchmund)
(St) M.** March 19
d. *c* 800 Prince of the royal house of Northumbria, who after many years of exile among the Picts of Scotland met his death in Shropshire in circumstances which lead to his being venerated as a martyr, first at Lilleshall and then at Derby.

Alcmund (St) Bp. OSB. Sept 7
d. 781 The seventh bishop of Hexham.

Alcober (John) (Bl) OP. Dec 30
See John Alcober.

**Alcuin (Flaccus Albinus)
(Bl) Ab. OSB.** May 19
c 735–804 A native of York, who was educated at the monastic cathedral of that city and became a monk there. Eventually he was ordained deacon and appointed headmaster of his old school. He travelled to Italy to obtain the *pallium* for his bishop and at Parma met Charlemagne who forthwith enlisted his services in the cause of education. The monk became, in fact, the "Minister of Education" of the Frankish empire and founded and directed the school (*schola palatina*) where Charlemagne himself became a pupil. In his old age Alcuin was given, among others, the abbey of St Martin of Tours, where he presided as abbot and restored the monastic observance with the help of St Benedict of Aniane. He was a very prolific writer, chiefly on theology and liturgy. Many martyrologies list his name as *beatus*.

**Alda (Aldobrandesca)
(Bl) W. OSB. Hum.** Apr 26
1249–1309 A Sienese maiden who married a very pious husband and lived with him in conjugal continency. Upon the death of her husband Alda joined the third order of the Humiliati and devoted her life to almsdeeds and mortification. She is greatly honoured at Siena. Variants of her name are Aude, Blanca and Bruna.

Aldate (Eldate) (St) C. Feb 4
6th cent.? A Briton who lived in W. England and became celebrated for his patriotism in stirring up his fellow-countrymen to resist the heathen invaders of the land. In some legends he is given as bishop of Gloucester. Many churches bear his name as their titular saint, but trustworthy data of his life are lacking.

**Aldebrandus (Hilderbrand)
(St) Bp.** May 1
1119–1219 Born at Sorrivoli, diocese of Cesena, he became provost of Rimini, where he was known for his brave, outspoken stand against all licentiousness: once indeed he had to flee for his life on account of his frank preaching. In 1170 he became bishop of Fossombrone of which town he is now the principal patron saint.

Aldegund (St) V. Abs. OSB. Jan 30
630–684 Sister of St Waldetrudis, abbess of Mons. She became the foundress and first abbess of Maubeuge.

Aldemar (St) Ab. OSB. March 24
d. *c* 1080 Surnamed "the Wise". Born at Capua, he became a monk at Montecassino. He was sent as a director to St Laurence's nunnery at Capua; but he was so much talked about on account of his miracles that he was recalled to Montecassino. He founded the abbey of Bocchignano in the Abruzzi and several other houses which he ruled with much success. He was a great lover of animals.

**Aldericus (Aldric,
Audry) (St) Bp.** Jan 7
d. 856 Chaplain to the emperor Louis the Pious, and bishop of Le Mans (832). He excelled alike as a saintly prelate and as an able administrator of public affairs. Some of his works are still extant.

**Aldericus (Aldric, Audri)
(St) Bp. OSB.** Oct 10
790–841 Born in the Gatinais, he became a Benedictine at Ferrières. The archbishop of Sens attached him to the clergy of the archdiocese. Then he was summoned to the palace as "master and chancellor" (*magister et cancellarius*). Lastly he became archbishop of Sens (828). He was a zealous fosterer of ecclesiastical studies.

**Aldetrudis (Adeltrudis)
(St) V. Abs. OSB.** Feb 25
d. *c* 696 Daughter of SS Vincent Madelgarus and Waldetrudis, and a niece of St Aldegund of Maubeuge, she was confided to her aunt's care at this nunnery, of which she became second abbess.

**Aldhelm (Adhelm,
Aldelmus) (St) Bp. OSB.** May 25
639–709 A native of Wessex who became a monk at Malmesbury. He was educated partly at Malmesbury and partly under St Adrian at Canterbury. He was given charge of the school at Malmesbury and in 675 was made abbot. Lastly, in 705 he was named first bishop of Sherborne. Aldhelm was the first Anglo-

Saxon to attain distinction as a scholar and a Latin poet. None of his English poems are extant. His love of books is one of the most attractive traits of his character. He has been described as the first English librarian.

Aldo (Bl) OSB.   March 31
d. late 8th cent.   Count of Ostrevant, he became a monk at Hasnon abbey in Belgium, which had been founded by his brother John. Aldo was chosen second abbot.

Aleman   Sept 16
See Louis Allemand.

Alena (St) VM.   June 18
d. *c* 640   Born of pagan parents near Brussels, Alena was baptized without their knowledge. She was put to death while secretly journeying to a celebration of the eucharist.

Aleth (Bl) W.   Apr 4
d. 1105   Wife of Tecolin and mother of several saintly children, the most famous of whom is St Bernard of Clairvaux. In 1250 her relics were transferred to Clairvaux.

Alexander (St) Bp. M.   Jan 11
? A native of Fermo, near Ancona, who became bishop of his native city, and was martyred under Decius. His relics are enshrined in the cathedral.

Alexander Akimetes (St) Ab.   Jan 15
d. 430   A Greek who became a monk in Syria and eventually founded a *laura* by the Ephrates, where he soon had some four hundred monks under his rule. He was a somewhat restless archimandrite, fond of new places and faces. He is best known as the founder of the "sleepless" (*akoimetoi*) monks who sang the divine office in relays without intermission day and night. One of these houses he established at Constantinople.

Alexander (St) M.   Jan 30
3rd cent.   The pre-1970 RM. described him as a martyr under Decius "glorious for his venerable age". Some writers have identified him with St Alexander of Jerusalem (see March 18).

Alexander (St) M.   Feb 9
? A martyr of Rome who wa accompanied in his confession and death by thirty-eight others. On this same day the pre-1970 RM. mentioned another St Alexander, martyred at Soli in Cyprus together with St Ammonius. See Ammonius and Alexander.

Alexander of Lugo (Bl) M. OP.   Feb 10
d. 1645   A Spanish Dominican martyred by the Turks.

Alexander (St) M.   Feb 18
See Maximus, Claudius, etc.

Alexander of Adrumetum (St) M.   Feb 21
d. *c* 434   A martyr of the group Verulus, Secundinus, etc., q.v.

Alexander of Alexandria (St) Bp.   Feb 26
c 250–328   Patriarch of Alexandria, who, as such, convicted of heresy and condemned Arius, one of his own clergy, and on the other hand realized the great gifts of Athanasius, whom he made his deacon and favoured with his confidence. Both the patriarch and his deacon attended the council of Nicea (325) where Arius was again condemned. Alexander died shortly after his return to Alexandria.

Alexander, Abundius, Antigonus, and Fortunatus (SS) MM.   Feb 27
? A group of martyrs who suffered either in Rome (the pre-1970 RM.) or in Thessaly (according to the Ven. Bede), when and how is not known.

Alexander (St) M.   March 10
See Caius and Alexander.

Alexander and Theodore (SS) MM.   March 17
? Their names are mentioned both in the Hieronymian and in the Roman Martyrologies. It has been conjectured that they should be identified with SS Alexander and Theodulus, commemorated in the pre-1970 RM. on May 3.

Alexander of Jerusalem (St) Bp. M. March 18
d. 251   A fellow-student with Origen at Alexandria, he became bishop of his native city in Cappadocia and was imprisoned for the faith under Severus. On his release he journeyed to Jerusalem where he was made coadjutor to Narcissus, the bishop of the holy city — the first recorded example of an episcopal translation and coadjutorship. Here he received Origen, now an exile, and founded for him a library and a school. Alexander died in chains at Caesarea in Palestine under Decius.

Alexander (SS) MM.   March 24
Two martyrs of the same name included in the group Timolaus and Comp., q.v.

Alexander (St) M.   March 27
3rd cent.   A soldier, described in the pre-1970 RM. as having suffered as a Christian in Pannonia under Maximian Herculeus.

It seems that he should be identified with the anonymous martyr of Thrace of May 13.

Alexander (St) M.   March 28
See Priscus, Malchus and Alexander.

Alexander Rawlins (Bl)
Priest M.   Apr 7
d. 1595   A secular priest born in Gloucestershire (?) educated at Reims and ordained in 1590. He was captured while labouring in the York mission and martyred. Beatified in 1929.

Alexander and Comp.
(SS) MM.   Apr 24
d. 178   A Greek by birth and the friend and companion of St Epipodius of Lyons. He was arrested. Thirty-four others suffered at the same time.

Alexander, Eventius and
Theodulus (SS) MM.   May 3
d. c 113   Three Roman martyrs buried on the Via Nomentana. The pre-1970 RM. erroneously identifies the Alexander of this group with Pope St Alexander I. Cult confined to local calendars since 1969.

Alexander I (St) Pope   May 3
Pope from c 107 to c 113. See the preceding notice. See S. Quirinus (March 30).

Alexander and Antonina
(Antonia) V. (SS) MM.   May 3
d. 313   The *laus* of the pre-1970 RM. was as follows: "At Constantinople the birthday of the martyrs SS Alexander, the soldier, and Antonina, a virgin. In the persecution of Maximian she was condemend to the stews by Festus the Governor. But she was secretly delivered by Alexander, who changed garments with her and remained there in her place. She was afterward commanded to be tortured with him; and both were together cast into the flames, with their hands cut off, and were crowned after ending a mighty contest."

Alexander (Bl) Mk. OSB.
Cist.   May 3
c 1180–1229   Born in Scotland a descendant of Scottish kings, he entered as a lay-brother the Cistercian abbey of Foigny (*Fusciniacum*), diocese of Laon.

Alexander Vincioli (Bl)
Bp. OFM.   May 3
d. 1363   Born at Perugia, he joined the Franciscans. Pope John XXII chose him as his penitentiary and named him bishop of Nocera in Umbria. Bl Alexander died at Sassoferrato.

Alexander (St) M.   May 20
See Thalelaeus, Asterius, etc.

Alexander (St) M.   May 29
See Sisinius, Martyrius and Alexander.

Alexander (St) M.   June 2
See Photinus (Pothinus), Sanctius, etc.

Alexander (St) Bp.   June 4
8th cent.   A bishop of Verona, of whom nothing further is known.

Alexander (St) Bp. M.   June 6
d. 590   Bishop of Fiesole in Tuscany, a brave defender of the church against the kings of Lombardy. His opponents waylaid him and drowned him in the R. Reno, near Bologna.

Alexander of Noyon (St)
M.   June 6
See Amantius, Alexander, etc.

Alexander (St) M.   July 9
See Patermuthius, Copres and Alexander.

Alexander (St) M.   July 10
One of the Seven Brothers, q.v.

Alexander (St) M.   July 21
See Victor, Alexander, etc.

Alexander (St) M.   Aug 1
See Leontius, Attius, etc.

Alexander (St) Bp.   Aug 11
d. 270   Surnamed Carbonarius (charcoalburner) from the trade he was following when appointed bishop of Comana in Pontus on the recommendation of St Gregory Thaumaturgus. He was a philosopher who adopted this trade through humility. He was burnt at the stake.

Alexander (St) M.   Aug 26
? Patron of Bergamo, where a church has been dedicated to him from the fourth century. A later manuscript makes him a centurion of the Theban legion who escaped from prison but was retaken.

Alexander (St) Bp.   Aug 28
d. ?336   Patriach ? or bishop of Constantinople from 313 to 336, i.e. during the period of the struggle of the church against Arianism. He assisted at the first council of Nicea (325) and took a firm stand against Arius. Indeed, the pre-1970 RM. added "by the power of his (Alexander's) prayers Arius, condemned by the judgment of God, brake in the midst and his bowels poured out".

Alexander (St) M.   Sept 9
See Hyacinth, Alexander and Tiburtius.

Alexander (St) Bp. M.   Sept 21
2nd cent.   A bishop in the neighbourhood of

Rome. His miracles attracted the attention of the people and he was arrested and martyred on the Claudian Way, some twenty miles from Rome. St Damasus translated his relics and enshrined them in one of the Roman churches.

Alexander (St) M.   Sept 28
See Mark, Alphius, etc.

Alexander (St) M.   Oct 5
3rd cent. One of the "innumerable multitude" put to death at Trier by the prefect Rictiovarus during the persecution of Diocletian.

Alexander Sauli (St) Bp.
Barn.   Oct 11
1534–1593 A native of Milan who joined the Barnabites in 1550. Ordained priest, he became a zealous preacher and confessor and was for many years director of St Charles Borromeo. He was elected general of his congregation, and, in 1569, bishop of the Corsican diocese of Aleria which he completely reformed during his 20 years' rule. In 1592 Pope Gregory XIV commanded him to accept the transfer to Pavia, where he died the following year in the course of his first pastoral visitation. Beatified in 1741–1742 and canonized in 1904.

Alexander (St) M.   Oct 17
See Victor, Alexander and Marianus.

Alexander, Heraclius
and Comp. (SS) MM.   Oct 22
? Alexander, a bishop, made by his preaching such an impression on the multitude that many, both Jews and pagans, became Christians. He was arrested and tortured, and such was his constancy that Heraclius, one of the soldiers of the guard, was at once converted. Others followed his example. All were put to death together with St Alexander. Neither place nor year is recorded.

Alexander (St) M.   Nov 9
4th cent. A martyr of Salonica under Maximian Herculeus.

Alexander (St) M.   Nov 24
d. 361 A martyr at Corinth under Julian the Apostate.

Alexander Briant (St)
Priest M. SJ.   Dec 1
d. 1581 A secular priest, who was admitted into the Society of Jesus in prison, cruelly tortured to make him disclose the whereabouts of Father Parsons SJ and martyred at Tyburn together with SS Ralph Sherwin and Edmund Campion SJ for complicity in a fictitious plot. He was only twenty-five years of age. Beatified

in 1886. Canonized in 1970 as one of the Forty Martyrs of England and Wales, q.v.

Alexander (St) M.   Dec 12
See Epimachus.

Alexandra, Claudia, Euphrasia, Matrona, Juliana, Euphemia, Theodosia, Derphuta and a Sister of Derphuta (SS) MM. March 20
d. c 300 Christian women, natives of Amisus in Paphlagonia, burnt to death under Diocletian.

Alexandra (St) VM.   May 18
See Theodotus, Thecusa, etc.

Alexandria (Martyrs of)
The pre-1970 RM. makes mention of the following anonymous groups of martyrs put to death for Christ at Alexandria in Egypt:

                                        Jan 28
d. 356 A great number of Catholics were ordered to be put to death by an Arian officer while they were in church celebrating the holy sacrifice with St Athanasius. St Athanasius himself was able to escape.

                                        Feb 28
d. 260 The *laus* of the pre-1970 RM. concerning this group of martyrs read as follows: "At Alexandria...the commemoration of the holy priests, deacons, and many others who, in the time of the emperor Valerian, when a most deadly pestilence was raging, freely met their death whilst ministering to the sick; whom the religious faith of pious persons is wont to honour as martyrs."

                                        March 17
d. 390 During the reign of the emperor Theodosius, a heathen mob of worshippers of Serapis massacred a multitude of Christians who refused to join in the sacrifices to the pagan idol. Theodosius had the temple of Serapis destroyed and a Christian church built on its site.

                                        March 21
d. 342 The pre-1970 RM. read: "At Alexandria the commemoration of the holy martyrs who were slain on Good Friday under the emperor Constantius and Philagrius the Prefect, when the Arians and heathens rushed into the churches." St Athanasius who escaped from the tumult has left a description in his Second Apology.

                                        May 13
d. 372 A great number of Catholics of both

sexes were put to death or exiled from Alexandria when, for the fifth time, St Athanasius had been driven from his flock under the Arian emperor Valens. The pre-1970 RM. made special mention of those massacred in the church of Theonas.

Aug 10

c 257   The pre-1970 RM. had this *laus*: "At Alexandria the commemoration of the holy martyrs who in the persecution of Valerian, under Emilian the Governor, were long tormented with various and sharp tortures, and obtained the crown of martyrdom by divers kinds of deaths". St Dionysius of Alexandria has left a graphic account of them all.

Alexandrina di Letto (Bl)
Abs Poor Clare   Apr 3
1385-1458   Born at Sulmona, she joined the Poor Clares when fifteen years of age and after some twenty-three years founded a convent of her order at Foligno of which she became first abbess. Here she initiated a new Franciscan reform, which was blessed and encouraged by Pope Martin V.

Alexius Falconieri (St) C.   Feb 17
One of the Seven Holy Founders of the Servite Order, q.v.

Alexius (Bl) M. OP.   June 1
d. 1622   A Japanese catechist and novice of the Dominican missionaries in Japan. He was burnt alive on the day of the great martyrdom, Sept 10, at Nagasaki. Beatified in 1867.

Alexius Delgado (Bl) M. SJ.   July 15
1556-1570   A native of Elvas in Portugal, he became a Jesuit novice, and was only fourteen years old when he was killed by Calvinist French pirates near Palma on his way to the W. Indies with a group of Jesuits under the leadership of Bl. Ignatius de Azevedo, q.v. Beatified in 1854.

Alexius (Alexis) (St) C.
formerly July 17
d. early 5th cent.   A saint originally distinguished with the anonymous title of "the man of God", at a later period he was named Alexis or in Latin, Alexius. This was probably in confusion with a certain holy person, Mar Riscia of Edessa. The legend of his life came from the East and spread throughout the West in the tenth century, when the Greek monks were given the Benedictine abbey of St Boniface on the Aventine, which they renamed SS Boniface and Alexius. The *laus* of the pre-1970 RM. summed up the legend somewhat as follows: Alexius the son of a Roman senator, in order to serve God in humility, on his wedding day fled from his parental home

disguised as a beggar. He set sail for Edessa where after seventeen years an image of our Lady proclaimed him "the man of God". Alexius fled again and eventually returned to Rome and for years lived unrecognized as a beggar in his own home. After his death a mysterious voice again proclaimed him "the man of God". This attractive legend made St Alexius one of the most popular of "popular saints". However, only this seems certain: that Mar Riscia was a holy person in Edessa. All else is legend. Cult suppressed in 1969. In art he is shown holding a ladder, or supine beneath a staircase.

Alexius Nacamura (Bl)
M.   Nov 27
1619   A Japanese layman, born in Figen, of the royal family of Firando. Beheaded with ten companions at Nagasaki. Beatified in 1867.

Aleydis (St) V.   June 15
Otherwise Adelaide, q.v.

Alfanus (Alphanus) (St)
Bp. OSB.   Oct 9
d. 1085   A monk of Montecassino, who was made at Rome archbishop of Salerno in 1058. It was he who assisted Pope St Gregory VII on his deathbed.

Alferius, (Alpherius, Adalfericus) (St) Ab.
OSB.   Apr 12
930-1050   A Norman by origin, he was born at Salerno and belonged to the family of Pappacarbone. Sent as an ambassador to France, he fell ill at the abbey of Chiusa, and on his recovery betook himself to Cluny and was professed under St Odilo. The duke of Salerno asked for his return, and Alferius settled at Mt Fenestra, near Salerno, and there founded the abbey of La Cava, under the Cluniac observance. Soon the abbey counted its affiliated houses by hundreds and became a potent civilizing influence in S. Italy. Cult confirmed in 1893.

Alfonso
Note. This is the modern spelling of Alphonsus in Spanish, Portuguese and Italian; the French spell it Alphonse. The old Spanish spelling is Alonso, and the Portuguese Alonzo. All are derivatives of the original Spanish name Ildephonsus or Aldephonsus. See Alphonsus.

Alfred (St) Bp. OSB.   Aug 15
Otherwise Altfrid, q.v.

Alfred the Great (St)
King C.   Oct 26
849-899   King of Wessex. A patron of learn-

ing, he encouraged education especially of the clergy, and himself translated into English such works as the Dialogues of Gregory the Great and Boethius's Consolation of Philosophy. He also defeated the Danes, which ensured the growth of the church in England. His memory has been held in great veneration as the pattern of Christian kingship.

Alfreda (Elfreda, Ethelfreda) (St) V. OSB   Aug 2
Otherwise Etheldritha, q.v.

Alfrick (St) Bp. OSB.   Nov 16
d. 1005   Monk and abbot of Abingdon, and afterwards, successively, bishop of Wilton (990) and archbishop of Canterbury (995). He governed the church very ably in the critical times of the Danish invasion of Kent.

Alfwold (St) Bp. OSB.   March 26
d. 1058   A monk of Winchester who was chosen bishop of Sherborne in 1045. He was known for his great devotion to SS Cuthbert and Swithun, whose cult he propagated.

Algeric (St) Bp.   Dec 1
Otherwise Agericus, q.v.

Alice (St) V.   Feb 5
Otherwise Adelaide (or Adelhid), q.v.

Alice Rich (Bl) V.OSB.   Aug 24
c 1270   Sister of St Edmund, archbishop of Canterbury. She joined the Benedictine nuns of Catesby, and became their prioress.

Alipius (Alypius) (St) Bp.   Aug 15
d. c 430   Disciple and lifelong friend of St Augustine. They were baptized together at Milan on Easter Eve, 387. Upon their return to Africa they spent some time in solitude as religious. St Alipius then visited Palestine. About the year 393 he became bishop of Tagaste and was St Augustine's chief assistant in all his public work.

Aliprandus (or Leuprandus) (St) Ab. OSB.   July 24
8th cent.   An abbot of the monastery of St Augustine in Ciel d'Oro (*in coelo aureo*) at Pavia. He was related to the royal family of the Lombards.

Alix le Clerc (Bl) V.
Foundress   Jan 9
1576–1622   Born of noble parents in Lorraine, at first she led a frivolous life, but soon gave herself to God, under the guidance of St Peter Fourier. She founded under his direction the Congregation of Canonesses of St Augustine devoted to the teaching of poor children. A great mystic as well as an active

foundress, she was described by one of her spiritual daughters as "the child of silence". Beatified in 1947.

Alkeld (or Athilda) (St) V.   March 27
? 10th cent.   Two Yorkshire churches are dedicated to this saint, of whom nothing else is known, except that an ancient painting represents her being strangled by Danish pirates.

Alkmund (St) M.   March 19
Otherwise Alcmund, q.v.

Allan (Allen) (St) C.   Jan 12
Otherwise Elian, q.v.

Alleaume (Aleaume) (St) Ab.   Jan 30
The French form of Adelelmus, q.v.

Alloyne (St) C.   Oct 1
Otherwise Bavo, q.v.

Allucio (St) C.   Oct 23
d. 1134   Born in the diocese of Pescia in Tuscany, Allucio started life as a herdsman. Eventually his fellow citizens entrusted him with the direction of an almshouse at Val di Nievole, near Pescia, and he became in fact the second founder of that charity. He had some followers who were named the Brethren of St Allucio. Cult confirmed by Pius IX.

Allyre (St) Bp.   July 7
Otherwise Illidius, q.v.

Almachius (or Telemachus), St. HM.   Jan 1
d. 391   A hermit who came to Rome from the East, and publicly protested against the gladiatorial combats in the Roman amphitheatre. He was seized and cut to pieces by order of the prefect Alipius. As a consequence, the emperor Honorius is said to have abolished such spectacles. (Theodoret, *History of the Church* 5,26)

Almedha (Eled, Elevetha) (St) VM.   Aug 1
6th cent.   A descendant of King Brychan of Brecknock. The tradition is that she suffered martyrdom on a hill near Brecon.

Almirus (Almer, Almire) (St) Ab.   Sept 11
d. c 560   A native of Auvergne, he was educated at Menat, where he met SS Avitus and Carilefus. With them he went to Maine. After a short stay at Micy, St Almirus lived as a hermit at Gréez-sur-Roc, where he died.

Almus (Alme, or Alanus) (St) Ab. OSB. Cist.   June 28
d. 1270   Cistercian monk of Melrose who

became the first abbot of the Scottish monastery of Balmerino, founded in 1229 by Ermengardis, widow of William I of Scotland.

Alnoth (St) M. Nov 25

d. *c* 700   A cowherd attached to St Werburg's monastery at Weedon (Northants). Later he lived as a hermit at Stowe, near Bugbrooke. He was put to death by robbers and venerated as a martyr.

Alodia (St) VM. Oct 22

See Nunilo and Alodia.

Alonso or Alonzo

Otherwise Alphonsus, q.v.

Alorus (St) Bp. Oct 26

See Alanus and Alorus.

Aloysius, or Ludovicus

Note. These are two Latin forms of the French Louis, radically identical with Chlodovicus and Clovis. The modern languages have usually derived variants from both forms: thus in Italian: Luigi, Lodovic; in Spanish: Luis, Ludovico; in Portuguese: Luiz, Ludovico; in Catalan: Lluis, Ludovic; in German: Aloys, Ludwig; in English: Lewis (Aloysius), Ludovic.

Aloysius Rabata (Bl) C. OC. May 11

c 1430–1490   A Sicilian friar of the Carmelite monastery of Randazzo. He died from the effects of a blow on the head from an assailant whom he refused to bring to justice. Cult confirmed by Gregory XVI.

Aloysius Gonzaga (St) C. SJ. GC. June 21

1568–1591   Born in the castle of Castiglione in Lombardy, he served as a page at the courts of Tuscany, Mantua and Spain, and in his eighteenth year entered the Society of Jesus, after having overcome the opposition of his family. Within six years he fell sick while nursing the plague-stricken and died. He was beatified in 1605 and canonized in 1726. Benedict XIII declared him special protector of young students and Pius XI proclaimed him patron of Christian Youth. Over-sentimental biographies and cheap art have rather obscured his attractive personality.

Alpais (Bl) V. Nov 3

d. 1211   Born in the small village of Cudot, diocese of Sens, of a peasant family, she helped her parents in the fields until, still very young, she became bed-ridden with leprosy. It is said that for a long time her only food was the eucharist. Her patience and gentleness made a great impression on her contemporaries. Cult confirmed by Pius IX in 1874.

Alphaeus (St) C. May 26

1st cent.   Mentioned in Matt. 10:3 as the father of St James the Less. The Greek liturgy commemorates him on this day. The apocryphal books have embellished his life, but they deserve no credence.

Alphaeus and Zachaeus (SS) MM. Nov 17

d. 303   Alphaeus was a reader and exorcist at Caesarea in Palestine, and Zachaeus, his cousin, a deacon at Gadara beyond the Jordan. They were beheaded at Caesarea under Diocletian.

Alphage or Alphege (St) Bp. M. OSB. Apr 19

Alphege the Elder (St) Bp. OSB. March 12

d. 951   Also surnamed "the Bald", probably on account of his monastic tonsure. From being a monk he was made bishop of Winchester (935). He induced many to become monks, notably his young kinsman St Dunstan, whom he ordained priest. St Ethelwold too received the priesthood from St Alphege, on the same day as St Dunstan.

Alphege the Martyr (St) Bp. OSB. Apr 19

954–1012   A Benedictine of Deerhurst abbey in Gloucestershire, then abbot of a monastery near Bath, he was ordained bishop of Winchester in 984, and became archbishop of Canterbury in 1006. He was greatly loved by his flock, and during the Danish invasion of 1011 he was urged to escape. He declined, and was taken prisoner and put to death at Greenwich for refusing to ransom himself with the money of the poor. He was killed by being pelted with the bones of an ox at a wild banquet of the heathen. His relics were enshrined at St Paul's, and later on the north side of the high altar at Canterbury until the Reformation.

Alphanus (St) Bp. OSB. Oct 9

Otherwise Alfanus, q.v.

Alpherius (St) Ab. OSB. Apr 12

Otherwise Alferius, q.v.

Alphius, Philadelphus and Cyrinus (SS) MM. May 10

d. 251   Sicilian saints, said to have been brothers. They appear to have suffered under Decius. They are held in great veneration in Sicily (chiefly at Lentini, of which town they are patron saints) and also among the Greeks.

Alphius (St) M. Sept 28

See Mark, Alphius, etc.

Alphonsus Leziniana
(Bl) M. OP. Jan 22
d. 1745 A Spanish Dominican who was one of the companions of Bl Francis Gil in Tonkin, and was martyred with him.

Alphonsus of Astorga
(St) Bp. OSB. Jan 26
9th cent. A bishop of Astorga who retired and became a monk at the abbey of St Stephen de Ribas de Sil, in Spanish Galicia.

Alphonsus de Rojas (Bl)
C. OFM. March 21
d. 1617 Successively professor at Salamanca, tutor to a young duke, canon of Coria and a Franciscan friar. His feast at Coria is kept on March 26.

Alphonsus Navarrete
(Bl) M. OP. June 1
d. 1617 Born at Valladolid, he entered the Dominican order and worked first as a missionary in the Philippine Islands, whence, in 1611, he was sent to Japan where he was appointed provincial vicar. He converted, we are told, many thousands to Christianity. He was beheaded on the isle of Tacaxima. Beatified in 1867.

Alphonsus de Mena
(Bl) M. OP. June 1
d. 1622 (Sept 10) Born at Logroño, in Spain, he became a Friar Preacher at Salamanca. He was a nephew of Bl Peter Navarrete, whom he accompanied to Japan. Here he was burnt alive at Nagasaki with the group led by Bl Charles Spinola, SJ. Beatified in 1867.

Alphonsus de Vaena (Bl)
M. SJ. July 15
d. 1570 Born at Toledo, he entered the Society of Jesus as a coadjutor. He belonged to the band of Jesuit martyrs led by Bl Ignatius de Azevedo. Beatified in 1854.

Alphonsus Pacheco (Bl)
M. SJ. July 25
1550–1583 Born at Minayá in Catalonia, he joined the Jesuits in 1566 and was sent to Goa, where he was ordained priest. After a very laborious apostolate among the Goanese he was killed with Bl Rudoph Acquaviva at Salsette, near Goa. Beatified in 1893.

Alphonsus Mary Liguori
(St) Bp. Dr. Founder
CSSR. GC. Aug 1
1696–1787 Born near Naples of a distinguished family, he became a barrister, but soon abandoned this promising career and became a priest in 1726. He joined a society of priests engaged in catechizing the peasants of the country districts, and this led him to the foundation of the Congregation of the Most Holy Redeemer, which was approved in 1749. In 1762 an order of the pope forced the saint to accept the bishopric of Sant' Agata de' Goti, which he held until 1775, when he was compelled to resign through ill-health. He returned to live with the members of his own congregation. Throughout all these years he produced a steady output of ascetical, theological and historical works. Canonized in 1839, and declared Doctor in 1871.

Alphonsus de Orozco
(Bl) C. OSA Erem. Sept 19
1500–1591 Born at Oropesa in Castile, he studied at the university of Salamanca, where as an undergraduate he was drawn to the Augustinian hermits by the sermons of St Thomas of Villanueva. After his profession Bl Alponsus became preacher at the court of Philip II of Spain. He was a prolific writer and his works are reckoned among the classics of Spanish literature. Beatified in 1882.

Alphonsus Rodriguez
(St) C. SJ. Oct 30
1531–1617 Born at Segovia in Spain, he became a merchant and married, but lost his wife and children, and at the age of 44 was received into the Society of Jesus as coadjutor and sent to Palma in Majorca. From 1580 to 1604 he was doorkeeper of the college of Montesión. In this office he edified the whole island. A sonnet by G. M. Hopkins celebrates his humility. Beatified in 1825 and canonized in 1888.

Alpinian (St) C.
June 30
See Martial, Alpinian and Austriclinian.

Alrick (St) C.
June 30
12th cent. An English hermit associated with St Godric, who was with him at his death.

Altfrid (St) Bp. OSB.
Aug 15
d. 874 Monk and headmaster of the school at the abbey of Corvey in Saxony. In 851 he became bishop of Hildesheim. He was known throughout the Frankish empire as a fosterer of peace and goodwill, a champion of his Benedictine brethren, an upholder of the ecclesiastical canons, and devoted to our Lady.

Altheus (St) C.
Dec 26
Otherwise Tathai, q.v.

Althryda (Alfrida, Etheldrytha) (St) V. OSB.
Aug 2
Otherwise Etheldritha, q.v.

Altigianus and Hilarinus
(SS) MM. OSB.   Aug 23
d. 731   Two monks killed by the Saracens at
Saint-Seine, diocese of Langres, Côte d'Or.

Altinus (Attinus (St) Bp.
M.   Oct 19
1st or 4th cent.   An alleged disciple of our
Lord, founder of the churches of Orleans and
Chartres. Others state that he was a martyr of
the fourth century.

Altman (St or Bl) Bp.   Aug 8
c 1020–1091   Born in Westphalia, he studied
at Paris, became a canon regular, chaplain to
the emperor Henry III and finally bishop of
Passau in 1065. He upheld the authority of St
Gregory VII against Henry IV and was driven
from his see, but he continued to exercise
great influence throughout the Germanies. He
was buried at the Benedictine abbey of Göttweig in Austria, which he had founded. Cult
confirmed by Leo XIII.

Alto (St) Ab. OSB.   Feb 9
d. c 760   A monk, probably Irish, who cros-
sed over into Germany (c 743) and settled as a
hermit in a wood near Augsburg. King Pepin
made him a grant of that place, and there the
saint founded an abbey, since called Altomünster (Alto's monastery). St Boniface dedicated
its church in 750.

Aluinus (St) Bp. OSB.   Sept 5
Otherwise Alvitus, q.v.

Alvarez, Bartholomew
(Bl) M. SJ.   Jan 12
See Bartholomew Alvarez.

Alvarez, Emmanuel (Bl)
M. SJ.   July 15

Alvarez, Francis (Bl) M.
SJ.

Alvarez, Gaspar (Bl) M.
SJ.
Three Jesuit martyrs belonging to the group of
Bl Ignatius de Azevedo, q.v.

Alvaro (Alvarez)
of Cordoba (Bl) C. OP.   Feb 9
d. c 1430   He became a Dominican at Cor-
doba in 1368 and worked with great success
in Andalusia, France and Italy. He was chosen
by the queen-mother of Spain, Catherine,
daughter of John of Gaunt, as her adviser and
as tutor of her son John II. Bl Alvaro opposed
the Avignon pope, Peter de Luna. His priory
near Cordoba became a centre of learning and
piety. Cult confirmed in 1741.

Alvaro Garcia (Bl) M.   June 11
See Peter Rodriguez and Comp.

Alvitus (Avitus, Aluinus,
Albinus) (St) Bp. OSB.   Sept 5
d. c 1063   He was born in Spanish Galicia
and belonged to the family of Rudesind, the
great abbot-bishop of Mondoñedo. St Alvitus
became a Benedictine at Sahagún (Cluniac
observance) and in 1057 was appointed bishop
of León by King Ferdinand I. He transfered
the relics of St Isidore from Seville to León.

Alypius (St) C.   Nov 26
4th cent.   One of the early ascetics who lived
on top of a column for extended periods. In the
east Alypius is resorted to by barren women, in
the hope that his prayers will vouchsafe a
pregnancy. In art he is depicted as an old man
carrying a swaddled infant, often perched on a
pillar. His legend is identical with that of St
Stylianos, kept in the east on Nov 28 (q.v.).

Amabilis (St) V.   July 11
d. c 634   According to tradition she was a
daughter of an Anglo-Saxon king. She became
a nun of Saint-Amand at Rouen.

Amabilis (St) C.   Nov 1
d. 475   It seems that he was precentor of the
cathedral at Clermont and afterwards parish
priest of Tiom in Auvergne. He is invoked as a
protector against fire and snakes.

Amadeus of Clermont
(Bl) C. OSB. Cist.   Jan 14
d. c 1150   Lord of Hauterives (Drôme), he
left the world with sixteen of his vassals
(c 1119) and entered the Cistercian abbey of
Bonnevaux. Later he spent some time at Cluny
to attend to the education of his son Bl
Amadeus of Lausanne. He founded four
monasteries: Léoncel, Mazan, Montperoux
and Tamis. Returned to Bonnevaux where he
died.

Amadeus (Bl) Bp. OSB.
Cist.   Jan 28
c 1110–1159   Son of Bl Amadeus of Cler-
mont, he was educated at Cluny and afterwards
served in the court of the emperor Henry V. In
1125 he became a monk at Clairvaux under St
Bernard, by whom he was sent in 1139 to
govern as abbot the abbey of Hautecombe in
Savoy. In 1144 the pope put him under
obedience to accept the bishopric of Lausanne. During the last years of his life he was
also co-regent of Savoy and chancellor of
Burgundy. Cult approved by St Pius X.

Amadeus IX of Savoy
(Bl) C.   March 30
1435–1472   Born at Thonon, son of the
Duke of Savoy, he began to rule in 1455. He
suffered from epilepsy, but nevertheless governed in such a way as to endear himself to all

his subjects, until compelled to resign in favour of his wife. He was proclaimed a saint immediately after his death, but was beatified only in 1677. He was an ancestor of the royal house of Savoy, which chose him for its patron.

Amadeus of Portugal
(Bl) C. OFM.   Aug 10
See Amedus of Portugal.

Amador, Amadour
(*several*)
Otherwise Amator, q.v.

Amaethlu (Maethlu) (St)
C.   Dec 26
6th cent. A Welsh saint who has left his name to Llanfaethlu, a church founded by him in Anglesey.

Amandus of Elnon (St)
Bp.   Feb 6
c 675   Born near Nantes, he lived for fifteen years as a solitary at Bourges. At the age of thirty-three he journeyed to Rome and received from the pope his commission as a missionary bishop. As such he preached in Flanders, to the Slavs in Carinthia and the Basques in Navarre. He founded many monasteries in all these places, of which the best known is Elnon, near Tournai, where he retired in his old age and died a nonagenarian. In art he is represented carrying a church in his hand.

Amandus (St) Bp.   June 18
d. *c* 431   Successor of St Delphinus as bishop of Bordeaux (*c* 404). He is chiefly known from the works of St Paulinus of Nola, whom St Amandus converted and prepared for baptism.

Amandus and Anselm
(SS) Abbots OSB.   Nov 18
Amandus d. 708: Anselm later in the 8th cent.   St Amandus succeeded St Aigulphus as abbot of Lérins in 676 and ruled the monastery with a firm hand. St Anselm, another abbot of Lérins, lived later in the eighth century.

Amandus or Amantius
(Amatius)
Note. There are a number of other saints of this name, belonging to the fourth, fifth, sixth and seventh centuries, of whom only the bare fact of their existence is known. Among these, the following are likely identifications: (1) Amandus, abbot-founder of Moissac, d. 644, feast Feb 6. (2) Abbot-founder of Nantes, 7th cent., feast id. (3) Count of Grisalba, near Bergamo, d. Apr 6, 515, feast Apr 6. (4) Abbot-founder of Saint-Amand-de-Boixe, feast May 22. (5)

A Scottish hermit at Beaumont, diocese of Reims, 6th cent., feast June 16. (6) Abbot-founder of Saint-Amand de Coly (Dordogne), diocese of Limoges, 6th cent., feast June 25. (7) A hermit in a solitude at the meeting of the rivers Glanne and Vienne, diocese of Limoges, 5th cent., feast Oct 16. (8) The first bishop of Strasburg, d. 346, feast Oct 26. (9) A bishop of Worms, 4th cent., feast id. (10) A bishop of Rodez (otherwise Amantius) 4th cent. He was mentioned in the pre-1970 RM. on Nov 4. (11) A bishop of Avignon, id. (12) A bishop of Rennes, 4th cent., feast Nov 13.

Amantius (St) M.   Feb 10
See Zoticus, Irenaeus, etc.

Amantius (St) C.   March 19
See Landoald and Amantius.

Amantius (St) Bp.   Apr 8
d. 440   Successor of St Provinus in the see of Como. He is still held in veneration in his diocese.

Amantius, Alexander,
and Comp. (SS) MM.   June 6
? Said to have been four brothers, priests. Amantius is given as bishop of Noyon, who evangelized Cannes, diocese of Carcassonne, where he was martyred with the other three.

Amantius (St) M.   June 10
See Getulius, Cerealis, etc.

Amantius (St) C.   Sept 26
d. *c* 600   A priest of Città di Castello (*Tiphernum*) near Perugia, who was personally known to St Gregory the Great and held in veneration by the holy pontiff. He is the patron saint of Città di Castello.

Amarand (St) Bp. OSB.   Nov 7
d. *p.*700   Abbot of Moissac, who became bishop of Albi sometime between 689 and 722.

Amaranthus (St) M.   Nov 7
3rd cent.   A martyr venerated at Albi in S. France. The fact of his martyrdom is attested by St Gregory of Tours. Other data are lacking.

Amarinus (St) M. Ab.
OSB.   Jan 25
d. 676   Abbot of a monastery in the Vosges. Companion in martyrdom of St Praejectus (St Priest), bishop of Clermont. The valley of Saint-Amarian in Alsace is named after him.

Amasius (St) Bp.   Jan 23
d. 356   A Greek, driven from the East by the Arians, who became second bishop of Teano in 346. His cult is still flourishing in several dioceses of central Italy.

Amaswinthus (St) Ab. Dec 22
d. 982 Monk and abbot for forty-two years
of a monastery at Silva de Málaga in Andalusia.

Amata (St) V. Poor Clare Feb 20
d. *c* 1250 A niece of St Clare of Assisi,
healed by her aunt of a disease and thereby
converted to the life of the cloister. Her name
is in the Franciscan martyrologies.

Amata (Bl) V. OP. June 10
d. 1270 A Dominican nun of San Sisto in
Rome. A co-foundress of the convent of St
Agnes at Valle di Pietro, Bologna.

Amator (Amador) (St) C. March 27
? A Portuguese hermit, of the diocese of
Guarda, to whom several churches are dedicated in his country. He has often been
confused with St Amator of Rocamadour (see
below, Aug 20).

**Amator, Peter and Louis
(SS)** MM. Apr 30
d. 855 Amator was born at Martos, near
Cordoba, in which latter city he studied and
was ordained priest. He, together with a monk,
Peter by name, and a lay-man called Louis was
put to death by the Saracens for having
publicly confessed Christ.

**Amator (Amatre,
Amadour) (St)** Bp. May 1
d. 418 Bishop of Auxerre. He had been
married to a holy woman venerated locally as
St Martha. St Amator ordained as a priest his
successor St Germanus, who has left us the
biography of his predecssor.

**Amator (Amadour) (St)
C.** Aug 20
? An incorrupt body was found buried beneath the church of Our Lady at Rocamadour
in 1166, and thus originated "St Amadour".
Various identifications, including one with the
publican Zacchaeus, have been made, but
beyond a general agreement since the seventeenth century that he was a hermit of an
unknown date, no information can be given.

Amator (St) Bp. Nov 26
3rd cent. Bishop of Autun. There is nothing
further known for certain about him.

Amatus Ronconi (Bl)
Mk. OSB. May 8
d. 1292 Born near Rimini, after having four
times made the pilgrimage to Compostella he
became a lay-brother at the abbey of San
Giuliano near his native town.

Amatus (St) Bp. Aug 31
d. 1093 He was bishop of Nusco near
Naples. He has been claimed as a monk of

Montevergine, but the date of his death
renders this impossible.

**Amatus (Amat, Amé,
Aimé, Amado) (St)** Ab. OSB. Sept 13
c 567–630 Born at Grenoble, he entered as a
boy the abbey of St Maurice of Agaune in
Switzerland where he lived as a monk hermit
for over thirty years. St Eustace induced him to
migrate to Luxeuil. Here he turned the heart
of St Romaricus to God, and when this
nobleman founded the abbey of Habendum
(*Remiremont: Romarici mons*) in 620, under the
Benedictine rule, St Amatus was made its first
abbot. Here he lived until his death.

Amatus (St) Bp. OSB. Sept 13
d. 690 Abbot of Agaune, he became the
tenth bishop of Sion in Valais — *Sedunensis*,
not *Senonensis* (Sens). As a result of a false
accusation, he was banished to the abbey of
Péronne, and then to that of Breuil, diocese of
Arras, where he lived as one of the monks, and
where he died.

**Ambicus, Victor and
Julius (SS)** MM. Dec 3
4th cent. Christians martyred at Nicomedia
under Diocletian, whose imperial residence
was in that city.

Ambrose Fernandez (Bl)
M.SJ. March 14
1551–1620 Born at Sisto in Portugal, he
went to Japan to seek his fortune, which he
found in 1577 by entering the Society of Jesus
as a lay-brother. He died in the horrible
prison of Suzota (Omura) of apoplexy, aged
69. Beatified in 1867.

Ambrose (St) C. March 17
d. *c* 250 A rich nobleman of Alexandria,
who befriended and helped Origen financially.
He suffered imprisonment for the faith under
Maximinus, but was released and died a
confessor.

Ambrose Sansedoni (Bl)
C. OP. March 20
1220–1287 Born at Siena, he joined the
Dominicans in 1237 and was a fellow student
of St Thomas Aquinas under St Albert the
Great. He excelled as a preacher, and in the
performance of this office he travelled through
Germany, France and Italy. He was also
Master of the Sacred Palace. His death was
hastened by the vehemence of his preaching.
In art he is represented as holding in his hand a
model of his native city. Cult confirmed in
1622.

Ambrose Kibuka (St) M. June 3
d. 1886 Page to King Mwanga of Uganda;

he was baptized on Nov 17, 1885, and burnt alive the following year. See Charles Lwanga and Comps.

Ambrose Autpertus (St)
Ab. OSB.   July 19
d. *c* 778   Born in Gaul, he was Charlemagne's tutor at the court of Pepin the Short. He went to Italy as the king's envoy and visited the Benedictine abbey of St Vincent by the river Volturno, in the duchy of Benevento, and forthwith entered there as a monk. Eventually he became abbot. He was an able exegete and his works were considered as authoritative as those written by the greatest of the Latin Fathers. In fact, though not in title, he is one of the Doctors of the Church.

Ambrose (St) M.   Aug 16
d. *c* 303   A centurion put to death under Diocletian at Ferentino in central Italy. His *Acta* are preserved only in a MS. of the fourteenth century.

Ambrose Piccolomini and Patrick de' Patrizi
(BB) Mks OSB. Oliv.   Aug 21
d. ? 1347   With Bl Bernard Tolomei they were co-founders of Montoliveto Maggiore, near Siena. They are always called *Beati* by the Olivetans.

Ambrose (St) Bp.   Aug 28
d. *p.* 450   A bishop of Saintes, whose episcopate lasted for about fourteen years. He is mentioned in the life of his successor, St Vivian, and is honoured together with him in the diocese of La Rochelle.

Ambrose (St) Bp.   Sept 3
d. *c* 455   Bishop of Sens, of whom nothing else is known.

Ambrose Edward Barlow
(St) M. OSB.   Sept 11
d. 1641   Baptized a Catholic, he was educated a Protestant, but was reconverted to the faith and studied for the priesthood at Douai and Valladolid. In 1615 he was professed a monk at St Gregory's, Douai, now Downside; but he asked to be affiliated to the Spanish abbey of Celanova; and the community granted his petition. He was sent to the English mission in his native Lancashire, where he laboured for twenty-four years. Four times he was imprisoned and released, the fifth time he was executed at Lancaster. Beatified in 1929. Canonized in 1970 as one of the Forty Martyrs of England and Wales, q.v.

Ambrose (St) Bp.   Oct 16
d. *c* 752   The thirteenth bishop of Cahors. Eventually he resigned and lived as a recluse.

After a pilgrimage to Rome he died at Ernotrum (now Saint-Ambroise-sur-Arnon), in Berry.

Ambrose (St) Ab.   Nov 2
523 and 582   There were two abbots of this name of the abbey of Agaune, St Moritz, Switzerland. The former, who had formerly been abbot of Ste Barbe, near Lyons, is the one commemorated by the pre-1970 RM.; the latter died in 582.

Ambrose Traversari (Bl)
Ab. OSB. Cam.   Nov 20
1376–1439   Born at Portico, near Florence, he studied under the Greek humanist Chrysoloras at Venice, and became a typical Renaissance scholar. In 1400 he joined the Camaldolese at Santa Maria degli Angeli, at Florence; here he continued his studies, wrote much, chiefly in Greek, and collected a large library. He was the soul of the council of Florence for the reunion of the Greeks. In 1431 he became abbot-general. He was both a great churchman and a great scholar.

Ambrose (St) Bp. Dr.   GC. Dec 7
c 339–397   Born in Gaul, where his father, who belonged to the Roman nobility, was praetorian prefect. Still very young, Ambrose became a barrister at Rome and before his thirty-fifth year was appointed governor of Liguria and Aemilia with his headquarters at Milan. The whole province was rent by the Arian controversy. When in 374 the bishop of Milan died, Ambrose, as governor, went to the cathedral to ensure peace and order in the new election, with the result that he himself, though a catechumen, was elected by acclamation, after a child had been suddenly heard to cry out "Ambrose for bishop". Ambrose's objections were overruled and he was ordained on Dec 7, 374 (the day on which his feast is now kept). He proved to be one of the greatest and most beloved bishops of all time. He excelled as an administrator, as a writer, as a protector of the poor, as the "hammer of Arianism". He was prompt and outspoken in withstanding the tyranny of the emperors. His courage in reproving Theodosius the Great was a noble example of Christian heroism. He died on Good Friday, Apr 4, 397. He is one of the four great Latin Fathers and Doctors. His symbol is a scourge; or a beehive (to represent the sweetness of his eloquence).

Amé, Aimé (St)
Otherwise Amatus, q.v.

Amedeo (St) C.   Feb 17
One of the Seven Holy Founders of the Servite Order, q.v.

Amedeus IX (Bl) C. March 30
d. 1472 The third Duke of Savoy. His cult was authorized by Innocent XI.

Amedeus of Portugal (St) C. Aug 9
1420–1482 Of a noble Portuguese family, he became a Hieronymite, but later decided to become a Franciscan. After much opposition, he was allowed to enter as a lay-brother at Assisi. His life was quasi-eremetical, but later he was made a priest, and founded several houses "of the regular observance". Sixtus IV treated him with great honour. In 1568, his houses were united to those of the Franciscan observants.

Amelberga
Note. Variant forms of this name are: Amalberga, Amalburga, Amalia, Amelia.

Amelberga (St) V. OSB. July 10
d. *c* 772 She was a nun of Münsterbilsen in Flanders, receiving the veil from St Willibrord. Her relics were transferred to the abbey church of St Peter at Ghent in 1073.

Amelberga (St) W. OSB. July 10
d. 690 Born in Brabant, she was a niece, or sister, of Bl. Pepin of Landen. She was married to Count Witger and mother of SS Gudula, Emebert, and Reineldis. When Witger became a Benedictine monk at Lobbes, she joined the nunnery of Maubeuge under the same rule. Often confused with the preceding.

Amelberga (St) Abs. OSB. Nov 21
d. *p.*900 Abbess of Susteren. She educated in her convent two daughters of the king of Lorraine.

Amicus and Amelius (SS) MM. Oct 12
d. 773 French knights who took part in Charlemagne's campaign against the Lombards in Upper Italy, where they were killed, or fell in battle, and have been venerated as martyrs ever since at Mortara in Lombardy.

Amicus (St) Mk. OSB. Nov 2
d. *c* 1045 Born near Camerino, he became a secular priest, then a hermit and finally a monk of St Peter's at Fonteavellana, founded by St Dominic of Sora in 1025 (not that governed by St Peter Damian). St Peter's was at that time a daughter-house of Montecassino, and for this reason St Amicus is often called a monk of Montecassino, and was held in special veneration at that abbey.

Amicus (St) Ab. OSB. Nov 2
Early 11th cent. Abbot of Rambara.

Amidaeus (Amidei, Amadio) (St) C. OSM. Feb 17
One of the Seven Holy Founders of the Servite Order, q.v.

Ammia (St) Matron Aug 31
See Theodotus, Rufina and Ammia.

Ammianus (St) M. Sept 4
See Theodore, Oceanus, etc.

Ammon, Emilian, Lassa and Comp. (SS) MM. Feb 9
? A band of forty-four Christians martyred at Membressa in Africa.

Ammon and Comp. (SS) MM. Sept 1
d. *c* 322 Ammon, a deacon, was put to death under Licinius at Heraclea in Thrace, together with forty young women, his converts. The executioner killed St Ammon by placing a red-hot helmet on his head. Both the Greeks and the Latins commemorate their passion.

Ammon, Theophilus, Neoterius and Comp. (SS) MM. Sept 8
? These three, together with twenty-two more Christians, suffered at Alexandria. The Bollandists give the names of all, but no other data are known.

Ammon the Great (St) Ab. Oct 4
d. *c* 350 Of a wealthy Egyptian family, Ammon married, and for eighteen years he and his wife lived as brother and sister. Then by mutual agreement they embraced the religious life. Ammon retired to the Nitrian desert and eventually had under his charge from four to five thousand monks or hermits. In his later years Ammon ate only once every three or four days. He is one of the earliest and greatest hermit-monks. St Athanasius mentioned him in his life of St Antony.

Ammon, Zeno, Ptolemy, Ingen, and Theophilus (SS) MM. Dec 20
d. 249 The first four were soldiers. They, together with Theophilus, were present when a Christian on trial at Alexandria showed signs of wavering. They forthwith encouraged him and were beheaded on that account.

Ammonaria, Mercuria, Dionysia, and a second Ammonaria (SS) MM. Dec 12
c 250 A band of holy women of Alexandria martyred under Decius. Mercuria is described as an aged woman, Dionysia as the mother of many children and the two Ammonarias as young girls.

Ammonius (St) M.   Jan 18
See Moseus and Ammonius.

**Ammonius and Alexander
(SS)** MM.   Feb 9
? Two Christians martyred at Soli in Cyprus.

Ammonius (St) M.   Feb 12
See Modestus and Ammonius.

Ammonius (St) M.   Feb 14
See Dionysius and Ammonius.

Ammonius (St) M.   March 26
See Theodore, Irenaeus, etc.

Ammonius (St) M.   Nov 26
See Faustus, Didius, etc.

**Amnichad (Amnuchad)
(Bl)** H. OSB.   Jan 30
d. 1043   Born either in Ireland or in Scotland, he travelled to Germany and became first
a monk, and then a recluse, at Fulda.

Amo (Amon) (St) Bp.   Oct 23
4th cent.   Second known bishop of Toul, the
successor of St Mansuetus in that see.

Amoes (St) H.   Jan 17
See Achillas and Amoes.

Amor (Amour) (St) M.   Aug 9
? Venerated in the Franche-Comté together
with St Viator. Their relics are enshrined at
Saint-Amour, in Burgundy.

**Amor (Amator, Amour)
(St)** Ab. OSB.   Aug 17
8th cent.   Companion of St Pirmin in the
evangelization of Germany. Abbot-founder of
Amorbach in Franconia.

**Amor (Amour) of
Aquitaine (St)** H.   Oct 8
9th cent.   Born in Aquitaine, he lived as a
recluse at Maestricht. Eventually he founded
Münsterbilsen nunnery, in the diocese of
Liège. He has been wrongly identified with St
Amor, founder of Amorbach.

Amos (St) Prophet   March 31
8th cent B.C.   One of the earliest of the
minor prophets, a shepherd of Tekoa near
Bethlehem, who was a dresser of sycamore
trees. He savagely attacked social injustice and
warned of God's Judgement on "the Day of
the Lord".

Ampelius (St) M.   Feb 11
See Saturninus, Dativus, etc.

Ampelius (St) Bp.   July 7
d. c 672   Bishop of Milan during the Lombard period. He wielded a great influence for
good among the invading Lombards.

Ampelus and Gaius (SS)
MM.   Nov 20
d. c 302   They are presumed to have been
Sicilians, martyred at Messina under Diocletian. Actually nothing is known about them.

**Amphianus (Appian,
Apian) (St)** M.   Apr 2
d. c 305   A young Christian of Lycia, Asia
Minor, who entered the governor's house
when the latter was on the point of offering
sacrifices to idols and boldly reproached him
for his idolatry. He was forthwith arrested and
most cruelly tortured to death.

Amphibalus (St)   June 24
? The supposed fellow-martyr of St Alban of
Verulam. In the original *Acta* it is only said that
St Alban put on the priest's cloak (*amphibalus*)
and was arrested *instead* of the priest who had
taken refuge in his house — not *with* the priest.
Geoffrey of Monmouth took the word *amphib-
alus* to be the name of the priest.

Amphilochius (St) M.   March 27
See Philetus, Lydia, etc.

Amphilochius (St) Bp.   Nov 23
c 340–395   Fellow-student of St Basil under
Libanius, a successful lawyer at Constantinople, a hermit, and finally one of the group of
Cappadocian bishops, friends of St Basil,
appointed by the latter to counteract Arianism
in Cappadocia. Amphilochius was appointed
to the see of Iconium 373. He opposed the
Macedonian heretics, against whom he wrote
a work on the Holy Spirit highly commended
by St Jerome. He presided at the synod of Side
which condemned the Messalians, who asserted that prayer is the only means of salvation.
He was a cousin of St Gregory Nazianzen.

Amphion (St) Bp.   June 12
d. p.325   The pre-1970 RM. described him
as "an excellent confessor in the time of
Galerius Maximian". He was then bishop of
Epiphania in Cilicia. During the Arian
troubles he was elected by the Catholic party to
Nicomedia. Amphion was one of the "illustrious confessors" who attended the council
of Nicea. St Athanasius approved of his writings.

**Ampliatus, Urban and
Narcissus (SS)** MM.   Oct 31
1st cent.   St Paul mentions these three saints
in Romans 16:8 sqq: "Salute Ampliatus, most
beloved by me in the Lord. Salute Urban our
helper in Jesus Christ. Salute them that are of
Narcissus's household who are in the Lord".
Later, chiefly Greek traditions have made

Ampliatus a bishop, and all three disciples of our Lord and preachers of the gospel with St Andrew in the Balkan countries. The RM. added "they were slain by Jews and Gentiles". All we know for certain is contained in the extract from Romans above.

Amulwinus (Amolvinus)
(St) Ab. Bp. OSB.   Feb 7
d. *c* 750   He was an abbot-bishop (*chorepisc-opus*) of Lobbes, successor of St Erminus (d. 737).

Amunia (St) W. OSB.   March 11
d. *c* 1069   The mother of St Aurea (Oria), whom she joined in her widowhood as a recluse under the obedience of the abbot of San Millán de la Cogolla, in La Rioja, Spain.

Anacharius (Aunacharius, Aunachaire, Aunaire) (St) Bp.   Sept 25
d. 604   Born near Orleans and educated at the court of King Guntram of Burgundy, he became bishop of Auxerre in 561. He ordered the Litany of the Saints to be sung daily in the chief centres of population by rotation and enforced the recitation of the divine office in all churches of the diocese.

Anacletus (Anencletus)
(St) Pope
Identical to St Cletus q.v. Nothing definite is known about him. He is the traditional successor of St Linus as leader of the Roman church. Cult suppressed in 1969. His name is in the first eucharistic prayer.

Ananiah, Azariah and Mishael (SS)   Dec 16
7th cent B.C.   Named otherwise Shadrach, Meshach and Abednego, they were the three youths cast into the fiery furnace at the behest of Nebuchadnezzar. All that we know of them is in the Book of Daniel.

Ananias (St) M.   Jan 25
1st cent.   The disciple at Damascus who baptized St Paul (Acts 9), and who, according to tradition, evangelized Damascus, Eleutheropolis and other places, and was ultimately martyred.

Ananias and Comp. (SS)
MM.   Feb 25
d. *c* 298   A martyr-priest of Phoenicia under Diocletian. Thrown into prison, he converted his gaoler, Peter, and seven soldiers of the guard. All were put to death together.

Ananias (St) M.   Apr 21
See Simeon, Abdechalas, etc.

Ananias (St) M.   Dec 1
? A layman, martyred at Arbela, either the

Persian or the Assyrian (Erbel) town of that name.

Anastasia the Patrician
(St) VH.   March 10
6th cent.   Her life is counted as a pious legend, the first of many historiettes. She belonged to the nobility of Byzantium, and found favour in the eyes of the emperor Justinian, thus exciting the empress's jealousy. Anastasia escaped first to a nunnery near Alexandria, and after the empress's death, when the emperor instituted a search for her, she disguised herself in male attire and lived in Scythia as a monk-hermit for twenty-eight years. The Greeks keep her feast on March 10.

Anastasia (St) M.   Apr 15
See Basilissa and Anastasia.

Anastasia and Cyril (SS)
MM.   Oct 28
d. ? 253   All that we know concerning these two saints was given in the pre-1970 RM.: "At Rome, the passion of SS Anastasia the Elder, the Virgin, and Cyril, Martyrs. The former was bound with chains in Valerian's persecution under the Prefect Probus, tortured...her breasts cut off, her nails torn out, her teeth broken, her hands and feet cut off, and being beheaded...she passed to her Spouse; Cyril, who offered her water when she begged thereof, received martydom for his reward". The whole *passio* is a fictitious composition and it is doubtful that the saints ever existed.

Anastasia (St) M.   Dec 25
d. *c*? 304   Well known in the Middle Ages as her name was commemorated in the second mass of Christmas and her name occurs in the first eucharistic prayer. It was also in the litany before its revision in 1979. Little is known about her. According to legend she suffered at Sirmium in Dalmatia, her relics were translated to Constantinople and her cult spread to Rome under the influence of Byzantine officials who dwelt in the aristocratic quarters by the Forum where there is a basilica dedicated in her honour, the ancient *titulus Anastasiae*. The *Acta* of her martyrdom are worthless.

Anastasius (St) M.   Jan 6
4th cent.   A martyr at Syrmium, Pannonia.

Anastasius, Jucundus, Florus, Florianus, Peter, Ratites, Tatia, and Tilis
(SS) MM.   Jan 6
4th cent.   Martyred at Syrmium, Pannon-halma.

Anastasius (St) Bp.   Jan 7
d. 977   Archbishop of Sens from 968 to 977, he began the building of the cathedral, and greatly favoured the monks of Saint-Pierre-le-Vif, in whose church he was buried.

Anastasius (St) M.   Jan 9
See Julian, Basilissa, etc.

Anastasius (St) Ab. OSB.   Jan 11
d. c 570   A notary of the Roman church, who became monk and abbot of Suppentonia (Castel Sant' Elia), diocese of Nepi, near Mt Soracte. St Gregory the Great narrates that, at the summons of an angel, St Anastasius and his monks died in quick succession.

Anastasius the Persian
(St) M.   Jan 22
d. 628   Magundat had been a soldier in the army of Chosroes, the Persian king. Baptised as Anastasius, he became a monk at Jerusalem. He was arrested at Caesarea in Palestine, tortured and taken to the Persian king in Assyria, who ordered his execution. His head was brought to Rome and enshrined in a church dedicated to him and St Vincent, the Spanish martyr. Hence his wide-spread cult in the West in the Middle Ages. Since 1969 his cult is confined to local calendars only.

Anastasius (St) M.   March 20
d. c 797   The archimandrite (superior) of the *laura* of St Sabas, at Jerusalem. The *laura* (a cluster of hermitages) was attacked by robbers and all its monks massacred with the archimandrite at their head. The Greeks keep their feast on the anniversary of their death.

Anastasius the Sinaite
(St) C.   Apr 21
d. c 700   A Palestinian who eventually became abbot at Mt Sinai, hence his surname "the Sinaite". He took part in all the Christological controversies of his time, in Syria, in Egypt, and elsewhere. He has left ascetical and theological writings of considerable value, although we no longer possess unaltered texts, even of the "Hodegos" or Guide, his most famous work.

Anastasius I (St) Patriarch   Apr 21
d. 599   Often confused with his name-sake "the Sinaite". He was patriarch of Antioch and a resolute opponent of the imperial politico-theological rule. For this reason he was threatened with deposition by Justinian, and actually banished from his see after twenty-three years by Justin II. He was restored to Antioch by St Gregory the Great and the emperor Maurice.

Anastasius and Comp.
(SS) MM.   May 11
d. 251   Anastasius, a tribune in the army of the emperor Decius, was converted to Christianity on witnessing the courage of the martyrs whom in his capacity of tribune he was torturing to death. A few days after his conversion he was arrested and beheaded with all his family and servants. Their relics are venerated at Camerino in central Italy.

Anastasius (St) C.   May 11
? The patron saint of the city of Lérida in Spanish Catalonia. He is probably to be identified with one of the many *Anastasii* martyrs listed here, although the people of Lérida assert that their Anastasius was a native of that city.

Anastasius (St) Bp.   May 20
d. 610   Bishop of Brescia in Lombardy. He greatly contributed to the conversion of the Lombards from Arianism. St Charles Borromeo solemnly translated his relics in 1581.

Anastasius (St) Bp.   May 30
d. 680   A convert from Arianism, who became bishop of Pavia in Lombardy 668–680. He is commonly called Anastasius II, to distinguish him from one of his predecessors in the see.

Anastasius, Felix and
Digna (SS) MM. OSB.   June 14
d. 853   Anastasius was a deacon of the church of St Acisclus at Cordoba, who became a monk of the double abbey of Tábanos, near the same city. Felix was born at Alcalá (*Complutum*) of a Berber family, was professed a monk in Asturias but joined the community of Tábanos, being desirous of martyrdom. Digna belonged to the nunnery of the double abbey. The three were among the first to confess Christ at Cordoba, and were beheaded by order of the Caliph.

Anastasius (St) M.   June 29
See Marcellus and Anastasius.

Anastasius (SS) Cc.   Aug 13
See Maximus, Homologetes and Comp.

Anastasius (St) Bp.   Aug 14
11th cent.   Benedictine abbot (996–1006) of Pannonhalma in Hungary, and then second archbishop of Eszterzom and primate of Hungary.

Anastasius (St) Bp.   Aug 17
d. ? 553   Bishop of Terni at the time of the invasion of Totila. Said to have come from Syria and to have been a hermit near Perugia. The Bollandists state that there has been a confusion between a hermit martyr and a

bishop of Terni. St Anastasius the bishop did not find a place in the RM. until 1518.

Anastasius Cornicularius
(St) M.   Aug 21
d. 274   A military tribune (*cornicularius*, sub-officer) converted to Christ on beholding the courage of the young St Agapitus. This happened at Salone, twelve miles from Palestrina, near Rome. the pre-1970 RM., however, gave Salona in Dalmatia as the place of martyrdom. The story itself is a duplication of that of St Anastasius of Camerino (May 11) and, as regards its location in Dalmatia, of that of St Anastasius the Fuller (see below, Sept 7). All is very confused.

Anastasius the Fuller
(St) M.   Sept 7
d. 304   A fuller of Aquileia, not far from Venice. He crossed into Dalmatia and continued to ply his trade at Salona and to profess his religion openly, painting a conspicuous cross on his door. He was seized and drowned. He is now commonly identified with the Anastasius of August 21.

Anastasius, Placid,
Genesius and Comp. (SS)
MM.   Oct 11
? The pre-1970 RM. had this entry: "The passion of SS Anastasius, a priest, Placid, Genesius, and their companions". And this is all we know about them.

Anastasius of Cluny (St)
Mk. OSB.   Oct 16
c 1020–1085   A native of Venice and a man of considerable substance and learning, he became a monk of Mont-Saint-Michael in Normandy, but left the abbey, being dissatisfied with the abbot, who was accused of simony. In 1066 St Hugh of Cluny made his acquaintance and invited him to join Cluny. After about seven years Gregory VII ordered him to to go Spain to preach to the Moors. He did so, but after another seven years returned to Cluny; then he lived for a time as a recluse near Toulouse, recalled again to Cluny, he died on the way.

Anastasius II (St) Pope   ? Nov 19
d. 498   He was pope for only two years: 496–498. On account of his conciliatory attitude towards the Acacian schism of Constantinople he was maligned by the intransigents. As a result his memory remained under a cloud for centuries, and this led Dante to give the pontiff a place in Hell (Inferno, 9, 4). The pope's name is found with the title of Saint in many calendars on Sept 8.

Anastasius (St) M.   Dec 5
? The *laus* of the pre-1970 RM. was as follows: "The passion of St Anastasius the martyr, who in his ardent desire for matyrdom gave himself up, of his own accord, to the persecutors". Nothing else is known about him.

Anastasius (St) M.   Dec 19
See Cyriacus, Paulillus, etc.

Anastasius I (St) Pope   Dec 19
d. 401   The pre-1970 RM. had this *laus*: "At Rome, the death of Pope St Anastasius I, a man of extreme poverty and apostolic solicitude. St Jerome in his writings saith that Rome did not deserve to possess him for long..." This pope is given similar praises by SS Augustine and Paulinus of Nola. He stopped the spread of errors attributed to Origen by convening a synod in 400.

Anastasius II the Younger
(St) Patriarch, M.   Dec 21
d. 609   In 599 he succeeded St Anastasius I in the see of Antioch. During his episcopate there took place at Antioch a rising of the Syrian Jews against the tyranny of the emperor Phocas, and Anastasius was murdered by the mob and was looked on as a martyr.

Anathalon (St) Bp.   Sept 24
1st cent.   The oldest catalogues give him as the first bishop of Milan, sent there by St Barnabas whose disciple he was. As first bishop of Milan he evangelized the surrounding district, including Brescia, where he died.

Anatole Kiriggwajjo (St)
M.   June 3
d. 1886   He came from a tribe of herdsmen and was one of the young pages of King Mwanga of Uganda. Martyred together with several others. See Charles Lwanga and Comps.

Anatolia and Audax (SS)
MM.   July 9
d. *c* 250   There are two *legenda* connnected with these martyrs, who suffered under Decius. The martyrology of St Jerome makes Anatolia a Roman maiden, denounced with her sister Victoria, by their rejected lovers. They were confined to a prison near Rieti, where their miracles converted Audax, one of the guards. The pre-1970 RM., however, does not mention Victoria, and places the scene of the martyrdom at Thora, in the diocese of Rieti, not far from the small village now called Sant' Anatolia. Otherwise the two stories agree.

Anatolius (St) Bp.   Feb 3
9th cent.   A Scottish bishop who went as a

pilgrim to Rome and settled as a hermit at Salins in the Jura, where at a later date a church was built in his honour. Another completely different legend makes him a fourth century bishop of Galicia.

Anatolius (St) Bp. Feb 7
? A supposed bishop of Cahors whose relics were venerated at the abbey of Saint-Mihiel, diocese of Verdun. The whole account of his life bristles with inaccuracies.

Anatolius (St) M. March 20
See Photina, Joseph, etc.

Anatolius (St) Bp. July 3
d. *c* 282 Head of the Aristotelian school at Alexandria, his native city. He excelled as a philosopher and a mathematician. About the year 269 he was chosen bishop of Laodicea. St Jerome commends his works.

Anatolius (St) Bp. July 3
d. 458 Patriarch of Constantinople from 449 to 458. The Bollandists have vindicated his claims to sanctity. His feast is kept by the Byzantine Catholics.

Anatolius (St) M. Nov 20
See Eustace, Thespesius and Anatolius.

Ancina, Juvenal (Bl) Aug 31
See Juvenal Ancina.

Andéol (St) Bp. Oct 15
Otherwise Antiochus, q.v.

Andeolus (St) M. May 1
d. 208 A subdeacon of Smyrna sent to France by St Polycarp. He is said to have been martyred near Viviers on the Rhône.

Andochius, Thyrsus and Felix (SS) MM. Sept 24
2nd cent. Andochius, a priest, and Thyrsus, a deacon of Smyrna, sent to Gaul by St Polycarp. They established themselves at Autun where they converted their host, a rich merchant, by name Felix. All three were martyred together. Their cult was widespread throughout Gaul.

Andrew (St) ? Bp ? M. ? Jan 13
d. ? 235 The supposed twelfth bishop of Trier whom some chroniclers make also a martyr.

Andrew of Peschiera (Bl) C. OP. Jan 19
d. 1485 Called "the Apostle of the Valtellina". He was born at Peschiera on the southern shore of Lake Garda, diocese of Verona. At the age of fifteen he became a Friar Preacher at Brescia, studied at San Marco in Florence, and afterwards for forty-five years carried out a most successful apostolate in the Valtellina district on the borders of Switzerland and Italy.

Andrew of Segni (Bl) C. Feb 1
d. 1302 Born at Anagni of the noble family of Conti, he became a Franciscan and then a recluse in the Apennines. Troubled in life by demons, he became celebrated for his assistance to those who invoked his aid against them. Cult confirmed in 1724.

Andrew Corsini (St) Bp. OC. Feb 4
1302–1373 Born in Florence of the illustrious Corsini family. After wasting his early years in dissipation, he joined the Carmelites in 1318, and embarked on a life of the most austere penance. He studied in Paris and at Avignon, and was made prior at Florence. Bishop of Fiesole from 1360, he continued his extraordinary life of penance, was a father of the poor, and mediator between the quarrelsome Italian states of that time. He died on Jan 6. Since 1969 his cult has been confined to local or particular calendars.

Andrew of Elnon (Bl) Ab. OSB. Feb 6
d. *c* 690 Monk and disciple of St Amandus at Elnon, whom he succeeded as abbot. His relics were enshrined together with those of St Amandus in 694.

Andrew and Aponius (SS) MM. Feb 10
1st cent. Martyred at Bethlehem, it is said, during the persecution mentioned in Acts 12, in which St James the Great was put to death.

Andrew Conti (Bl) C. OFM. Feb 15
d. 1302 (Feb 1) Andrew of the counts of Segni, or Andrew of Anagni, as he is called from his birthplace, was a nephew of Pope Alexander IV. He became a Franciscan lay-brother and remained in that position although offered a cardinal's hat by Pope Boniface VIII. He was beatified in 1724.

Andrew of Florence (St) Bp. Feb 26
d. *c* 407 The successor — according to Gams, the predecessor — of St Zenobius in the see of Florence. Gams lists a second Andrew as a successor — with an interrogation mark.

Andrew of Strumi (Bl) Ab. OSB. Vall. March 10
d. 1097 Born at Parma, he was the disciple

and chief supporter of the deacon St Arialdo in the campaign against simony at Milan. After his master's martyrdom, Andrew became a Vallumbrosan monk, and was made abbot of San Fedele at Strumi on the Arno. He excelled as a peacemaker between Florence and Arezzo.

Andrew de' Gallerani
(Bl) C.   March 19
d. 1251 He was a distinguished Sienese soldier, who accidentally killed a man whom he had heard blaspheming. Exiled from Siena, he led a life of extraordinary penance and charity until he was allowed to return to his native city, where he founded the Brothers of Mercy, which lasted until 1308.

Andrew of Montereale
(Bl) C. OSA. Erem.   Apr 12
1397–1480 Born at Mascioni, diocese of Rieti, at the age of fourteen he became an Augustinian hermit at Montereale. Ordained priest, he preached and laboured for fifty years throughout Italy and France, disciplining himself by severe fasts. He was for a time provincial of his order in Umbria. Cult confirmed in 1764.

Andrew Hibernon (Bl)
C. OFM.   Apr 18
1534–1602 Born at Alcantarilla, near Murcia, in Spain, of noble but poor parents, he worked in order to help his sister financially, but was robbed of his savings and, disillusioned, joined the Conventual Franciscans as a lay-brother. In 1563 he passed over, at Elche, to the Alcantarine Reform. He converted many Moors by his frank simplicity. He died while helping to introduce the reform at Gandia. Beatified in 1791.

Andrew Fournet (St) C.   May 13
1752–1834 Born at Maillé, near Poitiers. After several false starts, he was ordained and appointed parish priest of his native town, which he served unremittingly, even at the risk of his life, during the French Revolution. In 1807 he, with Elizabeth des Anges, founded the congregation of the Daughters of the Cross for nursing and teaching. Beatified in 1926 and canonized in 1933.

Andrew (St) M.   May 15
See Peter, Andrew, etc.

Andrew Abellon (Bl)
COP.   May 15
1375–1450 A Dominican friar, prior of the royal monastery of St Mary Magdalen at Saint-Maximin, in France. Cult confirmed in 1902.

Andrew Bobola (St)
M. SJ.   May 16
1592–1657 (May 16) Called by the schismatics *Duszochwat* (robber of souls). He was a Pole, who joined the Society of Jesus at Vilna in 1611 and spent his whole life reconciling the Orthodox with the Holy See. For this reason he was cruelly tormented and partially flayed alive and finally put to death by a gang of Cossacks at Janov, near Pinsk. Beatified in 1853, canonized in 1938.

Andrew Franchi (Bl) Bp.
OP.   May 30
1335–1401 Of the family dei Franchi Boccagni. He was born at Pistoia, where he took the Dominican habit and eventually (1378) was chosen bishop. One year before his death he resigned and retired to his old friary. Cult confirmed in 1921.

Andrew Tocuan (Bl) M.   June 1
d. 1619 (Nov 18) A Japanese layman, born at Nagasaki, he was a member of the Confraternity of the Holy Rosary, and was burnt alive together with Bl Leonard Kimura because he had sheltered the missionaries. Beatified in 1867.

Andrew Tshochinda (Bl)
M.   June 1
d. 1617 (Oct 1) A Japanese layman and member of the Confraternity of the Holy Rosary. Martyred at Nagasaki for having given shelter to the Dominican missionaries. Beatified in 1867.

Andrew Caccioli (Bl)
C.OFM.   June 3
d. 1254 (or 1264) Born at Spello, near Assisi, he was ordained priest and was possessed of considerable wealth. He gave it all to charity and became one of the first seventy-two followers of St Francis. He favoured a strict interpretation of the Franciscan rule, against the innovations of Brother Elias, and was for this reason persecuted and imprisoned. He died at Spello, where he had founded a friary. Cult confirmed by Clement XII.

Andrew Kagwa (St) M.   June 3
d. 1886 A native of Uganda and royal bandmaster of King Mwanga. Baptized in 1881, he was condemned to death for the faith, and after his right arm had been severed from his body he was beheaded in 1886. See Charles Lwanga and Comps.

Andrew of Crete (St) Bp.   July 4
c 660–740 Surnamed also "of Jerusalem". He was born at Damascus, became a monk of Mar Saba and then of the Holy Sepulchre at

Jerusalem, a deacon of St Sophia at Constantinople, and finally archbishop of Gortyna in Crete. He excelled as a writer of homilies and panegyrics of saints; he is also considered to be the initiator of the *Kanon* of the Byzantine Liturgy: his Great Kanon contains 250 strophes.

Andrew Wouters (St) M.   July 9

d. 1572   One of the martyrs of Gorkum (see under Gorkum). He was a secular priest at Heinot near Dortrecht in Holland. He led a scandalous life, but when the Calvinists tried to compel him to renounce the Catholic faith, he expiated his past by a brave confession, was imprisoned at Briel with the other martyrs and hanged with them. Beatified in 1675, canonized in 1867.

Andrew of Rinn (Bl) M.   July 12

1459–1462   A boy, aged three, alleged to have been put to death by Jews out of hatred of Christ at Rinn, near Innsbruck. The facts are very doubtful. Benedict XIV allowed the continuation of the local *cultus* but refused to proceed to Andrew's canonization.

Andrew Nam-Thuong
(St) M.   July 15

c 1790–1855   A native catechist of Vietnam and mayor of his village. He died on the way to exile at Mi-Tho, Vietnam. Canonized in 1988.

Andrew Zorard (St) M.   July 17

d. *c* 1010   A hermit of Polish origin, he lived on Mount Zobar, in Hungary, near a Benedictine monastery, under whose influence he trained St Benedict of Szkalka (q.v.). His life was written by Bl Maur OSB. Canonized 1083.

Andrew the Tribune and
Comp. (SS) MM.   Aug 19

d. *c* 303   An officer in the army of Maximian Galerius, who took part in an expedition against the Persians. Accused with a number of his comrades of being a Christian, he and they were expelled from the army and took refuge in the Taurus mountains in Cilicia, but were tracked and put to death.

Andrew of Tuscany (St)
Ab. OSB.   Aug 22

d. *c* 880   An Irish or Scottish pilgrim to Rome, who settled at Fiesole and became the abbot-restorer of San Martino in Mensula. These seem to be the only trustworthy facts in his life, which has come down to us largely embellished with fiction.

Andrew (St) M.   Aug 29

See Hypatius and Andrew.

Andrew Dotti (Bl) C.
OSM.   Sept 3

1256–1315 (Aug 31)   Born at Borgo San Sepolcro, Italy, from being a military captain he followed St Philip Benizi into the Servite order and accompanied him on his preaching expeditions. He retired to the solitude of Montevecchio, where he died. Cult confirmed in 1806.

Andrew Kim (St) M.   GC. Sept 20

d. 1846   Of one of the noblest families of Korea, he was ordained at Macao, S. China, and returned to Korea as the first native priest, and was arrested almost immediately and put to death. Beatified with many others in 1925, and canonised in 1984 as leader of the Korean Martyrs q.v.

Andrew, John, Peter, and
Antony (SS) MM   Sept 23

d. *c* 900   According to the Greek Menology these saints were deported from Syracuse to Africa by the Saracens, at that time masters of Sicily. They were there subjected to savage tortures and put to death.

Andrew Chakichi
(Bl) M.   Oct 2

d. 1622   A Japanese boy, aged eight, son of BB. Louis and Lucy Chakichi and brother of Francis. He was beheaded with his mother and his brother Francis; their father was burnt at the stake. The four were beatified together in 1867.

Andrew the Calabyte
(St) M.   Oct 20

d. 766   A native of Crete, and a monk there, who went to Constantinople and openly denounced the emperor Constantine Copronymus for heresy on account of the latter's edict against the veneration of images. The emperor ordered the brave monk to be put to the torture and finally abandoned him to the mob, who led him through the streets in derision and stabbed him to death.

Andrew of Baudiment
(Bl) Ab. OSB. Cist.   Nov 10

d. 1142   A Cistercian monk of Pontigny, he became the abbot-founder of Chablis (*Caroli-loci*).

Andrew Avellino (St) C.
Theatine   Nov 10

1521–1608   Born near Naples and christened Lancelot. Ordained priest, he was at first an ecclesiastical lawyer and as such was entrusted with the reform of a certain nunnery, being nearly killed in the enterprise. He then joined the Theatine Clerks Regular and took the name of Andrew. He worked with great success, chiefly in Lombardy where he became a personal friend and advisor of St Charles Borromeo. He died at Naples in his eightieth year, at the foot of the altar. Beatified in 1624 and canonized in 1712. Cult confined to particular calendars since 1969.

Andrew Trong (St) M.   Nov 28

1817–1835 A native soldier of Vietnam attached to the Society of Foreign Missions of Paris. He was arrested with other Christians in 1834. His mother was present at his execution at Hué and received his falling head in her lap. Canonized in 1988.

Andrew (St) M.   Nov 28

See Stephen, Basil, etc.

Andrew the Apostle (St)
M.   GC. Nov 30

1st cent. A native of Bethsaida in Galilee, elder brother of St Peter and like him a fisherman. He was a disciple of St John the Baptist and the first to be called to Christ's apostleship. He is said to have evangelized Asia Minor and Greece and to have been crucified at Patras in Achaia. The *Acta* of his martyrdom seem to date from the fourth century. His alleged relics, stolen from Constantinople in 1210, rest now at Amalfi in S. Italy. St Andrew is the patron saint of Scotland, Russia and Greece; his name occurs in the first eucharistic prayer. His emblem in art is the traditional cross of his martyrdom — shaped like an X: sometimes he also holds a fish.

Andrew of Antioch (Bl)
C. OSA   Nov 30

1268–1348 A descendant of Robert Guiscard, he was born at Antioch of Norman parents. He joined the Canons Regular of the Holy Sepulchre at Jerusalem and was sent into Europe to collect funds for the Eastern houses of his order. In this quest he died at Annecy (March 27).

Andrew Dung Lac
(Bl) M.   Dec 21

1785–1839 A native priest of Vietnam. Arrested with St Peter Thi, both were beheaded on Dec 21. Canonized in 1988.

Andronicus and Junias
(SS) MM.   May 17

1st cent. Disciples of St Paul, who makes mention of them in Romans 16:7, "Salute Andronicus and Junias, my kinsmen and fellow-prisoners, who are of note among the Apostles, who also were in Christ before me". This is all we know about them. The Greeks celebrate their feast on May 17.

St Andrew, Nov 30

Andronicus and Athanasia
(SS) HH. Oct 9

5th cent. Husband and wife, citizens of Antioch in Syria, where the former was a silversmith or banker. On the death of their two children they agreed to separate and live as hermits in Egypt. Years later they met and occupied adjoining cells, Andronicus not recognizing his wife until after her death. They are particularly venerated in Egypt and Ethiopia.

Andronicus (St) M. Oct 11
See Tharacus, Probus and Andronicus, etc.

Anectus (St) M. March 10
See Condratus, Dionysius, etc.

Anectus (Anicetus) (St)
M. June 27

d. 303 Nothing really is known about him. Baronius, who wrote the *laus* for the pre-1970 RM., places him at Caesarea in Palestine under Diocletian, but remarks that the Greek *Acta* are very vague.

Anempodistus (St) M. Nov 2
See Acindynus, Pegasius, etc.

Anesius (St) M. March 31
See Theodulus, Anesius, etc.

Aneurin (or Gildas) and
Gwinoc (SS) CC. Oct 26

6th cent. Welsh monks, father and son. The latter has left some Celtic poems of a certain literary value.

Angadresima (Angadrisma,
Angadreme) (St) Abs. OSB. Oct 14

d. *c* 695 Cousin to St Lambert of Lyons, monk of Fontenelle. She herself received the veil at the hands of St Ouen. Eventually she became abbess of the Benedictine nunnery of Oröer-des-Vierges, near Beauvais.

Angela of Foligno (Bl) W.
Tert. OFM. Jan 4

c 1248–1309 Born at Foligno of good family, she led a worldly self-indulgent life in the married state, until her conversion when she became a Franciscan tertiary. After the death of her husband and children she gave herself up completely to God and to penance and became the leader of a large group of tertiaries, men and women. At the request of her confessor, Friar Arnold, she dictated to him an account of her visions and ecstasies in which she reveals herself as one of the greatest of mystics. Cult confirmed in 1693.

Angela de' Merici (St) V.
Foundress GC. Jan 27

1474–1540 (Jan 24) Born at Desenzano on Lake Garda, diocese of Verona, she devoted herself to the education of girls and the care of sick women. She was joined by several companions, and this led to the foundation of the Institute of St Ursula in 1535, the first specifically teaching order of women established in the church. Canonized in 1807.

Angelelmus (St or Bl) Bp.
OSB? July 7

d. 828 He is said to have been abbot of SS Gervase and Protase at Auxerre. He was bishop there from *c* 813 to 828.

Angelico (Bl) C. OP. Feb 18
1387–1455 His baptismal name was John. Born in the province of Mugello near Florence, he became a Dominican in 1407 at Fiesole. He resided for a time at San Marco in Florence, which he decorated with his wonderful paintings, and died at the Dominican friary of La Minerva at Rome. He is one of the best known and admired religious painters of all times. Beatified on the 3 Oct 1982 by Pope John Paul II, he was declared Patron of Artists in 1984.

Angelina of Marsciano
(Bl) W. Tert. OFM. July 15

1377–1435 Born at Montegiove in Umbria, she married in her fifteenth year and was left a widow at seventeen. She was inspired to found a convent of regular tertiaries of St Francis at Foligno. It was finished in 1397, and before her death there were a hundred and thirty-five such houses under her direction as superior general. Cult confirmed in 1825.

Angelus
Note. This is the Latin form of a name which is very common in Latin countries: Angelo in Italian; Ange in French; Angel in Spanish; Anjo in Portuguese.

Angelus of Furci (Bl) C.
OSA. Feb 6

1246–1327 Born at Furci in the Abruzzi, diocese of Chieti, he joined the Augustinians at an early age, studied in Paris where he became lector of theology, and on his return to Italy spent the rest of his life as professor of theology at Naples. Without giving up his teaching he became for a time provincial of his order and refused several bishoprics. Cult confirmed in 1888.

Angelus of Gualdo (Bl)
C. OSB. Cam. Feb 14

c 1265–1325 (Jan 25) A native of Gualdo, diocese of Nocera, on the borders of Umbria. In his youth he travelled barefoot from Italy to

Compostella. He was professed a Camaldolese lay-brother and for forty years lived as a hermit walled up in his cell. All his life he was distinguished for his extreme simplicity, innocence and gentleness. Cult confirmed in 1825.

Angelus of Borgo San Sepolcro (Bl) C.
OSA. Erem.   Feb 15
d. c 1306   A native of Borgo San Sepolcro in Umbria, and a scion of the family of Scarpetti. He entered the order of Augustinian friars and became a fellow-student of St Nicholas of Tolentino. It is said that Bl Angelus worked in England and founded several friaries there. He was famed as a wonder-worker: once, it was narrated, he asked pardon for a man condemned to death and was refused this request, but after the man's execution he raised him to life again. Cult approved in 1921.

Angelus Portasole (Bl)
Bp. OP.   Feb 22
c 1296–1334   A native of Perugia, he was elected bishop of Iglesias, in Sardinia, in 1330. He died at Ischia.

Angelus Carletti, of Chivasso (Bl) C. OFM.   Apr 12
d. 1495   Born at Chivasso, diocese of Ivrea, near Turin, he studied law at Bologna and practised at Monferrato. Elected a senator, he left all to become a Friar Minor at Genoa. In the order he filled important offices; preached among the Saracens and the Waldensians and against usurious money-lenders; wrote a book of "Moral Cases" (the *Summa Angelica*), and effected many conversions. Cult approved by Benedict XIV.

Angelus of Jerusalem
(St) M. OC.   May 5
1145–1220   Born in Jerusalem of convert Jewish parents. He was one of the early friar-hermits of Mt Carmel (1203). Commissioned to obtain the approval of Honorius III for the rule written by St Albert for the use of the new friars, he journeyed to Rome and shortly after went to preach in Sicily, where he was killed by a man whose crimes he had denounced.

Angelus of Massaccio
(Bl) M. OSB. Cam.   May 8
d. 1458   A Camaldolese monk of Santa Maria di Serra in the Marches of Ancona. He was put to death by the heretics, called Fraticelli or Bertolani, on account of his vehement preaching in defence of the Catholic faith.

Angelus Agostini Mazzinghi (Bl) C. OC.   Oct 30
1377–1438   Born at Florence, a member of the Agostini family, he was professed a Carmelite in his native city. After his ordination he was professor of theology, prior at Frascati and Florence, and provincial. He died in retirement, revered by all as a model religious. Cult approved in 1761.

Angelus of Acquapagana
(Bl) C. OSB. Cam.   Aug 19
1271–1313   He became a Camaldolese at Val di Castro and then lived as a hermit near Acquapagana, diocese of Camerino, under the authority of the Silvestrines. Cult confirmed in 1845.

Angelus of Foligno (Bl)
C. OSA. Erem.   Aug 27
1226–1312   Born at Foligno, at the age of twenty he became an Augustinian friar, and like Bl Angelus of Borgo San Sepolcro, he was linked in friendship with St Nicholas of Tolentino. He founded three houses of the order in Umbria. Cult confirmed in 1891.

Angelus Orsucci (Bl) M.
OP.   Sept 10
1573–1622   A native of Lucca, in Italy, he became a Dominican there and passed over to Valencia in Spain to finish his studies. Eventually he went to the missions of the order in the Philippine Islands and Japan. Here he was arrested and for four years languished in the horrible prison of Omura until he was burnt alive at Nagasaki. Beatified in 1867.

Angelus (St) M.   Oct 10
See Daniel, Samuel, etc.

Angelus of Acri (Bl) C.
OFM. Cap.   Oct 30
1669–1739   Born at Acri, diocese of Bisignano, in Calabria. Twice he attempted unsuccessfully to become a religious. The third time, after a tempestuous novitiate, he was professed as a Capuchin. His public life as a preacher was again quite unsuccessful in the beginning and "tempestuously successful" afterwards. Beatified in 1825.

Angelus Sinesius (Bl) Ab.
OSB.   Nov 27
d. c 1386   Born at Catania, he joined the Benedictines at the abbey of San Nicolo del' Arena and eventually was chosen abbot of San Martino della Scala at Palermo, whence he influenced all the Sicilian Benedictine abbeys in restoring monastic observance.

Angilbert (St) Ab. OSB.   Feb 18
c 740–814   Nicknamed "Homer" at the court of Charlemagne, because he was a fluent verse-writer. His early life was worldly, if not

dissipated. He excelled, however, as a minister and filled several important offices. As a reward Charlemagne gave him the abbey of St Riquier (*Centula*) and Angilbert became a model abbot. He introduced the continuous chanting of the office, using his three hundred monks and one hundred boys in relays, enriched the library and completed the buildings. He has always been venerated with a public cult.

Anglinus (St) Ab. OSB.   Oct 28
d. *c* 768   The tenth abbot of Stavelot-Malmédy, in the province of Liège, Belgium.

Angus of Keld (St)   March 11
Otherwise Aengus, q.v.

Anianus (St) Bp.   Apr 25
1st cent.   According to the Acts of St Mark and Eusebius, he was a disciple and immediate successor of St Mark in the see of Alexandria. He is said to have been a shoemaker.

Anianus (St) M.   Nov 10
See Demetrius, Anianus, etc.

Anianus (Aignan) (St)
Bp.   Nov 17
d. 453   Fifth bishop of Orleans. He is best known in history as the prelate who organized the defence of his episcopal city at the time of the invasion of the Huns under Attila and interviewed the latter on his approach to Orleans, thus saving the city.

Anianus (Agnan) (St) Bp.   Dec 7
5th cent.   Fifth bishop of Chartres. We know nothing else about him.

Anicetus (St) Pope   formerly Apr 17
d. 160   A Syrian by descent, he was Bishop of Rome from about 152 till 160. During this period St Polycarp of Smyrna visited Rome to settle with him the question of the date of Easter. Anicetus took a firm stand against the Gnostics. He was not a martyr, although deemed one for centuries. Cult suppressed in 1969.

**Anicetus, Photinus
(Photius) and Comp.
(SS)** MM.   Aug 12
c 305?   Martyrs of Nicomedia under Diocletian? Anicetus and Photinus were closely related by blood. They are only known through Acts of no historical value.

Aninus (St) H.   March 16
? A Syrian hermit famous for his austerities and his miracles; his date is uncertain.

Anna the Prophetess (St)
W.   Sept 1
All that is known of her is to be found in St

Luke's Gospel, 2:36–38. Her feast in some Eastern calendars is Feb 3rd.

**Annam (Vietnam)
(Martyrs of) (SS)** MM.   Nov 24
1798–1853 and 1736–1861   The two major beatifications of 1900 and 1909 comprise martyrs who suffered between these dates in Indo-China, most of them between 1833 and 1840 or between 1859 and 1861. There are sixty-four in the first group and twenty-eight in the second. Each receives a special notice in this book. See also Dominican Martyrs. Canonized in 1988.

Anne Line (St) M.   Feb 27
d. 1601   A gentlewoman, née Higham, born at Dunmow in Essex. A convert, she was hanged at Tyburn for harbouring priests. Beatified in 1929. Canonized in 1970 as one of the Forty Martyrs of England and Wales q.v.

**Anne of St Bartholomew
(Bl)** V. OCD.   June 7
1549–1626   Anne Garcia was born at Almendral, diocese of Avila, Spain, the daughter of poor shepherds. A shepherdess herself in her early years, she was the first to join St Teresa's reform at Avila as a lay-sister. Eventually she became St Teresa's secretary and companion in her foundations throughout Spain. In 1606 she was sent to establish the reform in France, was made a choir sister, and appointed prioress at Pontoise and Tours. She was the foundress of the convent at Antwerp, primarily intended for English refugees. She has left some delightful religious verse. Beatified in 1917.

Anne Mary Taigi (Bl)
Matron   June 9
1769–1837   Born at Siena, daughter of a druggist named Giannetti, whose business failed, she was brought to Rome and worked for a time as a domestic servant. In 1790 she married Dominic Taigi, a butler of the Chigi family in Rome, and lived the normal life of a married woman of the working class. In the discharge of these humble duties and in the bringing up of her seven children she attained a high degree of holiness. Endowed with the gift of prophecy, she read thoughts and described distant events. Her home became the rendezvous of cardinals and other dignitaries who sought her counsel. Beatified in 1920.

Anne Mary Javouhey (Bl)
V. Foundress   July 15
1779–1851   Her childhood took place dur-

St Anne, July 26

ing the years of the French Revolution and she was accustomed to hide persecuted priests, and to care for them. After the persecution she founded at Cabillon the Institute of St Joseph of Cluny, and seven years later, in 1812, moved it to Cluny. Fired with apostolic zeal she sent her nuns to work in far distant regions, and herself laboured for several years in French Guiana, with heroic courage. Beatified in 1950.

Anne Pelras and Anne Mary Thouret (BB.) VV. MM. OC.   July 17
See Carmelite Nuns of Compiègne.

Anne (St) VH.   July 23
c 840–918   Called also Susanna. A maiden of Constantinople who, while in her first youth, was left an orphan with a large fortune and was importuned to marry by unsuitable suitors. She refused, spent her money in the service of the poor, and finally lived half a century as a solitary on the Leucadian promontory of Epirus.

Anne (St) Mother of Our Lady.   GC. July 26
1st cent.   The Gospels do not mention the names of our Lady's parents. Tradition gives them as Joachim and Anne (Hannah — "Grace"). St Anne's *cultus* already appears in the sixth century in some of the Eastern liturgies and in the eighth in the West, but it did not become general till the fourteenth century was well advanced. St Anne is usually represented as teaching her little daughter to read the Bible, or greeting St Joachim, her husband, at the Golden Gate.

Anne Mary Erraux and Anne Joseph Leroux (BB.) VV. MM. OS. Ursulae.   Oct 23
See Ursuline Nuns.

Anne or Euphemianus (St) W. H.   Oct 29
d. 820   Born at Constantinople, a maiden of good family, she was married against her will but, after the death of her husband, under the name of Euphemianus and in male attire, became a monk at an abbey on Mt Olympus. Here she made rapid progress in virtue, and was asked to take charge of an abbey built by the patriarch of Constantinople. She declined, and died instead in a small out-of-the-way monastery. The Greeks keep her feast.

Annemundus (St) Bp.   AC. Sept 28
d. 657   Called in French either Annemond or Chamond, and by St Bede, in error, Dalphinus. He was archbishop of Lyons and friend and patron of the young St Wilfrid of York, to whom he gave shelter for three years in his diocese. St Wilfrid was present when Annemundus was murdered at Châlon-sur-Saône by order of Ebroin.

Anno (Hanno, Annon) (St) BP.   May 13
d. 780   A native of Verona, who became bishop there and is remembered chiefly in connection with the translation of the relics of SS Firmus and Rusticus.

Anno (Bl) Mk. OSB.   Sept 29
See Catholdus, Anno, etc.

Annon (St) Bp.   Dec 4
c 1010–1075   Son of a poor knight, he eventually became archbishop-elector of Cologne (1056) in spite of the hostility of his flock who thought him insufficiently well-born for their see. After a crowded career, full of political events, in which he took a great, and often leading, albeit not uniformly edifying part, he retired to the Benedictine abbey of Siegburg, which he had founded, and spent there the last twelve months of his life in rigorous penance.

Annobert (Alnobert) (St)
Bp. OSB.   May 16
d. *p.*689 Monk of Almenèches, who was
ordained bishop of Séez about the year 685.

Ansanus (St) M.   Dec 1
c 304 A scion of the Anician family of Rome
he became a Christian when twelve years old.
His own father accused him to the authorities,
but the boy contrived to escape, and converted
so many pagans, first at Bagnorea and then at
Siena, that he was called "the Baptizer". He
was at last arrested and beheaded.

Ansbald (St) Ab. OSB.   July 12
d. 886 Born in Luxemburg of the counts of
Querry, he became a monk of Prüm, and
afterwards abbot of Saint-Hubert in the Ardennes, and finally of Prüm in 860. In 882 his
abbey was burnt down by the Normans, and he
succeeded in restoring it with the help of
Charles the Fat.

Ansbert (St) Bp. OSB.   Feb 9
d. *c* 700 From being chancellor at the court
of Clotaire III he became a monk at Fontenelle
under St Wandrille. He was chosen the third
abbot and in 683 was made bishop of Rouen.
Pepin of Heristal banished him to the monastery of Hautmont on the Sambre, where he
died.

Ansegisus (St) Ab. OSB.   July 20
c 770–833 Monk of Fontenelle at eighteen,
he was soon chosen by Charlemagne to be the
restorer of several abbeys, and he ruled successively those of St Sixtus at Reims, St Meuge
near Châlons, St Germer at Flaix, Luxeuil and
Fontenelle. He excelled as a canonist, and
wrote a collection of capitularies, which
became the official law-book of the Empire.

Anselm (St) Ab. OSB.   March 3
d. 803 Brother-in-law of the Lombard
King Aistulph, and duke of Friuli, Anselm
became a monk and founded the abbey of
Fanano, near Modena, and a second at Nonantola. To both he attached sundry hospitals
and hostels. Aistulph's successor, King Desiderius, banished him to Montecassino, but
after seven years he was restored to Nonantola
by Charlemagne.

Anselm of Lucca (St) Bp.
OSB.   March 18
1036–1086 Born at Mantua. His uncle Pope
Alexander II nominated him bishop of Lucca;
but Anselm refused to accept investiture from
the emperor Henry IV. Later, counselled by
Gregory VII, he accepted investiture, took
possession of his see and then had scruples
and withdrew to the Cluniac abbey of Polizone
where he was professed as a Benedictine.

St Anselm, Apr 21

Gregory VII recalled him to Lucca and the
saint obeyed. He tried to reform the canons,
who raised a revolt, and Anselm again withdrew. A man of great learning, he excelled as a
canonist. He was Gregory VII's staunch supporter. Before his death at Mantua he became
apostolic legate in Lombardy.

Anselm (St) Abp. Dr.
OSB.   GC. Apr 21
c 1033–1109 Born at Aosta in Piedmont, he
became a Benedictine at Bec in Normandy
under Bl Herluin. He became abbot at Bec
and succeeded Lanfranc in the see of Canterbury in 1093. For his resistance to King
William Rufus's encroachments on ecclesiastical rights he was exiled to the Continent. In
1098 he was present at the council of Bari,
and, at the pope's request, resolved the theological doubts of the Italo-Greek bishops. On
Rufus's death Anselm returned to Canterbury, at the invitation of the new king Henry I,
whom, however, he had also to oppose on the
question of investitures. Hence a second exile,

terminating in a triumphal return (1106). In spite of his somewhat stormy career, Anselm was one of the gentlest of saints. He stands out also in church history as the link between St Augustine of Hippo and St Thomas Aquinas. He was officially declared a Doctor of the Church in 1720. Several of his philosophical and spiritual works are still important. His life was written by his own secretary, the monk Eadmer of Christ Church, Canterbury. In art he is shown as an archbishop or a Benedictine monk, admonishing an evildoer; or with our Lady appearing to him; or with a ship.

Anselm (St) Ab. OSB.   Nov 18
c 750   Abbot of Lérins. Mentioned in most menologies together with St Amandus of Lérins.

Ansfridus (St) Bp. OSB.   May 3
d. 1010   Count of Brabant and a knight in the service of the emperors Otto III and Henry II. In 992 he built the convent of Thorn for his daughter and wife, being himself desirous of becoming a monk. He was appointed instead archbishop of Utrecht. As such, he founded the Benedictine abbey of Hohorst (Heiligenberg) and, when stricken with blindness, he retired there and realized his ambition of taking monastic vows. There too he ended his days.

Ansgar (St) Bp. OSB.   Feb 3
Otherwise Anschar q.v.

Ansgar, (Anschar, Scharies) (St) Bp. OSB.   GC. Feb 3
801–865   Born near Amiens, he was received as a boy by the Benedictines of Old Corbie in Picardy, and educated there under St Adelard as abbot and St Paschasius Radbert as headmaster. After his monastic profession he was transferred to New Corbie in Saxony, whence he was taken by King Harold of Denmark to evangelize the heathen Danes. For thirteen years he worked there as first archbishop of Hamburg and legate of the Holy See; his mission extended to Sweden, Norway and N. Germany. The success achieved by his personal efforts was unfortunately not lasting and most of those northern churches relapsed into paganism.

Ansilio (St) Mk. OSB.   Oct 11
d. late 7th cent.   A monk whose relics were enshrined at the Benedictine abbey of Lagny, diocese of Meaux.

Ansovinus (St) Bp.   March 13
d. 840   A native of Camerino in Italy, who from being a hermit at Castel Raimondo, near Torcello, was ordained bishop of his native town. He accepted the office on condition that his see should be exempt from the service of recruiting soldiers, then imposed upon most bishops in their capacity of feudal lords.

Anstrudis (Austrude, Austru) (St) V. OSB.   Oct 17
d. 688   Daughter of SS Blandinus and Salaberga, the founders of the nunnery of St John the Baptist at Laon. Mother and daughter were successively the first two abbesses. She had to suffer much at the hands of Ebroin, the mayor of the palace and oppressor of all the saints of that period.

Ansuerus and Comp. (SS) MM. OSB.   July 17
d. *p.*1066   He belonged to the nobility of Schleswig and was a monk and abbot of the Benedictine monastery of St Georgenberg, near Ratzeburg in Denmark, whence he and his monks evangelized that country. Ansuerus and twenty-eight of his community were stoned to death in the anti-christian reaction which took place among the Wends after the emperor Henry III's death.

Ansurius (Aduri, Asurius, Isauri) (St) Bp. OSB.   Jan 26
d. 925   He was bishop of Orense in Spanish Galicia and helped in the foundation of the Benedictine abbey of Ribas de Sil. He was elected to the see in 915, and in 922 he resigned and became a monk at the above-mentioned monastery. After his death he was venerated there, together with seven other bishops who had followed his example.

Anthelmus (St) Bp. O. Cart.   June 26
1105–1178   A Savoyard nobleman who, ordained priest early in life, went on a chance visit to the charterhouse of Portes and stayed there as a monk. In 1169 he was chosen prior of the Grande Chartreuse, and it is owing to his efforts that the Carthusians, from being more or less a branch of Benedictine Monachism, became definitely a new religious order. In 1163 he accepted the bishopric of Belley under obedience to the pope, and so much did he endear himself to the people that, after his death, the city was called for a time Anthelmopolis. He was sent to England to try to bring about a reconciliation between King Henry II and St Thomas Becket. To the end of his life his heart was in his beloved charterhouse which he revisited on every possible occasion.

Antheros (St) Pope.   Jan 3
d. 236   A Greek who was pope only a few weeks. It is not certain whether he died a martyr, as his name is not mentioned in the

Depositio Martyrum. He was buried in the catacomb of St Callistus, the first pope to be so. Parts of his funerary inscription still exist.

Anthes (St) M.   Aug 28
See Fortunatus, Caius, and Anthes.

Anthia (St) M.   Apr 18
See Eleutherius and Anthia.

Anthimus (St) Bp. M.   Apr 27
d. 303   Bishop of Nicomedia, where he was beheaded for the faith under Diocletian. His death was followed by a wholesale slaughter of the Christian communities of the district.

Anthimus (St) M.   May 11
d. 303   A priest of Rome, who is said to have converted the pagan husband, a prefect, of the Christian matron Lucina, well known for her charity to her imprisoned fellow-Christians. The martyr, thrown into the Tiber but miraculously rescued by an angel, was afterwards recaptured and beheaded.

Anthimus (St) M.   Sept 27
d. *c* 303   Mentioned in the legendary *Acta* as a companion martyr of SS Cosmas and Damian, q.v.

Antholian (Anatolianus) (St) M.   Feb 6
c 265   Mentioned by St Gregory of Tours as one of the martyrs of Auvergne under Valerian and Gallienus. Fellow-sufferers were SS Cassius, Maximus, Liminius and Victorinus.

Antholin (St) Ab.   Jan 17
Otherwise Antony, q.v.

Anthonius (St) M.   May 11
Otherwise Anthimus, q.v.

Anthony
Note. From the Greek Anthonios and the Latin Anthonius or Antonius. The usual modern forms are: in Italian and Portuguese: Antonio; in Spanish: Antonio or Anton; in Catalan: Antoni; in French: Antoine; in German: Anton; in English: Antony, q.v.

Anthusa (St) V.   July 27
8th cent.   First a recluse, and then abbess of a nunnery near Constantinople. Known for her open veneration of the images of saints. For this reason she had to appear before the emperor Constantine Copronymus, by whose orders she was put to the torture. The empress, however, befriended Anthusa, who lived to an advanced age.

Anthusa the Elder (St) M.   Aug 22
See Athanasius, Anthusa, etc.

Anthusa (St) VM.   Aug 27
? Called St Anthusa the Younger, to distinguish her from St Anthusa of Seleucia (Aug 22). She was probably a Persian and suffered in that country. She is said to have been sewn up in a sack and drowned in a well.

Antidius (Antel, Antible, Tude) (St) Bp. M.   June 17
d. *c* 265   Disciple and successor of St Froninus in the see of Besançon. He was put to death by a horde of Vandals at a place called Ruffey.

Antigonus (St) M.   Feb 27
See Alexander, Abundius, etc.

Antimus (St) Ab. OSB.   Jan 28
8th cent.   He was, it seems, one of the first abbots of Brantôme, an abbey founded by Charlemagne in 769 and destroyed by the Normans in 817.

Antinogenes (St) M.   July 24
See Victor, Stercatius and Antinogenes.

Antioch in Syria (Martyrs of) (SS)
The following anonymous groups of martyrs put to death at Antioch in Syria were given in the pre-1970 RM.:

                                         March 11
c 300   "Many holy martyrs...under Maximian set upon red hot gridirons and condemned not to death but continued torture," while others were afflicted with other cruel torments.

                                         Nov 6
d. 637   "Ten holy martyrs, who are said to have suffered at the hands of the Saracens," i.e., after their seizure of Antioch. Some records put their number at forty or more.

                                         Dec 24
d. 250   Forty Christian maidens put to death under Decius.

Antiochus (St) M.   May 21
See Nicostratus, Antiochus and Comp.

Antiochus and Cyriacus (SS) MM.   July 15
3rd cent.   The pre-1970 RM. had this *laus*: "At Sebaste the passion of St Antiochus the physician who was beheaded under the governor Hadrian; and when milk flowed forth from the severed head in place of blood, Cyriacus, the executioner, was converted to Christ, and himself also suffered martyrdom."

Antiochus (Andeol) (St) Bp.   Oct 15
5th cent.   When St Justus, bishop of Lyons,

joined the solitaries in Egypt, the priest Antiochus was sent to seek him out and induce him
to return to his see. The priest's efforts were in
vain, and on his own return to Lyons he was
himself chosen bishop.

Antiochus (St) M.   Dec 13
d. *c* 110   A martyr of Solta (*Sulci*), a small
island near Sardinia, under the emperor Hadrian. The island is now also known as the *Isola
di Sant' Antioco.*

Antipas (St) M.   Apr 11
d. *c* 90   The martyr referred to in Rev 2:13
as a "faithful witness" put to death at Pergamum. Details of his martyrdom are not reliable, and it is very unlikely that he was bishop
of Pergamum, as his legend states. All we
really know is given in Revelations.

Antoninette
French diminutive form of the names Antonia,
Antonina, q.v.

Antoinette Roussel (Bl)
V. OCD.   July 17
See Carmelite Nuns of Compiègne.

Antonia of Florence (Bl)
W. OFM.   Feb 28
1400–1472   Born in Florence, she was left a
widow in early life and joined the Franciscan
tertiaries. Chosen superioress at Aquila, she
adopted the original rule of the Poor Clares.
She contracted a painful disease, which afflicted her for fifteen years, but this and other
trials she bore bravely under the guidance of St
John Capistran. Cult confirmed in 1847.

Antonia (St)
VM.   Apr 29
See Agapius and Comp.

Antonia of Brescia (Bl)
V. OP.   Oct 27
1407–1507   Having entered as a young girl at
the Dominican convent of Brescia, she was, at
the age of sixty-six, chosen prioress of St
Catherine's Convent at Ferrara, which she
ruled justly but rigorously. She was deposed
and underwent other trials, always with much
patience and humility.

Antonina (St) VM.   May 3
See Alexander and Antonina.

Antoninus of Sorrento
(St) Ab. OSB.   Feb 14
d. 830   A Benedictine monk in one of the
daughter houses of Montecassino. Forced to
leave his monastery by the wars raging in the
country, he became a hermit, until he was
invited by the people of Sorrento to live among
them. He did so as abbot of St Agrippinus. He

is now venerated as the patron saint of the
town.

Antoninus (St) M.   Apr 20
See Victor, Zoticus, etc.

Antoninus (St)
Bp. OP.   May 10
1389–1459 (May 2)   A Florentine of the
Pierozzi family, he joined the Friars Preachers
at Fiesole, and while still very young was made
prior of the Minerva at Rome. In 1436 he
founded San Marco at Florence, and in 1446
he was against his will appointed archbishop of
that city. He was the "people's prelate" and
"the protector of the poor". He also distinguished himself as a writer on moral theology
and international law. Canonized in 1523.
Cult confined to local calendars since 1969.

Antoninus (St) M.   July 6
See Lucy, Antoninus, etc.

Antoninus (St) M.   July 29
See Lucilla, Flora, etc.

Antoninus (St) M.   Aug 22
d. 186   A converted executioner at Rome
under Commodus. However, see Eusebius,
Pontian, etc. (Aug 25).

Antoninus (St) M.   Sept 2
?   It is not certain whether the Pamia mentioned in the pre-1970 RM. is a town named
Apamea in Syria or Pamiers in France. In both
places there are traditions connected with a
martyr named Antoninus.

Antoninus (St) M.   Sept 3
See Aristaeus and Antoninus.

Antoninus (St) M.   Sept 30
3rd cent.   A soldier of the Theban Legion,
martyred on the banks of the Trebbia, near
Piacenza, in Italy. His blood, kept in a phial, is
said to have the same miraculous properties as
that of St Januarius.

Antoninus (St) M.   Oct 25
See Marcellinus, Claudius, etc.

Antoninus (St) Bp.   Oct 31
d. 660   Surnamed Fontana. He was arch-
bishop of Milan for one year. In 1581 St
Charles Borromeo enshrined his relics beneath a magnificent altar in the church of St
Simplician.

Antoninus, Zebinas,
Germanus and Ennatha
(SS) MM.   Nov 13
d. 297   Martyrs under Galerius at Caesarea

St Antony, Jan 17

in Palestine. St Ennatha, a virgin, was burnt alive; her male fellow-sufferers were beheaded.

Antony (St) M.   Jan 9
See Julian, Basilissa, etc.

Antony Mary Pucci (St)
C. OSM.   Jan 12
1819–1892   A native of Poggiole, Tuscany, he made his profession as a Servite in 1843. Appointed pastor of Viareggio, he devoted himself to teaching the catechism, administration of the sacraments and solicitude for the poor, the sick and the plague-stricken. Canonized in 1962.

Antony (St) Ab.   GC. Jan 17
c 251–356   The patriarch of all monks. Born at Coma in Upper Egypt, at the age of twenty he gave away his property, which was considerable, to the poor and lived as a hermit near his native place. About the year 305 he established a community at Fayum and another shortly after at Pispir. Thus he was the first to establish the religious life as we know it today, by gathering together large groups of hermits into loose communities. Soon he became famous throughout Egypt and beyond, and was in great demand as an advisor by people of every rank. He was a personal friend of St Athanasius and his staunch supporter against the Arians, whom he arraigned as heretics in a public sermon preached at Alex-

andria at the invitation of Athanasius, when he was ninety years old. Athanasius himself became St Antony's biographer. St Antony died in his hermitage on Mt Kolzim, near the Red Sea. In art he is frequently shown with a T-shaped cross and a pig. The latter, perhaps originally the symbol of evil, became associated with a privilege of the Hospital Brothers of St Antony, founded in the seventeenth century. St Antony's fire was apparently an epidemic form of erysipelas against which the saint's intercession was involved: another of his symbols is a torch, to represent this affliction.

Antony, Merulus and John (SS) Mks. OSB.   Jan 17
6th cent.   Three monks of St Andrew's on the Coelian Hill, Rome. St Gregory the Great, who was their abbot, has left us an account of their virtues and miraculous power.

Antony Fatati (Bl) Bp.   Jan 19
c 1410–1484 (Jan 9)   Born at Ancona, he held successively the office of archpriest of Ancona, vicar-general of Siena, canon of the Vatican at Rome, bishop of Teramo and bishop of Ancona. His feast is celebrated in all these places. Cult approved by Pius VI.

Antony of Amandola (Bl)
C. OSA. Erem.   Jan 28
c 1355–1450   A native of Amandola in the Marches of Ancona, he joined the Augustinian Hermits and followed in the footsteps of St Nicholas of Tolentino, with whom he was on terms of friendship. His cult was confirmed in 1759, and he is honoured chiefly at Ancona.

Antony Manzoni (or Manzi) (Bl) C.   Feb 1
c 1237–1267   Surnamed "the Pilgrim". Born at Padua of a wealthy family, he gave all his patrimony to the poor and spent the rest of his life living on alms and tramping his way to Loreto, Rome, Compostella and Palestine. On account of his wandering habits, his relatives, especially his two sisters who were nuns, looked on him with marked disfavour.

Antony Deynan (St) M.   Feb 6
d. 1597   Born at Nagasaki of Japanese parents, he was an altar boy (thirteen years old) and a tertiary of St Francis, when he was crucified for the faith at his native town. Beatified in 1627, canonized in 1862. See Paul Miki and Comps.

Antony of Stroncone (Bl)
C. OFM.   Feb 7
1391–1461   Antony dei Vici became a Franciscan lay-brother in his twelfth year. Notwithstanding his humble status, he was chosen

to assist Bl Thomas of Florence in an important mission on behalf of the Holy See. After more than ten years combating the heresy of the Fraticelli, he was recalled to the friary of the Carceri, in Umbria, where he lived and practised rigorous penance for the rest of his life. Cult confirmed in 1687.

Antony Cauleas (St) Bp.   Feb 12
829–901 Born near Constantinople, he became monk and then abbot of a monastery of that city. Eventually he became patriarch, the second after Photius, the effects of whose schism he laboured to remove.

Antony of Saxony, Gregory of Tragurio, Nicholas of Hungary, Thomas of Foligno, and Ladislas of Hungary (BB) MM. OFM.   Feb 12
d. 1369 Franciscan friars put to death for the faith by King Bazarath at the village of Widdin (in modern Yugoslavia) and in the presence of the heretic monk by whom they had been arrested.

Antony (St) M.   Feb 14
See Bassus, Antony and Protolicus.

Antony (St) Mk. OSB.   March 9
10th cent. A monk of Luxeuil, who became a recluse at Froidemont, in Franche-Comté.

Antony of Milan (Bl) OFM.   March 15
See Monaldus of Ancona, etc.

Antony Fuster (Bl) C. OP.   Apr 5
14th cent. A disciple of St Vincent Ferrer, he was called "the Angel of Peace". He is highly honoured at Vich in Catalonia.

Antony Pavoni (Bl) M. OP.   Apr 9
1326–1374 Born at Savigliano, he joined the Dominicans and became their prior in his native town, and finally inquisitor-general for Liguria and Piedmont. On Low Sunday, 1374, he preached a vigorous sermon against heresy at Brichera, and on leaving the church was killed by heretics. Cult confirmed in 1856.

Antony Neyrot (Bl) M. OP.   Apr 10
d. 1460 A native of Rivoli, diocese of Turin, in Piedmont, he was professed a friar preacher. He was captured by Moorish pirates and carried off to Tunis, where he apostatized to Islam and married. After a few months he repented, put on the Dominican habit, publicly confessed Christ, and was stoned to death. Cult approved by Clement XIII.

Antony, John and Eustace (SS) MM.   Apr 14
d. 1342 Officials of the court of the grand duke of Lithuania, at Vilna. Antony and John, who were brothers, were crucified for having refused to eat meat on an abstinence day. Eustace became a Christian on witnessing their heroic fortitude, and was himself martyred for the faith. They are the patron saints of Vilna.

Antony de' Patrizzi (Bl) C. OSA. Erem.   Apr 27
d. 1311 Born at Siena, Antony became a hermit friar of St Augustine at the friary of Monticiano, of which he eventually became superior. Cult confirmed in 1804.

Antony (St) Ab. OSB.   May 4
6th cent. A supposed disciple of St Benedict and companion of St Maurus on his mission to France. He was the abbot-founder of Saint-Julian at Tours. He is surnamed "du Rocher" because he ended his days as a recluse on a spot called le Rocher. The story of St Maurus's mission to France is now discarded by all historians.

Antony Middleton (Bl) M.   May 6
d. 1590 Born at Middleton Tyas, Yorks, he was educated at Reims for the secular clergy. He was hanged, drawn and quartered at Clerkenwell, London. Beatified in 1929.

Antony of Foligno (Bl) C.   May 13
d. c 1398 A pilgrim from Hungary, and Franciscan tertiary, he was noted for his works of mercy. His relics are preserved in the Cathedral of Foligno.

Antony Mary Gianelli (St) Bp.   June 7
1789–1846 Born at Cerreto near Genoa, he was ordained priest in 1812 and, after twelve years spent as a devoted parish priest, was ordained bishop of Bobbio in 1838. As a parish priest he organized a congregation of missioners and another of teaching sisters. Canonized in 1951.

Antony of Padua (St) C. Dr OFM.   GC. June 13
1195–1231 A native of Lisbon and christened Ferdinand, he joined the Canons Regular at an early age, but a few years later (1212) passed over to the recently founded Friars Minor at Coimbra. Bent on martyrdom he sailed for Africa, but illness and storm brought him to Italy, where under the guidance of St Francis he began his career as a preacher — against heresy — and as a wonder-worker. He died at Padua and was canonized by Gregory

St Antony of Padua, June 13

IX in the following year. He is popularly invoked to help in the finding of lost objects. In art he is usually represented bearing the Child Jesus in his arms and holding a lily: often the child sits or stands on an open book.

Antony Mary Zaccaria
(St) C. Founder   GC. July 5
1502–1539 Born at Cremona he studied medicine, but changed his mind and became a secular priest. His zeal, moulded on that of St Paul, knew no bounds. In 1530 he founded the congregation of clerks regular under the patronage of St Paul, called Barnabites from their headquarters at the church of St Barnabas at Milan. It was approved in 1533. He died as a result of his unceasing apostolic toil. Canonized in 1897.

Antony van Hornaer and Antony van Werden (SS)
MM   July 9
See Gorkum, Martyrs of.

Antony Francisco (Bl)
M. SJ.   July 15
d. 1583   Born at Coimbra in Portugal. After his profession as a Jesuit in 1570, he was sent to India, and after his ordination he took charge of the mission of Arlin on the peninsula of Salsette, near Goa. He was martyred with Bl Rudolph Acquaviva, q.v.

Antony Correa, Antony Fernandez and Antony Suarez (BB) MM. SJ.   July 15
d. 1570   Three Jesuits — companions of Bl Ignatius de Azevedo, q.v.

Antony Turriani (or Turriano, of Torre) (Bl)
C. OSA. Erem.   July 24
d. 1694   Born at Milan, he studied medicine at Padua and practised at Milan. Then he became an Augustinian friar hermit. After several apostolic journeys, including three years at Compostella in Spain, he died at Aquila in the kingdom of Naples. Cult confirmed in 1759.

Antony della Chiesa (Bl)
C. OP.   July 28
1394–1459 (Jan 22)   Born at San Germano, near Vercelli, in Piedmont, he belonged to the family of the Marquis della Chiesa. He became a Dominican and ruled, as prior, the friaries of Como, Savona, Florence and Bologna, sharing in the apostolic labours of St Bernadine of Siena. Cult confirmed in 1819. Bl Antony was a collateral ancestor of Pope Benedict XV.

Antony Peter Dich (St)
M.   Aug 12
d. 1838   A wealthy native farmer of Vietnam, attached to the Foreign Missions of Paris. He was beheaded for sheltering St James Nam, a priest. Canonized in 1988.

Antony Primaldi and Comp. (BB) MM.   Aug 14
d. 1480   An aged artisan, eminent for his piety, of the city of Otranto in Italy. When the Turks raided that city in 1480, they gave the inhabitants the choice between death and apostasy. Antony became the leader and spokesman of eight hundred citizens, all men who chose death for Christ, and were accordingly hacked to pieces. Cult approved in 1771.

Antony of St Francis (Bl)
M.   Aug 17
d. 1627   A Japanese catechist, who was burnt at Nagasaki. A co-worker with Bl Francis of Saint Mary, q.v.

Antony Dshmananda (Bl) M.   Aug 19
d. 1622   A Japanese sailor on board the ship of Bl Joachim Firaiama. He was beheaded at Nagasaki. Beatified in 1867.

Antony Ixida and Comp. (BB) MM.   Sept 3
d. 1632   A Japanese Jesuit, famed for his learning and eloquence, who with five Franciscan and Augustinian friars was tortured for thirty-three days, by the application of scalding water, in a vain effort to make them apostatize. Finally they were burnt alive at Nagasaki. Beatified in 1867.

Antony of St Bonaventure (Bl) M. OFM   Sept 8
1588–1628   A native of Tuy in Galicia, Spain, he studied at Salamanca, became a Franciscan, and was appointed to the mission of Manila in the Philippines. Here he was ordained and crossed over to Japan, where it is on record that he reconciled over 2700 apostates. He was burnt alive at Nagasaki. Beatified in 1867.

Antony of St Dominic (Bl) M.   Sept 8
d. 1628   A Japanese man of twenty years, tertiary of St Dominic, companion of Bl Dominic Castellet. He was beheaded at Nagasaki. Beatified in 1867.

Antony Kiun (Bl) M. SJ.   Sept 10
1572–1622   A native of the province of Mikata in Japan, he was received into the Society of Jesus at Omura, and burnt alive at Nagasaki. Beatified in 1867.

Antony of Korea (Bl) M.   Sept 10
d.1622   Born in Korea, catechist under the Jesuits in Japan, he was beheaded at Nagasaki. Beatified in 1867.

Antony Sanga (Bl) M.   Sept 10
d. 1622   A Japanese catechist beheaded with Bl Charles Spinola, q.v.

Antony Vom (Bl) M.   Sept 10
d. 1622   Son of Bl Clement Vom. Beheaded at Nagasaki with his father. Beatified in 1867.

Antony (St) M.   Sept 23
See Andrew, John, etc.

Antony Mary Claret (St)
Bp. Founder   GC. Oct 24
1807–1870   Born at Sallent in Catalonia, he started life as a weaver, but soon became a student for the secular priesthood. He was

ordained in 1835 and devoted himself to missionary work among the people, helped by a group of priests, whom he formed into the institute of the Missionary Sons of the Immaculate Heart of Mary — Claretians. Antony was ordained bishop of Santiago de Cuba, and in 1856 was made confessor to Queen Isabella II and was exiled with her in 1868. Both in Cuba and in Spain he encountered the hostility of the Spanish liberal (i.e. anti-clerical) politicians. He had the gifts of prophecy and miracles. Canonized in 1950.

Antony (St) M.   Nov 7
See Melasippus, Antony and Carina.

Antony Baldinucci (Bl)
C. SJ.   Nov 7
1665–1717   Born at Florence, he became a Jesuit in 1681. He worked as a missionary chiefly in the Colli Albani near Rome, adopting very unconventional methods of preaching and calling people to penance. Beatified in 1893.

Antony Nam-Quynh (St)
M.   Nov 24
1768–1840   A native catechist and physician of Vietnam, who became attached to the Foreign Missions of Paris. He was imprisoned for the faith in 1838, and strangled two years later. Beatified in 1900. Canonized in 1988.

Antony Kimura (Bl) M.   Nov 27
1595–1619   A Japanese of the royal family of Firando, aged twenty-three, a relative of Bl Leonard Kimura. He was beheaded with ten companions at Nagasaki. Beatified in 1867.

Antony Bonafadini (Bl)
C. OFM.   Dec 1
1400–1482   Born at Ferrara, he joined the Franciscan Friars of the Observance and was sent to the mission of the Holy Land. He died at Cotignola, diocese of Faenza. Cult confirmed in 1901.

Antony Grassi (Bl) C.
Orat.   Dec 13
d. c 1672   Priest of the Oratory at Fermo in the Italian Marches, and its superior from 1635 until his death. In 1621 he was struck by lightning, but this only seemed to increase his marked serenity of manner. He had the gift of reading consciences and excelled as a director of souls. Beatified in 1900.

Antony (St) M.   Dec 15
See Irenaeus, Antony, etc.

Antony of Lérins (St) H.   Dec 28
d. c 520   Born in Lower Pannonia, he served God as a recluse in several places north of the Alps until he found rest for the last two years of his life as a monk at Lérins.

Anysia (St) M.   Dec 30
d. 304   A maiden of Salonika, put to death by a soldier when she resisted an attempt to drag her to a pagan sacrifice, according to her legend.

Anysius (St) Bp.   Dec 30
d. c 407   The successor of St Ascolus in the see of Salonika. He was a friend of St Ambrose, vicar apostolic of Pope Damasus in Illyria, and loyal defender of St John Chrysostom.

Aout (St) C.   Oct 7
Otherwise Augustus, q.v.

Apelles (Apellius), Lucius (Luke) and Clement
(SS) MM.   Apr 22 and Sept 10
1st cent.   Apelles and Lucius were described by the pre-1970 RM. as "from among the first disciples of Christ". They are usually identified with the "Apelles, approved in Christ" and "Lucius, my kinsman" mentioned by St Paul (Rom. 16:10,21). These names are duplicated in the pre-1970 RM., in the second entry (Sept 10) a third name Clement being added. Tradition adds that St Apelles was bishop of Smyrna, and Lucius bishop of Laodicea.

Aper (St) Bp.
Otherwise Aprus, q.v.

Aphraates (St) H.   Apr 7
4th cent.   A Persian hermit who settled at Edessa in Mesopotamia, and later on removed to Antioch in Syria, where he valiantly opposed Arianism during the reign of Valens. Some authors have endeavoured to identify him with the famous "Aphraates the Syrian", the ecclesiastical writer.

Aphrodisius (St) M.   March 14
See Peter and Aphrodisius.

Aphrodisius, Caralippus, Agapius, and Eusebius
(SS) MM.   Apr 28
1st cent.   A French legend, now universally rejected, makes this Aphrodisius an Egyptian who sheltered the Holy Family during their flight into Egypt. He is alleged to have been martyred with the other three in Languedoc. Their story is told by Gregory of Tours.

Aphrodisius and Comp.
(SS) MM.   Apr 30
? An Egyptian priest put to death at Alexandria with a group of some thirty of his flock.

Aphthonius (St) S.   Nov 2
See Acindynus, Pegasius, etc.

Apian
Otherwise Amphianus, Apphianus, Appianus, Appian, Apphian. Here we adopt the spelling Appian, q.v.

Apodemius (St) M.   Apr 16
See Saragossa, Martyrs of.

Apollinaris Syncletica
(St) V.   Jan 5
The heroine of a religious romance who disguised herself in boy's clothes and lived undiscovered in an Egyptian hermitage as a disciple of one of the Saints Macrius.

Apollinaris the Apologist
(St) Bp.   Jan 8
d. *c* 180 Claudius Apollinaris, a bishop of Hierapolis in Phrygia, is now only known from the *Apologia* for the Christian faith which he dedicated to Marcus Aurelius towards the middle of the second century.

Apollinaris (St) Bp. M.   June 21
See Cyriacus and Apollinaris.

Apollinaris (St) Bp. M.   July 23
? 1st cent. He is mistakenly described as a disciple of St Peter due to some fictitious seventh century *Acta*. He certainly was the first bishop of Ravenna and was reputedly put to the torture for the faith and died of its effects. The exact date is not known. His shrine at the Benedictine abbey of Classe at Ravenna became famous throughout Christendom. Cult confined to local calendars since 1969.

Apollinaris and
Timothy (SS) MM.   Aug 23
3rd cent. Apollinaris was once thought to be the executioner in the gaol at Reims, who became a Christian on witnessing the fortitude of St Timothy under repeated torture. Both were beheaded for Christ and their tomb became famous in that district: but it is now thought that Apollinaris is Apollinaris of Ravenna (see previous entry) and Timothy is the Martyr of Rome (q.v., Aug 22). The legend arose to explain why both these saints were kept on the same day at Reims.

Apollinaris Sidonius (St)
Bp.   Aug 23
See Sidonius Apollinaris.

Apollinaris Franco and
Comp. (BB) MM. OFM.   Sept 10
d. 1622 Born at Aquilar del Campo in Old Castile, he studied law at Salamanca, entered the Franciscan Order of the Observance, and eventually was sent to Japan (1614) as com-missary general of the missions of his order there. He was arrested in 1617 and detained in the horrible prison of Omura until he was burnt alive on Sept 10. The "Companions" include Japanese martyrs of various dates, beatified in 1867. See Japan, Martyrs of.

Apollinaris (Aiplonay)
(St) Bp.   Oct 5
d. *c* 520 Elder brother of St Avitus of Vienne, he became bishop of Valence, where he died after a glorious and indefatigable apostolate. He is the patron saint of the diocese.

Apollinaris (Bl or St) Ab.
OSB.   Nov 27
d. 828 The fourteenth abbot of Montecassino, he governed the archabbey for eleven years. He has always been venerated at Montecassino.

Apolline (St) VM.   Feb 9
Otherwise Apollonia, q.v.

Apollo (St) Ab.   Jan 25
c 316–395 An Egyptian hermit who, after forty years of solitude in the Thebaid, became the abbot of over five hundred monks near Hermopolis. He left the desert in order to withstand Julian the Apostate.

Apollo, Isacius and Crotates
(Codratus) (SS) MM.   Apr 21
d. *c* 302 Three servants at the palace of Alexandra, wife of Diocletian, described as martyrs at Nicomedia. Alexandra, however, never existed and the story is part of the legend of St George.

Apollonia (Apolline) (St)
VM.   Feb 9
d. 249 An aged deaconess of Alexandria, martyred under Decius. Her teeth were broken with pincers, and for this reason she is invoked against toothache and is represented in art holding a tooth in pincers. Finally she was led to a kindled pyre to be burnt alive unless she renounced Christ, and "of her own accord leaped into the pyre, being kindled within by the greater fire of the Holy Spirit" (pre-1970 RM.). Since 1970 her cult has been restricted to local usages only.

Apollonius (St) M.   Feb 14
See Proculus, Ephebus and Apollonius.

Apollonius (St) M.   March 8
See Philemon and Apollonius.

Apollonius and Leontius
(or Leontinus) Bps. MM.   March 19
? Neither the see nor the date of martyrdom of these two bishops is known. Their names,

St Apollonia, Feb 9

however, already occur in the martyrology of St Jerome. The Portuguese have claimed them for their see of Braga.

Apollonius and Comp (SS) MM.   Apr 10
? A priest and five companions martyred at Alexandria under Decius.

Apollonius the Apologist (St) M.   Apr 18
d. c 190   A Roman senator, denounced as a Christian by one of his own slaves and condemned to be beheaded. His eloquent defence of the faith (*Apologia*) delivered before the Senate at his trial is one of the most priceless documents of Christian antiquity. It was discovered in an Armenian text in 1874.

Apollonius (St) M.   June 5
See Marcian, Nicanor, etc.

Apollonius (St) Bp.   July 7
? A bishop of Brescia in Lombardy. He is mentioned in the acts of SS Faustinus and Jovita which, however, cannot be relied upon. His supposed relics are enshrined in the cathedral of Brescia.

Apollonius (St) Bp.   July 8
d. p.326   Bishop of Benevento. He went into hiding during the last persecution under Diocletian.

Apollonius (St) M.   July 10
d. Early 4th cent.   A native of Sardis in Lydia, Asia Minor, he was scourged and crucified at Iconium.

Apollonius and Eugene (SS) MM.   July 23
? Roman martyrs, the former was pierced with arrows at the stake, the latter was beheaded.

Aponius (St) M.   Feb 10
See Andrew and Aponius.

Apphia (St) M.   Nov 22
See Philemon and Apphia.

Appian (St) Mk. OSB.   AC. March 4
d. c 800   Born in Liguria, he became a Benedictine at the abbey of St Peter of Ciel d'Oro at Pavia. Eventually he became a recluse at Commacchio on the shores of the Adriatic, and evangelized that country.

Appian (St) M.   Apr 2
d. 306   A martyr at Caesarea in Palestine in the persecution of Galerius and Maximian.

Appian and Comp. (SS) MM.   Dec 30
See Mansuetus, Severus, etc.

Apronia (Evronie) (St) V.   July 15
5th and 6th cent.   Born near Trier. Sister of St Aprus (Evre), bishop of Toul, at whose hands she received the veil. She died at Troyes.

Apronian (St) M.   Feb 2
d. c 304   A Roman executioner who was converted to Christianity when taking the martyr St Sisinnius before the tribunal, and was himself thereupon put to death.

Aprus (Aper, Apre, Epvre, Evre) (St) Bp.   Sept 15
d. 507   Born near Trier, he became a very able and just lawyer. He gave up this profession to be ordained priest, and in time was chosen bishop of Toul, which see he governed for seven years. Some authorities reject the tradition of his having been a lawyer.

Apuleius (St) M. Oct 7
See Marcellus and Apuleius.

Aquila (St) M. Jan 23
See Severian and Aquila.

Aquila (St) M. March 23
See Domitius, Pelagia, etc.

Aquila (St) M. May 20
d. 311 An Egyptian, torn to pieces with iron combs under Maximinus Daza. The prefect Arianus, who had ordered this torture, subsequently became a Christian and a martyr in the same persecution.

Aquila and Priscilla (SS) July 8
1st cent. Husband and wife, belonging to the Jewish diaspora, who worked as tentmakers at Rome, whence they were banished with all other Jews under Claudius. They settled at Corinth, where they received St Paul into their house (Acts 18:3). Under Nero they returned to Rome and St Paul sent greetings to them. There is a tradition in Rome that they were martyred there.

Aquila (St) M. Aug 1
See Cyril, Aquila, etc.

Aquilina (St) VM. June 13
d. 293 A young girl — said to have been no more than twelve years old — who was tortured and beheaded at Byblus in Syria. The account of her passion is not trustworthy.

Aquilina (St) M. July 24
See Niceta and Aquilina.

Aquilinus, Geminus, Eugene, Marcian, Quintus, Theodotus and Tryphon (SS) MM. Jan 4
c 484 A band of martyrs put to death in Africa under the Arian Hunneric, king of the Vandals. Their acts are now lost, but it seems that Ven. Bede had access to them in the eighth century.

Aquilinus (St) M. Jan 29
d. 650 A Bavarian by birth who, flying from the prospect of high ecclesiastical preferment at Cologne, went to Paris and then to Milan, preaching against Arianism. On this account he was assassinated by the Arians. His relics are venerated at Milan.

Aquilinus, Geminus, Gelasius, Magnus and Donatus (SS) MM. Feb 4
? 3rd cent. Martyrs at Forum Sempronii, which has been interpreted very doubtfully as Fossombrone in central Italy. No details survive.

Aquilinus and Victorian (SS) MM. May 16
? Martyrs in the Province of Isauria, in Asia Minor and, as such, registered by Ven. Bede in his martyrology. Nothing else is known about them.

Aquilinus (St) M. May 17
See Heradius, Paul, etc.

Aquilinus (St) Bp. Oct 19
c 620–695 A native of Bayeux, he spent forty years in the service of Clovis II. On his return from the war against the Visigoths, he and his wife agreed to give themselves up to works of charity. They retired to Evreux, and Aquilinus was soon made bishop of that city. He managed, however, to live more as a hermit than a pastor.

Arabia (Martyrs of) Feb 22
By the term Arabia is here understood, conformably to the usage of the period, the countries, mainly desert, east of the Jordan, and the mountainous districts south of the Dead Sea. The pre-1970 RM. had this entry: "In Arabia, the memory of many holy martyrs, who were cruelly slain under the emperor Galerius Maximian".

Arabia (St) M. March 13
See Theusetas, Horres, etc.

Araldus (Bl) Mk. OSB. Cist. Nov 11
d. c 1250 A lay-brother of the Cistercian abbey of Isenhagen.

Arator, Fortunatus, Felix, Silvius and Vitalis (SS) MM. Apr 21
? St Arator is said by the pre-1970 RM. to have been a priest of Alexandria in Egypt, put to death with the other Christians named above in one of the earlier persecutions. No particulars are now extant.

Arator (St) Bp. Sept 6
d. c 460 The fourth bishop of Verdun.

Arbogast (St) Bp. July 21
d. c 678 Born in Aquitaine not, as has been maintained, in Ireland or Scotland. He was living as a recluse in Alsace when King Dagobert II forced on him the see of Strasburg, which he ruled with great humility and wisdom. At his own request he was interred in the place set apart for the burial of criminals. A church was soon built over his tomb. In art he is represented as walking dryshod over a river.

Arcadius (St) M. Jan 12
d. c 302? A prominent citizen of Caesarea in

Mauretania (near Algiers) who under Maximianus Herculeus was slowly and barbarously mutilated until he died under the torture.

Arcadius (St) Bp. M. March 4
See Basil, Eugene, etc.

Arcadius (St) Bp. Aug 1
d. *c* 549 Bishop of Bourges, he took part in the council of Orleans in 538. Buried at Saint Ursin.

Arcadius, Paschasius, Probus, Eutychian and Paulillus (SS) MM. Nov 13
d. 437 All of these were Spaniards, exiled to Africa by the Vandal Arian king Genseric, where they became the protomartyrs of the Vandal persecution. Paulillus was only a boy, the little brother of SS Paschasius and Eutychian. "As he could not be turned from the Catholic Faith he was long beaten with rods, and condemned to the basest servitude" (pre-1970 RM.).

Arcanus (St) Ab. OSB. Sept 1
See Giles and Arcanus.

Archangela Girlani (Bl) V. OC. Feb 13
1461–1494 A native of Trino, in the Monferrato, Italy, she became a Carmelite at Parma and, at the request of the Gonzagas, was sent to found a new Carmel at Mantua. She was its first prioress, a living pattern of perfection. Cult confirmed in 1864.

Archangelus Canetuli (Bl) C. OSA. Apr 16
d. 1513 Born at Bologna, he became an Augustinian Canon Regular, conspicuous for his gifts, natural and supernatural. He died as archbishop-elect of Florence.

Archangelus of Calafatimi (Bl) C. OFM. July 30
d. 1460 Born at Calafatimi in Sicily, he was a hermit at the time when Pope Martin V suppressed the Sicilian hermitages. He then joined the Franciscans of the Observance and was a great promoter of this new branch throughout Sicily. Cult confirmed in 1836.

Archelais, Thecla and Susanna (SS) VV. MM. Jan 18
d. 293 Three Christian maidens of the Romagna who retired to Nola in the Campagna in order to escape death; but there too they were accused of being Christians, tortured, taken to Salerno and beheaded.

Archelaus, Cyril and Photius (SS) MM. March 4
Nothing is known about these martyrs.

Archelaus (St) M. Aug 23
See Quiriacus, Maximus, etc.

Archelaus (St) Bp. Dec 26
d. *c* 278 Bishop of Kashkar in Mesopotamia. He seems to have been a formidable opponent of Manicheism during his life, but the writings against these heretics attributed to him are not his work.

Archippus (St) March 20
1st cent. St Paul calls him "my fellow-soldier" (Philem. 2) and mentions him also in his letter to the Colossians (4:17). Tradition, basing itself on St Paul's words, has made Archippus the first bishop of Colossae.

Arcontius (St) Bp. M. Jan 19
8th (or 9th) cent. Bishop of Viviers, killed by a mob for having upheld the rights of his church.

Arcontius (St) M. Sept 5
See Quintius, Arcontius and Donatus.

Ardalion (St) M. Apr 14
d. *c* 300 An actor who suddenly proclaimed himself a Christian while engaged in ridiculing Christianity on the stage. He was roasted alive in the public square.

Ardanus (Ardaing, Ardagne, Ardagnus, Ardan) (St) Ab. OSB. Feb 11
d. 1058 The thirteenth abbot of the Benedictine monastery of Tournus, now in the diocese of Autun. He restored the monastic buildings and was a father to the people during the famine of 1030–1033.

Ardo (St) Ab. OSB. March 7
d. 843 A native of Languedoc, he changed his baptismal name of Smaragdus on entering the abbey of Aniane under its first abbot, St Benedict. He became director of the schools attached to the abbey, St Benedict's travelling companion and secretary — and eventually also his biographer — and his successor at Aniane when St Benedict went to reside at Aachen. His cult was well established at Aniane at an early date.

Arduinus (Ardwyne, Ardoin) (St) July 28
? 7th cent. He is patron saint of Trepino in S. Italy. An improbable legend makes him one of four English pilgrims who died in this region in the seventh century.

Arduinus (St) Aug 15
d. 1009 A priest of Rimini who lived first as

a hermit and ended his days in the monastery of San Gudenzio, but did not however take vows there.

Aredius (Arige, Aregius, etc.) (St) Abp.   Aug 10
d. *p.*614 An outstanding archbishop of Lyons; his political activities have come down to us in an unfavourable light.

Aredius (Yrieix, Yriez) (St) Ab.   Aug 25
d. 591 Born at Limoges, after a period of service at the court of the Frankish kings he became the abbot-founder of the abbey of Atane in the Limousin, which later on was called after him, as was also the village of Saint-Yrieux which grew up around the abbey. He was famous for his evangelical travels throughout Gaul. Other variants are: Yriel, Ysary, Ysère, Yséry.

Aregloe, Aregle, (St) Bp.   March 17
Otherwise Agricola, q.v.

Aresius, Rogatius and Comp. (SS) MM.   June 10
? A band of seventeen African martyrs, particulars concerning whom have been lost. Some martyrologies class them with the Roman martyrs, Basilides and others, commemorated on the same day.

Aretas and Comp. (SS) MM.   Oct 1
? According to the pre-1970 RM. St Aretas suffered at Rome with five hundred and four others. The first to mention this number was Usuardus. Some try to identify this group with that mentioned on Oct 24. See Nagran, Martyrs of.

Aretas (St) M.   Oct 24
See Nagran, Martyrs of.

Aretius (Arecius, Aregius) and Dacian (SS) MM.   June 4
? Roman martyrs who were buried in the catacombs on the Appian Way.

Argariarga (St) V.   Sept 9
Otherwise Osmanna, q.v.

Argeus, Narcissus and Marcellinus (SS) MM.   Jan 2
d. 320 Three brothers said to have been enrolled as soldiers in the army of the emperor Licinius and who suffered martyrdom at Tomi in Pontus, on the Black Sea. Marcellinus was only a boy enrolled as a recruit, who, on refusing to perform military service, was first flogged most cruelly, then kept long in prison, and lastly thrown into the sea. His brothers were beheaded.

Argymirus (St) M. Mk.   June 28
d. 858 A native of Cabra, near Cordoba, who held high official position among the Muslims of that city. He was deprived of his office on account of his Christian faith and became a monk. Shortly after he openly renounced his belief in Islam and confessed Christ and was beheaded.

Ariadne (St) M.   Sept 17
d. *c* 130 A Christian woman slave of a Phrygian prince, who was flogged for refusing to join in the heathen rites celebrated on the anniversary of her master's birthday; it is said that she took refuge in a chasm in the rock which miraculously opened before her and closed on her entering, thus affording her a tomb and the crown of martyrdom.

Arialdus (St) M.   June 27
d. 1066 A deacon of Milan, who distinguished himself for his zeal against the rampant simony of his time, chiefly at Milan. For this reason he was first excommunicated and, after much persecution, killed by the party of the simoniac archbishop of Milan. Cult approved in 1904.

Arian, Theoticus and Comp. (SS) MM.   March 8
c 311 Arian, governor of Thebes, in Egypt, with Theoticus and three others was converted to Christianity on witnessing at Alexandria the martyrdom of SS Apollonius and Philemon. The judge ordered them to be drowned in the sea.

Arigius (St) Bp.   May 1
535–604 Bishop of Gap for twenty years, he was one of the great pastors of the time. Cult confirmed by St Pius X.

Arilda (St) VM.   Oct 30
? A maiden of Gloucestershire who met her death in defence of her chastity. The church at Oldbury-on-the-Hill is dedicated to her.

Aristaeus and Antoninus (SS) MM.   Sept 3
? Aristaeus is said to have been bishop of Capua, but modern research inclines rather to identify him with the Egyptian martyr of the same name, venerated by the Greeks on Sept 3. Similarly the child-martyr, Antoninus, seems to be a duplicate of St Antoninus of Apamea, commemorated in the pre-1970 RM. on Sept 2. At Capua there is no record of either saint.

Aristarchus (St) Bp. M.   Aug 4
1st cent. A native of Salonika and a companion of St Paul in his travels (Acts 20:4, 27:2). He was arrested with the apostle at Ephesus,

and shared his imprisonment. He is described as "his fellow-worker" (Philem. 24). Tradition makes him the first bishop of Salonika and adds that he was beheaded in Rome with St Paul.

Aristides (St)   Aug 31
2nd cent.   An Athenian philosopher, famous for his *Apologia* for Christianity, which he presented to the emperor Hadrian in 125. The text, long lost, has now been recovered in Syriac, Armenian and Greek. See Barlaam and Josaphat.

Ariston (St) M.   Feb 22
1st cent.   Traditionally one of the seventy-two disciples of our Lord. He is said to have preached in Cyprus and died there a martyr, at Salamis. Others assert that he was martyred at Alexandria.

Aristobulus (St) M.   March 15
1st cent.   Traditionally one of the seventy-two disciples of our Lord. Perhaps he is the Aristobulus mentioned by St Paul (Rom. 16:11). He has been identified with Zebedee, the father of SS James and John, and Britain has been allotted to him as the place of his labours and martyrdom — all without the slightest foundation.

Ariston, Crescentian, Eutychian, Urban, Vitalis, Justus, Felicissimus, Felix, Marcia, and Symphorosa (SS) MM.   July 2
d. *c* 285   A band of martyrs put to death in the Campagna, S. Italy, under Diocletian. Nothing more is known about them.

Aristonicus (St) M.   Apr 19
See Hermogenes, Caius, etc.

Armagillus (Armel) (St) C.   Aug 16
d. *c* 550   Said to have been born in S. Wales, a cousin of St Samson. A Cornish church was dedicated to him — St Erme. He crossed over to Brittany and founded Saint-Armel-des-Boscheaux and Plou-Ermel (Ploermel). Like all the Celtic names of that period, Armel has taken countless variants. Here are a few: Ermel, Erme, Ermin, Arthmael, Armail, Arzel, Armahel, Hermel, Thiarmail. In Latin it is translated as Armagillus. In art he holds the Devil on a chain, and often wears a suit of armour under his vestments. Sometimes he binds the Devil with his stole.

Armand (St) C.   Jan 23
Otherwise Ormond, q.v.

Armel (St) C.   Aug 16
Otherwise Armagillus, q.v.

Armentarius (St) Bp.   Jan 30
d. *p.*451   First bishop of Antibes in Provence. An old church is dedicated in his name at Draguignan.

Armentarius (St) Bp.   Jan 30
d. *c* 711   Bishop of Pavia. During his episcopate the see of Pavia was withdrawn from the jurisdiction of the metropolitan see of Milan and directly attached to the Roman church.

Armogastes and Comp. (SS) MM.   March 29
d. *p.*460   Armogastes and Saturus, high officers at the palace, suffered in Africa during the Arian persecution under the Vandal king, Genseric. First they were tortured, then sent to labour in the mines, then condemned to slavery as cowherds near Carthage. They were not put to death "lest the Romans should venerate them as martyrs". The other names given in the pre-1970 RM., Archimimus and Masculas, thought to be martyrs of this group, apparently refer to Armogastes, with the meaning "President of the Theatre, a native of Mascula" or possibly we should understand "Archimimus, the Masculan".

Armon (St) Bp.   July 31
Otherwise Germanus of Auxerre, q.v.

Arnold Janssen (Bl)
Founder   Jan 15
Born in Goch, Germany in 1837. After priestly ordination he founded the Society of the Divine Word in 1875 in Steyl, Holland, and two Congregations of Sisters. He died in 1909 and was beatified in 1975.

Arnold (Arnald, Arnaud) (Bl) Ab. M. OSB.   March 14
d. 1254   Born at Padua of the noble family de' Cattanei, he became a Benedictine at St Justina, Padua, and eventually its abbot. The tyrant Ezzelino da Romano, after persecuting him for a long time, imprisoned him at Asolo and loaded him with chains. He bore it all patiently for eight years and died in prison at the age of seventy.

Arnold (St) C.   July 8
d. *p.*800   A Greek by birth, attached to the court of Charlemagne. He was famed for his charity to the poor. He has left his name to the village, Arnold-Villiers (Arnoldsweiler) near Jülich.

Arnold (Bl) Ab. OSB.   Nov 30
d. 1155   A Benedictine of the abbey of St Nicasius at Reims, who became abbot of Gemblours.

Arnulf (Arnulphus, Arnulph, Arnoul) (Bl) Mk.

OSB. Cist. June 30

d. 1228 Surnamed "Cornibout" or "of Villers". He was born at Brussels, and after a pleasure-loving youth, he became a lay-brother at the Cistercian abbey of Villers in Brabant, where he atoned for his past by long years of prayer and penance. He attained to a high degree of mystical prayer.

Arnulf (St) Bp. M. July 1

d. 1160 Archbishop of Mainz from 1153. He was murdered by his own diocesans and is venerated as a martyr.

Arnulf (St) Bp. July 18

d. c 640 A courtier of high standing in the palace of the Austrasian kings, he determined to become a monk at Lérins. His wife took the veil and Arnulf was just on the point of retiring to Lérins when he was made bishop of Metz (c 616). A few years before his death he resigned and retired to a hermitage near the abbey of Remiremont.

Arnulf (St) Bp. OSB. Aug 15

c 1040–1087 Born in Flanders, after some years in the armies of Robert and Henry I, kings of France, he became a Benedictine at the abbey of St Medard at Soissons. After his profession he lived as a recluse under the abbot's obedience. In 1082 he was obliged to accept the bishopric of Soissons. Some time after he resigned and founded the abbey of Oudenbourg in Flanders, where he died.

Arnulf (St) H. Aug 22

9th cent. The relics of this saint were venerated at Arnulphsbury, or Eynesbury (Cambs). He has been described as an English hermit of that district, but he is probably a duplicate of St Arnulf of Metz.

Arnulf (St) Bp. OSB. Sept 19

d. 1070 Born at Vendôme, he became a Benedictine at the abbey of Holy Trinity in his native city. In 1063 Pope Alexander II consecrated him bishop of Gap. As such he restored the cathedral of his episcopal city. He is the principal patron saint of Gap.

Arnulf (St) M. OSB. Oct 31

d. c 840 A monk of Novalese, in Piedmont, who was put to death by the Saracens.

Arnulf (St) Bp. Nov 15

d. 871 Bishop of Toul from 847 to 871. He was a firm and outspoken opponent of the divorce of King Lothair.

Arontius (Orontius) (St)

M. Aug 27 and Sept 1

See Honoratus, Fortunatus, etc.

Arpinus (St) Bp. Nov 9

Otherwise Agrippinus, q.v.

Arsacius (Ursacius) (St)

C. Aug 16

d. 358 A Persian soldier in the Roman army, who on his conversion retired to live as a recluse in a high tower overlooking Nicomedia. He forewarned its inhabitants of the impending destruction of their city by the great earthquake of 358. Some survivors found refuge in the tower, where Arsacius had already died in the attitude of prayer.

Arsenius (St) Bp. Jan 19

d. 959 A native of Constantinople of Jewish descent, he became the first bishop of Corfu, of which he is now venerated as the principal patron.

Arsenius the Great (St)

H. July 19

d. c 449 Surnamed also "the Roman" and "the deacon", being actually a Roman deacon. He was summoned by Theodosius the Great to Constantinople to become the tutor of Arcadius and Honorius, the emperor's sons (c 383). After ten years in that thankless office (c 393) he abandoned the court and retired to the desert of Skete as a hermit. A hermit he remained for the rest of his life, living in various places in Egypt and ever weeping over the feebleness of Arcadius and the foolishness of Honorius. He breathed his last at the rock of Tröe, near Memphis.

Arsenius (St) M. OSB. Aug 30

See Pelagius, Arsenius and Sylvanus.

Arsenius (St) M. Dec 14

See Heron, Arsenius, etc.

Artaldus (Arthaud, Artaud) (Bl) Bp. O. Cart.

Oct 7

1101–1206 Served at the court of Amadeus III of Savoy, and then became a Carthusian at Portes (1120). In 1140 he founded the charterhouse of Arvières-en-Valromey in Savoy. He was an octogenarian when he was appointed bishop of Belley (1188) but resigned after two years (1190) and returned to Val-romey where he died. Cult approved in 1834.

Artaxus, Acutus, Eugenda, Maximianus, Timothy, Tobias and Vitus

(SS) MM. Jan 2

3–4th cent. Martyrs at Syrmium, Pannonia.

Artemas (St) M. Jan 25

? Said to have been a boy of Pozzuoli (Puteoli) who was stabbed to death with iron pens by his pagan school-fellows. It seems, however, that the whole story is a pious romance.

Artemas (St) Bp.   Oct 30
1st cent. One of St Paul's disciples, he is mentioned by the apostle in his letter to Titus (3:12). A later tradition has made him a bishop of Lystra. He is venerated by the Greeks.

Artemius (Arthemius)
(St) Bp.   Jan 24
d. 396 An imperial legate who, on his way to Spain, fell sick in Gaul and settled at Clermont, in Auvergne, where eventually he became bishop.

Artemius (St) Bp.   Apr 28
d. 609 A native of Sens where he became bishop. He admitted to public penance a Spaniard named Baldus (in modern French, Bond), whom he trained in the spiritual life and who was also declared a saint.

Artemius, Candida and
Paulina (SS) MM.   June 6
d. 302 Artemius, gaoler of one of the Roman prisons, with his wife Candida and daughter Paulina, was converted to Christ by St Peter the exorcist and baptized by St Marcellinus. Artemius was beheaded, and his wife and daughter buried alive under a pile of stones.

Artemius (St) M.   Oct 20
d. 363 An officer of high rank under Constantine the Great. A pronounced Arian, he was made by Constantius prefect of Egypt and, as such, persecuted St Athanasius and harassed the Catholics, nor is there any record of his having renounced Arianism. He was beheaded as a Christian under Julian the Apostate. He is called by the Greeks the Megalo-martyr.

Artemon (St) M.   Oct 8
d. c 305 A priest of Laodicea (in Phrygia) burnt to death under Diocletian.

Arthelais (St) V.   March 3
6th cent. One of the patron saints of Benevento, whither she is said to have fled from Constantinople to escape the attentions of the emperor Justinian.

Arthen (St)
? This saint seems untraceable. He appears to be one and the same with the St Arvan or Aroan who has left his name at St Arvans and Cwmcarvan in Wales. Stanton's Menology, following Challoner, identifies St Arvan with Maruanus, a companion of SS Banca (or Breaca) and Sennen (sixth century).

Arwald (SS) MM.   Apr 22
d. 686 Two brothers, sons of Arwald, a prince in the Isle of Wight, whose proper names are lost. They were put to death by soldiers of King Ceadwalla, then a pagan, on the day after their baptism.

Asaph (St) Bp.   May 1
d. c 600 One of St Kentigern's monks in N. Wales. He is believed to have succeeded St Kentigern as abbot and bishop, leaving his own name to the see now in Clwyd. Many of his kinsfolk — Deiniol, Tysilo, etc. — are also venerated as saints.

Ascelina (St) V. OSB.   Aug 23
1121–1195 A relative of St Bernard and early Cistercian mystic. She entered the convent of Boulancourt (Haute-Marne).

Asclas (St) M.   Jan 23
d. c 287 Martyred under Diocletian by being thrown into the Nile at Antinoe.

Asclepiades (St) Bp. M.   Oct 18
d. 217 St Serapion's successor in the see of Antioch, from 211 to 217. He is usually given the title of martyr, probably on account of all that he underwent during the persecution of Severus.

Asclepiodotus
(Asclepiadorus) (St) M.   Sept 15
See Maximus, Theodore and Asclepiodotus.

Asella (St) V.   Dec 6
d. c 406 St Jerome, who became her panegyrist, calls her "a flower of the Lord", and tells us that this Roman maiden took the veil at the age of ten and retired to a small cubicle at twelve, where she lived for long years until she became "the mother of many virgins". Pallasius visited her in Rome, where she had her community.

Asicus (Ascicus, or
Tassach) (St) Bp.   Apr 27
d. c 490 One of the earliest disciples of St Patrick, by whom he was placed at the head of the monastery and diocese of Elphin, of which he is now venerated as the patron saint. He excelled as a coppersmith, and some remarkable specimens of his handiwork yet remain.

Aspasius (St) Bp.   Jan 2
d. c 560 A bishop of Eauze — now Auch — who took part in the councils of Orleans, 533, 541 and 549, besides holding a provincial council at Aauze in 551. He is honoured in the diocese of Meaux, and especially at Melun.

Aspren (Aspronas) (St)
Bp.   Aug 3
1st cent. The tradition concerning this saint, dating from time immemorial, was recorded by the pre-1970 RM. as follows: "At Naples in Campania, the birthday of St Aspren the

bishop, who was cured of infirmity by St Peter the Apostle, and afterwards baptized and ordained bishop of that city". It seems however that he should not be dated before the end of the second or beginning of the third century.

Asteria (Hesteria) (St)
VM.   Aug 10
d. *c* 307   A martyr venerated according to a Passio of doubtful validity, at Bergamo in Lombardy. She was a sister of St Grata, and both were associated in the burial of the martyr, St Alexander (Aug 26).

Astericus (Astricus, Ascrick) (St) Bp. OSB.   Nov 12
d. *c* 1035   A native of Bohemia, he became a monk and accompanied St Adalbert to the Bohemian mission. He became the first abbot of Brevnov, but had to flee to Hungary where he was appointed the first abbot of Pannonhalma, recently founded by King Stephen and the archbishop of Kalocsa. Anastasius was the king's ambassador, sent to negotiate the recognition of the new Hungarian kingdom by Pope Sylvester II. He brought the Holy Crown of Hungary to St Stephen.

Asterius (St) M.   March 3
See Marinus and Asterius.

Asterius (St) M.   May 20
See Thalelaeus, Asterius, etc.

Asterius (St) Bp.   June 10
d. *p.* 362   Formerly an Arian who, after his conversion, became bishop of Petra in Arabia and earned the hatred of the heretics by publishing the story of their intrigues at the council of Sardica (347). Banished to Libya by Constantius, but recalled by Julian the Apostate, he was presented at the council of Alexandria in 362, and was chosen to be the bearer of the letter from the council to the Church of Antioch. He died shortly after.

Asterius (St) M.   Aug 23
See Claudius, Asterius, etc.

Asterius (St) M.   Oct 21
d. *c* 223   A Roman priest under Pope St Callistus, whose body he secretly buried. For this reason he was cast into the Tiber at Ostia by order of the emperor Alexander. The Christians recovered his body and buried it at Ostia, where it is now enshrined in the cathedral.

Asterius (St) Bp.   Oct 30
d. *c* 400   Bishop of Amasea in Pontus, Asia Minor. He was renowned as a preacher; twenty-one of his sermons are still extant.

Astius (St) Bp. M.   July 7
See Peregrinus, Lucian, etc.

Asyncritus (St) Bp.   Apr 8
See Herodion, Asyncritus and Phlegon.

Athan (St)
See Tathai (Dec 26).

Athanasia (St) W.   Aug 14
d. 860   Born in the island of Aegina of an ancient Greek family. Her first husband died fighting against the Saracens; her second husband, with her consent, left her to become a monk. She turned her house into a convent, and numerous disciples gathered around her whom she ruled as an abbess.

Athanasia (St) H.   Oct 9
See Andronicus and Athanasia.

Athanasius (St)   Jan 3
See Zozimus and Athanasius.

Athanasius (St) Bp.   Jan 26
? He is honoured at Sorrento in S. Italy. Nothing is known about him. Perhaps he is to be identified with St Athanasius of Naples (July 15).

Athanasius (St) Bp.   Jan 31
d. *c* 885   A native of Catania in Sicily. During the invasion of the Saracens he fled to Patras in Peloponnesus, became a Basilian monk, and eventually also bishop of Modon.

Athanasius (St) Ab.   Feb 22
d. *c* 818   Born at Constantinople, he became abbot of the Paulo-Petrian monastery, near Nicomedia. He had to suffer much at the hands of the iconoclast emperor, Leo the Armenian.

Athanasius (St) Bp. Dr.   GC. May 2
c 296–373   History has given him the titles, amply deserved, of "Father of Orthodoxy", "Pillar of the Church", and "Champion of Christ's Divinity". A native of Alexandria, he began his public career when a deacon; he denounced Arius as a heretic. He accompanied his bishop to the council of Nicea, and on his return to Alexandria (328) was made patriarch of that city, which he governed for over forty years. His life-work was the defeat of Arianism and the vindication of the divinity of Christ. For this cause he was five times exiled from his see: 336 to Trier; 339–346 to Rome; 356–362 to the desert; 362–363 and a second time during four months of 363 again to the desert: 365–366 was the last of his exiles. Through it all he managed to guide his flock and to write for them most illuminating treatises on Catholic dogma. One of his most

attractive characteristics was his unfailing humour, which often proved a deadly weapon against his adversaries. He is revered in the universal church as one of the four great Greek Doctors, and in the East as one of the three Holy Hierarchs. He was an outstanding theologian.

Athanasius Badzekuketta
(St)) M.   June 3
d. 1886 (May 17) A page to King Mwanga of Uganda and a Keeper of the Royal Treasury. He was baptized in 1885 and martyred by the king's soldiers in the following year. See Charles Lwanga and Comps.

Athanasius (St) M.   July 5
d. 452 A deacon of Jerusalem. He denounced the heretic Theodosius, who had supplanted the Catholic St Juvenal in the see of Jerusalem. For this act he was seized by the soldiery and beheaded.

Athanasius the Athonite
(St) Ab.   July 5
c 920–1003 Born at Trebizond, he embraced the monastic life in Bithynia, whence he migrated to Mt Athos. Here he found a *laura* (961), which became the first nucleus of what has ever since been a wholly monastic republic. At the time of his death he ruled as abbot-general over some sixty communities of hermits and monks living on Mt Athos.

Athanasius (St) Bp.   July 15
d. 872 Son of the duke of Naples, he was made bishop of that city at the age of eighteen. After he had ruled it for twenty years he began to suffer from the exactions of relatives, in whose hands rested the civil authority of Naples. Imprisoned, and then exiled, he died at Veroli and was buried at Montecassino, whence his body was transferred to Naples.

Athanasius, Anthusa
and Comp. (SS) MM.   Aug 22
d. c 257 Athanasius was bishop of Tarsus in Cilicia. Anthusa, a noble lady of Seleucia, was baptized by him together with two of her slaves, Charisius and Nephytus. The three men were martyred under Valerian; Anthusa survived twenty-three years. The Acts of St Anthusa which relate this story closely resemble those of St Pelagia of Tarsus.

Athelm (St) Bp. OSB.   Jan 8
d. 923 Paternal uncle of St Dunstan. A monk, and then abbot, of Glastonbury, he was appointed first bishop of Wells in Somerset, and in 914 transferred to the see of Canterbury.

Athenodorus (St) Bp. M.   Oct 18
d.c 269 A native of Neo-Caesarea in Cappa-

docia and a brother of St Gregory the Wonder-Worker (Thaumaturgus). After their conversion the two brothers studied under Origen at Caesarea and then became bishops, Athenodorus of an unnamed see in Pontus. He suffered martyrdom under Aurelian.

Athenodorus (St) M.   Nov 11
d. c 304 A martyr of Mesopotamia under Diocletian, who, according to the pre-1970 RM. "was tormented with fire and tried with other punishments...at length he was condemned to capital punishment, but when the executioner fell to the ground, and none other dared smite him with the sword, he fell asleep in the Lord in prayer".

Athenogenes (St) Bp.
M.   Jan 18, July 16
? On Jan 18 the pre-1970 RM. had: "In Pontus, the birthday of St Athenogenes, an aged theologian, who, when about to consummate his martyrdom by fire, sang a hymn of joy, which he left in writing to his disciples". The martyr is to be identified, it seems, with the bishop who suffered at Sebaste in Armenia with ten disciples, under Diocletian (pre-1970) RM. July 16). The hymn referred to above is, according to St Basil, the beautiful *Phos hilaron*, feature of the vespers service in the Byzantine liturgy.

Atheus (St) C.   Dec 26
Otherwise Tathai, q.v.

Athilda (St) VM.   March 27
Otherwise Alkeld, q.v.

Attala (Attalus) (St) Ab.
OSB.   Apr 3
d. c 800 A Benedictine monk and abbot of a monastery at Taormina in Sicily.

Attalas (St) Ab.   March 10
d. 627 Born in Burgundy, he was professed a monk at Lérins, whence he passed over to Luxeuil under St Columbanus, whom he followed to Bobbio in N. Italy, helping him in the foundation of the abbey and succeeding him as abbot (615). It was during his abbacy that most of the monks stood out against the severity of the Columbanian Rule.

Attalia (Attala) (St) Abs.
OSB.   Dec 3
c 697–741 A niece of St Ottilia. She became a Benedictine nun and abbess of St Stephen's nunnery at Strasburg.

Attalus (St) M.   June 2
See Photinus, Sanctius, etc.

Attalus (St) M. Dec 31
See Stephen, Pontian, etc.

Atticus (St) Bp. Jan 8
d. 425 (Oct 10) A convert from heresy, he opposed St John Chrysostom and was intruded as bishop of Constantinople during the latter's second banishment. However, he repented of his opposition and submitted to Pope Innocent's ruling. Afterwards he lived as an eminently virtuous bishop.

Atticus (St) M. Nov 6
? The pre-1970 RM. had: "In Phrygia St Atticus, Martyr". Nothing else is known about him.

Attilanus (St) Bp. OSB. Oct 5
c 939–1009 A native of Tarazona, near Saragossa, he became a Benedictine at Moreruela under St Froilan, who chose him as prior of the abbey. The two sees of León and Zamora becoming vacant, Froilan was appointed to the former and Attilanus to the latter, and they were ordained together on Whit-Sunday, 990. St Attilanus was canonized in 1089.

Attius (St) M. Aug 1
See Leontius, Attius, etc.

Atto (Attho) (St) Bp. OSB. Vall. May 22
d. 1153 Born at Badajoz in Spain — some Italian writers claim him for Florence in Italy. He became a Benedictine at Vallumbrosa, and eventually abbot-general of the congregation and bishop of Pistoia. He wrote the lives of St John Gualbert and of St Bernard of Parma and a work on Compostella in Spain.

Atto (St) Bp. OSB. June 1
d. c 1044 Benedictine monk at Oña, in Old Castile, under St Enneco. Afterwards bishop of Oca-Valpuesta.

Atto (St) Ab. OSB. Nov 19
d. p.1010 First abbot of Tordino, near Teramo, a house founded by Montecassino in 1004.

Attracta (Athracht) (St) V. Aug 11
? 5th cent. She seems to have been a contemporary of St Patrick. She certainly was a recluse, first at Killaraght, on Lough Gara, and then at Drum, near Boyle. Both places eventually grew into nunneries under her direction. She is venerated throughout Ireland.

Aubert (*several*)
Otherwise Autbert, q.v.

Aubierge (St) V. July 7
Otherwise Ethelburga, q.v.

Aubin (Aubyn) (St) Bp. March 1
Otherwise Albinus, q.v.

Aucejas and Luceia (SS) MM. June 25
See Lucy and Comp.

Auctus, Taurion and Thessalonica (SS) MM. Nov 7
? Martyrs at Amphipolis in Macedonia. Nothing else is known of them.

Audactus (Adauctus) (St) M. Oct 24
See Felix, Audactus, etc.

Audas (or Abdas) (St) Bp. M. May 16
d. 420 A Persian bishop, martyred together with seven priests, nine deacons and seven virgins. Their death marked the beginning of a widespread persecution of Christians throughout the kingdom.

Audax (St) M. July 9
See Anatolia and Audax.

Audifax (St) M. Jan 19
See Marius, Martha, etc.

Audöenus (St) Bp. Aug 24
Otherwise Ouen, q.v.

Audomarus (St) Bp. Sept 9
Otherwise Omer, q.v.

Audrey (Awdrey) (St) V. June 23
Otherwise Etheldreda, q.v.

Augulus (Augurius, Aule) (St) Bp. M. Feb 7
d. c 303 His name appears in the martyrology of St Jerome as a bishop. Others describe him as a martyr put to death in London under Diocletian. French writers usually identify him with St Aule of Normandy.

Augurus (St) M. Jan 21
See Fructuosus, Augurius and Eulogius.

Augusta (St) VM. March 27
5th cent. Daughter of the Teuton duke of Friuli. Her conversion to Christianity so enraged her father that he killed her with his own hand. She has been venerated from time immemorial at Serravalle, near Treviso, in N. Italy.

Augustalis (Autal) (St) Bp. Sept 7
? c 450 A bishop in Gaul, probably at Arles.

Augustina Pietrantoni (Bl) V. SC. Nov 12
Born near Tivoli in 1864 she became a Sister of Charity, serving God and the sick. She was stabbed to death by a patient at the Hospital of

Santo Spirito: her dying words asked for mercy for him. Beatified in 1972.

Augustine Schöffler (St)
M.   May 1
1822–1851 Born at Mittelbronn in Lorraine, he joined the Paris Society of Foreign Missions and was sent to Vietnam where he was beheaded. Canonized in 1988.

Augustine Webster (St)
MO. Cart.   May 4
d. 1535 Prior of the charterhouse of Axholme, England; he was arrested at the London charterhouse and executed at Tyburn. Canonized in 1970 as one of the Forty Martyrs of England and Wales, q.v.

Augustine of Nicomedia
(St) M.   May 7
See Flavius, Augustus and Augustine.

Augustine Novello (Bl)
C. OSA. Erem.   May 19
d. 1309 Born at Taormina, in Sicily. After taking his doctorate in law at Bologna, he was appointed chancellor to King Manfred of Sicily. Left for dead on the battlefield at Benevento, after his recovery he joined the Augustinian friars as a lay-brother with the name Augustine. His gifts were soon discovered and he was commanded to accept presbyteral ordination. Eventually he became prior-general of the order, confessor to the pope, and legate. Cult confirmed in 1759. In art he is shown as a Benedictine monk or a bishop, and holding an icon of the Holy Face.

Augustine of Canterbury
(St) Bp. OSB.   GC. May 27
d. 604 He shares with St Gregory the Great the title of Apostle of the English. He was prior of St Andrew's on the Caelian Hill when he was sent by Pope Gregory the Great with a band of forty companions to evangelize England. The missionaries landed at Ebbsfleet near Ramsgate, Thanet, in 597. Soon Augustine had converted the king of Kent with thousands of his subjects to the Faith. He was ordained bishop at Arles (597) and established his see at Canterbury. He was not so successful in his relations with the Celtic missionaries. He died shortly after St Gregory the Great. Whether he followed the Benedictine rule has been questioned.

Augustine Huy (St) M.   June 13
d. 1839 A native soldier of Vietnam, sawn asunder with St Nicholas The. Canonized in 1988.

Augustine Tchao (Bl) M.   July 9
d. 1815 He was among the soldiers who

St Augustine of Canterbury, May 27

escorted Bl John Gabriel Dufresse to Pekin, and was converted by his behaviour. Ordained priest, he laboured in the Province of Su-Tchuen. He was arrested while on his ministry, and being already sick, died of ill-usage, in prison. Beatified 1900.

Augustine Fangi (Bl) C.
OP. July 22
d. 1493   He was born at Biella, where he joined the Dominicans. After a crowded apostolic life and great bodily sufferings he died at Venice. Cult approved in 1872.

Augustine Gazotich (Bl)
Bp. OP. Aug 3
1262–1323   A native of Trau in Dalmatia, he became a Friar Preacher at the age of twenty. Eventually he was sent to preach among the Slavs and Hungarians and in 1303 was chosen bishop of Zagreb in Croatia. Later he was translated to Lucera (Nocera) in Italy. His characteristic was gentleness, and he had the gift of healing. Beatified by Clement XI.

Augustine Cannini (Bl)
M. OSM. Aug 11
See Laurence Nerucci, etc.

Augustine of Hippo (St)
Bp. Dr Founder GC. Aug 28
Nov 13, 354–Aug 28, 430   A native of Tagaste in N. Africa. In spite of his early training by his mother, St Monica, he spent his youth in vice and all but became a Manichaean. A professor of rhetoric by profession, he taught successively at Tagaste, Carthage, Rome (383) and Milan (384–386). Under the influence of St Ambrose, of St Paul's Letters and of some neoplatonist writings, he was converted and was baptized at thirty-two by St Ambrose at Easter 387. The same year he left for Africa, his mother dying at Ostia. From 388 to 391 he lived a sort of monastic life with a few friends near Tagaste. In 391 he was ordained priest at Hippo and three years later coadjutor-bishop of the same city. From this time on he devoted all his energy and extraordinary intellectual gifts to the defence of Christian faith and morals and to the refutation of heresy and schism, thus opposing Manichaeans, Priscillianists, Donatists, Pelagians and Semipelagians, and Arian Vandals. His leading ideas and principles on religious life are still followed by numerous canons, friars, hermits and nuns. He is one of the most prolific, and certainly the most influential, of all the Doctors. His two works, the *Confessions* and the *City of God*, are reckoned among the world's classics. In his life he is a miracle of divine grace, since even the child of his sin, Adeodatus, is now venerated as a saint. His relics are enshrined in the basilica of S. Pietro in Ciel d'Oro, Pavia.

Augustine Ambrose Chevreux (Bl) M. OSB.
Sept 2
d. 1792   The last superior-general of the French Benedictine congregation of St Maur

St Augustine of Hippo, Aug 28

— the Maurists. He was imprisoned with a numerous band of ecclesiastics at the Carmelite monastery of Paris (*Les Carmes*) and put to death in the general massacre of Sept 2. Beatified in 1931.

Augustine, Sanctian and Beata (SS) MM.
Sept 6
d. 273   Three Spanish Christians, who fled to Gaul in time of persecution and were martyred near Sens, where they are still venerated.

Augustine Ota (Bl) M.
SJ. Sept 25
1622 (Aug 10)   A native of Firando, Japan, who helped the missionaries as a catechist, was imprisoned at Iki, received into the Society of Jesus in prison, and beheaded at Iki. Beatified in 1867.

Augustine and Paulinus
(SS) Mks. OSB.   Nov 5
6th cent. According to the Cassinese tradition, they were monks sent by St Benedict to the foundations of Terracina.

Augustine Moi (St) M.   Dec 19
d. 1839 A poor day-labourer in Vietnam, a Dominican tertiary, he was strangled because he refused to trample on the crucifix. Beatified in 1900, Canonized in 1988.

Augustus Chapdelaine
(Bl) M.   Feb 27
1814–1856 Born in France, the ninth child of a peasant. After his ordination to the priesthood in the Paris Society of Foreign Missions, he served as a curate, and then went to China to work as a missionary priest in the apostolic vicariate of Kwang-si. He was put to death with every refinement of cruelty. Beatified in 1900.

Augustus (St) M.   May 7
See Flavius, Augustus, and Augustine.

Augustus (St) C.   Sept 1
See Priscus, Castrensis, etc.

Augustus (St) C.   Oct 7
6th cent. An abbot of Bourges in France, friend of St Germanus of Paris. He is chiefly notable for having discovered the body of St Ursinus, apostle of that district.

Aulaire (St) VM.   Feb 12
Otherwise Eulalia of Barcelona, q.v.

Auld (St) Bp.   Feb 4
Otherwise Aldate, q.v.

Aunaire (St) Bp.   Sept 25
Otherwise Anacharius, q.v.

Aurea (Oria) (St) V. OSB.   March 11
d. *c* 1069 An anchoress attached to the Benedictine abbey of San Millán de la Cogolla in the old kingdom of Navarre, Upper Ebro, Spain. She lived under obedience of the abbot and was directed by St Dominic of Silos. She died at the age of twenty-seven.

Aurea (Aura) (St) WM.   July 19
d. 856 Born at Cordoba, daughter of infidel parents, in her widowhood she became a Christian and a nun at Cuteclara, where she remained for more than twenty years. She was then denounced as a Christian by her own family and beheaded.

Aurea (St) VM.   Aug 24
d. *c* 270 The Acts of St Aurea's martyrdom are described as a "hagiographical romance", but her existence is vouched for by the early cultus at her shrine at Ostia.

Aurea (St) Abs.   Oct 4
d. 666 A Syrian lady, placed by St Eligius at the head of the nunnery of St Martial at Paris (633). She governed the community thirty-three years and died of the plague, together with one hundred and sixty of her nuns.

Aurea (St) Abs.   Oct 6
8th cent. A young girl of Amiens who retired to Boves and eventually became the abbess of a numerous community.

Aurelia and Neomisia
(SS) VV.   Sept 25
? Born in Asia, they visited Palestine and Rome. At Capua they were maltreated by the Saracens (?) but escaped under cover of a thunderstorm. They took shelter at Macerata, near Anagni, where they died.

Aurelia (St) V. OSB.   Oct 15
d. 1027 A French princess who spent fifty-five years as a recluse at Strasburg under the obedience of a Benedictine abbey. Her name has been associated with that of St Wolfgang.

Aurelia (St) M.   Dec 2
See Eusebius, Marcellus, etc.

Aurelian (St) Bp.   May 10
1st (or 3rd) cent. Disciple of St Martial of Limoges, and eventually bishop of that city.

Aurelian (St) Bp.   June 16
d. *c* 550 He became the bishop of Arles in 546 and was appointed papal legate in Gaul by Pope Vigilius. He founded two monasteries, one for monks and one for nuns, and drew up for each a monastic rule, based on that of St Caesarius.

Aurelian (St) Bp. OSB.   July 4
d. 895 Monk and abbot of Ainay and afterwards archbishop of Lyons.

Aurelius (St) Bp.   July 20
d. 429 Bishop of Carthage, metropolitan, friend and fellow-worker of St Augustine of Hippo. He was among the first to detect and oppose Pelagianism. He was forced by the violence of his adversaries to invoke the civil power against them, much against his own will.

Aurelius of Cordoba (St)
M.   July 27
See George, Aurelius, and the translation of their relics to Paris, in the pre-1970 RM. Oct 20.

Aurelius and Publius
(SS) Bps. MM.   Nov 12
2nd cent. Two bishops who wrote against

the Montanists or Cata-Phrygians. They were martyred, probably in Asia, according to others in N. Africa.

Aureus, Justina and Comp. (SS) MM. June 16
? During an invasion of the Huns, St Aureus, bishop of Mainz, was driven from his see and was followed by his sister, Justina, and others. On their return, while the bishop was celebrating the eucharist, he and the others were murdered in the church.

Ausonius (St) Bp. M. May 22
1st (or 3rd) cent. Supposed to have been a disciple of St Martial of Limoges, and first bishop of Angoulême.

Auspicius (St) Bp. July 8
d. *c* 130 Said to have been the fourth bishop of Trier and successor of St Maternus (*c* 130). It seems, however, that he should be identified with a first-century bishop of Toul of the same name.

Auspicius (St) Bp. July 8
d. *c* 475 According to Sidonius Apollinaris, he was bishop of Toul. He was buried at Saint-Mansuy.

Auspicius (St) Bp. Aug 2
Before 4th cent. Said to have been the first bishop of Apt.

Austell (St) C. June 28
6th cent. A disciple of St Mewan or Mevan of Cornwall. He lived probably in the district where a place-name preserves his memory. Some modern writers conjectured that Austell (Hawystill) is a woman saint, one of the daughters of the famous Brychan of Wales, who has perhaps left her name to Aust or Awst in Gloucestershire.

Austin (St)
Otherwise Augustine (especially St Augustine of Canterbury).

Austindus (St) Bp. OSB. Sept 25
d. 1068 A native of Bordeaux, he became a monk and then abbot of Saint-Orens, at Auch, where he introduced the Cluniac observance. In 1041 he was elected archbishop of Auch and proved a brave upholder of the rights of his church against simoniacal customs.

Austreberta (Eustreberta) (St) V. Abs. OSB. Feb 10
630–704 Born near Thérouanne, in Artois, daughter of St Framechildis and the count palatine Badefrid. She received the veil at the hands of St Omer in the nunnery of Abbeville (Port-sur-Somme) of which she became abbess. As abbess she governed Pavilly in Normandy and proved to be most successful.

Austregildis (St) W. Apr 18
Otherwise Agia, q.v.

Austregisilus (Aoustrille, Outrille) (St) Bp. May 20
551–624 Born at Bourges, he was educated as a courtier, but preferred the life of a monk and entered the abbey of Saint-Nizier at Lyons, where he became abbot. In 612 he was elected bishop of Bourges. He has always been honoured as a saint.

Austremonius (Stremoine) (St) Bp. Nov 1
1st (or 3rd) cent. One of the seven missionaries sent from Rome to evangelize Gaul. He preached in Auvergne and was the first bishop of Clermont-Ferrand.

Austriclinian (St) C. June 30
See Martial, Alpinian and Austriclinian.

Astrude (St) V. Oct 17
Otherwise Anstrudis, q.v.

Autbert (St) Mk. OSB. Feb 1
d. 1129 A Benedictine monk of Landevenec in Brittany, who became chaplain to the nuns of St Sulpice, near Reims. He is honoured liturgically at Reims.

Autbert (St) Bp. Sept 10
d. *p.*709 A bishop of Avranches, famous because he founded the abbey-church and monastery of Mont-St-Michel *in periculo maris* on the Normandy coast.

Autbert (St) Bp. Dec 13
d. *c* 669 Bishop of Cambrai-Arras. As such he was a great fosterer of monastic life and the founder of monasteries, among others, of the great abbey of St Vedast (Saint Vaast) at Arras. He does not seem, however, to have been a monk himself. Under him Hainault and Flanders became a vast monastic colony.

Autbodus (St) C. Nov 20
d. 690 An Irish missionary who preached in Artois, Hainault, and Picardy, and died as a hermit near Laon.

Autel (St) Bp. Sept 7
Otherwise Augustalis, q.v.

Authaire (Oye) (St) C. Apr 24
7th cent. A courtier at the palace of King Dagobert I of France and father of St Ouen of Rouen. He is the patron saint of the village La-Ferté-sous-Jouarre, where he usually resided.

Authbertus (Audbert, Aubert, Albert) (*several*)
Otherwise Autbert, q.v.

Autonomus (St) Bp. M.   Sept 12
d. *c* 300   Said by the Greeks to have been an
Italian bishop who, to escape the fury of the
persecution under Diocletian, fled into Bithynia in Asia Minor, where he made many
converts and afterwards was martyred.

Autor (Adinctor, Auteur)
(St) Bp.   Aug 9
5th cent.   The thirteenth bishop of Metz. In
830 his relics were translated to the abbey of
Marmoutier.

Auxanus (St) Bp.   Sept 3
d. 568   Known in Milan as Sant' Ansano.
He was bishop of that city, where he has always
been held in great veneration.

Auxentius (St) H.   Feb 14
d. *c* 470   Born in Syria, of Persian parents,
he served as a soldier in the guards of the
emperor Theodosius the Younger. Later he
retired to live as a hermit in Bithynia. He was
accused of heresy at the council of Chalcedon,
but most successfully vindicated his orthodoxy.

Auxentius (St) M.   Dec 13
See Eustratius, Auxentius, etc.

Auxentius (St) Bp.   Dec 18
d. *p*.321   A soldier in the army of the emperor Licinius, he had to suffer for refusing to
take part in idolatrous practices. However, he
survived the persecution and became a priest
and lastly bishop of Mopsuestia in Cilicia.

Auxibius (St) Bp.   Feb 19
1st cent.   Said to have been baptized by St
Mark and ordained by St Paul as first bishop of
Soli in Cyprus.

Auxilius (St) B.   March 19
d. *c* 460   A companion of St Patrick, he was
made bishop and resided at Killossey.

Auxilius (St) M.   Nov 27
See Basileus, Auxilius and Saturninus.

Auxilius, Isserninus and
Secundinus (SS) Bps.   Dec 6
5th cent.   Fellow-workers under St Patrick in
the evangelization of Ireland. The decree
signed by the four, reminding the Irish clergy
that appeals from the judgment of Armagh
may be made to Rome, is still extant.

Ava (or Avia) (St) Abs.
OSB.   Apr 29
d. *p*.845   A niece of King Pepin, in her
childhood and youth she was blind, but was
cured miraculously by St Rainfredis. She
entered a nunnery at Denain in Hainault,
where she became abbess.

Aventinus of Chartres
(St) Bp.   Feb 4
d. *c* 520   Bishop of Chartres, in which office
he succeeded his brother, St Solemnis.

Aventinus of Troyes (St)
H.   Feb 4
c 538   Born in central France, he acted as
almoner to St Lupus, bishop of Troyes, until
he retired to live as a hermit. The spot where
he thus lived is now called Saint-Aventin.

Aventinus (St) M.   June 7
d. 732   Born at Bagnères in the Pyrenees, he
became a recluse in the valley of Larboush,
where the Saracens discovered him and put
him to death.

Avertanus (St) C. OC.   Feb 25
d. 1380   A native of Limoges, where he was
professed as a Carmelite lay-brother. He died
outside Lucca while on a pilgrimage to Palestine.

Avitus (St) M.   Jan 27
? The pre-1970 RM. mentions a martyr of
this name in Africa, who is probably to be
identified with the St Avitus venerated in the
Canary Islands as their apostle and first
bishop.

Avitus of Vienne (St) Bp.   Feb 5
d. *c* 520   Born in Auvergne and brother to St
Apollinaris, bishop of Valence. Their father St
Isychius, a Roman senator, had been bishop of
Vienne. Avitus succeeded him. As a bishop he
commanded the respect of his flock, as also of
the pagan Franks and the Arian Burgundians.
He converted the Burgundian king, Sigismund. St Avitus was also an elegant writer.

Avitus II of Clermont
(St) Bp.   Feb 21
d. 689   Bishop of Clermont in Auvergne
from 676 to 689. He was one of the great
bishops who defended and developed the
church training of the epoch.

Avitus (Avy) (St) Ab.   June 17
d. *c* 530   First a monk of Menat in Auvergne, then abbot of Micy, near Orleans, finally a
hermit in the French province of Perche,
where he was forced by numerous followers to
build, and govern, a new monastery.

Avitus I of Clermont (St)
Bp.   Aug 21
d. *c* 600   Eighteenth bishop of Clermont,
contemporary of St Gregory of Tours, whom
he ordained deacon.

Avitus (or Adjutus) (St)
Ab.   Dec 19
? The pre-1970 RM. called him Adjutus. It

seems that he was an abbot of Micy, near Orleans. If so, there must have been two of the same name, and almost contemporaries, in the same abbey (see Avitus, June 17).

Aybert (St) H. OSB.   Apr 7
Otherwise Aibert, q.v.

Aye (St)   Apr 18 or Sept 1
Otherwise Agia, q.v.

Aymard (Bl) Ab. OSB.   Oct 5
d. 965   He succeeded St Odo in the abbacy of Cluny (942); but, after about ten years he became blind and resigned his office to St Majolus, giving to all during the rest of his life an example of wonderful resignation. Many writers call him saint.

Azadanes and Azades
(SS) MM.   Apr 22
d. 341–342   The former a deacon, the latter an officer of high standing at the court of the Persian king, Shapur II. They were martyred together with Abdesus and others.

Azariah (St)   Dec 16
6th cent. B.C.   One of the three youths cast into the fiery furnace at Babylon by order of Nebuchadnezzar. The Babylonian officials gave him the name of Abednego.

Azas and Comp. (SS)
MM.   Nov 19
d. c 304   About one hundred and fifty Christian soldiers martyred in Isauria, Asia Minor, under Diocletian.

B

Babylas, Urban, Prilidian and Epolonius (SS) MM. Jan 24

d. *c* 250 Babylas was bishop of Antioch, the most celebrated occupant of that see after St Ignatius. St John Chrysostom preached two homilies in his praise, in one of these he asserts that Babylas refused admission to his church to an emperor, who is held to have been Philip the Arabian. The other three were his pupils. Babylas died in chains awaiting execution under Decius and his relics were enshrined near a temple of Apollo, to the chagrin of Julian the Apostate. The three youths were put to death.

Babilla (St) VM. May 20

Otherwise Basilla, q.v.

Barbolenus (St) Ab. June 26

d. *c* 677 Monk of Luxeuil under St Columbanus, and afterwards first abbot of St Peter, later St Maur-des-Fossés, near Paris. He was helped by St Fursey in the erection of many churches and hospitals in the diocese of Paris.

Barbolenus (St) Ab. OSB. Aug 31

d. *c* 640 Fourth abbot of Bobbio in Italy, where he introduced the Benedictine rule in place of that of St Columbanus.

Bacchus (St) M. Oct 7

See Sergius and Bacchus.

Badarn (Padarn) (*several*)

Otherwise Paternus, q.v.

Bademus (St) M. Apr 10

c 380 A native of Persia, founder and abbot of a monastery near Beth-Lapat in his own country. He suffered martyrdom under Shapur II.

Badilo (St) Ab. OSB. Oct 8

d. *c* 870 A Benedictine monk of Vezelay (Yonne), who became abbot of Leuze (*Lutsa*) in Hainault.

Badulfus (Badour, Badolf) (St) Ab. OSB. Aug 19

d. *c* 850 Monk and abbot of Ainay, Lyons. The *Proprium* of Lyons has a commemoration on Aug 19.

Baglan (SS)

? There are two Welsh saints of this name, both attributed to the fifth century, but beyond the fact of there being existing churches dedicated to their honour, and a mention in an ancient litany, nothing is known of them.

Bain (Bainus, Bagnus) (St) Bp. OSB. June 20

d. *c* 710 Monk of Fontenelle under St Wandrille. In 685 he was made bishop of Thérouanne, which then included Calais. After twelve years he resigned and went back to Fontenelle, and three years later became its abbot. Towards the end of his life he had to govern, in addition, the abbey of Fleury which Pepin had just restored. He is the principal patron saint of Calais.

Baisil (St)

? Patron of a church in the Llandaff diocese. There is no record of such a saint in Welsh hagiology. It may be that *Baisil* is only a misspelling of some other appellative.

Baithin (St) Ab. June 9

d. *c* 598 Also called Comin or Cominus, and described as first cousin to St Columba, whom he succeeded as abbot of Iona. He is said to have died on the anniversary of the death of St Columba.

Bajulus (St) M. Dec 20

See Liberatus and Bajulus.

Balbina (St) VM. March 31

d. *c* 130 The pre-1970 RM. had this *laus*: "At Rome, the birthday of St. Balbina the Virgin, daughter of blessed Quirinus the martyr; she was baptized by Pope Alexander, and chose Christ as her Spouse in her virginity; after completing the course of this world she was buried on the Appian Way near her father". Later on, her relics were enshrined in the church dedicated in her name on the Aventine. Modern writers query the truth of all the above statements, admitting merely that there was a Roman virgin of this name.

Balda (St) Abs. OSB. Dec 9

d. late 7th cent. Third abbess of Jouarre in the diocese of Meaux. Her relics were enshrined in the abbey church of Nesle-la-Reposte, diocese of Troyes.

Baldegundis (St) Abs.   Feb 10
c 580   Abbess of Saint-Croix, Poitiers, one of the most ancient of French nunneries.

Balderic (Baudry) (St)
Ab.   Oct 16
7th cent.   He and his sister, St Bova, were children of Sigebert I, king of Austrasia. Eventually he became the abbot-founder of Montfaucon in Champagne as well as the founder and protector of a nunnery at Reims where his sister took the veil.

Baldomerus (or Galmier)
(St) Mk.   Feb 27
d. c 650   By trade a locksmith at Lyons, later in life he retired to the monastery of St Justus under Abbot Viventius, and was ordained sub-deacon. He is the patron saint of locksmiths, and is represented in art carrying pincers and blacksmith's tools.

Baldred (St) Bp.   March 6
8th cent.   A Scottish bishop alleged to have been the successor of St Kentigern or Mungo at Glasgow, and to have ended his life as a hermit on the coast of the Firth of Forth. Some identify him with St Balther, the hermit of Tinningham.

Baldus (St) H.   Oct 29
Otherwise Baud, Baudin, or Bond. See Bond.

Baldwin (St) Ab. OSB.
Cist.   July 15
d. 1140   An Italian, who became a monk of Clairvaux under St Bernard and one of the most beloved disciples of the holy founder. He was sent back to Italy as abbot of San Pastore in the diocese of Rieti. He is the principal patron saint of Rieti.

Baldwin (Balduinus,
Baudoin) (St) M.   Oct 16
d. c 680   Son of St Salaberga and brother of St Anstrude, abbess at Laon. He was archdeacon at Laon, and was murdered in circumstances which have led to his being honoured as a martyr.

Balin (Balanus, Balloin)
(St)   Sept 3
7th cent.   Said to have been the brother of St Gerald (March 13) and one of the four sons of an Anglo-Saxon king. He and his brothers, after accompanying St Colman of Lindisfarne to Iona, retired into Connaught in Ireland and settled at Tecksaxon, "the house of the Saxons", in the diocese of Tuam.

Balsamus (Bl) Ab. OSB.   Nov 24
d. 1232   Tenth abbot of Cava, which he governed from 1208 to 1232. He is described by John of Capua, as "the gem of the priest-

hood and the crown of prelates". Cult approved in 1928.

Balthasar (St)   Jan 6
One of the Magi, q.v.

Balthasar de Torres (Bl)
M. SJ.   June 20
1563–1626   Born at Granada, he became a Jesuit (1579), was sent to India (1586), taught theology at Goa and Macao, and passed over to Japan (1606) where he remained during the terrible persecution which broke out soon after. He was burnt alive at Nagasaki. Beatified in 1867.

Balthasar of Chiavari
(Bl) C. OFM.   Oct 17
d. 1492   A Friar Minor and fellow preacher with Bl Bernadinus of Feltre. He is venerated in the diocese of Pavia. Cult confirmed in 1930.

Balther (Baldred,
Balredus) (St) Mk. OSB.   March 6
d. 756   A monk-priest of Lindisfarne, who became an anchorite at Tinningham on the Scottish border, where he lived on Bass Rock, near North Berwick, surrounded by the sea. His relics were enshrined at Durham, with those of St Bilfrid, the anchorite.

Bandaridus (Banderik,
Bandery) (St) Bp.   Aug 9
d. 566   Bishop of Soissons from 540 to 566 and founder of Crépin abbey. He was banished by Clotaire I and worked for seven years, without making himself known, as a gardener in an English abbey. At length Clotaire discovered his place of refuge and recalled him to his see. He was buried in the abbey he had founded.

Banka (St) V.   June 4
Otherwise Breaca, q.v.

Baptist or Baptista
(*several*)
See under John Baptist.

Barachisius (St) M.   March 29
See Jonas, Barachisius, and Comp.

Baradates (St) H.   Feb 22
d. c 460   Theodoret in his *Philotheus* gives a glowing acount of this Syrian solitary, whom he calls "the admirable Baradates". The emperor Leo I of Constantinople wrote to consult Baradates regarding the council of Chaldedon.

Barat, Magdalen (St)   May 25
See Mary-Magdalen Sophie Barat.

Barbara (St) VM.   formerly Dec 4
?   According to the extant legend, first told by

Metaphrastes in the tenth century, she was
shut up in a tower by her father, who himself
killed her for being a Christian, whereupon he
was struck dead by lightning. According the
the pre-1970 RM. this happened at Nicomedia under Maximinus Thrax. But the
whole legend is obviously spurious, and she
never existed. She was the patron saint of
firework makers, artillerymen, architects,
founders, stonemasons, grave-diggers, forti-
fications, magazines, and a protectress against
lightning, fire, sudden death and impenitence.
In art she is usually represented holding a
tower, and with the palm of martyrdom, or a
chalice or feather, and trampling on a Saracen.
Cult suppressed in 1969.

Barbasymas (Barbascemin)
and Comp. (SS) MM.   Jan 14
d. 346 Bishop of Seleucia-Ctesiphon in
Persia. Under Shapur II he was incarcerated
for eleven months with sixteen companions in
an infected prison. After being tortured, they
were all put to death.

Barbatian (St) C.   Dec 31
5th cent. A priest of Antioch who came to
Rome and there attracted the attention of the
empress Placidia Augusta. She induced him to
fix his residence at Ravenna, near the imperial
court, where she built for him a monastery. By
his prudent advice he rendered great services
to the state.

Barbatus (Barbas) (St)
Bp.   Feb 19
c 612–682 A native of Benevento where, as a
priest and later as a bishop (663), he rendered
signal services to his native town, especially
when it was besieged by the emperor Constans
II of Byzantium. He assisted at the sixth
general council, held at Constantinople, at
which the Monothelites were condemned.

Barbe (St) VM.   Dec 4
The French for Barbara, q.v.

Barbea (St) M.   Jan 29
See Sarbelius and Barbea.

Bardo (St) Bp. OSB.   June 10
982–1053 Born at Oppershofen and educated at Fulda, where he received the Benedictine habit and became a dean. In 1029 he was
chose abbot of Werden on the Ruhr, in 1031
abbot of Hersfeld, and in the same year archbishop of Mainz. He was for a time the chancellor and grand almoner of the Empire. He was
noted for his love of the poor, the destitute, and
of animals. He was also noted for his austerities,
which Pope St Leo IX considered too severe
and advised him to relax.

St Barbara, formerly Dec 4

Bardomian, Eucarpus
and Comp. (SS) MM.   Sept 25
? Twenty-eight martyrs of Asia Minor in one
of the early persecutions.

Barhadbesciabas (St) M.   July 20
d. 355   A deacon of Arbela in Persia
beheaded under Shapur II.

Barlaam (St) M.   Nov 19
d. *c* 304   A martyr of Caesarea in Cappadocia under Diocletian. His memory has been
preserved in one of St Basil's homilies,
preached in his honour.

**Barlaam and Josaphat
(SS)**   Nov 27
? These two supposed saints are the protagonists of a Christian version of a Buddhist
romance — perhaps the adaption was by St
John Damascene for it was he who popularized
the present Greek text which dates from the
seventh century. By a piece of great good
fortune the entire text of the apology for
Christianity of Aristides, the Athenian, was
embodied in the romance and has thus come
down to us.

Barnabas (St) Apostle M.
                                   GC. June 11
1st cent.   A native of Cyprus and a very early
disciple. He is one of the most attractive
characters of the New Testament, and the
early chapters of the Acts of the Apostles are
full of his name and deeds. It was he who
"introduced" St Paul to the Apostles and thus
to the church. He was not one of the twelve,
but has always been honoured as an apostle.
An old tradition has it that he died a martyr in
Cyprus. Another, that he was first bishop of
Milan. His name is in the first eucharistic
prayer. In art he is often depicted as standing
on or near a pile of stones, holding a book.

Barnabas of Poland (St)
H. OSB. Cam.   July 9
See Justus of Poland.

Barnard (St) Bp. OSB.   Jan 23
777–841   Born in the Lyonnais, he was educated at the court of Charlemagne. He restored the abbey of Ambournay and became a
monk therein and finally abbot. In 810 he was
ordained bishop of Vienne, and became one of
the most influential bishops of his age. As
archbishop he founded the abbey of Romans
(*c* 837) where he was buried. Cult as a saint
approved in 1907.

Barnoch (St) C.   Sept 27
Otherwise Barrog, q.v.

**Barontius and Desiderius
(SS)** Mks. OSB.   March 25
c 725   Barontius was a gentleman of Berry
who became a monk at Lonrey, diocese of
Bourges. As a result of a vision he asked
permission to become a hermit, set out for
Italy, and established himself in the district of

St Barnabas, June 11

Pistoia. There he lived a most austere life with
another monk, Desiderius by name, who is
also honoured as a saint.

**Barr (Finbar, Barrocus)
(St)** Bp.   Sept 25
6th cent.   A native of Connaught, who
founded, and presided over, a monastic school
at Lough Eire, thus originating the city of
Cork, of which he became first bishop. He
died at Cloyne.

**Barrfoin (Bairrfhionn,
Barrindus) (St)**   May 21
6th cent.   Said to have had charge of the
church founded by St Columba at Drum
Cullen Offaly, and afterwards to have lived at
Killbarron, near Ballyshannon, in Donegal. It
is added that he reached America on one of his
missions by sea, and informed St Brendan the
Navigator of his discovery. By some he is said

to have been a bishop. The details of his life are vague.

Barrog (Barrwg, Barnoch) (St) H.   Sept 27

7th cent. A reputed disciple of the great Welsh St Cadoc, he has left his name (often spelled Barruc or Barnoch) to Barry Island, off the coast of Glamorgan, where he lived as a hermit.

Barsabas and Comp. (SS) MM.   Oct 20

d. c 342 A Persian abbot and his eleven monks put to death under Shapur II near the ruins of Persepolis.

Barsabas (St) M.   Dec 11

d. c 342 A Persian abbot, who, with several of his monks, suffered under Shapur II. Some identify him with St Barsabas of Oct 20, others with St Simeon Barasbae, commemorated on Apr 21.

Barsanuphius (St) H.   Apr 11

d. c 540 An anchorite near Gaza, in Palestine, greatly venerated among the Greeks, who keep his feast on Feb 6. He became by letter the counsellor of the entire region.

Barsenorius (St) Ab. OSB.   Sept 13

7th cent. Successor of St Leutfrid (Leufroy) as abbot of La-Croix-Saint-Leuffroi, in the diocese of Evreux. His relics are at Fécamp.

Barses (Barso, Barsas) (St) Bp.   Jan 30

d. c 379 A bishop of Edessa in Syria, banished to W. Egypt on the frontiers of Libya by the Arian emperor Valens. He died in exile.

Barsimaeus (Barsamja) (St) Bp.   Jan 30

? According to the pre-1970 RM., a bishop of Edessa, who, after converting many to the faith, suffered under Trajan. The story of his martyrdom, however, is now rejected.

Bartholomaea Bagnesi (Bl) V. OP.   May 27

1511–1577 Born at Florence, she became a Dominican nun in 1544, and until her death was afflicted with many and varied sufferings, including diabolical obsessions. Cult approved by Pius VII.

Bartholomaea Capitanio (St) V. Foundress   July 27

1807–1836 Together with St Vincenza Gerosa (q.v.) she founded the Italian Sisters of Charity of Lovere. In spite of her extreme youth, she was the real driving force in her institute throughout her short life. The institute was approved in 1840.

Bartholomew Alvarez (Bl) M. SJ.   Jan 12

d. 1737 A Portuguese, born near Braganza, who joined the Jesuits at Coimbra in 1723. He was sent to Tonkin, where he was arrested in March 1736 and beheaded the following year.

Bartholomew Alban Roe (Bl) M. OSB.   Jan 21

See Alban Bartholomew Roe.

Bartholomew Aiutami-Cristo (Bl) H. OSB. Cam.   Jan 28

d. 1224 He received the surname Aiutami-Cristo ("Christ help me") because this ejaculation was always on his lips. He was born at Pisa, and became a Camaldolese lay-brother at the monastery of San Frediano in his native city. Cult approved in 1857.

Bartholomew Laurel (St) M. OFM.   Feb 6

d. 1627 Born at Mexico City, he became a Franciscan lay-brother and in 1609 was sent to Manila, where he studied medicine. In 1622 he crossed over to Japan and a few years later was burnt alive at Nagasaki. He is venerated on Feb 6 as one of the companions of St Paul Miki q.v.

Bartholomew (Hugh) Amidei (St)   Feb 12

See Seven Holy Founders.

Bartholomew of Cervere (Bl) M. OP.   Apr 21

1420–1466 Born at Savigliano in Piedmont. He taught theology at Turin and afterwards was appointed inquisitor in Piedmont. For his zeal in exercising his office he was killed by heretics at Cervere, diocese of Fossano. Cult approved by Pius IX.

Bartholomew Pucci-Franceschi (Bl) C. OFM.   May 23

d. 1330 (May 6) A wealthy married lay-man of Montepulciano, who, with his wife's consent, became a Franciscan friar, and is usually described as having become "a fool for Christ's sake". Cult confirmed in 1880.

Bartholomew of Durham (or of Farne) (St) H. OSB.   June 24

d. c 1193 A native of Whitby who, after being ordained a priest in Norway, became a Benedictine at Durham and was subsequently given leave by the abbot to lead an eremitical life on Farne Island, in the cell consecrated of old by St Cuthbert. There he spent forty-two years and there he died.

Bartholomew de Vir (Bl) Bp. OSB. Cist.   June 26

d. 1157 As bishop of Laon (1113–1151) he

helped St Norbert in the foundation of Prémontré. In 1121 he built the Cistercian abbey of
Foigny, where he became a monk in 1151.

Bartholomew Sonati (Bl)
M. OSM.   Aug 11
See Laurence Nerucci, etc.

Bartholomew Monfiore
(Bl) M.   Aug 19
d. 1622   A Japanese sailor in the ship of Bl
Joachim Firaiama. He was beheaded at Nagasaki. Beatified in 1867.

Bartholomew (St)
Apostle M.   GC. Aug 24
1st cent.   One of the Twelve, he is identified
with Nathanael (John I). He is said to have
preached in Asia Minor, N.W. India and Greater Armenia, and to have been flayed alive. His
alleged relics are enshrined in Rome on the
island in the Tiber called after him, Isola di San
Bartolomeo. He is depicted as an elderly man
holding a flaying knife and a human skin.

Bartholomew Gutierrez
(Bl) M. OSA.   Sept 3
1538–1632   A native of Mexico, he joined
the Augustinian friars (1596), was ordained at
Puebla and sent to Manila in 1606. In 1612 he
went to Japan as prior of Ukusi. He worked
most zealously, though his life was in continual
danger. At last, in 1629 he was betrayed,
imprisoned for three years at Omura, and
burnt alive at Nagasaki. Beatified in 1867.

Bartholomew Xikiemon
(Bl) M.   Sept 10
d. 1622   A Japanese layman, beheaded at
Nagasaki. He belongs to the group of Bl
Charles Spinola, q.v.

Bartholomew of Braganza
(Bl) Bp. OP.   Oct 23
c 1200–1271   Born at Vicenza, he received
the Dominican habit at the hands of St
Dominic himself at Padua. In 1233 he
founded a sort of military order — the *Fratres
Gaudentes* — for the preservation of public
order. In 1252 he was sent to Cyprus as bishop
of Nimesia, whence he was translated to
Vicenza (1256). Cult approved in 1793.

Bartholomew of
Marmoutier (Bl) Bp.
OSB.   Nov 11
d. 1067   Abbot of Marmoutier, and archbishop of Tours from 1052 to 1067. He was a
tireless worker in the face of many difficulties.
He strove unavailingly to bring back Berengarius to the Catholic faith.

Bartholomew of Rossano
(St) Ab.   Nov 11
d. 1065   Of Greek extraction, he was born at

St Bartholomew, Aug 24

Rossano, in Calabria. He followed St Nilus to the foundation of Grottaferrata, at Frascati, near Rome, under St Basil's rule and in the Greek rite. St Bartholomew is rightly considered its second founder. He excelled as a composer of Greek hymns. It was he who persuaded Pope Benedict IX to reform his life and do penance at Grottoferrata.

Bartholomew Xeki (Bl) M. Nov 27
d. 1619 A Japanese layman of the royal family of Firando, beheaded at Nagasaki. Beatified 1867.

Bartholomew Fanti (Bl)
C. OC. Dec 5
1443–1495 Born at Mantua, where he joined the Carmelites. He was the instructor of St John Baptist Spagnuolo, and was famous as a preacher and director as well as for his gift of healing. Cult confirmed in 1909.

Bartholomew (Bartolo)
Buonpedoni (Bl) C. Dec 14
d. 1300 Born near San Geminiano, in Italy. He was first a lay-servant at the Benedictine abbey of San Vito, at Pisa. Later he became a Franciscan tertiary. When he was thirty years of age the bishop of Volterra ordained him priest, and he served the village of Peccioli, near Volterra. The last twenty years of his life he spent as a leper ministering to his fellow-sufferers with infinite patience. Cult confirmed in 1910.

Barulas (St) M. Nov 18
See Romanus and Barula.

Barypsabas (St) M. Sept 10
1st cent. A hermit from the East who suffered martyrdom in Dalmatia. A Greek legend has it that Barypsabas had carried to Rome a vessel containing some of the precious blood which flowed from the side of our Lord on the cross.

Basil (St) Bp. Jan 1
c 475 A priest of Arles who became second bishop of Aix, in Provence.

Basil the Great (St)
Bp. Dr. GC. Jan 2
c 330–379 (Jan 1) Born at Caesarea in Cappadocia. His parents, his paternal grandparents, his two brothers and one sister, are all honoured as saints. After his studies at Constantinople and Athens, Basil visited the monastic colonies of Egypt, Palestine and Syria, and founded one himself on the river Iris, in Pontus, for which he wrote his Rules, still the standard works of their kind in the East. In 370 he was made metropolitan of Caesarea, and at once entered upon his brave fight for orthodoxy against Arians and Macedonians, who had the support of the imperial authorities at Byzantium. Nothing daunted, Basil saved the whole of Cappadocia for the Catholic faith. For this purpose he spent himself in preaching and writing doctrinal works, in both of which activities he excelled as much as in the administration of his diocese. His work on the Holy Spirit is still unsurpassed in Catholic theology. He edited also the eucharistic liturgy which bears his name. In the East Basil is the first of the three Holy Hierarchs; in the West, one of the four Great Doctors.

Basil and Procopius (SS)
CC. Feb 27
d. c 750 Two courageous defenders of the veneration of images against the emperor Leo the Isaurian.

Basil, Eugene, Agathodorus, Elpidius, Aetherius, Gapito, Ephrem, Nestor and
Arcadius (SS) Bps. MM. March 4
4th cent. Missionary bishops: the first seven preached in the Crimea and S. Russia; the last two in Cyprus. All are honoured by the Greeks, on March 7, as martyrs.

Basil (St) Bp. March 6
d. 335 Ordained bishop of Bologna by Pope St Sylvester, he ruled his diocese for twenty years, 315–335.

Basil of Ancyra (St) M. March 22
d. 362 A priest of Ancyra in Galatia, who distinguished himself as a staunch upholder of orthodoxy against Arianism. Under Julian the Apostate he was cruelly martyred. His Acts appears to be genuine.

Basil the Younger (St) H. March 26
d. 952 An anchorite near Constantinople who was seized as a spy and put to the torture by the imperial officers. Miracles proved his sanctity, and he continued to live and exercise his gift of prophecy. His life was written by his disciple, Gregory, who shared his solitude.

Basil and Emmelia (SS) May 30
d. c 370 Parents of SS Basil the Great, Gregory of Nyssa, Peter of Sebaste and Macrina the Younger. They were exiled under Galerius Maximinus, but returned after the peace of the church to their native city of Caesarea in Cappadocia. St Basil was educated by his grandmother, St Macrina the Elder.

Basil (St) M. Nov 28
See Stephen, Basil, etc.

Basileus (St) M. March 2
See Jovinus and Basileus.

Basileus (St) Bp. M.   Apr 26
d. 319   Bishop of Amasea in Pontus, martyred by drowning in the sea under Licinius.
The pre-1970 RM. added that one of his
disciples, by name Elpidiphorus, instructed by
an angel, recovered the body and gave it
Christian burial.

Basileus (St)) M.   May 23
See Epitacius and Basileus.

**Basileus, Auxilius and
Saturninus (SS)** MM.   Nov 27
? Basileus, a bishop of an unknown see, was
put to death at Antioch in Syria together with
Auxilius and Saturninus. Nothing further is
known about them.

Basilian (St) M.   Dec 18
See Theotimus and Basilian.

**Basilides, Tripos, Mandal
and Comp. (SS)** MM.   June 10
270–275   A group of twenty-three Christians
martyred at Rome on the Aurelian Way, under
Aurelian. Probably to be identified with the
next group (June 12).

**Basilides, Cyrinus,
Nabor and Nazarius (SS)**
MM.   formerly June 12
? The pre-1970 RM. had this *laus:* "At Rome
on the Aurelian Way, the birthday of the holy
martyrs Basilides, Cyrinus, Nabor, and Nazarius, soldiers who were cast into prison in the
persecution of Diocletian and Maximian,
under the prefect Aurelius for the confession
of the Christian name, scourged with scorpions and beheaded." It seems, however, more
likely that this group is the result of confusion
of names in the martyrologies: Basilides is
probably the Roman martyr of June 10: Cyrinus (or Quirinus) the martyr of June 4; Nabor
and Nazarius, two Milanese martyrs, of whom
nothing can be ascertained. Cult suppressed in
1969, due to these confusions and lack of
reliable data.

Basilides (St) M.   June 30
d. 205   A soldier of the guard of the prefect
of Egypt, told to execute St Potamiana, whom
he defended from the insults of the mob. He
was rewarded with the gift of faith, for which
he was martyred shortly after under Septimius
Severus.

**Basilides and Comp.
(SS)** MM.   Dec 23
See Theodulus, Saturninus, etc.

Basiliscus (Basilicus) (St)
M.   March 3
See Cleonicus, Eutropius and Basiliscus.

Basiliscus (St) M.   May 22
d. 312   Bishop of Comana in Pontus, Asia
Minor. He was beheaded under Maximin the
Thracian and his body thrown into a river near
Nicomedia. It was recovered and translated to
Comana. This was the martyr who appeared to
St John Chrysostom on the eve of the holy
Doctor's death.

Basilissa (St) VM.   Jan 9
See Julian, Basilissa, etc.

Basilissa (St) M.   March 22
See Callinica and Basilissa.

**Basilissa and Anastasia
(SS)** MM.   Apr 15
d. c 68   Noble Roman ladies, disciples of the
Apostles Peter and Paul, whose bodies they
buried. They were martyred themselves under
Nero. Some modern writers have cast doubts
on their existence.

Basilissa (St) VM.   Sept 3
d. c 303   The pre-1970 RM. had this story:
"At Nicomedia, the passion of St Basilissa
virgin and martyr; though she was only nine
years of age, yet by the power of God, she
overcame scourges, fire and the beasts under
the persecution of the emperor Diocletian; by
this she converted the governor to the faith of
Christ, and at length she gave up her spirit to
God, while she was at prayer outside the city."
Perhaps it is all fictitious.

Basilissa (St) Abs. OSB.   Dec 5
d. c 780   A Benedictine abbess at the nunnery of Oehren (*Horreum*) in the diocese of
Trier.

Basilla (St) M.   May 17
See Adrio, Victor and Basilla.

Basilla (St) VM.   May 20
d. 304   Alleged to have been a Roman
maiden, betrothed to a pagan patrician, whom
she refused to marry on becoming a Christian.
Forced to choose between her bridegroom and
death, she at once chose the latter and was
accordingly martyred for Christ. This summary of her *Acta* shows that they conform to a
type common in hagiological literature.

Basilla (St) V.   Aug 29
? A holy woman, who, according to the
pre-1970 RM., died at Smyrna. Other martyrologies, instead of Smyrna, have Sirmium in
Pannonia (now Mitrovica).

Basinus (St) Bp. OSB.   March 4
d. c 705   Monk and abbot of the Benedictine
monastery of St Maximin at Trier, he succeeded St Numerian as bishop of the city. In
this capacity he greatly helped the English

missionaries, notably St Willibrord. He died at St Maximin, whither he had again retired in his old age.

Basolus (Basle) (St) H.   Nov 26
c 555–620 A native of Limoges, he became a monk at Verzy, near Reims, and then a hermit, living for forty years on the top of a hill overlooking the city. He was celebrated as a wonder-worker.

Bassa (St) M.   March 6
See Victor, Victorinus, etc.

Bassa, Paula and Agathonica (SS) VV. MM.   Aug 10
? Three Christian maidens registered in the accepted lists as having been martyred at Carthage.

Bassa, Theogonius, Agapius and Fidelis (SS) MM.   Aug 21
d. 304 Bassa, wife of a pagan priest, was martyred with her three sons at Edessa (Larissa) in Greece under Diocletian. Like the mother of the Maccabees, she chose to suffer last in order to encourage her children in their agony. Their cult is ancient, though the *Acta* are untrustworthy.

Bassian (St) Bp.   Jan 19
d. 413 A Sicilian by birth, he became bishop of Lodi in Lombardy. He was held in high esteem by his friend St Ambrose of Milan, with whom he attended the council of Aquileia (381) and whom he assisted at his death (390).

Bassian (St) M.   Feb 14
See Cyrion, Bassian, etc.

Bassian (St) M.   Dec 9
See Peter, Successus, etc.

Bassus, Antony and Protolicus (SS) MM.   Feb 14
? A group of martyrs who were cast into the sea at Alexandria in Egypt. Some ancient accounts add nine fellow-sufferers to this group.

Bassus (St) M.   May 11
See Maximus, Bassus and Fabius.

Bassus, Dionysius, Agapitus and Comp. (SS) MM.   Nov 20
? A band of forty-three Christians put to death at Heraclea in Thrace.

Bassus (St) Bp. M.   Dec 5
d. *c* 250 Bishop of Nice in Gaul. He was martyred under Decius by having his body transfixed with two huge nails.

Bathildis (St) Queen, OSB.   Jan 30
d. 680 An English girl sold as a slave to the mayor of the palace of the kingdom of Neustria. King Clovis II married her in 649, and she became the mother of three future kings. After her husband's death she was for eight years regent of France (656–664). When Clotaire III came of age, she entered the nunnery of Chelles, which she had founded, and lived there as a simple nun. Her biography was written by a contemporary.

Bathus, Wereka and Comps. (SS) MM.   March 26
d. 370 They were Goths who embraced Christianity to the great irritation of their king, Jungerich or Athanaric. They were all burnt to death in a church.

Baudacarius (St) Mk. OSB.   Dec 21
d. 650 Monk of Bobbio, in N. Italy. His relics were solemnly translated in 1483.

Baudelius (St) M.   May 20
2nd (or 3rd) cent. A native of Orleans, a married man, who worked zealously in the cause of Christianity. He was martyred at Nîmes. His cult spread throughout France and N. Spain: there are some four hundred churches dedicated in his honour.

Baudry (St) C.   Oct 16
Otherwise Balderic, q.v.

Bavo (St) H. OSB.   Oct 1
c 589–654 Born in Brabant, in the district of Liège, in his early years he led a very irregular life. Left a widower, he was converted by a sermon of St Amandus and entered upon a course of canonical penance. Next he founded the abbey of St Peter on his estate at Ghent (later called St Bavo's), and became a monk under St Amandus. Finally he lived as a recluse in the forest of Malmédun, and in a cell by St Peter's.

Baya and Maura (SS) VV.   Nov 2
?10th cent. Recluses in Scotland, St Baya being the instructress of St Maura, and the latter in her turn the abbess of a community which attached itself to her. Some authors identify St Baya with St Begha or Bee. Possibly they should be identified with SS Maura and Britta, q.v.

Bean (St) Bp.   Oct 26
d. *p*.1012 Bishop of Mortlach in Banff, from which see he was later transferred to Aberdeen.

Beata (St) M.   March 8
See Cyril, Rogatus, etc.

Beata (St) M.   Sept 6
See Augustine, Sanctian.

Beatified Martyrs of England and Wales (BB)
MM   May 4
About 160 Blessed Martyrs who gave their lives in defence of the Catholic faith in England and Wales in the sixteenth and seventeenth centuries. Many have individual entries in this book.

Beatrix II of Este (Bl) N.
OSB.   Jan 18
d. 1262   A niece of Bl Beatrix I of Este (see May 10). Being bereft of her husband (or fiancé) at an early age, she founded, in the teeth of much opposition, the Benedictine convent of St Antony at Ferrara and became a nun there. Cult confirmed in 1774.

Beatrix of Lens (Bl) N.
OSB. Cist.   Jan 19
d. p.1216   Born at Lens, in the diocese of Arras. She founded the Cistercian monastery of Epinlieu near Mons, and became a nun there.

Beatrix d'Ornacieux (Bl)
NO. Cart.   Feb 13
d. 1309 (Nov 25)   A Carthusian nun of Parménie, and one of the foundresses of the Esmue nunnery of the same order. For many years she had remarkable mystical experiences as well as diabolic persecutions. Cult confirmed in 1869.

Beatrix I of Este (Bl) VN.
OSB.   May 10
1206–1226   Daughter of the Marchese Azzo d'Este, she was left an orphan at the age of six. When she was fourteen she secretly left her home and, against the wishes of her relatives, became a Benedictine nun at Solarola, near Padua. Shortly afterwards she was transferred to Gemmola, where she died a victim of loving self-immolation. Cult confirmed in 1763.

Beatrix (St) M.   July 29
See Simplicius, Faustinus and Beatrix.

Beatrix (Brites) da Silva
(St) Abs. OSB. Cist.   Aug 16
1424–1490   Born in Portugal, a daughter of the count of Viana. At the age of twenty she accompanied Princess Isabel of Portugal to the Spanish court. Soon after she entered the Cistercian nunnery of St Dominic of Silos at Toledo. Later she founded the Congregaton of the Immaculate Conception (Conceptionists) under the Benedictine rule. After St Beatrix's death Cardinal Cisneros gave them the rule of St Clare. Cult confirmed in 1926. Canonized in 1976.

Beatus (St) Mk.   Feb 19
d. 789   A native of Asturias, in Spain, monk and priest of Liébana, famous for his firm stand against Helipandus, archbishop of Toledo and other Adoptionists. When the Adoptionists were condemned, the saint retired to the monastery of Valcavado, where he wrote his commentary on the Apocalypse.

Beatus (St) Bp.   March 8
Otherwise Beoadh, q.v.

Beatus (St) H.   May 9
? An early hermit, venerated as the apostle of Switzerland. His hermitage was at the place now called Beatenberg, above the lake of Thun.

Becan (Began) (St) Ab.   Apr 5
6th cent.   One of the "twelve Apostles of Ireland". He was connected by blood with St Columba. He founded a monastery at Kill-Beggan, Westmeath, which centuries later became a Cistercian abbey. He also gave its name to the church and parish of Imleach-Becain, Meath.

Becan (St) H.   May 26
6th cent.   An Irish hermit in the time of St Columba. He lived in the neighbourhood of Cork.

Beche, John (Bl) M.   Dec 1
See John Beche.

Bede the Younger (St)
Mk. OSB.   Apr 10
d. 883   One of the chief officials at the court of Charles the Bald of France, who became a Benedictine at the abbey of Gavello, near Rovigo, in N. Italy. He refused several bishoprics. His relics were translated to Subiaco in the nineteenth century.

Bede the Venerable (St)
Dr. OSB.   GC. May 25
673–735   Born at Wearmouth, he was offered as a child to the double abbey of SS Peter and Paul at Wearmouth-Jarrow, was professed there under the founder St Benedict Biscop, and there he spent his whole life, "always writing, always praying, always reading, always teaching". He was ordained by St John of Beverley. The Bible was his principal study, and then history. His *Ecclesiastical History of the English People* has earned for him the title of Father of English History. His works *De Temporibus* and *De Temporum Ratione* helped to establish the idea of dating from the incarnation. He also wrote works on hagiography, chronology metre and other subjects. He is the type of the Benedictine scholar of all periods, and has been declared a Doctor of the Church. He died on Ascension Eve, and his dying words were *Gloria Patri et Filio et Spiritui Sancto*. In art he is depicted as an old monk,

St Bede, May 25

with a book and pen, or a jug, or writing at a desk; or dying amidst his community.

Bee (St) V.   Oct 31
Otherwise Bega, q.v.

Bega (Begh, Bee) (St) V.   Oct 31
7th cent.   An Irish maiden who founded a nunnery on the promontory of St Bee's Head, in Cumberland, which still perpetuates her memory, as does also the name of the village, Kilbees, in Scotland. Two other saints of the same name are mentioned by hagiographers, a nun in Yorkshire and an abbess at Kilbees.

Begga (St) W. Abs. OSB.   Dec 17
d. 698   Daughter of Bl Pepin of Landen and of St Ida, and sister of two other saints. She married Angisilus (Ansegis), son of St Arnulf of Metz, and of their union was born Pepin of Heristal, the founder of the Carolingian dynasty. After her husband's death St Begga founded a nunnery at Andenne on the Meuse, which she governed as abbess.

Belina (St) VM.   Feb 19
d. 1135   A peasant girl of the district of Troyes (France) who, threatened by the feudal lord of the territory, died in defence of her chastity. Canonized in 1203.

**Bellatanus and Savinus
(BB)** HH. OSB. Cam.   May 19
? Camaldolese hermits of Montacuto in the neighbourhood of Perugia.

Bellinus (St) Bp. M.   Nov 26
d. 1151   A bishop of Padua who suffered death in the faithful discharge of pastoral duties, and was canonized three centuries later by Pope Eugene IV.

Benedict
Note. In Latin: Benedictus; in Italian: Benedetto; in French: Benoît; in Spanish: Benito; in Portuguese: Bento; in Catalan: Benet (accent on the second syllable); in German: Benedikt; in English: Benet and Benedict.

Benedict Biscop (St) Ab.
OSB.   Jan 12
c 628–c 690   A Northumbrian by birth, Biscop Baducing made two pilgrimages to Rome early in life, and after the second became a monk at Lérins. After a third journey to Rome he returned to England and founded the abbey of Wearmouth and Jarrow (674–682). Twice more he visited Rome, whence he brought the precentor of the Vatican to train the English monks in the Roman ways. He was the spiritual father of the Venerable Bede, a bibliophile and a scholar in his own right.

Benedict Ricasoli (Bl) H.
OSB. Vall.   Jan 20
d. 1107   Born at Coltiboni, in the diocese of Fiesole. He entered the monastery founded by his parents for the monks of Vallumbrosa on a mountain near Coltiboni. Later he became a hermit in a cell nearby. Cult confirmed in 1907.

Benedict of Aniane (St)
Ab. OSB.   Feb 11
c 750–821   A Visigoth, by name Witiza, born in Languedoc, he served as a cup-bearer at the court of Pepin and Charlemagne. In 773 he became a monk at Saint-Seine, near Dijon, and was appointed cellarer. In 779 he founded an abbey on his native estate, in Languedoc, by the brook Aniane. The emperor ordered him to undertake the oversight of all the abbeys of Languedoc, Provence and Gascony, and eventually also the reform of all the French and German houses. As a kind of model abbey St Benedict, with the help of Louis the Pious, founded the abbey of Kornelimünster, near Aachen. At Aachen he presided over a meeting of all the abbots of the empire (817) — a turning point in Benedictine history.

Benedict Revelli (St) Bp.
OSB.   Feb 12
c 900   He is said to have been a Benedictine monk of Santa Maria dei Fonti, and then a hermit on the island of Gallinaria, in the Gulf

of Genoa. In 870 he was chosen bishop of Albenga towards the western end of the Ligurian riviera. Cult confirmed by Pope Gregory XVI.

Benedict (Manettus) Dell' Antella (St)   Feb 12
See Manettus.

Benedict of Cagliari (St)
Bp. OSB.   Feb 17
d. p.1112   Monk of the monastery attached to the basilica of St Saturninus, at Cagliari, in Sardinia. He was bishop of Dolia, also in Sardinia, from 1107 to 1112. In his old age he resigned and returned to his abbey, where he died shortly after.

Benedict Crispus of Milan (St) Bp.   March 11
d. 725   Archbishop of Milan, he governed his see for forty-five years. He composed the epitaph for the tomb of Ceadwaller, king of Wessex, buried in old St Peter's, Rome.

Benedict of Campania (St) H.   March 23
d. c 550   A contemporary of St Benedict of Montecassino, and a hermit in the Campagna, who was delivered by a miracle from death by burning at the hands of Totila the Goth.

Benedict the Moor (St)
C. OFM.   Apr 4
1526–1589   Called in Italian "il Moro " – "the Black". He was in fact born of Negro parents, serfs near Messina in Sicily. He first became a hermit and then joined the Friars Minor of the Observance at Palermo as a lay-brother. Nevertheless, he was appointed guardian and novice-master of the friary and he excelled in both offices. His heart, however, was in the kitchen, whither he returned in his old age. Beatified in 1743 and canonized in 1807.

Benedict (Bénézet) the Bridge-builder (St) C.   Apr 14
d. 1184   A shepherd boy of Avignon who, as the result of a vision, asked the blessing and help of the bishop of the city to build a bridge at a dangerous ford over the Rhône. A series of miracles accompanied the carrying out of the work.

Benedict Joseph Labre (St)
C.   Apr 16
1748–1783   A native of Amettes, then in the diocese of Boulogne-sur-Mer. He came of a family of small shopkeepers and was educated by an uncle, a priest. He tried without success to join the Trappists. Then he found his vocation as a pilgrim-beggar, tramping from shrine to shrine throughout Europe, living on alms, and spending long hours before the Blessed Sacrament. He died in Rome during Holy Week. He was beatified in 1860 and canonized in 1883.

Benedict of Urbino (Bl)
C. OFM. Cap.   Apr 30
1560–1625   Born at Urbino, of the family de' Passionei, he was a lawyer at Urbino before he joined the Capuchin friars at Fano (1584). He was the companion of St Laurence of Brindisi, whom he followed to Austria and Bohemia. He died at the monastery of Fossombrone. Beatified in 1867.

Benedict of Szkalka (St)
M.   May 1
d. 1012   A hermit on Mount Zobor in Hungary near the Benedictine monastery. He was trained by St Andrew Zorard (q.v.). Renowned like his master for his austerity and gifts of contemplation, he was killed by marauders in 1012. Canonized in 1083.

Benedict II (St) Pope   May 8
d. 685   A Roman by birth, he was chosen pope in 683, but his consecration was delayed a year awaiting the arrival of the confirmation from Constantinople. He governed the church eleven months.

Benedict XI (Bl) Pope, OP.   July 7
1240–1304   A native of Treviso, Nicholas Boccasini, as he was called in baptism, joined the Dominicans and became their ninth master-general. Eventually he was created cardinal-bishop of Ostia and papal legate. He was elected pope in 1303. He continued to the end his religious observances and penances. Beatified in 1736.

Benedict d'Alignan (Bl)
Bp. OFM.   July 8
d. 1268   A Benedictine abbot who was chosen bishop of Marseilles. He made a pilgrimage to the Holy Land, and on his return resigned the bishopric and joined the Friars Minor.

Benedict (St) Ab.
Founder   GC. July 11
c 480–550   Born in the district of Nurcia, in Umbria, central Italy, he was sent to Rome for his studies; but left there and joined (c 500) a sort of community of ecclesiastical students at Affile. Shortly after he retired to a cave near Subiaco — now the Sacro Speco — to live as a hermit. Here his sanctity was soon discovered and many disciples flocked to him; for these he built a *laura*, composed of twelve small monasteries, himself retaining the command over all. About the year 530 he left Subiaco for Monte-

St Benedict, July 11

cassino, where on the road to Naples he founded the great arch-abbey and where he lived till his death, famous as a wonder-worker. Here too, he promulgated his rule, which is justly considered one of the most potent factors in building up the civilization of Christian Europe. Eventually it became the norm for all western monks, and was simply called "The Holy Rule". The little we know of St Benedict's own personality shows him to us as a strong but lovable character. He died standing in prayer before the altar. It is generally considered that he may have been a deacon, but not a priest. His life was written by St Gregory the Great, Dialogues Bk II. The French tradition maintains that the remains of St Benedict were translated to Fleury in 703. This is contested by the monks of Montecas-ino where excavations made possible by the wanton destruction of the abbey in the last war yielded up substantial remains, regarded as those of Benedict and Scholastica. His symbols are a raven with a bun in its beak. He often holds a book with a broken chalice, or a sieve. Sometimes he carries an open copy of his own rule, open at the first word, "Ausculta". Proclaimed Patron of Europe by Paul VI in 1964.

Benedict (St) Bp.   July 15
d. *c* 820   Bishop of Angers in the reign of Louis the Pious.

Benedict de Castro (Bl)
M. SJ.   July 15
d. 1570   A native of Chacim, diocese of Miranda in Portugal. He belonged to the group of Jesuit martyrs under the leadership of Bl Ignatius Azevedo, q.v., killed by Calvinistic pirates.

Benedict of Arezzo (Bl)
C. OFM.   Aug 31
d. 1281   One of the first companions of St Francis of Assisi, and subsequently one of the first Franciscan provincials. He was sent to Greece, Rumania, the Holy Land and Constantinople, where he gave the Franciscan habit to the emperor.

Benedict of Macerac (St)
Ab.   Oct 22
d. 845   A Greek abbot who fled from Petras and settled at Macerac, in the diocese of Nantes. His relics were later transferred to the abbey of Redon.

Benedict of Sebaste (St)
Bp.   Oct 23
d. *c* 654   An alleged bishop of Sebaste in Samaria, who had to escape to Gaul during the persecution of Julian the Apostate. He built a hermitage near Poitiers which later became the abbey of St Benedict of Quincay. Not all the above details, however, are above suspicion.

Benedict, John, Matthew, Isaac and Christinus (Christian) (SS) MM. OSB.   Nov 12
d. 1005   Italian Benedictines who followed

St Adalbert of Prague to the mission among the Slavs, and were massacred by robbers at their monastery near Gnesen (May 11). They were canonized by Julius II.

Benedict de Ponte (Bl)
C. OP.   Nov 22
13th cent. Dominican missionary among the Tartars. He died immediately after preaching a sermon.

Benedicta (St) VM.   Jan 4
See Priscus, Priscillian and Benedicta.

Benedicta (St) V.   May 6
6th cent. A nun of the convent founded in Rome by St Galla, of whom St Gregory the Great narrates that her death was foretold to her by St Peter in a vision.

Benedicta (St) VM.?   June 29
? The pre-1970 RM. styled her simply "a virgin in the territory of Sens". Later legends add that she was a sister of SS Augustine and Sanctian, all three natives of Spain, and that they passed into France and were martyred under Aurelian.

Benedicta and Cecilia
(SS) Abs. OSB.   Aug 17
10th cent. These two daughters of the king of Lorraine became nuns and successive abbesses of Susteren in the Rhineland.

Benedicta (St) VM.   Oct 8
? The pre-1970 RM. had only this *laus*: "In the country of Laon (the birthday) of St Benedicta, Virgin and Martyr". Further details, added by later writers, are conflicting.

Benedictine Martyrs (BB)   Dec 1
See Richard Whiting, Hugh Faringdon and John Beche.

Bénézet (St) C.   Apr 14
See Benedict the Bridge-Builder.

Benignus (St) M.   Feb 13
d. *c* 303 A priest of Todi in Umbria, put to death under Diocletian.

Benignus (St) Ab. OSB.   March 20
d. 725 Monk and abbot of Fontenelle, he was exiled from the abbey and retired to Flay where the monks asked him to be their abbot. After the victory of Charles Martel, he returned to Fontenelle, retaining the government of Flay, and died shortly after.

Benignus (St) M.   Apr 3
See Evagrius and Benignus.

Benignus (St) Mk. OSB.
Cist.   June 20
13th cent. Cistercian monk at Breslau, in Silesia, martyred by the Tartars with many

other members of his abbey. The Cistercian menologies commemorate him on June 20.

Benignus (St) Bp. M.   June 28
6th cent. This bishop is mentioned in a decretal of Pope Pelagius II as desirous of resigning his see. He appears to have retired to Utrecht; at any rate the pre-1970 RM. placed him there, and his relics were there rediscovered in 996.

Benignus Visdomini (Bl)
Ab. OSB. Vall.   July 17
d. 1236 A Florentine priest, who fell into sin, repented and entered the abbey of Vallombrosa. He became abbot-general but, always conscious of his past guilt, resigned and died as a hermit.

Benignus (St) Mk. OSB.   July 21
See John and Benignus.

Benignus (St) M.   Nov 1
2nd cent. A martyr venerated at Dijon from early times, over whose tomb there was erected the magnificent abbey church — now cathedral — of St Benignus. His alleged connection with St Polycarp of Smyrna is rejected by modern writers.

Benignus (Benen) (St) Bp.   Nov 9
d. *c* 466 "Benen, son of Sessenen, St Patrick's Psalmsinger". A favourite disciple of St Patrick, whom he succeeded as chief bishop of the Irish church. He preached, it is said, chiefly in Clare and Kerry and founded a monastery at Drumlease. His connexion with Glastonbury has no historical foundation.

Benignus (St) Bp.   Nov 20
d. *c* 477 Archbishop of Milan, during whose pontificate the Heruli, under Odoacer, occupied the city.

Benildis (St) M.   June 15
d. 853 A woman of Cordoba, who was so moved by the fortitude displayed by St Athanasius, a Spanish priest, during his martyrdom at the hands of the Moors, that she braved death at the stake on the following day. Her ashes were thrown into the Guadalquivir.

Benildus (St) C.   Aug 13
1805–1862 Peter Romancon of Thuret, diocese of Clermont, France, joined the Brotherhood of Christian Schools and combined the work of education with a life of prayer and devotion to his religious rule. Beatified April 4 1948. Canonized in 1967.

Benincasa (Bl) Ab. OSB.   Jan 10
d. 1194 Eighth abbot of La Cava, near Salerno, from 1171 to 1194. It was during his abbacy that a hundred monks were sent from

Cava to staff the new monastery of Monreale, founded by the king of Sicily in that island. Cult confirmed in 1928.

Benincasa (Bl) C. OSM. May 11

1376–1426 A native of Florence, who joined the Servites at Montepulciano. He spent his whole life as a hermit, first at Montagnata, near Siena, and then in the almost inaccessible cave of Montechiello. Cult confirmed in 1829.

Benjamin (St) M. March 31

c 421 A Persian deacon who, having been imprisoned for the faith, and refusing as a condition of his release to cease preaching Christianity, was tortured to death under Isdegerdes.

Benno (St) Bp. June 16

1010–1106 Born at Hildesheim and educated at the abbey of St Michael in his native city. He became canon of Gozlar, chaplain to the emperor Henry III and finally bishop of Meissen. He is one of the protagonists in the quarrel between Pope Gregory VII and Henry IV. He upheld the former but not at all times with equal zeal. In later years he preached to the Wends. His canonization in 1525 roused Luther to fury.

Benno (Bl) Bp. OSB. July 12

d. 1088 A Swabian, he was educated and professed as a Benedictine at Reichenau, where he was taught by Bl Herman the Cripple. He became the headmaster at Gozlar in Hanover, and finally of the cathedral school of Hildesheim. He was also the official architect to Henry III. He was archbishop of Osnabrück (1067) and as such always upheld the pope's cause. He founded Iburg abbey where he retired to die.

Benno (Bl) Bp. OSB. Aug 3

d. 940 A Swabian, canon of Strasburg, he became a hermit on Mt Etzel, in Switzerland, St Meinrad's former hermitage. He lived there with a few disciples, thus becoming the founder of the abbey of Einsiedeln, which still exists. In 927 he was called to the see of Metz. Striving to remedy abuses, he was attacked and blinded by those whom he had rebuked. He resigned and returned to Einsiedeln, which had already grown into a numerous community.

Bentivoglio de Bonis (Bl) C. OFM. Jan 2

d. 1232 (Dec 25) Born at San Severino, in the Italian Marches, he was one of St Francis's earliest disciples, and as such he is mentioned in the *Fioretti*. Cult confirmed by Pius IX.

Benvenuta Bojani (Bl) V. Tert. OP. Oct 30

d. 1292 The seventh of seven daughters, christened by her parents Benvenuta, although they had asked for a son. Having become a Dominican tertiary at an early age, she spent her whole life at her home in Cividale, N. Italy, busy with her domestic duties, praying, and working miracles. Cult approved in 1763.

Benvenutus Scotivoli (St) Bp. OFM. March 22

d. 1282 Born at Ancona, he studied law at Bologna, where he was a fellow-student of St Sylvester. Soon he was appointed archdeacon of Ancona, and finally bishop of Osimo. Before his episcopal ordination he professed the Franciscan rule and donned the Franciscan habit. Canonized by Martin IV.

Benvenutus of Recanati (Bl) C. OFM. May 21

d. 1289 Born at Recanati, near Loreto, of the Mareni family. He joined the Friars Minor as a lay-brother and was mostly employed in the kitchen, where he was constantly favoured with ecstasies and visions. Cult confirmed by Pius VII.

Benvenutus of Gubbio (Bl) C. OFM. June 27

d. 1232 An uncouth soldier, he was received into the Franciscan order by St Francis himself. At his own request the new friar was allowed to tend lepers, a task which he carried out with the utmost charity. Cult authorized by Gregory IX.

Beoadh (Beatus) (St) Bp. March 8

d. between 518 and 525 Aeodh (Aidus), an Irish saint, acquired the prefix *Bo* on account of the greatness of his virtues, and was appointed bishop of Ardcarne (Roscommon). The "Bell of St Beoadh", a beautiful work of art, was long venerated as a relic of the saint.

Beoc (Beanus, Dabeoc, Mobeoc) (St) Ab. Dec 16

5th (or 6th) cent. He founded a monastery on an island in Lough Derg, Donegal.

Beocca, Ethor and Comp. (SS) MM. OSB. Apr 10

d. 870 The Danes, in their continuous raids on England, singled out the Anglo-Saxon abbeys as the special object of their ferocity. Thus at Chertsey abbey in Surrey, they put to death SS Beocca, abbot, Ethor, monk-priest, and some ninety monks; at Peterborough, they killed St Hedda, abbot, and others of his community; at Thorney abbey, St Torthred and others. All were justly venerated as martyrs.

Berach (Barachias, Berachius) (St) Ab. Feb 15

6th cent. From his birth he was placed under the care of his uncle, St Freoch. He afterwards became St Kevin's disciple, and founded an abbey at Clusin-Coirpte, in Connaught. He is the patron saint of Kilbarry, County Dublin.

Berachiel Apr 20

See Seven Angels who stand before the throne of God.

Berardus, Peter, Otto, Accursius and Adjutus (SS) MM. OFM. Jan 16

d. 1220 Sent by St Francis to evangelize the Muslims of the West, these friars travelled from Italy to Aragon, then to Coimbra in Portugal, to Seville and finally to Morocco, where they were beheaded. Berardus, Peter and Otto were priests, Adjutus and Accursius lay-brothers. Canonized in 1481.

Berarius (St) Bp. Oct 17

d. c680 Bishop of Le Mans. During his episcopate part of St Scholastica's relics were translated from Montecassino to Le Mans.

Bercham (St) Bp. Apr 6

Otherwise Berthanc, q.v.

Bercharius (St) Ab. M. OSB. Oct 16

d. 696 Monk of Luxeuil and first abbot of Hautvilliers, which had been founded by St Nivard, bishop of Reims. St Bercharius himself founded two new houses, Moutier-en-Der for monks, and Puelle-moutier for nuns. He went on pilgrimage to Rome and Palestine and on his return settled at Moutier-en-Der. A young monk, whom he had corrected, fatally stabbed him by night. Bercharius died, forgiving his murderer, and is venerated as a martyr.

Berchtold of Ratisbon (Bl) OFM. Dec 14

13th cent. A Franciscan missionary who worked in Germany, Austria and Hungary, and converted thousands by his ardent sermons.

Bercthun (Bertin) (St) Ab. OSB. Sept 24

d. 733 A disciple of St John of Beverley and by him appointed first abbot of Beverley, where he died.

Berctuald (St) Ab. OSB. Jan 9

Otherwise Brithwald, q.v.

Bere, Richard (Bl) M. May 4

d. 1537 Born at Glastonbury and educated at Oxford and the Inns of Court, he was starved to death with another Carthusian monk of the London charterhouse in Newgate prison, Aug–Sept 1537.

Beregisus (St) C. Oct 2

d. p.725 A priest, confessor of Pepin of Heristal, with whose help he founded the abbey of Saint-Hubert, in the Ardennes. It is not certain if he was himself a monk, although some writers call him abbot.

Berencardus (Berenger) (St) C. OSB. May 26

d. 1293 Born near Toulouse, he became a Benedictine at the abbey of St Papoul in Languedoc. After his ordination he filled the offices of novice-master, almoner and master of works (operarius) of the abbey. He was noted for his kind charity and patience.

Berengarius (Bl) Ab. OSB. Oct 29

d. 1108 First abbot of the Benedictine abbey of Formbach in Bavaria (1094–1108).

Berenice (St) M. Oct 4

See Domnina, Berenice and Prosdoce.

Berlinda (Berlindis, Bellaude) (St) V. OSB. Feb 3

d. 702 A niece of St Amandus, she became a Benedictine nun of St Mary's convent, at Moorsel, near Alost, in Belgium, and afterwards a recluse at Meerbeke.

Bernardette (Bernardetta) Bernada (St) V. Apr 16

1844–1879 Born at Lourdes, Bernardette Soubirous was the daughter of a miller in very poor circumstances. When she was fourteen years of age, she was favoured with a series of apparitions of our Lady, who chose the uneducated peasant girl to reveal to the world the healing shrine at Lourdes. In 1866 she joined the Institute of the Sisters of Notre Dame at Nevers, where her one desire was to remain hidden and forgotten by the world. Canonized in 1933.

Bernard of Corleone (Bl) C. OFM. Cap. Jan 19

1605–1667 Born at Corleone in Sicily, Philip Latini, a shoemaker by trade, was reckoned the best swordsman of Sicily. After mortally wounding another man, he fled from the police and took sanctuary in the church of the Capuchin friars at Palermo. He joined them as a lay-brother (1632) and henceforth became a prodigy of austerity till his death. Beatified in 1768.

Bernard of Lippe (Bl) Bp. OSB. Cist. Jan 23

d. 1217 Count of Lippe in Westphalia. He professed the Cistercian rule and was made abbot of Dünemunde, and later bishop of Semgallen in Kurland.

Bernard Scammacca (Bl)
C. OP.   Feb 16
d. 1486   A native of Catania, he belonged to
a wealthy family, and in his youth gave himself
up to riotous living until, having been gravely
wounded in a duel, he came to reflect on his
folly, changed his ways and joined the friars
preachers. As a friar he atoned by a life of
continuous penance for his former evil co-
urses. Cult approved in 1825.

Bernard of Carinola (St)
Bp.   March 12
d. 1109   A native of Capua, he was appointed bishop of Forum Claudii in 1087 by Pope
Victor III. He transferred the see (1100) to
Carinola in Campania. St Bernard died in
extreme old age. He is now the principal
patron saint of Carinola.

Bernard of Thiron (or of Abbeville) (St) Ab. OSB.
Abbeville) (St) Ab. OSB.   Apr 14
1046–1117   Born near Abbeville, Bernard
professed the Benedictine rule at St Cyprian's,
Poitiers, and later was appointed prior of St
Sabinus. After some twenty years in this office
he retired as a recluse to Craon. He was next
made abbot of St Cyprian's, but soon retired
again to the forest of Thiron in Picardy where
he founded the congregation of that name, of
which the main feature was hard manual
labour. The congregation spread rapidly throughout France, England and Scotland. Cult as
a saint confirmed in 1861.

Bernard the Penitent (Bl)
Mk. OSB.   Apr 19
d. 1182   A native of Provence who, owing to
some horrible crime which he had committed,
was sentenced by the bishop of Maguelone to
seven years public penance. He performed this
penance loaded with seven heavy iron bands,
which he dragged from shrine to shrine —
Compostella, Rome, Palestine — until he came
to the abbey of St Bertin (Sithin), where he first
lived as a hermit and then ventured to ask the
monks to receive him into their community.

Bernard of Menthon (St)
C. OSA.   May 28
d. c 1081   For forty years he served the
bishop of Aosta as vicar-general of the diocese,
visiting every mountain and valley in the Alps,
and taking particular care of travellers. For this
purpose he established two hospices on the
great and little passes which bear his name,
placing them under Augustinian canons regular. Pius XI named him patron saint of mounta-
ineers.

Bernard, Mary and Gracia (Grace) (SS) MM. OSB. Cist.
(Grace) (SS) MM. OSB. Cist.   June 1
d. c 1180   Children of Almanzor, the Muslim caliph of Lérida in Catalonia. Their
Moorish names were respectively Achmed,
Zoraida and Zaida. Achmed was converted to
Christianity and became a Cistercian monk at
Poblet (Populetum) near Tarragona, under
the name of Bernard. He in his turn converted
his two sisters, who were in some way affiliated
to the Cistercian order. As a result of their
endeavour to convert their brother Almanzor,
they were handed over by him to the executioners and martyred in odium fidei. They are the
patron saints of Alcira, in Valencia, Spain.

Bernard of Baden (Bl) C.
                                         July 15
1428–1458   Margrave of Baden, he renounced the rights of his title in favour of his
brother and offered himself to several European courts to organize a crusade against the
Turks. He died without having attained his
object. Cult confirmed in 1481 and again in
1769.

Bernard of Rodez (de Ruthenis) (Bl) Card.
Ruthenis) (Bl) Card.
OSB.   July 19
d. 1079   Abbot of St Victor at Marseilles
(1064). A fast friend of SS Gregory VII, Hugh
of Cluny and William of Hirschau, he zealously fostered the Cluniac observance. He was
made cardinal and sent as papal legate to
Germany (1077) and Spain (1078).

Bernard Due (St) M.
                                          Aug 1
1755–1838   A native priest of Vietnam, after
labouring for many years on the mission, he
was living in retirement but spontaneously
offered himself to the pagan soldiers as a
Christian priest, and was beheaded at the age
of eighty-three. Canonized in 1988.

Bernard of Clairvaux (St)
Ab. Dr. OSB. Cist.   GC. Aug 20
1090–1153   Born near Dijon, at the age of
twenty-two he joined (1112) the recently
founded struggling abbey of Citeaux, after
having persuaded thiry other young noblemen
to follow him thither. Scarcely had he finished
his novitiate when he was sent as abbot-
founder to Clairvaux (1115) and as such
became the real founder of the Cistercians.
During his lifetime he established sixty-eight
Cistercian houses; was the adviser of popes,
kings and councils; the preacher of the second
crusade (which, however, was a failure); and
the arbiter of Europe who, as has been said,
"carried the twelfth century on his shoulders".
In the theological field, he confuted Abelard;
wrote profusely on the love of God; commen-
ted for his monks on the Song of Songs; sent a
noble treatise, De consideratione, to his former
monk, Pope Eugene III; and produced many
other works. His Treatise on the Love of God is

St Bernard, Aug 20

considered the best. Canonized in 1174 and declared a Doctor in 1830. His symbol is a white dog; or the saint, clad in a white Cistercian habit, is shown seeing a vision of our Lady.

Bernard of Valdeiglesias
(St) Mk. OSB. Cist.   Aug 20
d. *p*.1155   A monk of Valdeiglesias in Spanish Galicia. He is the patron saint of Candelada. Possibly but not certainly a Cistercian.

Bernard Tolomei (Bl)
Founder, OSB. Oliv.   Aug 21
1272–1348   Born at Siena, he was educated by his uncle, a Dominican friar. He studied law and filled several municipal offices, including that of *podestà* (mayor). In 1313 he withdrew to a place ten miles from the city and there he became the founder of the abbey and congregation of Montoliveto. He was summoned to Avignon to give an account of this new foundation, and received papal approval (1324). After years spent in wonderful deeds of charity, he died of the pestilence whilst nursing the sick, together with a large number

of his monks. Cult officially approved in 1644. Among the Olivetans he is usually given the title of Saint.

Bernard of Offida (Bl) C.
OFM. Cap.   Aug 22
1604–1694   An Italian peasant, born at Appignano, diocese of Ascoli-Piceno. He took his vows as a Capuchin lay-brother at Offida and here, and at the friary of Fermo, he became famous for his wisdom and miracles.

Bernard of Arce (St) C.   Oct 14
9th cent.   Either an Englishman or a Frenchman, who undertook a pilgrimage to the Holy Land and Rome and then lived as a recluse at Arpino in the Campagna. His relics are enshrined at Rocca d'Arce.

Bernard of Bagnorea (or of Castro) (St) Bp.   Oct 20
d. *p*.800   A native of Bagnorea, he was chosen bishop of Vulcia in Tuscany, whence he transferred the see to Ischia di Castro.

Bernard Calvo (St) Bp.
OSB. Cist.   Oct 24
d. 1243   A native of Manso Calvo, in Catal-

St Bernardine of Siena, May 20

onia, he became a Cistercian and eventually the first abbot of Santas Creus, near Tarragona. In 1233 he was chosen bishop of Vich.

Bernard de la Tour (Bl)
C. O. Cart.   Oct 30
d. 1258 A Carthusian monk of Portes, diocese of Belley, who became the thirteenth superior-general of the order.

Bernard of Hildesheim
(St) Bp.   Nov 20
Otherwise Bernward, q.v.

Bernard of Toulouse (Bl)
M. OP.   Dec 3
d. 1320 A Dominican friar, who in his campaign against the Albigenses was seized by them, put to torture and sawn in two.

Bernard degli Uberti (St)
Bp. OSB. Vall.   Dec 4
d. 1133 A native of Florence, he was professed a monk at Vallombrosa. He was appointed successively abbot of San Salvi, general of Vallombrosa, cardinal (1097), papal legate and finally bishop of Parma (1106), at that time the storm-centre of the anti-pope's supporters. Twice he was exiled, but he proved a most successful bishop.

Bernard (or Berard)
Paleara (St) Bp. OSB.   Dec 19
d. 1122 A monk of Montecassino, chosen bishop of Teramo in 1115. He is venerated as the principal patron saint of Teramo.

Bernardine of Siena (St)
C. OFM.   GC. May 20
1380–1444 Born on Sept 8 at Massa Mari-

tima near Siena, of the family degl'Albizzeschi. He took the Franciscan habit (Sept 8, 1402), and was ordained priest (Sept 8, 1404) and, having preached his first sermon (Sept 8, 1417), his career as a preacher ended only with his life. He was accounted the foremost Italian missioner of the fifteenth century. He was particularly eloquent when preaching on the Holy Name of Jesus, devotion to which he spread far and wide. He was also responsible for the revival of discipline among the Franciscans, and from 1438 to 1442 he was vicar-general of the order. Canonized in 1450. In art he is shown holding up a sign bearing the legend IHS, from which rays shine forth. Habited as a friar, he stands with three mitres at his feet.

Bernardine Realino (St)
SJ.   July 2
1530–1616 A native of Modena, he became a lawyer, but when aged thirty-four joined the Society of Jesus. He worked for ten years at Naples and was then appointed rector of the college at Lecce, where he died. Canonized in 1947.

Bernardine of Feltre (Bl)
C. OFM.   Sept 28
c 1439–1494 A native of Feltre, his baptismal name was Martin Tomitani. He took his vows as a Franciscan and was first employed as a teacher in various houses of the order, but developed before long into a tempestuous preacher, the terror of all evil-doers, but especially of usurers. To protect the people against these he suggested the establishment of *monti di pietà*, of which he organized over thirty in various Italian cities. Beatified in 1728.

Bernardine of Fossa (Bl)
C. OFM.   Nov 27
d. 1503 Bernardino Amici was born at Fossa, diocese of Aquila in central Italy. In 1445 he received the Franciscan habit, and after filling sucessfully several offices in the order, he embarked on a career of mission-preaching throughout Italy, Dalmatia and Bosnia, being still engaged in this apostolate when he died at Aquila.

Berno (St) Ab. OSB.   Jan 13
d. 927 A native of Burgundy and a monk of St Martin, Autun. He was abbot restorer of Baume-les-Messieurs, where he gave the habit to St Odo in 909, and the abbot-founder of Gigny, Bourg-Dieu, Massay and finally of Cluny (910), which he governed till 926. In that year he resigned and was succeeded by St Odo. History, whether sacred or profane, has

done less than justice to St Berno for his great work for the church and for civilization.

Bernold (Bl) Mk. OSB.   Nov 25
d. c 1050 A monk-priest of Ottobeuren in Bavaria, renowned as a wonder-worker, especially after his death.

Bernward (Berward) (St)
Bp. OSB.   Nov 20
d. 1022 Bernward is one of the most attractive figures of medieval Germany — a German St Dunstan, He excelled as an architect, painter, sculptor, decorator and metal-smith. He was also the tutor of the emperor Otto III. In 993 he was made bishop of Hildesheim. He died after having been clothed in the habit of St Benedict. Canonized in 1193.

Beronigus, Pelagia and Comp. (SS) MM.   Oct 19
? A group of fifty-one Christians put to death at Antioch in Syria in one of the early persecutions.

Bertellin (St) C.   Sept 9
Otherwise Bettelin, q.v.

Bertha (St)
d. 612 The first Christian queen in England, she was the daughter of the king of the Franks. On her marriage to the pagan Ethelbert of Kent, she brought with her the saintly Luidhard as her chaplain. Their influence no doubt prepared her husband for his kind reception of St Augustine in 596. She has always been regarded as a saint in Kent, but no ancient dedications or days seem associated with her.

Bertha (Bl) Abs. OSB.
Vall.   March 24
d. 1163 Born in Florence, a member of the Alberti family (she is often wrongly called de'Bardi). She became a nun at the Vallombrosan convent of St Felicitas at Florence, whence Bl Qualdo Galli, the general of the Vallombrosans, sent her to Cavriglia in the Valdardo, as abbess. She died ten years later, on Easter Sunday.

Bertha (St) M.   May 1
d. p.680 Abbess-foundress of Avenay, diocese of Châlons-sur-Marne. She was perfidiously put to death and is venerated as a martyr.

Bertha (St)   May 15
See Rupert and Bertha.

Bertha (St) W. OSB.   July 4
d. c 725 A lady of high station, who after her husband's death entered the nunnery of Blangy, in Artois, which she had founded, and became its abbess.

Bertha of Marbais (Bl)
W. OSB. Cist.   July 18
d. 1247 A near relative of the count of Flanders, she married the chatelain of Molembais. Left a widow, she became a Cistercian at Ayvrières. Her family founded the nunnery of Marquette, whither she was sent as abbess. She has a liturgical cult in the diocese of Namur.

Berthaldus (Bertaud) (St) H.   June 16
d. c 540 A hermit in the Ardennes who was ordained priest by St Remigius.

Berthanc (Berchan) (St)
Bp.   Apr 6
d. c 840 A Scottish saint, who is said to have been a monk of Iona and later bishop of Kirkwall in the Orkneys. He seems to have died in Ireland, and his tomb was shown at Inishmore in Galway Bay. Hence perhaps his surname of Fer-da-Leithe (the man of two parts or countries).

Bertharius (St) Bp.
See Betharius.

Bertharius (St) Ab. M.
OSB.   Oct 22
d. c 884 A scion of the royal house of France, he was professed at Montecassino and chosen as its abbot in 856. While kneeling in prayer he was martyred, with several of his monks, by a band of invading Saracens. He is the author of homilies, poems, etc. One of the altars of Montecassino is consecrated in his name.

Berthoald (St) Bp.   Oct 13
7th cent. Fifth bishop of Cambrai Arras.

Berthold (St) C. OC.   March 29
d. c 1195 A Frenchman and a brilliant student at the university of Paris, he set out for Palestine as a crusader. There he joined the group of hermits who dwelt on Mt Carmel and eventually was appointed by his brother Aymeric, Latin patriarch of Antioch, their first superior-general. For all practical purposes he may be considered the founder of the Carmelite order.

Berthold of Scheda (Bl)
C. O. Praem.   July 13
d. c 1214 Founder of the Premonstratensian abbey of Frodenburg (Vrundeberg). He was a brother of Bl Menrich of Lübeck.

Berthold of Garsten (Bl)
Ab. OSB.   July 27
1090–1142   Born on the shores of the lake of
Constance, Berthold belonged to the family of
the counts of Bogen. After a short period of
married life he was left a widower at the age of
thirty and at once joined the Benedictines of
Blasien in the Black Forest. He became their
prior, and then prior of Göttweig in Austria
and abbot of Garsten in Styria, where he
founded a hospice for the poor. He enjoyed a
great reputation as a confessor.

Berthold (Bertoldo) (St)
C. OSB.   Oct 21
d. 1111   An Anglo-Saxon by descent, his
parents having fled from England at the
Norman Conquest, Berthold was born at
Parma. He spent his whole life as a lay-brother
in the service of the nuns of St Alexander in
that city.

Berthold (Bl) Ab. OSB.   Nov 3
d. 1197   A monk of Engelberg in Switzerland, who excelled as a transcriber of books.
He became the third abbot of the monastery
(1178). His memory is liturgically celebrated
at Einsiedeln and Engelberg.

Bertilia (St) V.   Jan 3
d. c 687   A noble maiden who together with
her husband took a vow of perpetual continence, and on the death of the latter lived as a
recluse near a church she had founded at
Maroeuil (Marolles) in Flanders.

Bertilla (Mary)
Boscardin (St) V.   Oct 20
1888–1922   Born at Brendola (Vincenza) in
Northern Italy. St Mary Bertilla, more widely
known as St Bertilla among her people, was a
member of the congregation entitled Teachers
of St Dorothy, Daughters of the Sacred
Hearts. She earnestly devoted her life of
obedience to the service of the sick and of
children. Canonized in 1961.

Bertilla (St) V. OSB.   Nov 5
d. c 705   A nun at Jouarre, near Meaux,
where she held the offices of infirmarian,
headmistress of the convent school and prioress. When St Bathildis restored the nunnery
of Chelles, St Bertilla was made its first abbess
and she governed it for half a century. Great
numbers flocked to her convent, including
many Anglo-Saxon girls.

Bertilo (Bl) M. OSB.   March 26
d. c 878 — 888   Abbot of St Benignus, at
Dijon. The Normans sacked his abbey and
massacred him and several of his community
at the foot of the altar.

Bertin the Younger (Bl)
C. OSB.   May 2
d. c 699   Monk of Sithin under its founder,
St Bertin the Great.

Bertin (St) Ab. OSB.   Sept 5
d. c 709   Born near Constance, he became a
monk at Luxeuil under St Waldebert, who had
introduced there the Benedictine rule. He was
sent to help St Omer, bishop of Thérouanne,
by whom he was made abbot of Sithin (afterwards called St Bertin). Under his government
the community increased in a remarkable
manner, and he was obliged to establish
several new houses. His usual emblem is a
boat or small ship.

Bertoara (St) Abs.   Dec 4
d. p.614   Abbess of Notre-Dame-de-Sales,
in Bourges (612–614) under the Columbanian
rule.

Bertram (St) C.   Sept 9
Otherwise Bettelin, q.v.

Bertrand (Bertram, Bertran, Ebertram) (St)
Ab. OSB.   Jan 24
7th cent.   One of St Bertinus's disciples, and
one of St Omer's helpers in the evangelization
of N. France and Flanders. At a later date he
was made abbot of Saint-Quentin.

Bertrand (St) Bp. M.   June 6
1260–1350   Born near Cahors, he became
dean of the cathedral chapter of Angoulême;
later he became bishop of Aquileia. He met his
death in defence of the rights of his church.
Cult approved by Benedict XIV.

Bertrand (Bertichramnus) (St) Bp.   June 30
d. 623   A native of Autun, he was educated
by St Germanus at Paris, and appointed
archdeacon of that city and some time later
bishop of Le Mans. He took a great interest in
agriculture and wine-growing. He was especially noted for his benefactions to the poor.

Bertrand of Garrigue (Bl) C. OP.   Sept 6
d. 1230   A native of Garrigue, diocese of
Nîmes. He was already a secular priest when
he became a disciple of St Dominic and helped
him in his first foundation at Paris. He was the
constant companion of the holy founder until
his appointment as provincial of the Dominicans in Provence. Cult confirmed by Leo XIII.

Bertrand of Comminges (St) Bp.   Oct 16
d. 1123   The most celebrated of the bishops
of Comminges (now included in the diocese of
Toulouse), he may be considered as the

second founder of his episcopal city. He was its pastor for fifty years — energetic, fearless, enterprising, zealous. Canonized by Alexander III.

Bertrand of Grandselve (Bl) Ab. OSB. Cist.   Oct 23

d. 1149 (July 11) Cistercian abbot of Grandselve for twenty years. He was often favoured with heavenly visions.

Bertuin (St) Bp. OSB.   Nov 11

d. c 698   An Anglo-Saxon monk of the small abbey of Othelle. He was ordained a missionary bishop, left for Rome where he spent two years, and finally became the abbot-founder of the abbey of Malonne, in the territory of Namur, henceforward the centre of his missionary labours.

Berthulph (Bertulfus) (St) Ab. OSB.   Feb 5

d. 705   Born in Pannonia, a pagan, he migrated to Flanders, where he became a Christian and a priest. Count Wambert entrusted to him the administration of his estate, and gave him the land of Renty. Here the saint founded an abbey whither he retired after his benefactor's death.

Bertulph (St) Ab.   Aug 19

d. 640   Of Frankish origin, he entered the abbey of Luxeuil and was professed there under St Eustace. Then he migrated to Bobbio, where he was chosen abbot on St Attalas's death (627). As abbot of Bobbio he is best remembered for having obtained from Pope Honorius I the exemption of his abbey from episcopal jurisdiction, the first case recorded in history.

Besas (St) M.   Feb 27

See Julian, Cronion and Besas.

Bessarion (St) H.   June 17

d. c 400   One of the fathers of the Egyptian desert, greatly venerated among the Greeks, who keep his feast on June 6.

Betharius (St) Bp.   Aug 2

d. c 623   He was bishop of Chartres from 595 to 623 and was present at the council of Sens. His life is of doubtful authenticity.

Bettelin (Bethlin, Bethelm) (St) H. OSB.   Sept 9

8th cent.   Disciple of St Guthlac of Croyland. After the death of his master, Bettelin and his companions lived on at Croyland under Kenulphus, first abbot of the monastery founded there by King Ethelbald of Mercia. A saint of the name of Bettelin was patron of the town of Stafford, the base of whose shrine still exists at Ilam, Staffs.

Betto (St) Bp. OSB.   Feb 24

d. 918   A Benedictine monk of the abbey of Sainte-Colombe, at Sens, who became bishop of Auxerre in 889.

Beuno (St) Ab.   Apr 21

d. c 640   A Welshman by birth, he was the founder of monasteries at Llanfeuno in Herefordshire and Llanymynech; but his name is chiefly connected with that of Clynnog Fawr in Gwynedd. Legend makes him the uncle of St Winefride and claims that he restored her to life.

Beuve (St) V. OSB.   Apr 24

Otherwise Bova, q.v.

Bianor and Sylvanus (SS) MM.   July 10

4th cent.   Martyrs beheaded in Pisidia, in Asia Minor. Their extant Greek Acts are untrustworthy.

Bibiana (Vibiana, Vivian) (St) VM.   Dec 2

?   A virgin martyred at Rome. This is all that is certain about her. Her *Acta* are a medieval romance, much read and admired throughout Europe, and especially in Germany and Spain, as witness the great number of churches dedicated in her honour. They gave rise to a number of spurious entries in the pre-1970 RM.; see St Dafrosa, and SS Priscus, Priscillian and Benedict. Since 1969 her cult has been confined to her basilica on the Esquiline.

Biblig (Peblig) (St)   July 3

Otherwise Byblig, q.v.

Biblis (or Biblides) (St) M.   June 2

One of the martyrs of Lyons. See Photinus, Sanctius, etc.

Bicor (St) M.   Apr 22

A bishop martyr under Shapur II.

Bieuzy (St) M.   Nov 24

7th cent.   A native of Britain who followed St Gildas to Brittany. We have no particulars of his life or of the martyrdom which closed it.

Bilfrid (Billfrith) (St) H. OSB.   March 6

8th cent.   A monk-hermit of Lindisfarne and an expert goldsmith, who bound in gold the Lindisfarne copy of the Gospels, written and illuminated by bishop Eaddfrid. The discovery of his alleged relics in the 11th century and their enshrining at Durham strengthened his cult.

Bilhild (St) W. OSB.   Nov 27

c 630–c 710   Born near Würzburg, Bilhild

married the duke of Thuringia. After the death of her husband, she became the abbess-foundress of the nunnery of Altenmünster in Mainz.

Birgitta (St) W.   Oct 8
Otherwise Brigid of Sweden, q.v.

Birillus (St) Bp.   March 21
d. *c* 90 Said to have been ordained first bishop of Catania in Sicily by St Peter the Apostle, with whom he had travelled from Antioch. He died in extreme old age. Nothing factual can be established.

Birinus (St) Bp.   Dec 3
d. *c* 650 A Roman missionary priest commonly said to have been a monk, who offered himself for the foreign missions and was sent by Pope St Honorius to Britain. He was ordained bishop at Genoa and on his arrival in England converted Cynegils, king of the West Saxons, and was given Dorchester in Oxfordshire for his see. He is known as the "Apostle of Wessex".

Birnstan (Birrstan, Brynstan) (St) Bp. OSB.   Nov 4
d. *c* 934 Successor of St Frithestan in the see of Winchester and a disciple of St Grimbald. He was fond of reciting prayers for the faithful departed.

Biteus (St) C.   July 22
Otherwise Movean, q.v.

Bitheus and Genocus (SS) CC.   Apr 18
6th cent. Two British monks who accompanied St Finian of Clonard to Ireland, and there attained a great reputation for sanctity.

Blaan (St) Bp.   Aug 10
Otherwise Blane, q.v.

Bladus (St) Bp.   July 3
? According to tradition, one of the early bishops of the Isle of Man.

Blaesilla (St) W.   Jan 22
d. 383 Daughter of St Paula and a disciple of St Jerome. In her widowhood she consecrated herself to God. She died in Rome aged twenty.

Blaise (Blasius, Blase) (St) Bp. M.   GC. Feb 3
d. *c* 316 According to his legendary acts, which became widely known in W. Europe at the time of the crusades, Blaise was a physician who became bishop of Sebaste in Armenia, where he was martyred. One of his miracles was the saving of the life of a boy who had half swallowed a fish-bone which could not be extricated; hence the rite of the *Blessing of St*

St Blaise, Feb 3

Blaise, incorporated in the Roman ritual, against infections of the throat. His feast is observed with much solemnity throughout the East, as was also the case, in ancient times, in the West. His symbol is a wool comb, sometimes made of iron rather than of wood, with which a legend states he was martyred.

Blaise of Auvergne (Bl) C. OP.   Apr 5
14th cent. A disciple of St Vincent Ferrer, and like him an impassioned Dominican preacher.

Blaise and Demetrius (SS) MM.   Nov 29
? Martyrs of Veroli in central Italy. Their connexion with St Mary Salome is discarded nowadays.

Blaithmaic (Blathmac, Blaithmale) (St) M.   Jan 15
d. *c* 823 An Irish abbot, who, desirous of martyrdom, crossed over to England, then a prey to heathen Danes. He was murdered by the Danes on the altar steps of the abbey church at Iona. Walafrid Strabo narrates his life in verse.

Blanca (Bl) W.   Apr 26
Otherwise Alda, q.v.

Blanche (*several*)
Otherwise Gwen, q.v.

Blanda (St) M.   May 10
See Calepodius, Palmutius, etc.

Blandina (St) M.   June 2
See Photinus (Pothinus), Sanctius, etc.

Blandinus (St) H.   May 1
See Salaberga.

Blane (Blaan, Blain) (St)
Bp.   Aug 10
6th cent. A Scottish bishop, disciple of SS
Comgall and Canice in Ireland, who flourished in the sixth century, and was buried at
the place now called Dunblane. There has
been much controversy over the actual dates of
his life; but the above summary is now commonly agreed upon by scholars.

Blath (Flora) (St) V.   Jan 29
d. 523 In the Irish martyrologies several
saints are registered under the name Blath
(latinized Flora). The one best remembered
was a lay-sister, the cook in St Brigid's
nunnery at Kildare, where she earned a great
reputation for sanctity.

Bledrws (St)
? There is a church in Dyfed named after St
Bledrws, but is has not been found possible to
identify the saint.

Bleiddian (Blewdian)
(St) Bp.   July 29
Otherwise Lupus of Troyes, q.v.

Blenwydd (St)
? The dedication of a chapel to this saint in the
Isle of Anglesey is all that perpetuates his
memory.

Blidulf (Bladulph) (St) Mk.   Jan 2
d. c 630 A monk of Bobbio, who courageously denounced the heresy of the Lombard
king Ariovald.

Blinlivet (Blevileguetus)
(St) Bp.   Nov 7
9th cent. The twenty-fifth bishop of Vannes
in Brittany. Before his death he resigned and
became a monk at Quimperlé.

Blitharius (Blier) (St) C.   June 11
7th cent. A native of Scotland, who passed
over into France with St Fursey, and settled at
Seganne in Champagne, where he is still held
in great veneration.

Blitmund (St) Ab.   Jan 3
d. 660 ? Monk of Bobbio under St Attalas.
He followed St Walaricus (St Valéry) to
France, where they founded the abbey of
Leucone (later on called Saint-Valéry; now the

village of the same name). St Blitmund survived his master and ruled the abbey as its
second abbot.

Boadin (St) H. OSB.   Jan 11
? An Irishman who passed over to France and
became a Benedictine monk there.

Bobinus (St) Bp. OSB.   Jan 31
d. c 766 A native of Aquitaine, monk of
Moutier-la-Celle, which was enriched by his
benefactions when he became bishop of
Troyes (760).

Bobo (Beuvon) (St) H.   May 22
d. c 985 A knight of Provence, who fought
bravely against the invading Saracens and then
retired as a hermit to lead a life of penance. He
died at Pavia in Lombardy while on a pilgrimage to Rome.

Bodagisil (St) Ab.   Dec 18
d. 588 A Frankish courtier, who later
became the founder and first abbot of an abbey
on the banks of the Meuse. St Venantius
Fortunatus and St Gregory of Tours are loud
in his praises.

Bodfan (Bobouan) (St)   June 2
7th cent. The patron saint of Abern in
Gwynedd. The only extant tradition about him
is that the great inundation that formed Beau-
maris Bay impelled him, with his father and
other relations, to embrace the religious life.

Bodo (St) Bp. OSB.   Sept 11
d. p.670 A native of Toul, brother to St
Salaberga. He married, but by mutual consent
both he and his wife became religious. He
entered an abbey at Laon, which, however, he
was forced to leave in order to become bishop
of Toul. He founded Etival, Bon-Moutier,
and Affonville abbeys.

Boetharius (St) Bp.   Aug 2
7th cent. Chaplain of King Clotaire II, and
afterwards bishop of Chartres (c 595).

Boethian (St) M. OSB.   May 22
7th cent. A disciple of St Fursey and an
Irishman by birth. He built the monastery of
Pierrepont, near Laon, in France, and was
eventually murdered by those whom he had
felt bound to rebuke. His shrine is still a place
of pilgrimage.

Boethius (Bl) C.   Oct 23
See Severinus Boethius.

Bogumilus (i.e.
Theophilus) (St) Bp.
OSB. Cam.   June 10
d. 1182 A native of Dobrow, a little Polish
town on the Wartha. After his studies at the
university of Paris he was appointed parish

priest of Dobrow, and then archbishop of Gnesen. As such he founded the Cistercian abbey of Coronowa. In spite of his wisdom and zeal his clergy paid little heed to his admonitions. He resigned in 1172 and became a Camaldolese monk at Uniejow. Cult approved in 1925.

Boisil (St) Ab.   Feb 23
Otherwise Boswell, q.v.

Bolcan (Olcan) (St) Bp.   Feb 20
d. c 480   Baptized by St Patrick and sent by him to study in Gaul, Bolcan was subsequently by the same saint ordained bishop of Derkan in N. Ireland. His school there was one of the best equipped in the island. Another St Bolcan is venerated in the diocese of Elphin. He is known as St Olcan of Kilmoyle.

Bolonia (St) VM.   Oct 16
d. 362   A maiden of fifteen who was martyred under Julian the Apostate, and who has left her name to the village of Saint Boulogne in the Haute Marne.

Bona (St) V.   Apr 24
Otherwise Bova, q.v.

Bonajuncta (St) C.   Feb 17
i.e. Buonagiunta, one of the Seven Holy Founders of the Servite Order, q.v.

Bonannus (Bl) C. OSB. Cel.   Jan 1
d. c 1320   A Benedictine of the Celestine congregation, monk of the monastery of St Laurence in the Abruzzi.

**Bonaventure of Meaco
(Bl)** M. Tert. OFM.   Feb 6
d. 1597   A native of Meaco in Japan, this saint became a Franciscan tertiary and helped the Franciscan missionaries as a catechist. He was crucified at Nagasaki. Beatified in 1862. He is one of the Companions of St Paul Miki, q.v.

Bonaventure Tornielli (Bl)
C. OSM.   March 31
1411–1491   Born at Forli, he became a Servite in 1448. At the order of the pope Sixtus IV he preached continually throughout the papal states and S. Italy. He was for some years vicar-general of the Servites. Cult confirmed in 1911.

**Bonaventure Baduario
of Peraga (Bl)** C. OSA. Erem.   June 10
1332–1386   A native of Peraga, near Padua, where he was professed as an Augustinian hermit. After having been general of the order he was created cardinal-priest of St Caecilia — the first of the order to attain that honour.

He was killed in Rome by an arrow, probably in retaliation for his defence of the rights of the church.

Bonaventure (St) Bp. Dr.
OFM.   GC. July 15
1221–1274   Born at Bagnorea, near Viterbo. His baptismal name was John. The name Bonaventure (good fortune) was given to him by St Francis of Assisi, who cured him miraculously when he was a small child, and exclaimed: *O buona ventura!* At the age of twenty he became a Franciscan, and at thirty-six minister-general of the order. He was nominated archbishop of York, but refused the honour. Finally in 1273 he was created cardinal bishop of Albano. He died during the general council of Lyons. A disciple of Alexander of Hales and a friend and admirer of St Thomas Aquinas, Bonaventure is known as the "Seraphic Doctor", and was officially given the title of Doctor of the Church by Sixtus V. Besides theological and philosophical works, St Bonaventure has left us sundry ascetical treatises, and a touchingly beautiful life of St Francis of Assisi written with the aim of promoting unity among the Friars Minor. Canonized in 1482.

Bonaventure Grau (Bl)
C. OFM.   Sept 11
1620–1684   Born at Riudoms, near Barcelona, left a widower after a short period of married life, he joined the Friars Minor at Escornalbou. To escape notoriety for his mystical gifts he went to Rome where he was made doorkeeper at St Isidore. He founded several retreat-convents in the Roman province of his order. His advice was sought by popes and cardinals. Cult approved in 1906.

**Bonaventure of Potenza
(Bl)** C. OFM.   Oct 26
1651–1711   A native of Potenza in Lucania. He entered the Franciscan order at Nocera and spent his life as a missioner in S. Italy, chiefly at Amalfi, and as a novice master. He died in an ecstasy singing psalms.

**Bonaventure Buonaccorsi
(Bl)** C. OSM.   Dec 14
d. 1313   A native of Pistoia in Tuscany and the leader of the Ghibellines there, he was converted in 1276 by St Philip Benizi, who was acting as a peace-maker between the parties. He followed St Philip into the Servite order and as a Servite friar went about preaching peace. The people called him "*il Beato*" even during his lifetime. Cult approved in 1822.

Bonaventure Tolomei (Bl)
C. OP.   Dec 27
d. 1348   Born at Siena in Tuscany. As a

child he was favoured with divine charismata, but in early manhood he abandoned himself for four years to a life of impurity and sacrilege. He repented, visited on foot all the celebrated shrines and subsequently entered the Dominican order. He died while tending the plague-stricken in Siena.

Bonavita (Bl) C. Tert.
OFM.   March 1
d. 1375   A blacksmith of Lugo, near Ravenna. He was a Franciscan tertiary, wholly devoted to prayer and good works.

Bond (Baldus) (St) H.   Oct 29
7th cent.   A penitent hermit venerated at Sens in France. See Arthemius (Apr 28).

Bonet (Bont) (St) Bp.   Jan 15
Otherwise Bonitus, q.v.

Bonfilius Monaldi (St)   Feb 17
One of the Seven Holy Founders of the Servite order, q.v.

Bonfilius (St) Bp. OSB.   Sept 27
1040–1125   A native of Osimo in Piceno, he became a monk, and then abbot, of the monastery of Our Lady, at Storace. In 1078 he was made bishop of Foligno: but in 1096, after a pilgrimage to the Holy Land, he resigned and retired to the abbey of Santa Maria della Fara, diocese of Cingoli, where he died.

Boniface of Lausanne (St)
Bp.   Feb 19
d. 1265   Born in Brussels and educated by nuns of La Cambre (Camera S. Mariae), near his native city. He then studied at Paris, where he taught dogma, afterwards transferring his chair to the university of Cologne. About the year 1230 he was made bishop of Lausanne, but resigned (1239) and henceforth lived at the Cistercian convent, La Cambre, as chaplain to the nuns. The Cistercians claim him for their order.

Boniface of Savoy (Bl)
Bp. O. Cart.   March 13
d. 1270   A member of the ducal house of Savoy, who became a Carthusian monk (and prior) and then bishop of Valence, and finally archbishop of Canterbury (1241). Besides his fame as a saint, the fact that he was uncle to Henry III's wife explains the appointment, which, however, proved very unpopular in England. He died in Savoy and was buried at Hautecombe. Cult confirmed in 1830.

Boniface Curitan (St) Bp.   March 14
d. c 660   A bishop of Ross, very likely a Roman by birth, who evangelized the Picts and Scots, one of the chief features of his mission being the introduction of Roman discipline

and observance, as opposed to the Celtic usages. He is said to have founded a very great number of churches.

Boniface of Valperga (Bl)
Bp.   Apr 25
d. 1243   Monk of the Benedictine abbey of Fruttuaria, who was chosen prior of the Augustinian canons regular of St Ursus at Aosta (1212) and finally bishop of Aosta (1219–1243).

Boniface IV (St) Pope   May 8
d. 615   Born at Valeria in the Abruzzi, he became, according to a tradition which cannot, however, be substantiated, a Benedictine monk of St Sebastian, in Rome. He was pope from 608 to 615 and is best remembered for his dedication of the Pantheon to our Lady and all the saints. St Columbanus addressed to him a famous — or notorious — letter.

Boniface of Tarsus (St)
M.   formerly May 14
d. c 307   A martyr beheaded at Tarsus in Cilicia, whither, his fictitious acts add, he had gone from Rome to recover the bodies of certain martyrs. His own relics are enshrined in the church of SS Alexius and Boniface on the Aventine. Cult suppressed in 1969.

Boniface (St) Bp.   May 14
6th cent.   Bishop of Ferentino in Tuscany at the time of the emperor Justin. He is commemorated by St Gregory the Great.

Boniface (Bl) Mk. OSB.
Cist.   June 4
d. c 1280   Monk and prior of the great Cistercian abbey of Villers in Brabant.

Boniface (St) Bp. M.
OSB.   GC. June 5
680–754   An Anglo-Saxon, whose baptismal name was Winfrid, born at Crediton in Devon. At the age of five he entered a monastery at Exeter, there to become a Benedictine monk. He was transferred to Nutshulling, diocese of Winchester, where he became head of the abbey school and was ordained priest in 710. In 716 he set out for Germany on his first missionary expedition, which proved a failure. In 718 he left England again, this time for Rome, to get the pope's blessing on his enterprise, and forthwith evangelized Bavaria, Hesse, Friesland, Thuringia and Franconia. In 723 Gregory II ordained him regionary bishop with full jurisdiction over the Germanies. In 731 he was made by the pope metropolitan beyond the Rhine, in 738 papal legate, and in 747 archbishop of Mainz. A few years before his death he founded the abbey of

St Boniface, June 5

Fulda (where his body now rests) as the focus of German missionary activities. Before this he had already established a great number of abbeys and nunneries, with attached schools, and to staff them he had invited bands of monks and nuns from England. He was martyred in his old age, with fifty-two companions at Dokkum. He was responsible for the organization of the Frankish church. Always on the best of terms with the Carolingians, he became their mentor and support. He is rightly styled the Apostle of Germany. Among the apostles of all time he stands on a par with St Paul and St Francis Xavier. His symbol is a book, pierced with a sword or an axe, or he is shown felling an oak tree.

Boniface (St) M. OSB.   June 19
Otherwise Bruno of Querfurt. See Bruno-Boniface.

Boniface (St) M.   Aug 17
See Liberatus, Boniface, etc.

Boniface and Thecla (SS)
MM.   Aug 30
d. *c* 250 Their *Passio* makes them the parents of the "twelve brothers" commemorated on Sept 1. They are supposed to have been martyred under Maximian (though their *Passio*

does not say this) at Hadrumetum, i.e. Soussa in Tunisia.

Boniface I (St) Pope   Sept 4
d. 422 A Roman priest who was elected pope in 418. He was opposed by the anti-pope Eulalius and later on was troubled by the ever-recurring claims of the patriarch of Constantinople. Gently but firmly he defended the rights of the Roman see. St Augustine dedicated to him several treatises against Pelagianism.

Boniface (St) M.   Oct 5
Said to be the name of one of the martyrs who suffered with St Palmatius and Comp., q.v.

Boniface (St) M.   Dec 6
See Dionysia, Dativa, etc.

Boniface (St) M.   Dec 29
See Callistus, Felix and Boniface.

Bonitus (Bont) (St) Bp.
OSB.   Jan 15
623–*c* 710 A native of Auvergne who became successively chancellor to King Sigebert III, governor of Provence, and bishop of Clermont in Auvergne. After ten years as bishop, he resigned, owing to a scruple of conscience, and retired to the Benedictine

abbey of Manlieu, where he became a monk and died in extreme old age.

Bonitus (St) Ab. OSB.   July 7
d. c 582   Fourth successor of St Benedict as abbot of Montecassino. During his abbacy the Lombards under Zoto of Benevento plundered and destroyed the arch-abbey (c 581). The monks saved themselves by flight and were housed in the Lateran in Rome. Bonitus died shortly after.

Bonizella (Bl) W.   May 6
d. 1300   The wife of Naddo Piccolomini of Siena. In her widowhood she devoted herself and all her wealth to the service of the poor in the district of Belvederio.

Bononius (St) Ab. OSB.
Cam.   Aug 30
d. 1026   A native of Bologna and a Benedictine monk of St Stephen's in the same city. He became a disciple of St Romuald, by whom he was sent to preach the gospel in Egypt and Syria. On his return he was made abbot of Lucedio in Piedmont.

Bonosa (St) M.   July 15
See Eutropius, Zosima and Bonosa.

**Bonosus and Maximian
(SS)** MM.   Aug 21
d. 362   Two officers of the Herculean Cohort at Antioch, under Julian the Apostate. They were tortured and beheaded for refusing to change Constantine's Christian banner — the *labarum* — for a new idolatrous standard.

**Bonus, Faustus, Maurus
and Comp. (SS)** MM.   Aug 1
d. ?   Bonus, a priest, with Faustus, Maurus and nine companions, was martyred at Rome under Valerian.

Boris and Gleb (SS) MM.   July 24
d. 1010   Sons of St Vladimir, Duke of Muscovy. Their zeal for the propagation of the faith led to their martyrdom at the hands of their heathen fellow countrymen. Boris is the patron saint of Moscow. In the West they were sometimes called Romanus (Boris) and David (Gleb).

Bosa (St) Bp. OSB.   March 9
d. 705   Monk of Whitby under St Hilda, he was ordained bishop of York by St Theodore (678) when the titular of that see, St Wilfrid, was in exile. St Bede praises St Bosa in the following words: "a man beloved by God...of most unusual merit and sanctity." He served as bishop 678–686 and later 691–705.

Boswell (Boisil) (St) Ab.   Feb 23
d. c 661   Abbot of Melrose. He counted SS

Cuthbert and Egbert among his monks. Both had a great admiration for him, as had also St Bede. His favourite reading was the Gospel of St John.

**Botulph and Adulph
(SS)** CC. OSB.   June 17
7th cent.   Brothers, sons of noble Saxon parents. They were educated, and received the Benedictine habit in Belgian Gaul. Adulph is said to have been made a bishop. Botulph returned to England and became one of the foremost missionaries of the seventh century. He founded an abbey at Ikanhoe, formerly thought to be near Boston in Lincolnshire, but now generally supposed to be Iken in Suffolk. More than seventy English churches were dedicated to St Botulph, including four at the gates of the city of London.

Botwid (St) M.   July 28
d. 1100   A Swede, converted to the faith in England, who became an apostle in his own country. He was murdered by a Finnish slave whom he thought he had converted and whom he had set free.

Bova and Doda (SS) VV.
OSB.   Apr 24
7th cent.   St Bova was a sister, and St Doda a niece, of St Balderic (Baudry), the founder of Montfaucon and of the nunnery of St Peter at Reims. He appointed Bova first abbess of this convent and she was succeeded by Doda.

**Bradan and Orora
(Crora) (SS)**   Oct 20
?   Two saints venerated in the Isle of Man. In the church of St Bradan, Kirk-Braddan, near Douglas, Mark, the bishop of Sodor, held a synod in 1291. In a map of the sixteenth century, reference is made to the churches of SS Patrick and Crora.

Brandan (St) Ab.   Jan 11
5th cent.   An Irishman who crossed into Britain and had to suffer much there at the hands of the Pelagians. He took refuge in a monastery of Gaul, of which he eventually became abbot.

Brannock (St) Ab.   Jan 7
?   A saint who appears to have migrated from S. Wales into Devon, and to have founded a monastery at Braunton, near Barnstaple. The traditions concerning him are very untrustworthy. See also Brynach.

Branwallader (St) Bp.   Jan 19
?   6th cent.   Said to have been a bishop in Jersey. King Athelstan, who founded Milton abbey in Dorset, had a portion of this saint's relics translated there in 935.

Braulio (St) Bp. March 26
d. 646 A monk of St Engratia's monastery, Saragossa, he was sent to Seville to study under St Isidore. He was ordained priest by his own brother, John, whom he succeeded as archbishop of Saragossa. He was a ready writer and excelled chiefly as a hagiographer.

Breaca (St) V. June 4
5th–6th cent. A disciple of St Brigid who is said to have gone from Ireland to Cornwall (c 460) with several companions and to have landed on the eastern bank of the river Hayle. Variants of her name are: Breague, Branca, Banka, etc.

Bregwin (St) Bp. OSB. Aug 26
d. 764 The twelfth archbishop of Canterbury (761–765). His life was written by Eadmer. Letters of his to St Lullus of Mainz are still extant.

Brenach (St) H. Apr 7
Otherwise Brynach, q.v.

**Brendan the Voyager
(St)** Ab. May 16
c 486–c 575 or c 583 One of the three most famous saints of Ireland. He was born on Fenit peninsula, Kerry, and educated for five years under St Ita, becoming afterwards a disciple of St Finian at Clonard and of St Gildas at Llancarfan in Wales. He was a great founder of monasteries, the chief of which was Clonfert. To his monks he gave a rule of remarkable austerity. He is best known in history for his voyages, in which, it is said, he reached the American continent. His voyaging has nevertheless had some influence on history, since legends of St Brendan's journey to discover the Isles of the Blessed were popular throughout Europe. St Brendan is most fittingly venerated as the patron saint of sailors.

Brendan of Birr (St) Ab. Nov 29
d. c 573 A contemporary of St Brendan the Voyager, and his fellow-disciple under St Finian at Clonard. His abbey of Birr was somewhere near Parsonstown in Offaly. He was the great friend and adviser of St Columba, who in a vision saw the soul of St Brendan carried by angels to heaven at the moment of his death.

Bretannion (St) Bp. Jan 25
d. c 380 Bishop of Tomi in Scythia on the Black Sea, near the mouth of the Danube. The Arian emperor, Valens, exiled him for his brave defence of Christ's divinity, but was compelled by popular discontent to recall him.

Briarch (St) Ab. Dec 17
d. c 627 An Irishman who became a monk in Wales under St Tudwal, whom he accompanied to Brittany. He built a monastery at Guingamp. He died at Bourbiac.

**Briant, Alexander (Bl)
M.** Dec 1
See Alexander Briant.

Briavel (Brevile) (St) H. June 17
? The name of this saint (possibly a variant of Ebrulfus) is perpetuated as that of the patron saint of the parish of St Briavels in the Forest of Dean in Gloucestershire; but no record of his life is extant.

**Brice (Britius, Brixius)
(St)** Bp. Nov 13
d. 444 A disciple of St Martin of Tours, but, unlike his master, a proud, ambitious and even licentious cleric. Nevertheless, he was chosen to be St Martin's successor at Tours, and during twenty years he continued to be a very unsatisfactory ecclesiastic, being for this reason eventually driven from his see. He went to Rome, repented, and was reinstated at Tours, and such was his change of manners that his flock proclaimed him a saint immediately after his death. His cult spread throughout N. Europe.

Brictius (St) Bp. July 9
d. c 312 Bishop of Martola near Spoleto in Umbria, imprisoned for the faith under Diocletian. He escaped death, and died a confessor under Constantine.

Bridget
(several)
Otherwise Brigid, q.v.

**Brieuc (Briocus, Brioc)
(St)** Bp. May 1
c 420–510 Born in Dyfed, he was educated in France by St Germanus of Auxerre. He laboured very successfully first in his native land, and then in Brittany, where he founded two abbeys, one near Tréguier, and the other where the town of St Brieuc now stands. He is venerated in Cornwall.

Brigid (Briga) (St) V. AC. Jan 21
6th cent. Known as St Brigid of Kilbride and venerated in the diocese of Lismore. It is recorded that her famous namesake of Kildare visited her more than once at Kilbride.

Brigid and Maura (SS) Jan 28
? Venerated as daughters of a Scottish chieftain, said to have been martyred in Picardy while on a pilgrimage to Rome. They are most probably to be identified with SS Maura and Britta (q.v.).

St Bridget of Sweden, July 23

Brigid (Bridget, Bride, Ffraid) (St) V. Foundress Feb 1

c 450–*c* 525   Born at Faughart, near Dund-
alk, she took the veil in her youth and founded
the nunnery of Kildare, the first to be erected
on Irish soil. Around her name there have
been formed hundreds of legends, the keynote of them all being mercy and pity for the
poor. In art St Brigid is represented holding a
cross, with a flame over her head, and sometimes with a cow near her, since she is reputed
to be the protectress of those engaged in dairy
work. A greatly venerated saint, she is the
patron of Ireland after St Patrick.

Brigid (St) V. Feb 1

9th cent.   Alleged sister of St Andrew, abbot
of St Donatus at Fiesole in Tuscany. It is said
that she was carried by angels to her brother's
deathbed. She died as a recluse in the Apennines. Most modern writers discard all this as a
fiction.

Bridget of Sweden (Brigid, Birgitta) (St) W. Foundress GC. July 23

1303–1373   Born of a noble Swedish family,
Bridget married, before she was fifteen, a
Swedish prince, with whom she lived happily
for twenty-eight years, and to whom she bore
eight children. She proved to be a busy,
home-loving wife. In her widowhood she
founded the monastery of Wadstena (1344),
thus instituting the Order of the Most Holy
Saviour, known as "the Bridgettines". She is
also famous for the visions and revelations with
which she was favoured by God, and which she
recorded in writing. She died in Rome on her
return from Jerusalem (July 23) and was
canonized eighteen years later (1391). In art
she is represented clothed in the religious
habit of her order; bearing a pilgrim's staff,
holding a heart marked with a cross and with
our Saviour near her, or holding a chain or a
pilgrim's flask.

Brinstan (St) Bp. Nov 4

Otherwise Birnstan, q.v.

Brioc (Briocus) (St) Bp. May 1

Otherwise Brieuc, q.v.

Brithwald (Brihtwald, Berthwald, Berctuald) (St) Bp. OSB. Jan 9

d. 731   An Anglo-Saxon, educated probably
at Canterbury; afterwards monk and abbot of
Reculver in Kent. He was elected archbishop
of Canterbury in 692 and governed that see for
thirty-seven years.

Brithwold (St) Bp. OSB. Jan 22

d. 1045   A monk of Glastonbury. He was
chosen bishop of Ramsbury (1005), whence he
removed the see to Old Sarum. He was a great
benefactor of Malmesbury and Glastonbury,
where he was buried.

Brito (Britonius) (St) Bp. May 5

d. 386   Bishop of Trier. A stout opponent of
the Priscillian heretics, whom he nevertheless
always refused to hand over for punishment by
the state.

Britwin (Brithwin, Brithun) (St) Ab. OSB. May 15

d. *c* 733   Abbot of Beverley. He received his
great friend and patron, St John of Beverley,
into his monastery, after the latter had resigned the bishopric of York.

Brixius (St) Bp.   Nov 13
Otherwise Brice, q.v.

Brocard (St) C. OC.   Sept 2
d. 1231   St Berthold's successor as prior of
the Frankish hermits of Mt Carmel. At his
request St Albert, patriarch of Jerusalem,
drew up for them the rule under which they
developed in the West into the Order of Mt
Carmel. He was highly respected by the
Muslims.

Bron (St) Bp.   June 8
d. c 511   A disciple of St Patrick, ordained
bishop of Cassel-Irra, near the town of Sligo.

Bronach (Bromana) (St)
V.   Apr 2
? Called the Virgin of Glen-Seichis and regis-
tered in the martyrologies of Tallaght and
Donegal. Glen-Seichis is the old name of
Kilbrony or Kilbronach, in Co. Down, which
takes its present appellation from her.

Bronislava (Bl) V. O.
Praem.   Aug 30
d. 1259   A cousin of St Hyacinth of Poland.
She was a professed Premonstratensian nun in
Poland, but died a recluse. Cult confirmed in
1839.

**Brothen and Gwendolen
(SS)**   Oct 18
? 6th cent.   Welsh saints, of whom nothing is
known but the names and the fact that they
were given a public cult in Wales. St Brothen is
still the patron saint of Llanbrothen. Dolwyd-
delen and Llanwyddelan suggest a St Gwendolen; this and similar names are diminutives
of Gwen (white) and are equivalent to our
Blanche and its allied forms.

Bruno and Comp. (SS)
MM.   Feb 2
See Ebsdorf, Martyrs of.

Bruno (St) Bp.   May 27
d. 1045   Appointed bishop of Würzburg in
1033 and best remembered as the fosterer of
church-building throughout the diocese, on
which work he spent all his private fortune.
While he was dining with the emperor Henry
III at Bosenburg on the Danube, a gallery gave
way, killing the saintly bishop on the spot.

Bruno Seronkuma (St)
M.   June 3
d. 1885   A soldier of King Mwanga of
Uganda. He was baptized on Nov 18, 1885,
and burnt alive a few weeks later, having
refused a drink on the road to martyrdom. See
Charles Lwanga and Comps.

Bruno-Boniface (St) M.
OSB. Cam.   June 19 and Oct 15
d. 1009   Born at Querfurt, and educated
at the cathedral-school of Magdeburg. He accompanied Otto III to Italy (996) and there he
received the Camaldolese habit from St Romuald. He was made archbishop of Mersburg,
and sent to evangelize Prussia and Russia. He
was martyred with eighteen companions (Feb
14). Note that St Boniface of the pre-1970
RM. on June 19 and St Bruno on Oct 15 are
one and the same person. Bruno was the
baptismal, and Boniface the monastic name of
the saint.

Bruno of Segni (St) Bp.
OSB.   July 18
1049–1123   Born at Solero (Asti) in Piedmont, he studied in the monastery of St Perpetuus at Asti, and at Bologna. He first
became known as the opponent of Berengarius. In 1079 Gregory VII made him bishop of
Segni; but he left the see and became a monk,
and then abbot, of Montecassino. The pope,
however, although allowing him to become a
monk, had not definitely accepted his resignation of the see, and eventually Bruno had to
return to it. Among other offices held by the
saint were those of librarian of the Holy
Roman See and cardinal legate. He was a
profound theologian, and his work on the holy
eucharist was a standard work for centuries.
Canonized in 1183.

Bruno (St) Founder   GC. Oct 6
c 1032–1101   Born at Cologne, he studied at
Reims and Paris, and became chancellor of the
diocese of Reims. In 1084 he retired with six
companions to La Grande Chartreuse, near
Grenoble, and there he founded his order, or
rather a monastery of monk-hermits, under
the Benedictine rule, which at a later period
grew into the Carthusian order. Bl Urban II,
who had been St Bruno's student at Reims,
called the saint to Rome, to be a papal
counsellor. Even here, though never fully
released from the pope's service, St Bruno
managed to establish another charterhouse at
La Torre in Calabria, whither he was allowed
to retire. He refused the see of Reggio. St
Bruno excelled as a biblical exegete, writing on
the psalms and on St Paul's letters.

Bruno (St) Bp.   Oct 11
c 925–965   Called "the Great", a title which
nowadays would seem rather to belong to the
founder of the Carthusians. This Bruno was
the youngest son of the emperor, Henry the
Fowler, and St Matilda. From childhood, we
are told, he was devoted to learning; Prudentius was his bedside book. In 953 he was made

bishop of Cologne, being already commendatory abbot of Lorsch and Corvey. As archbishop his political influence was a factor in the consolidation of the German states.

Bruno (Bl) C. OSB.   Dec 24
d. *c* 1050   A Benedictine lay-brother of the abbey of Ottobeuren in Bavaria.

Brychan (St)   Apr 6
Nothing is known for sure about his life, but in legends he is a saintly king in Wales with a large number of saintly children: the usual quoted number is twenty-four. Other saints are meant to be descendents of him in later generations such as Enoder, q.v. All have separate entries in this book.

Brynach (Bernach, Bernacus) (St) C.   Apr 7
? 5th cent.   A Celt who settled in Wales, where he built a cell and a church at a place called Carn-Englyi (Mountain of Angels), overhanging Nefyn, Gwynedd. Some authors identify him with St Brannock of Braunton.

Brynoth (St) Bp.   May 9
d. 1317 (Feb 6)   A Swede, bishop of Scara in W. Gothland. Canonized in 1498.

Budoc (Budeaux) (St) Bp.   Dec 9
? 7th cent.   A Breton, educated in Ireland, where he became abbot of Youghal. Returning afterwards to Brittany, he succeeded SS Samson and Maglorius in the see of Dol. He has given his name to several places in Devon and Cornwall.

Buithe (Buite, Boethius) (St) C.   Dec 7
d. 521   A Scot, who spent some years in Italy and elsewhere on the Continent and, returning to Scotland, evangelized the Picts. From him it seems that Carbuddo (Castrum Butthi) takes its name.

Bulgaria (Martyrs of) (SS)   July 23
9th cent.   During the war between the Greek emperor, Nicephorus, and the Bulgars, not as yet Christians, many Catholics, besides those slain in battle, were put to death on account of their faith. There is much uncertainty as to the exact circumstances, but they have always been reckoned as martyrs.

Burchard (Bl) Ab. OSB. Cist.   Apr 19
d. 1164   A favourite monk and disciple of St Bernard at Clairvaux. He was appointed successively abbot of Balerne (1136) and of Bellevaux (*c* 1157).

Burchard (Bl) Ab. OSB.   June 25
d. 1122   Monk of the Benedictine abbey of St Michael at Bamberg, and first abbot of Mallersdorf in Bavaria.

Burchard (Bl) Bp. OSB.   Aug 20
d. 1026   A native of Hesse who, after studying at Coblentz, became a monk at Lobbes. In 1006 he was compelled by the emperor Otto to accept the bishopric of Worms. He is famous as a compiler of canons and decretals.

Burchard (St) Bp. OSB.   Oct 14
d. *c* 754   An English priest and monk who joined the German mission under St Boniface (*c* 732). He was ordained first bishop of Würzburg (Herbipolis), and founded there several Benedictine abbeys of which the most important was St Andrew's, afterwards called after him. About the year 753 he resigned his bishopric to a monk of Fritzlar and spent the remaining months of his life in monastic retirement.

Burginus and Guilminus (BB) Mks. OSB.   Nov 18
d. *p*.1065   Two Benedictine monks who were among the pioneers of the priory of Thouacé in Anjou, founded by St Florentius.

Burgundofara (or Fara) (St) Abs. OSB.   Apr 3 and Dec 7
d. 657   Blessed by St Columbanus in her infancy, Burgundofara early developed a religious vocation in spite of the fierce opposition of her father, a noble Frankish courtier. In the end he had to give way and founded for her the nunnery of Brige (Brie) or *Evoriacum* — later called Faremoutiers, i.e. Fara's Monastery — over which she ruled for thirty-seven years. Many English nun-saints were trained under her.

Buriana (St) V.   June 4
6th cent.   An Irishwoman who lived as a recluse in Cornwall. The place-name St Buryan, opposite the Scilly Islands, perpetuates her memory.

Buzad Banfy (Bl) M., OP.   Dec 8
d. 1241   A Hungarian count who became a famous friar preacher. Killed in front of the altar by the Tartars when they invaded Pesth.

Byblig (Biblig, Peblig, Piblig, Publicius)   July 3
? 5th cent.   A holy man connected with Carnarvon and honoured with a cult in parts of Wales, of whom, however, nothing certain is known.

Cadell (St)   ?
7th cent. A Welsh saint, giving the name to Llangadell in Glamorgan.

Cadfan (St) Ab.   Nov 1
d. early 6th cent. A native of Brittany, who came over to Wales and founded several monasteries. His name is chiefly associated with those of Towyn in Gwynedd and Bardsey Island (Ynys Enlli).

Cadfarch (St)   Oct 24
6th cent. A Welsh saint, disciple of St Illtyd, and member of a family of saints. He is said to have founded churches at Penegoes and Abererch.

Cadoc (Docus, Cathmael, Cadvael) (St) Bp. M.   Jan 24
d. c 580 A Welsh monk, founder of the great monastery of Llancarfan not far from Cardiff, which became a veritable house of saints. Accompanied by St Gildas, St Cadoc later continued his religious life on an island off the coast of Vannes in Brittany. He returned to Britain and is said to have taken spiritual charge of the Britons, his compatriots, in the eastern counties, during their last struggle with the conquering Saxons, by whom he was martyred near Weedon.

Cadog (Gadoga) (St)   ?
5th cent. The titular saint of Llangadock in Dyfed, not to be confused with the later St Cadoc or Docus.

Cadroe (Cadroel) (St) Ab. OSB.   March 6
d. 976 The son of a Scottish prince, he was sent to Ireland to be educated at Armagh. He came to England and is said to have saved London from destruction by fire. Then he passed over to France and took the Benedictine habit at Fleury. Shortly after he was made abbot of the new foundation of Waulsort on the Meuse and finally called to Metz to restore St Clement's.

Cadwallader (St) King   Nov 12 (Oct 9)
d. c 682 A chieftain in Wales of the ancient British race, not to be confused with the Anglo-Saxon St Ceadwalla.

Caecilia Caecilianus, Caelestine
More frequently written Cecilia, Cecilanus, Celestine, and sometimes Coelestine.

Caecilian (St) M.   Apr 16
See Saragossa, Martyrs of.

Caecilian (St) C.   June 3
Otherwise Caecilius, q.v.

Caecilius (St) Bp.   May 15
See Torquatus, Cresiphon, etc.

Caecilius (Caecilian) (St) C.   June 3
3rd cent. A priest of Carthage, who, according to the pre-1970 RM., brought St Cyprian to the faith of Christ. St Cyprian never ceased to revere Caecilius's name, adding it to his own, and on Caecilius's death taking charge of his wife and children.

Caedmon (St) Mk. OSB.   Feb 11
d. c 680 A Northumbrian, attached first as a farm-servant and then as a lay-brother to the community of Whitby under St Hilda. He was the first of the Anglo-Saxons to write in verse.

Caelian (St) M.   Dec 15
See Faustinus, Lucius, etc.

Caellainn (Caoilfionn) (St) V.   Feb 3
? 6th cent. An Irish saint listed in the Martyrology of Donegal. A church in Roscommon perpetuates her memory.

Caerealis, Pupulus, Gaius and Serapion (SS) MM.   Feb 28
? Martyrs at Alexandria in Egypt. Some ancient MSS read Cerulus or Celerius for Caerealis. Gaius was added to the group by Baronius.

Caerealis (St) M.   June 10
See Getulius, Caerealis, etc.

Caerealis and Sallustia (SS) MM.   Sept 14
d. 251 Caerealis, a soldier, and his wife Sallustia were instructed in the faith by Pope St Cornelius, and martyred at Rome under Decius.

Caesarea (St) V.   May 15
? An Italian maiden, who in defence of her virtue took refuge in a cave near Otranto, S. Italy, and lived therein as a recluse. This cave is now a place of popular pilgrimage.

Caesareus (St) M.   Apr 20
See Victor, Zoticus, etc.

Caesaria (St) V.   Jan 12
d. c 530 Sister of St Caesarius of Arles, and abbess of the great nunnery founded by her brother in that city. According to the testimony of her contemporaries, Gregory of Tours and Venantius Fortunatus, she was a person of outstanding gifts.

Caesarius (St) C.   Jan 29
1st cent. Deacon of Angoulême under its first bishop, St Ausonius.

Caesarius of Nazianzus (St) C.   Feb 25
d. 369 Brother of St Gregory Nazianzen and physician at the imperial court of Byzantium, even under Julian the Apostate, who endeavoured unsuccessfully to drag Caesarius back to paganism. The saint, however, remained a catechumen nearly all his life, and was baptized only after a narrow escape from death in an earthquake at Nicea in Bithynia. We owe all these details to the funeral oration delivered by his brother, Gregory.

Caesarius of Arles (St) Bp.   Aug 27
470–543 A native of Châlon-sur-Saône, at the age of twenty he became a monk at Lérins, and at the age of thirty (500) was chosen bishop of Arles. A great churchman, he presided over several councils, notably over that of Orange (529) which condemned Semi-pelagianism. He founded the great nunnery afterwards called by his name at Arles, for which he drew up a monastic rule and of which his sister St Caesaria became abbess. He was zealous for decorum in liturgical worship. He excelled as a preacher, and his homilies may still be read with much profit. His people looked upon him as their leader even in social and political affairs, and he always proved worthy of their trust. During the distress caused by the siege of Arles in 508 he sold the treasures of his church to relieve the poor. He is said to have been the first archbishop in Western Europe to receive the *pallium* from the pope.

Caesarius and Julian (SS) MM.   Nov 1
? The former was an African deacon, the latter a priest. Both were martyred at Terracina, and their names appear in the earliest martyrologies. The church of St Caesarius on the Appian Way in Rome, now a title of one of the cardinal deacons, is dedicated to St Caesarius the African.

Caesarius, Dacius and Comp. (SS) MM.   Nov 1
? A group of seven martyrs who suffered at Damascus.

Caesarius (St) Bp.   Nov 1
d. p.627 The nineteenth or the twenty-second bishop of Clermont.

Caesarius (St) M.   Nov 3
See Germanus, Theophilus, etc.

Caesarius (St) M.   Dec 28
d. 309 Father of a notorious Arian, Eudoxius by name, his own past life had not been above reproach; but he atoned for it all by his heroic death at the stake at Arabissus in Armenia, under Galerius Maximian.

Caesidius and Comp. (SS) MM.   Aug 31
3rd cent. Known only from the unreliable *Acta* of St Rufinus (Aug 11), in which he is said to have been the son of that saint, and to have been martyred with a group of Christians on the shores of Lake Fucino, sixty miles east of Rome.

Cagnoald (St) Bp.   Sept 6
d. c 635 Brother of St Faro and St Burgundofara. He became a monk at Luxeuil under St Columbanus, and afterwards the sixth bishop of Laon.

Caian (St)   Sept 25
5th cent. A son or grandson of King Brychan of Brecknock. His church at Tregaian in Anglesey perpetuates his memory.

Caidoc and Fricor (Adrian) (SS) HH.   Apr 1
7th cent. Two Irishmen who evangelized the country of the Morini in N. France. St Ricarius, the future founder of Centula (Saint-Riquier), was one of their converts. Their relics are still venerated at the parish church of Saint-Riquier, diocese of Amiens.

Caillin (St) Bp.   Nov 13
7th cent. Associated with St Aedan (Maidhoc) of Ferns. It is narrated of him that he turned certain unbelieving Druids into stone.

Caimin (Cammin) of Inniskeltra (St) Ab.   March 24 or 25
d. 653 An Irish recluse who had led a life of great austerity on an island in Lough Derg, to which his reputation for sanctity attracted many disciples. Later in life he founded a monastery and church on the island of the Seven Churches. He was a fellow-worker with

St Senan. A fragment of the psalter of St Caimin, copied with his own hand, still exists.

Cairlon (Caorlan) (St)
Bp.   March 24
6th cent. An Irish abbot, said to have died and to have been restored to life by St Dageus. Afterwards, when St Cairlon had been made archbishop of Cashel, St Dageus placed himself and his monks under his rule.

Cairnech (St)   May 16
Otherwise Carantac, q.v.

Caius
Otherwise written Gaius q.v.

Cajetan (Gaetano) (St)
Founder   GC. Aug 7
1480–1547 Born at Vicenza, in Lombardy, a scion of the family of the counts of Thienna (Tiene). He renounced the posts offered him in Rome in order to devote his life to the service of the sick and the poor at Vicenza. Later, with Peter Caraffa (afterwards Pope Paul IV), he founded the congregation of clerks usually called *Theatines*, from Theate (Chieti), in the Abruzzi, where Caraffa was bishop. The institute, characterized by absolute trust in divine providence, played a part in the counter-Reformation. St Cajetan died at Naples; he was canonized in 1671.

Calais (St) Ab.   July 1
Otherwise Carilefus, q.v.

Calanicus (St) M.   Dec 17
See Florian, Calanicus, etc.

Calepodius, Palmatius, Simplicius, Felix, Blanda and Comp. (SS) MM.   May 10
d. 222–232 A number of Roman martyrs who suffered under Alexander Severus during the pontificate of Callistus I. Calepodius, a priest, was the first to suffer; he has given its name to a Roman catacomb. St Palmatius, of consular rank, died with his wife and children and forty-two of his household. St Simplicius, a senator, was martyred with sixty-five of his family and dependents. SS Felix and Blanda were husband and wife. All were victims of an outburst of fury on the part of the heathen mob.

Caletricus (St) Bp.   Sept 4
529–c 580 Born at Chartres he became bishop of that city after the death of St Lubinus (c 557).

Calimerius (St) Bp. M.   July 31
d. c 190 A Greek, educated in Rome by

Pope St Telesphorus, he became bishop of Milan. He was the apostle of the valley of the Po. Under the emperor Commodus he was martyred by being cast headlong into a deep well. He is buried under the high altar of his church at Milan.

Calimerius of Montechiero (Bl) C. OP.   Nov 28
d. 1521 A Friar Preacher who spent his life preaching throughout Italy. When a nonagenarian and unable to climb into the pulpit he persuaded others to lift him into it in order that he might preach.

Calixtus (*several*)
Otherwise Callistus, q.v.

Callinica and Basilissa (SS) MM.   March 22
d. 250 Rich ladies of Galatia in Asia Minor, who spent their fortune in succouring the Christians imprisoned for their faith. Both were martyred on that account.

Callinicus (St) M.   Jan 28
See Thyrsus, Leucius and Callinicus.

Callinicus (St) M.   July 29
? 3rd cent. A native of Gangra, the chief town of Paphlagonia in Asia Minor. He was burnt to death. Metaphrastes gives full details of his martyrdom, and he is held in high esteem in the Eastern churches.

Calliope (St) M.   June 8
d. ? 250 An Eastern martyr, beheaded for Christ. Neither the place nor the exact date of her martyrdom is known. Her acts are untrustworthy.

Calliopus (St) M.   Apr 7
d. c 303 A martyr who, under Diocletian, was crucified head downwards at Pompeiopolis in Cilicia.

Callista (St) M.   Sept 2
See Evodius, Hermogenes and Callistus.

Callisthene (St) V.   Oct 4
See Adauctus and Callisthene.

Callistratus and Comp. (SS) MM.   Sept 26
d. c 300 A body of fifty African soldiers put to death at Constantinople under Diocletian. They were sewn up in sacks and cast into the sea.

Callistus, Charisius and Comp. (SS) MM.   Apr 16
3rd cent. Nine Christians of Corinth, martyred by being thrown into the sea.

Callistus I (St) Pope M.   GC. Oct 14
d. c 222 A Christian slave of Rome, who

was made deacon by Pope St Zephyrinus, whom he succeeded as pope (217). For his lenient attitude towards repentant sinners he incurred the wrath of the rigorists — notably SS Hippolytus, Tertullian and Novatian. He condemned Sabellianism and other heresies and was forgiving and tolerant to those whom rigorists regarded as sinners. As deacon he had superintended the Christian cemetery on the Appian Way, which is still known by his name. He was probably martyred. He is honoured as a martyr at Todi on Aug 14.

Callistus (St) M.   Oct 15
d. 1003   A native of Huesca, in Aragon, who, together with St Mercurialis, passed over to France and died there fighting against the Saracens. They are still venerated in the diocese of Tarbes.

Callistus, Felix and Boniface (SS) MM.   Dec 29
? Roman martyrs, whose names are listed in all the Western martyrologies, but about whom nothing is known.

Callixtus, Calixtus
(*several*)
Otherwise Callistus, q.v.

Calminius (Calmilius) (St) H.   Aug 19
d. *c* 690   A hermit in Gaul who founded the abbeys of Villars (*Calminiacum, Saint Chaffe*) and Mauzac, near Riom.

Calocerus (St) Bp.   Feb 11
d. *c* 130   A disciple of St Apollinaris, whom he succeeded in the see of Ravenna.

Calocerus (St) M.   Apr 18
? Nothing reliable is known about this martyr. His acts, which belong to a much later period, connect him with SS Faustinus and Jovita, and make him an officer of the emperor Hadrian at Brescia in Lombardy.

Calocerus and Parthenius (SS) MM.   May 19
d. 250   Two brothers, eunuchs in the palace of Tryphonia, wife of the emperor Decius. They were martyred at Rome in the Decian persecution.

Calogerus the Anchoret (St) M.   June 18
d. *c* 486   A Greek who received the monastic habit at the hands of the pope at Rome, and lived for thirty-five years as a recluse near Girgenti in Sicily, after having evangelized the isles of Lipari.

Calogerus (St) Ab.   June 18
See Gregory, Demetrius and Calogerus.

Calupan (St) H.   March 3
d. 575   Monk of Meallet in Auvergne, and afterwards a recluse in a neighbouring cave.

Camelian (St) Bp.   July 28
d. *c* 525   Successor of St Lupus in the see of Troyes (478–*c* 525).

Camerinus (St) M.   Aug 21
See Luxorius, Cisellus and Camerinus.

Camilla (St) V.   March 3
d. *c* 437   A native of Civitavecchia who became a disciple of St Germanus of Auxerre at Ravenna and accompanied his corpse to Auxerre. She settled near that place as a recluse and died there.

Camilla Gentili (Bl) V.   May 18
d. 1486   A maiden of holy life who is venerated in the church of the Dominican friars at San Severino. Cult approved in 1841.

Camilla Varani (Bl) Abs.
Poor Clare.   May 31
d. 1527   Abbess of a convent founded by her father at Camerino, in Italy. Cult confirmed in 1843.

Camillus de Lellis (St)
Founder.   GC. July 14
1550–1614   A native of the Abruzzi in central Italy who, after some years of soldiering, tried to join the Capuchins, but had to leave them on account of a disease of the leg, which proved incurable. Ultimately he found his vocation in the service of the sick, for whom he founded the nursing congregation of the Ministers of the Sick, approved in 1591. Before this, St Camillus had been ordained priest by Thomas Goldwell of St Asaph, the last English bishop of the old hierarchy. Canonized in 1746, and declared by Leo XIII patron saint of the sick and of their nurses.

Camillus Constanzi (Bl)
M. SJ.   Oct 12
1572–1622   An Italian Jesuit and a missionary in Japan, who was banished from that country as a Christian, but returned was was burnt to death over a slow fire at Firando (Sept 15). Beatified in 1867.

Camin or Inniskeltra (St)
Ab.   March 24 or 25
Otherwise Caimin, q.v.

Campania (Martyrs of) (SS)   March 2
6th cent.   Christians put to death by the Lombards. They numbered several hundreds (the pre-1970 RM. mentioned eighty). As to their claim to the title of martyrs, we have the

testimony of St Gregory the Great, their contemporary.

Campion, Edmund (St)
M. SJ. Dec 1
See Edmund Campion, SJ.

Candida (St) W. Jan 27
d. *c* 798 Mother of St Emerius, the founder of the abbey of St Stephen of Bañoles. She died as a recluse near the monastery, in the diocese of Gerona, Spain.

Candida (St) June 1
? Her relics still exist in their original shrine at Whitchurch Canonicorum, Dorset: the only one to survive the Reformation in a parish church in England. In 1900 an examination of the bones showed that she was about forty at her death. She was perhaps slain by the Vikings, but nothing else is known. Pilgrims still worship at the shrine, and she has a holy well nearby at Morcombe lake.

Candida (St) M. June 6
See Artemius, Candida and Paulina.

Candida (St) VM. Aug 29
? One of a group of martyrs who suffered on the Ostian Way, outside the gates of Rome. In the ninth century Pope St Paschal I enshrined her relics in the church of St Praxedes.

Candida the Elder (St)
VM. Sept 4
d. *c* 78 An aged woman who is said to have welcomed St Peter when passing through Naples on his way to Rome and to have been miraculously cured by him of a malady. In her turn she converted St Aspren, who became the first bishop of Naples.

Candida the Younger (St) Sept 10
d. ? 586 A married woman of Naples, who sanctified herself by fulfilling perfectly her duties as a wife and as a mother. The pre-1970 RM. described her as "famous for her miracles".

Candida (St) VM. Sept 20
d. *c* 300 A martyred maiden of Carthage under Maximian Herculeus. The date of her martyrdom is contested; see the Bollandists on this controversy.

Candida (St) M. Dec 1
See Lucius, Rogatus, etc.

Candidus of Rome (St) M. Feb 2
See Fortunatus, Felician, etc.

Candidus (St) M. March 10
One of the Forty Armenian Martyrs, q.v.

Candidus, Piperion and
Comp. (SS) MM. March 11
d. *c* 254–259 Twenty-two African martyrs who suffered either at Carthage or at Alexandria, most probably under Valerian and Gallienus. Particulars are lost.

Candidus (St) M. Sept 22
See Theban Legion.

Candidus (St) M. Oct 3
? A Roman martyr, buried on the Esquiline Hill, in the place called "*ad Ursum Pileatum*".

Candidus (St) M. Dec 15
See Faustinus, Lucius, etc.

Candres (St) Bp. Dec 1
5th cent. A regionary bishop who evangelized the territory of Maestricht. He is still liturgically commemorated in the diocese of Rouen.

Canice (Canicus,
Cainnech, Kenny,
Kenneth) (St) Ab. Oct 11
c 525–*c* 599 Born in N. Ireland, he was trained to the monastic life under St Finian of Clonard, and St Cadoc in Wales. Then he went to Glasnevin. He founded the monastery of Agahanoe and perhaps of Kilkenny, and later preached in Scotland under St Columba and was the first to build a church in the place now known as St Andrews. He has always been very popular in Ireland; the city of Kilkenny is named after him.

Canion (St) C. Sept 1
See Briscus, Castrensis, etc.

Cannatus (St) Bp. Oct 15
5th cent. Bishop of Marseilles after St Honoratus.

Cannera (Cainder,
Kinnera) (St) V. Jan 28
d. *c* 530 An Irish maiden who lived as a recluse near Bantry. She died after visiting St Senan and receiving holy communion at his hands. She was buried on St Senan's island of Enniscorthy.

Canog (Cynog) (St) M. Oct 7
d. *c* 492 Eldest son of King Brychan of Brecknock. He met his death as a result of an inroad of barbarians at Merthyr-Cynog. Several churches in Wales were dedicated to him. In Brittany he is known as St Cenneur.

Cantian and Cantianilla
(SS) MM. May 31
See Cantius, Cantian, etc.

Cantidius, Cantidian
and Sobel (SS) MM. Aug 5
? Egyptian martyrs of whom nothing is known except the fact of their martyrdom.

Cantius, Cantian, Cantianilla and Protus (SS) MM.   May 31

d. *c* 304   Two brothers and their sister, said to have belonged to the Roman family of the Anicii. They were martyred at Aquileia, whither they had retired, together with their tutor, Protus by name, under Diocletian. We have still a panegyric preached in their honour by St Maximus of Turin.

Canute (Knud) Lavard (St) M.   Jan 7

d. 1133   A nephew of St Canute, king of Denmark, with whom he is sometimes confused. He was duke of Schleswig, and his life was spent mostly in war against the Viking pirates. He was slain as a result of a conspiracy of the Danes, headed by a kinsman of his, pretender to the throne. Canonized in 1171 and venerated as a martyr.

Canute (Knud) (St) King, M.   Jan 19

d. 1086   Natural son of Sweyn III, king of Denmark, and great-nephew of Canute, king of England, he succeeded to the Danish throne as Canute IV. He displayed a warlike zeal for the spreading of the gospel in Denmark itself, and in Courland, Livonia and elsewhere. He was prevented by treachery from helping the Anglo-Saxons against their Norman conquerors. Though well liked by his people, he was killed in a church by a party of malcontents, headed by his brother Olaf (July 10). As this crime was prompted by opposition to the laws he had enacted to enforce the payment of tithes, he was considered a martyr and as such was canonized by the Holy See, at the request of Eric III, king of Denmark, in 1101. Venerated on local calendars only since 1969.

Capito (St) Bp. M.   March 4
See Basil, Eugene, etc.

Capito (St) M.   July 24
See Meneus and Capito.

Capitolina and Erotheis (SS) MM.   Oct 27

d. 304   A Cappadocian lady and her handmaid, martyred under Diocletian.

Cappadocia (Martyrs of) (SS)   May 23

d. 303   A group of martyrs, put to death in Cappadocia, under Galerius, after having suffered exquisite tortures.

Caprasius (St) Ab.   June 1

d. *c* 430   A native of Gaul, he retired to the island of Lérins to live as a hermit. Thither he was followed by SS Honoratus and Venantius, and together they went to the East to visit the monastic colonies there. Venantius died in Greece; the other two returned to Lérins, where St Honoratus founded the famous abbey, and on his being appointed bishop of Arles, he was succeeded by Caprasius as abbot.

Caprasius (St) M.   Oct 20

d. 303   A native of Agen in S. France, who, owing to fear, concealed himself during the persecution of Diocletian; but on hearing of the courage of St Faith at the stake, he came forth and boldly confessed his religion. He was forthwith beheaded.

Caradoc (St) Ab.   Apr 13

d. 1124   A Welshman, harpist at the court of King Rhys of S. Wales, who became a monk at Llandaff, and then lived as a hermit in different places — on Barry Island, at St Issels, etc. — in S. Wales. He had much to suffer during the English invasion under Henry I. He was buried with great honour in the cathedral of St David's: his shrine is extant there.

Caralippus (St) M.   Apr 28
See Aphrodisius, Caralippus, etc.

Carantac (Carantog, Cairnach, Carnath) (St)   May 16

5th cent.   A Welshman who laboured under St Patrick in the evangelization of Ireland.

Carantock (St) Ab.   May 16

6th cent.   A Welsh abbot, founder of the church of Llangranog. He is associated with Crantock in Cornwall and Carhampton in Somerset. He is also highly venerated in Brittany. Some writers identify him with St Carantac.

Caranus (St) Bp.   Dec 24

7th cent.   A saint commemorated in the Aberdeen breviary. He belonged to E. Scotland.

Caraunus (Ceraunus, Cheron) (St) M.   May 28

5th cent.   A Christian of Roman descent, he preached the gospel in Gaul, and was killed by robbers near Chartres. A church and monastery were built over his tomb.

Cardeña, Martyrs of
See Stephen of Cardeña.

Carilefus (Carilephus, Carileff, Calais) (St) Ab.   July 1

d. *c* 536   A French monk, friend and companion of St Avitus. He was the abbot-founder of the abbey of Anisole in Maine. His cult is found chiefly at Blois.

Carina (St) M.   Nov 7
See Melasippus, Antony and Carina.

Carissima (St) V.   Sept 7
5th cent. A native of Albi, in France. She retired to a forest near the city, then to the nunnery of Viants (Vious). She is liturgically commemorated at Albi.

Caritas (St) VM.   Aug 1
Otherwise Charity. See Faith, Hope and Charity.

Carloman (Bl) Mk. OSB.   Aug 17
707–755 Eldest son of Charles Martel, and brother of Pepin the Short. On his father's death he became king of Austrasia. As such, he promoted the foundation of the abbeys of Fulda, Lobbes, Stavelot, etc., helped St Boniface in the evangelization of the Germanies, and endeavoured to remedy the injustice done by Charles Martel with regard to ecclesiastical property. On St Boniface's advice he left the kingdom to his brother, received the Benedictine habit at the hands of Pope St Zachary and was a monk first on Mt Soracte and then at Montecassino, where he was employed in the kitchen and as the shepherd of the abbey. Having been sent to maintain peace between Pepin and the Lombards, he died in a monastery at Vienne.

**Carmelite Nuns of
Compiègne (BB)** MM   July 17
d. 1794 Sixteen nuns of the Carmel of Compiègne, guillotined in Paris during the French Revolution. They went to the scaffold singing the *Salve Regina*. Beatified in 1906. Each is given a separate notice in this book.

Carmes (Martyrs des) (BB)   Sept 2
See September, Martyrs of.

**Carnath or Carnech (St)
Ab.**   May 16
Otherwise Carantac, q.v.

Caron (St) ? Bp.   March 5
? The title saint of Tregaron in Dyfed. Nothing is known about him.

**Carponius, Evaristus
and Priscian (SS)** MM.   Oct 14
d. c 303 Three brothers who, with their sister St Fortunata, were among the Christians martyred under Diocletian at Caesarea in Palestine. Their relics were translated to Naples.

**Carpophorus, Exanthus,
Cassius, Severinus,
Secundus and Licinius
(SS)** MM.   Aug 7
d. c 295 Christian soldiers who were put to death at Como in N. Italy, under Maximian Herculius.

Carpophorus (St) M.   Aug 27
See Ruphus and Carpophorus.

Carpophorus (St) M.   Nov 8
See Four Crowned Martyrs.

**Carpophorus and
Abundius (SS)** MM.   Dec 10
d. 290–300 A priest and his deacon who suffered under Diocletian. Rome, Spoleto and Seville have been given as the place of their martyrdom.

**Carpus, Papylus,
Agathonica, Agathodorus
and Comp. (SS)** MM.   Apr 13
d. 150 (or 250) Carpus was the bishop of Thyatira, Papylus, his deacon, Agathonica, the latter's sister, and Agathodorus, their servant. They were martyred with many others at Pergamos in the time of Marcus Aurelius or of Decius.

Carpus (St)   Oct 13
1st cent. The Carpus of Troy on the Hellespont with whom St Paul (II Tim. 4:13) says "he had left his cloak". Nothing more is known about him. Some Greek writers make him a bishop.

Carterius (St) M.   Jan 8
d. 304 A priest of Caesarea in Cappadocia, who suffered under Diocletian. He is venerated by the Greeks.

**Carterius, Styriacus,
Tobias, Eudoxius, Agapius
and Comp. (SS)** MM.   Nov 2
d. c 315 Ten Christian soldiers in the army of the emperor Licinius, burnt at the stake at Sebaste in Armenia.

**Carthage the Elder (St)
Bp.**   March 5
d. c 540 The successor of St Kieran in the see of Ossory. He is said to have been the son or grandson of King Aengus.

**Carthage (Carthach
Mochuda) the Younger
(St)** Bp.   May 14
d. c 637 Born in Kerry, he founded (c 590) an abbey at Rathin in Westmeath, of which he was abbot-bishop, and for which he wrote a monastic rule in verse. Shortly before his

St Casimir of Poland, March 4

death (*c* 635) he and his community were expelled. He led his monks to the banks of the Blackwater and there established the monastery-school of Lismore. Cult confirmed in 1903.

Carthusian Martyrs (BB) May 4
1535–1540 Eighteen monks of the Carthusian order in England, put to death for their allegiance to the Holy See under Henry VIII. Beatified in 1886. Each is given a separate notice in this book.

Casdoe (St) M. Sept 29
See Dadas, Casdoe and Gabdelas.

Casilda (St) V. Apr 9
d. *c* 1050 A native of Toledo and said to have been of Moorish parentage. She became a Christian and led the life of an anchoress near Briviesca in the province of Burgos. She is greatly venerated throughout Spain, chiefly in the provinces of Burgos and Toledo.

Casimir of Poland (St)
C. GC. March 4
1460–1483 The second son of King Casimir IV of Poland. His father wished him to seize the crown of Hungary which was offered to him by a powerful party among the Hungarians: but the prince refused to employ force

and was imprisoned by his father for three months. The remainder of his life he devoted to prayer and study. He died of consumption in 1483. He is the patron saint of Poland and Lithuania. In art he is often shown crowned, and holding a lily.

Caspar (Gaspar) (St) Jan 6
One of the Magi, q.v.

Caspar Cratz (Bl) M. SJ. Jan 12
See John Caspar Cratz.

Caspar Sadamazu (Bl)
M. SJ. June 10
d. 1626 A native of Omura in Japan, he was received into the Society of Jesus at Bungo 1582. He acted as secretary to several provincials, the last being Bl Francis Pacheco, with whom he was buried alive at Nagasaki. Beatified in 1867.

Caspar de Bono (Bl) C.
Minim. July 14
1530–1604 A native of Valencia in Spain, he became a silk merchant, then a trooper and finally a Minim friar. After his ordination in 1561 he was twice appointed corrector provincial of the Spanish province of Minims. Beatified in 1786.

Caspar Alvarez (Bl) M. SJ. July 15
d. 1570 Born at Oporto in Portugal, he became a Jesuit lay-brother, and was one of a band of martyrs who suffered with Bl Ignatius de Azevedo. Beatified in 1854.

Caspar and Mary Vaz (BB)
MM. Aug 17
d. 1627 Husband and wife, natives of Japan and tertiaries of St Francis, martyred at Nagasaki. Caspar was burnt alive and his wife beheaded. Beatified in 1867.

Caspar Cotenda (Bl) M. Sept 11
d. 1622 A Japanese belonging to the royal family of Firando. He was martyred at Nagasaki. Beatified in 1867.

Caspar Fisogiro (Bl) M. Oct 1
d. 1617 A Japanese Christian, member of the Confraternity of the Holy Rosary. He was beheaded at Nagasaki for having befriended Bl Alphonsus Navarrete, OP. Beatified in 1867.

Caspar del Bufalo (St)
Founder Dec 28
1786–1836 A native of Rome, who studied for the priesthood at the Roman College, and was ordained in 1808. He was exiled to Corsica for refusing to swear allegiance to Napoleon. On his return in 1814 he founded

at Giano, diocese of Spoleto, the first house of the Missioners of the Most Precious Blood for mission work at home. After much opposition it received the approval of the Holy See, but by that time Caspar was already dead. Canonized in 1955.

Cassia (St) M.   July 20
See Sabinus, Julian, etc.

Cassian (St) M.   March 26
See Peter, Marcian, etc.

Cassian (St) Ab.   July 23
Otherwise John Cassian, q.v.

Cassian of Autun (St) Bp.   Aug 5
d. c 350   Bishop of Autun 314–350, he succeeded St Reticius, and was famous for miracles. A life composed in the ninth century makes him an Egyptian by origin.

**Cassian Vaz López-Neto
(Bl)** OFM. Cap.   Aug 7
1607–1638   Born at Nantes in France but of Spanish descent, he took the Capuchin habit at Angers, and was sent to Egypt to preach to the Copts, together with Bl Agathangelus, q.v. He was stoned to death on entering Abyssinia. Beatified in 1904.

**Cassian of Benevento
(St)** Bp.   Aug 12
d. c 340   Bishop of Benevento in S. Italy. His relics are enshrined in the church of St Mary in the same city.

Cassian of Imola (St) M.   Aug 13
250 ?   The *laus* of the pre-1970 RM. read as follows: "The birthday of holy Cassian the martyr. When he refused to worship idols, the persecutor summoned certain boys who hated Cassian as their schoolmaster, and afforded them the opportunity of killing him. As their efforts were puny, so was his suffering bitter above the ordinary and his death protracted". The story is from Prudentius. Since 1969 his cult is confined to local calendars.

**Cassian of Todi (St)
Bp. M.**   Aug 13
4th cent.   A convert of St Pontian, bishop of Todi, in Central Italy, and his successor in that see. He was martyred under Maximian Herculeus. It is possible that St Cassian of Imola was celebrated at Todi, and this gave rise to the notion of a second saint.

Cassian (St) M.   Dec 1
See Lucius, Rogatus, etc.

Cassian (St) M.   Dec 3
d. 298   During the trial of St Marcellus (Oct 30) at Tangier under Diocletian, Cassian, as the *exceptor* (official shorthand-writer or recorder) of the court, was taking down the *acta* of the proceedings. Indignant at the injustice done to the martyr, he threw down his pen and declared himself a Christian. He was arrested and a few weeks later he too suffered martyrdom. His acts are quite authentic; he is also mentioned in one of the hymns of Prudentius.

**Cassius, Victorinus,
Maximus and Comp.
(SS)** MM.   May 15
d. c 264   A group of martyrs of Clermont in Auvergne, who suffered at the hands of Chrocas, chief of the invading Teutonic barbarians.

Cassius of Narni (St) Bp.   June 29
d. 558   Bishop of Narni from 537 to 558. St Gregory the Great has left on record the virtues of this holy man.

Cassius (St) M.   Aug 7
See Carpophorus, Exanthus, etc.

**Cassius, Florentius and
Comp. (SS)** MM.   Oct 10
d. 303   Christians put to death by the emperor Maximian Herculeus at Bonn in Germany.

**Castor and Dorotheus
(SS)** MM.   March 28
? Two martyrs who suffered at Tarsus in Cilicia in one of the early persecutions.

Castor and Stephen (SS)
MM.   Apr 27
? Two martyrs who suffered at Tarsus in Cilicia in one of the early persecutions. Some writers identify them with the preceding pair.

Castor (St) Bp.   Sept 2
d. c 420   A native of Nîmes, who married a wife and settled at Marseilles. After a short time they separated by mutual consent and both became religious. Castor founded the monastery of Manauque, and shortly after was chosen bishop of Apt. St John Cassian wrote the *De Institutis Coenobiorum* at Castor's request.

**Castor, Victor, and
Rogatian (SS)** MM.   Dec 28
? African martyrs of whom the names only are known.

Castora Gabrielli (Bl) W.   June 14
d. 1391   A Franciscan tertiary, wife and widow of Santuccio Sanfonerio, a lawyer at Sant' Angelo in Vado in Umbria. She sanctified herself by the daily practice of the domestic virtues.

Castorius (St) M.   July 7 and Nov 8
See Claudius, Nicostratus, etc., and Four Crowned Martyrs.

Castrensis (St) Bp.   Sept 1 and Feb 11
See Priscus, Castrensis, etc.

Castritian (St) Bp.   Dec 1
d. 137   The predecessor of St Calimerius in
the see of Milan. He governed that see for
forty-two years.

Castulus (St) M.   Jan 12
See Zoticus, Rogatus, etc.

Castulus (St) M.   Feb 15
See Saturninus, Castulus, etc.

Castulus (St) M.   March 26
d. 288   An officer of the palace in Rome of
the emperor Diocletian. For having sheltered
some of his fellow Christians he was put to the
torture and buried alive. A cemetery was
named after his burial place on the Via
Labicana.

**Castulus and Euprepis
(SS)** MM.   Nov 30
? Roman martyrs of whom nothing is known.

Castus and Emilius (SS)
MM.   May 22
d. c 250   Two African martyrs who suffered
under Decius. They at first gave way under
torture, but repented, and on being seized a
second time, were burned to death. Their
contemporary, St Cyprian, and also St Augustine are loud in their praise of these two
martyrs.

**Castus and Secundinus
(SS)** Bps.   July 1
c 305   Two saints much venerated in S. Italy.
The martyrologies register them as of Sinu-
essa (Mondragone) near Caserta.

Castus (St) M.   Sept 4
See Magnus, Castus and Maximus.

Castus (St) M.   Oct 6
See Marcellus, Castus, etc.

Cataldus (St) Bp.   May 10
7th cent.   Born in Munster, Ireland, he was
first a pupil, and then the headmaster, of the
monastic school of Lismore. On his return
from a pilgrimage to the Holy Land, he was
chosen bishop of their city by the people of
Taranto, in S. Italy. He is the titular of the
cathedral of Taranto and the principal patron
saint of the diocese.

Catellus (St) Bp   Jan 19
9th cent.   Bishop of Castellamare, south of
Naples. He was an intimate friend of St
Antoninus, OSB. He is venerated as the
principal saint of the city and diocese of
Castellamare.

Cathaldus (Cathal) (St)
Bp.   May 10
Otherwise Cataldus, q.v.

**Cathan (Catan, Chattan,
Cadan) (St)** Bp.   May 17
6th or 7th cent.   He seems to have been
bishop in the Isle of Bute, often called after
him Kil-Cathan. His tomb is shown at Tam-
lacht near Londonderry, but the Scots contend that he rests in the Isle of Bute. Possibly
there were two saints of the same name.

Catherine dei Ricci (St)
V. OP.   Feb 2
1522–1590   Born at Florence, she became in
1535 a regular tertiary of St Dominic, and
filled the offices of novice-mistress and prioress. She was famous for her ecstasies in which
she beheld and enacted the scenes of our
Lord's passion. It is narrated that she met in
vision St Philip Neri, still alive in Rome. Three
future popes were among the thousands who
flocked to her convent to ask her prayers.
Canonized in 1746.

**Catherine of Bologna
(St)** V. Poor Clare.   March 9
1413–1463   Born at Bologna, she was a maid
of honour to Margaret d'Este. At the age of
thirteen, she joined an Augustinian community at Ferrara. Later they became Poor
Clares. Catherine was appointed novice-mistress and then abbess of a daughter convent of
Poor Clares at Bologna. Here she spent her
life praying for sinners, favoured by God with
amazing visions, and committing to writing her
mystical experiences. Canonized in 1712.

Catherine of Sweden (St)
Bridg.   March 24
1331–1381   Born in Sweden, the fourth
child of St Bridget, she married Eggard
Lydersson, a life-long invalid, with whom she
lived in continency, and whom she tended with
great devotion. With the consent of her husband she joined her mother St Bridget in
Rome, and accompanied her to Jerusalem.
After the death of her husband and mother she
returned to Sweden and became abbess of
Vadstena. In 1375–1380 she was again in
Rome, obtaining the approval of the Salvato-
rian order (the Bridgettines) and promoting
the canonization of her own mother. Cult
confirmed in 1484.

Catherine Tomas (St) V.
OSA.   Apr 5
1533–1574   Born on the island of Majorca.
She joined the Canonesses Regular of St
Augustine at Palma and there she spent her
whole life, subject to a great number of strange

St Catherine of Siena, Apr 29

phenomena and mystical experiences; during the last years of her life she was continually in ecstasy. Canonized in 1930.

Catherine of Pallanza
(Bl) V. OSA.   Apr 6
c 1437–1478   A native of Pallanza, diocese of Novara. At fourteen years of age she began to live the life of a recluse in the mountain district above Varese, near Milan. Disciples gathered

round her and she formed them into a community under the rule of St Augustine. Cult confirmed in 1769.

Catherine Tekakwitha (Bl)   Apr 17
See Kateri Tekakwitha (Bl).

Catherine of Siena (St) V.
Tert. Dr. OP.   GC. Apr 29
1347–1380   Born at Siena in Tuscany, the

twenty-fifth child of a wool-dyer, Catherine Benincasa received the habit of the third order of St Dominic at the age of sixteen, continuing, however, to live at home. Soon her sanctity attracted a number of persons, clerical and lay, round her — the *Caterinati* — of whom she was a sort of leader. She worked among the poor of Siena and was most active and successful in the conversion of hardened sinners. She had especially at heart the unity and welfare of the church and was instrumental in persuading Pope Gregory XI to abandon Avignon and return to Rome. She tried to heal the great schism of the West, rallying all Italy around Pope Urban VI. In 1378 she was summoned by the pope to Rome and there died, fighting still in the cause of the true pope. She has left over four hundred letters and a *Dialogue* which is one of the most remarkable mystical works of all time. Canonized in 1461; declared patron saint of Italy in 1939; and Doctor of the Church by Paul VI on Oct 4, 1970. In art she is shown clad as a Dominican, holding a heart, and wearing a crown of thorns.

Catherine of Parc-Aux-Dames (Bl) V. OSB. Cist. May 4

13th cent. A daughter of Jewish parents of Louvain, her name was Rachel. The chaplain of the duke of Brabant was a frequent visitor to her home, and the little Rachel was an eager listener when he would defend the Catholic religion against the attacks of her Jewish father. When she was twelve years old she secretly left her home, received baptism and joined the Cistercian nuns at Parc-aux-Dames, near Louvain, where she lived till her death.

Catherine of Cardona (Bl) V. May 21

1519–1577 Born at Naples of a noble Spanish family, she lived for a time at the court of Philip II of Spain; then she retired to live as a recluse near Roda in S. Spain. She remained there for twenty years until she was received into a Carmelite convent where, however, she continued to live as an anchoress. St Teresa speaks very highly of her.

Catherine Tanaca (Bl) M. July 12

d. 1626 Wife of Bl John Tanaca. Both were beheaded at Nagasaki, Japan. Beatified in 1867.

Catherine Soiron (Bl) VM. July 17

d. 1794 She, and her sister Teresa, were the door-keepers (*tourières*) for the Carmelite nuns at Compiègne and were guillotined with them at Paris. They were not in vows. Beatified in 1904.

Catherine Mattei (Bl) V. Tert. OP. Sept 4

d. 1547 Born at Racconigi in the diocese of Cuneo, daughter of a poor working man. She took the Dominican habit of the third order and tried faithfully to imitate her namesake of Siena. She, too, is said to have been favoured with signal mystical experiences. Cult confirmed in 1810.

Catherine (Bl) M. Sept 10

d. 1622 A Japanese widow. She was beheaded at Nagasaki together with Bl Charles Spinola and his fifty-one companions. Beatified in 1867.

Catherine of Genoa (St) W. Sept 15

1477–1510 Born in Genoa, of the noble Fieschi family, she married Julian Adorno when she was sixteen. She led a life of active charity, devoting herself to the service of others both at home and in the hospitals and poor quarters of the city. At first her work was made exceedingly difficult by the attitude of her profligate husband, whom she succeeded in converting to better ways. A book *Vita e dottrina* published in 1551 contains her spiritual testimony: it is possible that she herself was not responsible for this final form. Canonized in 1737.

Catherine of Alexandria (St) VM. formerly Nov 25

According to a legend she was a maiden martyred at Alexandria under Maxentius but there is no evidence for this before the 9th century. Her alleged relics have been enshrined for the last thousand years in the Orthodox monastery of Mt Sinai. In art she is represented with the spiked wheel of her martyrdom, or arguing with the pagan philosophers. Nothing definite seems to be known about her life: she was very popular in the Middle Ages. Cult suppressed in 1969.

Catherine Labouré (St) V. Nov 28

1806–1875 Born in the Côte d'Or, daughter of a yeoman farmer, she became a Sister of Charity of St Vincent de Paul in 1830, and spent her whole life much as the ordinary Sister of Charity spends it, except for a series of visions with which she was favoured by God. The first "miraculous medal" was struck as the result of one of these visions. She died in the convent of Enghien-Reuilly and was canonized in 1947.

St **Catherine of Alexandria**, formerly Nov 25

Catholdus, Anno and Diethardus (BB) Mks.
OSB. Sept 29
d. late 8th cent. Three Benedictine monks who preached the gospel in the diocese of Eichstätt. Catholdus was a monk of Herrieden (built in 790).

Catulinus (Cartholinus), Januarius, Florentius, Julia and Justa (SS) MM. July 15
? Carthaginian martyrs. Their bodies were enshrined in the basilica of Fausta at Carthage. Of St Catulinus, a deacon, we have a panegyric preached by St Augustine. Nothing else is known about them.

Catus (St) M. Jan 19
See Paul, Gerontius, etc.

Cawrdaf (St) Dec 5
6th cent. The son and successor of Caradog, chieftain of Brecknock and Hereford. He ended life as a monk under St Illtyd.

Ce
Note. In many names this syllable is often written Cae, or Che, or Ke, or Kae, etc.

Ceadda (St) Bp. March 2
Otherwise Chad, q.v.

Ceadwalla (Cadwalla) (St)
King. Apr 20
d. 689 King of Wessex who, while yet a pagan, showed himself not less cruel and crafty than other conquerors of his race and time. He was converted by St Wilfrid and journeyed to Rome, where he was baptized by Pope St Sergius and died while yet wearing the white robe of the neophytes. There is no evidence of an ancient cult.

Ceallach (Kellach) (St)
Bp. May 1
6th cent. A disciple of St Kieran of Clonmacnoise, who became bishop of Killala but ended his life as a hermit, by some accounts as a martyr. There are several other saints of the same name.

Cearan (Ciaran) (St) Ab. June 14
d. 870 An Irish abbot of Bellach-Duin, now Castle-Kerrant, Co. Meath, surnamed The Devout.

Cecilia, Cecily
Otherwise Caecilia.

Cecilia (Bl) V. OP. June 9
See Diana, Cecilia and Amata — the first Dominican nuns.

Cecilia (St) Abs. OSB. Aug 17
See Benedicta and Cecilia.

Cecilia (St) VM. GC. Nov 22
2nd–3rd cent. One of the most famous of martyred Roman maidens. Having suffered for Christ, she was buried in the cemetery of St Callistus. Her name is in the first eucharistic

St Cecilia, Nov 22

prayer. At about the same time SS Valerian and Tiburtius suffered at Rome and were

buried in the cemetery of Praetextatus. What connexion they had with St Cecilia, it is difficult now to ascertain. The alleged relics of all three are believed to rest at present beneath the high altar of the basilica of St Cecilia in Trastevere. As early as the fourth century St Cecilia was already celebrated as one of the greatest Roman martyrs. The acts, however, which we now possess, cannot be admitted as history. St Cecilia is the patron saint of musicians. In art she is represented playing a musical instrument; her earliest representations show her wearing a wreath of roses, and carrying a sword.

Cecilia of Ferrara (Bl) V.
OP.   Dec 19
d. 1511   Married to a very virtuous husband, they separated by mutual consent to become religious, and she joined the Dominican nuns at Ferrara.

Cedd (St) Bp. OSB.   Jan 7
d. 664 (Oct 26)   Brother of St Chad of Lichfield. He was a monk of Lindisfarne who evangelized the midlands of England and afterwards was made bishop of the East Saxons. He founded the abbeys of Tilbury and of Lastingham. At the synod of Whitby he abandoned the Celtic for the Roman observances. In his old age he retired to his own foundation at Lastingham in Yorkshire to die under monastic obedience.

Ceitho (St)   Nov 1
6th cent.   One of five brothers, saints of the great Welsh family of Cunedda. A church at Pumpsant was dedicated to the five brothers. That at Llangeith, in Dyfed, was founded by St Ceitho.

Cele-Christ (St) Bp.   March 3
d. *c* 728   St Cele-Christ, otherwise *Christicola* (worshipper of Christ), for many years led an eremitical life but ultimately was forced to accept a bishopric in Leinster.

Celerina (St) M.   Feb 3
See Laurentinus, Ignatius and Celerina.

Celerinus (St) M.   Feb 3
d. *p.*250   An African who, without shedding his blood, earned the title of martyr on account of the sufferings he endured under Decius during a visit to Rome. Set at liberty, he returned to Carthage where he was ordained deacon by St Cyprian. A church was dedicated in his name at Carthage.

Celestine (St) M.   May 2
See Saturninus, Neopolus, etc.

Celestine V (St) Pope   May 19
Otherwise Peter Celestine, q.v.

Celestine I (St) Pope.   formerly July 27
d. 432 (Aug 1)   Born in the Campagna, he
joined the Roman clergy and succeeded St
Boniface I as pope (422). Three great events
stand out in his pontificate: he supported the
campaign of St Germanus of Auxerre against
Pelagius; he sent St Palladius to preach in
Ireland shortly before St Patrick's mission
there; and he condemned Nestorianism, presiding, through his legates, over the council of
Ephesus (431). His feastday was on April 6
until 1922: from then until 1969, when it was
suppressed, it was July 27.

**Cellach (Ceilach,
Keilach — latinized as
Celsus).**
Note. Colgan enumerates no less than thirty-
three Celtic saints named Cellach. Most of
them, however, are evidently the same person.

**Cellach (Ceilach,
Keilach) (St)** Bp.   Apr 1
9th cent.   Archbishop of Armagh, possibly
before his ordination as abbot of Iona and
founder of the abbey of Kells.

Cellach (Celsus) (St) Bp.   Apr 1
d. 1129   Cellach McAedh, a native of Ireland, seems to have been a Benedictine of
Glastonbury. He certainly was for a time at
Oxford, and in 1106 was ordained archbishop
of Armagh. He proved to be a great prelate,
restorer of ecclesiastical discipline throughout
the island. When dying he sent his pastoral
staff to St Malachy, then bishop of Connor,
who in fact became his successor. He was the
last hereditory archbishop of Armagh.

Celloch (St) Ab.   March 26
Otherwise Mochelloc, q.v.

Celsus (*several*)
Otherwise Cellach, q.v.

Celsus of Antioch (St) M.   Jan 9
See Julian, Basilissa, etc.

Celsus (St) M.   July 28 and May 10
See Nazarius and Celsus.

Celsus and Clement (SS)
MM.   Nov 21
? Roman martyrs of whom the names only
have come down to us.

Censurius (St) Bp.   June 10
d. 486   The successor of St Germanus in
the see of Auxerre. He governed that see from
448 to 486. He was buried in the church of St
Germanus, which he himself had built.

Centolla and Helen (SS)
MM.   Aug 13
d. ? c 304   Two Spanish maidens who suffered martyrdom near Burgos.

Ceolfrid (Geoffrey) (St)
Ab. OSB.   Sept 25
642–716   A Northumbrian who became a
monk at Gilling in Yorkshire, whence he
migrated to Ripon, where St Benedict's Rule
was observed. After a visit to Canterbury, he
became novice-master at Ripon, but later
migrated to Wearmouth at St Benet Biscop's
invitation (672). Eventually he became abbot
of Wearmouth-Jarrow, which he governed for
twenty-six years. He was a great abbot and
deserves a special recognition for the help he
gave to St Bede, who was one of his monks. He
is to be remembered as the instigator of the
production of the *Codex Amiatinus*, the great
Bible written in uncials, the oldest known copy
of the Vulgate in one complete volume, which
he intended as a gift for the pope. It is now
preserved in Florence, and a witness of the
spirituality and culture of its sponsor and his
abbey. In 716 he resigned and died at Langres
in Champagne on his way to Rome.

Ceollach (St) Bp.   Oct 6
? 7th cent.   An Irish prelate who for a short
time governed as bishop the diocese of the
Mercians or Mid-Angles. Thence he retired
to Iona but returned to die in his native
country.

Ceolwulph (St) King, Mk.
OSB.   Jan 15
d. 764   King of Northumbria, fosterer of
learning of the monastic life. To him St Bede
dedicated his *Ecclesiastical History*. He ended
his days as a monk at Lindisfarne.

**Cera (Ciar, Cyra, Cior,
Ceara) (St)** V.   Jan 5
7th cent.   An Irish abbess, a native of Tipper-
ary, who governed two nunneries, one at
Kilkeary and the other at Tech Telle, now
Tehelly.

Ceratius (Cérase) (St)
Bp.   June 6
d. c 455   Bishop of Grenoble in France. Cult
confirmed in 1903.

Ceraunus (Ceran) (St)
Bp.   Sept 27
c p.614   Bishop of Paris. His relics were
formerly enshrined in the church of St Genev-
ière.

Cerbonius (St) Bp.   Oct 10
d. c 580   One of the African bishops driven
from their sees by the Arian Vandals. He
settled at Piombino (*Populonium*) in Tuscany and is said to have become a bishop
there.

Cerbonius (St) Bp.   Oct 10
d. ? *c* 400   Bishop of Verona in Italy, of
whom nothing is known.

Cerneuf (St) M.   Feb 23
Otherwise Sirenus, q.v.

Ceslas (Bl) C. OP.   July 17
d. 1242   A native of Poland, who received
the habit of the Friars Preachers together with
St Hyacinth, from the hands of St Dominic
himself. He acted as spiritual director to the
duchess St Hedwig of Poland. The successful
resistance of the people of Breslau in Silesia to
the Mongols in their great invasion of 1240, is
attributed to the prayers of the saint.

Cettin (Cethagh) (St) Bp.   June 16
5th cent.   A disciple of St Patrick, consecrated bishop to assist him in his apostolic
work. Some authorities distinguish Cethagh
from Cettin.

Cewydd (St)   July 1
6th cent.   A Welsh saint who flourished in
Anglesey.

Ch
Note. Saint's names beginning with Ch should
also be looked for under Ca, Co, or K, the
spelling being frequently very uncertain and
variable.

Chad (Ceadda) (St) Bp.   March 2
d. 673   Brother of St Cedd. Educated at
Lindisfarne under St Aidan, and in Ireland.
On returning to England, he was made abbot
of Lastingham, where at that time, i.e., before
the synod of Whitby, St Columba's Rule was
strictly observed. During one of St Wilfrid's
absences in France, St Chad was made archbishop of York, but was removed by St
Theodore of Canterbury. St Chad readily
withdrew, and St Theodore arranged for him
to exercise his episcopate in Mercia. The saint
fixed his residence at Lichfield and there he
died shortly after. His relics are preserved in
the cathedral dedicated to him in Birmingham.
In art he is shown as a bishop holding a church
and/or a vine.

Chaeremon (St) M.   Oct 4
See Caius, Faustus, etc.

**Chaeremon and Comp.
(SS)** MM.   Dec 22
d. *p.*250   Bishop of Nilopolis in Egypt. He
was already a very old man when the Decian
persecution broke out. He was forced to flee to
the mountainous district of the Arabian desert
with several companions, and they were never
seen again.

St Chad, March 2

Chaffre (St) Ab. OSB.   Oct 19
Otherwise Theofrid, q.v.

**Chainoaldus (Chagnoald,
Cagnou) (St)** Bp.   Sept 6
d. 633   Brother of St Faro and of St Fara. A
disciple of St Columbanus, whom he accompanied to Bobbio and helped in the foundation
of the abbey there. Afterwards he became
bishop of Laon.

**Chalcedon (Martyrs of)
(SS)**   Sept 24
d. 304   A band of forty-nine martyrs who
suffered at Chalcedon under Diocletian. They
seem to have been the choir of singers of the
church of Chalcedon.

**Chamond (Annemond)
(St)** Bp. M.   Sept 28
d. 657   A courtier in the palace of King
Clovis II who became archbishop of Lyons.
The arch-tyrant Ebroin, mayor of the palace,
caused the saint to be assassinated. St Wilfrid
of York took part in the ceremony of the
enshrining of the relics of the martyr.

Charalampias and Comp. (SS) MM. Feb 18

d. 203 Martyrs of Magnesia in Asia Minor in the persecution under Septimius Severus. St Charalampias was a priest. With him suffered two soldiers and three women.

Charbel (St) M. Sept 5

d. 107 A martyr of the Antiochene Church under Trajan. Feast kept by the Maronites on the above date.

Charbel Maklhouf (St) Dec 24

Born in 1828 he became a monk in the Maronite rite at the age of twenty at the abbey of Annaya. He spent twenty-three years as a hermit; his influence on all the district, including the Muslims, was profound. He had a great love of the holy eucharist. He died in 1898, was beatified in 1965 and canonized in 1977.

Charisius (St) M. Apr 16

See Callistus, Charisius, etc.

Charisius (St) M. Aug 22

See Athanasius, Anthusa and Comp.

Charitina (St) VM. Oct 5

d. c 304 A Christian maiden who breathed forth her soul in the torture chamber. She suffered under Diocletian and probably at Amisus on the Black Sea.

Chariton (St) M. Sept 3

See Zeno and Chariton.

Charity (St) VM. Aug 1

Otherwise Caritas or Agape. See Faith, Hope, and Charity.

Charlemagne (Bl) Emperor. Jan 28

742–814 Son of Pepin the Short. King of the Franks in 768, on Christmas Day of the year 800 he was crowned first Holy Roman Emperor by Pope St Leo III. Popular devotion to Bl Charlemagne took root chiefly at the time of the great quarrel between the pope and Frederick Barbarossa; in France it was made compulsory by the state in 1475. Benedict XIV confirmed, or allowed, the title of Blessed given to the emperor. His feast is still observed in several German dioceses.

Charles of Sezze C. OFM. Jan 6

1613–1670 A native of Sezze in the Roman Campagna. He professed the Franciscan rule as a lay-brother at Rome. His was a life of great mystical experiences, and it is narrated that his heart was pierced by a ray of light proceeding from the Sacred Host, which left a visible wound. Canonized in 1959.

Charles of Sayn (Bl) Ab. OSB. Cist. Jan 29

d. 1212 A soldier who became a Cistercian at Hemmerode (1185). In 1189 he was chosen prior of Heisterbach and in 1197 abbot of Villers in Brabant. In 1209 he resigned and returned to Hemmerode to prepare for death. He has always been venerated as a *beatus*, at any rate by the Cistercians.

Charles the Good (Bl) M. March 2

d. 1127 Son of St Canute of Denmark. He fought in the second crusade and on his return succeeded Robert II as count of Flanders. His rule was a continuous defence of the poor against the profiteers of his time, both clerical and lay. He was called "the Good" by popular acclamation and was done to death in the church of St Donatian at Bruges as a result of a conspiracy of the rich people whom he had offended. Cult confirmed in 1883.

Charles Lwanga and Comps (SS) MM. GC. June 3

St Charles died in 1886. A servant of King Mwanga of Uganda. He was baptized in Nov 1885, and burnt alive the following June at Namuyongo. His companions were twenty-one other boys and young men aged between thirteen and thirty, mostly pages of the despotic King Mwanga of Uganda. All were martyred between 1885–1887 with horrible cruelty. They were converts of the White Fathers. They were canonized in 1964. Each has a separate entry in this book.

Charles de la Calmette Sept 2–3

See September Martyrs.

Charles Spinola (Bl) M. SJ. Sept 11

d. 1622 Though born at Prague he belonged to the Italian noble house of Spinola. He became a Jesuit in 1584 and in 1594 was sent to the missions of Japan. He worked there until 1618 when he was arrested and kept in prison for four years. He was then burnt to death with twenty-four companions. Each of them is given separate notice in this book. Beatified in 1867.

Charles of Blois (Bl) C. Sept 29

1316–1364 Nephew of Philip VI of France. He married Joan of Brittany in 1341 and claimed her dukedom against John de Montfort. This led to the war in which he was engaged for the rest of his life, except for nine years spent as a prisoner in the Tower of London. He fell in battle in 1364. Cult confirmed in 1904.

Charles Borromeo (St)

C. Bp.   GC. Nov 4

1538–1584   Son of Count Gilbert Borromeo by a Medici mother. His uncle, Pope Pius IV, appointed him archbishop of Milan and cardinal when he was aged only twenty-two. He did not receive priestly or episcopal orders until the year 1563. He was the most imposing and influential figure of the counter-reformation in Italy. He was a model bishop — zealous, selfless, prodigal even of his life. An attempt was made on his life by evildoers. Canonized in 1610.

Charles Steeb (Bl)   Dec 15

1775–1856   Born at Tübingen of a wealthy Lutheran family. He became a Catholic whilst studying at Verona, and then was ordained a priest. After a life in the service of the sick, the penitent and those in need of education he founded, with Sister Luigia Poloni, the Institute of the Sisters of Mercy. He died in Verona on Dec 15. Beatified in 1975.

Chef (St) Ab.   Oct 29

Otherwise Theodore, q.v.

Cheledonius (St) M.   March 3

See Hemiterius and Cheledonius.

Chelidonia (St)

V. OSB.   Oct 13

d. 1152   Born at Ciculum in the Abruzzi, she early fled into the mountains above Tivoli, near Subiaco, where she dwelt as a recluse in a cave, now called Morra Ferogna. From Cuno, cardinal of Frascati, she received the Benedictine habit in the abbey church of St Scholastica at Subiaco, but continued to live as a recluse under the obedience of the abbot. Her body now reposes in the church of St Scholastica. She is one of the patron saints of Subiaco.

Chely (St) Bp.   Oct 25

Otherwise Hilary of Mende, q.v.

Cheron (St) M.   May 28

Otherwise Caraunus, q.v.

Cherubinus Testa of

Avigliana (Bl) C. OSA.   Dec 17

1449–1479   An Augustinian friar-hermit of Avigliana in Piedmont. Cult approved by Pius IX.

Chilian (St) Bp. M.   July 8

See Kilian, Colman and Totnan.

Chillien (Killian,

Chilianus) (St)   Nov 13

7th cent.   An Irishman, kinsman of St Fiacre, who became a missionary in Artois. His body was enshrined at Aubigny, near Arras.

China (Martyrs of)

In addition to individual martyrs, there have been various group beatifications: (1) in 1893 a group of five Dominicans; (2) 1900, thirteen martyrs included with the Annamite martyrs 1798–1856; (3) seven martyrs included in a similar decree of 1909; (4) twenty-nine Franciscan martyrs during the Boxer Rising, beatified in 1496. See also Annam, Korea and individual articles.

Chionia (St) VM.   Apr 3

See Agape and Chionia.

Chl

Note. Names so beginning are often spelt Cl or Kl.

Chr

Note. Names so beginning are often spelt Cr.

Christeta (St) M.   Oct 27

See Vincent, Sabina and Christeta.

Christian (Bl) Ab. OSB.

Cist.   March 18

d. 1186   His Celtic name was Giolla Croist O'Conarchy. An Irish priest, who professed the Cistercian rule at Clairvaux under St Bernard and eventually was sent back to Ireland (1142) to introduce the Cistercians there. He was in fact the abbot-founder of Mellifont abbey. It is said that he became bishop of Lismore and papal legate in Ireland.

Christian (Bl) C.   Apr 7

? A priest of Douai, whose relics are in the church of St Albinus.

Christian (St) Bp.   June 12

d. 1138   Croistan O'Morgair, brother of St Malachy of Armagh. He was made bishop of Clogher (1126) and obtained several privileges from the Holy See for his diocese.

Christian (Christinus)

(St) M. OSB.   Nov 12

See Benedict, John, etc.

Christian (Bl) Bp.   Nov 22

d. c 873   Thirty-seventh bishop of Auxerre.

Christian (Bl) C. OP.   Dec 1

13th cent.   One of the first disciples of St Dominic, whom he helped in the foundation of the friary at Perugia.

Christian (Bl) Bp. OSB. Cist.   Dec 4

d. 1245   A Cistercian monk, probably belonging to the great abbey of Oliva, near Danzig. He went to Prussia as a missionary (1207), and was nominated bishop in 1215. He was instrumental in introducing the Teutonic Knights there. His efforts to convert Prussia were only partially successful.

Christiana of the Cross
(Bl) V.   Jan 10
Otherwise Oringa, q.v.

Christiana (St) V.   July 24
7th cent. Said to have been the daughter of an Anglo-Saxon king. She crossed over to Flanders where she lived until her death. She is the patron saint of Termonde in Belgium.

Christiana (St) V.   Dec 15
Otherwise Nino, q.v.

Christicola (St) Bp.   March 3
Otherwise Cele-Christ, q.v.

Christina Ciccarelli (Bl)
V. OSA.   Jan 18
1481–1543 A native of Luco in the Abruzzi and a nun and prioress of the Augustinian hermits, who died at Aquileia. Cult confirmed in 1841.

Christina of Spoleto (Bl)
Penitent   Feb 13
1435–1458 Christina Camozzi (wrongly called Visconti) was born near Lake Lugano, the daughter of a physician. After a few years spent in frivolity she embraced a life of extreme bodily mortifications. She died at Spoleto aged twenty-three. Cult confirmed in 1834.

Christina (St) VM.   March 13
? A Persian maiden who was scourged to death.

Christina (St) VM.   July 24
? A maiden, perhaps a native of Rome, who was put to death near the Lake of Bolsena in Tuscany. Her legendary acts have been confused with those of a St Christina of Tyre, whose very existence, however, is very doubtful. In art she is shown holding an arrow, or pierced by arrows, or holding a millstone, whilst trampling on a pagan. Cult confined to local calendars since 1969.

Christina the Astonishing
(Mirabilis) **(Bl) V.**   July 24
1150–1224 Born near Liège. In 1182, after a cataleptic fit, she was the subject of a life-long series of most astonishing experiences, recorded by a contemporary Dominican. She died in the convent of St Catherine at Trond. Cult never officially confirmed.

Christina of Stommeln
(Bl) V.   Nov 6
1242–1312 Christina Bruzo, or Bruso, was born at Stommeln, near Cologne. Like her namesake of Belgium, she too could be styled "the Astonishing", since her life is a continuous record of most extraordinary phenomena which indeed tax the faith of the reader. They were recorded by a contemporary Friar Preacher. Cult confirmed in 1908.

Christina (St) V. OSB.   Dec 5
d. 1160 Nun and recluse of Markgate under the obedience of the abbot of St Alban's. Her spiritual director was Bl Roger of St Alban's.

Christinus (St) M. OSB.   Nov 12
See Benedict, John, etc.

Christopher
Note. The Latin Christophorus means the Christ-Bearer. It was one of the most popular names during the Middle Ages. Its variants are numerous: Cristoforo, Christophe, Cristobal, Tobal, Cristobalón, Kester, Kitt, etc.

Christopher of Milan
(Bl) C. OP.   March 1
d. 1484 A Friar Preacher who, true to his profession, preached with extraordinary success throughout Liguria and the Milanese. At Taggia, as a result of his preaching, the people built a friary and the saint was made its first prior. He died there. Cult confirmed in 1875.

Christopher Bales (Bl)
M.   March 4
d. 1590 Born at Coniscliffe, Durham. He was educated at Rome and Reims and ordained priest at Douai (1587). In 1588 he crossed over to England and two years later was seized, condemned, and hanged, drawn and quartered in Fleet Street, London. Beatified in 1929.

Christopher Macassoli
(Bl) C. OFM.   March 11
d. 1485 Born at Milan, he joined the Franciscans and eventually founded a friary at Vigevano, in the province of Milan, where thousands sought his help and advice. Cult confirmed in 1890.

Christopher (St) M.   July 25
? The pre-1970 RM. made him a martyr of Lycia under Decius, but beyond the fact of his martyrdom, nothing is known about him. Many legends, however, some of them very beautiful but others unbelievable and absurd, have grown up around his name. The most graceful is that of his carrying an unknown child across a ford, and being borne down by its weight, despite his own gigantic stature and great strength: the child was Christ, carrying in His hand the weight of the whole world. This episode led to the usual representa-

St Christopher, July 25

tion of the saint in art. He was one of the Fourteen Holy Helpers, q.v. Venerated in local calendars since 1969.

Christopher (St) M.   Aug 20
See Leovigild and Christopher.

Christopher of Guardia
(St) M.   Sept 25
d. *c* 1490   A boy of Guardia, near Toledo, in Spain, who at the age of three years was stolen by Jews at Toledo and crucified at Guardia, under Ferdinand and Isabella. His cult was officially confirmed, with the title of saint, by Pius VII in 1805. He is the principal patron saint of Guardia.

Christopher Buxton (Bl)
M.   Oct 1
d. 1588   Born at Tideswell in Derbyshire, educated at Reims and Rome, and ordained priest in 1586. Two years later he was hanged, drawn and quartered for his faith at Canterbury. Beatified in 1929.

Christopher of Romagnola
(Bl) C. OFM.   Oct 31
c 1172–1272   A parish priest in the diocese of Cesena, who resigned his office, and joined St Francis of Assisi. He was sent to establish the order in Gascony, where he died at Cahors. Cult approved in 1905.

Christopher (Bl) M.   Nov 12
d. *c* 1500   A Portuguese knight of the Order of Christ (under the Cistercian rule), who was beheaded for the faith by a Muslim prince of Ceylon.

Chrodegang (St) Bp.   March 6
d. 766   A near relative of Pepin, he became the chief minister to Charles Martel and ultimately bishop of Metz (742). He played a major part in nearly all the important affairs of his time, and took part in several councils. He is known for the rule he wrote for the secular clerks whom he gathered together in chapters of canons with common life. He also introduced the Roman liturgy and chant into his diocese and thus into N. Europe.

Chromatius (St) C.   Aug 11
3rd cent. Said to have been prefect of Rome
and father of St Tiburtius the martyr.

Chromatius (St) Bp.   Dec 2
d. *c* 406 Bishop of Aquileia, near Venice,
from 387 to 406. St Jerome styles him "a most
learned and most holy man", and dedicated to
him several of his works. Chromatius was also
a friend of St John Chrysostom and of
Rufinus. We still posses part of his commentary on St Matthew.

Chronan (St) Ab.   Apr 28
Otherwise Cronan, q.v.

**Chrysanthus and Daria
(SS) MM.**   Oct 25
d. 283? Chrysanthus, an Egyptian, with his
wife Daria, a Greek, were distinguished in
Rome for their zealous profession and practice
of the Christian religion. This led to their
martyrdom under Numerian and Carinus. In
ancient times they were celebrated each on a
differing day. Since 1969 the information
about their lives has been regarded as a legend.
All that is known for sure is that they were early
martyrs buried on the Via Salaria. Since 1969
their cult has been confined to particular
calendars.

Chrysogonus (St) M.   formerly Nov 24
d. *c* 304 A martyr who suffered at Aquileia.
His name occurs in the first eucharistic prayer.
His association with the martyr St Anastasia of
Sirmium is now rejected. His cult continues
only in his own basilica in Rome.

Chrysolius (St) Bp. M.   Feb 7
4th cent. An Armenian who evangelized
N.E. Gaul, where, it is said, he was ordained
bishop. He had left Armenia during the
persecution of Diocletian, but won the crown
of martyrdom in Flanders. His relics are
venerated at Bruges.

Chrysologus (St) Bp.   Dec 2
See Peter Chrysologus.

Chrysophorus (St) M.   Apr 20
See Victor, Zoticus, etc.

Chrysostom (St) Bp. Dr   Jan 27
See John Chrysostom.

Chrysotelus (St) M.   Apr 22
See Parmenius, and Comp.

**Chuniald and Gislar (SS)
CC.**   Sept 24
7th cent. Missionaries, probably of Irish or
Scottish origin, who evangelized S. Germany
and Austria, under the leadership of St Rupert
of Salzburg.

Cian (St) C.   Dec 11
6th cent. A Welsh saint who ended his life as
a hermit. He is sometimes described as a
servant of St Peris.

Cianan (St) Bp.   Nov 24
Otherwise Kenan, q.v.

Ciaran (St) Bp.   March 5
Otherwise Kieran, q.v.

Ciaran (St) Bp.   Sept 9
Otherwise Kieran, q.v.

Cicely (St) VM.   Nov 22
Otherwise Cecilia, q.v.

**Cicco of Pesaro (Bl) C.
Tert. OFM.**   Aug 4
d. 1350 A native of Pesaro, and a tertiary of
St Francis, who led the life of a recluse near
Pesaro. Cult confirmed by Pius IX.

Cilinia (St) Matron   Oct 21
d. *p*.458 Mother of St Principius, bishop of
Soissons, and of St Remigius, bishop of
Reims. She died at Laon.

Cillene (St) Ab.   July 3
d. *c* 752 An Irish monk who migrated to
Iona and was there elected abbot in 726.

Cindeus (St) M.   July 11
d. *c* 300 A priest of Pamphylia in Asia
Minor who was burnt at the stake under
Diocletian.

Cinnia (St) V.   Feb 1
5th cent. A princess of Ulster converted by
St Patrick, who also gave her the veil.

Cisellus (St) M.   Aug 21
See Luxorius, Cisellus and Camerinus.

Cissa (St) H. OSB.   Sept 23
Late 7th cent. Monk-recluse in Northumbria, most probably at Lindisfarne.

Ciwa (St) V.   Feb 8
Otherwise Kigwe, q.v.

Clair (St) M.   Nov 4
The French spelling of Clarus, q.v.

**Clare Agolanti of Rimini
(Bl) W. Tert. OFM.**   Feb 10
1282–1346 She belonged to the nobility of
Rimini and was twice married. During her
married life she wasted her time in sinful
dissipations. On the execution of her father
and brother, as a result of civil disturbances,
she completely changed her life. She became a

St Clare, Aug 11

Franciscan tertiary and founded a nunnery, but never became a nun herself. She practised rigorous penances, some of which were considered extravagant even by her contemporaries. Cult sanctioned in 1784.

Clare Gambacorta (Bl)
W. Op.   Apr 17
1362–1419   Daughter of the head of the state of Pisa. Being left a widow at fifteen, she wished to become a Poor Clare. Her father strongly opposed this at first, but eventually relented and built for her a nunnery where she introduced the strict Dominican observance. As a superior she was continually beset by financial troubles.

Clare of Assisi (St) V.
Foundress   GC. Aug 11
c 1194–1253   Born at Assisi. At the age of eighteen she was irresistibly drawn to the ideal of Christian poverty preached by St Francis. She ran away from home and took the veil from St Francis himself, who provided a refuge for her with the Benedictine nuns of San Paolo and finally at San Damiano, where the first convent of Poor Clares was established under her guidance. She governed it for forty years, and popes, cardinals and bishops came to consult her. She was indeed as much

instrumental in the rapid spreading of the Franciscan movement as St Francis himself. She was canonized two years after her death. In art she is usually represented with a monstrance in her hand in memory of her having in this attitude miraculously saved her convent from assault.

Clare of Montefalco (St)
V. OSA.   Aug 17
c 1268–1308   Surnamed Clare of the Cross. She was a native of Montefalco, in the diocese of Spoleto who joined a convent of Franciscan tertiaries. In 1290 she became abbess of Holy Cross Convent with the rule of St Augustine. There is some doubt as to what rule she followed. Her distinctive devotion was the Passion of Christ: a cross was found depicted on the flesh of her heart after her death. Canonized in 1881.

Clare Xamada (Bl) M.   Sept 10
d. 1622   A Japanese matron, wife of Bl Dominic Xamada. Both were beheaded at Nagasaki, in Japan.

Claritus (Chiarito) Voglia
(Bl) C.   May 25
d. 1348   A Florentine, who in 1342 founded a convent of Augustinian nuns at Florence. His wife became a nun there, and he remained in the convent as a manservant till his death.

Clarentius (St) Bp.   Apr 26
d. c 620   The successor of St Etherius in the see of Vienne.

Clarus (St) Ab. OSB.   Jan 1
d. c 660   A monk of the abbey of St Ferreol, who was chosen abbot of the monastery of St Marcellus at Vienne in Dauphiny. He was the spiritual director of the convent of St Blandina, where his own mother had taken the veil. Cult confirmed in 1907.

Clarus (St) H. OSB.   Feb 1
d. c 1048   A monk of Seligenstadt, in the diocese of Mainz. He lived for thirty years as a recluse, given to great austerities. His motto was: "Christ, and Him crucified".

Clarus (St) Bp. M.   June 1
?   A regionary bishop, said to have been sent from Rome to preach the gospel in Aquitaine, where he was martyred. He is not to be confused with St Clarus, bishop of Nantes (Oct 10).

Clarus (St) Bp.   Oct 10
?   Bishop of Nantes. Some writers make him a disciple of St Peter and the first apostle of Armorica (Brittany). Others place his apostolate in the third century.

Clarus (St) M. OSB.   Nov 4
d. *c* 875 He is described as a native of
Rochester, who crossed over to France, where
he was first a monk and then a hermit in the
diocese of Rouen. He was murdered at the
instigation of a woman whose advances he had
rejected. The village Saint-Clair-sur-Epte is
named after him.

Clarus (St) H.   Nov 8
d. 397 Born at Tours in France, he joined
the community of Marmoutier under St
Martin. He was ordained priest and henceforth lived as a hermit near the same abbey.

Classicus (St) M.   Feb 18
See Lucius, Sylvanus, etc.

Clateus (St) Bp.   June 4
d. *c* 64 One of the earliest bishops of Brescia, who suffered martyrdom under Nero.

Claud or Claude (*several*)
Otherwise Claudius, q.v.

Claudia (St) M.   March 20
See Alexandra, Claudia, etc.

Claudia (St) VM.   May 18
See Theodotus, Thecusa, etc.

Claudia (St) W.   Aug 7
1st cent. A woman mentioned by St Paul in
his second letter to Timothy (4:21). A much
later tradition asserts that she was a Briton, the
wife of Aulus Pudens, a senator, and the
mother of SS Praxedes and Pudentiana. This
however, is but a pious fiction.

Claudian (St) M.   Feb 25
See Victorinus, Victor, etc.

Claudian (St) M.   Feb 26
See Papias, Diodorus, etc.

Claudian (St) M.   March 6
See Victor, Victorinus, etc.

**Claudius (Claude) de la
Colombière (Bl)** C. SJ.   Feb 15
1641–1682 Born near Grenoble, he became
a Jesuit in 1659 at Avignon. While superior of
the Jesuits at Paray-le-Monial he was the
spiritual director of St Margaret Mary Alacoque and was instrumental in spreading devotion to the Sacred Heart. Sent to England in
1676 as chaplain to the Duchess of York, he
was arrested and banished for alleged complicity in the imaginary "Popish Plot". Beatified
in 1929.

Claudius (St) M.   Feb 18
See Maximus, Claudius, etc.

Claudius (St) M.   June 3
See Lucillian, Claudius, etc.

**Claudius of Besançon
(St)** Bp. OSB.   June 6
d. *c* 699 A native of Franche-Comté, he was
trained to bear arms, but decided to be a priest
and eventually was appointed canon of Besançon. He next became a monk, and abbot of
Condat abbey in the Jura mountains, where he
introduced, or enforced, the rule of St Benedict. In 685 he was chosen bishop of Besançon
but retained the direction of the abbey, to
which he retired again before his death. The
abbey was afterwards known as Saint-Claude.

**Claudius, Nicostratus,
Castorius, Victorinus
and Symphorian (SS)**
MM.   July 7
d. *c* 288 Described in the very untrustworthy Acts of St Sebastian as having suffered
martyrdom at the same time as that saint. They
are very likely identical with the group of saints
honoured on Nov 8 with the Four Crowned
Martyrs, q.v.

**Claudius, Justus, Jucundinus
and Comp. (SS)** MM.   July 21
d. 273 A group of eight martyrs who suffered with St Julia at Troyes in Gaul, under
Aurelian. Their bodies were enshrined in the
Benedictine nunnery of Jouarre, near Meaux.

**Claudius, Asterius,
Neon, Donvina and
Theonilla (SS)** MM.   Aug 23
d. 303 The first three were brothers who
were accused to the magistrate of Aegea in
Cilicia by their step-mother, who hoped to
inherit their estate. They were crucified or,
according to another account, decapitated. It
is not certain that the two women were
fellow-sufferers; Donvina is a mistake for
Domina.

Claudius (St) M.   Oct 25
See Marcellinus, Claudius, etc.

**Claudius, Lupercus and
Victorius (SS)** MM.   Oct 30
d. *c* 300 Three brothers, sons of the centurion, St Marcellus. They were martyred at
Léon in Spain under Diocletian. They are the
titular saints of St Claudius in Galicia, one of
the earliest Benedictine abbeys in Spain.

**Claudius, Nicostratus
and Comp. (SS)** MM.   Nov 8
These saints belong to the group of the Four

Crowned Martyrs, q.v. They are probably the same group as that mentioned on July 7. See Claudius, Nicostratus, etc. above (July 7).

Claudius, Hilaria, Jason, Maurus (Maris) and Comp. (SS) MM. Dec 3

d. ? 283 This group of martyrs, consisting of Claudius, a military tribune, Hilaria his wife, their two sons, and seventy soldiers, belong to the larger group figuring in the legendary acts of SS Chrysanthus and Daria.

Claudius, Crispin, Magina, John and Stephen (SS) MM. Dec 3

? African martyrs, of whom nothing is known.

Clear (Cleer, Clether) (St) Bp. Oct 10

Otherwise Clarus, q.v.

Cledog (Clydog, Cleodicus) (St) Oct 23

Otherwise Clether, q.v.

Cledwyn (Clydwyn) (St) C. Nov 1

5th cent. Patron saint of Llangedwyn in Clwyd. Alleged to have been the eldest son of King Brychan, and to have succeeded him as ruler of part of his dominions.

Clement (St) Bp. M. Jan 23

d. 309 Bishop of Ancyra in Galatia, martyred under Diocletian.

Clement (St) Ab. OSB. March 5

c 800 Abbot of Santa Lucia, in Syracuse, the oldest Benedictine monastery in Sicily.

Clement Mary Hofbauer (St) C. C.SS.R. March 15

1751–1820 A Slav, born in Moravia, whose real name was John Dvorak. He was the son of a grazier, and he himself started life as a baker and then became a hermit. While on a pilgrimage to Rome he received the habit as a recluse at the hands of the bishop of Tivoli, the future pope Pius VII, who changed John's name into that of Clement Mary. In 1784 he joined the recently founded Redemptorists at Rome and four years later was sent to Warsaw to establish the first house of the congregation beyond the Alps. There the untiring zeal of the Redemptorists met with signal success, though the development of the institute was retarded by the Napoleonic wars. Clement spent the last twelve years of his life at Vienna, firmly planting the Redemptorist institute in German lands, whence it spread throughout the world. Canonized in 1909.

Clement (Bl) Bp. OP. March 19

d. 1258 He received the habit from St Dominic himself and preached in Scotland into which country he introduced the Dominicans. He became bishop of Dumblane.

Clement of Elpidio (Bl) C. OSA. Apr 8

d. 1291 A native of Osimo and a hermit friar of St Augustine. In 1270 he was chosen general of the order and as such he drew up its constitutions, which were approved in 1287. For this reason he is considered the second founder of the order. Cult approved in 1572.

Clement (St) M. June 27

d. c 298 A martyr of Cordoba, in Spain, under Diocletian. He belongs to the group led by St Zoilus, q.v.

Clement of Okhrida (St) C. July 17

See Seven Apostles of Bulgaria.

Clement (St) M. Sept 10

See Apelles, Lucius and Clement.

Clement Vom (Bl) M. Sept 10

d. 1622 A Japanese layman, martyred at Nagasaki. He belongs to the group of Bl Charles Spinola, q.v.

Clement Kingemon (Bl) M. Nov 1

d. 1622 A native of Arima in Japan. He was the servant of Bl Paul Navarro, whose life he wrote. He was burnt alive with his master at Ximabarra. Beatified in 1867.

Clement (St) M. Nov 21

See Celsus and Clement.

Clement I (St) Pope, M. GC. Nov 23

d. c 101 The third successor of St Peter in the see of Rome, he governed the church there for about ten years. In his capacity as pope, he wrote to the church of Corinth to settle some disputes there; the letter is one of the most important documents of the sub-apostolic age. He is venerated as a martyr, but his martyrdom cannot be proved, much less the legends attached to it. He is mentioned in the first eucharistic prayer. His memory is perpetuated in Rome by the magnificent church of San Clemente, which possibly is on the same site as his own dwelling.

Clement (St) Bp. Nov 23

? The first bishop of Metz, sent directly from Rome to evangelize that district of Roman Gaul.

Clement of Alexandria (St) C. Dec 4

d. c 217 Titus Flavius Clemens succeeded Panthenus as the head of the catechetical school of Alexandria, where he had Origen as

St Clement, Nov 23

one of his pupils. He has left numerous writings. His name was listed in the RM. up to 1751.

Clementia (Bl) N. OSB.   March 21
d. 1176 Daughter of Adolph, count of Hohenburg. A model wife, she became in her widowhood a nun at Oehren, Trier.

Clementinus, Theodotus and Philomenus (SS) MM.   Nov 14
? Martyrs of Heraclea in Thrace. Nothing else is known about them.

Cleomenes (Leomenes) (St) M.   Dec 23
See Theodulus, Saturninus, etc.

Cleonicus, Eutropius and Basiliscus (SS) MM.   March 3
d. c 308 These saints belong to a group of martyrs put to death in the province of Pontus on the Black Sea, under Diocletian. Most of the group — some forty to fifty — seem to have been soldiers in the imperial army; several, however, were crucified, the punishment reserved for slaves. Their martyrdom was closely connected with that of St Theodore (Feb 7).

Cleopatra (St) W.   Oct 19
d. 319 A widow of Palestine who succeeded

in securing the body of St Varus, martyred under Diocletian, and enshrined it at her home at Deráá in Syria. On the day of the dedication of the church her twelve-year-old son died, and he and St Varus appeared in a vision to comfort her.

Cleophas (St) M.   Sept 25
1st cent. One of the two disciples whom Christ met on the way to Emmaus (Luke 24). The pre-1970 RM. states that he was murdered by the Jews in the house in which he entertained our Lord on that first Easter day. He was sometimes identified, without any real grounds, with Clopas or Alpheus, the father of St James the Less (Mt 10:3, Jn 19:25). Hegesippus adds that he was a brother of St Joseph.

Clerus (St) M.   Jan 7
d. c 300 A Syrian deacon, martyred at Antioch.

Clether (Cleer, Clydog, Scledog. Latinized: Clitanus or Cleodius) (St)   Oct 23
d. c 520 One of the saints descended from King Brychan of Brecknock, or at least of his clan. He left Wales and went to Cornwall. Several dedications of churches — for in-

stance, St Clear, near Liskeard — perpetuate his memory. Another Clether, or Cledog, is commemorated on Nov 3. He is alleged to have died a martyr in Herefordshire.

Cletus (St) Pope   formerly Apr 26
Nothing definite can be said about him as he is really the same person as Anacletus q.v. Cletus is an accepted abbreviation which caused later writers to distinguish two persons when only one existed. Cult suppressed 1969.

Clicerius (St) Bp.   Sept 20
d. *c* 438 Bishop of Milan, of whom no record is extant.

Clinius (St) Ab. OSB.   March 30
? A Greek and a Benedictine of Montecassino, who was made superior of the daughter-house of St Peter, near Pontecorvo, where his relics are venerated.

Clodoaldus. French:
Clous (St) Ab.   Sept 7
d. *c* 560 Grandson of King Clovis and of St Clotilde. When his two brothers were murdered he was taken to safety in Provence. Afterwards he became a priest, a recluse, and the abbot-founder of Nogent-sur-Seine, near Versailles, now called after him, Saint-Cloud.

Clodulphus. French:
Clou (St) Bp.   June 8
605–696 Son of St Arnulf, bishop of Metz. He too became bishop of Metz, succeeding his father in 656 and ruling over his diocese for forty years.

Clotilde (St) Queen   June 3
c 474–545 Born at Lyons, daughter of Chilperic, king of Burgundy, she married Clovis, king of the Salian Franks, and was the means of leading her husband to embrace Christianity (496). She had much to suffer on account of the quarrels between her three sons. In old age she retired to Tours, where she died.

Clotilde Paillot (Bl) M.   Oct 23
1739–1794 Born at Bavay, professed as an Ursuline in 1756, superior of the house of Valenciennes. She was guillotined at Valenciennes. She belongs to the group of the Ursuline martyrs beatified in 1920, q.v.

Clotsindis (Clotsend) (St) Abs. OSB.   June 30
c 635–714 Daughter of St Adalbald and of St Rictrudis, later the abbess-foundress of Marchiennes in Flanders. She was educated at Marchiennes by her mother, the abbess-foundress, whom she succeeded as second abbess (688).

Clou (St) Bp.   June 8
Otherwise Clodulphus, q.v.

Cloud (St) Ab.   Sept 7
Otherwise Clodoaldus, q.v.

Clydog (St)   Oct 23
Otherwise Clether, q.v.

Clytanus (Clitanus) (St)   Oct 23
Otherwise Clether, q.v.

Cocca (Cucca, Cuach) (St) V.   June 6
? Patroness of Kilcock on the borders of Cos. Meath and Kildare.

Cocha (Coecha) (St) V.   June 29
6th cent. Said to have cared for St Kieran of Saighir in his infancy. She was afterwards abbess of Ross-Benchuir.

Codratus (Chuadratus), Dionysius, Cyprian, Anectus, Paul and Crescens (SS) MM.   March 10
d. *c* 258 Greek martyrs, beheaded at Corinth, under Valerian. Prior to this Codratus, then a child, appears to have been driven into the woods to escape from the persecution under Decius (250).

Codratus (St) M.   March 26
Otherwise Quadratus, q.v.

Coemgen (St) Ab.   June 3
Otherwise Kevin, q.v.

Cogitosus (St)   Apr 18
? 8th cent. He appears to have been a monk of Kildare. If the tradition representing him as the author of the life of St Brigid be trustworthy, we are indebted to him for much interesting information regarding that saint and her times.

Cointha (Quinta) (St) M.   Feb 8
d. 249 An Egyptian lady — some say a young maiden — martyred under Decius. She was fastened to the tail of a horse, and dragged by her feet through the streets of Alexandria till she died.

Colan (St)   May 21
The Cornish form of the name of the Welsh Gollen, q.v.

Colette (St) V. Poor Clare.   March 6
1381–1447 Nicolette Boilet was born at Corbie, in Picardy, a carpenter's daughter. She tried her religious vocation with the Beguines and the Benedictines, but failed. Next she became a recluse at Corbie, and finally she found her vocation in reviving the Franciscan spirit among the Poor Clares. She was made superioress of the whole order, and her reform spread throughout France, Savoy,

Germany and Flanders, many convents being restored and seventeen new ones founded by her. She helped St Vincent Ferrer in the work of healing the papal schism. She died at Ghent, and was canonized in 1807.

Colgan (St) Ab.   Feb 20
d. *c* 796 Surnamed "the Wise" and "the Chief Scribe of the Scots". Abbot of Clonmacnoise, in Offaly. He was a friend of Bl Alcuin.

Colman. Latin: Colmanus
Note. Probably the most popular baptismal name in the early Irish church. There are ninety-six saints of this name in the martyrology of Donegal, two hundred and nine in the Book of Leinster and many others. Holweck lists seventy-one; several, however, are evidently duplicates.

Colman of Lismore (St)
Bp.   Jan 23
d. *c* 702 Abbot-bishop of the monastery of Lismore, in the government of which he succeeded St Hierlug (Zailug) in 698. Under his rule the fame of Lismore reached its peak.

Colman of Lindisfarne
(St) Bp.   Feb 18
d. 676 A native of Connaught and a monk of Iona, he was chosen third abbot-bishop of Lindisfarne. His reluctance to accept the Roman traditions prescribed for England at the synod of Whitby (664) led him to withdraw with his monks to Ireland. Here he founded a monastery on Innisboffin Island, but later was compelled to establish another (Mayo of the Saxons) on the mainland for his English monks as they were not on good terms with their Irish brethren. He is praised by St Bede and by Bl. Acluin.

Colman of Armagh (St)
C.   March 5
5th cent. A disciple of St Patrick. He died during the lifetime of his master, by whom he was buried at Armagh.

Colman Mc O'Laoighse
(St) Ab.   May 15
6th cent. Named also Columbanus. He was a disciple of St Columba and of St Fintan of Clonenagh. He founded, and governed, a monastery at Oughaval.

Colman of Dromore (St)
Bp.   June 7
6th cent. A native of Argyll or of Ulster (there are two traditions) who settled in Ireland and became the abbot-founder and bishop of Dromore in Co. Down. He is said to

have been the teacher of St Finnian of Clonard. Cult approved in 1903.

Colman McRoi (St) Ab.   June 16
6th cent. A deacon, disciple of St Columba, and himself abbot-founder of a monastery at Reachrain, now Lambay Island, Dublin.

Colman (Colomannus)
(St) M.   July 8
See Kilian, Colman and Totnan.

Colman Elo (St) Ab.   Sept 26
d. *c* 610 A nephew of St Columba and the abbot-founder of monasteries at Lynally (Land-Elo, Lin-Alli) and at Muckamore. He is credited with the authorship of the *Alphabet of Devotion*.

Colman of Stockerau
(St) M.   Oct 13
d. 1012 An Irish, or Scottish, pilgrim who passing through Austria on his way to the Holy Land, was seized as a spy, racked and hanged with a couple of malefactors at Stockerau, near Vienna. Miracles were wrought by his dead body and he was venerated as a saint. He is honoured as one of the patron saints of Austria.

Colman of Kilroot (St)
Bp.   Oct 17
6th cent. A disciple of St Ailbe of Emly, and abbot-bishop of Kilroot, near Carrickfergus.

Colman of Senboth-Fola
(St) Ab.   Oct 27
d. *c* 632 An Irish abbot of Senboth-Fola, in the diocese of Ferns, and associated with St Aidan, bishop of that see.

Colman of Kilmacduagh
(St) Bp.   Oct 29
d. *c* 632 A son of the Irish chieftain, Duac. He was first a recluse at Arranmore and at Burren in Co. Clare; then he founded the monastery of Kilmacduagh i.e. the church of the son of Duac, and governed it as abbot-bishop. Cult approved in 1903.

Colman of Cloyne (St)
Bp.   Nov 24
522–*c* 600 Born in Cork, a poet and a royal bard at the court of Cashel. In middle age he was baptized by St Brendan, embraced the monastic life, was ordained priest and preached in Limerick and Cork. Finally he founded the church of Cloyne and was ordained its first bishop. Cult approved in 1903.

Colman of Glendalough
(St) Ab.   Dec 12
d. 659 An abbot of Glendalough, mentioned in the Irish calendars.

Colmoc (Macholmoc)
(St) Bp.   June 7
Otherwise Colman of Dromore, q.v.

Coloman de Ungvar (Bl)
C.   June 28
d. *c* 1510   A Hungarian Pauline monk in
Ungvár. He healed the blind, the lame and the
lepers.

Columba (Colum, Colm, Columbkill, Columcille, Columbus, Combs) (St)
Ab.   June 9
c 521–597   The most famous of the saints of
Scotland. He was a native of Garton, in Co.
Donegal, studied at Moville and Clonard,
embraced the monastic life at Glasnevin, was
ordained priest, and forthwith embarked upon
his life's work of founding monasteries and
churches, first in Ireland, and after 563 in
Scotland. On Whitsun eve of that year he
landed with twelve companions on the island
of Iona (Holy Island) where he established the
greatest and most celebrated of his monasteries, which became thenceforward the most
potent factor in the conversion of Picts, Scots,
and the Northern English. The description
given of him by his biographer and successor,
Adamnan, is famous: "He had the face of an
angel; he was of an excellent nature, polished
in speech, holy in deed, great in counsel...lov-
ing unto all". His relics were transferred to
Dunkeld in 849, and his "Cathach", a copy of
the psalms in his own hand, is still extant.

Columba (St) Ab.   Dec 12
d. 548   A native of Leinster and disciple of
St Finian. He governed the monastery of
Tyrdaglas in Munster.

Columba of Rieti (Bl) V.
Tert. OP.   May 20
1467–1501   Angelella Guardagnoli was born
at Rieti in Umbria. She became a Dominican
of the third order at Perugia and won the
confidence of all in that city, so that even the
magistrates would ask her advice. She is said to
have been ruthlessly persecuted by Lucrezia
Borgia. Beatified in 1627.

Columba (St) VM.   Sept 17
d. 853   A native of Cordoba and a nun at
Tábanos, whence she was driven by the
Moorish persecution of 852. She took refuge
at Cordoba, where at a later date, being called
upon to deny Christ, she openly reviled
Mohammed and thereupon was beheaded.

Columba (St) VM.   Nov 13
? Said to have been a Christian maiden put to
death by a heathen king of Cornwall. She is the
patron saint of two parishes in Cornwall.

Columba of Sens (St)
VM.   Dec 31
d. 273   A Spanish girl who abandoned her
country in order to avoid being denounced as a
Christian. She went to France with other
Spanish Christians and all were put to death
near Meaux, under Aurelian. Her shrine was
at Sens, and she was formerly venerated
throughout France.

Columbanus (St) H.   Feb 2
d. 959   An Irish recluse whose hermitage
was near the church of Saint-Bavo at Ghent.

Columbanus Junior (St)
M.   Nov 21
d. *p*.616   A disciple of St Columbanus and a
monk at Luxeuil.

Columbanus (St) Ab.   GC. Nov 23
c 543–615   A native of Leinster and a monk
of Bangor. In 580 he left Ireland with a band of
monks and worked first in England, then in
Brittany and finally in the Vosges district
where he founded the great abbey at Luxeuil
which he governed for twenty-five years. His
outspoken protest against the disorders of the
Frankish court led to his exile. He ended his
days in N. Italy, in the abbey of Bobbio which
he founded shortly before his death. He came
into conflict with both civil and religious
authorities from time to time due to the Celtic
observances kept in his monasteries. His rule
was very austere, although very influential.
Through the numerous abbeys, founded by
himself and by his disciples, especially after
they had become Benedictine, he exerted a
determining and lasting influence on the civilization of Western Europe.

Columbinus (St) Ab. OSB.   Sept 13
d. *c* 680   Successor of St Deicola as abbot of
Lure.

Columbus (Bl) C. OP.   Nov 8
d. 1229   Dominican prior of Toulouse and
Montpellier. He died while preaching at
Fréjus: his relics are in the cathedral there.

Combs (St) Ab.   June 9
A corrupt form of the name Columbkill or
Columba, q.v.

Comgall (Comgallus)
(St) Ab.   May 10
c 516–601   Born in Ulster, he became a
monk under St Fintan and eventually the
abbot-founder of Bangor (Ben-Chor) where
he was teacher of St Columbanus and the
band of monks who evangelized Central
Europe. He wrote a rather severe rule for his

St Columba, June 9

monks. It seems that he lived some time in Wales, Cornwall and Scotland.

Comgan (St) Ab.   Feb 27
d. *c* 565   Abbot of Glenthsen or Killeshin. He was assisted in death by St Utha of Munster.

Comgan (St) Ab.   Oct 13
8th cent. An Irish prince, brother of St Kentigern, who embraced the monastic life in Scotland and was buried on Iona.

Cominus (St)
There are several saints of this name, and they have been confused by hagiographers. The following are the most important:

                  May 1
A martyr of Catania in Sicily.

                  June 3
A companion of St Photinus (Pothinus), martyr of Lyons.

                  June 12
An Irish abbot, patron saint of Ardcavan. See also Baithin (June 9).

Companius (Compagno, Company) (Bl) Ab. OSB. Cam.   Oct 8
12th cent. First abbot of the Camaldolese abbey of our Lady of Porzia in Italy.

Conald (St) C.   Sept 24
Otherwise Chuniald, q.v.

Conall (Coel, Conald) (St) Ab.   May 22
7th cent. Abbot of the monastery of Inniscoel, Donegal, where there is a holy well called after him.

Conan (St) Bp.   Jan 26
d. ?*c* 648   A native of Ireland and a monk of Iona, said to have been a bishop in the Isle of Man.

Concessa (St) M.   Apr 8
? A martyr anciently venerated at Carthage.

Concessus (St) M.   Apr 9
See Demetrius, Concessus, etc.

Concordia (St) VM.   Aug 13
See Hippolytus, Concordia and Comp.

Concordius (St) M.   Jan 1
d. 175   A subdeacon put to death at Spoleto, central Italy, under Marcus Aurelius.

Concordius (St)   June 23
See John.

Concordius (St) M.   Sept 2
See Zeno, Concordius and Theodore.

Concordius (St) M.   Dec 16
See Valentine, Concordius, etc.

Condedus (Condé, Condède) H. OSB.   Oct 21
d. *c* 690   An Englishman who became a hermit at Fontaine-de-Saint-Valéry, on the Somme, France. There he heard of the abbey of Fontenelle and asked to be received into the community (*c* 673). After some years as a monk he obtained leave to preach, while residing as a recluse on an island in the Seine, near Caudebec.

Congan (St) Ab.   Oct 13
Otherwise Comgan, q.v.

Conindrus (St) Bp.   Dec 28
See Romulus and Conindrus.

Conleth (St) Bp.   May 4
d. *c* 519   An Irish recluse at Old Connell on the Liffey. St Brigid came to know him and made him the spiritual director of her nuns at Kildare, where eventually he became the first bishop. He was a metal-worker and very skilled as a copyist and illuminator.

Connat (Comnatan) (St) V.   Jan 1
d. *c* 590   Abbess of St Brigid's convent in Kildare.

Conogan (Gwen — latinized into Albinus) (St) Bp.   Oct 16
d. 460   The successor of St Corentin in the see of Quimper, in Brittany. His memory is still held in great veneration.

Conon (St) M.   Feb 26
See Papias, Diodorus, etc.

Conon (St) M.   March 6
d. 250   A Christian from Nazareth in Ga-

lilee who worked as a poor gardener at Mandona (Carmel), in Pamphylia, martyred under Decius.

Conon (St) Ab.   March 28
d. 1236   A Basilian monk and abbot of the Greek monastery of Nesi in Sicily.

Conon, Father and Son (SS) MM.   May 29
d. 275   Both were martyred at Iconium in Asia Minor under Aurelian. The boy was only twelve years of age. They were roasted before a slow fire and then racked to death.

Conrad of Mondsee (Bl) Ab. M. OSB.   Jan 16
d. 1145   Conrad Bosinlother was born near Trier and became a Benedictine at Siegburg. In 1127 he was appointed abbot of Mondsee (*Lunaelacensis*) in Upper Austria. His firmness in reclaiming the alienated possessions of the abbey led some nobles to murder him at Oberwang near Mondsee. From the time of his death he was publicly venerated at his abbey as a martyr.

Conrad of Bavaria (Bl) OSB. Cist.   Feb 15
1105–1154   Son of Henry the Black, duke of Bavaria. While a student at Cologne he was drawn to the monastic life by St Bernard, who professed him at Clairvaux. After some years he was granted permission to visit the Holy Land and on his return journey he died near Molfetta in Apulia. Cult approved in 1832.

Conrad of Piacenza (St) C. Tert. OFM.   Feb 19
1290–1354   A nobleman of Piacenza who once, when out hunting, caused a great conflagration for which a poor man was unjustly accused and condemned to death. Conrad confessed his guilt and forfeited all his fortune to make restitution. After this he and his wife decided to become religious: she was professed as a Poor Clare, he joined the third order of St Francis as a hermit. He passed the last thirty years of his life as a recluse in Sicily. Cult approved, with the title of Saint, by Paul III.

Conrad of Hildesheim (Bl) C. OFM.   Apr 14
c 1190–?   An Italian by birth and one of the first followers of St Francis, by whom he was sent to establish the order in N. Germany. He did so at Hildesheim, where his *cultus* survived till the Reformation.

Conrad Miliani of Ascoli (Bl) C. OFM.   Apr 19
1234–1289   A native of Ascoli Piceno, he

joined the Franciscans together with Jerome Masci, afterwards Pope Nicholas IV, whose future he foretold. Conrad was sent to evangelize Libya in N. Africa, whence he was recalled to act as advisor to Jerome Masci, when the latter became a cardinal.

Conrad of Parzham (St)
C. OFM. Cap.   Apr 21
1818–1894   Born of poor parents at Parzham near Passau in Bavaria, he joined the Capuchins as a lay-brother at the age of thirty-one and spent more than forty years as doorkeeper at his friary. He was endowed with the gift of prophecy and the power to read hearts. Beatified in 1930 and canonized in 1934.

Conrad of Seldenbüren
(Bl) M. OSB.   May 2
d. 1126   A scion of the royal house of Seldenbüren and founder of the Swiss abbey of Engelberg in Unterwalden where he was professed as a Benedictine lay-brother. He was sent to Zurich to defend the rights of his abbey and was murdered there by his opponents. He is venerated as a martyr.

Conrad (Cuno) of Trier
(St) Bp. M.   June 1
d. 1066   Of the noble family of Pfullingen in Swabia. His uncle, St Annon, archbishop of Cologne, appointed him bishop of Trier in defiance of the right of election of the Chapter. Conrad was seized on his way to Trier and cast from the battlements of the castle of Uerzig. He is venerated as a martyr.

Conrad of Hessen (Bl)
Ab. OSB. Cist.   June 1
d. c 1270   Conrad of Herlesheim in Ober-Hessen entered the Cistercian order and belonged to the abbey of Haina in which he was cellarer for at least sixteen years.

Conrad of Ottobeuren
(Bl) Ab. OSB.   July 27
d. 1227   Abbot of Ottobeuren abbey in Bavaria from 1193 till his death. He is described as a "lover of the brethren and of the poor".

Conrad Nantwin
(Antvin) (Bl) M.   Aug 1
d. 1286   While making a pilgrimage to Rome he was unjustly accused and burnt at the stake at Wolfrathshausen, near Munich. His cult was approved by Boniface VIII, and a church is dedicated to him.

Conrad of Zähringen
(Bl) Card. Bp. OSB. Cist.   Sept 30
d. 1227   A member of the family of the counts of Seyne. In early life he was made a canon of St Lambert's, Liège; then he passed

over to the Cistercians at Villers in Brabant. Subsequently he became successively abbot of Villers (1209), of Clairvaux (1214), of Cîteaux (1217), cardinal-bishop of Porto and Santa Rufina (1219) and papal legate in Languedoc (1224–1226). He died at Bari. The Cistercians have always given him the title of Saint.

Conrad of Frisach (Bl) C.
OP.   Nov 24
d. 1239   A doctor at the university of Bologna whom St Dominic received into the order and sent to Germany. He died at Magdeburg singing the psalm, *Cantate Domino canticum novum.*

Conrad of Heisterbach
(Bl) C. OSB. Cist.   Nov 25
d. c 1200   A soldier and a minister to the Margraves of Thuringia until his fiftieth year, and then a Cistercian at Heisterbach.

Conrad of Constance
(St) Bp.   Nov 26
d. 975   Bishop of Constance in Switzerland from 934 till his death. Three times he made the pilgrimage to the Holy Land, and in an age when most bishops were continually involved in secular politics, he succeeded in attending exclusively to ecclesiastical interests. Canonized in 1123.

Conrad of Offida (Bl) C.
OFM.   Dec 14
c 1241–1306   A native of Offida, diocese of Ascoli Piceno. When fourteen years of age he joined the Franciscans and throughout his life as a Minorite, he favoured the "spiritual" and eremitical tendencies in the order. He died at Bastia in Umbria while preaching a sermon. Cult confirmed in 1817.

Conradin of Brescia (Bl)
C. OP.   Nov 1
d. 1429   Born at Bornato, in the diocese of Brescia, he was professed a Friar Preacher at Padua (1413) and was chosen prior of Bologna. Here he was twice imprisoned for defending the pope.

Conran (St) Bp.   Feb 14
The legend of a holy bishop of the Orkney Islands so-named lacks all historical foundation.

Consortia (St) V.   June 22
d. ? 570   Said to have been the foundress of a convent generously endowed by King Clotaire out of gratitude for her having miraculously healed his dying daughter. She was venerated at Cluny, but nothing certain is known about her.

Constabilis (St) Ab. OSB. Feb 17
1060–1124 A native of Lucania, he became
a Benedictine under St Leo at the abbey of
Cava near Salerno, and in 1122 was chosen its
fourth abbot. He built the town of Castelab-
bate, where he is now venerated as the principal patron saint. Canonized in 1893.

Constant (St) M. Nov 18
d. 777 An Irish priest-hermit at Lough
Erne who died under circumstances which led
to his being venerated as a martyr.

Constantia (St) M. Sept 19
See Felix and Constantia.

Constantian (St) Ab. Dec 1
d. 570 A native of Auvergne, monk at Micy
(Orleans) and abbot-founder of Javron abbey.

Constantine (St) March 11
? The pre-1970 RM. said: "At Carthage, St
Constantine, confessor". Nothing is known of
him.

Constantine (St) M. March 9
d. 576 Said to have been a king of Cornwall,
who after a career of vice and greed, led a
penitent's life in Wales and Ireland, whence he
went as a missionary to Scotland. There he
was put to death by pirates. There is little
serious historical foundation for this story.
Two places in Cornwall perpetuate his name.

Constantine (St) King, M. Apr 2
d. 874 Constantine II, king of Scotland, was
slain in a battle against heathen invaders of his
country and was henceforth locally honoured
as a martyr. He was buried at Iona.

Constantine (St) Bp. Apr 12
d. 529 The first bishop of Gap in France,
about whom nothing else is known.

Constantine (St)
Emperor May 21
d. 337 The son of Constantius Chlorus and
St Helena (q.v.), he was trained at the court of
Diocletian, and at the death of his father at
York in 306, proclaimed emperor, defeating
his rival Maxentius at the battle of the Milvian
bridge. His armies marched behind the labarum, he having adopted Christianity. Thus
followed the Peace of the Church. Unbaptized
until on his deathbed, he presided over church
councils such as Nicaea and tried to reconcile
contending forces inside and outside the
church. His laws and policies embodied
Christian principles, and he was a great builder of churches. In the East he is venerated as
the "Thirteenth Apostle".

Constantine (St) Bp. June 15
d. *c* 706 Said to have been a monk under St

St Constantine, May 21

Philibert at Jumièges, and then bishop of Beauvais.

Constantine (St) Ab. OSB.   July 21
d. *c* 560   Disciple and first successor of St Benedict at Montecassino.

Constantine (St) M.   July 27
One of the Seven Sleepers, q.v.

Constantinople (Martyrs of)
Three anonymous groups of martyrs put to death at Constantinople were commemorated in the pre-1970 RM, viz. —

Feb 8
d. 485   The community of monks of St Dius martyred at the time of the Acacian schism for their fidelity to the Holy See.

March 30
d. 351–359   A great number of people who suffered under the Arian emperor Constantius.

July 8
d. 832   The Abrahamite monks, put to death under the iconoclast emperor Theophilus.

Constantius and Comp. (SS) MM.   Jan 29
d. 170   Constantius, first bishop of Perugia, was put to death with numerous Christians of his flock, under Marcus Aurelius. The Acts of these martyrs are far from trustworthy. See Simplicius, Constantius and Victorian (Aug 26).

Constantius of Fabriano (Bl) C. OP.   Feb 25
d. 1481   Constantius Bernocchi was born at Fabriano in the Marches of Ancona and at the age of fifteen entered the Dominican order. He had as masters Bl Conradin and St Antoninus. Appointed prior of the friary of San Marco at Florence, he achieved there a complete reform. He was renowned for his gift of prophecy. Beatified in 1811.

Constantius (St) M.   Aug 26
See Simplicius, Constantius and Victorian.

Constantius (St) Bp.   Sept 1
d. *c* 520   Bishop of Aquino. He is mentioned with great honour by St Gregory the Great in his Dialogues.

Constantius (St) C.   Sept 23
6th cent.   Sacristan of the ancient church of St Stephen at Ancona. He is still greatly venerated in that city.

Constantius (St) C.   Nov 30
5th cent.   A priest of Rome who strongly opposed the Pelagians, at whose hands he had much to endure.

Constantius (St) M.   Dec 12
See Maxentius, Constantius, etc.

Contardo of Este (St) C.   Apr 16
d. 1249   Surnamed "the Pilgrim". He belonged to the Este family of Ferrara. He set out on a pilgrimage to Compostella, but died at Broni, diocese of Tortona, in extreme poverty.

Contardo Ferrini (Bl) C.   Oct 17
1859–1902   He was born at Milan and studied at the university of Pavia. After taking degrees in civil and canon law he taught at Messina, Mutina and finally Pavia. A Franciscan tertiary, a member of the Society of Saint Vincent de Paul, and a friend of Mgr Achilles Ratti (later Pope Pius XI), he was the model of a Catholic professor, and remarkable for his "inexhaustible desire for prayer". He died comparatively young at Suna on the shore of Lake Maggiore. Beatified in 1947.

Contestus (St) Bp.   Jan 19
d. *c* 510   Bishop of Bayeux in Normandy from 480 till his death.

Conus (St) Mk. OSB.   June 3
d. *c* 1200   Benedictine monk of Cardossa in Lucania. His relics were enshrined in the neighbouring village of Diano (1261), the saint's native place.

Convoyon (St) Ab. OSB.   Jan 5
d. 868   A Breton by birth, he became successively archdeacon of Vannes, recluse, monk at Glanfeuil, and lastly abbot-founder of the great Benedictine monastery of St Saviour (831) near Redon, in Brittany. He was driven from his abbey by the Norsemen and died in exile. Cult confirmed, with the title of saint, in 1866.

Conwall (Conval) (St) C.   Sept 28
d. *c* 630   An Irish priest, disciple of St Kentigern, who preached and died in Scotland.

Copres (St) M.   July 9
See Patermuthius, Copres, etc.

Corbican (St) C.   June 26
8th cent.   An Irish recluse in the Low Countries who spent part of his day helping and instructing the peasants.

Corbinian (St) Bp.   Sept 8
670–730   A Frank who spent fourteen years as a hermit and then went to Rome, where Pope Gregory II ordained him bishop and sent him to evangelize Germany. Corbinian established his residence at Freising in Bavaria. His last years were made very trying by Duke

Grimoald, whose incestuous marriage the saint had denounced.

Corbmac (St) Ab. June 21
6th cent. A disciple of St Columba, placed by him over the monastery he had founded at Durrow.

Cordula (St) VM. formerly Oct 22
d. *c* 453 An apocryphal saint who belongs to the legendary group of St Ursula and her eleven thousand virgins. Cult suppressed in 1969.

Corea (Martyrs of) Sept 22
See Laurence Imbert, etc.

Corebus (St) M. Apr 18
c 117–138 A prefect of Messina in Sicily converted to Christ by St Eleutherius and martyred under the emperor Hadrian. It seems, however, that the Acts of St Eleutherius and Anthia are entirely fictitious.

Corentinus (Cury) (St)
Bp. Dec 12
d. *c* 490 The first bishop of Cornouaille, now Quimper, in Brittany. He had been a recluse at Plomodiern. His cult spread throughout S.W. England, where he was known as St Cury.

Corfu (Martyrs of) Apr 29
1st cent. Known as "the Seven Holy Thieves". Seven criminals converted to Christ, it is said, by St Jason, a disciple of our Lord (Acts 17:5). Their names are given as Saturninus, Inischolus, Faustian, Januarius, Massalius, Euphrasius, and Mannonius. They were martyred in the island of Corfu. The story is from a Greek Menology.

Cormac (St) Bp. Sept 14
d. 908 Probably the first bishop of Cashel. He is likewise known as king of Munster and was slain in battle. The "Psalter of Cashel" compiled by him is still extant.

Cormac (St) Ab. Dec 12
6th cent. An Irish abbot, friend of St Columba.

Cornelia (St) M. March 31
See Theodulus, Anesius, etc.

Cornelius (St) Bp. Feb 2
1st cent. The centurion of the Italic cohort, baptized at Caesarea in Palestine by the apostle St Peter (Acts 10). Tradition makes him the first bishop of Caesarea; and as such he was described in the pre-1970 RM.

Cornelius (St)
Bp. OSA. June 4
c 1120–1176 Cornelius Mc Conchailleach,

St Cornelius, Sept 16

an Irishman by birth, joined the Augustinian canons regular at Armagh in 1140, was chosen abbot there in 1151, and finally became archbishop of that city in 1174. He died at Chambèry in Savoy on his return from a pilgrimage to Rome and is still held in great veneration there.

Cornelius (St) M. OFM. July 9
d. 1572 Born at Dorestat near Utrecht, he took the Franciscan habit at Gorkum, Holland, and was hanged by Calvinists at Briel with eighteen companions. (See Gorkum Martyrs.)

Cornelius (St) Pope M. GC. Sept 16
d. 253 The violent persecution suffered by the Roman church under Decius resulted in the delay of over a year before Cornelius could be chosen as bishop by the Christians there. During this persecution many had fallen away and Cornelius favoured a pastorally sensitive and forgiving approach to their readmission. However Novatian, a talented cleric in Rome, set himself up as a rival bishop, denying the right of the church to forgive those who had lapsed. Cyprian of Carthage and others supported Cornelius, and eventually Novatian was excommunicated, and the more moderate policy enacted. A revival of persecution entailed Cornelius' banishment to Centumcellae

(Civita Vecchia), where his sufferings probably hastened his death: St Cyprian later refers to him as a martyr. His tomb in the crypt of Lucina in the cemetery of Callixtus is still extant, and his name was included in the first eucharistic prayer. In art he is shown vested as a pope holding a cow's horn, or with a cow near him.

Cornelius (St) M.   Dec 31
See Stephen, Pontian, etc.

Corona (Bl) V. OSB.   Apr 24
? A Benedictine nun of the convent of Elche, near Valencia in Spain.

Corona (St) M.   May 14
See Victor and Corona.

**Cosmas Tachegia
(Zaquira) (St)** M. Tert.
OFM.   Feb 6
d. 1597 A Japanese Franciscan tertiary who served the Franciscan missionaries as interpreter. He was crucified with St Peter Baptist and twenty-four companions at Nagasaki. Beatified in 1627: canonized in 1862. See St Paul Miki and Comps.

Cosmas Taquea (Bl) M.   June 1
d. 1619 (Nov 18) A layman, native of Korea, taken to Japan as a prisoner of war. There he became a member of the Confraternity of the Rosary and gave shelter to Bl John of St Dominic. He was in consequence burnt alive. Beatified in 1867.

Cosmas (St) Bp. M.   Sept 10
d. 1160 Born at Palermo in Sicily, he was appointed bishop of Aphrodisia and ordained by Eugene III. The Saracens captured his episcopal city and he died as a consequence of maltreatment at their hands. Cult approved by Leo XIII.

**Cosmas and Damian
(SS)** MM.   GC. Sept 26
d. c 303 Twin Arab brothers, physicians by profession, who were martyred at Cyrrhus, traditionally under Diocletian. They practised their profession without taking payment from their patients, and on this account they are surnamed in the East *Anargyroi* (the moneyless ones). Their relics were brought to Rome, whence their cult spread throughout the West. They are mentioned in the first eucharistic prayer. In the Middle Ages their cult was extremely popular and many beautiful legends grew up around them; they were often used as subjects by artists and iconographers. They are usually depicted as doctors of medicine with robes and surgical instruments contemporary with each depiction.

St Cosmas, Sept 26

**Cosmo di Carbognano
(Bl)**   Nov 5
Otherwise Gomidas, q.v.

Cottam (Thomas) (Bl)
M.   May 30
See Thomas Cottam.

**Cottidus, Eugene and
Comp. (SS)** MM.   Sept 6
? Cappadocian martyrs, whose *Acta* have not

come down to us. St Cottidus is described as a deacon.

Cottolengo (Joseph-Benedict) (St)   Apr 29
See Joseph-Benedict Cottolengo.

Craton and Comp. (SS)
MM.   Feb 15
d. *c* 273   Craton, a philosopher and professor of rhetoric, was converted to Christ by St Valentine, bishop of Terni. He was martyred in Rome together with his wife, and family.

Credan (St) Ab. OSB.   Aug 19
d. *c* 780   Eighth abbot of Evesham in the time of King Offa of Mercia.

Crementius (St) M.   Apr 16
See Caius and Crementius.

Crescens (St) M.   March 10
See Codratus, Dionysius, etc.

Crescens (St) M.   Apr 15
? A martyr of Myra in Lycia, Asia Minor, who perished at the stake.

Crescens, Dioscorides, Paul and Helladius (SS)
MM.   May 28
d. *c* 244   Roman Christians who were burnt to death. Helladius does not seem to have belonged to this group.

Crescens (St) Bp. M.   June 27
2nd cent.   The disciple of St Paul mentioned by him (2 Tim. 4:10) as having gone into Galatia. He is stated to have been appointed bishop of the Galatians. Tradition tells us of his apostolate in France and also that he founded the see of Mainz in Gaul. Then he returned to the east and was martyred under Trajan. It is certain that the Crescens who was first bishop of Vienne and the Crescens who worked at Mainz were not the disciples of St Paul, even if they did really exist.

Crescens (St) M.   July 18
See Symphorosa and Comp.

Crescens (St) M.   Oct 1
See Priscus, Crescens and Evagrius.

Crescens (St) Bp.   Nov 28
See Valerian, Urban, etc.

Crescentia Hoss (Bl) V.
Tert. OFM.   Apr 5
1682–1744   Born at Kaufbeuren in Bavaria. In 1703, at the request of the Protestant mayor of the town, she was admitted to the convent of the Franciscan regular tertiaries, but the nuns neglected and even persecuted her because she had entered without a dowry. Her holiness, however, overcame their hostility, and

eventually she was made novice-mistress, and superioress. Beatified in 1900.

Crescentia (St) VM.   June 15
See Vitus, Modestus and Crescentia.

Crescentian (St) M.   May 31
d. *c* 130   A martyr who suffered at Sassari, in Sardinia, at the same time as SS Gabinus and Crispulus, in the reign of the emperor Hadrian. He is still held in great veneration there.

Crescentian (St) M.   June 1
d. *c* 287   A soldier beheaded at Saldo, near Città di Castello (*Tiphernum*) in Italy. His historical existence is doubtful.

Crescentian (St) M.   July 2
See Ariston, Crescentian, etc.

Crescentian (St) M.   Aug 12
See Hilaria, Digna, etc.

Crescentian, Victor, Rosula, and Generalis
(SS) MM.   Sept 14
d. *c* 258   African martyrs, alleged to have suffered at the same time and place as St Cyprian.

Crescentian (St) M.   Nov 24
d. 309   A martyr who suffered at Rome in company with SS Cyriacus, Largus and Smaragdus, expiring on the rack in their presence under Maxentius.

Crescentian (St) Bp.   Nov 28
See Valerian, Urban, etc.

Crescentiana (St) M.   May 5
5th cent.   Beyond the fact that as early as the time of Pope Symmachus (498–514) a church in Rome was dedicated to her, nothing is known of this martyr.

Crescentio (St) M.   Sept 17
See Narcissus and Crescentio.

Crescentius (St) C.   Apr 19
d. *c* 396   A subdeacon of Florence, a disciple of St Zenobius and of St Ambrose.

Crescentius (St) M.   Sept 14
d. *c* 300   A boy, only eleven years of age, the son of St Euthymius, q.v., who, in the persecution of Diocletian, was brought from Perugia to Rome, bravely confessed Christ under torture, and was beheaded.

Crescentius (St) M.   Dec 12
See Maxentius, Constantius, etc.

Crescentius (St) Bp.
Otherwise Crescens (June 27) q.v.

Crescentius (St) M.   Dec 29
See Dominic, Victor, etc.

Cresconius (St) Bp. M.   Nov 28
See Valerian, Urban, etc.

Crete (Martyrs of)   Dec 23
For this group of ten martyrs, who suffered in
Crete, see Theodulus, Saturninus, etc.

Crewenna (St)   Feb 1
5th cent. This saint accompanied St Breaca
from Ireland to Cornwall. There is no record
of him beyond the place-name Crowan near St
Erth.

Crispin (St) Bp.   Jan 7
Two bishops of this name, both saints, served
the see of Pavia in Lombardy: one in the first
half of the third century occupied the see for
thirty-five years, the second was bishop during
the reign of Pope St Leo the Great and in 451
subscribed the acts of the council of Milan. It
is apparently the second who is commemorated on Jan 7.

**Crispin of Viterbo (St) C.
OFM. Cap.**   May 23
1668–1750 A native of Viterbo, who joined
the Capuchins as a lay-brother and was employed as a cook in the friaries of Viterbo,
Tolfa, Rome and Albano. He loved to call
himself "the little beast of burden of the
Capuchins". Beatified in 1806. Canonized in
1982.

**Crispin and Crispinian
(SS) MM.**   Oct 25
d. c 285 Two brothers, shoemakers by
trade, who were beheaded at Soissons in
France under Diocletian. They were held in
great popular veneration throughout the
Middle Ages (see in this connection Shake-
speare's Henry V, Act IV, Scene 3) and are still
the patron saints of shoemakers. An English
tradition popular until well after the Reformation held that they had lived for a while in
Faversham, Kent, during a persecution. In art
they are shown holding shoes, or cobbling
equipment.

Crispin (St) Bp. M.   Nov 19
4th cent. Bishop of Ecija (*Astiagis*) in Andalusia, beheaded under Maximian Herculeus.
He is honoured with a special office in the
Mozarabic breviary.

Crispin (St) M.   Dec 3
See Claudius, Crispin, etc.

Crispin (St) M.   Dec 5
See Julius, Potamia, etc.

Crispina (St) M.   Dec 5
d. 304 A wealthy matron of Thebeste in

Numidia. She was tortured, forced to undergo
the most shameful indignities and ultimately
beheaded. We have still a glowing panegyric
preached by St Augustine in her honour.

Crispulus (St) M.   May 30
See Gabinus and Crispulus.

**Crispulus and Restitutus
(SS) MM.**   June 10
1st cent. Martyrs believed to have suffered
under Nero, and probably in Rome. Baronius,
however, following Rabanus Maurus, assigns
them to Spain. No account of them is extant.

Crispus (St) M.   Aug 18
See John and Crispus.

**Crispus and Gaius (SS)
MM.**   Oct 4
1st cent. Saints of the apostolic age, the only
two whom St Paul baptized at Corinth (1 Cor.
1: 14). Crispus was ruler of the synagogue in
that city (Acts 18:8). Gaius in all likelihood is
the same person whom the apostle styles "my
host" (Rom. 16:23), and also the "dearly
beloved Gaius" to whom St John addressed
his third epistle. According to traditions, both
became bishops: the former of the island of
Aegina, the latter of Thessalonica.

Cristiolus (St)   Nov 3
7th cent. A Welsh saint, brother of St Sulian
and founder of churches, including one in
Anglesey.

**Croidan, Medan and
Degan (SS)**   June 4
6th cent. Three disciples of St Petroc, q.v.

Cronan Beg (St) Bp.   Jan 7
7th cent. A bishop of ancient Aendrum, Co.
Down, mentioned in connection with the
paschal controversy in 640.

Cronan the Wise (St) Bp.   Feb 9
? 8th cent. Surnamed "the wise" on account
of his ability in systematizing Irish canon law.
He is probably identical with St Roman,
bishop of Lismore.

**Cronan of Roscrea (St)
Ab.**   Apr 28
d. c 626 Born in Munster, founder of several religious houses in various parts of Ireland, chief among them being that of Roscrea.

Cronan (St)   June 3
d. 617 Surnamed "the Tanner". A disciple
of St Kevin.

Cronidas (St) M.   March 27
See Philetus, Lydia, etc.

Cronion (St) M.   Oct 30
See Julian, Cronion, etc.

Cross (St)

Churches dedicated to St Cross are dedicated not to a person but to the Cross of Our Lord Jesus Christ. In this case St stands for "Holy". The medieval hospital of St Cross at Winchester founded by Henry of Blois (1129–1171) is an example. In the American continent places called Vera Cruz derive their names from relics of the True Cross being enshrined there.

Crotates (St) M.   Apr 21
See Apollo, Isacius, etc.

Croyland (Martyrs of) (SS) OSB.   Apr 9
See Theodore and Comp.

Crummine (St) Bp.   June 28
5th cent.   A disciple of St Patrick, placed by him over the church of Leccuine (Lackan) Co. Westmeath.

Ctesiphon (St) Bp.   May 15
See Torquatus, Ctesiphon, etc.

Cuan (St) Ab.   Jan 1
6th cent.   An Irish abbot, called Mochua or Moncan, who founded many churches and monasteries, and who lived to close upon his hundredth year.

Cuaran (Curvinus, Cronan) (St) Bp.   Feb 9
d. p.700   An Irish bishop, surnamed like several others, "the Wise", who concealed his identity in order to become a monk at Iona, where, however, he was recognized by St Columba.

Cuby (St)   Nov 8
See Cybi (Cuby).

Cucuphas (Cucufate, Cugat, Guinefort, Qoqofas) (St) M.   July 25
d. 304   A son of noble parents of Punic descent resident at Scillis in Africa. He crossed over to Spain and was martyred near Barcelona at the place where some centuries later arose the Benedictine abbey of St Cugat del Valles. He is one of the most celebrated of the Spanish martyrs. Prudentius composed some exquisite stanzas in his honour. Part of his relics were venerated at Paris.

Culmatius (St) M.   June 19
See Gaudentius and Culmatius.

Cumgar (Cungar, Cyngar) (St) C.   Nov 7
6th (or 8th) cent.   A native of Devon, founder of monasteries at Budgworth, Congresbury (Somerset) and at Llangennith (West Glamorgan). He is to be identified with St Docuinus,

or Doguinus. This seems to be the name which was later corrupted into Oue and Kew. St Cumgar was buried at Congresbury, to which town he has given his name.

Cumine the White (St) Ab.   Feb 24 or Oct 6
d. 669   An abbot of Iona of Irish descent, who wrote a life of St Columba.

Cummian (Cumian, Cummin) (St) Bp. OSB.   June 9
1st half 8th cent.   An Irish bishop who in his wanderings through Italy visited Bobbio and remained there as a monk. By this time Bobbio was already a Benedictine abbey.

Cummian Fada (St) Ab.   Nov 12
d. 662   An Irish monk who had charge of the monastic school at Clonfert and became the abbot-founder of the monastery at Kilcummin, where he strenuously defended the Roman computation of Easter against his Celtic brethren.

Cuncolim (Martyrs of)   July 27
See Rudolph Acquaviva and Comp.

Cunegund (St) V. OSB.   March 3
d. 1039   Wife of Henry II, Holy Roman Emperor, with whom she lived in conjugal virginity and is, for this reason, venerated as a virgin. She founded the Benedictine nunnery of Kaufungen, which she entered on the first anniversary of her husband's death (1024) and where she earnestly endeavoured to forget her past social position. Canonized in 1200.

Cunegund (Bl) V. OSB.   May 4
d. p.1052   A Benedictine nun of the convent of Niedermunster in Ratisbon.

Cunegund (Bl) V.   July 24
Otherwise Kinga, q.v.

Cunera (St) V.   June 12
? A saint venerated more particularly in Germany, but said to have been of British birth. The traditions relating to her are most untrustworthy.

Cuniald and Gislar (SS)   Sept 24
7th century Confessors.

Cunibert (St) Ab. OSB.   Sept 16
d. c680   Successor of St Humbert as abbot of Maroilles, in the diocese of Cambrai.

Cunibert (St) Bp.   Nov 12
d. c663   A Frankish courtier who became successively archdeacon of Trier and archbishop of Cologne. He filled the office of chief minister during the minority of King Sigebert

of Australasia. He was an untiring builder of churches and monasteries.

Curcodomus (St) C.   May 4
3rd cent.   A Roman deacon, sent by the pope to attend St Peregrinus, first bishop of Auxerre, on his mission into Gaul.

Curé d'Ars (St) C.   Aug 9
See John Baptist Vianney.

Curig (St) Bp.   June 16
6th cent.   Stated to have been bishop of Llanbadarn in Wales, in which country several churches are dedicated in his honour. There is, however, great difficulty in distinguishing him from other saints bearing similar names.

Curitan (St) Bp.   March 14
Otherwise Boniface, q.v.

Curonotus (St) Bp. M.   Sept 12
d. c 258   A bishop of Iconium in Lycaonia, Asia Minor, martyred under Valerian.

Cury (St) Bp.   Dec 12
Otherwise Corentinus, q.v.

Cuthbert (St) Bp. OSB.   Sept 4
d. 687   A Briton who in his youth tended his father's sheep until he embraced the monastic life at Melrose. When Ripon abbey was founded he was sent there as guest-master, then he became prior of Melrose. Finally, after the council of Whitby, he was asked to go to Lindisfarne, now under the new Benedictine observance, and was made prior of the abbey. In March, 685, he was ordained abbot-bishop of Lindisfarne by St Theodore at York. After his death his body was found to be incorrupt. When the hostile incursions of the Vikings ended monastic life at Lindisfarne in 875, his shrine was transported across England until it reached Durham by 995. St Cuthbert is one of the most famous of English saints. He was moreover the wonder-worker of England, and his shrine at Durham was one of the most frequented in the Middle Ages: it was already an ancient shrine before St Thomas of Canterbury was born. His relics remain at Durham: they were incorrupt when the body was examined from time to time in the Middle Ages. At the destruction of the shrine in the sixteenth century his relics were reburied on the spot where it had stood. In 1828 a further examination took place and the pectoral cross, vestments and ancient coffin were removed and may still be seen at Durham. The shrine was last opened in March 1899. In art St Cuthbert is shown as a bishop, holding the crowned head of St Oswald, and sometimes accompanied by swans and otters. In medieval times his feast was March 20. It has been

St Cuthbert, Sept 4

changed to Sept 4 in modern times so as to keep it out of Lent. Sept 4 was in ancient days celebrated as the feast of the translation of his relics.

Cuthbert (St) Bp. OSB.   Oct 26
d. 758   A monk of Lyminge in Kent who became bishop of Hereford (c 736) and archbishop of Canterbury (c 740). He is best remembered as one of the English correspondents of St Boniface.

Cuthbert Mayne (St) M.   Nov 29
1544–1577   Born near Barnstaple in Devonshire, he was educated as a Protestant, but he was converted to Catholicism while an undergraduate at St John's, Oxford. He was ordained at Douai and sent to the English mission (c 1575). He laboured in Cornwall, but before a year had elapsed was captured and condemned for the crime of celebrating the mass. He was executed at Launceston. Beatified in

1886, he is the protomartyr of the English seminaries. Canonized in 1970 as one of the Forty Martyrs of England and Wales q.v.

Cuthburga (St) Abs. OSB.   Aug 31
d. *c* 725   Sister to King Ina of Wessex. She married Aldfrid of Northumbria (688) who allowed her to enter as a nun at Barking under St Hildelid. Some time after 705 she founded, with her sister St Queenburga, Wimborne abbey in Dorset, which she governed as abbess. From this nunnery came forth the band of missionary nuns who helped in the evangelization of Germany.

Cuthman (St) H.   Feb 8
9th cent.   A south of England saint who lived a holy life as a shepherd near Steyning in Sussex. The old church of that place was dedicated in his honour. Later his relics were transferred to Fécamp in France.

Cutias (St) M.   Feb 18
See Maximus, Claudius, etc.

Cybar (St) Ab.   July 1
Otherwise Eparchius, q.v.

Cybi (Cuby) (St)   Nov 8
6th cent.   A Welsh saint who was an abbot, and with St Seiroil is one of the most highly venerated saints in Anglesey. He was the founder of a monastery there, called Caer Gybi (the fortress of Cybi) as it is within the confines of an old Roman fortress. He is the patron saint of Llangibby (Monmouth) and of Llangybi (Gwynedd), and in Cornwall of Tregony, Landulph and Cuby. As with all the Celtic saints, legends grew up about his name. The above facts, however, seem certain.

Cyndeyrn (St) Bp.   Jan 14
Otherwise Kentigern, q.v.

Cynfarch (St)   Sept 8
Otherwise Kingsmark, q.v.

Cynfran (St) C   Nov 11
5th cent.   A Welsh saint, one of the sons of the chieftain Brychan of Brecknock and founder of a church in Gwynedd. There is also a St Cynfran's well.

Cynibild (St) C.   March 2
7th cent.   A brother of SS Chad and Cedd who also laboured in the evangelization of the Anglo-Saxons.

Cynidr (Kenedrus) (St) Ab.   Apr 27
Otherwise Enoder, q.v.

Cynllo (St)   July 17
5th cent.   A Welsh saint, in whose honour several churches are dedicated.

St Cyprian, Sept 16

Cynog (St) M.   Oct 7
Otherwise Canog, q.v.

Cynwl (St) H.   Apr 30
6th cent.   The brother of St Deiniol, first bishop of Bangor. He lived an austere life in N. Wales, and after his death churches were dedicated in his honour.

Cyprian (St) M.   March 10
See Codratus, Dionysius, etc.

Cyprian (St) Bp.   Apr 21
d. 582   Bishop of Brescia in Lombardy. His relics are enshrined in the church of San Pietro in Oliveto at Brescia.

Cyprian (St) M.   July 11
See Sabinus and Cyprian.

Cyprian (St) Bp. M.   GC. Sept 16
c 200–258   Thascius Cecilianus Cyprianus

was born in proconsular Africa, became a lawyer, was converted to Christianity and was ordained bishop of Carthage (248). It is as a bishop that he played a most important part in the history of the Western church. As such he produced numerous treatises on various theological subjects, one of the most important being *De Unitate Catholicae Ecclesiae* (251) and wrote numerous letters. He is in fact, like Tertullian, a pioneer of Latin Christian literature. His writings are distinguished, like his life, by his compassion, discretion and pastoral zeal. He seconded Pope St Cornelius's teaching on the reconciliation of fallen Christians. He erred, however, on the doctrine of the validity of baptism conferred by heretics. Nevertheless, the Roman church has always been grateful to his memory and mentions his name in the first eucharistic prayer. Cyprian went into hiding during the persecution of Decius, but was arrested and beheaded under the first edict of Valerian. The Acts of his martyrdom are of great charm and interest. In art he is shown as a bishop holding a palm and a sword. His church at Clarence Gate, London, is of exquisite beauty.

Cyprian and Justina (SS)
MM.   formerly Sept 26
The legend is that Cyprian, a pagan necromancer and astrologer, was converted to Christianity by the virgin Justina whom he had tried to lead astray. In the persecution under Diocletian they were both arrested and beheaded at Nicomedia. There is no evidence whatever to justify the belief that these two persons ever existed. The story is merely a moral fable. Cults suppressed in 1969.

Cyprian (St) Bp.   Oct 3
6th cent.   Monk of St Victor at Marseilles, and bishop of Toulon (516). He was a staunch opponent of Semi-Pelagianism. He has left us the life of his master St Caesarius of Arles.

Cyprian (St) M.   Oct 12
See Felix and Cyprian.

Cyprian (St) Ab.   Dec 9
d. 586   A monk of Périgueux, France, who ended his life as a hermit on the banks of the Dordogne. St Gregory of Tours has left an account of St Cyprian's life and miracles.

Cyr (St) M.   June 16
See Quiricius and Julitta.

Cyra (St)   Aug 3
See Marana and Cyra.

Cyrenia and Juliana (SS)
MM.   Nov 1
d. 306   Two Christian women burnt to death at Tarsus in Asia Minor under Maximian.

Cyria (St) M.   June 5
See Zenais, Cyria, etc.

Cyriaca, Cyriacus, etc.
Note. These names, common to many saints, are often found written Quiriacus, Quiriaca, etc. Sometimes they are replaced by their equivalent Latin forms, Dominicus, Dominica, etc. Less frequently, the spelling Kyriacus, Kiriacus, etc., is met with.

Cyriaca (St) M.   March 20
See Photina, Joseph, etc.

Cyriaca and Comp. (SS)
VV. MM.   May 19
d. 307   Six Christian maidens who perished at the stake at Nicomedia under Galerius.

Cyriaca (Dominica) (St) M.   Aug 21
d. 249   A wealthy Roman widow, who sheltered the persecuted Christians and to whose house St Laurence, the deacon and martyr, was accustomed to repair to distribute his alms. The Roman Church of St Mary in *Dominica* perpetuates her name.

Cyriacus (St) M.   Jan 31
See Tarcisius, Zoticus, etc.

Cyriacus (St) M.   Feb 8
See Paul, Lucius and Cyriacus.

Cyriacus and Comp.
(SS) MM.   Apr 7
? Eleven Christians, martyred at Nicomedia in Asia Minor.

Cyriacus (St) M.   May 2
See Exuperius, Zoe, etc.

Cyriacus (Quiriacus) (St)
M. Bp.   May 4
? Most probably a bishop of Ancona in Italy, who while making his pilgrimage to the Holy Land, was martyred under Julian the Apostate. Others assert that he was a bishop of Jerusalem put to death under Hadrian.

Cyriacus (St) M.   June 5
See Florentius, Julian, etc.

Cyriacus and Julitta (SS)
MM.   June 16
Otherwise Quiricus and Julitta, q.v.

Cyriacus and Paula (St)
MM.   June 18
d. 305   Two Christians, stoned to death at

Málaga in Spain under Diocletian. St Paula is registered as a virgin-martyr.

Cyriacus (St) M.   June 20
See Paul and Cyriacus.

Cyriacus and Apollinaris
(SS) MM.   June 21
? African martyrs, registered in the martyrologies, but whose Acts have been lost.

Cyriacus (St) M.   June 24
See Orentius, Heros, etc.

Cyriacus (St) M.   July 15
See Antiochus and Cyriacus.

Cyriacus, Largus,
Smaragdus and Comp.
(SS) MM.   Aug 8
d. 304   A group of twenty-four martyrs who suffered in Rome under Diocletian. At their head was St Cyriacus, a deacon, who at a later period gave his name to a church. The Acts are worthless, and the only certain fact is that Cyriacus gave his name to the church. All that is known for certain is that the martyrs were buried near the seventh milestone on the Ostian Way. Cult confined to particular calendars since 1969.

Cyriacus (St) H.   Sept 29
d. 556   Hermit and abbot in Palestine. He died in the *laura* of St Sabas. His life was written by St Cyril of Scythopolis.

Cyriacus (St) Bp.   Oct 27
d. 606   Administrator, and afterwards patriarch, of Constantinople. The Greeks commemorate him on Oct 29.

Cyriacus, Paulillus,
Secundus, Anastasius,
Sindimius and Comp. (SS)
MM.   Dec 19
d. 303   A group of Christians, martyred at Nicomedia under Diocletian. No other particulars are extant.

Cyril and Methodius
(SS) CC.   GC. Feb 14
d. 869 and 885   Two brothers who are venerated as the "Apostles of the Slavs". Cyril, or Constantine, was a secular priest and Methodius a monk in a Greek monastery. In 863 they began to evangelize Moravia. They met with opposition there from German missionaries and came to Rome to ask the apostolic blessing on their work. Cyril now became a monk at SS Boniface and Alexius on the Aventine, and died shortly after. Methodius was ordained bishop and returned to preach in Moravia and Pannonia with permission to celebrate the liturgy in Slavonic. This conces-

sion turned the German bishops against his work, and they even put him in prison. His apostolate, however, met with signal success. He translated most of the Bible into Slavonic. Pope John Paul II, on 31 Dec 1980, proclaimed them co-patrons of Europe, with St Benedict.

Cyril (St) M.   March 4
See Archelaus, Cyril and Photius.

Cyril of Constantinople
(St) C. OC.   March 6
d. 1235   Born of Greek parents at Constantinople, he was ordained priest and was noted as a teacher of true sanctity. At the age of forty-six he became a Carmelite in Palestine and was prior general for seventeen years.

Cyril, Rogatus, Felix,
another Rogatus, Beata,
Herenia, Felicitas,
Urban, Silvanus, and
Mamillus
(SS) MM.   March 8
? African martyrs — Cyril is described as a bishop — registered in all the ancient lists, but of whom nothing is known.

Cyril of Jerusalem (St)
Bp. Dr.   GC. March 18
c 315–386   Born near Jerusalem, he became a priest in 345, and patriarch of the city from c 350 till his death. Seventeen years of his patriarchate he spent in exile, driven out by the Arians. His name is forever connected with his work as a catechist: his instructions on Christian doctrine, addressed to the catechumens before baptism, are gems of theological literature. He was declared Doctor of the Church by Leo XIII in 1882.

Cyril (St) M.   March 20
See Paul, Cyril, etc.

Cyril (St) M.   March 29
d. c 362   A deacon of Heliopolis in the Lebanon, who suffered under Julian the Apostate.

Cyril (St) Bp.   May 19
5th cent.   A bishop of Trier, whose relics were enshrined in the abbey church St Matthias in that city.

Cyril (St) M.   May 29
d. ? 251   A boy of Caesarea in Cappadocia, who embraced Christianity without his father's knowledge. He was turned out of his home, arrested and put to death.

Cyril of Alexandria (St)
Bp. Dr.   GC. June 27
c 376–444   A native of Alexandria who

became patriarch of that city in 412. His name in history is famous as the untiring opponent of Nestorianism, which he denounced to Pope St Celestine I. The pope appointed him to preside at the council of Ephesus in 431, at which Nestorius was definitely condemned. Stressing the truth of Christ's divinity, St Cyril employs a terminology that sometimes seems to favour Monophysitism, and this is the reason why Monophysite Copts, Syrians and Ethiopians venerate him as their chief teacher. He was declared Doctor of the Church by Leo XIII.

Cyril (St) Bp. M.   July 9
d. 250   An aged bishop of Gortyna in Crete, tortured and beheaded under Decius.

Cyril (St) Bp.   July 22
d. c 300   The successor of Timaeus (280) in the patriarchate of Antioch. He had much to endure in the persecution of Diocletian, but appears to have died in peace.

Cyril, Aquila, Peter, Domitian, Rufus, and Menander (SS) MM.   Aug 1
This group of martyrs had a local feast at Philadelphia in Arabia. They were not martyred there, and Peter is apparently the Apostle, Rufus of Rome, and Cyril of Times.

Cyril (St) M.   Oct 2
See Primus, Cyril and Secundarius.

Cyril (St) M.   Oct 28
See Anastasia and Cyril.

Cyrilla (St) M.   July 5
d. c 300   An aged widow of Cyrene, condemned to death, but who appears to have expired in the torture chamber. Several other martyrs suffered at the same time.

Cyrilla (St) VM.   Oct 28
d. 268–270   The daughter of St Tryphonia and a sharer in the good works of that saintly

Roman widow. She was put to death under the emperor Claudius II.

Cyrinus, Primus, and Theogenes (SS) MM.   Jan 3
d. 320   Soldiers in the imperial army who were martyred at Cyzicus on the Hellespont under the emperor Licinius.

Cyrinus (St) M.   May 10
See Alphius, Philadelphus and Cyrinus.

Cyrinus (St) M.   June 12
See Basilides, Cyrinus, etc.

Cyrinus (St) M.   Oct 25
3rd cent.   A Roman martyr under Diocletian of whom mention is made in the Acts of St Marcellinus, pope and martyr, whose cult is now suppressed.

Cyrion, Bassian, Agatho and Moses (SS) MM.   Feb 14
? A group of martyrs of Alexandria, listed together because all perished at the stake. Cyrion was a priest, Bassian a lector, Agatho an exorcist, and Moses a layman.

Cyrion and Candidus (SS) MM.   formerly March 9
The two most conspicuous among the Forty Armenian Martyrs, q.v. Their cult was suppressed in 1969.

Cyrus and John (SS) MM.   Jan 31
d. c 303   Two physicians of Alexandria who went to Canopus to assist a woman and her three daughters who were being persecuted as Christians. All were martyred together.

Cyrus of Carthage (St) Bp.   July 14
? St Possidius, the biographer of St Augustine, speaks of a sermon delivered by the latter on the feast of St Cyrus. Probably he meant St Cyprian.

Cythinus (St) M.   July 17
One of the Scillitan Martyrs, q.v.

Dabeoc (St) Ab.   Jan 1
Otherwise Beoc, q.v.

Dabius (Davius) (St) C.   July 22
? An Irish priest who worked in Scotland,
where he is the titular of several churches. He
may be identical with St Movean or Biteus,
disciple of St Patrick.

Dacian (Datianus) (St) M.   June 4
See Aretius and Dacian.

Dacius (St) M.   Nov 1
See Caesarius, Dacius and Comp.

Dadas (St) M.   Apr 13
See Maximus, Quintilian and Dadas.

**Dadas (Didas), Casdoe,
and Gabdelas (SS)** MM.   Sept 29
c 310–368   Dadas, a noble Persian, Casdoe,
his wife, and Gabdelas, probably their son,
were of the number of the many martyrs who
suffered under Shapur II, to whom Dadas was
kinsman.

Dafrosa (Affrosa) (St) M.   Jan 4
? According to the untrustworthy Acts of St
Bibiana, St Dafrosa, her mother, was martyred
under Julian the Apostate. It is probably all a
fiction.

Dagan (St) M.   Aug 27
Otherwise Decuman, q.v.

Dagobert II (St) King M.   Dec 23
d. 679   Son of St Sigebert III, and king of
Austrasia. He was exiled to a monastery in
656, recalled in 675 and murdered by order of
Ebroin, mayor of the palace. His death has
been traditionally regarded as a martyrdom.

**Daig Maccairill
(Dagaeus, Daganus)** Bp.   Aug 18
d. 586   Son of Cayrill, he was a disciple of St
Finian and founded a monastery at Inis Cain
Dega (Iniskeen). He was bishop and abbot.
The Book of Leinster makes him "one of the
Three Master Craftsmen of Ireland".

**Dallan Forgaill (of
Cluain Dallain) (St)** M.   Jan 29
d. 598   A kinsman of St Aidan of Ferns,
born in Connaught, and a great scholar.
Through his application to study he became

blind. He is best remembered for his poem in
honour of St Columba, called *Ambra Choluim
Kille*. He was murdered at Inis-coel by pirates.

Dalmatius (St) C.   Aug 3
d. *c* 440   An Archimandrite, venerated at
Constantinople. He took a lively part in defending the Catholic bishops against the intrigues of the Nestorians.

Dalmatius Moner (Bl) C.
OP.   Sept 26
1291–1341   Born near Gerona, in Spain, he
joined the friars preachers. His life among
them was uneventful as regards titles and
offices, which he constantly refused, but was a
living pattern of fidelity to the rule. Cult
confirmed in 1721.

Dalmatius (St) Bp.   Nov 13
d. 580   Bishop of Rodez, in France, from
524 to 580. He had much to suffer at the hands
of the Arian Visigoth King Amalric.

Dalmatius (St) Bp. M.   Dec 5
d. 304   Born at Monza of pagan parents he
preached, after his conversion, in Gaul and N.
Italy until his election as bishop of Pavia. He
was martyred under Maximian Herculeus
within a year of his election.

**Damascus (Martyrs of)
(BB)** MM.   July 10
See Emmanuel Ruiz and Comp.

Damasus (St) Pope   GC. Dec 11
d. 384   A Spaniard by descent, but probably
born in Rome, he served as deacon the
Spanish church of St Laurence in that city. He
was chosen pope in 366 and after this he
greatly increased the prestige of the Roman
see. He successfully opposed the Arians and
Apollinarians; commissioned his great friend
St Jerome to correct the Latin Bible; developed the Roman liturgy; and restored many
sacred buildings and the tombs of the martyrs,
composing beautiful inscriptions for them
which have become famous. St Jerome styles
him "an incomparable man".

Damhnade (St) V.   June 13
? An Irish virgin greatly venerated in Cavan,

Fermanagh, etc. Colgan identifies her with St Dympna, the martyr of Gheel in Belgium. Nothing certain is known of her life or date.

Damian (SS) MM.   Feb 12
? The Bollandists distinguish two saints of this name under the date Feb 12: one a soldier, martyred in Africa, probably at Alexandria; the other a Roman martyr whose relics were found in the catacombs of St Callistus and sent to Salamanca in Spain. Other particulars are lacking.

Damian, Peter (St) Bp.
Dr.   Feb 23
See Peter Damian.

Damian (St) Bp.   Apr 12
d. 710   Bishop of Pavia in Lombardy, elected to that office in 680. He vigorously opposed the Monothelites, and acted successfully as peacemaker between the Emperor of Byzantium and the Lombards.

Damian (St) M.   May 26
Otherwise Dyfan, q.v.

Damian Vaz (Bl) M.   June 11
d. 1242   A Portuguese knight of St John, put to death by the Moors at Tavira, Algarbes, Portugal (see Peter Rodriguez).

Damian Yamiki (Bl) M.   Sept 10
d. 1622   A Japanese layman, beheaded at Nagasaki. He belongs to the group of Bl Charles Spinola, q.v.

Damian (St) M.   Sept 26
See Cosmas and Damian.

Damian dei Fulcheri (Bl)
C. OP.   Oct 26
d. 1484   A native of Finale (*Finarium*) near Savona, in Liguria, he took the Dominican habit at Savona, and preached in nearly all the cities of Italy. He died at Reggio d'Emilia. Cult approved in 1848.

Daniel (St) M.   ·   Jan 3
d. 168   A deacon, said to have been of Jewish extraction, who aided St Prosdocimus, first bishop of Padua, in his apostolate in N.E. Italy. He was martyred in 168. His body was discovered many centuries later and solemnly enshrined Jan 3, 1064.

Daniel (Bl) Ab. OSB. Cist.   Jan 20
d. 1232   The third abbot of the Cistercian monastery of Cambron, in Hainault.

Daniel (St) M.   Feb 16
See Elias, Jeremiah etc.

Daniel and Verda (SS)
MM.   Feb 21
d. 344   Persian martyrs, greatly honoured in

St Damian, Sept 26

the East, who suffered under King Shapur II. The first was a priest, the second a woman.

Daniel (St) H. OSB. Cam.   March 31
d. 1411   A German merchant who, through travelling to Venice on business, came to know the Camaldolese monks of Murano. He lived a hermit's life under their direction and rule, but in his own house, and was wont to spend long periods with them. He was killed by robbers in his cell.

Daniel (St) M.   Apr 29
9th cent.   A hermit-martyr, the titular of the

abbey-church of the Benedictine nuns at Gerona in Spain. According to the legend, which defies all historical verification, he was a native of Asia Minor, and flourished in the times of Charlemagne.

Daniel (St) M.   July 10
See Leontius, Maurice, etc.

Daniel (St) Prophet   July 21
? One of the four great prophets of the O.T. The book of Daniel as we now receive it seems to have been written about 168 B.C. The pre-1970 RM. mentioned Babylon as the place of his death. His relics are said to have been translated first to Alexandria and then to Venice. His emblems are his lions; or he holds a scroll with words of prophecy.

Daniel, Samuel, Angelus (Angeluccio), Domnus, Leo, Nicholas and Hugolinus (SS) MM. OFM.   Oct 10
d. 1221   This band of Franciscan missionaries was sent by St Francis himself to preach the gospel to the Moors in Morocco. The leader of the band was Brother Daniel, provincial of Calabria. On their arrival at Ceuta the friars were first treated as madmen, but on their refusal to apostatize to Islam, they were beheaded, having been in the country less than three weeks. Canonized in 1516.

Daniel the Stylite (St)   Dec 11
d. 493   After St Simeon the Elder, the greatest and best known of the pillar-saints. He was a monk near Samosata, on the Upper Euphrates. When travelling with his abbot he came to know of St Simeon Stylites, who lived on the top of a pillar near Antioch. He forthwith determined to follow the same way of life at a spot near Constantinople. Here the emperor Leo I built for him a series of pillars, and here too he was ordained priest by St Gennadius. From the top of his pillar he became the oracle of the whole city. He lived on his pillar for thirty years, during which time he came down only once from it in order to rebuke the usurping emperor Basiliscus for supporting the Monophysites.

Daniel (Bl) C. OSB. Cist.   Dec 26
Late 12th cent.   Monk and cellarer of the great Cistercian abbey of Villers in Brabant. He is listed as a *beatus* in the Cistercian catalogues.

Darerca (St) W.   March 22
? 5th cent.   St Patrick's sister. Her name, derived from the Irish *Diar-Sheare*, means constant and firm love. She is reputed to have left fifteen sons, some ten of whom became bishops.

Daria (St) M.   Oct 25
See Chrysanthus and Daria.

Darius, Zosimus, Paul and Secundus (SS) MM.   Dec 19
? A group of martyrs who suffered at Nicaea, of whom nothing else is known.

Darlugdach (Dardulacha, Derlugdach) (St) V.   Feb 1
d. c 524   Successor of St Brigid and second abbess of Kildare.

Dasius, Zoticus, Gaius and Comp. (SS) MM.   Oct 21
d. c 303   A group of fifteen soldiers who suffered martyrdom at Nicomedia under Diocletian.

Dasius (St) M.   Nov 20
d. c 303   A Roman soldier who refused to take part in heathen orgies at Saturnalia, and was for this reason martyred at Dorostorum in Mysia, Asia Minor.

Dathus (Datus) (St) Bp.   July 3
d. 190   Bishop of Ravenna. His election was due to the miraculous appearance of a dove hovering over his head, according to legend. He governed his see during the reign of the emperor Commodus.

Datius (St) Bp.   Jan 14
d. 552   Bishop of Milan, being elected to that see some time after 530. His whole diocese was overrun by the Arian Ostrogoths, and he had to flee to Constantinople, where he spent the rest of his life. Here he defended Pope Vigilius in the dispute about the "Three Chapters".

Datius, Reatrus (Restius) and Comp., and Datius (Dativus), Julian, Vincent and 27 Comp. (SS) MM.   Jan 27
? Two groups of African martyrs; the second group suffered under the Arian Vandals. The Arian persecution lasted a century (427–531).

Dativa (St) M.   Dec 6
See Dionysia, Dativa, etc.

Dativus (St) M.   Feb 11
See Saturninus, Dativus, etc.

Dativus (St) Bp. M.   Sept 10
See Nemesian, Felix, etc.

David (St) Bp.   March 1
d. c 600   Born in S. Wales. He founded a monastery at Mynyw (Menevia) in the far west of Dyfed and is honoured as the first bishop of the place now called St Davids. The monks followed an exceedingly austere rule and their

St Daniel, July 21

monastery became a veritable nursery of saints. He attended the synod of Brefi *c* 545. The foundation of a dozen monasteries and many miracles are attributed to him, but the biography of St David, as handed down to us, is full of anachronisms. It was written by Rhygyvarch, around 1090. As bishop of St Davids he was concerned to claim as much independence from Canterbury as possible and so may have slanted materials in his life of St David to that end. Pope Callistus II in 1120 approved of his cult and decreed that two pilgrimages to his shrine were equivalent to one to Rome. His relics still survive and are enshrined in the cathedral. He is the principal patron saint of Wales. In art he is shown as a bishop with a dove near him, or touching his mouth with its beak; he often stands on a small hill. The leek and daffodil are also associated with him, the latter perhaps because of the similarity of its name to his in Welsh (Dafydd).

David (St) H.   June 26
? 5th cent. Said to have been a native of Mesopotamia who settled in a solitary place outside Thessalonica, where he served God for seventy years. His relics were translated to Pavia in 1054.

David Gonson (Bl) M.   July 12
d. 1541 Son of Vice-Admiral Gonson (or Gunston), and a knight of St John. He was hanged, drawn and quartered at Southwark. Beatified in 1929.

David of Sweden (St) Bp.
OSB.   July 15
d. *c* 1080 Tradition makes him an English Benedictine, who had a passionate desire to give his life to Christ by martyrdom. When he heard of the death of St Sigfrid's three nephews he offered himself to the saint and was sent to Sinenga. Eventually he founded a Benedictine abbey, afterwards called Monkentorp, which he governed as abbot. He is said to have been the first bishop of Västeräss.

David (Gleb) (St) C.   July 24
See Romanus and David.

David Lewis (St) M. SJ.   Aug 27
1616–1679 David Lewis (*alias* Charles Baker) was born in Monmouthshire and educated at Abergavenny. He was converted to the faith, studied for the priesthood at Rome and became a Jesuit in 1645. He worked in S. Wales for thirty-one years. He was martyred at

Usk. Beatified in 1929 and canonized in 1970 as one of the Forty Martyrs of England and Wales, q.v.

David of Himmerode (Bl)
Ab. OSB. Cist.   Dec 11
d. 1179   A native of Florence, who took the Cistercian habit at Clairvaux under St Bernard (1131). In 1134 he was sent to Germany as abbot-founder of Himmerode, in the diocese of Trier.

David (St) King and Prophet   Dec 29
d. c 970 B.C.   David "the beloved" and "the man after God's own heart". He is one of the types of Christ in the O.T., and indeed one of the most lovable characters in history. His story is fully told in Kings (Samuel) Bks I and II and in Chronicles. The Greeks keep his feast, together with those of all the other saints who were ancestors of our Lord, on Dec 19. He is depicted as a lad with a sling or carrying the head of Goliath, or as a king playing the harp.

Davinus (St) C.   June 3
d. 1051   A native of Armenia who set out on a pilgrimage to Rome and Compostella. On his way he stopped at Lucca, where he succumbed to a fatal malady and was venerated as a saint.

Davy (John) (Bl) M.   June 6
See John Davy.

Day (Dye) (St) Ab.   Jan 18
? This saint, otherwise unknown, to whom a Cornish church near Redruth is dedicated, may possibly be St Deicola, abbot, q.v.

Dé (St) Bp.   Jan 31
Breton form of the name St Aidan (or Eden) of Ferns.

Declan (St) Bp.   July 24
5th cent.   A disciple of St Colman who became a bishop in the district of Ardmore.

Decorosus (St) Bp.   Feb 15
d. 695   For thirty years bishop of Capua, St Decorosus was one of the bishops at the council of Rome under Pope St Agatho (680).

Decuman (Dagan) (St) M.   Aug 27
d. 706   A Welsh saint who lived as a recluse in Somersetshire, where he was murdered, according to a much later biography.

Deel (Deille) (St) Ab.   Jan 18
Otherwise Deicola (Dichul), q.v.

Degadh (St)   Aug 18
Otherwise Dagaeus, q.v.

Degenhard (Bl) H. OSB.   Sept 3
d. 1374   A native of Bavaria and a monk of

Niederaltaich. After some years in the abbey he retired to live as a recluse under BB Otto and Hermann, also Benedictine monks of Niederaltaich, in their cell at Frauenau, in the Bavarian Forest, and afterwards at Breitenau on the Danube.

**Deicola (Deicolus,
Desle, Dichul, Deel,
Delle, Deille, etc.) (St)**
Ab.   Jan 18
d. c 625   A monk of Bangor who followed St Columbanus to Burgundy, where he helped in the foundation of Luxeuil. When St Columbanus was compelled to go elsewhere by Queen Brunehaut, Deicola, too old to travel, remained behind and founded the abbey of Lure (Lutra) in the Vosges.

Deifer (St) Ab.   March 7
6th cent.   A Welsh saint, abbot-founder of Bodfari in Clwyd.

Deiniol (Daniel) (St) Bp.   Sept 11
d. 584   Ordained first bishop of Bangor by St Dyfrig. The cathedral of Bangor and other churches are dedicated in his name.

Delphina (Bl) V. Tert. OFM.   Dec 9
1283–1358   Born at Château-Puy-Michel in Languedoc, she became the wife of St Elzear, and is said to have been a member of the third order of St Francis. After her husband's death she lived in retirement at the court of Naples. Cult approved by Urban VIII.

Delphinus (St) Bp.   Dec 24
d. 404   Bishop of Bordeaux. He is best remembered as having been instrumental in the conversion of St Paulinus of Nola, and as an untiring opponent of the Priscillianists.

Demetria (St) VM.   June 21
d. 363   An alleged sister of St Bibiana and daughter of SS Flavian and Dafrosa, q.v. Her life is probably fictitious.

Demetrian (St) Bp.   Nov 6
d. c 912   A native of Cyprus who became monk and *hegoumenos* of St Antony's and finally bishop of Khytri, both in his native island. He is one of the most venerated of Cypriot saints.

Demetrius of Tiflis (Bl) M.   Apr 9
See Thomas of Tolentino and Comp.

**Demetrius, Concessus,
Hilary and Comp. (SS)**
MM.   Apr 9
? A group composed of martyrs from different

St David (with Goliath's head), Dec 29

localities, but about whom no particulars are extant.

Demetrius (St) C.   June 18
See Gregory, Demetrius, etc.

Demetrius (St) M.   Aug 14
? A martyr of whose death neither the place nor circumstances can be verified. The pre-1970 RM., however, described him as an African martyr.

Demetrius (Dimitri) (St)
M.   Oct 8
Early 4th cent. Surnamed by the Greeks
"the Megalomartyr", he is, after St George,
the most famous military martyr of the East.
His military career, however, is a legend. He
was probably a deacon who suffered at Sirmium in Dalmatia, under Diocletian, though the
centre of his cult was at Salonika, where a
magnificent basilica was erected in his name.
He is mentioned to this day in the preparation
of the Byzantine liturgy.

Demetrius (St) Bp.   Oct 9
d. 231 or 232 The twelfth patriarch of
Alexandria, during whose episcopate the catechetical school of that city attained its highest
fame. He was a close friend of Origen, whom
later he had to banish from the diocese in 231
for being irregularly ordained.

Demetrius, Anianus,
Eustosius and Comp.
(SS) MM.   Nov 10
? A band of twenty-three martyrs registered as
having suffered at Antioch in Syria. St Demetrius is described as a bishop and St Anianus as
his deacon.

Demetrius and Honorius
(SS) MM.   Nov 21
? Old Roman manuscripts describe these
saints as martyrs who suffered at Ostia at the
mouth of the Tiber.

Demetrius (St) M.   Nov 29
See Blaise and Demetrius.

Demetrius, Honoratus
and Florus (SS) MM.   Dec 22
? These martyrs are stated to have suffered at
Ostia at the mouth of the Tiber. They probably are to be identified with SS Demetrius
and Honorius of Nov 21.

Democritus, Secundus
and Dionysius (SS) MM.   July 31
? Martyrs, some say of Phrygia, some of
Africa. Nothing really is known about them.

Denis, Dennis, Denys
(*several*)
French forms of the name Dionysius, q.v.

Denis, Rusticus and
Eleutherius (SS) MM.   GC. Oct 9
d. *c* 250 According to St Gregory of Tours,
Denis or Dionysius was born in Italy and was
sent with five other bishops from Rome to
Gaul: he became the first bishop of Paris. He
and his two companions were beheaded under
Decius; and the abbey of St Denis, later the
place of the sepulchres of the kings of France,

St Denis, Oct 9

was built over their tomb. However, in the
ninth century Hilduin, the abbot of St Denis,
linked Denis to St Dionysius the Areopagite
(q.v.) by attributing to this Biblical figure the
works of a fifth century ecclesiastical writer
called the Pseudo-Dionysius. Three disparate
persons and traditions were thus united in the
popular mind: the cult spread far and wide in
the Middle Ages. All that we really know of
Denis comes from Gregory of Tours. In art he
is shown as a headless bishop, carrying his own
mitred head, and with a palm, sword or book.
His vestments may be covered with fleurs-de-
lys.

Denise (*several*)
French form of the name Dionysia, q.v.

Dentlin (Dentelin, Denain) (St) C.   March 16
7th cent. The little son of St Vincent Madelgarus (q.v.) and of St Waldetrudis. He was only seven years old when he died. A church in the duchy of Cleves is dedicated in his honour.

Deochar (Theutger or Gottlieb) (St) Ab. OSB.   June 7
d. 847 A hermit in the wilds of Franconia, for whom Charlemagne founded the abbey of Herriedon under the Benedictine rule, Deochar becoming its first abbot. In 802 he was appointed *missus regius*. In 819 he took part in the translation of St Boniface's relics to Fulda.

Deodatus (St) Mk. OSB.   Feb 3
8th cent. A monk of Lagny in the archdiocese of Paris.

Deodatus (St) Ab.   Apr 24
d. *c* 525 A hermit, or abbot, in the neighbourhood of Blois. At a later period the town of Saint-Dié grew up round his cell (or monastery).

Deodatus (Dié, Didier, Dieu-Donné, Adéodat) (St)
Bp. OSB.   June 19
d. *p.*680 A bishop who founded (*c* 660) and was abbot of the monastery of Vallis-Galilaea (Val-de-Galilée — Jointures abbey).

Deodatus (St) Bp.   June 19
d. 679 Bishop of Nevers in 655 and then a solitary in the Vosges. Later he was abbot-founder of Ebersheimmünster, near Strasburg. He is often confused with St Deodatus of Vallis-Galilaea.

Deodatus (St) Bp.   June 27
d. 473 Deacon to St Paulinus, bishop of Nola, and his successor in that see. His relics were brought to Benevento in 839.

Deodatus (St) M. (or C.)   Sept 27
? A saint of Sora (central Italy) whose relics were enshrined in the cathedral of Sora in 1621.

Deogratius (St) Bp.   March 22
d. 457 Ordained bishop of Carthage in 456, fourteen years after the death of his predecessor, St Quodvultdeus, who had been driven into exile by the Arian Vandals. The Vandal king, Genseric, having brought many Italian captives to Carthage, St Deogratias sold all that he or his church possessed, even the sacred vessels, to ransom them. He was bishop only one year.

Derfel-Gadarn (St)   Apr 5
6th cent. A Welsh saint, a soldier and afterwards a solitary at Llanderfel in Gwynedd. He was greatly venerated by the Welsh in the Middle Ages. His image, carved of wood and showing him armed and mounted on a horse, was a great focus of pilgrimages. It was burned at Smithfield on 22 May 1538 with Bl John Forest, q.v. by order of Thomas Cromwell.

Dermot (Diarmis, Diarmaid) (St) Ab.   Jan 10
6th cent. The spiritual director and teacher of St Kieran of Clonmacnois and later abbot-founder of a monastery on Innis-Clotran Island.

Derphuta (St) M.   March 20
See Alexandra, Claudia, etc.

Deruvianus (St) M.   May 26
Otherwise Dyfan, q.v.

Derwa (St) M.   ?
The patron saint of Menadarva (Merthyr-Dava, i.e. the Martyr Derwa) near Camborne in Cornwall. Nothing is known about this saint. Probably he is no other than St Dyfan (Damian or Deruvianus), one of the legendary missionaries sent to Britain in the second century by Pope St Eleutherius.

Desideratus (Désiré) (St)
Bp.   Feb 10 and 11
6th cent. Successor of St Avitus as bishop of Clermont in Auvergne.

Desideratus (St) H. AC.   Apr 30
d. *c* 569 A French solitary who lived at Gourdon, near Châlon-sur-Saône.

Desideratus (St) Bp.   May 8
6th cent. Successor of St Arcadius in the bishopric of Bourges.

Desideratus (St) Mk. OSB.   Dec 18
d. *c* 700 Son of St Waningus, the founder of Fécamp abbey, he became a monk of Fontenelle. His relics were enshrined at Ghent.

Desiderius (Didier) (Bl)
Bp.   Jan 20
d. 1194 The thirty-third bishop of Thérouanne and founder of the Cistercian abbey of Blandecques (Blandyke) near Saint-Omer. At the end of his life he resigned and prepared for death in a Cistercian monastery. He is usually styled a saint and is claimed by the Cistercians as one of their own. Cult not yet officially confirmed.

Desiderius (St) Bp. M.   Feb 11
d. 608 A native of Autun, educated at Vienne, where he became archdeacon and then bishop. An intrepid defender of Christian

morality, he was persecuted by Queen Brun-hildis, who was also instrumental in securing his murder at the place now called Saint-Didier-sur-Chalaronne.

Desiderius (St) M.   March 25
See Barontius and Desiderius.

Desiderius (St) Bp. M.   May 23
407 ? Said to have been a native of Genoa who preached in and became bishop of Lang-res in France. He was killed at the time of a Vandal invasion while pleading for his people.

Desiderius (St)
Pope, OSB.   Sept 16
Otherwise Victor III, q.v.

Desiderius (St) M.   Sept 19
See Januarius and Comp.

Desiderius (St) Mk. OSB.   Oct 19
d. *c* 705 A monk of Lonrey, and a disciple of St Sigiranus, who became a recluse at La Brenne (*Ruriacus*) in the diocese of Bourges, France.

Desiderius (St) Bp.   Oct 27
d. *c* 625 The successor of St Anacharius (Aunaire) in the bishopric of Auxerre. He has often been confused with St Desiderius of Vienne (Feb 11).

Desiderius (St) Bp.   Nov 15
d. 655 The successor of his own brother, St Rusticus, as bishop of Cahors (630–655).

Deusdedit (St) Bp. OSB.   Jan 14
d. 664 An Anglo-Saxon, Frithona by name. He was the first of his race to occupy the primatial see of Canterbury as the successor of St Honorius in 655.

Deusdedit (St) C.   Aug 10
6th cent. A poor shoemaker in Rome, con-temporary of St Gregory the Great, who relates that he gave away to the poor every Saturday all that he earned at his trade during the week.

Deusdedit (St) Ab. M. OSB.   Oct 9
d. 836 Monk of Montecassino, chosen abbot about the year 830. He was especially noted for his generous almsgiving. To extort money from him the tyrant, Sicard of Bene-vento, ill-treated and imprisoned him. He died in prison of hunger and misery. He is venerated as a martyr.

Deusdedit (Adeodatus I)
(St) Pope   Nov 8
d. 618 A Roman by birth, he became pope in 615. During his pontificate a pestilence raged in Rome and he worked untiringly for the plague-stricken. In all ancient Benedictine menologies he is called a Benedictine monk, but there is no certain evidence for it: he seems rather to have preferred secular clergy to religious.

Deusdedit of Brescia (St)
Bp.   Dec 10
d. *c* 700 A bishop of Brescia who played a leading part in the councils convened against the Monothelite heretics.

Devereux (St) Bp.   Nov 13
Otherwise Dubricius, q.v.

Devinicus (Denick,
Teavneck) (St) Bp.   Nov 13
6th cent. A native of N. Scotland who in his old age associated himself with the missionary work of SS Columba and Machar and evan-gelized Caithness. He is reputed to have been a bishop.

Devota (St) VM.   Jan 27
d. 303 A maiden of Corsica who expired on the rack in the persecution of Diocletian. Her relics are at Monaco on the Riviera di Ponente. She is the patron saint of both Corsica and Monaco.

Dewi (St) Bp.   March 1
Otherwise David of Wales, q.v.

Deyniolen (St)   Nov 22
d. 621 Also known as St Deiniol (Daniel) the Younger. He was abbot of Bangor at the time of the slaughter of his monks and the destruction of their monastery by King Aet-helfrith of Northumbria (616). The saint appears to have escaped the massacre of his two thousand monks.

Diaconus (St) M.   March 14
6th cent. So described on account of his office of deacon, which he held in the church of the Marsi in central Italy. St Gregory narrates of him that together with two monks he was put to death by the Lombards.

Diana, Cecilia and
Amata (BB) VV. OP.   June 10
13th cent. The three first members of the first house of Dominican nuns at Bologna. Diana, of the ancient family of the Carbonesi, was a native of Bologna. After a very worldly youth she embraced religion against the wish of her family; she died in 1236. The other two later became nuns of the Roman convent of San Sisto. Beatified in 1891.

Dichu (St)   Apr 29
5th cent. The first convert made by St Patrick in Ulster. He was originally a swineherd. After his conversion, we are told,

he continued to the end faithful to Christ and St Patrick.

Dichul (St) Ab.   Jan 18
Otherwise Deicola, qv.

Dictinus (St) Bp.   July 24
d. 420 An adherent of Priscillianism, he was converted by St Ambrose and recanted his errors at the council of Toledo (400). Soon after he was made bishop of Astorga in Spain.

Didacus (Diego) de Azevedo (Bl) Bp. OSB.
Cist.   Feb 6
d. 1207 (Dec 30) Provost of the cathedral of Osma, in Old Castile, where he obtained a canonry for St Dominic Guzmán. In 1201 he became bishop of Osma. He was sent to Rome by King Alphonsus of Castile and took St Dominic as a companion on his journey: this was the occasion of the founding of the Dominican order. Didacus became a Cistercian in order to join the crusade against the Albigenses. He has always been styled a *beatus*, or a saint, by the Cistercians.

Didacus Carvalho (Bl)
M. SJ.   Feb 25
1578–1624 Born at Coimbra in Portugal, he joined the Jesuits in 1594. He was sent to India in 1600, where he was ordained priest. In 1609 he migrated to Japan. Here he worked untiringly until 1623, when he was arrested with a number of his flock and carried off to Sendai, suffering many indignities on the way. The story of their martyrdom is a miracle of endurance. Beatified in 1867.

Didacus (Diego, Diaz) (Bl)
C. OFM. Cap.   March 24
1743–1801 A native of Cádiz, he joined the Capuchins at Seville in 1759, and after his ordination began to preach throughout Spain, but chiefly in Andalusia, of which province he is called "the Apostle". Most of his time which remained over from preaching he spent in the confessional. Beatified in 1894.

Didacus Perez (Bl) M. SJ.   July 15
d. 1570 A Jesuit novice who formed one of the band of missionaries led by Bl Ignatius de Azevedo, whose martyrdom he shared.

**Didacus (Diego, Diaz)
(St)** C. OFM.   Nov 13
c 1400–1463 Born of poor parents in the diocese of Seville, he joined the Franciscans as a lay-brother at Arrizafa. He was appointed, on account of his remarkable ability and goodness, guardian of the principal friary in the Canary Islands, at Fuerteventura (1445).

Later he was recalled to Spain, and after a pilgrimage to Rome in 1450, died at the friary of Alcalà, in Castile. Canonized in 1588. Cult confined to local calendars since 1969.

Didier (St) Bp. M.   May 23
Otherwise Desiderius, q.v.

Didius (St) M.   Nov 26
See Faustus, Didius, etc.

Didymus (St) M.   Apr 28
See Theodora and Didymus.

Didymus (St) M.   Sept 11
See Diodorus, Diomedes, etc.

Dié (St) Bp.   June 19
Otherwise Deodatus, q.v.

Diego (*several*)
Otherwise Didacus, q.v.
Note. Diego is really a corrupt form of the Spanish name for St James, viz. Santiago (Sant-Iago, San Tiego, San Diego). Only in modern times has Diego been latinized into Didacus.

Diemut (Diemuda) (Bl)
H. OSB.   March 29
d. c 1130 A nun at the Benedictine monastery of Wessobrunn in Bavaria, who was granted leave to live as a solitary under the obedience of the monastery. She spent her time in copying manuscripts, some of which are still extant.

Diethardus (Bl) Mk. OSB.   Sept 29
See Catholdus, Anno, etc.

Dietrich (St) Bp. M.   Feb 2
See Bruno and Comp.

Dieudonné (*several*)
The French form for Deusdedit or Adeodatus, q.v.

Digain (St) C.   Nov 21
5th cent. A son of Constantine, king or chieftain of Cornwall. Llangernw, in Clwyd, perpetuates his memory.

Digna (St) M.   June 14
See Anastasius, Felix and Digna.

Digna (St) V.   Aug 11
4th cent. A maiden of Todi in Umbria, who lived as a solitary in the mountains near her native city during the persecution of Diocletian.

Digna (St) M.   Aug 12
See Hilaria, Digna, etc.

Digna and Emerita (SS)
VV. MM.   Sept 22
d. c 259 Roman maidens martyred under

Valerian. They expired standing before their judges and praying. Their relics are enshrined in the church of St Marcellus at Rome.

Diman (Dimas, Dima) (St)
Bp.   Jan 6
d. 658 Surnamed *Diman Dubh* (Diman the Black). A monk under St Columba, and afterwards abbot and bishop of Connor. He is one of the bishops to whom (640) the Roman church, after the death of Pope Honorius, addressed the letter on the Paschal controversy and on Pelagianism.

Dimitri (St) M.   Oct 8
Otherwise Demetrius, q.v.

Dingad (St) C.   Nov 1
5th cent. A son of the chieftain Brychan of Brecknock, who led a monastic or eremitical life at Llandingad, i.e. Llandovery, in Dyfed.

Diocles (St) M.   May 24
See Zöellus, Servilius, etc.

Diocletius (St) M.   May 11
See Sisinius, Diocletius, etc.

Diodorus (St) M.   Feb 26
See Papias, Diodorus, etc.

Diodorus and Rhodopianus (SS) MM.   May 3
Early 4th cent. Two deacons martyred under Diocletian in the province of Caria, Asia Minor.

Diodorus (St) M.   July 6
See Lucy, Antoninus, etc.

Diodorus, Diomedes and Didymus (SS) MM.   Sept 11
? Martyrs of Laodicea (Kulat-el-Husn or Ladhikijeh) in Syria.

Diodorus, Marianus and Comp. (SS) MM.   Dec 1
d. 283 Roman martyrs under Numerian. They are described as being very numerous. In fact, it appears to have been a case of a Christian congregation surprised while assembled at prayer in the catacombs and disposed of by having the entrance to their subterranean oratory blocked up.

Diogenes (St) M.   Apr 6
See Timothy and Diogenes.

Diogo (*several*)
The Portuguese form of James or Didacus, q.v. (Cf. note on Diego.)

Diomedes (St) M.   Aug 16
d. 300–311 ? A native of Tarsus in Cilicia,

by profession a physician, and a zealous propagator of Christianity. He was arrested at Nicaea in Bithynia and martyred under Diocletian.

Diomedes, Julian, Philip, Eutychian, Hesychius, Leonides, Philadelphus, Menalippus and Pantagapes (SS) MM.   Sept 2
? Some perished at the stake, others were drowned, beheaded or crucified. Place and other circumstances unknown.

Diomedes (St) M.   Sept 11
See Diodorus, Diomedes, etc.

Diomma (St)   May 12
5th cent. An Irish saint, said to have been the teacher of St Declan of Ardmore and other saints. He is now venerated as the patron saint of Kildimo, Co. Limerick.

Dion (St) M.   July 6
See Lucy, Antoninus, etc.

Dionysia, Dionysius
Note. These Greco-Latin names became very popular in the Middle Ages under the corresponding French forms of Denise, Denis, Denys. Sydney in English is a corrupt form of St Denys.

Dionysia (St) M.   May 15
See Peter, Andrew, etc.

Dionysia, Dativa, Leontia, Tertius, Emilian, Boniface and Comp. (SS) MM.   Dec 6
d. 484 African martyrs under the Arian Vandal king, Hunneric. We have a quite genuine account of their martyrdom from Victor of Utica. According to him Dionysia, a widow, perished at the stake with her little child, Majoricus (q.v.), and her sister Dativa. Emilian, a physician, and Tertius, a monk, were flayed alive. The fanatics seem to have amused themselves by devising strange kinds of death for the rest of the heroic band.

Dionysia (St) M.   Dec 12
See Ammonaria, Mercuria, etc.

Dionysius, Emilian and Sebastian (SS) MM.   Feb 8
? The pre-1970 RM. described them as Armenian monks. We know nothing about them, save their names. St Emilian is honoured at Trevi on Jan 28.

Dionysius and Ammonius (SS) MM.   Feb 14
? Martyrs beheaded, it seems, at Alexandria in Egypt.

Dionysius of Augsburg
(St) Bp. MM.   Feb 26
d. *c* 303   Venerated as first bishop of Augsburg in Germany. He is said to have been
converted to Christ, baptized and later ordained bishop by St Narcissus. He was martyred
under Diocletian. The story, however, is from
the Acts of St Afra (Aug 5 q.v.) which date
from the eighth century.

Dionysius Fugixima (Bl)
M. SJ.   March 5
d. 1622 (Nov 1)   A Japanese, born of noble
parents at Aitzu, Arima, who became a Jesuit
novice and worked under Bl Paul Navarro,
with whom he was burnt alive at Ximabara.
Beatified in 1867.

Dionysius (St) M.   March 10
See Codratus, Dionysius, etc.

Dionysius the Carthusian
(Bl) C. O. Cart.   March 12
1402–1471   Born at Ryckel, near Loos, in
Flanders, he gained his doctorate at the
university of Cologne in his twenty-second
year. In 1423 he entered the Carthusian order.
He excelled as a mystical writer and on this
account has been given the title of *Doctor
Ecstaticus*. He is commemorated as a *beatus* in
several martyrologies.

Dionysius (St) M.   March 16
See Hilary, Tatian, etc.

Dionysius (SS) MM.   March 24
Two of the same name who suffered together.
See Timolaus and Comp.

Dionysius of
Corinth (St) Bp.   Apr 8
d. *c* 170   A bishop of Corinth who was a
leader of the church in the second century.
Several of his letters to various churches are
still extant: especially noteworthy is that in
which he records the martyrdom of SS Peter
and Paul in Rome. The Greeks venerate him
as a martyr (Nov 20).

Dionysius (St) M.   Apr 19
See Socrates and Dionysius.

Dionysius (St) Bp.   May 8
d. *p.*193   Said to have been one of the ten
missionaries sent with St Peregrinus into Gaul
by Pope Sixtus I, early in the second century.
He succeeded St Justus in the bishopric of
Vienne in Dauphiné. Some have erroneously
described him as a martyr.

Dionysius (St) M.   May 12
d. 304   An Asiatic by birth and uncle of the

youthful martyr St Pancras, to whom he acted
as guardian. They came together to Rome,
were converted to Christianity, and martyred
under Diocletian, Dionysius dying in prison.

Dionysius of Milan (St) Bp.   May 25
d. *c* 359   The successor of St Protasius in
the see of Milan in 351. In 355 he was
banished to Cappadocia by the Arian emperor
Constantius for having upheld the cause of St
Athanasius. He died in exile, but St Ambrose
had his remains translated to Milan.

Dionysius (St) M.   June 3
See Lucillian, Claudius, etc.

Dionysius Sebuggwao
(St) M.   June 3
d. 1885   A servant of King Mwanga of
Uganda; he was pierced with a lance by the
king because he was caught teaching the
catechism — the first victim of the persecution. See Charles Lwanga and Comp.

Dionysius (St) M.   July 27
One of the Seven Sleepers, q.v.

Dionysius (St) M.   July 31
See Democritus, Secundus and Dionysius.

Dionysius and Privatus
(SS) MM.   Sept 20
? Martyrs of Phrygia in Asia Minor.

Dionysius, Faustus,
Gaius, Peter, Paul and
Comp. (SS) MM.   Oct 3
d. 257   A group of Christians from Alexandria in Egypt, banished to Libya under
Decius (250) and again brought to trial and
martyred at Alexandria under Valerian. There
is much confusion as to the identity of each of
these martyrs.

Dionysius (St) Bp. M.   Oct 9
1st cent.   This is Denis the Areopagite who
was converted at Athens by St Paul (Acts
17:34). Early writers say that he became first
bishop of Athens and died a martyr (*c* 95).
Unfortunately, at a much later period he was
identified with St Dionysius or St Denis, q.v.
of Paris, and the works of an ecclesiastical
writer of the fifth century — the pseudo-
Dionysius — were falsely attributed to him. All
that is really known of St Dionysius is in the
Book of Acts.

Dionysius, Rusticus and
Eleutherius (SS) MM.   GC. Oct 9
See Denis, Rusticus and Eleutherius, above.

Dionysius of Alexandria
(St) Bp.   Nov 17
d. 265   Called also Dionysius the Great. A

native of Alexandria, he studied under Origen, whom he succeeded as a master of the catechetical school. In 248 he became patriarch of Alexandria, but two years later, under Decius, was banished to Libya, whence he continued to govern his diocese. He returned to Alexandria, but was again driven from it under Valerian. He was restored under Gallienus. He was a great theologian; St Athanasius styles him "the teacher of the whole Church".

Dionysius (St) M. Nov 20
See Bassus, Dionysius, etc.

Dionysius and Redemptus (BB) MM. OC. Nov 29
d. 1638 Dionysius of the Nativity (Peter Berthelot) was a French shipmaster and trader who became a Carmelite at Goa in 1635 and was ordained in 1638. This same year he was sent on an embassy to Sumatra. A Carmelite lay-brother, Redemptus of the cross (Thomas Rodriguez da Cunha), a Portuguese by birth, was given him as a companion. The embassy proved a failure, and both friars were put to death by the Sumatrans. Beatified in 1900.

Dionysius (St) Pope Dec 26
d. 268 A Roman priest who was chosen bishop of Rome in 259 and very energetically and successfully restored the Roman church after the persecution of Valerian. He opposed Sabellius and condemned Paul of Samosata. He was buried in the cemetery of Callistus.

Dioscorides (St) M. May 10
? A martyr of Smyrna in Asia Minor.

Dioscorides (St) M. May 28
See Crescens, Dioscorides, etc.

Dioscorus (St) M. Feb 25
See Victorinus, Victor, etc.

Dioscorus (St) M. May 18
d. c 305 A reader of the church of Kynopolis in Egypt. He was burnt with hot irons and he died under the torture.

Dioscorus (St) M. Dec 14
See Heron, Arsenius, etc.

Dioscorus (St) Dec 21
See Themistocles and Dioscorus.

Diruvianus (St) M. May 26
Otherwise Dyfan, q.v.

Disibod (Disibode, Disen) (St) Bp. OSB. Sept 8
d. c 700 An Irishman — a bishop — who

passed over to the Continent with several companions and founded a monastery on a hill in the valley of the Nahe, near Bingen, which became known as Disibodenberg or Disenberg, *Mons Disibodi*. It became famous in a later age on account of the residence there of St Hildegarde.

Dismas (St) March 25
The name given by tradition to the Good Thief, q.v.

Diuma (St) C. Sept 7
7th cent. An Irish priest sent with St Cedd to convert Mercia; later he was bishop in Mercian territories. Bede speaks highly of him.

Dizier (St) Bp. M. May 23
Otherwise Desiderius, q.v.

Docanus or Docco (St) Ab. Nov 7
Otherwise Cumgar (or Cungar), q.v.

Dochow (Dochau, Dogwyn) C. Feb 15
? 473 According to the Vita Samsonis he travelled from Wales to Cornwall and founded a monastery there. In the Ulster Annal he is styled bishop.

Docus (St) Bp. M. Jan 24
Otherwise Cadoc, q.v.

Doda (St) V. OSB. Apr 24
See Bova (Bona) and Doda.

Dodo (Bl) C. H. March 30
d. 1231 A hermit at Asch in Frisia, who practised astonishing austerities. He is reputed to have received the stigmata.

Dodo (St) Ab. OSB. Oct 1
d. c 750 Born in the territory of Laon. Placed from childhood under St Ursmar, he became a monk at Lobbes and eventually was made abbot of Wallers-en-Faigne.

Dodolinus (St) Bp. Apr 1
7th cent. Bishop of Vienne in Dauphiné, France.

Dogfan (Doewan) (St) M. July 13
5th cent. A Welshman, one of the descendants of the chieftain Brychan. He is said to have been put to death by heathen invaders of Dyfed where a church was built to his memory.

Dogmael (St) C. June 14
5th–6th cent. A Welsh monk of the house of Cunedda. He founded several cells in Dyfed, Brittany and Anglesey.

Domangard (Donard) (St) C. March 24
d. c 500 The patron of Maghera, Co.

Down, who in the time of St Patrick lived as a hermit on the mountain now called after him Slieve-Donard.

Dometius and Comp.
(SS) MM. Aug 7
Otherwise Domitius, q.v.

Dominator (St) Bp. Nov 5
d. ? 495 The fourteenth bishop of Brescia in Lombardy.

Dominic
Note. Dominicus, Dominica are latinized forms of Cyriacus (*Kuriakos*) and Cyriaca (*Kuriake*). The Latin Dominicus has the following derivatives in modern languages: in Italian, Domenico; in Spanish and Portuguese, Domingo; in French, Dominique; in English, Dominic.

Dominic of Sora (St) Ab.
OSB. Jan 22
d. 1031 Born at Foligno in Etruria, he became a Benedictine and eventually the abbot-founder of several monasteries — at Scandrilia, Sora, Sangro, and elsewhere in the old kingdom of Naples. He died at Sora in Campania when eighty years old.

Dominic Savio (St) C. March 9
1842–1857 He was the son of a peasant blacksmith in Piedmont, and became a pupil of St John Bosco, who wrote his life. He died shortly before his fifteenth birthday, having given proof of his high virtue. He is the youngest non-martyr to receive official canonization in the history of the church. Canonized in 1954.

Dominic Jorjes (Bl) M. March 14
d. 1619 A Portuguese soldier, born at Aguilar de Sousa, who settled in Japan, where he gave shelter to Bl Charles Spinola. For this reason he was burnt alive at Nagasaki (Nov 18). Beatified in 1819.

Dominic Tuoc (St) M. OP. Apr 2
d. 1839 A native of Vietnam, and a priest of the third order of Friars Preachers. He died of his wounds in prison. Canonized in 1988.

Dominic Vernagalli (Bl)
Mk. OSB. Cam. Apr 20
d. 1218 A native of Pisa who was professed a Camaldolese at the abbey of St Michael in his native city. He founded a hospital attached to the monastery. Cult confirmed in 1854.

Dominic and Gregory
(BB) CC. OP. Apr 26
d. 1300 Two Spanish Dominicans who preached in the villages of the Somontano, at the foot of the Pyrenees near Barbastro, in Aragon. They were killed near Perarúa by the fall of a rock, under which they had sought refuge during a thunderstorm. Their relics are enshrined at Besians, diocese of Barbastro. Cult confirmed by Pius IX.

Dominic de la Calzada
(St) H. May 12
d. c 1109 Born at Victoria in Biscay, he tried unsuccessfully his religious vocation at Valvanera and then became a hermit in Rioja. He devoted his days to making a road — *Calzada* (causeway) — for pilgrims on their way to Compostella. The spot where he lived, now the township of La Calzada, became a great pilgrimage shrine.

Dominic of the Holy
Rosary (Bl) M. Op. June 1
d. 1622 A Japanese catechist and novice of the Dominican order. He was beheaded on the day of the great martyrdom — Sept 10, 1622 — at Nagasaki. Beatified in 1867.

Dominic of Fiunga (Bl)
M. June 1
d. 1622 (Sept 12) A Japanese catechist, of the third order of Friars Preachers, burnt alive at Omura with Bl Thomas Zumarraga and companions. Beatified in 1867.

Dominic Castellet (Bl)
M. OP. June 1
1592–1628 (Sept 8) A native of Esparraguera, province of Barcelona. He took the Dominican habit at Barcelona and was sent to the Dominican mission of Japan, of which he was vicar provincial at the time of his martyrdom. He was burnt alive at Nagasaki. Beatified in 1867.

Dominic Tomaki (Bl) M. June 1
d. 1628 (Sept 8) Son of Bl John Tomaski, beheaded at the age of sixteen with his father and brothers at Nagasaki. Beatified in 1867.

Dominic Nifaki (Bl) M. June 1
d. 1628 (Sept 8) A child, two years old, beheaded at Nagasaki with his father, Bl Louis Nifaki, and his brother Francis. Beatified in 1867.

Dominic Xibioje (Bl) M. June 1
d. 1628 (Sept 26) A Japanese layman, of the third order of Friars Preachers, who sheltered the missionaries. Beheaded at Nagasaki. Beatified in 1867.

Dominic of Comacchio
(Bl) Mk. OSB. June 21
d. p.820 A Benedictine monk of Comac-

chio, near Venice. According to the legend, it was he who in 820 went as a pilgrim to the Holy Land and brought the relics of St Mark from Alexandria to Venice.

Dominic Henares (St)
Bp. M. OP.   June 25
d. 1838   A Spaniard by birth and a Dominican friar by profession, he became in 1803 bishop-coadjutor to St Ignatius Delgado, vicar apostolic of Vietnam. He was beheaded with his catechist, St Francis Chien, during the Vietnamese persecution. Canonized in 1988.

Dominic Fernandez (Bl)
M. SJ.   July 15
d. 1570   A Jesuit lay-brother. Born at Villa Viciosa in Portugal. A companion of Bl Ignatius de Azevedo, q.v.

Dominic Nicholas Dat
(St) M.   July 18
d. 1839   A native soldier in Vietnam, who was strangled during the persecution of the Christians in Vietnam. Canonized in 1988.

Dominic Van Hanh Dieu
(St) M. OP.   Aug 1
d. 1838   A native of Vietnam, and a priest of the Dominican order. He was executed in his sixty-seventh year. Canonized in 1988.

Dominic de Guzman (St)
Founder OP.   GC. Aug 8
1170–1221   A native of Calaruega, province of Burgos, in Old Castile, and an Augustinian canon regular at the cathedral of Osma. In 1203 he accompanied his bishop, Bl Diego de Azevedo, to S. France, where the Albigenses were at that time devastating the country. Dominic began his life-long apostolate among the heretics, and in 1206 succeeded in opening a convent at Prouille for nun-converts from Albigensianism. This was the germ of his order of friars known as the friars preachers, whom Dominic sent everywhere to preach and teach. The order was approved in 1216 and within a few years it had spread throughout Europe. The Order of Preachers, with that founded by St Francis and known as the Friars Minor, marks the culminating point of that powerful tide of Christian asceticism which had begun with Cluny and been continued by Cîteaux. By his personal charm St Dominic won the enthusiastic affection of his followers. He died at Bologna, and was canonized in 1234. In art, clad in the habit of his order, a white tunic and scapular and black cloak, he holds a lily. Often a star shines above his head. With him may be a dog and a globe, with fire: he may carry a rosary and hold a tall cross.

St Dominic de Guzman, Aug 8

Dominic Barberi of the Mother of God (Bl) C.
CP.   Aug 27
1792–1849   A native of the Viterbo (Rome) countryside, he entered the Congregation of the Passion and was ordained priest in 1818. Chosen by his superiors as head of the Pas-

sionist English Mission, Dominic reached England in 1841 and worked unsparingly until his death at Reading. Cardinal Newman was the most prominent of the distinguished converts Bl Dominic received into the church. Beatified in 1963.

Dominic del Val (St) M.   Aug 31
d. 1250   In Spain he is usually called San Dominguito — Little Dominic. He was a seven-year-old altar boy at the cathedral of Saragossa, who was kidnapped by Jews and nailed against a wall. His feast is celebrated throughout Aragon.

Dominic of Nagasaki
(Bl) M. OFM.   Sept 8
d. 1628   A Japanese catechist. He received the Franciscan habit in the prison at Omura from Bl Antony of St Bonaventure and was burnt alive at Nagasaki. Beatified in 1867.

Dominic Nacano (Bl) M.   Sept 10
d. 1622   Son of Bl Matthias Nacano. He was behead at Nagasaki. Beatified in 1854.

Dominic Xamada and
Clare, his wife (BB) MM.   Sept 10
d. 1622   Japanese laypersons, beheaded at Nagasaki. Beatified in 1854.

Dominic Trach (St) M. OP.   Sept 18
1792–1842   A native priest of Vietnam, and a member of the Dominican third order. He was beheaded for his faith. Canonized in 1988.

Dominic Spadafora (Bl)
C. OP.   Oct 3
d. 1521   A native of Palermo, who, after having finished his studies at Padua, joined the friars preachers and spent his life in continuous preaching throughout Italy and Sicily. Cult confirmed in 1921.

Dominic Loricatus (the
Mailed) (St) H. OSB.   Oct 14
995–1060   Born in Umbria. By means of a bribe his father had him ordained priest in contravention of canon law, and on learning this, the saint determined to do penance for it during the rest of his life. He first became a hermit and then a Benedictine monk under St Peter Damian at Fontavellana. He is surnamed "the Mailed" because he wore for years a rough iron coat-of-mail next to his skin.

Dominic Doan Xuyen
(St) M. OP.   Nov 26
1788–1839   A native of Vietnam, and a member of the Dominican order, beheaded with St Thomas Du. Canonized in 1988.

Dominic Uy (St) M.   Dec 19
1813–1839   A native catechist of Vietnam,

who belonged to the third order of St Dominic. He was strangled at the age of twenty-six. Beatified in 1900, Canonized in 1988.

Dominic of Brescia (St)
Bp.   Dec 20
d. c612   The successor of St Anastasius in the see of Brescia. St Charles Borromeo translated and enshrined his relics.

Dominic of Silos (St) Ab.
OSB.   Dec 20
c1000–1073   Born at Cañas — then Spanish Navarre, now Rioja–he became a Benedictine at San Millán de la Cogolla. As prior of this great abbey he came into conflict with King Garcia III of Navarre by whom he was exiled from the kingdom. King Ferdinand I of Old Castile received him kindly and sent him as abbot to restore the old monastery of St Sebastian — now St Dominic — of Silos. The saint was most successful in this task and was responsible for a virtual rebuilding of the abbey. He was a lover of the arts, and the scriptorium of his abbey produced under his inspiration the best specimens of Spanish Christian art. The cloisters of the abbey — a gem of Romanesque architecture — stand to this day as the best monument to his enterprise. He was also renowned for rescuing Christian slaves from the Moors. He is one of the best beloved of Spanish saints. At his shrine Bl Aza de Guzmán obtained the child whom she called Dominic, after the abbot of Silos, and who became the founder of the Dominican Friars.

Dominic, Victor, Primian,
Lybosus, Saturninus,
Crescentius, Secundus,
and Honoratus (SS) MM.   Dec 29
? African martyrs whose Acts have been lost.

Dominica (St) VM.   July 6
? Said to have been a martyr in Campania under Diocletian. Possibly she is to be identified with St Cyriaca — Dominica, venerated on this day in the East as a martyr at Nicomedia.

Dominica (St) M.   Aug 21
Otherwise Cyriaca, q.v.

Dominica Ongata (Bl) M.   Sept 10
d. 1622   A Japanese woman, beheaded at Nagasaki. See Bl Charles Spinola.

Dominican Martyrs of
Vietnam (SS)   Nov 24
1856–1862   Between these years the per-

secution of the church by the King Tu-Duc raged with particular severity in the Dominican vicariates of Central Tonkin. Five martyrs were beatified in 1906 and in 1917 no less than 2078 causes were introduced. In 1951 a representative group of twenty-five of these were selected for immediate beatification. These were: Joseph Diaz Sanjurjo OP., Vic. Ap.; Melchior Garcia Sampedro, OP., Vic. Ap.; Dominic Ninh; Laurence Ngon; Dominic An-Kham; Luke Cai-Thin; Joseph Cai-Ta; Dominic Mao; Vincent Tuong; Dominic Nguyen; Andrew Tuong; Dominic Nhi; Peter Da; Joseph Tuan; Peter Dung; Peter Tuan; Vincent Duong; Dominic Mau, priest OP.; Dominic Toai; Dominic Huyen; Joseph Tuan, priest OP.; Dominic Cam, priest and Dominican tertiary; Thomas Khuong, priest and Dominican tertiary; Paul Duong; Joseph Tuc. Canonized in 1988.

Domitian (St) Bp.   May 7
d. *c* 560   Bishop of Maestricht, and apostle of the Meuse valley. His relics are venerated at Huy.

Domitian and Hadelin
(SS) Mks. OSB.   June 15
d. *c* 686   Two disciples of St Landelinus at the abbey of Lobbes. They were connected also, it seems, with Crépin abbey.

Domitian (St) Ab.   July 1
c 347–440   Born in Rome and left an orphan at an early age, he passed into Gaul and became a monk and a priest at Lérins. Later he founded the monastery of Bebron, now St Rambert de Joux. The sources, however, of St Domitian's life are very unreliable.

Domitian (St) M.   Aug 1
See Cyril, Aquila, etc.

Domitian of Châlons (St)
Bp.   Aug 9
4th cent. ?   The third bishop of Châlons-sur-Marne in France, in which he succeeded his master, St Donatian.

Domitian (St) M.   Dec 28
See Eutychius and Domitian.

Domitilla (St) VM.   formerly May 2
More correctly Flavia Domitilla, q.v.

Domitius, Pelagia,
Aquila, Esparchius and
Theodosia (SS) MM.   March 23
d. 361   St Domitius was a Phrygian who died by the sword under Julian the Apostate, probably at Caesarea in Palestine. He is said to have publicly attacked the errors of heathenism in the circus, where the pagans were gathered for the festival games held in honour of the gods. Several others were martyred with him.

Domitius (St) M.   July 5
d. 362   A Persian, or a Phrygian monk, stoned to death under Julian the Apostate, in much the same circumstances as St Domitius of March 23.

Domitius (Domestius)
and Comp. (SS) MM.   Aug 7
4th cent.   The entry in the pre-1970 RM. was "At Nisibis in Mesopotamia St Dometius, a Persian monk who with two of his disciples was stoned to death under Julian the Apostate." This Domitius is probably identical with the preceding two of March 23 and July 5.

Domitius (St) C.   Oct 23
8th cent.   A priest, or a deacon, of the diocese of Amiens, who retired to a solitude and lived as an anchorite.

Domna (St) VM.   Dec 28
See Indes, Domna, etc.

Domneva (Domna Eva)
(St) W. OSB.   Nov 19
Otherwise Ermenburg, q.v.

Domnina and Comp.
(SS) VV. MM.   Apr 14
69 ?   Maidens who were martyred at Terni, in Umbria, at the same time, it is said, as the bishop St Valentine.

Domnina, Berenice and
Prosdoce (SS) MM.   Oct 4
d. 303–310   St Domnina and her two daughters were martyred in Syria during the persecution of Diocletian. They are commemorated by several contemporary Greek writers.

Domnina (St) M.   Oct 12
d. 303   A Christian woman who, after cruel torments, died in prison at Anazarbus under the prefect Lysias.

Domninus (St) M.   March 21
See Philemon and Domninus.

Domninus, Victor and
Comp. (SS) MM.   March 30
c 304   St Domninus appears to have suffered at Thessalonica under Maximian Herculeus, together with Philocalus, Achaicus and Palotinus. He is to be identified with St Domninus of Oct 1 (see below), on which day he is venerated by the Greeks. St Victor and his companions, some ten in number, suffered elsewhere, the name of the place being no longer known.

Domninus (St)   Apr 20
See Marcellinus, Vincent and Domninus.

Domninus (St) M.   Oct 1
The same as Domninus commemorated on
March 30, q.v.

Domninus (Donnino)
(St) M.   Oct 9
d. 304 A native of Parma, who, while trying
to escape in time of persecution, was overtaken
and beheaded on the Via Claudia or Aemilia, a
few miles out of Parma at a place now called
after him Borgo san Donnino, where his relics
are held in great veneration.

Domninus,
Theotimus, Philotheus,
Sylvanus and Comp.
(SS) MM.   Nov 5
? St Domninus, a young physician, and St
Sylvanus, a Syrian bishop, were together con-
demned to work in the mines. The former was
burnt alive somewhere in Palestine, the latter
was martyred much later. The rest seem to
have suffered under Maximian.

Domninus (St) Bp.   Nov 5
4th cent. This St Domninus is given as the
first bishop of Grenoble in France.

Domnio and Comp. (SS)
MM.   Apr 11
? According to an old legend, Domnio, one of
the seventy-two disciples of Christ, was sent
from Rome by St Peter to evangelize Dalmatia, where he was martyred as first bishop of
Salona. A more probable version states that he
was martyred during the persectuion of Diocletian.

Domnio (St) M.   July 16
d. c 295 A martyr of Bergamo in Lombardy
under Diocletian.

Domnio (St) C.   Dec 28
4th cent. A Roman priest, of whom his
contemporaries SS Jerome and Augustine
speak in glowing terms.

Domnoc (St)   Feb 13
Otherwise Modomnock, q.v.

Domnolus (St) Bp.   May 16
d. 581 Abbot of the monastery of St Laurence, near Paris. In 543 he was chosen bishop
of Le Mans. He was the founder of many
monasteries, hospitals and churches.

Domnus (St) M. OFM.   Oct 13
See Daniel, Samuel, etc.

Domnus of Vienne (St) Bp.   Nov 3
d. 657 Successor of St Desiderius the
martyr in the bishopric of Vienne. He was most
zealous in ransoming the captives taken in the
incessant wars of that period.

Donald (Donivald) (St) C.   July 15
8th cent. A holy man of Scotland who with
his nine daughters — the "Nine Maidens", led
the life of a religious at Ogilvy in Forfarshire.

Donard (St)   March 24
Otherwise Domangard, q.v.

Donas (St) Bp.   Oct 14
Otherwise Donatian, q.v.

Donat (Dunwyd) (St)   Aug 7
The patron saint of St Donat's or Llandun-
wyd, Glamorgan. This from the English Menology. Nothing more is discoverable.

Donata (St) M.   July 17
One of the Scillitan Martyrs, q.v.

Donata, Paulina, Rustica,
Nominanda, Serotina,
Hilaria and Comp. (SS) MM.   Dec 31
? A band of Roman women martyred in one of
the early persecutions and whose relics were
enshrined in the catacombs of the Via Salaria.

Donatian and Rogatian
(SS) MM.   May 24
d. 299 Two brothers of Nantes in Brittany
put to death by Rictiovarus under Diocletian.

Donatian (St) Bp.   Aug 7
? 4th cent. Second bishop of Châlons-
sur-Marne.

Donatian, Praesidius,
Mansuetus, Germanus,
Fusculus and Laetus (SS)
MM.   Sept 6
5th cent. Some of the more prominent
among the Catholics driven from Africa into
exile by Hunneric, the Arian king of the
Vandals. An account of them is given by Victor
of Utica in his history of that persecution. It is
said that the number of exiles reached nearly
five thousand in a single year.

Donatian (Donas) (St) Bp.   Oct 14
d. 390 A Roman by birth and bishop of
Reims from 360 to 390. His relics were
translated to Bruges in the ninth century. He
has since been venerated as the patron saint of
Bruges.

Donatilla (St) VM.   July 30
See Maxima, Donatilla and Secunda.

Donatus, Sabinus and
Agape (SS) MM.   Jan 25
? Martyrs whose names are listed in the pre-
1970 RM. but of whom no record is extant.

Donatus (St) M.   Feb 4
See Aquilinus, Geminus, etc.

Donatus (St) M.   Feb 9
See Primus and Donatus.

**Donatus, Secundian,
Romulus and Comp.
(SS)** MM.   Feb 17
d. 304   A group of eighty-nine martyrs who
suffered under Diocletian. They were put to
death at Porto Gruaro (*Concordia*), not far from
Venice.

**Donatus, Justus, Herena
and Comp. (SS)** MM.   Feb 25
3rd cent.   A band of fifty martyrs who suffered in Africa under Decius.

Donatus (St) M.   March 1
See Leo, Donatus, etc.

Donatus (St) M.   Apr 7
See Epiphanius, Donatus, etc.

Donatus (St) Bp.   Apr 30
d. late 4th cent.   Bishop of Euraea in Epirus
(Albania). His sanctity is recorded by Sozomen and other Greek writers.

Donatus (St) M.   May 21
See Polyeuctus, Victorius, and Donatus.

**Donatus and Hilarinus
(SS)** MM.   Aug 7
4th cent.   St Donatus was the second bishop
of Arezzo. Through confusion with another
Donatus he was thought to be a martyr. He
had no connection with St Hilarinus, a martyr
of Ostia. Cult confined to local calendars since
1969.

Donatus (St) Bp. OSB.   Aug 7
d. *c* 660   A monk of Luxeuil. Bishop of
Besançon in 624. He was a most zealous
fosterer of monasticism and founded at Besançon the abbey of St Paul. His *Regula ad
Virgines* combines elements of the rules of St
Benedict and of St Columban.

Donatus (St) Mk. OSB.   Aug 17
1179–1198   Born at Ripacandida, in the diocese of Rapallo. He became a monk of the
Benedictine congregation of Montevergine at
St Onofrio at Petina (1194). He is now the
principal patron saint of Ripacandida.

Donatus (St) C.   Aug 19
d. *c* 535   A native of Orleans, who lived as a
hermit on Mt Jura near Sisteron in Provence.

Donatus of Antioch (St)
M.   Aug 23
See Restitutus, Donatus, etc.

Donatus and Felix (SS)
MM.   Sept 1
Two of the Twelve Holy Brothers, so-called,
q.v.

Donatus of Capua (St) M.   Sept 5
See Quintius, Arcontius and Donatus.

Donatus (St) M.   Oct 5
See Placid, Eutychius, etc.

Donatus of Fiesole (St)
Bp.   Oct 22
d. 874   An Irishman who, while passing
through Tuscany on his return from a pilgrimage to Rome, was made bishop of Fiesole near
Florence. He was a poet and a scholar, and
solicitous for pilgrims.

Donatus of Corfu (St) C.   Oct 29
?   All we know of this saint is that, about the
year 600, St Gregory the Great directed that
his relics, brought to Corfu by a refugee priest
from Asia Minor, should be enshrined in one
of the churches of the island.

Donatus (St) M.   Dec 12
See Hermogenes, Donatus, etc.

**Donatus of Alexandria
(St)** M.   Dec 30
See Mansuetus, Severus, etc.

**Donnan (Dounan) and
Comp. (SS)** MM.   Apr 17
d. 618   St Donnan was a monk of Iona under
St Columba. He eventually became the abbot-
founder of a monastery on Eigg Island in the
Inner Hebrides, off the west coast of Scotland.
He and his fifty-two monks were massacred by
heathen raiders on Easter Sunday.

Donvina (St) M.   Aug 23
See Claudius, Asterius, etc.

Dorbhene (St) Ab.   Oct 28
d. 713   Abbot of Iona, descended from a
brother of St Columba. A copy of St Adamnan's life of the latter written by St Dorbhene
is still in existence.

Dorcas (St) W.   Oct 25
Otherwise Tabitha, q.v.

Doris (*several*)
Otherwise Dorothy, q.v.

Dorotheus (St) M.   March 28
See Castor and Dorotheus.

Dorotheus of Tyre (St) M.   June 5
d. *c* 362   A priest of Tyre, who was exiled
under Diocletian. On his return he was chosen
bishop of Tyre, and as such attended the
council of Nicaea. Under Julian the Apostate

he was beaten to death at Varna on the Black Sea. All the above details, however, are more or less guess-work.

Dorotheus the Archimandrite (St) Ab.   June 5

d. *c* 640   A monk of Gaza, who became archimandrite of an unknown monastery. His writings were greatly admired by Abbot de Rancé.

Dorotheus the Younger (St) Ab.   June 5

11th cent.   Born at Trebizond, he was first a monk at Samsun on the Black Sea and afterwards abbot-founder of a monastery at Khiliokomos nearby.

Dorotheus and Gorgonius (SS) MM.   Sept 9

d. 303   Favourites of the emperor Diocletian and officials of his bodyguard at Nicomedia. The emperor had them hanged for their faith. Eusebius of Caesarea, a contemporary, records their martyrdom. Since 1969 the cult has been confined to particular calendars.

Dorothy (Dora, Dorothea) (St) VM.   formerly Feb 6

d. *c* 300   A virgin-martyr of Caesarea in Cappadocia who suffered under Diocletian. Her *Acta* are apocryphal, but beautiful. In art she is shown crowned with roses, or holding a bunch of roses, or a basket of fruit and roses: often she holds a palm. Cult suppressed in 1969.

Dorothy (St) VM.   Sept 3

See Euphemia, Dorothy, etc.

Dorothy of Montau (St) W.   Oct 30

1336–1394   A peasant girl of Montau in Prussia, who married a wealthy swordsmith named Albert. She bore him nine children and by her gentle patience completely changed his surly disposition. After his death Dorothy lived as a recluse at Marienwerder. Though she was never canonized her cult is still to be found in Central Europe.

Dorymedon (St) M.   Sept 19

See Trophimus, Sabbatius and Dorymedon.

Dositheus (St) Mk.   Feb 23

d. *c* 530   A rich young man who became a Christian at Jerusalem and, shortly after, a monk at Gaza. His poor health prevented him from fasting, and moreover he did not work any miracles: these facts scandalized his fellow monks. His abbot, however, considered him a great saint, since he had completely given up

St Dorothy, formerly Feb 6

his own will. This has been the verdict of history, which has canonized him.

Dotto (St) Ab.   Apr 9
? 6th cent. Said to have been abbot of a monastery in the Orkney Islands.

Douai (Martyrs of) (BB)   Oct 29
More than a hundred and sixty "seminary priests" from the English College at Douai were martyred in England and Wales during the century following its foundation in 1568. Over eighty of them were beatified in 1929. Each receives here a special notice. A collective feast is kept in their honour in several English dioceses.

**Drausinus (Drausius)
(St)** Bp.   March 7
d. *c* 576   Bishop of Soissons. A great fosterer of monastic life, he even enlisted the services of the tyrant Ebroin for the building of a convent near Soissons. For this reason he is invoked against the machinations of enemies, and St Thomas Becket is said to have visited his shrine before returning to England for the last time.

Dreux (St) H.   Apr 16
Otherwise Drogo, q.v.

Drillo (St) C.   June 15
Otherwise Trillo, q.v.

Drithelm (St) H.   Aug 17
d. *c* 700   A Northumbrian who, terrified by a vision, embraced the monastic life at Melrose, where he lived a life of great austerity in a special cell near the abbey. Bede's *History* gives us the main details of his remarkable life.

**Droctoveus (Droctonius
— in French Drotté) (St)**
Ab.   March 10
d. *c* 580   A disciple of St Germanus of Paris, then abbot of the monastery of St Symphorian at Autun and afterwards called by his old master to Paris as first abbot of the new monastery of St Vincent and the Holy Cross — afterwards renamed Saint-Germain-des-Prés.

Drogo (Bl) Mk. OSB.   Apr 2
10th cent. After a worldly life, Drogo entered the Benedictine abbey of Fleury-sur-Loire, and afterwards migrated to that of Baume-les-Messieurs, where he was engaged in tending the flocks of the abbey.

**Drogo (Dreux, Druon)
(St)** H.   Apr 16
d. 1186   A Fleming by birth and an orphan,

at twenty years of age he disposed of all his property and served as a shepherd in France. Nine times he made the pilgrimage to Rome. Stricken with a most unsightly bodily affliction, he built himself a hut under the shadow of the church of Sebourg in Hainault, where he died aged eighty-four.

Drostan (St) Ab.   July 11
d. *c* 610   An Irishman by birth, a monk under St Columba, and first abbot of Deer in Aberdeenshire. He is venerated as one of the apostles of Scotland. His holy well is near Aberdour.

**Drusus, Zosimus and
Theodore (SS)** MM.   Dec 14
? Christians martyred in Syria, probably at Antioch. Some MSS have Drusina for Drusus. St John Chrysostom has left a homily preached on their festival day.

Drusus (St) M.   Dec 24
See Lucian, Metrobius, etc.

Druthmar (St) Ab. OSB.   Feb 15
d. 1046   A Benedictine of Lorsch, who in 1014 was appointed by the emperor St Henry II abbot of Corvey in Saxony. Fervour and good observance were marks of his rule.

**Dubricius (Dubric, Dyfrig,
Devereux) (St)** Bp.   Nov 14
d. *c* 545   One of the founders of monastic life in Wales. His chief centres of monachism were at Henllan and Moccas, whence he established many other religious houses in what is now Herefordshire and Gwent and the Wye Valley. He had jurisdiction over Caldey Island and appointed St Samson abbot of the monastery there, and later ordained him bishop. A later legend makes St Dubricius archbishop of Caerleon. He died on the Isle of Bardsey.

Dubtach (St) Bp.   Oct 7
d. *c* 513   Archbishop of Armagh from 497 to *c* 513.

Dula (St) VM.   March 25
? The slave of a pagan soldier at Nicomedia in Asia Minor. She suffered death at his hands in defence of her chastity.

Dulas (St) M.   June 15
d. 300   A Christian of Zepherinum in Cilicia, martyred after having undergone the most frightful tortures.

Dulcardus (St) H.   Oct 25
d. 584   Monk of Micy (Saint-Mesmin) in Orleans, and afterwards a hermit near

Bourges, where now stands the village of Saint-Doulchard (Cher).

Dulcidius (Dulcet, Doucis) (St) Bp. Oct 16
d. *c* 450 Successor of St Phoebadius in the bishopric of Agen in France.

Dulcissima (St) VM. Sept 16
? Nothing is really known about this saint, but from time immemorial she has been venerated at Sutri, formerly in the Papal States, as a virgin-martyr and as the principal patron saint of the town and diocese.

Dumhaid (St) Ab. May 25
Otherwise Dunchadh, q.v.

Dunchadh (St) Ab. May 25
d. 717 Abbot of Iona in Scotland from 710 till his death. In his time the Roman customs — tonsure, date of Easter, Benedictine rule — were finally adopted by the Celtic monks in Scotland.

Dunchaid O'Braoin (St) Ab. Jan 16
d. 988 Born in Westmeath, he was an anchorite near the monastery of Clonmacnoise until the year 969, when he was chosen abbot of that place. In his old age he retired to Armagh, where he died.

Dunstan (St) Bp. OSB. May 19
909–988 One of the great figures in English history — abbot, archbishop, statesman, and saint. An Anglo-Saxon by origin, he was born near Glastonbury, where he was also educated and became a monk. In 943 he was made abbot, and under his rule the monastery became the greatest centre of learning in England. He himself excelled as a goldsmith, an illuminator, embroiderer and also as a musician. He was summoned to court to be a royal counsellor, but was forced into exile by King Edwy, whom he had rebuked. Dunstan now spent one year at Ghent, then a great centre of monastic restoration. He was recalled to England by King Edgar and became his chief adviser, being ordained bishop of Worcester (957) and of Canterbury (961). Moreover, Pope John XII appointed Dunstan his legate in England (961). He now achieved, together with SS Ethelwold of Winchester and Oswald of York, a thorough monastic and ecclesiastical reform throughout England and initiated a vigorous policy of national unification and moral restoration. Active and energetic to the very end, he died peacefully at Canterbury, in his cathedral of Christ Church. In art he is shown as a bishop holding the Devil by a pair of pincers, often by the nose.

St Dunstan, May 19

Duthac (St) Bp. March 8
d. 1065 An Irishman by birth, he became bishop of Ross in Scotland, where his memory is preserved in several place-names, e.g., Kilduthie, etc. Several picturesque legends are attached to his name.

Dwynwen (St) V. Jan 25
d. *c* 460 A Welsh saint of the family of

Brychan of Brecknock. The maxim "nothing wins hearts like cheerfulness" is attributed to her. Churches dedicated to her are to be found in Wales and Cornwall. Her holy well and shrine in Anglesey (at Llanddwyn) were great centres of pilgrimage until the Reformation, especially attracting those seeking guidance in affairs of the heart.

Dwynwen (St) W.   July 18
Otherwise Theneva, q.v.

Dyfan (Deruvianus, Damian) (St) M.   May 26
2nd cent. Said to have been one of the missionaries sent to the Britons by Pope St Eleutherius at the instance of King St Lucius. His church of Merthyr Dyfan shows the popular tradition that he ended his days by martyrdom: but it is all a legend.

Dyfnan (St) C.   Apr 24
5th cent. A son of the Welsh chieftain, Brychan. He founded a church in Anglesey.

Dyfnog (St) C.   Feb 13
7th cent. A Welsh saint of the family of Caradog. He was formerly held in local veneration in Clwyd.

Dyfrig (St) Bp.   Nov 14
Otherwise Dubricius, q.v.

Dympna (Dymphna) (St) VM.   May 15
? Popular legend makes her the daughter of an Irish chieftain who escaped to Belgium accompanied by her chaplain, St Gerebern. Their relics were discovered at Gheel, near Antwerp, in the thirteenth century, and since then numberless cases of insanity, epilepsy, etc., have been cured at their shrine. The asylum built at Gheel in the same century still stands, equipped with all up-to-date improvements. St Dympna is invoked as the patroness of lunatics.

Note. Saints' names beginning with the letter E are often found written with the diphthong AE, or OE, as the initial letter.

Eadbert (St) Bp. OSB.   May 6
d. 698   A monk of Lindisfarne who succeeded St Cuthbert as abbot-bishop of the island. He was remarkable for his knowledge of holy scripture. Bede speaks of his great learning. His relics were removed to Durham after 875.

Eadburga (*several*)
Otherwise Edburga, q.v.

Eadfrid (St) Mk. OSB.   Oct 26
d. *c* 675   A Northumbrian monk-priest who preached in Mercia and founded, and was the first superior of Leominster priory.

Eadgith (*several*)
Otherwise Edith, q.v.

Eadnot (St) Bp. OSB.   Oct 19
d. 1016   Monk of Worcester and abbot of Ramsey. In 1006 he became bishop of Dorchester. As such he helped and seconded St Oswald of York. He died in a battle against the Danes, and is sometimes termed a martyr.

Eadsin (St) Bp.   Oct 28
d. 1050   Archbishop of Canterbury. He crowned St Edward the Confessor on the restoration of the Anglo-Saxon line in England. He resigned his see some years before his death.

Eanfleda (St) W. OSB.   Nov 24
d. *c* 700   Daughter of King St Edwin of Northumbria and of his wife St Ethelburga of Kent, baptized as an infant by St Paulinus. She was a great benefactress of St Wilfrid. In her widowhood she became a nun at Whitby under her own daughter, St Elfleda.

Eanswith (Eanswida) (St)
Abs. OSB.   Sept 12
d. *c* 640   Granddaughter of King St Ethelbert of Kent. She was the abbess-foundress (630) of a nunnery on the coast near Folkestone. Her convent was destroyed by the Danes but re-founded for Benedictine monks in 1095. Part of it was swallowed up by the sea, and it was removed to Folkestone. Its successor is now the church of SS Mary and Eanswith. In 1885 restoration of the church resulted in the rediscovery of St Eanswith's relics hidden during the Reformation. These are now suitably enshrined in the north wall of the chancel. In art she is robed as a nun, and crowned; she holds a fish, or a church.

Easterwine (St) Ab. OSB.   March 7
Otherwise Esterwine, q.v.

Eata (St) Bp. OSB.   Oct 26
d. *c* 686   An Englishman educated by St Aidan in the Celtic observance at Ripon. When St Wilfrid arrived at this abbey, Eata left it for Melrose, where he became abbot. After the council of Whitby, however, he adopted fully the Roman observances and was made abbot of Lindisfarne. In 678 he became bishop of the Bernicians, being consecrated by St Theodore, with his see first at Lindisfarne and then at the Benedictine abbey of Hexham.

St Eanswith, Sept 12

Ebba the Younger and Comp. (SS) VV. MM.

OSB.   Aug 23

d. *c* 870 Abbess of the great Benedictine nunnery of Coldingham, on the Scottish border, founded two centuries earlier by St Ebba the Elder. During a Danish incursion St Ebba, fearing for her virginity, mutilated her face and invited her nuns to do the same. The Danes set fire to the nunnery and all the community perished in the flames. This story is found only in Matthew Paris's *Chronica Majora*.

Ebba the Elder (St) Abs.

OSB.   Aug 25

d. 683   Sister of SS Oswald and Oswy, kings of Northumbria. She took the veil from St Finan at Lindisfarne and founded the double monastery of Coldingham, on the coast of Northumberland, near Berwick, of which she was first abbess. The organization of the abbey resembled that of Whitby in most points. Ebba, we are told, was personally a very holy abbess, but not a great success as an administrator.

Ebbo (St) Bp. OSB.   Aug 27

d. 740   A native of Tonnerre and a Benedictine monk of Saint-Pierre-le-Vif, at Sens. About the year 709 he was made bishop of Sens. In 725 he saved the city when it was besieged by Saracens.

Eberhard (*several*)

Note. This Teutonic name, when transliterated into other languages, is often softened into Everhard, Everard, Evard, Erhard, Erard, etc.

Eberhard (Bl) Mk. OSB.

Cist.   March 20

d. *c* 1150   Count of Mons in Belgium. In expiation of a crime committed as a soldier, he went on pilgrimage to Rome and Compostella and finally asked to be hired as a swineherd at the Cistercian abbey of Morimond. When his identity was discovered, he was induced to continue his life of penance as a monk, and accordingly took the vows. In 1142 he founded Einberg and then Mont-Saint-George. He is officially venerated by the Cistercians.

Eberhard of Schaffhausen

(Bl) Mk. OSB.   Apr 7

1018–1078   Eberhard III, count of Nellenburg, was a relative of Pope St Leo IX and the emperor St Henry II. In 1050 he founded the Benedictine abbey of Schaffhausen in Switzerland — now a town — and took the habit there.

Eberhard (Bl) O. Praem.   Apr 17

d. 1178   Premonstratensian monk of Roth, later provost of Marchtal in Swabia when it was handed over to the Premonstratensians in 1166.

Eberhard of Salzburg

(St) Bp. OSB.   June 22

1085–1164 (June 11)   Born at Nuremberg and educated by the monks of Michelberg at Bamberg, he obtained a canonry at Bamberg, which, however, he gave up in order to become a Benedictine at Prüfening (1125). In 1133 he was made abbot of Biburg, and in 1147 archbishop of Salzburg. He was the greatest supporter of the pope in Germany during the investiture controversy.

Eberhard of Einsiedeln

(Bl) Ab. OSB.   Aug 14

d. 958   One of the ducal family of Swabia. He was already provost of the cathedral chapter at Strasburg when, in 934, he joined his friend Bl Benno at Einsiedeln. After Bl Benno's death he was acknowledged as the first abbot of Einsiedeln. During his rule, the abbey was built and the church dedicated.

Ebontius (Pontius Ponce, Ebon) (St) Bp.

OSB.   Oct 3

d. 1104   Born at Comminges, Haute Garonne, France, and a Benedictine of Sainte-Foi of Tomières, he became abbot of St Victorian (Asán), near Ainsa, in Upper Aragon, and first bishop of Babastro after its recapture from the Moors. It is doubtful, however, whether the fact of his cultus can be proved.

Ebregesilus (St) Bp. M.   Oct 24

Otherwise Evergislus, q.v.

Ebrulfus (Evroult) (St) Ab.   July 25

d. *c* 600   Born at Beauvais in France, he became a hermit and afterwards abbot-founder of Saint-Fuscien-aux-Bois.

Ebrulfus (Evroult) (St)

Ab.   Dec 29

626–706   A native of Bayeux in Normandy, he became a courtier at the palace of King Childebert I. He left the court to become a monk at the abbey of Deux Jumeaux, diocese of Bayeux, and later the abbot-founder of Ouche and of other smaller houses. The historian Ordericus Vitalis was a monk of St Evroult.

Ebsdorf (Martyrs of) (SS) Feb 2
d. 880   In the winter of 880 Duke St Bruno led the army of King Louis III against the invading Norsemen. On the marshy heath of Luneberg, at Ebsdorf in Saxony, the army was caught in ice and snow and defeated by the Norsemen. Bruno, with four bishops, eleven noblemen, and many others were slain and forthwith venerated as martyrs.

Ecclesius (St) Bp. July 27
d. 532   Bishop of Ravenna from 521 till 532. He began the building of San Vitale, at Ravenna, where there is a figure of him in mosaic.

Echa (Etha) (St) H. OSB. May 5
d. 767   An Anglo-Saxon priest and monk-hermit at Crayk, near York.

Edan (St) Bp. Jan 31
Otherwise Aidan, q.v.

Edana (Etaoin) (St) V. July 5
? An Irish saint, patron of parishes in W. Ireland. A famous holy well bears her name. She appears to have lived near the confluence of the rivers Boyle and Shannon. Some have thought her to be one and the same with St Modwenna, who is also commemorated on July 5.

Edbert (St) Bp. May 6
Otherwise Eadbert, q.v.

Edbert (St) King, OSB. Aug 20
d. 768   The successor of St Ceolwulph on the throne of Northumbria. After a prosperous reign of twenty years he resigned and retired to the abbey of York, where he spent a further ten years in prayer and seclusion.

Edburga (several)
Note. The name is spelt in many different ways: Iderberga, Edberga, Eadburga, Ideberga, Idaberga, etc.

Edburga of Winchester (St) Abs. OSB. June 15
d. 960   Daughter of Edward the Elder and granddaughter of Alfred the Great, she was placed as a child in the nunnery which King Alfred's widow had founded at Winchester. Her shrine at Pershore in Worcestershire was famous for its miracles.

Edburga of Bicester (St) N. OSB. July 18
Late 7th cent.   The daughter of the pagan Penda, king of Mercia, a nun at Aylesbury, Buckinghamshire, from whence her relics were transferred to Bicester and later to Flanders. Parts of her shrine remain at Stanton Harcourt, Oxfordshire.

Edburga of Thanet (St) Abs. OSB. Dec 12
d. 751   Of the royal family of Wessex. A disciple of St Mildred, whom she probably succeeded as abbess of Minster-in-Thanet in 716. She was a friend and correspondent of St Boniface, whom she helped with books, altar vestments and other gifts. She had a new church built for her convent at Minster.

Edburga (St) N. OSB. Dec 13
7th cent.   A nun of Lyminge in Kent.

Edeyrn (St) H. Jan 6
6th cent.   The patron saint of a church in Brittany. The legend describes him as a Briton, associating him with King Arthur, and making him end his days as a hermit in Armorica.

Edgar the Peaceful (St) King. July 8
d. 975   The great friend of St Dunstan, whom he took as his adviser. His reign is marked by a strong religious revival in England. Though he enjoyed a local cultus at Glastonbury, he would not nowadays be reckoned a likely candidate for canonization due to his amorous attachment to two nuns, one of whom bore him a daughter, Edith of Wilton, q.v.

Edilburga (St) V. July 7
Otherwise Ethelburga, q.v.

Ediltrudis (St) V. June 23
Otherwise Etheldreda, q.v.

Edistius (St) M. Oct 12
d. c 303   A martyr of Ravenna under Diocletian.

Edith of Polesworth (St) W. OSB. July 15
d. ? 925   There is much confusion as to the identity of this St Edith. She was certainly the widow of a king of Northumbria and died as a nun — probably abbess — of Polesworth in Warwickshire.

Edith Stein (Bl) Aug 9
See Teresa Benedicta of the Cross.

St Edith, Sept 16

Edith of Wilton (St) N.
OSB.   Sept 16
961–984   Daughter of King Edgar and of St
Wilfrida. Taken to Wilton abbey shortly after
birth, she never left it, so that, in the words of
the pre-1970 RM. "she rather knew not this
world than forsook it". She was professed
before her fifteenth year, her father being
present. She declined to accept the government of three abbeys, preferring to remain a
simple nun at Wilton. When her father died,
she was offered and refused the throne. She
died at the age of twenty-two, St Dunstan
attending her in her last illness.

Edmund Arrowsmith
(St) M. SJ.   Aug 28
d. 1628   Born at Haydock, near St Helens,
in Lancashire, of a recusant yeoman family.
He was educated at Douai, ordained priest
(1612), and sent to the English mission, where
he worked from 1613 to 1628, being received
into the Society of Jesus in 1623. He was
hanged, drawn and quartered at Lancaster,
where he exercised his apostolate. Beatified in
1929. Canonized in 1970 as one of the Forty
Martyrs of England and Wales, q.v.

Edmund Rich (St) Bp.   Nov 20
1180–1242   Born at Abingdon, he studied at
Oxford and Paris, and became professor of
philosophy at Oxford (1219–1226), canon of
Salisbury, and archbishop of Canterbury
(1233). His uncompromising stand in favour
of good discipline, monastic observance and
justice in high quarters, brought him into
conflict with King Henry III, with several
monasteries and with his own chapter. He was
moreover opposed by the papal legate. In 1240
he retired to the Cistercian abbey of Pontigny,
where, according to the Cistercian tradition,
he lived and died in the Cistercian habit.
Canonized in 1246.

Edmund (St) King M.   Nov 20
849–869   King of the East Angles from 855.
In the Danish inroad of 870 he was taken
prisoner and savagely done to death at Hoxne
in Suffolk. He expired with the name of Jesus
on his lips. His shrine gave its name to the
Benedictine abbey and town of Bury St Edmund's. Although it has been contended that
he was slain at Hellesdon in Norfolk, the tradition that he died in Suffolk is supported by the
recent discovery that a tract of land near
Bradfield St Clare was called Hellesdon as late
as 1840. In art, St Edmund is depicted as
crowned and robed as a king, pierced by
arrows, or holding sceptre, orb and arrows, or
a quiver.

St Edmund, Nov 20

Edmund Campion (St)
M. SJ.   Dec 1
c 1540–1581 "The Pope's Champion". Born in London and educated at Christ's Hospital, he was a brilliant student at Oxford. Reconciled to the Catholic church, he passed on to Douai and then to Rome, where he joined the Jesuits. Next he worked in Bohemia, and finally, for one year, on the English mission. His extraordinary success caused him to be hunted down relentlessly. He was betrayed, racked and martyred at Tyburn. Canonized as one of the Forty Martyrs of England and Wales, q.v.

Edmund Genings (St) M.   Dec 10
d. 1591   Born at Lichfield, and a convert from Protestantism, he studied and was ordained priest at Reims (1590). He passed on to the English mission and was condemned to death the following year. He was hanged, drawn and quartered at Gray's Inn Fields, London. Beatified in 1929. Canonized in 1970 as one of the Forty Martyrs of England and Wales, q.v.

Edward Waterson (Bl)
M.   Jan 7
d. 1593   Born in London and a convert. He studied at Reims and was ordained in 1592. The following year he was executed at Newcastle. Beatified in 1929.

Edward Stransham (Bl)
M.   Jan 21
d. 1586   Born at Oxford, and educated there at St John's College. He studied for the priesthood at Douai and Reims, was ordained in 1580, and sent to the English mission in 1581. He worked in London and in Oxford. He was condemned and executed at Tyburn. Beatified in 1929.

Edward the Martyr (St)
King M.   March 18
d. 979   The son of Edgar the Peaceful, and king of England at the age of thirteen, after his father's death (975). In 979 he was murdered at Corfe at the instigation of his stepmother Elfrida and buried at Wareham in Dorsetshire. He was forthwith popularly acclaimed as a martyr. In art he is shown as king holding a dagger and a cup, or with a dagger and falcon, or a sceptre and sword.

Edward Oldcorne (Bl)
M. SJ.   Apr 7
d. 1606   A native of York, he was ordained

priest at Rome and received into the Society of Jesus in 1587. He worked in the Midlands from 1588 to 1606, and was condemned to death at Worcester for alleged complicity in the Gunpowder Plot. Beatified in 1929.

Edward Catherick (Bl)
M.   Apr 13
d. 1642   Born at Carlton, near Richmond, Yorks. He was educated at Douai and laboured as a missionary priest in England from 1635 till his death. He was executed at York. Beatified in 1929.

Edward Jones (Bl) M.   May 6
d. 1590   Born in the diocese of St Asaph in Wales and a convert. He studied for the priesthood at Reims, and was ordained in 1588. He was captured and executed in Fleet Street. Beatified in 1929.

Edward Fulthrop (Bl) M.   July 4
d. 1597   A gentleman of Yorkshire executed at York for having been reconciled to the Catholic church. Beatified in 1929.

Edward Powell (Bl) M.   July 30
d. 1540   A Welshman who became a canon of Salisbury and a fellow of Oriel and was well known in Europe as the author of various treatises against Luther. He was chosen by Queen Catherine of Aragon as one of her counsel. After six years in prison he was hanged, drawn and quartered at Smithfield, London, for denying the king's spiritual supremacy. Beatified in 1886.

Edward Shelley (Bl) M.   Aug 30
d. 1588   A gentleman of Warminghurst, Sussex, hanged at Tyburn for harbouring priests. Beatified in 1929.

Edward Barlow (St) M.
OSB.   Sept 10
Otherwise Ambrose Edward Barlow, q.v.

Edward James (Bl) M.   Oct 1
d. 1588   A native of Breaston, near Derby, and an undergraduate of St John's College, Oxford. After his conversion he studied at Reims and Rome. Ordained priest in 1583, he was condemned and executed at Chichester. Beatified in 1929.

Edward Campion (Bl) M.   Oct 1
d. 1588   Born at Ludlow in Shropshire, he studied at Jesus College, Oxford. After his conversion he was trained for the priesthood at Reims and ordained in 1587. He was condemned and executed at Canterbury. Beatified in 1929.

Edward the Confessor
(St) King   Oct 13
1003–1066   Born at Islip, near Oxford, the

St Edward the Confessor, Oct 13

son of King Ethelred the Unready. He became king of England in 1042. Considerate, just, gentle and unselfish, his reign was one of peace, prosperity and good government. Some of the nobility opposed him, but the commoners were all for "good King Edward". He was much given to prayer and hunting. In commutation of a vow to go on pilgrimage to Rome he rebuilt Westminster abbey, where he was buried. He was canonized in 1161, and his relics solemnly enshrined on Oct 13, 1162, on which day his feast was celebrated throughout Christendom until 1969, though the date of his death was Jan 5. His relics, although removed for a time at the Reformation, remain almost undisturbed since then behind the high altar of the abbey. In art, he is depicted as an elderly king richly robed holding a ring, offering it to St John disguised as a beggar. Cult confined to particular calendars since 1969.

Edward Coleman (Bl) M.   Dec 3
d. 1678   A gentleman of Suffolk, educated at Peterhouse, Cambridge, and a convert to the Catholic faith. He was secretary to the Duchess of York, and was executed at Tyburn on a false charge of conspiring with a foreign power to restore the Catholic church in England. He was the first victim of the "Titus Oates Plot". Beatified in 1929.

Edwen (St) V.   Nov 6
7th cent. The alleged patron saint of Llanedwen, Anglesey. She is described as having been a daughter of King Edwin of Northumberland.

Edwin (St) King M.   Oct 12
d. 633   King of Northumbria from 616. He married as his second wife Ethelburga of Kent and was baptized by her chaplain bishop, St Paulinus (627). He fell in battle at Hatfield Chase fighting against the pagan Mercians and Welsh. Hence he was venerated as a martyr.

Edwold (St) C.   Aug 29
9th cent. Brother of St Edmund the Martyr, king of East Anglia. He lived as a recluse at Cerne in Dorsetshire.

Efflam (St) C.   Nov 6
d. c 700   Son of a British prince who, crossing to France, became abbot of a monastery he had founded in Brittany.

Egbert (St) Mk. OSB.   March 18
d. c 720   A monk, probably of Ripon, where his relics were venerated from about the year 1000.

Egbert (St) Mk.   Apr 24
d. 729   An English monk of Lindisfarne who migrated to Ireland and lived at Rathelmigisi in Connaught. Here he trained several bands of monks for the German mission. He passed over to Iona to induce the monks to adopt the Roman usages. He succeeded at last: in fact, on the day of his death Easter was for the first time celebrated at Iona according to the Roman reckoning.

Egdunus and Comp. (SS)
MM.   March 12
d. 303   Martyrs at Nicomedia under Diocletian. They were eight in number: they were suspended head downwards over a fire and suffocated by its smoke.

Egelnoth (St) Bp. OSB.   Oct 30
See Ethelnoth, q.v.

Egelred (St) M. OSB.   Sept 25
d. c 870   A monk-martyr of Croyland abbey, put to death with his abbot and many others of the community by the heathen Danes.

Egelwine (St) C.   Nov 29
7th cent. A prince of the house of Wessex who lived at Athelney in Somersetshire.

Egidius (*several*)
Otherwise Giles, q.v.

Egilhard (St) M. OSB.   May 25
d. 881   The eighth abbot of Cornelimünster, near Aachen. He was killed by the Normans at Bercheim.

Egilo (Egilon, Eigil) (St)
Ab. OSB.   June 28
d. 871   Monk of Prüm, near Trier, and then abbot there. As abbot he gave the habit to St Humphrey at Prüm. In 860 the emperor Charles the Bald directed him to restore Flavigny, in the diocese of Dijon. Later on he founded the abbey of Corbigny, Yonne.

Egino (Egon) (St) Ab. OSB.   July 15
d. 1122   Born at Augsburg and received as a child-oblate at the abbey of SS Ulric and Afra in the same city. In the conflict between the pope and the emperor he sided with the former, and was for this reason expelled by his abbot, being welcomed at the abbey of St Blasien (Blaise). In 1106 he was recalled to Augsburg and appointed abbot in 1109. He had to suffer much at the hands of the simoniacal bishop Herimann and fled to Rome in 1120. On his return home he died at Pisa in the monastery of his Camaldolese brethren.

Egwin (St) Bp. OSB.   Dec 30
d. 717   Consecrated to God in his youth, he eventually became the third bishop of Worcester (692) and perhaps the founder of the abbey of Evesham. Twice he made the pilgrimage to Rome; once, indeed, to appeal to the pope against some of his flock, whose enmity he had incurred for his severity against vice.

Egypt (Martyrs and Confessors of) (SS)
The pre-1970 RM. listed two groups of anonymous martyrs and confessors of Egypt, as follows:

                                    Jan 5
d. 303   "In Egypt the commemoration of many holy martyrs, who were slain in the Thebaid...under Diocletian".

May 21
d. *c* 357 "At Alexandria, the memory of the holy bishops and priests who were sent into exile by the Arians, and merited to be joined to the holy confessors".

Eigil (Aeigilus) (St) Ab.
OSB.   Dec 17
d. 822   A monk of Fulda, he became abbot in 817, succeeding Rutgar, who had been deposed by Charlemagne on account of excessive and imprudent severity. Eigil restored peace and union among the large community and had the consolation of paving the way for the abbacy of his great successor St Rabanus Maurus.

Eigrad (St) C.   Jan 6
6th cent.   A brother of St Samson of York, trained by St Illtyd, and founder of a church in Anglesey.

Eilan (St) C.   Jan 12
Otherwise Elian, q.v.

Eingan (Einion, Eneon, Anianus) (St) H.   Feb 9
6th cent.   A British prince who came from Cumberland into Wales and finished his days as a hermit at Llanengan, near Bangor. He is said to have been a son of the chieftain Cunedda, whose family claims no less than fifty saints.

Einhildis and Roswidna (SS) Ns. OSB.   Dec 13
8th cent.   Nuns of Hohenburg under St Ottilia. St Roswinda seems to have been St Ottilia's sister. St Einhildis became abbess of Niedermünster, near Hohenburg.

Ekbert (Egbert) (Bl) Ab.
OSB.   Nov 25
d. 1075   Monk of Gorze and afterwards abbot of Münsterschwarzach in Bavaria.

Ekhard (Bl) Ab. OSB.   June 28
d. 1084   Canon of the cathedral of Magdeburg and first abbot of Huysburg.

Ela (Bl) W.   Feb 1
d. 1261   The widow of William Longsword, she placed herself under the direction of St Edmund Rich. She founded a monastery of Carthusians at Hinton and a convent of Augustinian nuns at Laycock. She became abbess in the latter.

Elaeth the King (St)   Nov 10
6th cent.   A Briton from the North driven into Wales by the Picts. He became a monk under St Seiriol in Anglesey. Some poems of his are still extant.

Elaphius (St) Bp.   Aug 19
d. 580   Bishop of Châlons-sur-Marne. According to Gregory of Tours, he was sent as ambassador to Spain and died en route. A later writer of his life states he went to Spain to seek the relics of St Eulalia at Merida.

Eldate (Eldad) (St) C.   Feb 4
Otherwise Aldate, q.v.

Eldrad (St) Ab. OSB.   March 13
Otherwise Heldrad, q.v.

Eleazar (St) M.   Aug 1
See Machabees.

Eleazar (St) M.   Aug 23
See Minervus, Eleazar, etc.

Eleazar (St) C.   Sept 27
Otherwise Elzear, q.v.

Elefreda (St) V. OSB.   Aug 2
Otherwise Etheldritha, q.v.

Elerius (St) C.   Nov 3
6th cent.   A Welsh saint, mentioned in the legends concerning St Winefred. He is supposed to have presided over a monastery in N. Wales.

Elesbaan (St) King   Oct 27
d. *c* 555   Called by the Abyssinians Calam-Negus. He was a Christian king of Ethiopia, who successfully fought the Jewish usurper Dhu-newas, a persecutor of Christianity. After an eventful reign, during which he showed more than once his cruel and revengeful disposition, he died as an exemplary monk at Jerusalem. It seems, however, that he always remained a Monophysite.

Elesmes (St) Ab. OSB.   Jan 30
Otherwise Adelelmus, q.v.

Eleuchadius (St) Bp.   Feb 14
2nd cent.   A Greek by origin, he was converted by St Apollinaris of Ravenna, and in his absence he governed the church there. He succeeded St Adheritus as third bishop of that see.

Eleusippus (St) M.   Jan 17
See Speusippus, Eleusippus, etc.

Eleutherius (St) Bp. M.   Feb 20
d. *c* 310   Said to have been bishop of Byzantium and a martyr. Most writers, after the Bollandists, identify him with St Eleutherius commemorated on Aug 4, q.v.

Eleutherius of Tournai (St) Bp. M.   Feb 20
d. 532   A native of Tournai, bishop of that city from 486, who evangelized the Franks then settled in and near Tournai and died

from wounds inflicted by the Arian heretics of that district.

Eleutherius and Anthia
(SS) MM.   Apr 18
d. 117–138   Eleutherius, a bishop of Illyria, his mother Anthia and eleven others, are said to have been martyred in Illyria under the emperor Hadrian. The whole story has been proved to be merely a pious romance of Greek origin.

Eleutherius (St) Pope
formerly May 26
d. 189   A Greek who became a deacon of the Roman church. He succeeded St Soter as pope in 175. Very little is known about him. The story of his sending missionaries to Britain is abandoned by modern scholars. Cult suppressed in 1969.

Eleutherius (St) C.   May 29
? An English pilgrim, said to have been the brother of SS Grimwald and Fulk, who died at Rocca d'Arce, near Aquino, in S. Italy. He is venerated there as principal patron saint.

Eleutherius (St) M.   Aug 4
d. c 310   He was a martyr of Tarsus, and his tomb there became a centre of pilgrimage. He had a basilica at Constantinople. The *Passio* resumed by the pre-1970 RM. is unreliable.

Eleutherius and Leonides
(SS) MM.   Aug 8
? Martyrs burnt to death at Constantinople.

Eleutherius (St) Bp.   Aug 16
d. 561   Bishop of Auxerre, 532–561.

Eleutherius (St) Ab. OSB.   Sept 6
d. c 590   Mentioned several times by St Gregory the Great as a well-known wonder-worker. He was abbot of St Mark at Spoleto, whence he migrated to St Gregory's own abbey in Rome, where he lived for many years as a monk.

Eleutherius and Comp.
(SS) MM.   Oct 2
d. c 303   A soldier-martyr of Nicomedia under Diocletian. The story told in the pre-1970 RM. is wholly untrustworthy.

Eleutherius (St) M.   Oct 9
See Dionysius, Rusticus and Eleutherius.

Elevetha (St) VM.   Aug 1
Otherwise Almedha, q.v.

Elfeda (Ethelfleda, Edilfleda, Elgiva) (St)
Abs. OSB.   Feb 8
d. 714   Daughter of Oswy, king of North-umbria. She was offered to God as a tiny child at the nunnery of Hartlepool under St Hilda in thanksgiving for the overthrow of the pagan Penda in battle by her father, which occurred in 654. She migrated to Whitby with St Hilda and succeeded her as abbess there. She was one of the most influential personages of her time and was instrumental in reconciling SS Theodore and Wilfrid.

Elfleda (St) N. OSB.   Oct 23
d. c 936   An Anglo-Saxon princess who lived as a recluse at Glastonbury under the obedience of the abbey. She was held in great veneration by St Dunstan.

Elfleda (St) Abs. OSB.   Oct 29
d. c 1000   Daughter of Earl Ethelwold, founder of Ramsey, where she became a nun and eventually abbess.

Elfric (St) Bp. OSB.   Nov 16
Otherwise Alfrick, q.v.

Elgar (St) H.   June 14
d. c 1100   Born in Devonshire. After some years of captivity in Ireland, he settled as a hermit in the isle of Bardsey off the coast of Carnarvon.

Elgiva (St) W. OSB.   May 18
d. 944   The mother of Kings Edwy and Edgar, and wife of King Edmund (921–946). She retired to the nunnery at Shaftesbury where she ended her days. William of Malmesbury praised her virtues.

Elian (Eilan, Allan) (St) H.   Jan 13
6th cent.   A Cornish or Breton saint of the family of St Ismael. He has given his name to Llanelian in Anglesey and Llanelian in Clwyd and was titular of St Allen's church in Cornwall. His name is often confused with that of St Hilary.

Elian ap Erbin (St) C.   Jan 13
? 5th cent.   This name appears in some Welsh calendars.

Elias
This name is often also spelt Elijah.

Elias, Jeremiah, Isaiah, Samuel and Daniel (SS)
MM.   Feb 16
d. 309   Five Egyptians who, on their return journey from visiting some of their fellow-Christians condemned to the mines of Cilicia, were themselves arrested at Caesarea in Palestine and beheaded. The graphic accounts of their martyrdom is given by Eusebius who at that time was living at Caesarea.

Elias (Bl) Ab. OSB.   Apr 16
d. 1042   An Irishman who became monk

and abbot (1020) of the Scottish abbey of St Martin the Great at Cologne. The archbishop placed also under his care the abbey of St Pantaleon.

Elias, Paul and Isidore
(SS) MM. Apr 17
d. 856 Elias, a priest of Cordoba, was put to death by the Moors in his old age together with SS Paul and Isidore, two young men under his spiritual direction. St Eulogius, an eye-witness, has left us an account of their martyrdom.

Elias of Bourdeilles (Bl)
Bp. OFM. July 5
1407–1484 Born in Périgord, of the family of the counts of Bourdeilles, he took the Franciscan habit at the age of ten. He was successively bishop of Périgueux (1437), archbishop of Tours (1468) and cardinal (1483), being also confessor of King Louis XI. He is best known in history for his written defence of Joan of Arc. The process of his beatification was begun in 1526, but never finished.

Elias of Jerusalem (St)
Bp. July 20
See Flavian and Elias.

Elias (St) Bp. OSB. Aug 26
d. 660 A Benedictine monk of Sicily, who died bishop of Syracuse.

Elias (St) Bp. M. Sept 19
See Peleus, Nilus, etc.

Eligius (Eloi, Eloy) (St) Bp. Dec 1
588–660 A native of Limoges, he became a very skilful metal-smith. Some examples of his great skill survived until the French Revolution. He was appointed master of the mint at Paris under King Clotaire II. In 640 he abandoned this office to become a priest and soon after was ordained bishop of Noyon. He evangelized the districts round Antwerp, Ghent and Courtrai, founded Solignac abbey and many other monasteries and convents. He was one of the most lovable of saints and most "popular" throughout the Middle Ages. His emblems are those of metal working contemporary with the picture, e.g. a hammer and horseshoe, or a shod horse's leg; or he wears armour and stands on an anvil or he is dressed as a bishop and holds one of these emblems or with the finer instruments of a goldsmith.

Elijah
A name often spelt Elias.

Elijah (St) Prophet July 20
9th cent. B.C. The great prophet of the Old Law, the account of whose eventful life is given in 1 and 2 Kings. His association with Mt Carmel is also to be found there. The Carmelite order liturgically commemorates this great prophet as its principal patron saint. In art, he is shown as an old man in a cave being fed by ravens, or at prayer before a burning altar.

Elilantius (Bl or St) OSB. July 10
See Lantfrid, Waltram, etc.

Elined (St) VM. Aug 1
Otherwise Almedha, q.v. The name is also written Ellyw, and the saint is probably the one whose memory is perpetuated in the Welsh place-names of Llanelly and Llanelieu, besides perhaps the Breton Lanhelen.

Eliphius (Eloff) (St) M. Oct 16
d. 362 An Irishman — or Scot — by birth, who suffered at Toul in France under Julian the Apostate. His relics were translated in the tenth century to Cologne.

Elisha (St) Prophet June 14
9th cent. B.C. The holy man on whom fell the mantle of Elijah, and who continued the work of that great prophet, as is described in 1 and 2 Kings. The feast of St Elisha is liturgically observed in the Carmelite order, and also generally in the East. The Greek form of his name is Eliseus.

Elizabeth Anne Bayley
Seton (St) W. Foundress Jan 4
1774–1821 She was born in New York and grew up as a devout Episcopalian until her thirty-first year when, widowed by the death of her husband William M. Seton and with full responsibility for her five children, she was received into the church in 1805 and was confirmed in 1806 by John Carroll, bishop of Baltimore. She is the foundress of the first American sisterhood, the Sisters of Charity of St Joseph, and is considered by some as the initiator of the American parochial school system. Beatified in 1963. Canonized in 1975.

Elizabeth Salviati (Bl)
Abs. OSB. Cam. Feb 11
d. 1519 Camaldolese nun and abbess of the convent of San Giovanni Evangelista at Boldrone. Pope Urban VIII allowed pictures of her with the title of *beata* underneath to be printed in Rome.

Elizabeth Bartholomea
Picenardi (Bl) V. OSM. Feb 20
1428–1468 Born at Mantua in Italy. After her mother's death she joined the third order of the Servites. Several young girls of the noble

families of Mantua banded themselves together to live in community under her direction. Beatified in 1804.

Elizabeth of Hungary, the Younger (St) V. OP.   May 6

d. 1338 Daughter of King Andrew III of Hungary. She refused to marry Wenceslaus, the son of the king of Bohemia, and became a Dominican nun. She died in the Swiss convent at Töss, the last of the dynasty of St Stephen.

Elizabeth of Schönau (St) Abs. OSB.   June 18

1126–1164 At the age of twelve she entered the Black Benedictine — not the Cistercian — convent of Schönau, about sixteen miles N.E. of Bonn. She was professed in 1147, and shortly after she became subject to extraordinary supernatural manifestations. In 1157 she was made abbess of Schönau. Her brother Egbert, who governed the Benedictine monks at the same place, wrote her Life.

Elizabeth of Portugal (St) Queen, Tert. OFM.   GC. July 4

1271–1336 Born in Aragon, Spain, Elizabeth was the daughter of King Peter III of that kingdom, and was married at twelve years of age to the dissolute and selfish but capable King Denis of Portugal. She distinguished herself as a peacemaker between the kings of Portugal, Castile and Aragon. After the death of her husband she retired to a Poor Clare convent as a Franciscan tertiary. She was canonized in 1625.

Elizabeth Bichier des Ages (Bl) V. Foundress   Aug 26

1773–1832 Of noble rank, she was born in the diocese of Bourges. After the French Revolution she entrusted herself to the guidance of St Andrew Fournet (q.v.), and in spite of grave difficulties at the outset founded the Congregation of the Daughters of the Cross for teaching and service in hospitals. She died at Le Pay, Poiters. Beatified in 1947.

Elizabeth (St) W.   Nov 5

1st cent. The mother of St John the Baptist. All that we know about her is limited to what we find in the first chapter of St Luke's gospel. In art she is shown clad as an elderly lady, holding the infant St John the Baptist; or pregnant and greeting Our Lady.

Elizabeth of Hungary (St) Queen, Tert. OFM.   GC. Nov 17

1207–1231 Born at Presburg, the daughter

St Elizabeth of Hungary, Nov 17

of King Andrew II of Hungary and a niece of St Hedwig. At the age of fourteen she was married to Louis IV, landgrave of Thuringia, and bore him three children. Hers was a very happy married life until 1227 when her husband went to the crusade and died at Otranto. She then became a Franciscan tertiary and devoted herself to the relief of the destitute, living a life of voluntary poverty until her death at twenty-four. She was canonized three years later (1235). She is shown performing an act of charity; or weaving a crown and holding two others. Her cloak may be full of roses and she may bear a basket of provisions.

Elizabeth the Good (Bl) V. Tert. OFM.   Nov 25

1386–1420 Born at Waldsee in Würtemberg, she lived her whole life in a small community of Franciscan tertiaries close by. She was subject to mystical experiences including the stigmata, and went for long periods without any natural food. Cult confirmed in 1766.

Elizabeth-Rose (St) Abs. OSB.   Dec 13

d. 1130 A nun of Chelles near Paris, and afterwards abbess-foundress of the nunnery of Sainte-Marie-du-Rozoy, near Courtenay, Loiret.

Elleher (St) M. OSB.   June 5
See Waccar, Gundekar, etc.

Ellidius (Illog) (St) C.   Aug 8
7th cent.   Patron saint, it would appear, of
Hirnant, Powys, and of a church in the Scilly
Isles.

Ellyn (St) VM.   Aug 1
Otherwise Almedha, q.v.

Elmo (Bl) C.   Apr 15
Otherwise Peter Gonzalez, q.v. But the name
Elmo usually stands for an abbreviation of that
of St Erasmus (June 2).

Eloff (Elophius) (St) M.   Oct 16
Otherwise Eliphius, q.v.

Eloi (St) Bp.   Dec 1
Otherwise Eligius, q.v.

Eloquius (Eloque) (St)
Ab. OSB.   Dec 3
d. *p.*66   Disciple and successor of St Fursey
as abbot of Lagny (*Latiniacensis*).

Elphege
See Alphege.

Elpidephorus (St) M.   Nov 2
See Acindynus, Pegasius, etc.

Elpidius (St) Bp. M.   March 4
See Basil, Eugene, etc.

Elpidius (St) M.   Sept 1
See Priscus, Castrensis, etc.

Elpidius (St) Ab.   Sept 2
4th cent.   A hermit in Cappadocia who lived
for twenty-five years in a cave and gathered
round him numerous disciples. His relics were
brought to a village in the Marches of Ancona,
now called Sant' Elpidio. His emblem in art is
a vine in leaf in winter.

Elpidius (St) Bp.   Sept 2
d. 422   The successor of St Antiochus in the
see of Lyons. His relics were enshrined in the
church of St Justus.

**Elpidius, Marcellus,
Eustochius, and Comp.**
(SS) MM.   Nov 16
d. 362   Elpidius, a dignitary at the court of
the emperor Constantius, was degraded by
Julian the Apostate and, with several companions, dragged at the tail of wild horses. Finally
they were burnt at the stake.

Elpis (St) VM.   Aug 1
See Faith, Hope (Elpis) and Charity.

Elric (St) Bp.   Jan 7
Otherwise Aldericus, q.v.

Elsiar (St) Mk. OSB.   June 4
d. *c* 1050   A Benedictine of the abbey of
Saint-Savin in Lavedan.

Elstan (St) Bp. OSB.   Apr 6
d. 981   Monk of Abingdon under St Ethelwold, celebrated as a model of blind obedience. He succeeded St Ethelwold both as
abbot of Abingdon and bishop of Winchester.

Elvan and Mydwyn (SS)   Jan 1
2nd cent.   Said to have been the two Britons
sent by King St Lucius to Pope St Eleutherius
to beg for missionaries to be sent to Britain
(see St Eleutherius, pope). Their story had no
basis in fact.

Elvis (St) C.   Feb 22
Otherwise Elwyn, or Alleyn, or Allan, or Elian.
See below under Elwin.

Elwin (St) C.   Feb 22
6th cent.   Said to have been one of the holy
men who accompanied St Breaca from Ireland
to Cornwall, and perhaps the title saint of St
Allen's church in that country. But the traditions are very perplexing.

Elzear (Eleazarus) (St) C.
Tert. OFM.   Sept 27
1285–1323   A native of Provence, where he
inherited the barony of Ansuis as well as the
county of Ariano in the kingdom of Naples.
Married to St Delphina of Glandèves, he was
the perfect type of Christian gentleman. He
went to Naples as tutor to Prince Charles and
as ambassador, and was for a time regent of the
kingdom. According to an old tradition both
he and his wife, St Delphine (q.v.), were
Franciscan tertiaries.

Emebert (Ablebert) (St)
Bp.   Jan 15
d. *c* 710   Said to have been a brother of SS
Reineldis and Gudula. He was bishop of
Cambrai in Flanders.

Emerentiana (St) VM.   Jan 23
d. 304?   According to legend, Emerentiana,
the foster-sister of St Agnes, while as yet only a
catechumen, was discovered by the pagan mob
praying at the tomb of the recently martyred St
Agnes, and was stoned to death. In point of
fact St Emerentiana is a Roman martyr of

unknown date. Her cult is very ancient. Cult confined to local calendars since 1969.

Emeric (Bl) Bp.   Aug 1
d. 1318   Bishop of Aosta (1301–1318). Cult approved in 1881.

Emeric (St) C.   Nov 4
1007–1031   Son of St Stephen, the first Christian king of Hungary. He was educated by St Gerard Sagredo of Czanad and gave promise of being a model king, but died before inheriting the crown. He was canonized with his father in 1083.

Emerita (St) VM.   Sept 22
See Digna and Emerita.

Emeritus (St) M.   Feb 11
See Saturninus, Dativus, etc.

Emerius (St) Ab. OSB.   Jan 27
8th cent.   A Frenchman by birth, he founded, and ruled as first abbot, the Benedictine abbey of St Stephen of Bañoles, near Gerona, in Spanish Catalonia.

Emeterius (St) M.   March 3
Otherwise Hemiterius, q.v.

Emidius (St) Bp. M.   Aug 5
Otherwise Emygdius, q.v.

Emilas and Jeremiah (SS)
MM.   Sept 15
d. 852   Two Spanish youths, of whom the former was a deacon, imprisoned and beheaded at Cordoba under the caliph Abderrahman.

Emilian (Aemilio) (St)
Mk. OSB.   Jan 7
d. 767   A native of Vannes, and a monk of Saujon, near Saintes, he died as a recluse in the forest of Combes, Bordeaux.

Emilian (St) M.   Feb 8
See Dionysius and Emilian.

Emilian (St) M.   Feb 9
See Ammon, Emlian, etc.

Emilian (or Eminian)
(St) Ab. OSB.   March 10
d. 675   An Irishman who became a monk, and then abbot, of Lagny in France.

Emilian (St) M.   Apr 29
See Agapius and Comp.

Emilian (St) M.   July 18
d. 362   A martyr of Silistria in Bulgaria under Julian the Apostate.

Emilian (St) Bp.   Aug 8
d. c 820   A bishop of Cyzicus, an island off the southern shore of the sea of Marmora. He died in exile for his firm stand against the Iconoclasts.

Emilian (St) Bp.   Sept 11
d. 520   A N. Italian hermit who, after forty years as a recluse, was raised to the see of Vercelli in Piedmont, where he died a centenarian.

Emilian (St) C.   Oct 11
? According to the pre-1970 RM. he was a hermit at Rennes in Brittany. No saint of this name can be found in the Breton records. Possibly he has been confused with St Melanius, bishop of Rennes (d. 567).

Emilian (St) Ab.   Nov 12
d. 574   A poor shepherd in La Rioja, in the old kingdom of Spanish Navarre. He became a hermit and eventually was ordained priest by his bishop (of Tarazona) who put him in charge of the parish of Berceo. The saint, however, returned to his solitude and there gradually gathered round him a large number of disciples of whom he became the abbot. This gave rise to the great abbey of La Cogolla, which afterwards adopted the Benedictine Rule. He is a minor patron saint of Spain where he is known as San Millan de la Cogolla — the cowled St Emilian. In art he is usually represented on horseback fighting the Moors.

Emilian (St) M.   Dec 6
See Dionysia, Dativa, etc.

Emiliana (St) V.   Jan 5
6th cent.   A Roman lady and the paternal aunt of St Gregory the Great, from whom we know of her saintly life, visions and death.

Emiliana (St) M.   June 30
? She is stated to have been a Roman maiden who died a martyr.

Emilius (St) M.   May 22
See Castus and Emilius.

Emilius, Felix, Priam
and Lucian (SS) MM.   May 28
? Churches are dedicated to these saints in Sardinia; otherwise nothing is known concerning them.

Emilius (St) M.   Oct 6
See Marcellus, Castus, etc.

Emily de Vialar (St) V.

Foundress   June 17

1797–1856 Born at Gaillace, in the diocese of Albi, S. France, she was early bereaved of her mother, and while giving herself to prayer and works of charity, managed her father's house until she was thirty-five. Then, on receiving a large legacy, she decided to devote herself to the foundation of a religious institute, viz., the Sisters of St Joseph of the Apparition (i.e. the apparition of the Angel Gabriel to St Joseph). Great trials befell her, and, losing both her money and her reputation in the diocese of Albi, she established the mother-house at Marseilles. When she died there in 1856, she left behind her houses of the Institute in Europe, Africa and Asia. Canonized in 1951.

Emily Bicchieri (Bl) V. OP.   Aug 19

1238–1314 A native of Vercelli, who induced her father to build a convent, where she professed the Dominican rule. She was a great success as the first prioress of the convent. Cult confirmed in 1769.

Emily de Rodat (St)

Foundress   Sept 19

1787–1852 A native of Château Druelles, near Rodez, in southern central France. In 1816, under the direction of Mgr Marty, later vicar general of Rodez, she started a new teaching institute which has since developed into the present-day Religious Congregation of the Holy Family of Villefranche. Canonized in 1950.

Emma (several)

Otherwise Gemma q.v.

Emmanuel (several)

Note. A popular name in the Latin countries: Emmanuele in Italian; Manuel in Spanish, Portuguese and Catalan.

Emmanuel d'Abreu (Bl)

M. SJ.   Jan 12

1708–1737 A Portuguese born at Arouca, he entered the Jesuit order in 1724 and was sent to China; arrested at Tonkin in 1736, he was martyred in 1737 with three companions.

Emmanuel (Bl) Bp.   Feb 27

d. 1198 Bishop of Cremona (1190–1195). Some writers make him a Cistercian monk of Adwerth, in Frisia, before his episcopate; but Adwerth was only founded in 1192. In 1195 Bl Emmanuel indeed retired to Adwerth, where he died, possibly in the Cistercian habit.

Emmanuel (St) M.   March 26

See Quadratus, Theodosius, etc.

Emmanuel Ruiz and

Comp. (BB) MM.   July 10

d. 1860 During the rising of the Druses against the Christians in the Lebanon, the Franciscan community of Damascus, eight in all, and three Maronite laymen, were offered the alternative of accepting Islam or death; they refused the former and were slain in their own friary. The guardian of the friary was Bl Emmanuel Ruiz, a Spaniard, as were most of the other friars. Beatified in 1926.

Emmanuel Alvarez (Bl)

M. SJ.   July 15

d. 1570 A Jesuit lay-brother, companion of Bl Ignatius de Azevedo, q.v.

Emmanuel Fernández

(Bl) M. SJ.   July 15

d. 1570 A native of Celorico, diocese of Cuarda, Portugal, and a Jesuit cleric, companion of Bl Ignatius de Azevedo, q.v.

Emmanuel Pacheco (Bl)

M. SJ.   July 15

d. 1570 A native of Zeita, in Portugal, and a Jesuit novice, companion of Bl Ignatius de Azevedo, q.v.

Emmanuel Rodríguez

(Bl) M. SJ.   July 15

d. 1570 A native of Alconchel, Portugal, and a Jesuit cleric, companion of Bl Ignatius de Azevedo, q.v.

Emmanuel Phung (St) M.   July 31

c 1796–1859 Born at Dan-nuoc, in Vietnam, he worked as catechist, and was for this reason garrotted near Chaudoc. Canonized in 1988.

Emmanuel Trieu (St) M.   Sept 17

c 1756–1798 Born in Vietnam of Christian parents, he joined the army, but was afterwards ordained priest at Pong-King and worked under the priests of the Foreign Missions of Paris. While visiting his mother he was arrested and beheaded. Canonized in 1988.

Emmelia (St) Matron   May 30

See Basil and Emmelia.

Emmeramus

(Haimhramm) (St) Bp. M.

OSB.   Sept 22

d. c 690 A native of Poitiers, he migrated to Bavaria where he became abbot of a monastery at Regensburg, and then bishop of that city. While on his way to Rome he was attacked by assassins, and died from the injuries received. His relics were enshrined in the great Benedictine abbey dedicated to his name at Regensburg, where he is venerated as a martyr.

Emygdius (Emidius) (St)
Bp. M.   Aug 5
d. *c* 303   His relics are kept at Ascoli, whither they were transported between 996 and 1052. His legend is historically worthless.

Encratia (Encratis, Encratide, Engracia) (St)
VM.   Apr 16
d. ? 304   A Spanish maiden who suffered at Saragossa, where the church now stands dedicated in her name. She is famous for "her ardour in suffering for Christ". Though counted a martyr, she apparently outlived her torments.

Enda (Endeus, Enna) (St)
Ab.   March 21
d. *c* 530   Brother of St Fanchea and was the earliest founder of monasteries in Ireland, of which the principal was on Inishmore. SS Kieran and Brendan, among others, were his disciples.

Endellion (St) V.   Apr 29
? 6th cent.   Sister of St Nectan of Hartland. Many beautiful legends surround her name. All that is known is that she was one of the many saintly children of Brychan. Part of her shrine at St Endellion in Cornwall is still extant. Around her church also survive a complete and unique set of houses for her prebendaries, the only set to survive from medieval times.

Eneco (Enneco, Spanish: Iñigo) (St) Ab. OSB.   June 1
d. 1057   Born at Calatayud, and a monk of San Juan de la Peña, in Aragon, where the Cluniac observance had been just then introduced. After much entreaty, King Sancho the Great of Navarre induced him to accept the abbacy of Oña in Old Castile. Under Iñigo's rule the abbey rose to great splendour, and on his death he was much lamented by Christians, Jews and Saracens alike. Canonized in 1259.

Engelbert (St) Ab.   Feb 18
Otherwise Angilbert, q.v.

Engelbert (St) Bp. M.   Nov 7
1186–1225   A typical medieval prince-prelate. Early in his career he gained possession uncanonically of benefices, and thereby incurred excommunication. When this was lifted he became archbishop of Cologne (1216). In this position he was a great success: zealous for the discipline of his clergy, fosterer of monastic life and of learning. He was appointed tutor to the emperor's son and chief minister of the empire. While defending the rights of a nunnery he was killed by hired assassins, and hence he is venerated as a martyr.

Engelmer (St) M.   May 14
d. 1096   The son of a poor Bavarian labourer, he became a hermit near Passau. He was murdered by a visitor who hoped to find his treasure.

Engelmund (St) Ab. OSB.   June 21
d. *c* 739   An Englishman by birth and education, he received the Benedictine habit at a very early age, and became priest and abbot. He crossed over to Friesland, where he worked most successfully under St Willibrord, at Velsen, six miles north of Haarlem.

Enghenedl (St)   Sept 30
7th cent.   A Welsh saint to whom a church in Anglesey was dedicated. Nothing is now known about his life.

England (Martyrs of) (BB)   May 4
1535–1681   British-born Catholics, put to death between these two dates. Fifty-four were beatified by Leo XIII in 1886, nine in 1895, and one hundred and thirty-seven by Pius XI in 1929: their common feast is held on May 4. Each of these martyrs who has already been officially acknowledged as Saint or Blessed, receives a separate notice in this book.

Englatius (Englat, Tanglen) (St) Bp.   Nov 3
d. 966   A Scottish saint, said by some to have been a bishop, who lived at Tarves in Aberdeenshire.

Engratia (St) H.   Oct 25
See Fructus, Valentine and Engratia.

Enguerrammus (Angilram) (Bl) Ab. OSB.   Dec 9
d. 1045   Of a humble family, he was educated at the abbey of Saint-Riquier (*Centula*), where eventually he became a monk and abbot (1022). By his contemporaries he was surnamed "the Wise" or "the learned Abbot". He was a very fluent Latin verse-writer.

Ennatha (St) VM.   Nov 13
See Antoninus, Zebinas, etc.

Ennodius (St) Bp.   July 17
473–521   Magnus Felix Ennodius was a Gallo-Roman by birth and a professor of rhetoric who, after his conversion, became (*c* 514) bishop of Pavia in Lombardy. The pope entrusted him with two missions to Byzantium in connection with the Eutychian controversy. He is now best remembered as a Christian poet, whose writings, chiefly hymns, are full of interest.

Enoch (St) V. March 25
Otherwise Kennocha, q.v.

Enoder (Cynidr or Keneder) (St) Ab. Apr 27
6th cent. A grandson of the Welsh chieftain Brychan. Llangynidr in Powys perpetuates his memory, as also possibly St Enoder or Enodoc in Cornwall. Very likely he is to be identified with St Enodoch, q.v. In Breton he is called St Quidic.

Enodoch (Wenedoc) St March 7
d. *c* 520 A Welsh saint of the Brychan race. Some writers identify him with St Enoder, q.v., others state that she was a daughter — instead of a son — of Brychan and call her St Qwendydd. The traditions are very confused.

Enogatus (St) Bp. Jan 13
d. 631 The fifth successor of St Malo in the see of Aleth in Brittany.

Eoban (St) M. OSB. June 5
d. 754 A Benedictine monk-priest said to have been of Irish descent, who worked under SS Willibrord and Boniface in the German mission and shared in the latter's martyrdom at Dokkum.

Eochod (St) Jan 25
d. 597 One of St Columba's twelve companions, chosen by him to evangelize N. Britain. He is called the apostle of the Picts of Galloway.

Eogan (St) Bp. Aug 23
Otherwise Eugene, q.v.

Epagathus (St) M. June 2
See Photinus (Pothinus), Sanctus, etc.

Epaphras (St) Bp. M. July 19
1st cent. "The most beloved fellow-servant" of St Paul (Col 1:7). He is traditionally said to have been bishop of Colossae and to have suffered martyrdom there. But beyond what we read in the New Testament (Col 1:7; 4:12 and Philem 23) we know nothing of his life.

Epaphroditus (St) Bp. March 22
1st cent. St Paul mentions him as an apostle sent to the Philippians (Phil 2:25). Hence, St Epaphroditus is reputed first bishop of Philippi in Macedonia. Two saints of the same name are listed in ancient catalogues: one as the first bishop of Andriacia in Lycia, and another as the first bishop of Terracina in Italy. The three are said to have been among the seventy-two disciples of Christ. Very likely they are the same person, with different local veneration.

Eparchius (St) Bp. March 23
See Domitius, Pelagia, etc.

Eparchius (French: Cybar) (St) AB. July 1
504–581 Born duke of Périgord in France, he renounced his title to become a monk of Sessac. After his ordination to the priesthood he was "walled-up" at Angoulême (542) where he lived for the rest of his life, directing a community who established themselves in the neighbourhood for that purpose.

Ephebus (St) M. Feb 14
See Proculus, Ephebus and Apollonius.

Ephesus (Martyrs of) (SS) Jan 12
d. *c* 762 Forty-two monks of a monastery at Ephesus, put to death by the emperor Constantine Copronymus for their firm stand against the iconoclasts. This entry was made by Baronius, but his source is uncertain. See Stephen, Basil, etc. (Nov 28); in their Acts is mention of thirty-eight martyr monks.

Ephraem (St) Bp. M. March 4
See Basil, Eugene, etc.

Ephraem the Syrian (St) Dr. GC. June 9
c 306–373 Surnamed also "the Deacon" and "the Harp of the Holy Ghost". He was a native of Nisibis in Mesopotamia and very likely the head of the catechetical school of that city before it was captured by the Persians. Afterwards he became a monk near Edessa and a deacon. Here he spent most of his long life writing copious commentaries on the Bible and composing hymns. He wrote the hymns in his native Syriac so that his people could make use of them and thus retain their Catholic faith and keep free from Arianism. He excelled in his Mariological hymns, which are an important contribution to Catholic dogma. In the terrible famine which raged throughout Mesopotamia a few years before St Ephraem's death the saint was the leader in organizing relief and help for the sick. He died in his monastic cell, revered both in the East and in the West. Benedict XV officially declared him a Doctor of the Church in 1920.

Ephysius (St) M. Jan 15
d. 303 A martyr said to have been put to death in Sardinia under Diocletian. He is still greatly venerated in the island.

Epicharis (St) M. Sept 27
d. *c* 300 She is said to have been the wife of

a Roman senator and to have been martyred at New Rome (Byzantium) under Diocletian.

Epictetus, Jucundus, Secundus, Vitalis, Felix and Comp. (SS) MM.   Jan 9

d. ? 250   Twelve African martyrs probably of the Decian persecution. Epictetus was a bishop mentioned by St Cyprian.

Epictetus (St) M.   Aug 22

See Martial, Saturninus, etc.

Epigmenius (St) M.   March 24

d. c 300   A Roman priest martyred under Diocletian. Possibly to be identified with St Pigmenius (q.v.).

Epimachus (St) M.   May 10

d. 250   A native of Alexandria in Egypt, burnt there at the stake under Decius. He is commemorated also on Dec 12 with his fellow-sufferer, St Alexander.

Epiphana (St) M.   July 12

? She is mentioned in the Acts of St Alphius, which are wholly unreliable. Nothing really is known about her.

Epiphanes and Isidore (SS) MM.   Aug 4

? Two martyrs, venerated at the cathedral of Besançon up to the time of the French Revolution. Nothing is known of them.

Epiphania (St) N. OSB.   Oct 6

d. c 800   A Benedictine nun in the convent of Santa Maria della-Caccia — *Sancta Maria Venationum* — at Pavia in Lombardy. An old tradition adds that she was a daughter of King Ratchis, who himself became a monk at Montecassino.

Epiphanius (St) Bp.   Jan 21

439–497   Born at Pavia and elected bishop of that city in 467. During his episcopate Odoacer destroyed Pavia and Epiphanius was largely responsible for the rebuilding of the city. In order to ransom some of his flock who were held captive he travelled to Burgundy and so contracted the fever of which he died.

Epiphanius, Donatus, Rufinus and Comp. (SS) MM.   Apr 7

The pre-1970 RM. reproduced the names from the martyrology of Usuard, who introduced that of Rufinus. There were thirteen fellow-martyrs, but we have no details, except that Epiphanius was an African bishop.

Epiphanius of Salamis (St) Bp.   May 12

c 315–403   A native of Palestine and a monk from his earliest youth. He became abbot at Eleutheropolis, where he wrote and preached against all heretics, but chiefly against Arianism in imperial circles. He was acclaimed "the oracle of Palestine". In 367 he was made bishop of Salamis in Cyprus, where he continued his vehement defence of orthodoxy. In his old age he acted occasionally in a very headstrong way. His writings were his most important contribution to the Catholic cause.

Epipodius and Alexander (SS) MM.   Apr 22

d. 178   Two young friends, citizens of Lyons, put to death under Marcus Aurelius. St Epipodius was decapitated; for Alexander, see Alexander and Comp.

Epistemis (St) M.   Nov 5

See Galation and Epistemis.

Epitacius and Basileus (SS) MM.   May 23

1st cent.   The former is said to have been first bishop of Tuy in Spanish Galicia, and the latter first bishop of Braga in present-day Portugal — both in the apostolic age.

Epolonius (St) M.   Jan 24

See Babilas, Urban, etc.

Eppo (Bl) Ab. OSB.   June 27

d. 1143   Monk, and second abbot (1122) of Mallersdorf in Bavaria.

Epvre (Eure) (St) Bp.   Sept 15

Otherwise Aprus, q.v.

Equitius (St) Ab.   Aug 11

d. c 540   A contemporary of St Benedict, and the founder of a number of monasteries in the province of Valeria (a district east of Rome). St Gregory the Great gives all we know about him in the first book of his Dialogues.

Erasma (St) VM.   Sept 3

See Euphemia, Dorothy, etc.

Erasmus (Elmo, Erarmo, Ermo) (St) Bp. M.   June 2

d. c 303   Stripped of all the later legendary additions our knowledge of this saint is reduced to the fact that he was a bishop of

St Erasmus, June 2

Formiae in Campania, martyred under Diocletian, and that his relics were transferred to Gaeta in 842. The legend of his "Acts" made him patron of sailors (hence "St Elmo's fire") and one of the Fourteen Holy Helpers (q.v.), greatly revered throughout Europe in the Middle Ages. Traditionally martyred by disembowelment, he is shown with his intestines being wound around a windlass; or vested as a bishop he holds a winch or windlass. Since 1969 his cult has been confined to local calendars.

Erasmus (St) M.   Nov 25
? A Syrian, martyred at Antioch. It is probable that he is a duplicate of St Erasmus of June 2.

Erastus (St) Bp. M.   July 26
1st cent.   The treasurer of the city of Corinth (Rom 16:23) converted by St Paul, and one of his helpers in the apostolate (Acts 19:22), especially at Corinth (2 Tim 4:20). The Greek tradition is that he became bishop of Philippi Paneas in Palestine: that of the Latins is that his see was Philippi in Macedonia and that he was a martyr.

Erbin (Ervan, Erbyn, Erme or Hermes) (St)   Jan 13
? 5th cent.   A Cornish saint who seems to have been related to one of the Cornish or Devonshire chieftains. Churches were dedicated to him in Cornwall.

Erbo (Bl) Ab. OSB.   Aug 27
d. 1162   A disciple of St Theoger and a monk under him at St George's in the Black Forest. In 1121 he was chosen by St Otto, bishop of Bamberg, to succeed St Erminold in the abbacy of Prüfening, which he governed for forty years, the observance being that of Cluny-Hirschau.

Ercongotha (St) V. OSB.   July 7
d. 660   Daughter of King Erconbert of Kent and of St Sexburga. She was a nun at Faremoutiers-en-Brie under her aunt, St Ethelburga. At Faremoutier her feast was Feb 21. She died very young.

Erconwald (Erkenwald) (St) Bp. OSB.   Apr 30
d. 693   An East-Anglian of royal blood. He retired to the kingdom of the East Saxons where he founded two houses — Chertsey abbey, in Surrey, for men; and Barking nunnery, in Essex, for women. He became the abbot of the former and his sister St Ethelburga the abbess of the latter. In 675 he was chosen bishop of London by St Theodore. His shrine at St Paul's cathedral was a focal point for the devotion of Londoners and a place of miracles until its destruction during the Reformation.

Erembert (St) Bp. OSB.   May 14
d. c 672   Born at Wocourt near Passy, he became a Benedictine at Fontenelle (c 640) and bishop of Toulouse (c 656) which he ruled for twelve years. In his old age he resigned and went back to die at Fontenelle.

Erembert I (Bl) AB. OSB.   Jan 24
d. p.1050   Abbot of Kremsmünster, in Austria, to which office he was elected in 1050.

Eremberta (St) Abs. OSB.   Oct 16
Late 7th cent.   Niece of St Wulmar and first abbess of the nunnery of Wierre, which he built for her.

Erentrudis (Ermentrude) (St) Abs. OSB.   June 30
d. c 718   A sister — or niece — of St Rupert, the apostle of Salzburg. She was the first abbess of Nonnberg in Salzburg, a nunnery founded for her by Rupert.

Erfyl (Eurfyl) (St) V.   July 5
? A British maiden, foundress of the church of Llanerfyl, Powys.

Ergnad (Ercnacta) (St) V.   Jan 8
5th cent. A native of Ulster who is said to
have received the veil from St Patrick.

Ergoule (St) V.   Jan 8
Otherwise Gudula, q.v.

Erhard (St) Bp.   Jan 8
d. *c* 686 He is described as an Irishman,
who passed over to the Continent and laboured as a missionary bishop in Bavaria, chiefly in
and around Regensburg.

Eric (Henry) (Bl) C.   March 13
d. 1415 The son of the king of Scandinavia,
he inherited the crown on the death of his
father, but fled into solitude to lead a life of
penance. He went on pilgrimage to Rome and
died at Perugia, where he is venerated.

Eric (Henry) (St) King, M.   May 18
d. 1160 Eric IX became king of Sweden in
1150 and at once began to exert all his
influence to spread the gospel throughout the
country. He codified the laws of his kingdom
in the same spirit, and is for this reason called
"the Lawgiver". He also laboured for the
conversion of the heathen Finns. He was
murdered as he was leaving a church after the
eucharist.

Erizzo (Bl) Ab. OSB. Vall.   Feb 9
d. 1094 A native of Florence, and the first
disciple of St John Gualbert. At a later period
he became the fourth general of the Vallumbrosans. Cult confirmed in 1600.

Erkemboden (St) Bp. OSB.   Apr 12
d. 714 A monk of Sithin at Saint-Omer,
who succeeded the founder, St Bertinus, as
abbot, and then became bishop of Thérouanne, continuing to rule the abbey. He was
bishop for twenty-six years.

Erlafrid (St) Ab. OSB.   Nov 6
d. *p.*830 Count of Calw in Swabia. Founder
of Hirschau abbey, where he became a monk.

Erluph (St) Bp. M.   Feb 10
d. 830 A Scottish missionary in Germany
who later became bishop of Werden, and was
martyred by pagans.

**Ermel (Armel, Erme)
(St)** Ab.   Aug 16
Otherwise Armagillus, q.v.

**Ermelinda (Ermelindis)
(St)** V.   Oct 29
d. *c* 595 A Belgian recluse who lived at
Meldaert, near Tirlemont.

Ermenburga (St) W. OSB.   Nov 19
d. *c* 700 Otherwise known as Domna Ebba
(Lady Ebba), abbreviated into Domneva. She
was a Kentish princess married to the king of
Mercia, and the mother of SS Mildred, Milburga and Mildgytha. In her old age she
founded the nunnery of Minster in Thanet,
around the year 670, where the place-name
Ebbsfleet still perpetuates her memory.

Ermenfridus (St) Ab. OSB.   Sept 25
d. *c* 670 A courtier then a monk at Luxeuil
under its third abbot, St Waldebert. Later he
became the abbot-founder of Cusance.

Ermengardis (Bl) W.
OSB. Cist.   June 1
c 1067–1147 A native of Angers and wife of
the duke of Brittany (1092). Before her death
she received the Cistercian habit at the hands
of St Bernard (*c* 1130).

Ermengol (St) Bp.   Nov 3
Otherwise Hermengaudius, q.v.

Ermengytha (St) V. OSB.   July 30
d. *c* 680 A sister of St Ermenburga (Domneva). She lived under the latter's obedience
as a nun at Minster in Thanet.

**Ermenilda (Ermengild)
(St)** W. OSB.   Feb 13
d. *c* 700 Daughter of King Erconbert of
Kent and of St Sexburga. She married Wulf-
here, the king of Mercia, and exercised a truly
Christian influence over him and the kingdom.
On his death, she joined her mother at
Minster in Sheppey, eventually succeeding
her as abbess. She then migrated to Ely where
also she became abbess.

Erminold (St) M. Ab. OSB.   Jan 6
d. 1121 He was offered to God at the abbey
of Hirschau as a child and educated and
professed there. In 1110 he was chosen abbot
of Lorsch; but fearing that this appointment
might have been the result of simony he
resigned and returned to Hirschau. In 1114 he
was chosen the first prior of Prüfening and in
1117 its first abbot. One of the lay-brothers of
the community struck him with a piece of
timber and caused his death. He has always
been venerated as a martyr.

Erminus (St) Bp. OSB.   Apr 25
d. 737 Born at Laon. After his ordination he
professed the Benedictine rule at Lobbes
under St Urmar, who appointed him his
successor both as abbot and as regionary
bishop.

Ernan (Ernin) (*several*)
There are various Irish saints of this or a similar name. Perhaps the most notable among them is one described as a nephew of St Columba.

Ernest (St) Ab. OSB.   Nov 7
d. 1148   Benedictine abbot of Zwiefalten in Germany who joined the crusaders and preached in Persia and Arabia. He was taken prisoner and tortured to death at Mecca.

Erney (St)
? The patron saint of a church at Landrake in Cornwall.

Erotheis (St) M.   Oct 27
See Capitolina and Erotheis.

Erotis (Eroteis) (St) M.   Oct 6
4th cent.   A martyr who perished at the stake. The martyrdom seems to have taken place in Greece, though by some Erotis is identified with St Erotheis of Cappadocia, who suffered with St Capitolina.

Erth (Herygh, Urith) (St)   Oct 31
6th cent.   Brother of St Uny and St Ia (Ives). He crossed from Ireland to Cornwall, where a church is dedicated in his name. He has given his name also to the village of St Erth.

Ervan (St)   May 29
Otherwise Erbin, q.v.

Ervan (St) Ab.   Aug 16
Otherwise Armagillus, q.v.

Esdras
See Ezra, q.v.

Eskill (St) Bp. M.   June 12
d. c 1080   A fellow-missionary of St Sigfrid in Sweden by whom he was ordained bishop. Both were English. St Eskill was stoned to death for protesting against a heathen festival at Strengnäss.

Esterwine (St) Ab. OSB.   March 7
d. 688   A noble Northumbrian who spent his early years at court and then entered the monastery of Wearmouth, where he was professed under his kinsman St Benedict Biscop, the founder of the abbey. He succeeded St Benet as abbot and ruled four years, dying before the founder. He was celebrated for his gentleness.

Eternus (St) Bp.   July 15
d. p.660   The ninth bishop of Evreux in France.

Etha (St) H. OSB.   May 5
Otherwise Echa, q.v.

Ethbin (St) Ab.   Oct 19
d. c 600   A Briton educated in France by St Samson. When a deacon, he retired to the abbey of Taurac (554), where he remained till the dispersion of the community through a raid by the Franks (556). He then crossed over to Ireland, and there led the life of a hermit near Kildare.

Ethelbert of Kent (St)
King.   Feb 25
560–616   Husband of Bertha, a Christian princess from France, he was reigning in Kent when St Augustine arrived in Thanet. Ethelbert protected the missionaries from the start, and received baptism on Whit-Sunday, 597. Though he never tried to force his subjects into Christianity, hundreds followed his example. He was the founder of the abbeys of Christ Church, and SS Peter and Paul, Canterbury, and of St Andrew's, Rochester.

Ethelbert (St) M.   May 20
d. 794   King of East Anglia. He was treacherously murdered at the instigation of the wife of Offa of Mercia. He has always been venerated as a martyr, especially at Hereford, where portions of his shrine remain to this day.

Ethelbert and Ethelred
(SS) MM.   Oct 17
d. 670   Great-grandsons of St Ethelbert of Kent, cruelly put to death at Eastry near Sandwich. Their shrine was finally set up at Ramsey abbey in Huntingdonshire. Robed and crowned as kings, they stand on the supine forms of their murderers.

Ethelburga (St) W. OSB.   Apr 5
d. c 647   Daughter of King St Ethelbert of Kent, she married King St Edwin of Northumbria. She went there accompanied by St Paulinus as her chaplain. After Edwin's death she returned to Kent and founded the nunnery of Lyminge, where she became a nun and abbess.

Ethelburga (St) Abs. OSB.   July 7
d. c 664   The daughter of Anna, king of the East Angles. She became a nun at Faremoutiers-en-Brie, in France, where she succeeded, as abbess, the foundress herself, St Fara. She is known in France as St Aubierge.

Ethelburga (St) Queen.   Sept 8
See Ina and Ethelburga.

Ethelburga (St) Abs. OSB.   Oct 11
d. c 675   Sister of St Erconwald of London, who founded for her the nunnery of Barking in Essex. She was made abbess; but as she was quite inexperienced, St Hildelid was fetched

St Ethelreda, June 23

from a French nunnery to train her. Eventually she governed alone and proved a great abbess.

Etheldreda (Ethelreda, Ediltrudis, Audrey) (St)

Abs. OSB.   June 23
d. 679   At one time the most popular of Anglo-Saxon women saints. A native of Suffolk, she was a daughter of King Anna of East Anglia and a sister to SS Sexburga, Ethelburga and Withburga. Twice married, she remained a virgin. She took the veil at Coldingham under St Ebba and then migrated to Ely where she was chosen abbess of the double monastery. It was a rich and royally endowed establishment wherein she lived a life of great holiness and simplicity. Her body remained incorrupt after death: her hand is preserved in the Catholic church at Ely. Depicted as an abbess, wearing a crown, she holds a crozier and a budding rod or lily.

Etheldritha (or Ethelfreda, Alfreda, Althryda) (St)

V. OSB.   Aug 2
d. 834   Daughter of King Offa of Mercia. She lived as a recluse on Croyland Island, in the desolate marshes of Lincolnshire. Her shrine remained until Croyland was sacked in 870.

Etheldwitha (Ealsitha)

(St) W. OSB.   July 20
d. 903   An Anglo-Saxon princess, wife of

King Alfred. After his death she retired to a nunnery which she founded at Winchester.

Ethelfleda (St) N. OSB.   Oct 23
Otherwise Elfleda, q.v.

Ethelgitha (St) Abs. OSB.   Aug 22
d. c 720   Abbess of a convent in Northumbria.

Ethelgiva (St) Abs. OSB.   Dec 9
d. 896   Daughter of King Alfred the Great and abbess of Shaftesbury.

Ethelhard (St) Bp.   May 12
d. 805   He was archbishop in 793 at a time of great political upheaval, which led to his flight abroad. The primacy of Canterbury in England was restored by Pope Leo III after the abolition of Lichfield as a metropolitical see. Ethelhard died at Canterbury in 805, and his cult was of some importance there but died out after the time of Lanfranc.

Ethelnoth (St) Bp.   Oct 30
d. 1038   Surnamed "the Good". Monk of Glastonbury, and archbishop of Canterbury from 1020 till his death.

Ethelred (St) Ab.   Jan 12
Otherwise Aelred, q.v.

Ethelred (St) King, Ab. OSB.   May 4
d. 716   A king of Mercia, who resigned the crown to become a monk at Bardney, where he was afterwards elected abbot.

Ethelred (St) M.   Oct 17
See Ethelbert and Ethelred.

Ethelwald (Oidilwald)

(St) H. OSB.   March 23
d. 699   A monk of Ripon who succeeded St Cuthbert as a hermit on Farne Island, where he lived for twelve years. He was buried at Lindisfarne.

Ethelwin (St) Bp.   May 3
8th cent.   The second bishop of Lindsey. He was a devoted friend of St Egbert, whom he accompanied to Ireland, where he died.

Ethelwold (Aedilauld)

(St) Bp.   Feb 12
d. c 740   One of St Cuthbert's chief helpers. He was prior and then abbot of Old Melrose in Scotland and finally succeeded to the see of Lindisfarne.

Ethelwold (St) Bp. OSB.   Aug 1
912–984   A native of Winchester. When St Dunstan became abbot of Glastonbury in 943 and restored there the Benedictine observance, Ethelwold, already a priest, took the habit and was made one of the deans. In 955 he became abbot of Abingdon and in 963 bishop

of Winchester. Together with St Dunstan and St Oswald of York he was a leader in the monastic revival of that century, replacing secular canons by Benedictines, founding or restoring abbeys — Newminster, Milton Abbas, Chertsey, Peterborough, Thorney, Ely, etc. He was indeed worthy of the name given him, "The Father of Monks". He was also a skilled craftsman. In his time the Winchester School of Illumination flourished, as did the musical and liturgical aspects of worship. He was the author of the *Regularis Concordia* which regularized monastic observance in England.

Ethenia and Fidelmia
(SS) VV.   Jan 11
d. 433   Daughters of King Laoghaire, and among the first converts made by St Patrick. They received the veil from his hands, and the tradition is that they died immediately after receiving holy communion from him.

Etherius (Aetherius) (St)
Bp. M.   March 4
See Basil, Eugene, etc.

Etherius (St) Bp. C.   June 14
d. *c* 6th cent.   Bishop of Vienne in France.

Etherius (St) M.   June 18
d. *c* 303   A martyr who suffered at Nicomedia under Diocletian.

Etherius (St) Bp. C.   July 27
d. 573   Bishop of Auxerre, 563–573.

Etherius (Alermius) (St)
Bp. C.   Aug 27
d. 602   The bishop of Lyons to whom St Gregory the Great recommended St Augustine when the latter was on his way to England.

Ethernan (St) Bp.   Dec 3
? A native of Scotland who studied in Ireland, and was there ordained bishop. He then went back to evangelize his country.

Ethernascus (St) Bp.   Aug 18
Otherwise Ernan, q.v.

Ethor (St) M.   Apr 10
See Beocca, Ethor and Comp.

Etto (Hetto) (St) Bp. OSB.   July 10
d. *c* 670   Said to have been a native of Ireland. He laboured as a missionary abbot-bishop in Belgium, using St Peter's abbey at Fescau as his headquarters.

Eubulus (St) M.   March 7
See Adrian and Eubulus.

Eucarpius (St) M.   March 18
See Trophimus and Eucarpius.

Eucarpus (St) M.   Sept 25
See Bardomian, Eucarpus, and Comp.

Eucharius (St) Bp.   Dec 8
1st cent.   Said to have been the first bishop of Trier in apostolic times.

Eucherius (St) Bp. OSB.   Feb 20
d. 743   Born at Orleans, he received a good education, especially in theology, and entered the Benedictine abbey of Jumièges on the Seine, in the diocese of Rouen, about the year 714. In 721 he became bishop of Orleans. He opposed Charles Martel for the latter's high-handed distribution of ecclesiastical property, and was exiled to Cologne in 737. Here he became very popular, and was sent to Liège. He spent the rest of his life in the abbey of St Trond, near Maestricht.

Eucherius (St) Bp.   Nov 16
d. 449   A Gallo-Roman by birth and the father, by his wife Galla, of two sons who became bishops. He himself retired to Lérins in 422, while Galla took the veil. He spent his retirement in praying and writing, several of his ascetical works being still extant. In 434 he was made bishop of Lyons, where he laboured till his death. In 441 he presided at the synod of Orange with St Hilary.

Eudo (Eudon, Eudes
Odo) (St) Ab. OSB.   Nov 20
d. *c* 760   Abbot-founder of the monastery of Corméry-en-Velay (Charmillac, afterwards Saint-Chaffre). Before entering upon his duties as abbot he went to Lérins to be instructed in the monastic observance.

Eudocia (St) M.   March 1
d. 98–117   A native of Heliopolis in Coele-Syria and a Samaritan by blood who led at first a profligate life, but was converted to Christianity and died a penitent. She was beheaded under Trajan.

Eudoxius, Zeno, Marcarius
and Comp. (SS) MM.   Sept 5
c 311   A body of Christian soldiers, said to have been more than a thousand in number, martyred at Melitene in Armenia under Constantius I.

Eudoxius (St) M.   Nov 2
See Carterius, Styriacus, etc.

Eufridus (St) Mk. OSB.   Oct 11
7th cent.   Monk of the diocese of Asti, venerated in the cathedral of Alba in Piedmont.

Eugendus (Oyend) (St) Ab.   Jan 1
450–*c* 510   The fourth abbot of Condat, near

Geneva, called after him Saint-Oyend, but later Saint-Claude. He entered the abbey at the age of seven and lived there until his death at sixty-one.

Eugene (*several*)

Note. The Latin form Eugenius is often used also in English.

Eugene (St)   Jan 4
See Aquilinus, Geminus, etc.

Eugene (St) M.   Jan 24
See Mardonius, Musonius, etc.

Eugene (St) M.   March 4
See Basil, Eugene, etc.

Eugene (St) M.   March 20
See Paul, Cyril, etc.

Eugene (St) Bp. M.   May 2
See Vindemialis, Eugene and Longinus.

Eugene I (St) Pope.   June 2
d. 657 A Roman priest, who acted as vicar for Pope St Martin I during the latter's exile in the Chersonese. After St Martin's death in 655, Eugene was chosen to succeed him. Gentle and affable with the poor, he firmly opposed the Monothelite emperor of Byzantium, who threatened to roast St Eugene alive.

Eugene III (Bl) Pope
OSB. Cist.   July 8
d. 1153 A native of Montemagno, between Lucca and Pisa, of the Pignatelli family, he was called Peter in baptism, Bernard in religion, and Eugene as pope. He was an official in the ecclesiastical curia of Pisa when he entered Clairvaux (1135) and was professed under St Bernard. He was appointed first abbot of Tre Fontane (St Anastasius) near Rome, and in 1145 was chosen pope. His pontificate was a troubled one, the greater part of it being passed at a distance from Rome owing to the hostility of the citizens. St Antoninus fittingly called him "one of the greatest and one of the most afflicted of popes". Cult confirmed in 1872.

Eugene, Salutaris, Muritta and Comp. (SS)
MM.   July 13
d. 505 Eugene was made bishop of Carthage in 481 and was shortly afterwards expelled by the Arian Vandals with many of his flock, some of them young boys who served as lectors in the church. They were banished to the desert of Tripoli, where they had to undergo much hardship. In 488 they were allowed to return to Carthage, but Eugene was banished again some eight years later and died at Albi.

They are called martyrs on account of their sufferings.

Eugene (St) M.   July 18
See Symphorosa and Comp.

Eugene (St) M.   July 23
See Apollonius and Eugene.

Eugene (St) M.   July 29
See Lucilla, Flora, etc.

Eugene (Eoghan, Euny, Owen) (St) Bp.   Aug 23
6th cent. An Irishman who laboured as a missionary in England and on the Continent, and then returned to his native country, where he became first bishop of Ardstraw in Tyrone, a see now replaced by that of Derry.

Eugene (St) M.   Sept 6
See Cottidus, Eugene, and Comp.

Eugene (St) M.   Sept 25
See Paul, Tatta, etc.

Eugene II of Toledo (St)
Bp.   Nov 13
d. 657 A Spanish Goth, born at Toledo, where he was a cleric under St Helladius. He became a monk of St Engracia at Saragossa, and the archdeacon of St Braulio there. Finally, in 646, he was bishop of the primatial see of Toledo. He was a gifted poet and musician, and most zealous for all that pertained to divine worship.

Eugene (St) Bp. M.   Nov 15
? A fellow-labourer of St Dionysius, archbishop of Paris, martyred, it is said, somewhere near the city. The pre-1970 RM. wrongly calls him archbishop of Toledo. His relics were, it is said, translated to Toledo many centuries afterwards.

Eugene (St) C.   Nov 17
d. 422 A deacon of the church of Florence under the bishop, St Zenobius. He had been a disciple of St Ambrose at Milan.

Eugene (St) M.   Dec 13
See Eustratius, Auxentius, etc.

Eugene and Macarius
(SS) MM.   Dec 20
d. 362 Two priests who were scourged, banished into the desert of Arabia, and on their return put to the sword under Julian the Apostate.

Eugene (St) Bp.   Dec 30
? A bishop of Milan, of whose life no record remains.

Eugenia (St) Abs. OSB.   Sept 16
d. 735 Daughter of Adalbert, duke of
Alsace, she succeeded her aunt St Ottilia, as
abbess of Hohenburg.

Eugenia (Bl) Abs. OSB.   Nov 22
d. c 1093 Abbess of the convent of SS Lucy
and Agatha at Matera in S. Italy.

Eugenia (St) V. M.   Dec 25
d. ? 257 A Roman maiden, martyred under
Valerian and buried in the cemetery of Apron-
ian on the Via Latina. At a later period she was
described quite groundlessly as a woman who
disguised herself as a monk and who was
accused of a crime she could not commit.

Eugenian (St) Bp. M.   Jan 8
4th cent. He is stated to have been bishop of
Autun in France, a staunch defender of the
Catholic faith against Arianism, and a martyr.

Eugraphus (St) M.   Dec 10
See Mennas, Hermogenes and Eugraphus.

Eugyppius (St) C.   Jan 15
d. c 511 An African who was ordained
priest at Rome, he was a companion of St
Severinus of Noricum, whose life he wrote.

Eulalia of Barcelona (St)
VM.   Feb 12
d. c 304 A maiden born at Barcelona who
suffered martyrdom under Diocletian. In all
probility she is identical with St Eulalia of
Mérida (see Dec 10) though the Catalonians
stoutly deny it. Under the names of Aulaire,
Aulazie, Olalla, etc., she is greatly venerated
throughout Spanish and French Catalonia.

Eulalia (St) VM.   Dec 10
d. c 304 The most celebrated virgin martyr
of Spain. Prudentius wrote a long hymn
describing her martyrdom, and she is mentioned by St Augustine and others. A native of
Mérida, at thirteen years of age, she was burnt
at the stake in her native city under Diocletian,
according to her legend.

Eulampia (St) VM.   Oct 10
See Eulampius, Eulampia and Comp.

**Eulampius, Eulampia
and Comp. (SS)** MM.   Oct 10
d. 310 Two young children, brother and
sister, martyred at Nicomedia under Gallienus. According to legend their courage
led to the conversion and martyrdom of two
hundred soldiers.

**Eulogius of Tarragona
(St)** M.   Jan 21
See Fructuosus, Augurius and Eulogius.

Eulogius of Cordoba (St)
M.   March 11
d. 859 A prominent priest of Cordoba in the
middle of the ninth century, when the Moorish
persecution was at its height. An outstanding
personality for his erudition and courage, he
encouraged the Christians of the province in
their sufferings, and wrote *The Memorial of the
Saints* for their benefit. He himself suffered
martyrdom for having protected St Leocritia, a
girl converted from Islam.

Eulogius of Edessa (St)
Bp.   May 5
d. p.381 A priest of Edessa, banished to the
Thebaid for his firm stand against Arianism,
and chosen bishop of his native town on his
return after the death of Valens (375).

Eulogius and Comp. (SS)
MM.   July 3
d. 364–370 A group of Catholics martyred
at Constantinople under the Arian emperor
Valens.

**Eulogius of Alexandria
(St)** Bp.   Sept 13
d. 607 A Syrian by birth and a monk from
early youth, Eulogius was chosen patriarch of
Alexandria in 579. He was a great friend of St
Gregory the Great, who wrote to tell him about
the new mission for the conversion of England.

Eumenes (St) Bp.   Sept 18
3rd cent. Bishop of Gortyna in Crete, who
died in exile. He is one of those whom on
account of their many miracles, the Greeks
surname "the Wonder-Worker".

Eunan (St) Bp.   Sept 23
7th cent. Identical with St Adamnan of Iona,
q.v.

Eunician (St) M.   Dec 23
See Thedulus, Saturninus, etc.

Eunomia (St) M.   Aug 12
See Hilarla, Digna, etc.

Eunus (St) M.   Oct 30
See Julian, Cronion, etc.

Euphebius (St) Bp.   May 23
? A bishop of Naples, about whom nothing is
known.

Euphemia (St) M.   March 20
See Alexandra, Claudia, etc.

Euphemia (Bl) Abs. OSB.   June 17
d. 1180 Daughter of the count of Andechs,
she became a nun and abbess of Altomünster
in Bavaria.

Euphemia, Dorothy, Thecla and Erasma (SS)

VV. MM.   Sept 3

? 1st cent.   A group of maidens, martyred at Aquileia. They are venerated at Venice and at Ravenna.

Euphemia (St) VM.   Sept 16

d. 307?   A maiden said to have been burnt at the stake at Chalcedon. She is one of the most venerated of virgin-martyrs in the Greek church. Her *Acta* are a fiction. Cult confined to local calendars since 1969.

Euphrasia (St) V.   March 13

d. c 420   Born at Constantinople and connected by blood with the imperial family. She was brought up in a convent in Egypt, and when at a later date she was asked by the emperor to marry a senator she refused and remained in the convent for the rest of her life. An early life of her is in the *Acta Sanctorum*.

Euphrasia (St) M.   March 20

See Alexandra, Claudia, etc.

Euphrasia Pelletier (St)

Foundress   Apr 24

1796–1868   A native of Noxmontier, in W. France, at eighteen she joined the Institute of Our Lady of Charity founded by St John Eudes, and in 1829 founded at Angers the first convent of the Good Shepherd. St Euphrasia visited London in 1844. She died at Angers in her seventy-second year, and was beatified in 1933 and canonized in 1940.

Euphrasia (St) VM.   May 18

See Theodotus, Thecusa, etc.

Euphrasius (St) Bp.   Jan 14

? Perhaps identical with Eucrathius, a correspondent of St Cyprian; or else, a bishop martyred in Africa by the Arian Vandals.

Euphrasius (St) M.   Apr 29

See Corfu, Martyrs of.

Euphrasius (St) Bp. M.   May 15

See Torquatus, Ctesiphon, etc.

Euphronius (St) Bp.   Aug 3

d. p.475   Bishop of Autun in France, friend of St Lupus of Troyes. A letter of his written with St Lupus survives (PL LVIII, col 66–67).

Euphronius (St) Bp.   Aug 4

530–573   Bishop of Tours from 556 till his death. During his episcopate the city was burnt, and he worked most strenuously and successfully to rebuild it.

Euphrosyne (St) VM.   Jan 1

? According to the legend, St Euphrosyne was a maiden of Alexandria in Egypt, who lived there as a monk in a monastery, her sex not being discovered till her death many years later. It is only a replica of similar stories; see SS Pelagia (Oct 8), Eugenia (Dec 25) etc. It is doubtful whether St Euphrosyne ever existed.

Euphrosyne (St) VM.   May 7

See Flavia Domitilla, Euphrosyne and Theodora.

Euplus (St) M.   Aug 12

d. 304   A Christian of Catania in Sicily who was found with a copy of the gospels in his possession, against Diocletian's edict. He was cruelly racked and martyred on this account. His Acts are genuine.

Euporus (St) M.   Dec 23

See Theodulus, Saturninus, etc.

Euprepia (St) M.   Aug 12

See Hilaria, Digna, etc.

Euprepis (St) M.   Nov 30

See Castulus and Euprepis.

Euprepius (St) Bp.   Aug 21

1st cent.   The first bishop of Verona in N. Italy. The tradition (now abandoned) was that he was sent there by St Peter.

Euprepius (St) M.   Sept 27

d. c 303   Mentioned in the legendary *Acta* as a companion martyr of SS Cosmas and Damian, q.v.

Eupsychius (St) M.   Apr 9

d. 362   A youth of Caesarea in Cappadocia, martyred under Julian the Apostate as leader of a group of Christians accused of having destroyed the temple of Fortune in that city.

Eupsychius (St) M.   Sept 7

d. c 130   A martyr of Caesarea in Cappadocia who suffered under Hadrian.

Eurfyl (St) V.   July 5

Otherwise Erfyl, q.v.

Eurgain (St) V.   June 30

6th cent.   A daughter of the chieftain Caradog in Glamorgan, foundress of Cor-Eurgain, afterwards Llantwit.

Eurosia (Orosia) (St) VM.   June 25

d. 714   According to the legend, she was a native of Bayonne — a more florid version makes her a native of Bohemia — who was martyred by the Saracens at Jaca in the Aragonese Pyrenees, close to the French frontier. She is to this day venerated as the patron saint of the diocese of Jaca, and her cult has spread throughout S. France and N. Italy.

Leo XIII officially confirmed it in 1902. However, her very existence is doubtful.

Eusebia (St) Abs. OSB.   March 16
d. c 680   Eldest daughter of SS Adalbald and Rictrudis, she was placed by her mother in the abbey of Hamage (Hamay) which had been founded by her grandmother St Gertrude. St Eusebia succeeded as abbess at the age of twelve, whereupon she was summoned by her mother to Merchiennes; she went with all her community, but later was allowed to return to Hamage and continued to rule her nunnery in peace.

Eusebia (St) Abs. M. OSB.   Sept 20
d. c 731   Abbess of a nunnery at Marseilles. She, with some forty nuns of her community, was put to death by the Saracens at Saint-Cyr.

Eusebia (St) VM.   Oct 29
Late 3rd cent.   A maiden of Bergamo, in Lombardy, niece of St Domnio, q.v., martyred under Maximian Herculeus.

Eusebius (Bl) Founder.   Jan 20
d. 1270   At first a canon of Esztergom, he became a hermit in the mountains of Pilis. Gathering disciples there he founded the Pauline Order of Hermits, after St Paul, the first hermit (Jan 15 q.v.). The constitutions were written by St Thomas Aquinas and received papal approval. He died in Pilis and has always been venerated as Blessed in Hungary.

Eusebius (St) H.   Jan 23
d. 4th cent.   A Syrian hermit who lived on Mt Coryphe, near Antioch.

Eusebius (St) M. OSB.   Jan 31
d. 884   An Irish pilgrim who took the Benedictine habit in the Swiss abbey of St Gall. Eventually he obtained leave to live as a recluse on Mt St Victor in the Vorarlberg. When he was denouncing some godless peasants, one of them struck him with a scythe and killed him. Hence his veneration as a martyr.

Eusebius (Bl) H. OSB.
Cam.   Feb 10
d. 1501   A member of the Spanish nobility who was sent as ambassador to the Republic of Venice. Here, he left all things to don the Camaldolese habit at San Michele, on the isle of Murano.

Eusebius (St) H.   Feb 15
5th cent.   A hermit of Aschia in Syria, venerated in the East.

Eusebius and Comp. (SS)
MM.   March 5
? A group of ten martyrs who suffered in Africa.

Eusebius (St) Ab.   March 5
d. c 423   A native of Cremona and an intimate friend of St Jerome whom he followed to Rome and to the East. Here he succeeded the holy Doctor as abbot of Bethlehem, and was involved, like his friend, in bitter disputes on Origenism. The tradition that he founded the abbey of Guadalupe in Spain cannot be substantiated.

Eusebius, Neon, Leontius, Longinus and Comp. (SS)
MM.   Apr 24
? According to the Greek menologies, these were eight bystanders who became Christians on witnessing the martyrdom of St George and were for this reason put to death. The legend should be studied in connection with that of St George.

Eusebius (St) M.   Apr 28
See Aphrodisius, Caralippus, etc.

**Eusebius of Samosata
(St)** Bp. M.   June 21
d. c 380   Bishop of Samosata in Syria from the year 361, he was a great friend of SS Basil and Gregory of Nazianzos, and a brave defender of orthodoxy against the Arians. He was for this reason banished to Thrace in 374, but recalled four years later. He was killed by an Arian woman who threw a tile at his head.

Eusebius of Vercelli (St)
Bp.   GC. Aug 2
c 283–371   A native of Sardinia, he joined the Roman clergy and in 340 became bishop of Vercelli in Piedmont. He fought Arianism with all the ardour of his Sardinian temperament, and with Dionysius of Milan and Lucifer of Cagliari was banished to the East. Before returning to Italy under Julian he visited St Athanasius at Alexandria. St Jerome wrote: "on the return of Eusebius, Italy put off her mourning". He was the first bishop who lived with his clergy under a rule, an example which was followed by St Augustine. He died in peace at Vercelli on Aug 1, 371, although he has at times been called a martyr for his sufferings.

Eusebius of Milan (St) Bp.   Aug 12
d. 465   Probably a Greek by birth, he suc-

ceeded St Lazarus in the see of Milan and governed it for sixteen years. He helped Pope St Leo the Great to repress Eutychianism.

Eusebius (St) C.   Aug 14
4th cent.   A Roman priest, belonging to the patrician order, who founded the "parish church" called after him the *titulis Eusebii*. The Acts of Eusebius, according to which he publicly preached against Pope Liberius, are entirely spurious. Since 1969 his cult has been confined to his church in Rome.

Eusebius (St) Pope.   Aug 17
d. 310   A Greek by birth, he was pope for a few months only, and died in exile in Sicily.

Eusebius, Pontian, Vincent and Peregrinus (SS) MM.   Aug 25
d. 192?   The only certain fact is that the relics of SS Eusebius and Pontian were sought from Pope Nicholas I and taken to Vienne in 863. The *Passio* which mentioned other Christians, including Vincent, Peregrinus, Julius and Antony (or Antoninus) is untrustworthy.

Eusebius, Nestabus and Zeno (SS) MM.   Sept 8
d. 362   Martyrs massacred by the mob at Gaza in Palestine for having helped in the destruction of a pagan temple there.

Eusebius (St) M.   Sept 21
?   A martyr of Phoenicia, who appears to have given himself up voluntarily as a Christian.

Eusebius of Bologna (St) Bp.   Sept 26
d. *c* 400   A bishop of Bologna from about the year 370. He was a great friend of St Ambrose of Milan, and an ardent opponent of Arianism. During his pontificate the relics of the martyrs SS Vitalis and Agricola were discovered.

Eusebius (St) M.   Oct 4
See Gaius, Faustus, etc.

Eusebius (St) M.   Oct 22
See Philip, Severus, etc.

Eusebius (St) M.   Nov 5
See Felix and Eusebius.

Eusebius, Marcellus, Hippolytus, Maximus, Adria, Paulina, Neon, Mary Martana and Aurelia (SS) MM.   Dec 2
d. 254–259   Roman martyrs under Valerian. Eusebius, a priest, Marcellus, his deacon, Neon and Mary were beheaded; Adria and Hippolytus scourged to death; Paulina died in

the torture-chamber; and Maximus was thrown into the Tiber.

Euseus (St) H.   Feb 15
14th cent.   A hermit who lived and died near Serravalle in Piedmont. He is regarded as a patron of cobblers, since he plied that trade.

Eusignius (St) M.   Aug 5
d. 362   An old soldier of the army of Constantius Clorus who, surviving to the age of 110, refused to sacrifice to idols at the bidding of Julian the Apostate and was scourged and beheaded at Antioch in Syria.

Eustace (*several*)
Note. The Latin forms of this name, viz., Eustachius and Eustathius, are also used in English.

Eustace (Eustasius) (St) Ab.   March 29
d. 625   A favourite disciple and monk of St Columbanus, whom he succeeded as second abbot of Luxeuil. He ruled over about six hundred monks, and during his abbacy the monastery was a veritable seedbed of bishops and saints.

Eustace (St) M.   Apr 14
See Antony, John and Eustace.

Eustace (Eustathius) (St) M.   July 28
?   A martyr of Galatia who after torture appears to have been cast into a river.

Eustace (St) Ab. OSB. Cist.   Sept 7
d. 1211   Born in the Beauvais, he became a priest of the diocese of Beauvais. He later entered the Cistercian abbey of Flay (Saint-Germer) and was eventually its abbot. Under Pope Innocent III he was apostolic legate in England and on the Continent against the Albigenses. He is greatly honoured by the Cistercians.

Eustace, Theopistes, Agapitus and Theopistus (SS) MM.   formerly Sept 20
d. 118   Said to have been a Roman family of distinction — Eustace, an officer, Theopistes, his wife, and Agapitus and Theopistus, their two sons, who were martyred under Hadrian. Eustace owed his conversion to the vision of a stag with a crucifix between its antlers seen by him while hunting. Actually, however, nothing certain is known about him or his supposed

St Eustace, formerly Sept 20

family, and their acts are wholly untrustworthy. Shown with a stag bearing a crucifix between its antlers: or carrying his children through a flood. Cults suppressed in 1969.

Eustace (St) M. (or C.)   Oct 12
? Hagiologists are in complete disagreement as to who this St Eustace was. The pre-1970 RM. describes him as a priest and confessor in Syria; the Bollandists make of him an Egyptian martyr.

Eustace, Thespesius and Anatolius (SS) MM.   Nov 20
d. 235   Martyrs of Nicaea in Asia Minor under the emperor Maximinus the Thracian.

Eustace (St) M. Bp.   Nov 28
See Valerian, Urban, etc.

Eustace White (St) M.   Dec 10
d. 1591   Born at Louth, in Lincolnshire, he became a convert and was educated for the priesthood at Reims and Rome. Ordained in 1588, he was condemned to death and executed at Tyburn. Canonized in 1970 as one of the Forty Martyrs of England and Wales, q.v.

Eustadiola (St) Abs. OSB.   June 8
d. 690   A native of Bourges who married early in life. Having been left a widow she spent all her fortune in building a nunnery in her native town — Moyenmoutier *Medianum monasterium* — whither she retired and became abbess.

Eustathius (St) Bp.   July 16
d. *c* 335   A native of Side in Pamphylia and a confessor during the last persecution, he was made bishop of Beroea in Syria and then transferred to the patriarchal see of Antioch (324–330). He was present at the council of Nicaea, and from that time never ceased to oppose Arianism in preaching and writing. The Arians succeeded in deposing and banishing him, and he died in exile.

Eusterius (St) Bp.   Oct 19
5th cent. The fourth bishop of Salerno, of whom only the name is known.

Eustochia (St) V.   Sept 28
Otherwise Eustochium, q.v.

**Eustochium Calafato
(St)** Poor Clare.   Jan 20
1437–1468 Daughter of the Countess Matilda of Calafato, she was born at Messina in Sicily, where she became a Poor Clare and eventually (1446) founded a convent of stricter observance at a place called *Monte delle Vergini* (Maidens' Hill). Canonized in 1988.

**Eustochium of Padua
(Bl)** N. OSB.   Feb 13
1444–1469 The Cinderella of the Cloister. She was the daughter of a nun of Padua who had been seduced, and her baptismal name was Lucrezia Bellini. Gentle and pious, she became a nun in 1461 and for four years was subject to violent hysteria. She was treated as one diabolically possessed by being exorcized, kept in prison, fed on bread and water, or even deprived of food. When in her right mind she bore her treatment with heroic patience and humility. She died after her profession, aged twenty-five, and the name of Jesus was found cauterized on her breast. She is liturgically honoured at Padua.

Eustochium (St) V.   Sept 28
c 370–419 The third and best loved daughter of St Paula, the Roman matron who followed St Jerome to Palestine. She joined her mother at Bethlehem, where she collated manuscripts for St Jerome's translation of the Bible. She succeeded her mother in 404 in the direction of the nunnery at Bethlehem.

Eustochium (St) VM.   Nov 2
d. 362 A maiden of Tarsus in Cilicia condemned to death under Julian the Apostate. She was barbarously tortured, and as a consequence died in prison, while engaged in prayer.

Eustochius (St) Bp.   Sept 19
d. 461 The successor (444) of St Brice in the see of Tours.

Eustochius (St) M.   Nov 16
See Elpidius, Marcellus, etc.

Eustolia and Sopatra (SS)
VV.   Nov 9
7th cent. It is uncertain whether both of these virgins were daughters of the emperor Maurice of Constantinople (582–602) or only

one of them. They were from the first revered as saints.

Eustorgius (St) M.   Apr 11
d. ? 300 A priest of Nicomedia in Asia Minor, martyred, probably under Diocletian.

Eustorgius II (St) Bp.   June 6
d. 518 A Roman priest who became bishop of Milan in 512. He spent large sums of money in ransoming many of his flock taken prisoners by the barbarians.

Eustorgius I (St) Bp. M.   Sept 18
d. p.331 A Greek by birth, he was raised in 315 to the see of Milan, where he exerted all his influence against the Arians.

Eustosius (St) M.   Nov 10
See Demetrius, Anianus, etc.

**Eustratius, Auxentius,
Eugene, Mardarius and
Orestes (SS)** MM.   Dec 14
d. c 302 Martyrs under Diocletian at Sebaste in Armenia. Eustratius was burnt to death in a furnace; Orestes, a soldier, roasted on a gridiron; the others were martyred in various ways.

Eustreberta (St) V.   Feb 10
Otherwise Austreberta, q.v.

Euthalia (St) VM.   Aug 27
? A virgin martyr of Leontini in Sicily. The Bollandists consider her very existence to be hardly proved.

Euthymius the Great (St)
Ab.   Jan 20
378–473 An Armenian, born at Melitene. He was a priest charged with the supervision of all the monasteries of the district. At the age of twenty-nine he became a monk near Jerusalem, retiring afterwards to Jericho and further into the desert, where he established several *lauras*. He opposed Nestorianism and Eutychianism alike, and induced the empress Eudoxia to give up the latter. He is highly revered throughout the East.

Euthymius of Sardis (St)
Bp. M.   March 11
d. 840? A monk who was made bishop of Sardis in Lydia and bravely opposed the iconoclasts. He was banished by the emperor Nicephorus, and although he was several times given permission to return on condition of his becoming an iconoclast, he always refused and remained in exile for twenty-nine years. He was scourged to death.

Euthymius (St) M.   May 5
? A deacon of Alexandria, martyred there.

Euthymius (St) C.   Aug 29
4th cent. A Roman who fled to Perugia with
his wife and his child, St Crescentius, during
the persecution of Diocletian. He died at
Perugia and is venerated there. The *Passio* is
untrustworthy.

**Euthymius the
Thessalonian (St)** Ab.   Oct 15
d. 886 Surnamed also "the New". Before
his twentieth year he became a monk at Mt
Olympus in Bithynia. Later he migrated to Mt
Athos and finally restored the monastery of St
Andrew, and established a new nunnery, near
Salonika. He returned to Mt Athos to die.

Euthymius (St) M.   Dec 24
d. 303 A Christian of Nicomedia, foremost
in encouraging his fellow-believers during the
persecution of Diocletian, and a martyr himself under the same emperor.

Eutropia (St) VM.   June 15
See Lybe, Levnis and Eutropia.

Eutropia (St) W.   Sept 15
5th cent. Said to have lived in Auvergne,
France. She is first mentioned by Sidonius
Apollinaris.

Eutropia (St) M.   Oct 30
d. ? 253 An African martyr, probably under
Valerian.

Eutropia (St) VM.   Dec 14
See Nicasius, Eutropia, etc.

Eutropius (St) M.   Jan 12
See Tigris and Eutropius.

Eutropius (St) M.   March 3
See Cleonicus, Eutropius and Basiliscus.

Eutropius (St) Bp. M.   Apr 30
? One of the alleged companions of St Dionysius of Paris. He is honoured as the first bishop
of Saintes, and as a martyr.

Eutropius (St) Bp.   May 27
d. *p.*475 A native of Marseilles who succeeded St Justin in the see of Orange, in
France, at a time when the diocese had been
laid waste by the Visigoths.

**Eutropius, Zosima and
Bonosa (SS)** MM.   July 15
d. *c* 273 Martyrs of Porto, near Rome,
under Aurelian.

Eutyches (St) M.   Apr 15
See Maro, Eutyches and Victorinus.

Eutychian (St) M.   July 2
See Ariston, Crescentian, etc.

Eutychian (St) M.   Aug 17
See Straton, Philip and Eutychian.

Eutychian (St) M.   Sept 2
See Diomedes, Julian, etc.

Eutychian (St) M.   Nov 13
See Arcadius, Paschasius, etc.

Eutychian (St) Pope M.   Dec 8
d. 283 A native of Etruria or Tuscany. In
275 he succeeded St Felix I as pope. He is
venerated as a martyr but nothing certain is
known about him.

Eutychius (St) M.   Feb 4
4th cent. A Roman martyr under Diocletian.
From St Damasus's inscription on the tomb of
the martyr we learn that he was left for twelve
days in prison without food and then thrown
into a well.

**Eutychius and Comp.
(SS)** MM.   March 14
d. 741 A considerable number of martyrs
put to death at Carrhes by the Muslims in
Mesopotamia for refusing to deny Christ.

**Eutychius of Alexandria
and Comp. (SS)** MM.   March 26
d. 356 Eutychius was a subdeacon of the
church of Alexandria who, for his stand
against Arianism, was condemned to slavery in
the mines, but perished from exhaustion on
the road thither. His companions were other
leading Catholics of Alexandria, four of whom
were seized and scourged (but not executed)
for showing sympathy for him.

**Eutychius of
Constantinople (St)** Bp.   Apr 6
d. 582 Appointed patriarch of Constantinople in 552, he opposed the emperor Justinian's interference in theological controversies.
He was for this reason exiled for twelve years.
He is honoured in the East.

Eutychius (St) M.   Apr 15
? A martyr of Ferentino in the Roman Campagna. According to the Dialogues of St
Gregory he appeared in a vision to St Redemptus.

Eutychius (St) M.   May 21
See Timothy, Polius and Eutychius.

**Eutychius and
Florentius (SS)** CC.   May 23
6th cent. Two monks who successively governed a monastery in Valcastoria, near Norcia,
Italy. St Gregory the Great has left a glowing
account of their virtues and miracles.

Eutychius (St)   Aug 24
1st cent.   A Phrygian, disciple of St John the
Evangelist (according to the apochryphal *Acta*
of St John). He is sometimes identified with
the young man raised from the dead by the
apostle Paul at Troas (Acts 20).

Eutychius (St) M.   Sept 19
See Januarius and Comp.

**Eutychius, Plautus and
Heracleas (SS)** MM.   Sept 29
? Martyrs in Thrace.

Eutychius (St) M.   Oct 5
See Placid, Eutychius, etc.

Eutychius (St) M.   Nov 21
See Honorius, Eutychius and Stephen.

Eutychius (St) M.   Dec 11
4th cent.   A Spanish martyr — San Oye —
martyred at Mérida, or at Cádiz. Nothing
certain is known about him.

**Eutychius and Domitian
(SS)** MM.   Dec 28
? A priest and his deacon, martyred at Ancyra,
in Galatia.

Euvert (St) Bp.   Sept 7
Otherwise Evortius, q.v.

Eva of Liège (Bl) V.   March 14
d. *c* 1266   A recluse of Liège who lived
under the Cistercian rule, and who on the
death of Bl Juliana of Cornillon successfully
continued her work in favour of the institution
of the liturgical feast of *Corpus Christi*. Cult
confirmed in 1902.

Evagrius (St) Bp.   March 6
d. *c* 380   In 370, after the Arians had occupied the see of Constantinople for twenty years,
the Catholics chose Evagrius for that see; but a
few months later he was banished by the
emperor Valens, and remained in exile till his
death.

**Evagrius and Benignus
(SS)** MM.   Apr 3
? Martyrs at Tomi on the Black Sea.

Evagrius (St) M.   Oct 1
See Priscus, Crescens and Evagrius.

**Evagrius, Priscian and
Comp. (SS)** MM.   Oct 12
? A group of martyrs who suffered either in
Rome or, more probably, in Syria.

Eval (Uvol, Urfol)   Nov 20
6th cent.   A British bishop in Cornwall, from
whom a village in that county is named.

Evan (Inan) (St) H.   Aug 18
9th cent.   A Scottish hermit in Ayrshire,
where churches are still dedicated to him.

**Evangelist and Peregrinus
(BB)** CC. OSA.   March 20
d. *c* 1250   These two saints were born at
Verona, became friends at school, entered
together the order of the Augustinian friars,
were both endowed with similar miraculous
gifts, and died within a few hours of each
other. Their cult was approved in 1837.

Evaristus (St) M.   Oct 14
See Carponius, Evaristus and Priscian.

Evaristus (St) Pope M.
                                    formerly Oct 26
d. *c* 107   Traditionally of an Hellenic-
Jewish background. Nothing is certain
of this very early pope, even the length of his
pontificate. Along with all the early popes, he
was honoured as a martyr. Cult suppressed in
1969.

Evaristus (St) M.   Dec 23
See Theodulus, Saturninus, etc.

Evasius (St) Bp. M.   Dec 1
d. ? 362   Said to have been the first bishop
of Asti in Piedmont, whence he was driven by
the Arians, and finally to have been put to
death under Julian the Apostate at Casale
Monferrato. The accounts given of him are
very untrustworthy.

Evasius (St) Bp.   Dec 2
? First bishop of Brescia.

Eve (St)   Dec 24
See Adam and Eve.

Evellius (St) M.   May 11
d. *c* 66   Said to have been a counsellor of
Nero, converted to Christ on witnessing the
patience of the martyrs, and himself martyred
at Pisa.

Eventius (St) M.   Apr 16
See Saragossa, Martyrs of.

Eventius (St) M.   May 3
See Alexander, Eventius and Theodulus.

Everard (*several*)
Otherwise Eberhard, q.v.

Everard Hanse (Bl) M.   July 30
d. 1581   A native of Northamptonshire who
was educated at Cambridge and became a

Protestant minister. After his conversion he was ordained priest at Reims (1581). A few months after he was martyred at Tyburn; when dying he was heard to exclaim: "Oh happy day!" Beatified in 1886.

Evergislus (Ebregesilus) (St) Bp. M.   Oct 24
? 5th cent. A bishop of Cologne, and a martyr at the hands of heathen robbers. Very probably he died at a much later period and not as a martyr.

Everildis (Averil) (St) Abs. OSB.   July 9
d. late 7th cent. This saint received the veil from St Wilfrid at York at a spot called "the Bishop's Farm", afterwards Everildsham, now Everingham, where she became abbess of a large community. Her two first companions were SS Bega and Wulfreda.

Evermarus (St) M.   May 1
d. c 700 A pilgrim, murdered by robbers at Rousson, near Tongres, in Belgium.

Evermod (St) Bp. O. Praem.   Feb 17
d. 1178 A Premonstratensian canon under St Norbert, who preached to the Wends, and eventually was chosen abbot of Gottesgnaden, then abbot of Magdeburg, and finally bishop of Ratzeburg.

Evermund (Ebremundus) (St) Ab. OSB.   June 10
d. c 720 A native of Bayeux and a courtier. He married and, with his wife's consent, founded several religious houses, the chief of which was Fontenay-Louvet, in the diocese of Séez, where he became monk and abbot. His wife entered one of his foundations as a nun.

Evilasius (St) M.   Sept 20
See Fausta and Evilasius.

Evodius, Hermogenes and Callista (SS) MM.   Apr 25
? The pre-1970 RM. mentioned this group three times. On Aug 2 they are given as the three sons of Theodota, martyred at Nicea in Bithynia. On the other two dates their martyrdom is placed at Syracuse, and in each of these places the third name is given as Callista, indicating a sister and not a third brother. There is no *Passio* of the martyrs of Syracuse, and it is possible that they suffered at Nicea. See Theodota.

Evodius (St) Bp. M.   May 6
d. c 67 The successor of St Peter in the see of Antioch. Tradition makes him a martyr and one of the seventy-two disciples of our Lord.

Evodius (St) Bp.   Oct 8
5th cent. A native of Rouen and bishop of that see. His relics were translated to Braine, near Soissons.

Evodius (St) Bp.   Nov 12
d. p.560 Bishop of Le Puy in France.

Evortius (St) Bp.   Sept 7
d. c 340 A Roman who became bishop of Orleans. The abbey of Saint-Euvert (St Evortius) was founded to enshrine his relics.

Evroul (St) Ab.   Dec 29
Otherwise Ebrulfus, q.v.

Ewald the Fair and Ewald the Dark (SS) Mks. OSB.   Oct 3
d. c 695 Two brothers of Northumbrian stock who became monks and priests and followed St Willibrord to Frisia. After a short apostolate they were martyred together at Aplerbeke, near Dortmund.

Exanthus (St) M.   Aug 7
See Carpophorus, Exanthus, etc.

Expeditus of Melitene (St) M.   Apr 19
See Hermogenes, Gaius, Expeditus, etc.

Exuperantia (St) V.   Apr 26
? A saint whose relics are venerated at Troyes in France. Nothing else is known about her.

Exuperantius (St) Bp.   Jan 24
5th cent. Bishop of Cingoli near Ancona, in Italy. He is believed to have been a native of Africa.

Exuperantius (St) Bp.   May 30
d. 418 Bishop of Ravenna from 398 to 418.

Exuperantius (St) M.   Dec 30
See Sabinus, Exuperantius, etc.

Exuperia (St) M.   July 26
See Symphronius, Olympius, etc.

Exuperius (Hesperius), Cyriacus and Theodulus (SS) MM.   May 2
d. c 127 A family of slaves — husband, wife and two sons — owned by a rich pagan of Attalia in Pamphylia. They were martyred for refusing to take part with their master in idolatrous rites.

Exuperius (St) M.   Sept 22
See the Theban Legion.

Exuperius (French: Soupire) (St) Bp.   Aug 1
? 4th cent. A bishop of Bayeux, who appears to have lived in the fourth century, and is honoured at Corbeil under the name of St Spire.

**Exuperius (French:
Soupire) (St)** Bp.   Sept 28
d. 411 Bishop of Toulouse, a benefactor
and friend of St Jerome, noted for his generosity in sending large contributions to the poor
of Palestine and Egypt.

Exuperius (St) M.   Nov 19
See Severinus, Exuperius and Felician.

Ezechiel (St) Prophet   Apr 10
? 6th cent. B.C.   One of the three greater
prophets and the writer of a canonical book of
Scripture. The tradition is that he was put to
death, while in captivity in Babylon, by one of
the Jewish judges who had turned pagan, and
that he was buried there in the tomb of Shem.
His grave was for the early Christians a place
of pilgrimage.

Ezra (Esdras) (St) Prophet.   July 13
4–5 cent. B.C.   A Jewish scribe and priest,
born in Babylon during the captivity. Around
397 B.C. he obtained permission to lead a
group of exiles back to Jerusalem. He had the
walls of the city built, and on the completion of
the work concluded a solemn pact between
God and the people. Two books of the Vulgate
Bible bear his name (Ezra and Nehemiah in
the A.V.) although he is not their author. Two
others, known as the third and fourth books of
Esdras, are apocryphal.

Fabian (St) Pope M. GC. Jan 20

d. 250 In 236 Fabian succeeded St Antheros as Pope and was bishop of Rome for fourteen years, until his martyrdom under Decius. St Cyprian, his contemporary, describes him as an "incomparable man" and adds that the glory of his death corresponded with the purity and goodness of his life. Part of his relics were taken to the Basilica of St Sebastian; thereafter the two martyrs were honoured with one feast until 1969, when they were separated liturgically.

Fabian (St) M. Dec 31

See Stephen, Pontian, etc.

Fabiola (St) W. Dec 27

d. 399 A Roman patrician maiden who was married to a very young man of equal rank but of dissolute habits, whom she divorced. She then united herself with another man, causing great scandal in Rome. After the latter's death she performed public penance, and devoted her great wealth to the care of the sick in a hospital which she established in Rome — the first of its kind in the West — associating herself in this work with St Pammachius. In 395 she visited her friend St Jerome in the Holy Land, wishing to enter the convent at Bethlehem; but was dissuaded by St Jerome. She returned accordingly to Rome and founded, and superintended, a hostel for pilgrims near the city. The veneration in which she was held in Rome was demonstrated by the great concourse of people at her funeral.

Fabius (St) M. May 11

See Maximus, Bassus and Fabius.

Fabius (St) M. July 31

d. 300 A soldier beheaded at Caesarea in Mauretania, under Diocletian, for refusing to carry a standard bearing idolatrous emblems.

Fabrician and Philibert (SS) MM. Aug 22

? Said to have been martyred in Spain. They are honoured at Toledo.

Fachanan (St) Bp. Aug 14

d. late 6th cent. Probably the first bishop of Ross, in Ireland. He founded the monastic

St Fabian, Jan 20

school at what is now Rosscarbery, in Co. Cork, and placed there St Brendan as one of the teachers. He is venerated as the patron saint of the diocese of Ross.

Faciolus (St) Mk. OSB. Sept 7
d. *c* 950 A Benedictine monk of the abbey of St Cyprian at Poitiers.

Facundinus (St) Bp. Aug 28
d. *c* 620 Bishop of Taino in Umbria, where he is still venerated.

Facundus and Primitivus (SS) MM. Nov 27
d. *c* 300 Born at Léon in Spain and beheaded by the River Cea, where the town of Sahagun now stands. At a later period the great Benedictine abbey of Sahagun, round which grew the present township of that name, was called after St Facundus (Sant'Facun-Sahagun).

Fagan (St) May 26
Otherwise Fugatius, q.v.

Fagildus (St) Ab. OSB. July 25
d. 1086 Benedictine abbot of the monastery of St Martin de Anteltares, at Compostella in Spain. The epitaph on his tomb ends with this line: "A saint, he left the world to live with the saints."

Failbhe the Little (St) Ab. March 10
d. 754 For seven years abbot of Iona, where he died at the age of eighty.

Failbhe (St) Ab. March 22
d. *c* 680 An abbot of Iona. He was an Irishman and brother to St Finan of Rath. There are some twenty other saints of the same name commemorated in the Irish and Scottish menologies.

Faina (St) M. May 18
See Theodotus, Thecusa, etc.

Faith, Hope and Charity (SS) VV. MM. Aug 1
The English equivalent of the Greek Pistis, Elpis, Agape, and of the Latin Fides, Spes, Caritas. The legend is that they were three young girls, aged respectively twelve, ten and nine years, daughters of St Wisdom (Sophia, Sapientia) with whom they were martyred in Rome under Hadrian. The story is fiction.

Faith (Foi) (St) VM. Oct 6
3rd cent. A Maiden of Agen in S. France, burnt to death in the same city (under Maximian Herculeus). Her shrine at the abbey of Conques was very famous during the Middle Ages. A portion of her relics was taken to Glastonbury; hence her place in the Sarum calendar and the dedication to her of several English churches. Her golden shrine at Conques still exists and is the centre of an active cult. Her existence is historical but her legends are fables. In art she is shewn as a damsel, often crowned, holding a gridiron or a metal bedstead.

Fal (Fele) (St) C. May 16
Otherwise Fidolus, q.v.

Falco (St) Bp. Feb 20
d. 512 Bishop of Maestricht from 495 till his death.

Falco (Bl) Ab. OSB. June 6
d. 1146 Falco received the Benedictine habit at Cava, at the hands of St Peter, abbot of that monastery. Shortly after he was sent to rule the daughter house of St Mary at Cirzosimo, and in 1141 he succeeded Bl Simon as abbot of Cava. Cult confirmed in 1928.

Falco (Bl) H. Aug 9
d. 1440 A native of Calabria, who led a hermit's life in the Abruzzi. His shrine is to be found at Palena. Cult approved in 1893.

Famianus (Quardus) (St) H. OSB. Cist. Aug 8
1090–1150 A native of Cologne, who made the pilgrimage to the Holy Land, to Rome and Compostella, and finally settled near the last named place as a hermit, living for twenty-five years at San Placido on the River Minho. When the Cistercian abbey of Osera was built in the neightbourhood he joined the community and professed the rule. However, he obtained leave to visit the Holy Land once more and, on his return, died at Gallese in Umbria.

Fanchea (Garbh) (St) V. Jan 1
d. *c* ?585 A native of Clogher and sister of St Endeus (Enda). She was the abbess-foundress of a convent at Rossory in Fermanagh, and was buried at Killane.

Fandilas (St) Mk. M. June 13
d. 853 An Andalusian by birth, he was a priest and abbot of the monastery of Peñamelaria, near Cordoba. He was beheaded at Cordoba by order of the emir Mohammed.

Fantinus (St) Ab. Aug 30
d. *p.*980 A Basilian monk of Calabria, and abbot of the Greek monastery of St Mercury. He was already an old man when his abbey was destroyed by the Saracens. He then travelled to the East, where he died.

Fara (St) Abs Apr 3 and Dec 7
Otherwise Burgundofara, q.v.

Farannan (St) Ab. Feb 15
d. *c* 590 An Irish disciple of St Columba at

Iona. Eventually he returned to Ireland to lead the life of a hermit at All-Farannan, now Allernan, Sligo, where he probably died.

Faro (St) Bp.   Oct 28
d. *c* 675   A brother of SS Fara and Cognoaldus. He gave up the office of chancellor which he held at the court of Dagobert I and became a monk (either at Luxeuil or at Rebais), a priest, and finally bishop of Meaux (626). In this capacity he was a great fosterer of monasticism.

Fastred (Bl) Ab. OSB. Cist.   Apr 21
d. 1163   Fastred de Cavamiez was a native of Hainault who received the Cistercian habit from St Bernard at Clairvaux. In 1148 he was dispatched with a colony of monks to be abbot-founder of Cambron, in the diocese of Cambrai. In 1157 he was transferred to the abbacy of Clairvaux and in 1162 to that of Cîteaux.

Fausta and Evilasius
(SS) MM.   Sept 20
d. 303   St Fausta, a girl of about thirteen, was being cruelly treated by order of Evilasius, a heathen magistrate, when, impressed by her constancy, the latter also confessed Christ. Both were martyred together at Cyzicum in Pontus under Diocletian.

Fausta (St) W.   Dec 19
3rd cent.   The reputed mother of St Anastasia of Sirmium.

Faustian (St) M.   Apr 29
See Corfu, Martyrs of.

Faustina (St) V.   Jan 18
See Liberata (Jan 18).

Faustinian (St) Bp.   Feb 26
4th cent.   Said to have been the second bishop of Bologna. He reorganized the diocese which had suffered much during the persecution of Diocletian, and lived to be a firm defender of the faith against Arianism.

Faustinus and Jovita (SS)
MM.   formerly Feb 15
2nd cent.   Two brothers, belonging to the nobility of Brescia, in Lombardy, and zealous preachers of Christianity, who were beheaded in their native city, under the emperor Hadrian. The details of their Passion are doubtful but their cult was ancient and widespread. Cult suppressed in 1969.

Faustinus (St) Bp.   Feb 16
d. 381   The successor of St Ursicinus, about the year 360, in the see of Brescia, in Lombardy. He is said to have been a collateral descendant of SS Faustinus and Jovita and to have compiled their Acts.

Faustinus and Comp.
(SS) MM.   Feb 17
? A group of forty-five martyrs, of whom nothing whatever is known. The pre-1970 RM. placed them at Rome.

Faustinus, Timothy and
Venustus (SS) MM.   May 22
d. *c* 362   Roman martyrs under Julian the Apostate.

Faustinus (St) M.   June 5
See Florentius, Julian, etc.

Faustinus (St) M.   July 29
See Simplicius, Faustinus and Beatrix.

Faustinus (St) C.   July 29
4th cent.   A disciple of St Felix, bishop of Martano, or Spello, near Spoleto, and his attendant at his martyrdom. St Faustinus himself suffered much for Christ before passing away peacefully at Todi in Umbria.

Faustinus, Lucius,
Candidus, Caelian, Mark,
Januarius and Fortunatus
(SS) MM.   Dec 15
? African martyrs, about whom nothing is known.

Faustus (St) Ab.   Feb 15
6th cent.   An alleged disciple of St Benedict at Montecassino, and companion and biographer of St Maurus, according to the legendary *Vita Sancti Mauri* of Abbot Odo of Glanfeuil.

Faustus and Comp. (SS)
MM.   June 24
? Twenty-four Roman martyrs, whose Acts have been lost. They are very probably to be identified with the group of Roman martyrs commemorated on June 25 (see Lucilla, Flora, etc.).

Faustus (St) M.   July 16
d. 250   A martyr of the Decian persecution, who, crucified and transfixed with arrows, is said to have lingered in his agony for five days.

Faustus (St) M.   Aug 1
See Bonus, Faustus, etc.

Faustus (St) C.   Aug 3
5th cent.   Said to have been the son of St Dalmatius but the history is of later origin. Faustus became a monk.

Faustus (St) M.   Aug 7
d. *c* 190   According to tradition, this St Faustus was a soldier martyred at Milan under Commodus.

Faustus, Macarius and Comp. (SS) MM. Sept 6
d. 250 A group of twelve martyrs, beheaded at Alexandria in Egypt under Decius.

Faustus (St) Ab. Sept 6
d. c 607 Abbot of the monastery of Santa Lucia, at Syracuse, where he taught Zosimus, the future bishop of Syracuse.

Faustus (St) M. Sept 8
See Timothy and Faustus.

Faustus (St) Bp. Sept 28
c 408–490 Born in Brittany, Faustus became a monk at Lérins and later the abbot (433) of that monastery. About 459, he was chosen bishop of Riez. He combated with great energy and success both Arianism and Pelagianism; though in his writings he himself is not exempt from semi-Pelagianism. He was one of the most influential bishops of his time.

Faustus (St) M. Oct 3
See Dionysius, Faustus, etc. This Faustus is identified by the pre-1970 RM. with those of Oct 4 and Nov 19.

Faustus (St) M. Oct 4
See Gaius, Faustus, etc.

Faustus (St) M. Oct 5
See Placid, Eutychius, etc.

Faustus, Januarius and Martial (SS) MM. Oct 13
d. 304 Martyrs of Cordoba under Diocletian, Prudentius calls them "the Three Crowns of Cordoba".

Faustus (St) M. Nov 19
4th cent. The deacon of St Dionysius of Alexandria and his companion in exile. He survived his master and in extreme old age died a martyr under Diocletian. See Dionysius, Faustus, etc., and Gaius, Faustus, etc.

Faustus, Didius, Ammonius, Phileas, Hesychius, Pachomius, Theodore and Comp. (SS) MM. Nov 26
d. c 311 Egyptian martyrs under Maximian Galerius. It is said that their total number was six hundred and sixty. Phileas, Hesychius, Pachomius and Theodore were bishops; Faustus, a priest of Alexandria.

Fazzio (Fatius, Fazius, Facius) (St) C. Jan 18
1190–1272 A native of Verona and a goldsmith. He founded a charitable society at Cremona, called the Order of the Holy Spirit. He made several pilgrimages on foot to Rome and to Compostella.

Febronia (St) VM. June 25
d. 304 A young nun, barbarously mutilated and finally put to death under Diocletian at Nisibis in Mesopotamia (not at Sybapolis in Syria). The legend adds many ghastly details; but there is good reason to doubt the very existence of this saint.

Fechin (St) Ab. Jan 20
d. c 665 A native of Connaught, and the abbot-founder of several Irish monasteries. His name is particularly connected with that of Fobhar (Fore) in Westmeath. Ecclefechan and St Vigean's, near Arbroath in Scotland, also perpetuated his memory.

Fedlemid (St) Bp. Aug 9
Otherwise Phelim, q.v.

Feighin (St) Ab. Jan 20
Otherwise Fechin, q.v.

Felan (St) Ab. Jan 9
Otherwise Foelan, q.v.

Fele (St) C. May 16
Otherwise Fidolus, q.v.

Felicia de Montmorency (Bl) V. OV. June 6
1600–1666 Born at Rome of French parents, Marie Félicie des Ursins became a nun of the Visitation at Autun, during the life-time of the foundress, St Jane Frances de Chantal.

Felicia Meda (Bl) Poor Clare Oct 5
1378–1444 A native of Milan, who joined the Poor Clares at the convent of St Ursula in that city (1400). In 1425 she was made abbess, and after fourteen years she was sent to Pesaro to establish a new house which she ruled with equal success. Cult approved in 1812.

Felician (St) Bp. M. Jan 24 and Oct 20
d. 251 A native of Foligno, who was consecrated bishop of that city by Pope St Victor I and governed his diocese for more than fifty years, meanwhile evangelizing the whole of Umbria. He was arrested under Decius, and died on his way to martyrdom at Rome.

Felician, Philappian and Comp. (SS) MM. Jan 30
? A band of one hundred and twenty-six African martyrs.

Felician (St) M. Feb 2
See Fortunatus, Felician, etc.

Felician (St) M. June 9
See Primus and Felician.

Felician (St) M. July 21
See Victor, Alexander, etc.

Felician (St) M.   Oct 29
See Hyacinth, Quintius, etc.

Felician (St) M.   Nov 11
See Valentine, Felician and Victorinus.

Felician (St) M.   Nov 19
See Severinus, Exuperius and Felician.

Felicinus (St) Bp.   July 19
Otherwise Felix of Verona, q.v.

Felicissima (St) VM.   Aug 12
See Gracilian and Felicissima.

**Felicissimus, Heraclius
and Paulinus (SS)** MM.   May 26
d. 303   Martyrs under Diocletian. They suffered in all probability at Todi in Umbria,
where their relics are still venerated.

Felicissimus (St) M.   July 2
See Ariston, Crescentian, etc.

Felicissimus (St) M.   Aug 6
See Sixtus II and Comp.

Felicissimus (St) M.   Oct 26
See Rogatian and Felicissimus.

Felicissimus (St) M.   Nov 24
d. c 303   A martyr who suffered at Perugia,
probably under Diocletian.

Felicitas (St) M.   March 7
See Perpetua, Felicitas, etc.

Felicitas (St) M.   March 8
See Cyril, Rogatus, etc.

Felicitas (St) V.   March 26
9th cent.   A nun, in all probability of the
Benedictine order, who professed the rule in a
convent on the Colli Euganei, or else in that of
SS Cosmas and Damian at Padua. Her relics
are now at St Justina, Padua.

Felicitas (St) M.   Nov 23
d. 165   A Roman widow martyred at Rome
with her sons under Marcus Antoninus. The
pre-1970 RM. identified her sons with the
seven brothers, commemorated July 10 (see
Seven Brothers). This is now discredited.
This Felicitas may be the saint named in the
first eucharistic prayer rather than the companion of St Perpetua, as usually supposed. All
that is really known about her is that she was an
early martyr buried on this date at the cemetery of Maximus on the Via Salaria in Rome.
Cult confined to local calendars since 1969.

Felicity
Saints called Felicity are often spelt Felicitas,
q.v.

Felicula (St) M.   Feb 14
See Vitalis, Felicula and Zeno.

Felicula (St) VM.   June 13
d. c 90   A Roman maiden of the apostolic
age, according to a legend the foster sister of St
Petronilla. After the latter's martyrdom under
Domitian she was left for a fortnight in her
prison without food or drink, and then was
thrown into a ditch to die. Her body was
recovered by St Nicomedes. The whole story
seems to be a fiction.

Felinus and Gratian (SS)
MM.   June 1
d. 250   Soldiers in the imperial army martyred at Perugia under Decius. Their relics
were translated to Arona near Milan in 979.

Felix (*several*)
Note. This name is one of the most common in
Christian hagiology. In the following notices
we list only the best known among them.

Felix of Bourges (St) Bp.   Jan 1
d. c 580   Bishop of Bourges in France. He
took part in the council of Paris in 573. He is
still venerated at Bourges.

Felix and Januarius (SS)
MM.   Jan 7
?   Said to have suffered martyrdom at Herac-
lea, a name common to several ancient cities.

Felix (St) M.   Jan 9
See Epictetus, Jucundus, etc.

Felix of Nola (St)   Jan 14
d. c 250   The son of a Romano-Syrian soldier who had settled at Nola, near Naples.
Felix was ordained a priest and devoted himself to the service of his bishop, St Maximus,
especially during the persecution which broke
out under Decius. On account of his sufferings during the persecution, he was sometimes
referred to as a martyr. St Paulinus, bishop of
Nola, has left a glowing account of the popular
veneration for St Felix. Cult confined to local
calendars since 1969.

Felix (St) C.   Jan 14
?   A Roman priest, venerated also on Jan 14,
and often confused with St Felix of Nola.

Felix O'Dullany (Bl)
Bp. OSB. Cist.   Jan 24
d. 1202   An Irish Cistercian monk, probably
of Jerpoint, Kilkenny. In 1178 he was made
bishop of Ossory, residing at Aghaoe. He is
venerated by the Cistercians as a *beatus*.

**Felix, Symphronius
(Sempronius), Hippolytus
and Comp. (SS)** MM.   Feb 3
?   A group of martyrs who suffered probably in
proconsular Africa.

Felix of Lyons (St) Bp.   Feb 3
See Lupicinus and Felix.

Felix of Africa (St) M.   Feb 11
See Saturninus, Dativus, etc.

Felix of Adrumetum (St)
M.   Feb 21
See Verulus, Secundinus, etc.

Felix of Metz (St) Bp.   Feb 21
2nd cent. Described as the third bishop of
Metz, which see he is alleged to have occupied
for over forty years in the sub-apostolic age.

Felix of Brescia (St) Bp.   Feb 23
d. *c* 650 The twentieth bishop of Brescia.
He governed the diocese for over forty eventful years during which he was occupied in
combating Lombard Arians and other heretics.

Felix (St) M.   Feb 26
See Fortunatus, Felix and Comp.

Felix III (or II) (St) Pope   March 1
d. 492 A Roman, an ancestor of St Gregory
the Great. He was pope from 483 till his death.
The nine years of his pontificate were occupied with controversy against Monophysitism
and Eutychianism as also in remedying the
evils caused in Africa by numerous apostasies
during the Vandal persecution.

Felix, Luciolus, Fortunatus,
Marcia, and Comp. (SS)
MM.   March 3
? A group of forty martyrs conjectured to have
suffered in N. Africa.

Felix of Rhuys (St) Ab.
OSB.   March 4
d. 1038 A native of the diocese of Quimper
in Brittany who became a hermit on Ouessant
Island and afterwards a Benedictine at Fleury
(Saint-Benoit-sur-Loire). The abbot of
Fleury sent him to restore Rhuys abbey, the
great Breton monastery founded by St Gildas,
which had been destroyed by the Normans.

Felix (St) M.   March 8
See Cyril, Rogatus, etc.

Felix of Dunwich (St) Bp.   March 8
d. 647 A native of Burgundy who became a
bishop in Gaul and who offered himself to
work for the conversion of the East Angles. In
630 Sigebert, their king, came back from exile
and work began. St Felix undertook the
mission with the approval of St Honorius of
Canterbury, and placed his episcopal see at
Dunwich, now washed away by the sea. He
preached with great success in Norfolk, Suffolk and Cambridgeshire, opening schools on
the French model. He is the veritable apostle
of the East Angles. In art he is shewn as vested

as a bishop: he has three rings on his right
hand.

Felix of Aquileia (St) M.   March 16
See Hilary, Tatian, etc.

Felix of Gerona (St) M.   March 18
See Narcissus and Felix.

Felix and Comp. (SS)
MM.   March 23
5th cent. A group of twenty-one martyrs.
Unless their proximity in the pre-1970 RM. to
SS Victorian and Comp. implies that they
suffered in the same persecution of the Van-
dals, we can only say that they suffered in
Africa.

Felix of Montecassino
(Bl) Mk.   March 23
d. *c* 1000 A Benedictine of Montecassino,
who spent all his life in one of the daughter-
houses of the abbey. On account of the many
miracles wrought at his tomb the bishop of
Chieti enshrined his relics for veneration.

Felix of Trier (St) Bp.   March 26
d. *c* 400 Consecrated bishop of Trier by his
friend, St Martin of Tours, in 386. Owing to
the fact that this took place under the usurping
emperor Maximus, the legality of his election
was questioned by the papacy and St Ambrose,
and he consequently resigned. Contemporary
writers, particularly St Sulpicius Severus,
speak very highly of his virtues.

Felix (St) M.   March 31
See Theodulus, Anesius, etc.

Felix of Saragossa (St)
M.   Apr 16
See Saragossa, Martyrs of.

Felix of Alexandria (St)
M.   Apr 21
See Arator, Fortunatus, etc.

Felix, Fortunatus and
Achilleus (SS) MM.   Apr 23
d. 212 St Felix, a priest, and his two
deacons, Fortunatus and Achilleus, were sent
by St Irenaeus of Lyons to evangelize the
district of Vienne, in France. After a most
successful apostolate they were martyred. The
Acta are of much later composition.

Felix of Seville (St) M.   May 2
? A deacon, martyred in all probability at
Seville, where he is held in great veneration.

Felix of Rome (St) M.   May 10
See Calepodius, Palmatius, etc.

Felix and Gennadius
(SS) MM.   May 16
? Two martyrs venerated from ancient times

in the city of Uzalis in proconsular Africa, where their relics were enshrined.

Felix of Spoleto (St) Bp. M.　　May 18
d. *c* 304　A bishop, either of Spoleto or of the neighbouring town of Spello (*Hispellum*) in Umbria. He was martyred under Diocletian.

Felix of Cantalice (St)
OFM. Cap.　　　　　　　　May 18
1513–1587　A native of Cantalice, near Rieti, in Apulia, the child of peasant farmers, he started life as a farm labourer, and at the age of thirty joined the Capuchins in Rome as a lay-brother; thereafter for forty years he begged the daily alms for his friary. He was a friend of St Charles Borromeo, and an intimate of St Philip Neri. He was nicknamed *Deo Gratias* on account of his habitual use of this ejaculation. His characteristic virtue was spiritual joy. Canonized in 1724 — the first Capuchin friar to attain this honour.

Felix of Istria (St) M.　　　May 24
See Zöellus, Servilius, etc.

Felix of Sardinia (St) M.　　May 28
See Emilius, Felix, etc.

Felix (St) H.　　　　　　　May 29
See Votus, Felix and John.

Felix I (St) Pope　　formerly May 30
d. 274　A Roman by birth and pope from 269 to 274. He was the first to condemn the heresy of Paul of Samosata. He is said to have died a martyr under Aurelian; but this appears to be an error, due to confusion with another Felix. Cult suppressed in 1969.

Felix of Nicosia (Bl)
OFM. Cap.　　　　　　　　June 1
1715–1787　A native of Nicosia in Sicily. He began life as an apprentice to a shoe-maker; then he sought to become a religious, but failed several times. At last he was professed as a lay-brother, and in the course of his begging expeditions on behalf of his friary at Nicosia, reclaimed numerous sinners and helped the poor and the sick. Beatified in 1888.

Felix of Fritzlar (St) M.
OSB.　　　　　　　　　　June 5
d. *c* 790　A Benedictine monk of Fritzlar in Germany and a martyr probably at the hands of the heathen Saxons.

Felix and Fortunatus
(SS) MM.　　　　　　　　June 11
d. 296　Two brothers, born at Vicenza in N Italy, who suffered under Diocletian at Aquileia.

Felix of Cordoba (St) M.　　June 14
See Anastasius, Felix and Digna.

Felix and Maurus (SS)
CC.　　　　　　　　　　　June 16
6th cent.　Natives of Palestine, father and son, who after a pilgrimage to Rome settled at a place now called San Felice near Narni, in central Italy.

Felix of Apollonia (St) M.　　June 17
See Isaurus, Innocent, etc.

Felix of Sutri (St) M.　　　June 23
d. 257　A priest of Sutri in Tuscany, scourged to death under the emperors Valerian and Gallienus.

Felix of Cîteaux (Bl) Mk.
OSB. Cist.　　　　　　　　June 23
d. 1113　A Cistercian monk, listed in the menologies of the order as a *beatus*.

Felix (St) M.　　　　　　　July 2
See Ariston, Crescentian, etc.

Felix of Nantes (St) Bp.　　　July 7
d. 584　A great bishop of Nantes for about thirty-three years. He died on Jan 8; July 7 is the anniversary of the translation of his relics.

Felix (St) M.　　　　　　　July 10
One of the Seven Brothers, q.v.

Felix (St) M.　　　　　　　July 10
See Januarius, Marinus, etc.

Felix of Milan (St) M.　　　July 12
See Nabor and Felix.

Felix of Como (St) Bp.　　　July 14
d. *c* 390　Said to have been the first bishop of Como. He was an intimate friend of St Ambrose.

Felix of Pavia (St) Bp. M.　　July 15
? A martyr, of whom nothing is known. Some identify him with St Felix of Spoleto (May 18).

Felix (St) M.　　　　　　　July 17
One of the Scillitan Martyrs, q.v.

**Felix (Felicinus) of
Verona (St)** Bp.　　　　　　July 19
? A bishop of Verona, venerated from ancient times as a saint.

**Felix of Manfredonia
(St)** M.　　　　　　　　　July 25
See Florentius and Felix.

Felix of Cordoba (St) M.　　July 27
See George, Aurelius, etc.

**Felix, Julia and Jucunda
(SS)** MM.　　　　　　　　July 27
? The pre-1970 RM. erroneously assigns these martyrs to Nola. As to St Felix, the reference would simply be the date of the

consecration of St Felix, bishop of Nola (see Nov 15). SS Jucunda and Julia are in older MSS assigned to Nicomedia in Asia Minor.

Felix II (St)   July 29
d. 365   The accounts of the life of this Felix are very conflicting: he does not seem to have been either a pope or a martyr although the pre-1970 RM. listed him as such. He certainly was intruded into the see of Rome in the year 355, when Pope Liberius was exiled by the Arian emperor Constantius II. Since 1969 his cult has been confined to local calendars, as nothing is known for sure of him beyond his name and his burial in Rome.

Felix (Fedlimid) (St) Bp.   Aug 9
Otherwise Phelim, q.v.

Felix of Porto (St) M.   Aug 22
See Martial, Saturninus, etc.

Felix of Pistoia (St) H.   Aug 26
9th cent.   A hermit of Pistoia in Tuscany, venerated as a saint, about whom, however, almost nothing is known.

Felix (St) M.   Aug 28 and Sept 1
See Septiminus, Januarius and Felix, a group among the Twelve Holy Brothers.

Felix and Adauctus (SS)
MM.   Aug 30
d. c 304   Martyrs beheaded in Rome under Diocletian. St Felix was a priest; as he was being led to execution, a bystander confessed Christ and was put to death with him. Because this second martyr's name was not known, he was called *Adauctus*, i.e., the one added. All this is legend: the only known facts are their names and their place of burial on the Ostian Way. Cult confined to local calendars since 1969.

Felix (St) M.   Sept 1
See Donatus and Felix.

Felix and Augebert (SS)
MM.   Sept 6
7th cent.   Two English slaves sold in France and ransomed by St Gregory the Great, who directed that they should be received and educated in a monastery with a view to their becoming missionaries in their native country. Felix was ordained priest, and Augebert deacon; but unfortunately they were killed by pagans in Champagne before they could undertake their mission.

Felix and another Felix
(SS) Bps. MM.   Sept 10
See Nemesian, Felix, etc.

Felix and Regula (SS) MM.   Sept 11
3rd cent.   Brother and sister who at the time

of the martyrdom of St Maurice under Maximian Herculeus, took refuge in Switzerland, where they were eventually found and martyred near Zurich.

Felix and Constantia
(SS) MM.   Sept 19
1st cent.   Martyrs under Nero, at Nocera, between Naples and Salerno.

Felix III (IV) (St) Pope   Sept 22
d. 530   Less accurately, Felix IV. (See above, St Felix II, July 29.) His pontificate lasted from 526 till 530 and his best remembered deed as pope was the building of the church of SS Cosmas and Damian. He was greatly loved in Rome for his simplicity and generosity to the poor.

Felix of Auton (St) M.   Sept 24
See Andochius, Thyrsus and Felix.

Felix and Cyprian (SS)
MM. Bps.   Oct 12
d. c 484   Two African bishops, leaders of a great multitude of Catholics — the number of four thousand nine hundred and sixty-six is usually given by historians — driven out to starvation and death in the Sahara desert by the Arian Vandal king, Hunneric. We have the account of their sufferings from Victor of Utica, a contemporary writer.

Felix (Africanus),
Audactus (Adauctus),
Januarius, Fortunatus and
Septimus (SS) MM.   Oct 24
d. 303   Felix was a bishop of Thibiuca in Africa who was put to death for refusing to deliver up the sacred books. He was one of the first victims of Diocletian's persecution. The accounts we have of the other martyrs mentioned with him are not trustworthy.

Felix and Eusebius (SS)
MM.   Nov 5
? 1st cent.   Alleged martyrs of Terracina, an Italian city between Rome and Naples.

Felix of Fondi (St) Mk. OSB.   Nov 6
6th cent.   A monk of a Benedictine house at Fondi in S. Italy — a contemporary of St Gregory the Great, by whom he was greatly revered.

Felix of Thynissa (St) M.   Nov 6
? An African martyr who suffered at Thynissa, near Hippona (Bona). He was found dead in prison the day before he was to be executed. St Augustine preached a sermon on the martyr's feast day.

Felix of Nola (St) Bp. M.   Nov 15
d. 287   Said to have been the first bishop of
Nola, near Naples, and to have been put to
death for Christ with thirty companions.

Felix of Valois (St) C.   Nov 20
1127–1212?   His legend states that he lived
first as a hermit in a forest near Meaux. It is
said that he, with St John of Matha, organized
the Trinitarians in France, a religious order
founded for the purpose of ransoming captives
from the Moors. Any details of his life are
legendary and of little historical value. Cult
confined to particular calendars since 1969.

Felix (St) Bp.   Nov 28
See Valerian, Urban, etc.

Felix of Bologna (St) Bp.   Dec 4
d. 429   A deacon of the church of Milan
under St Ambrose, and afterwards the fifth
bishop of Bologna.

Felix (St) M.   Dec 5
See Julius, Potamia, etc.

Felix of Rome (St) M.   Dec 29
See Callistus, Felix and Boniface.

Feock (St) V.   Feb 2
?   A saint otherwise unknown, whose name is
perpetuated by a church dedication in Corn-
wall. Possibly she was an immigrant from
Ireland. Some have it that Feock is only a
variant of the name of St Fiace, the friend of St
Patrick; others identify St Feock with St
Vougas of Brittany.

Ferdinand III (St) King   May 30
1198–1252   King of Castile in 1217, and of
Léon in 1230. For twenty-seven years he was
engaged in an almost uninterrupted crusade
against the Muslims in Spain, from whom he
recaptured Cordoba (1236), Murcia, Jaen,
Cadiz, and finally Seville (1249). He was a
wise ruler, and was wont to say that he "feared
more the curse of one old woman that the
whole army of the Moors". He was the
founder of the university of Salamanca and of
the cathedral of Burgos. By his second wife he
was the father of Eleanor, wife of Edward I of
England. Canonized in 1671.

**Ferdinand of St Joseph
Ayala (Bl)** M. OSA.   June 1
1575–1617   Born at Ballesteros, diocese of
Toledo, Spain, he took the Augustinian habit
at Mentilla, and in 1603 was sent to Mexico,
and thence to Japan (1605) as vicar provincial.
He worked at Ozaka with great success until
his capture and execution at Omura. Beatified
in 1867.

**Ferdinand of Portugal
(Bl)** M.   June 5
1402–1443   Surnamed "the Constant" or
"the Standard-bearer" (*El Abanderado*), son of
King John I of Portugal, he was born at
Santarem, and his leanings towards the religious life led him to become the master-general
of the military order of Aviz, an order dependent on Cîteaux. In this capacity he led an
expedition against the Moors in Africa, but
was defeated at Tangier and given up as a
hostage. He was imprisoned at Arzilla and
remained a prisoner, with never a word of
complaint, for five years, finally dying there of
neglect. Cult approved in 1470.

Ferdinand of Aragon (St)
Bp.   June 27
13th cent.   Related to the royal family of
Aragon, then the rulers of the Two Sicilies, he
became the fifth bishop of Cajazzo, in that
kingdom. His relics are now venerated at
Cornello, in Sicily.

Ferdinand Sanchez (Bl)
M. SJ.   July 15
d. 1570   Born in Castile, and a Jesuit novice,
he suffered martyrdom under the leadership
of Bl Ignatius de Azevedo, q.v.

Feredarius (St) Ab.   May 18
d. *p.*863   An Irishman by birth, chosen abbot
of Iona in 863. During his abbacy the relics of
St Columba were removed to Ireland, for fear
of the Danes.

Fergna (St) Ab.   March 2
d. 637   Surnamed "the White", a kinsman
and disciple of St Columba and his successor
as abbot of Iona.

**Fergus (Fergustus,
Ferguisius) (St)** Bp.   March 30
6th cent.   A bishop of Downpatrick; but the
traditions concerning him are vague in the
extreme, and he may possibly be identified
with St Fergus of Scotland (Nov 27).

Fergus (St) Bp.   Nov 27
d. *c*721   An Irish bishop who preached in
Perthshire, Caithness, Buchan and Forfarshire. He signed the Acts of the Roman
council of 721, describing himself a a Pict. In
the Aberdeen breviary he is called Fergustian.

Fernanado (*several*)
The Spanish and Portuguese form of Ferdin-
and, q.v.

Ferran (*several*)
The old Castilian and Catalan form of Ferdin-
and, q.v.

Ferreolus (St) Bp.   Jan 4
d. 581   A native of Narbonne, who became
bishop of Uzès. He devoted himself in particular to converting the Jews of his diocese
and is said to have been exiled by King
Childebert on that account. He was the
founder of a monastery, for which he wrote a
monastic rule.

Ferreolus (Fergéol) (Bl)
Bp. M.   Jan 16
d. c 670   Said to have been bishop of Grenoble in France. Cult confirmed in 1907.

Ferreolus and Ferrutio
(SS) MM.   June 16
d. c 212   Ferreolus, a priest, and Ferrutio, a
deacon, are said to have been brothers and
natives of Asia Minor. They were sent by St
Irenaeus of Lyons to evangelize the country
round Besançon, where they worked for thirty
years and then were martyred.

Ferreolus (St) M.   Sept 18
3rd cent.   An officer of the imperial army,
martyred at Vienne in Gaul, under Diocletian.
One tradition makes him superior officer to St
Julian of Auvergne.

Ferreolus (St) Bp.   Sept 18
d. c 591   Fifth bishop of Limoges in France.
He is mentioned with great veneration by St
Gregory of Tours.

Ferrutio (St) M.   June 16
See Ferreolus and Ferrutio.

Ferrutius (St) M.   Oct 28
? A Roman soldier stationed at Mainz in
Germany, who demanded his discharge from
the army rather than take part in idolatrous
worship. He was cast into prison, where he
died of ill-treatment and hunger.

Festus (St) M.   June 24
Otherwise Faustus, q.v.

Festus (St) M.   Sept 19
See Januarius and Comp.

Festus (St) M.   Dec 21
See John and Festus.

Fiace (Fiech) (St) Bp.   Oct 12
5th cent.   An Irish bishop, friend and disciple
of St Patrick, in whose honour he wrote a
hymn which is still extant.

Fiachan (Fianchine) (St)
C.   Apr 29
7th cent.   A native of Munster in Ireland, a
monk at Lismore and disciple of St Carthage
the Younger.

**Fiacre (Fiacrius, Fiaker,
Fèvre) (St)** Ab.   Aug 30
d. c 670   An Irishman, he was given land for

a hermitage by St Faro of Meaux. Here he
lived for the rest of his life, attracting many
disciples for whom he built the abbey of
Breuil. St Fiacre's shrine is still a place of
pilgrimage. As patron of gardeners, he is often
represented carrying a shovel.

Fibitius (St) Bp.   Nov 5
d. c 500   Abbot of a monastery at Trier, and
the twenty-first bishop of that city.

Fidelis (St) Bp.   Feb 7
d. c 570   Eastern by origin, he travelled to
Spain with some merchants and settled at
Mérida, where he was trained by St Paul,
bishop of the city, whom he succeeded in that
office.

Fidelis (St) M.   March 23
? An African martyr. Some writers place him
in the same group of African martyrs as St
Felix and his twenty-four companions (March
23).

Fidelis of Sigmaringen
(St) M. OFM. Cap.   GC. Apr 24
1577–1622   Mark Rey, born at Sigmaringen,
in S. Germany, practised as a lawyer, and came
to be known as the "advocate of the poor". In
1612 he joined the Capuchins, receiving the
new name of Fidelis, and after his ordination
the newly founded Roman Congregation of
Propaganda sent him as a missionary to the
Swiss Protestants in the Grisons. Incensed at
his success, the Calvinists raised the peasants
against him by inventing the story that he was a
politcal agent of the Austrian emperor. He was
stabbed to death in the church at Seewis in
Switzerland.

Fidelis of Edessa (St) M.   Aug 21
See Bassa, Theogonius, etc.

Fidelis of Como (St) M.   Oct 28
d. c 304   A soldier martyred in Lombardy
under Maximian Herculeus. His body was
translated by St Charles Borromeo to Milan,
but some of his relics are venerated at Como.

Fidelmia (St) V.   Jan 11
See Ethenea and Fidelmia.

Fidentian (St) M.   Nov 15
See Secundus, Fidentian and Varicus.

Fidentius and Terence
(SS) MM.   Sept 27
? The relics of these martyrs were discovered
in the twelfth century at Todi in central Italy,
where they are venerated. Nothing else is
known about them. The legend of their martyrdom is quite untrustworthy.

Fidentius (St) Bp.   Nov 16
2nd cent.   Some make this saint a confessor,

others a martyr, Baronius a bishop. Tradition assigns him to Padua and to the second century. All this is mere surmise and nothing is known about him.

Fides (St) VM.   Aug 1
Otherwise Faith, q.v.

Fidharleus (St) Ab.   Oct 1
d. 762   An Irish saint, the restorer of Rathin abbey.

Fidleminus (St) Bp.   Aug 9
Otherwise Phelim, q.v.

Fidolus (French: Phal)
(St) Ab.   May 16
d. c 540   The son of a Roman official in Auvergne, France. Taken prisoner by the soldiers of Clovis and sold into slavery, he was ransomed by Aventinus, abbot of Aumont, near Troyes. At a later period Fidolus was himself abbot of the abbey, which was afterwards called Saint-Phal.

Fidweten (Fivetein,
Fidivitanus) (St) Mk. OSB.   Dec 11
d. c 888   A Benedictine monk, disciple of St Convoyon at the abbey of Redon, in Brittany.

Fiech (St) Bp.   Oct 12
Otherwise Fiace, q.v.

Fillan (St) Ab.   Jan 9
Otherwise Foelan, q.v.

Fina (St) V.   March 12
Otherwise Seraphina, q.v.

Finan (St) Bp.   Feb 17
d. 661   An Irish monk of Iona, who succeeded St Aidan in the government of the Northumbrian church. Attended by St Cedd and other fellow-missionaries he evangelized parts of southern England.

Finan (Finnian) (St) Ab.   Apr 7
6th cent.   A native of Munster and a disciple of St Brendan, at whose wish he founded and governed a monastery at Kinnitty in Offaly of which place he is patron.

Finbar (St) Ab.   July 4
6th cent.   An Irish abbot of Innis-Doimhle, Wexford.

Finbarr (Fion-Bharr, i.e.
White Head) (St) Bp.   Sept 25
Otherwise Barr, q.v.

Findan (or Fintan) (St)
H. OSB.   Nov 15
d. 879   A native of Leinster in Ireland who

was carried off as a slave to the Orkneys by Norse raiders, but managed to escape to Scotland. He then undertook a pilgrimage to Rome and became a Benedictine at the abbey of Farfa in Sabina. Thence he migrated to the abbey of Rheinau in Switzerland, where he was allowed to live as a recluse for twenty-two years. His relics are extant.

Findbarr (St) Bp.   Sept 10
Otherwise Finian, q.v.

Fingar (Gwinnear),
Phiala and Comp. (SS)
MM.   Dec 14
5th cent.   Fingar and Phiala, brother and sister, left their native Ireland and crossed over to Cornwall, but they were put to death at Hayle, near Penzance, by a pagan chief. Their attendants shared their crown.

Finian (St) Ab.   March 16
d. ? c 560   A disciple of St Columba, by whom he is said to have been made abbot of Swords, near Dublin. The records of his life are most conflicting.

Finian (Findbarr, Winnin)
(St) Bp.   Sept 10
c 493–579   Born near Stangford Lough, he became a monk in Scotland, and was ordained in Rome. On his return to Ireland he brought with him biblical manuscripts which led to the famous incident of the psalter of St Columba. He was the founder and first abbot-bishop of the monastery of Moville in Co. Down. Wrongly identified with St Frigidian of Lucca.

Finian (Fintan Munnu)
(St) Ab.   Oct 21
d. c 635   A disciple of St Columba at Iona, and at a later period the abbot-founder of the monastery of Taghmon in Co. Wexford. In Scotland he is called St Mundus. He bore a terrible skin disease with patience.

Finian of Clonard (St)
Bp.   Dec 12
d. c 549   Born at Myshall in Co. Carlow, early in life he became a monk in Wales, and after a long sojourn there returned to Ireland and founded a great number of churches, monasteries and schools. Clonard was the greatest, and it was here that Finian had as pupils many of the so-called Twelve Apostles of Ireland, among whom was St Columba. Finian indeed became known as the "Teacher of the Irish Saints", Clonard was the greatest school of its period, renowned chiefly for its biblical studies.

Finlugh (Finlag) (St) Ab.   Jan 3
6th cent.   A brother of St Fintan (Jan 3) who
crossed to Scotland, where it is thought that he
became one of St Columba's disciples. Returning to Ireland he was made abbot of a
monastery established by St Columba in Co.
Derry.

Fintan (St) Ab.   Jan 3
6th cent.   A disciple of St Comgall at Bangor.
He is honoured as the patron saint of Doon in
Limerick. His holy well is still venerated there.

Fintan (St) Ab.   Feb 17
d. 603   A disciple of St Columba, he led the
life of a hermit at Clonenagh in Leix. Soon
numerous disciples attached themselves to
him and he became their abbot. Such was the
austerity of the life led at Clonenagh that
neighbouring monasteries protested.

Fintan (St) H. OSB.   Nov 15
Otherwise Findan, q.v.

Fionnchu (St) Ab.   Nov 28
6th cent.   The successor of St Comgall in the
abbey of Bangor.

Firmatus (St) M.   Oct 5
See Placid, Eutychius, etc.

**Firmatus and Flaviana
(SS) MM.**   Oct 5
? Firmatus, a deacon, and Flaviana, a virgin,
are venerated on Oct 5 at Auxerre in France.
Their names appear already in St Jerome's
martyrology, as venerated in France long
before the legendary martyrdom of St Placid,
Eutychius and Companions (with whom they
were once linked).

**Firmian (Fermanus,
Firminus) (St) Ab. OSB.**   March 11
d. c 1020   A Benedictine abbot of the mon-
astery of San Sabino Piceno, near Fermo, in
the Marches of Ancona.

Firmina (St) VM.   Nov 24
d. c 303   A Roman maiden tortured to death
at Amelia (Ameria) in Umbria, under Diocletian.

Firminus (St) Bp.   Jan 19
? Third bishop of Gabales (Gévaudan),
Mende, in France.

Firminus (St) Ab.   March 11
? It seems that Baronius became confused
between St Firmian (or Firminus), abbot in
the Marches of Ancona (March 11) and
Firminus, bishop of Amiens (Sept 1). No
abbot-saint of the name of Firminus has ever
been venerated at Amiens.

Firminus (St) Bp.   March 29
6th cent.   Bishop of Viviers, in France.

**Firminus of Armenia
(St) M.**   June 24
See Orentius, Heros, etc.

**Firminus of Metz (St)
Bp.**   Aug 18
d. 496   Greek, or Italian, by origin, he was
bishop of Metz for eight years.

**Firminus of Amiens (I and
II) (SS) Bps.**   Sept 25
4th cent.   Two bishops of the name Firminus
are venerated at Amiens: one on Sept 1, said to
have been the third bishop of that city, and
another on Sept 25, the supposed first bishop
of Amiens. The latter is described as a native
of Pampeluna in Spanish Navarre and a
convert of St Saturninus, bishop of Toulouse.
The former, viz. the third bishop of Amiens, is
alleged to have been the son of one of the
converts of St Firminus, the first bishop of that
city. Some writers consider them to have been
one and the same person.

Firminus of Uzès (St) Bp.   Oct 11
d. 553   A native of Narbonne in S. France,
he was educated by his uncle the bishop of
Uzès, whom he succeeded as bishop at the age
of twenty-two. He died at the age of thirty-
seven.

Friminus (St) Bp.   Dec 5
d. 6th cent.   The seventh bishop of Verdun.

Firmus of Rome (St) M.   Feb 2
See Fortunatus, Felician, etc.

Firmus (St) M.   March 11
See Gorgonius and Firmus.

Firmus (St) M.   June 1
d. c 290   An Eastern martyr who suffered
under Maximian.

Firmus (St) M.   June 24
See Orentius, Heros, etc.

**Firmus of Tagaste (St)
Bp.**   July 31
? Of him St Augustine writes that he was *firm*
by name but *firmer* yet by faith. Put to the
torture, he endured the most frightful sufferings rather than betray the hiding-place of one
of his flock. This notice of St Augustine led
Baronius to insert St Firmus's name in the
RM.

**Firmus and Rusticus
(SS) MM.**   Aug 9
d. c 290   Two kinsmen, prominent citizens

of Bergamo in Lombardy, who suffered at Verona under Maximian. Their *Passio* is not authentic; it seems possible that the relics of two martyrs of these names were translated from Africa to Verona.

First Martyrs of the See of Rome (SS) MM.   GC. June 30

d. 64 Otherwise known as the Protomartyrs of the See of Rome. The old RM. read "at Rome, the birthday of very many holy martyrs who, under the Emperor Nero, were falsely charged with the burning of the city and by him were ordered to be slain by divers kinds of cruel deaths; some were covered with the skin of wild beasts, and cast to the dogs to be torn asunder; others were crucified, and when daylight failed were used as torches to illuminate the night. All these were disciples of the Apostles and the first fruits of the martyrs whom the Holy Roman church sent to their Lord before the Apostles' death". All the above facts are historically certain. It is not known if Nero himself set fire to the city.

Fisher, John (St) Bp. M.   June 22
See John Fisher.

Flannan (St) Bp.   Dec 18
7th cent. An Irish monk ordained bishop by Pope John IV. He was the first bishop of Killaloe and worked also in the Hebrides and elsewhere, and in spite of all this toil, he managed, we are told, to recite daily the entire psalter. He is patron of Killaloe diocese.

Flavia Domitilla, Euphrosyna and Theodora (SS) VV. MM.   formerly May 12
2nd cent. Flavia Domitilla was a great-niece of the emperors Domitian and Titus, and also of St Flavius Clemens. She became a Christian, and on refusing to marry a pagan, was banished from Rome and eventually martyred with her foster sisters, Euphrosyna and Theodora, at Terracina. The Roman liturgy associates her name with those of SS Nereus and Achilles, who were buried in the cemetery of Domitilla in the Via Ardeatina. Probably there were two Roman ladies named Flavia Domitilla and both martyrs — the one described above and her own niece by marriage. Cult suppressed in 1969.

Flavia (St) VM.   Oct 5
See Placid, Eutychius and Comp.

Flavian (St) M.   Jan 28
d. *c* 304 A deputy-prefect of Rome who suffered martyrdom at Civita Vecchia, under Diocletian.

Flavian of Constantinople (St) Bp. M.   Feb 18
d. 449 Appointed patriarch of Constantinople in 446. He refused to give the customary bribe on his accession to the see, and it was not long before he was compelled to denounce the heresy of Eutyches, a favourite of the imperial court. Pope Leo the Great approved his condemnation of Eutychianism by sending him the famous "Dogmatic Letter". At "the Robber Synod" of Ephesus in 449, Flavian appealed to the pope, whereupon he was exiled and maltreated, dying shortly after of his injuries. The council of Chalcedon (451) proclaimed him a saint and a martyr.

Flavian (St) M.   Feb 24
See Montanus, Lucius, etc.

Flavian and Elias (SS) Bps.   July 20
d. (respectively) 512 and 518 St Flavian was patriarch of Antioch, and St Elias patriarch of Jerusalem. Both were exiled by the Monophysite emperor Anastasius (491–518) for strenuously upholding the decrees of the council of Chalcedon. This is the reason for their joint commemoration.

Flavian (Flavinian, Flavius) of Autun (St) Bp.   Aug 23
7th cent. The twenty-first bishop of Autun in France. The fifteenth bishop of Autun also called Flavius (d. *c* 544) has also a local cult.

Flavian (St) M.   Dec 22
d. 362 Said to have been an ex-prefect of Rome, branded on the forehead as a slave and exiled to the small village of Acquapendente in Tuscany by order of Julian the apostate. At Acquapendente he died while in prayer.

Flaviana of Auxerre (St) VM.   Oct 5
See Firmatus and Flaviana.

Flavius, Augustus and Augustine (SS) MM.   May 7
d. *c* 300 Flavius, bishop of Nicomedia, and his two brothers, were martyred in that city under Diocletian.

Flavius Clemens (St) M.   June 22
d. *c* 96 Brother of the emperor Vespasian and uncle of Titus and Domitian, whose niece, Flavia Domitilla, he married. In the year 95 he held the consular office together with Domitian. The following year Domitian had him beheaded as a Christian.

Flavius of Autun (St) Bp.   Aug 23
Otherwise Flavian, q.v.

Flocellus (St) M.   Sept 17
2nd cent. A youth martyred at Autun in
France under the emperor Marcus Aurelius
(161–180). After having been put to the
torture he was flung, half-dead, to the wild
beasts in the amphitheatre.

Flora (St) V.   Jan 29
Otherwise Blath, q.v.

Flora of Beaulieu (Bl) V.   June 11
d. 1347 Born in Auvergne, Flora, at the age
of fourteen, entered the order of Hospitallers
of St John of Jerusalem at Beaulieu, near
Rocamadour. Her spiritual trials and the
physico-mystical phenomena which accompanied them make her life of absorbing interest.

Flora (St) VM.   July 29
See Lucilla, Flora, etc.

Flora and Mary (SS) VV.
MM.   Nov 24
d. 856 Two Christian maidens of Cordoba,
in Spain, who gave themselves up to the
Moors, and were beheaded by order of Abderrahman II.

Florence (*several*)
Otherwise Florentina, Florentia or Florentius,
q.v.

Florentia (Florence) (St)
M.   Nov 10
See Tiberius, Modestus and Florentia.

Florentian (St) Bp.   Nov 28
See Valerian, Urban, etc.

Florentina (Florence)
(St) Abs.   June 20
d.c 636 A native of Carthagena in Spain, and
the only sister of SS Leander, Fulgentius and
Isidore. Losing her parents at an early age, she
was placed under the guardianship of St
Leander. She retired to a convent for which St
Leander wrote a rule. Eventually she governed
it as abbess.

Florentinus and Hilary
(SS) MM.   Sept 27
? Two French solitaries, put to death in Gaul
by some invading barbarians. Several places
have been suggested as the place of their
martyrdom. Pseudun, now Sémont in the
diocese of Autun; Sion in the Valais; Suint, in
Charollais; and Simond in the diocese of
Dijon.

Florentinus of Trier (St)
Bp.   Oct 16
4th cent. The successor of St Severianus in
the see of Trier. There is much controversy
about him and about his reputed predecessor
St Severinus.

Florentius of Vienne (St)
Bp. M.   Jan 3
? The pre-1970 RM. spoke of him as bishop
of Vienne martyred under Gallienus about
275. The local feast also is of a bishop and
martyr. But the episcopal catalogues of Vienne
place Florentius in the fourth century, and he
is said to have attended the council of Valence
(374).

Florentius of Seville (St)   Feb 23
d. c485 A saint much venerated in Seville
and its neighbourhood.

Florentius, Geminianus
and Saturus (SS) MM.   Apr 6
? 4th cent. Martyrs of Sirmium, Pannonia.

Florentius of Osimo (St)
M.   May 11
See Sisinius, Diocletius and Florentius.

Florentius of Nursia (St)
Mk.   May 23
See Eutychius and Florentius.

Florentius, Julian,
Cyriacus, Marcellinus and
Faustinus (SS) MM.   June 5
d. 250 These martyrs suffered under
Decius, being beheaded at Perugia in central
Italy.

Florentius of Carthage
(St) M.   July 15
See Catulinus, Januarius, etc.

Florentius and Felix (SS)
MM.   July 25
d. 235 Two soldiers of the Roman imperial
army put to death under Maximinius the
Thracian, at Furcona, an ancient town near
Aquila in S. Italy. They belong to the group of
eighty-three soldiers commemorated on July
24.

Florentius (St) C.   Sept 22
5th cent. A Bavarian by birth and a disciple
of St Martin of Tours, by whom he was
ordained priest and sent to evangelize Poitou.
He eventually retired as a hermit to Mt Glonne
in Anjou, where he was followed by numerous
disciples. He built for them the monastery
afterwards known as Saint-Florenti-le-Vieux.
Here he died in extreme old age.

Florentius (St) M.   Oct 10
See Cassius, Florentius, etc.

Florentius (St) M.   Oct 13
d. 312   A martyr of Thessalonica who died at the stake, under the emperor Maximinus Daza.

Florentius of Orange (St)
Bp.   Oct 17
d. c 526   The eighth bishop of Orange in S. France.

Florentius (St) M.   Oct 27
3rd cent.   A martyr who suffered at Trois-Châteaux in Burgundy.

Florentius of Strasburg
(St) Bp.   Nov 7
d. c 693   An Irishman by birth, he left his country for Alsace and settled in the wilds of Haselac, where he built a monastery. About the year 678 he was made bishop of Strasburg, where he founded another monastery — St Thomas's — chiefly for his own countrymen.

Florentius of Carracedo
(St) Ab. OSB.   Dec 10
d. 1156   Abbot of the Black Benedictine monastery of Carracedo, in the Bierzo Mountains, province of Léon, Spain. He was greatly revered by King Alphonsus VII of Léon. After the saint's death the abbey adopted the Cistercian observance. St Florentius is still greatly venerated in his native province.

Florentius (Flann) (St)
Ab.   Dec 15
7th cent.   An abbot of Bangor in Ireland.

Florian (St) M.   May 4
d. 304   A high Roman officer (princeps officiorum) in Noricum, now Upper Austria, who was drowned in the R. Enns (Anisus), near Lorch, under Diocletian. He is the patron of Upper Austria and Poland.

Florian, Calanicus and
Comp. (SS) MM.   Dec 17
d. c 637   A band of sixty martyrs, slain by the Moslem invaders at Eleutheropolis (Beit Jibrin) in Palestine.

Floribert (St) Bp.   Apr 27
d. 746   Bishop of Liège, described as "vehement in correcting". He has been confused with St Floribert, abbot of Ghent.

Floribert (Florbert) (St)
Ab. OSB.   Nov 1
d. c 660   Appointed by St Amandus abbot of the new monasteries of Ghent, Mont-Blandin and Saint-Bavon.

Florius of Nicomedia
(St) M.   Oct 26
See Lucian, Florius, etc.

Florus, Laurus, Proculus
and Maximus (SS) MM.   Aug 18
2nd cent.   A Greek tradition, which is called in question by some writers, described Florus and Laurus as twin brothers, stone masons by trade, and Proculus and Maximus as their employers. They handed over a temple on which they had been working to Christian worship, and as a punishment were drowned in a well. This is said to have happened in Illyria.

Florus (French: Flour) of
Lodève (St) Bp.   Nov 3
d. 389   First bishop of Lodève in Languedoc. He has given his name to the town where his relics are enshrined.

Florus (St) M.   Dec 22
See Demetrius, Honoratus and Florus.

Flos (St) M.   Dec 31
See Stephen, Pontian, etc.

Flosculus (French: Flou)
(St) Bp.   Feb 2
d. p.480   Bishop of Orleans, a contemporary of Sidonius Apollinaris.

Flou (St) Bp.   Feb 2
Otherwise Flosculus, q.v.

Flour (St) Bp.   Nov 3
Otherwise Florus of Lodève, q.v.

Foellan (Foilan, Fillan)
(St) C.   Jan 9
8th cent.   A native of Ireland who accompanied his mother, St Kentigerna, and his kinsman, St Comgan, to Scotland, where he became a missionary monk. The place where he died is now called Strathfillan.

Foila (Faile) (St) V.   March 3
6th cent.   Said to have been the sister of St Colgan. The two were patrons of the parishes of Kil-Faile (Kileely) and Kil-Colgan, in Galway. Kil-Faile has been a noted place of pilgrimage.

Foillan (St) Ab. OSB.   Oct 31
d. c 655   Brother of SS Fursey and Ultan. They left Ireland, their native country, and worked in E. Anglia. St Foillan became the abbot of Burghcastle, near Yarmouth, but when this monastery was destroyed by the Mercians, he crossed over to Belgium. Bl Ita of Nivelles gave him some land at Fosses, where he founded the abbey of that name. He was the religious leader of Nivelles and evangelized Brabant. He was killed by robbers and is venerated as a martyr.

Forannan (St) Bp. OSB.   Apr 30
d. 982   An Irish bishop who left his native

country and, arriving at the abbey of Waulsort on the Meuse, joined the community as a monk and in 962 became its abbot. He spent some time at Gorze to study the monastic observance established there by St John (Feb 27) in order to introduce it at Waulsort, which he did most successfully.

Fort (St) Bp. M.　　　　　　　May 16
? 1st cent. Venerated as the first bishop of Bordeaux and as a martyr.

Fortchern (St) C.　　　　　　Feb 17
? 6th cent. Said to have been converted by St Lornan. He succeeded him for a short time as bishop of Trim, and then became a recluse.

Fortis Gabrielli (Bl) H. OSB.　　May 13
d. 1040 A native of Gubbio in Umbria, and a hermit in the mountains near Scheggia, under the guidance of Bl Ludolph, founder of Fontavellana. Later he entered that monastery and was professed there as a monk-hermit. Cult approved in 1756.

Fortunata (St) VM.　　　　　　Oct 14
d. 303 A maiden martyred at Caesarea in Palestine under Diocletian. Her relics have been venerated at Naples since the eighth century. The legend adds that her three brothers, SS Carponius, Everistus and Priscian, suffered with her.

Fortunata Viti (Bl)　　　　　　Nov 20
See Mary Fortunata Viti.

**Fortunatus of Smyrna
(St)** M.　　　　　　　　　　　Jan 9
See Vitalis, Revocatus and Fortunatus.

**Fortunatus, Felician,
Firmus and Candidus
(SS)** MM.　　　　　　　　　　Feb 2
? The names have been transferred from the martyrology of Usuard, but nothing is known of them.

Fortunatus (St) M.　　　　　　Feb 21
See Verulus, Secundinus, etc.

**Fortunatus, Felix and
Comp. (SS)** MM.　　　　　　Feb 26
? A group of twenty-nine martyrs of whom nothing is known.

Fortunatus (St) M.　　　　　　Feb 27
See Alexander, Abundius, etc.

Fortunatus (St) M.　　　　　March 3
See Felix, Luciolus, etc.

**Fortunatus and Marcian
(SS)** MM.　　　　　　　　　　Apr 17
? Martyrs, perhaps of Antioch in Syria, but more probably of some town in Africa.

**Fortunatus of Alexandria
(St)** M.　　　　　　　　　　　Apr 21
See Arator, Fortunatus, etc.

**Fortunatus of Valence
(St)** M.　　　　　　　　　　　Apr 23
See Felix, Fortunatus and Achilleus.

Fortunatus (St) C.　　　　　　June 1
d. c 400 A parish priest at a place near Spoleto, in Umbria, conspicuous for his charity to the poor.

**Fortunatus of Aquileia
(St)** M.　　　　　　　　　　　June 11
See Felix and Fortunatus.

**Fortunatus and Lucian
(SS)** MM.　　　　　　　　　　June 13
? African martyrs, whose Acts have been lost. Most martyrologies register six or more other names.

**Fortunatus the
Philosopher (St)**　　　　　　June 18
d. c 569 An Italian bishop driven from his see in N. Italy by the Lombards. He was much esteemed by St Germanus of Paris. He must not be confused with the better known St Venantius Fortunatus, his contemporary in France.

Fortunatus (St) M.　　　　　　July 12
See Hermagoras and Fortunatus.

**Fortunatus, Gaius
and Anthes (SS)** MM.　　　　Aug 28
d. 303 Martyred near Salerno under Diocletian. Their relics were enshrined at Salerno in 940, and since then the three have been held in great popular veneration. Their Passion has no historical foundation. Fortunatus may be the martyr included in the "Twelve Holy Brothers".

Fortunatus (St) M.　　　　　　Sept 1
See Honoratus, Fortunatus, etc. (Sept 1), and the Twelve Holy Brothers.

**Fortunatus of Todi (St)
Bp.**　　　　　　　　　　　　Oct 14
d. 537 A bishop of Todi, who saved the city from being sacked by Totila the Goth.

Fortunatus (St) M.　　　　　　Oct 15
d. ? 537 A Roman martyr.

Fortunatus (St) M.　　　　　　Oct 24
See Felix, Audactus, etc.

**Fortunatus, Venantius
(St)** Bp.　　　　　　　　　　Dec 14
See Venantius Fortunatus.

The Forty Martyrs, formerly March 10

Fortunatus (St) M. Dec 15
See Faustinus, Lucius, etc.

**Forty Armenian Martyrs
(SS)** formerly March 10
d. 320 Forty soliders put to death by the
emperor Licinius at Sebaste (Sivas) in Lesser
Armenia. They were exposed naked on the ice
of a frozen lake, a warm bath being on the bank
as a temptation to apostatize. One fell, but his
place was taken by one of the guards who was
converted by the heroism of the rest. On the
morrow all were dead, save the youngest
among them. His brave mother carried her
child after the corpses of the rest until he too
expired in her arms, and then laid his body by
their side. Many ecclesiastical writers of that
period speak of this group of martyrs — SS
Basil, Gregory of Nyssa, Gaudentius of Brescia, Sozomen, etc. They are still greatly venerated in the East. In art they are shewn as near
naked, and standing on the frozen lake. Cult
suppressed in 1969.

**Forty Martyrs of England
and Wales (SS)** MM. Oct 25
A group of martyrs canonised by Pope Paul VI
on Oct 25 1970. All have separate entries in
this book. Their names are:
Alban Roe (Jan 21), Alexander Bryant (Dec 1),
Ambrose Barlow (Sept 11), Anne Line (Feb
27), Augustine Webster (May 4), Cuthbert
Mayne (Nov 29), David Lewis (Aug 27),
Edmund Arrowsmith (Aug 28), Edmund
Campion (Dec 1), Edmund Gennings (Dec
10), Eustace White (Dec 10), Henry Morse
(Feb 1), Henry Walpole (Apr 7), John Almond
(Dec 5), John Boste (July 24), John Houghton
(May 4), John Jones (July 12), John Kemble
(Aug 22), John Lloyd (July 22), John Payne
(Apr 2), John Plessington (July 19), John Rigby
(June 19), John Roberts (Dec 9), John Stone
(May 12), John Southworth (June 27), John
Wall (Aug 22), Luke Kirby (May 30), Mar-
garet Clitherow (Oct 21), Margaret Ward
(Aug 30), Nicholas Owen (Mar 2), Philip
Evans (July 22), Philip Howard (Oct 19),

Polydore Plasden (Dec 10), Ralph Sherwin (Dec 1), Richard Gwyn (Oct 17), Richard Reynolds (May 4), Robert Lawrence (May 4), Robert Southwell (Feb 21), Swithun Wells (Dec 10), Thomas Garnet (June 26). The dates in parentheses refer to local calendars.

Foster (St) Bp.   Feb 6
The old English form of the name Vedast or Waast. See Vedast.

Four Crowned Martyrs
(SS)   Nov 8
There are two groups of martyrs called the Four Holy Crowned Ones — *Sancti Quatuor Coronatia*: one group suffered at Albano *c* 305, viz, Secundus, Severian, Carpophorus and Victorinus; the other group met their death in Pannonia about the same time: Claudius, Nicostratus, Symphorian and Castorius, to whom a fifth named Simplicius is added. The Pannonian group were sculptors who refused to carve a statue of the god Aesculapius and were martyred at the request of the retired emperor Diocletian. Their *Acta* are documents of very high value. Relics of four of the martyrs were brought to Rome and so the cult of four, not five, originated and they were later confused with the Albano group. Cult confined to local or particular calendars since 1969.

Fourteen Holy Helpers,
The (SS)   formerly Aug 8
A collective feast is celebrated in several places, chiefly in Germany, in honour of fourteen saints, each of whom is believed to grant a special form of help. The usual fourteen are: Acacius (June 22), Barbara, Blaise (Feb 3), Catherine of Alexandria, Christopher (July 25), Cyriacus (Aug 8), Dionysius of Paris (Oct 9), Erasmus (June 2), Eustace (Sept 20), George (Apr 23), Margaret (July 20), Pantaleon, Vitus — all martyrs — and Giles (Sept 1). See their respective notices. Feast suppressed in 1969.

Fragan and Gwen
(Blanche) (SS)   July 5
5th cent. Refugees from Britain in the troublesome times consequent upon the departure of the Romans, and parents of SS Winwalöe, Jacut and Guithern. Churches in Brittany are dedicated to each of them.

Franca Visalta (St) OSB.
Cist.   Apr 26
1170–1218 A native of Piacenza in Italy. At the age of seven she was offered to God in the Benedictine convent of St Syrus. She was professed at fourteen and soon, though very

St Frances of Rome, March 9

young, made abbess. She seems to have been over severe, and she was in fact deposed. After some years she was made abbess of the Cistercian nunnery of Pittoli. Cult confirmed, with the title of Saint, by Gregory X.

Frances of Rome (St) W.
OSB.   GC. March 9
1384–1440 A native of Rome, she married in 1396 Lorenzo de Ponziani, with whom she lived for forty years, succeeding during all this time in never once annoying him. Her life was a model of fidelity and devotedness to her domestic duties; she patiently bore many severe trials, among them being the death of her children, her husband's banishment and the confiscation of their estates. In 1433 she

founded the community of Benedictine Oblates of Tor de' Specci, but it was not until 1436, after the death of husband, that she could join it. Her biography, with many particulars of visions and revelations, of her devotion to her angel guardian, whom she often saw walking by her side and guiding her, was written by John Matteotti, who had been her confessor during the last ten years of her life. Canonized in 1608. She is patron saint of motorists. She is shewn habited in black with a white veil, and accompanied by her angel guardian. Often she carries a basket of food.

Frances Lanel (Bl) M.   June 26

1745–1794   A native of Eu, diocese of Rouen, she became a Sister of Charity at Rouen, and was later stationed at Cambrai and Arras. She, with three other sisters, was guillotined at Cambrai. Beatified in 1920.

Frances de Croissy and Frances Brideau (BB) MM. OC.   July 17

d. 1794   Frances de Croissy was born at Paris in 1745 and was professed a Carmelite nun at Compiègne in 1764. She was prioress from 1779 to 1787 and at the time of her death was novice-mistress. Frances Brideau was born at Belfort in 1752 and professed at Compiègne in 1771. She was the sub-prioress. Both were guillotined at Paris with the rest of the community in 1794. Beatified in 1906.

Frances Bizzocca (Bl) M.   Aug 17

d. 1627   A Japanese, the wife of Bl Leo, she belonged to the third order of friars preachers. She was condemned to death for sheltering missionaries in her house, and was burnt alive at Nagasaki. Beatified in 1867.

Frances d'Amboise (Bl) OC.   Nov 4

1427–1485   Reared at the court of Brittany, Frances became the wife of Duke Peter of Brittany, and spent her life in endeavouring to please and pacify her jealous husband — no light task — and in charitable works. She was a great benefactress of the Carmelite Bl John Soreth, and herself became a Carmelite in her widowhood (1470) at the convent which she had founded at Nantes. Beatified in 1863.

Frances Xavier Cabrini (St) Foundress   Dec 22

1850–1917   Born at Sant' Angelo Lodigiano in Lombardy, the thirteenth child of Augustine and Stella Cabrini. In 1874 she was asked by the parish priest to teach in an orphanage at Codogno, diocese of Lodi. In 1877 the orphanage became the mother-house of a new institute, founded by Mother Frances under the title of Missionary Sisters of the Sacred Heart. She made her own profession at the hands of the bishop of Lodi, who in 1880 officially approved the new congregation as a diocesan institute. Mother Cabrini's dream was to send her sisters to China, but on the advice of Pope Leo XIII she dispatched them instead to the United States. In 1889 she herself accompanied the first batch of missionary sisters to New York, and from that time almost every year she crossed the sea at the head of new bands of missionaries. During her life-time she founded as many as sixty-seven religious houses — schools, orphanages, hospitals, etc. — in N. and S. America, Italy, Spain, England, etc. She died in one of the American foundations, Columbus Hospital, Chicago. Earlier, she had become an American citizen. Canonized in 1946.

Francis Ferdinand de Capillas (Bl) M. OP.   Jan 15

1606–1648   A native of Vacherim de Campos in Old Castile, Francis joined the Dominicans at Valladolid and was sent to the missions in China. He laboured in Fokien with great success, but political and religious troubles arose in the province, and Francis was executed as a spy. Beatified in 1909, and proclaimed the protomartyr of China.

Francis Gil de Frederich (St) M. OP.   Jan 22

1702–1745   A native of Tortosa, Spain, he became a friar preacher at Barcelona and was sent to the Philippines. Thence he went to Tonkin in 1732 where after long apostolic labours, he was imprisoned for several years and beheaded at Checo. Canonized in 1988.

Francis of Sales (St) Bp. Dr. Founder   GC. Jan 24

1567–1622   Born near Annecy, in Savoy, the eldest son of the Seigneur de Nouvelles. He read for the law at Paris and Padua, but abandoned his legal studies and became a priest in 1593. At once he set out for his apostolate among the Calvinists of the Chablais, where he is said to have made within two years over eight thousand converts. In 1599 he was chosen coadjutor to the bishop of Geneva, whom he succeeded in 1602. Two years later he met St Jane Frances of Chantal, with whom he founded the Order of the Visitation. He was indefatigable in the discharge of his office as a bishop; organized conferences for the clergy, directed them to teach the catechism in simple words; insisted on unadorned straightforward preaching; and established a seminary at

Annecy which he visited regularly. He excelled as an ascetical writer, and his treatise *Introduction to the Devout Life* remains a classic. His people loved him and styled him "The Gentle Christ of Geneva". Canonized in 1665; declared a Doctor of the Church in 1877, and patron saint of journalists in 1923.

Francis Xavier Bianchi
(St) Barn.   Jan 31
1743–1815 A native of Arpino in Italy who became a Barnabite clerk regular and was ordained priest in 1767 — in the teeth of opposition from his family. Owing to overwork and to his austere life, he ruined his health and lost the use of his legs. He was considered and acclaimed as the "Apostle of Naples" for his work for the poor and abandoned and for preserving girls from the danger of an immoral life. Canonized in 1951.

Francis Blanco (St) M.
OFM.   Feb 6
d. 1597 A native of Monterey, in Spanish Galicia. He studied at Salamanca, and was professed as a Franciscan at Villalpando. He first laboured at Churubusco in Mexico, and in 1594 reached Japan from Manila. He was crucified at Nagasaki. Canonized in 1862. See Paul Miki and Comps.

Francis of St Michael
(St) M. OFM.   Feb 6
d. 1597 Born at Parilla, near Valladolid. He became a Franciscan lay-brother and in 1593 accompanied St Peter Baptist from Manila to Japan. He was arrested with him at Ozaka (1596) and crucified. Canonized in 1862. See Paul Miki and Comps.

Francis of Nagasaki (St)
M.   Feb 6
d. 1597 A Japanese physician from Macao and a member of the third order of St Francis. He served the missionaries as a catechist and was for this reason crucified at Nagasaki. Canonized in 1862. See Paul Miki and Comps.

Francis Regis Clet (Bl)
M. CM.   Feb 17
1748–1820 Born at Grenoble, he joined the Lazarists and was sent to China as a missionary in 1791. Here he laboured for thirty years, in the face of incredible difficulties, and at last, in his seventy-second year, was cruelly tortured and strangled near Hankow. Beatified in 1900.

Francis of Fermo (Bl) M.
OFM.   March 15
See Monaldus of Ancona, etc.

Francis of Nostra (Bl)
Mk.   March 18
d. 1433 A Hungarian Pauline monk of the famous convent of Maria Nostra, he was meek and modest in outward appearance. His body is reputed to have remained incorrupt after death. Venerated by his order as Blessed, though his cult has not been officially confirmed. Called also Francis the Pious.

Francis of Paola (St)
Founder   GC. Apr 2
1416–1507 Born at Paola in Calabria. At the age of fourteen he settled as a hermit on the sea coast near Paola. Many disciples followed him and eventually their community at Paola grew into the new order of Minim Friars — *Minimi*, i.e., the least of all friars. The order was approved by Sixtus IV in 1474. It was this same pope who directed St Francis to travel to France (1482) in order to visit, at Plessis-les-Tours, the dying King Louis XI. At the request of that king's successors Francis remained in France for the rest of his life and died at Plessis. Canonized in 1519 and made Patron of Seafarers in 1943.

Francis Page (Bl) M. SJ.   Apr 20
d. 1602 Born at Antwerp, he belonged to an English Protestant family of Harrow-on-the-Hill. He was reconciled to the church, educated at Douai, ordained in 1600, sent to the English mission, captured, received in prison into the Society of Jesus and executed at Tyburn. Beatified in 1929.

Francis Venimbene of
Fabriano (Bl) C. OFM.   Apr 22
1251–1322 Born at Fabriano, the son of a physician. He joined the Franciscans in 1267 and was a disciple of St Bonaventure. He founded the first Franciscan library.

Francis Colmenario (Bl)
C.   Apr 24
d. 1590 A Spanish missionary priest who evangelized the West Indies. He preached also in Guatemala.

Francis Dickenson (Bl)
M.   Apr 30
d. 1590 A native of Yorkshire and a convert, he was educated for the priesthood at Reims, ordained in 1589 and sent to the English mission, where the following year he was hanged, drawn and quartered at Rochester. Beatified in 1929.

Franics Jerome (de Geronimo) (St) C. SJ. May 11

1642–1716 Born near Taranto in S. Italy, and ordained priest in 1666, he entered the Society of Jesus in 1670. From this time on he spent his whole life preaching throughout S. Italy, where his sermons were attended by huge congregations. Canonized in 1839.

Francis Patrizi (Bl) C. OSM. May 12

d. 1328 A native of Siena, he was converted by a sermon of the Servite friar, Bl Ambrose Sansedoni, and was himself received into the Servite order by St Philip Benizi. He was favoured by God with the grace of reconciling enemies. He died at Siena. Cult approved in 1743.

Francis Ronci (Bl) C. OSB. Cel. June 4

1223–1294 Born at Abri in S. Italy, he was one of the first disciples of St Peter Celestine and his companions at the hermitages of Orfente and Morrone. In 1285 he became prior of Santo Spirito and Majella and the first General of the Congregation until 1294. It seems probable that he was created cardinal in Sept 1294; he died the following month.

Francis Caracciolo (St) C. Founder June 4

1563–1608 A scion of the noble Neapolitan family of Caracciolo, he was born in the Abruzzi and during his early years was afflicted with a disease akin to leprosy, of which he was cured on deciding to become a priest. He did so, and in 1588 founded with John Augustine Adorno the order of Minor Clerks Regular, with perpetual adoration of the Eucharist as one of its main duties. Francis was the first General of the order and spent his life in governing it and in preaching. Canonized in 1807. Since 1969 this cult has been confined to local or particular calendars.

Francis Pacheco and Comp. (Bl) MM. SJ. June 20

1566–1626 A native of Ponte da Lima in Portugal. In 1586 he became a Jesuit and was sent to Macao (1592) where he was ordained priest. He laboured at Macao and in Japan and held the office of rector, provincial, vicar general and administrator of the diocese. He was burnt alive at Nagasaki, together with two other Jesuits from Europe, a Japanese Jesuit, four Japanese laymen and a Korean. All were beatified in 1867.

Francis Chieu (St) M. June 25

1796–1838 A Chinese catechist, arrested

with St Dominic Henares and beheaded in Vietnam. Canonized in 1988.

Francis Rod (St) M. OFM. July 9

d. 1572 Born at Brussels, he took the Franciscan habit at Gorkum, Holland. Shortly after his ordination he was hanged by the Calvinists at Briel.

Francis Solano (St) C. OFM. July 14

1549–1610 A native of Andalusia in Spain. He professed the Franciscan rule among among the Observants (1569) and after twenty years of apostolic activities in Spain, he went to Peru (1589). Here and elsewhere in S. America he laboured for another twenty years until his death at Lima. Canonized in 1726.

Francis Alvarez (Bl) M. SJ. July 15

d. 1570 A native of Covilhao in Portugal, who became a Jesuit lay-brother. He was martyred with Bl Ignatius de Azevedo, q.v.

Francis Aranha (Bl) M. SJ. July 15

d. 1583 A native of Braga in Portugal who came to Goa with his uncle, and there joined the Society of Jesus (1571) as a coadjutor. He served the mission on the islet of Salsette, where he was martyred with Bl Rudolph Acquaviva, q.v.

Francis Magallanes (Bl) M. SJ. July 15

d. 1570 A native of Alcázar do Sal, in Portugal, who became a Jesuit cleric and shared the martyrdom of Bl Ignatius de Azevedo and companions, q.v.

Francis Perez Godoy (Bl) M. SJ. July 15

d. 1570 A native of Torrijos, diocese of Toledo, in Spain. He was a Jesuit novice and a companion in martyrdom of Bl Ignatius de Azevedo, q.v.

Francis of St Mary and Comps. (BB) MM. Aug 1

d. 1627 Francis of St Mary was a Spanish friar minor who was burnt alive at Nagasaki on Aug 17, 1627, together with Br Bartholomew Laurel, another Franciscan, of Mexican origin, and a doctor, Gaspar Vaz, a Japanese tertiary in whose house Fr Francis of St Mary was taken, and Br Antony of St Francis, a native catechist. With them were beheaded the wife of Gaspar Vaz, named Mary, and six Franciscan tertiaries: Louis Soyeman, a neighbour; Francis Coufioye, baptized in prison; Thomas Wo Jonyemon, formerly a servant of the Jesuits; Luke Kiyemon, a builder of hiding places; Michael Kizayemon, another carpenter; and Martin Gomez de Facato, who had hidden Franciscan friars. On the same or the preceding day were burnt four Dominican tertiaries: Francis Curobioye, catechist; Gaius Jiyemon, formerly a bonze of Korea; Magdalen Kista, of royal blood; and Frances Bizocca. All were beatified in 1867.

Francis (Ceco) of Pesaro
(St) Tert. OFM.   Aug 13
d. 1350   An early Franciscan tertiary who lived with others in community. Cult confirmed in 1859.

Francis Culoye (Bl) M.   Aug 17
d. 1627   A Japanese tertiary of St Francis, beheaded for having sheltered missionaries. Beatified in 1867.

Francis Curobioye (Bl)
M.   Aug 17
d. 1627   A native Japanese Christian, and a Dominican tertiary, burnt alive at Nagasaki. Beatified in 1867.

Francis de la Rochefoucauld
(Bl) Bp. M.   Sept 2–3
See September Martyrs.

Francis of Jesus Ortega
(Bl) M. OSA.   Sept 3
d. 1632   A native of Villamediana in Spain. In 1614 he took the habit of the Hermits of St Augustine at Valladolid. In 1622 he was sent to Mexico, and thence with Bl Vincent Carvalho, to Manila, and in 1623 to Japan. He was burnt alive at Nagasaki. Beatified in 1867.

Francis Nifaki (Bl) M.   Sept 8
d. 1628   A native boy of five years of age, beheaded at Nagasaki with his father, Bl Louis Nifaki, and his brother Dominic. Beatified in 1867.

Francis de Morales (Bl)
M. OP.   Sept 10
d. 1622   A native of Madrid who became a Dominican and worked for twenty years in the Japanese mission of Satzuma. In 1608 he returned to Fuximi, and in 1614 to Nagasaki where he was burnt alive with Bl Charles Spinola and companions. Beatified in 1867.

Francis Taquea (Bl) M.   Sept 11
d. 1622   A Japanese boy of twelve years of age, a son of Bl Thomas Tacquea, beheaded with Bl Caspar Cotenda at Nagasaki. Beatified in 1867.

Francis of St Bonaventure
(Bl) M. OFM.   Sept 12
d. 1622   Born in Musaxi, Quanto, Japan. A native catechist who worked under Bl Apollinaris Franco. He was burnt alive at Omura. Beatified in 1867.

Francis of Calderola (Bl)
C. OFM.   Sept 13
d. 1407   A native of Calderola, diocese of Camerino. He embraced the Franciscan rule and was a very successful preacher, with the special gift for reconciling enemies. He died at Colfana. Cult approved by Gregory XVI.

Francis of Camporosso
(St) C. OFM. Cap.   Sept 16
1804–1866   An Italian peasant born near Ventimiglia, who became a lay-brother in the Capuchin friary of the Immaculate Virgin at Genoa. He spent forty years there and died while nursing cholera victims. Canonized in 1962.

Francis de Posadas (Bl)
C. OP.   Sept 20
1644–1713   Born at Cordoba in Spain, he took the Dominican habit at Aracoeli in 1663, and spent the rest of his life giving missions throughout S.W. Spain. He died at Aracoeli. Beatified in 1818.

Francis Jaccard (St) M.   Sept 21
1799–1838   Born at Onnion in Savoy. He entered the Seminary for Foreign Missions in Paris and was sent to Vietnam in 1826, where he was later strangled. Canonized in 1988.

Francis Chakichi (Bl) M.   Oct 2
d. 1622   A Japanese boy of four years of age, son of BB Louis and Lucy Chakichi. He was beheaded with his mother and his brother Andrew (their father was burnt at the stake) at Nagasaki. Beatified in 1867.

Francis of Assisi (St)
Founder   GC. Oct 4
1181–1226   "The Poor Little Man" — *il Poverello* — one of the best known and loved of saints. A native of Assisi in Umbria, the son of a merchant. In his youth he loved pleasure, until a series of providential happenings led him, in 1209, to found the order of Friars Minor, characterized by a loving, joyous worship of Christ, and by a profession of poverty which was both individual and collective. The appeal of the new order to that generation may be gauged from the fact that at the General Chapter of 1219 five thousand friars were present. This same year Francis sailed for Palestine and tried to evangelize the Muslims, but this mission was a failure. Meanwhile, the new order was passing through a period of painful internal difficulties. Francis returned to Italy, sent friars into all western European countries, with instructions to establish them-

St Francis of Assisi, Oct 4

selves preferably in university centres. His rule was approved by Innocent III, and his life and message received a direct sanction from Christ in 1224, when on September 14 Francis received the stigmata of the Passion on Mt Alvernia. He died in deacon's orders and was canonized two years after his death. He is depicted in the habit of his order, grey, brown or any drab colour: usually he has the stigmata,

with a winged crucifix before him, or preaching to the birds; or propping up a tottering church; or kneeling before a crib.

Francis Titelmans (Bl)
C. OFM. Cap.   Oct 4
d. 1537   A student of Louvain who joined the Capuchins and ended his days tending the sick in the hospital of St James in Rome.

Francis Trung (St) M.   Oct 6
1825–1858   A native of Vietnam and a corporal in the army there. Born at Phan-xa, beheaded in An-hoa. Canonized in 1988.

Francis Borgia (St) C. SJ.   Oct 10
1510–1572   Born at Gandia, near Valencia, in Spain, of the noble family of de Borja. He was reared at the court of Charles V, married very young, and up to the time of his wife's death (1546) devoted himself to the discharge of his duties at the emperor's court and on his own estates as Duke of Gandia. In 1546 he left all, and joined the Society of Jesus. As General of the Society, he was one of the greatest saints of the counter-reformation. Under him the Society spread throughout Europe and the foreign missions. Austere with himself, Francis was the typical saint of the Spanish nobility — courteous, refined, kind, humble and generous, yet most determined and enterprising. He died at Ferrara, while travelling on an embassy from Pope St Pius V, his great friend, to the kings of France and Spain. Canonized in 1671. Cult confined to particular calendars since 1969.

Francis Isidore Gagelin
(St) M.   Oct 17
1799–1833   A native of Montperreux, diocese of Besançon. He belonged to the Society of Foreign Missions of Paris, and was sent to Vietnam in 1822, where on his arrival he was ordained priest. He worked zealously until the persecution broke out, when he gave himself up to the Mandarin of Bongson and was strangled. Canonized in 1988.

Francis Diaz (Bl) M. OP.   Oct 20
d. 1748   A Spanish Dominican missionary in Fo-Kien, China. He was strangled in prison with Bl Francis Serrano at Futsheu. Beatified in 1893.

Francis Serrano (Bl) M. OP.   Oct 20
d. 1748   Born in Spain and sent as a missionary to China, to the province of Fo-Kien. He was arrested with Bl Peter Sanze (1746). Whilst in prison at Futsheu he was elected titular bishop of Tipasa. He was strangled with three other Dominicans. Beatified in 1893.

Francis Néron (Bl) M.   Nov 3
See Peter-Francis Néron.

Francis Xavier Can (St) M.   Nov 20
1803–1837 Born at Sou-Mieng, in Vietnam, he was a catechist attached to the fathers of the Foreign Missions of Paris. He was strangled in prison. Canonized in 1988.

Francis Xavier (St) C. SJ.   GC. Dec 3
1506–1552 Born at the family castle of Javier, in Spanish Navarre, Francis inherited the best characteristics of his race — generosity, love of culture and adventure. He was studying with distinction at the university of Paris when he met St Ignatius Loyola, and in 1534 they took their first religious vows at Montmartre. In obedience to St Ignatius's order, Francis set out on his first journey to the Far East in 1540, landing at Goa in 1542. He visited India, Ceylon, Malaya, Japan, and other Far Eastern islands, dreaming all the time of his longed-for apostolate in China. The difficulties he met with in his missionary labours were well-nigh insurmountable: they proceeded chiefly from the politically-minded European traders. However, he was favoured with such extraordinary graces from heaven, that his mission proved from the start a signal success: it is reckoned that in Japan alone, some forty years afterwards, there were 400,000 Christians. Indeed, Francis Xavier is perhaps the greatest individual missionary the church has produced since St Paul. Francis died at Sancian, when about to enter China. Canonized in 1602, and proclaimed by St Pius X patron of all foreign missions.

Francis Galvez (Bl) M.
OFM.   Dec 4
1567–1623 A native of Utiel in New Castile. He joined the Friars Minor at Valencia (1591), went to Manila (1609) and thence to Japan (1612). During the persecution he returned to Manila (1614); at Macao he blackened his face in order to be able to enter Japan anew (1618). He preached with great courage, and finally was burnt alive at Yeddo. Beatified in 1867.

Francis Fasani (St) C.
OFM.   Dec 9
1681–1742 Antony Fasani was born at Luceria and after a devout childhood entered the Franciscan order under the name of Francis. Ordained in 1775 he rose to be provincial and introduced salutary reforms. In prayer he was sometimes raised from the ground. He worked mainly at Luceria and died there in 1742. Beatified in 1951. Canonized in 1986.

Francis Xavier Mau (St)
M. Tert. OP.   Dec 19
d. 1839 A native catechist of Vietnam, strangled with four companions. Beatified in 1900.

Franciscan Martyrs of
China (BB)   July 9
d. 1900 A group of twenty-nine martyrs, mostly Franciscans or tertiaries, put to death in the Boxer Rising under the Dowager Empress Tz'u-hsi, and beatified as a representative group of the 100,000 Christians estimated to have been put to death in that persecution. They were nearly all slaughtered in the courtyard of the palace of Yu Sun, viceroy of Tay-yüan-fu of the Scien-fu province. Their names were: (1) Bishop Gregory Grassi, vicar apostolic of Northern Scian-si; Bishop Francis Fogolla, his coadjutor; Elias Facchini, Theodore Balat, Andrew Bauer — all friars minor; Sisters Mary Emiliana Grivot, Mary of Peace Guiliani, Mary Clare Nanette, Mary of Sainte Nathalie Kerguin, Mary of St Justus Moreau, Mary Amandina Jeuris, Mary Adolphine Dierk — all Franciscan Missionaries of Mary; John Tciang, John Van, Philip Tciang, Patrick Tun, another John Tcaing — all seminarists; Thomas Sen, Simon Tcing, Peter U-Ngan-Pau, Francis Tciang-Iun, Mathias Fun-Te, James Ien-Kutun, Peter Tchang-Pau-Nien, James Tciao-Tcieum-Sin, Peter Van-al-man — members of the bishop's household. (2) Bishop Antoninus Fantosanti, vicar apostolic of Hunan (now Hengchow) and Joseph Mary Gambaro, both friars minor, tortured to death at Hengchow on July 7. (3) Caesidius Giacomantonio OFM., burned alive at Wanshawan on July 4. Beatified 1946.

Franco (Francus) (St) H.
OSB.   June 5
d. c 1275 A native of Castel Regni, near Asserigo, in the Abruzzi. He became a Benedictine at the monastery of Colimento, and after twenty years as a cenobite, spent the last fifteen years of his life as a hermit near Asserigo.

Franco Lippi (Bl) C. OC.   Dec 11
d. 1291 A native of Grotton, near Siena. Early in life he fell in with evil companions and became their leader. A fugitive from justice, he joined a band of *condottieri* and excelled them all in crime until about his fiftieth year. Then he became blind, repented, went on a pilgrimage to Compostella, received back his sight, was absolved by Gregory X, and admitted to the Carmelite order as a lay-brother. He was already over sixty-five, but managed to earn the title of Saint by his fervour in his new life.

Francoise Lacroix (Bl)
M.   Oct 23
One of the Ursuline Nuns, q.v.

Francoveus (Franchy)
(St) Mk.   May 16
7th cent. Monk of St Martin de la Breton-
nière, he had to suffer much from the jealousy
of his fellow-monks. The monastery being
destroyed, he lived as a hermit in the Nivernais.

Fraternus (St) Bp. M.   Sept 29
d. c 450 Bishop of Auxerre in France.
Tradition makes him also a martyr.

Fredegand (Fregaut) (St)
Ab. OSB.   July 17
d. c 740 Said to have been an Irish companion of St Foillan. Monk and abbot of Ker-
kelodor, near Antwerp. It seems probable that
he was a fellow-worker with St Willibrord.

Frederick of Arras (Bl)
Mk. OSB.   Jan 6
d. 1020 Son of Geoffrey le Barbu, count of
Verdun. In 997 he handed over his patrimony
to the bishop of Verdun, set out for Palestine,
and on his return was admitted to the Benedictine abbey of St Vanne. His friend Bl
Richard, abbot of St Vanne, was transferred to
the abbey of St Vedast at Arras, and Bl
Frederick followed him as prior.

Frederick (Bl) Ab. O.
Praem.   March 3
d. 1175 Born at Hallum in Frisia he became
the abbot-founder of the Premonstratensian
abbey of Mariengart in Holland.

Frederick (Bl) Ab. OSB.   May 7
d. c 1070 A native of Swabia and a monk of
Einsiedeln in Switzerland, he was sent with
twelve monks to restore discipline in the abbey
of Hirschau (1066). He was calumniated by
evil-minded monks and deposed by the Count
of Calw, owner of Hirschau, in 1069. He
retired to Ebersberg where he died.

Frederick (St) Bp.   May 27
d. 1121 Chosen bishop of Liège in 1119 in
the room of the deposed simoniacal bishop
Alexander. He was an excellent bishop, but
had to suffer much and in the end, it is said,
was poisoned by Alexander's supporter, the
count of Louvain.

Frederick (Fridrich) (St)
Bp. M.   July 18
d. 838 Grandson of Radbod, king of the
Frisians. In 820 he was appointed bishop of
Utrecht and devoted himself especially to
combating the evil custom of incestuous mar-

riages, for which reason he was murdered in
church at Maestricht.

Frederick of Regensburg
(Bl) OSA.   Nov 29
d. 1329 Born at Regensburg of poor par-
ents. He was received as a lay-brother into the
order of Augustinian Hermits at Regensburg
and was employed there as carpenter and
wood-chopper. Cult approved in 1909.

Frediano (Frigidanus,
Frigdianus) (St) Bp.   March 18
d. 588 An Irishman who went on pilgrimage
to Rome and settled in Italy as a hermit on
Monte Pisano. In 566 he was elected bishop of
Lucca and formed the clergy of the city into a
community of canons regular. He rebuilt the
cathedral after it had been burnt by the
Lombards. He is greatly venerated at Lucca.

Fremund (St) M.   May 11
d. 866 An Anglo-Saxon hermit, who seems
to have been killed by the Danes and to have
been honoured as a martyr. His remains were
enshrined at Dunstable.

Friard (St) H.   Aug 1
d. c 577 Hermit on the isle of Vindomitte,
near Nantes. With him is mentioned St
Secundel.

Fricor (Adrian) (St) H.   Apr 1
See Caidoc and Fricor.

Frideswide
(Fredeswinda) (St) V. OSB.   Oct 19
d. c 735 According to a twelfth-century Life
she was the daughter of Didan, prince (subreg-
ulus) of a district bordering the Upper
Thames. She was the abbess-foundress of the
nunnery of St Mary's under the rule of St
Benedict on the site of what is now Oxford. It
is said that from her childhood she took for her
maxim: "Whatsoever is not God is nothing".
She is the patroness of the city and university
of Oxford. Her relics are extant although
disturbed at the Reformation. In art, she is
shown as a nun with a crown, crozier and
sceptre, and with an ox beside her.

Frigidand (St) Ab. OSB.   July 17
Otherwise Fredegand, q.v.

Fridolin (St) Ab. OSB.   March 6
d. c 540 A priest of Irish origin, he is said to
have become a monk of Luxeuil. Later he
founded the abbey of Säckingen. He is venerated as the apostle of the Upper Rhine.

Frigidian (Fridan, Finnian)
(St) Bp.   March 18
Otherwise Frediano, q.v.

Frithbert (Fridebert, Frithubeorht) (St) Bp. OSB.   Dec 23
d. 766   The successor of St Acca in the bishopric of Hexham, which church he served for thirty-four years.

Frithestan (St) Bp. OSB.   Sept 10
d. 933   A disciple of St Grimbald, ordained bishop of Winchester by St Plegmund. He was bishop for twenty-three years.

Frodobert (St) Ab. OSB.   Jan 8
d. c 673   A monk of Luxeuil under the third abbot St Waldebert. Abbot-founder of Moutier-la-Celle, near Troyes, where he led a life of continuous prayer and great austerities.

Frodulphus (Frou) (St) H. OSB.   Apr 21
d. c 750   A disciple of St Medericus (Merry), he became a monk at St Martin's, Autun, from whence he was driven by the Saracen invasion and settled at Barjon, Côte d'Or, where he died.

Froilan (St) Bp. OSB.   Oct 3
d. 1006   A native of Lugo in Galicia, at the age of eighteen he undertook, together with his companion Attilanus (q.v.), the reorganization of monastic observance at Moreruela, on the river Esla in Old Castile. After a very successful career as abbot he was ordained bishop of Léon. He and St Attilanus were the great restorers of Benedictine monasticism in W. Spain.

Fromundus (St) Bp. OSB.   Oct 24
d. p.690 Monk and abbot, and then bishop of Coutances.

Fronto (St) H.   Apr 14
? 2nd cent.   A solitary in the desert of Nitria in Egypt.

Fronto (St) M.   Apr 16
See Saragossa, Martyrs of.

Fronto and George (SS) Bps.   Oct 25
? Apostles of Périgueux in France at some early period. Worthless legends have completely obscured their true story.

Frowin (Bl) Ab. OSB. Cist.   Feb 17
d. 1165   A Cistercian of Bellevaux in Savoy and the abbot-founder of Salom in the diocese of Constance. He was a companion of St Bernard when the latter was preaching his crusade.

Frowin II of Engelberg (Bl) Ab. OSB.   March 7
d. 1178   A Benedictine of St Blasien in the Black Forest who was made abbot of Engelberg in Switzerland (1143). He founded the monastic school at Engelberg, a library, etc., and was himself the chronicler of the abbey and an ascetical writer of distinction.

Fructulus (St) M.   Feb 18
See Lucius, Sylvanus, etc.

Fructuosa (St) M.   Aug 23
See Restitutus, Donatus, etc.

Fructuosus, Augurius and Eulogius (SS) MM.   Jan 21
d. 259   Fructuosus, bishop of Tarragoña in Spain, with his two deacons, Augurius and Eulogius, were burnt at the stake under Valerian. When the fire had burnt through their bonds, they stretched out their arms in the form of a cross and thus expired. The account of their official examination is still extant and seems to be authentic.

Fructuosus (St) Ab. Bp.   Apr 16
d. 665   Born in Spain, the son of a military officer belonging to the royal house of the Visigoths. He became a monk, and then a hermit in the Vierzo Mts, whither he was followed by crowds of disciples. His rule was based on the rule of St Benedict. Fructuosus was eventually forced to accept the bishopric of Dumium and later became archbishop of Braga.

Fructus (Frutos), Valentine and Engratia (SS) HH.   Oct 25
d. c 715   Two brothers and their sister who were living at Sepúlveda in Old Castile at the time of one of the Saracen raids. Valentine and Engratia were killed by the Moors, but Frutos escaped and died a hermit. They are now venerated as the patron saints of Segovia where their relics are enshrined.

Frugentius (St) M. OSB.   Sept 3
d. 675   A Benedictine of Fleury, killed with St Aigulphus, abbot of Lérins, q.v.

Frumentius and another Frumentius (SS) MM.   March 23
See Victorian, Frumentius, etc.

Frumentius (St) Bp.   Oct 27
d. c 380   A native of Tyre, who in the course of a voyage on the Red Sea, was wrecked on the Ethiopian coast with another young man — perhaps his brother — St Aedesius. Both were taken to the king's palace at Axum, and attained high offices at court. Eventually Frumentius applied to St Athanasius for the appointment of a bishop for Ethiopia. St Athanasius complied by ordaining him. Frumentius and Aedesius preached the gospel with signal success and are for this reason venerated as the apostles of Ethiopia.

Fugatius and Damian (SS) May 26
? 2nd cent. The alleged missionaries sent by Pope St Eleutherius to Britain. Their names are also written, Phaganus and Diruvianus, Fagan and Deruvian, Ffager and Dyfan. It is all a fiction. See Dyfan.

Fulbert (St) Bp. Apr 10
c 960–1028 Fulbert was an Italian by birth, who became a student at the Benedictine abbey of Reims, under Gerbert (Pope Silvester II). He directed as headmaster the cathedral school of Chartres, of which city he was made bishop in 1007. A poet and scholar, he identified himself whole-heartedly with the Cluniac movement of reform. A polymath and a saint, Fulbert was an outstanding person.

Fulcran (St) Bp. Feb 13
d. 1006 A bishop of Lodève in Languedoc, famous for his vigorous asceticism and energetic rule. He was ordained bishop in 949 and ruled his diocese for over half a century.

Fulgentius (St) Bp. Jan 1
462–527 or 468–533 An African, belonging to a family of senatorial rank. Early in life he embraced the monastic life and was elected abbot of his monastery; but he had to flee owing to the Vandal persecution. In 502 or 507 he was chosen bishop of Ruspe; but was again exiled by the Vandals. He spent his exile in Sardinia where he wrote his numerous works, which are still of the greatest importance for the history of the Arian persecutions. In 523 he returned to Africa. He was a good bishop and a follower of St Augustine.

Fulgentius (St) Bp. Jan 16
d. c 633 Brother of SS Isidore and Leander of Seville and of St Florentina. He was bishop of Ecija, in Andalusia, and one of the leaders of the Spanish church of that time. He is often confused with St Fulgentius of Ruspe (see Jan. 1).

Fulgentius (Bl) Ab. OSB. Dec 10
d. 1122 A Walloon by birth, he was professed a Benedictine at the abbey of St Airy, Verdun. The community of this monastery had to disband, owing to the struggle between Gregory VII and Henry IV. Fulgentius repaired to the abbey of Afflighem in Belgium, where later he was elected abbot.

Fulk (Foulques, Fulco) (Bl) C. March 2
d. 1201 Parish priest of Neuilly-sur-Marne in France, commissioned by Innocent III to preach the third crusade, in which Richard Coeur de Lion took part. He died before setting out for the Holy Land.

Fulk (St) C. May 22
d. p.600 A pilgrim to Rome who gave his life in the service of the plague-stricken at Santopadre or Castrofuli, near Arpino, in S. Italy. He is venerated as the patron saint of that district. Cult approved in 1572. The legend is extremely doubtful, but he is certainly the patron saint of Castrofuli.

Fulk (St) Ab. OSB. Oct 10
d. 845 The twenty-first abbot of Fontenelle in Normandy.

Fulk (St) Bp. Oct 26
1164–1229 Born at Piacenza of Scottish parents, he was appointed to a canonry there. Then, after his studies in Paris, he became archpriest and bishop of Piacenza. Six years later he was transferred by Honorius III to the see of Pavia, which he occupied for thirteen years.

Fulk (Folquet) (Bl) Bp. OSB. Cist. Dec 25
c 1155–1231 A Genoese by birth, and a minstrel by profession, he entered the Cistercian abbey of Thoronet, of which he became abbot in 1200. In 1206 he was made bishop of Toulouse and greatly helped St Dominic in the founding of the friars preachers. He was known as "the Minstrel Bishop". He is venerated by the Cistercians.

Fulrad (St) Ab. OSB. July 16
d. 784 An Alsatian by origin, he became a Benedictine at the abbey of St Denis near Paris, and in 750 was elected its abbot. From this time his life is identified with that of the Carolingian court, at which he held the offices of councillor, court chaplain, grand-almoner, ambassador to the pope, etc. His was a crowded life in the service of the church and of the Holy Roman Empire.

Fursey (St) Ab. OSB. Jan 16
d. c 648 An Irish monk, who established a monastery at Rathmat, whence he passed over to England and founded another at Burgh Castle, near Yarmouth, in East Anglia. He finally crossed over to France and became the abbot-founder of Lagny, near Paris. He was buried in Picardy and his shrine survived until the French Revolution. His life is also famous for his remarkable ecstasies, of which St Bede and others write.

Fusca V. and Maura (SS) MM. Feb 13
d. c 250 Two martyrs of Ravenna under Decius. Fusca was a young girl and Maura her nurse.

Fuscian (St) M.   Dec 11
See Victoricus, Fuscian and Gentian.

Fusculus (St) Bp. M.   Sept 6
See Donatian, Praesidius, etc.

Fymbert (St) Bp.   Sept 25
7th cent. A bishop in the W. of Scotland,
said to have been ordained by St Gregory the
Great.

Fyncana and Fyndoca
(SS) VV. MM.   Oct 13
? Two martyrs listed in the Aberdeen Brevi-
ary, of whom nothing is known.

Gabdelas (St) M.   Sept 29

See Dadas, Casdoe and Gabdelas.

Gabinus (St) M.   Feb 19

d. 295 (or 296) A Roman Christian and martyr related to the emperor Diocletian, brother of Pope St Gaius and father, in the legend, of the martyr St Susanna. His Acts, however, are quite untrustworthy.

Gabinus and Crispulus (SS) MM.   May 30

d. *c* 130 The proto-martyrs of Sardinia. They suffered at Torres, where they had preached the gospel, under Hadrian.

Gabriel de Duisco (St) M.   Feb 6

d. 1597 One of the group of twenty martyrs who were crucified at Nagasaki. He was a Japanese Franciscan tertiary. See Paul Miki and Comps.

Gabriel of our Lady of Sorrows (St) CP.   Feb 27

1838–1862 Francis Possenti was born at Assisi and educated at Spoleto under the Jesuits. After two serious illnesses he suddenly developed a religious vocation and joined the Passionists at Morovalle, near Macerata (1856). Six years later (1862) the young man died of consumption at Isola, in the Abruzzi. He attained perfection by heroic self-denial in small things. Canonized in 1920. Cult confined to local or particuler calendars since 1969.

Gabriel Mary (Bl) C. OFM.   Aug 27

1463–1532 Gabriel's baptismal name was Gilbert Nicolas, and he was born near Clermont. He was refused admission to several houses of the Franciscan Observants, but finally was received at Notre-Dame-de-la-Fon, near Rochelle. He co-operated with St Jane of Valois, whose confessor he was, in the foundation of the order of the Annonciades (1532). Cult approved in 1647.

Gabriel of St Magdalen (St) M. OFM.   Sept 3

d. 1632 A native of Fonseca in New Castile, and a Francsican lay-brother. In 1612 he was sent to Manila, where he studied medicine. In 1622 he passed over to Japan and, at the risk of his own life, ministered to the sick during the persecutions. He was at last captured and burnt alive at Nagasaki. Beatified in 1867.

Gabriel Perboyre (Bl) M.   Sept 11

1802–1840 Born at Peuch, in the diocese of Montauban, he joined the Vincentians in 1818 and after his ordination (1825) taught theology at Saint-Flaur (1825–1835). Here he received the news of the death of his brother, a missionary in China, and offered to replace him. He arrived in China in 1836 and worked in the mission of Honan. In 1840, after a long incarceration and many tortures, he was strangled at the cross. Beatified in 1889.

Gabriel John Taurin Du-Fresse (Bl) M.   Sept 14

1750–1815 Born at Ville-de-Lezoux, diocese of Clermont, he entered the seminary for foreign missions in 1774, and arrived in China in 1777. In 1800 he was ordained titular bishop of Tabraca and after fifteen years of continual danger was betrayed by a native Christian and beheaded. Beatified in 1900.

Gabriel the Archangel (St)   GC. Sept 29

St Gabriel is mentioned in the Book of Daniel (8:16; 9:21) and was the angel sent to Zechariah (Luke 1: 11–19) and especially to our Lady, to tell her that she was chosen to be the Mother of God (Luke 1: 26–38). He is for this reason called "The Angel of the Annunciation". He is usually depicted as an archangel, young, and vested with an alb and girdle, kneeling and holding a scroll emblazoned with Ave Maria, etc.

Gabriel Ferretti (Bl) C. OFM.   Nov 12

1385–1456 A native of Ancona, and a scion of the family of the counts Ferretti. He became a Friar Minor at Ancona, and eventually provincial of Piceno (Marches). Cult confirmed in 1753.

Gabriel Bourla (Bl) M.   Oct 17

1746–1794 Her name in religion was Marie-Ursule, and she belonged to the group

St Gabriel, Sept 29

of Ursuline Nuns, martyrs of Valenciennes, q.v.

Gaiana (St) VM.   Sept 29
See Rhipsime, Gaiana, etc.

Gaius (St) M.   Jan 4
See Hermes, Haggai and Gaius.

Gaius Francis (St)
M. Tert. OFM.   Feb 6
d. 1597 A Japanese soldier, recently baptized and received as a Franciscan tertiary, who insisted on being arrested with the friars. He was crucified with twenty-five companions at Nagasaki. Beatified 1627, canonized in 1862. See Paul Miki and Comps.

Gaius (St) M.   Feb 28
See Caerealis, Pupulus, etc.

Gaius and Comp. (SS)
MM.   March 4
d. 254–259 Gaius, an officer of the imperial palace was, with twenty-seven (some MSS have thirty-seven) other Christians, thrown into the sea at Nicomedia.

Gaius and Alexander
(SS) MM.   March 10
d. c 172 Two Christians martyred at Apamea in Phrygia under Marcus Aurelius. They had previously distinguished themselves as firm opponents of the Montanists.

Gaius and Crementius
(SS) MM.   Apr 16
d. 304 Martyrs or (according to Fortunatus) confessors of the faith at Saragossa, they belong to the group "Martyrs of Saragossa". See Saragossa.

Gaius of Melitene (St) M.   Apr 19
See Hermogenes, Gaius, etc.

Gaius (St) Pope   formerly Apr 22
d. 296 Nothing definite is known about the life of this pope. According to the *passio* of St Susanna he hailed from Dalmatia: but this legend, as well as that of St Sebastian, in which he figures, are not reliable. Neither is he called a martyr in early sources. Fragments of his epitaph, in the cemetery of Callistus, are extant. Cult suppressed in 1969.

Gaius Xeymon (Bl) M.
Tert. OP.   June 1
d. 1627 A Japanese born of Christian parents on the isle of Amakus. He became a Dominican tertiary and helped the friars in their missionary work. He was burnt alive at Nagasaki (Aug 17). Beatified in 1867.

Gaius and Leo (SS) MM.   June 30
? Martyrs either in Africa or in Rome. Gaius was a priest and Leo a subdeacon.

Gaius of Salerno (St) M.   Aug 28
See Fortunatus, Gaius and Anthes.

Gaius of Milan (St) Bp.   Sept 27
1stcent. He is said to have been the successor of St Barnabas the Apostle in the see of Milan, which he governed for twenty-four years. He is also said to have baptized the martyr, St Vitalis, and his sons SS Gervase and Protase. St Charles Borromeo enshrined his relics in the church of St Francis at Milan (1571).

Gaius (St) M.   Oct 3
See Dionysius, Faustus, etc.

Gaius of Corinth   Oct 4
See Crispus and Gaius.

Gaius, Faustus, Eusebius, Chaeremon, Lucius and Comp. (SS) MM.   Oct 4

3rd cent. Victims at Alexandria of the persecution under Valerian (257). Gaius and Faustus are probably the saints of those names commemorated on Oct 3 with St Dionysius of Alexandria, their bishop. Eusebius, a deacon, survived to become bishop of Laodicea, and died in 269. Chaeremon, who had already suffered under Decius, was sent into exile. Of Lucius nothing certain is known.

Gaius (St) M.   Oct 21
See Dasius, Zoticus, etc.

Gaius of Korea (Bl) M.   Nov 15
d. 1627 A former Korean bonze who fled from his country to Nagasaki, where he harb-oured Dominican friars. A tertiary OP.

Gaius (St) M.   Nov 20
See Ampelus and Gaius.

Gajan (St) M.   Apr 10
? 4th cent. A deacon martyred in Dacia.

Galata (St) M.   Apr 19
See Hermogenes, Gaius, etc.

Galation (Galacteon) and Epistemis (SS) MM.   Nov 5

d. 251 According to the legend, Galation, already a Christian, converted his wife, upon which each retired to a monastery. They were martyred under Decius at Emessa in Phoenicia. It is now generally agreed that these two martyrs never existed: they are simply the hero and heroine in what may be described as the Christian continuation of the romance of Clitophon and Leucippe.

Galdinus (St) Bp.   Apr 18
1100–1176 A native of Milan and a member of the Della Scala family. After his ordination he was chancellor and archdeacon of the archdiocese. In 1161 he fled on the approach of the emperor Barbarossa; but, though absent, was elected archbishop of Milan and created cardinal (1165). He returned to Milan and was instrumental in rebuilding the city that had been razed to the ground by Barbarossa. He died immediately after having preached a sermon in his cathedral. The Milanese always invoke him after SS Ambrose and Charles Borromeo.

Galganus (St) C.   Dec 5
d. 1181 A native of Siena who at first led a worldly life, but was converted to better ways and became a hermit at Monte Siepe in Tuscany, where he died. He was canonized by Alexander III. In 1196 a church was built on the site of his hermitage which was handed over to the Cistercians in 1201. It is probably for this reason that the Cistercians have always claimed him as one of their own.

Gall (St) Bp.   July 1
c 489–554 A native of Auvergne who became a monk but after being ordained deacon by St Quinctian, bishop of Clermont, was sent to represent him at the court of King Thierry. In 527 he succeeded St Quinctian. He was uncle and teacher of St Gregory of Tours.

Gall (St) Ab.   Oct 16
c 550–645 An Irishman and a monk of Bangor who accompanied St Columbanus to England and France, where he helped in the foundation of Luxeuil. He was banished, together with St Columbanus, and settled in Switzerland at a place on the Steinach, where the great abbey and town of Saint-Gall sprang up at a later period. He is venerated as one of the apostles of Switzerland. The abbey library was very important and many of its manuscripts still survive.

Galla (St) W.   Oct 5
d. c 550 A Roman lady, daughter of Symmachus the younger and sister-in-law of Böethius. After her husband's death she led the life of a recluse in a small cottage on the Vatican Hill, where she died of cancer of the breast. Her life and death are briefly described by St Gregory the Great.

Gallgo (St) Ab.   Nov 27
6th cent. A Welsh saint, founder of Llanallgo in Anglesey.

Gallicanus (St) M.   June 25
d. c 362 Described as a high officer in the army of Constantine and consul at Rome, who in the year 330, retired to Ostia, where he founded a hospital and ministered to the sick. The pre-1970 RM. makes him a martyr at Alexandria under Julian the Apostate; but both his banishment to Alexandria and his martyrdom are denied by historians.

Gallicanus (St) Bp.   June 25
d. p.541 The fifth bishop of Embrun, in France.

Gallus (St)   July 1
Otherwise Gall, q.v.

Galmier (St)   Feb 27
The French form of Baldomerus, q.v.

Galnutius (St) Ab.   March 3
Otherwise Winalöe, q.v.

Gamaliel (St)   Aug 3
1st cent. The Jewish doctor of the law, at

whose feet St Paul sat (Acts 22:3) and whose counsel saved Peter and John (ib. 5:34–39). A doubtful tradition makes him a convert to Christianity. The pre-1970 RM. commemorates the finding of his body, together with those of SS Stephen, protomartyr, Nicodemus and Abibo (415).

Gamelbert (St) C.   Jan 27
720–800 Son of rich Bavarian parents, Gamelbert went to Rome on pilgrimage, was ordained priest, and laboured for over fifty years as parish priest of Michaelsbuch. Cult approved in 1909.

Gamo (St) Ab. OSB.   May 30
8th cent. Monk and then abbot of Brétigny near Noyon.

**Gandulphus of Binasco
(Bl)** C. OFM.   Apr 3
d. 1260 Born at Binasco, near Milan, he became a Friar Minor during the lifetime of St Francis, and spent all his life praying and preaching in Sicily.

Gangulphus (St) M.   May 11
d. 760 A Burgundian and a courtier, who retired from public life to lead the life of a recluse and was killed by his wife's paramour.

Garbh (St) V.   Jan 1
Otherwise Franchea, q.v.

Garbhan (St) Ab.   March 26
7th cent. The Irish saint who appears to have left his name to Dungarvan. Nothing certain is known about him.

Garcia Gonzalez (St) M.
OFM.   Feb 6
d. 1597 A Spanish Franciscan and missionary in Japan, crucified at Nagasaki. Beatified in 1627, and canonized in 1862. See Paul Miki and Comps.

Garcia (St) Ab. OSB.   Sept 29
d. c 1073 A native of Quintanilla, near Burgos, in Old Castile. He became monk and abbot (1039) of Artanza, in Old Castile, and was the counsellor and companion of King Ferdinand I of Castile, whom he more than once followed into battle.

Gardiner, German (Bl)
M.   March 7
See Jermyn Gardiner.

Garembert (St) Ab.   Dec 31
Otherwise Walembert, q.v.

Garibaldus (St) Bp. OSB.   Jan 8
d. 762 First bishop of Regensburg, who was

ordained by St Boniface c 740. He had probably been abbot of St Emmeran at Regensburg.

Garmier (Germier) (St)   Feb 27
Otherwise Baldomerus, q.v.

Garmon (St) Bp.   July 31
A French form of the name of St Germanus of Auxerre, q.v.

Garnat (St)   Nov 8
Otherwise Gervadius, q.v.

Gaspar (*several*)
Otherwise Caspar, q.v.

Gaston (St) Bp.   Feb 6
A French form of Vedast, q.v.

Gatian (St) Bp.   Dec 18
d. ? c 337 Venerated as one of the disciples of St Dionysius of Paris and the founder and first bishop of the diocese of Tours, in France.

**Gaucherius (Gaultier,
Walter) (St)** Ab.   Apr 9
d. 1140 The abbot-founder of the monastery of St John at Aureil in the Limousin, for Augustinian canons regular. He was also a great benefactor of St Stephen of Gramont at Muret.

**Gaudentia and Comp.
(SS)** VV. MM.   Aug 30
? St Gaudentia, a Roman maiden, is said to have suffered with three other Christians; but the more ancient martyrologies do not rank her among the martyrs.

**Gaudentius of Gnesen
(St)** Bp. OSB.   Jan 5
d. c 1004 Younger brother of St Adalbert of Prague and his fellow-monk at the Benedictine abbey of Sant' Alessio, on the Aventine, Rome, and again his companion on his mission to Prussia. He escaped the massacre in which his brother was martyred and in 1000 was appointed first archbishop of Gnesen by Otto III.

**Gaudentius of Novara
(St)** Bp.   Jan 22
d. 417 A priest of Ivrea, near Turin, who was befriended first by St Laurence of Novara and then by St Eusebius of Vercelli. He succeeded the former as bishop of Novara, and governed the diocese twenty years.

**Gaudentius of Verona
(St)** Bp.   Feb 12
d. c 465 Bishop of Verona. His relics are

enshrined at Verona in the ancient basilica of St Stephen.

Gaudentius of Ossero
(St) Bp. OSB.   June 1
d. 1044   Bishop of Ossero in Istria. He was appointed to that see in 1030. Two years later he journeyed to Rome to appeal against his persecutors. On his way back he fell ill at Ancona and, on his recovery, resigned his see (1042) and became a Benedictine under St Peter Damian.

Gaudentius and Culmatius
(SS) MM.   June 19
d. 364   Gaudentius, a bishop, and Culmatius, his deacon, are stated in the pre-1970 RM. to have been martyred at Arezzo in Tuscany under Valentinian I. With them suffered Andrew, a layman, with his wife and children and a group of fifty-three companions.

Gaudentius of Rimini
(St) Bp. M.   Oct 14
d. c 360   An Asiatic, who joined the Roman clergy (332) and in 346 became bishop of Rimini. He suffered much at the hands of the Arians, who dominated the council of 357, and was by them done to death.

Gaudentius of Brescia
(St) Bp.   Oct 25
4th–5th cent.   A pupil of St Philastrius, bishop of Brescia, he became a monk at Caesarea in Cappadocia, but was recalled to Brescia to succeed St Philastrius as bishop and was ordained by St Ambrose (c 387). In 405 he was sent to the East to defend the cause of St John Chrysostom and was imprisoned near Thrace. He died shortly after.

Gaudiosus of Brescia
(St) Bp.   March 7
d. 445 ?   Bishop of Brescia where his relics are venerated.

Gaudiosus of Salerno
(St) Bp.   Oct 26
7th cent.   A bishop of Salerno, whose relics are venerated at Naples.

Gaudiosus of Naples (St)
Bp.   Oct 27
d. c 455   Surnamed "the African". He was in fact a bishop of Abitina in N. Africa, exiled by the Arian Vandal king Genseric (440). He took refuge at Naples where he founded a monastery of which, later, St Agnellus became abbot.

Gaudiosus of Tarazona
(St) Bp.   Nov 3
d. c 585   A monk of Asan in the Aragonese Pyrenees, near Benasque, under St Victorian. About the year 565 he was made bishop of Tarazona (*not* Tarragona) in the province of Saragossa.

Gaufridus (Bl) Ab. OSB.   Sept 9
d. 1139   A disciple of Bl Vitalis, and his successor as abbot of Savigny (1122–1139). Under him the new Benedictine congregation of Savigny spread to Normandy, England, Ireland and numbered some twenty-nine houses.

Gaugericus (Gau, Géry)
(St) Bp.   Aug 11
d. c 625   Gaugericus was born in the diocese of Trier, was ordained priest by the bishop of that diocese and later was made bishop of the united dioceses of Cambrai and Arras, which he served for over thirty-nine years.

Gausmarus (Bl) Ab. OSB.   June 3
d. 984   Abbot of St Martin of Savigny (954–984).

Gebetrude
(Gertrude) (St) Abs.
OSB.   Nov 7
d. c 675   Third abbess of Remiremont (Habend). Her relics were enshrined and her cult approved by Leo IX in 1051.

Gebhard (St) Bp.   Aug 27
d. 995   Bishop of Constance (979–995). He founded the great Benedictine abbey of Petershausen, near Constance (983), where he was buried.

Gebizo (St) Mk. OSB.   Oct 21
d. c 1087   A native of Cologne, he became a monk of Montecassino under abbot St Desiderius (Pope Victor III) in 1076. He was sent to Croatia by Pope St Gregory VII, to crown King Zwoinimir.

Gebuinus (St) Bp.   Apr 18
d. 1080   Archbishop of Lyons. He is patron of the cathedral-chapter of Langres.

Gedeon (St) Bp.   Aug 8
d. c 796   The thirteenth bishop of Besançon (790–796).

Gelasinus (Gelasius) (St)
M.   Aug 26
d. 297   An actor at Heliopolis in Phoenicia who, having to burlesque the ceremony of baptism, suddenly declared himself a Christian and was stoned to death by the mob. Probably identical with St Genesius (Aug 25).

Gelasius II (St) Pope OSB.   Jan 29
c 1058–1119   A monk of Montecassino, he

became cardinal and counsellor of Pope Pascal II. He was elected pope in 1118 and carried on the struggle with the emperor Henry V and his anti-pope. But he died soon after at Cluny. Baronius said that no pontiff, except the martyrs, had suffered so much for the church.

Gelasius (St) M.   Feb 4
See Aquilinus, Geminus, etc.

Gelasius (Gioua-Mac-Liag) (St) Bp.   March 27
d. 1174   Abbot of Derry. He was ordained as archbishop of Armagh in 1138, and is said to have been the first Irish bishop to whom the pallium was sent. In 1162 he ordained St Laurence O'Toole archbishop of Dublin.

Gelasius I (St) Pope.   Nov 21
d. 496   An African by descent, he was elected bishop of Rome in 492. He showed himself a vigorous pontiff, in fact one of the greatest in that century of great bishops. Although he is not the author of the Sacramentary which goes under his name, some of his work may appear in the Leonine Sacramentary.

Gelasius (St) M.   Dec 23
See Theodolus, Saturninus, etc.

Gemellus (St) M.   Dec 10
d. 362   Crucified for the faith at Ancyra in Galatia (Asia Minor) under Julian the Apostate.

Geminian of Modena (St) Bp.   Jan 31
d. 348   Deacon to the bishop of Modena and his successor in the see. He gave shelter to St Athanasius when that great bishop passed through Italy on his way to his exile in Gaul. Geminian bravely opposed Jovinianism.

Geminian (St) M.   Sept 16
See Lucy and Geminian.

Geminus (St) M.   Jan 4
See Aquilinus, Geminus, etc.

Geminus of Fossombrone (St) M.   Feb 4
See Aquilinus, Geminus, Gelasius, etc.

Geminus (St) Mk.   Oct 9
d. ? 815   A monk of Sanpaterniano de Fano, diocese of Narni, in Umbria. He is claimed both by the Basilians and the Benedictines for their respective orders. He is the patron saint of San Gemini.

Gemma Galgani (St) V.   Apr 11
1878–1903   Born at Camigliano, near Lucca, in Tuscany. Her mother died when she was seven years old, and from that time her life was one of domestic trials and intense suffering both spiritual and physical. Through it all, however, she remained at peace and was the subject of various extraordinary supernatural phenomena — especially periodically recurring stigmata between 1899 and 1901. She was directed by the Passionists. Her physical infirmities prevented her becoming a Passionist nun, as she ardently desired. She died on Holy Saturday. Beatified in 1933 and canonized in 1940, in the teeth of strong opposition based on the extraordinary nature of her religious experiences.

Gemma (Bl) V.   May 12
d. 1249   A shepherdess, and afterwards for forty-two years a recluse at Goriano Sicoli, diocese of Sulmona in the Abruzzi. Cult approved in 1890.

Gemma (Hemma, Emma) (St) W. OSB.   June 29
d. 1045   A near relative of the emperor St Henry II. Left a widow, she became the foundress of the double monastery of Gurk in Carinthia, and took the veil among the nuns.

Gemus (St) Mk. OSB.   March 19
? Monk, probably of Moyenmoutier in Alsace. His relics were enshrined at Hürbach.

Genebald of Laon (St) Bp.   Sept 5
d. c 555   A bishop of Laon related to St Remigius. For a fault he committed he is said to have performed a seven years' continuous penance.

Genebrard (St) M.   May 15
Otherwise Gerebern, q.v.

Generalis (St) M.   Sept 14
See Crescentian, Victor, etc.

Generosa (St) M.   July 17
One of the Scillitan Martyrs, q.v.

Generosus (St) Ab. OSB.   July 16
d. c 682   An abbot of Saint-Jouin-de-Marnes in Poitou.

Generosus (St) M.   July 17
? Venerated at Tivoli, where his relics are enshrined under the high altar in the cathedral, but nothing is known about him.

Genesius (St) Bp.   June 3
d. 662   Bishop of Clermont in Auvergne. He is described as learned, benevolent, surpassingly good, beloved by old and young, rich and poor.

Genesius the Comedian
(St) M.   **Aug 25**

d. *c* 300 An actor at Rome who, while taking part in a burlesque of Christian baptism in the theatre, was suddenly converted and forthwith martyred. The same story is told of at least three other martyrs. Probably this Genesius is the same as the saint of Arles, to whom a popular story has been applied. (Cf. Gelasinus above.)

Genesius (Genès) of
Arles (St) M.   **Aug 25**

d. *c* 303 A notary of Arles in S. Gaul who, having refused to put on record an imperial decree against Christians and declaring that he himself believed in Christ, was martyred under Maximian Herculeus.

Genesius (St) M.   Oct 11
See Anastasius, Placid, etc.

Genesius (St) Bp.   Nov 1

d. *c* 679 From being prior at Fontenelle he was chosen abbot-chaplain of the palace by Queen Bathildis, and in 658 was made bishop of Lyons. He died at the nunnery of Chelles while on a visit there.

Genistus (St) M. OSB.   Apr 30

c 1100 A Benedictine monk of Beaulieu in the Limousin, diocese of Limoges. Killed by his nephew at Aynac-en-Quercy. He is venerated as a martyr and as patron saint of Aynac.

Geneviève (St) V.   Jan 3

c 422–500 Born at Nanterre near Paris. In her seventh year she happened to become known to St Germanus of Auxerre, who befriended her. When fifteen years old she received the veil from the bishop of Paris, and gave herself up to penance and the exercise of charity. When Paris was occupied by the Franks and afterwards threatened by Attila and his Huns, St Geneviève encouraged the people to defend the city. She has always been considered the special protectress and patroness of Paris. There has been in recent times a lively controversy over the authenticity of her life, of which the above is a resumé. In art, shown as a shepherdess, usually holding a candle, a devil attempting to extinguish it whilst an angel guards it. She may have a coin suspended around her neck.

Gengulphus (St) M.   May 11
Otherwise Gangulphus, q.v.

Genitus (St)   Jan 17
See Genulfus and Genitus.

Gennadius (St) M.   May 16
See Felix and Gennadius.

Gennadius (St) Bp. OSB.   May 25

d. *c* 936 A monk at Argeo, near Astorga, in Spain, abbot-restorer of San Pedro de Montes, and a zealous propagator of St Benedict's Rule throughout N.W. Spain. About the year 895 he was made bishop of Astorga, which he resigned five years before his death, returning to live as a monk-hermit in his beloved San Pedro.

Gennard (St) Ab. OSB.   Apr 6

d. 720 Educated at the court of Clotaire III, he became a monk at Fontenelle under St Wandrille, and eventually abbot of Flay (Saint-Germer) in the diocese of Beauvais, Before his death he resigned and returned to die at Fontenelle.

Gennaro (St) M.   Sept 19
The Italian form of Januarius, q.v.

Gennys (Genewys) (St)
Bp.   **July 31**
Otherwise Germanus of Auxerre, q.v.

Genocus (St) C.   Apr 18
See Bitheus and Genocus.

Genovefa (St) V.   Jan 3
Otherwise Geneviève, q.v.

Gentian (St) M.   Dec 11
See Victoricus, Fuscian and Gentian.

Gentilis (Bl) M. OFM.   Sept 5

d. 1340 A native of Matelica in the Marches, Piceno, where he joined the Friars Minor. He spent some time on Mt Alvernia and then went as a missionary among the Muslims of Egypt and Persia. He was martyred at Toringa in Persia. Cult approved by Pius VI.

Genuinus (Ingenuinus)
and Albinus (SS) Bps.   **Feb 5**

7th cent. A bishop of the small town of Sabion (which has since disappeared) near Brixen in the Tyrol. With him is commemorated on the same day St Albinus, bishop of Brixen in the 11th century.

Genulfus (Genou) and
Genitus (SS)   **Jan 17**

? 3rd cent. They are said to have been two holy monks who lived at Celle-sur-Naton in France. Another St Genulfus is honoured at Cahors as the first bishop of that see.

Geoffrey (Godfrey) (St)
Ab.   **June 21**
Otherwise Agofredus, q.v.

Geoffrey (St) Ab.   Sept 25
The Norman form of the Saxon name Ceolfrid, q.v.

Geoffrey (*several*)
Otherwise Godfrey, q.v.

George Haydock and Comps. (BB) MM. May 4

d. 1584–1679 This group of eighty-five martyrs who were put to death for their faith between these two dates in England, Wales and Scotland were beatified on Nov 22 1987 by Pope John Paul II. They comprise one Dominican friar, five Franciscan friars, two Jesuits, sixty-three secular clergy and twenty-two of the faithful. Their names and dates of martyrdom are George Haydock (1584), William Carter (1584), Marmaduke Bowes (1585), Hugh Taylor (1585), Francis Ingleby (1586), John Fingley (1586), Robert Bickerdike (1586), Alexander Crow (1586), William Thompson (1586), John Sandys (1586), Richard Sargeant (1586), John Lowe (1586), Robert Dibdale (1586), John Adams (1586), Nicholas Woodfen (1586), Edmund Sykes (1587), Stephen Rowsham (1587), Thomas Pilcher (1587), John Hambley (1587), George Douglas (1587), Richard Simpson (1588), Edward Burden (1588), Henry Webley (1588), William Lampley (1588), Nicholas Garlick (1588), Robert Ludlam (1588), Robert Sutton (1588), Richard Flower (Lloyd) (1588), William Spenser (1589), Robert Hardesty (1589), Thomas Belson (1589), Richard Yaxley (1589), George Nichols (1589), Humphrey Pritchard (1589), Nicholas Horner (1590), Richard Hill (1590), John Hogg (1590), Alexander Blake (1590), Edmund Duke (1590), Richard Holliday (1590), Robert Thorpe (1591), Thomas Watkinson (1591), George Beesley (1591), William Pike (1591), Mountford Scott (1591), Joseph Lambton (1592), Thomas Pormort (1592), William Davies (1593), Antony Page (1593), Edward Osbaldeston (1594), William Knight (1596), William Gibson (1596), George Errington (1596), Christopher Robinson (1597), John Bretton (1598), Ralph Grimstow (1598), Peter Snow (1598), Christopher Wharton (1600), Edward Thwing (1600), Thomas Palaser (1600), John Talbot (1600), Robert Nutter (1600), John Norton (1600), Roger Filcock (1600), Thomas Hunt (1600), Thomas Sprott (1600), Robert Middleton (1601), Thurston Hunt (1601), Robert Grissold (1604), John Sugar (1604), Robert Drury (1607), Matthew Flathers (1608), Roger Cadwallador (1610), Thomas Atkinson (1616), Roger Wrenno (1616), John Thules (1616), William Southerne (1618), Thomas Bullaker (1642), Henry Heath (1643), Arthur Bell (1643), Edward Bamber (1646), John Woodcock (1646), Thomas Whittaker (1646), Nicholas Postage (1679), Charles Meeham (1679).

George of Lodève (St)

Bp. OSB. Feb 19

d. *c* 884 Born near Rodez and a Benedictine at Saint-Foi-de-Conques in Rouergue. After the destruction of the monastery by the Norsemen (862) he became a monk at Vabres, diocese of Rodez. When quite old he was elected to the see of Lodève.

George of Amastris (St)

Bp. Feb 21

d. *c* 825 A native of Kromna, near Amastris, on the Black Sea. He was first a hermit on Mt Sirik, then a monk of Bonyssa, and lastly bishop of Amastris. He deserved well of his people during the Saracen attacks, against which he successfully defended his episcopal city.

George the Younger (St)

Bp. Apr 7

d. *c* 816 Bishop of Mitilene, the capital of Lesbos. He is called "the Younger" because two of his predecessors in the see and of that century, also named George, are venerated as saints.

George Gervase (Bl) M.

OSB. Apr 11

d. 1608 A native of Bosham, Sussex. In his youth he had a very adventurous career under Drake in the West Indies. He was educated for the priesthood at Douai and ordained priest in 1603. At Douai, too, he was received into the Benedictine order. Sent to the English mission, he was condemned and suffered at Tyburn. Beatified in 1929.

George of Antioch (St)

Bp. M. Apr 19

d. 814 A monk who became bishop of Antioch in Pisidia. He was one of the Fathers of the second council of Nicea (787) against the Iconoclasts. Banished by the emperor Leo V, the Armenian, he died in exile.

George the Great (St)

M. GC. Apr 23

d. *c* 300 It is now almost universally agreed that St George was a martyr who suffered at Diospolis (Lydda, Ludd) in Palestine, probably under Diocletian. All the other legends which have grown up around his name may safely be regarded as fictitious, including the story of the dragon, which seems to have originated in Italy at a comparatively recent period. The crusaders certainly gave great

St George, Apr 23

impetus to devotion to St George in the West, though he was venerated there as early as the seventh century. He is venerated in the East as one of the fourteen Holy Helpers and, universally, as the model of knighthood and avenger of women. He is the acknowledged patron saint of England, Aragon, Portugal and Germany, also of Genoa and Venice, and protector of Ferrara. In the East he is especially honoured as the patron of soldiers. His veneration as protector of England was officially approved by Pope Benedict XIV. His cult is bound up with British history, traditions and popular culture, and his life has always been a source of inspiration to artists. He is shown as a youth in armour, often mounted, and slaying, or having slain, a dragon, his shield and lance pennant being a red cross on a white ground.

George Swallowell (Bl)
M.   July 26
d. 1594   Born near Durham, he became a Protestant minister and schoolmaster. He was condemned to death for being reconciled to the church, and was executed at Darlington. Beatified in 1929.

George, Aurelius and Natalia, Felix and Liliosa
(SS) MM.   July 27
d. c 852   Martyrs who suffered at Cordoba in Spain under the Caliph Abderrahman II. Aurelius and Felix, with their wives, Natalia and Liliosa, were Spaniards; but the deacon George was a monk from Palestine, who, though offered pardon as a foreigner, preferred to throw in his lot with the others.

George Limniotes (St)
M.   Aug 24
d. c 730   A hermit of Mt Olympus in Asia Minor, who had reached the age, it is said, of ninety-five, when he was martyred under Leo the Isaurian for defending the worship of sacred images.

George and Aurelius
(SS) MM.   Oct 20
See George, Aurelius, etc., July 27. The relics of SS Aurelius and George were translated to the abbey church of St Germain at Paris. The anniversary of this translation is celebrated on Oct 20.

George of Périgueux (St)
Bp.   Oct 25
See Fronto and George.

George of Vienne (St) Bp.   Nov 2
? A bishop of Vienne in France, who flourished probably at the beginning of the eighth century, though some put Nov 2, 699 as the date of his death. Canonized in 1251.

George Napper (Bl) M.   Nov 9
d. 1610   Born at Holywell Manor, Oxford, and educated at Corpus Christi College, Oxford. He studied at Douai, where he was

ordained in 1596. Sent to the English mission he laboured in Oxfordshire and was finally condemned and executed at Oxford. Beatified in 1929.

Georgia (St) V. Feb 15
d. *c* 500 A maiden who became a recluse near Clermont in Auvergne, France.

Gerald (St) Bp. OSB. Feb 6
d. 1077 From being prior at Cluny Gerald was ordained bishop of Ostia by Pope Alexander II as successor to St Peter Damian. He was papal legate to France, Spain and Germany, and was arrested and imprisoned by the German emperor, Henry V. He is the principal patron saint of Velletri.

Gerald (St) Ab. March 13
d. 732 A Northumbrian monk who followed St Colman from Lindisfarne to Ireland and became his successor in the English house built at Mayo for the English monastic colony. He lived to an old age and must have witnessed the introduction of the Roman observances into his abbey.

Gerald of Sauve-Majeure
(St) Ab. OSB. Apr 5
d. 1095 A native of Corbie, he was educated and became a monk and cellarer at the famous abbey of his native town. He was taken by his abbot to Rome and Montecassino, and at Rome Pope Leo IX ordained him priest. He suffered from acute headaches but on his return to Corbie, he was cured by St Adalard. He then went to Palestine before being chosen abbot of St Vincent's at Laon and of St Medard at Soissons; but, being expelled by a usurper, he founded Sauve-Majeure, which became the centre of a widespread Benedictine congregation. Canonized in 1197.

Gerald (St) Bp. OSB. May 29
d. 927 A monk of Brou. He became bishop of Mâcon but after some forty years in the episcopate he returned to his old abbey to die.

Gerald of Aurillac (St) C. Oct 13
855–909 Gerald, count of Aurillac, led a life of great virtue at a period when it was difficult for one of his rank to do so. He founded a Benedictine abbey on his estate and endowed it in princely fashion. He is the patron saint of Upper Auvergne.

Gerald (Bl) Ab. OSB. Cist. Oct 16
d. 1177 A native of Lombardy and professed at the Cistercian monastery at Fossanu-

ova in the Roman Campagna, being eventually chosen abbot. He was later elected abbot of Clairvaux (1170) and was killed by an unruly monk while on a canonical visitation to Igny.

Gerald of Beziers (St)
Bp. Nov 5
d. 1123 A canon regular who became bishop of Beziers in S. France. He spent all his revenues in relieving the distress of the poor of the diocese.

Gerald (St) Bp. OSB. Dec 5
d. 1109 Born near Cahors in Gascony, he took the Benedictine habit at Moissac. He accompanied archbishop Bernard of Toledo to Spain, and was eventually made archbishop of Braga in Portugal (1100).

Gerard (Bl) D. OSB. Cist. Jan 30
d. 1138 The second and favourite brother of St Bernard of Clairvaux. He was not of the party of thirty who accompanied St Bernard to Cîteaux. He was then soldiering and, on being wounded, made up his mind to become a monk. He entered Cîteaux and followed his brother to Clairvaux where he excelled as a cellarer. St Bernard mourned him deeply when he died.

Gerard (Bl) C. OSB. Cam. Apr 1
1280–1367 At the age of nine Gerard received the Camaldolese habit at the abbey of the Holy Cross, at Sassoferrato. After his ordination he was entrusted with the care of the parish, which he served with untiring zeal. He died on Nov 18; but his feast is kept by the Camaldolese on Apr 1.

Gerard of Orchimont
(Bl) Ab. OSB. Apr 23
d. 1138 A Benedictine monk, afterwards abbot of Florennes (1126–*c* 1136).

Gerard of Toul (St) Bp. Apr 23
d. 994 A native of Cologne, who became bishop of Toul in 963. He rebuilt the cathedral and established religious houses in which teaching was given by Greek and Irish monks to the great furtherance of religion and learning in the diocese. He was canonized by Pope Leo IX, his successor in the see.

Gerard (St) C. Apr 28
639? One of four English pilgrims — the other three were Ardwine, Bernard and Hugh — who died at Galinaro in S. Italy. Many scholars doubt their very existence.

Gerard of Bourgogne
(Bl) Ab. OSB. Cist.   Apr 28
d. 1172 The successor of St Fastred as
abbot of the Cistercian monastery of Cambron.

Gerard of Villamagna
(Bl) C.   May 13
1174–1242 A native of Tuscany who, as
esquire to a knight, took part in the crusades
and was taken prisoner. On being ransomed,
he returned to Italy, joined the third order of
St Francis and lived as a recluse for the rest of
his life. Cult approved in 1833.

Gerard de Lunel (St) C.   May 24
1275–1298 Said to have been a French
pilgrim, belonging to the third order of St
Francis, who died at Monte Santo, near
Ancona, on his return from Palestine. His cult
was approved by Benedict XIV and Pius VI,
and he is now honoured as the patron saint of
Monte Santo.

Gerard Tintorio (Bl) C.   June 6
d. 1207 A young citizen of Monza in Lombardy, belonging to the upper middle class,
who expended his wealth in founding a hospital, where he served the sick, especially
lepers. Cult approved in 1582.

Gerard Sagredo (St) Bp.
M. OSB.   Sept 24
d. 1046 Apostle of Hungary, where he is
venerated as St Collert. Venetian by birth, he
was a Benedictine monk and abbot of San
Giorgio Maggiore in his native city. On a
pilgrimage to Palestine he was stopped when
passing through Hungary by King St Stephen
and persuaded to work among the Magyars.
He became the tutor of Prince St Emeric and,
in 1035, first bishop of Csanad. Gerard
worked most zealously, but during the pagan
reaction after St Stephen's death he was
martyred at Buda, and his body cast into the
Danube.

Gerard of Brogne (St)
Ab. OSB.   Oct 3
d. 959 Born in the county of Namur, and
trained for the army, as a page of the count of
Namur he was sent on a special mission to the
French court (918). He stayed in France and
joined the Benedictines of St Denis. After
some eleven years he was ordained priest, and
left for Belgium in order to found a new abbey
on his own estate of Brogne. He was its abbot
for twenty-two years and during that period
was instrumental in introducing St Benedict's
rule into numerous houses in Flanders, Lorraine and Champagne. He was noted for his
engaging sweetness of temper.

Gerard Majella (St) C.
C.SS.R.   Oct 16
1725–1755 A native of Muro in S. Italy, he
was apprenticed to a tailor before asking to be
received by the Redemptorists as a lay-
brother. He continued his trade in the monastery, where he soon attracted the attention of
St Alphonsus de Liguori, who shortened his
novitiate. His wonderful and well authenticated life was a series of supernatural phenomena — bilocations, reading of consciences,
prophecies, multiplying of food, etc. Canonized in 1904.

Gerard of Potenza (St)
Bp.   Oct 30
d. 1119 A native of Piacenza, who was enrolled among the clergy of Potenza, in S. Italy,
and elected bishop there at an advanced age.
Canonized by Pope Callistus II.

Gerard de Bazonches
(St) Mk. OSB.   Nov 4
d. 1123 A Benedictine monk-priest of St
Aubin, at Angers.

Gerard (St) Ab. OSB.   Dec 6
d. 1109 First prior of the Cluniac house of
La-Charité-sur-Loire, in the diocese of
Namur. He founded several more Cluniac
houses in France and elsewhere and finally
governed the abbey of Soigny, but resigned
and returned to La-Charité to end his days as a
choir monk.

Gerard Cagnoli (Bl) C.
OFM.   Jan 2
1270–1345 He was born of noble parents at
Valenzo near Pavia; after the death of his
mother he became a hermit on Mt Etna in
Sicily. After some years he entered the Franciscans as a lay brother and fulfilled the office of
cook. He was the recipient of many extraordinary divine favours. Cult confirmed 1908.

Gerardesca (Bl) W. OSB.
Cam.   May 29
d. c 1260 A native of Pisa, who married a
citizen of that city. After some years of married
life she induced her husband to become a
Camaldolese monk at San Salvio, while she
lived nearby as a recluse, under the obedience
of the abbey. Cult confirmed in 1856.

Gerasimus (St) Ab.   March 5
d. c 475 A monk first in Lycia, Asia Minor,
and afterwards in Palestine. Eventually he

founded a *laura* on the banks of the Jordan, near Jericho, which grew to be second only to that of St Sabas. "St Jerome's Lion" really belonged to St Gerasimus.

Gerbald, Reginhard, Winebald and Worad (BB) MM. OSB.   May 25

d. 862   The first two were monks, the two latter deacons of the abbey of St Bertin, all martyred by the Danes.

Gerbold (St) Bp. OSB.   Dec 5

d. *c* 690   Monk of Ebriciacum under Abbot Alnobert, and afterwards abbot-founder of the abbey of Livray (*Liberiacum*). Eventually he became bishop of Bayeux.

Gerbrand (Bl) Ab. OSB. Cist.   Oct 13

d. 1218   Second abbot of the Cistercian monastery of Klaarkamp in Frisia, and founder of Bloemkamp (1191). He died at Foigny, in the Laonnais, when returning from a general chapter, and has been venerated there ever since.

Gerebald (St) Bp.   June 12

d. 885   Bishop of Châlons-sur-Seine (864–885).

Gerebern (Gerebrand) (St) M.   May 15

7th cent.   The aged Irish priest who accompanied St Dympna (q.v.) to Belgium and shared in her martyrdom. He is the patron saint of a village in the Rhineland, where his relics are enshrined.

Geremarus (Germer) (St) Ab. OSB.   Sept 24

d. *c* 658   A native of Beauvais, attached to the court of Dagobert I. With the consent of his saintly wife he retired to the abbey of Pentale on the Seine, near Brionne, of which he eventually became abbot. He was over-severe, with the result that some of his monks made an attempt on his life, whereupon he resigned and retired to a cave near the abbey to live as a hermit. In 655 he founded Flay abbey, between Beauvais and Rouen, which was afterwards called Saint-Germer.

Gereon (St) M.   Oct 10

3rd cent.?   Two pairs of martyrs, one at Xanten and the other at Bonn, become confused with the passage of time. One of the two, probably named Gereon, may have been a martyred soldier. A large number of people, or any association with the Theban legion, is not now considered possible.

Gerinus (Garinus, Werinus) (St) M.   Oct 2

d. 676   Brother of St Leodegarius (Leger) and, like him, persecuted by Ebroin, mayor of the palace. He was stoned to death near Arras.

Gerius (St) C.   May 24

Otherwise Gerard de Lunel, q.v.

Gerlac (St) H.   Jan 5

d. *c* 1170   A Dutch soldier of licentious life who, after the death of his wife, experienced a moral conversion and led thenceforth a life of most austere penance, living in a hollow tree near Valkenberg, his native place. He had a kind of spiritual pact with St Hildegard.

Gerland (St) Bp.   Feb 25

d. 1104   Said to have been born at Besançon in France, and to have been related to Robert Guiscard, the Norman conqueror of Sicily. He was certainly ordained bishop of Girgenti, in Sicily, by Urban II, and laboured for the restoration of Christianity in Sicily after the expulsion of the Saracens.

Gerland (St) C.   June 18

13th cent.   A knight — either a Templar or a Hospitaller — whose relics are venerated at Caltagirone in Sicily.

German Gardiner (Bl) M.   March 7

Otherwise Jermyn Gardiner, q.v.

Germana (St) M.   Jan 19

See Paul, Gerontius, etc.

Germana (French: Germaine) Cousin (St) V.   June 15

c 1579–1601   Born at Pibrac, near Toulouse, daughter of a poor farmer. She suffered from scrofula, was neglected by her father and treated with much harshness by her step-mother. Sent to tend the sheep, she spent her short life in the fields, communing with God in prayer and practising charity towards others poorer than herself. She died all alone on her straw bed at the age of twenty-two. Canonized in 1867.

Germanicus (St) M.   Jan 19

d. 156   A youth of Smyrna thrown to the wild beasts in the amphitheatre at the public games. The letter describing his martyrdom — together with that of St Polycarp — is one of the most authentic documents of early ecclesiastical history.

Germanus and Randoald (SS) MM. OSB.   Feb 21

d. *c* 677   Germanus was born at Trier and

became a monk at Remiremont. Thence he
migrated to Luxeuil under its third abbot, St
Waldebert, who introduced the Benedictine
rule into the abbey. At a later date he was made
abbot of Granfield in the Val Moutier. He and
his prior, St Randoald, were put to death by
the duke of that district while interceding with
him on behalf of the poor.

Germanus (St) M.   May 2
See Saturninus, Neopolus, etc.

Germanus (St) Bp. M.   May 2
d. *c* 460   Of Irish or Scottish origin, he was
converted by St Germanus of Auxerre whose
name he took. He was martyred in Normandy.

Germanus of
Constantinople (St) Bp.   May 12
c 634–1732   A churchman of senatorial rank
who, from being bishop of Cyzicus, was made
patriarch of Constantinople (715). He bravely
opposed the iconoclast emperor, Leo III, the
Isaurian and was forced to resign (732). He
died in exile. Several of his writings are still
extant.

Germanus of Paris (St)
Bp.   May 28
c 496–576   Born near Autun, he was
ordained priest and became abbot of a monastery. In 555 he was made bishop of Paris. He
cured King Childebert I in the body and
converted him from a licentious life. The king
built for him the abbey of St Vincent, now
known as Saint-Germain-des-Prés. St Germanus is one of those bishops to whom history
has given the title of "father of the poor".

Germanus (St) Bp.   July 3
d. *c* 474   Said to have been a nephew of St
Patrick and a missionary monk in Ireland,
Wales and Brittany. Eventually he was sent as a
bishop to the Isle of Man, where his memory is
still preserved in several place-names under
the forms "Germain" and "Jarman".

Germanus (St) M.   July 7
See Peregrinus, Lucian, etc.

Germanus of Auxerre
(St) Bp.   July 31
c 378–448   A native of Auxerre, he studied
civil law in Rome, and governed part of Gaul.
In 418 he became bishop of Auxerre. He had
relations with the church in Britain, whither he
came twice (in 429 and 447) and where he
succeeded in completely stamping out Pelagianism. He led the Britons to their great

St Germanus of Auxerre, July 31

"Alleluia" victory over the Saxons. He died at
Ravenna in Italy on a mission which he
undertook on behalf of his people. Vested as a
bishop, he often carries a knife, or tramples on
his judge.

Germanus (St) Bp. M.   Sept 6
See Donation, Praesidius, etc.

Germanus of Besançon
(St) Bp. M.   Oct 11
d. *c* 390   Successor of St Desideratus in the
see of Bresançon. He is said to have been
martyred by the Arians.

Germanus (St) M.   Oct 23
See Servandus and Germanus.

Germanus of Capua (St)
Bp.   Oct 30
d. *c* 545   Bishop of Capua, and a great friend
of St Benedict. He seems to have been sent to
Constantinople as papal legate to heal the
Acacian schism and to have met with ill-
treatment at the hands of the schismatics. St
Benedict saw his soul being carried to heaven.

Germanus of Montfort
(St) Mk. OSB.   Nov 1
c 906–1000   Born at Montfort, he studied at
Paris and was ordained. Afterwards he entered
the abbey of Savigny and was made prior of
Talloires. He ended his life as a recluse. His

relics were enshrined by St Francis of Sales in 1621.

Germanus, Theophilus, Caesarius and Vitalis
(SS) MM.   Nov 3
d. 250   Martyrs of Caesarea in Cappadocia under Decius.

Germanus (St) M.   Nov 13
See Antoninus, Zebinas, etc.

Germerius (St) Bp.   May 16
d. ? 560   Bishop of Toulouse for fifty years. His cult is very ancient.

Germoc (St) C.   June 24
6th cent.   An Irish chieftain, brother of St Breaca, who settled in Cornwall, near Mount's Bay.

Gerold (St) H.   Apr 19
d. 978   A member of the Rhetian family of the counts of Saxony. He bestowed his lands upon the abbey of Einsiedeln where his two sons, Cuno and Ulric, were monks, and retired to a village near Mitternach. Here he lived as a hermit, under the obedience of the abbot of Einsiedeln.

Gerold (St) Bp. OSB.   June 14
d. 806   One of Charlemagne's courtiers who became a monk of Fontenelle and in 787 was made bishop of Evreux. At a later period he resigned and returned to Fontenelle, where he died.

Gerold (Bl) M.   Oct 7
13th cent.   A pilgrim from Cologne killed by robbers near Cremona and honoured as a martyr at both places.

Gerontius (St) M.   Jan 19
See Paul, Gerontius, etc.

Gerontius (St) Bp. M.   May 9
c 501   A bishop of Cervia, near Ravenna, who was murdered at Cagli on the Flaminian Way, under circumstances which led to his being honoured as a martyr.

Gerontius (Geraint) (St)
King M.   Aug 10
d. ? 508   Son of Erbin and king of Damnonia (Devon). He fell in battle against the Saxons. He and his wife Enid have been the subject of much romantic legend. Another St Gerontius, king of Cornwall, died in 596. St Gerrans in Cornwall and St Géran in Brittany have one or the other of these for patron saint. Nothing is known for sure about either.

Gertrude van Oosten (Bl)
V.   Jan 6
d. 1358   Gertrude began life as a servant girl at Delft in Holland. Having been jilted by her lover she entered the *béguinage* in her native town. In her new life she rapidly advanced in the way of perfection and was rewarded with the stigmata. "Van Oosten" is said to be a nickname she earned by her frequent repetition of the hymn "*Het daghet in den Oosten*". "The day breaks in the East".

Gertrude of Nivelles (St)
Abs. OSB.   March 17
626–659   Younger daughter of Pepin of Landen and of Bl Ida. Ida founded the nunnery of Nivelles for herself and her daughter, but insisted on Gertrude being the first abbess. Though then only twenty years of age, Gertrude performed her duties admirably. At the age of thirty she resigned in favour of her niece Wilfetrudis. She befriended the Irish saints SS Foillan and Ultan.

Gertrude of Altenberg
(Bl) Abs. O. Praem.   Aug 13
1227–1297   Daughter of Louis IV, landgrave of Thuringia and of St Elizabeth of Hungary. She was educated and became a nun at the nunnery of Altenberg. She was chosen abbess very young and ruled the house for half a century. Cult authorized by Clement VI.

Gertrude of Remiremont
(St) Abs. OSB.   Nov 7
d. c 690   Sister of St Adolphus and granddaughter of St Romaricus. She was educated at the nunnery of Saint-Mont, near Remiremont, where she took the veil and was abbess after her aunt, St Clare (c 654). Cult authorized by St Leo IX (1051).

Gertrude the Great (St)
N. OSB.   GC. Nov 16
c 1256–1302   She was born at Eisleben in Germany, and as a child of five years old was offered to God at Hefta in Saxony, a Black Benedictine nunnery which in its early days had for political reasons been fictitiously designated Cistercian. Gertrude had her first mystical experience in 1281, and from that year her life was a continuous familiar communing with Christ, especially during the Divine Office. Her mystical writings did much to spread the once popular devotion to the Sacred Heart. Her feast was extended to the whole church in 1677. St Teresa of Avila had a great devotion to her. St Gertrude is patroness of the West Indies. She is depicted clad as an

abbess holding a flaming heart: a mouse or mice may accompany her.

Gertrude the Elder (St)
W. OSB.   Dec 6
d. 649 A widow, who founded and was the first abbess of the nunnery of Hamaye (Hamay, Hamage) near Douai.

Gerulph (St) M.   Sept 21
d. c 746 A Flemish youth, heir to a vast estate, who was treacherously murdered by a relative who hoped to succeed to his inheritance. At the time of his death Gerulph was returning home after having received confirmation. He died with words of pardon on his lips.

Geruntius of Milan (St)
Bp.   May 5
d. c 470 Successor of St Eusebius in the see of Milan (c 465–470).

Geruntius of Italica (St)
Bp. M.   Aug 25
d. c 100 A missionary in Spain in the apostolic age, said to have been bishop of Talco (Italica, near Seville) and a martyr. A special hymn in the old Mozarabic breviary commemorates him.

Gervadius (Gernard, Garnet) (St) C.   Nov 8
10th cent. An Irish saint, who crossed over to Moray and afterwards became a recluse near Elgin.

Gervase and Protase
(SS) MM.   June 19
? 2nd cent. In 386, during the episcopate of St Ambrose, there were discovered at Milan the relics of SS Gervase and Protase, whom the saintly bishop styled the protomartyrs of the city. Even then next to nothing was remembered about them, except their names and the fact of their martyrdom in one of the early persecutions. Their supposed *Acta* have no historical value. Cults confined to local calendars since 1969.

Gervinus (St) Ab. OSB.   March 3
d. 1075 Born near Reims and educated at the episcopal school, Gervinus became a canon of that city. Subsequently he entered the Benedictine abbey of St Vannes at Verdun, and became abbot of Saint-Riquier. He enjoyed the friendship of St Edward the Confessor. He is described as great in his love of the Divine Office, great in preaching, and great in collecting Greek and Latin MSS.

This last was, after the service of God, the great passion of his life.

Gervinus (Bl) Ab. OSB.   Apr 17
d. 1117 A monk of Saint-Winnoc, and then a hermit at Munster in Aldenburg. He was finally chosen abbot (1095) of Aldenburg (Oudenburg) in Flanders.

Gery (St) Bp.   Aug 11
Otherwise Gaugericus, q.v.

Getulius, Caerealis, Amantius and Primitivus
(SS) MM.   June 10
d. c 120 Getulius, a Roman, is said to have been the husband of St Symphorosa. He and his brother Amantius, and the two officers sent to capture him and converted by him, were clubbed to death at Tivoli under Hadrian.

Gezelin (Ghislain, Gisle, Joscelin) (St) H.   Aug 6
? A hermit honoured at Slebusrode near Cologne.

Gherardino (Manettus) Sostegni (St)   Feb 12
See Seven Holy Founders.

Gibardus (St) Ab. OSB. M.   Apr 7
d. c 888 Abbot of Luxeuil at the time of the invasion of the Huns. He and his monks fled from the abbey, but the barbarians found them and put them to death.

Gibitrudis (St) N. OSB.   Oct 26
d. c 655 A nun at Faremoutiers-en-Brie under St Fara.

Gibrian (St) C.   May 8
d. ? c 515 An Irish hermit, the eldest of five brothers and three sisters, all alleged to have migrated to Brittany and to have become saints there. Their names are given as Tressan, Helan, Germanus, Abran (or Gibrian), Petran, Franca, Promptia and Possenna.

Gideon (St)   Sept 1
11th cent. B.C. The Judge of Israel (Judges 6,7), commemorated with Joshua by the Greek and Latin churches on Sept 1. The Copts keep his feast on Dec 16; the Armenians on the second Saturday of August.

Gilbert of Sempringham
(St) C. Founder.   Feb 4
1083–1189 A native of Sempringham in Lincolnshire, who became parish priest of that village in 1123. A group of seven ladies of his parish wishing to live in community, he drew

for them a set of rules. This developed into the Gilbertine order, which came to comprise monks under the Augustinian rule as well as nuns under that of St Benedict. He was their first master-general until he became blind. The order, unique in being founded by an Englishman, counted twenty-two houses in England at the time of the Reformation. Canonized in 1202.

Gilbert (St) Bp.   Apr 1
d. 1245   For twenty years bishop of Caithness, of which diocese he built the cathedral. He was a valued servant of the Scottish kings and a zealous upholder of Scottish independence against the archbishop of York.

Gilbert (Bl) Ab. O. Praem.   June 6
d. 1152   The abbot-founder of the Premonstratensian monastery of Neuffons (Neufontaines).

Gilbert (Bl) Ab. OSB.   Aug 21
d. 1185   A monk at Saint-Crespin-en-Chaie, Soissons, and then the second abbot of the monastery of St John the Baptist at Valenciennes. He suffered persecution at the hands of the Count of Hainault.

Gilbert of Hexham (St)
Bp.   Sept 7
Otherwise Tilbert, q.v.

Gilbert (Bl) Ab. OSB. Cist.   Oct 17
d. 1167   An Englishman by birth who became a Cistercian, probably at Ourscamp, of which he was made abbot in 1147. In 1163 he was elected abbot of Cîteaux. The Cistercian writers surname him "the Great", or "the Theologian".

Gildard (Godard) (St)
Bp.   June 8
d. c 514   Bishop of Rouen for about fifteen years. The pre-1970 RM. unfortunately re-echoes a later fable, according to which Gildard was a brother of St Medard of Soissons "born on the same day, ordained bishops on the same day, and on the same day withdrawn from his life". In fact Gildard had been dead at least five years when St Medard was ordained.

Gildas the Wise (St) Bp.   Jan 29
d. c 570   Often called Badonicus, because born in the year the Britons defeated the Saxons at Bath. He was trained by St Illtyd and towards the end of his life, crossing over to Brittany, he lived as a hermit on the island of Rhuys. St Gildas is famous for a Latin work on the miseries of his fatherland, *De excidiis*

Britanniae. It was very influential in the early Middle Ages, and by its quotations and references reveals something of the classical and early Christian literature available in England at this period.

Gilduin (St)   Jan 27
1052–1077   A devout and very young canon of Dol, in Brittany. He was elected bishop, but humbly declined the post, arguing his case before Gregory VII, who accepted his decision. He died whilst travelling home from Rome. His tomb was the source of many miracles.

Giles (*several*)
Note. Giles is the English form of the Latin name Aegidius. It was a very common name in the Middle Ages. The other Western European variants are as follows: Italian, Egidio; French, Gilles; Spanish and Portuguese, Gil.

Giles of Lorenzana (Bl)
C. OFM.   Jan 28
c 1443–1518   A native of Lorenzana, in the kingdom of Naples, who began life as a farmhand. Later he became a Franciscan lay-brother and was allowed to live as a hermit in the garden of the friary. He is famous for his love of animals. Cult approved in 1880.

Giles Mary of St Joseph
(Bl) C. OFM.   Feb 7
d. 1812   Born at Taranto in S. Italy, and a rope-maker by trade. He joined the Alcantarine Franciscans at Naples. He spent the rest of his life as porter of the Neapolitan friary. Beatified in 1888.

Giles of Assisi (Bl) C. OFM.   Apr 23
d. 1262   The third follower of St Francis of Assisi and one of the most delightful figures of the *Fioretti*. He went to preach to the Muslims in Tunis, but his mission was a failure. The rest of his life he spent in Italy, being eagerly consulted by all sorts of people on spiritual matters. He died at Perugia.

Giles of Saumur (Bl) Bp.   Apr 23
d. 1266   Chaplain to St Louis, king of France, with whom he went on a crusade. In 1243 he became bishop of Damietta, and in 1245 archbishop of Tyre. He died at Dinant in Belgium.

Giles of Santarem (Bl) C.
OP.   May 14
1185–1265   A native of Vaozela in Portugal who became a medical student and, it is said, practised necromancy. After his conversion he

St Giles, Sept 1

joined the Dominicans at Palencia, resided a long time at Santarem, and was made provincial for Spain.

Giles (St) Ab. OSB.   Sept 1
8th cent. Many legends have been woven round the memory of this saint. Giles was probably a Provençal by birth, and abbot of a monastery on the Rhône, where the city of Saint-Gilles now stands. He became one of the most "popular" saints of the Middle Ages, and his shrine a much frequented place of pilgrimage. Over one hundred and sixty churches were dedicated in his name in

England alone. He is venerated as the patron saint of cripples, beggars, and blacksmiths. Nothing certain is known now about him. His emblem is a hind, which accompanies him; sometimes he is shown with an arrow piercing his breast or leg. Since 1969 his cult has been confined to local calendars.

Giles and Arcanus (SS)
OSB.   Sept 1
d. c 1050 Giles was of Spanish birth and, together with the Italian St Arcanus, founded an abbey under the Benedictine rule to enshrine the relics which they had brought from Palestine. This grew into the present-day Borgo San Sepolcro in central Italy.

Giles of Castañeda (Bl)
Ab. OSB. Cist.   Sept 1
d. c 1203 Cistercian abbot of the monastery of Castañeda in the Asturias. He is now greatly venerated in the diocese of Astorga, in Spain.

Girald (Girard, Giraud)
(St) Ab. OSB.   Dec 29
d. 1031 A Benedictine monk at Lagny and afterwards abbot of Saint-Arnoul. Richard IV, duke of Normandy, enlisted his services as abbot of Fontenelle, where he was murdered by an unruly monk.

Gisella (Gizella, Gisele)
(Bl) W.   May 7
d. c 1095 First Queen of Hungary, wife of St Stephen, sister of St Henry, emperor of Germany. After a saintly life of good works she retired to the convent at Passau, where she died and is buried.

Gislar (St) C.   Sept 24
See Chrenrald and Ghislar.

Gislenus (Ghislain,
Guislain) (St) Ab. OSB.   Oct 9
d. c 680 A Frankish recluse living in a forest at Hainault, whither he was followed by numerous disciples. He built for them the abbey of SS Peter and Paul, now Saint-Ghislain near Mons, which he governed for thirty years.

Gistilian (Gistlian) (St)
C.   March 2
5th–6th cent. The uncle of St David and a monk of Menevia, or St Davids.

Gladys (St) W.   March 29
5th cent. A Welsh saint, daughter of Brychan of Brecknock. She became the wife of St Gundleus and mother of St Cadoc.

Glaphyra (St) V.   Jan 13
d. *c* 324   A female slave in the service of
Constantia, wife of the emperor Licinius. In
order to safeguard her chastity she fled to St
Basil, bishop of Amasea in Pontus. She was
recaptured and condemned to death. She died
on the way to martyrdom.

Glastian (St) Bp.   Jan 28
d. 830   The patron saint of Kinglassie in
Fife. As mediator between the Picts and Scots,
he did much to alleviate the lot of the former
when subjugated by their foes.

Gleb (St)   July 24
See Boris and Gleb.

Glodesind (St) Abs. OSB.
Otherwise Clotsindis, q.v.

Glodesind (St) Abs.   July 25
d. *c* 608   Betrothed to a courtier who was
arrested on their wedding day and afterwards
executed. She took the veil in a nunnery at
Metz, of which she became abbess.

Glunshallaich (St) C.   June 3
7th cent.   An Irish penitent, converted by St
Kevin and buried in the same grave with him at
Glendalough.

Gluvias (Glywys) (St) C.   May 3
6th cent.   Brother of St Cadoc of Llancarfan,
and possibly sent by him into Cornwall, where
he made a monastic foundation. A parish in
Cornwall perpetuates his name.

Glyceria (St) VM.   May 13
d. *c* 177   A Roman maiden, living with her
father at Trajanopolis in Greece, who was
martyred at Heraclea in the Propontis.

Glycerius (St) Bp.   Sept 20
d. *c* 438   Archbishop of Milan.

Glycerius (St) M.   Dec 21
d. 303   A priest of Nicomedia in Asia Minor,
burnt at the stake under Diocletian.

Glywys (St) C.   May 2
Otherwise Gluvias, q.v.

Goar (St) C.   July 6
d. *c* 575   A secular priest of Aquitaine, who
led the life of a hermit near Oberwesel on the
Rhine. His extant life is most untrustworthy.
Charlemagne built a stately church over St
Goar's hermitage.

Goban Gobhnena (St) C.   May 23
6th or 7th cent.   Supposed to be the Goban
mentioned in the life of St Laserian as governing the monastery of Old-Leighlin, from
which he migrated to Tascaffin, in the present
Co. Limerick.

Goban (Gobain) M. OSB.   June 20
d. *c* 670   An Irishman by birth, and a disciple
of his countryman, St Fursey, under whom he
became a monk at Burgh-Castle in Suffolk.
He followed his abbot to France and both took
to the solitary life in the great forest near the
Oise. He was murdered by barbarian marauders at the place now called Saint-Gobain.

Gobert (Bl) Mk. OSB.   Aug 20
d. 1263   Count of Apremont. After fighting
as a crusader in Palestine he became a Cistercian at Villers in Brabant.

Gobnata (Gobnet) (St) V.   Feb 11
? 6th cent.   St Abban is said to have founded
a convent in Ballyvourney, Co. Cork, and to
have placed St Gobnet over it as abbess. A well
(called after her) still exists there.

Gobrain (St) Bp.   Nov 16
d. 725   A Breton monk who became bishop
of Vannes, and at the age of eighty-seven
resigned his see to retire to a hermit's cell,
where he died.

Godard (St) Bp. OSB.   May 4
Otherwise Godehard, q.v.

Godard (St) Bp.   June 8
Otherwise Gildard, q.v.

Godebertha (St) Abs.   Apr 11
d. *c* 700   Born in the diocese of Amiens. In
657 she received the veil from St Eligius,
bishop of Noyon, who also composed a rule for
her nunnery there. She was the first abbess.

**Godehard (Godard,
Gothard) (St) Bp. OSB.**   May 4
d. 1038   A Bavarian, whose father was
employed in the service of the canons of
Niederaltaich. Godehard joined them and
became their provost. He was instrumental in
reintroducing the Benedictine rule at
Niederaltaich and was commissioned by the
emperor St Henry to revive the Benedictine
observance in several German dioceses.
Tegernsee, Hersfeld and Kremsmünster
received abbots from Niederaltaich. In 1022
the saint was made bishop of Hildesheim and
did much to foster religion and culture.
Canonized in 1131.

**Godeleva (Godliva) (St)
M.**   July 6
d. 1070   Married very young to Bertulf of
Ghistelles, who after ill-treating her for two
years had her strangled. She has been venerated as a martyr ever since.

Godfrey (*several*)
Note. This name in Latin, Godefridus, is

variously spelt in English: Godefrid, Geoffrey, Gotfrid, Goffry, etc. In other languages the spelling is: Gottfried, Geoffroy, Gioffredo, Gaufrid, Geofroi, Goffredo, Gofrido, etc.

Godfrey of Cappenberg
(Bl) C. O. Praem.   Jan 13
1097–1127   Born at Cappenberg Castle in Westphalia where, besides being a count, he owned large estates. He made the acquaintance of St Norbert and in the teeth of violent opposition from his relatives made over his lands to the holy founder; turned his castle into a Premonstratensian abbey; and himself joined the order with his brother, while his wife and two sisters took the veil in a nunnery which he founded for them. He died at the age of thirty.

Godfrey of Duynen
and Godfrey of Merville
(SS) MM.   July 9
d. 1572   The former was a secular priest and at one time rector of a school in Paris; the latter was custos of the Franciscan house at Gorkum, Holland, and a painter. Both were hanged with others by the Calvinists at Briel. The group is known as the martyrs of Gorkum. See Gorkum.

Godfrey of Loudun (Bl)
Bp.   Aug 3
d. 1255   Bishop of Mans from 1234, he was a man of intense activity, and he took a full part in the ecclesiastical affairs of the time. He founded the Charterhouse of Parc d'Orgues, where he was buried. He died at Anagni on a visit to the pope.

Godfrey (St) Bp. OSB.   Nov 8
c 1066–1115   Born in the province of Soissons and placed at the age of five at the abbey of Mont-Saint-Quentin, where in due course he was professed and ordained. In 1096 he was elected abbot of Nogent-sous-Coucy in Champagne and in 1104 bishop of Amiens. He was rigidly austere, both with himself and with others. In spite of this, when he wished to resign and become a Carthusian his people would not allow it. He was a lifelong opponent of simony and incontinency.

Godo (Gaon) (St) Ab.
OSB.   July 24
d. c 690   A native of Verdun and a nephew of St Wandrille, under whom he was professed at Fontenelle. Afterwards he was the abbot-founder of Oye Abbey, near Sezanne-en-Brie.

Godric (St) H. OSB.   May 21
1069–1170   A native of Walpole in Norfolk who, after years of adventurous seafaring and of many pilgrimages, became a hermit at Finchale in Co. Durham under the obedience of the prior of Durham. There he lived for sixty years, remarkable for his austerities, his supernatural gifts and also for his familiarity with wild animals. His remarkable and fascinating life was recorded by Reginald of Durham. Some of Godric's poems survive.

Godwin (St) Ab. OSB.   Oct 28
d. c 690   Abbot of the great Belgian monastery of Stavelot-Malmédy.

Goeric (St) Bp.   Sept 19
d. 647   Also called Abbo. The successor of St Arnulf in the bishopric of Metz.

Goeznoveus (St) Bp.   Oct 25
d. 675   A Cornish saint, brother of St Maughan, who crossed into Brittany and became bishop of Léon.

Gorfor (St) C.   May 9
?   A Welsh saint, patron of Llanover in Gwent.

Gohardus (St) Bp. M.   June 25
d. 843   Bishop of Nantes, slain by raiding Normans while celebrating Mass; many monks and priests were killed with him.

Gollen (Collen, Colan)
(St) C.   May 21
?   7th cent.   A saint who has given his name to Llangollen in Clwyd. His name is connected in legend with Wales, Glastonbury and Rome.

Golvinus (Golwen) (St)
Bp.   July 9
?   7th cent.   A Breton saint, but of British origin, whose fame for sancity led to his being appointed to the see of St Pol-de-Léon. He died at Rennes where his relics are still enshrined.

Gomer (St)   Oct 11
Otherwise Gummarus, q.v.

Gomidas (Bl) M.   Nov 5
c 1656–1707   Gomidas Keumurjian, an Armenian by descent, was born at Constantinople, married at the age of twenty and was ordained a priest of the Armenian church. In 1696, he and his family made their submission to Rome. This angered the Armenians, who approached the Turkish authorities and unjustly accused Gomidas of being an agent of hostile Western powers. As a result, he was beheaded at Parmark-Kapu, on the outskirts of Constantinople. Beatified in 1929.

Goneri (St) C.   July 18
6th cent.   An exile from Britain to Brittany, where he led an eremitical life near Tréguier.

**Gonsalvo of Amaranthe
(Bl) C.** Jan 16
Otherwise Gundisalvus, q.v.

Gontram (St) King March 28
Otherwise Gunthamnus, q.v.

Gonzaga Gonza (St) M. June 3
d. 1886 Having spent a long time in prison,
he was put to death by King Mwanga of
Uganda. See Charles Lwanga and Comps.

Good Thief, The (St) March 25
1st cent. The repentant thief, to whom the
dying Saviour promised paradise. The name
of Dismas has been given him by tradition, and
a number of legends have grown up around his
name; but except for the episode recorded in
the gospel, nothing is known about him.

Goran (Woranus) (St) C. Apr 7
6th cent. Several Cornish churches are
dedicated in his honour. He lived at Bodmin
before St Petroc.

Gorazd (St) C. July 17
See Seven Apostles of Bulgaria.

**Gordian an Epimachus
(SS) MM.** May 10
d. 250 and 362 Epimachus was martyred at
Alexandria under Decius, and his relics were
taken to Rome. Gordian suffered at a later
date, very probably under Julian the Apostate,
and was buried in the same tomb. Their *Acta*
are not trustworthy. Cult confined to local
calendars since 1969.

Gordian (St) M. Sept 17
See Valerian, Macrinus and Gordian.

Gordius (St) M. Jan 3
d. 304 A soldier of Caesarea in Cappadocia,
dismissed from the army on acount of his
religion. He retired to the desert, but during
the persecution under Diocletian gave himself
up and was beheaded.

Gorgonia (St) Dec 9
d. *c* 375 Daughter of St Gregory Nazianzen
senior and of St Nonna, and sister of St
Gregory Nazianzen junior, the great Greek
theologian. She married and was a model
Christian matron.

**Gorgonius and Firmus
(or Firminus) (SS) MM.** March 11
3rd cent. Martyrs, either of Nicaea in Bithynia, or of Antioch in Syria.

Gorgonius (St) M. Sept 9
See Dorotheus and Gorgonius.

**Gorkum (Martyrs of)
(SS)** July 9
d. 1572 A group of nineteen martyrs — ten

Franciscans, two Premonstratensians, a Dominican, a canon regular, four secular priests
and a layman — put to death with unspeakable
cruelty by the Calvinists at Gorkum, near
Dordrecht in Holland. Each receives a separate notice in this book. Canonized in 1867.

Gorman (St) Bp. OSB. Aug 28
d. 965 A Benedictine of Reichenau, who
went to preach the gospel in the North and
became bishop of Schleswig in Denmark.

Gormcal (St) Ab. Aug 5
d. 1016 An Irish abbot of the monastery of
Ardoilen in Galway.

Gosbert (St) Bp. OSB. Feb 13
d. *c* 859 The fourth bishop of Osnabruck
and a disciple of St Ansgar. His was a
particularly laborious episcopate.

**Goscelinus (Goslin,
Gozzelinus) (St) Ab.
OSB.** Feb 12
d. 1153 Second abbot of San Solutore, near
Turin (1147–1153). The solemn translation
of his relics took place in 1472.

Goswin (St) Ab. OSB. Oct 9
d. 1165 A native of Douai and a student at
Paris, he first taught theology in his native city
where he held a canonry; then he professed
the Benedictine rule at Anchin (1113), where
he eventually became abbot (*c* 1130): one of
the greatest abbots of that great abbey.

Goswin (Bl) OSB. Cist. Oct 27
d. 1203 A Cistercian monk, first at Clairvaux and then at Chemnion.

Gothard (St) Bp. May 4
Otherwise Godehard, q.v.

Gotteschalk (St) M. June 7
d. 1066 A Wendish prince who renounced
Christianity because his father had been murdered by Christian Saxons. As the husband of
Canute's grandniece he came to England and
returned to the faith, which he henceforth
fostered with great zeal. He was murdered at
Lenzen by assassins in the service of his
brother-in-law. Many doubt whether he has a
true claim to the title of either saint or martyr.

**Govan (Goven, Cofen)
(St)** June 20
6th cent. A hermit who lived halfway down a
cliff at St Govan's Head, Dyfed, where his
stone hut can still be seen. It is a very
remarkable place, full of interest. He is probably buried under the altar in the hut, which
later became a small chapel. It still attracts

many visitors. Govan was probably a disciple of St Ailbe.

Grace and Probus (SS)   July 5
See Probus and Grace.

Gracia (St) M. OSB. Cist.   June 1
See Bernard, Mary, etc.

Gracilian and Felicissima (SS) MM.   Aug 12
d. c 304   According to the legend, which is untrustworthy, Gracilian, a Christian of Faleria, while in prison awaiting martyrdom, restored the sight of a blind girl and converted her to Christ. They were beheaded on the same day.

Graecina (St) VM.   June 16
See Actinea and Graecina.

Grata (St) W.   May 1
4th (or 8th) cent.   A holy woman of Bergamo, zealous in securing Christian burial for the bodies of the martyrs. The evidence regarding her life is very conflicting.

Gratia of Cattaro (Bl) C. OSA.   Nov 16
1438–1509   A native of Cattaro in Dalmatia. For thirty years he was a fisherman in the Adriatic and then professed the Augustinian rule as a lay-brother. He was famous for the gift of infused knowledge. Cult approved in 1889.

Gratian (St) Bp.   Dec 18
Otherwise Gatian, q.v.

Gratinian (Gratian) (St) M.   June 1
See Felinus and Gratian.

Gratus (St) Bp.   Sept 7
d. c 470   Bishop of Aosta. He is now its patron saint.

Gratus (St) Bp.   Oct 8
d. c 652   A French bishop of Châlons-sur-Saône.

Gratus (St) Bp.   Oct 11
d. c 506   The first bishop of the ancient see, long suppressed, of Oloron, in S. France.

Gratus (St) M.   Dec 5
See Julius, Potamia, etc.

Gredifael (St) C.   Nov 13
7th cent.   A Breton or Welsh saint who accompanied St Paternus from Brittany to Wales. He is said to have been abbot of Whitland in Dyfed.

Gregory Nazianzen the Elder (St) Bp. C.   Jan 1
c 276–374   A native of Nazianzos in Cappa-docia, Asia Minor. A state functionary and a pagan, he was converted (325) by his wife, St Nonna. They had three children — all saints: Gregory Nazianzen, junior, the great Father of the church, Caesarius and Gorgonia. Gregory senior became bishop of his native city (c 328) and attached himself to some heretical sect, but was converted to orthodoxy (361) by his more gifted son, Gregory junior, who, in 372, became his coadjutor. He died when nearly one hundred years of age.

Gregory Nazianzen (St) Bp. Dr.   GC. Jan 2
329–389   A native of Arianzos in Cappadocia and eldest son of St Gregory Nazianzen the Elder (q.v.). He read law for ten years at Athens and then joined his friend St Basil in his monastic solitude in Pontus. In 361 he was ordained priest, and in 372 ordained bishop of the small township of Sasima. This see he refused to accept, acting instead as coadjutor to his father at Nazianzos until, in 380, he was prevailed to accept the see of Constantinople. He was there only one month, after which he resigned and retired to Arianzos where he died in 390. The tragedy of his life was his ordination as a bishop, since his character was not fitted for a life of action. On the other hand, as a writer he stands far above most other Greek Doctors. In fact, he is surnamed by the Greeks "the Divine" — *o Theologos*. He is venerated in East and West as a Doctor of the Church. His feast was formerly on May 9. Since 1969 it has been celebrated with that of St Basil on January 2.

Gregory of Langres (St) Bp.   Jan 4
d. 539   A leading citizen (*comes*) of the district round Autun and a firm and severe civil governor of the city. Later in life he lost his wife, was ordained priest and became bishop of Langres and, as such, gained a reputation for gentleness and understanding. He was the father of St Tetricus (q.v.), and great-uncle of St Gregory of Tours.

Gregory X (Bl) Pope   Jan 9
1210–1276   Theobald Visconti was a native of Piacenza in Italy who became archdeacon of Liége, in Belgium. While holding this office he was entrusted with the preaching of the last crusade. He accompanied the crusaders to Palestine, and he was still there when elected pope in 1271. He was not then a priest. The outstanding event of his pontificate was the holding of the council of Lyons, at which the Eastern orthodox became reconciled, unhappily for only a short time, to the Catholic

church. Beatified 1713. His name was inserted in the pre-1970 RM. by Benedict XIV and his feast was, until 1963, on January 10.

Gregory II (St) Pope — Feb 11
669–731 Roman born and educated at the Lateran, he held the offices of librarian and archivist of the Roman church, when he was elected pope in 715. He devoted much of his time to the affairs of the Eastern church, and his pontificate is also famous for the spreading of the gospel among the Teuton races, to whom he sent as missionaries St Boniface and St Corbinian. He fostered Benedictine life everywhere and restored several Italian abbeys, notably Montecassino. An old tradition makes him in fact a Benedictine monk, and his office figured for centuries in several Benedictine *Propria*. He opposed Iconoclasm and checked the advancing Lombards. King Ine of Wessex became a monk in Rome in his pontificate. Some record his feast day as February 13.

Gregory of Tragurio (Bl)
OFM — Feb 12
See Antony of Saxony.

Gregory of Nyssa (St) Bp. — March 9
d. *c* 395 A younger brother of St Basil the Great. After his marriage he practised as a professor of rhetoric but abandoned this profession for the priesthood. In 372 his brother Basil nominated him bishop of Nyssa, a small township in Lower Armenia. It was a somewhat unfortunate choice as Gregory was not a man of affairs, and the Arians were predominant in the diocese. After a period of exclusion from his diocese he regained it in 378 and after his brother's death he was the mainstay of orthodoxy throughout Cappadocia. His writings are remarkable for depth of thought and lucidity of expression. Of the three "great Cappadocians" — Basil, Gregory Nazianzen, Gregory of Nyssa — he is the least prolific but the most profound.

Gregory Makar (St) Bp. — March 16
d. *c* 1000 He is described as an Armenian who became a monk and was elected bishop of Nicopolis in Armenia. He is said to have fled to France and settled as a hermit at Pithiviers in the diocese of Orleans.

Gregory of Elvira (St) Bp. — Apr 24
d. *c* 394 Bishop of Elvira, in S. Spain — a see which has since been translated to Granada. He was one of the champions of the faith against Arianism, and one of the few bishops who at Rimini (359) consistently refused to compromise with the heretics. In all good faith he sided with the party of Lucifer of Cagliari, but never left the communion of the Roman see.

Gregory of Besians (Bl)
COP. — Apr 26
See Dominic and Gregory.

Gregory Celli of Verucchio
(Bl) C. OSA. — May 4
d. 1343 A native of Verucchio, in the diocese of Rimini. His mother founded a monastery for the Augustinians in his native town, and Gregory took the habit there. After a time he was dismissed for some unjust reason, but was charitably received by the Franciscans of Monte Carnerio, near Rieti, where he died. Cult confirmed in 1769.

Gregory of Ostia (St) Bp.
OSB. — May 9
d. *c* 1044 A Benedictine cardinal, bishop of Ostia, who exercised legatine powers in the old kingdoms of Spanish Navarre and Old Castile. He died at Logroño. He is still greatly venerated throughout Navarre and Rioja. His life, however, as handed down to us, is full of conflicting statements.

Gregory VII (St) Pope, OSB. — May 25
c 1021–1085 A native of Soana, in Tuscany. His baptismal name was Hildebrand. He was sent very young to Rome, where his uncle was superior of the Cluniac abbey of St Mary on the Aventine, and there Hildebrand professed the Benedictine rule. He accompanied the deposed Pope Gregory VI to Germany, but returned to Rome with St Leo IX and became abbot of St Paul-outside-the-Walls (1059). From this date begins his close association with the popes, five of whom he served as archdeacon. In 1073 he himself was elected pope and continued his life-long struggle against lay investiture, simony and clerical concubinage. He succeeded in imposing his will on his persistent and childishly cunning enemy, the emperor Henry IV of Germany, but nevertheless a few years later he was driven into exile at Salerno, where he died. Few men have been so admired by their friends and reviled by their foes. Canonized in 1606.

Gregory Barbarigo
(Barbardico) (St) Bp. — June 17
1625–1697 Venetian-born, he was first bishop of Bergamo and then of Padua, and was created cardinal in 1660. He was equally distinguished both as a churchman and a statesman. His charities were on a princely scale and his benefactions to Padua numerous

and lasting. He was an earnest worker for the reconciliation of the churches of East and West. Canonized 1960. Cult confined to local calendars since 1969.

Gregory, Demetrius and Calogerus (SS) CC.   June 18
d. 5th cent. Rspectively a bishop, an archdeacon and an abbot in N. Africa, whence they were driven by Arian Vandals. They settled down at Fragalata, near Messina, in Sicily, and preached the gospel there. They are now honoured as the patron saints of Fragalata.

Gregory Escrivano (Bl) M. SJ.   July 15
d. 1570   Born at Logroño, in Old Castile, he was a Jesuit coadjutor and a companion of Bl Ignatius de Azevedo q.v.

Gregory Lopez (Bl) H.   July 20
1542–1596   A native of Madrid, where he served as page to Philip II. In 1562 he migrated to Mexico and lived as a hermit among the Indians near Zacatecas and later near the capital. His cult spread all over Mexico, but the process of his beatification, begun in 1752, still continues.

Gregory of Nonantula (Bl) Ab. OSB.   Aug 3
d. 933   A Benedictine abbot of the great Italian abbey of Nonantula, near Modena.

Gregory of Utrecht (St) Ab. OSB.   Aug 25
c 703–776   A native of Trier. When a child he met St Boniface, under whom he became a monk. The old apostle loved him as a son and made him abbot of St Martin's at Utrecht. Without relinquishing his office of abbot, St Gregory administered the diocese as well for twenty-two years. During his abbacy St Martin's became a great missionary centre and a nursery of saints.

Gregory the Great (St) Pope, Dr.   GC. Sept 3
c 540–604   Born in Rome of patrician parents, he became the prefect — *praetor* mayor — of the city. He soon resigned the office, turned his ancestral home on the Caelian Hill into a monastery and became a monk there. Next he was sent to Constantinople as *apocrisarius* — papal nuncio. On his return he was chosen pope (590), and what he achieved in his fourteen years' pontificate makes him one of the most commanding figures in world history. First in importance was his mission to England, whither he sent St Augustine and some

St Gregory the Great, Sept 3

forty of his monks from the Caelian Hill; this was important not only on account of the conversion of England itself, but also because of the spreading of the Benedictine rule among the new races of W. Europe. He promoted likewise the conversion of the Lombards in Italy and of the Goths in Spain; upheld the rights of the Roman see against Constantinople; embellished the liturgy in its sacramentary and in its chant; defended and befriended monachism; and cared for the poor in Rome, at Ravenna and on his estates in Sicily. He was moreover a prolific writer; his dialogues, comprising the only extant life of St Benedict, and his *Regula Pastoralis* are classics in ascetical literature. Indeed, the *Regula Pastoralis* was translated into English by King Alfred himself. He is depicted as vested as a pope and carrying a double barred cross. A dove sits on his shoulder, or hovers near his ear. He may be writing or reading; or kneeling before an altar with our Lord and all the emblems of His Passion appearing behind it.

Gregory the Illuminator (St) Bp.   Sept 30
c 240–332   Also surnamed "the apostle of Armenia". Unfortunately his life, as given by tradition, is not well authenticated. The following main facts seem certain: he began to preach to the Armenians and converted their king, Tiridates; he had himself ordained

bishop and set up his see at Ashtishat, whence his apostolate spread far and wide. Armenian legends about St Gregory run to several volumes and are obviously fictitious.

Gregory of Burtscheid
(St) Ab. OSB.   Nov 4
d. 999 A Basilian monk at Cerchiara, in Calabria, who fled from the Saracens and met the emperor Otto III in Rome. The emperor befriended him, invited him to Germany and built for him the abbey of Burtscheid, near Aachen, under the Benedictine rule.

Gregory of Einsiedeln
(St) Ab. OSB.   Nov 8
d. 996 An Anglo-Saxon who, on a pilgrimage to Rome, received the Benedictine cowl on the Caelian Hill. On his way home he stayed at the Swiss abbey of Einsiedeln and joined the community (949). He was elected abbot and his rule coincided with the period of the greatest monastic splendour of the abbey.

Gregory Thaumaturgus
(St) Bp.   Nov 17
c 213–270 A native of Pontus and a disciple of Origen. He was made bishop of Neocaesarea in 240. It is related that on his accession to the see he found just seventeen Christians, and that when he died he left only seventeen pagans. His title of "the Wonder-Worker" explains itself. He is also an ecclesiastical writer. Cult confined to particular calendars since 1969.

Gregory of Tours (St) Bp.   Nov 17
540–594 This saint was born in Auvergne, and was baptized George Florentius, but took the name Gregory when he was made bishop of Tours in 573. He was a great bishop, much revered by St Gregory the Great. He excelled, however, as a historian, and his writings are now the best historical source of the Merovingian period.

Gregory Decapolites (St)
C.   Nov 20
9th cent. So-called from his birthplace in Asia Minor. He opposed the Iconoclasts zealously and suffered much at their hands.

Gregory of Girgenti (St)
Bp.   Nov 23
d. c 638 A Sicilian of the Byzantine rite who, after a protracted sojourn in the Eastern *lauras*, was nominated by St Gregory the Great bishop of Girgenti (*Agrigentum*), his native town. His interesting commentary on the book of Ecclesiastes is still extant.

Gregory III (St) Pope   Dec 10
d. 741 A Syrian who was pope from 731 to 741. His was a very stormy pontificate, troubled in the beginning by the foolish excesses of the Iconoclasts and at the end by the incursions of the Lombards. Gregory sought the aid of Charles Martel against the latter, thus establishing a connection with the Franks which was to prove of historic importance.

Gregory of Terracina (St)
C. OSB.   Dec 12
d. c 570 A disciple of St Benedict and, with his brother St Speciosus, monk at Terracina. St Gregory the Great speaks of him in the Dialogues Bk. II.

Gregory of Auxerre (St)
Bp.   Dec 19
d. c 540 The twelfth bishop of Auxerre. He governed the see for thirteen years and died aged eighty-five.

Gregory of Spoleto (St)
M.   Dec 24
A priest said to have been martyred under Maximinian Herculeus. His *Acta* are not reliable and doubt has been thrown on his very existence.

Grignon de Montfort
(Bl) C.   Aug 19
See Louis Mary Grignon de Montfort.

Grimbald (St) Ab. OSB.   July 8
d. 901 A Benedictine monk and prior of Saint-Bertin. In 885 King Alfred, then on his way to Rome, invited him to England. Grimbald came, but declined the see of Canterbury offered to him by the king. Eventually he was made abbot of the new minster at Winchester. He was a restorer of learning in England.

Grimoaldus (St) C.   Sept 29
d.*p.*1137 Archpriest of Pontecorvo, near Aquino, in S. Italy. Some writers state that he was an Englishman.

Grimonia (Germana)
(St) VM.   Sept 7
4th cent. Said to have been an Irish maiden, martyred in Picardy in defence of her virtue.

Grwst (St) C.   Dec 1
7th cent. The Welsh saint whose memory is perpetuated by the placename Llanrwst, Clwyd.

Guala (Bl) C. OP.   Sept 3
d. 1244 One of the first disciples of St Dominic in Italy and the first Dominican prior

of Brescia and Bologna. In 1228 he was made bishop of Brescia, but resigned in 1242 on account of civil strife and retired to the Vallumbrosans of San Sepolcro d'Astino, where he died. Cult approved in 1866.

Gualfardus (Wolfhard)
(St) H. OSB. Cam.   May 11
d. 1127   A native of Augsburg and a saddler, who plied his trade in Verona, till the people began to look upon him as a saint. Then he retired to live as a monk-hermit in the Camaldolese priory of San Salvatore, near Verona.

Gualterus (several)
Otherwise Walter, q.v.

Guarinus (Guerin) (St)
Bp. OSB. Cist.   Jan 6
1065–1150   Originally a monk of Molesmes, he was made abbot of Aulps, near Geneva. At his request his community was affiliated to Clairvaux. Afterwards he became bishop of Sion in the Valais.

Guarinus (St) Bp. OSA.   Feb 6
d. 1159   A native of Bologna, who joined the Augustinian canons regular. After forty years of religious life he was elected bishop of Pavia, but nothing could induce him to accept the post. However, Lucius II created him cardinal bishop of Palestrina. Canonized by Alexander III.

Guasacht (St) Bp.   Jan 24
4th cent.   Son of Maelchu, the master under whom St Patrick worked as a slave in Ireland. Guasacht was converted by Patrick, whom he helped as bishop of Granard (Longford), in the evangelization of Ireland.

Gudelia (St) M.   Sept 29
d. c 340   A maiden martyred in Persia under Shapur II.

Gudula (Goule) (St) V.   Jan 8
d. 712   Daughter of St Amelberga, she was trained by St Gertrude at Nivelles, and afterwards lived a life of great holiness at home. She is the patroness of Brussels. In art she is often shown with a lantern.

Gudwall (Curval) (St)
Bp.   June 6
6th cent.   A Welsh bishop who founded monasteries in Devon and Cornwall. By many he is supposed to be the Gurval who succeeded St Malo at Aleth in Brittany. His relics are venerated at Ghent.

Guenhael (St) Ab.   Nov 3
d. c 550   Guenhael means "white Angel". He was born in Brittany and educated at Landevenec under St Winwalöe, where in due course he became abbot.

Guenninus (St) Bp.   Aug 19
7th cent.   A bishop of Vannes in Brittany, whose relics are enshrined in the cathedral.

Guerembaldus (St) Mk.
OSB.   Nov 10
d. 965   A Monk of Hirschau, who, through humility, renounced the bishopric of Spire.

Guerricus (Bl) Ab. OSB.
Cist.   Aug 19
?1080–?1155   Born at Tournai, he studied there and became canon and headmaster of the cathedral school. He visited Clairvaux to see St Bernard, and stayed there. In 1138 St Bernard sent him as first abbot of Igny, in the diocese of Reims. He was a prolific ascetical writer; some of his writings indeed have been attributed to St Bernard. Cult approved 1889.

Guesnoveus (Gouernou)
(St) Bp.   Oct 25
d. 675   A bishop of Quimper in Brittany and founder of a monastery near Brest, where he died.

Guethenoc (Gwenthenoc)
(St)   Feb 6
See Jacut and Guethenoc.

Guevrock (Gueroc),
Kerric) (St) Ab.   Feb 17
6th cent.   A Briton who followed St Tadwal to Brittany and succeeded him as abbot of Loc-Kirec. He helped St Paul of Léon in the rule of the diocese.

Guibertus (St) Mk. OSB.   May 23
d. 962   A noble of Lorraine who served with distinction in several campaigns. He then lived the life of a hermit on his own estate of Gembloux, in Brabant, but eventually he turned it into a monastery before retiring to the Benedictine abbey of Gorze. Several times, however, he had to leave the peace of Gorze in order to defend the rights of his foundation at Gembloux. He died at Gorze.

Guido (several)
Otherwise Guy, q.v.

Guier (St) H.   Apr 4
? Priest and hermit in Cornwall, where a church perpetuates his name.

Guilminus (Bl) Mk. OSB.   Nov 18
See Burginus and Guilminus.

Guingar (St) M.   Dec 14
Otherwise Fingar, q.v.

**Guingaloc (Guignole,
Guinvaloeus)**   March 3
Otherwise Winwalöe, q.v.

Guinizo (St) Mk. OSB.   May 26
d. c 1050   A native of Spain who professed
the Benedictine rule at Montecassino, and
remained as a hermit on the holy mountain
after one of the destructions of the abbey.

Guinoc (St) Bp.   Apr 13
d. c 838   A Bishop in Scotland, commemorated in the Aberdeen breviary.

Guislain (St) Ab.   Oct 9
Otherwise Gislenus, q.v.

Guitmarus (St) Ab. OSB.   Dec 10
d. c 765   Fourth abbot of Saint-Riquier
(Centula) in France.

**Gulstan (Gustan, Constans)
(St)** Mk. OSB.   Nov 29
d. c 1010   A Benedictine of the abbey of St
Gildas of Rhuys, in Brittany, under St Felix.

**Gumesindus and
Servusdei (SS)** MM.   Jan 13
d. 852   Two Spanish martyrs, one a
parish-priest, the other a monk, who suffered
at Cordoba under Abderrahman II.

Gummarus (Gomer) (St) H.   Oct 11
c 717–774   A courtier of King Pepin who
married a wife of extravagant and tiresome
disposition. After long and patient endurance
of her perversity he was at last obliged to
separate from her and died a recluse. The
present Flemish town of Lierre (Lier) has
grown up and around his hermitage.

**Gundebert (Gumbert,
Gondelbert) (St)** Bp.
OSB.   Feb 21
d. c 676   A Frankish bishop (of Sens) who
resigned and retired into the Vosges, where he
founded the abbey of Senones (c 660).

Gundebert (St) M.   Apr 20
8th cent.   Tradition describes this saint as a
Frankish courtier who married St Bertha
(q.v.), and was the brother of St Nivard. He
separated from his wife, became a monk,
crossed over to Ireland and was killed there by
heathen marauders.

Gundechar (Bl) Bp.   Aug 2
1019–1073   Bishop of Eichstätt. The Pontifical which he drew is still preserved and is of

great historical interest. He had been chaplain
to Empress Agnes.

**Gundekar (Kundekar)
(St)** M. OSB.   June 5
See Waccar, Gundekar, etc.

**Gundelindis
(Guendelindis)** V. OSB.   March 28
d. c 750   A daughter of the duke of Alsace
and a niece of St Ottilia, whom she succeeded
as abbess in the nunnery of Niedermünster.

Gundenis (St) VM.   July 18
d. 203   A maiden martyred at Carthage,
under Septimius Severus.

Gundisalvus (Bl) C. OP.   Jan 16
1187–1259   A native of Vizella in the diocese
of Braga, in Portugal. After his ordination to
the priesthood he led the life of a solitary at
Amaranthe and later entered the Dominican
order. Cult approved in 1560.

Gundisalvus Garcia (St)
M. OFM.   Feb 6
1556–1597   Born in the East Indies of Portuguese parents, he first served the Jesuits as a
catechist, then opened a flourishing business
in Japan and finally (1591) joined the Franciscans at Manila as a lay-brother. He returned to
Japan as an interpreter to St Peter Baptist, with
whom he was crucified at Nagasaki. Canonized in 1862. See Paul Miki and Comps.

Gundisalvus (Bl) Ab.
OSB. Cist.   June 6
d. 1466   Cistercian abbot of Azebeyro, in
Spanish Galicia.

**Gundisalvus Hendriquez
(Bl)** M. SJ.   July 15
d. 1570   A Portuguese deacon and a Jesuit
scholastic, companion of Bl Ignatius de
Azevedo, q.v.

Gundisalvus Fusai (Bl)
M. SJ.   Sept 10
1582–1622   A Japanese who held a high
office at court but, after baptism, attached
himself to the Jesuit missionaries. He was put
in gaol at Omura, and there received into the
Society of Jesus by Bl Charles Spinola, with
whom he was burnt alive at Nagasaki. Beatified in 1867.

Gundisalvus (St) OSB. Cist.   Oct 10
d. c 1163   First abbot, or prior, of the Cistercian abbey of Las Junias in Portugal, founded
from Osera in 1135.

Gundisalvus of Lagos
(Bl) C. OSA. Oct 21
d. 1422 A native of Lagos in Portugal. He
became an Augustinian, and excelled as a
preacher. Cult approved in 1778.

Gundisalvus (Gonzalo)
(Bl) Mk. OSB. Dec 20
d. c 1073 Monk of the Benedictine abbey of
Silos, in Old Castile, under its great abbot, St
Dominic.

Gundulphus (St) Bp. June 17
6th cent. A bishop somewhere in Gaul, who
is said to have died at Bourges.

Gunifort (St) M. Aug 22
? Said to have been a Northerner — Irish,
Scottish or English — martyred at Pavia. His
legend resembles that of St Richard the King.

Gunther (Bl) Mk. OSB. Oct 9
955–1045 A cousin of St Stephen of Hungary. He began life full of worldly ambition,
but was brought to better ways by St Godehard
of Hildesheim and became a monk at Niederaltaich in Bavaria. But his ambitious nature
asserted itself once more and he had himself
made abbot of Göllingen, but proved a failure.
Made wise by experience, he resigned and
lived as a hermit for twenty-eight years in the
mountains of Bakory, Hungary.

Gunthiern (St) H. July 3
d. c 500 A Welsh prince who adopted the
solitary life in Brittany.

Gunthildis (St) V. OSB. Dec 8
d. c 748 An English nun of Wimborne who,
at the request of St Boniface, passed over to
Germany, where she was abbess of a nunnery
in Thuringia and inspector of all the schools
founded by the English nuns in the Germanies.

Gunthrammus (Gontram)
(St) King March 28
d. 592 King of Burgundy. Having divorced
his wife and over-hastily ordered the execution of his physician, he was overcome with
remorse and lamented these sins for the rest of
his life. On his death he was at once proclaimed a saint.

Gurias and Samonas
(SS) MM. Nov 15
d. 305 Martyrs beheaded at Edessa in Syria
under Diocletian.

Gurlöes (St) Ab. OSB. Aug 25
d. 1057 A Benedictine monk, prior of

Redon abbey who in 1029 became abbot of
Sainte-Croix of Quimperlé in Brittany.

Gurval (St) Bp. June 6
Otherwise Godwall, q.v.

Guthagon (St) C. July 3
8th cent. An Irishman who crossed over into
Belgium, where he became a recluse.

Guthlac (St) H. OSB. Apr 11
673–714 From being a warrior in the army of
Ethelred, king of Mercia, Guthlac entered the
Benedictine abbey of Repton, a double house
under the abbess Elfrida, where he was duly
professed. Afterwards he asked to leave to
become a recluse in the heart of the Lincolnshire fens, where he spent the last fifteen years
of his life. At a later period the abbey of
Crowland was erected on the site of his cell.

Guy
Note. This is the English form of the Latin
Vitus and also of Guido. Variants in other
languages are: Gui, Gwin, Guidone, Viton,
Wido, Witen, Wit, Wye, Wyden.

Guy (Guido) (St) Ab. OSB. March 31
d. 1046 Born near Ravenna, Guy became a
Benedictine at the abbey of St Severus in that
city, of which he was chosen abbot. Afterwards
he went to the abbey of Pomposa, near
Ferrara. He loved sacred learning and at his
request St Peter Damian delivered lectures on
the scriptures to his monks for two years.
Towards the end of his life he was fiercely,
though unjustly, persecuted by the bishop of
Ravenna.

Guy of Vicogne (Bl) O.
Praem. March 31
d. 1147 Founder of the Premonstratensian
abbey of Vicogne, in the diocese of Arras,
whither he retired and was superior of the
community.

Guy de Gherardesca (Bl)
H. May 20
d. 1099 A native of Pisa, who led the life of a
solitary at Campo in the diocese of Massa
Maritima, in Italy.

Guy of Acqui (Bl) Bp. June 2
d. 1070 Bishop of Acqui in Monferrato,
Piedmont, from 1034 till 1070. Cult confirmed in 1853.

Guy Vignotelli (Bl) C.
Tert. OFM. June 16
c 1185–1245 A rich citizen of Cortona who
gave up his wealth on hearing a sermon by St
Francis of Assisi. He was received into the
third order of St Francis by the holy founder

himself. Ordained a priest, he lived the rest of his life as a recluse near Cortona.

Guy (St) Ab. OSB. June 18
d. *p.*940 The successor of Bl Berno in the abbey of Baume. About the year 940 he resigned and retired to a hermitage near Fay-en-Bresse.

Guy Maramaldi (Bl) C. OP. June 25
d. 1391 A native of Naples who became a Dominican, taught philosophy and theology, established a friary at Ragusa, and died as the General Inquisitor for the kingdom of Naples. Cult confirmed in 1612.

Guy (St) C. Sept 12
d. *c* 1012 Surnamed "the Poor Man of Anderlecht". He was a native of Brabant and the sacrist of Our Lady of Laken and afterwards for seven years a pilgrim in the Holy Land. On his return he was admitted to the public hospital at Anderlecht, near Brussels, where he died.

Guy of Durnes (Bl) Ab.
OSB. Cist. Sept 23
d. *c* 1157 A monk of Clairvaux and one of St Bernard's most beloved disciples. He was sent to be abbot-founder of Our Lady of Cherlieu, in the diocese of Besançon. At the request of St Bernard he revised the Cistercian liturgical chant, which was approved in the general chapter of 1150.

Guy of Casauria (Bl) Ab.
OSB. Nov 23
d. 1045 A Benedictine of Farfa, who was elected abbot of Casauria, near Chieti.

Gwen (Blanca, Blanche)
(St) July 5
See Fragan and Gwen.

Gwen (St) W. Oct 18
5th cent. Said to have been the sister of St Nonna and therefore aunt to St David of Wales. She is alleged to have been the mother of SS Cyby and Cadfan.

Gwen (Candida, Blanche)
(St) WM. Oct 18
d. *c* 492 Reputed to have been a daughter of Brychan of Brecknock, she was murdered by the heathen Saxons at Talgarth.

Gwendoline (St) V. OSB. March 28
Otherwise Gundelindis, q.v.

Gwendoline (Gwendolen)
(St) V. Oct 18
See Brothen and Gwendolen.

Gwenhael (St) Ab. Nov 3
Otherwise Guenhael, q.v.

Gwerir (St) H. Apr 4
? A hermit near Liskeard in Cornwall, at whose grave King Alfred is said to have been cured of a serious malady. St Gwerir's cell was after his death occupied by St Neot.

Gwinoc (St) C. Oct 26
See Aneurin and Gwinoc.

Gwynllyw (St) H. March 29
d. *c* 500 Gwynllyw is anglicized as Woollos. He is said to have been the husband of St Gladys, the father of St Cadoc, and to have ended his life as a hermit in Wales. There is an Anglican cathedral dedicated to him at Newport, in Gwent.

Gyavire (St) M. June 13
d. 1886 Known as the "good runner of messages". He was put to death by order of King Mwanga of Uganda. See Charles Lwanga and Comps.

H

Note. Names beginning with a vowel to which by some an aspirate is prefixed, by others not, will be found either under the letter H or under the initial vowel, according as the one or the other form may appear the more usual or the more authentic.

Habakkuk (St) Prophet   Jan 15
7th cent. B.C. One of the twelve lesser prophets. He prophesied in Judaea during the time of captivity. The reason why his name was inserted in the pre-1970 RM. is the alleged finding of his relics by bishop Zebenus of Eleutheropolis under Theodosius the Great (379–395). Churches have been dedicated to him in the Holy Land.

Habakuk (St) M.   Jan 19
Otherwise Abachum. See Marius, Martha, etc.

Habentius (St) M.   June 7
See Peter, Wallabonsus, etc.

Haberilla (Habrilia) (Bl)
V. OSB.   Jan 30
d. *c* 1100 A virgin who became a recluse under the obedience of the abbot of Mehrerau, in Switzerland. Mehrerau at that time was a Black Benedictine monastery.

Habet-Deus (St) Bp. M.   Feb 17
d. *c* 500 Bishop of Luna in Tuscany, an ancient city now in ruins. He was martyred by the Arian Vandals (?), and is now venerated at Sarzana.

Hadelin (St) Ab. OSB.   Feb 3
d. *c* 690 A native of Gascony who followed St Remaclus first to Solignac and then to Maestricht and Stavelot. He became the founder of Chelles, in the diocese of Liège. He lived as a hermit near Dinant on the Meuse.

Hadelin (St) Ab. OSB.   June 15
See Domitian and Hadelin.

Hadelin (Adelheim) (St)
Bp. OSB.   Nov 10
d. *c* 910 Monk and abbot of Saint-Calais, and then bishop of Séez from *c* 884 till 910.

Hadeloga (St) V. OSB.   Feb 2
Otherwise Adeloga, q.v.

Hadrian
(*several*)
See Adrian.

Haduin (Harduin) (St)
Bp.   Aug 20
d. *c* 662 A bishop of Le Mans, founder of several monasteries including Notre-Dame-d'Evron.

Hadulph (St) Bp. OSB.   May 19
d. *c* 728 A prelate who simultaneously held the offices of abbot of Saint-Vaast and bishop of Arras-Cambrai.

Hadulph (St) M. OSB.   June 5
Otherwise Hathawulf. See Waccar, Gundekar, etc.

Haggai (St) Prophet.   July 4
6th cent. B.C. He was the tenth of the Minor Prophets. He belongs to the period after the exile, and the purpose of his divine message was to forward the rebuilding of the Temple in Jerusalem.

Halward (Hallvard) (St)
M.   May 14
d. *c* 1043 A scion of the royal family of Norway. He is said to have met his death while defending from ill-usage a woman who had appealed to him for help. He is the patron saint of Oslo.

Hananiah, Azariah and Mishael (SS)
See Ananiah, Azariah and Mishael.

Hardoin (St) Bp.   Nov 29
7th cent. Bishop of St Pol-de-Léon in Brittany. The name is variously written: Ouardon, Wardon, Hoarzon, Huardo, etc.

Harduin (Bl) Mk. OSB.   Apr 20
d. 811 Born in the diocese of Rouen he became a Benedictine at Fontenelle (749). After a time he asked leave to live as a recluse near the abbey, and spent his leisure time copying the writings of the Fathers.

Hardulph (St)   Aug 21
? The church at Breedon-on-the-Hill in

Leicestershire was dedicated to this saint, of whom nothing is known. He may be identical with the hermit of Bredon (or Breedon) mentioned in the life of St Modwenna, q.v.

Harmon (St) Bp.   July 31
Otherwise Germanus of Auxerre, q.v.

Harold (St) M.   March 25
d. 1168   A child said to have been put to death by Jews in Gloucester.

Hartmann (Bl) Bp.   Dec 23
d. 1164   A native of Polling in Austria who was educated by the Augustinians of Passau, and became dean of the cathedral at Salzburg (1122) and eventually bishop of Brixen. He was highly respected by emperors and popes as well as by the poor people of his diocese. He did much for the canons regular, but was also a great benefactor of other religious, notably of the Benedictines. Cult confirmed in 1784.

Hartwig (Bl) Bp.   June 14
d. 1023   Twenty-first archbishop of Salzburg (991–1023).

Haruch (St) Bp.OSB.   July 15
d. c 830   Abbot and regionary bishop in the territory of Werden.

Hatebrand (St) Ab. OSB.   July 30
d. 1198   A native of Frisia who professed the Benedictine rule of St Paul's, in Utrecht. In 1183 he became abbot of Olden-Klooster in his native land, and as such he revived the Benedictine life throughout Frisia.

Hathawulf (St) M. OSB.   June 5
See Waccar, Gundekar, etc.

Hatto (Bl) Mk. OSB.   July 4
d. 985   Born of a noble Swabian family, he left all his property to the Benedictine abbey of Ottobeuren and became a monk therein. Afterwards he lived as a recluse; but the abbot thought that he was showing too much attachment to his old property and recalled him back to community life — a call which he at once obeyed.

Hebed Jesus (St) M.   Apr 22
Otherwise Abdiesus, q.v.

Hedda and Comp. MM.
OSB.   Apr 9
d. c 870   Hedda was the abbot of Peterborough (Medehampstead). He and eighty-four monks of his community were slain by the Danes, and thenceforward venerated as martyrs.

Hedda (St) Bp. OSB.   July 7
d. 705   An Anglo-Saxon monk and abbot, probably of Whitby, who in 676 was made bishop of the divided diocese of Wessex. He resided first at Dorchester, near Oxford, whence he removed to the see of Winchester. He was a great benefactor of Malmesbury and King Ina's chief adviser. He ruled the diocese for about forty years.

Hedwig (Bl) Queen   Feb 28
1371–1399   She succeeded her father Louis on the throne of Poland at the age of thirteen. She was married to Jagiello of Lithuania, but she made it conditional on him becoming a Christian, which he did. Afterwards she was instrumental in bringing to the faith many Lithuanians. She is venerated throughout Poland with a popular cult.

Hedwig (Hadwigis) (Bl)
Abs. OSB.   Sept 13
d. c 887   A niece of Bl Warinus of Corvey. She became a Benedictine nun and abbess of Herford (*Herivordien*) in Westphalia.

Hedwig (Jadwiga) (St) W.
OSB. Cist.   GC. Oct 16
c 1174–1243   Born at Andechs in Bavaria, but of Moravian descent, she was the daughter of the duke of Croatia and Dalmatia, and the aunt of St Elizabeth of Hungary. She was educated by the Benedictine nuns of Hitzingen in Franconia and at the age of twelve was married to the duke of Silesia, head of the Polish royal family. She bore him seven children, who were in after-life the cause of great anxiety to their parents. The king and the queen were at one in fostering the religious life in their kingdom. Among other houses, they founded the Cistercian nunnery of Trebnitz, whither Hedwig retired in her widowhood. She was canonized in 1266.

Hegesippus (St) C.   Apr 7
d. c 180   A Jew and a native of Jerusalem who spent twenty years of his life in Rome. He is considered the father of ecclesiastical history and the first to trace the succession of bishops of Rome from St St Peter to his own day. Only a few chapters of his work remain. It was warmly commended by Eusebius and by St Jerome, who knew it well and made use of it.

Heimrad (St) Mk. OSB.   June 28
d. 1019   A priest of Baden who after many pilgrimages, lived as a monk at Hersfeld, and then as a hermit at Hasungen in Westphalia. In his wanderings throughout Europe he was often taken for a lunatic rather than a pilgrim. His cult has never been officially confirmed.

Heldrad (Eldrad) (St) Ab.
OSB.   March 13
d. 842   A native of Provence who spent his

large fortune in good works and then set out on a pilgrimage to Rome. He heard from other pilgrims of the Benedictine abbey of Novalese, at the foot of the Alps, and joined that community. After a time he was made abbot and ruled the house for thirty years. The library was his special care. He was moreover a great builder, and had an hospice erected at the highest point of Mt Cenis pass. Cult approved in 1904.

Helanus (St) H. — Oct 7

6th cent. An Irishman who crossed over to France, it is said, with six brothers and three sisters, and settled near Reims. He became a priest and ministered to the people of the neighbourhood.

Helen of Poland (Bl) W.

Poor Clare — March 6

d. 1298 Daughter of Bela IV of Hungary. In 1256 she married Boleslas V of Poland, after whose death (1129) she lived as a Poor Clare at Gnesen. Cult approved in 1827.

Helen Valentini (Bl) W. — Apr 23

d. 1458 A lady of Udine noted by her contemporaries both for her devotion to the duties of married life for twenty-five years and for her charity and austerities as an Augustinian tertiary after her husband's death. Cult confirmed in 1848.

Helen (St) V. — May 22

d. p.418 A maiden mentioned in the Acts of St Amator of Auxerre as present with him at his death.

Helen (Helena) (St) VM. — June 24

Otherwise Alena, q.v.

Helen of Sköfde (St)

WM. — July 31

d. c 1160 A noble Swedish lady who, left a widow, spent her fortune in the service of the poor and the church. She was barbarously put to death in a family feud. Canonized in 1164.

Helen (St) M. — Aug 13

See Centolla and Helen.

Helen (St) Empress — Aug 18

c 250–330 An Asiatic by birth, a native of Bithynia (certainly not of Britain), who became the wife of Constantius Chlorus, to whom she bore a child who became Constantine the Great. Helen became a Christian after the Edict of Milan (313), and spent the rest of her life in the East and in Rome. She helped in the building of several Roman basilicas and many

St Helen, Aug 18

churches in the Holy Land. Her name is chiefly associated with the discovery of the True Cross in a rock-cistern near Mt Calvary. Geoffrey of Monmouth recorded the important legend that she was of Celtic origin and the daughter of King Coel of Colchester. Her porphyry sarcophagus is still extant (Vatican Museum). Depicted as garbed as an Empress, she holds or supports a cross, which itself may vary in form.

Helen Duglioli (Bl) W.   Sept 23
1472–1520   A native of Bologna who, to please her mother, married against her own inclinations and lived a happy married life for thirty years. After her husband's death she devoted herself completely to works of charity. Already revered as a saint during her life, she was venerated as such after her death. Cult confirmed in 1828.

Helen Enselmini (Bl) V.
Poor Clare   Nov 4
d. 1242   A native of Padua who at the age of twelve received the veil of the Poor Clares from St Francis himself at Arcella, near her native city. It is narrated of her that her only food for months was the Eucharist. Before her death she became blind and dumb. Cult approved in 1695.

Helen (Ilona) of Hungary
(Bl) V. OP.   Nov 9
d. c 1270   A Dominican nun in Veszprem, and novice mistress of St Margaret of Hungary. She is reputed to have been marked with the stigmata. Venerated as Blessed in Hungary and in the Dominican order.

Helen Guerra (Bl) V.
Foundress   Dec 23
1835–1914   The foundress of the Sisters of St Zita, also called the Handmaids of the Holy Spirit, was born at Lucca (Tuscany). Her life was characterized by zealous devotion to the Holy Spirit and to the propagation of the faith. Her congregation is prominent in mission territories. St Gemma Galgani was a pupil in her schools. Beatified 1959.

Helen (Heliada) (St) Abs.
OSB.   June 20
d. c750   A Benedictine abbess of the nunnery of Ohren (*Horreum*) at Trier.

Heliconis (Helconides)
(St) M.   May 28
d. ? 250   A woman of Thessalonica, who was arrested at Corinth and beheaded during the persecution of Decius.

Helier (Helerous) (St) M.   July 16
6th cent.   A native of Tongres (Limburg),

who lived as a hermit in the island of Hersey and was murdered by heathen whom he was endeavouring to convert.

Helimenas (St) M.   Apr 22
See Parmenius, and Comp.

Helinand (Elinandus)
(Bl or St) C. OSB. Cist.   Feb 3
d. 1237   A native of Pronleroy (Oise) in the diocese of Beauvais, who from being a court singer was converted and became a Cistercian at Froidmont. The Cistercians venerate him as a saint.

Heliodorus, Desan and
Marjab (SS) MM.   Apr 9
c 355   Heliodorus was a bishop in Mesopotamia who, with two priests and many faithful, were put to death in the persecution of Shapur II.

Heliodorus, Venustus
and Comp. (SS) MM.   May 6
3rd cent.   A group of seventy-seven martyrs who suffered under Diocletian. Heliodorus and seven others seem to have been martyred in Africa; St Ambrose claims the greater part of the rest for Milan.

Heliodorus (St) Bp.   July 3
c 332–390   A Dalmatian who, early in life, became an intimate friend of St Jerome, whom he followed to Palestine and helped financially and otherwise in the preparation of the Vulgate. Later he settled in Aquileia and was made bishop of Altinum, a small town since destroyed, near Venice. He was a great bishop and a brave opponent of Arianism.

Heliodorus, Dausa,
Mariahle, Abdiso and
Comp. (SS) MM.   Aug 20
d. 362   A group of 9000 Christians were deported by the Persians, 300 of whom were set aside by Shapur and invited to renounce their faith. Two hundred and seventy-five refused and were martyred. To this number belongs Abdicius (q.v.), Apr 22.

Heliodorus (St) M.   Sept 28
See Mark, Alphius, etc.

Heliodorus and Comp.
(SS) MM.   Nov 21
d. c270   A group of martyrs, who suffered under Aurelian in Pamphylia.

Helladius (St) M.   Jan 8
See Theophilus and Helladius.

Helladius of Toledo (St)
Bp.   Feb 18
d. 632   A native of Toledo and a minister of

the court of the Visigothic kings. He loved to pay frequent visits to the abbey of Agali (Agallia) near Toledo on the banks of the Tagus, until one day he joined the community and eventually was made its abbot (605). In 615 he was made archbishop of Toledo.

Helladius of Auxerre (St)
Bp.   May 8
d. 387 Bishop of Auxerre in France for thirty years. He converted his own successor, St Amator, to a devout life.

Helladius (St) M.   May 28
See Crescens, Diosorides, etc.

Helpers, Fourteen Holy
See under Fourteen Holy Helpers.

Helwisa (Bl) H. OSB.   Feb 11
d. *p.*1066 A recluse under the obedience of the Benedictine abbey of Coulombs in Normandy.

Hemiterius and
Cheledonius (SS) MM.   March 3
? 4th cent. Two Spanish martyrs, believed to have been soldiers, who suffered at Calahorra in Old Castile. Their Acts have been lost but both Prudentius and St Gregory of Tours have handed down to us the few details we have of them.

Hemma (*several*)
Otherwise Gemma, q.v.

Henedina (St) M.   May 14
See Justa, Justina and Henedina.

Henry
Note. A Teuton name latinized into Henricus. The most common variants in other languages are — German, Heinrich; French, Henri; Danish, Eric; Spanish and Portuguese, Enrique; Hungarian, Emeric; Italian, Enrico (Arrigo, Amerigo — whence America) etc.

Henry (St) H.   Jan 16
d. 1127 A Dane by birth, he renounced his own country and lived as a recluse on Coquet Island, off the coast of Northumberland, under the obedience of the monks of Tynemouth to whom the island belonged. Tynemouth itself was a daughter-house of St Alban's. He was buried at Tynemouth.

Henry of Uppsala (St) Bp. M.   Jan 19
d. *c* 1156 An Englishman who accompanied Nicholas Breakspear (later Pope Adrian IV) to Sweden and Norway. Made bishop of Upsala in Sweden (1152) he was helped in his apostolate by King St Eric IX. He then went to Finland as a member of an expedition led by the same king. He was murdered by a Finn whom he had excommunicated. He was canonnized in 1158 and is venerated as a martyr and as the patron saint of Finland.

Henry Morse (St) M. SJ.   Feb 1
1549–1645 A native of Brome (Suffolk) and a convert, who after being a member of the Inns of Court, studied for the priesthood at Douai in Rome. He entered the Society of Jesus in 1626 and worked in London. An engaging character, he worked selflessly for those stricken down by the plague of 1636, catching it and then recovering. Imprisoned in 1638 on the word of an informer, he was released, worked in various parts of the country, and re-arrested nine years later. He was martyred at Tyburn; beatified in 1929, and canonized in 1970 as one of the Forty Martyrs of England and Wales, q.v.

Henry Suso (Bl) C. OP.   March 2
c 1295–1366 A native of Bihlmeyer, near Constance, who joined the Friars Preachers at an early age, was prior in several houses of the order and excelled as a spiritual director. He is one of the greatest Dominican mystics and his *Book of the Eternal Wisdom* is still in print, a classic of German Mysticism. Cult approved in 1831.

Henry of Gheest (Bl) C.
OSB. Cist.   Apr 4
d. *c* 1190 A Cistercian monk at Villers, in the diocese of Namur. His relics were solemnly enshrined in 1599.

Henry Walpole (St) M. SJ.   Apr 7
1558–1595 A native of Docking, Norfolk, who was educated at Norwich, Cambridge (Peterhouse) and Gray's Inn. He was received into the church and studied for the priesthood at the English College, Rome, there entering the Society of Jesus (1584). Ordained in 1588, he worked at York. Here also he was martyred. Beatified in 1929. Canonized in 1970 as one of the Forty Martyrs of England and Wales, q.v.

Henry the Shoemaker
(Bl) C.   ?June 9
d. 1666 Henry Michael Bucke—"der gute Heinrich" — was a native of Luxemburg and a shoemaker by trade. In 1645 he settled at Paris and, with the help of Baron de Renti, founded the confraternity of SS Crispin and Crispinian (Frères Cordonniers) for his fellow-craftsmen. He is usually called "saint" or "blessed" but there is no evidence of cult.

Henry of Treviso (Bl) C.   June 10
d. 1315 Usually called in Italy, San Rigo (a diminutive form of Arrigo). He was born at Bolzano in the Tyrol, but lived at Treviso where he earned his daily bread as a hired

labourer (*facchino*). In his old age he lived on alms. Cult approved by Benedict XIV.

Henry (Heric) (Bl) C.
OSB.   June 24
d. *c* 880 A native of Hery (Yonne), who became a Benedictine and the headmaster of the monastic school at Saint-Germain d'Auxerre. He was also a hagiographer.

Henry Zdick (Bl) Bp. O.
Praem.   June 25
d. 1150 A son of King Wratislas I of Bohemia who was elected bishop of Olmütz in 1126. In 1137 he went to Palestine and donned the Premonstratensian habit at Jerusalem. On his return to his diocese he introduced the Premonstratensians in many places and founded for them the abbey of Strahov.

Henry of Albano (Bl) Bp.
Card. OSB. Cist.   July 4
d. 1188 Usually surnamed "Henricus Gallus". He was a French Cistercian who became cardinal bishop of Albano in 1179, and died at Arras.

Henry Abbot (Bl) M.   July 4
d. 1597 A native of Howden, in Yorkshire. He was a layman and a convert and was, for this reason, hanged at York. Beatified in 1929.

Henry II (St) Emperor   GC. July 13
973–1024 Henry the Good was born in Bavaria and was educated by St Wolfgang of Regensburg. From being duke of Bavaria he ascended the imperial throne in 1002. He was crowned as Holy Roman Emperor by the pope in 1014. With his wife St Cunegundis, he was providentially raised up to protect the church in that troublous period. Henry, though very much a political and temporal ruler, had always at heart the welfare of religion, and readily co-operated with the Benedictine abbeys of that time — Cluny, Montecassino, Camaldoli, Einsiedeln, St Emmeran, Verdun, Gorsch — in the restoration of ecclesiastical and social discipline. He himself tried to become a Benedictine and was, for this reason, officially declared the patron saint of Benedictine Oblates by Pius X. Canonized in 1146.

Henry of Cologne (Bl) C.
OP.   Oct 23
d. 1225 One of the first Dominicans recruit ed from among the students of the university of Paris, who became the first prior of the friary at Cologne. He was a friend of Bl Jordan.

Henry of Zwiefalten (Bl)
C. OSB.   Nov 4
d. *p.*1250 A Benedictine monk of the abbey of Zwiefalten, who became prior of Ochsenhausen. Both monasteries were in Swabia.

Heraclas (St) Bp.   July 14
d. 247 An Egyptian, brother of St Plutarch the martyr. He was at first a pupil and afterwards the successor of Origen as head of the catechetical school of Alexandria. He became patriarch in 231.

Heracleas (St) M.   Sept 29
See Eutychius, Plautus and Heracleas.

Heraclides (St) M.   June 28
See Plutarch, Serenus, etc.

Heraclius (St) M.   March 2
See Paul, Heraclius, etc.

Heraclius and Zosimus
(SS) MM.   March 11
d. *c* 263 African martyrs who suffered at Carthage under Valerian and Gallienus.

Heraclius (St) M.   May 26
See Felicissimus, Heraclius and Paulinus.

Heraclius of Sens (St)
Bp.   June 8
d. *c* 515 The fourteenth bishop of Sens. He was present in the cathedral of Reims at the baptism of Clovis (Dec 25, 496). He built the abbey of St John the Evangelist at Sens, where he was buried.

Heraclius (St) M.   Sept 1
See Prisucs, Castrensis, etc.

Heraclius (St) M.   Oct 22
See Alexander, Heraclius and Comp.

Heradius, Paul, Aquilinus
and Comp. (SS) MM.   May 17
d. 303 Five martyrs put to death at Nyon (*Noviodunum*) on the lake of Geneva, under Diocletian.

Herais (St) VM.   Sept 22
Otherwise Irais, q.v.

Herbert (St) H.   March 20
d. 687 A priest, friend of St Cuthbert, who lived as a solitary on the island named after him on Lake Derwentwater. The two saints were granted their prayer to die on the same day.

Herbert Hoscam (St) Bp.   Aug 20
d. 1180 An Englishman by birth, who became archbishop of Conze, in the Basilicata, Italy. He is venerated as the principal patron saint of Conza.

Herbert (Haberne,
Herbern) (St) Bp. OSB.   Oct 30
? Abbot of Marmoutier, and afterwards archbishop of Tours.

Herculanus of Piegare
(Bl) C. OFM.   June 1
d. 1541   A native of Piegare, near Perugia, he joined the Franciscans and became one of their foremost preachers. Beatified in 1860.

Herculanus of Brescia
(St) Bp.   Aug 12
d. c 550   A bishop of Brescia in Lombardy.

Herculanus (St) M.   Sept 5
d. ? c 180   A martyr who suffered at Porto, near Rome, probably under Marcus Aurelius.

Herculanus (St) M.   Sept 25
2nd cent.   A Roman soldier, mentioned in the untrustworthy Acts of St Alexander I as having been converted by the pontiff and martyred shortly afterwards.

Herculanus (St)
Bp.   Nov 7 and March 1
d. 549   A bishop of Perugia, beheaded by the soldiers of Totila, the marauding leader of the Ostro-Goths.

Herebald (Herband) (St)
C.   June 11
8th cent.   A native of Britain who embraced the solitary life in Brittany, where a church is dedicated to him.

Herena (St) M.   Feb 25
See Donatus, Justus, etc.

Herenia (St) M.   March 8
See Cyril, Rogatus, etc.

Hereswitha (St) W. OSB.   Sept 3
d. c 690   A Northumbrian princess, sister of St Hilda and mother of SS Sexburga, Withburga and Ethelburga. She spent the closing years of her life as a nun at Chelles in France.

Heribaldus (St) Bp. OSB.   Apr 25
d. c 857   A Benedictine monk and abbot of the monastery of St Germanus, at Auxerre, who was bishop of the same city.

Heribert (St) Bp.   March 16
d. 1022   Born at Worms and educated by the Benedictines of Gorze, he became chancellor to the emperor Otto III and (998) archbishop of Cologne. He was an outstanding churchman, learned, zealous and enterprising. He built the Benedictine abbey of Deutz on the Rhine, where he was buried.

Herlindis and Relindis
(SS) Abs. OSB.   Oct 12
d. c 745 and 750   Daughters of Count Adelard, who built for them the nunnery of Maaseyk, on the Meuse, of which they became respectively first and second abbesses. They were friends of SS Willibrord and Boniface. See Relindis.

Herluin (Bl) Ab. OSB.   Aug 26
d. 1078   A native of Normandy who was bred to the profession of arms and served as a knight at the court of the count of Brionne. He left it to found a monastery on his own estate at Bonneville, of which he became the abbot. In 1040 the community moved to a new site on the banks of the little river Bec. One of the first novices was Bl Lanfranc; shortly afterwards came St Anselm. Under these three great men Bec became the foremost school of Christendom. Herluin has always been given the title of *Beatus*. His relics are extant at Bec.

Hermagoras and
Fortunatus (SS) MM.   July 12
d. c 66   According to tradition, St Hermagoras was a disciple of St Mark, by whom he was appointed first bishop of Aquileia. After a fruitful apostolate he and his deacon Fortunatus were beheaded under Nero.

Herman of Zähringen
(Bl) Mk. OSB.   March 25
d. 1074   Margrave of Zähringen, who became a monk at Cluny.

Herman Joseph (Bl) C.
O. Praem.   Apr 7
c 1150–1241   A native of Cologne who, at an early age, began to have mystical experiences which made him famous throughout the Germanies. He joined the Premonstratensians at Steinfeld and has left some remarkable mystical writings. He had a special devotion to St Ursula.

Herman of Heidelberg
(Bl) H. OSB.   Sept 3
d. c 1326   A Benedictine monk professed at Niederaltaich in Bavaria in 1320, who lived as a hermit. An altar is dedicated to him in the parish church of Rinchnach.

Herman the Cripple
(*Contractus*) (Bl) Mk. OSB.   Sept 25
1013–1054   His nickname "the Cripple" describes his physical condition. He was offered as a child of seven to the abbey of Reichenau on the Rhine, and became the most famous religious poet of his age. He has always been given the title of *Beatus*.

Herman (Bl) Ab. O. Praem.   Dec 23
d. c 1200   A Jew, born in Cologne, who became a Christian and joined the Premonstratensians. He was elected first abbot of Scheda in the archdiocese of Cologne.

Hermas (St) Bp. May 9
1st cent.   A Roman, whom St Paul mentions in his Epistle to the Romans (16:14). A Greek tradition makes him bishop of Philippi and a martyr.

Hermas, Serapion and Polyaenus (SS) MM. Aug 18
? Roman martyrs who were dragged by their feet over rough ground till they expired; they were the victims of the infuriated mob. It seems that their biographer has united their stories quite arbitrarily into one. Hermas may be Hermes (Aug 28).

Hermas (St) M. Nov 4
See Nicander and Hermas.

Hermellus (St) M. Aug 3
The same as Hermylus, q.v.

Hermenegild (St) M. Apr 13
d. 586   Son of the Visigothic king of Spain, Leovigild, and brought up an Arian at the court of Seville. He became a Catholic on his marriage to the daughter of Sigebert of Austrasia. His father disinherited him on account of this change, whereupon he rose in arms, was defeated, captured, and on refusing to give up the Catholic faith, was put to death at the instigation of his stepmother. Cult confined to local calendars since 1969.

Hermenegild (St) Mk. OSB. Nov 5
d. 953   A Spanish Benedictine of Salcedo in the diocese of Tuy, in Spanish Galicia — one of those who helped in the spreading of Benedictinism throughout N.W. Spain under St Rudesind.

Hermengaudius (Armengol) (St) Bp. Nov 3
d. 1035   Bishop of Urgell, in the Spanish Pyrenees, from 1010 till 1035. He built the cathedral and gave its canons a rule of life based on that of St Augustine.

Hermenland (Hermeland, Herbland, Erblon) (St) March 25
d. c 720   A native of the diocese of Noyon, he served in his youth as royal cup-bearer. Then he withdrew to Fontenelle and became a monk under St Lambert. He was ordained priest and sent, with a band of twelve monks, to establish a new abbey on the island of Aindre, in the estuary of the Loire.

Hermes Haggai and Gaius (SS) MM. Jan 4
d. c 300   There is some uncertainty as to where these martyrs suffered. The pre-1970 RM. said at Bologna, under Maximian; this could be Bologna, a town of Mesia in Asia Minor. The feast day in their honour at Bologna, Italy, was abolished in 1914. Bononia on the Danube is another possibility.

Hermes and Adrian (SS) MM. March 1
d. c 290   Martyrs who suffered under Maximian Herculeus. The pre-1970 RM. said "at Marseilles" but most writers now identify this group of martyrs — Hermes and Adrian are only the first in a list of twenty-six — with "the Massylitan martyrs on whose birthday St Augustine delivered a discourse". The original reading of the martyrology was *Massylis* (Marula) in Numidia, the spelling of which is very similar to the Latin *Massilia* (Marseilles).

Hermes and Comp. (SS) MM. Aug 28
d. c 120   Roman martyrs who perished under the judge Aurelian, and are mentioned in the very dubious Acts of Pope St Alexander. Although their Acts are not trustworthy, the cult of St Hermes was both ancient and widespread. Cult confined to local calendars since 1969.

Hermes (St) M. Oct 22
See Philip, Severus, etc.

Hermes (St) M. Nov 2
See Publius, Victor, etc.

Hermes (St) M. Dec 31
d. c 270   A cleric, of the rank of exorcist, who is believed to have suffered under Aurelian. He may be the same as the martyr commemorated on Jan 4.

Hermias (St) M. May 31
d. 170   A veteran soldier, martyred at Comana in Cappadocia — not in Pontus, as Baronius thought. He has a prominent place in the Greek liturgy.

Hermione (St) V. Sept 4
d. c 117   One of the daughters of Philip the Deacon, mentioned in the Acts of the Apostles (21:9) as a prophetess. She is said to have died a martyr at Ephesus.

Hermippus (St) M. July 27
See Hermolaus, Hermippus and Hermocrates.

Hermocrates (St) M. July 27
See Hermolaus, Hermippus and Hermocrates.

Hermogenes (St) M. Apr 17
See Peter and Hermogenes.

**Hermogenes, Gaius,
Expeditus, Aristonicus,
Rufus and Galata (SS)**
MM. Apr 19
4th cent. Armenian martyrs who are believed to have suffered at Melitene. The cult of
St Expeditus (whose name appears in some
documents as Elpidius) dates from the 17th
century, and is of German origin.

Hermogenes (St) M. Apr 25
See Evodius, Hermogenes and Callistus.

Hermogenes (St) M. Dec 10
See Mennas, Hermogenes and Eugraphus.

**Hermogenes, Donatus
and Comp. (SS) MM.** Dec 12
? Twenty-four martyrs, said to have been
driven into a marsh and there left to perish of
cold and exhaustion.

Hermogius (St) Bp. OSB. June 26
d. c 942 A native of Tuy and founder of the
abbey of Labrugia (915) in Spanish Galicia.
He was taken captive by the Moors and
brought to Cordoba, but was subsequently
given his freedom; his nephew, the boy St
Pelagius, being retained there as a hostage. St
Hermogius resigned his see and retired to
Ribas del Sil.

**Hermolaus, Hermippus
and Hermocrates (SS) MM.** July 27
d. c 305 St Hermolaus, an aged priest of
Nicomedia, having succeeded in converting St
Pantaleon, the imperial physician, was martyred with him and with the two brothers
Hermippus and Hermocrates.

**Hermylus and
Stratonicus (SS) MM.** Jan 13
d. 315 Hermylus, a deacon of *Singidunum*
(Belgrade) and Stratonicus his servant, were
drowned in the Danube under Licinius. The
value of the *Life* however has been questioned.

Hernan (St) C. Sept 15
6th cent. A native of Britain, who took refuge
in Brittany at the time of the Anglo-Saxon
conquest. He lived as a solitary at a place called
after him Loc-Harn, and he is the patron saint
of that village.

**Herodion, Asyncritus
and Phlegon (SS) MM.** Apr 8
1st cent. Herodion, whom St Paul styles his
kinsman (Rom 16:11) with Asyncritus and
Phlegon, likewise mentioned by the apostle,
are said to have become bishops, Herodion of
Patras, Asyncritus of Marathon and Phlegon
of Hyrcania, and to have been done to death at
the instigation of the Jews. Apart from the
N.T. references, it is probably all a legend.

Heron (St) M. June 28
See Plutarch, Serenus, etc.

Heron (St) Bp. M. Oct 17
d. c 136 The disciple, and successor of St
Ignatius in the see of Antioch, which he served
for twenty years (c 116–136). He died a martyr.

**Heron, Arsenius, Isidore
and Dioscorus (SS) MM.** Dec 14
d. 250 The three first named were burnt to
death at Alexandria in Egypt under Decius.
Dioscorus, a boy, was whipped and then
dismissed.

Heros (St) M. June 24
See Orentius, Heros, etc.

**Herulph (Hariolfus) (St)
Bp. OSB.** Aug 13
d. 785 A son of the count of Ellwangen. He
became a Benedictine at St Gall and afterwards founded the abbey of Ellwangen (764)
in the diocese of Augsberg. He later became
bishop of Langres.

Herundo (St) V. July 23
See Romula, Redempta and Herundo.

**Herveus (Hervé) of
Tours (St) C.** Apr 16
d. 1021 A native of Touraine, he became
treasurer of the abbey of St Martin of Tours,
and lived for a time as a hermit, but died
among the canons of St Martin.

Herveus (Hervé) (St) Ab. June 17
d. c 575 A Welsh saint and singer, blind
from his childhood. He was taken very young
to Brittany, where he grew up to become a
teacher and minstrel. Though blind he
became abbot of Plouvien, whence he
migrated with part of his community to
Lanhouarneau. He is still a most popular saint
in Brittany. In art he is represented as blind,
being led about by a wolf.

Herveus (Bl) H. July 18
d. 1130 A native of the British Isles, he led
the life of an anchorite on the island of
Chalonnes, in Anjou.

Hesperius (St) M. May 2
Otherwise Exuperius, q.v.

**Hesso (Esso) (Bl) Ab.
OSB.** Dec 27
d. 1133 Benedictine monk and procurator
of Hirschau under St William. He was sent to
Beinwil in Switzerland as its first abbot (1085).

Hesychius (St) Bp. May 15
See Torquatus, Cresiphon, etc.

Hesychius (St) M. June 15
d. c 302 A Roman soldier martyred at

Dorostorum (Silistria) in Maesia, together with the veteran St Julius.

Hesychius (St) M.   July 7
See Peregrinus, Lucian, etc.

Hesychius (St) M.   Sept 2
See Diomedes, Julian, etc.

Hesychius (St) H.   Oct 3
d. *c* 380   A disciple of St Hilarion, under whom he became a monk at Majuma, near Gaza, in Palestine. He followed his master from solitude to solitude and when St Hilarion fled to Sicily, St Hesychius spent three years searching for him. At St Hilarion's death (371) he conveyed the remains back to Majuma, where he lived until his own death.

Hesychius (St) M.   Nov 7
See Hieron, Nicander, etc.

**Hesychius of Antioch
(St)** M.   Nov 18
d. *c* 303   A Roman soldier who cast away his military belt (the *cingulum militare*) proclaiming himself a Christian. As a punishment for this he was drowned in the River Orontes.

Hesychius (St) Bp. M.   Nov 26
See Faustus, Didius, etc.

Hewald (SS) MM.   Oct 3
Otherwise Ewald, q.v.

Hia (Ia, Ives) (St) V.   Feb 3
Otherwise Ia, q.v.

Hidulphus (St) Mk. OSB.   June 23
d. *c* 707   Count of Hainault and a courtier at the royal palace of Austrasia. He married St Aye, but by mutual consent they became religious, Hidulphus entering the abbey of Lobbes, which he had helped to found.

Hidulphus (St) Bp. OSB.   July 11
d. 707   A native of Regensburg who became a monk of the abbey of Maximinus, at Trier. At a later date he was ordained a regionary bishop; but about the year 676 he resigned and founded the Benedictine abbey of Moyen-moutier. When he died he was abbot both of Moyenmoutier and Bonmoutier (Galilaea, afterwards called Saint-Dié).

Hierlath (St) Bp.   Feb 1
Otherwise Jarlath, q.v.

Hiero (Iero) (St) M.   Aug 17
d. 885   An Irish missionary in Holland, where he died a martyr.

**Hieron, Nicander,
Hesychius and Comp.
(SS)** MM.   Nov 7
d. *c* 300   A group of thirty-three Armenian martyrs who suffered at Mitilene under Diocletian.

**Hieronides, Leontius,
Serapion, Seleucus (Selesius),
Valerian and Straton (SS)
MM.**   Sept 12
d. *c* 300   Martyrs cast into the sea at Alexandria under Diocletian. Hieronides was a deacon far advanced in years; Leontius and Serapion were brothers. The name Selesius should be Seleucus.

Hierotheus (St) Bp.   Oct 4
? The alleged teacher and friend of St Dionysius the Areopagite. Modern writers either deny his existence or postdate him to the fourth or fifth century. See the entry for Dionysius above.

Hieu (St) V.   Sept 2
d. *c* 657   A Northumbrian maiden who received the veil from St Aidan, by whom she was made abbess of Tadcaster in Yorkshire. St Hieu is thought by some to be one and the same with St Bega or Bee.

**Hilaria, Digna, Euprepia,
Eunomia, Quiriacus, Largio,
Crescentian, Nimmia,
Juliana and Comp. (SS)** MM.   Aug 12
d. *c* 304   Hilaria is alleged to be the mother of St Afra of Augsburg (q.v.). She and her three maids were seized while visiting the tomb of St Afra and burnt alive. The others (Quiriacus, etc., twenty-five in all) were Roman martyrs buried on the Ostian Way.

Hilaria (St) M.   Dec 3
See Claudius, Hilaria, etc.

Hilaria (St) M.   Dec 31
See Donata, Paulina, etc.

Hilarinus (St)   Aug 7
See Donatus and Hilarinus.

Hilarinus (St) M.   Aug 23
See Altigianus and Hilarinus.

Hilarion (St) M.   July 12
See Proclus and Hilarion.

Hilarion (St) Ab.   Oct 21
c 291–371   A native of Gaza in Palestine, Hilarion became a Christian while studying at Alexandria and took St Antony the Great as his model. On his return to Gaza he introduced there the eremitical life. Disciples soon flocked around him and he founded several monasteries in Palestine. The latter part of his

life is the story of his escapes from the crowds who followed him on account of his miracles. He lived on Mt Sinai, and in Egypt, Sicily, Dalmatia, Paphos and Cyprus, where he died at the age of eighty. Cult confined to particular calendars since 1969.

Hilary (St) Bp. Dr. GC. Jan 13
315–368 Born at Poitiers of pagan patrician parents, he studied rhetoric and philosophy and married early in life. Shortly after he became a Christian and in 353 was elected bishop of Poitiers. At once he began his masterly campaign against Arianism, and for this reason was exiled to Phrygia by the Arian emperor Constantius. But in Phrygia he was even more objectionable to the Arians, who clamoured for his recall. He returned to Poiters in 360. Hilary is the Doctor of the Divinity of Christ. He was officially declared a Doctor of the Church in 1851.

Hilary (Hilarus) (St) Pope Feb 28
d. 468 A Sardinian by birth, given high office in the Roman curia by St Leo the Great, who sent him as his legate to the "Robber Synod of Ephesus" from which he escaped with difficulty (449). He was made pope in 461 and worked energetically against the Nestorians and Eutychians, as well as in consolidating the church in Sandi, Africa and Gau. He was a great benefactor of churches in Rome.

Hilary, Tatian, Felix, Largus and Denis (SS)
MM. March 16
d. c 284 Hilary was a bishop of Aquileia, Tatian his deacon, and the rest laymen. All were beheaded under Numerian.

Hilary (St) M. Apr 9
See Demetrius, Concessus, etc.

Hilary (St) Bp. May 5
c 400–449 Born in Lorraine, while still a pagan he gained high office in the local administration. His relative and friend, St Honoratus, invited him to the monastery recently founded at Lérins. Hilary received baptism there and joined the community. When St Honoratus became bishop of Arles he took Hilary as his secretary. St Hilary succeeded to the see and showed himself a zealous prelate, though not always prudent. In fact, he was twice reproved by the Holy See. His sanctity, however, won for him popular veneration in life and after death.

Hilary (St) Ab. May 15
d. 558 A hermit near the River Ronco in Italy. Joined by others he built the monastery called Galeata, afterwards known as Sant'-

Ilaro, which at a later period was handed over to the Camaldolese.

Hilary (St) Bp. May 16
d. 376 Bishop of Pavia. One of the prelates of N. Italy who fought Arianism.

Hilary (St) Bp. May 20
4th cent. Bishop of Toulouse.

Hilary (St) Bp. June 3
? 4th cent. Bishop of Carcassonne.

Hilary (St) M. Sept 27
See Florentinus and Hilary.

Hilary of Mende (St) Bp. Oct 25
d. 535 Born at Mende, the ancient *Gavallus*, in S. France, he received baptism on coming to man's estate, became a hermit on the banks of the Tarn, a monk of Lérins, and finally bishop of Mende.

Hilary of Viterbo (St) M. Nov 3
See Valentine and Hilary.

Hilary (St) Ab. OSB. Nov 21
d. c 1045 A native of Matera in S. Italy, he became abbot of San Vincenzo at Volturno (1011–1045). He revived the ancient glory of his monastery.

Hilda (St) Abs. OSB. Nov 17
614–680 A native of Northumbria and a kinswoman of King St Edwin. She was baptized when a child by St Paulinus (631) and at the age of thirty-three joined the nuns of Hartlepool, by the River Wear in Northumberland, of whom soon after she became the abbess. Later on, she migrated also as abbess to the double monastery of Whitby at Streaneshalch. Her influence was certainly one of the decisive factors in securing unity in the English church. Although she and her double community had professed and favoured the Celtic rule and observances, they gave them up after the council of Whitby (convened by St Hilda herself) in 664, when the Roman observances, including the monastic rule of St Benedict, were definitely adopted throughout England. Five of her monks, including St Wilfrid of York and St John of Beverley, became bishops. Hilda is one of the greatest Englishwomen of all time. She was also a patroness of learning and culture — under her aegis the poet Caedmon was inspired to write his verses in the vernacular.

Hildebert (St) Ab. M. OSB. Apr 4
d. 752 Abbot of the Benedictine monastery of St Peter at Ghent. He was killed by some fanatics for his defence of holy images, and was venerated as a martyr.

Hildebrand (Bl) M.   Apr 11
See Stephen and Hildebrand.

Hildebrand (St) Pope
OSB.   May 25
Otherwise Gregory VII, q.v.

Hildegard (Bl) Empress   Apr 30
d. 783   A daughter of the duke of Swabia. In
771 she was married to Charlemagne. Hildegard bore him eight children during the twelve
years of their married life. She befriended
monks and nuns, among whom she had a
special predilection for St Lioba. She is
considered to be the foundress of Kempten
abbey, where she was buried.

Hildegard (St) Abs. OSB.   Sept 17
1098–1179 Surnamed "the Sibyl of the
Rhine". Born at Bockelheim, she joined the
Benedictines at Diessenberg when she was
only eight years old, and in early womanhood
was chosen abbess of the place. She removed
the community to Rupertsberg, near Bingen
(c 1147), and founded another daughter-
house in the neighbourhood. Her claim to
fame, however, rests on her amazing writings.
"Hildegard was the first of the great German
mystics, a poetess and a prophetess, a physician and a political moralist, who rebuked popes
and princes, bishops and lay-folk, with complete fearlessness and unerring justice" (Attwater). Accused by her numerous enemies,
she was defended by St Bernard and by his
pope-disciple Bl Eugene III. There has been
much interest in her works among modern
scholars. Some of her writings have been
translated into English, and her music and
poetry recorded and performed. She is an
outstanding figure of the twelfth century
renaissance.

Hildegrin (St) Bp.   June 19
d. c 827   Younger brother of St Ludger, q.v.,
and his fellow-worker in the evangelization of
the Saxons. At a later period (802?) he was
made bishop of Châlons-sur-Marne. It is
usually stated that towards the end of his life
he became a monk and abbot of the Benedictine monastery of Werden.

Hildegund (St) W. O.
Praem.   Feb 6
d. 1183   Wife of Count Lothair. In her
widowhood she turned her castle of Meer,
near Cologne, into a Premonstratensian nunnery and entered there with her daughter, in
the teeth of fierce family opposition. Hildegund became the prioress of the new foundation.

**Hildegund, or Joseph
(Bl)** N. OSB. Cist.   Apr 20
d. 1188   The Cistercian menology states
"Hildegund, died a novice at the abbey of
Schönau, disguised in male apparel and calling herself Brother Joseph. She died most
holily and is famous for her miracles." Hers is
a romantic story. She was born in the Rhineland and, dressed as a boy, she accompanied
her father to the Holy Land. On her return she
joined the Cistercian monks at Schönau, her
sex being discovered after her death. Of the
several women of whom similar stories are
related, Hildegund is almost the only one in
whose story there seems to be a measure of
truth. Her cult is, however, only a popular one.

**Hildelith (Hildilid,
Hildeltha) (St)** Abs. OSB.   March 24
d. c 712   A younger Anglo-Saxon princess
who took the veil either at Chelles or at
Faremoutiers-en-Brie, in France. She was
recalled to England by St Erconwald to train
her sister Ethelburga of Barking. When the
latter became abbess Hildelith stayed on as
one of her nuns and eventually succeeded her
as abbess. She won the admiration of SS
Aldhelm, Bede and Boniface. She was a great
and wise abbess, and a very cultured woman.

Hildemar (Bl) M. OSA.   Jan 13
d. 1097(8)   German by origin, he was a court
chaplain to William the Conqueror in England. Then he became a hermit at Arrouaise in
Artois. He was joined by many disciples for
whom he founded the monastery of Arrouaise
under the Augustinian rule of canons regular.
He was killed by an assassin who posed as a
novice.

Hildemar (St) Bp. OSB.   Dec 10
d. p.844   A monk of Corbie who was appointed bishop of Beauvais in 821.

Hildemarca (St) Abs. OSB.   Oct 25
d. c 670   A nun of St Eulalia at Bordeaux,
who was invited by St Wandrille to govern his
new monastery at Fécamp.

**Hilduard (Hilward,
Garibald) (St)** Bp. OSB.   Sept 7
d. c 750   A missionary in Flanders, founder
of St Peter's abbey at Dickelvenne, between
Ghent and Audenarde, in the Schelde.

Hillonius (St) C.   Jan 7
Otherwise Tillo, q.v.

Hilsindis (Bl) Abs. OSB.   May 4
d. 1028   Of the family of the dukes of Lorraine. In her widowhood she was the abbess-
foundress of the nunnery of Thorn, on the
Marne.

Hiltrude (St) V. OSB. Sept 27
d. *c* 790 A recluse in a cell near the abbey of Liessies, under the obedience of its abbot, who was her own brother, Gundrad.

Hiltutus (St) Ab. July 7
Otherwise Illtyd, q.v.

Himelin (St) C. March 10
d. *c* 750 An Irish, or Scottish, priest, who died at Vissenaeken, near Tirlemont, in Belgium, on his return from a Roman pilgrimage. He is still venerated at Vissenaeken.

Himerius (St) Bp. June 17
d. *c* 560 A native of Calabria, who was firstly a monk and then bishop of Ameila (*Ameria*) in Umbria. He is described as a very austere man, first with himself and then with others. In 995 his relics were translated to Cremona, where he is venerated as one of its principal patron saints.

Himerius (Imier) (St) Ab. Nov 12
d. *c* 610 A monk-hermit and a missionary in the district of the Swiss Jura, now called after him Immertal, Val-Saint-Imier.

Hipparchus (St) M. Dec 9
See Samosata Martyrs.

Hippolytus (St) M. Jan 30
? A martyr renowned at Antioch. The details given in the pre-1970 RM. are borrowed from the story of St Hippolytus of Rome.

Hippolytus (St) M. Feb 3
See Felix, Symphronius, etc.

Hippolytus Galantini (Bl)
C. March 20
1565–1619 A native of Florence, and a silk-weaver by trade. From his twelfth year he assisted priests in teaching Christian doctrine to the children. This practice was imitated by others, whom Bl Hippolytus formed into the congregation of Italian Doctrinarians. It soon spread throughout Italy. Beatified in 1825.

**Hippolytus, Concordia
and Comp. (SS)** MM. GC. Aug 13
d. *c* 235 A native of Rome who became a member of the Roman clergy, among whom he was known for his rigoristic learnings. He censured Pope St Callistus I, causing himself to be elected anti-pope. He was exiled to Sardinia and there reconciled to the church before his martyrdom. He is one of the most important ecclesiastical writers of his time. His story has been overlaid by legends. One connects him with the death of St Laurence, and St Concordia (a genuine martyr of whom, however, nothing is known) is worked into the story. The legend of Hippolytus of Porto has

no basis beyond the fact that this Hippolytus was venerated with a basilica at Porto. St Hippolytus alone of this group is kept, with St Pontian, on Aug 13. The cult of the others was suppressed in 1969.

Hippolytus of Porto (St)
Bp. M. formerly Aug 22
? d. *c* 236 This saint is confused with St Hippolytus of Rome, commemorated on Aug 13. The confusion arose through this saint having a basilica dedicatd to him at Rome. The pre-1970 RM. makes him a bishop of Porto, martyred by drowning under Alexander. Cult suppressed in 1969.

Hippolytus (St) Bp. OSB. Nov 28
d. *c* 775 Abbot-bishop of Saint-Claude, in France.

Hippolytus (St) M. Dec 2
See Eusebius, Marcellus, etc.

**Hirenarchus, Acacius
and Comp. (SS)** MM. Nov 27
d. *c* 305 Martyrs of Sebaste in Armenia. They include Acacius, a priest, seven women, and Hirenarchus, converted on witnessing the courage of the other martyrs.

Homobonus (St) C. Nov 13
d. 1197 A merchant of Cremona, who throughout his life practised the most scrupulous honesty and was conspicuous for his charity to the poor. He died during the celebration of the Eucharist. Two years after his death his fellow-citizens petitioned the Holy See for his canonization and their petition was granted at once (1199).

Honestus (St) M. Feb 16
d. 270 A native of Nimes, who was ordained priest and sent into Spain by St Saturninus to preach the gospel, which he did very fruitfully. He appears to have been martyred at Pampeluna in Spanish Navarre.

Honorata (St) V. Jan 11
d. *c* 500 The sister of St Epiphanius, bishop of Pavia. She was a nun at Pavia when Odoacer, the king of the Heruli, dragged her into captivity. She was ransomed by her brother and returned to Pavia.

Honoratus of Arles (St) Bp. Jan 16
c 350–429 Born probably in Lorraine of a Roman consular family, he renounced paganism in his youth and went to the East to study monasticism. Returning to France, he founded on the Mediterranean islet of Lérins the abbey of that name. In 426 he was forced to accept the archbishopric of Arles, but died only three years later.

Honoratus of Fondi (St)
Ab. ?OSB.　　　　　　　　　　Jan 16
6th cent.　The abbot-founder of the monastery of Fondi on the confines of Latium and Campania. St Gregory the Great gives a pleasing, though all too short, account of his life (Dialogues Bk I).

Honoratus of Milan (St)
Bp.　　　　　　　　　　　　Feb 8
d. 570　Appointed bishop of Milan in 567, at a time when much trouble was being caused by the Arian disputes and by the Lombard invasion. He was driven from his see by barbarians, and died in exile.

Honoratus of Amiens (St)
Bp.　　　　　　　　　　　May 16
d. *c* 600　A native of Ponthieu who became bishop of Amiens. The church and thoroughfare of Saint-Honoré, in Paris, take their name from him.

Honoratus, Fortunatus, Arontius (Orontius), Sabinian (Savinian) (SS)
MM.　　　　　　Aug 27 and Sept 1
d. 303　Martyrs beheaded at Potenza under Maximian. They are one of the groups commemorated under the title of The Twelve Holy Brothers, q.v.

Honoratus of Vercelli (St)
Bp.　　　　　　　　　　　Oct 28
c 330–415　A native of Vercelli who was trained in the monastic and the ecclesiastical life by St Eusebius. He accompanied his master into his exile at Scythopolis (355), and in his wanderings through Cappadocia, Egypt and Illyricum. In 396 he was elected bishop on the recommendation of St Ambrose, to whom he administered the sacrament of anointing the sick at his deathbed.

Honoratus of Toulouse
(St) Bp.　　　　　　　　　Dec 21
d. 3rd cent.　Born in Spanish Navarre, he succeeded St Saturninus in the see of Toulouse. He ordained St Firminus II bishop of Amiens.

Honoratus (St) M.　　　　　Dec 22
See Demetrius, Honoratus and Florus.

Honoratus (St) M.　　　　　Dec 29
See Dominic, Victor, etc.

Honoré (St) Bp.　　　　　　May 16
Otherwise Honoratus of Amiens, q.v.

Honorina (St) VM.　　　　　Feb 27
? One of the early martyrs of Gaul. Her Acts have been lost. Her cult is most ancient in Normandy.

Honorius of Buzancais
(St or Bl) M.　　　　　　　　Jan 9
d. 1250 (?)　Born at Buzancais in Berry, France, Honorius was a rich and charitable cattle merchant. On his return from a journey he found that he had been robbed by his servants. When he remonstrated with them they killed him, at Parthenay in Poitou, where he is venerated as a martyr. Canonized in 1444.

Honorius of Brescia (St)
Bp.　　　　　　　　　　　Apr 24
d. *c* 586　A hermit near Brescia, who was chosen bishop of that city (*c* 577).

Honorius of Canterbury
(St) Bp. OSB.　　　　　　　Sept 30
d. 653　A Roman by birth and a Benedictine by profession, he succeeded St Justus as archbishop of Canterbury (627). He was ordained bishop at Lincoln by St Paulinus, and himself ordained as bishops St Felix for the East Angles and St Ithamar, the first English-born bishop, for Rochester. His emblem is a baker's peel, often with loaves upon it.

Honorius (St) M.　　　　　Nov 21
See Demetrius and Honorius.

Honorius, Eutychius and Stephen (SS) MM.　　　　　Nov 21
d. *c* 300　Spanish martyrs who suffered at Asta, in Andalusia, under Diocletian.

Honorius (St) M.　　　　　Dec 30
See Mansuetus, Severus, etc.

Hope (St) VM.　　　　　　Aug 1
See Faith, Hope, and Charity.

Hormisdas (St) Pope　　　　Aug 6
d. 523　Born at Frosinone in Latium, he succeeded St Symmachus in 514. He is best remembered for the confession of faith called the Formula of Hormisdas, which was accepted in the East (519) and thus ended the Monophysite schism of Acacius. His son, St Silverius, became pope in 536.

Hormisdas (St) M.　　　　　Aug 8
d. 420　A noble Persian youth who refused to apostatize and was degraded by King Varannes to the rank of an army camel-driver and subsequently executed.

Horres (St) M.　　　　　　March 13
See Theusetas, Horres, etc.

Hortulanus (St) Bp. M.   Nov 28
See Valerian, Urban, etc.

Hosanna of Cattaro (Bl)
V. Tert. Op.   Apr 27
d. 1565   Her baptismal name was Catherine
Cosie, and she was the daughter of Orthodox
parents in Montenegro. She was converted at
Cattaro and became a Dominican tertiary,
taking the new name of Hosanna. Cult confirmed in 1928.

Hosanna of Mantua (Bl)
V. Tert. Op.   June 18
1449–1505   A native of Mantua, daughter of
the patrician, Andreasio. She spent her large
fortune in the service of the poor as a Dominican tertiary. Cult confirmed by Leo X and
Innocent XII.

Hosea (St) Prophet   July 4
8th cent. B.C.   A prophet among the ten
tribes of Israel. He seems to have been a
younger contemporary of Amos. His prophecy
was directed to his compatriots of Samaria, of
which kingdom he foretells the destruction.

Hospitius (St) H.   May 21
d. c 580   A hermit at the place now called
after him, Cap-Saint-Hospice, between Vil-
lefrance and Banlieu. His relics were translated to Lérins on May 21, the day on which
his feast is now celebrated.

Hroznata (Bl) M. O. Praem.   July 19
1160–1217   A member of a noble family of
Bohemia, who married and lost by sudden
death his wife and only child. He then founded
the Premonstratensian abbey of Tepl in
Bavaria, and was himself professed therein.
He died of starvation in a dungeon, into which
he had been thrown by robbers. Cult approved
in 1897.

Hubert (St) Bp.   Nov 3
d. 727   A courtier of Pepin of Heristal who,
having lost his wife, devoted his life to religion.
According to a late legend his conversion
happened while he was hunting, in circumstances similar to those narrated of St Eustace
and others. He is also said by some writers to
have joined the community of Stavelot. Eventually he succeeded St Lambert as bishop of
Maestricht (c 706) whence he transferred the
see to Liège. He is venerated as the patron
saint of hunters. He shares with St Eustace,
q.v. the emblem of a stag bearing a crucifix
between its antlers.

Hubert (Hugbert) of
Bretigny (St) C. OSB.   May 30
d. c 714   At the age of twelve he entered, in
spite of much opposition from his family, the
abbey of Brétigny, near Noyon. There his life
was an uninterrupted series of portentous
happenings.

Hugh of Fosse (Bl) O.
Praem.   Feb 10
1164   Born at Fosse, near Namur in Belgium, he was ordained priest and in 1119
joined St Norbert, the founder of the Premonstratensians, whose companion and assistant
he became, and whom he succeeded as abbot
of Prémontré and superior general of the
order. Cult confirmed in 1927.

Hugh dei Lippi-Uguccioni
(St) C. OSM.   Feb 17
d. 1282   A Florentine by birth. One of the
Seven Founders of the Servite Order. He
accompanied St Philip Benizi to France and
Germany and was vicar-general of the order in
Germany for eight years. He died on Mt
Senario.

Hugh of Vaucelles (Bl)
OSB. Cist.   March 29
d. 1239   From being dean of the church at
Cambrai he became a monk at the Cistercian
abbey of Vaucelles.

Hugh of Grenoble (St)
Bp. OSB.   Apr 1
1053–1132   A native of Dauphine who,
although a layman, was at the age of twenty-
five a canon of Valence. He was appointed
bishop of Grenoble in 1080. Convinced of his
own inefficiency, he retired to the austere
abbey of Chaise-Dieu and received the Benedictine habit. Pope Gregory VII, however,
ordered him back to Grenoble. He gave to St
Bruno the land of La Grande Chartreuse. He
was canonized in 1134, two years after his
death.

Hugh of Bonnevaux (Bl
or St) Ab. OSB. Cist.   Apr 1
d. 1194   A nephew of St Hugh of Grenoble
who became a Cistercian at Mezières. In 1163
he was made abbot of Léoncel, and in 1169
went to Bonnevaux. He was possessed of
singular powers of divination and exorcism,
but he is chiefly remembered as the mediator
between Alexander III and Barbarossa (1177).

Hugh of Rouen (St) Bp.
OSB.   Apr 9
d. 730   At a very early age he became a
monk, either at Fontenelle or Jumièges. Then
he was called to be *primicerius* of Metz and
shortly after was made bishop of Rouen (722)
as well as of Paris, being at the same time abbot
of Fontenelle and Jumièges. He made use of

St Hubert, Nov 3

all these offices to foster piety and learning. Before his death, however, he resigned them all and died at Jumièges as a choir monk.

Hugh of Anzy-le-Duc (St)
C. OSB.   Apr 20
d. *c* 930   A native of Poitiers, he was trained from infancy at the Benedictine abbey of Saint-Savin, Poitou, where he became a monk. Later he was sent to several houses to revive monastic observance, including the newly founded abbey of Cluny, where he helped Bl Berno. He died as prior of Anzy-le-Duc. His relics were enshrined in 1001.

Hugh the Great of Cluny
(St) Ab. OSB.   Apr 29
1024–1109   Born at Samur, he made his profession at Cluny (1039), was ordained

priest at twenty and elected abbot at twenty-five. He was abbot from 1049 till 1109 and during this period he was the adviser of nine popes; consulted and revered by all the sovereigns of Europe; and the ruler of over 1000 monasteries and dependent houses. The abbey church at Cluny, whose altar was blessed in 1095 by Pope Urban II, himself a monk of Cluny, was 555 ft (169 metres) long, the biggest in Europe at the time. He and his Cluniac monk, St Gregory VII, were instrumental in promoting the powerful revival of spiritual life throughout W. Europe which characterizes the eleventh century. He founded a hospital at Marcigny in which he loved to wait upon the lepers with his own hands. Few men have been so universally esteemed or so influential. Canonized in 1120.

Hugh of Marchiennes
(Bl) Ab. OSB.   June 11
d. 1158   Born at Tournai and educated at
Reims, he became a Benedictine at St Martin,
Tournai, and abbot of Marchiennes in 1148.

Hugh of Montaigu (Bl)
Bp. OSB.   Aug 10
d. 1136   A nephew of St Hugh of Cluny,
under whom he was educated and professed a
Benedictine at Cluny. In 1096 he was made
bishop of Auxerre.

Hugh (Little) (St) M.   Aug 18
d. 1255   A boy of Lincoln, aged nine, who
was said to have been put to death by Jews.
King Henry III conducted the judicial investi-
gations which unfortunately resulted in eighteen Jews being hanged for the crime. Little
Hugh is shown as a boy bound with cords,
often kneeling before Our Lady. This feast is
now not kept, being an example of popular
anti-semitism rather than the result of individual sanctity.

Hugh Green (Bl) M.   Aug 19
d. 1642   A Londoner, educated at Peterhouse, Cambridge. After his conversion he
studied for the priesthood at Douai, and was
ordained there in 1612. He worked in Dorset
and was hanged at Dorchester for his faith.

Hugh More (Bl) M.   Aug 28
d. 1588   Born at Grantham in Lincolnshire,
he was educated at Oxford (Broadgates Hall)
and Gray's Inn. He became a convert at Reims
and was hanged for this at Lincoln's Inn
Fields. Beatified in 1929.

Hugh of Sassoferrato (Bl)
C. OSB. Silv.   Sept 19
d. c 1290   Born at Serra San Quirico in the
diocese of Camerino, he studied at Bologna.
He received the monastic habit from St Silvester, of whom he was a devoted disciple. He
died at Sassoferrato. Cult approved in 1747.

Hugh Canefro (St or Bl) C.   Oct 8
1168–1230   Chaplain of the knights of St
John of Jerusalem at Genoa.

Hugh of Macon (Bl) Bp.
OSB. Cist.   Oct 10
d. 1151   A Cistercian under St Stephen, and
then abbot of Pontigny (1114). In 1137 he was
elected bishop of Auxerre, the first Cistercian
to be made a bishop.

Hugh of Ambronay (St)
Ab. OSB.   Oct 21
9th–10th cent.   Third abbot of the Benedictine monastery of Ambronay in the diocese of
Belley.

Hugh Faringdon (Bl) Ab.
M. OSB.   Nov 15
d. 1539   Hugh Faringdon (vere Cook)
became abbot of Reading in 1520. He was an
intimate friend of Henry VIII, but at the
dissolution he refused to surrender his abbey.
He was martyred at Reading with two prebendaries of the abbey (doubtless monks).

Hugh of Noara (St) Ab.
OSB. Cist.   Nov 17
d.p. 1172   First abbot of the Cistercian abbey
of Noara in Sicily, founded in 1172 by the
community of Sambucina.

Hugh of Lincoln (St) Bp.
O. Cart.   Nov 17
1140–1200   A native of Burgundy and a
canon regular who at the age of twenty joined
the Carthusians. In 1175 he was invited by
King Henry II to found the first English
Charterhouse at Witham in Somerset, which
he did in the face of obstacles of all kinds. In
1181 he was chosen to be bishop of Lincoln,
and governed zealously and wisely; the present
cathedral of Lincoln was begun during his
episcopate. He died, aged sixty, deeply lamented by all, especially by the Jews, whom he had
always defended and befriended. At his
magnificent funeral the kings of England and
Scotland helped to carry the bier. He was
canonized in 1220. He is usually shewn vested
as a bishop, sometimes as a Carthusian. In
either case he is accompanied by a swan, or
with seven stars about him (in mistake for St
Hugh of Grenoble).

Hugolinus of Gualdo (Bl)
C. OSA.   Jan 1
d. 1260   A hermit of St Augustine who
ruled, as prior, a monastery of that order at
Gualdo, in Umbria. Cult approved in 1919.

Hugolinus Zefferini (Bl)
C. OSA.   March 22
d. c 1470?   An Augustinian hermit friar who
lived at Cortona (or perhaps Mantua). Cult
confirmed in 1804.

Hugolinus (St) M. OFM.   Oct 10
See Daniel, Samuel, etc.

Hugolinus Magalotti (Bl)
C. Tert. OFM.   Dec 11
d. 1373   A native of Camerino who lived as a
hermit after having joined the third order of
the Friars Minor. Cult confirmed in 1856.

Humbeline (St) Abs.
OSB.   Feb 12
1092–1135   A younger sister of St Bernard

of Clairvaux. She married a rich man and was leading a worldly life when a visit to her brother in Clairvaux resulted in her spiritual conversion. She asked and obtained her husband's consent to become a nun, and entered the Black Benedictine nunnery of Jully-les-Nonnais, near Troyes, of which she became abbess. She founded Tart nunnery for the Cistercians, but she herself remained a Black Benedictine at Jully, where she died in St Bernard's arms. Cult approved in 1763.

Humbert of Savoy (Bl) C.   March 4
1136–1188   Humbert III was king of Savoy, and was three, perhaps four times married. Coming to the throne at the age of thirteen he learnt holiness and the art of government from Bl Amedius of Lausanne. Ever just and pious, in his old age he retired to the Cistercian abbey of Haute Combe, where he died in the Cistercian habit. Cult confirmed in 1838.

Humbert (St) Ab. OSB.   March 25
d. c 680   A disciple of St Amandus who became the joint founder and first abbot of the abbey of Marolles in Flanders.

Humbert of Romans (Bl) C. OP.   July 14
d. 1277   The fifth master general of the Dominicans. He was particularly successful in the development of the foreign missions, and in the definitive planning of studies among the Friars Preachers.

Humbert (Bl) C. OSB.   Oct 26
d. 7th or 8th cent.   Monk of Fritzlar in Hesse and prior of Buraburg.

Humbert (Bl) Ab. OSB. Cist.   Dec 7
d. 1148   A monk of Chaise-Dieu who went over to Clairvaux in 1117. St Bernard made him prior and then sent him as abbot to Igny (1127). Humbert sought to return to Clairvaux, but St Bernard ordered him back to Igny under pain of monastic excommunication. On Humbert's death St Bernard delivered a most touching homily to his brethren at Clairvaux.

Humiliana de'Cerchi (Bl) Tert. OFM.   May 19
1220–1246   Daughter of a Florentine family, she married at the age of sixteen. After the early death of her husband she became the first cloistered Franciscan tertiary at Florence. Cult approved by Innocent XII.

Humilis of Bisignano (Bl) C. OFM.   Nov 27
1582–1637   A native of Bisignano in Calab-

ria and a Franciscan lay-brother. He became so widely known for his sanctity that he was called to Rome, where both Gregory XV and Urban VIII consulted him. Beatified in 1882.

Humilitas (or Rosanna) (St) Abs. OSB. Vall.   May 22
1226–1310   Born at Faenza, in the Romagna, at fifteen years of age she was compelled to marry a frivolous young man named Ugoletto. After nine years of married life he became seriously ill, and on his recovery consented to become a religious and allowed Humilitas to receive the veil. She first lived as a recluse near the Vallumbrosan church of St Apollinaris where her husband was a monk. Later, persuaded by the general of the Vallumbrosans, she founded and ruled two houses for Vallumbrosan nuns.

Humphrey (St) H.   June 12
Otherwise Onuphrius, q.v.

Humphrey (Hunfrid) (St) Bp. OSB.   March 8
d. 871   A monk of the Benedictine abbey of Prüm, in the Ardennes, at the time of its greatest splendour. He became bishop of Therouanne and ruled at the same time the abbey of St Bertin. He was a source of strength and comfort to the people during the Norman invasion. He had the feast of the Assumption of Our Lady kept with especial splendour in his diocese.

Humphrey Middlemore (Bl) M. O. Cart.   June 19
d. 1535   A Carthusian monk, belonging to the London Charterhouse, who was hanged at Tyburn with two others of his brethren. Beatified in 1886.

Huno (St) C. OSB.   Feb 13
d. c 690   A monk-priest at Ely under St Etheldreda, whom he helped in her last moments, afterwards retiring to a hermitage in the Fens, where he died.

Hunegund (St) N. OSB.   Aug 25
d. c 690   According to her biographer she was compelled to marry against her wish. She prevailed on her bridegroom to accompany her to Rome, where she received the veil at the hands of Pope St Vitalian. They returned to their country and Hunegund entered the nunnery of Homblières, while her former betrothed served there as chaplain.

Hunger (St) Bp.   Dec 22
d. 866   Bishop of Utrecht from 856. During

the Norman invasion he fled to Prüm, where he died.

Hunna (St) W.   Apr 15
d. 679   The wife of an Alsatian nobleman. Her neighbours called her "the holy washer-woman" because she was wont to help them all in that capacity. Canonized in 1520.

Hyacinth (St) M.   Feb 10
See Zoticus, Irenaeus, etc.

Hyacinth (St) M.   July 3
d. *c* 120   A chamberlain of the emperor Trajan at Caesarea in Cappadocia. He was imprisoned and offered as sustenance only meat consecrated to idols. This he constantly refused and died in consequence of starvation.

Hyacinth (St) M.   July 17
? A martyr of Amastris in Paphlagonia, put to death for having cut down a tree consecrated to an idol.

Hyacinth (St) M.   July 26
d. ? *c* 110   A martyr under Trajan. His existence is certain, but his Acts are thoroughly untrustworthy.

Hyacinth (St) C. OP.   Aug 17
1185–1257   Surnamed "the Apostle of Poland". Silesian by birth, and a canon of Cracow, he received the Dominican habit from St Dominic himself. In three apostolic journeys he is said to have travelled through Poland, Pomerania, Denmark, Sweden, Norway, Russia, and as far as Tibet and China. However, the details of his life are very uncertain. He died at Cracow and was canonized in 1594. Since 1969 his cult is confined to particular calendars.

Hyacinth, Alexander and Tiburtius (SS) MM.   Sept 9
? Martyrs who are said to have suffered at some place in the Sabine country, about thirty miles from Rome.

Hyacinth Orfanel (Bl) M.
OP.   Sept 10
1578–1622   A native of Llana, Valencia, Spain. He joined the Dominicans at Barcelona and was sent to the missions of Japan. He was burnt alive at Nagasaki after many years of apostolic labours. Beatified in 1867.

Hyacinth (St) M.   Sept 11
See Protus and Hyacinth.

Hyacinth, Quintus, Felician and Lucius (SS) MM.   Oct 29
? Martyrs of Lucania in S. Italy.

Hyacinth Castañeda (St)
M. OP.   Nov 7
d. 1773   Born at Sétavo in the diocese of Valencia, Spain. After his profession as a Friar Preacher and his ordination, he was sent first to China, then to Vietnam, where he was beheaded. Canonized in 1988.

**Hyacinth of Mariscotti
(St)** Tert. V. OFM.   Jan 30
1585–1640   A lady of Viterbo, who, at the age of twenty, was passed over by the Marquis Cassizucchi in favour of her younger sister, whom he married. Hyacinth became so very troublesome that her family almost forced her into the convent of Franciscan tertiaries at Viterbo. Here, she began by scandalously ignoring or transgressing the rule, was then converted to better ways, but relapsed. Finally, over a period of twenty-four years, she gave herself up to a life of heroic humility, prayer, patience and penance. Canonized in 1807.

Hydroc (St) C.   May 5
5th cent.   The patron saint of Lanhydroc in Cornwall.

**Hygbald (Hugbald, Higbald,
Hybald) (St)** H. OSB.   Sept 18
d. *c* 690   An abbot in Lincolnshire to whom several churches are dedicated.

Hyginus (St) Pope   formerly Jan 11
d. *c* 142   The probable dates of his pontificate are 138 to 142, but even this is uncertain. It is also doubtful whether he died a martyr. Cult suppressed in 1969.

Hypatius (St) M.   June 3
See Lucillian, Claudius, etc.

Hypatius (St) C.   June 17
d. *c* 450   Born in Phrygia, at the age of nineteen he embraced the solitary life, first in Thrace and then at Chalcedon in Bithynia, where he became abbot of a flourishing *laura*. He was a determined opponent of Nestorianism.

Hypatius (St) M.   June 18
See Leontius, Hypatius and Theodulus.

Hypatius and Andrew (SS)
MM.   Aug 29
d. 735   Natives of Lydia. Hypatius was a bishop and Andrew a priest. They were martyred at Constantinople under Leo the Isaurian for their defence of the veneration of sacred images.

Hypatius (St) Bp. M.   Nov 14
d. *c* 325   A bishop of Gangra in Paphlagonia, who attended the council of Nicaea and was a prominent defender of the divinity of Christ.

While on his return from Nicaea, he was attacked by a band of heretics and stoned to death.

Hyperechios (St) C.   Aug 7

? An Egyptian desert father. A collection of 160 sayings attributed to him were published by Rosweyde's *Vitae Patrum*.

Hywyn (St) C.   Jan 6

d. *p.*516 Probably a companion of St Cadfan on his return journey (516) from Brittany to Cornwall and Wales. He is said to have been the founder of Aberdaron in Gwynedd. Several churches in W. England known as St Owen's or St Ewen's possibly have him for their titular saint.

Ia (Hia, Ives) (St) VM.   Feb 3
d. 450   An Irish maiden, sister of St Ercus, who crossed into Cornwall with SS Fingar, Piala and other missionaries, and there suffered martyrdom at the mouth of the Hayle river. She has left her name to St Ives in Cornwall.

Ia and Comp. (SS) MM.   Aug 4
d. 360   A Greek slave, who suffered martyrdom in Persia with many other Christian captives (the figure usually given is nine thousand) during the persecution of King Shapur II. The name signifies "violet", and the circumstances attending his martyrdom are not known.

Iago (St) Apostle   July 25
Note. An antiquated Spanish form of the name of St James. Iago is now always used with the prefixed hagiological title of Sant (Saint) in this way: Santiago.

Ibar (Iberius, Ivor) (St) C.   Apr 23
5th cent.   One of the missionaries — among them SS Kiaran, Ailbe, Declan, etc. — who evangelized Ireland at the time of, or as some writers hold, shortly before, St Patrick. St Ibar preached chiefly in Leinster and in Meath.

Ida of Argensolles (Bl) Abs. OSB. Cist.   Jan 13
d. 1226   A Black Benedictine nun of St Leonard's, Liège, who was elected abbess of the Cistercian nunnery of Argensolles, in the diocese of Soissons.

Ida of Hohenfels (Bl) N. OSB.   Feb 24
d. *c* 1195   Wife of Eberhard, count of Spanheim and, after his death, a Benedictine nun at Bingen.

Ida of Boulogne (Bl) W.   Apr 13
1040–1113   A daughter of Godfrey IV, duke of Lorraine, descended from Charlemagne. She was the mother of Godfrey and Baldwin de Bouillon. After the death of her husband she endowed several monasteries in Picardy, herself living as a Benedictine oblate under the obedience of the abbot of St Vaast.

Ida of Louvain (Bl) N. OSB. Cist.   Apr 13
d. *c* 1300   A native of Louvain. She joined the Cistercians at the nunnery of Rossendael, near Malines, where she was favoured by God with a life-long series of amazing supernatural charismata.

Ida of Nivelles (Bl) N. OSB.   May 8
d. 652   She is also named Itta or Iduberga. She was the wife of Pepin of Landen, after whose death (640) she became a Benedictine at Nivelles under her own daughter, St Gertrude.

Ida of Herzfeld (St) W.   Sept 4
d. *c* 813   Great-granddaughter of Charles Martel. She married and was very happy in her married life; but lost her husband very young. She then founded the nunnery of Herzfeld in Westphalia, devoted herself to good works, and died at the convent.

Ida of Toggenburg (Bl) N. OSB.   Nov 3
1156–1226   She married a Count Henry of Toggenburg, to whom she bore no child and from whom she suffered much persecution. She escaped, and at last succeeded in obtaining her husband's consent to her becoming a nun in the Benedictine convent of Fieshingen.

Idaberga (*several*)
Otherwise Edburga, q.v.

Idesbald (Bl) Ab. OSB. Cist.   Apr 18
1100–1167   Born in Flanders, he spent his youth at the court of the count of Flanders. In 1135 he was made canon of Furnes, but resigned his office to become a Cistercian at the abbey of Our Lady of the Dunes on the sand-hills between Dunkirk and Nieuport. He became the third abbot and ruled for twelve years. Cult confirmed in 1894.

Idus (St) Bp.   July 14
5th cent.   A disciple of St Patrick by whom he was baptized and appointed bishop of Alt-Fadha in Leinster.

Ignatius of Antioch (St)
Bp. M.   GC. Oct 17
d. *c* 107   Surnamed Theophorus (the God-bearer). Bishop of Antioch in Syria for forty years. Under Trajan he was carried to Rome, where he was thrown to the wild beasts in the amphitheatre during the public games. On his way to Rome he wrote seven letters, which are still extant and are of great doctrinal value. His relics are kept at St Peter's, Rome, and his name is mentioned in the first eucharistic prayer.

Ignatius of Africa (St) M.   Feb 3
See Laurentinus, Ignatius and Celerina.

Ignatius de Laconi (St)
C. OFM. Cap.   May 11
1701–1781   Vincent de Laconi was born in Sardinia of parents of modest means. His childish devotion was remarkable, for he would be at the church doors before dawn waiting in prayer for them to be opened. Received with some difficulty into the Franciscan order, he made profession as Br Ignatius in 1722. He passed his lfe in menial tasks and in begging for his convent at Cagliari. Illiterate, he loved to listen to the gospels, especially the Passion of Christ being read, and was favoured with the gifts of prophecy and miracles. Canonized 1951.

Ignatius Delgado (St) Bp.
M. OP.   July 12
1761–1838   A Spaniard by birth, Ignatius Delgado y Cebrián professed the Dominican rule and was sent to the missions in Vietnam. He laboured for nearly fifty years and was appointed vicar apostolic of E. Tonkin and ordained bishop. He died from hunger and exposure in a cage. Beatified in 1900, Canonized in 1988.

Ignatius de Azevedo and Comp. (BB) MM. SJ.   July 15
d. 1570   A band of forty Portuguese and Spanish Jesuit missionaries who were put to death by the Huguenot skipper, Jacques Sourie, near the Canary Islands, while on their way to the West Indies. Ignatius was the superior and leader of the band. He was born at Coimbra, where he joined the Society of Jesus in 1548. He was a religious of outstanding ability, highly revered by all. Cult officially confirmed in 1854.

Ignatius of Loyola (St)
Founder   GC. July 31
1491–1556   Iñigo de Recalde de Loyola was born on the estate of his family at Loyola in the Basque province of Guipuzcoa (Spain) and, after some time as a page at court, joined the army and was grievously wounded at the siege of Pampeluna in 1521. On his recovery he turned his mind to the service of the church. He prepared himself by a retreat at Montserrat and Manresa, where he wrote his epoch-making classic, *The Book of Spiritual Exercises*. At Paris he gathered nine companions and together they took their first vows at the church of Montmartre. Ignatius's aim was simply this: to work for the greater glory of God under the obedience of the pope. In 1537 he called his little band the Society of Jesus and, in April 1541, all took their final vows in the Benedictine basilica of St Paul-outside-the-Walls, Rome. Ignatius was naturally elected the first general and ruled the Society until his death. Before this time the original band had already become a veritable army scattered throughout the world — from Japan in the Far East to the furthermost West Indies. Ignatius was canonized in 1622.

Ignatius Jorjes (Bl) M.   Sept 10
d. 1622   The four-year-old son of Dominic Jorjes and Isabel Fernandez. He was beheaded with his mother at Nagasaki (see Charles Spinola).

Ignatius of Constantinople (St) Bp.   Oct 23
c 799–877   Son of the Byzantine emperor Michael, he was successively monk, priest, abbot and patriarch (842) of his native Constantinople. He stood firm against intrigue and corruption, even in high places, and openly refused holy communion to Bardas Caesar on account of his public incest. Ignatius was driven from the see, and Photius intruded. After nine years Ignatius was recalled and was patriarch until his death.

Ildephonsus (St) Bp.   Jan 23
607–667   Nephew of St Eugene of Toledo. He was also born at Toledo; studied at Seville under St Isidore; became monk and abbot of Agli (Agalia) on the Tagus near Toledo; and was made archbishop of that city in 657. He was responsible for the unification of the Spanish liturgy and excelled as a writer, chiefly on Our Lady.

Illadan (Illathan, Iolladhan) (St) Bp.   June 10
6th cent. Bishop of Rathliphthen (now Rathlihen) in Offaly, Ireland.

Illidius (Allyre) (St) Bp.   July 7
d. 385   The fourth bishop of Clermont, France. St Gregory of Tours had a great veneration for him.

Illog (St) C.   Aug 8
Otherwise Ellidius, q.v.

Illtyd (Illtut) (St) Ab.   Nov 6
d. *c* 505   One of the most celebrated of the
Welsh saints, though unfortunately the details
of his life have not reached us in trustworthy
form. He embraced the monastic life under St
Cadoc and later founded the great abbey of
Llan-Illtut, or Llantwit, whence issued most of
the Welsh saints of that period. According to
some the original foundation was on Caldey
Island. He is said to have died in Brittany.

Illuminata (St) V.   Nov 29
d. *c* 320   A maiden of Todi, in Italy, where
she is still held in great veneration.

Illuminatus (St) Mk. OSB.   May 11
d. *c* 1000   A Benedictine monk of the abbey
of San Mariano, in his native township of
Sanseverino in the Marches of Ancona.

Illuminatus (St) C. OFM.   May 11
d. *c* 1230   Said to have been a disciple of St
Francis of Assisi. He is often confused with his
homonym of Sanseverino.

**Imana of Loss (Imaina,
Himmanna, Imaine) (Bl)**
Abs. OSB.   Oct 21
d. 1270   Cistercian abbess of Salzinnes,
near Namur, and afterwards of Flines, in the
diocese of Cambrai.

Imelda Lambertini (Bl)
V. OP.   May 12
d. 1333   Daughter of Count Egano Lambertini of Bologna, she was a pupil at the
Dominican convent of that city and "is stated
to have received her first holy communion
miraculously at the age of eleven, and to have
died immediately after" (Attwater). Cult confirmed in 1826.

Imelin (St) Ab.   March 10
Otherwise Emilian, q.v.

Imma (Immina) (St) Abs.
OSB.   Nov 25
c 700–752   A native of Würzburg and abbess
of a nunnery at Karlburg in Franconia.

Ina and Ethelburga (SS)   Sept 8
d. 727   Ina was king of Wessex from 688 till
726. As such he is best remembered as the
restorer of Glastonbury. About the year 726 he
resigned and, with his wife Ethelburga, journeyed to Rome, where he ended his days in
practices of piety and penance as a monk.

Inan (St) H.   Aug 18
Otherwise Evan, q.v.

Indaletius (St) Bp.   May 15
See Torquatus, Ctesiphon, etc.

**Indes, Domna, Agapes
and Theophila (SS) MM.**   Dec 28
d. 303   A group of martyrs who suffered at
Nicomedia under Diocletian.

Indract (St) M.   Feb 5
d. *c* 710   An old legend makes him a Irish
chieftain who, on his return from a Roman
pilgrimage, was put to death with his sister St
Dominica (Drusa) and others, by heathen
Saxons, near Glastonbury, where their relics
were enshrined. A still later legend has made
them contemporaries of St Patrick.

Inés de Beniganim (Bl)
V. OSA. Erem.   Jan 21
1625–1696   Born near Valencia, in Spain,
she entered the nunnery of Augustinian her-
mitesses at Beniganim with the new name of
Josepha Maria. In Spain she is usually called
by her baptismal name, as above. Beatified in
1888.

Inés, Inez (*several*)
Note. The Spanish and Portuguese forms
respectively of the name Agnes, q.v.

Ingen (St) M.   Dec 20
See Ammon, Zeno, etc.

Ingenuinus (St) Bp.   Feb 5
Otherwise Genuinus, q.v.

Iñigo (St) Ab. OSB.   June 1
Otherwise Eneco, q.v.

Inischolus   Apr 29
See Corfu, Martyrs of.

**Injuriosus and
Scholastica (SS)**   May 25
d. *c* 550   A married couple of Auvergne who
lived the whole of their married life as brother
and sister, "*Les Deux Amants*".

Innocent of Tortona (St)
Bp.   Apr 17
d. *c* 350   He was a confessor under Diocletian, being scourged and just escaping death.
After Constantine's peace, he was ordained a
priest and then bishop of Tortona in Italy
(*c* 326).

Innocent (St) M.   June 17
See Isaurus, Innocent, etc.

Innocent (St) Bp.   June 19
d. 559   Bishop of Le Mans, in France, for
over forty years.

The Holy Innocents, Dec 28

Innocent I (St) Pope   formerly July 28
d. 417 A native of Albano, near Rome, St
Innocent was pope from 402 till 417. The
outstanding event in his pontificate was the
sack of Rome by the Goth, Alaric, in 410. He
firmly maintained the supremacy of the
Roman see, both in the West in the case of the
African synods against Pelagianism, and in the
East as witness the appeal of St John Chrysostom. Cult suppressed in 1969.

Innocent V (Bl) Pope OP.   June 22
1245–1277 Born at Tarentaise in Burgundy, he entered the Dominican order and
acquired great fame as a theologian and as a
preacher. In 1272 he was made archbishop
of Lyons, and during his episcopate the general council was held in that city, in which he
took a prominent part. Created cardinal of
Ostia, he was made pope in 1276, but died
only a few months later. Beatified in 1898.

Innocent XI (Bl) Pope   Aug 12
1611–1689 Born at Como, he was elected
pope in 1676. He was outstanding for charity,
evangelical simplicity and poverty. He withstood the autocracy of Louis XIV of France,
strove to check nepotism, stirred up exemplary
life among the clergy and encouraged catche-
tical instruction. He condemned Jansenism,
Quietism and the errors of Molinos. Beatified
1956.

**Innocent, Sebastia (Sabbatia)
and Comp. (SS)** MM.   July 4
? A group of thirty-two martyrs who suffered
at Sirmium, now Mitrovica, in the Balkans.

Innocent (St) M.   Sept 22
See Theban Legion.

Innocents, The Holy (SS)
MM.   GC. Dec 28
1st cent. From a very early date the male
children in Bethlehem and all the area around
it, murdered by Herod (Matt. 2:1–18), have
been liturgically venerated as martyrs. Prudentius most fittingly styles them *Flores Martyrum*. Their number is not known, and this has
led to the multiplication of their relics in many
churches. In art they are shown as a large
number of small boys being slain by soldiers in
various ways; their helpless mothers bewailing
the scene.

Iphigenia (St) V.   Sept 21
1st cent. Alleged to be a maiden of Ethiopia
converted by St Matthew the apostle and
evangelist.

Irais (Herais, Rhais) (St)
VM.   Sept 22
d. *c* 300 An Egyptian maiden of Alexandria,
or of Antinöe, beheaded under Diocletian.

Irchard (St) Bp.   Aug 24
7th cent. An apostle of the Picts and disciple of St Ternan, born in Kincardineshire and said to have been ordained bishop in Rome by St Gregory the Great.

Irenaeus (St) M.   Feb 10
See Zoticus, Irenaeus, etc.

Irenaeus of Sirmium (St)
Bp. M.   March 25
d. 304 A bishop in Pannonia (Hungary), who suffered martyrdom under Diocletian at Sirmium (Mitrovica). His Acts are authentic and most touching.

Irenaeus (St) M.   March 26
See Theodore, Irenaeus, etc.

Irenaeus (St) M.   Apr 1
See Quintian and Irenaeus.

**Irenaeus, Peregrinus
and Irene (SS)** MM.   May 5
d. *c* 300 Martyrs of Thessalonica, burnt at the stake under Diocletian.

Irenaeus of Lyons (St)
Bp. M.   GC. June 28
c 130–200 A native of Asia Minor and a disciple of St Polycarp, who was a pupil of St John the apostle. He migrated to Gaul, and became bishop of Lyons (*c* 177). Tradition adds that he was a martyr, but of this we have no proof. St Irenaeus is the first great ecclesiastical writer of the West. His work against Gnosticism is a witness to the apostolic tradition, derived from St John. His theological writings emphasise the importance of both old and new testaments, the unity of the gospels and the idea of the recapitulation of our human nature in Christ's nature. His writings are a very early testimony to the clear teaching of the apostles and the traditions of the early church.

**Irenaeus and Mustiola
(SS)** MM.   July 3
d. 273 Irenaeus, a deacon, and Mustiola, a noble lady, were martyred at Chiusi in Tuscany under Aurelian for having ministered to other martyrs and buried their bodies.

**Irenaeus and Abundius
(SS)** MM.   Aug 26
d. *c* 258 They were Roman martyrs. According to their *Passio* they were drowned in the public sewers during the persecution of Valerian.

**Irenaeus, Antony, Theodore,
Saturninus, Victor and
Comp. (SS)** MM.   Dec 15
d. *c* 258 A group of twenty-two martyrs who suffered under Valerian.

Irene (St) VM.   Apr 5
d. 304 The sister of SS Agape and Chionia, q.v.

Irene (St) M.   May 5
See Irenaeus, Peregrinus, etc.

Irene (St) M.   Sept 18
See Sophia and Irene.

Irene (St) VM.   Oct 20
d. *c* 653 Long revered as a nun of Portugal, especially revered in Santarem. She is now regarded as a duplicate of the St Irene of April 5, q.v.

Irenion (St) Bp.   Dec 16
d. 389 A bishop of Gaza in Palestine in the time of Theodosius the Great.

Irmengard (Bl) Abs. OSB.   July 16
d. 866 Daughter of King Louis the German, grandson of Charlemagne. By her father she was appointed abbess, first of Buchau and then of Chiemsee. Cult confirmed in 1928.

Irmina (St) Abs. OSB.   Dec 24
d. 708 Daughter of Dagobert II. At the age of fifteen she was given in marriage but on the day of her wedding her betrothed died. She then persuaded her father to build for her the nunnery of Oehren (*Horreum*) near Trier, under the Benedictine rule. She was a generous benefactress of both Celtic and Saxon monks and built Echternach for St Willibrord (698). She died at the monastery of Weissenburg, another foundation of her father's.

Isaac (St) H.   Apr 11
d. *c* 550 A Syrian monk who fled from the Monophysite persecution and founded a *laura* at Monteluco, near Spoleto, in Umbria. He was one of the restorers of eremitical life in 6th century Italy.

Isaac (Isacius) (St) M.   Apr 21
See Apollog, Isacius and Crotates.

Isaac (St) Ab.   May 30
d. *c* 410 A brave defender of the Catholic faith against the Arian emperor Valens, whom he publicly denounced. He narrowly escaped death and became a monk, and eventually abbot, of a large monastery at Constantinople.

Isaac (St) M.   June 3
d. 852 Born at Cordoba, in Spain, he

became very proficient in Arabic and was made a notary under the Moorish government. He resigned this office to embrace the monastic life at Tabanos, about seven miles from Cordoba. In a public debate at Cordoba he denounced Mohammed and was put to death at the age of twenty-seven.

Isaac the Great (St) Bp.   Sept 9
c 350–440 Son of the Armenian patriarch (or katholikos) St Nerses the Great, to whose office he succeeded. He is the real founder of the Armenian church. He translated a large part of the Bible, founded monasteries, and was practically the only ruler — ecclesiastical and civil — of the Armenians.

Isaac (Isacius) (St) Bp. M.   Sept 21
? An Eastern martyr, honoured chiefly in Cyprus, of which he was bishop.

Isaac Jogues (St) M. SJ.   GC. Oct 19
d. 1646 (Oct 18) A Jesuit missionary who arrived in Canada in 1636 and, after several heroic adventures, was tomahawked by the Mohawks in an Iroquois village. Canonized in 1930. See John de Brebeuf and Comps.

Isaac (St) M. OSB.   Nov 12
See Benedict, John, etc.

Isabel Fernandez (Bl) M.   Sept 10
d. 1622 A Spanish lady, widow of Dominic Jorjes, beheaded with her son Ignatius at Nagasaki, for having given shelter to Bl Charles Spinola, q.v. Beatified in 1867.

Isabella (St) Queen   July 8
Otherwise Elizabeth, q.v.

Isabelle of France (Bl) V.
Poor Clare   Feb 26
d. 1270 The only sister of St Louis of France. She declined marriage with the emperor of Germany and after the death of her mother, Blanche of Castile, founded the convent of Poor Clares at Longchamps, near Paris, where she lived as a nun, without, however, taking vows. Beatified in 1520.

Isacius (Isaac)   Apr 21
See Apollo, Isacius and Crotates.

Isaiah (St) Prophet   July 6
8th cent. B.C. One of the four greater prophets of the O.T. Tradition tells us that he was sawn in two by order of King Manasses of Juda, and buried under an oak tree. His tomb was still venerated in the 5th century A.D. In art he is shown as an elderly man, bearing a scroll inscribed "Ecce Virgo Concipiet", or being sawn in two, or holding a saw.

St Isaiah, July 6

Isaias, Sabas and Comp. (SS) MM.   Jan 14
d. 309 Thirty-eight monks on Mt Sinai, massacred by pagan Arabs. This massacre was followed by several others in the neighbourhood of the Red Sea.

Isaias Boner (Bl) C. OSA.   Feb 8
d. 1471 Born at Cracow, where he studied theology. He joined the Augustinians and was employed chiefly in teaching scripture, which he did with extraordinary zeal and success.

**Isarnus (Ysarn) of
Toulouse (St)** Ab. OSB.   Sept 24
d. 1048 Born at Marseilles, he was edu-

cated locally at St Victor's, where he became a monk and an abbot. He was famous for his charity, chiefly towards criminals.

Isaurus, Innocent, Felix, Jeremias and Peregrinus (SS) MM.
June 17

? Athenians, who during one of the persecutions, concealed themselves in a cave at Apollonia in Macedonia. On being discovered they were beheaded.

Isberga (Itisberga) (St) V. OSB.
May 21

d. *c* 800 A supposed sister of Charlemagne. She was a nun at Aire (*Aria*) in the Artois. She is venerated as the patroness of Artois.

Ischyrion and Comp. (SS) MM.
June 1

d. 250 Ischyrion was an Egyptian official who was impaled for the faith under Decius. The Ischyrion commemorated in the pre-1970 RM. on June 1 is identical with the one mentioned on Dec 22.

Isidora (St) V.
May 1

c 365 A nun in an Egyptian monastery who, to escape being honoured in the cloister, fled to a desert hermitage, where she died.

Isidore of Antioch (St) Bp. M.
Jan 2

Baronius introduced this saint into the pre-1970 RM. on the strength of a notice in the martyrology of St Jerome which read: *In antiochia Siridoni episcopi eiusdem loci.* No such bishop is known.

Isidore of Nitria (St) Bp.
Jan 2

4th cent. Mentioned by St Jerome as "a holy venerable bishop" who had welcomed him to Egypt. Some think that he is identical with St Isidore of Pelusium (Feb 4).

Isidore the Egyptian (St) C.
Jan 15

d. 404 An Egyptian priest who was in charge of the hospice for pilgrims at Alexandria. He defended St Athanasius and suffered much at the hands of the Arians. Accused of Origenism by St Jerome, Isidore went to Constantinople where he was befriended by St John Chrysostom.

Isidore of Pelusium (St) C.
Feb 4

d. *c* 450 An Egyptian abbot of a monastery at Pelusium. He was much esteemed by St Cyril of Alexandria. A great number of his letters are still extant.

Isidore (St) M.
Feb 5

The pre-1970 RM. placed him at Alexandria,

but he is probably a duplicate of Isidore of Chios (May 15), q.v.

Isidore of Seville (St) Bp. and Dr.
GC. Apr 4

c 560–636 A native of Cartagena, in Spain, and brother to SS Leander, Fulgentius and Florentina. He was educated by St Leander whom he succeeded in the see of Seville in 600. He presided over several synods; reorganized the Spanish church; encouraged monastic life; completed the Mozarabic liturgical rite; was responsible for the decree of the council of Toledo in 633; and was himself an encyclopaedical writer on theology, scripture, biography, history, geography, astronomy and grammar. Declared Doctor of the Church by Benedict XIV. He is often shown as a bishop holding a pen and with a swarm of bees around him, or a hive near him.

Isidore (St) M.
Apr 17

See Elias, Paul and Isidore.

Isidore the Farmer (St) C.
May 10

d. 1170 A native of Madrid, he spent his whole life working in the fields on an estate just outside the city. He was married to St Mary de la Cabeza. Canonized in 1622 and venerated as the patron saint of Madrid.

Isidore of Chios (St) M.
May 15

d. ? 251 A martyr of Chios under Decius.

Isidore (St) M.
Aug 4

See Epiphanes and Isidore.

Isidore (St) M.
Dec 14

See Heron, Arsenius, etc.

Ismael (St) Bp.
June 16

6th cent. A disciple of St Teilo, and by him ordained bishop. Several Welsh churches are dedicated to him.

Ismael (St) M.
June 17

See Manuel, Sabel and Ismael.

Isnard de Chiampo (Bl) C. OP.
March 22

d. 1244 A native of Chiampo, diocese of Vicenza, he received the Dominican habit at the hands of St Dominic in 1219 and was the founder and first prior of the friary at Pavia. It is narrated of him that, in spite of his mortified life, "he was excessively fat and people used to ridicule him about it when he was preaching" (Attwater). Cult confirmed in 1919.

Issell (Issey) (St) Bp.
Feb 9

Otherwise Teilo, q.v.

Isserninus (St) Bp.
Dec 6

See Auxilius, Isserninus and Secundinus.

St Isidore the Farmer, May 10

Issey (St) Ab. Feb 9
Otherwise Teilo, q.v. Perhaps also a Cornish
variant of Ita.

Ita (Ytha, Meda) (St) V. Jan 15
d. *c* 570 In popular veneration among the
Irish she is second only to St Bridget. She was
a native of Drum in Co. Waterford. She
founded the nunnery of Hy Conaill in Co.
Limerick and soon attracted thither large
numbers of maidens. Her life is full of incredible anecdotes.

Ithamar (St) Bp. June 10
d. *c* 656 A native of Kent. He was the first
Anglo-Saxon to be made a bishop, succeeding
St Paulinus at Rochester.

Itta (Iduberga) (Bl) N.
OSB. May 8
Otherwise Ida of Nivelles, q.v.

Ivan (St) H. June 24
9th cent. A hermit in Bohemia, who had
renounced a brilliant position at court. He was
buried by St Ludmilla, duchess of Bohemia.

Ive (Ives) (St) VM. Feb 3
Otherwise Ia, q.v.

Ives (St) Bp. Apr 24
Otherwise Ivo, q.v.

Ivetta (Jutta) (Bl) W. Jan 13
1158–1228 A Dutch mystic who was left a
widow and the mother of two children at the
age of eighteen. Consecrating her widowhood
to God, she undertook the care of lepers, till
she took to the solitary life at Huy, near
Leyden. She spent more than forty years as a
solitary and was famous for discernment of
spirits and gifts of counsel.

Ivo (St) Bp. Apr 24
? According to the medieval legend he was a
Persian bishop who became a hermit in Huntingdonshire. The town of St Ives in Huntingdonshire takes its name from him (but not that
in Cornwall).

Ivo (Yvo) Hélory (St) C. May 19
1253–1303 A native of Brittany, born near
Tréguier. He studied at Paris and Orleans and
practised law in his native city, both in the
ecclesiastical and in the civil courts. He
defended the poor and unprotected as well as
the rich and was called "the Advocate of the
Poor". Canonized in 1347 and venerated by
lawyers as their patron saint.

Ivo of Chartres (St) Bp.
OSA. May 23
c 1040–1115 The provost of the Augustinian canons regular of Saint-Quentin, who in
1091 was made bishop of Chartres. He was
renowned for his knowledge of canon law and
was consulted by King Philip of France on
difficult canonical questions. Upright and just,
Ivo opposed the rapacity of ecclesiastical dignitaries. He wrote much on canon law.

Ivor (St) Bp. AC. Apr 23
Otherwise Ibar, q.v.

Jacob of Nisibis (St) Bp. July 15

4th cent. Not much is known for sure about him, but he is an important figure in the traditions of the Syriac church. Theodoret mentions the important part he took in the council of Nicaea (325) which in itself betokens a high standard of theological and intellectual attainment. He is second only to St Ephraem amomg the Syrian Fathers.

Jacobinus de' Canepaci (Bl) C. OC. March 3

1438–1508 A native of the diocese of Vercelli, in Piedmont, and a Carmelite lay-brother there. Cult approved in 1845.

Jacopone da Todi (Bl) C. OFM. Dec 25

c 1230–1306 Jacopone Benedetti was a native of Todi, who read law at Bologna, married, and lived in easy circumstances. In 1268 he lost his wife and his sorrow knew no bounds. He became a "fool for Christ's sake" and eventually joined the Friars Minor. Unfortunately his tempestuous temperament led him to join the party of the Franciscan Spirituals; he wrote against the pope and was put in prison. He is the alleged author of the *Stabat Mater*, etc. Cult never widespread; today it is centred on Todi.

Jacut and Guethenoc (SS) CC. Feb 8

5th cent. Sons of SS Fragan and Gwen, and brothers of the more celebrated St Gwenaloe or Winwaloe. They became disciples of St Budoc, and like him were driven from Britain by the invading Saxons.

Jader (St) Bp. M. Sept 10

See Nemesian, Felix, etc.

Jadwiga (*several*)

Otherwise Hedwig, q.v.

Jambert (St) Bp. OSB. Aug 12

d. 792 Abbot of St Augustine's, Canterbury and chosen to succeed St Bregwin as archbishop in that see (766).

James (*several*)

Note. James is the English form of the Hebrew Jacob, latinized into Jacobus. Hence the modern variants in different languages: in Italian, Giacomo; in French, Jacques; in Spanish, Santiago, Iago, Jaime, Diego; in Portuguese, Iago, Diogo; in Catalan, Jaume.

James of Tarentaise (St) Bp. Jan 16

d. ? 429 A Syrian by origin he became a monk and a disciple of St Honoratus at Lérins and was venerated at Chambéry as an apostle of Savoy and the first bishop of Tarentaise.

James the Hermit (St) C. Jan 28

6th cent. The pre-1970 RM. said: "In Palestine the memory of St James the Hermit, who, after a lapse from the faith, lay hid long in a tomb for penance, and, renowned for miracles, passed to the Lord." A later legend changes the "lapse from the faith" into one of homicide, committed under most romantic circumstances.

James the Almsgiver (Bl) C. or M. Jan 28

d.1304 Born near Chiusi in Lombardy, Bl James studied law, but on attaining manhood became a priest and restored a ruined hospital, where he tended the sick and gave legal advice gratuitously. Having discovered that the former revenues of this hospital had been unjustly appropriated, he found it necessary to sue the bishop of Chiusi in the courts where he won his case. The bishop retaliated by hiring assassins who murdered the saint.

James Kisai (St) M. SJ. Feb 6

d. 1597 A native of Japan, temporal coadjutor of the Society of Jesus, and catechist at Ozaka. He was crucified at Nagasaki at the age of sixty-four. Canonized in 1862. See Paul Miki and Comps.

James Salès and William Saultemouche (BB) MM. SJ. Feb 7

d. 1593 James Salès was born in 1556 and joined the Society of Jesus. In 1592, in company with William Saultemouche, a temporal coadjutor, he was sent to preach at Aubenas in the Cévennes. His sermons, in which he attacked the teaching of the Protestants, were a great success. Early in February 1593, a band of Huguenot raiders dragged the Jesuits before an improvised court of Calvinist ministers. After a heated theological discussion Salès was shot, while Saultemouche was stabbed to death. Both were beatified in 1926.

James Fenn (Bl) M.   Feb 12
d. 1584   A native of Montacute, near Yeovil, Somerset, he was educated at Oxford (Corpus Christi College and Gloucester Hall), became a schoolmaster and married. On his wife's death he studied at Reims and was ordained priest (1580). Four years later he was martyred at Tyburn. Beatified in 1929.

James of Viterbo (Bl) C.
OSA. Erem.   Feb 13
d. 1308   He became an Augustinian hermit in his native city and taught theology with considerable renown, being known as *Doctor Speculativus*. He became bishop of Benevento, and was transferred to Naples in 1303. Cult confirmed by Pius X.

James Carvalho and Comp. (BB) MM. SJ.   Feb 25
d. 1624   A Portuguese Jesuit who laboured as a missionary in the Far East. Together with sixty other Christians he was slowly martyred by exposure to cold at Sendai in Japan. They were beatified 1867.

James Capocci (Bl) Bp.
OSA.   March 14
d. 1308   Born at Viterbo. From being an Augustinian friar he became in 1302 bishop of Benevento and in 1303 transferred to Naples. Cult approved in 1911.

James Bird (Bl) M.   March 25
d. 1593   A native of Winchester who, at the age of nineteen, was hanged in that city for being reconciled to the church. Beatified in 1929.

James of Padua (Bl) M.
OFM.   Apr 9
See Bl Thomas of Tolentino and Comp.

James of Certaldo (Bl) C.
OSB. Cam.   Apr 13
d. 1292   James Guidi was born at Certaldo, the son of a knight of Volterra. He joined the Camaldolese Benedictines at the abbey of SS Clement and Justus at Volterra. He spent sixty years there, during forty of which he acted as parish priest of the abbey church. His father and his brother joined the abbey as lay-brothers. Twice he refused the abbacy.

James of Cerqueto (Bl)
C. OSA.   Apr 17
d. 1367   A native of Cerqueto, near Perugia.

He joined the Augustinian friars in the latter city. Cult approved in 1895.

James D'Oldo (Bl) C.
Tert. OFM.   Apr 19
d. 1404   A native of Lodi who married and for a time gave himself up to pleasure and good living. He was converted to higher things during a time of pestilence when, with his wife, he became a Franciscan tertiary, turned his house into a church, and eventually was ordained.

James Duckett (Bl) M.   Apr 19
d. 1602   A native of Gilfortrigs, Skelsmergh, Westmorland, who became a convert and settled as a bookseller in London. After several terms of imprisonment, amounting altogether to nine years, for printing and selling Catholic books, he was hanged at Tyburn for the same reason. Beatified in 1929.

James Bell (Bl) M.   Apr 20
d. 1584   A native of Warrington, Lancs, and educated at Oxford. He was ordained under Queen Mary, conformed to the state church under Elizabeth, but repented and was reconciled to the Roman church. For this he was hanged at Lancaster in his sixty-fourth year. Beatified in 1929.

James of Persia (St) M.   Apr 22
4th cent.   A priest martyred under Shapur II.

James of Bitetto (Bl) C.
OFM.   Apr 27
d. c 1485   Surnamed also "of Sclavonia", or "of Illyrium", or "of Zara", or "of Dalmatia". He was a native of Sebenico in Dalmatia, and donned the Franciscan habit as a lay-brother at Zara; but spent most of his life at the friary of Bitetto, near Bari, in S. Italy. Cult approved by Innocent XII.

James of Numidia (St) M.   Apr 30
See Marianus, James, etc.

James the Less (St)
Apostle   GC. May 3
d. c 62   James the Less (*Jacobus Minor*) or "the Younger", surnamed also "the Just", was a cousin of our Lord, and one of the Twelve. After the Resurrection he became the first bishop of Jerusalem. He is the author of one of the canonical letters. He was martyred at Jerusalem by being thrown from a pinnacle of the temple and then stoned to death according to tradition. His emblem is a fuller's club: he often also holds a book.

James Walworth (Bl) M.
O. Cart.   May 11
d. 1537   A monk of the London charter-

St James the Less, May 3

house, hanged in chains at York under Henry VIII. Beatified in 1886.

James of Nocera (Bl) C.
OSB.   May 27
d. 1300 A native of Nocera in Umbria, and a monk of Santa Croce di'Fontavellana.

James Bertoni (Bl) C.
OSM.   May 30
c 1444–1483 A native of Faenza. At the age of nine he joined the Servites, whom he served as procurato of the friary from the time of his ordination till his death. Cult confirmed in 1766.

James Salomone (Bl) C.
OP.   May 31
1231–1314 A native of Venice who joined the Dominicans at Santa Maria Celeste in that city, and held office in several houses of the order until he died of cancer at Forli. Cult approved in 1526.

James of Strepar (Bl) Bp.
OFM.   June 1
c 1350–1411 Of Polish birth, he joined the Franciscans and worked very successfully as vicar-general of the Franciscan missions among the orthodox and pagans of W. Russia. In 1392 he was appointed archbishop of Halicz in Gallicia. Cult approved in 1791.

James Buzabaliao (St) M.   June 3
d. 1886 Son of the royal bark-cloth maker and a soldier of King Mwanga of Uganda. He was baptized in 1885 and burnt alive at Namuyongo in the following year. See Charles Lwanga and Comps.

James of Toul (St) Bp.   June 23
d. 769 Born probably at Bertigny in Haute Marne. It is commonly asserted that he was a monk of Hornbach in the diocese of Metz, before he became bishop of Toul (756). He was a great benefactor of the Benedictines. He died at Dijon, praying before the tomb of St Benignus, while on his return from a pilgrimage to Rome.

James Lacop (St) M. O.
Praem.   July 9
d. 1572 A native of Oudenarden, Flanders. He was a Norbertine at Middelburg and in 1566 he apostatized, wrote and preached against the church. Then he repented, returned to his abbey and was martyred by the Calvinists with the group of Gorkum martyrs, q.v. Canonized in 1867.

James of Voragine (Bl)
Bp. OP.   July 13
c 1230–1298 A native of Varezze (Voragine), in the diocese of Savona, he took the Dominican habit (1244), was provincial of Lombardy (1267–1286), and finally was consecrated archbishop of Genoa at Rome (1292). His highest title to fame is the compilation of the *Legenda Aurea Sanctorum*, a classic now known everywhere as *The Golden Legend*, a major source-book for study of the medieval mind

and for all sorts of strange and fascinating information. Beatified in 1816.

James Andrade (Bl) M. SJ.   July 15

d. 1570 Born at Pedrogao in the diocese of Coimbra, Portugal. He was a Jesuit priest and a companion of Bl Ignatius de Azevedo, whose martyrdom he shared. Beatified in 1854.

James the Greater (St)
Apostle   GC.July 25

d. 44 The son of Zebedee and Salome and brother of St John the Evangelist, called with him to the apostolate by our Lord. He was the first of the Twelve to be martyred (Acts 12:2) under King Herod Agrippa. A 9th-century legend makes him apostle of Spain and points to Compostella as the place where his body is enshrined. The legend grew, under Cluniac influence, and spread throughout W. Europe, so that Compostella became, after Jerusalem and Rome, the most famous place of pilgrimage in Christendom. St James is the patron saint of Spain. He is depicted as elderly and bearded, with a hat with a scallop shell thereon; or with a shell or shells about him; and dressed as a pilgrim with a wallet and a staff.

James Gerius (Bl) C.
OSB. Cam.   Aug 5

d. 1345 A Camaldolese monk of Florence who died aged thirty-three. His great devotion was the "Sacred Will of God".

James the Syrian (St) C.   Aug 6

d. p.500 A Syrian by birth, who led a solitary life in the environs of Amida (Diarbekir) in Mesopotamia.

James Nam (St) M.   Aug 12

d. 1838 A native Vietnamese priest attached to the Society of Foreign Missions of Paris. Beheaded with St Antony Dich, his host, and St Michael My. Canonized in 1988.

James the Deacon (St) C.
OSB.   Aug 17

7th cent. An Italian monk and deacon, companion of St Paulinus in his mission to Northumbria, where he remained in spite of the pagan reaction which set in after the death of St Edwin.

James Guengoro (Bl) M.   Aug 18

d. 1620 A native Japanese child, aged two, son of BB Thomas and Mary Guengoro, with whom he was crucified at Cocura. Beatified in 1867.

James Denxi (Bl) M.   Aug 19

d. 1622 A Japanese sailor on board the ship of Bl Joachim Firaiama, q.v. He was beheaded at Nagasaki. Beatified in 1867.

James of Mevania (Bl) C.
OP.   Aug 23

d. 1301 James Bianconi was a native of Mevania — now Bevagna — in the diocese of Spoleto, and the founder and first prior of the Dominican friary in his native city. Cult approved in 1400 and again in 1674.

James Claxton (Bl) M.   Aug 28

d. 1588 Born in Yorkshire and educated at Reims, where he was ordained in 1582. He was hanged at Isleworth. Beatified in 1929.

James Fayaxida (Bl) M.
Tert. OP.   Sept 8

d. 1628 A Japanese who became a Dominican tertiary and was beheaded at Nagasaki. Beatified in 1867.

James Chastan (Bl) Mk.   Sept 22
See Lawrence Imbert, etc.

James Griesinger (Bl) C.
OP.   Oct 11

1407–1491 Born at Ulm in Swabia, he joined the army but abandoned this profession to take the Dominican habit as a lay-brother at Bologna (1441). For the rest of his life he was employed in painting on glass, in which art he excelled. Beatified in 1825.

James the Persian (St) M.   Nov 1
See John and James.

James of Sasseau (St) C.
OSB.   Nov 19

d. c 865 A native of Constantinople and an army officer. After many travels he came to Gaul, was ordained at Clermont and joined the Benedictines near Bourges, whence at a later date he retired to the solitude of Sasseau (*Saxiacum*).

James Benfatti (Bl) Bp. OP.   Nov 26

d. 1338 A native of Mantua and a Friar Preacher. He was a master in theology and in 1303 was chosen bishop of Mantua, in which office he merited the title of "Father of the Poor". Cult confirmed in 1859.

James Intercisus (St) M.   Nov 27

d. 421 A Persian officer of high rank who apostatized to keep the favour of King Yezdegird; but repented, and under King Varanes V was martyred by being cut into twenty-eights parts. Hence his surname of *Intercisus* (cut into pieces). Many other Christians suffered with him.

James della Marca (St) C.
OFM.   Nov 28

1391–1475 James Gangala was born in the

March of Ancona (the ancient Picenum). He studied law, but abandoned that career to join the Friars Minor. He became a fellow-missionary of St John Capistran, and for forty years he never let a day pass without preaching the word of God.

James Thompson (alias Hudson) (Bl) M.   Nov 28

d. 1582   Born at York and educated for the priesthood at Reims, he was ordained in 1581 and hanged the following year at York. Beatified in 1895.

James (St) M.   Dec 9
See Samosata Martyrs.

Jane (*several*)
The English feminine form of John. The variants in other modern languages are numerous. In hagiology, however, the principal are: in Italian, Giovanna; in French, Jeanne; in Spanish, Juana; in Portuguese and Catalan, Joana. Another English form is Joan.

Jane of Bagno (Bl) V.
OSB. Cam.   Jan 16
d. 1105   Born at Fontechiuso in Tuscany, she became a Camaldolese lay-sister at Santa Lucia, near Bagno, in Tuscany. Cult approved in 1823.

Jane de Lestonnac (St)
Foundress   Feb 2
1556–1640   She was born at Bordeaux, the daughter of a Calvinist mother, and a niece of Montaigne. After the death of her husband, in her forty-seventh year she entered the Cistercian novitiate which she had to leave on account of ill-health. She now felt called to found a new religious institute for the education of girls with the object of stemming the tide of Calvinism. Her scheme was approved by Paul V in 1607 and the first house was opened at Bordeaux. The order spread rapidly, some thirty houses being established, all of which she ruled as superioress general. But as the result of a calumny and intrigue on the part of one of the sisters she was deposed, and spent some years in seclusion. Her character was completely vindicated before she died. Canonized 1949.

Jane of Valois (St)
Foundress   Feb 4
1461–1504   The daughter of Louis XI of France, who married her to the duke of Orleans, afterwards King Louis XII. Her husband obtained a decree of nullity of marriage and she retired to Bourges where, together with the Franciscan Bl Gabriel Mary, she founded the order of nuns of the Annunciation — known as *Les Annonciades*. Canonized 1949.

She is shewn crowned and in the habit of her order, with a symbol of the corporal works of mercy, e.g. bread and wine.

Jane Mary Bonomo (Bl)
V. OSB.   March 1
1606–1670   Born at Asiago, diocese of Vicenza, in N. Italy and educated by the Poor Clares at Trent. She became a Benedictine at Bassano in 1622 and fell into ecstasy for the first time at the ceremony of profession. She held the offices of novice mistress, abbess (three times) and prioress. She was bitterly persecuted by some members of her own community. Beatified in 1783.

Jane Mary de Maillé (Bl)
V. Tert. OFM.   March 29
1331–1414   The daughter of the Baron de Maillé, she married the Baron de Silly, with whom she lived in virginity for sixteen years. After his death (1362) she joined the Franciscan tertiaries and retired to Tours, where she spent the rest of her life in much poverty and privation due to the persecution of her husband's relatives. Cult confirmed in 1871.

Jane of Toulouse (Bl) V.
Tert. OC.   March 31
d. 1286   A native of Toulouse, she was affiliated to the Carmelite order as a tertiary by St Simon Stock, and is for this reason venerated as the foundress of the Carmelite third order. She spent her time and substance in training young boy-candidates for the Carmelite friars. Cult confirmed in 1895.

Jane of Portugal (Bl) V. OP.   May 12
1452–1490   Born at Lisbon, a daughter of King Alphonsus V of Portugal. In 1473 she entered the Dominican convent at Aveiro, but her family would not allow her to take her vows until 1485, when the Portuguese succession was secured. She had to suffer much annoyance on this account. Cult confirmed in 1693.

Jane of Arc (St) V.   May 30
Otherwise Joan of Arc, q.v.

Jane Gerard (Bl) M.   June 26
d. 1794   One of the Sisters of Charity of Arras in France, who were arrested in 1792, and guillotined at Cambrai. Beatified in 1920.

Jane Scopelli (Bl) V. OC.   July 9
c 1428–1491   A native of Reggio d'Emilia, Italy. She was the foundress and first prioress of the Carmelite nunnery at Reggio, for which she refused all endowments except those freely given to the nuns as alms. Cult confirmed in 1771.

Jane of Orvieto (Bl) Tert.
OP.   July 23
d. 1306   Usually called Vanna, an Italian derivative of Giovanna (Jane). She was born at Carnajola, near Orvieto, where also she took the Dominican habit of the third order. Cult approved in 1754.

Jane of Aza (Bl) W. OP.   Aug 8
d. c 1190   Born at the family castle of Aza, near Aranda, in Old Castile, she married Felix de Guzman, to whom she bore two sons and a daughter and finally — in answer to prayer before the shrine of St Dominic of Silos — the Dominic who became the founder of the Friars Preachers. Cult approved in 1828.

Jane Delanoue (St) V.
Foundress   Aug 16
1666–1732   Jane Delanoue was the twelfth child of a man who ran a small business in the village of Fenet, near Saumur, in the diocese of Angers. After a pious childhood, her father being dead, she continued to run the business and became somewhat remiss in her piety. Recalled by grace and granted an extraordinary vision, she began to serve the poor women and sick persons. For their care she founded the institute of the Sisters of St Anne, taking herself the name of Jane of the Cross. After practising heroic virtue and founding several houses of the institute, she died at Fenet. Beatified 1947. Canonized in 1982.

Jane Antide Thouret (St)
V. Foundress   Aug 24
1765–1828   Born near Besançon, the daughter of a tanner. In 1787 she joined the Sisters of Charity of St Vincent de Paul, but on the outbreak of the French Revolution she was forced to return home. She now (1798) started at Besançon, a school of her own for poor girls. Soon her helpers in this and in other works of charity were so numerous as to lead her to found a new Institute of Daughters of Charity which was approved by the Holy See before the foundress's death. Canonized by Pius XI.

Jane-Elizabeth Bichier des Ages (St) V. Foundress   Aug 26
1773–1832   Of noble rank, she was born in the diocese of Bourges. After the French Revolution she entrusted herself to the guidance of St Andrew Fournet (q.v.), and in spite of grave difficulties at the outset founded the Congregation of the Daughters of the Cross for teaching and service in hospitals. She died at Le Pay, Poitiers. Canonized 1947.

Jane Soderini (Bl) V.
Tert. OSM.   Sept 1
1301–1367   Born at Florence and educated by St Juliana Falconieri, under whom she became a Servite tertiary. Beatified in 1827.

Jane-Louise Barré and Jane-Reiné Prin (BB)
MM.   Oct 17
d. 1794   Two Ursuline nuns called in religion, respectively, Sister Cordula and Sister Laurentina, guillotined at Valenciennes. They formed part of a group of martyrs listed in this book under the title Ursuline Nuns, MM., q.v.

Jane of Segna (Bl) V.   Nov 17
d. 1307   Born at Segna, near Florence, she tended sheep. Both the Vallumbrosans and the Franciscans claim her as one of their tertiaries. Cult approved in 1798.

Jane of Cáceres (Bl) Abs.
OSB. Cist.   Dec 8
d. 1383   Cistercian abbess of the nunnery of St Benedict, at Castro, near Cáceres, in W. Spain. She was killed by marauding soldiers.

Jane Frances Frémiot de Chantal (St) W. Foundress GC. Dec 12
1572–1641 (Dec 13)   Jane Frances Frémiot was born at Dijon, in Burgundy, and in 1592 married the Baron de Chantal. They spent eight years of happy married life together and had four children; then the Baron died as the result of a hunting accident. St Jane now found her spiritual father and friend in St Francis de Sales, under whose guidance she founded the new Order of the Visitation, chiefly for widows and ladies who could not stand the austerities of the older orders. Sixty-six convents were established during her lifetime. Her last years were a period of intense suffering in body and mind. St Frances described her as "the perfect woman". She died at Moulins, but her remains rest at Annecy in Savoy.

Januaria (St) M.   March 2
See Paul, Heraclius, etc.

Januaria (St) M.   July 17
See Scillitan Martyrs.

Januarius (St) M.   Jan 7
See Felix and Januarius.

Januarius (St) M.   Jan 19
See Paul, Gerontius, etc.

Januarius, Maxima and Macaria (SS) MM.   Apr 8
?   African martyrs of whom nothing further is known. The names are sometimes given as SS Januarius, Maximus and Maccarius.

Januarius (St) M.   Apr 29
See Corfu, Martyrs of.

Januarius (St) M.   July 10
See Seven Brothers.

**Januarius, Marinus,
Nabor and Felix (SS)**
MM.   July 10
? African martyrs, of whom nothing further is
known.

**Januarius and Pelagia
(SS)** MM.   July 11
d. 320 Martyrs beheaded at Nicopolis in
Lesser Armenia, under Licinius.

Januarius (St) M.   July 15
See Catulinus, Januarius, etc.

Januarius (St) M.   Aug 6
See Sixtus II and Comp.

Januarius (St) M.   GC. Sept 19
d. 304 Januarius, bishop of Benevento, was
beheaded at Pozzuoli, under Diocletian. The
body of St Januarius (Gennaro) was eventually
enshrined at Naples, of which city he has
become the patron saint. The yearly liquefac-
tion of some of his blood preserved in a phial is
a well-known phenomenon, of which there are
records for the past four hundred years. No
natural explanation has been found, although
many have been advanced. A legend, now
discredited, but popular in the Middle Ages,
linked with St Januarius the following people:
Festus, his deacon; Desiderius, lector or
reader; Sosius, deacon of the church of Mis-
enum; Proculus, deacon of Pozzuoli and two
other Christians, Eutyches and Acutius. Their
existence however is very doubtful and their
cults suppressed in 1969.

Januarius (St) M.   Oct 13
See Faustus, Januarius and Martial.

Januarius (St) M.   Oct 24
See Felix (Africanus), Audactus, etc.

Januarius (St) M.   Oct 25
See Protus and Januarius.

Januarius (St) M.   Dec 2
See Severus, Securus, etc.

Januarius (St) M.   Dec 15
See Faustinus, Lucius, etc.

**Japan (Martyrs of) (SS.
BB)** MM.   Feb 6
d. 1597 and 1614 and the following years.

There are two main groups of Japanese
martyrs: the first comprises St Paul Miki and
his companions, q.v. Their feast day is Feb 6.
The second group is formed of thirty-six
Jesuits, twenty-six Franciscans, twenty-one
Dominicans, and five Augustinians, and one
hundred and seven lay victims. They were
martyred between 1614 and 1644 and were
beatified by Pius IX and Leo XIII at different
dates. Most of the religious were Spanish;
most of the lay people, native Japanese. Each is
given a separate notice in this book.

Jarlath (Hierlath) (St) Bp.   Feb 1
d. c 480 One of St Patrick's disciples, who
succeeded St Benignus in the see of Armagh.

Jarlath (St) Bp.   June 6
d. c 550 The founder and first abbot-
bishop of Tuam, in Connaught, Ireland,
where he established a monastic school which
became famous. St Brendan of Clonard and St
Colman of Cloyne were pupils there.

Jarman (St) Bp.   July 3
Otherwise Germanus, q.v.

Jason (St)   July 12
1st cent. The Acts of the Apostles (17:5-9)
say that St Paul stayed at Jason's house in
Thessalonica. St Paul mentions him in his
Epistle to the Romans (16:21). In the Greek
legend he is described as a bishop of Tarsus in
Cilicia, going to Corfu, evangelizing that
island, and dying there. The pre-1970 RM.
wrongly identifies him with the Mnason mentioned in the Acts (21:16) "a Cyprian, an old
disciple", with whom St Paul was staying in
Jerusalem and whom tradition makes bishop
of Tamasus in Cyprus.

Jason (St) M.   Dec 3
See Claudius, Hilaria, etc.

Jehudiel   Apr 20
See Seven Angels.

Jeremiah (St) M.   Feb 16
See Elias, Jeremiah etc.

Jeremiah (St) Prophet   May 1
7th cent. B.C. The second of the greater
prophets. The tradition concerning him is that
at the age of fifty-five he was stoned to death in
Egypt by the Jews who shared his captivity. His
feast is observed chiefly at Venice, where some
of his alleged relics are enshrined.

Jeremias (St) M.   June 7
See Peter, Wallabonsus, etc.

Jeremias (St) M.   June 17
See Isaurus, Innocent, etc.

Jeremias (St) M. Sept 15

See Emilas and Jeremias.

Jermyn (German) Gardiner (Bl) M. March 7

d. 1544 Educated at Cambridge, he became secretary to Stephen Gardiner, bishop of Winchester, and was executed at Tyburn with BB John Larke and John Ireland, for denying the royal supremacy. Beatified in 1886.

Jerome Lu (Bl) M. Jan 28

c 1810–1858 Born at Mao-Cheu in China. He worked as a native catechist and was beheaded in his native town. Beatified in 1909.

Jerome Emiliani (St) C. GC. Feb 8

1481–1537 A Venetian who in his youth served in the army of the Republic. Being taken prisoner he was miraculously set free after praying to our Lady. He took holy orders and devoted himself to charitable works. In 1532 he founded a congregation of clerks regular vowed to the care of orphans. They were called *Somaschi*, from the little town in Lombardy — Somasca — where they started. Jerome died of a contagious malady caught while tending the sick. Canonized in 1767, and in 1928 declared the patron saint of orphans and abandoned children.

Jerome of Vallumbrosa (Bl) C. OSB. Vall. June 18

d. 1135 A Vallumbrosan monk who retired to the hermitage of the abbey called *Masso delle celle*, where he spent thirty-five years, living all the time, it is said, only on bread and water.

Jerome of Werden (St) M. OFM. July 9

1522–1572 A native of Werden in Holland, who spent several years in Palestine as a Franciscan missionary. He was a powerful preacher against Calvinism. At the time of his martyrdom he was the vicar of the friary at Gorkum under St Nicholas Pieck (see Gorkum, Martyrs of).

Jerome of Pavia (St) Bp. July 19

d. 787 Bishop of Pavia, 778–787.

Jerome of the Cross de Torres M. Tert. OFM. Sept 3

d. 1632 A Japanese secular priest, educated in the seminary of Arima and ordained at Manila. he returned to Japan (1628), was arrested (1631) and burnt alive at Nagasaki. Beatified in 1867.

Jerome (St) C. Dr. GC. Sept 30

c 341–420 Eusebius Hieronymus Sophronius was born at Stridonium in Dalmatia. He studied in Rome, particularly the classics for which he developed a life-long passion. He travelled extensively in Italy and Gaul, lived as a hermit in Palestine, then returned to Rome where, after his ordination, he joined the Roman clergy and acted as secretary to the pope. Finally, having come to be on bad terms with those who surrounded him, he went back to Palestine and settled at Bethlehem. He spent the rest of his life translating, and commenting on the Bible, and became the most learned biblical scholar of his day. Appreciating this fact he was apt to resent any opposition to his way of thinking. However, he acknowledged his own shortcomings, particularly his shortness of temper, with a rather tempestuous but virile humility. His place as an exponent of Catholic dogma is still the highest ever allotted to a biblical scholar. He died at Bethlehem and is officially venerated as a Doctor of the Church. In art he is shown as robed as a cardinal, with a lion in attendance; or stripped of his robes and beating his breast with a stone; or as a scholar writing, or with pen and inkwell.

Jerome Hermosilla (St) M. Bp. OP. Nov 1

d. 1861 A native of La Calzada, in Old Castile, who after his profession in the Dominican order was sent to Manila, where he was ordained priest and in 1828 appointed to the mission of Vietnam. He succeeded St Ignatius Delgado as vicar-apostolic and was ordained bishop. Arrested in 1861 he was tortured and beheaded. Canonized 1988.

Jerome de Angelis (Bl) M. SJ. Dec 4

d. 1623 A native of Castrogiovanni in Sicily, who became a Jesuit at Messina and was sent to the missions of the Far East. He worked for twenty-two years in various parts of Japan and finally, betrayed to the persecutors, was martyred by burning at Yeddo, together with BB Simon Yempo and Francis Gálvez. Beatified in 1867.

Jerome Ranuzzi (Bl) C. OSM. Dec 12

d. 1455 Born at Sant' Angelo in Vado (Urbino), he took his religious vows as a Servite and eventually became the personal adviser of Duke Frederick of Montefeltro, of Urbino. On this account he was surnamed

St Jerome, Sept 30

"the Angel of Good Counsel". Cult approved in 1775.

Joachim Saccachibara
(St) M. Tert. OFM.   Feb 6
d. 1597   A native of Japan, doctor of the Franciscans. He was crucified at Nagasaki with twenty-four companions. Beatified in 1627. Canonized in 1862. See Paul Miki and Comps.

Joachim of Fiore (de Floris) (Bl) Ab. OSB. Cist.   March 30
c 1130–1202   Born at Celico in Calabria, after a pilgrimage to Palestine, he joined the Cistercians at Sambucina and in 1176 was made abbot of Corazzo; about the year 1190 he inaugurated at Fiore a new Cistercian congregation. He was a prolific ascetical and biblical writer, and his commentary on the Apocalypse gave him the title of "the Prophet" by which he is described by Dante: "the Calabrian abbot Joachim, endowed with prophetic spirit" (Paradiso, XII). Unfortunately, after his death the Franciscan Spirituals made use of his books to uphold their heretical tendencies. The holy abbot, however, has always been given the title of *Beatus*.

Joachim Piccolomini (Bl)
C. OSM.   Apr 16
d. 1305   A member of the illustrious Piccolomini family of Siena, he joined the Servites as a lay-brother under St Philip Benizi. Beatified by Paul V.

Joachim (St) Patriarch   GC. July 26
1st cent. B.C.   Joachim is now the usual name given to the father of our Lady. Other names attributed to him are: Heli, Cleopas, Eliacim, Jonachir, Sadoc. Nothing is known about him. Liturgically, he has been honoured in the East from time immemorial; in the West, only since the sixteenth century. The traditions concerning him rest only on the apocryphal Gospel of James.

Joachim Firaiama-Di z
(Bl) M.   Aug 19
d. 1622   A Japanese captain of a ship at Manila. When bringing Bl Peter Zuñiga and Louis Flores to Japan his ship was captured by Dutch Protestant pirates and brought to

Firando. He and his crew, all members of the confraternity of the Holy Rosary, were beheaded at Nagasaki. Beatified in 1867.

Joachim Royo (Bl) M. OP.   Oct 28
d. 1748   A Spanish missionary of the Dominican order, who was sent to China to work under Bl Peter Sanz and was ordained there. He was strangled in prison at Fu-tsheu. Beatified in 1893.

Joachim Ho (Bl) M.   Nov 24
d. 1839   A Chinese, martyred at Kouei-Tcheou. Beatified in 1900.

Joan of Arc (St) V.   May 30
1412–1431   Called "the Maid of Orleans" — *La Pucelle*. She was born at Domrémy in Lorraine, the daughter of a peasant. When she was seventeen, while minding her father's sheep, she heard supernatural voices commanding her to take up arms and lead the French army against the English invaders of France. Accordingly, Charles VII entrusted her with an armed force, and Joan's rapid successes enabled him to be crowned at Reims. However, as Joan herself had predicted, she was captured by the Burgundians and handed over to the English. She was tried by an ecclesiastical court presided over by the bishop of Beauvais, and condemned to be burnt alive at the stake as a heretic. The sentence was executed at Rouen, May 31, 1431. In 1456 the case was re-tried and Joan was declared innocent. After centuries of popular veneration she was beatified in 1909 and canonized in 1920. Problems exist, however, as to the "heavenly" inspiration of her warlike career. She claimed that St Margaret of Antioch and St Catherine of Alexandria spoke to her, but these persons never existed. In 1922 she was declared a patroness of France. In art she is shown as a bareheaded girl in armour, with a sword, lance or banner. She may wear an unvisored helm.

Joanna (St) W.   May 24
1st cent.   The wife of Chuza, steward of Herod Antipas, tetrarch of Galilee. She is mentioned by St Luke (8:3) in his Gospel as one of the holy women who ministered to our Lord.

Joannicius (St) H.   Nov 4
750–846   A native of Bithynia who, after serving as a soldier, retired at the age of forty to lead a solitary life near Mt Olympus. Popular veneration, however, drove him from one solitude to another. He was a strenuous opponent of Iconoclasm. His memory is held in high honour among the Greeks.

St Joan of Arc, May 30

Joanninus de San Juan (Bl)
M.   July 15
d. 1570   A nephew of the captain of the ship which carried Bl Ignatius de Azevedo (q.v.) and his companions. He voluntarily joined the martyrs and was thrown into the sea by the French Calvinist pirates.

Joaquina Vedruna de
Mas (St) W. Foundress   May 19
1783–1854   A Spanish lady, wife of Theodore de Mas, of the Spanish nobility, who died in the Napoleonic wars. Joaquina then retired

to Vich, where she founded the Institute of the Carmelite Sisters of Charity, now spread throughout Spain and S. America. She died at Barcelona during a cholera epidemic. Canonized 1959.

Joavan (St) Bp.　　　　　　　March 2
d. *c* 570　A Romano-Briton who passed over to Brittany to live under his uncle St Paul of Léon, from whom he received episcopal ordination as coadjutor.

Job (St) Patriarch　　　　　　　May 10
? The man "simple and upright and fearing God and avoiding evil", whose patience forms the subject matter of a canonical book of Scripture. (See also James 5:11.) His liturgical cult obtains chiefly in the East. The book was probably written about 400 B.C.

Jodoc (Judocus, Josse,
Jost) (St) C.　　　　　　　　Dec 13
See Judocus.

Joel (Bl or St) Ab. OSB.　　　　Jan 25
d. 1185　A disciple of St John of Matera, founder of the Benedictine congregation of Pulsano. St Joel was its third general.

Joel (St) Prophet　　　　　　　July 13
? B.C.　One of the twelve minor prophets. His body is said to be enshrined under the high altar of the cathedral of Zara in Dalmatia. Nothing is known of his life or the date of the work bearing his name.

John
Note. This is the most popular proper name in Christendom. The original Hebrew form has been Hellenized and Latinized into Joannes, whence the numerous variants in all languages. For hagiological purposes we mention only the following: Italian, Giovanni; French, Jean; Spanish, Juan; Portuguese, Xuan; Catalan, Jean; Dutch, Jan; German, Johann; Russian, Iwan, Ivan. There are also numerous diminutive forms, e.g., Italian, Giovannino, Nanino; Spanish, Juanito; French, Jeanin; Old English, Johnikin, etc. Moreover, especially in the Latin countries, the name is very often used in combination with others, as follows: Gianpier, Gianluigi, Jean-Benoît, Jean-François, Juan-José, Juan-Maria, etc.

John Baptist Turpin Du
Cormier and Comps
(BB) MM.
See Martyrs of Laval.

John Nepomucene
Neumann (St) Bp. C.SS.R.
Founder　　　　　　　　　　　Jan 5
1811–1860　From Bohemia, his native soil, missionary zeal led him to America in 1836, where he laboured in the district of Niagra until 1840 when he became a Redemptorist. As superior, and even more fully with his ordination as bishop of Philadelphia, he devoted himself to the ministry of the word; the education of youth; the building of churches; the decorum of divine worship and, above all, to the care of orphans and the needy. He also founded the Sisters of the Third Order of St Francis. Beatified 1963. Canonized in 1977.

John de Ribera (St) Bp.　　　　Jan 6
1532–1611　A native of Seville, and the son of the duke of Alcalá, viceroy of Naples. He was educated at the university of Salamanca, was ordained priest in 1557, and remained at the university as professor of theology. His gifts became widely known and gained him the esteem of Pope Pius V and of Philip II of Spain. He was appointed bishop of Badajoz, but transferred shortly after to the archbishopric of Valencia, with the added title of Viceroy of that province. While all may not regard him as an enlightened statesman, one cannot but admire his conscientious devotion to duty and his heroic patience in bearing the responsibilities of his office. Canonized 1959.

John Camillus the Good
(St) Bp.　　　　　　　　　　　Jan 10
d. *c* 660　Bishop of Milan. The Lombard invasion forced the bishops of Milan to live for eighty years away from that city. With John Camillus the line of resident bishops recommenced. He worked successfully against Arianism and Monothelitism.

John of Ravenna (St) Bp.　　　Jan 12
d. 494　Bishop of Ravenna from 452 to 494. He is said to have saved his flock from the fury of Attila the Hun, and mitigated its sad lot when the city was taken by Theodoric, king of the Ostro-Goths.

John Gaspard Cratz (Bl)
M. SJ.　　　　　　　　　　　Jan 12
d. 1737　A German Jesuit born at Duren, near Cologne. He entered the order at Macao in 1730. Sent to China with three Portuguese companions, he was arrested at Tonkin in 1736 and martyred in the following year.

John Calabytes (St) H.　　　　Jan 15
d. *c* 450　Born at Constantinople, he disappeared from home and, at the age of twelve, became a monk at Gomon on the Bosphorus. After some years he returned home so changed in appearance that his parents did not recognize him. He lived on their charity in a small hut — Calybe in Greek, whence *Kalaby-*

tes — near their home until his death, so runs the legend, which is remarkably reminiscent of that of St Alexis of Rome and other saints.

John of Rome (St) C. OSB.   Jan 17
See Antony, Merulus and John.

John the Almoner (St) Abp.   Jan 23
d. ? 616 A Cypriot, who became patriarch of Alexandria (c 608). He set himself to redress social evils by means of almsgiving. He compiled a list of the 7500 poor of the diocese, and one of his first episcopal acts was the distribution of 80,000 pieces of gold to hospitals and monasteries. He followed this policy systematically till his death.

John Grove (Bl) M.   Jan 24
d. 1697 A layman, servant of Bl William Ireland, SJ., with whom he was martyred at Tyburn for alleged complicity in the Oates Plot. Beatified in 1929.

John of Warneton (Bl) Bp.   Jan 27
d. 1130 Born at Warneton, in French Flanders, a disciple of St Ivo of Chartres. He became a canon regular at Mont-Saint-Eloi, near Arras, and was eventually made bishop of Thérouanne, which he accepted only under a papal order. He was a great founder of monasteries. Though he had a reputation for strictness, he showed himself extremely gentle when dealing with certain individuals who had conspired against his life.

John of Reomay (Réomé)
(St) Ab.   Jan 28
425–539 Born at Dijon, he was first a solitary at Reomay. When disciples gathered round him he escaped in secret and became a monk of Lérins. Here he learnt the traditions of St Macarius, and when summoned back to Reomay, he regulated his monastery according to them. He was one of the pioneers on monastic life in the West.

John (St) M.   Jan 31
See Cyrus and John.

John Angelus (Bl) C.
OSB.   Jan 31
d. c 1050 A native of Venice and a Benedictine at Pomposa in the diocese of Ferrara, under St Guy, q.v.

John Bosco (St) Founder   GC. Jan 31
1815–1888 Born at Becchi, Castelnuovo d'Asti, in Piedmont, son of a peasant. After his ordination in 1841 he began at Turin his lifelong work of educating boys. From the first he had a clear programme of education in his mind — viz., to educate through love, to induce the boys to love their teachers, their studies, and all the conditions which surround

their education. A group of willing helpers offered themselves to Don Bosco and in 1860 the new institute was approved by the Holy See. St John placed it under the protection of Our Lady Help of Christians and of St Francis of Sales — *Salesians*. It grew rapidly and spread throughout Europe and the foreign missions. He also formed on the same lines a new sisterhood, the Daughters of Mary Auxiliatrix, for the education of girls. Canonized in 1934.

John of the Grating
(St) Bp. OSB. Cist.   Feb 1
1098–1163 Surnamed *de Craticula* "of the Grating", from the metal railings that surrounded his shrine. He was a Breton who entered Clairvaux and was professed under St Bernard. He returned to Brittany as abbotfounder of Buzay and Bégard and finally was made bishop of Aleth, which see he transferred to Saint-Malo. He introduced Canons Regular into the diocese, and some sources treat him as a canon, and a friend of St Bernard, but not a monk under him.

John Nelson (Bl) M. SJ.   Feb 3
d. 1578 A native of Skelton, near York. He began his studies for the priesthood at Douai at the age of forty and was ordained in 1575. He was sent to London, but was soon arrested and subsequently executed at Tyburn. He became a Jesuit shortly before his death.

John Zakoly (Bl) Bp.   Feb 3
d. 1494 Bishop of Csanad in Hungary, he entered the Pauline order and died prior of the monastery of Diosgyör.

John Speed (Bl) M.   Feb 4
d. 1594 *Alias* Spence. A layman, born at Durham and martyred, also at Durham, for befriending priests. Beatified in 1929.

John de Britto (St) M. SJ.   Feb 4
1647–1693 A native of Lisbon, he joined the Society of Jesus in 1662 and was soon after sent to the missions of the Far East. He worked in Malabar, Tanjore, Marava and Madura. He joined the Brahmin caste in an endeavour to reach the nobility, and his methods were in many other respects unconventional and enlightened. He was captured and tortured and ordered to leave the country; but he refused and was martyred at Oreiour in India. Canonized 1947.

John Morosini (Bl) Ab.
OSB.   Feb 5
d. 1012 A native of Venice who became a Benedictine at Cuxá in the Catalonian Pyrenees. At a later period he returned to Venice where he founded and was the first

abbot of San Giorgio Maggiore (*c* 982). Most writers call him *beatus*, although there is no evidence of a cult.

John Soan de Goto (St)
M. SJ.　　　　　　　　　　　　Feb 6
d. 1597　A Japanese temporal-coadjutor of the Society of Jesus, and catechist at Ozaka. Crucified at Nagasaki in his nineteenth year, with many companions. Canonized in 1862. See Paul Miki and Comps.

John Kisaka (or Kimoia)
(St) M. Tert. OFM.　　　　　　Feb 6
d. 1597　A Japanese silk-weaver, born at Meaco. He was baptized and received into the third order of St Francis shortly before his crucifixion at Nagasaki with twenty-five others. See Paul Miki and Comps.

John of Matha (St)
Founder　　　　　　　　　　　Feb 8
1160–1213 (Dec 17)　A native of Faucon in Provence, who studied at Paris and later founded the order of Trinitarians for the redemption of captives, which was approved by Pope Innocent III. It is said that John himself ransomed many captives at Tunis, but of this and many other episodes of his life there are no trustworthy records. He died at Rome. He used to be on the General Calendar before 1969; since then hs is venerated on local calendars.

John Charles Cornay (St)
M.　　　　　　　　　　　now Sept 20
1809–1837　Born at Loudun, in the diocese of Poitiers, France. He belonged to the Paris Society of Foreign Missions and worked in Vietnam. He was seized at Ban-no, and kept in a cage for three months, being put often in irons and brutally beaten. He was finally beheaded (Sept 20). Canonized in 1988.

John Buonagiunta (St)　　　　Feb 12
See Seven Holy Founders.

John Nutter and John Munden (BB) MM.　　　　　Feb 12
d. 1584　John Nutter was born near Burnley, Lancs, and was a fellow of St John's College, Cambridge. He studied for the priesthood at Reims and was ordained in 1581. John Munden, a native of Coltley, S. Maperton, Dorset, studied at New College, Oxford, became a schoolmaster, went to Reims and to Rome for his ecclesiastical training and was ordained in 1582. They were martyred at Tyburn with three other priests. Beatified in 1929.

John Lantrua of Triora (Bl)
M. OFM.　　　　　　　　　　Feb 13
1760–1816　A native of Triora in Liguria, who at the age of seventeen joined the Friars Minor. After having been guardian of Velletri, near Rome, he volunteered for the Chinese missions, where at that time a fierce persecution was raging. He arrived there in 1799 and worked with great success in spite of many obstacles. At length he was seized and martyred by strangulation at Ch'angsha Fu. Beatified in 1900.

John Baptist of the Conception (St) C.　　　　Feb 14
1561–1613　A native of Almodovar, Toledo, Spain. He entered the Trinitarian order at Toledo and seventeen years later joined the party of reform in that order. As superior, he inaugurated such a revival at Valdepeñas in 1597. The reform, called the Discalced Trinitarians, was approved by Rome and John had to endure on this account the bitter opposition of the "unreformed". At the time of his death thirty-four houses had adopted his reform. Beatified in 1819. Canonized 1975.

John Pibush (Bl) M.　　　　Feb 18
d. 1601　Born at Thirsk, Yorks, and educated at Reims. Ordained in 1587, he was sent to the English mission, where he spent his time mostly in prison and was finally executed at Southwark. Beatified in 1929.

John Peter (Néel) (Bl)　　　Feb 18
1832–1862　A French missionary priest working in Kuy-tsheu, China, who was arrested, dragged while tied to a horse's tail by his hair, and finally beheaded at Kuy-tsheu. Beatified in 1909.

John the Saxon (Bl) M.　　　Feb 22
d. 895　Apparently a native of Old Saxony and a monk in some French abbey who was invited by King Alfred to restore religion and learning in the English abbeys after the devastation of the Danes. The king appointed him abbot of Athelingay. John worked zealously in furthering the king's wishes. Two French monks of his own community murdered him one night in church.

John of Hungary (Bl) OFM.　　Feb 23
d. 1287　Of French origin, he was the first Franciscan to work in Hungary. In the chronicle of his order he is styled "saint".

John Theristus (St) Mk.
OSB.　　　　　　　　　　　Feb 24
d. 1129　Of Calabrian parentage, he was born in Sicily, whither his mother had been carried as a slave by the Saracens. He contrived to escape to Calabria while still a child,

and there he became a Benedictine. Theristus means harvester, a reference to a miraculous harvesting supposed to have been performed by the saint.

John of Gorze (St) Ab. OSB.   Feb 27

d. *c* 975   Born at Vandières, near Metz. After some years spent in administering his large estates, he made a pilgrimage to Rome and on his return restored, and entered, the abbey of Gorze (933). The emperor Otto I sent him as his ambassador to the Caliph Abd-er-Rahman of Cordoba, where he stayed for two years. In 960 he was made abbot of Gorze, and the wise reforms which he introduced spread even to distant Benedictine abbeys. The saint is said to have been gifted with a prodigious memory.

John-Joseph of the Cross
(St) C. OFM.   March 5

1654–1734   Carlo Gaetano was born on the island of Ischia, off the coast of Naples. In 1670 he joined the Franciscan-Alcantarines and was given the new name of Gianguiseppe (John-Joseph). He held various offices in the order and finally that of superior of the new Italian branch of the Alcantarines. Canonized in 1839.

John Larke and John
Ireland (BB) MM.   March 7

d. 1544   Both were secular priests. John Larke was rector of St Ethelburga's, Bishopsgate, then of Woodford, Essex, and finally of Chelsea, to which he was nominated by St Thomas More. John Ireland, after being chaplain to the same saint, was made rector of Eltham, Kent. Both were martyred at Tyburn, with Bl Jermyn Gardiner. John Larke was beatified in 1886 and John Ireland in 1929.

John of God (St)
Founder   GC. March 8

1495–1550   Born at Montemoro Novo, diocese of Evora, in Portugal, John followed various vocations for the first forty years of his life — shepherd, soldier, pedlar, superintendent of slaves in Morocco, vendor of religious books in the district near Gibraltar, etc. He was led to a more perfect life by a sermon of Bl John of Avila, but the fervour of his conversion produced in him such extravagant behaviour that he was taken for a madman. Finally, in 1540, he settled at Granada and founded a hospital where he tended the sick. This was the beginning of the new order of Brothers Hospitallers (Brothers of St John of God). St John was canonized in 1690 and declared patron of the sick and of hospitals in 1886.

John of Vallumbrosa (Bl)
C. OSB. Vall.   March 10

d. *c* 1380   A Florentine monk of the Holy Trinity in his native city. As a result of poring over forbidden books night and day, he took secretly to the practice of the Black Art and became a necromancer and a slave to vice and depravity. On being found out, he was summoned before the abbot-general of Vallumbrosa and, after first denying, ultimately confessed his guilt and was imprisoned in a pestilential gaol. This proved his salvation: he became truly penitent and by voluntary fasting reduced himself to a skeleton, so that his fellow monks implored him to return to community life. He, however, preferred to remain in prison till his death, living as a hermit to a very old age and attaining to great sanctity. He was an elegant writer, and a great friend of St Catherine of Siena, who often appeared to him.

John Ogilvie (St) M. SJ.   March 10

d. 1615   Born at Drum-na-Keith, Banffshire, and brought up a Calvinist, he was received into the church at Louvain (1596) at the age of seventeen. He joined the Society of Jesus (1599) and worked in Austria and in France till 1613. He then returned to his native Scotland where he was beginning to make converts when he was betrayed and imprisoned. For eight days and nights on end he was forcibly kept from sleep so that he should reveal the names of other Catholics. He resisted his persecutors and was hanged at Glasgow. Beatified in 1929. Canonised Oct 17 1976.

John Righi of Fabriano
(Bl) C. OFM.   March 11

1469–1539   John Baptist Righi was a native of Fabriano, province of Ancona, who professed the Franciscan rule and lived a hermit's life at Massaccio. Cult approved in 1903.

John Sordi, or Caccia-
fronte (Bl) Bp. M. OSB.   March 16

d. 1183   A native of Cremona who joined the abbey of St Lawrence in his native city, and became abbot in 1155. He is described as most loyal to, and gentle with his monks. He sided with the pope against the emperor Barbarossa, by whom he was banished from his abbey. He lived as a hermit near Mantua and, in 1174, the bishop of this city being deposed by the pope, Bl John was raised to the see. But, some three years afterwards, the former bishop repented and Bl John asked permission to resign in his favour, being himself transferred to

Vicenza (1177). Here he was killed by a man whom he had rebuked for embezzling episcopal revenues.

John Amias (or Anne)
(Bl) M.   March 16
d. 1589   Born near Wakefield, he began life as a clothier. He married but, on his wife's death, studied for the priesthood at Reims and was ordained in 1581. He was executed at York, together with Bl Robert Dalby. Beatified in 1929.

John Sarkander (Bl) M.   March 17
1576–1620   Born in Austrian Silesia, he became a parish priest of Holleschau in Moravia. He converted many Hussites and Bohemian Brethren but, as a result, was unjustly accused by the heretics of conspiring to bring Polish troops into the country, and was ordered to reveal what he heard in confession from his penitent, the baron of Moravia. On refusing, he was cruelly racked and left to die in prison. Beatified in 1859.

John the Syrian of Pinna
(St) H.   March 19
6th cent.   According to the pre-1970 RM. he was a Syrian monk who settled at Pinna, near Spoleto, where for forty-four years he was abbot of a large monastic colony. It is probable that he was a refugee from Monophysite persecution.

John Baptist Spagnuolo
(Bl) C. OC.   March 20
1448–1516   Usually called *Baptista Mantuanus*. His family name *Spagnuolo* denotes his Spanish origin. He was, however, born at Mantua, studied at Padua, joined the Carmelites (1464) and in 1513 became their prior-general. He is famous as a Latin poet — he wrote over 50 000 lines of Latin verse — and he is considered one of the most eminent representatives of Christian Humanism in Italy. Beatified in 1885.

John of Parma (Bl)
C. OFM.   March 20
1209–1289   A native of Parma, who after his profession in the Franciscan order and his ordination, taught theology at Bologna and Naples. In 1247 he was elected seventh minister general of the Franciscans and held the office until 1257. He visited the Franciscan provinces of different countries, including England. He was sent to Constantinople as papal legate. His final years he lived in retirement at Greccio. Cult approved in 1777.

John, Sergius and Comp.
(SS) MM.   March 20
d. 796   A group of twenty monks of the *laura* of St Sabas, near Jerusalem, who were killed in one of the anti-Christian Arab raids. Many more were wounded, and a few escaped. One of the last category, Stephen the poet, has left a detailed account of the event.

John del Bastone (Bl) C.
OSB. Silv.   March 24
d. 1290   One of the first disciples of St Silvester at Monte Fano.

John of Lycopolis (St) H.   March 27
c 305–394   Surnamed "The Egyptian" or "the Prophet of the Thebaid". He was born near Assiut, in Egypt, and was a carpenter by trade. At the age of twenty-five he journeyed to a mountain near Lycopolis and lived there for forty years as a recluse. He was consulted by the emperor Theodosius and greatly admired by his contemporaries SS Jerome, Augustine, Cassian, Palladius, etc. He was remarkable for his gift of prophecy.

John Climacus (St) Ab.   March 30
c 570–649   Called "*Climacus*" from the title of his book *The Climax*, or *Ladder of Perfection*, which is a classic in ascetical literature. He was born in Palestine and, at the age of sixteen, became a monk on Mt Sinai and afterwards a solitary in different places in the Arabian Desert. He was already seventy-five when he was made abbot of Sinai, but four years later he resigned and died as a hermit. Some writers give his dates as c 525–605.

John of Penna (Bl) C. OFM.   Apr 3
d. 1271   A native of Penna San Giovanni in the diocese of Fermo who, after being ordained, joined the Franciscans at Recanati and founded several houses in Provence, where he lived for twenty-five years. (See his life in ch. 45 of the *Little Flowers of St Francis*.) Cult approved by Pius VII.

John Baptist de la Salle
(St) Founder   GC. Apr 7
1651–1719   A native of Reims and a canon of the cathedral chapter (1667), before he was ordained (1678). His life-work was the foundation on new, original and revolutionary educational principles of the congregation of the Brothers of the Christian Schools. In the teeth of extreme opposition, he succeeded in establishing his system and his new institute on solid foundations. He died in retirement at Saint-Yon. Canonized in 1900.

John of Vespignano (Bl) C.   Apr 9
d. 1331   Born at Vespignano in the diocese

of Florence. During the civil wars he devoted himself to works of charity among the refugees who flocked to Florence. Cult approved by Pius VII.

John of Cupramontana (Bl) C. OSB. Cam.   Apr 11
d. 1303   A Camaldolese monk-hermit who lived many years in the cave of Cupramontana, on Mt Massaccio.

John Lockwood (Bl) M.   Apr 13
d. 1642   John Lockwood, *alias* Lascelles, was born at Sowerby, Yorks, and studied for the priesthood at Rome. Ordained in 1597, he was sent to the English mission, where he worked from 1598 till 1642. At the age of eighty-one he was hanged, drawn and quartered at York. Beatified in 1929.

John of Vilna (St) M.   Apr 14
See SS Antony, John and Eustace.

John of Grace-Dieu (Bl) Ab. OSB. Cist.   Apr 20
d. 1280   A Benedictine monk of St Denis, who passed over to the Cistercians and became successively abbot of Igny, of Clairvaux (1257) and of Grace-Dieu (*c* 1262).

John Finch (Bl) M.   Apr 20
d. 1584   A yeoman farmer of Eccleston in Lancashire, who suffered at Lancaster for being reconciled to the church and for harbouring priests. Beatified in 1929.

John Payne (St) M.   Apr 20
d. 1582   Born in the diocese of Peterborough, he was educated for the priesthood at Douai, where he was ordained in 1576. He worked on the English mission at Ingatestone in Essex until his martyrdom at Chelmsford. Beatified in 1886. Canonized in 1970 as one of the Forty Martyrs of England and Wales, q.v.

John of Valence (Bl) Bp. OSB. Cist.   Apr 26
d. 1146   A native of Lyons, he was a canon of that city, and after a pilgrimage to Compstella, entered Clairvaux under St Bernard. In 1117 he was sent to found Bonneval (*Bona Vallis*) on the Loire, and proved to be an excellent abbot. In 1141 he was made bishop of Valence, but had to be carried by main force to the altar to be ordained. Cult approved in 1901.

John of Constantinople (St) Ab.   Apr 27
d. 813   Abbot of the monastery called *Cathares* at Constantinople, a staunch opponent of the Iconoclast emperor Leo the Armenian by whom he was imprisoned and exiled.

John Baptist Thanh (St) M.   Apr 28
d. 1840   A native catechist in Vietnam, attached to the Society of Foreign Missions. Canonized in 1988.

John-Louis Bonnard (St) M.   May 1
1824–1852   A missionary priest, a native of France, who belonged to the Paris Society of Foreign Missions and was beheaded in Annam (Vietnam). Canonized in 1988.

John Houghton (St) M. O. Cart.   May 4
d. 1535   A native of Essex and prior of the London charterhouse. As such, he was the first to oppose Henry VIII's Acts of Succession and Supremacy, giving to his monks and the whole of England a magnificent example of fidelity to the Catholic faith, for which he was martyred at Tyburn, with four companions. He is the proto-martyr of the post-reformation English martyrs. Beatified in 1886. Canonized in 1970 as one of the Forty Martyrs of England and Wales, q.v. He is shown as a Carthusian, carrying a noose.

John Haile (Bl) M.   May 5
d. 1535   A secular priest, vicar of Isleworth, Middlesex. He was martyred with Bl John Houghton, q.v.

John of Beverley (St) Bp. OSB.   May 7
d. 721   He was born at Harpham in Yorkshire and studied at Canterbury under SS Adrian and Theodore; then he became a monk at Whitby. Eventually he was ordained bishop of Hexham, whence he was transferred to York as metropolitan. As such he ordained St Bede to the priesthood. He was the founder of Beverley abbey, to which he retired in his old age.

John of Châlon (St) Bp.   May 9
d. *c* 475   The third bishop of Châlon-sur-Saône. He was ordained by St Patiens of Lyons.

John of Avila (St) C.   May 10
d. 1569   Born at Almodovar, in New Castile, he studied law at Salamanca and theology at Alcalá (*Complutum*). After his ordination he was preparing to sail for the missions of the West Indies and Mexico, but was detained by the archbishop of Seville. He spent the forty years of his priestly career evangelizing Andalusia — preaching, writing, directing people (among others SS Teresa, Francis Borgia, John of God, Louis of Granada) and converting sinners. His ascetical writings, chiefly his letters, rank high among the Spanish classics. He is usually called "the Apostle of Andalusia". Beatified in 1894. Canonized in 1970.

St John Houghton, May 4

John Rochester (Bl) M.
O. Cart.   May 11
d. 1537   He was born at Terling, Essex, and
was a professed Carthusian of the London
Charterhouse. He was martyred at York, with
Bl James Walworth. Beatified in 1886.

John Stone (St) M. OSA.   May 12
d. 1538   An Augustinian friar at Canter-

bury, martyred there for denying the royal
supremacy. Canonized in 1970 as one of the
Forty Martyrs of England and Wales, q.v.

John the Silent (St) Bp.   May 13
454–558   Born at Nicopolis in Armenia,
before his twentieth year he had already
founded a monastery and become a monk in
his native city. At the age of twenty-eight he
was chosen bishop of Colonia (Taxara). He
resigned after nine or ten years, and hiding his
identity, entered the *laura* of St Sabas near
Jerusalem. Here he spent the rest of his life,
part of it as a "walled-up" recluse.

John Nepomucen (St) M.   May 16
c 1340–1393   A native of Nepomuk, in
Bohemia, he became canon of Prague and
eventually court chaplain and confessor to
Queen Sophie, second wife of the dissolute
Wenceslaus IV. He was of a retiring disposition and repeatedly refused bishoprics which
were offered to him. In 1393, or according to
another tradition 1383, he was, by order of
Wenceslaus, thrown into the river Moldau and
drowned. A tradition, still widely credited in
Central Europe, attributes his martyrdom to
his refusal to reveal to the king what he had
heard from the queen in sacramental confession. Canonized in 1729.

John I (St) Pope M.   GC. May 18
d. 526   A Tuscan, who was ordained for the
Roman clergy, became archdeacon and finally
pope (523). In 526 he went to Constantinople
on an embassy from Theodoric, the Arian king
of the Ostro-Goths. On his return Theodoric
cast the pope into prison on suspicion of
having conspired with the emperor Justin. The
pope died there of want and hardship.

John of Parma (St) Ab. OSB.   May 22
d. c 982   He was born at Parma and early in
life was made canon of the cathedral in that
city. He is said to have made six pilgrimages to
Jerusalem and to have taken the Benedictine
habit there. He was abbot of St John's, at
Parma (973–c 982) then under the Cluniac
observance. He is a minor patron of Parma.

John of Cetina (Bl) M. OFM.   May 22
d. 1397   A Spanish Franciscan, who with Bl
Peter de Dueñas (q.v.) was commissioned to
evangelize the Moors at Granada and was
martyred in the attempt.

John Forest (Bl) M. OFM.   May 22
d. 1538   Born in all probability at Oxford
where, after his profession as a Friar Minor, he
was also educated in the Franciscan college.
He was stationed at Greenwich when he
became confessor to Queen Catherine of
Aragon. He opposed the queen's divorce and

the king's supremacy in matters spiritual, and was for this cause burnt to death at Smithfield under conditions of most revolting cruelty. Beatified in 1886.

John Baptist Machado
(Bl) M. SJ.   May 22
1580–1617   Born at Terceira, in the Azores, he became a Jesuit at Coimbra, and in 1609 was dispatched to the Japanese missions. He was beheaded at Nagasaki with two companions. Beatified in 1867.

John Baptist de Rossi (St)
C.   May 23
1698–1764   Born at Voltaggio, diocese of Genoa, he studied at the Roman College and, after his ordination in 1721, remained in Rome as a member of the Roman clergy. In 1737 he was made canon of Santa Maria in Cosmedin at the foot of the Aventine. His main work as missioner and catechist was among the teamsters, farmers and herdsmen of the Campagna, and among the sick and prisoners. Canonized in 1881.

John of Montfort (Bl)
Knight   May 24
d. 1177(8)   A Knight Templar of Jerusalem. Wounded in a battle against the Saracens he was taken to Cyprus, where he died at Nicosia. His feast was for a long time celebrated at Cyprus on May 25.

John del Prado (St) M.
OFM.   May 24
d. 1636   Born at Morgobresio, Léon, Spain. While following his theological course of Salamanca he joined the barefooted Franciscans of the Strict Observance. Eventually he was sent to Morocco with special ecclesiastical powers, and was martyred there with two other Spanish friars.

John Hoan (St) M.   May 26
c 1789–1861   Born at Kim-long, in Vietnam, he was ordained priest and worked zealously until his martyrdom by beheading under King Yu-Duc near Dougl Hoi. Beatified in 1909, canonized in 1988.

John Shert (Bl) M.   May 28
d. 1582   Born   at   Shert   Hall,   near Macclesfield, Cheshire and educated at Brasenose College, Oxford. After his conversion he studied at Douai and Rome and was ordained in 1576. In 1579 he began his work on the English mission. He suffered at Tyburn with BB Thomas Ford and Robert Johnstone. Beatified in 1886.

John de Atarés (St) H.   May 29
d. c 750   A hermit in the diocese of Jaca, in the Aragonese Pyrenees, whose cell was situated under a huge rock, where at a later time the Benedictine abbey of St John de la Peña (of the Rock) was built. The saint and the place are famous in Spanish history, since the abbey of La Peña became the cradle of the Christian kingdoms of Navarre and Aragon.

John Pelingotto (Bl) C.
Tert. OFM.   June 1
1240–1304   A native of Urbino, the son of a merchant. He was received into the Franciscan third order and devoted his whole life to prayer and works of charity. Cult approved in 1918.

John Storey (Bl) M.   June 1
d. 1571   He was born in N. England and educated at Oxford, where he received the degree of Doctor of Law and subsequently was appointed president of Broadgate Hall and first Regius Professor of civil law. He married (after 1547), became a member of parliament, and opposed several laws against the Catholic faith, enacted under Edward VI and Elizabeth. He was imprisoned and managed to escape abroad but, followed by Elizabeth's secret agents he was kidnapped, brought back to England and martyred at Tyburn for alleged treason.

John de Ortega (St) H.   June 2
d. c 1150   A priest of the diocese of Burgos, in Spain, who after sundry pilgrimages to Palestine, Rome and Compostella, became a hermit in a small village near Burgos, and helped St Dominic de la Calzada (q.v.) in the work building bridges and hospices, opening roads, etc. His feast is liturgically observed in the diocese of Burgos.

John Mary Mzec (St) M.   June 3
d. 1887   A negro of Uganda who baptized many in the hour of death. Beheaded in January 1887. Beatified in 1912. Canonized in 1964. See Charles Lwanga and Comps.

John Grande (Bl) C.   June 3
1546–1600   Born at Carmona in Andalusia, Spain, he worked in the linen trade but abandoned that occupation to become a hermit at Marcena. From this time up to his death, punning on his Spanish surname — *Grande*, i.e. Great — he always called himself *Juan Grande Pecador* — John the Great Sinner. He left his cell to work in the prisons and hospitals at Xeres, where a recently opened hospital was entrusted to his care. This he handed over to St John of God, taking the

habit of the latter's new order at Granada. he died at Xeres while still caring for the prisoners and the sick. Beatified in 1853.

John Maria Muzeyi (St) M.   June 3

d. 1886   He practised the corporal works of mercy until his martyrdom by order of King Mwanga of Uganda. See Charles Lwanga and Comps.

John of Verona (St) Bp.   June 6

7th cent.   The successor of St Maurus in the see of Verona, in N. Italy.

John Davy (Bl) M. O. Cart.   June 6

d. 1537   A Carthusian monk, professed at the London Charterhouse, and later starved to death at Newgate, where he was imprisoned for resisting Henry VIII's spiritual supremacy. He suffered with a group of six other Carthusians. Beatified in 1886.

John Rainuzzi (Bl) C. OSB.   June 8

d. ? 1330   A Benedictine monk of St Margaret's monastery, at Todi. His charity earned for him the title of "John the Almsgiver", by which he is often called.

John Dominic (Bl) Bp. OP.   June 10

1356–1418   Born at Florence, he entered the Dominican order, in which he distinquished himself as one of the leaders in the restoration of discipline. In 1408 he was named archbishop of Ragusa and created cardinal. He was one of those who worked most successfully for the healing of the Great Schism of the West and, as papal legate for Hungary and Bohemia, converted many Hussites. Cult confirmed in 1832.

John of Sahagun (of St Facundo) (St) C. OSA.   June 12

1419–1479   Born at Sahagun, province of Léon in Spain, and educated by the Benedictines at the great abbey of his native town, and then at Salamanca and Burgos. While still quite young he held several benefices in the diocese of Burgos, but eventually he surrendered all but one. In 1463 this too he gave up to become an Augustinian at Salamanca, where he held the offices of novice-master and prior. By his fearless preaching he effected a great change in the social life of Salamanca. Canonized in 1690. Since 1969 his cult has been confined to local calendars.

John of Pulsano (of Matera) (St) Ab. OSB.   June 20

d. 1139   A native of Matera in the Basilicata, who early in life entered a Benedictine monastery, where his austerity was not looked upon with much favour. He next joined the monks of Montevergine under St William, the founder, but left him to become a popular preacher at Bari. Finally he settled at Pulsano, near Monte Gargano, where he established an abbey, the first of a series of foundations which coalesced into a new Benedictine congregation. He died at Pulsano. He is often called, from his birthplace, St John of Matera.

John Baptist Zola (Bl) M. SJ.   June 20

1576–1626   Born at Brescia in Italy, he became a Jesuit (1595) and was sent to India (1602) and thence to Japan (1606). He settled at Tacacu but in 1614 was banished to China. On his return to Japan he was captured and burnt alive at Nagasaki. Beatified in 1867.

John Kinsaco (Bl) M. SJ.   June 20

d. 1626   A native of Ocinozu in Japan, who became a Jesuit novice and was arrested and burnt alive at Nagasaki. Beatified in 1867.

John Fenwick and John Gavan (BB) MM. SJ.   June 20

d. 1679   John Fenwick was born at Durham and educated at Saint-Omer. He became a Jesuit in 1656. John Gavan, a Londoner by birth, was also educated at Saint-Omer and received into the Society of Jesus in 1660. Both were martyred at Tyburn, with three other Jesuits, for alleged complicity in the Oates Plot. Beatified in 1929.

John Rigby (St) M.   June 21

d. 1600   A layman, born at Harrock Hall, near Wigan, Lancs, who was condemned for being reconciled to the Catholic church and executed at Southwark. Beatified in 1929. Canonized in 1970 as one of the Forty Martyrs of England and Wales q.v.

John Fisher (St) Card. Bp. M.   GC. June 22

1469–1535 (June 22)   Born at Beverley in Yorkshire, the son of a draper. He was educated at Cambridge and ever afterwards was connected with the life of the university, of which he eventually became chancellor. As such he did much to further the growth and progress of his Alma Mater, of which he may justly be considered the second founder. In 1504 he was appointed bishop of Rochester and proved to be the most faithful of the English bishops of that period: he upheld the cause of the queen against her adulterous husband, Henry VIII, and refused to take the Oath of Supremacy. He was for this reason beheaded on Tower Hill. Shortly before his death he had been created cardinal by the pope. He died with the words *Te Deum* on his lips. Canonized in 1935. In art he is robed as a

St John Fisher, June 22

cardinal, with drawn, ascetic features; with an axe, or his hat at his feet.

John I of Naples (St) Bp.   June 22
5th cent. The bishop of Naples who translated the body of St Januarius from Puteoli to Naples.

John IV of Naples (St) Bp.   June 22
d. 835 Locally known as *San Giovanni d'Acquarola*, or "the Peacemaker". Bishop of Naples, where he is now venerated as one of the patron saints of the city.

John (St) M.   June 23
d. 362 A Roman priest beheaded under Julian the Apostate. The relic venerated as the head of John the Baptist at San Silvestro in Capite, the English church in Rome, is supposed to be in reality the head of this martyred priest.

John the Baptist (St)
Prophet M.   GC. June 24 and Aug 29
1st cent. "The man sent from God", the voice crying in the wilderness: "Prepare ye the way of the Lord", of whom Christ said "among those that are born of women there is not a greater prophet". His career as a forerunner of the Messiah is fully described in the four Gospels. Patristic tradition maintains that St John was freed from original sin and sanctified in his mother's womb: hence from the earliest time the church has liturgically celebrated the nativity of St John. His martyrdom under Herod is also commemorated (August 29). St John has always been, and still is, one of the most popular of saints. His life in the desert appealed to many of the earliest monks and so he has always been a major patron of the monastic orders. He is depicted as lean and ascetic, with a rough robe and carrying a lamb or with a lamb near him, and a tall staff often ending in a cross; or carrying his own head.

John of Tuy (St) H.   June 24
9th cent. A native of Spanish Galicia, who lived as a hermit near Tuy. His body is now enshrined in the Dominican church at Tuy.

John the Spaniard (Bl) C.
O. Cart.   June 25
1123–1160 A native of Almanza in Spain who, when still a boy, travelled to France and studied at Arles. He became a Carthusian at Montrieu, was transferred to the Grande Chartreuse under St Anthelmus and finally sent as founder and first prior of the charter-

house of Reposoir, near Lake Geneva. He was the first to draw up constitutions for the Carthusian nuns. Cult approved in 1864.

John and Paul (SS) MM. June 26
? Roman martyrs who suffered at Rome but not, as traditionally asserted, under Julian the Apostate. Their names occur in the first eucharistic prayer and there is a stately basilica erected in their name on the Coelian Hill. Their Acts, however, are held by most scholars to be merely a pious fiction. Since 1969 their cults are confined to the calendar of their titular church.

John of the Goths (St) Bp. June 26
d. *c* 800 A bishop of the Goths in S. Russia, noted for his defence of the veneration of images. He was driven from his see by the invading Khazars and died in exile.

John of Chinon (St) H. June 27
6th cent. A native of Brittany who became a hermit at Chinon in Touraine, where he was the spiritual adviser of Queen St Radegund.

John Southworth (St) M. June 28
d. 1654 A Lancashire man who became a student at Douai. He was ordained in 1619 and sent to the English mission, where his ministrations during the plague of 1636 were specially noteworthy. He was arrested and imprisoned as early as 1627, but was subsequently released. He was executed at Tyburn under the Commonwealth. Beatified in 1929. Canonized 1970 as one of the Forty Martyrs of England and Wales, q.v. His relics are enshrined in Westminster cathedral, London.

**John Cornelius SJ. and
John Carey (BB) MM.** July 4
d. 1594 Bl John Cornelius was born at Bodmin of Irish parents. He became a fellow of Exeter College, Oxford, and a student at Reims and then at Rome, where he was ordained in 1583. He worked for ten years on the English mission at Lanherne and became a Jesuit only in 1594. Bl John Carey was a layman, an Irish servant of Bl Thomas Bosgrave and a fellow-servant of Bl Patrick Salmon. The four were martyred at Dorchester in Oxfordshire. Beatified in 1929.

John of Cologne (St) M. OP. July 9
d. 1572 A native of Cologne who became a Dominican and parish priest of Horner, Holland. He was hanged with the other Gorkum martyrs, q.v. They were canonized in 1867.

**John of Osterwick (St)
M. OSA.** July 9
d. 1572 A native of Holland who joined the Augustinians at Briel and was director and

St John the Baptist, June 24

confessor of a community of Augustinian nuns at Gorkum when the town was taken by the Calvinists. He suffered with the group of Gorkum martyrs, q.v.

John of Bergamo (St) Bp. July 11
d. *c* 690 A bishop of Bergamo (*c* 656 to *c* 690) renowned for his learning and great success in combating Arianism. The letters BM. appended to his name, instead of being read *Bonae Memoriae*—"of good memory", were wrongly taken for *Beati Martyris*—"of the Blessed Martyr" — and he was in consequence formerly considered to have been a martyr.

John the Georgian (St) Ab. July 12
d. *c* 1002 This John is usually surnamed "the Iberian", i.e., the Georgian, and also "the Hagiorite". With his wife's consent, he and his son St Euthymius became monks on Mt Olympus in Bithynia. Thence they migrated to Mt Athos in Macedonia, where they founded the monastery of Iviron (Iweron — the Iberian), which still exists.

John Gualbert (St) Ab.
OSB. Vall. July 12
d. 1073 A Florentine by birth, of the noble family of the Visdomini. As a young man he spent his time in worldly amusements, until one Good Friday, having pardoned his brother's murderer, he saw the image of the crucifix miraculously bow its head in acknowledgement of Gualbert's good action. Thereupon John became a Benedictine at San Miniato del Monte, at Florence. When it seemed likely that he would be appointed abbot he left the abbey for a more secluded spot and founded the monastery of Vallumbrosa — *Vallis Umbrosa* — near Fiesole, under St Benedict's rule. His foundation soon grew into a powerful congregation spread chiefly through Tuscany and Lombardy. St John died at Passignano, one of his own foundations, and was canonized in 1193. Since 1969 his cult has been confined to local or particular calendars.

John Jones (St) M. OFM. July 12
d. 1598 John Jones, *alias* Buckley, was born at Clynog Fawr, Gwynedd. He became a Franciscan Observant at Rome and worked on the London mission from 1592 till 1597. He was martyred for his priesthood at Southwark. Beatified in 1929. Canonized 1970 as one of the Forty Martyrs of England and Wales, q.v.

John Naisen (Bl) M. July 12
d. 1626 A wealthy Japanese layman from Arima. When the persecutors threatened him with the prostitution of his wife, his constancy gave way for a time, but he repented and was burnt alive at Nagasaki. Beatified in 1867.

John Tanaca (Bl) M. July 12
d. 1626 A Japanese layman who gave shelter to Bl Balthasar de Torres. After a long imprisonment at Omura he was burnt alive at Nagasaki. Beatified in 1867.

The following six saints all belonged to the Society of Jesus; the first two were clerics and the rest temporal-coadjutors. All suffered martyrdom with Bl Ignatius de Azevedo and comp., q.v.

John Fernandez, born at Lisbon.
John of San Martin, born at Toledo.
John de Baeza, a Spaniard by birth.
John de Zafra, born at Toledo.
John de Mavorga, born in Aragon.
and
John Fernandez (BB) MM.
SJ. July 15
d. 1570 Born at Braga, Portugal.

John Plesington (St) M. July 19
d. 1697 Born at Dimples, near Garstang, Lancs, and educated at Valladolid, he worked on the mission in Cheshire and was hanged at Chester. Beatified in 1929. Canonized in 1970 as one of the Forty Martyrs of England and Wales, q.v.

John of Edessa (St) H. July 21
6th cent. A Syrian monk of Edessa and an associate of St Simeon Salus.

John and Benignus (SS)
OSB. July 21
d. 707 Said to have been twin brothers and monks of Moyenmoutier under St Hidulphus.

John Lloyd (St) M. July 22
d. 1679 A native of Powys who received his priestly education at Valladolid and then served the Welsh mission. He was executed at Cardiff with Bl Philip Evans, SJ. Beatified in 1929. Canonized in 1970 as one of the Forty Martyrs of England and Wales, q.v.

John Cassian (St) Ab. July 23
c 360-433 An Eastern monk who received his monastic training in Egypt and afterwards established himself at Marseilles, where he founded the abbey of St Victor and a nunnery, ruling both from Lérins. His *Conferences* and his *Institutes* were commended by St Benedict as authoritative treatises on the training of monks, and in consequence have exerted a lasting influence in the Christian world.

John of Tossignano (Bl) Bp. July 24
d. 1446 John Tavalli was born at Tossignano, near Imola, and after his studies at the university of Bologna, joined the order of the Gesuati. In 1431 he became bishop of Ferrara.

He is best remembered as the translator of the Bible into Italian. Cult confirmed by Benedict XIV.

John Boste (St) M. July 24
d. 1594 Born at Dufton in Westmorland and educated at Queen's College, Oxford and, after his conversion, at Reims. He was ordained in 1581 and laboured in the northern counties for twelve years until his martyrdom at Durham. Beatified in 1929. Canonized in 1970 as one of the Forty Martyrs of England and Wales, q.v.

John Ingram (Bl) M. July 26
d. 1594 Born at Stoke Edith, Herefordshire. He became a convert, studied at New College, Oxford, and afterwards at Reims and Rome. After his ordination in 1589 he worked in Scotland. He was condemned, and suffered at Gateshead.

John Baptist Lo (Bl) M. July 29
1825–1861 A Chinese servant beheaded at Tsin-gai. Beatified in 1909.

John Soreth (Bl) C. OC. July 30
c 1420–1471 A native of Caen in Normandy. He joined the Carmelites and was their prior-general from 1451 to 1471. He was a forerunner of St Teresa in his efforts to return to the primitive observance and to admit nunneries into the order. Cult approved in 1865.

John Colombini (Bl)
Founder July 31
c 1300–1367 A native of Siena who became a prominent citizen, held the office of *Gonfalionere* (first magistrate), and is described as an ambitious, avaricious and bad-tempered man. While reading the story of the conversion of St Mary of Egypt, he was suddenly converted and eventually formed a small society of lay persons devoted to penance and deeds of charity. They were called *Gesuati* and were approved in 1367. Bl John was beatified by Gregory XIII.

John Baptist Vianney (St)
C. GC. Aug 4
1786–1859 More often called "the Curé d'Ars". Born at Dardilly, near Lyons, he was a farm-hand and aged nineteen when he began his studies for the priesthood, which he completed only with considerable difficulty. He was, however, ordained in 1815 and three years after was appointed parish priest of Ars, a small village near Lyons, where he worked for the rest of his life, and for which he won world-wide fame. His chief work was administering the Sacrament of Reconciliation: his confessional was thronged with all classes of persons who flocked to him from far and wide, and during the last ten years of his life he spent in the confessional from sixteen to eighteen hours a day. He was gifted with discernment of spirits, prophecy and hidden knowledge, and was often tormented by evil spirits. Canonized in 1925 and declared patron saint of parish-priests.

John Felton (Bl) M. Aug 8
d. 1570 Born at Bermondsey, of a Norfolk family. He was living at Southwark when the Bull of Pope St Pius V excommunicating Queen Elizabeth reached London, and he bravely affixed a copy to the door of the bishop of London's house. For this he was martyred in St Paul's churchyard. Beatified in 1886.

John of Salerno (Bl) C. OP. Aug 9
c 1190–1242 A native of Salerno, who received the religious habit from St Dominic and became the founder of the Dominican friary of Santa Maria Novella at Florence (1221). Cult approved in 1783.

John of Alvernia (Bl) C. OFM. Aug 9
1259–1322 Born at Fermo, he joined the Friars Minor in 1272, and thereafter lived a semi-eremitical life on Mt Alvernia, whence he evangelized the surrounding district. He was famous for his gift of infused knowledge. Cult approved in 1880.

John of Rieti (Bl) C. OSA. Erem. Aug 9
d. c 1350 John Bufalari was a native of Castel Porziano, near Rome, and an Augustinian friar-hermit at Rieti. Cult approved in 1832.

John and Peter Becchetti (BB) CC. OSA. Erem. Aug 11
13th cent. Descendants of the family of St Thomas Becket (Becchetti) from a branch that settled at Fabriano, in Italy. Both belonged to the Augustinian hermits, and Bl John is said to have taught at Oxford. Cult approved in 1835.

John Baptist Petrucci (Bl) M. OSM. Aug 11
See Laurence Nerucci, etc.

John Berchmans (St) C. SJ. Aug 13
1599–1621 Born at Diest in Brabant, the son of a master-shoemaker. He studied at Malines and there also he entered the Society of Jesus at the age of seventeen and was sent to Rome for his novitiate. His short life of twenty-two years was remarkable for the heroic fidelity with which he kept the minutest points of regular observance. He was canonized in 1888, and is venerated as patron of young servers at the eucharist.

John of Saint Martha (Bl)
M. OFM.   Aug 16
1578–1618   Born at Prados, near Tarragona,
in Spain. After his ordination (1606) he was
sent to Japan, where he is said to have gained a
perfect mastery of the language. Arrested at
Meaco in 1615, he was beheaded after being
imprisoned for three years. Beatified in 1867.

John of Monte Marano
(St) Bp. OSB.   Aug 17
d. 1094   A Benedictine monk, probably of
Monte Cassino. He was nominated bishop of
Monte Marano by Gregory VII (1074) while
that pope was in exile at Salerno. His cult was
approved in 1906, and he is venerated as the
principal patron saint of Monte Marano.

John and Crispus (SS)
MM.   Aug 18
According to the pre-1970 RM. they were
Roman priests who devoted themselves to
recovering and burying the bodies of the
martyrs, for which they themselves suffered
martyrdom. Their names are taken from the
untrustworthy Acts of SS Simplicius, Faustinus and Beatrix.

John Nangata, John Yano and John Foiamon (BB)
MM.   Aug 19
d. 1662   The two first-named were sailors in
the ship on which Bl Peter Zuñiga (q.v.) was a
traveller, and the last-named was a scribe on
the same ship. They were beheaded at Nagasaki. Beatified in 1867.

John Eudes (St) Founder   GC. Aug 19
1601–1680   A native of Ri, France, who after
his ordination (1625) entered the French
Oratory and devoted himself wholeheartedly
to the parochial work, twice risking his life in
attending victims of the plague. In 1641 he
founded the Sisterhood of our Lady of Charity
of the Refuge to care for women of ill repute,
and in 1643 the Society of Jesus and Mary —
Eudists — for the education of priests. He was
moreover the originator of the liturgical cult of
the Sacred Heart. He died at Caen, and was
canonized in 1925.

John Kemble (St) M.   Aug 22
1599–1679   A native of Herefordshire. After
his studies and ordination at Douai, he served
the missions of Monmouthshire and Herefordshire for fifty-three years (1625–1679). In
his eighty-first year he was hanged, drawn and
quartered at Hereford. Beatified in 1929.
Canonized in 1970 as one of the Forty Martyrs
of England and Wales, q.v.

John Wall (St) M. OFM.   Aug 22
d. 1679   Born near Preston, in Lancs, he

was educated at Douai and in Rome. Here he
joined the Friars Minor with the new name of
Fr Joachim of St Anne (1651). In 1656 he
joined the Worcester mission which he served
until the year of his martyrdom at Worcester.
Beatified in 1929. Canonized in 1970 as one of
the Forty Martyrs of England and Wales, q.v.

John of Caramola (Bl) C.
OSB. Cist.   Aug 26
d. 1339   A native of Toulouse who became a
hermit on Mt Caramola in the Basilicata, Italy,
and afterwards a Cistercian lay-brother at the
abbey of Sagittario, near Chiaramonte,
Naples.

John Bassand (Bl) C.
OSB. Cel.   Aug 26
1360–1445   A native of Besançon, where he
joined the Canons Regular of St Paul. Shortly
after, however, he passed over to the Celestine
Benedictines at Paris. He held important
offices in the congregation and was spiritual
director of St Colette. He made great efforts to
establish his congregation in England and
Aragon.

John (St) M.   Aug 27
See Marcellinus, Mannea, etc.

John (St) Bp.   Aug 27
d. 813   Bishop of Pavia, in Lombardy,
801–813.

John Roche (Bl) M.   Aug 30
d. 1588   John Roche (*alias* Neale) was an
Irish waterman who was condemned to death
for rescuing a priest. He suffered at Tyburn
with five companions, including Bl Richard
Leigh. Beatified in 1929. As depicted, he
always wears Elizabethan working man's
dress, and carries an oar or a small boat.

John du Lau (Bl) Bp. M.   Sept 2
d. 1792   Archbishop of Arles. During the
French Revolution he was imprisoned in the
Carmelite church in the rue de Rennes at
Paris, and later martyred by the mob, with the
approval of the Legislative Assembly, for
refusing the oath and constitution of the clergy
which had been condemned by the Holy See.
He forms part of the group, September
(Martyrs of), q.v.

John of Perugia and Peter of Sassoferrato
(BB) MM. OFM.   Sept 3
d. 1231   These two Franciscan friars were
sent by St Francis of Assisi in 1216 to preach
to the Muslims in Spain. They worked in
the district between Teruel and Valencia.
They were seized in a mosque at Valencia,
and, on refusing to apostatize, they were beheaded. Cult approved in 1783.

John of Nicomedia (St) M.   Sept 7
d. 303   A Christian of rank who, when the
edict of persecution against the Christians was
first published at Nicomedia, removed it and
tore it to pieces. He was burnt alive.

John of Lodi (St) Bp. OSB.   Sept 7
d. 1106   A native of Lodi Vecchio in Lombardy who, after being a hermit for some years,
entered the abbey of Fontavellana, where he
professed the Benedictine rule under St Peter
Damian. In 1072 he was chosen prior of the
abbey and in 1105 bishop of Gubbio. He wrote
the life of St Peter Damian.

John Maki (Bl) M.   Sept 7
d. 1627   An adopted son of Bl Louis Maki.
He was burnt alive at Nagasaki. Beatified in
1867.

John Duckett (Bl) M.   Sept 7
d. 1644   A kinsman of Bl James Duckett, the
bookseller, (q.v.). He was born at Under-
winder, near Sedbergh, Yorks, educated for
the priesthood at Douai and ordained in 1639.
He ministered to the Catholics at Durham.
Martyred at Tyburn with Bl Ralph Corby.
Beatified in 1929.

John Tomaki and John Inamura (BB) MM. Tert. OP.   Sept 8
d. 1628   Japanese laymen and Dominican
tertiaries, beheaded at Nagasaki for helping
the missionaries. Bl John Tomaki was a very
active Christian and the father of four martyr
sons. Beatified in 1867.

John Kingocu (Bl) M. SJ.   Sept 10
d. 1622   Born at Amanguchi in Japan, he
was a catechist of Bl Charles Spinola, by whom
he was received into the Society of Jesus in the
prison at Omura. He was beheaded at Nagasaki. Beatified in 1867.

John of Korea (Bl) M.   Sept 10
d. 1622   A boy of twelve, son of Bl Antony of
Korea and his wife Mary, beheaded at Nagasaki. Beatified in 1867.

John-Gabriel Perboyre (Bl) M.   Sept 11
See Gabriel Perboyre.

John Chrysostom (St) Bp. Dr.   GC. Sept 13
c 347–407 (Sept 14)   Surnamed *Chrysostom*
("Golden Mouthed") on account of his great
eloquence. He was born at Antioch, tried the
monastic life in his youth and ruined his
health, and was then ordained priest. It was as
a priest at Antioch that he delivered the series
of sermons which made him famous throughout the East. In 398, much against his own will,

he became Patriarch of Constantinople, where
his ardent zeal, which knew no compromise,
brought down upon him the imperial wrath. In
403, at a gathering of bishops known as the
Synod of the Oak, he was deposed and
banished, but public opinion was so strongly in
his favour that the court was unable to prevent
his triumphant return. Two months later,
however, on account of another of his outspoken denunciations of vice, he was exiled
again to Armenia, in defiance of the pope who
strenuously espoused the saint's cause. John
died in exile on Sept 14. Besides being the
most prolific of the Greek Doctors, St John
was famous for his revision of the Greek
Liturgy.

John the Dwarf (St) H.   Sept 15
5th cent.   John, nicknamed *Kolobos*, "the
Dwarf", was a native of Basta in Lower Egypt.
He became a disciple of St Poemen in the
desert of Skete, and is described as short-
tempered and conceited by nature, but gentle
and humble by grace. He was also famous for
his absentmindedness. In obedience to orders
he watered a walking stick, and when it
sprouted, it was called "the tree of obedience".

John (St) M.   Sept 16
See Abundius, Abundantius, etc.

John de Massias (St) C. OP.   Sept 18
1585–1645   A native of Ribera, in Estremadura, Spain, who crossed over to S. America
and worked on a cattle ranch before becoming
a Dominican at Lima. He was employed as the
doorkeeper of the friary to the end of his life.
Beatified in 1837. Canonized 1975.

John Eustace (Bl) Ab. OSB. Cist.   Sept 20
d. 1481   A Canon Regular at Mons who
became a Cistercian and eventually was made
first abbot of Jardinet, in the diocese of
Namur. He was deputed to restore discipline
in several other houses.

John (St) M.   Sept 23
See Andrew, John, etc.

John of Meda (St) Ab. OSB.   Sept 26
d. 1159 (?)   A native of Meda, and a
member of the clergy of Milan, who about the
year 1134 joined the *Humiliati* and advised
them to adopt St Benedict's rule, which they
did, although they continued to call themselves canons. Canonized by Alexander III.

John Mark (St) Bp.   Sept 27
1st cent.   The pre-1970 RM. made this John
Mark (see Acts 12:25) a bishop of Byblos in
Phoenicia. Nowadays most biblical scholars
identify him with St Mark the evangelist, first
bishop of Alexandria.

John of Cordoba (St) M.   Sept 27
See Adolphus and John.

John Cochumbuco (Bl) M.   Sept 28
d. 1630   A tertiary of St Augustine and a
native catechist to Bl Bartholomew Gutierrez.
Beheaded at Nagasaki and beatified in 1867.

John de Montmirail (Bl)
C. OSB. Cist.   Sept 29
1165–1217   Besides other titles of nobility he
was Seigneur de Montmirail on the Marne.
Originally a soldier, he was married and had
several children, but as soon as he could win
his wife's consent he became a Cistercian at
Longpoint, where he died. He is venerated
liturgically by the Cistercians and in several
French dioceses.

John of Ghent (Bl) C. OSB.   Sept 29
d. 1439   A Benedictine of the abbey of
Sainte-Claude on the Jura Mountains. A
collaborator with St Joan of Arc, he is known
as "the Hermit of St Claude".

John of Dukla (Bl) C. OFM.   Oct 1
d. 1484   A native of Dukla in Polish Galicia
who became a Franciscan Conventual at Lem-
berg and, at the instigation of St John of
Capistrano, passed over to the Observants and
worked successfully among the Ruthenians.
Cult approved in 1739.

John Robinson (Bl) M.   Oct 1
d. 1588   Born at Ferrensby, Yorks. Having
become a widower he went to Reims to study
for the priesthood and was ordained there in
1585. He was executed at Ipswich. Beatified in
1929.

John Hewitt (Bl) M.   Oct 5
d. 1588   *Alias* Weldon and Savell. A native
of Yorkshire, he was educated at Caius College, Cambridge and studied for the priesthood at Reims. He was ordained in 1586 and
hanged at Mile End Green in London.
Beatified in 1929.

John Leonardi (St)
Founder   GC. Oct 9
c 1550–1609   A native of Diecimo in the
diocese of Lucca. While serving as an apprentice to a pharmacist at Lucca he studied for the
priesthood and was ordained in 1571. He
worked with great zeal among the prisoners
and in hospitals and, with the help of two
laymen and some priests, founded the Institute of Clerks Regular of the Mother of God,
approved in 1593. He is reckoned one of the
founders also of the College of Propaganda
Fide in Rome, and was appointed visitor of the
Vallombrosans and Monteverginians.

John of Bridlington (St)
C. OSA.   Oct 11
d. 1379   John Thwing, a student at Oxford
university, joined the community of Augustinian canons at Bridlington and in due course
ruled it as prior for seventeen years. Canonized in 1403. Nothing else is known about
him.

**John de Brébeuf and
Comps (SS) MM. SJ.**   GC. Oct 19
1596–1649   Born at Condé in France, he was
ordained and sent to Quebec in 1615. He
worked among the Huron Indians for thirty-
four years. He was martyred by the Iroquois in
1649. With Isaac Jones, Antony Daniel, Gabriel Lalement, Charles Garnier, Noel Chab-
anel, John Lalande and René Goupil, all
Jesuits, he was working among the Indians,
and they, like him, were martyred with prolonged and indescribable cruelty by the
Iroquois, mortal enemies of the Hurons. Their
bodies, or what remained of them, were eaten
by the Iroquois. See also Isaac Joques.

John of Capistrano (St)
C. OFM.   GC. Oct 23
1386–1456 (Oct 23)   A native of Capistrano
in the Abruzzi, he began life as a lawyer and
was made governor of Perugia in the Papal
States. When he was thirty he was left a
widower and became a Franciscan and a life-
long friend of St Bernardine of Siena. His
whole religious life was spent as papal legate to
various states, Palestine, Milan, France, Sicily,
Austria, Bavaria, Poland, Bohemia, and Silesia. The most important was that to Bohemia,
where his conduct in connection with the
Hussite movement has been adversely criti-
cized. St John played a large part in inspiring
the heroic resistance of the Hungarians to the
Turks. Canonized in 1724.

John of Syracuse (St) Bp.
OSB.   Oct 23
d. c 609   Bishop of Syracuse from 595 till
c 609.

John Buoni (Bl) C. OSA.
Erem.   Oct 23
d. 1249   A native of Mantua who in early life
was a licentious jester at various Italian courts.
In 1208, after a severe illness, he changed his
life completely and retired to do penance as a
hermit near Cesena, whither a number of
disciples followed him. They were given the
Augustinian rule (*Boniti*) by Innocent IV, and
soon they coalesced with similar hermits to
form the order of Augustinian hermit friars.
Cult approved in 1483.

John Angelo Porro (Bl)
C. OSB. Oct 24
d. 1504 A native of Milan who joined the Servites and, after a time spent at Monte Senario, returned to Milan where he worked to the end of his life. Cult approved in 1737.

John Dat (St) M. Oct 28
1764–1798 A native of Vietnam, ordained in 1798. After three months' captivity he was beheaded in the same year. Canonized in 1988.

John of Autun (St) Bp. Oct 29
? A bishop-saint venerated at Autun, of whom no particulars are extant.

John Slade (Bl) M. Oct 30
d. 1583 A native of Manston, Dorset (?) and a student at New College, Oxford. He became a schoolmaster and was martyred at Winchester for denying the royal supremacy in spiritual matters. Beatified in 1929.

John and James (SS) MM. Nov 1
d. c 344 Persian martyrs who suffered under King Shapur II. John is described as a bishop.

John Bodey (Bl) M. Nov 2
d. 1583 Born at Wells, Somerset, and a fellow of New College, Oxford. He became a convert and studied law at Douai. He returned to England and became a schoolmaster. He was condemned for repudiating the royal supremacy in spiritual matters and was hanged at Andover. Beatified in 1929.

John Zedazneli (St) Ab. Nov 4
6th cent. The leader of the group of Syrian monks who evangelized Georgia (Iberia) and introduced the monastic life there.

John Baptist Con (St) M. Nov 8
1805–1840 A married native of Vietnam who was beheaded. Canonized in 1988.

John of Ratzeburg (St)
Bp. M. Nov 10
d. 1066 A native of Scotland, who became a missionary in Germany. He was appointed bishop of Ratzeburg and evangelized the Baltic coastal region, where he was martyred.

John of Poland (St) M. OSB. Nov 12
See Benedict, John and Comp.

John Cini "della Pace"
(Bl) C. Tert. OFM. Nov 12
d. 1433 Surnamed "the Soldier", or "Stipendario", or from his domicile, "*de Porta pacis*", "*della pace*". He was a native of Pisa who, in 1396, became a Franciscan tertiary and founded several charitable organizations and a confraternity of flagellants. Cult approved in 1856.

John Licci (Bl) C. OP. Nov 14
1400–1511 Born at Caccamo in the diocese of Palermo, in Sicily. He joined the Dominican order and died at the age of one hundred and eleven years. Cult confirmed in 1753.

John Thorne (Bl) M. OSB. Nov 15
d. 1539 A Benedictine at Glastonbury and treasurer of the abbey at the time of the dissolution. He was executed at Glastonbury with his abbot, Bl Richard Whiting and a brother-monk, Bl Roger James. The charge against John Thorne was that of *sacrilege*, the sacrilege consisting in his having hidden various treasures of the abbey church to save them from the rapacious hands of the king. Beatified in 1895.

John Eynon and John
Rugg (BB) MM. OSB. Nov 15
d. 1539 John Eynon was priest in charge of St Giles, at Reading, and John Rugg a prebendary of Chichester living at Reading abbey. Both were executed at Reading with the abbot Bl Hugh Faringdon. They are generally considered to have been monks of the abbey. Beatified in 1895.

John Xoun (Bl) M. Nov 18
d. 1619 A Japanese, born at Meaco and baptized by the Jesuits at Nagasaki. He was a member of the confraternity of the Holy Rosary. Burnt alive at Nagasaki. Beatified in 1867.

John Angeloptes (St) Bp. Nov 27
d. 433 Bishop of Ravenna, 430–433. He was appointed by the pope metropolitan of Aemilia and Flaminia. The nickname *Angeloptes* means "the man who saw an angel": it was given him because, according to the legend, an angel visible to him alone once came and helped him to celebrate the eucharist.

John Ivanango and John
Montajana (BB) MM. Nov 27
d. 1619 Japanese laymen, both belonging to the royal family of Firando. They were beheaded at Nagasaki with eight companions. Beatified in 1867.

John of Vercelli (Bl) C. OP. Dec 1
d. 1283 Born at Mosso Santa Maria, near Vercelli, he studied at Paris and taught law at Paris and Vercelli. He then joined the friars preachers, among whom he held several offices, ending with that of master-general (1264–1283). He was commissioned by the pope to draw up the *Schema* for the second ecumenical council of Lyons. Cult approved in 1903.

John Beche (Bl) Ab. M.
OSB.   Dec 1
d. 1539   As a young Benedictine Beche took
his D.D. at Oxford (1515) and eventually
became abbot of St Werburgh at Chester
whence in 1533 he went to be abbot of
Colchester. He was a great friend of SS John
Fisher and Thomas More, and opposed
Henry VIII's ecclesiastical policy. He took the
oath of supremacy, but when in 1538 his abbey
was dissolved, he openly denied the king's
right to do this. Within the year he was charged
with treason and executed at Colchester.
Beatified in 1895.

John Ruysbroeck (Bl) C.
OSA.   Dec 2
1293–1381   A native of Ruysbroeck, near
Brussels, who after his ordination was
appointed to a canonry at Sainte-Gudule. In
1343 he founded, and ruled as first prior, the
monastery of Groenendael, for Augustinian
canons. It was here that he composed his
numerous spiritual works, which have entitled
him to a prominent place among medieval
mystical writers. Cult confirmed in 1908.

John Armero (Bl) C. OP.   Dec 2
d. 1566   A Dominican lay-brother at Baeza,
Spain, who was directed by his superiors to
take holy orders. His two great interests in life
were study and prayer. He is the object of a
popular cultus.

John (St) M.   Dec 3
See Claudius, Crispin, etc.

John Damascene (St) C.
Dr.   GC. Dec 4
c 676–749   A native of Damascus, where his
father was the Logothete, or representative of
the Christians at the court of the caliph. He
was educated by Cosmos, a Sicilian monk who
had been brought into Syria as a slave. After
succeeding his father as Logothete, he retired
to the *laura* of St Sabas at Jerusalem and
embraced there the monastic life. He boldly
resisted the Iconoclast emperor, Leo the Isaurian, but he is best remembered as a theologian. He was the author of the first real
compendium of theology, the *Fountain of
Wisdom*, as well as of numerous liturgical
hymns. He was the last of the Greek fathers
and the first of the Christian Aristotelians. Leo
XIII proclaimed him Doctor of the Church in
1890.

John the Wonder-Worker
(St) Bp.   Dec 5
d. *p.*750   Bishop of Polybotum in Phrygia,
one of the most strenuous champions of
orthodoxy against the emperor Leo, the

Image-Breaker. Such was his fame as a
wonder-worker that the emperor did not dare
to interfere with him.

John Gradenigo (Bl) H.
OSB.   Dec 5
d. 1025   A Venetian nobleman who was pro-
fessed as a Benedictine at Cuxa, in the
Catalonian Pyrenees, together with his friend
St Peter Urseolo. After a life of manifold
vicissitudes, he died as a hermit near Monte
Cassino.

John Almond (St) M.   Dec 5
d. 1612   A native of Allerton, near Liver-
pool, and educated at Much Woolton, Reims,
and Rome. Ordained in 1598, he worked on
the English mission from 1602 till 1612. He
was put to death at Tyburn. Beatified in 1929.
Canonized in 1970 as one of the Forty Martyrs
of England and Wales, q:v.

John Roberts (St) M.
OSB.   Dec 9
c 1577-1610   Born at Trawsfynydd in
Gwynedd, he was brought up nominally a
Protestant, but was always a Catholic at heart.
At the age of nineteen he went up to St John's
College, Oxford, and in 1598 was entered at
the Inns of Court as a student of law. This
same year, travelling on the Continent on
holiday, he was received into the church at
Notre Dame, Paris, and went to Valladolid in
October for his ecclesiastical course. While
there he joined the Benedictines at San Benito
el Real (1599), and was professed the following year at Compostella. In December 1602,
after his ordination, he set out for the English
mission. His resourcefulness and courage
made him an outstanding figure even among
the priests of the English mission. Six or seven
times he was imprisoned and released; during
the plague of 1603 his services to the sick in
London made his name known throughout the
land. Meanwhile, he was the chief assistant of
Dom Augustine Bradshaw in the founding of
St Gregory's at Douai (now Downside abbey).
He was captured in his priestly vestments at
the eucharist and executed at Tyburn.
Beatified in 1929. Canonized in 1970 as one of
the Forty Martyrs of England and Wales, q.v.

John Mason (Bl) M.   Dec 10
d. 1591   A native of Kendal, Westmorland.
He was a layman and was hanged at Tyburn
for succouring priests. He suffered with four
companions. Beatified in 1929.

John Marinoni (Bl) C.   Dec 13
1490–1562   A Venetian, canon of St Mark's
cathedral, who gave up his canonry to join
(1530) St Cajetan, the founder of the

Theatines. He was a ubiquitous preacher, the exclusive theme of his sermons being Christ crucified. He refused the archbishopric of Naples, the city in which he died. Cult approved in 1762.

John of the Cross (St) Dr. OC.   GC. Dec 14

1542–1591 Juan de Yepes was born at Fontiberos in Old Castile, the son of a weaver. He joined the Carmelites at Medina (1562) and from 1564 to 1567 was a student of theology at Salamanca. He now fell under the influence of St Teresa and was her first "half-friar" of the first house of the reform, founded for men, at Duruelo. From 1572 to 1577 he was the confessor of St Teresa at Avila. There followed a most trying period of ill-treatment, calumny and imprisonment at Toledo, until the Discalced were definitely separated from the Calced Carmelites in 1578. St John was now made prior successively of several houses and, in 1585, visitor of Andalusia. The last years of his life were again a period of intense humiliation, misunderstanding and physical suffering. He died in obscurity at Ubeda. St John's highest title to fame are his mystical writings (*The Ascent of Mount Carmel, The Dark Night of the Soul, The Spiritual Canticle, etc.*) which, besides being superb masterpieces of Spanish literature, contain a thorough exposition of Catholic mysticism. St John was canonized in 1726 and declared a Doctor of the Church in 1926.

John Bread-and-Water (Bl) C. OSB. Cist.   Dec 14

d. *p.*1150 A Cistercian lay-brother of the abbey of Sagramenia (*Sacra Moenia*) in Spain, founded in 1142. On account of Bl John's life-long fasting on bread and water the people nicknamed him Brother John Bread-and-Water. (*Pan y Agua*).

John and Festus (SS) MM.   Dec 21

? Martyrs honoured in Tuscany.

John Vincent (St) Bp. OSB.   Dec 21

d. 1012 A native of Ravenna who became a Benedictine at St Michael of Chiusa, and then a hermit on Monte Caprario; finally he was made bishop of a diocese in the neighbourhood.

John Cirita (Bl) H. OSB.   Dec 23

d. *c*1164 A Spanish Benedictine who was first a hermit in Galicia and then a monk at Toronca in Portugal. He was instrumental in handing over the abbey to the Cistercians, and is said to have written the rule of the Knights of Avis.

John of Kenty (St) C.   GC. Dec 23

c 1390–1473 (Dec 24) Born at Kenty in Silesia, he graduated at the university of Cracow and was appointed to the chair of theology. For some time he took charge of a parish but, fearing the responsibility, returned to his biblical teaching, which he carried on until his death. He made a practice of sharing his earnings with the poor. Canonized in 1767.

John (St) Apostle and Evang.   GC. Dec 27

d. *c*100 Often surnamed in English the Divine i.e. the theologian. A Galilean, the son of Zebedee and brother of St James the Greater, John was a fisherman by profession until called by Christ to be an apostle. He became in fact "the Disciple whom Jesus loved," whom our Lord, dying on the cross, made the guardian of His mother. He wrote the fourth gospel, chiefly to express Christ's divinity, three canonical letters and, by tradition, the Book of Revelation (Apocalypse). After the resurrection he spent most of his time at Ephesus. A very ancient legend holds that he was cast into a cauldron of boiling oil at Rome under Domitian, but was preserved unhurt and banished to Patmos. This tradition used to be liturgically commemorated in the Western church on May 6 — St John before the Latin Gate, *ante Portam Latinam*. St John died at Ephesus at a great age. He has several symbols in art. In medieval times his statue always appeared on the rood beam in churches, whilst he is represented as holding a chalice from which a snake or dragon is proceeding; or as a young man with a book; or as an eagle, or with an eagle. With reference to the legend described above, he is sometimes shown naked in a large pot of bubbling oil.

John Alcober (Bl) M. OP.   Dec 30

1694–1748 Born at Gerona, in Spain. After his profession in the Dominican order, he was sent to China (1728) and for sixteen years he worked in the province of Fo-kien. Arrested in 1746, he was strangled in the prison at Futsheu. Beatified in 1893.

John-Francis Regis (St) C. SJ.   Dec 31

1597–1640 Born at Font-Couverte in the diocese of Narbonne, in Languedoc. At the age of eighteen he entered the Society of Jesus at Béziers; was ordained in 1631; and from that moment knew no rest, spending himself in preaching the gospel to unlettered farming folk of Languedoc and Auvergne; providing for prisoners and fallen women; establishing confraternities of the Bl Sacrament; and effecting everywhere numerous conversions among

St John, Dec 27

the Huguenots. He died while preaching a mission (Dec 30) and was canonized in 1737.

John *(several)*
Note. There are some two hundred or more other saints, named John — e.g. John Thauler, John Gelibert, John Wagner, John Duns Scotus, John of Jesus-Mary, John of Lerida, etc. — who are usually called *Beati* in their respective orders or nations, but there is no evidence of their being the object of any cult, whether official or popular.

John Charles Cornay (St)
See page 301.

Jolenta of Hungary (Bl)
W. Poor Clare   March 6
Otherwise Helen of Poland, q.v.

Jonah (St) Prophet.   Sept 21
? 6th cent. B.C.   A companion or disciple of St Dionysius of Paris, who preached in the neighbourhood of that city, and was martyred.

Jonas (St) H.   Feb 11
4th cent.   A monk of Demeskenyanos in Egypt under St Pachomius. He was the gardener of the community for eighty-five years, working in his capacity during the day, and at night plaiting ropes and singing psalms.

**Jonas, Barachisius and
Comp. (SS)** MM.   March 29
d. 327   Jonas and Barachisius were brothers, born at Beth-Asa in Persia. They suffered martyrdom under Shapur II. We have an eye-witness's account of their passion: the brutal inventiveness of the persecutors in devising new tortures was only surpassed by the quiet heroism of the martyrs. Some nine companions suffered at the same time.

Jonas (Yon) (St) M.   Sept 22
3rd cent.   A companion or disciple of St Dionysius of Paris, who preached in the neighbourhood of that city, and was martyred.

Jonatus (St) Ab. OSB.   Aug 1
d. *c* 690   A monk of Elnone under St Amandus. He was abbot first of Marchiennes (*c* 643–652), and then of Elnone (*c* 652–659).

Jorandus (St) H. OSB.   Nov 2
d. 1340   A monk-hermit at Kergrist and later Saint-Juhec in Pédernec.

Jordan of Saxony (Bl) C.
OP.   Feb 15
d. 1237   Jordan joined the Dominican order under St Dominic himself in 1220, and while yet a novice attended the first general chapter of the order at Bologna. He was later elected second master-general and under him the new order advanced apace, spreading throughout Germany and reaching Denmark. He was a powerful preacher and one of his sermons won

St Albert the Great for the order. He was shipwrecked and drowned when on a voyage to the Holy Land. Cult confirmed in 1828.

Jordan of Pisa (Bl) C. OP.   March 6
d. 1311   Bl Jordan received the Dominican habit at Pisa in 1280. After having studied at Paris he returned to Italy and became a preacher of very great renown at Florence. It was he who began to make use of the Italian vernacular, instead of Latin, in his sermons, and he is reckoned as one of the creators of the Italian language. Cult approved in 1833.

Jordan Forzatei (Bl) Ab. OSB.   Aug 7
1158–1248   A native of Padua, where he became a monk and then abbot of the Benedictine abbey of St Justina. He was entrusted with the government of the city by Frederick II. The tyrant Count Ezzelino cast him into prison where he remained for three years. He died at Venice. His feast is observed at Padua, Treviso, Praglia, etc.

Jordan of Pulsano (Bl) Ab. OSB.   Sept 5
d. 1152   A monk of Pulsano under the founder St John of Pulsano, whom he succeeded as abbot general of the congregation (1139–1152).

Josaphat (St) Bp. M.   GC. Nov 12
1584–1623   A native of Vladimir in Poland who, at the age of twenty, became a monk of the Byzantine rite and abbot of Vilna. He devoted himself unsparingly to the work of reuniting separated Christians with the Holy See. In his thirty-ninth year he was ordained archbishop of Polotsk in Lithuania, where he continued his labours, refusing to be dragged into politics. He was martyred by a mob of sectaries. He was the first of the Uniates to be formally canonized in Rome (1687).

Josaphat (St) M.   Nov 27
See Barlaam and Josaphat.

Joscius (Josbert, Valbebertus) (Bl) C. OSB.   Nov 30
d. 1186   A Benedictine monk of Saint-Bertin (Saint-Omer) in the diocese of Arras, renowned for his devotion to the *Ave Maria*. The legend adds that, after his death, a rose tree grew out of his mouth and that the name of Mary was written on the leaves of one of the roses!

Joseph (*several*)
Note. The spelling is the same in most modern languages, excepting the Italian: Giuseppe, and the Spanish: José. In both Italy and Spain the name is frequently joined to that of our Lady, viz. Giuseppe Maria, José Maria. The feminine form takes the following variants: Italian: Giuseppa, Giuseppina; Spanish: Josefa, Josefina; French: Josephine.

Joseph Mary Tommasi (St) Card.   Jan 1
1649–1713   A son of the duke of Palermo. He joined the Theatines and was stationed in Rome, where he devoted his great natural gifts to the methodical study of the liturgy and produced several very valuable works on this subject. He was the confessor of Cardinal Albani who, on being elected pope (Clement XI), was ordered by Joseph to accept the papacy under pain of mortal sin. The pope retaliated by appointing Joseph cardinal! He was wont to teach the catechism to the children in his titular church. Beatified in 1803. Canonized 12 Oct 1986 by Pope John Paul II.

Joseph of Freising (Bl) Bp. OSB.   Jan 17
d. 764   A Benedictine who in 752 founded the monastery of St Zeno at Isen. In 764 he became third bishop of Freising. His relics are at Isen.

Joseph of Leonissa (St) C. OFM. Cap.   Feb 4
1556–1612   A native of Leonissa, in the States of the church, who became a Capuchin (1574). He was sent as a missionary to Turkey, chiefly to care for the Christian galley-slaves. During his stay at Constantinople he suffered both imprisonment and torure. He returned to Italy and died after an operation for cancer. Canonized in 1745.

Joseph (Josippus) of Antioch (St) M.   Feb 15
?   A deacon who, with seven others, is stated to have suffered martyrdom at Antioch.

Joseph Tshang-ta-Pong (Bl) M.   March 12
c 1754–1815   A Chinese catechist martyr. Beatified in 1909.

Joseph of Arimathaea (St) C.   March 17
1st cent.   "The noble counsellor" (Mark 15:43), mentioned in the gospels in connexion with our Lord's burial. Later legends concerning him are numerous: in the sacristy of San Lorenzo, Genoa, is the *Sacro Catino*, in which Joseph is said to have caught the blood of Christ at the crucifixion; in England there is the well-known story which connects St Joseph with Glastonbury. None of these legends have any evidence to support them. He is depicted as a very old man carrying a pot

St Joseph, March 19

father of our Lord. All that we know of him is to be found in Matt. 1:2 and Luke 1:2. He is described with the all-embracing phrase "a just man" (Matt. 1:9). From the circumstance of his not being mentioned in the history of the passion, it is believed that he was then already dead. Devotion to him as a saint, widespread in the East from early ages, has, since the fourteenth century, grown in the West to such an extent that Pope Pius IX formally constituted him the patron of the universal church. Besides the feast of his *Transitus* on March 19, he has now a second feast, St Joseph the Workman, on May 1. He is shown as an old man carrying a lily and some symbol of carpentry such as a set square; or the Holy Infant.

Joseph Oriol (St) C.   March 23
1650–1702   The son of humble parents, citizens of Barcelona, Joseph Oriol succeeded in his ambition to become a priest, took the degree of doctor of theology and was appointed canon of Santa Maria del Pino in his native city. He lived on bread and water for twenty-six years, carrying on at the same time a very active apostolate, being particularly successful with soldiers and children. Canonized in 1909.

Joseph of Persia (St) M.   Apr 22
d. 376   A priest martyr under Shapur II: he suffered with St Acepsimas.

Joseph Benedict Cottolengo (St) C.   Apr 30
1786–1842   Born at Bra, near Turin, where he became canon of the church of *Corpus Domini*. In 1827 he opened a small house near his church for the sick and derelict which in 1832 was transferred to Valdocco, and called the Little House of Divine Providence. The *Piccola Casa* soon grew into a veritable township, comprising asylums, orphanages, hospitals, schools, workshops, almshouses of all descriptions, and catering for all needs. To meet the large daily expenditure required to keep up all these institutions the saint continued to depend almost entirely on alms: he kept no books of accounts and made no investments and his trust in Divine Providence never once failed him. Throughout his life he was first and foremost a man of prayer and from his time to this the *Piccola Casa* has cared for a vast number of people. Canonized in 1934.

Joseph Luu (St) M.   May 2
c 1790–1854   A native catechist, born at Cai-nhum, Vietnam, who died in prison at Vinh-long. Canonized in 1988.

Joseph Mukasa (St) M.   June 3
d. 1886   Major-domo to King Mwanga of

of ointment, or a flowering staff, or a pair of altar cruets.

Joseph (St) Patriarch   GC. March 19
1st cent.   Spouse of our Lady and foster-

Uganda, who ordered him to be put to death. See Charles Lwanga and Comps.

Joseph the Hymnographer (St) Bp.
June 14

c 810–886   Bishop of Salonica, brother of St Theodore Studites. He bravely opposed the Iconoclast emperor, Theophilus. He is one of the great liturgical poets of the Byzantine church.

Joseph Cafasso (St) C.
June 22

1811–1860   Born at Castelnuovo d'Asti, he was ordained in 1833 and three years later was appointed professor of moral theology at the ecclesiastical college at Turin. Ten years later he was appointed superior of the college and remained in that position till his death. He led a very penitential life and was renowned as a confessor. Canonized 1947.

Joseph Yuen (or Uen) (Bl) M.
June 24

1765–1815   A native priest of Tonkin, he suffered a year's imprisonment and was finally strangled. Beatified in 1900.

Joseph Hien (St) M. OP.
June 27

d. 1840   A native Dominican priest of Vietnam, who was beheaded at Nam-Dinh. Canonized in 1988.

Joseph Peter Uyen (St) M. Tert. OP.
July 3

1778–1838   A native catechist, born in Vietnam, who died in prison. Canonized in 1988.

Joseph Barsabas (St) Disciple
July 20

1st cent.   Surnamed "the Just" (Acts 1:23). He was the competitor of St Matthias for the twelfth place among the apostles left vacant by Judas Iscariot. He is often shewn as a child holding stones or loaves, or blowing soap bubbles.

Joseph of Palestine (St) C.
July 22

d. *c* 356   A Jew belonging to the biblical school of Tiberias. After prolonged interior resistance he became a Christian and was much favoured by the emperor Constantine, who bestowed on him the title of *Comes* (count). He devoted himself to building churches and spreading the gospel in the Holy Land. He was the host of St Eusebius of Vercelli, St Epiphanius and others.

Joseph Fernandez (St) M. OP.
July 24

1775–1838   A Spaniard and a professed friar of the Dominican order. He was sent to Vietnam in 1805 and, having been ordained, was appointed provincial vicar in Tonkin,

where later he was beheaded. Beatified in 1900, canonized in 1988.

Joseph Tshang (Bl) M.
July 29

c 1832–1861   A young native seminarian, born in the province of Su-tchuen, China. He was beheaded at Tsin-gai with three companions. Beatified in 1909.

Joseph Nien Vien (St) M.
Aug 21

1786–1838   A priest in Vietnam, beheaded at Hung-An. Canonized in 1988.

Joseph Calasanctius (St) Founder
GC. Aug 25

1556–1648   Joseph Calasanz was born at Peralta, near Barbastro, in Aragon. Ordained in 1583, he was engaged in pastoral work until in a vision he learned that he was to go to Rome. He did so in 1592 and at once joined the Confraternity of Christian Doctrine for the free schooling of neglected children. He gradually organized it into a religious order, called *Le Scuole Pie* (Religious Schools), whose members were, and are still, known as *Scolopi*, or Piarists. The new congregation had to pass through a period of violent persecution, mainly from other religious engaged in similar work. In his old age Joseph was unjustly accused, brought before the Holy Office and removed from control of the congregation. Later, however, he was restored. Canonized in 1767.

Joseph Canh (St) M. Tert. OP.
Sept 5

1765–1838   A native physician of Vietnam and a Dominican tertiary, beheaded in 1838. Canonized in 1988.

Joseph of Volokolamsk (St)
Sept 9

1440–1515   After some years of monastic life he was elected abbot at Borovsk and then instituted his reform at a new monastery at Volokolamsk. Strict discipline, fasting, obedience and elaborate liturgies, as well as learning and active works of charity, characterised his reform.

Joseph of St Hyacinth (Bl) M. OP.
Sept 10

d. 1622   A native of Villareal in the Spanish Mancha. He was provincial vicar of the Dominican missions in Japan and spoke Japanese perfectly. He was burnt alive at Nagasaki. Beatified in 1867.

Joseph Abibos (St) Ab.
Sept 15

d. *c* 590   Abbot of Alaverdi in Georgia; one of the thirteen Syriac disciples of St John Zedazneli.

Joseph of Cupertino (St)
C. OFM. Sept 18
1602–1663   Joseph Desa was born at Cupertino, near Brindisi. He tried his vocation in several places, but was summarily dismissed on account of his poor intelligence. Finally he was received by the Conventual Franciscans of Grotella as a stable-hand and a lay tertiary. On account, however, of the rare spiritual gifts which now began to be manifest in him, he was professed as a friar and duly ordained priest. From this time on his life is an amazing and perfectly authenticated succession of preternatural phenomena. The most remarkable of these was his power of levitation: he would fly straight from the church door to the altar over the heads of the worshippers. Once he flew to an olive tree and remained kneeling on a branch for half an hour. Happenings like these were almost every day occurrences, witnessed by hundreds of persons. Withal he was a simple, gentle, humble follower of St Francis. His brethren, however, resented so much publicity and on this account the saint had much to suffer from them. Canonized in 1767. Cult confined to particular calendars since 1969.

Joseph Thi (St) M. Oct 24
d. 1860   A native captain in the army of King Tu-duc of Vietnam. He was garroted at Anhoa. Canonized in 1988.

Joseph Nghi (St) M. Nov 8
d. 1840   A native priest of Vietnam, attached to the Society of Foreign Missions of Paris. He was beheaded. Canonized in 1988.

Joseph Pignatelli (St) C.SJ. Nov 11
1737–1811   A native of Saragossa and a scion of one of the noblest Aragonese families, who at the age of fifteen joined the Jesuits at Tarragona. After his profession he taught at Manresa, Bilbao and Saragossa. After the banishment of the Jesuits from Spain he went to Corsica and thence to Ferrara, in charge of the young Jesuits. Finally, after the suppression of the Society in 1773, he resided at Bologna for twenty years, contributing to the temporal support of his religious brethren, and strengthening their courage with brotherly advice. At the same time he worked hard for the restoration of his beloved Institute. In 1799 he was allowed to open a quasi-novitiate, and in 1804 he became the first Italian provincial of the restored order—"the link between the old and the new Society". Pius XI described him as a priest of "manly and vigorous holiness". Canonized in 1954.

Joseph Moscati (Bl) Nov 16
d. 1927   Born at Benevento in 1880, he became a celebrated doctor in Naples. He excelled in medical research and was a professor at Naples university. He gave his time, care and earnings to the poor of the slums. Beatified in 1975. Canonized in 1987.

Joseph Khang (St) M.
Tert. OP. Nov 6
1832–1861   Born at Tra-vi, province of Nam-Dinh, Vietnam, he was a servant of St Jerome Hermosilla, whom he tried to deliver from prison. Caught in the attempt, he was punished with one hundred and twenty lashes and after other most cruel tortures, was beheaded. Canonized in 1988.

Joseph Marchand (St) M. Nov 30
1803–1835   Born at Passavant in the diocese of Besançon, in France. He joined the Missionary Seminary of Paris and was sent to Vietnam, where he died while the flesh was being torn from his body with red-hot tongs. Canonized in 1988.

Josepha-Maria of St Agnes
(Bl) V. OSA. Jan 21
Otherwise Bl Inés de Beniganim, q.v.

Josephine (Ann-Joseph)
Leroux (Bl) VM. Oct 23
1747–1794   Born at Cambrai, she became an Ursuline nun at Valenciennes under the name of Josephine. When the convents were closed by the French Revolution she retired to Mons in Hainault, but returned to Valenciennes in 1793. The following year she was captured and guillotined with ten other Ursulines. Beatified in 1920.

Joshua (St) Patriarch Sept 1
c 1200 B.C.   The leader of the Israelites into the land of Canaan. All that we know of him is to be found in the Pentateuch and in the canonical book which bears his name, which was written perhaps in the sixth century B.C. but which contains older material. He figures, with Gideon, in both the Eastern and Western martyrologies.

Josse (Jost, Joder) (St) Dec 13
Otherwise Judocus, q.v.

Jovinian (St) M. May 5
d. c 300   A fellow missioner with St Peregrinus of Auxerre, whom he served as reader (lector). He is believed to have survived his bishop, and to have died a martyr.

Jovinus and Basileus
(SS) MM. March 2
d. c 258   Two martyrs, who suffered in Rome under Gallienus and Valerian and were buried on the Latin Way.

Jovinus (St) M.   March 26
See Peter, Marcian, etc.

Jovita (St) M.   Feb 15
See Faustinus and Jovita.

Jucunda (St) M.   July 27
See Felix, Julia and Jucunda.

Jucunda (St) V.   Nov 25
d. 466   A virgin of Reggio in Aemilia, Italy, a
spiritual daughter of St Prosper, bishop of that
city.

Jucundian (St) M.   July 4
? An African, who was martyred by being cast
into the sea.

Jucundinus (St) M.   July 21
See Claudius, Justus, etc.

Jucundus (St) M.   Jan 9
See Epictetus, Jucundus, etc.

Jucundus of Bologna (St)
Bp.   Nov 14
d. 485   A bishop of Bologna who flourished
in the fifth or sixth century.

Jude (Thaddaeus) (St)
Apostle   GC. Oct 28
1st cent.   One of the Twelve, brother of St
James the Less and therefore related by blood
to our Lord. He is the writer of one of the
canonical letters. The tradition is that he
preached in Mesopotamia, and afterwards,
together with St Simon, in Persia, where he
was martyred. His feast is kept with St Simon,
and Jude is regarded as the patron of difficult
or hopeless cases or problems. He is depicted
as a bearded man, holding an oar, boat or boat
hook, or a club; and a book.

Judgoenoc (Judganoc,
Jouven) (St)   Dec 13
Otherwise Judocus, q.v.

Judicäel (St) King   Dec 17
d. 658   King of Brittany, much beloved by
his people. After a victorious reign he abdi-
cated and spent the last twenty years of his life
in the monastery of Gäel, near Vannes.

Judith (St) OSB.   June 29
See Salome and Judith.

Judocus (Judganoc,
Josse, etc.) (St) H.   Dec 13
d. c 668   A priest, brother of King Judicäel
of Brittany and, on the abdication of the latter
for some months, occupant of the throne.
After a pilgrimage to Rome, he left Brittany
and retired to Villiers-Saint-Josse, near Saint-
Josse-sur-Mer, where he ended his life as a

St Jude, Oct 28

solitary. He was popular in medieval England: some relics were enshrined at Winchester.

Julia of Certaldo (Bl) V.
OSA.   Feb 15
d. 1367   Julia began life as a domestic servant, but in her nineteenth year she joined the third order of St Augustine at Florence. Returning to her native city of Certaldo, she lived as an anchoress beside the church of SS Michael and James. She died aged forty-eight, on Jan 9. Cult confirmed in 1819.

Julia Billiart (St) V.
Foundress   Apr 8
1751–1816   Marie Rose Julia Billiart was born at Cuvilly in Picardy, the daughter of a peasant farmer. At the age of fourteen she took a vow of chastity and gave herself up to the service and instruction of the poor. Soon her health completely broke down and she remained a helpless cripple until miraculously cured in 1804. During the French Revolution (1794–1804) pious friends gathered round her couch seeking to give a permanent shape to their works of charity. Thus developed the Institute of Notre Dame, for the Christian education of girls, which was definitely established at Amiens in 1804. Beatified in 1906. Canonized in 1970.

Julia of Saragossa (St) M.   Apr 16
See Saragossa, Martyrs of.

Julia (St) VM.   May 22
5th cent.   A noble maiden of Carthage sold into slavery by the Vandal conquerors. The ship on which she was being taken to Gaul touched at Corsica. A heathen festival was just being observed by the islanders and when Julia refused to join in it, she was forthwith nailed to a cross.

Julia (St) M.   July 15
See Catulinus, Januarius, etc.

Julia Louise of Jesus (Bl)
M. OC.   July 17
Otherwise Rose Chrétien, q.v.

Julia of Troyes (St) VM.   July 21
d. p.272   A maiden of Troyes, France, seized by the soldiers of the emperor Aurelian after his victory over the usurper Tetricus. Committed to the charge of Claudius, an officer of the army, she succeeded in converting him to Christ and both were beheaded at Troyes under the same Aurelian.

Julia of Nicomedia (St) M.   July 27
See Felix, Julia and Jucunda.

Julia of Lisbon (St) M.   Oct 1
See Verissimus, Maxima and Julia.

Julia (St) VM.   Oct 7
d. c 300   A martyr, either in Egypt or in Syria, under Diocletian.

Julia of Mérida (St) VM.   Dec 10
d. c 304   A fellow-sufferer with St Eulalia at Mérida in Spain, under Diocletian.

Julia (Bl) V.OSB. Cam.   Dec 15
?   A Camaldolese nun in St Benedict's convent at Arezzo, Italy.

Julian of Cagliari (St) M.   Jan 7
?   A martyr honoured at Cagliari in Sardinia, whose relics were discovered and enshrined in 1615. Locally he is often styled *Comes* (Count), but nothing is now known of his history.

Julian (St) M.   Jan 8
See Lucian, Maximian and Julian.

Julian, Basilissa, Antony, Anastasius, Celsus, Marcionilla and Comp. (SS)
MM.   Jan 9
d. c 302   Julian and Basilissa, a married couple, took vows of continence and turned their house into a hospital for the poor and indigent. Antony was a priest; Anastasius, a new convert; Marcionilla, a married woman and Celsus her little son. All except Basilissa were put to death at Antioch — which Antioch it is not known — under Diocletian. The very existence, however, of Julian and Basilissa is questioned.

Julian Sabas the Elder (St)
C.   Jan 17 and Oct 18
d. 377   A Mesopotamian solitary who did much to encourage the Christians when persecuted by Julian the Apostate. He was called on to go to Antioch to visit the triumphant Arian party. St John Chrysostom and Theodoret have left us an account of his life.

Julian (St) M.   Jan 27
See Datius, Reatrus, etc.

Julian of Sora (St) M.   Jan 27
d. c 150   A Dalmatian, arrested, put to the torture and beheaded at Sora in Campanis, under Antoninus Pius (138–161).

Julian of Le Mans (St) Bp.   Jan 27
?   3rd cent.   Honoured as the first bishop of Le Mans in France. Various English churches and places dating from Norman and Plantagenet times have this Julian for their titular.

Julian of Cuenca (St) Bp.   Jan 28
1127–1208   A native of Burgos in Spain who,

on the recapture of Cuenca in New Castile from the Moors by King Alphonsus IX, was appointed bishop of that city. In his longing to help the poor he is said to have spent all his spare time earning money for them by the work of his hands. He is the principal patron saint of the diocese of Cuenca.

Julian Maunoir (Bl) C.SJ.   Jan 28
1606–1683 Born at Saint-Georges-de-Reitembault in France, he was piously brought up by his parents, entered the Society of Jesus and took vows in 1625. Being ordained in 1637 he desired to go on the Canadian mission but was destined to become an apostle in Brittany. He mastered the language and preached so effectively that he is said to have recalled 30 000 to God within two years. He laboured thus for forty years, being joined by a number of secular priests, and finally died worn out with his labours in the town of Plévin. Beatified in 1951.

Julian (St) M.   Feb 12
See Modestus and Julian.

Julian the Hospitaller (St)
C.   Feb 12
? Also surnamed "the Poor". The legend, which is included in *The Golden Legend* and was very popular in the Middle Ages, runs as follows: Julian in error slew his own parents; in penance he and his wife went to Rome to obtain absolution and, on their return home, built a hospice by the side of a river, where they tended the poor and the sick and rowed travellers across the river. Julian is for this reason venerated as patron saint of boatmen, innkeepers and travellers. Probably the whole story is fictitious. It may be a variant of that of St Julian of Jan 9 (q.v.).

Julian of Lyons (St) M.   Feb 13
? A martyr registered in the pre-1970 RM. as having suffered at Lyons in France, though many maintain that he was martyred at Nicomedia.

Julian of Egypt and
Comp. (St)   Feb 16
? It is said that this saint Julian was the leader of 5000 martyrs who suffered in Egypt. Nothing, however, is known of him and his fellow-sufferers. One text substitutes *militibus* for *millibus* i.e. five soldiers not five thousand persons.

Julian of Caesarea (St) M.   Feb 17
d. 308 According to Eusebius, this St Julian was a native of Cappadocia who happened to be present at Caesarea in Palestine at the martyrdom of St Pamphilus and ten companions. He instantly offered himself to the

executioners to make up the number of twelve and was roasted to death at a slow fire.

Julian (St) M.   Feb 19
See Publius, Julian, etc.

Julian (St) M.   Feb 24
See Montanus, Lucius, etc.

Julian, Cronion
(surnamed Eunus) and
Besas (SS) MM.   Oct 30
d. 250 Martyrs at Alexandria in Egypt under Decius. Julian, too infirm to walk, was carried to the court by his two slaves, both Christians. One apostatized through fear, the other, Eunus, bravely shared his master's lot. They were carried on camels through Alexandria, scourged, and finally burnt to death. Besas, a sympathetic soldier, was killed by the mob for having sought to shield them. We have these particulars from St Dionysius of Alexandria.

Julian of Toledo (St) Bp.   March 8
d. 690 Monk of Agali under St Eugene, whom he succeeded first as abbot in the same monastery and then (680) as archbishop of Toledo. He was the first bishop to exercise the primacy over the whole Iberian peninsula. Besides presiding over several national councils and revising and developing the Mozarabic liturgy, he was a voluminous writer. He was an outstanding churchman in the Spain of his day.

Julian of Anazarbus (St) M.   March 16
d. c 302 A Christian of senatorial rank of Anazarbus in Cilicia who suffered under Diocletian. After being tortured he was taken to the coast, sewn up in a sack half-filled with scorpions and vipers and cast into the sea. His body was recovered and enshrined at Antioch, where St John Chrysostom delivered a sermon in his praise.

Julian (St) M.   March 23
? The pre-1970 RM. styled him a confessor but it appears certain that he was also a martyr. Nothing more is known about him.

Julian of St Augustine
(Bl) C. OFM.   Apr 8
d. 1606 Born at Medinaceli in the diocese of Segovia, in Castile. After being twice rejected he was finally admitted to the Franciscan order as a lay-brother at Santorcaz. He accompanied the Franciscan preachers on their missions and it was his custom to ring the bell through the streets to summon people to the sermon. Beatified in 1825.

**Julian Cesarello de Valle
(Bl) C. OFM.** May 11
? Born and died at Valle in Istria where his
tomb is venerated. Cult approved in 1910.

Julian (St) M. May 23
See Quintian, Lucius, etc.

Julian of Perugia (St) M. June 5
See Florentius, Julian, etc.

Julian (St) C. June 9
d. c 370 A captive from the West who was
sold into slavery in Syria. On regaining his
freedom he entered a monastery in Mesopotamia under St Ephraem.

Julian (St) M. July 18
One of the alleged sons of St Symphorosa, q.v.

Julian (St) M. July 20
See Sabinus, Julian, etc.

Julian (St) M. Aug 7
See Peter, Julian, etc.

**Julian, Marcian and
Comp. (SS) MM.** Aug 9
d. 730 A group of about ten citizens of
Constantinople (among them a patrician lady,
named Mary) who opposed by force the
attempts of the Iconoclasts to deface the icon
of our Lord set up over the Brazen Gate of the
city. They were put to death by order of Leo
the Isaurian.

Julian (St) M. Aug 12
See Macarius and Julian.

Julian (St) M. Aug 25
? Baronius describes him as a Syrian priest,
but nothing certain is known about him.

Julian of Auvergne (St) M. Aug 28
3rd cent. A native of Vienne in France, an
officer in the imperial army, and secretly a
Christian. On the outbreak of persecution,
probably under Decius, he fled but gave
himself to his pursuers and was martyred near
Brionde. His feast day was fixed by St Germanus of Auxerre.

Julian (St) M. Sept 2
See Diomedes, Julian, etc.

**Julian (Renatus or René)
Massey (Bl) M. OSB.** Sept 2
d. 1792 Julian (his baptismal name was
René) Massey was a Benedictine monk of St
Melanis of Rennes, of the Congregation of St
Maur. He was martyred at Paris with the
September martyrs, q.v. Beatified in 1926.

Julian (St) M. Sept 4
See Theodore, Oceanus, etc.

Julian (St) M. Sept 13
See Macrobius and Julian.

Julian Majali (Bl) Ab. OSB. Oct 4
d. 1470 A Benedictine of San Martino delle
Scale in Sicily. He was held in high esteem by
popes and kings. Six years before his death he
became a recluse.

**Julian, Eunus, Macarius
and Comp. (SS) MM.** Oct 30
d. c 250 Martyrs of Alexandria in Egypt. St
Julian and St Eunus are identical with the
martyrs of that name commemorated on Feb
27; St Macarius is again mentioned on Dec 8.
The duplication was caused by the insertion in
the pre-1970 RM. of another group of sixteen
martyrs, which includes the above-mentioned.
This larger group is commemorated in the
Greek calendar on this day.

Julian (St) M. Nov 1
See Caesarius and Julian.

Julian of Apamea (St) Bp. Dec 9
3rd cent. Bishop of Apamea in Syria. He
distinguished himself in the controversies with
the Montanist and Kata-Phrygian heretics.

Juliana of Bologna (St) W. Feb 7
d. 435 A matron of Bologna in Italy whose
piety and charity are extolled by St Ambrose of
Milan. Her husband, having with her consent
left her to become a priest, she devoted herself
to bringing up her four children and to the
service of the church and the poor.

Juliana (St) VM. Feb 16
d. 305 The pre-1970 RM. described this
virgin martyr as having suffered at Nicomedia
in Asia Minor, but it is more probable that she
was martyred in the neighbourhood of Naples,
perhaps at Cumae, where her relics are supposed to be enshrined. She is depicted as a
maiden standing or sitting on a dragon; or
binding the same with chain, or chaining and
scourging the Devil.

Juliana (St) VM. March 20
See Alexandra, Claudia, etc.

**Juliana of Cornillon (Bl)
V. OSA.** Apr 6
1192–1258 Born at Retinnes near Liège she
became an Augustinian nun and prioress at Mt
Cornillon. As such she promoted the institution of the feast of *Corpus Christi*, her greatest
achievement. On this account she was reviled
as a visionary and driven from Cornillon.
Recalled by the bishop of Liège she was
expelled definitely from her convent in 1248.
She took refuge at the Cistercian nunnery of
Salzinnes, and when this place was burnt

down she retired to Fosses, where she lived as a recluse. Cult confirmed in 1869.

Juliana of Norwich (Bl)
H. OSB.   May 13
d. c 1423   Dame Juliana of Norwich is one of the most celebrated of English mystics. She was a recluse at Norwich and was under the spiritual direction of the Benedictines of that city. Her book, *Revelations of Divine Love* is still in print and is one of the most popular and beautiful spiritual works in English. She has never been formally beatified.

Juliana Falconieri (St) V.
Tert. OSM.   June 19
1270–1341   A lady of Florence who at the age of sixteen embraced the rule of the Servite Friars, of whom her uncle St Alexis Falconieri, was a co-founder. In 1304 the community of Servite Tertiaries known as the "Mantellate", of which she was the first superior, was formally established and admitted into the order by St Philip Benizi. Canonized in 1737. Cult confined to local calendars since 1969.

Juliana (St) M.   Aug 12
See Hilaria, Digna, etc.

Juliana Puricelli (Bl) V.
OSA.   Aug 14
1427–1501   A native of Busto-Arizio in upper Italy who, as an Augustinian nun, was the first companion of Bl Catherine da Pallanza at the Sacro Monte sopra Varese, where she died. Cult approved in 1769.

Juliana (St) VM.   Aug 17
See Paul and Juliana.

Juliana (St) M.   Aug 18
See Leo and Juliana.

Juliana of Collalto (Bl) V.
OSB.   Sept 1
d. 1262   Born near Treviso of the noble Collalto family. At the age of ten she became a Benedictine at Salarola whence, in 1222, she migrated with Bl Beatrix of Este, to Gemmola. In 1226 she became the abbess-foundress of SS Biagio and Cataldo at Venice. Cult approved by Gregory XVI.

Juliana of Pavilly (St)
Abs. OSB.   Oct 11
d. c 750   A servant girl who became a nun at Pavilly in Normandy under St Benedicta, and finally abbess of the same nunnery. She is called "the Little Sister of Jesus".

Juliana (St) M.   Nov 1
See Cyrenia and Juliana.

Julie Billiart (Bl) V.   Apr 8
French form for Julia Billiart, q.v.

Juliette Verolot (Bl) M. OC.   July 17
d. 1794   Called in religion Sister St Francis Xavier. She was born in the diocese of Troyes and became a Carmelite nun at Compiègne, the last Carmelite to be professed there (Jan 12, 1789) before the outbreak of the French Revolution. She was guillotined with her community at Compiègne. Beatified in 1906.

Juliot (St) M.
See Quiricus and Julitta.

Julitta (St) VM.   May 18
See Theodotus, Thecusa, etc.

Julitta (St) M.   June 16
See Quiricus and Julitta.

Julitta (St) M.   July 30
d. 303   A rich lady of Caesarea in Cappadocia who, after losing her property, was condemned to be burnt at the stake.

Julius (St) M.   Jan 19
See Paul, Gerontius, etc.

Julius of Novara (St) C.   Jan 31
d. p.390   Julius was a priest and his brother Julian a deacon. They were authorized by the emperor Theodosius to devote themselves to converting the heathen temples into Christian churches.

Julius I (St) Pope.   Apr 12
d. 352   A Roman who ruled the church from 337 to 352. He received the appeal of St Athanasius, whom he defended against his Arian accusers. The letter he wrote to the East on this occasion is one of the most momentous pronouncements of the Roman see. He built several churches in Rome, and ranks as one of Rome's most distinguished bishops.

Julius of Dorostorum (St)
M.   May 27
d.c 302   A veteran soldier of the Roman army put to death at Dorostorum on the Danube (now Silistria in Roumanis) under Diocletian. Other soldiers of his legion were martyred about the same time.

Julius and Aaron with
others (SS) MM.   July 1
d. c 305   According to tradition these martyrs met their death at Caerleon-upon-Usk under Diocletian. They are included in Bede's martyrology.

Julius (St) M.   Aug 19
d.c 190   A Roman senator mentioned in the unreliable *Passio* of SS Eusebius, Pontian, etc. There is no archaeological evidence of his existence.

Julius (St) M.   Dec 3
See Ambicus, Victor and Julius.

Julius, Potamia, Crispin, Felix, Gratus and Comp. (SS) MM.   Dec 5
d. 302 Twelve African martyrs who suffered at Thagura in Numidia, under Diocletian.

Julius (St) M.   Dec 20
? A martyr registered in the martyrologies as having suffered at Gelduba (Gildoba) in Thrace.

Junian (St) Ab.   Aug 13
d. 587 Founder and first abbot of Mairé (*Mariacum*) in Poitou, France, and then a recluse at Chaulnay.

Junian (St) H.   Oct 16
5th cent. A hermit at Commodoliacus — now Saint-Junien (Haute Vienne), in the diocese of Limoges, France.

Junias   May 17
See Andronicus and Junias.

Jurmin (St) C.   Feb 23
7th cent. An E. Anglian prince, son or, more probably, nephew of King Anna (634–654). His relics were eventually enshrined at Bury St Edmunds.

Just (St)
The titular saint of a parish in Cornwall. He may be identical with Justus (or Justin), a boy-martyr commemorated on Oct 18, or with the Justus commemorated on Aug 12.

Justa, Justina and Henedina (SS) MM.   May 14
d. c 130 Saints said to have been venerated in Sardinia, where they were martyred under Hadrian (117–138), either at Cagliari or at Sassari.

Justa (St) M.   July 15
See Catulinus, Januarius, etc.

Justa and Rufina (SS) VV. MM.   July 19
d. 287 Two sisters of Seville, in Spain, potters by trade, who suffered under Diocletian. They are greatly honoured in the Mozarabic liturgy and are now venerated as principal patron saints of Seville. It is to be noted that in the early MSS Justa is given as Justus.

Justin of Chieti (St) C.   Jan 1
d. c ?540 This saint has been from time immemorial venerated at Chienti. Some writers describe him as a bishop of that city.

Justin the Philosopher or Justin Martyr (St) M.   GC. June 1
c 100–165 Born at Nablus in Palestine of pagan parents. He was converted to Christ when about thirty years of age by reading the scriptures and witnessing the heroism of the martyrs. His two *Apologies for the Christian Religion* and *Dialogue with the Jew Trypho* are among the most instructive second-century writings which we possess. He was beheaded in Rome with other Christians. The records of his trial still exist.

Justin (St) M.   July 18
One of the alleged sons of St Symphorosa, q.v.

Justin de Jacobis (St) Bp. C.   July 31
1800–1860 He was a great apostle of Africa and the true founder of the Abyssinian mission. Born at San Fele in Lucania, he was noted for his youthful piety. He became a Vincentian and was chosen by the Congregation de Propaganda Fide as Prefect Apostolic for Abyssinia. In 1838 he left for his mission field with a few companions. There he adapted his whole way of life to that of the country, and amid persecution, prison and hardship laboured with indefatigable zeal; he founded missions and a native clergy; his converts are reckoned at 12 000, among them Bl Ghebre Michael. In 1849 he was constrained to accept the title of vicar-apostolic and episcopal ordination. Beatified in 1939. Canonized 1975.

Justin (St) M.   Aug 1
d. c 290 A child said to have been martyred at Louvre, near Paris. He may be identical with Justus, the boy-martyr of Beauvais, commemorated on Oct 18. At any rate his story appears to have been taken from the same source.

Justin (St) M.   Sept 17
d. 259 A priest who devoted himself to burying the bodies of martyrs, and was eventually martyred himself. His relics were transferred to Frisingen in Germany.

Justin (St) M.   Dec 12
See Maxentius, Constantius, etc.

Justina Bezzoli (Bl) N. OSB.   March 12
d. 1319 Francuccia (in religion, Justina) Bezzoli was born at Arezzo, and at the age of thirteen entered the Benedictine convent of St Mark in her native city, whence she migrated to that of All Saints, also Benedictine, at Arezzo. Later she lived as a recluse at Civitella, and finally returned to community life at All Saints. Cult confirmed in 1890.

Justina (St) M.   May 14
See Justa, Justina and Henedina.

Justina (St) M.   June 16
See Aureus, Justina, etc.

Justina (St) VM.   Sept 26
See Cyprian and Justina.

Justina (St) VM.   Oct 7
d. *c* 300   A virgin-martyr of Padua under
Diocletian. A medieval forgery associates her
with St Prosdocimus "a disciple of blessed
Peter". Her cult spread throughout Italy on
account of the Benedictine abbey dedicated in
her name at Padua, which became the cradle
of the Cassinese Congregation of St Justina. In
art she is depicted as a damsel with both
breasts pierced by one sword, along with the
usual emblems of martyrdom, crown, palm
and sword.

Justina (St) VM.   Nov 30
? A maiden martyred at Constantinople.

Justinian (Iestin) (St) M.   Dec 5
6th cent.   A hermit, a native of Brittany, who
became a recluse on the Isle of Ramsey off the
coast of S. Wales, where he was murdered by
evildoers and was thenceforward venerated as
a martyr. Many legends surround his name.

Justus (St) M.   Feb 25
See Donatus, Justus, etc.

Justus (St) M.   Feb 28
See Macarius, Rufinus, etc.

Justus of Urgell (St) Bp.   May 28
d. *p.* 527   The first recorded bishop of Urgell
in Spanish Catalonia. He is numbered by St
Isidore among the "viri illustres", of whom he
wrote the lives. St Justus has left us a very
interesting commentary on the *Song of Songs*.

Justus (St) M.   July 2
See Ariston, Crescentian, etc.

Justus of Poland (St) H.
OSB. Cam.   July 9
d. 1008   One of the four Polish brethren —
viz. SS Benedict, Andrew, Barnabas and
Justus. All were Camaldolese monks.

Justus (St) M.   July 14
? A Roman soldier in the imperial army
martyred at Rome (or perhaps at New Rome,
i.e. Constantinople).

Justus (St) M.   July 21
See Claudius, Justus, etc.

Justus and Pastor (SS)
MM.   Aug 6
d. *c* 304   Two brothers, aged respectively
thirteen and nine years, who were scourged
and beheaded at Alcalá under Diocletian.
Prudentius numbers them among the most
glorious martyrs of Spain.

Justus (St)   Aug 12
Otherwise Ust, q.v.

Justus of Lyons (St)
Bp.   Sept 2 and Oct 14
d. 390   A deacon of Vienne who was bishop
of Lyons in 350. In 381 he attended the
council of Aquileia and then instead of returning to his see, repaired to Egypt where, in spite
of remonstrances, he lived as a hermit till his
death.

Justus of Beauvais (St) M.   Oct 18
d. 287   A child-martyr, aged nine, who is
alleged to have suffered at Beauvais. He is
probably identical with some other saint of this
name, and certainly his Acts, as we now
possess them, are pure fiction.

Justus of Trieste (St) M.   Nov 2
d. 303   A citizen of Trieste martyred under
Diocletian by being cast into the sea. He is still
much honoured at Trieste.

Justus of Canterbury (St)
Bp. OSB.   Nov 10
d. 627   A Roman Benedictine, one of those
sent by St Gregory the Great in 601 to
reinforce the mission to the Anglo-Saxons. In
604 St Augustine of Canterbury ordained him
bishop of Rochester, and in 624 he succeeded
St Mellitus at Canterbury itself. Pope Boniface V, in sending Justus the *Pallium*, writes to
him in words of high appreciation. In art he is
shown as an archbishop, carrying the Primatial
cross.

Justus and Abundius (SS)
MM.   Dec 14
d. 283   Spanish martyrs who suffered under
Numerian. After a futile attempt to burn them
at the stake, they were beheaded. The Mozarabic liturgy has a solemn office in their honour.

Juthware (St) V.   July 1
7th cent.   Sister of St Sidwell. They were
probably of British lineage and appear to have
lived in Devonshire before the Anglo-Saxons
of Wessex penetrated into that county. Many
odd legends surround her name. In art she
carries her own head, having been decapitated
according to a legend, or she carries a cheese.

Jutta (Bl) W.   Jan 13
Otherwise Bl Ivetta, q.v.

Jutta (St) W.   May 5
d. 1250   A Thuringian of noble family
whose husband lost his life crusading in the
Holy Land and who, after providing for her
children, became a recluse near Kulmsee in
Prussia. She is venerated as patroness of
Prussia.

Jutta (Julitta) (Bl) Abs.
OSB. Cist.   Nov 29
d. *c* 1250 Foundress and first abbess
(1234–*c* 1250) of the Cistercian nunnery of
Heiligenthal.

Jutta (Judith) (Bl) Abs.
OSB.   Dec 22
d. 1136 Sister of the count Palatine of
Spanheim, she became a recluse in a cell near
the monastery-church of Disenberg (*Disibodi
Mons*). Here she was entrusted with the education of St Hildegarde. Other disciples
gathered round her and she formed them into
a Benedictine community, which she ruled for
twenty years.

Juvenal of Narni (St) Bp.   May 3
d. 369 First bishop of Narni, in central Italy,
ordained, it is said by Pope St Damasus. His
biographers have confused him with other
saints of the same name, with the result that we
have no certainty as to the details of his career.
Cult confined to local calendars since 1969.

Juvenal of Benevento
(St) Bp.   May 7
d. *c* 132 A saint of Narni. His reputed
shrine is at Benevento.

Juvenal Ancina (Bl) Bp.   Sept 12
1545–1604 Born at Fossano in Piedmont,
he became professor of medicine at the university of Turin and as such he accompanied
the ambassador of Savoy to Rome as his
private physician (1575). At Rome he came
under the influence of St Philip Neri and
joined the oratory in 1575. He was duly
ordained and sent to Naples to open a new
oratory there. He was noted especially for his
work for the poor. Finally, in 1602 he was
made bishop of Saluzzo and at once set out on
his first episcopal visitation. On his return he
was poisoned by a friar whose evil life he had
rebuked. Beatified in 1869.

Juventinus and Maximus
(SS) MM.   Jan 25
d. 363 Officers in the army of Julian the
Apostate. For criticizing the laws against
Christians and refusing to sacrifice to idols,
they were degraded, imprisoned, scourged
and finally beheaded at Antioch in Syria.

Juventius of Pavia (St)
Bp.   Feb 8 and Sept 12
1st cent. (?) The tradition is that St Hermagoras, bishop of Aquileia, the disciple of St
Mark, despatched SS Syrus and Juventius to
evangelize Pavia (*Ticinum*), of which city the
latter became the first bishop. The pre-1970
RM. commemorated him a second time with
St Syrus on Sept 12.

Juventius (St) M.   June 1
? A Roman martyr, whose relics were translated in the sixteenth century to the Benedictine abbey of Chaise-Dieu, Évreux, France.

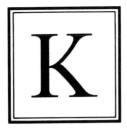

Note. For Katherine and similar names sometimes written with an initial K, see also C and CH.

Kanten (Cannen) (St) C. Nov 5
8th cent. A Welsh saint. Founder of Llanganten abbey (Powys).

Karantoc (St) Jan 16
Probably identical with St Carantac of May 16, q.v.

Kateri (Catherine) Tekákwitha (Bl) V. Apr 17
1656–1680 Born of an Iroquois father and a Christian Algonquin mother in the present state of New York, she was orphaned at the age of four. Missionaries instructed her and she was baptized in 1676. Presecuted by her kinsfolk she fled 400 miles to Quebec French Mission. Taking a vow of virginity, the rest of her short life was spent in hard work, prayer and sacrifice. She died on April 17. Beatified on 22 June 1980.

Kea (Kay, Kenan) (St) Bp. Nov 5
6th cent. A British saint who has left his name to Landkey in Devon. He passed some of his life in Brittany, where he is venerated as St Quay. The details of his life are very uncertain.

Kebius (St) Bp. Nov 8
Otherwise Cuby (Cyby), q.v.

Kellach (St) Bp. May 1
Otherwise Ceallach, q.v.

Kenan (Cianan) (St) Bp. Nov 24
d. c 500 An Irish bishop. He was, with St Patrick, a disciple of St Martin of Tours. He was the first bishop in Ireland to build his cathedral (Damleag or Duleek, in Meath) of stone.

Kenelm (St) King M. July 17
d. 821 Said to have been a Mercian prince who at the age of seven succeeded to the throne of his father, King Coenwulf. According to legend he was murdered in the forest of Clent by order of his sister, Cynefrith. However, the historical facts confirm that he was indeed the son of King Coenwulf (796–821)

but that he appears to have died, perhaps in battle, before his father. His place of burial was at Winchcombe abbey, where the legend originated. A sarcophagus deemed to be his was discovered at the east end of the ruined abbey in 1815. In medieval England Kenelm was venerated as a saint and martyr and he is mentioned in *The Canterbury Tales*. In art he is

St Kenelm, July 17
(19th century conception of a boy saint)

shown as a boy in royal robes, holding a lily, or trampling on his cruel sister.

Kennera (St) VM.   Oct 29
4th cent. A recluse at Kirk-Kinner, Galloway, Scotland. She had been educated with St Ursula and also with St Regulus of Patras.

Kenneth (Kined) (St) H.   Aug 1
6th cent. A Welsh hermit, the son of a chieftain. He made his cell among the rocks in the peninsula of Gower, at a place later called Llangenydd.

Kenneth (St) Ab.   Oct 11
Otherwise Canice (or Canicus), q.v.

**Kennocha (Kyle, Enoch)
(St)** V.   March 25
d. 1007 A Scottish nun belonging to a convent in Fife. Formerly she was held in great veneration in Scotland, especially in the district round Glasgow.

Kenny (St) Ab.   Oct 11
Otherwise Canice, q.v.

Kentigern Mungo (St) Bp.   Jan 13
d. 603 The surname *Mungo* means "darling". He began his missionary labours at Cathures, on the Clyde, on the site of the present city of Glasgow, and was ordained first bishop of the Strathclyde Britons. Driven into exile, he preached around Carlisle and then went to Wales, where he is said to have stayed with St David at Menevia. Tradition credits him with having founded the monastery of Llanelwy (St Asaph), but it is now thought that he was not the founder, but merely the abbot of that monastery for a time. Returning to Scotland, he continued his missionary labours, making Glasgow his centre. He is venerated as the apostle of N.W. England and S.W. Scotland.

Kentigerna (St) W.   Jan 7
d. 734 Daughter of Kelly, prince of Leinster and mother of St Coellan. After her husband's death she left Ireland and became a recluse on the island of Inchebroida, in Loch Lomond, where a church is dedicated in her name.

Keric (St) Ab.   Feb 17
Otherwise Guevrock, q.v.

Kerrier (St)   March 5 and Sept 9
A variant of the name Kieran, q.v., Piran, Queranus.

Kessog (Mackessog) (St)
Bp.   March 10
d. c 560 Born at Cashel, Tipperary. Even as a child he is said to have worked miracles. He

became a missionary and laboured in Scotland, where he was ordained bishop. It is not certain where he died: according to one tradition he was martyred at Bandry. He is the patron of Lennox.

Kester (St) M.   July 25
Otherwise Christopher, q.v.

Keverne (St)   Nov 18
6th cent. A Cornish saint, friend of St Kieran or Piran, with whom indeed some identify him.

**Kevin (Coemgen,
Caoimhghin) (St)** Ab.   June 3
d. c 618 The name has been Latinized as Coemgenus. A native of Leinster, he was educated by St Petroc of Cornwall who was then in Ireland. He is best remembered as the abbot-founder of Glendalough, one of the most famous names in Irish history. His extant biographies abound in romantic but untrustworthy legends which, however, may be based on actual facts. He is one of the patron saints of Dublin.

**Kevoca (Kennotha,
Quivoca) (St)**   March 13
7th cent. She is honoured at Kyle in Scotland. Possibly she should be identified with St Mochoemoc.

Kewe (Kwya, Ciwa) (St)   Feb 8
Otherwise Kigwe, q.v.

**Keyna (Keyne, Ceinwen)
(St)** V.   Oct 8
5th cent. A Welsh saint, an alleged daughter of Brychan of Brecknock (Powys). She lived as a recluse in Cornwall. Camden, and various later writers and hagiographers deemed that Keynsham in Somerset was named after her, but more recent research has demonstrated this to be false. A church in Cornwall bears her name.

Kiara (Chier) (St) V.   Jan 5 (Oct 16)
d. c 680 A Irish maiden, directed in the religious life by St Fintan Munnu. She lived near Nenagh, Co. Tipperary, at a place now called after her, Kilkeary.

**Kieran (Kiernan, Kyran,
Ciaran) (St)** Bp.   March 5
d. c 530 Styled "the first-born of the saints of Ireland". A native of Ossory, he was probably ordained bishop by St Patrick. He has certainly been venerated from time immemorial as the first bishop of Ossory and as founder of the monastery of Saighir. He is wrongly identified with St Piran of Cornwall.

Kieran (Kyran, Latin: Queranus) (St) Ab.   Sept 9
d. *c* 556 (?) Surnamed "The Younger". He
was born in Connacht, and was trained in the
monastic life by St Finian of Clonard, where
he was one of the "Twelve Apostles of Ireland". At a later date he became the abbot-
founder of Clonmacnois in West Meath, on
the Shannon, and gave his monks an extremely
austere monastic rule, known as "the Law of
Kieran".

Kigwe (Kewe) (St) V.   Feb 8
? She is probably the same as St Ciwa, a sixth-
or seventh-century saint venerated in Gwent.
The name is also spelt Ciwg, Cwick, Kigwoe,
etc.

Kilda (St)
An unidentified saint whose name has been
given to an island off the Scottish coast, in
which there is a well-known St Kilder's or St
Kilda's Well.

**Kilian (Chilianus), Colman
and Totnan (SS)** MM.   July 8
d. *c* 689 Irish missionary monks who evangelized Franconia and East Thuringia, where
they were martyred after a successful apostolate. Kilian was bishop of Wurzburg: he is still
greatly honoured there.

Kilian (St) Ab.   July 29
7th cent. An Irish abbot of a monastery on
the island of Inishcaltra, and author of a life of
St Brigid.

Kilian (St) C.   Nov 13
Otherwise Chillien, q.v.

Kinga (St) V. Tert. OFM.   July 24
d. 1292 A niece of St Elizabeth of Hungary
and great-niece of St Hedwig. She shared with
her husband, Prince Boleslaus of Poland, the
sufferings to which the Tartar invasion subjected that land. She died a Franciscan tertiary
in the nunnery she had founded at Sandez.
Her name is also given as Cunegunde, Kioga,
Zinga, etc.

Kingsmark (Cynfarch) (St)
C.   Sept 8
5th cent. Said to have been a Scottish chieftain who lived in Wales, where some churches
are dedicated to him.

Kinnia (St) V.   Feb 1
5th cent. An Irish maiden, baptized by St
Patrick, and by him also consecrated to God.
She is greatly venerated in Co. Louth.

Kitt (St) M.   July 25
Otherwise Christopher, q.v.

Kizito (St) M.   June 3
d. 1886 At fourteen, he was the youngest of
the martyrs put to death by King Mwanga of
Uganda. See Charles Lwanga and Comps.

"Klaus" (St)   Dec 6
A corrupt form of the name Nicholas (Nik-
laus), q.v.

Korean Martyrs (SS)
MM.   GC. Sept 20
The church in Korea flourished under lay
leadership in the eighteenth century. In 1839,
1846 and 1867 severe persecution broke out.
One hundred and three Catholics and some
French missionaries were martyred. St
Andrew Kim Taegon, who has a separate
entry in this book, was the first native priest to
die; another prominent victim was Paul Chong
Hasang, a layman. Men, women and children
of all ages and stations comprise this group of
saints, some being the subjects of separate
entries. These martyrs were canonized in
Korea in 1984 by Pope John Paul II.

Kybi (St) Bp.   Nov 8
Otherwise Cuby, q.v.

**Kyneburga, Kyneswide
and Tibba (SS)**
OSB.   March 6
d. *c* 680 Kyneburga and Kyneswide were
daughters of Penda of Mercia, famous for his
fierce opposition to Christianity. The former
became the abbess-foundress of Dormancas-
ter, now Castor, in Northamptonshire, and
was succeeded by her sister as abbess. Tibba
may have been their kinswoman, who joined
them at the convent. Their relics were
enshrined together at Peterborough abbey,
although they were removed to Thorney for a
while.

Kyneswide (St) V. OSB.   March 6
See Kyneburga, Kyneswide and Tibba.

Kyran (St) Ab.   Sept 9
Otherwise Kieran, q.v.

Kyrin (Kyrstin) (St) Bp.   March 14
Otherwise Boniface, q.v.

Lactan (Lactinus) (St) Ab.　March 19
d. 672　Born near Cork, in Ireland, he was educated at Bangor under SS Comgall and Molua. St Comgall sent him to be abbot-founder of Achadh-Ur, now Freshford in Kilkenny.

Ladislas (Bl) M. OFM.　Feb 12
See Antony of Saxony, etc.

Ladislas Bathory (Bl)　Feb 27
d. c 1484　A Pauline hermit on the mount-ains of Buda. He translated the Bible into Hungarian. Not officially beatified.

Ladislas (Lancelot) (St)
King　June 27
1040–1095　Son of Bela, king of Hungary, to which kingdom, after his accession in 1077, he added Dalmatia and Croatia. His enlightened government, with regard both to church and state affairs, makes him one of the great national heroes of Hungary. He fought suc-cessful wars against the Poles, Russians and Tartars. He died while preparing to take part, as commander-in-chief, in the first crusade. Canonized in 1192. The Hungarians call him Laszlo.

Ladislas of Gielniow (Bl)
C. OFM.　Sept 25
1440–1505 (May 4)　A Pole by birth, he joined the Observant Franciscans at Warsaw and eventually became their Minister Provin-cial. As such he sent Franciscan missionaries to Lithuania. He himself was an untiring preacher and travelled the whole length and breadth of Poland evangelizing the country. Beatified in 1586.

Laetantius (St) M.　July 17
See Scillitan Martyrs.

Laetus (St) M.　Sept 1
See Vincent and Laetus.

Laetus (St) Bp. M.　Sept 6
See Donatian, Praesidius, etc.

Laetus (St) Priest　Nov 5
d. 533　Honoured in the diocese of Orleans, his relics being enshrined in the village of St Lié in that diocese. He is said to have em-braced the monastic state at the age of twelve years.

Laicin (St) Ab.　Jan 20
Otherwise Molagga, q.v.

Lamalisse (St) H.　March 3
7th cent.　A Scottish hermit who has left his name to an islet (Lamlash) off the coast of the isle of Arran.

Lambert of Lyons (St)
Bp. OSB.　Apr 14
d. 688　Born in N. France and reared at the court of Clotaire III, he became a monk at Fontenelle under St Wandrille whom he suc-ceeded as abbot in 666. In 678 he became bishop of Lyons.

**Lambert of Saragossa
(St)** M.　Apr 16
d. c 900　A servant, killed near Saragossa in Spain, by his Saracen master during the Moorish occupation. His cult was promoted by Pope Hadrian VI.

Lambert Péloguin (St)
Bp. OSB.　May 26
c 1080–1154　He was born in the diocese of Riez, France, and became a Benedictine at Lérins. In 1114 he was made bishop of Vence in Provence, and ruled his diocese for forty years. His relics are still enshrined at Vence.

Lambert (Bl) Ab. OSB.　June 22
d. 1125　From childhood he was trained in the monastic life at the Benedictine abbey of Saint-Bertin, of which he eventually became the fortieth abbot. He completed the abbey church and introduced the Cluniac observ-ances.

Lambert (Bl) Ab. OSB.
Cist.　July 12
d. 1163　He became a Cistercian monk at Morimond and afterwards was successively abbot of Clairfontaine, Morimond and Cîteaux (1155–1161). The last two years of his life he spent in retirement at Morimond, where he died.

Lambert (Bl) Ab. OSB.
Cist.　Aug 22
d. 1151　A brother of St Peter of Tarentaise

and, like him, a Cistercian monk at Bonne-vaux. In 1140 he was sent to govern as abbot-founder over the new abbey of Chézery, in the diocese of Belley, France.

Lambert (St) Bp. OSB.   Sept 17
d. 709   Born at Maestricht, he became bishop of that city in 668, but in 674 he was driven from his see by the tyrant, Ebroin. He then lived as a monk for seven years at the Benedictine abbey of Stavelot. He was recal-led to his see by Pepin of Heristal, and did much to foster the apostolate of St Willibrord. He was murdered in the then village of Liège, and has ever since been venerated as a martyr.

**Lambert and Valerius
(Bellère, Berlher) (SS)**
CC. OSB.   Oct 9
d. c680   Disciples of St Gislenus and his fellow-workers in preaching the gospel.

Landelinus (St) Ab. OSB.   June 15
c625–686   Born near Bapaume, in N. France, Landelinus, though carefully brought up by St Aubert of Cambrai, was for a time led astray and turned robber, but repented and became a monk. Afterwards he was ordained and founded the abbeys of Lobbes (*Lanbacum*) in 654, Aulne (656), Walers (657) and Crespin (Crepy, *Crespiacum*) in 670, which he governed till his death.

Landericus (Landry) (St)
Bp. OSB.   Apr 17
7th cent.   The eldest son of SS Madelgarus and Waldetrudis. From 641 to 650 he was bishop of Meaux, but on the death of his father, the abbot of Soignies, Landericus resigned his see in order to take his place as abbot.

Landericus (St) Bp.   June 10
d. c661   Bishop of Paris from 650 to his death. He is best remembered as the founder of the first hospital — *Hôtel-Dieu* — in Paris.

Landericus (St) M. OSB.   June 10
d. 1050 (?)   A Benedictine monk of Novalese in Savoy, drowned in the R. Arc by some malefactors whom he had reprimanded.

**Landoald and Amantius
(SS)** CC.   March 19
d. c668   Said to have been a Roman priest and his deacon, sent by the pope to evangelize what is now Belgium and N.E. France. They founded the church at Wintershoven.

Landrada (St) V. OSB.   July 8
d. c690   Foundress and first abbess of the nunnery of Münsterbilsen, in Belgic Luxem-burg.

Landulf Variglia (St) Bp.
OSB.   June 7
1070–1134   Born at Asti in Piedmont, he took the Benedictine habit at San Michele in Ciel d'Oro at Pavia and became bishop of Asti in 1103.

**Lanfranc of Canterbury
(Bl)** Bp. OSB.   May 28
c1005–1089   Born of a family of senatorial rank at Pavia, he studied at Bologna, taught civil law at Pavia, and in 1042 became a Benedictine at Bec in Normandy, where he founded the school which was to become famous throughout Christendom. He left Bec to be the first abbot of St Stephen's at Caen and in 1070 became archbishop of Canter-bury. Both as a zealous churchman and as a theological writer he left his mark on the ecclesiastical as well as on the civil history of his time. He has always been given the title of *Beatus*, although he does not seem to have been honoured with a public cult.

Lanfranc Beccaria (Bl)
Bp. OSB. Vall.   June 23
d. 1194   He was born near Pavia, and in 1178 was made bishop of that city. During his episcopate he was troubled much by heretics and rapacious civil magistrates. He left the city and joined the monks of St Sepolcro, but was recalled. At the time of his death he had definitely determined to become a Vallumbro-san.

**Lantfrid, Waltram and
Elilantus (BB) or (SS)**
OSB.   July 10
d. p.770   Three brothers who became founders of Benediktbeuren in Bavaria and succeeded one another as abbots of the monastery. St Lantfrid, the first to be abbot, was still alive in 770.

Lanuinus (Bl) C. O. Cart.   Apr 14
d. 1120   A disciple of St Bruno, who accom-panied the saint to Calabria, where he suc-ceeded him as prior of the charterhouse which he founded at Torre in the diocese of Squil-lace. He was also appointed visitor-apostolic of all the monastic houses in Calabria. Cult confirmed in 1893.

Lanzo (Bl) Mk. OSB.   Apr 1
d. c1100   Described by William of Malmes-bury as "the most perfect religious of his century", Lanzo was a monk of Cluny who became prior of St Pancras, in Lewes.

Largio (St) M.   Aug 12
See Hilaria, Digna, etc.

Largus of Aquileia (St) M.   March 16
See Hilary, Tatian, etc.

Largus of Rome (St) M.   Aug 8
See Cyriacus, Largus, etc.

Lasar (Lassar, Lassera) (St) V.   March 29
6th cent.   An Irish nun, niece of St Forchera. She was in early life placed under the care of SS Finan and Kiernan at Clonard. Her name means "Flame".

Laserian (St) Bp.   Apr 18
d. 639   Otherwise Molaisse, and (probably) Lamliss. He was an Irishman by birth and the founder of the monastery and bishopric of Leighlin. He was appointed by Pope Honorius I apostolic legate to Ireland where he strenuously upheld the Roman observance. He was prominent at the synod of Whitefield (635).

Lassa (St) M.   Feb 9
See Ammon, Emilian, etc.

Laszlo (St) King   June 27
Magyar form of Ladislas, q.v.

Latinus of Brescia (St) Bp.   March 24
d. 115   Flavius Latinus is said to have been a successor of St Viator (q.v.) and third bishop of Brescia (84–115). he is said to have suffered imprisonment and torture with other Christians.

Laudo (St) Bp.   Sept 22
Otherwise Lauto, q.v.

Laura (St) Abs. M.   Oct 19
d. 864   A native of Cordoba, in Spain. In her widowhood she became a nun at Cuteclara. Condemned as a Christian by the Moorish conquerors she was thrown into a cauldron of molten lead.

Laurence Wang (Bl) M.   Jan 28
1811–1858   A Chinese catechist, born at Kuy-yang and beheaded at Mao-Ken. Beatified in 1909.

Laurence of Canterbury (St) Bp. OSB.   Feb 2
d. 619   One of the Benedictines sent by Pope St Gregory the Great to convert England. St Augustine sent him back to Rome to report to St Gregory on the progress of the English mission and to bring back reinforcements for the work. Succeeding to the archbishopric of Canterbury in 604, he had much to suffer during the pagan reaction in Kent under Eadbald and thought of escaping to France, but was forcibly rebuked by St Peter in a dream and in the end succeeded in converting Eadbald. The Irish Stowe Missal commemorates him by name in its eucharistic

prayer. In art he is shown as a bishop and holding a scourge, or displaying the marks received from scourging.

Laurence the Illuminator (St) Bp.   Feb 3
d. 576   A Syrian Catholic, driven by the Monophysite persecution to Italy, where he was ordained and founded a monastery near Spoleto. Chosen bishop of that city, he held the see for twenty years: he then resigned and founded the famous abbey of Farfa in the Sabine hills near Rome. St Laurence was renowned as a peacemaker. His title, it is said, derives from his gift of healing blindness, both spiritual and physical.

Laurence of Siponto (St) Bp.   Feb 7
d. c 546   Surnamed Majoranus. Bishop of Siponto from 492 to his death. He is said to have built the sanctuary of St Michael on Mt Gargano.

Laurence Huong (St) M.   Apr 27
c 1802–1856   A native priest of Vietnam, beheaded near Ninh-biuh, Beatified in 1909, canonized in 1988.

Laurence of Novara and Comp. (SS) MM.   Apr 30
d. c 397   Said to have come from the West (Spain or France?) and to have assisted St Gaudentius, bishop of Novara, in Piedmont. He was put to death with a group of children whom he was instructing.

Laurence Richardson (vere Johnson) (Bl) M.   May 30
d. 1582   A native of Great Crosby in Lancashire, he was educated at Brasenose College, Oxford, and after his conversion, studied for the priesthood at Douai. He was ordained in 1577 and was sent to the English mission, where he worked in Lancashire. He was martyred at Tyburn. Beatified in 1886.

Laurence of Villamagna (Bl) C. OFM.   June 6
1476–1535   Born at Villamagna, in the Abruzzi, of the noble family dei Mascoli, he joined the Franciscan order and became a most powerful and successful preacher. Cult approved in 1923.

Laurence Humphrey (Bl) M.   July 7
1571–1591   A native of Hampshire and a convert, he was only twenty years of age when he was hanged, drawn and quartered at Winchester for his conversion to the Catholic faith. Beatified in 1929.

Laurence of Brindisi (St)
C. Dr. OFM. Cap.   GC. July 21

1559–1619 A native of Brindisi who joined
the Capuchins and was sent to Germany as
one of the pioneers of the Capuchin order in
that country. He preached throughout Central
Europe, and was appointed chaplain to the
forces of the Archduke Matthias fighting
against the Turks. He contributed to the
success of the Christian army by his prayers
and shrewd military advice. He died at Lisbon
during one of his diplomatic missions. Canonized in 1881. He was made a Doctor of the
Church in 1959.

Laurence of Rome (St)
M.   GC. Aug 10

d. 258 The *Passio* of St Laurence was written at least a century after his death and is
consequently unreliable. It claims that St
Laurence, one of the deacons of Pope Sixtus
II, was put to death three days after the
martyrdom of that pope, by being roasted alive
on a gridiron. See Sixtus II (Aug 7). Most
modern scholars maintain that, like Sixtus, he
was beheaded. Whatever may be said of the
historical value of his Acts the fact remains that
Laurence has always been venerated, both in
the West and in the East, as the most celebrated of the numerous Roman martyrs —
witness the writings of SS Ambrose, Leo the
Great, Augustine and Prudentius. His martyrdom must have deeply impressed the Roman
Christians. His death, says Prudentius, was
the death of idolatry in Rome, which from that
time began to decline. He was buried on the
Via Tiburtina, at the *Campus Veranus*, where
his basilica now stands, and his name is
mentioned in the first eucharistic prayer. He is
depicted vested as a deacon, and holding a
gridiron, or tied to the same.

Laurence Nerucci, Augustine Cennini, Bartholomew Donati, and John Baptist Petrucci
(BB) MM. OSM.   Aug 11

d. 1420 Four Servite friars sent from Siena
to Bohemia by Pope Martin V to combat the
Hussite heresy. With sixty other Servites they
were burnt in a church at Prague while singing
the *Te Deum*. Cult approved in 1918.

Laurence Loricatus (Bl)
H. OSB.   Aug 16

d. 1243 Born at Fanello, near Lido di
Siponto, Apulia, trained as a soldier and,
having accidentally killed a man, undertook a
pilgrimage to Compostella. On his return in
1209 he joined the Benedictines at Subiaco

St Laurence of Rome, Aug 10

and obtained leave to live as a recluse in the
ruins of one of the twelve monasteries founded
there by St Benedict. His name, Loricatus,
was given to him on account of a coat of mail
which he wore next his skin. His relics are
enshrined at the Sagro Speco, Subiaco. Cult
approved in 1778.

Laurence Rocouyemon
(Bl) M.   Aug 19

d. 1622 A Japanese merchant on the ship of

Bl Joachim Firaiama. He was beheaded at Nagasaki. Beatified in 1867.

Laurence Giustiniani (St)
Bp.   Sept 5
1381–1455 A scion of the noble Venetian family of the Giustiniani, who at the age of nineteen joined the canons regular of San Giorgio in Alga, of whom in due time he became the general. In 1433 he was forced to accept the see of Castello, and in 1451 was translated to that of Grado which (with its patriarchal title) was transferred at the same time from Grado to Venice. His writings on mystical contemplation are sublime in their simplicity. Canonized in 1690. Since 1969 his cult has been confined to local calendars.

Laurence Jamada (Bl) M.   Sept 8
d. 1628 A Dominican tertiary, son of Bl Michael Jamada. He was beheaded at Nagasaki. Beatified in 1867.

Laurence Imbert, Bp.
Peter Maubant, James
Chastan and Comp.
(SS) MM.   GC. Sept 20
d. 1839–1846 These martyrs perished in the persecution of the Christians which raged in Korea from 1839 till 1846. Imbert, a native of Aix-en-Provence, was a member of the Paris Society of Missions. He worked first as a missionary priest in China and then as a bishop in Korea. With Maubant and Chastan, missionary priests of the same society, he was exiled and cruelly tortured to death in 1839. With them were beatified in 1925 seventy-six native converts who suffered death in the next few years with heroic constancy. All were canonized in Korea in 1984. See Korean Martyrs.

Laurence Ruiz and
Comps. (SS) MM.   GC. Sept 28
Born in Manila in the Philippines c. 1600/10, he was a pious married layman. He accompanied a secret Dominican mission to Japan. A storm drove him and his companions, Bl Michael Aozaraza, Bl Antony Gonzales, Bl William Cowtet, Bl Vincent Shiwozuka and Bl Lazarus of Kyoto to Okinawa. All were put to death with terrible tortures by the Japanese. Beatified in Manila by Pope John Paul II in 1981. Canonized 18 Oct 1987.

Laurence of Africa (St) M.   Sept 28
See Martial, Laurence, and Comp.

Laurence of Rippafratta
(Bl) C. OP.   Sept 28
d. 1457 Born at Rippafratta in Tuscany, he joined the friars preachers at Pisa under Bl John Dominic, and was made novice-master at Cortona. St Antoninus and BB Benedict of Mugello and Fra Angelico were his novices. Cult approved in 1851.

Laurence Xizo (Bl) M.   Sept 28
d. 1630 A native of Japan and a tertiary of St Augustine. He was condemned to death for having sheltered the Augustinian fathers and was beheaded at Nagasaki. Beatified in 1867.

Laurence O'Toole (St)
Bp. OSA.   Nov 14
1128–1180 Lorcan O'Tuathail was born in Leinster and at the age of twelve became an Augustinian canon at Glendalough, of which he was made abbot at the age of twenty-five. Eight years later he was made archbishop of Dublin. In 1179 he attended the Lateran Council at Rome and was made papal legate in Ireland. He carried out many reforms in his diocese and was much engaged in negotiating on behalf of the Irish with King Henry II of England. It was while on an embassy to the latter that he died at the Augustinian abbey of Eu in Normandy. Canonized in 1226.

Laurence Pe-Man (Bl) M.   Nov 24
d. 1856 A Chinese labourer and convert of Bl Augustine Chapdelaine. He was beheaded after torture at Su-Lik-Hien (Province of Kwang-Si). Beatified in 1900.

Laurentia (St) M.   Oct 8
See Palatias and Laurentia.

Laurentinus, Ignatius
and Celerina (SS) MM.   Feb 3
3rd cent. African martyrs, of whom St Cyprian writes movingly in his 34th Epistle. SS Laurentinus and Ignatius were uncles, and St Celerina, an aunt, of the deacon St Celerinus (q.v.), who is commemorated on the same day.

Laurentinus Sossius (Bl)
M.   Apr 15
d. 485 A boy aged five, said to have been killed by the Jews on Good Friday at Valrovina in the diocese of Vicenza, in Italy. Cult approved in 1867.

Laurentinus (St) M.   June 3
See Pergentinus and Laurentinus.

Laurianus (St) M.   July 4
d. ? c 544 Said to have been Hungarian by birth, he was ordained deacon in Milan and later appointed archbishop of Seville. The place of his supposed martyrdom is given as Bourges, in France. All these details are open to grave doubt.

Laurus (St) M.   Aug 18
See Florus, Laurus, etc.

Laurus (Léry) (St) Ab.   Sept 30
7th cent. A native of Wales, who crossed over to Brittany and became the abbot-founder of the monastery afterwards called after him, Saint-Léry, on the R. Doneff.

Lauto (Laudo, Laudus, Lô) (St) Bp.   Sept 22
d. c 568 Bishop of Coutances in Normandy for forty years (528–568). He appears to have been one of the most energetic prelates of that period. His family estate has become the village of Saint-Lô.

Lawdog (St)   Jan 21
6th cent. Titular of four churches in the diocese of St David's, Wales, and perhaps identical with St Lleuddad (Laudatus), abbot of Bardsey.

Lazarus of Milan (St) Bp.   Feb 11
d. c 450 (March 14) An archbishop of Milan who was the support of his flock during the invasion of the Ostrogoths. His feast was translated to Feb 11, in deference to the Milanese custom of not keeping saints' days in Lent, now generally followed in the most recent revision of the Roman rite.

Lazarus (St) C.   Feb 23
d. c 867 Surnamed Zographos (the Painter). He was a monk of Constantinople, and a skilled painter, who in the time of Theophilus (829–842), one of the iconoclast emperors, occupied himself in restoring the sacred pictures defaced by the heretics. For this he was cruelly tormented by the emperor. Later he was restored to honour and sent as ambassador to Rome.

Lazarus (St) M.   March 27
See Zanitas, Lazarus, etc.

Lazarus (St)   June 21
The poor man in our Lord's parable (Luke 16). The military order of St Lazarus, founded during the crusades (one of whose duties was to take care of lepers), was named after him. Hence also the words Lazaretto, for a hospital, Lazarone, for a poor man of the street, etc. The Ethiopians keep his feast on June 21.

Lazarus (St) Bp.   July 29
1st cent. The disciple and friend of our Lord raised by Him from the dead (John II). The Greek tradition states that he died bishop of Kition in Cyprus. The French legend which connects him with Marseilles is first heard of in the eleventh century, and has no historical foundation whatever: it is probably due to confusion with an early bishop of Aix, also called Lazarus. Since the 1970 revision of the calendar of the saints a feast of Martha, Mary

and Lazarus has been kept by the Benedictines on this date.

Lea (St) W.   March 22
d. 384 A Roman lady who, after the death of her husband, joined the community of St Marcella, where she spent her life serving the nuns.

Leafwine (St) C. OSB.   Nov 12
Otherwise Lebuin, q.v.

Leander (St) Bp.   Feb 27
550–600 The elder brother of SS Fulgentius, Isidore and Florentina. He entered a monastery in his early youth and was later sent to Constantinople on a diplomatic mission. There he met St Gregory the Great, whose close friend he became and whose Moralia was published at his request. On his return to Spain Leander was appointed archbishop of Seville. He proved himself a great bishop. He revised and unified the Spanish liturgy; converted St Hermenegild; was instrumental in winning the Visigoths from Arianism; and was responsible for the holding of two national synods at Toledo (589 and 590). He founded the episcopal school of Seville. In Spain he is liturgically honoured as a Doctor. His emblem is a flaming heart.

Lebuin (Leafwine) (St) C. OSB.   Nov 12
d. c 773 A Benedictine of Ripon who crossed over to Holland and took part in the missionary work inaugurated by St Boniface. He worked with St Marcellinus (July 14) under St Gregory of Utrecht and founded the church at Deventer. From there he went forth to preach to the Saxons and Frisians.

Lebuinus (St) Bp. M.   Nov 12
Otherwise Livinus, q.v.

Leger (St) Bp. M.   Oct 2
Otherwise Leodegarius, q.v.

Lelia (St) V.   Aug 11
? An Irish maiden, who seems to have lived at a very early period and to have been connected with the dioceses of Limerick and Kerry. Several placenames in Ireland perpetuate her memory.

Leo Carasuma (St) M.   Feb 5
d. 1597 A native of Korea who, after being a pagan priest, was converted to the faith and was the first to be received into the third order of St Francis in Japan. As a catechist of the Franciscans, he was crucified at Nagasaki. Beatified in 1627 and canonized in 1862. See Paul Miki and Comps.

Leo and Paregorius (SS)
MM.   Feb 18
d. *c* 260   Martyrs of Patara in Lycia, greatly
venerated in the East. Their alleged Acts may
be merely a pious romance.

Leo of Catania (St) Bp.   Feb 20
703–787   Known in Sicily as St Leo *"il
Maraviglioso"*, the wonder-worker. He was a
priest of Ravenna who became bishop of
Catania in Sicily. He was highly esteemed for
his learning. The story of his life has been
embellished with many delightful, though unreliable, anecdotes.

Leo of Saint-Bertin (Bl)
Ab. OSB.   Feb 26
d. 1163   Of noble Flemish birth, Leo was
appointed abbot of Lobbes where he succeeded in making good the ravages of war. In
1138 he was given charge of the great abbey of
Saint-Bertin, which he ruled for twenty-five
years. In 1146 he joined the second crusade
and reached Jerusalem and on his return
brought with him the alleged relic of our
Lord's blood which ever since has been wor-
shipped at Bruges. The abbey of St Bertin was
destroyed by fire in 1152, but Bl Leo was
energetic in its rebuilding.

Leo, Donatus, Abundantius, Nicephorus and Comp. (SS) MM.   March 1
?   A group of thirteen martyrs, believed to have
laid down their lives for Christ in Africa.

Leo of Rouen (St) Bp. M.   March 1
c 856–900   Born at Carentan in Normandy,
he is said to have been bishop of Rouen, and
afterwards to have resigned in order to preach
the gospel in Navarre and the Basque provinces — both French and Spanish — devastated
by the Saracen invasion. Pirates beheaded him
near Bayonne, of which city he is now the
patron saint. The whole story is untrustworthy.

Leo Luke (St) Ab. C.   March 1
d. *c* 900   He became abbot of a Basilian
monastery of Corleone in Sicily, and is honoured also in Calabria. He died a centenarian
after eighty years of monastic life.

Leo (St) Bp. M.   March 14
?   The pre-1970 RM. had the following
entry: "At Rome, in the Agro Verano, St Leo,
bishop and martyr." This is all that is known
about him. He may have been a victim of the
Arians.

Leo IX (St) Pope   Apr 19
1002–1054   A cousin of the emperor Conrad
the Salic, born in Alsace, and in baptism
named Bruno. He was made bishop of Toul in
1026 and constrained to accept the papal
office in 1048. He took with him to Rome, as
his spiritual adviser, Hildebrand, the future
Gregory VII, and the reform of the Roman
curia now began in earnest. Leo combated
simony; condemned Berengar, and his eucharistic doctrine; strove to prevent the schism
between the Eastern and the Western
churches; and corresponded with the patriarch, Michael Cerularius. While at Benevento, a city belonging to the Holy See, he
was taken prisoner by the Normans, against
whom he was engaged in active warfare. He
was released, but shortly after died before the
high altar in St Peter's.

Leo of Sens (St) Bp.   Apr 22
d. 541   Bishop of Sens for twenty-three
years. He defended the rights of his own see
against the pretensions of King Childebert.

Leo of Troyes (St) Ab.   May 25
d. *c* 550   A monk who succeeded St Romanus in the government of the monastery of
Mantenay, near Troyes.

Leo Tanaca (Bl) M.   June 1
d. 1617   A Japanese catechist to the Jesuits.
Beheaded at Nagasaki, and beatified in 1867.

Leo III (St) Pope   June 12
d. 816   A Roman by birth, who became pope
in 795. While attempting to suppress the
unruly factions of Rome he was himself seized
and put to the torture. He then called to his
help Charlemagne, who re-established order
in Rome. Subsequently, in St Peter's, Charlemagne was crowned emperor of the West by
Pope Leo (800), thereby founding the Holy
Roman Empire and laying the foundations of
the Middle Ages. Leo refused to add the
"filioque" to the Nicene creed. He was also
concerned with the affairs of the church in
England.

Leo (St) M.   June 30
See Gaius and Leo.

Leo II (St) Pope   July 3
d. 683   A Sicilian who became pope in 681.
He governed the church for only two years and
the outstanding event of his pontificate was the
condemnation of Pope Honorius I for having
been remiss in formally denouncing the
Monothelites. He was a musician, and he
restored several churches.

Leo of Lucca (St) Ab. OSB.   July 12
d. 1079   Born at Lucca in Tuscany, he en-

tered the Benedictine abbey of La Cava, near Naples, under its founder St Alferius, whom he succeeded as abbot in 1050. He stood in great favour with Duke Gisulf II of Salerno. Cult approved — as a saint in 1579 and again in 1893.

Leo IV (St) Pope OSB. July 17
d. 855 A Roman and a monk of the Benedictine abbey of San Martino, he was chosen pope in 847. He enclosed the whole Vatican city with a wall (the Leonine city), and, through his prayers and exhortations to the soldiers, the Saracens from Calabria were utterly routed at Ostia. His benefactions to churches take up twenty-eight pages in the *Liber Pontificalis*. The English king Alfred visited Rome during his pontificate (853) and Leo stood godfather for him at his confirmation.

Leo and Juliana (SS) MM. Aug 18
? Leo was martyred at Myra, in Lycia, and Juliana at Strobylum. Juliana may be identified with the martyr of Ptolemais. (See Paul and Juliana).

Leo Sucheiemon (Bl) M. Aug 19
d. 1622 A native Japanese, pilot of the ship of Bl Joachim Firaiama. Beheaded at Nagasaki. Beatified in 1867.

Leo II of Cava (Bl) Ab. OSB. Aug 19
1239–1295 The fifteenth abbot of the Benedictine abbey of La Cava, near Naples. He ruled from 1268 to 1295. Cult approved in 1928.

Leo Combioge (Bl) M. Sept 8
d. 1628 A Japanese catechist, member of the third order of St Dominic. Beheaded at Nagasaki. Beatified in 1867.

Leo Satzuma (Bl) M. Sept 10
d. 1622 A Japanese catechist, and a Franciscan tertiary. He was burnt alive at Nagasaki with Bl Charles Spinola (q.v.), on the day of the great martyrdom.

Leo (St) M. OFM. Oct 10
See Daniel and Comp.

Leo the Great (St)
Pope and Dr. GC. Nov 10
d. 461 Born probably in Tuscany. He joined the Roman clergy, becoming archdeacon under Celestine I and Sixtus III, and bishop of Rome in 440. Ever conscious of his supreme jurisdiction and responsibility as the successor of St Peter, he combated Pelagians, Manicheans, Priscillianists and, especially, the Eutychians and Nestorians. His celebrated *Tomos*, or Dogmatic Letter, addressed to Flavian, patriarch of Constantinople, in which

he defined the exact Catholic belief in the twofold nature and one person in Christ, marks an epoch in Catholic theology. It was acclaimed as the teaching of the church at the council of Chalcedon (451). The most famous action of his pontificate was his meeting with Attila outside the gates of Rome, which resulted in the salvation of the city (452), but he was unable to stop Genseric the Vandal from pillaging it in 455. He was proclaimed a Doctor of the Church in 1754.

Leo of Melun (St) C. Nov 10
? A saint held in veneration from time immemorial at Melun, near Paris. He is now identified by scholars with St Leo the Great, who died on Nov 10.

Leo of Nonantula (St)
Ab. OSB. Nov 20
d. 1000 Monk and abbot of the Benedictine monastery of Nonantula, near Modena.

Leo Nacanixi (Bl) M. Nov 27
d. 1619 A Japanese layman, born at Amangucchi, of the royal family of Firando. He was beheaded with ten companions at Nagasaki. Beatified in 1867.

Leobald (Leodebod) (St)
Ab. OSB. Aug 8
d. 650 Abbot-founder of Fleury, afterwards called Saint-Benoît-sur-Loire, in the diocese of Orleans. He had been a monk at Saint-Aignan, in the same diocese.

Leobard (Liberd) (St) C. Jan 18
d. 593 A recluse at Tours who shut himself up in a cell near the abbey of Marmoutier and lived there for twenty-two years under the direction of St Gregory of Tours.

Leobinus (Lubin) (St) Bp. Sept 15
d. c 556 Born near Poitiers, the son of a peasant family. Early in life he became a hermit, then a priest, abbot of Brou, and finally bishop of Chartres — one of the most distinguished occupants of that important see.

Leocadia (St) VM. Dec 9
d. c 303 According to the pre-1970 RM. she was a maiden of Toledo, who was condemned to death and died in prison, under Diocletian. Her cult at Toledo dates from the fifth century, at the latest. In Flanders she is known as St Locaie.

Leocritia (Lucretia) (St)
VM. March 15
d. 859 A maiden of Cordoba, Spain, born of Moorish parents, but early converted to Christianity and in consequence driven from her home. She was sheltered by St Eulogius, and both were flogged and beheaded.

Leodegarius (St) Bp. M.
OSB.   Oct 2
c 616–678 Nephew of the bishop of Poitiers
by whom he was educated. In 653 he was made
abbot of the monastery of St Maxentius, where
he introduced the Benedictine rule. On the
death of King Clovis II he assisted St Bathildis, the queen regent during the minority of
her son, Clotaire III. In 659 he became bishop
of Autun, in which capacity he reformed
church discipline and imposed on all the
monasteries the observance of the rule of St
Benedict. His connexion with the court
brought upon him the full fury of the tyrant
Ebroin, mayor of the palace, who had the saint
degraded, imprisoned, blinded and finally
murdered. He is widely venerated in France as
St Leger. In art he is shown as vested as a
bishop: he holds a drill, or his eyes, tongue etc.
on a plate or book; or holds a needle or
pronged hook, all emblems of his martyrdom.

Leomenes (St) M.   Dec 23
See Theodulus, Saturninus, etc.

Leonard of Avranches (Bl)
Bp. C.   March 4
d. *c* 614 In his early years he was a torment
to the countryside, but being converted,
largely by the prayers of his mother, he was
elected bishop of Avranches, and venerated by
the people as a saint.

Leonard Murialdo (St)
C. Founder   March 30
1828–1890 As a native of Turin he belongs
to the times and the distinguished quadrumvi-
rate of saintly men, John Bosco, Joseph
Cafasso, Joseph Cottolengo, with himself the
fourth as the guide of Christian social work. In
fact, "conservative Catholics" dubbed him "a
socialist" for advocating an eight-hour day for
workers in 1885. His congregation of St
Joseph continues to care for young appren-
tices. Beatified in 1963. Canonized May 3
1970.

Leonard (Bl) H. OSB. Cam.   May 15
d. *c* 1250 Monk-hermit at Camaldoli.

**Leonard Wegel (Wichel,
Vechel) (St)** M.   July 9
d. 1572 Born at Bois-le-duc, in Holland, he
studied at Louvain and was appointed parish
priest of Gorkum, where he was noted for his
opposition to Calvinism. He was one of the
group of the Gorkum martyrs, q.v. Canonized
in 1867.

Leonard of Cava (Bl) Ab.
OSB.   Aug 18
d. 1255 Eleventh abbot of La Cava, in S.

Italy, from 1232 till his death. Cult confirmed
in 1928.

**Leonard of Vandoeuvre
(St)** Ab.   Oct 15
d. *c* 570 A hermit, who became the abbot-
founder of Vandoeuvre, now Saint-Leonard-
aux-Bois, near Le Mans.

Leonard of Noblac (St) Ab.   Nov 6
?d. *c* 559 According to a legend he was a
French courtier converted by St Remigius of
Reims. On the advice of that saint, St Leonard
retired to the abbey of Micy near Orleans, and
later became a hermit in a neighbouring forest,
now called Noblac. His cult was widespread in
the West during the Middle Ages. Little is
known for sure about his life as no evidence for
it exists before the eleventh century. He is
depicted as vested as an abbot, holding chains,
fetters, or a lock as his emblems.

Leonard of Reresby (St) C.   Nov 6
13th cent. A native of Thryberg in Yorkshire. According to local tradition, he was a
crusader who, taken prisoner by the Saracens,
was miraculously set free and returned safely
home.

**Leonard Kimura and
Comp. (BB)** MM.   Nov 18
d. 1619 A Japanese nobleman, who after his
conversion became a temporal coadjutor in the
Society of Jesus and, with others of his
countrymen, was burnt to death at Nagasaki.

**Leonard of Port Maurice
(St)** C. OFM.   Nov 26
1676–1751 Born at Porto Maurizio, on the
Italian Riviera, he studied in the Roman
College and became a Franciscan of the
Strictest Observance in the convent of St
Bonaventure on the Palatine. Soon after his
ordination he began his career as a missionary,
spreading everywhere devotion to the Blessed
Sacrament, to the Sacred Heart, to the
Immaculate Conception and to the Stations of
the Cross: he is said to have established the
Way of the Cross in five hundred and seventy-
two places, including the Colosseum in Rome.
He was a prolific ascetical writer, his works
filling thirteen volumes. In 1744 he was sent to
restore discipline in Corsica. In 1751 he was
called to Rome by Benedict XIV but died on
the night after his arrival at his old friary of St
Bonaventure. Canonized in 1867.

Leonianus (St) C.   Nov 6
d. *c* 570 A Pannonian by birth, he was taken
as a captive to Gaul and, on regaining his
freedom, lived as a recluse near Autun. Later
he embraced the monastic life at the abbey of

St Leonard of Noblac, Nov 6

St Symphorianus, also at Autun. Cult approved in 1907.

Leonidas and Comp. (SS)
MM. Jan 28
d. 304 Egyptian martyrs, associated with SS Philemon and Apollonius (q.v.). All suffered under Diocletian.

Leonidas (St) M. Apr 22
d. 202 The father of Origen, and himself a distinguished philosopher. He was martyred at Alexandria, his native city, under Septimius Severus.

Leonides (St) M. Aug 8
See Eleutherius and Leonides.

Leonides (St) M. Sept 2
See Diomedes, Julian, etc.

Leonilla (St) M. Jan 17
See Speusippus, Eleusippus, etc.

Leonis (St) VM. June 15
See Lybe, Leonis and Eutropia.

Leonorious (Lunaire)
(St) Ab. Bp. July 1
d. c 570 A son of Hoel, king of Brittany, but born in Wales, educated by St Illtyd, and ordained bishop by St Dyfrig. Crossing to Brittany, then ruled by his brother Hoel II, he founded the monastery of Pontual, near Saint Malo.

Leontia (St) M. Dec 6
See Dionysia, Dativa, etc.

Leontius of Caesarea
(St) Bp. Jan 13
d. 337 Bishop of Caesarea in Cappadocia and one of the fathers of the council of Nicaea (325). He is specially praised by St Athanasius and described as "an angel of peace" by the Greeks.

Leontius (St) Bp. M. March 19
See Apollonius and Leontius.

Leontius (St) Bp. March 19
d. 640 Bishop of Saintes. A friend of St Malo, whom he received into his diocese when he was exiled from Brittany.

Leontius (St) M. Apr 24
See Eusebius, Neon, etc.

Leontius, Hypatius and
Theodulus (SS) MM. June 18
d. ? 135 Greeks martyred at Tripoli in Phoenicia at an early date.

Leontius, Maurice,
Daniel and Comp. (SS)
MM. July 10
d. c 320 A band of forty-five martyrs who suffered together at Nicopolis in Armenia under the emperor Licinius and were among the last martyrs of the great persecution.

Leontius the Younger
(St) Bp. July 11
c 510-565 A soldier who served against the Visigoths. He married and went to reside at Bordeaux, where he was forced to accept the see and government of that city, his wife taking the veil.

Leontius, Attius,
Alexander and Comp. Aug 1
d. c 300 Three Christians of Perga in Pamphylia who, together with six farm labourers, were martyred under Diocletian for having destroyed the altar of Artemis.

Leontius the Elder (St) Bp. Aug 21
d. c 541 Bishop of Bordeaux, the immediate predecessor of St Leontius the Younger (v. July 11).

Leontius (St) M. Sept 12
See Hieronides, Leontius, etc.

Leontius (St) M. Sept 27
Mentioned in the pre-1970 RM. as a companion in martyrdom of SS Cosmas and Damian, q.v.

Leontius (St) Bp. Dec 1
d. c 432 Bishop of Frégus in France from c 419 to c 432. He was a great friend of

Cassian, who dedicated to him his first ten conferences.

Leopardinus (St) Ab. M.   Nov 24
d. 7th cent.   Monk and abbot of the monastery of St Symphorian of Vivaris in the province of Berry, France. He perished at the hands of assassins and was forthwith venerated as a martyr.

Leopardus (St) M.   Sept 30
d. 362   A servant, or slave, in the household of Julian the Apostate. His execution probably took place in Rome.

Leopold of Gaiche (Bl)
C. OFM.   Apr 2
1732–1815 (Apr 15)   A native of Gaiche in the diocese of Perugia. He joined the Franciscans and, after his ordination, was professor of philosophy and theology and apostolic missionary for the Papal States. During the Napoleonic invasion he was compelled to put off his habit and became parish priest, although then seventy-seven years of age. Beatified in 1893.

Leopold the Good (St) C.   Nov 15
1073–1136 Born at Melk in Austria, a grandson of the emperor Henry III. In 1096 he succeeded his father as fourth Margrave of Austria. He married Agnes, daughter of Henry IV, by whom he had eighteen children. He ruled firmly and successfully for forty years, and was especially interested in the spread of religious institutions. He was the founder of Mariazell (Benedictine), Heiligenkreuz (Cistercian) and Klosterneuburg (Augustinian). He was buried in the last mentioned friary.

Leothadius (Léothade)
(St) Ab. OSB.   Oct 23
d. 718   Of noble Frankish family, Léothade became a monk and shortly after abbot of Moissac, in S. France. Later he was made bishop of Auch.

Leovigild and Christopher
(SS) MM.   Aug 20
d. 852   Leovigild was a monk of SS Justus and pastor of Cordoba, and Christopher of the monastery of St Martin de La Rojana, near Cordoba. They were martyred at Cordoba under Abderrahman II.

Lesbos (Martyrs of)   Apr 5
? Five maidens venerated by the Greeks as having suffered martyrdom in the island of Lesbos.

Lesmes (St) Ab. OSB.   Jan 30
The Spanish form of Adelelmus, q.v.

Letard (St) Bp.   Feb 24
Otherwise Liudhard, q.v.

Leu (St) Bp.   Sept 1
French form for Lupus of Sens, q.v.

Leuchteldis (Liuthild)
(St) V.   Jan 23
Otherwise Lufthild, q.v.

Leucius (St) M.   Jan 11
See SS Peter, Severus and Leucius.

Leucius of Brindisi (St) Bp.   Jan 11
d. c 180   Venerated as the first bishop of Brindisi whither he is said to have come as a missionary from Alexandria. Another saint of the same name, likewise bishop of Brindisi, who flourished at the beginning of the fifth century, is mentioned by St Gregory the Great.

Leucius (St) M.   Jan 28
See Thyrsus, Leucius and Callinicus.

Leudomer (Lomer) (St) Bp.   Oct 2
d. c 585   A French bishop of Chartres.

Leus (Leo) (St)   Aug 1
A priest of the fourth century whose relics were transported to Viguenza in the diocese of Ferrara.

Leutfrid (Leufroi) (St)
Ab. OSB.   June 21
d. 738   Abbot-founder of the monastery LaCroix-Saint-Ouen (afterwards Saint-Leufroy), near Evreux, which he governed for nearly fifty years. In art he is represented surrounded by a group of the poor children it was his delight to befriend.

Levan (St) C.   June 8
6th cent.   A Celtic saint who came to Cornwall and who has given his name (spelt also Levin — or Selyr) to a parish in that county.

Lewina (St) VM.   July 24
5th cent.   The first surviving record of this saint dates from 1058, when her relics were translated from Seaford in Sussex, where she is said to have been venerated, to Berg in Flanders. She is supposed to have been a British maiden martyred by the Saxon invaders.

Lezin (St) Bp.   Feb 13
Otherwise Lucinius, q.v.

Liafdag (St) Bp. M.   Feb 3
c 980   He was made bishop in Jutland to meet the needs of the growing number of Christians, but was soon put to death by the pagans.

Libentius (Liäwizo)
(St or Bl) Bp. OSB.   Jan 4
938–1013   Born in S. Swabia, he became
bishop of Hamburg in 988, professing at the
same time the Benedictine rule at the cathedral abbey of Hamburg. He is venerated as one
of the apostles of the Slavs.

Liberalis (St) C.   Apr 27
d. *c* 400   A priest of the district round
Ancona, who worked zealously for the conversion of the Arians and suffered much at their
hands. His relics are enshrined at Treviso.

Liberata (St) V.   Jan 16
5th cent.   Sister of St Epiphanius of Pavia
and St Honorata, she was a virgin, living
however in her parents' house.

Liberata (St) V.   Jan 18
d. 580   A maiden of Como, at which city she,
with her sister St Faustina, founded the
nunnery of Santa Margarita. Both died in 580.
Their relics are in Como cathedral.

Liberata (St) V.   July 20
Otherwise Wilgefortis, q.v.

Liberatus, Boniface,
Servus, Rusticus, Rogatus,
Septimus and Maximus
(SS) MM.   Aug 17
d. 483   Liberatus was abbot of a monastery
in Africa, the rest were his monks: Boniface, a
deacon; Servus and Rusticus, sub-deacons;
Rogatus and Septimus, monks; Maximus, a
child educated in the monastery. All were
martyred by the Arian king, Hunneric.

Liberatus da Loro (Bl) C.
OFM.   Sept 6
d. 1258   Born at San Liberato, in Piceno, of
the Brumforti family, he joined the Franciscans, among whom at a later date he introduced the initial austerity of the order, aided
by BB Humilis and Pacificus. His cult was forbidden in 1730, but restored in 1731 and again
approved in 1868.

Liberatus and Bajulus
(SS) MM.   Dec 20
? Martyrs venerated at Rome, of whom
nothing certain is known.

Liberius Wagner (Bl) M.   Dec 9
1593–1631 Born in the diocese of Wurzburg,
he was a Lutheran in his early years. After his
conversion he was ordained. During the
Thirty Years War he was cruelly martyred for
his faith. Beatified in 1974.

Liberius (St) Bp.   Dec 30
d. *c* 200   A bishop of Ravenna, venerated as
one of the founders of that see.

Libert (Liebert) (St) Bp.   June 23
d. 1076   Bishop of Cambrai from 1051 till
his death. He went on a pilgrimage to Palestine, but failing to reach the holy places he
built instead, on his return to his diocese, the
abbey of the Holy Sepulchre. He excommunicated the lord of Cambrai and was on that
account brutally persecuted.

Libert (St) M. OSB.   July 14
d. 783   Born at Malines, baptized and educated by St Rumoldus, from whom he received
the Benedictine habit. Afterwards he migrated
to the abbey of Saint-Trond, where he was put
to death by invading barbarians.

Liborious (St) Bp.   July 23
d. 390   Bishop of Le Mans from 348 to 390.
He is the patron saint of Paderborn, whither
his relics were translated in 836. Cult confined
to local calendars since 1969.

Licerius (Lizier) (St) Bp.   Aug 27
d. *c* 548   Born in Spain, probably at Lérida
(Ilerda). He went to France and in 506 was
chosen bishop of Couserans (now in the
diocese of Pamiers).

Licinius (St) M.   Aug 7
See Carpophorus, Exanthus, etc.

Licinius (Lesin) (St) Bp.   Nov 1
d. *c* 616   Count of Anjou under King Chilperic. He became a monk and afterwards was
chosen bishop of Angers (586), and ordained
by St Gregory of Tours. He wished to resign,
but his people would on no account allow him
to do so.

Lidanus (St) Ab. OSB.   July 2
1026–1118   A native of Antina in the Abruzzi
who became the abbot-founder of the Benedictine abbey of Sezze in the Papal States. He
deserves remembrance specially for his work
in draining the Pontine Marshes. In his old age
he retired to Montecassino. He is the patron
saint of Sezze.

Lidwina (St) V.   Apr 14
Otherwise Lydwina of Schiedam, q.v.

Lié (*several*)
French form of Laetus and Leo, q.v.

Liephard (St) Bp. M.   Feb 4
d. 640   An Englishman by birth and perhaps
a bishop, said to have been the companion of
King Cadwalla on the latter's pilgrimage to
Rome. While on his way back to England,
Liephard was done to death near Cambrai.

Ligorius (St) M.   Sept 13
? An eastern saint who met his death at the
hands of a pagan mob. His relics are enshrined
at Venice.

Liliosa (St) M.   July 27
See George, Aurelius, etc.

Limbania (St) V. OSB.   Aug 15
d. 1294 A Cyprian by birth who became a
Benedictine nun at Genoa, and then lived as a
recluse in a cave below the church of St
Thomas in that city. Cult approved by Paul V.
(*Note.* In 1509 the church of St Thomas was
handed over to the Augustinians and this is the
reason why Limbania is often described as an
Augustinian.)

Limnaeus (St) H.   Feb 22
See Thalassius and Limnaeus.

Linus (St) Pope   formerly Sept 23
d. c 79 The immediate successor of St Peter
in the see of Rome, which he ruled for twelve
years (67–79). He was traditionally venerated
as a martyr, but there is no evidence for his
martyrdom. His name is mentioned in the first
eucharistic prayer. Cult suppressed in 1969.

Lioba (St) Abs. OSB.   Sept 28
d. c 781 An Anglo-Saxon by birth and a
kinswoman of St Boniface, St Lioba professed
the Benedictine rule at Wimborne. In 748, at
the request of St Boniface, together with a
band of missionary nuns, she left England for
the German mission and was at once appointed abbess of Bischoffsheim and was given the
general supervision of all the daughter-houses
founded from that nunnery. She was greatly
loved by her nuns and was a close friend of the
empress St Hildegard, Charlemagne's wife,
while the tender affection which subsisted
between herself and St Boniface forms one of
the most charming episodes in church history.
St Lioba's convents were one of the most
powerful factors in the conversion of Germany
by the Benedictines. Life within them was
characterized by a truly Benedictine modera-
tion; intellectual studies, manual work and
prayer were the hallmarks of her abbeys.

Liphardus (Lifard) (St) Ab.   June 3
d. c 550 A prominent lawyer of Orleans who
at the age of fifty embraced the solitary life and
eventually became the abbot-founder of the
monastery of Meung-sur-Loire.

Litteus (St) M.   Sept 10
See Nemesian, Felix, etc.

Liudhard (St) Bp.   Feb 24
d. c 600 Frankish chaplain to Queen Bertha
of Kent. He is said to have been a bishop and
to have played an important in the conversion
of King Ethelbert, q.v. He was buried in the
abbey of SS Peter and Paul, at Canterbury.

Liutwin (St) Bp. OSB.   Sept 29
d. c 713 Founder and monk of Mettlach,
and then bishop of Trier.

**Livinus (Lebwin) (St) Bp.
M.**   Nov 12
d. c 650 An Irishman by birth, he was
ordained by St Augustine of Canterbury and
crossed over to Flanders, where for some years
he preached the gospel with great success. At
some time during this period he is said to have
been ordained bishop in Ireland. He was
martyred near Alost in Brabant. He is perhaps
to be identified with St Lebuinus.

Lizier (St) Bp.   Aug 27
Otherwise Licerius, q.v.

**Lleudadd (Laudatus) (St)
Ab.**   Jan 15
6th cent. A Welsh saint, abbot of Bardsey
(Gwynedd), who accompanied St Cadfan to
Brittany. By some scholars he is thought to be
no other than St Lô of Coutances.

**Llewellyn (LLywelyn)
and Gwrnerth (SS) CC.**   Apr 7
6th cent. Welsh monks at Welshpool and
afterwards at Bardsey.

Llibio (St) C.   Feb 28
6th cent. The patron saint of Llanlibio in the
isle of Anglesey.

Lô (St) Bp.   Sept 22
Otherwise Lauto, q.v.

Loarn (St) C.   Aug 30
5th cent. A native of W. Ireland and a
disciple of St Patrick. Some writers describe
him as a regionary bishop of Downpatrick.

Locaie (St) VM.   Dec 9
Otherwise Leocadia, q.v.

Lolanus (St) C.   Sept 2
d. c? 1034 A Scottish bishop. The legend
which makes him a native of Galilee who
preached the gospel in Scotland during the
fifth century deserves no credence.

Lollian (St)   Dec 9
See Samosata Martyrs.

Loman (Luman) (St) Bp.   Feb 17
d. c 450 Said to have been a nephew of St
Patrick and the first bishop of Trim, in Meath.

**Lombards (Martyrs
under the) (SS)**   March 2
d. c 579 A group of eighty martyrs slain by
the Lombards in Campania for refusing "to
adore the head of a goat" (pre-1970 RM.).
They are also mentioned by St Gregory the
Great.

Lomer (Laudomarus) (St)
Ab.   Jan 19
d. 593   A shepherd boy near Chartres, then
priest, he became a hermit. Disciples came
and with them he founded the monastery of
Corbion, near Chartres. He lived to be over a
hundred.

London (Martyrs of)
Three main groups of post-Reformation
martyrs may be listed under the above heading, namely: (I) those of 1582, executed for
being concerned in a spurious plot called the
conspiracy of Reims and Rome; (II) those of
1588, following on the defeat of the Armada;
(III) those of 1591, following on a stricter
enforcement of the laws against Catholics.
Each martyr receives in this book a special
notice.

Longinus (St) M.   March 15
1st cent.   This is the name given by tradition
to the soldier who pierced the side of our Lord
hanging on the cross (John 19:34). He is said
to have died a martyr in Cappadocia, his
alleged native country. In art he is clad as a
soldier but rarely in the uniform worn in the
first century; he carries the spear with which
he pierced the side of Christ. The centurion
who acknowledged Christ to be the son of
God, after the crucifixion, is also called Longinus (Matt. 27:54).

Longinus (St) M.   Apr 24
See Eusebius, Neon, etc.

Longinus (St) Bp. M.   May 2
See Vindemnialis, Eugene and Longinus.

Longinus (St) M.   June 24
See Orentius, Heros, etc.

Longinus (St) M.   July 21
See Victor, Alexander, etc.

Lonochilus (Longis, Lenogisil) and Agnofleda (SS)   Apr 2
d. 653 and 638   The first was a priest who
founded a monastery in Maine, France.
Agnofleda vowed her virginity to God and cast
herself on his protection. Both were calumniated as a result, but their innocence was
proved miraculously, according to their
legend.

Lorgius (St) M.   March 2
See Lucius, Absalom and Lorgius.

Lotharius (St) Bp. OSB.   June 14
c 756   Founder of a monastery in the forest of
Argentan, which was later called after him,
Saint-Loyer-des-Champs. Afterwards he was
bishop of Séez for thirty-two years.

St Longinus, March 15

Louis
See also under Aloysius.

Louis Ibarchi (St) M.   Feb 5
1585–1597   A Japanese boy of twelve who
was an altar server for the Franciscan missionaries in Japan. He was crucified at Nagasaki with twenty-five companions. Canonized
in 1867.

Louis Mary Grignon de Montfort (St) C.   Apr 28
1673–1716   Born in Brittany of poor parents.

Some charitable persons having defrayed the cost of his education, he was ordained in 1700. He became chaplain to a hospital at Nantes, where he founded the institute of Sisters of the Divine Wisdom. He now began his missionary activities throughout France, and in order to train helpers in his forceful methods of preaching he formed, shortly before his death, Missionaries of the Company of Mary. He was a Dominican tertiary, but never a professed member of that order. His writings were once quite popular: those on the Blessed Virgin Mary are hardly compatible with the teachings of the second Vatican council.

Louis of Cordoba (St) M.   Apr 30
See Amator, Peter and Louis.

Louis (Ludwig) von Bruck (St) M.   Apr 30
d. 1429 A boy born of Swiss parents at Ravensburg in Swabia, who was allegedly murdered by the Jews at Easter.

Louis Bonnard (Bl) M.   May 1
See John-Louis Bonnard.

Louis Mary Palazzolo (Bl) C. Founder   June 15
1827–1886 A native of Bergamo, he was ordained in 1880. A spirit akin to John Bosco, he also applied all his energy to the Christian education of both young people and adults; the care of girls, especially children of the working class; and the care of the sick and the poor. Heirs to these tasks are the congregations he established — the Poor Little Sisters, and the Brothers of the Holy Family. Beatified in 1963.

Louis Naisen (Bl) M.   July 12
1619–1626 A Japanese boy of seven years, son of BB John and Monica Naisen. He was beheaded at Nagasaki. Beatified in 1867.

Louis Correa (Bl) M. SJ.   July 15
d. 1570 A Jesuit student, born at Évora in Portugal. A companion of Bl Ignatius de Azevedo, q.v.

Louis Bertrán (Bl) M. OP.   July 29
d. 1629 Born at Barcelona a kinsman of St Louis Bertrán, the apostle of Colombia. After his profession in the Dominican order, he was sent to the Philippine Islands in 1618 and then to Japan, where he worked until his martyrdom. He was burnt alive with two companions at Omura. Beatified in 1867.

Louis Someyon (? Matzuo) (Bl) M.   Aug 17
d. 1627 A Japanese layman, of the third order of St Francis, beheaded at Nagasaki. Beatified in 1867.

Louis of Toulouse (St)
Bp. OFM.   Aug 19
1274–1297 Son of Charles II of Anjou, king of Naples, great-nephew of St Louis of France and of St Elizabeth of Hungary. He was born probably at Nocera and grew up in Provence. He spent seven years as a hostage for his father at Barcelona and in Tarragona. At the age of twenty-three he was ordained and joined the Friars Minor. Reluctantly he accepted the see of Toulouse, but died only six months later. Canonized in 1317.

Louis Flores (Bl) M. OP.   Aug 19
1570–1622 Born at Antwerp, he went with his parents to Mexico, where he joined the Dominicans. After serving as novice-master, he was sent in 1602 to the Philippine Islands. In 1620, while on a journey, he was captured by the Dutch, handed over to the Japanese, tortured, imprisoned for two years, and finally burnt alive at Nagasaki. Beatified in 1867.

Louis IX (St) King   GC. Aug 25
1214–1270 Born at Poissy, near Paris, he succeeded to the throne under the regency of his mother Blanche of Castile in 1226. He reigned for forty-four years. In his private life he was more austere and more prayerful than a religious; as a ruler he was energetic but considerate to his people, especially to the poor, and he was a brave warrior who knew how to lead his armies to victory, as when he defeated King Henry III of England at Taillebourg in 1242. He founded many monasteries and built the Saint-Chapelle in Paris to house his large collection of relics. He was the father of eleven children and a devoted husband. He led two crusades: in the first he was made prisoner in Egypt, and during the second he died of dysentery before Tunis. He was canonized, with the universal approbation of Western Christendom, in 1297. In art, clad in royal robes, often spangled with fleurs de lys, he holds a cross, crown of thorns, or other emblems of the Saviour's Passion.

Louis Sotelo (Bl) M. OFM.   Aug 25
d. 1624 Born of a noble family at Seville, in Spain, he became a Franciscan at Salamanca. After his ordination he was sent to Manila (1601) and then to Japan (1603). He was arrested and shipped back to Spain (1613), but after a visit to Rome he returned to Japan (1622). Again arrested at Nagasaki, he was burnt alive at Ximabara. Beatified in 1867.

Louis Sasanda (Bl) M.
OFM.   Aug 25
d. 1624 Son of Bl Michael Sasanda, a
martyr at Yeddo, Japan. In 1613, he accompanied Bl Louis Sotelo to Mexico, where he
became a Franciscan. In 1622 he was ordained
at Manila. Two years later he was burnt alive at
Ximabara, with Bl Louis Sotelo and Comp.
Beatified in 1867.

Louis Baba (Bl) M. Tert.
OFM.   Aug 25
d. 1624 A Japanese catechist. He accompa-
nied Bl Louis Sotelo to Europe. On his return
to Japan he was arrested, received the Franciscan habit in prison at Omura, and was burnt
alive at Ximabara. Beatified in 1867.

**Louis Barreau de la
Touche (Bl)** M. OSB.   Sept 2
d. 1792 A French Benedictine of the congregation of St Maur, monk of Saint-Florent-
de-Saumur, and nephew of Bl Augustine
Chevreux, with whom he was martyred in
Paris (see September, Martyrs of).

Louis Maki (Bl) M.   Sept 7
d. 1627 A Japanese layman, burnt alive at
Nagasaki for having allowed Bl Thomas
Tzughi to celebrate the eucharist in his house.
Beatified in 1867.

Louis Nifaki (Bl) M.
Tert. OP.   Sept 8
d. 1628 A Japanese Dominican tertiary be-
headed at Nagasaki with his two sons, Francis
and Dominic, for having sheltered the missionaries. Beatified in 1867.

Louis Cavara (Bl) M. SJ.   Sept 10
d. 1622 A page at the court of Arima, Japan,
who was later exiled by the apostate prince,
Michael. Received into the Society of Jesus by
Bl Charles Spinola, he was burnt alive at
Nagasaki. Beatified in 1867.

Louis (Ludwig) (Bl) C.   Sept 11
1200–1227 Landgrave of Thuringia and
husband of St Elizabeth of Hungary. An able
ruler and brave warrior, he died at Otranto
while following the emperor Frederick II to
the crusade. His cult has never been confirmed, but is certainly well deserved.

Louis the Great (Bl) C.   Sept 11
d. 1382 One of the greatest of the kings of
Hungary; later of Poland too. Fought for the
expansion of the church in the Balkans. Never
officially beatified, his cult is chiefly in Poland.

Louis Allemand (Bl) Bp.
Card.   Sept 16
d. 1450 Appointed archbishop of Arles in

1423 and cardinal shortly after, Louis was one
of the leaders of the "Council party" during
the troubled period of the Western Schism.
He was one of those who elected and remained
faithful to the antipope Felix V. On this
account he was deprived of the cardinalate and
excommunicated by Eugenius IV. Pope
Nicholas V restored him, and from this time
till his death Louis attended exclusively to the
government of his diocese. In his private life,
he was always a model of virtue.

Louis Chakichi (Bl) M.   Oct 2
d. 1622 A Japanese layman who released Bl
Louis Flores from prison at Firando. He was
burnt alive at Nagasaki. His wife and children
were beheaded. Beatified in 1867.

Louis Bertrán (St) C. OP.   Oct 9
1526–1581 A native of Valencia, in Spain,
and a blood relation of St Vincent Ferrer; like
him he was a Dominican. After filling very
successfully the office of novice-master, he
was in 1562 sent to evangelize S. America, and
for seven years worked in what are now
Colombia, Panama and some of the West
Indian islands. Under obedience he returned
to Spain, and served as prior in several houses.
Canonized in 1671.

Louis Morbioli (Bl) C.   Nov 16
1439–1495 A native of Bologna, who as a
young man was notorious for his loose living,
even after he had contracted marriage. He was
converted by sickness, became a Carmelite
tertiary, and went about teaching Christian
doctrine to the young and begging alms which
he gave to the poor. Cult confirmed in 1842.

**Louise degli
Albertoni (Bl)** W.   Jan 31
1474–1533 A Roman born, she married
James de Citara to whom she bore three
children. After his death she put on the habit
of the third order of St Francis and spent her
life in works of charity. Cult approved in 1671.

Louise de Marillac (St)
Foundress   March 15
1591–1660 Born in Paris. She wished to
become a nun but, on the advice of her
confessor, married Antony Le Gras. After his
death (1625), Louise spent the remainder of
her life in co-operating with St Vincent de
Paul in the establishment of the Sisters of
Charity. The sisters took their vows for the
first time in 1638, and Louise remained their
superioress till her death. Beatified in 1920,
canonized in 1934.

Louise of Savoy (Bl) W.
Poor Clare   July 24
1462–1503 Daughter of Bl Amadeus IX,

duke of Savoy, and cousin of Bl Joan of Valois. In 1479 she was married to Hugh of Châlons, who left her a widow when she was only twenty-seven. She now joined the Poor Clares at Orbe and was employed in collecting food for the community, which she did most graciously and cheerfully. Cult approved in 1839.

Louise of Omura (Bl) M.   Sept 8
d. 1628   A Japanese woman martyred at Omura.

Loup (St) Bp.   July 29
Otherwise Lupus of Troyes, q.v.

Louthiern (St) Bp.   Oct 17
6th cent.   An Irish saint, patron of St Ludgran in Cornwall, possibly identical with St Luchtighern, abbot of Ennistymon, associated with St Ita.

Lua (Lugid, Molua) (St) Ab.   Aug 4
554–609?   Originally from Limerick, he became a disciple of St Comgall and founder of many monasteries (the legendary number is 120). His rule was most austere, but he was of great tenderness to man and beast. He was probably a hermit at some time in his life.

Lubin (St) Bp.   Sept 15
Otherwise Leobinus, q.v.

Lucanus (St) M.   Oct 30
5th cent.   A martyr who is believed to have suffered at Lagny, near Paris, where his relics were enshrined.

Lucerius (St) Ab. OSB.   Dec 10
d. 739   While still a child he joined the Benedictines of Farfa, near Rome, under its restorer, St Thomas of Maurienne, whom he eventually succeeded as abbot.

Luchesius (Bl) C.   Apr 28
d. 1260   Born near Poggibonsi, in Umbria, he married Bl Bonadonna and was in business as a grocer, money changer and corn merchant. About the year 1221 he and his wife gave themselves to a life of alms-deeds and penance as Franciscan tertiaries. They are venerated as the first to have become tertiaries, but this is not quite established.

Luchtighern (St) Ab.   Apr 28
See under Louthiern.

Lucian of Antioch (St) M.   Jan 7
d. 312   A native of Edessa, where he distinguished himself as a scriptural scholar. He travelled to Antioch where he opened a school of exegesis, and then to Nicomedia, where he was martyred after nine years in prison. The Arians endeavoured to claim the authority of his name for their errors. He is highly praised by SS John Chrysostom and Jerome.

Lucian, Maximian and Julian (SS) MM.   Jan 8
d. c 290   Alleged to have been missionaries from Rome, martyred at Beauvais.

Lucian (St) M.   May 28
See Emilius, Felix, etc.

Lucian (St) M.   June 13
See Fortunatus and Lucian.

Lucian (St) M.   July 7
See Peregrinus, Lucian, etc.

Lucian, Florius and Comp. (SS) MM.   Oct 26
d. c 250   A group of martyrs who suffered at Nicomedia under Decius. Their Acts were fancifully embellished at a later date.

Lucian, Metrobius, Paul, Zenobius, Theotimus and Drusus (SS) MM.   Dec 24
? African martyrs who suffered at Tripoli.

Lucidius (St) Bp.   Apr 26
? A bishop of Verona, famous for his life of prayer and study.

Lucidus (St) H. OSB.   July 28
d. ? 938   Benedictine monk of St Peter's, near Aquara in S. Italy. He died as a recluse in the cell of Santa Maria del Piano.

Lucilla, Flora VV., Eugene, Antoninus, Theodore and Comp. (SS) MM.   July 29
d. c 260   A band of twenty-three martyrs who suffered under Gallienus. It seems that this group should be identified with the three groups commemorated on the following days: June 24 (SS Faustus, etc.), June 25 (SS Lucy and Comp.), July 6 (SS Lucy, Antoninus, etc.).

Lucilla (St) VM.   Aug 25
See Nemesius and Lucilla.

Lucillian, Claudius, Hypatius, Paul and Dionysius (SS) MM.   June 3
d. 273   Lucillian is said to have become a Christian in his old age. He was crucified at Byzantium, and on the same occasion the four youths mentioned above were beheaded. Another version of the story states that Lucillian was the father, the four youths his sons, and makes Paula (q.v.), a lady commemorated on the same day, their respective wife and mother.

Lucina (three of the same name) (St)   June 30
Some modern writers affirm that there were

three Roman saints of this name. (I) St Lucina of apostolic times, mentioned in the (spurious) Acts of SS Processus and Martinianus. (II) St Lucina who ministered to the martyrs under Decius (250). (III) St Lucina, connected with St Sebastian and other martyrs under Diocletian. The first is commemorated on June 30.

Lucinus (Lezin) (St) Bp.   Feb 13
d. c 618   A courtier who eventually became bishop of Angers.

Luciolus (St) M.   March 3
See Felix, Luciolus, etc.

Lucius (St) M.   Feb 8
See Paul, Lucius and Cyriacus.

Lucius and Comp. (SS)
MM.   Feb 11
d. 350   Lucius, bishop of Adrianople, played a leading part in the council of Sardica (347). Under the protection of Pope St Julius I he returned to Adrianople, but refused to be in communion with the Arian bishops condemned at Sardica. On this account he was martyred with a group of his faithful Catholics by order of the emperor Constantius.

Lucius (St) M.   Feb 15
See Saturninus, Castulus, etc.

Lucius, Silvanus, Rutulus, Classicus, Secundinus, Fructulus and Maximus
(SS) MM.   Feb 18
? African martyrs, whose names Baronius inserted in the pre-1970 RM. on the authority, he states, of reliable MSS.

Lucius (St) M.   Feb 24
See Montanus, Lucius, etc.

Lucius, Absolon and Lorgius (SS) MM.   March 2
The names are first met in the martyrology of Usuard. The pre-1970 RM. says they were martyred at Caesarea in Cappadocia.

Lucius I (St) Pope   formerly March 4
d. 254   He succeeded St Cornelius as pope in 253, and was at once sent into exile. On the death of the emperor Gallus he returned to his flock, but his pontificate lasted only eight months. Although referred to as a martyr by St Cyprian, there is no evidence or probability of his having been put to death; he was a confessor of the faith. He opposed the policies of the antipope Novatian. Portions of his epitaph remain in the cemetery of Callistus. Cult suppressed in 1969.

Lucius (St) M.   Apr 22
See Apelles, Lucius and Clement.

Lucius of Cyrene (St) Bp.   May 6
1st cent.   One of the "prophets and doctors" mentioned as being in the church at Antioch when Paul and Barnabas were set apart for their apostolate (Acts 13:1). He is stated to have been "of Cyrene", whence the tradition that he was the first bishop of that city in the Ptolemais (Africa).

Lucius (St) M.   May 23
See Quintian, Lucius, etc.

Lucius and Comp. (SS)
MM.   Aug 20
?   The story of Lucius is wrapped in obscurity. According to the pre-1970 RM. he came from Cyrene to Cyprus, and this may imply a confusion with Lucius of Cyrene (May 6).

Lucius (St) Bp. M.   Sept 10
See Nemesian, Felix, etc.

Lucius (St) M.   Oct 4
See Gaius, Faustus, etc.

Lucius (St) M.   Oct 19
See Ptolemy, Lucius, etc.

Lucius (St) M.   Oct 25
See Theodosius, Lucius, etc.

Lucius (St) M.   Oct 29
See Hyacinth, Quintus, etc.

Lucius, Rogatus, Cassian and Candida (SS) MM.   Dec 1
? Roman martyrs.

Lucius (St) King   Dec 3
? d. c 200   King of Britain. According to a tradition, first heard of in the sixth century, he asked Pope St Eleutherius (d. c 189) to send missionaries into Britain, where he founded the dioceses of London and Llandaff and whence he eventually set out as a missionary to the Grisons in Switzerland. Present-day scholars regard the whole story as fictitious: it is in fact based on a confusion with the story of Agbar IX, who was king of Edessa in Mesopotamia. He was also known as Lucius; and he sent to Pope St Eleutherius for missionaries to be sent to his country.

Lucius (St) M.   Dec 15
See Faustinus, Lucius, etc.

Lucretia (St) VM.   March 15
Otherwise Leocritia, q.v.

Lucretia (St) VM.   Nov 23
d. 306   A Spanish maiden, martyred at Mérida (Emerita) in W. Spain.

Lucy (Bl) VM.   Feb 19
1813–1862   A Chinese school-teacher beheaded at Kuy-tszheu. Beatified in 1909.

Lucy (Lucia) Filippini (St) V.   March 25

1672–1732 Born in Tuscany, she joined Rosa Venerini at Montefiascone and helped her in the work of training schoolmistresses. This was the origin of the Italian institute of the *Maestre Pie*, or Filippine, of which St Lucy is venerated as the co-foundress. Canonized in 1930.

Lucy (Lucia, Luceia) and twenty Comp. (SS) MM.   June 25

See the notice of SS Lucilla, etc., of July 29.

Lucy, Antoninus, Severinus, Diodorus, Dion and Comp. (SS) MM.   July 6

See the notice of SS Lucilla, etc., of July 29.

Lucy Bufalari (Bl) V. OSA.   July 27

d. 1350 Born at Castel Porziano, near Rome, a sister of Bl John of Rieti, she took the veil in the Augustinian convent of Amelia where she became prioress. She is venerated as patroness against diabolical possession. Cult confirmed in 1832.

Lucy de Freitas (Bl) M.   Sept 10

d. 1622 Of Japanese birth, but married to a Portuguese, Philip de Freitas. For having given shelter to the missionaries she was burnt alive at Nagasaki on the day of the great martyrdom. Beatified in 1867.

Lucy and Geminian (SS) MM.   formerly Sept 16

d. c 300 A Roman widow (said to have been 75 years old) and a neophyte, who were martyred together under Diocletian. Their Acts are untrustworthy. Cult suppressed in 1969.

Lucy of Caltagirone (Bl) V. OFM.   Sept 26

d. ? 1304 Born at Caltagirone in Sicily, she became a Poor Clare at Salerno. Cult approved in 1514.

Lucy Chakichi (Bl) M.   Oct 2

d. 1622 The wife of Bl Louis Chakichi, q.v. She was beheaded with her two boys, Andrew and Francis (q.v.), at Nagasaki. Beatified in 1867.

Lucy of Settefonti (Bl) V. OSB. Cam.   Nov 7

d. 12th cent. Born at Bologna, she took the Camaldolese habit in the convent of St Christina, at Settefonti, diocese of Bologna. The Camaldolese venerate her as the foundress of their sisterhoods.

Lucy Brocolelli (Bl) V. Tert. OP.   Nov 15

1476–1544 Born at Narni in Umbria, after three years of virginal wedlock she was allowed by her husband to become a Dominican regular tertiary at Viterbo, where she received the *Stigmata*. In 1499 she was sent as the first prioress of the convent of Ferrara, but she proved a very incapable superior and was deposed, treated with un-Christian cruelty by her successor, and forgotten by all. She lived thirty-nine years without ever complaining. Cult confirmed in 1710.

Lucy of Syracuse (St) VM.   GC. Dec 13

d. 304 A Sicilian maiden who suffered at Syracuse under Diocletian. She is one of the most famous of the Western virgin-martyrs. Her name occurs in the first eucharistic prayer. Although her Acta were written before the sixth century, they are unfortunately not trustworthy. Her relics are preserved at Venice, and were venerated by Pope John XXIII. In art she is depicted as a damsel carrying her eyes on a platter, book or shell; or with a gash in her neck, or a sword embedded in it; or carrying a sword and a palm.

Ludan (Luden, Loudain) (St) C.   Feb 12

d. c 1202 The saint of this name honoured at Scherkirchen in Alsace is said to have been a Scottish or Irish pilgrim who died in that country on his way back from Jerusalem.

Ludger (St) Bp. OSB.   March 26

d. 809 A Frisian by birth, educated under St Gregory in the abbey school of Utrecht and under Bl Alcuin in England. Returning to his fatherland as a missionary he worked chiefly in Westphalia, of which he is the apostle. His gentleness did more to attract the Saxons to Christ than all the armies of Charlemagne. He lived for a time at Montecassino, learning the Benedictine observance. He was the founder and the first bishop of Münster.

Ludmilla (St) M.   Sept 16

d. 921 Duchess of Bohemia, entrusted with the education of the young prince St Wenceslaus. She fell a victim to the jealousy of her daughter-in-law, by whose orders she was strangled by hired assassins at Tetin.

Ludolph (St) Bp. O. Praem.   March 29

d. 1250 A Premonstratensian canon who became bishop of Ratzeburg and had to endure much persecution at the hands of Duke Albert of Sachsen-Lauenberg.

Ludolph (St) Ab. OSB.   Aug 13

d. 983 Abbot of New Corvey in Westphalia

St Lucy of Syracuse, Dec 13

from 971 to 983. During his abbacy there was a marked revival of the monastic school and studies.

Ludovicus Pavoni (Bl) C.
Founder   Apr 1
1784–1849   From the cradle to the grave his life was lived in his native Brescia. Ordained in 1807 he did not spare himself in the fulfilment of his ministry, particularly in the care of the young. This ideal urged him to create the religious institute known as the Sons of Mary Immaculate. Beatified in 1947.

Ludwin (Leodwin, etc.)
(St) Bp. OSB.   Sept 29
d. 713   Born in Austrasia and educated under St Basinus, he married early in life. Left a widower, he founded the abbey of Mettlach (*Mediolacus*) and became a monk there. Later he became bishop of Trier.

Lufthild (St) V.   Jan 23
d. ? 850   A saint honoured in the neighbourhood of Cologne. She is said to have lived as an anchoress in that locality.

Luigi Orione (Bl)
Founder   March 12
1872–1940 (March 12)   The pupil of John Basco, Don Orione founded the Sons of Divine Providence, the Little Missionary Sisters of Charity, the Blind Sacramentive Sisters, and the Hermits of St Albert. He dedicated his life to those in suffering and misfortune. In 1936 he opened a House of Providence in Cardiff. This apostle of mercy died at San Remo and was beatified in 1980.

Luke (St) M.   Feb 6
See Silvanus, Luke, etc.

Luke the Younger (St)   Feb 7
d. *c* 946   A Greek farm labourer who was admitted as a novice to a monastery at Athens, and became a solitary on Mt Joannitza, near Corinth. He worked so many miracles in this place that it was known as *Soterion* (place of healing) and he himself as the thaumaturgus (the wonder-worker).

Luke Belludi (Bl) C. OFM.   Feb 17
1200–1285   He received the Franciscan habit from St Francis himself at Padua and became the intimate associate of St Antony of Padua. On his own death he was laid in the empty tomb from which the body of St Antony had been taken. Cult confirmed in 1927.

Luke (St) M.   Apr 22
See Parmenius and Comp.

Luke Kirby (St) M.   May 30
d. 1582   Born in N. England and educated, probably, at Cambridge. After his conversion he studied for the priesthood at Rome and Douai. On his return to England (1580) he was arrested and subjected in the Tower to the terrible torture known as the "Scavenger's daughter". He was finally martyred at Tyburn.

Canonized in 1970 as one of the Forty Martyrs
of England and Wales, q.v.

Luke Banabakiutu (St) M.   June 3
d. 1886 A Negro, baptized in 1881 and
burnt alive at Namuyongo in Uganda. See
Charles Lwanga and Comps.

Luke Loan (St) M.   June 5
1756–1840 An old priest, native of Vietnam,
beheaded for his faith. Canonized in 1988.

Luke Kiemon (Bl) M.   Aug 17
d. 1627 A native of Japan, and a Franciscan
tertiary, beheaded at Nagasaki. Beatified in
1867.

Luke Mellini (Bl) Ab.
OSB. Cel.   Aug 24
d. *c* 1460 A Benedictine monk of the Celestine congregation. Pope Nicholas V appointed
him general of the Celestines.

Luke Banfy (Bl) Bp. M.   Aug 28
d. *c* 1178 Primate of Hungary and archbishop of Esztergom, he defended the church
against royal despotism. His canonization,
started by Gregory IX, was interrupted by the
Tartar invasion of Hungary.

Luke (St) M.   Sept 10
See Apelles, Lucius and Clement.

Luke (St) Evangelist   GC. Oct 18
1st cent. A Greek of Antioch and a physician
by profession, who became the fellow worker
of St Paul and remained with him till the great
apostle's martyrdom. He wrote the third
gospel and the Acts of the Apostles. The later
tradition that he was a painter seems to be
based on the picturesque style of his narrative.
There is no evidence that he died a martyr. He
is shown in art as a bishop or a doctor of
medicine, and often accompanied by a winged
ox. He may be represented painting an icon of
our Lady.

Luke de Nostra (Bl) H.   Dec 5
14th cent. A Hungarian Pauline hermit,
friend and confessor of King Louis the Great
(1342–1382).

Lull (St) Bp. OSB.   Oct 16
d. 787 An Anglo-Saxon monk of Malmesbury, and a kinsman of St Boniface, whom he
joined in Germany, becoming his archdeacon
and chief assistant. In 751 he was sent to
Rome, and on his return Boniface ordained
him regionary bishop and his coadjutor in the
see of Mainz. After his master's martyrdom he
took his place. He was a founder of monasteries and a patron of the arts and of learning.

Lunaire (St) Bp.   July 1
Otherwise Leonorius, q.v.

St Luke, Oct 18

Luperculus (Luperculus)
(St) Bp. M. March 1
300 A French, or Spanish, martyr under Diocletian. He is venerated chiefly at Tarbes, near Lourdes.

Lupercus (St) M. Apr 16
See Saragossa, Martyrs of.

Lupercus (St) M. Oct 30
See Claudius, Lupercus and Victorius.

Luperius (St) Bp. Nov 15
6th (or 8th) cent. A bishop of Verona, of whom nothing further is known.

Lupicinus and Felix (SS)
Bps. Feb 3
5th cent. Described in the martyrologies as bishops of Lyons. To St Lupicinus is usually assigned the date 486. Nothing else is known of either saint.

Lupicinus (St) Ab. March 21
d. c 480 Brother of St Romanus of Condat (Feb 28), with whom he founded the abbeys of St Claud (Condat) in the Jura and Lauconne.

Lupicinus (St) Bp. May 31
5th cent. Bishop of Verona, described as "the most holy, the best of bishops".

Lupus (St) M. Aug 23
? A slave who gave his life for Christ.

Lupus of Châlons (St) Bp. Jan 27
d. c 610 Bishop of Châlons-sur-Saône, famous for his charity to the afflicted. We have a letter of St Gregory the Great addressed to him in 601.

Lupus of Troyes (St) Bp. July 29
384–478 A native of Toul who married the sister of St Hilary. After seven years husband and wife separated by mutual consent, Lupus becoming a monk at Lérins. In 426 he was made bishop of Troyes. In the course of his episcopate he accompanied St Germanus of Auxerre to Britain to rid the country of Pelagianism, and in 453 he succeeded in saving Troyes from being sacked by Attila. He died at the age of ninety-four. Some of these details may not be historically verifiable.

Lupus of Sens (St) Bp. Sept 1
d. 623 A monk of Lérins who became bishop of Sens in 609. He was slandered and banished from his see under Clotaire, but was recalled by his own people and his cause fully vindicated.

Lupus of Lyons (St) Bp. Sept 25
d. 542 A monk of a monastery near Lyons who became archbishop of that see. He had much to suffer in the political troubles which followed the death of St Sigismund, king of Burgundy.

Lupus (St) M. Oct 14
See Saturninus and Lupus.

Lupus of Soissons (St) Bp. Oct 19
d. c 540 A nephew of St Remigius of Reims who became bishop of Soissons.

Lupus of Bayeux (St) Bp. Oct 25
5th cent. A bishop of Bayeux, said to have flourished about the year 465.

Lupus of Verona (St) Bp. Dec 2
? A bishop of Verona of whom nothing is known save the name.

Lutgard (St) V. OSB.
Cist. June 16
1182–1246 Born at Tongres in Brabant, she became a Black Benedictine nun at the age of twenty, and in order to escape being made abbess some years later she migrated to the Cistercian nunnery of Aywières. Here she lived for thirty years a wonderful life, full of mystical experiences. She is an outstanding figure among the women mystics of the Middle Ages. She was blind for eleven years before her death.

Luxorius, Cisellus and Camerinus (SS) MM. Aug 21
d. c 303 Sardinian martyrs, beheaded under Diocletian. According to his *Passio* Luxorius had been a soldier in the imperial army; the other two were boys whom he encouraged to brave martyrdom.

Lybe, Leonis and Eutropia (SS) VV. MM. June 15
d. 303 Martyrs under Diocletian, at Palmyra in Syria. Lybe was beheaded; Leonis, her sister, died at the stake; and Eutropia, a girl of twelve was, by order of the judge, used as a target by archers.

Lybosus (St) M. Dec 29
See Dominic, Victor, etc.

Lycarion (St) M. June 7
? A martyr who suffered in Egypt.

Lydia (St) M. March 27
See Philetus, Lydia, etc.

Lydia Purpuraria (St)
Matron Aug 3
1st cent. A native of Thyatira (now Ak-Hissar), a city in Asia Minor famous for its dye-works, whence Lydia's trade — *purpuraria*, purple seller. She was at Philippi in Macedonia when she became St Paul's first convert in Europe and afterwards his hostess (Acts 16:14–15).

Lydwina of Schiedam (Bl) V.   Apr 14
1380–1433 In the words of her proper office
she was "a prodigy of human suffering and
heroic patience". The daughter of a labourer,
at the age of sixteen she met with an accident
and became completely bedridden. The disease increased in virulence up to the moment
of her death. Through it all she was favoured
by God with mystical experiences. She suffered greatly in union with the sufferings of
Christ.

Lyé (*several*)
Note. Both St Leo of Troyes (May 25) and St
Leo of Melun (Nov 10) are frequently called
Lié or Lyé, which is also a French form of
Laetus.

**Lyons and Vienne
(Martyrs of)**
See Photinus (Pothinus), Sanctius, etc.

**Lythan (Llythaothaw)
(St)**   Sept 1
? Titular saint of two Welsh churches in the
Llandaff diocese.

Lyutius (St) H. OSB.   July 28
d. *c* 1038 A monk of Montecassino, who
died as a hermit at La Cava. Some writers
identify him with St Lucidus, q.v.

Mabyn (St)   Sept 21
6th cent. Welsh and Cornish saints, Mabyn, Mabon, Mabenna, are associated with St Teilo, and have originated some placenames, but nothing definite can be stated in regard to them. One of the daughters of the chieftain Brychan of Brecknock is venerated as St Mabenna; and the placename Ruabon (Clwyd) perpetuates the name of another saint of similar name.

Macaille (St) Bp.   Apr 25
d. *c* 489 A disciple of Mel who became bishop of Croghan, Offaly. He assisted St Mel in receiving Brigid's vows. He should not be confused with St Maccai, also a disciple of St Patrick, venerated in the isle of Bute.

Macanisius (St) Bp.   Sept 3
d. 514 Or *Aengus Mc Nisse*. He is said to have been baptized as an infant by St Patrick, by whom he is also alleged to have been ordained bishop. He became the abbot-founder of a monastery, probably at Kells, which grew into the diocese of Connor.

Macaria (Macarius) (St) M.   Apr 8
See Januarius, Maxima, etc.

Macarius the Younger
(St) H.   Jan 2
d. *c* 408 Surnamed also "of Alexandria". He is said to have abandoned the trade of fruiterer to become a monk in the Thebaid in Upper Egypt, *c* 335. Thence passing into Lower Egypt, he took up his abode in the desert of Nitria. Lucius, the intruded Arian patriarch of Alexandria, banished him on account of his unflinching orthodoxy.

Macarius the Great (St) H.   Jan 15
c 300–390 Known also as "Macarius of Egypt" or "the Elder". Born in Upper Egypt, in his youth he retired to a solitary hut, where he combined assiduous prayer with the tending of sheep and the plaiting of baskets. To escape notice he migrated to the desert of Skete, where he was ordained and passed the remaining sixty years of his life. His chief duty was to celebrate the eucharist for the several thousand members of the monastic colony. He

was banished for a time for having upheld the Catholic faith against the Arians.

Macarius, Rufinus, Justus
and Theophilus (SS) MM.   Feb 28
d. *c* 250 Martyrs under Decius. The pre-1970 RM. claims them for Rome; other martyrologies for Alexandria. They are said to have been potters by trade.

Macarius of Jerusalem
(St) Bp.   March 10
d. *c* 335 Bishop of Jerusalem from 314 till his death. It is said that during his episcopate St Helen found the True Cross and that it was he who identified it. He planned Constantine's basilica of the Holy Sepulchre and of the Resurrection, which was completed before his death.

Macarius the
Wonder-worker (St) Ab.   Apr 1
d. 830 Abbot of Pelecete, near Constantinople. He was singled out as the special object of their persecution by the Iconoclast emperors Leo the Armenian and Michael the Stammerer. After several years in prison he died in exile.

Macarius of Antioch (St)
Bp.   Apr 10
d. 1012 Said to have been a native of Antioch in Pisidia, he was a bishop who travelled westward as a pilgrim and was received by the Benedictines of St Bavo, Ghent, in whose hospice he died of the plague then raging in Belgium.

Macarius (St) Bp.   June 20
d. *c* 350 A bishop of Petra in Palestine. He took part in the council of Sardica against the Arians, who succeeded in securing his banishment to Africa, where he died. His name was originally Arius, but he has been renamed Macarius to distinguish him from the founder of Arianism, whom Macarius opposed throughout his life.

Macarius and Julian (SS)
MM.   Aug 12
? Described by the pre-1970 RM. as martyrs

of Syria. The earlier martyrologies treat them as confessors; possibly they were monks.

Macarius (St) M. Sept 5
See Eudoxius, Zeno, etc.

Macarius (St) M. Sept 6
See Faustus, Macarius and Comp.

**Macarius and Comp.
(SS) MM.** Oct 30
d. *c* 250 The pre-1970 RM. places them at Alexandria but they seem to be identical with the group noticed under Feb 28.

Macarius (St) M. Dec 8
This Macarius, who suffered at Alexandria, also seems to be identical with those noticed under Feb 28 and Oct 30.

**Macarius the Scot (Bl)
Ab. OSB.** Dec 19
d. 1153 A Benedictine monk who crossed over to Würzburg from Scotland (or Ireland) and was elected first abbot of St James's monastery, founded by Bishop Embricho (1125–1146).

Macarius (St) M. Dec 20
See Eugene and Macarius.

**Macartan (Macartin,
Maccarthen) (St) Bp.** March 24
d. *c* 505 An early disciple and companion of St Patrick, by whom he is said to have been ordained bishop of Clogher. His name in Irish is Aedh mac Cairthinn.

Maccabean Martyrs (SS) Aug 1
See Machabees.

Maccaldus (St) Dec 28
Otherwise Maughold, q.v.

**Maccallin (Malcallan)
(St) Ab. OSB.** Jan 21
d. 978 An Irishman who made a pilgrimage to St Fursey's shrine at Péronne, and entered the Benedictine abbey of Gorze. Later he became a hermit and, later still, abbot of St Michael's monastery at Thiérache and Waulsort (*Valciodorum*), near Dinant, on the R. Meuse.

**Maccallin (Macallan,
Macculin Dus) (St) Bp.** Sept 6
d. *c* 497 An Irish bishop of Lusk, who is venerated also in Scotland, which country he is known to have visited.

Macdara (St)
The saint who has given its name to St Macdaras Island off the coast of Galway.

Macedo (St) M. March 27
See Philetus, Lydia, etc.

Macedonius (St) H. Jan 24
d. *c* 430 A Syrian hermit who wandered for forty years in Syria, Phoenicia and Cilicia, living all the time on barley; hence his surname of *Kritophagos*, "the barley-eater".

**Macedonius, Patricia
and Modesta (SS) MM.** March 13
d. *c* 304 A group of three martyrs, husband, wife and daughter, whom the pre-1970 RM. assigned to Nicomedia. Earlier martyrologies extend the group to twenty-two names.

Macedonius (St) Bp. Apr 25
d. 516 A patriarch of Constantinople who suffered deportation for his zeal in defence of the council of Chalcedon. He died in exile.

**Macedonius, Theodulus
and Tatian (SS) MM.** Sept 12
d. 362 Martyrs of Phrygia, roasted alive on gridirons at Mevos for having broken into the temple and destroyed the idols during the restoration of paganism under Julian the Apostate.

Maceratus (St) M.
See Peregrinus, Maceratus, etc.

Machabees (SS) MM. Aug 1
d. *c* 168 B.C. These were the only saints of the Old Testament liturgically venerated in the Western Church. Prominent among them were a scribe by name Eleazar, ninety years of age, and a mother with her seven sons (2 Mac 6 & 7). All were Jews and probably natives of Antioch, who were martyred under Antiochus IV Epiphanes for refusing to eat the flesh of swine, forbidden by the Jewish Torah. Their relics were said to be enshrined in the church of St Peter ad Vincula in Rome, but in recent times they were found to be certainly not genuine and removed. Cult confined to local calendars since 1969.

**Machabeo (Gilda-
Marchaibeo) (St) Ab.** March 31
1104–1174 An Irishman, abbot of the monastery of SS Peter and Paul at Armagh from 1134 till his death.

Machai (St) Ab. Apr 11
5th cent. A disciple of St Patrick, who founded a monastery in the isle of Bute.

Machan (St) Bp. Sept 28
? A Scottish saint trained in Ireland and ordained bishop in Rome.

**Machar (Macharius,
Mochumna) (St) Bp.** Nov 12
6th cent. An Irishman by birth, he was

baptized by St Colman and became a disciple of St Columba at Iona. Afterwards he was sent with twelve disciples to convert the Picts, near Old Aberdeen.

Machudd (Machell) (St) Ab.   Nov 15
7th cent.   Abbot-founder of Llanfechell (Anglesey).

Machutus (Maclovius) (St) Bp.   Nov 15
Otherwise Malo, q.v.

Mackessog (Kegsag) (St)   March 10
Otherwise Kessog, q.v.

Macra (St) VM.   Jan 6
d. 287   A maiden of Reims, martyred at Fismes in Champagne under the prefect Rictiovarus, before the outbreak of the persecution under Diocletian. In art she is usually represented with a pair of pincers in her hand, in memory of one of the fiendish tortures to which she was subjected.

Macrina the Elder (St) W.   Jan 14
d. c 340   The paternal grandmother of SS Basil and Gregory of Nyssa. In her youth she had been directed by St Gregory Thaumaturgus, and during the persecution of Diocletian she and her husband were forced to remain concealed for seven years or more in a hiding place on the shores of the Black Sea. They had much to suffer later under Licinius. Nevertheless they succeeded in rearing one of the most saintly families in Cappadocia.

Macrina the Younger (St) V.   July 19
c 327–379   Granddaughter of St Macrina the Elder (v. Jan 14) and eldest daughter of SS Basil and Emmelia. She was one of ten children among whom were SS Basil the Great and Gregory of Nyssa. She helped her parents in the training of her younger brothers and sisters and afterwards became a nun and abbess.

Macrina (St) VM.   July 20
Otherwise Margaret, q.v.

Macrinus (St) M.   Sept 17
See Valerian, Macrinus and Gordian.

Macrobius (St) M.   July 20
See Sabinus, Julian, etc.

Macrobius and Julian (SS) MM.   Sept 13
d. c 321   Martyrs who seem to have suffered under Licinius; Macrobius, a Cappadocian, at Tomis on the Black Sea, and Julian, a priest, in Galatia. It appears, however, that these two martyrs have been confused with those of Sept

17, Valerian, Macrinus (Macrobius) and Gordian (Julian).

Macull (St) Bp.   Apr 25
Otherwise Maughold, q.v.

Madalberta (St) V. OSB.   Sept 7
d. 706   Daughter of SS Vincent Madelgarus and Waldetrudis. She was educated by her aunt, St Aldegund, the foundress of Maubeuge, where she took the veil. About the year 697 she succeeded her sister, St Aldetrudis, as abbess.

Madeleine (*several*)
French form of Magdalen. See under Mary Magdalen.

Madelgisilus (French: Mauguille) (St) H. OSB.   May 30
d. c 655   An Irish monk, disciple and trusted confidant of St Fursey. After some years of monastic life at St Riquier, he retired, together with St Pulgan, to a solitude near Monstrelet, where he died.

Maden (Madern, Madron) (St) C.   May 17
d. c 545   A Breton hermit of Cornish descent, to whom many churches are dedicated, the most noted being that at St Madern's Well in Cornwall, the reputed site of his hermitage, and still a place of pilgrimage.

Madir (St) M.   March 3
Otherwise Hermiterius, q.v.

Madoes (Madianus) (St) C.   ? Jan 31
?   A saint who has left his name to a place in the Carse of Gowrie. Some identify him with St Modoc or Aidan of Ferns. Another tradition makes him a fellow missionary to Scotland with St Boniface Quiritinus or Curitan, who appears to have been sent from Rome to preach in N. Britain. It seems impossible to disentangle the facts from the legendary accretions.

Madrun (Materiana) (St) W.   Apr 9
5th cent.   A Welsh or Cornish saint to whom some Welsh churches are dedicated.

Maedhog (Aedhan, Mogue) (St) Ab.   Apr 11
6th cent.   An Irish abbot, whose chief monastery was at Clonmore. He was closely associated with SS Onchu and Finan.

Maedoc (Modoc, Aedan, Edan, Aidus) (St) Bp.   Jan 31
Otherwise Aidan, q.v.

Mael (Mahel) (St) C.   May 13
6th cent.   A disciple of St Cadfan with whom

The Magi, Jan 6

he came from Brittany into Wales. He became one of the solitaries of the isle of Bardsey.

Maelmuire (Marianus) (St) C.   July 3
d. *p.*1167 Maelmuire O'Gorman was an abbot of Knock (Louth), and is best known as a composer in Irish verse of an Irish menology.

Maelrhys (St) C.   Jan 1
6th cent. A saint of the isle of Bardsey, probably a Breton by birth, venerated in N. Wales.

Maelrubius (Maolrubha) (St) C.   Apr 21
d. *c*724 A member of St Comgall's community at Bangor, who migrated to Iona. He afterwards founded a church at Applecross on the N.W. coast of Scotland. Cult approved in 1898.

Maethlu (St) C.   Dec 22
Otherwise Amaethlu, q.v.

Mafalda (St) N. OSB. Cist.   May 2
1203–1252 Daughter of King Sancho II of Portugal. At the age of twelve she was married to King Henry I of Castile, but her marriage was declared null by the Holy See on account of consanguinity. She at once entered the Cistercian nunnery of Arouca in Portugal and there professed the Benedictine rule. Cult, as a saint, approved in 1793.

Magdalen (*several*)
See under Mary Magdalen.

Magdalveus (Madalveus, Mauvé) (St) Bp. OSB.   Oct 5
d. *c*776 Born at Verdun, he became a monk of St Vannes, and afterwards (*c*736) bishop of his native city.

Magenulpus (St) C.   Oct 5
Otherwise Meinuph, q.v.

Magi (Three Holy Kings): Balthasar, Caspar (Gaspar) and Melchior (SS)   Jan 6
1st cent. According to a very ancient, though not altogether constant tradition, the Wise Men from the East were three in number (Matt. 2). The idea, traced back to the sixth century, that they were kings, was almost certainly suggested by the passage in Psalm 72:10. Names were attributed to them as early as the eighth century. A magnificent medieval shrine in Cologne cathedral contains their reputed bones. In art they are shown as three kings of differing races and ages with gifts in their hands.

Magina (St) M.   Dec 3
See Claudius, Crispinus, etc.

Maginus (Catalan: Magí) (St) M.   Aug 25
d. *c*304 Born at Tarragona, in Spain, he

evangelized the people of the *Montes Brufagani* near his native city, and was finally beheaded under Diocletian.

Maglorius (St) Bp.   Oct 24
d. *c* 575   Maglorius, or Maelor, was born in S. Wales and educated under St Illtyd. He was a kinsman of St Samson, with whom he crossed over to Brittany, where they became abbots of two monasteries, St Samson of Dol and St Maglorius of Lammeur. St Samson became bishop of Dol and on his death he is said to have been succeeded by St Maglorius, who finally retired to the Channel Islands and built an abbey on Sark, where he died.

Magnericus (St) Bp.   July 25
d. 596   Of Frankish descent, he was the first of his race to be made bishop of Trier (*c* 566). He was an intimate friend of St Gregory of Tours and one of the most illustrious bishops of his time.

Magnoaldus (St) Ab.   Sept 6
Otherwise Magnus, q.v.

Magnobodus (Mainboeuf) (St) Bp.   Oct 16
d. *c* 670   A Frank of noble birth, appointed bishop of Angers at the demand of the people.

Magnus (St) M.   Jan 1
A martyr mentioned in the pre-1970 RM., of whom nothing is known.

Magnus (Mannus) (St) M.   Feb 4
See Aquilinus, Germinus, etc.

Magnus (St) M.   Feb 15
See Saturninus, Castulus, etc.

Magnus (St) M.   Apr 16
c 1076–1116   A native of the Orkneys, over which he was set as governor by the king of Norway, the then overlord of the islands. When his life was threatened by conspirators he escaped to the court of Scotland, where he gave himself up to a life of penance. In the end he was murdered by his cousin Hakon for political reasons, but has nevertheless been always venerated as a martyr. His relics are in Kirkwall cathedral. He is depicted as richly robed or in armour, carrying an axe or a club.

Magnus (St) M.   Aug 6
See Sixtus II and Comp.

Magnus of Anagni (St) Bp. M.   Aug 19
In the pre-1970 RM. he was described as a bishop martyred under Decius. Actually he seems to be a duplicate of St Andrew the Tribune, q.v. (Aug 19), surnamed by the

St Magnus, Apr 16

Greeks "the Megalomartyr" and listed in the matyrologies as *Andreas Tribunus Magnus Martyr*. Apparently a scribe put a comma after *Tribunus*, and thus made one martyr into two.

Magnus (St) Bp. OSB.   Aug 19
d. 660   Born at Avignon, he was appointed governor of the city. After his wife's death he joined the monks of Lérins, whither his son St Agricola had preceded him and where, in 656 he became bishop. His existence is doubtful, as he is first mentioned in a document of 1458 and his cult cannot be traced. There was, however, a bishop named Magnus at the council of Châlons-sur-Saône (630).

Magnus, Castus and Maximus (SS) MM.   Sept 4
? They probably belong to the group of seventeen martyrs (SS Rufinus, Silvanus, etc.) put to death at Ancyra in Galatia. Their names seem to have been separated from the remainder of the group whose entry occurs on the same day.

Magnus (Magnoaldus, Maginold, Mang, etc.) (St) Ab. OSB.   Sept 6

d. *c* 666   An alleged fellow-missionary with the Irish saints Columbanus and Gall: he became the abbot-founder of Füssen in Bavaria. Nothing is known for certain about him.

Magnus (St) Bp.   Oct 6

d. *c* 660   A Venetian born, who became bishop of Oderzo in the province of Treviso, on the Adriatic. In 638, owing to the incursions of the Lombards, he transferred his see to Citta Nuova, then called Heraclea in honour of the emperor Heraclius.

Magnus (St) Bp.   Nov 5

d. 525   Archbishop of Milan from *c* 520 to 525. Little further is known about him.

Maguil (St)   May 30

Otherwise Madelgisilus, q.v.

Maharsapor (St) M.   Oct 10

d. 421   A Persian who was martyred under Varanes V. After a three years' imprisonment he was thrown into a pit and left to die of starvation.

Maidoc (Madoc) (St) Bp.   Feb 28

There are several Welsh and Irish saints of this name: Aidnus, Aidan, Edan, Aldus, Edus, Eda, Maidoc, Maedoc, Modoc, Modog, Moedoc, Moeg, Mogue, Madog. The best known saints of this name are St Aidan of Ferns (Jan 31) and St Aidan of Lindisfarne (Aug 31). The St Maidoc assigned to Feb 28 may be the sixth century abbot-bishop after whom Llanmadog in Glamorganshire is called.

Maidoc (Mo-Mhaedog) (St) Ab.   March 23

5th cent.   An Irish abbot of Fiddown in Kilkenny.

Maildulf (St) Ab.   May 17

d. 673   An Irishman by birth who came to England and founded the great abbey of Malmesbury, where he had St Aldhelm among his disciples, and where he ended his days.

Maimbod (St) M.   Jan 23

d. *c* 880   An Irish missionary who was put to death by pagans while evangelizing the country people near Kaltenbrunn in Alsace, diocese of Besançon.

Mainard (Bl) Ab. OSB.   Dec 10

d. 1096   Abbot and founder of the monastery and Congregation of the Holy Cross at Sassovivo in the diocese of Foligno.

Maine (Mevenus, Mewan, Meen) (St) C.   June 21

d. 617   A Welsh or Cornish disciple of St Samson, whom he accompanied to Brittany. He founded there the monastery since known as Saint-Méon. He died at a great age.

Majolus (French: Maieul) (St) Ab. OSB.   May 11

c 906–994   Born at Avignon, he studied at Lyons and while still very young he was chosen archdeacon of Mâcon. He was offered the see of Besançon but he fled instead to Cluny and became a monk there. Shortly after, in 954, he was made abbot-coadjutor to St Aymard. In 965 he succeeded as the head of the Cluniac congregation, which under him grew and spread throughout W. Europe. He was the friend of emperors and popes and several times refused the papacy. He died at Souvigny.

Majoricus (St) M.   Dec 6

d. *c* 490   According to the pre-1970 RM. he was the son of St Dionysia, who encouraged him to suffer martyrdom and buried him in her own house. For the account given by Victor of Utica see Dionysia, Dativa, etc. The martyrdom took place in Africa under the Arian, Hunneric the Vandal.

Malachi (St) Prophet   Jan 14

c 450 B.C.   The last of the twelve minor prophets. The tradition is that he was a native of Sapha. "Malachi" means "my mesenger': it may not therefore be the actual name of the prophet.

Malachy O'More (St) Bp.   Nov 3

1094–1148   Maolmhaodhog ua Morgair was born at Armagh and ordained by St Cellach. He was successively vicar-general to St Cellach, abbot of Bangor, bishop of Connor and archbishop of Armagh (1132). He worked zealously to restore ecclesiastical discipline and succeeded in replacing once and for all the Celtic liturgy by the Roman. In 1138 he resigned the primatial see and made a pilgrimage to Rome, staying for a while at Clairvaux, then at the acme of its fame under St Bernard. He wished to remain a monk there, but this was not allowed by the pope. Instead he left at Clairvaux several young Irishmen who four years later were the pioneer monks of Mellifont abbey in Ireland. He made a second pilgrimage to Rome and on his way back died at Clairvaux in St Bernard's arms. He was formally canonized in 1190. The "prophecies of the popes" attributed to him were first found in Rome in 1590 — that is, over four centuries after his death.

Malard (St) Bp.   Jan 15
d. *p.*650   A bishop of Chartres who took part
in the council of Châlon-sur-Saône (650).

Malchus (St) M.   March 28
See Priscus, Malchus and Alexander.

Malchus (St) Bp. OSB.   Apr 10
d. 12th cent.   An Irishman who became a
monk of Winchester in England and was
ordained by St Anselm first bishop of Waterford. He was one of the preceptors of St
Malachy O'More. His life has been confused
with those of several among his contemporaries.

Malchus (St) H.   Oct 21
d. *c* 390   A Syrian monk at Chalcis, near
Antioch. After about twenty years of monastic
life he was kidnapped by the Bedouins, who
sold him for a slave. He was given an already
married woman to wife, but they lived as
brother and sister. After some seven years of
bondage they succeeded in escaping together
and Malchus returned to his monastery. St
Jerome knew him there and wrote his life.

Malcoldia (Bl) H. OSB.   March 15
d. *c* 1090   Benedictine nun and then a
recluse near the abbey church of St Anastasia,
at Asti.

Malo (Machutis, Maclou)
(St) Bp.   Nov 15
d. *c* 640   A Welshman who became a monk
under St Brendan and eventually migrated to
Brittany with a band of Welsh missionaries.
He settled at a place called Aleth, now St Malo
— of which he is recognized as the first bishop.
For a time he was banished and resided at
Saintes.

Malrubius (St) M.   Aug 27
d. *c* 1040   An anchorite in Merns (Kincardineshire) Scotland. He was martyred by
Norwegian invaders.

Mamas (Mammas,
Mamans) (St) M.   Aug 17
d. *c* 275   A shepherd of Caesarea in Cappadocia, martyred under Aurelian. He is greatly
venerated throughout the East. His *Acta* are
not reliable.

Mamelta (St) M.   Oct 17
d. *c* 344   Said to have been a heathen priest-
ess at Bethfarme in Persia who, on being
converted to Christ, was stoned and finally
drowned in a lake.

Mamertinus (St) Bp.   March 30
d. *c* 462   A convert of St Germanus, he

became a monk, and then abbot, of SS Cosmas
and Damian at Auxerre in France.

Mamertus (Mammertus)
(St) Bp.   May 11
d. 475   Archbishop of Vienne, 461–475. He
is best remembered as the originator of the
Rogation Days before the Ascension, which he
established in his diocese in consequence of
the many calamities which afflicted his people.

Mamilian (Maximilian)
(St) M.   March 12
?   A Roman martyr, of whom nothing definite
is known.

Mamillian (St) Bp.   Sept 15
d. 460   A bishop of Palermo in Sicily, said to
have been exiled to Tuscany by the Arian king
Genseric. His relics were eventually taken
back to Palermo.

Mamillus (St) M.   March 8
See Cyril, Rogatus, etc.

Mammea (St) M.   Aug 27
Otherwise   Mannea.   See   Marcellinus,
Mannea, etc.

Manaen (St)   May 24
1st cent.   Mentioned in the Acts of the
Apostles (13:1) as a courtier of King Herod
Antipas and as a prophet. He is supposed to
have died at Antioch in Syria.

Manakus (Manaccus) (St)
Ab.   Oct 14
6th cent.   A Welshman, abbot of Holyhead,
connected with St Cuby. He appears to have
died in Cornwall. Manaccan (Minster), near
Falmouth, is said to owe its name to him.

Mancius (St)   March 15
5th (or 6th?) cent.   Of Roman origin, he
appears to have been bought as a slave by
Jewish traders and taken to Evora in Portugal,
where he was martyred by his masters.

Mancius Araki (Bl) M.   July 8
d. 1626   A Japanese layman, brother of Bl
Matthew Araki. For giving shelter to the
missionaries he was imprisoned at Omura,
where he died of consumption. His body was
burnt at Nagasaki (July 12). Beatified in 1867.

Mancius of the Holy
Cross (Bl) M. OP.   July 29
d. 1629   An aged catechist, burnt alive at
Omura with Bl Louis Bertrán. Beatified in
1867.

Mancius of St Thomas
(Bl) M. OP.   Sept 12
d. 1622   A Japanese catechist imprisoned

and burnt alive with Bl Thomas Zumárraga and companions at Omura. Beatified in 1867.

Mancius Xizizoiemon
(Bl) M. Sept 25
d. 1630 A native of Japan and a tertiary of St Augustine, beheaded at Nagasaki. Beatified in 1867.

Mancus (St) May 31
See Winnow, Mancus and Myrbad.

Mandal (St) M. June 10
See Basilides, Tripos, etc.

Manehildis (Ménéhould)
(St) V. Oct 14
d. c 490 Born at Perthois, she was the youngest of seven sisters, all of whom are honoured as saints in different parts of Champagne. She is the patroness of Sainte-Ménéhould on the R. Aisne.

Manettus (Manetius, Manetto) (St) C. OSM. Feb 17
d. 1268 Benedict dell' Antella was a Florentine merchant who became one of the seven founders of the Servite order, q.v. From provincial of Tuscany he became general of the order. In 1246 he attended the council of Lyons, and at the request of St Louis introduced the order into France. He resigned his generalate to St Philip Benizi and retired to Monte Senario, where he died in the following year.

Manez (Mannes, Manes)
(Bl) C. OP. July 30
d. 1230 Manez de Guzmán, an elder brother of St Dominic, was born at Calaruega. He joined the original sixteen members of the order of Preachers in 1216 and later was prior of St James's in Paris, and the founder of a convent for nuns at Madrid. Cult approved in 1834.

Manirus (St) Bp. Dec 19
? One of the apostles of N. Scotland. His work seems chiefly to have been the promoting of good feeling and union among the newly converted Highlanders.

Mannea (St) M. Aug 27
See Marcellinus, Mannea, etc.

Mannonius (St) M. Apr 29
See Corfu, Martyrs of.

Mannus (St) M. Feb 4
Otherwise Magnus, q.v.

Mansuetus (St) Bp. Feb 19
d. c 690 A Roman by birth, he was appoint-ed to the see of Milan (c 672) and ruled it with vigour and wisdom. He wrote a treatise against the Monothelites.

Mansuetus (Mansuy)
(St) Bp. Sept 3
d. c 350 Bishop of Toul in France (c 338–350). His biography as it has come down to us is full of fictitious matter.

Mansuetus (St) M. Sept 6
See Donatian, Praesidius, etc.

Mansuetus (St) Bp. M. Nov 28
See Papinianus and Mansuetus.

Mansuetus, Severus, Appian, Donatus, Honorius and Comp.
(SS) MM. Dec 30
d. c 483 A group of ten martyrs who suffered at Alexandria in connexion with the troubles raised by the Monophysites.

Manuel (several)
The Spanish, Portuguese and Catalan form of Emmanuel, q.v.

Manuel Domingo y Sol
(Bl) C. Jan 25
Born in 1836 at Tortosa, Tarragona, he was ordained in 1860. He started the first Catholic Spanish newspaper directed at youth, called El Congregante, and built a sports and theatre complex to facilitate his apostolate with young men. He also founded three Congregations of Sisters, the Pontifical Spanish College in Rome (1896) and the Society of Diocesan Priests to foster vocations. He died in 1909 and was beatified in 1987.

Manuel, Sabel and Ismael (SS) MM. June 17
d. 362 Persian magnates sent to negotiate for peace with Julian the Apostate at Chalcedon. The tradition is that Julian, finding that they were Christians, had them beheaded. Theodosius the Great dedicated a church in their honour near Byzantium.

Maolruain (St) Ab. July 7
d. 792 Abbot-founder of the monastery of Tallaght in Ireland and compiler of the martyrology named after that place.

Mappalicus and Comp.
(SS) MM. Apr 17
d. 250 African martyrs who suffered at Carthage under Decius. They are highly praised by St Cyprian.

Maprilis (St) M. Aug 22
See Martial, Saturninus, etc.

Marana and Cyra (SS) MM.   Aug 3
5th cent. Two maidens who embraced the
eremitical life near Beroea in Syria. It is
recorded of them that they observed continuous silence throughout the year except on
Whit Sunday.

Marcella (St) W.   Jan 31
325–410 She belonged to the nobility of
Rome, and after the early death of her husband turned her house into a sort of "retreat"
for ladies of the aristocracy. St Jerome was her
guest for three years and under his direction
she devoted herself to the study of the Bible, to
prayer and to alms-deeds. When Alaric sacked
Rome, Marcella was cruelly scourged for
concealing, as the Goths thought, her wealth,
which she had already distributed to the poor.
She died shortly after from the effects of this
treatment.

Marcella (St) M.   June 28
See Plutarch, Serenus, etc.

Marcellian (St) M.   June 18
See Mark and Marcellian.

Marcellian (St) M.   Aug 9
See Secundian, Marcellian and Verian.

Marcellina (St) V.   July 17
c 330–398 Born in Rome, the elder sister of
St Ambrose of Milan and of St Satyrus. She
received the veil of a consecrated virgin from
the hands of Pope Liberius on Christmas Day,
353. She outlived both her brothers. Her
remains are enshrined at Milan.

Marcellinus (St) M.   Jan 2
See Argeus, Narcissus and Marcellinus.

Marcellinus of Ancona (St)   Jan 9
d. c 566 A native of Ancona, who was made
bishop there c 550. He is mentioned by St
Gregory the Great.

Marcellinus (St) M.   Apr 6
d. 413 Marcellinus was the imperial representative in Africa at the time of the Donatist
disturbances. He and his brother, the judge
Agrarius, endeavoured to enforce the deci-
sions of a conference at Carthage against those
heretics, but the Donatists resorted to false
accusation and the two brothers were put to
death without even the formality of a trial. St
Augustine was an intimate friend of Marcellinus, to whom the holy Doctor dedicated his
masterpiece "De civitate Dei".

**Marcellinus, Vincent
and Domninus (SS)**   Apr 20
d. c 374 African missionaries who crossed

over to Gaul and preached in Dauphiné. St
Marcellinus was ordained first bishop of
Embrun by St Eusebius of Vercelli. The relics
of the three saints are venerated at Digne, in
the Alps of Savoy.

Marcellinus (St) Pope.
                                    formerly Apr 26
Almost nothing definite is known about his
life, most of which was spent while the church
was free from persecution. It seems that
Marcellinus complied with the order of the
emperor Diocletian to worship pagan gods in
303; several prominent members of his clergy
also did so. Consequently his name was left
out of the list of popes compiled by Damasus I.
Later apologists over-compensated and invented the story of his remorse and subsequent martyrdom. No contemporary account
of such an event exists. His cult was suppressed in 1969.

**Marcellinus and Peter
(SS)** MM.   GC. June 2
d. 304 Marcellinus was a priest and Peter
probably an exorcist, both belonging to the
Roman clergy. Although their extant *Acta* are
unreliable, these two martyrs were certainly
greatly venerated by the Romans, since their
names occur in the first eucharistic prayer and
Constantine built a basilica over their tombs.

Marcellinus (St) M.   June 5
See Florentius, Julian, etc.

**Marcellinus (or
Marcellianus) (St)** M.   June 18
See Mark and Marcellian.

**Marcellinus (Marchelm,
Marculf) (St)** C.   July 14
d. c 762 An Anglo-Saxon who followed St
Willibrord to Holland. Together with St
Lebuin he preached the gospel to the people of
Over-Yssel. In 738 he accompanied St Boni-
face to Rome. He died at Oldensee (Olden-
zeel), but his remains were transferred to
Deventer.

**Marcellinus (or Marcellus),
Mannea, John, Serapion,
Peter and Comp. (SS)** MM.   Aug 27
d. c 303 According to their authentic *Acta*,
Marcellinus, a tribune, with his wife Mannea,
his three sons, John, Serapion and Peter, a
bishop, three clergy, eight laymen and another
woman — the entire Christian congregation of
a small place now said to be Oxyrinchus, in
Egypt, were taken to Thmuis and beheaded.
Marcellinus is often known as Marcellus.

Marcellinus of Ravenna
(St) Bp.   Oct 5
3rd cent. The second or third bishop of
Ravenna, said to have occupied that see in the
second half of the third century.

Marcellinus, Claudius, Cyrinus (Quirinus) and Antoninus (SS) MM.   Oct 25
d. 304   According to a story now shown to be
false, Claudius, Cyrinus and Antoninus are
named on this day as having been beheaded
together with Pope St Marcellinus. See April
26.

Marcellus (St) Pope   Jan 16
d. 309   St Marcellus was pope for one year
only (308–309). He seems to have been exiled
by Maxentius, but not to have died a martyr.
The story of his having been forced to work as
a slave in the stables seems to be legendary.
Cult confined to local calendars in 1969.

Marcellus (St) M.   Feb 19
Se Publius, Julian, etc.

Marcellus (St) Bp.   Apr 9
d. 474   A native of Avignon, he was educated by his own brother St Petronius, bishop
of Die (not of Saint-Dié), whom he succeeded
in the see, being ordained by St Mamertus,
bishop of Vienne. He suffered much from the
Arians, and died after a long episcopate.

Marcellus and Anastasius
(SS) MM.   June 29
d. 274   Roman missionaries sent into Gaul
to preach the gospel. They were put to death in
the neighbourhood of Bourges. Marcellus was
beheaded and Anastasius scourged to death.

Marcellus (St) Bp. M.   Aug 14
d. 389   A native of Cyprus, who from being a
conscientious civil magistrate was elected to
the see of Apamea in Syria. While supervising
the destructon of a pagan shrine, at Aulona, in
accordance with the edict of Theodosius the
Great, he was attacked and murdered by the
mob.

Marcellus (St) M.   Aug 27
Otherwise Marcellinus, q.v.

Marcellus (St) M.   Sept 4
d. c 178   A priest of Lyons who escaped
from prison and, being again arrested, was
buried up to the waist on the banks of the
Saône and left to die. It is said that he survived
three days.

Marcellus (St) Bp. M.   Sept 4
? A bishop of Trier (or of Tongres) listed in
the pre-1970 RM. His name seems to have
been invented in the tenth century.

Marcellus (St) Mk. OSB.   Sept 27
d. c 869 (?)   An Irishman (or Scot) by birth,
he became a monk at St Gall in Switzerland
and is best known as the tutor of Bl Notker
Balbulus.

Marcellus and Apuleius
(SS) MM.   Oct 7
? Martyrs of Capua, of whom no particulars
are extant. Venerated only in local calendars
since 1969.

Marcellus (St) M.   Oct 30
d. 298   A centurion of the Roman army
stationed at Tangier. During a festival in
honour of the birthday of the emperor he
refused to join in the celebrations, threw away
his arms and insignia and declared himself a
Christian. The notary, who refused to write
the official report of the case and who was in
consequence martyred, was St Cassian (v. Dec
3). The *Acta* of St Marcellus are quite reliable.

Marcellus (St) Bp.   Nov 1
d. c 430   A bishop of Paris, who was buried
in the old Christian cemetery outside the walls
of the city, where now is the suburb of Saint-
Marceau.

Marcellus (St) M.   Nov 16
See Elpidius, Marcellus, etc.

Marcellus (St) M.   Nov 26
d. 349   A priest of Nicomedia, in Asia
Minor, who during the reign of the emperor
Constantius was seized by the Arians and
killed by being hurled from a high rock.

Marcellus (St) M.   Dec 2
See Eusebius, Marcellus, etc.

Marcellus (St) Ab.   Dec 29
d. c 485   Surnamed "Akimetes" the "non-
rester". A native of Apamea in Syria, who
joined the monks called *Akimetes*, because they
recited the divine office in relays throughout
the day and night. He became the third abbot
of their chief abbey at Constantinople, and
under his rule the *Akimetes* grew in number
and influence. He was present at the council of
Chalcedon.

Marcellus (St) M.   Dec 30
See Sabinus, Exuperantius, etc.

Marcelo Spinola y Maestre
(Bl) Bp.   Jan 19
1835–1906   Born at San Fernando, Seville,
son of the Marquis de Spinola. He was
ordained in 1864, and care for the sick, poor
and friendless was to be the chief hallmark of
his life and apostolate. In 1880 he became

auxiliary bishop of Seville; bishop of Coria in 1844 (where he founded the Conceptionist Sisters of the Divine Heart, blending the active and contemplative charismata); bishop of Malaga in 1886, where he cared for education, young labourers etc.; and archbishop of Seville in 1896. In 1906 he was made a cardinal and died a few months later.

Marchelm (St)   July 14
Otherwise Marcellinus, q.v.

Marcia (St) M.   March 3
See Felix, Luciolus, etc.

Marcia (St) M.   June 5
See Zenais, Cyria, etc.

Marcia (St) M.   July 2
See Ariston, Crescentian, etc.

Marcian (St) M.   Jan 4
See Aquilinus, Geminus, etc.

Marcian (St) C.   Jan 10
d. *c* 471   A native of Constantinople, though connected with a Roman family. He was ordained and appointed treasurer of the church of St Sophia. In this capacity he superintended the building of several churches, notably that of the Anastasis. He was wrongly suspected of Novatianism and had to suffer much on this account.

Marcian (St) Bp.   March 6
d. 120   Said to have been a disciple of St Barnabas and first bishop of Tortona in Piedmont, where he is alleged to have been martyred under Hadrian, after an episcopate of forty-five years. The theory has been advanced that St Marcian of Tortona is to be identified with St Marcian of Ravenna.

Marcian (St) M.   March 26
See Peter, Marcian, etc.

Marcian (St) M.   Apr 17
See Fortunatus and Marcian.

Marcian of Auxerre (St)
Mk.   Apr 20
d. *c* 470   A native of Bourges, of humble birth, who was admitted as a lay-brother into the abbey of SS Cosmas and Damian at Auxerre. There he discharged menial duties and had charge of the abbey's cattle.

Marcian of Ravenna (St) Bp.   May 22
d. *c* 127   The fourth bishop of Ravenna, where he is known as San Mariano. He ruled the diocese from *c* 112 to *c* 127.

**Marcian, Nicanor,
Apollonius and Comp.
(SS) MM.**   June 5
d. *c* 304   According to the pre-1970 RM.

they were a group of Egyptian martyrs who suffered under Diocletian. Their *Acta* are, however, quite unreliable. It is more probable that Marcian and Nicander (not Nicanor) were soldiers in the Roman army, who suffered either in Bulgaria or Rumania.

Marcian of Syracuse (St)
Bp. M.   June 14
d. *c* 255   Said to have been "the first bishop of the West" having been, according to the Sicilian legend, sent to Syracuse by St Peter himself. It is more likely that Marcian was sent to Sicily by a pope of the third century. He is said to have been thrown from a tower by the Jews.

Marcian (St) M.   June 17
See Nicander and Marcian.

Marcian (St) Bp.   June 30
d. *c* 757   Bishop of Pampeluna, in Spanish Navarre. He signed the decrees of the sixth council of Toledo in 737.

Marcian (St) M.   July 11
d. 243   A youth martyred at Iconium in Lycaonia. He is specially notable for his courage in confessing Christ.

Marcian (St) M.   Aug 9
See Julian, Marcian, and Comp.

Marcian of Saignon (St) Ab.   Aug 25
d. 485   Born at Saignon (Vaucluse) he became the abbot-founder of St Eusebius at Apt, diocese of Avignon.

Marcian (St) M.   Sept 16
See Abundius, Abundantius, etc.

Marcian (St) M.   Oct 4
See Mark, Marcian, and Comp.

Marcian (St) M.   Oct 25
See Martyrius and Marcian.

Marcian (St) H.   Nov 2
d. 387   He left the emperor's court and gave up a brilliant military career in order to lead the solitary life in the desert of Chalcis. He had several illustrious disciples.

Marciana (St) VM.   Jan 9
d. *c* 303   A maiden of Mauritania. Accused of having shattered a statue of the goddess Diana she was thrown to the wild beasts in the amphitheatre, where she was gored to death by a bull. The Mozarabic office has a special hymn in her honour.

Marciana (St) M.   May 24
See Susanna, Marciana, etc.

Marciana (St) VM.   July 12
d. *c* 303   The pre-1970 RM. assigned this

virgin-martyr to Toledo in Spain, but she is almost certainly identical with St Marciana of Mauretania (v. Jan 9).

Marcionilla (St) M. Jan 9
See Julian, Basilissa, etc.

Marcius (Mark, Martin) (St) H. OSB. Oct 24
d. *c* 679   An Italian hermit at Montecassino, mentioned by St Gregory the Great in the life of St Benedict. The Cassinese tradition adds that Marcius (or Martin) became a monk at the abbey and then retired into a cave on Mount Massicus (Mondragone) where he died.

Marcolino of Forli (Bl) C. OP. Jan 24
1317–1397 (Jan 2)   Marcolino Amanni was born at Forli and became a Dominican in his early years. He was a model religious, but it was only after his death that his brethren realized his heroic sanctity. Cult confirmed in 1750.

Marculf (St) Ab. May 1
d. 558   The abbot-founder of a monastery of hermit-monks, on the Egyptian model, at Nanteuil. His relics were in 898 enshrined at Corbigny, diocese of Laon, and thither the kings of France resorted after their coronation. After touching the relics of the saint they healed those afflicted with "the king's evil" (scrofula).

Mard (St) Bp. June 8
Otherwise Medard, q.v.

Mardarius (St) M. Dec 13
See Eustratius, Auxentius, etc.

Mardonius, Musonius, Eugene and Metellus (SS) MM. Jan 24
d. ?   Four martyrs burnt at the stake somewhere in Asia Minor.

Mardonius (St) M. Dec 23
See Migdonius and Mardonius.

Mareas (St) Bp. M. Apr 22
d. 342   A Persian bishop martyred under King Shapur II. Together with him there suffered twenty-one other bishops, nearly two hundred and fifty clergymen, many monks and nuns, and a great number of lay people. The church of Persia was brought to the verge of extinction.

Margaret (*several*)
Note. The Latin, Spanish, Portuguese and Catalan form of this name is Margarita; the Italian Margherita and the French Marguer-ite. There are numerous diminutives of the same name in all languages.

Margaret of Ravenna (Bl) V. Jan 23
d. 1505   Born at Russi, near Ravenna, Margaret was from her youth almost blind and suffered much from want of sympathy on the part of those around her. Nevertheless, in course of time she gained many friends by her patience and humility. With the help of a priest she formed a religious association of persons living in the world, but this did not survive her. Her cult has never been officially confirmed.

Margaret of Hungary (St) V. OP. Jan 18
1252–1270   Daughter of Bela IV, king of Hungary. She founded a convent for Dominican nuns on an island in the Danube near Budapest and herself joined the community. Her life was most penitential. Canonized in 1943.

Margaret of England (St) M. OSB. Cist. Feb 3
d. 1192   Born in Hungary, probably of an English mother and related to St Thomas of Canterbury. She lost her mother in the holy land, made a pilgrimage to our Lady of Montserrat in Spanish Catalonia and joined the Cistercian nuns at Sauve-Benite, in the diocese of Puy-en-Velay. She was greatly venerated in that district.

Margaret of Cortona (St) Tert. OFM. Feb 22
1247–1297   Born at Laviano in Tuscany, a farmer's daughter, she was the mistress of a young nobleman for nine years. In his sudden death she saw a judgment from heaven and, publicly confessing her sins in the church of Cortona, she placed herself under the direction of the Franciscan friars. She became a tertiary herself and the foundress of a convent and a hospital where she and her nuns tended the sick. She suffered from calumny and obloquy, but God favoured her with supernatural charismata. Canonized in 1728.

Margaret of Città-di-Castello (Bl) V. Tert. OP. Apr 13
d. 1320   Born at Meldola, in the diocese of St Angelo in Vado, Italy, she was left a foundling at Città-di-Castello and was brought up by several families in the city, being usually occupied in looking after children. She died at the age of thirty-three, after passing her life in poverty, in blindness and in complete innocence of soul. Cult approved in 1609.

Margaret of Amelia (Bl)
V. OSB.   Apr 20
d. 1666   A Benedictine abbess of the nunnery of St Catherine at Amelia, possessed of
mystical gifts.

Margaret Pole (Bl) M.   May 28
d. 1541   Margaret Plantagenet was a niece
of Edward IV and Richard III. She married Sir
Reginald Pole, to whom she bore five children.
Left a widow she was created Countess of
Salisbury in her own right and appointed
governess to Princess Mary, daughter of
Henry VIII. When her son Cardinal Pole
opposed the royal supremacy and refused to
return to England, Henry revenged himself on
the cardinal's mother, lodging her in the
Tower of London for two years. Finally she
was condemned for high treason by Bill of
Attainder and beheaded on Tower Hill at the
age of seventy. Beatified in 1886.

Margaret of Vau-le-Duc
(Bl) V. OSB. Cist.   June 4
d. 1277   Daughter of Duke Henry II of
Brabant, she became a Cistercian nun and
second abbess of the convent of Vau-le-Duc in
Brabant, which had been founded by her
father. She has always been venerated as a
beata by the Cistercians.

Margaret or Marina (St)
VM.   formerly July 20
Said to have been a maiden of Antioch in
Pisidia martyred under Diocletian. This much
is probably true; everything else related in her
Acta is pure legend, including, of course, the
story of the fierce dragon which swallowed her
before she was beheaded. Nevertheless, she is
one of the most popular of maiden-martyr
saints and her cult is very ancient. In the East
she is known as Marina. In art she is shown as a
maiden trampling or standing on a dragon, or
issuing from its mouth, or piercing a dragon
with a cross-tipped spear. Cult suppressed in
1969.

Margaret of Faenza (Bl
or St) Abs. OSB. Vall.   Aug 26
d. 1330   A native of Faenza, she became a
Vallumbrosan nun under St Humilitas at the
convent of St John the Evangelist, near Florence, and eventually its second abbess.

Margaret the Barefooted
(St) W.   Aug 27
d. 1395   A poor girl of Sanseverino, near
Ancona, in Italy, who in her fifteenth year was
married to a man who ill-treated her. She bore
it all with patience for many years.

Margaret Ward (St) M.   Aug 30
d. 1588   A gentlewoman of Congleton,

Cheshire, hanged at Tyburn for rescuing a
priest. Beatified in 1929. Canonized 1970 as
one of the Forty Martyrs of England and
Wales, q.v.

Margaret of Louvain (Bl) V.   Sept 2
1207–1225   Surnamed in Belgium "Mar-
guerite la Fière". Born at Louvain, she worked
as a maid-servant at an inn in the same city.
She was murdered by robbers whom she had
seen kill and rob her employers. The Cistercian Caesarius of Heisterbach states that she
was about to become a Cistercian nun. Cult
approved in 1905.

Margaret Mary Alacoque
(St) V.   GC. Oct 16
1647–1690   Born at L'Hautecourt in Burgundy. In 1671 she joined the Order of the
Visitation at Paray-le-Monial. From a revelation made to her by our Lord in 1675 she was
led to enter upon her work, the spreading of
public and liturgical devotion to the Sacred
Heart. After violent opposition, met with
chiefly in Jansenistic milieus, the devotion
spread and became for a time extremely
popular in the church. St Margaret was canonized in 1920. She is depicted as clad in the
habit of her order, holding a flaming heart, or
kneeling before Our Lord, who exposes His
heart to her.

Margaret Clitherow (St) M.   Oct 21
1556–1586   Margaret Middleton was born
at York, married John Clitherow and shortly
after became a Catholic. For this she was
imprisoned for two years, and on her release
she began to shelter priests in her house. She
was again arrested and, refusing to plead, was
condemned to the horrible penalty of being
pressed to death. The sentence was carried
out at York. Beatified in 1929. Canonized in
1970 as one of the Forty Martyrs of England
and Wales (q.v.). She is depicted as an Elizabethan housewife, kneeling or standing on a
heavy wooden door.

Margaret Leroux (Bl) V.   Oct 23
d. 1794   An Ursuline nun of Valenciennes,
who formed part of the group of martyrs
guillotined on Oct 23. She was born at
Cambrai in 1747 and was professed in 1769.
Her name in religion was Ann-Joseph, or
Mother Josephine. See Ursuline Nuns.

Margaret of Lorraine
(Bl) W. Poor Clare   Nov 6
1463–1521   A daughter of Duke Frederick
of Lorraine, she married in 1488 René, duke

St Margaret or Marina, formerly July 20

of Alençon, who died in 1492 leaving her a widow with three children. She devoted herself exclusively to their upbringing and to works of charity. When they were of age, she founded a convent of Poor Clares at Argentan, and entered there in 1519. Cult confirmed in 1921.

Margaret of Scotland
(St) W.   GC. Nov 16

c 1045–1093 Granddaughter of King Edmund Ironside of England and of St Stephen of Hungary. In 1070 she married King Malcolm III of Scotland. She used her influence as queen for the good of religion

St Margaret Clitherow, Oct 21

and for the promotion of justice, ever having a special thought for the poor. She had six sons and two daughters, one of whom was Matilda (Maud), wife of Henry I. Among the foundations she made was the Benedictine abbey of Dunfermline, where she was buried. Canonized in 1251. In art she is shown robed as a queen with gifts for the poor.

Margaret of Savoy (Bl)
W. Tert. OP.   Nov 23
d. 1464   Born at Pinerolo, daughter of Duke Amadeo II of Savoy. In 1403 she married Theodore Paleologus, marquis of Montferrat, after whose death (1418) and influenced by St Vincent Ferrer, she joined the Dominican tertiaries. In 1426 she founded a house at Alba in Liguria, of which she became the first Dominican prioress. Cult confirmed in 1669.

Margaret of Hohenfels (Bl) V. OSB.   Dec 26
d. p.1150   She belonged to the family of the Hohenfels and became a Benedictine nun at Bingen under St Hildegard, by whom she was appointed prioress.

Margaret Colonna (Bl) V.
Poor Clare   Dec 30
d. 1284   Daughter of Prince Odo Colonna of Palestrina. She turned her family castle on the mountainside above Palestrina into a convent of Poor Clares, for whom her brother, Cardinal James Colonna, adapted a mitigated version of the Franciscan rule. Cult confirmed in 1847.

Marguerite Bourjeoys (St) V. Foundress   Jan 19
1620–1700   Born at Troyes, she went to Canada as tutor to the children of the French garrison of Montreal. In 1688 she founded the congregation of the Sisters of Notre Dame de Montreal, dedicated to the apostolate of Canada. She obtained from Louis XIV the royal patent to teach throughout Canada. Her congregation subsequently spread to the United States, receiving papal approval in 1889. Beatified in 1950. Canonized 1982.

Mari (St) Bp.   Aug 5
See Addai and Mari.

Maria Pilar (Mary) Martinez, Maria (Mary) Angeles Valtierra, Teresa Garcia y Garcia (BB) MM. OCD.   July 24
These Carmelite sisters were martyred by communist fanatics at Guadalajara in 1936 during the civil war. Sr Maria Pilar was born in

Tarazona, Zaragoza, and at fifty-eight years of age had been a nun for thirty-eight years. Sr Teresa was born at Mochales, Guadalajara, and was twenty-seven, having been a nun for nine years. Sr Maria Angeles, born at Getate, Madrid, was thirty-one and had been a nun for seven years. All three were beatified on 29 March 1987 by Pope John Paul II.

Maria Fortunata Viti (Bl)
V. OSB.   Nov 20
In her youth she was illiterate and had to bring up her large family after her mother's untimely death. At the age of twenty-four in 1851 entered the abbey of Sta. Maria dei Franconi as a lay sister. Her love of prayer, cheerfulness and unstinting work made her a paragon of monastic virtues. She died in 1922 and was beatified in 1967.

Mariana of Jesus (Bl) V.
O. Merc.   Apr 27
1565–1624 Surnamed "the Lily of Madrid". Mariana Navarra de Guevara was born in Madrid and joined the community of Discalced Mercedarians in the same city, where she distinguished herself by her life of penance. Beatified by Pius VI.

Mariana de Paredes (St) V.   May 26
1618–1645 Known as the "Lily of Quito". Her family name was Mariana de Paredes y Flores, but she chose to call herself Mariana of Jesus. She was born at Quito, in Ecuador, and was of Spanish descent. She tried her vocation as a religious, but failed. After this, she lived as a solitary in the house of her brother-in-law. During the earthquakes at Quito in 1645 she offered herself as a victim for the city and died shortly after. Canonized in 1950.

Marianus Scotus (Bl) Ab.
OSB.   Feb 9
d. 1088 His Irish name, Muirdach Mac-Robartaigh, was latinized as Marianus. He was born in Donegal. In 1067, while travelling with some companions on a pilgrimage to Rome, he was induced to become a Benedictine at Michelsberg, near Bamberg, whence he migrated to Upper Minster at Regensburg. In 1078 he founded and became the abbot of the abbey of St Peter, also at Regensburg, thus originating the congregation of Scottish monasteries in S. Germany. Throughout his life Bl Marianus occupied his free time in copying manuscripts.

Marianus (St) Mk.   Apr 20
Otherwise Marcian of Auxerre, q.v.

Marianus, James and
Comp. (SS) MM.   Apr 30
d. 259 Martyrs of Lambesa, an ancient town in Numidia (Algeria). Marianus was a reader and James a deacon. Their *Acta* are touching and authentic. The true day of their martyrdom was May 6.

Marianus (St) H.   Aug 19
d. c 515 A solitary in the forest of Entreaigues, near Evaux, in Berry, France. His life was written by St Gregory of Tours.

Marianus (St) M.   Oct 17
See Victor, Alexander and Marianus.

Marianus (St) M.   Dec 1
See Diodorus, Marianus, and Comp.

Marianus Scotus (Bl) H.
OSB.   Dec 22
d. 1086 Born in Ireland, his real name was Moelbrigte, i.e., servant of Brigid. After becoming a monk he migrated to Cologne (1056), then to Fulda, where for a time he lived as a recluse, and finally (1069) to Mainz. He wrote a *Chronicle of the World*.

Marie-Eugénie de Jésus
(Bl) V. Foundress   March 10
1817–1898 Born at Metz, Eugenie Milleret de Brou felt God's call during a course of sermons by Lacordaire in 1836. She founded a teaching institute adapted to contemporary needs, but with monastic observances. It became the Congregation of the Assumption, approved in 1888. She died at Antevil and was beatified in 1975.

Marie Louise Ducret
(Bl) M.   Oct 23
One of the Ursuline Nuns, q.v.

Marina (*several*)
Note. Marina is the Latin form of the Greek name Pelagia, a fact which has caused a few duplicates in our martyrologies.

Marina (St) VM.   June 18 (and July 17)
? In the ancient martyrologies this saint is variously named Maria, Marina, or even Marinus. Moreover, she is simply called *virgin*, not martyr. Some identify her with St Margaret (July 20); others with the Marina who lived in a monastery of men dressed as a boy, i.e., a duplicate of the Greek St Pelagia (Oct 8). Her life served as a model for the legends of SS Euphrosyne, Maria, Theodora, etc. The pre-1970 RM. made her a martyr at Alexandria.

Marina of Spoleto (Bl) V.
OSA.   June 18
d. c 1300 Marina Vallarina was an Augustinian nun of Spoleto in Umbria. Her cult at Spoleto seems to have died out.

Marina (St) VM.   July 18
? The pre-1970 RM. states that she was a
martyr of Orense in Spanish Galicia. All
records concerning her are lost. The name was
introduced into the Roman Martyrology by
Baronius (second revision).

Marinus (Amarinus) (St)
M. OSB.   Jan 25
See Amarinus.

Marinus (St) M.   Jan 29
Otherwise Maurus. See Papias and Maurus.

Marinus and Asterius
(SS) MM.   March 3
d. 262   Marinus was a Roman soldier stationed at Caesarea in Palestine who, when on
the point of being promoted to the rank of
centurion, was denounced as a Christian by a
jealous rival and forthwith martyred. Asterius,
or Astyrius, a senator, buried the body and it
seems, although it is not certain, that he too
died a martyr.

Marinus, Vimius and
Zimius (SS) CC. OSB.   June 12
d. *p.*1100   Surnamed the *"Tres Sancti*
Exules", the "Three Holy Exiles". They were
Benedictine monks of the Scots abbey of St
James at Regensburg, who, *c* 1100, became
hermits at Griesstetten.

Marinus, Theodotus and
Sedopha (SS) MM.   July 5
? Martyrs who suffered at Tomi on the Black
Sea.

Marinus (St) M.   July 10
See Januarius, Marinus, etc.

Marinus (St) M.   Aug 8
d. *c* 305   An aged man, martyred at Anazarbus in Cilicia under Diocletian.

Marinus (St) Ab. Bp. OSB.   Aug 19
c 800   A Benedictine abbot-bishop of the
monastery of St Peter at Besalu in Spanish
Catalonia.

Marinus (St) H.   Sept 4
4th cent.   He is said to have been born on an
island off the coast of Dalmatia and to have
been by profession a stonemason; to have been
ordained a deacon by Gaudentius, bishop of
Rimini; and finally to have died a hermit where
now stands the tiny Republic of San Marino,
which is called after him.

Marinus (St) M. OSB.   Nov 24
d. 731   Born in Italy, he became a Benedictine at Maurienne in Savoy, and afterwards a
hermit near the monastery of Chandor, where
he was put to death by the Saracens.

Marinus (Bl) Ab. OSB.   Dec 15
d. 1170   A Benedictine monk of La Cava in
S. Italy, where he held the office of treasurer
before he was elected abbot in 1146. He
received the abbatial blessing at Rome from
Pope Eugene III. He was a close friend both of
several popes and of the kings of Sicily, and he
acted as mediator between the two powers in
1156. Cult confirmed in 1928.

Marinus (St) M.   Dec 26
d. 283   He is described as a Roman, the son
of a senator, who was beheaded under Numerian, after having been miraculously delivered
from torture chambers, wild beasts, fire, water,
etc. His *Acta* are probably a pious romance.

Marius (Maris), Martha,
Audifax and Abachum
(SS) MM.   formerly Jan 19
d. *c* 270   The following legend survives.
Marius, a Persian nobleman, with his wife
Martha and their two sons, Audifax and
Abachum, journeyed to Rome to venerate the
tombs of the apostles. While in the holy city
they busied themselves in burying the bodies
of those who were then being martyred in the
persecution of Claudius II. They too were
arrested, the three men beheaded and St
Martha drowned. All that is known of them in
fact are their names and place and date of
burial, the cemetery Ad Nymphas, in Rome.
Cult suppressed in 1969.

Marius (St)   Jan 27
Otherwise Maurus, q.v.

Mark dei Marconi (Bl) C.   Feb 24
1480–1510   Born of a poor family at Milliar-
ino, near Mantua, he joined the Hieronymites
of Bl Peter of Pisa in the monastery of St
Matthew of Mantua, where he spent his life.
Cult approved in 1906.

Mark Barkworth (Bl) M.
OSB.   Feb 27
d. 1601   Bl Mark Barkworth (*alias* Lambert)
was born in Lincolnshire and educated at
Oxford. After his conversion he studied for the
priesthood at Rome and Valladolid and was
received into the Benedictine order at the
abbey of Our Lady of Hirache, near Estella, in
Spanish Navarre. He was the first to die at
Tyburn in the Benedictine habit after the
suppression of the monasteries.

Mark (St) M.   March 13
See Horres, etc.

Mark (St) M.   March 19
See Quintus, Quintilla, etc.

Mark of Montegallo (Bl)
C. OFM. March 20

1426–1497 Born at Montegallo, diocese of Ascoli Piceno, he became a physician. Though happily married, by mutual consent both he and his wife joined the Franciscans. Bl Mark was ordained and travelled the length and breadth of Italy preaching and establishing charitable pawnshops for the poor, known in Italy as *Monti di Pietá*.

Mark and Timothy (SS)
MM. March 24

d. *c* 150 Two Roman martyrs of post-apostolic times, mentioned by Pope St Pius I in a letter to the bishop of Vienne in Gaul.

Mark of Arethusa (St) M.
Bp. March 29

d. *c* 362 Bishop of Arethusa on Mt Lebanon. In 351 he was present at the synod of Sirmium where he produced a creed for which he was unjustly accused of Arianism by Baronius, who excluded his name from the RM. He has since been vindicated by the Bollandists. St Mark died a martyr under Julian the Apostate.

Mark Fantucci (Bl) C. OFM. Apr 10
1405–1479 Born at Bologna, he first studied law and in 1430 became a Friar Minor. He held several offices in the order and preached throughout Italy, Istria and Dalmatia, visiting also the friars in Austria, Poland, Russia and the Levant. He died at Piacenza. Cult approved in 1868.

Mark (St) Evangelist GC. Apr 25
d. *c* 75 He is generally thought to have been the young man who ran away when our Lord was arrested (Mark 14:51–52) and the "John whose other name was Mark" of Acts 12:25. He accompanied SS Paul and Barnabas on their first missionary journey. Afterwards he followed St Peter to Rome where, in the words of the pre-1970 RM., he was "the disciple and interpreter of St Peter", whose preaching he set down in writing in the gospel which bears his name. St Peter calls him "my son Mark" (1 Pet 5:13). According to tradition he afterwards went to Alexandria where he established the church and died a martyr. His body was in the ninth century translated to Venice and is enshrined in the magnificent cathedral dedicated to him. His main emblem is a winged lion; he is often shown writing or holding his gospel; he may have a halter around his neck.

Mark of Galilee (St) Bp. M. Apr 28
d. 92 Said to have been a Galilean by descent and the first missionary bishop and

St Mark, Apr 25

martyr in the province of the Marsi (Abruzzi) in Italy.

Mark of Lucera (St) Bp. June 14
d. *c* 328 A bishop locally venerated in S. Italy.

Mark and Marcellian
(SS) MM. June 18

d. *c* 287 Roman martyrs, twin brothers and deacons in legend, who suffered at Rome under Maximian Herculeus. Their basilica in the catacombs of St Balbina was rediscovered in 1902. Cult confined to local calendars since 1969.

Mark, Mucian, an unnamed boy, and Paul
(SS) MM.   July 3
? The entry in the pre-1970 RM. reads as follows: "The holy martyrs Mark and Mucian who were slain with the sword for Christ's sake. When a little boy called upon them with a loud voice that they should not sacrifice to idols, he was ordered to be whipped, and as he then confessed Christ more loudly, he was slain too, together with one Paul who was exhorting the martyrs."

Mark Caldeira (Bl) M. SJ.   July 15
d. 1570 A native of Feira, diocese of Oporto, Portugal, and a Jesuit novice. He was martyred with Bl Ignatius de Azevedo, q.v.

Mark Xineiemon (Bl) M.   Aug 19
d. 1622 A Japanese merchant on the ship of Bl Joachim Firaima (q.v.). He was beheaded at Nagasaki. Beatified in 1867.

Mark (St) M.   Aug 31
See Robustian and Mark.

Mark (St) M.   Sept 1
See Priscus, Castrensis, etc.

Mark, Stephen, SJ. and Melchior, SJ. (BB) MM.   Sept 7
d. 1619 Bl Mark Crisin (Körösy) was a Croat and a canon, Bl Stephen Pongracz a Hungarian Jesuit and Bl Melchior Grondech a Czech Jesuit. The three were most brutally massacred by the Calvinist soldiers at Körösi in Hungary. Beatified in 1905.

Mark of Modena (Bl) C. OP.   Sept 23
d. 1498 Born at Modena he joined the Friars Preachers and was a very successful preacher in N. and Central Italy. Cult approved in 1857.

Mark Criado (Bl) M. OS. Trin.   Sept 25
1522–1569 Born at Andujar, in Andalusia, in 1536 he joined the Trinitarians. He was tortured and slain at Almeria by the Moors. Cult approved by Leo XIII.

Mark (St) Bp.   Sept 27
Otherwise John Mark, q.v.

Mark, Alphius, Alexander and Comp. (SS) MM.   Sept 28
d. c 303 The pre-1970 RM. said: "At Antioch in Pisidia, the martyrs Mark, a shepherd, Alphius, Alexander and Zosimus, his brothers, Nicon, Neon, Heliodorus, and thirty soldiers, who through the miracles of blessed Mark believed in Christ, and were crowned with martyrdom in divers manners and places."

Mark, Marcian and Comp. (SS) MM.   Oct 4
d. 304 Egptian martyrs under Diocletian. Mark and Marcian were brothers. The rest are described as "victims of all ages and both sexes" and their number as "innumerable". They seem, however, to be duplicates of other groups.

Mark (St) Pope   Oct 7
d. 336 A Roman by birth, who was chosen pope in 336 and died within the year. Cult confined to local calendars since 1969.

Mark (St) Bp. M.   Oct 22
d. c 156 The first bishop of Jerusalem not of Jewish extraction. He is said to have ruled that see for twenty years and to have died a martyr: both statements are mere conjectures.

Mark (St)   Oct 24
Otherwise Marcius, q.v.

Mark (St) M.   Oct 25
See Theodosius, Lucius, etc.

Mark (Bl) Ab. OSB.   Nov 13
d. c 1280 A Benedictine abbot of Sant' Angelo di Scala, of the congregation of Montevergine.

Mark (St) M.   Nov 16
See Rufinus, Mark, etc.

Mark and Stephen (SS) MM.   Nov 22
d. c 305 Mark, with another martyr named Stephen, suffered at Antioch in Pisidia under Galerius.

Mark (St) M.   Dec 15
See Faustinus, Lucius, etc.

Marnock (Marnanus, Marnan, Marnoc) (St) Bp.   March 1
d. c 625 An Irish monk under St Columba at Iona and afterwards a missionary bishop, who died at Annandale and was much venerated in the neighbourhood of the Scottish border. He has given his name to Kilmarnock in Scotland. His feast is celebrated again on Oct 25.

Maro (St) Ab.   Feb 14
d. c 435 A Syrian hermit who lived on the bank of the R. Orontes between Homs and Apamea. He was greatly revered by St John Chrysostom and by Theodoret. The monastery of Beit-Marun, built around his shrine,

gave its name to the body of Syrian Catholics called Maronites.

Maro, Eutyches and Victorinus (SS) MM. Apr 15

d. *c* 99   According to the *Gesta Nerei et Achillei* they belonged to the entourage of St Flavia Domitilla, whom they accompanied in her exile to the island of Ponza. Eventually they returned to Rome and suffered martyrdom under Trajan. The pre-1970 RM. mentions Victorinus again on Sept 5 as a bishop, but little credence can be given to the legend of these martyrs.

Marolus (St) Bp. Apr 23

d. 423   A Syrian by origin, he was made bishop of Milan in 408. The Christian poet Ennodius wrote a poem in his honour.

Marotas (St) M. March 27

See Zanitas, Lazarus, etc.

Maroveus (St) Ab. OSB. Oct 22

d. *c* 650   Monk of Bobbio. Abbot-founder of the monastery of Precipiano, near Tortona.

Marquard (St) Bp. M. OSB. Feb 2

d. 880   A monk at New-Corbey in Saxony, he ruled the see of Hildesheim from 874 to 880 and fell in battle against the Norsemen at Ebsdorf. (See Bruno and Comp. MM. Feb 2.)

Martana (St) M. Dec 2

See Eusebius, Marcellus, etc.

Martha (St) M. Jan 19

See Marius, Martha, etc.

Martha (St) VM. Feb 23

d. 251   A Spanish maiden beheaded at Astorga under Decius. Her relics are enshrined in the old Benedictine abbey of Ribas de Sil and at Ters, diocese of Astorga.

Martha (St) V. GC. July 29

d. *c* 80   Sister of St Lazarus and of St Mary of Bethany (often identified in the West with St Mary Magdalen). She was the hostess of our Lord in their house at Bethany (Luke 10:38, John 11:2) who was "anxious and troubled about many things". For this reason she has become patron saint of housewives. The story of her subsequent journey to S. Gaul merits no credence. As depicted, dressed as a housewife, she often bears a distaff or any other emblem of housework, such as a bunch of keys.

Martha Wang (Bl) M. July 29

d. 1861   A native woman of Tonkin who carried letters from the imprisoned seminarians BB Joseph Tshang and Paul Tcheng to their bishop. She was arrested and beheaded with them at Tsingai. Beatified in 1909.

Martha, Saula and Comp. (SS) VV. MM. Oct 20

? The entry in the pre-1970 RM. read: "At Cologne the passion of the holy virgins Martha and Saula with many others." They are now usually assigned to the mythical cycle of St Ursula and her 11,000 virgins (Oct 21).

Martia (St) M. June 21

See Rufinus and Martia.

Martial (St) M. Apr 16

See Saragossa, Martyrs of.

Martial of Limoges, Bp. Alpinian and Austriclinian (SS) June 30

d. *c* 250   First bishop of Limoges, the reputed apostle of the Limousin and, according to St Gregory of Tours, one of the seven missionary bishops sent from Rome to preach the gospel in Gaul. His memory is still held in great veneration in the Limousin. Other legends connected with the saint are medieval forgeries. Alpinian and Austriclinian were priests who collaborated with him.

Martial (St) M. July 10

See Seven Brothers.

Martial, Saturninus, Epictetus, Maprilis, Felix and Comp. (SS) MM. Aug 22

d. *c* 300 ?   The names occur in the *Passio of St Aurea* (q.v.); otherwise unidentifiable.

Martial, Laurence and Comp. (SS) MM. Sept 28

? A group of twenty-two African martyrs who suffered in the province now called Algeria.

Martial (St) M. Oct 13

See Faustus, Januarius and Martial.

Martin of León (St) C. OSA. Jan 12

d. 1203   Born at León, in Old Castile, he joined the Augustinian canons regular, first at San Marcelo and then at St Isidore in his native city. He was a prolific ascetical writer.

Martin Manuel (St) M. Jan 31

d. 1156   Born at Auranca, near Coimbra, in Portugal. As archpriest of Soure he was captured by the Saracens and died in prison at Cordoba of ill-treatment at their hands.

Martin Loynaz of the Ascension (St) M. OFM. Feb 6

d. 1597   Born at Vergara, near Pampeluna, in Spanish Navarre, he studied at Alcalá, and became a Franciscan in 1586. He did missionary work in Mexico, Manila, and finally Japan. He was crucified at Nagasaki. Canonized in 1862. See Paul Miki and Comps.

Martin (Bl) M.   Feb 18
1815–1862   A native Chinese catechist and
host of Bl John Peter Néel. He was beheaded
at Kuy-tsheu. Beatified in 1909.

Martin of Braga (St) Bp.   March 20
520–580   Born in Pannonia, he became a
monk in Palestine and later travelled in Spanish Galicia where he preached to the pagan
Suevi. He was bishop first of Mondoñedo
(*Dumium*) and then of Braga, and introduced
monasticism through N.W. Spain. Several of
his highly interesting writings are still extant.

Martin I (St) Pope. M.   GC. Apr 13
d. 655   Born in Tuscany, he was elected
pope in 649. At once he convened a council
and condemned the Monothelites, of whom
the reigning emperor Constans II was one.
The imperial wrath now fell upon the pontiff,
who in 653 was deported by force to Naxos, in
the Aegean Sea. The following year he was
condemned to death at a mock trial at Constantinople, and finally taken as prisoner to the
Chersonese where he died of starvation. In art
he is vested as a pope; he has various emblems;
he holds money, or has geese around him (in
mistake for St Martin of Tours?).

Martin of Tongres (St) Bp.   June 21
d. *c* 350   He is said to have been the seventh
bishop of Tongres and is venerated as the
apostle of the Hesbaye district in Brabant.

Martin of Vienne (St) Bp.   July 1
d. *p.*132   Alleged third bishop of Vienne,
sent thither by Pope St Alexander.

Martin of Trier (St) Bp. M.   July 19
d. *c* 210   Listed in the episcopal records of
Trier as the tenth bishop of that see. There is
no conclusive evidence for his martyrdom.

**Martin Gómez (Bl) M.
Tert. OFM.**   Aug 17
d. 1627   A native Japanese, of Portuguese
descent, beheaded at Nagasaki. Beatified in
1867.

**Martin de Hinojosa (St)
Bp. OSB. Cist.**   Sept 3
d. 1213   A member of the illustrious Castilian family of the Hinojosas. He became a
Cistercian and eventually founded the abbey
of Huerta, by the R. Jalon, near Soria (1164),
of which he was the first abbot. In 1185 he
became bishop of Sigüenza, but resigned in
1192 to live again as a monk.

Martin (Bl) OSB. Cam.   Sept 13
d. 1259   Abbot and prior-general of Camaldoli (1248–1259). He is best known as the
compiler of the new constitutions of the order.

Martin (St) Ab. OSB.   Sept 28
See Willigod and Martin.

Martin Cid (St) Ab. OSB. Cist.   Oct 8
d. 1152   Born at Zamora, in Spain, he
became the abbot-founder of the Cistercian
abbey of Val-Paraiso, for which St Bernard
himself supplied the pioneer community. He
is still greatly venerated in the diocese of
Zamora and by the Cistercians.

Martin (St) C.   Oct 24
Otherwise Marcius, q.v.

Martin of Vertou (St) Ab.   Oct 24
d. 601   Abbot-founder of Vertou abbey,
near Nantes, of Saint-Jouin-de-Marnes and
of other monastic establishments. The particulars of his life, as they have come down to
us, are rather confused. He is venerated in the
province of Poitou.

Martin Porres (St) C. OP.   GC. Nov 3
1569–1639   Born at Lima, in Peru, son of a
Spanish knight of Alcantara and of a negro or
Indian mother from Panama. Martin became a
barber and studied surgery before entering the
Dominican friary of Lima as a lay-brother.
Here he nursed the sick and soon became
friends with stray animals, the destitute, ill-
treated slaves and all other unfortunates in the
city. When he was dying the Spanish Viceroy,
the Count of Chinchón, came to kneel by his
bed and ask for his blessing. Canonized in
1962.

**Martin Tinh and Martin
Tho (SS) MM.**   Nov 8
d. 1840   Martin Tinh was a native of Vietnam and a priest, martyred at the age of
eighty with his companion Martin Tho, a
tax-gatherer, also a native of Vietnam. Canonized in 1988.

Martin of Tours (St) Bp.   GC. Nov 11
c 316–397   Born in Upper Pannonia (now
Hungary), the son of a Roman officer. He was
educated at Pavia and at the age of fifteen
enrolled in the imperial cavalry. The episode
of his sharing his cloak with a poor beggar and
the subsequent heavenly vision which led to
his baptism has become famous. He left the
army and placed himself in the hands of St
Hilary, bishop of Poitiers, living for ten years
as a recluse and founding a community of
monk-hermits at Ligugé. In 372 he was made
bishop of Tours, but he accepted the office
with great reluctance and, establishing another
great monastic centre at Marmoutier, he continued to live there privately as a monk, while
publicly he devoted himself with burning zeal
to the discharge of his episcopal duties. He
opposed Arianism and Priscillianism, but be-

St Martin of Tours, Nov 11

friended the Priscillianists when they were persecuted and condemned the practice of invoking the civil power to punish heretics. He was the greatest of the pioneers of Western monachism before St Benedict, who had a particualr veneration for St Martin. His shrine at Tours was a great resort of pilgrims. In art, he is shown as a soldier, often on horseback, dividing his cloak with a beggar; as a bishop giving alms; or in armour, with episcopal symbols too.

Martin of Arades (St) C.
OSB.   Nov 26
d. 726 A monk of Corbie, in France, chaplain and confessor to Charles Martel.

Martin of Saujon (St) Ab.   Dec 7
d. *c* 400 A disciple of St Martin of Tours who, in his turn, became the abbot-founder of the monastery of Saujon, near Saintes.

Martina (St) VM.   Jan 30
d. 228 A Roman martyr under Alexander Severus. She has a basilica dedicated in her honour at the Roman forum, and there the sarcophagus containing her remains was found in 1634. Her "Passion" is entirely apocryphal and is borrowed from those of St Prisca and St Tatiana. Cult confined to her basilica in Rome since 1969.

**Martinian (Maternian)
(St)** Bp.   Jan 2
d. *c* 435 Bishop of Milan (423–*c* 435). He took part in the council of Ephesus and wrote against Nestorianism.

Martinian (St) H.   Feb 13
d. *c* 400 A hermit who lived near Caesarea in Palestine. Zoe, a woman of evil repute, tempted him to become her paramour; instead she was converted and persuaded to become a nun at Bethlehem. The story is questionable.

Martinian (St) M.   July 2
See Processus and Martinian.

**Martinian, Saturian and
Comp. (SS)** MM.   Oct 16
d. 458 Four Afro-Roman brothers, reduced to slavery in the house of an Arian Vandal in Mauretania. They were encouraged to suffer for Christ by Maxima, their fellow-slave. The four brothers were martyred under Genseric by being dragged to death by horses. Maxima died in peace, in a convent.

Martius (St) C.   Apr 13
d. *c* 530 A native of Auvergne, he lived an austere and primitive life on the mountainside, but later built a monastery for his disciples.

Martyrius (Martory) (St) M.   Jan 23
6th cent.   A solitary in the Abruzzi (Valeria),
whom St Gregory the Great extols in his
Dialogues (*Dial.* I, II).

Martyrius (St) M.   May 29
See Sisinius, Martyrius and Alexander.

**Martyrius and Marcian
(SS)** MM.   Oct 25
d. 351   Martyrius, a subdeacon, and Marcian, a chorister, were martyred at Constantinople under the Arian patriarch Macedonius
on a trumped-up charge of sedition.

Martyrs of Laval (BB) MM.   June 19
Victims of the anti-clerical feeling in France
during the disturbances resulting from the
Revolution of 1789, the Bl John Baptist
Turpin du Cormier and his companions,
clergy and religious, were maltreated and put
to death violently in 1794. Beatified by Pius
XII in 1955.

Maruthas (St) Bp.   Dec 4
d. *c* 415   One of the most prominent person-
alities of the Syrian church. He was bishop of
Maiferkat in Mesopotamia and devoted all his
energy to the reorganization of the church in
Persia and E. Syria, as well as to the preservation of the memory of the numerous Syrian
and Persian martyrs under Shapur. He collected their *Passiones*, and wrote liturgical hymns
in their honour. St John Chrysostom highly
valued his friendship.

Mary Christina (Bl)   Jan 31
1812–1836   Born at Cagliari in Sardinia,
daughter of Victor Emmanuel, king of Savoy
and of Mary Teresa, niece of the emperor
Joseph II. In 1832 she married Ferdinand II,
king of the two Sicilies, to whom she bore a son
before her death at the age of twenty-three.
Beatified in 1872.

Mary of Providence (Bl)
V. Foundress   Feb 7
1825–1871   Born at Lille, she founded the
congregation of the Helpers of the Holy Souls,
aided by the advice of the Curé d'Ars, to make
atonement on behalf of the souls in purgatory
by works of charity. Her congregation is active
in mission territories. Her boundless patience
under various trials, especially her sufferings
from incurable cancer, demonstrated more
clearly the great person she was. Beatified in
1957.

**Mary (Mileda, Mlada)
(Bl)** Abs. OSB.   Feb 8
d. 994   Daughter of Boleslas I, duke of
Bohemia. She became the abbess-foundress

of the nunnery of St George, at Prague (967).
She has always been venerated as a *beata*.

Mary (St) VM.   Feb 11
See Saturninus, Dativus and Comp.

Mary Mamala (Bl) W.
Poor Clare   March 31
d. 1453   A member of the Spanish family of
the dukes of Medina-Sidonia. She married
Henry de Guzmán, and in her widowhood
joined the Poor Clares at Seville.

Mary of Egypt (St) H.   Apr 2
? 5th cent.   An Egyptian by birth who
became an actress and then lived as a courtesan at Alexandria. After her conversion, which
took place it is said, at the Holy Sepulchre at
Jerusalem, she fled into the desert beyond the
Jordan, where she spent the remainder of her
life doing penance and where she was found
dead by two disciples of St Cyriacus. The story
is doubtful, and its elaborate additions may be
ignored. See also St Zosimus, H. She is
depicted naked, but covered with her long
hair, holding loaves, or with the lion that dug
her grave, or kneeling before a skull.

Mary of Clopas (St)   Apr 9
1st cent.   The wife of Clopas or Alpheus
(John 19:25) and the mother of the apostle St
James the Less. She was one of the "three
Marys" who followed our Lord from Galilee
and who stood at the foot of the cross on
Calvary. The legends which have grown up
around her name deserve no credence. She is
usually depicted carrying a pot of ointment or a
jar of spices.

**Mary Margaret Dufrost
de Lajemmerais d'Youville
(Bl)** W. Foundress   Apr 11
1701–1771   Born at Varennes, Canada, she
experienced the joys and hardships of a poor
backwoods home, the early loss of her father,
eleven years of married life and the untimely
death of her husband and four of her six
children. These trials did not break her spirit
but rather helped to develop a life of union
with God and of service to her neighbours,
especially those visited by suffering. She
founded the Sisters of Charity to serve the sick
and the needy. Beatified in 1959.

**Mary Bernard Soubirous
(St)** V.   Apr 16
Otherwise Bernadette Soubirous, q.v.

**Mary of the Incarnation
(Bl)** W. OC.   Apr 18
d. 1618   Barbara Avrillot, who in her young
days was styled "the beautiful Acarie", was

married to Peter Acarie, a French government official. After his death in 1613, Barbara joined the Carmelites as a lay-sister and took the new name of Mary-of-the-Incarnation. She introduced into France the Discalced Carmelites of St Teresa. Beatified in 1791.

Mary-Gabrielle Sagheddu (Bl) V. OCSO.   Apr 22

Born at Dorgali, Italy, in 1914, she entered the Trappestine monastery at Grottaferrata (now Viterbo), making profession in 1937. She offered her life in the cause of church unity, supported by the other nuns, who were influenced by the Abbé Couturier. Painful illnesses and severe spiritual trials were her lot. She died on April 23 1939, and was beatified by Pope John Paul II at St Pauls-outside-the-Walls on Jan 25 1983.

Mary Sainte-Euphrasie Pelletier (St) V.   Apr 24

Otherwise Euphrasia Pelletier, q.v.

Mary-Ann of Jesus   Apr 27

Otherwise Mariana of Jesus, q.v.

Mary Dominic Mazzarello (St) V. Co-Foundress   May 14

1837–1881   She was born at Mornese in the diocese of Acqui, N. Italy, of humble parents. After a devout childhood in which she worked in the fields, she joined the Pious Union of Mary Immaculate. First one and then other companions joined her in a life of regular piety, and so insensibly her institute, the Daughters of Mary Auxiliatrix came into being. Under the direction of St John Bosco it received full canonical formation and status, and undertook for girls what the Salesians were doing for boys. St Mary Dominic was obliged to become first superior general in 1874. She died in 1881 after a long illness, and was canonized in 1951.

Mary-Magdalen of Canossa (St) V.
Foundress   May 14

1774–1835   She was a daughter of the Marquis of Canossa. Her father died while she was a child and her mother married again, abandoning her children. She managed her late father's household till she was thirty-three. Then, after a brief period of serving hospitals in Venice in 1808, she founded the first house of her institute, the Daughters of Charity, at Verona, its scope being the education of poor girls, the service of hospitals and the teaching of the catechism in parishes. When the foundress died in 1835 she left several houses in N. Italy; since then many houses have been established in all parts of the world. Beatified in 1941. Canonized in 1988.

Mary-Magdalen Albrizzi (Bl) V. OSA.   May 15

d. 1465   Born at Como, she entered a nunnery at Brunate, near her native city, of which she became prioress. While prioress she affiliated the convent to the Augustinian friars. She was remarkable for her promotion of frequent communion among her nuns. Cult approved in 1907.

Mary Magdalen Sophie Barat (St) V. Foundress   May 25

1779–1865   Madeleine Sophie Barat was a native of Joigny, in Burgundy, and opened the first convent of her new congregation of nuns, called the Society of the Sacred Heart of Jesus, at Amiens in 1801. She was a lady of great charm and enterprise, and before her death she had established houses throughout Europe, America and Africa — one hundred and five foundations in all, during her lifetime. Canonized in 1925.

Mary-Magdalen de'Pazzi (St) V. OC.   GC. May 25

1566–1607 (May 25)   A native of Florence, where she became a Discalced Carmelite at the age of sixteen. Throughout her life she was subject to remarkable mystical experiences and was tried with many kinds of suffering — spiritual and physical. She filled various conventual offices with remarkable ability. Canonized in 1669.

Mary-Ann de Paredes (St) V.   May 26

Otherwise Mariana de Paredes, q.v.

Mary-Bartholomew Bagnesi (Bl)   May 27

Otherwise Bartholomaea Bagnesi, q.v.

Mary (St) M. OSB. Cist.   June 1

See Bernard, Mary, etc.

Mary-Magdalen of Carpi (Bl) V. OSM.   June 10

d. 1546   A Servite lay-sister at Carpi, collector of alms for her community.

Mary of Oignies (Bl) W.   June 23

d. 1213   Born at Nivelles in Belgium, she married early in life but persuaded her husband not to consummate the marriage. They then turned their house into a leper hospital, where they tended the sick. Finally Mary became a recluse in a cell near the church of Oignies, where she was favoured with supernatural charismata.

Mary-Magdalen Fontaine
(Bl) M.   June 26
1723–1794 Born at Etrépagny (Eure), she
entered the noviciate of the Sisters of Charity
of St Vincent de Paul in 1748, and from 1767
was the superior of the house of that institute
at Arras. She was guillotined at Cambrai
during the French Revolution, together with
three religious of her community. Beatified in
1920.

Mary (St) W.   June 29
1st cent. Mentioned in the Acts of the
Apostles (12:12), as the mother of John, surnamed Mark (q.v.). From the text it appears
that Mary's house was a place of assembly
for the apostles and the faithful generally.
Subsequent traditions about her are conflicting.

Mary Goretti (St) VM.   GC. July 6
1890–1902 Born at Corinaldo, near
Ancona, Italy, she showed marked signs of
youthful holiness although illiterate. She was
pursued by a youth inflamed with lustful
desires for her. Finally, when all were
working in the fields he came upon her
alone, but she died in defence of her chastity
under the repeated blows of his knife rather
than give way to him. Her canonization in
1950 was attended by her mother, family,
murderer and an enormous crowd. Some
thirty to forty miracles worked by her are on
record.

Mary Rose (Bl) M. OSB.   July 6
1741–1794 Her baptismal name was
Susanne-Agatha de Loye. She was born
at Sérignan, near Orange, and in 1762
became a Benedictine in the nunnery of
Caderousse. At the outbreak of the French
Revolution she was expelled from the convent, and in May 1794 she was arrested and
guillotined, the first of a band of thirty-one
martyrs put to death at Orange. Beatified in
1925.

Mary-Magdalen Postel
(St) V. Foundress   July 16
1756–1846 Born at Barfleur. Early in life
she opened a school for girls, but soon the
French Revolution stopped her work.
During that trying period she obtained
permission to administer the blessed
sacrament to the dying. In 1805 she reopened her school at Cherbourg and this
proved to be the origin of the Sisterhood of
Christian Schools which, after severe trials,
spread throughout the world. Canonized in
1925.

St Mary Magdalen, July 22

Mary St-Henry (Marguerite-Eléonore de Justamond) and Mary-Magdalen du St-Sacrement (Magdalen-Françoise de Justamond) (BB)

MM. OSB. Cist.   July 16

d. 1794 Sisters by blood and Cistercian nuns at the convent of St Catherine at Avignon. They were guillotined at Orange during the French Revolution. Beatified in 1925.

Mary Magdalen Lidoin (In religion: Mère Thérèse de St Augustine, Prioress), Mary Ann Piedcourt (Soeur de Jésus Crucifié), Mary Hanisset (Soeur Thérèse du Coeur de Marie), Mary Trésel (Soeur Thérèse de St Ignace), Mary Dufour (Soeur Sainte Marthe) (BB) MM. OC.   AC. July 17

d. 1794 They belong to the community of Carmelite Nuns of Compiègne, q.v., guillotined at Paris during the French Revolution. The first four were solemnly professed choir sisters; Bl Mary Dufour a lay-sister.

Mary Magdalen (St)   GC. July 22

1st cent. Mary Magdalen is mentioned in the four gospels as one of the most devoted followers of our Lord. Chiefly under the influence of St Gregory the Great's writings, the Western liturgies have often identified her with the unnamed sinner (Luke 7:37, Luke 8:2) and Mary the sister of Martha and Lazarus (John 1). This identification is challenged by Eastern tradition and by the writings of the Eastern fathers and has now also been repudiated both by scholarship and the new Roman Calendar. The story connecting St Mary Magdalen with France is a legend. In art she is shown with long unbound hair and carrying a pot of ointment.

Mary-Magdalen Martinengo (Bl)

V. OFM. Cap.   July 27

1687–1737 A native of Brescia, where she entered the convent of Capuchin nuns. She filled the post of novice-mistress and prioress with marked success. Beatified in 1900.

Mary the Consoler (St)   Aug 1

8th cent. Said to have been the sister of St Anno, bishop of Verona.

Mary the Blessed Virgin, Mother of God

(St)   GC. Aug 15 and as below

1st cent. The Virgin Mother of God is venerated with a special cult, called by St Thomas Aquinas, *hyperdoulia*, as the highest of God's creatures. The invocation of Mary pervades all Catholic and orthodox devotion, public and private. The principal events of the life of our Lady are the object of special liturgical feasts celebrated by the universal church and listed as follows: (1) Dec 8: her immaculate conception, viz., the singular privilege by which God preserved her from all stain of original sin at the first moment of her conception. (2) Sept 8: her birthday as a Jewish child and a lineal descendant of the royal family of David. (3) Nov 21: her presentation, i.e., the offering of her to God for the first time by her parents in the temple at Jerusalem. (4) March 25: the annunciation, when Gabriel the archangel was sent by God to declare unto her that she was chosen to be the mother of God, or Theotokos. (5) May 31: the visitation, viz. Mary's visit to her cousin St Elizabeth, the mother of St John the Baptist. (6) Aug 15: Mary's assumption soul and body into heaven. This last, and her solemnity on Jan 1, reflect the emphasis in the new Roman Calendar (1969) on her role in the incarnation and in redemption, stressing along with the constitution on the church of the second Vatican Council, her special dependence on her son and her role as a model of the church. Her cult is now seen in purely scriptural and patristic terms, and in recent times has developed along these lines in churches formerly hostile to it. Moreover, each nation and almost every diocese of the Catholic church venerates our Lady under some special title, thus literally fulfilling her prophecy: "All generations shall call me blessed" (Luke 1:48). She has countless iconographic attributes, relating to her various feasts and aspects. She is most frequently shown carrying her Son in the iconography of both the East and the West.

Mary-Magdalen Kiota

(Bl) M.   Aug 16

d. 1620 Wife of Bl Simon Kiota. She was crucified with her husband at Cocura, Japan. Beatified in 1867. (She is not to be identified with Bl Mary Magdalen Kiota of Nagasaki, q.v.)

Mary-Magdalen Kiota

(Bl) M. Tert. OP.   Aug 17

d. 1627 A Japanese princess, kinswoman to the king of Bungo, and a Dominican tertiary. She was burnt at Nagasaki for having sheltered the missionaries. Beatified in 1867.

Mary Vaz (Bl) M.   Aug 17

d. 1627 A Japanese woman, wife of Bl Caspar Vaz. She was a Franciscan tertiary. Beheaded at Nagasaki. Beatified in 1867.

Virgin Mary, Aug 15

Mary Guengoro (Bl) M.   Aug 18
d. 1620 A Japanese, wife of Bl Thomas
Guengoro. She was crucified at Cocura with
her husband and her son James. Beatified in
1867.

Mary de Matthias (Bl) V.
Foundress   Aug 20
1805–1866 She was born at Vallecorsa, S.
Italy. St Caspar del Bufalo chose her at the age
of seventeen to found a congregation for
women corresponding to that which he was
founding for teaching boys. In 1834 she
opened her first school at Acuto, and this
became the cradle of the new congregation,
the Adorers of the Most Precious Blood. By
the time of her death, her sisters were conducting about seventy schools. Beatified in 1950.

Mary-Michaela (St)
Foundress   Aug 24
1809–1865 Michaela Dermaisières, vis-
countess of Sorbalán, was born at Madrid. She
was educated by the Ursulines and afterwards
lived with her family at Guadalajara, where she
began her active life of charity. In 1848 she
founded the Institute of Handmaids of the
Blessed Sacrament and of Charity which was
approved in 1859. She died at Valencia from
the cholera, which she contracted in ministering to its victims. In Spain she is surnamed *La
Loca del S.mo Sacramento* — the mad-woman
of the blessed sacrament. Canonized in 1934.

Mary de la Cabeza (Bl)   Sept 9
d. *c* 1175 Born at Torrejon, she married St
Isidore the Farmer, q.v., after whose death she
retired to Caraquiz. Cult approved in 1697.

**Mary Tanaura, Mary
Tanaca, and Mary
Magdalen Sanga (BB) MM.**   Sept 10
d. 1622 Japanese women beheaded at
Nagasaki, the last two with their respective
husbands, BB Paul Tanaca and Antony Sanga.
Beatified in 1867.

**Mary Tocuan and Mary
Xoun (BB) MM.**   Sept 10
d. 1619 Japanese women martyred with
their husbands.

**Mary Victoria Fornaristrata
(Bl)** Foundress   Sept 12
1562–1617 Mary Victoria Fornari was born
at Genoa and married Angelo Strata, by whom
she had six children. In 1589 he died. After
Mary Victoria had educated and provided for
her children, she founded the congregation of
nuns called the Blue Annonciades, of whom
she was the first superior. Beatified in 1828.

Mary de Cerevellon (St)
V. O. Merc.   Sept 19
d. 1290 Also called, in her native Catalan,
Maria de Soćos, "Mary of help". She was born
at Barcelona and became one of the first nuns
of the Mercedarian order (our Lady of
Ransom) and the superioress of the convent at
Barcelona. Cult confirmed in 1690.

**Mary-Teresa Couderc
(St)** V. Foundress   Sept 26
1805–1885 At the age of twenty, under the
guidance of Father Terma, she founded the
Society of Our Lady of the Cenacle at La
Louvesc, France. The intention was to attract
pilgrims to the tomb of St John Francis Regis
there, and induce them to spend time in
recollection. The institute developed as one of
retreat houses for women and rapidly spread
throughout Europe and to America. Although
obliged in 1835 to resign the administration of
her institute through ill-health, she lived to the
age of eighty. Beatified in 1951, canonized in
1970.

Mary Frances (St) V.   Oct 6
1715–1791 Anna Maria Gallo was born at
Naples of a middle-class family. Her father
was brutal and avaricious and was especially
harsh towards her when she refused to marry
the man he had chosen for her. In 1731 she
became a Franciscan tertiary with the new
name of Mary Frances of the Sacred Wounds.
She continued to live at home until she got a
position as housekeeper to a priest, a post
which she filled for thirty-eight years. God
favoured her with extraordinary graces,
including mystical marriage.

**Mary-Desolata Torres
Acosta (St)** V. Foundress   Oct 11
1826–1887 This truly great woman was
born in a poor quarter of Madrid. She tried
unsuccessfuly to become a Dominican nun. In
1848 she responded to the call of a priest to
found an institute for the care of the sick in
their own homes. A subsequent priest-
director of the young institute (Handmaids of
Mary) removed her and appointed another
superior in her place, with the result that the
institute nearly perished. But after an examination by the bishop she was re-appointed and
lived to found forty-six houses. She died in
Madrid in 1887. Beatified in 1950. Canonized
in 1970.

**Mary-Magdalen dei
Panatieri (Bl)** V. OP.   Oct 13
1443–1503 Born at Trino, in the diocese of
Vercelli, in Piedmont, she modelled herself on
St Catherine of Siena, and like her became a
Dominican tertiary in her own home, devoted

to charitable works among her neighbours. Cult approved by Leo XIII.

Mary Magdalen Dejardin (in religion, Soeur Marie-Augustine) and Mary Louise Vanot (Soeur Natalie) (BB) MM.   Oct 17

d. 1794   Two Ursuline sisters belonging to the community of Valenciennes, guillotined in that town during the French Revolution together with nine others of the same community. Beatified in 1920. See also Ursuline Nuns.

Mary-Teresa de Soubiran
(Bl) V. Foundress   Oct 20

1834–1889   Born of noble parents in Castelnaudary, Carcassonne, she wished to become a Carmelite nun, but under the guidance of her uncle, a canon, she founded a Béguinage in 1855 and took the name of Mary-Teresa. In order to attain her apostolic ends more fully she transformed the Béguinage into the Institute of Mary Auxiliatrix, with the approval of the bishop. But through the machinations of one of her subjects she was driven from her own congregation, overwhelmed with calumnies and deprived of her property. Thus in 1868 she sought refuge in the Institute of Our Lady of Charity in which she was allowed to take vows and in which she persevered till her death. Only then did the truth come out. She enjoyed mystical gifts of a high order. Beatified in 1946.

Mary Salome (St)   Oct 22

1st cent.   One of the "three Marys". She was the wife of Zebedee, the mother of St James the Great and St John the Evangelist, and one of the holy women who ministered to our Lord during His public life. She also witnessed His death on the cross, burial and resurrection. She is depicted carrying a pot of ointment, or a cruse, or a pair of cruets.

Mary the Slave (St) M.   Nov 1

d. c 300   A slave-girl in the household of a Roman patrician who was venerated as a martyr on account of her sufferings during the persecution of Diocletian.

Mary (St) VM.   Nov 24
See Flora and Mary.

Mary (St) M.   Dec 2
See Eusebius, Marcellus, etc.

Mary of St Martin (Bl) N.
OSB. Cam.   Dec 4
d. 1240   A Camaldolese nun of the convent of Pugnano, near Pisa.

Mary-Joseph Rossello
(St) V. Foundress   Dec 7

1811–1888   Born at Albisola in the diocese of Savona of poor parents, Benedicta Rossello showed early signs of unusual virtue. Unable to enter a religious order for lack of a dowry or poor health, she became a Franciscan tertiary. In 1837 she laid the foundations of her new institute, the Daughters of Our Lady of Mercy, which spread through Italy and South America. Known in religion as Sister Mary-Joseph, she suffered from constant sickness, but ruled her institute with heroic courage amid many difficulties until her death in 1888. Canonized in 1949.

Mary Crucifixa di Rosa
(St) V. Foundress   Dec 15

1813–1885   She was born of a well-to-do business family. From her childhood she showed a lively piety and sympathy with the poor. When cholera broke out in 1836 she gave herself wholeheartedly to tending its victims, and in the course of this work gathered the first companions of her institute, the Servants of Charity. The society, formed in 1839, was approved by Pius IX in 1851. Her love for Christ crucified showed itself in the addition of the name Crucifixa. Canonized in 1954.

Mary of the Angels (Bl)
V. OC.   Dec 16

1661–1717   Mary Ann Fontanella was born at Baldinero, near Turin, the daughter of Count Fontanella. In 1676 she entered the Carmel of St Christina at Turin and soon her life was a replica of that of SS Teresa and Magdalen de' Pazzi. She founded the Carmel of Moncaglieri, which still exists. Beatified in 1865.

Mary of Pisa (Bl) W. Tert.
OP.   Dec 22
d. 1431   A member of the Mancini family of Pisa. She received extraordinary mystical favours from childhood, such as the apparition of her Guardian Angel. She married at the early age of twelve and was left a widow and the mother of two children at sixteen. She married again but lost her second husband eight years later. Mary then became a Dominican tertiary and later took charge of a new foundation of that order, noted for its strict observance. Cult confirmed by Pius IX.

Masculas (St) M.   March 29
See Armogastes and Comp.

Massa Candida (SS) MM.   Aug 24
d. c 260   The name Massa Candida (the white mass) denotes a group of martyrs who

suffered at Utica in N. Africa under Gallienus and Valerian. The pre-1970 RM. gave their number as three hundred but modern writers limit it to one hundred and fifty-three, the number mentioned in a sermon of St Augustine. According to the pre-1970 RM. they were called the "white mass" because they were thrown into a lime pit, their remains becoming conglomerated into one great white mass, but it now appears that *Massa Candida* was a locality near Utica.

Massalius (St) M.   Apr 29
See Corfu, Martyrs of.

Maternian (St) Bp.   Jan 2
Otherwise Martinian, q.v.

Maternus (St) Bp.   July 18
d. *c* 307   Bishop of Milan, chosen by popular acclamation in 295. He had much to suffer during the persecution of Diocletian, but survived it and died in peace.

Maternus (St) Bp.   Sept 14
d. *c* 325   The first bishop of Cologne about whom we have positive evidence. His name is in fact mentioned in connexion with the Donatist controversy. A medieval legend, which was still defended by St Peter Canisius, identifies this Maternus with the son of the widow of Naim and makes him a disciple of St Peter.

Mathias Mulumba (St) M.   June 3
d. 1886   Chief of several villages, he was martyred by King Mwanga of Uganda. See Charles Lwanga and Comps.

Mathildis (St) Queen   March 14
Otherwise Matilda, q.v.

Mathurin (Maturinus)
(St) C.   Nov 1
? Born in the district of Sens, he was converted and ordained by Polycarp, bishop of that city. In his turn he converted his own parents and evangelized his native district with signal success. This is a legend and not now regarded as factual.

Matilda of Spanheim
(Bl) V. OSB.   Feb 26
d. 1154   A German recluse, first at Mainz under the obedience of her brother, the abbot of St Albans's, Mainz; and then near Spanheim when he became abbot of a new abbey there.

Matilda (Mathildis,
Maud) (St) W.   March 14
d. 968   Wife of the German king Henry the Fowler. She was of a very generous disposition and founded, among others, the Benedictine

abbeys of Nordhausen, Pöhlde, Engern and Quedlinburg. She was a widow for thirty years and had to suffer much at the hands of her sons, Otto and Henry, by whom she was despoiled of most of her possessions. She died at Quedlinburg and the Benedictines venerate her as one of their oblates.

Matrona (St) VM.   March 15
d. *c* ?350   The serving-maid of a rich Jewess of Thessalonica, scourged to death at the orders of her mistress when she discovered that Matrona was a Christian. The *Acta* are not very reliable.

Matrona (St) M.   March 20
See Alexandra, Claudia, etc.

Matrona (St) H.   May 18
See Theodotus, Thecusa, etc.

Matronian (St) H.   Dec 14
? A native of Milan who became a hermit, and whose relics are said to have been enshrined by St Ambrose in the church of S. Nazario.

Matthew Alonso
Leziniana (St) M. OP.   Jan 22
d. 1745   Born at Navas del Rey in the diocese of Valladolid, Spain. After his profession in the Dominican order and his ordination he was sent to the Philippine Islands and thence to Tonkin, where he was eventually beheaded. Beatified in 1906. Canonized in 1988.

Matthew of Girgenti (Bl)
Bp. OFM.   Feb 3
d. 1450   Matthew Gimarra was born at Girgenti in Sicily and became a Conventual Franciscan. He afterwards migrated to the Observants and worked zealously under St Bernardine of Siena. Pope Eugene IV forced him to accept the bishopric of Girgenti, but as a result of much opposition he had to resign. He died in a Franciscan friary at Palermo. Cult confirmed in 1767.

Matthew of Beauvais (St)
M.   March 27
d. *c* 1098   A native of Beauvais who took the Cross under bishop Roger of Beauvais and joined the first crusade. He was taken prisoner by the Saracens and beheaded on refusing to renounce Christ.

Matthew Gam (Bl) M.   May 11
1812–1847   A native Vietnamese Christian who brought the missionaries of the Paris foreign missions from Singapore to Vietnam in his boat. He was imprisoned in 1846, tortured and beheaded. Canonized in 1988.

Matthew Phuong (St) M.   May 26
c 1801–1861   Born at Ke-lay in Vietnam,

he became a catechist, for which he was beheaded near Dong-hoi. Canonized in 1988.

Matthew Alvarez (Bl) M.

Tert. OP.   Sept 8
d. 1628   A Japanese catechist and Dominican tertiary who was beheaded at Nagasaki.
Beatified in 1867.

Matthew (Bl) H. OSB.

Cam.   Sept 11
d. 1303   A Camaldolese hermit, disciple of
Bl John of Massaccio, whose cave on Mt
Massaccio he inherited.

Matthew (St) Apostle   GC. Sept 21

1st cent.   Matthew, or Levi, as he was named
before being called by our Lord to be an
apostle (Matt 9:9), was a tax-gatherer at
Capernaum. We have a legendary account of
his career after the coming down of the Holy
Spirit, but the gospel narrative provides the
only trustworthy data concerning him. He is
the author of the first gospel. It is not known
where he preached or whether he died a
martyr. His main emblem is an angel, who may
hold pen, inkwell, etc. Matthew may be shown
holding money, a bag of coins, a money box, or
a sword.

Matthew Carreri (Bl) C. OP.   Oct 7

d. 1471   Born at Mantua, he joined the
Dominicans and spent his life in preaching
throughout Italy. Cult approved in 1483.

Matthew de Eskandely
(Bl) M.   Oct 8

d. c 1309   Born in Buda, Hungary, he went
as a missionary to the East, being apparently
the first Catholic missionary in China, where
he was martyred.

Matthew (St) M. OSB.   Nov 12

See Benedict, John, etc.

Matthew (Bl) Card. OSB.   Dec 25

d. 1134   A canon of Reims who became a
Cluniac monk at Saint-Martin-des-Champs
(1108) and prior there in 1117. In 1125 he was
created cardinal bishop of Albano and in 1128
papal legate in France and Germany. He was a
staunch upholder of the Cluniac ideal and a
great friend of St Peter the Venerable.

Matthew of Città della
Pieve (Bl) C. OSM.   ?

d. 1348   The ninth superior general of the
Servites (1344–1348). His cult has not yet
been confirmed.

Matthia del Nazarei (Bl)

Abs. OSB.   Dec 30
d. 1213   Born at Metalica in the March of

St Matthew, Sept 21

Ancona, she received the Benedictine veil at the nunnery of Santa Maddalena, at Metalica, of which she became abbess, a position wich she held for forty years. At a later date the convent adopted the rule of the Poor Clares, and for this reason Bl Matthia is often called a Poor Clare. Cult confirmed in 1756.

Matthias (St) Bp.   Jan 30
d. *c* 120   A bishop of Jerusalem of Jewish descent. He governed the see at a time when his flock was in great part dispersed.

Matthias of Meaco (St) M.   Feb 6
d. 1597   Born at Meaco, he became a Franciscan tertiary and was crucified at Nagasaki with St Peter Baptist and twenty-five companions. Canonized in 1862. See Paul Miki and Comps.

Matthias (St) Apostle   GC. May 14
1st cent.   He was chosen by lot by the Eleven to take the place of Judas Iscariot among the apostles (Acts I, 21–22). The traditions concerning his later life are not consistent. It seems however to have been believed that he died at Jerusalem, whence his supposed relics were removed by St Helena and are now venerated at St Matthias' Abbey, Trier. He is depicted as an elderly man holding, or being pierced by, a halberd or, more rarely, a sword.

Matthias of Arima (Bl) M.   May 22
d. 1622   A native Japanese catechist of the Jesuits and servant of the provincial. Because he would not betray his master he was subjected to a most revolting martyrdom. Beatified in 1867.

Matthias Murumba (St) M.   June 3
d. 1886   A negro judge in Uganda. He was first a Muslim, then a Protestant, and in 1881 became a convert to the Catholic faith. He was martyred on Kumpala hill. See Charles Lwanga and Comps.

Matthias Araki (Bl) M.   July 12
d. 1626   A Japanese person, brother of Bl Mancius Araki, q.v. He was burnt alive at Nagasaki for having sheltered the European missionaries. Beatified in 1867.

Matthias Cosaca and Matthias Nakano (BB)
MM.   Nov 27
d. 1619   Japanese men belonging to the royal family of Firando. They were imprisoned at Omura, their native place, and beheaded at Nagasaki. Beatified in 1867.

Maturinus (St) C.   Nov 1
Otherwise Mathurin, q.v.

Maturus (St) M.   June 2
See Photinus (Pothinus), Sanctus, etc.

Maud and Maude
Note. Saints of this name should be sought under other forms of the word, which is either a variant of Mechtilde, Matilda, or a diminutive of Magdalen (Maudlin).

Maughan (Mawgan, Morgan) (St)   Sept 26
Otherwise Meugant, q.v.

Maughold (Maccaldus) (St) Bp.   Dec 28
d. *c* 488   An Irishman said to have been a brigand, converted by St Patrick and by him sent to the Isle of Man, where his episcopate was very successful.

Maura (St) M.   Feb 13
See Fusca and Maura.

Maura (St) M.   May 3
See Timothy and Maura.

Maura (St) V.   Sept 21
d. 850   A maiden of Troyes in Champagne, who died at the age of twenty-three after a life of prayer and good works.

Maura (St) V.   Nov 2
See Baya and Maura.

Maura (St) VM.   Nov 30
? A maiden martyred at Constantinople. One of the Ionian islands is named after her.

Maura and Britta (SS) VV.   Jan 15
? 4th cent.   Two virgins whose life is not known, but whose relics were, according to St Gregory of Tours, found during the episcopate of his predecessor, St Euphronius.

Maurice Csaky (Bl) C. OP.   March 20
1281–1336   Maurice Csaky belonged to the royal house of Hungary. Some years after their marriage both he and his wife by mutual consent became religious, Maurice joining the Friars Preachers. Although never officially canonized or beatified, he is venerated in Hungary.

Maurice (St) M.   July 10
See Leontius, Maurice, etc.

Maurice and Comp. (SS)
MM.   Sept 22
See Theban Legion.

Maurice of Carnoet (St)
Ab. OSB. Cist.   Oct 13
c 1114–1191   Born in the district of Loudéac, in Brittany, and educated at Paris, he joined the Cistercians at Langonel, in his

St Maurice of Carnoet, Oct 13

native country (1144). In 1147 he was made abbot, and in 1177 he became the abbot-founder of Carnoet. As abbot both of Langonel and of Carnoet he was a great friend and adviser of the dukes of Brittany. Cult confirmed by Clement XI.

Maurilius (St) Bp. OSB.   Aug 9
d. 1067   A native of Reims, he became successively headmaster of the cathedral school at Halberstadt, a Benedictine monk at Fécamp in Normandy, abbot of St Mary's at Florence and archbishop of Rouen (1055). He was one of the leading churchmen of his day; he wrote against Berengarius.

Maurilius (St) Bp.   Sept 3
d. 580   Bishop of Cahors. It is recorded that he knew the whole Bible by heart.

Maurilius (St) Bp.   Sept 13
d. c 430   A native of Milan who migrated to France where he became a disciple of St Martin of Tours. About the year 407 he was ordained bishop of Angers.

Maurinus (St) Ab. M.   June 10
?   Abbot of a monastery — probably that of St Pantaleon — at Cologne. Venerated also as a martyr. All other data are lacking.

Mauritius (*several*)
Otherwise Maurice, q.v.

Maurontus (Maurontius, Mauruntius) (St) Ab. OSB.　　Jan 9
d. *c* 700　Abbot-founder of Saint-Florent-le-Vieil, in Anjou.

Maurontus (Mauront) (St) Ab. OSB.　　May 5
d. 701　Eldest son of SS Adalbald and Rictrudis, he was reared at the court and succeeded his father as lord of Douai. He was just on the point of marrying when he joined the Benedictines at Marchiennes. Eventually he became abbot-founder of Breuil-sur-lys, near Douai, of which town he is now the patron saint.

Maurontus (St) Bp. OSB.　　Oct 21
d. *c* 804　Abbot of St Victor at Marseilles, who became bishop of the same city *c* 767.

Maurus and Placid (SS) OSB.　　Jan 25
? Maurus and Placid were early disciples of St Benedict, patriarch of Western monasticism. With time, many legends grew about their names but all that may certainly be known about them is found in the second book of *The Dialogues* of St Gregory the Great. Their cults are relegated to local veneration since 1969, or particular calendars. In art, Maurus is shown habited as a monk saving Placid from drowning, a cowl floating in the air above.

Maurus (St) Bp. OSB.　　Jan 20
d. 946　A Roman, nephew of Pope John IX, who ordained him. Next he became monk and abbot of Classe at Ravenna (926), and finally bishop of Cesena (934). He built for himself a cell on a hill near the city, where he would spend part of his time in prayer. After his death the cell grew into the Benedictine abbey of Santa Maria del Monte.

Maurus (Marius, May) (St) Ab.　　Jan 27
d. *c* 555　Abbot-founder of Bodon in the diocese of Sisteron, France.

Maurus (St) M.　　Jan 29
See Papias and Maurus.

Maurus de Chak (Bl) OP.　　March 20
d. 1336　Son of the Count Chak, he left the wealth and dignity of his family to enter the Dominican order. He died in Gyor, where his tomb was destroyed by the Turks. His miracles were collected for the council of Ferrara but the Turkish invasion stopped the process of canonization.

Maurus (William) Scott (Bl) M. OSB.　　May 30
d. 1612　William (in religion, Maurus) Scott was born at Chigwell, in Essex, and became a student of law at Trinity Hall, Cambridge. By reading Catholic literature he was led to embrace Catholicism and was received into the church by Bl John Roberts, OSB., who sent him to the Benedictine abbey at Satagún, in Spain. He became a monk of this abbey (1604) and after his ordination was sent back to England as a missionary. Shortly after his arrival he witnessed the martyrdom of Bl John Roberts and not long afterwards he himself was captured and martyred for his faith at Tyburn. Beatified in 1929.

Maurus (St) M.　　June 16
See Felix and Maurus.

Maurus, Pantaleemon and Sergius (SS) MM.　　July 27
d. *c* 117?　Three martyrs venerated at Bisceglia on the Adriatic. Maurus is said to have been a native of Bethlehem, sent by St Peter to be the first bishop of Bisceglia. They are stated to have been martyred under Trajan, but their *Acta* are quite untrustworthy.

Maurus (St) M.　　Aug 1
See Bonus Faustus and Maurus.

Maurus and Comp. (SS) MM.　　Aug 22
? A group of fifty martyrs whose leader, Maurus, was a priest. All other data are uncertain. The pre-1970 RM. assigns them to Reims, and they seem to have suffered either under Valerian (*c* 260) or under Diocletian (*c* 300).

Maurus (Bl) Bp. OSB.　　Oct 25
d. *c* 1070　A Benedictine abbot who in 1036 became bishop of Pécs in Hungary. He wrote the lives of St Benedict Zorard and St Andrew Szkalka (q.v.).

Maurus (St) Bp.　　Nov 8
d. 383　Second bishop of Verdun (353–383). His relics were enshrined in the ninth century, when many miracles are said to have taken place at his tomb.

Maurus (St) Bp.　　Nov 21
d. *c* 600　Twelfth bishop of Verona, in N. Italy. Towards the end of his life he resigned and became a hermit.

Maurus (St) M.　　Nov 22
Born of Christian parents in proconsular Africa, he travelled to Rome, where he was martyred under Numerian. About ten different cities in Italy and France claimed to possess his relics.

Maurus (St) M.　　Dec 3
See Claudius, Hilaria, etc.

Maurus (Bl) Bp. OSB.　　Dec 4
d. *c* 1070　One of the Benedictine monks

whom St Stephen of Hungary invited to his kingdom. He was a member of the community of Pannonhalma until 1036, when he was made bishop of Pécs (*Quinque Ecclesiae*). He is notable too as a hagiographer. Cult approved in 1848.

Mavenus (Mavenna) (St)
Ab.   June 21
Otherwise Maine, q.v.

Mavilus (Majulus) (St) M.   Jan 4
d. 212   A martyr of Adrumetum in Africa, flung to the wild beasts in the arena, under Caracalla.

Mawes (Maudetus, Maudez) (St) Ab.   Nov 18
? 6th cent.   A Welshman, who lived first as a solitary near Falmouth in Cornwall, where a village still perpetuates his name, and then crossed over to Brittany where he is known as St Maudez, and where many churches are dedicated to him.

Mawgan (St)   Sept 26
Otherwise Meugant, q.v.

Maxellendis (St) VM.   Nov 13
d. *c* 670   She was stabbed to death at Caudry, near Cambrai, by Hardouin of Solesmes, in a fit of rage because she wished to be a nun and refused to marry him.

Maxentia (St) VM.   Nov 20
? An Irish or Scottish maiden who settled as a recluse near Senlis in France, where she was put to death at the place now called Pont-Sainte-Maxence. She is venerated at Beauvais.

Maxentiolus (Mezenceul) (St) Ab.   Dec 17
5th cent.   A disciple of St Martin of Tours, who became the abbot-founder of Our Lady of Cunault.

Maxentius (Maixent) (St) Ab.   June 26
c 448–515   Born at Agde in S. France, he was educated by St Severus and afterwards became a monk in a monastery of Poitou, now called after him Saint-Maixent, of which he eventually became abbot. He was highly esteemed by Clovis I and by the surrounding population whom he protected from the invading barbarians.

Maxentius, Constantius, Crescentius, Justin and Comp. (SS) MM.   Dec 12
d. *c* 287   Martyrs at Trier, at the beginning of the reign of Diocletian.

Maxima (St) M.   March 26
See Montanus and Maxima.

Maxima (St) M.   Apr 8
See Januarius, Maxima and Macaria.

Maxima (St) V.   May 16
? She is widely venerated in the diocese of Fréjus, in France, where several villages are called after her. Nothing, however, is known about her.

Maxima, Donatilla and Secunda (SS) VV. MM.   July 30
d. 304   Three maidens (Secunda was aged twelve), martyred at Tebourba in proconsular Africa under Diocletian.

Maxima (St) M.   Sept 2
d. 304   A Roman slave who expired under the lash during the persecution of Diocletian. She was condemned to death together with St Ansanus.

Maxima (St) M.   Oct 1
See Verissimus, Maxima, etc.

Maxima (St)   Oct 16
See Martinian, Saturian, and Comp.

Maximian of Beauvais (St) M.   Jan 8
See Lucian, Maximian, and Julian.

Maximian of Ravenna (St) Bp.   Feb 22
d. *c* 556   Ordained bishop of Ravenna by Pope Vigilius in 546. He built the splendid basilica of St Vitalis, which was dedicated with much pomp in the presence of the Emperor Justinian and his wife Theodora. Holding a jewelled cross, he is depicted there standing next to the Emperor in the magnificent mosaic on the north side of the sanctuary.

Maximian of Constantinople (St)   Apr 21
d. 434   A Roman by birth, he became a priest and finally patriarch at Constantinople. He was highly esteemed by Pope Celestine I.

Maximian of Syracuse (St) Bp. OSB.   June 9
d. 594   A Sicilian by birth and a monk of St Andrew's abbey on the Coelian Hill in Rome under St Gregory the Great. He served both Pope Pelagius and Gregory the Great as *Apocrisarius* in Constantinople. Recalled to Rome, he acted as minister to St Gregory, who finally appointed him bishop of Syracuse and apostolic legate in Sicily (591), where he died in the third year of his episcopate.

Maximian (St) M. Aug 21
See Bonosus and Maximian.

Maximian (St) Bp. Oct 3
d. 404 An African, a convert from Donatism, who was made bishop of Bagae (Bagaia) in Numidia. Finding his nomination displeasing to the people, he persuaded the Fathers of the council of Milevis to accept his resignation. Having deprived the Donatists of the basilica of Calvianum, he was grievously wounded and thrown from a tower by the heretics. Nursed back to life, he crossed over to Italy and obtained a decree of justification from the emperor Honorius.

Maximilian (St) M. March 12
d. 295 Otherwise Mamilian. The pre-1970 RM. appears to be wrong in placing his martyrdom at Rome. His Acts are genuine, and describe him as a young martyr who as a Christian refused to do military service and was therefore executed at Thebeste in Numidia.

Maximilian Kolbe (St) M. GC. Aug 14
Born in 1894 in Poland, he joined the Friars Minor Conventual whilst a youth. In poor health, he worked energetically to enliven the faith in Poland and Japan through a renewal of devotion to our Lady. During the Nazi occupation he harboured over two thousand Jews and refugees. Thrown into Auschwitz concentration camp he begged to be allowed to die in place of another: he encouraged his fellow victims with hymns and prayers, and died on August 14 1941. Canonized in 1982.

Maximilian (St) Bp. M. Oct 12
d. 284 A native of Novicum (the territory between the Inn and the Danube). He founded the church of Lorch (*Laurencum*), near Passau, and was martyred at Cilli in Styria, under Numerian. St Rupert of Salzburg erected churches in his name.

Maximilian (St) Bp. M. Oct 29
d. 284 A duplicate of St Maximilian of Lorch, coupled in the pre-1970 RM. with St Valentine, of whom nothing is known.

Maximinus (St) M. Jan 25
See Juventinus and Maximus.

Maximinus of Trier (St) Bp. May 29
d. c 349 Born at Silly near Poitiers and a brother of St Maxentius of Poitiers. In 333 he succeeded his teacher St Agrecius in the see of Trier, and became the valiant defender and host of St Athanasius of Alexandria and St Paul of Constantinople, exiled from their sees

by the Arian emperor. He was a prominent opponent of Arianism in the councils of Milan, Sardica and Cologne. St Jerome describes him as "one of the most courageous bishops of his time".

Maximinus of Aix (St) Bp. June 8
1st cent. (?) Venerated as the first bishop of Aix in Provence, and connected by legend with the mythical journey of St Mary Magdalen to Marseilles. Indeed, he is identified with the man born blind of John Ch. 9. All this of course is a fiction.

Maximinus (Mesmin) (St) Ab. Dec 15
d. c 520 First abbot of the monastery of Micy, founded near Orleans by King Clovis.

Maximus (St) Bp. Jan 8
d. 511 There were two bishops of Pavia of this name, both reputed as saints. The one honoured today is the second. He attended councils held at Rome under Pope Symmachus.

Maximus of Nola (St) Bp. Jan 15
d. p.250 Bishop of Nola. He ordained St Felix. During the persecution of Decius (250) he fled to the mountains, where he nearly died of exposure and hunger. He died at Nola worn out with the hardships he had endured for the faith.

Maximus (St) M. Jan 25
Otherwise Maximinus. See Juventinus and Maximus.

Maximus (St) M. Feb 18
See Lucius, Silvanus, etc.

Maximus, Claudius, Praepedigna, Alexander and Cutias (SS) MM. Feb 18
d. 295 These martyrs are supposed to have suffered under Diocletian, but their legend seems to be no more than a pious fiction.

Maximus, Quintilian and Dadas (SS) MM. Apr 13
d. 303 Three brothers of Dorostorum, now Silistria on the Danube, in Bulgaria, beheaded at Ozobia under Diocletian. Maximus was a lector.

Maximus (St) M. Apr 14
See Tiburtius, Valerian and Maximus.

Maximus and Olympiades (SS) MM. Apr 15
d. 251 Persian noblemen, martyred by being beaten to death with crowbars under Decius.

Maximus (St) M.   Apr 30
d. *c* 251   A citizen of Ephesus, a merchant by
profession, who on the publication of the edict
of Decius against the Christians in 250,
presented himself to the judge as a Christian
and was accordingly martyred. His proconsular *Acta* are still extant.

Maximus of Jerusalem
(St) Bp.   May 5
d. *c* 350   A confessor of the faith under
Diocletian. He survived the persecution, although a cripple for life, and eventually succeeded St Macarius as bishop of Jerusalem.
The Arians, taking advantage of his simplicity,
used him as a tool against St Athanasius, but
he afterwards made ample amends. The orthodox however do not venerate him.

Maximus, Bassus and
Fabius (SS) MM.   May 11
d. 304   Roman martyrs under Diocletian.

Maximus (St) M.   May 15
See Cassius, Victorinus, etc.

Maximus and Victorinus
(SS) MM.   May 25
d. *c* 384   Said to have been two brothers sent
from Rome by Pope Damasus to preach in
Gaul, and martyred by barbarians near
Evreux.

Maximus (St) Bp.   May 29
? 6th cent.   A bishop of Verona.

Maximus (St) Bp. M.   June 10
4th cent.   Tenth bishop of Naples (359). He
died in exile and is honoured as a martyr.

Maximus of Turin (St) Bp.   June 25
d. *c* 470   Bishop of Turin in the troublous
times of the barbarian inroads into N. Italy. He
is now best remembered for his homilies and
other ascetical writings, which are still extant.

Maximus (St) M.   July 20
See Sabinus, Julian, etc.

Maximus of Padua (St) Bp.   Aug 2
2nd cent.   Successor of St Prosdocimus as
bishop of Padua. His alleged relics were found
in 1053 and enshrined by Pope St Leo IX.

Maximus Homologetes
Ab. and Comp. (SS) CC.   Aug 13
580–662   A Greek of noble birth and a
courtier at Byzantium, who became a monk,
and later abbot, of Chrysopolis (Scutari). As
such he firmly opposed the Monothelite
heretics and upheld the authority of the bishop
of Rome. After attending the council of the
Lateran held at Rome in 649 he stayed there
for some years. In 655 he was seized by order
of the Monothelite emperor, taken to Constantinople, maimed and exiled. He died near
Batum in Transcaucasia. He was a prolific
theological and ascetical writer. Several of his
disciples, two of whom were named Anastasius, shared his exile and are honoured with
him.

Maximus (St)   Aug 17
See Liberatus, Boniface, etc.

Maximus (St) M.   Aug 18
See Florus, Laurus, etc.

Maximus (St) Ab.   Aug 20
d. *c* 470   Abbot founder of Chinon in the
diocese of Tours. A disciple of St Martin.

Maximus (St) M.   Aug 23
See Quiriacus, Maximus, etc.

Maximus (St) M.   Aug 25
Otherwise Maginus, q.v.

Maximus (St) M.   Sept 4
See Magnus, Castus, and Maximus.

Maximus, Theodore and
Asclepiodotus (SS) MM.   Sept 15
d. *c* 310   Three martyrs, natives of Marcianopolis, an ancient town in what is now Bulgaria, who suffered at Adrianopolis.

Maximus (St) M.   Sept 25
See Paul, Tatta, etc.

Maximus (St) M.   Sept 28
According to the best authorities, identical
with the St Maximus entered under April 30.

Maximus of Aquila (St) M.   Oct 20
d. *c* 250   A deacon of Aquila in S. Italy,
conspicuous for his zeal, who was martyred by
being cast down from an overhanging cliff near
his native city, during the persecution of
Decius. He is now venerated as the patron
saint of Aquila.

Maximus (St) M.   Oct 30
d. 304   According to the pre-1970 RM. he
was martyred at Apamea in Phrygia, under
Diocletian. More likely, the place of his martyrdom was Cuma (the ancient *Cumae*) in Campania.

Maximus of Mainz (St) Bp.   Nov 18
d. 378   The nineteenth bishop of Mainz of
which see he was pastor from *c* 354 to 378. He
suffered much at the hands of the Arians, and
was distinguished as a scholar and writer.

Maximus (St) M.   RM. Nov 19
d. *c* 255   A martyr who suffered in Rome
under Valerian.

Maximus of Riez (St) Bp.   Nov 27
d. 460   Appointed abbot of Lérins in 426

and made bishop of Riez much against his will in 434, being ordained by St Hilary. He was one of the most prominent prelates of the church of Gaul in his time.

Maximus (St) M.   Dec 2
See Eusebius, Marcellus, etc.

Maximus of Alexandria (St) Bp.   Dec 27
d. 282   A priest of Alexandria, who administered the patriarchate while St Dionysius was in exile (251–264) and finally succeeded him (265–282). He drove Paul of Samosata from Egypt.

Mazota (St) V.   Dec 23
? 8th cent.   One of a band of nineteen maidens who came over from Ireland to Scotland and founded a community at Abernethy on the Tay. Mazota seems to have been their leader.

Mbaga Tuzinde (St) M.   June 3
d. 1886   A page to King Mwanga of Uganda and adopted son of the chief executioner, he had to resist the pleas of his family up to the very moment of execution. He was burnt alive at Namuyongo. See Charles Lwanga and Comps.

Mechtild of Spanheim (Bl) H. OSB.   Feb 26
Otherwise Matilda of Spanheim, q.v.

Mechtild (Bl) V.   Apr 11
d. 1200   A virgin of Scottish origin who passed with her brother into France and spent her life as a recluse in the village of Lappion, diocese of Laon.

Mechtild of Diessen (St) Abs. OSB.   May 31
1125–1160   Born at Andechs in Bavaria, daughter of Count Berthold of Andechs. At the age of five she was placed in a convent at Diessen, where in due time she professed the Benedictine rule and became abbess. In 1153 she was entrusted by the bishop of Augsburg with the reform of the nunnery of Edelstetten, which she carried through in the teeth of fierce opposition, some of the nuns having in fact to be expelled. She was greatly revered by her contemporaries who credited her with the gift of miracles.

Mechtild of Magdeburg (Bl) V. OSB.   Oct 8
c 1210–c 1280   After living as a Béguine for forty years she became, towards the end of her life, a nun at Helfta, where she was professed under Abbess Gertrude of Hackeborn and was a fellow-religious of St Mechtild of Hackeborn and St Gertrude the Great. Mechtild of Magdeburg was the first of the Helfta nuns known to have been favoured with mystical experiences. Her book of visions survived but not in its original language.

Mechtild of Hackeborn (St) V. OSB.   Nov 19
d. 1298   A nun of Helfta, sister of the Abbess Gertrude of Hackeborn. She was the teacher and novice-mistress of St Gertrude the Great. She too had mystical experiences, which were written down by St Gertrude in the *Book of Special Grace*.

Meda (St) V.   Jan 15
Otherwise Ita, q.v.

Medan (St)   June 4
See Croidan, Medan, etc.

Medana (St) V.   Nov 19
8th cent.   An Irish maiden who passed over into Scotland and lived in Galloway. She is possibly identical with St Midnat venerated in West Meath on Nov 18.

Medard (St) Bp.   June 8
c 470–c 558   Born in Picardy, he was ordained when thirty-three years of age, and in 530 made bishop of Vermand, which he transfered to Noyon. At a later date he was entrusted also with the diocese of Tournai, which remained united with Noyon till 1146. See also St Gildard. A legend similar to that of St Swithun is attached to his name.

Medericus (Merry) (St) Ab. OSB.   Aug 29
d. c 700   Born at Autun, he was offered to God at the age of thirteen in the abbey of St Martin of Autun, of which he eventually became abbot. Later he resigned and lived as a hermit in a cell near Paris, where now stands the church of Saint-Merry.

Medrald (Mérald, Méraut) (St) Ab. OSB.   Feb 23
d. c 850   A monk of Saint-Evroult (Ebrulfus) of Ouche: he became abbot of Vendôme.

Medran and Odran (SS) CC.   July 7
6th cent.   Two brothers, disciples of St Kieran of Saghir, one of whom remained to the end with that holy man, while the other became the abbot-founder of a monastery at Muskerry.

Meen (St) Ab.   June 21
Otherwise Maine, q.v.

Megingaud (Mengold, Megingoz) (St) Bp. OSB.   March 16
d. 794   Born of a Frankish family, he

became a monk at Fritzlar (738), and after some years as teacher in the abbey school, was elected abbot. Later he succeeded St Burchard as bishop of Würzburg (c 754). In 787 he resigned and retired to the abbey of Neustadt, where he died.

Meginhard (Meginher, Meginard) (Bl) Ab. OSB.   Sept 26
d. 1059   A monk of Hersfeld in Germany who was chosen abbot in 1035. In 1037 he undertook the rebuilding of the monastery after it had been destroyed by fire. He was one of the best biblical scholars of the Middle Ages.

Meginratus (St) M.   Jan 21
Otherwise Meinrad, q.v.

Meingold (St)   Feb 8
10th cent.   There was a holy man, Meingold of Huy on the Meuse, who was venerated in Belgium after his death in the tenth century. Long afterwards he seems to have been confused with a certain Count Meingaud who was assassinated in 892.

Meingosus (Meingos) (Bl) Ab. OSB.   Apr 2
c 1200   Abbot of the great Benedictine abbey of Weingarten in Swabia from c 1188 to 1200.

Meinhard (Bl) Bp. OSA.   Apr 12
d. 1196   An Augustinian canon regular who went to preach in Latvia. In 1184 he was made bishop and fixed his residence at Yxkill on the Düna. (The see was transferred to Riga in 1201.)

Meinrad (St) M. OSB.   Jan 21
d. 861   Born at Solgen in Swabia, of the noble family of Hohenzollern, and educated, professed and ordained at the Benedictine abbey of Reichenau on the Rhine. Later he became a hermit in Switzerland, at the place where afterwards arose the abbey of Einsiedeln (i.e. Hermitage). He was a hermit for twenty-five years and was murdered by robbers who thought to find hidden treasures in his cell. He has always been venerated as a martyr.

Meinulph (St) C.   Oct 5
d. c 859   A godson of Charlemagne. He founded the abbey of Bödeken in Westphalia, where he died.

Meinwerk (Bl) Bp.   June 5
d. 1036   A relative of the emperor St Henry II by whom he became bishop of Paderborn in 1009. On account of his building activities, which occupied him throughout his episcopal career, he has been called "the bishop-builder" and "the second founder of Pader-

born". His cathedral school was famous all over N. Germany.

Mel (Melchno) (St) Bp.   Feb 6
d. c 490   Said to have been one of the four nephews of St Patrick (viz. Mel, Melchu, Munis and Rioch), sons of Conis and Darerca, St Patrick's sister. They are further stated to have accompanied St Patrick to Ireland as missionaries, St Mel becoming the first abbot-bishop of Ardagh. The evidence, however, concerning him and his brothers is hopelessly entangled and conflicting.

Melan (St) Bp.   June 15
d. p.549   Bishop of Viviers from 519 till some time after 549, in which year he sent his representatives to the council held at Orleans.

Melangell (Monacella) (St) V.   Jan 31
d. c 590   A virgin commemorated in certain Welsh calendars. She seems to have been a recluse in Powys. Her shrine, reconstructed from its fragmented parts, may be seen at Pennant Melangell.

Melania the Elder (St) W.   June 8
c 342–c 410   A patrician lady of Rome, of the family of the Valerii. She was interested in the holy land, which she was one of the first Roman matrons to visit. She founded a monastery on the Mount of Olives.

Melania the Younger and Pinian (SS)   Dec 31
c 383–438   This Melania was the granddaughter of St Melania the Elder. A Roman by birth, she belonged to the patrician family of the Valerii. She married her cousin St Pinian and they had two children who died young. About the year 410 husband and wife travelled to the East, the former entering a monastery and the latter a nunnery at Jerusalem. Melania outlived her husband, dying in 438.

Melanius (St) Bp.   Jan 6
d. c 535   A Breton by birth, he was bishop of Rennes at the critical period when the Franks were overrunning Gaul. He is said to have almost completely succeeded in extirpating idolatry from his diocese. He was highly revered by King Clovis.

Melanius (St) Bp.   Oct 22
Otherwise Mellonius, q.v.

Melantius (St) Bp.   Jan 16
Otherwise Melas, q.v.

Melas (Melantius) (St) Bp.   Jan 16
d. c 385   A humble ascetic who was made

bishop of Rhinocolura, a little town on the Mediterranean near the boundary between Egypt and Palestine. During the Arian troubles he underwent imprisonment and banishment for the Catholic cause.

Melasippus (St) Bp.   Jan 17
Otherwise Meleusippus, q.v.

Melasippus, Antony and Carina (SS) MM.   Nov 7
d. 360   Antony, or Antoninus, was the child of Melasippus and Carina. All three were martyred at Ancyra, under Julian the Apostate. The parents died under torture, and their child was beheaded.

Melchiades (St) Pope   Dec 10
Otherwise Miltiades, q.v.

Melchior (St)   Jan 6
One of the Magi, q.v. Depicted as a king bearing gifts.

Melchior (Bl) M. SJ.   Sept 7
See Mark, Stephen and Melchior.

Meldon (Medon) (St) Bp.   Feb 7
6th cent.   An Irishman who became an anchorite in France and died at Péronne, where he is the titular saint of several churches.

Meletius (St) Bp.   Feb 12
d. 381   Born at Melitene in Armenia he became bishop of Sebaste (358) and later, patriarch of Antioch (360), then in the throes of the Arian controversy. Within a month he was exiled by the Arian emperor. Recalled for a brief space, he was again banished and not fully reinstated till 378. In 381 he presided over the second general council of Constantinople, dying while the council was still sitting.

Meletius (St) M.   May 24
? The *laus* in the pre-1970 RM. read "The passion of the holy martyrs Meletius, a general of the army, and his 252 companions, who suffered martyrdom in various ways". Nothing more that is really trustworthy can be stated about them.

Meletius (St) Bp.   Sept 21
? The Menology of Basil associates the name of this St Meletius with that of St Isacius, who is styled a martyr. They are both described as bishops in Cyprus.

Meletius (St) Bp.   Dec 4
d. *c* 295   A bishop in Pontus, he suffered much during the persecution of Diocletian. Eusebius, who knew him personally, tells us that Meletius derived his name from *Mel Atticum*: ("Attic honey") a phrase used to describe his eloquence. If so, we do not know his real name.

Meleusippus (St) M.   Jan 17
See Speusippus, Eleusippus, etc.

Melior (Migliore, Millory) (Bl) H. OSB. Vall.   March 26
d. 1198   A monk and priest of Vallumbrosa, who after many years of cenobitical life, asked to become a recluse in the hermitage called *Massa delle Celle*, above Vallumbrosa. His relics are enshrined at Vallumbrosa in the "altar of the Ten Beati".

Melitina (St) M.   Sept 15
Mid. 2nd cent.   A maiden martyred at Marcianopolis in Thrace under Antoninus Pius. Her relics were translated to the isle of Lemnos.

Melito of Sardis (St) Bp.   Apr 1
d. *c* 180   A bishop of Sardis in Lydia and an ecclesiastical writer of the period of the Apologists. He had a great reputation, but very little of his work is extant.

Mella (St) W.   Apr 25
d. *c* 780   Born in Connaught, Mella became the mother of two saints, Cannech and Tigernach. After the death of her husband she embraced the religious life and died abbess of Doire-Melle, Leitrim.

Mellanius (St) Bp.   Oct 22
Otherwise Melanius, Mellonius, Mellon, Mellonus, Mello, Mullion, etc. In this dictionary we have adopted the form Mellon, q.v.

Mellitus (St) Bp.   Apr 24
d. 624   A Roman abbot, presumably from the monastery of St Andrew on the Coelian Hill, whom St Gregory the Great sent to England in the wake of St Augustine in 601 at the head of a second band of missionary monks. He spent three years in Kent, and then was sent to London as its first bishop. He was banished to France for refusing holy communion to the apostate sons of King Sigebert. In 619 he was recalled to Kent to succeed St Laurence as archbishop of Canterbury. He is depicted as an archbishop with a pallium.

Mellon (St) Bp.   Oct 22
d. 314   Said to have been a Briton, born near Cardiff in the district called St Mellon's, and to have been the first bishop of Rouen.

Melorius (St) M.   Oct 1
According to legend, son of a king of Armorican Cornwall, done to death when a child. He was at one time venerated at Amesbury in Wiltshire, and his cult still survives at Quimper in Brittany. Even in the early Middle Ages the true facts about him were lost.

Memmius (Menge, Meinge) (St) Bp. Aug 5

d. *c* 300 Founder and first bishop of the see of Châlons-sur-Marne, and the apostle of that district. He preached during the second half of the third century. The legend which makes him a disciple of St Peter is now discredited.

Memnon (St) M. Aug 20

See Severus, Memnon and Comp.

Memorius and Comp. (SS) MM. Sept 7

d. 451 Memorius, registered in the pre-1970 RM. as Nemorius and popularly known as St Mesmin, was a deacon of Troyes, under St Lupus, by whom he was sent with five companions to the camp of Attila, to implore the mercy of the barbarian leader. Attila had them all beheaded. The story is not trustworthy, though the relics of the martyrs are still the object of veneration.

Menalippus (St) M. Sept 2

See Diomedes, Julian, etc.

Menander (St) M. Apr 28

See Patrick, Acacius, etc.

Menander (St) M. Aug 1

See Cyril, Aquila, etc.

Menas (Mennas (St) Bp. Aug 25

d. 552 A native of Alexandria who became superior of the hospice of St Samson at Constantinople and later was made patriarch of the latter city in 536. He condemned Origenism, but subscribed to the decrees of the emperor Justinian on "the Three Chapters" and was for this reason excommunicated by Pope Vigilius in 551. He submitted at once, and died shortly after in full communion with the bishop of Rome.

Menedemus (St) M. Sept 5

One of the group Urban, Theodore, and Comp., q.v.

Menefrida (St) V. July 24

5th cent. Of the family of Brychan of Brecknock. She is the patron saint of Tredresick, in Cornwall.

Menehould (St) V. Oct 14

5th cent. Patron saint of the French town in the Argonne called after her. With her five sisters, likewise honoured as saints, she brought fame by her sanctity to the diocese of Châlons-sur-Marne.

Meneleus (French: Menele, Mauvier) (St) Ab. OSB. July 22

d. *c* 720 Born in Anjou, he became a monk of Carméry in Auvergne. Seven years afterwards he left the abbey and became the abbot-restorer of the monastery of Ménat, near Clermont.

Meneus (or Hymenaeus) and Capito (SS) MM. July 24

? Martyrs commemorated in both the Greek and the Latin menologies, of whom, however, nothing is known nowadays.

Menignus (St) M. March 15

d. 251 A martyr who suffered at Parium on the Hellespont under Decius. He was a dyer by trade. He tore down the imperial edict against the Christians. In punishment for this his fingers were cut off. Later he was beheaded for the faith.

Menna (Manna) (St) V. Oct 3

d. *c* 395 A maiden of Lorraine said to have been related by blood to SS Eucherius and Elaptius (MM.) and other saints. The particulars of her life as they have reached us are very unreliable.

Mennas (St) M. Nov 11

d. *c* 295 An Egyptian, martyred at Karm Aba-Mina, near Alexandria. He was said to have been an officer in the imperial army and was venerated as one of the great warrior saints, whose cult was so much in vogue during the Middle Ages. The legends woven around his name are as numerous as they are untrustworthy. Cult confined to local calendars since 1969. In art he is nearly always depicted with a camel near him.

Mennas (St) H. Nov 11

d. 6th cent. A Greek from Asia Minor who became a hermit in the Abruzzi, probably at Santomena (*Sanctus Menna*) in the diocese of Conza. St Gregory the Great (Dial., 3:26) enlarges upon his virtues and miracles.

Mennas, Hermogenes, and Eugraphus (SS) MM. Dec 10

d. *c* 312 Three martyrs who were beheaded at Alexandria under Diocletian. Their *Passio* is worthless; it has been falsely ascribed to St Athanasius.

Menodora, Metrodora and Nymphodora (SS) VV. MM. Sept 10

d. 306 Three sisters who were martyred under Maximian Galerius near the Pythian baths or hot springs in Bithynia. These bare facts are certain; but not so the later *Acta* based upon them.

Menulphus (Menou) (St)
Bp.   July 12
7th cent. Said to have been an Irish pilgrim
who became bishop of Quimper in Brittany
and died in the neighbourhood of Bourges
while on his return journey from Rome.

Mercolino Forli (Bl) C. OP.   Jan 24
Otherwise Marcolino of Forli, q.v.

Mecuria (St) M.   Dec 12
See Ammonaria, Mecuria, etc.

Mercurialis (St) Bp.   May 23
d. c 406 First bishop of Forli in central Italy.
He was a zealous opponent of paganism and
Arianism. His life became the subject of many
extravagant legends.

Mecurius (St) M.   Nov 25
d. c 250 An alleged Scythian officer in the
imperial army, martyred at Caesarea in Cap-
adocia under Decius. He forms one of the
group of "warrior saints".

Mercurius and Comp.
(SS) MM.   Dec 10
d. c 300 (?) A group of soldiers told to
escort Christian prisoners to their place of
execution at Lentini (*Leontium*) in Sicily. The
soldiers were so impressed with the behaviour
of the prisoners that they too declared themselves believers in Christ, and soldiers and
prisoners were beheaded together.

Merewenna (Merwenna,
Merwinna) (St) Abs.
OSB.   May 13
d. c 970 Abbess of Romsey, a nunnery in
Hampshire, restored under King Edgar the
Peaceful.

Merewenna (St) V.   Aug 12
? Titular saint of Marhamchurch, near Bude
in Cornwall. She is said to have been one of the
daughters of Brychan of Brecknock.

Meriadec (St) Bp.   June 7
d. c 886 (?) Probably a Welshman by birth.
He became a hermit-priest and later bishop of
Vannes in Brittany, where he is venerated. The
details of his life are of small historical
value.

Meriadec (St) Bp.   June 7
d. 1302 Born in Brittany, he was ordained
and retired to a solitude to live as a hermit, but
was forced to abandon it on being elected by
the clergy bishop of Vannes. He was known far
and wide for his charity to the poor.

Merinus (St) H.   Jan 6
6th cent. A disciple of Dunawd of Bangor
and titular saint of churches in Wales and
Brittany.

Merinus (Merryn,
Meadhran) (St) Bp.   Sept 15
d. c 620 A disciple of St Comgall at Bangor,
venerated both in Scotland and in Ireland.

Merililaun (Merolilaun)
(St) M.   May 18
8th cent. A British pilgrim who met his death
by violence near Reims while on his way to
Rome and who has since been popularly
venerated as a martyr.

Merri or Merry (St) Ab.   Aug 29
Otherwise Medericus, q.v.

Merryn (Meadhran) (St)   Sept 15
Otherwise Merinus, q.v.

Merulus (St) Mk. OSB.   Jan 17
See Antony, Merulus and John.

Merwenna (St) Abs. OSB.   May 13
Otherwise Merewenna, q.v.

Meshach (St)   Dec 16
See Mishael.

Mesme (St)   Aug 20
See Maximus.

Mesmin (St) M.   Sept 7
Otherwise Memorius, q.v.

Mesmin (St)   Dec 15
Otherwise Maximinus, q.v.

Mesopotamia (Martyrs
of) (SS) MM.   May 23
d. c 307 A group of martyrs who suffered in
Mesopotamaia under Maximian Galerius.

Mesrob (St) C.   Nov 25
c 345–440 Surnamed "the Teacher". A
native of the province of Taron in Armenia, he
became a disciple of St Nerses the Great and a
monk. For many years he was an auxiliary
bishop of the Patriarch Sahak, succeeding to
his office at the latter's death in 440, and dying
himself only six months later. The Armenians
attribute to him the invention of their alphabet
and the translation of the New Testament into
Armenian. He organized schools and studies
throughout the country. Indeed, he was one of
the most remarkable oriental churchmen of
his time.

Messalina (St) VM.   Jan 19
d. 251 A maiden of Foligno, who received
the veil from St Felician, bishop of that city.
She is said to have visited him in prison and to
have been thereupon delated as a Christian
and clubbed to death.

Messianus (St) M.   Jan 8
Otherwise Maximian. See Lucian, Maximian and Julian.

Metellus (St) M.   Jan 24
See Mardonius, Musonius, etc.

Methodius (St) Bp.   GC. Feb 14
See Cyril and Methodius.

Methodius the Confessor (St) Bp.   June 14
d. 847   A Sicilian who founded a monastery on the island of Chios. He was sent to Rome and on his return to Constantinople he was detained in prison for seven years. Finally in 842, the empress Theodora induced him to become patriarch of Constantinople. In this position he did excellent work in restoring the faith after thirty years of iconoclastic rule.

Methodius (St) Bp. M.   Sept 18
d. 311   Bishop of Olympus in Lycia, and then of Tyre in Phoenicia. He is generally supposed to have died a martyr at Chalcis. He is now better known as an ecclesiastical writer of distinction, especially for his *Banquet of the Ten Virgins*, an imitation of Plato's *Symposium*, and for his treatise on the resurrection.

Metranus (Metras) (St) M.   Jan 31
d. c 250   An Egyptian of Alexandria, martyred under Decius. St Dionysius of Alexandria, his bishop and contemporary, has left a vivid account of the martyrdom.

Metrobius (St) M.   Dec 24
See Lucian, Metrobius, etc.

Metrodora (St) VM.   Sept 10
See Menodora, Metrodora and Nymphodora.

Metrophanes (St) Bp.   June 4
d. 325   Bishop of Byzantium from 313 to 325, and supposed to have been the first occupant of that see. Very little, however, is known about him.

Meugant (Mawghan, Morgan) (St)   Sept 26
6th cent.   He appears to have been a disciple of St Illtyd, to have lived as a hermit in several places in W. Britain, and to have died on the isle of Bardsey. Several churches in Wales and Cornwall are dedicated to him.

Meuris and Thea (SS) MM.   Dec 19
d. c 307   Two maidens martyred at Gaza in Palestine. They are probably identical with the St Valentina and her anonymous fellow-martyr commemorated on July 25.

Mewan (St) Ab.   June 21
The Cornish form of the name Maine, q.v.

Mewrog (St) C.   Sept 25
? A Welsh saint, concerning whom no particulars are extant.

Micah (St) Prophet   Jan 15
8th cent. B.C.   One of the twelve Minor Prophets. His book contains the prophecy of Christ's birth in Bethlehem. His presence in the pre-1970 RM. is due to an alleged finding of his remains.

Michael Pini (Bl) H. OSB. Cam.   Jan 27
c 1445-1522   Born at Florence, he was in high favour at the court of Lorenzo de' Medici before becoming a Camaldolese hermit (1502). After ordination he was walled up in his hermitage, where he remained till his death.

Michael Cozaki (St) M.   Feb 6
d. 1597   A Japanese catechist and hospital nurse to the Franciscan missionaries. He was crucifed at Nagasaki with St Peter Baptist and other companions including his own son, St Thomas Cozaki. Beatified in 1627, and canonized in 1862. See Paul Miki and Comps.

Michael Cordero (Bl) FSC.   Feb 9
1854-1910   A native of Equador, and a de la Salle Brother, the first native vocation. A gifted teacher, he was much loved by his charges. Eventually, his literary and poetic works earned him membership of the Académie Française. A person full of charity and good humour, he led an intense life of personal prayer. He died near Barcelona. Due to Communist desecration in 1936 his intact body was taken back to Equador that year. He was beatified in 1977.

Michael of the Saints (St) C. O. Trin.   Apr 10
1591-1625   Born at Vich, in Spanish Catalonia, he joined the Calced Trinitarians at Barcelona in 1603, and took his vows at Saragossa in 1607. This same year he passed over to the Discalced Trinitarians and renewed his vows at Alcalá. After his ordination he was twice superior at Valladolid, where he died. Canonized in 1862.

Michael Ulumbijski (St) C.   May 7
6th cent.   One of the twelve companions of St John Zedazneli (Nov 7) in Georgia, q.v.

Michael Garicoits (St) Founder   May 14
1797-1863   Born near Bayonne, the son of a Pyrenean peasant, he acted as servant to his parish priest, and later to the bishop of Bayonne, in return for his education. He was

ordained in 1823; held a curacy for a short time; was appointed professor of philosophy; and eventually rector of the diocesan seminary. As such he founded in 1838 at Bétharram the congregation of Auxiliary Priests of the Sacred Heart, known as the Bétharram Fathers, for mission work among the people. After encountering many initial difficulties the congregation grew and spread beyond France and across the Atlantic. Canonized in 1947.

Michael Gedroye (Bl)
OSA.   May 4
d. 1485 Born near Vilna in Lithuania of noble parentage. He was a cripple and a dwarf. He took up his abode in a cell adjoining the church of the Augustinian canons regular at Cracow, and there he lived all his life, famous for his gifts of prophecy and miracles.

Michael Ho-Dinh-Hy (St)
M.   May 22
c 1808–1857 Born at Nhu-lam in Vietnam of Christian parents, he became a great mandarin and superintendent of the royal silk mills. For a long time he did not practise his religion, but eventually became leader and protector of his fellow-Christians. He was for this reason beheaded at An-Hoa, near Hué. Canonized in 1988.

Michael of Synnada (St) Bp.   May 23
d. c 820 A disciple of St Tarasius of Constantinople, by whom he was ordained bishop of Synnada in Phrygia. Tarasius also chose Michael as the bearer of his synodal letter to Pope St Leo III in Rome. Michael was a fearless opponent of the iconoclasts. He was for this reason banished to Galatia by the emperor Leo the Armenian.

Michael Tozo (Bl) M.   June 20
d. 1626 A native of Japan, catechist to Bl Balthassar Torres. He was burnt alive at Nagasaki. Beatified in 1867.

Michael My (St) M.   Aug 12
d. 1838 Born in Vietnam. He was mayor of Ke-Vinh, and a married man. He was martyred with Bl Antony Dich, his son-in-law, and St James Nam. Canonized in 1988.

Michael Kiraiemon (Bl)
M. Tert. OFM.   Aug 17
d. 1627 A native of Japan and tertiary of St Francis. Beheaded at Nagasaki. Beatified in 1867.

Michael Diaz (Bl) M.   Aug 19
d. 1622 A Spanish merchant on the Japanese ship of Bl Joachim Firaiama (q.v.).

He was beheaded at Nagasaki. Beatified in 1867.

Michael Carvalho (Bl) M.
SJ.   Aug 25
1577–1624 Born at Braga in Portugal, he entered the Society of Jesus in 1597 and was sent to Goa, where he was ordained and taught theology for fifteen years. He was next dispatched to Japan, which he reached after many adventures. In July 1623 he was arrested and finally roasted to death at Ximabura with BB Peter Vasquez, OP., Louis Sotelo, OFM. and two other Friars Minor. Beatified in 1867.

Michael Ghebre (Bl) M.
CM.   Sept 1
1791–1855 Born in Abyssinia, he became an orthodox monk in that country and was known for his zeal and scholarship. Contact with missionary fathers of St Vincent of Paul caused him to enter the Catholic church in 1844 and in 1851 he was ordained, having already joined the Vincentian Fathers. In 1855 a persecution was launched against the Ethiopian Catholics by their new *negus*, Theodore II. Michael was arrested and died from the ill-usage he received at the hands of his gaolers. Beatified in 1926.

Michael Jamada (Bl) M.
Tert. OP.   Sept 8
d. 1628 A Japanese and a Dominican tertiary, beheaded at Nagasaki. Beatified in 1867.

Michael Tomaki (Bl) M.   Sept 8
1613–1626 A Japanese boy of thirteen beheaded at Nagasaki with his father, Bl John Tomaki, and his three brothers. Beatified in 1867.

Michael Xumpo (Bl) M. SJ.   Sept 10
1589–1622 A Japanese who attached himself to the Jesuit missionaries when only eight years old. He was received into the Society of Jesus by Bl Charles Spinola in the prison at Omura and later burnt alive at Nagasaki. Beatified in 1867.

Michael Yamiki (Bl) M.   Sept 10
1617–1622 The five-year-old son of Bl Damian Yamiki, beheaded at Nagasaki with his father on the day of the great martyrdom. Beatified in 1867.

Michael Fimonaya (Bl)
M. Tert. OP.   Sept 16
d. 1628 A Japanese catechist and Dominican tertiary, beheaded at Nagasaki. Beatified in 1867.

Michael Kinoxi (Bl) M.
Tert. OSA.   Sept 28
d. 1630 A native of Japan, beheaded at

Nagasaki for having given shelter to the missionaries. He was an Augustinian tertiary. Beatified in 1867.

Michael the Archangel (St) GC. Sept 29

One of the three angels, Michael, Gabriel and Raphael, liturgically venerated by the church on this date, and also described as one of the seven angels who stand before the throne of God (q.v.). Holy scripture describes Michael as "one of the chief princes" (Dan. 10:13); and as the leader of the heavenly armies in their battle against the forces of hell (Rev. 12:7). He is mentioned also in the epistle of St Jude as "rebuking the devil". He has always been especially invoked by the Catholic church both in the East and in the West. His feast on Sept 29 is probably the anniversary of the dedication of a church of St Michael and All Angels on the Salarian Way at Rome in the sixth century. He is depicted as an archangel in full armour, with a sword and a pair of scales, and piercing a dragon or devil with his lance.

Michael Rua (Bl) Oct 29

Born in 1837 at Turin he was an early member of St John Bosco's Institute, succeeding him in 1888 as general. Nearly three hundred new Salesian houses were opened under his leadership. He was beatified in 1972.

Michael Takexita (Bl) M. Nov 27

d. 1619 A Japanese layman, of the royal family of Firando. He is described as a man of most amiable character. He was beheaded, at the age of twenty-five, at Nagasaki, with ten companions. Beatified in 1867.

Michael Nakaxima (Bl) M. SJ. Dec 25

d. 1628 Born at Maciai in Japan. He concealed the missionary priests in his house and was admitted to the Society of Jesus. From the year 1627 to September 1628 he was kept a prisoner in his own house. He was then taken to Ximabara and after many tortures brought to the hot springs of Mt Ungen where scalding water was poured upon him until he died. Beatified in 1867.

Michaela of the Most Holy Sacrament (St) Aug 26

Otherwise Mary-Michaela, q.v.

Michelina of Pesaro (Bl) W. Tert. OFM. June 20

1300–1356 Michelina Metelli was born at Pesaro, in the Duchy of Urbino, of the family of the counts of Pardi. At the age of twelve she married Duke Malatesta and was left a widow when she was twenty. On the death of her only child she determined to change her life, but met with opposition from her parents who shut her up as a lunatic. When set free she gave up her fortune, became a Franciscan tertiary, and lived as such till her death. Cult confirmed in 1737.

Mida (St) V. Jan 15

Otherwise Ita, q.v.

Midan (Nidan) (St) Sept 30

d. c610 A saint of Anglesey who flourished early in the seventh century.

Midnat (St) V. Nov 18

Otherwise Medana, q.v.

Migdonius and Mardonius (SS) MM. Dec 23

d. 303 High officials at the imperial court of Rome. When the persecution broke out under Diocletian in 303, they refused to renounce their Christian faith. Migdonius was for this reason burnt at the stake and Mardonius drowned in a well.

Miguel

See Michael, which is the spelling used in this book.

Milburga (St) Abs. OSB. Feb 23

d. 715 The elder sister of St Mildred of Thanet, and second abbess of Wenlock in Salop founded by her father Merewalh, king of Mercia. Archbishop St Theodore consecrated her as a nun and the nunnery is said to have greatly flourished under her rule. She had the gift of miracles and a mysterious power over birds. She is an attractive character.

Mildgytha (St) N. OSB. Jan 17

d. c676 The youngest of the three holy virgins of Thanet — Milburga, Mildred and Mildgytha. She either received the veil at Minster in Thanet, where her own mother, St Ermenburga, or Domneva, was abbess, or she entered a convent in Northumbria, where she died: these are two old traditions.

Mildred of Thanet (St) Abs. OSB. July 13

d. c700? One of the three daughters of St Ermenburga of Thanet. She was sent by her mother to be educated in the French nunnery of Chelles, and on her return, received the Benedictine habit from St Theodore of Canterbury at Minster in Thanet, where she eventually succeeded her mother as abbess. Her relics were first enshrined at Canterbury and afterwards removed to Deventer, Holland, whence a part of them have been in recent times brought back to Minster. Mildred was one of the most popular saints in medieval England. In her life she is described as "ever merciful, of easy temper and tranquil". Every

St Michael the Archangel, Sept 29

St Mildred of Thanet, July 13

year a pilgrimage takes place to Minster and her relics are venerated there. Her convent is one of the oldest continuously inhabited buildings in Britain. She is depicted habited as a Benedictine nun accompanied by a white hart.

Miles Gerard (Bl) M.   Apr 30
d. 1590 *Alias* William Richardson. He was born near Wigan and became a schoolmaster. Afterwards he studied for the priesthood at Reims and was ordained in 1583. He was martyred for his faith at Rochester. Beatified in 1929.

Milles (St) M.   Apr 22
d. 380 A Persian bishop martyred under King Shapur II.

Milo (Bl) Bp.   Feb 23
d. 1076 Born in Auvergne, he was made canon of Paris and dean of the chapter, and finally (1074) archbishop of Benevento in Italy. He died two years later.

Milo (Bl) Bp. O. Praem.   July 16
d. 1159 Milo of Selincourt was a disciple of St Norbert. He became abbot of Donmartin in

1123 and bishop of Thérouanne in 1131. He was one of the ablest opponents of Gilbert de la Porrée.

Milo (Bl) H. OSB.   Aug 18
d. *c* 740 His parents who were noble Franks both entered the cloister; Milo entered with his father at Fontenelle and later became a recluse.

Miltiades (St) Pope   Dec 10
d. 314 Wrongly spelt in the pre-1970 RM. and elsewhere, Melchiades. Perhaps an African by birth, he was pope from 311 to 314, during which period the emperor Constantine granted toleration to the church. St Miltiades was venerated as a martyr on account of his many sufferings during the persecution of Maximian. Cult confined to local calenders since 1969.

Minervinus (St) M.   Dec 31
See Stephen, Pontian, etc.

Minervius, Eleazar and Comp. (SS) MM.   Aug 23
3rd cent. The details of the passion of these martyrs are wanting, and those given in the chronicles are untrustworthy. It seems fairly clear that they suffered at Lyons. Eight children are said to have been included in their number, and these are alleged to have been the children either of Minervius or of Eleazar. Eleazar is believed by some to have been a woman, perhaps the wife of Minervius.

Minias (Italian: Miniato) (St) M.   Oct 25
d. *c* 250 A soldier, stationed at Florence, where he spread the faith among his comrades, and where he was martyred under Decius. The great abbey outside the city walls bears his name.

Minnborinus (St) Ab. OSB.   July 18
d. 986 An Irishman, who became abbot of St Martin at Cologne (974–986).

Miro (Bl) C. OSA.   Sept 12
d. 1161 An Augustinian canon regular at St John de las Abadesas, near Vich, in Spanish Catalonia.

Mirocles (St) Bp.   Dec 3
d. 318 Archbishop of Milan, one of the originators of the Ambrosian liturgy and chant.

Mishael (Meshach) (St)   Dec 16
7th cent. B.C. One of the three Hebrew youths cast into the fiery furnace at Babylon

and miraculously delivered unscathed therefrom (Dan. 3).

Mitrius (French: Mitre, Metre, Merre) (St) M. Nov 13
d. 314 A Greek slave belonging to a tyrannical master at Aix in Provence. He was savagely ill-used by his master and by his fellow-slaves, and finally beheaded.

Minason (St) July 12
Otherwise Jason, q.v.

Mo
Note. The syllable mo (my) often prefixed to the names of Irish saints has an honorific significance.

Mobeoc (Mobheoc) (St) Ab. Jan 1
Otherwise Beoc, q.v.

Mochoemoc (Mochaemhog, Pulcherius, Vulcanius) (St) Ab. March 13
d. *c* 656 He was born in Munster and brought up by his aunt, St Ita. He became a monk of Bangor in Co. Down under St Comgall, and later the abbot-founder of Liath-Mochoemoc. All other information we have about him is pure legend.

Mochelloc (Cellog, Mottelog, Motalogus) (St) March 26
d. *c* 639 Patron saint of Kilmallock in Limerick. Authentic particulars of his life are lacking.

Mochta (Mochteus) (St) Bp. Aug 19
6th cent. A Briton by birth, he founded the monastery of Louth in the East of Ireland. His life is a tissue of miraculous fables.

Mochua (St) Ab. Jan 1
Otherwise Cuan, q.v. Several Irish saints are honoured under the name of Mochua on various days.

Mochuda (St) Bp. May 14
Otherwise Carthage the Younger, q.v.

Modan (St) Ab. Feb 4
? 6th cent. The son of an Irish chieftain who preached at Stirling, Falkirk, and along the Forth, retiring in his old age to a solitude near Dumbarton.

Modanic (St) Bp. Nov 14
8th cent. A Scottish bishop whose feast was kept at Aberdeen, but of whom we have no reliable particulars.

Moderan (Moderamnus, Moran) (St) Bp. OSB. Oct 22
d. *c* 730 A native of Rennes who became bishop of that city in 703. About the year 720

he made a pilgrimage to Rome, resigned his see and ended his days as a monk-hermit in the abbey of Berceto, in the diocese of Parma.

Modesta (St) M. March 13
See Macedonius, Patricia and Modesta.

Modesta (St) Ab. OSB. Nov 4
d. *c* 680 Niece of St Mocoald, and first abbess of the nunnery of Oehren (*Horreum*) at Trier, to which office she was appointed by its founder, St Modoald.

Modestus (St) M. Jan 12
See Zoticus, Rogatus, etc.

Modestus (St) Bp. OSB. Feb 5
d. *c* 722 A monk under St Virgilius, abbot-bishop of Salzburg. He was appointed regionary bishop of Carinthia and was largely responsible for the evangelization of that country.

Modestus and Julian (SS) MM. Feb 12
? Modestus was martyred at Carthage, Julian at Alexandria (in 160). The former is venerated as the patron saint of Cartagena in Spain. Their association in the pre-1970 RM. was arbitrary.

Modestus and Ammonius (SS) MM. Feb 12
? Martyrs at Alexandria in Egypt. They are said to have been the children of St Damian, martyr (Feb 12). Nothing is known about them.

Modestus (St) M. Feb 12
d. *c* 304 A deacon, said to have been a native of Sardinia, martyred under Diocletian. His relics were brought to Benevento *c* 785.

Modestus (St) Bp. Feb 24
d. 489 Bishop of Trier from 486 to 489, that is, during the difficult period when the city came under Frankish rule. His relics are venerated in the church of St Matthias at Trier.

Modestus (St) M. formerly June 15
See Vitus, Modestus and Crescentia.

Modestus (St) M. Nov 10
See Tiberius, Modestus and Florentia.

Modoald (St) Bp. May 12
d. 640 A native of Gascony, related by blood and united in friendship with most of the saints of the Merovingian period. From being the adviser of King Dagobert I, he became bishop of Trier in 622, which he governed most successfully till his death.

Modoc (St) Bp. Jan 31
Otherwise Aidan of Ferns, q.v.

Modomnock (Domnoc, Dominic) (St) Bp. Feb 13
d. *c* 550 An alleged descendant of the Irish royal line of O'Neil. He was a disciple of St David in Wales, and afterwards a hermit at Tibraghny in Kilkenny, and, some writers add, a bishop.

Modwenna (St) V. July 5
7th cent. Also called Edana, Medana, Monyna, Merryn, and in French Modivene. Four or five saints of this name are listed in different menologies, but their lives are hopelessly confused. Two seem to have been more important than the rest: (1) St Modwenna who succeeded St Hilda as abbess of Whitby (d. *c* 695); and (2) St Modwenna, abbess of Polesworth in Warwickshire (d. *c* 900).

Moeliai (Moelray) (St) Ab. June 23
d. *c* 493 A native of Ireland, baptized by St Patrick, and by him set over the newly founded monastery of Nendrum, where he had SS Finian and Colman among his disciples.

Mogue (St) Bp. Jan 31
Otherwise Aidan, q.v.

Molagga (Laicin) (St) Ab. Jan 20
d. *c* 655 An Irishman, brought up in Wales under St David. He founded a monastery at Fulachmhin (Fermoy). He is venerated in Eire.

Molaisre (St) Bp. Apr 18
Otherwise Laserian, q.v.

Molling (Moling, Myllin, Molignus, or Dairchilla) (St) Bp. June 17
d. 697 Born in Wexford, he is said to have been a monk at Glendalough and afterwards abbot at Aghacainid (Teghmolin, St Mullins). Later, he succeeded St Aidan in the see of Ferns, having the whole of Leinster under his jurisdiction. He resigned some years before his death.

Moloc (Molluog, Murlach, Lugaidh) (St) Bp. June 25
d. *c* 572 A Scot, who was educated in Ireland and then returned to his native land as a missionary. His main work as a bishop was the evangelization of the Hebrides. He died at Rossmarkie, but his shrine was at Mortlach.

Molonachus (St) Bp. June 25
7th cent. A disciple of St Brendan who became bishop of Lismore in Argyle.

Molua (St) Ab. Aug 4
Otherwise Lua, q.v.

Mommolinus (St) Ab. OSB. Oct 16
Otherwise Mummolinus, q.v.

Mommolus (St)
Otherwise Mummolus, q.v.

Monacella (St) V. Jan 31
Otherwise Melangell, q.v.

Monaldus of Ancona, Antony of Milan and Francis of Fermo (BB) MM. OFM. March 15
d. 1286 Three Franciscan friars who were sent to Armenia to preach the gospel and were martyred there.

Monan (St) M. March 1
d. 874 A saint trained under St Adrian of St Andrew's, and a missionary in the country about the Firth of Forth. He was slain by the Danes, together with a great number of fellow-Christians.

Monas (St) Bp. Oct 12
d. 249 Bishop of Milan from 193 till his death, i.e., for fifty-six years. He lived through several persecutions.

Monegundis (St) July 2
d. 570 A woman of Chartres who, on the death of her two daughters, obtained the consent of her husband to become a hermit. She spent the better part of her life in a cell at Tours, where she died. Round her deathbed were gathered several nuns who had followed her example and who later united in forming the original community of Saint-Pierre-le-Puellier.

Monennaa (or Darerca) (St) V. July 6
d. 518 An Irish abbess at Sliabh Cuillin, where she died. Her regime was singularly austere.

Monessa (St) V. Sept 4
d. 456 Daughter of an Irish chieftain converted by St Patrick. The tradition is that she died on coming out of the baptismal font.

Monica (Bl) M. July 12
d. 1626 A native Japanese woman, wife of Bl John Naisen, with whom she was beheaded at Nagasaki for having given shelter to Bl John Baptist Zola. Beatified in 1867.

Monica (St) W. GC. Aug 27
332–387 Born at Carthage of Christian parentage, but married to a pagan husband, she was the mother of three children. Her husband's example led to the indifference of her elder son, St Augustine, the future Doctor of

the Church, to the faith. Through her patience and gentleness she converted her husband, and after his death her prayers and tears were rewarded by the return of Augustine to the practice of the Catholic faith. Monica followed him to Rome, where the longed-for conversion took place in 386. She died the same year at Ostia, near Rome, on the way back to Africa with Augustine. Her relics are preserved at his church in Rome near the Piazza Navona.

Monitor (St) Bp.   Nov 10
d. *c* 490   Twelfth bishop of Orleans.

Monon (St) M.   Oct 18
c 645   A Scottish pilgrim who crossed over to the Continent and lived as a hermit in the Ardennes. He was murdered at Nassogne, in Belgian Luxemburg, by some evil-doers whom he had reproved.

Montanus, Lucius, Julian, Victoricus, Flavian and Comp. (SS) MM.   Feb 24
d. 259   A group of ten African martyrs, disciples of St Cyprian of Carthage, who suffered in that city under Valerian. Their *Acta* are thoroughly authentic: the story of their imprisonment is told by themselves, and that of their martyrdom by eye-witnesses.

Montanus and Maxima (SS) MM.   March 26
d. 304   Montanus, a priest, and Maxima, said to have been his wife, were drowned as Christians in the R. Save at Sirmium, in Dalmatia, or Singidunum, Pannonia.

Montanus (St) M.   June 17
d. *c* 300   A soldier who was taken to the island of Ponza, off the Italian coast, and martyred there by being thrown into the sea with a heavy stone tied round his neck. Christians recovered his body and enshrined it at Gaeta.

Morandus (St) Mk. OSB.   June 3
d. *c* 1115   Born of noble parentage near Worms, he was educated there at the cathedral school, and after a pilgrimage at Compostella, received the Benedictine habit at Cluny from St Hugh the Great. Eventually he was sent to the new Cluniac foundation of St Christopher's at Altkirk, in Alsace, of which he was the first superior. He was greatly esteemed for his work as a missioner throughout the neighbouring countryside.

More, Thomas (St) M.   June 22
See Thomas More.

Moricus (Bl) C.   March 30
d. 1236   A religious of the order of the

Cruciferi, whose story is told by St Bonaventure in his life of St Francis of Assisi. The Franciscans claim him as the fifth recruit to join the Friars Minor. He is honoured chiefly at Orvieto and among the Franciscans.

Moroc (St) Bp.   Nov 8
9th cent.   Abbot of Dunkeld and afterwards bishop of Dunblane. He appears to have left his name to several churches, and was venerated with a solemn office in the old Scottish rite.

Morwenna (St) V.   July 8
5th cent?   A Cornish saint, to whom we owe several place-names. She is often confused either with the other saints of this name or with the Irish saints of the name of Moninne. Her emblem is a tall cross which she holds; or she teaches children to read.

Moses (St) Bp.   Feb 7
d. *c* 372   An Arab who retired into the desert around Mt Sinai, and there worked as bishop of a roaming Arab flock.

Moses (St) M.   Feb 14
See Cyrion, Bassian, etc.

Moses the Black (St) M.   Aug 28
d. *c* 395   An Abyssinian Negro, born in slavery and of such vicious propensities that his master drove him from his household, whereupon he became the chief of a gang of robbers. It was as a fugitive from justice that he took refuge among the hermits of Scete in Lower Egypt, by whom he was converted. He remained with them, was ordained and became famous for his supernatural gifts. In his old age he was murdered by Bedouins against whom he refused to defend himself.

Moses (St) Prophet   Sept 4
13th cent. B.C.?   The Hebrew leader and lawgiver. What we know of him we learn from the Bible, chiefly from the Book of Exodus. He died on the borders of the promised land. Where he was buried no man knows. In art he is shown as an old man holding the two tables of the law, and often with vestigial horns on his forehead.

Moses (St) M.   Nov 25
d. 251   A Roman priest, noted for his zeal in preaching the gospel and for his firm stand against Novatianism. He was one of the victims under Decius.

Moses (Moysetes) (St) M.   Dec 18
d. *c*? 250   An African martyr, who probably suffered under Decius.

Moseus and Ammonius
(SS) MM.   Jan 18
d. 250   Two soldier-martyrs sentenced to forced labour for life in the mines and later burnt alive at Astas (Asracus) in Bithynia.

Mount Ararat (Martyrs of)   June 22
See Acacius.

Mount Sinai (Martyrs of)   Jan 14
d. c 380   A group of monks on Mt Sinai, massacred by the marauding Bedouins. Another and larger group of solitaries done to death also by the Bedouins in the neighbouring desert of Raithu is commemorated on the same day in the pre-1970 RM.

Movean (Biteus) (St) Ab.   July 22
? A disciple of St Patrick and abbot of Inis-Coosery, Co. Down. He seems also to have worked in Perthshire, where he is thought to have died as a hermit.

Mucian (St) M.   July 3
See Mark, Mucian, etc.

Mucius (St) M.   Feb 6
See Silvanus, Luke, etc.

Mucius (St) M.   Apr 22
See Parmenius and Comp.

Mucius (St) M.   May 13
d. 304   A Roman by origin, but born at Byzantium, Mucius became a priest and was martyred under Diocletian for having, it is said, overturned a pagan altar.

Mugagga (St) M.   June 3
d. 1886   He was brought up and taught by the royal clothmaker. He was martyred by order of King Mwanga of Uganda. See Charles Lwanga and Comps.

Muirchu (Maccutinus)
(St) C.   June 8
7th cent.   An Irishman, who wrote a life of St Brigid and a life of St Patrick.

Mukasa Kiriwawanvu
(St) M.   June 3
d. 1886   He served at the royal table of King Mwanga of Uganda by whose orders he was put to death. See Charles Lwanga and Comps.

Mullion (St) Bp.   Jan 6
Otherwise Melanius, q.v.

Mummolinus
(Mommolenus, etc.) (St)
Bp. OSB.   Oct 16
d. c 686   A native of Constance in Switzerland, he became a monk at Luxeuil, and eventually was sent to St Omer and appointed superior of the Old Monastery (now Saint-

Mommolin). Thence he migrated to the New Monastery, viz. Sithin, which had been founded by his great friend and fellow-monk St Bertinus. Finally in 660 he was made bishop of Noyon-Tournai.

Mummolus (Mommolus, Mommolenus) (St) Ab. OSB.   Aug 8
d. c 678   Second abbot of Fleury. He caused perhaps a portion of the relics of SS Benedict and Scholastica to be translated from Montecassino to France, and for this reason Fleury began to be known as Saint-Benoît-sur-Loire.

Mummolus (Mumbolus, Momleolus, Momble)
(St) Ab. OSB.   Nov 18
d. c 690   An Irishman, companion of St Fursey, whom he succeeded as abbot of Lagny, in the diocese of Meaux.

Mun (St) Bp.   Feb 6
5th cent.   Described as a nephew of St Patrick, who allegedly ordained him a bishop. He is said to have ended his days as a solitary on an island in Lough Ree, Ireland.

Munchin (St) Bp. (?)   Jan 2
7th cent.?   Patron of the city and diocese of Limerick, St Munchin may have been first bishop of that see.

Mundus (Munde, Mund, Mond) (St) Ab.   Apr 15
d. c 962   A Scottish abbot who governed a large abbey and made several monastic foundations in Argyle. The details of his career are obscure.

Mungo (St) Bp.   Jan 13
Otherwise Kentigern, q.v.

Munnu (Mundus, etc.) (St)   Oct 21
Otherwise Fintan, q.v.

Mura McFeredach
(Muran, Murames) (St)
Ab.   March 12
d. c 645   Born in Donegal, he was appointed abbot of Fahan by St Columba. He is the special patron saint of Fahan in Co. Derry, where his cross still stands.

Muredhae (Bl) Ab. OSB.   Feb 9
Otherwise Marianus Scotus, q.v.

Muritta (St) M.   July 13
See Eugene, Salutaris, etc.

Murtagh (Muredach) (St)
Bp.   Aug 13
6th cent.?   A disciple of St Patrick, by whom he was ordained first bishop of Killala. He ended his life as a hermit in the island of

Innismurray: alternatively, he was known to St Columba. Both traditions cannot be correct.

Musa (St) V.   Apr 2
d. 6th cent. A child living in Rome who was favoured with visions and mystical experiences. She is spoken of by St Gregory the Great, her contemporary.

Musonius (St) M.   Jan 24
See Mardonius, Musonius, etc.

Mustiola (St) M.   July 3
See Irenaeus and Mustiola.

Mydwyn (St)   Jan 1
See Elvan and Mydwyn.

Myllin (St) Bp.   June 17
The Welsh form of the name Molling, q.v.

Mylor (St) C.   Oct 1
Otherwise Melorius, q.v.

Myrbad (St) C.   May 31
See Winnow, Mancus and Myrbad.

Myron (St) Bp.   Aug 8
c 250–350 Surnamed "the Wonder-worker". A bishop in Crete, who died a centenarian.

Myron (St) M.   Aug 17
d. c 250 A priest who boldly faced the persecutors when they came to destroy his church, and was martyred at Cyzicus on the sea of Marmora.

Myrope (St) M.   July 13
d. c 251 A native of Chios in the Grecian archipelago, whence she used to make pilgrimages to the shrines of the martyrs. Accused of having hidden the body of the martyr St Isidore, she admitted having done so. She was scourged and died in prison from the effects of the punishment.

Naal (St) Ab. Jan 27
Otherwise Natalis, q.v.

Nabor (St) M. June 12
See Basilides, Cyrinus, etc.

Nabor (St) M. July 10
See Januarius, Marinus, etc.

Nabor and Felix (SS) MM. July 12
d. *c* 304 Martyrs at Milan under Diocletian. They owe their celebrity to their solemn translation and enshrinement by St Ambrose, nearly a century later. Since 1969 their cult has been confined to local calendars.

Nagran or Najran (Martyrs of) (SS) Oct 24
d. 523 A large group of martyrs (the pre-1970 RM. gives their number as 340) massacred at Nagran (Najran) in S.W. Arabia by Jews and heathen Arabs under the Jew Dhu Nowas (Dunaan). The leader of the martyrs was the chief of the Beni Harith, Abdullah ibn Kaab (the "Aretas" of the RM.). "After these," added the RM., "a Christian woman was delivered to the flames, and her son of five years old in his lisping voice confessed Christ, and could not be moved from his purpose by promises or threats, but threw himself head-long into the fire where his mother was burning". The massacre of the Nagran martyrs made such a deep impression that they are even mentioned by Mohammed in the Koran (Šura 85).

Nahum (St) C. July 17
See Seven Apostles of Bulgaria.

Nahum (St) Prophet Dec 1
c 612 B.C. One of the minor prophets, supposed to have been a native of N. Palestine. His short prophecy of three chapters is directed against Niniveh. He lived to see the destruction of Niniveh (612 B.C.) which he had foretold.

Namadia (St) N. OSB. Aug 19
d. *c* 700 Wife of St Calminius, and in her widowhood a Benedictine nun at Marsat.

Namasius (Naamat, Namat, Namatius) (St) Bp. Nov 17
d. *c* 599 Twenty-second bishop of Vienne in France. Cult confirmed in 1903.

Namatius (Namace) (St) Bp. Oct 27
d. *p.*462 Ninth bishop of Clermont in France. He built the cathedral.

Namphanion and Comp. (SS) MM. July 4
d. *c*? 180 Namphanion, of Carthaginian descent, was martyred with several companions, his compatriots, at Madaura in Numidia. He is usually styled by the African writers "the Archmartyr".

Namphasius (Namphisius, Namphosius, Nauphary, Namphrase) (St) H. OSB. Nov 12
d. *c* 800 A friend of Charlemagne, and one of those who fought against the Saracens in S. France. He afterwards became a monk-recluse near Marcillac (Lot).

Nanterius (Nantier, Nantère) (Bl) Ab. OSB. Oct 30
d. *c* 1044 A Benedictine abbot of the monastery of Saint-Mihiel (*S. Michaelis ad Mosam*) in Lorraine, diocese of Verdun.

Narcissus (St) M. Jan 2
See Argeus, Narcissus, and Marcellinus.

Narcissus and Felix (SS) MM. March 18
d. *c* 307 A bishop and his deacon honoured as martyrs at Gerona in Spanish Catalonia. This is all that is certain about these martyrs; their alleged escape to, and their apostolate in Germany and Switzerland with the subsequent conversion of St Afra, is legendary.

Narcissus and Crescentio (SS) MM. Sept 17
d. *c* 260 They are mentioned in the Acts of St Lawrence the Martyr, which are only substantially authentic. St Lawrence used to distribute alms to the poor in the house of

Narcissus, and there he cured Crescentio of his blindness. On the Salarian Way a cemetery bore the name of Crescentio.

Narcissus (St) Bp.   Oct 29
d. *c* 222   A Greek who was appointed bishop of Jerusalem when he was already a very old man. He was summoned to a council at Jerusalem at which he favoured the Roman custom of celebrating Easter. He was for this reason calumniated and for a time retired from his see, but returned to it at the request of his people.

Narcissus (St) M.   Oct 31
See Ampliatus, Urban and Narcissus.

Narnus (St) Bp.   Aug 27
? The alleged first bishop of Bergamo, said to have been consecrated by St Barnabas.

Narses (St) Bp.   Jan 3
340?   Narses, bishop of Subogord in Persia, was arrested and martyred with his disciple Joseph. The date is uncertain.

Narses (St) M.   March 27
See Zanitas, Lazarus, etc.

Narseus (St) M.   July 15
See Philip, Zeno, etc.

Narzales (St) M.   July 17
See Scillitan Martyrs.

Natalia (St) M.   July 27
See George, Aurelius, etc.

Natalia (St) MW.   Sept 8
See Adrian and Natalia.

Natalia (St)   Dec 1
d. *c* 311   A woman of Nicomedia, who bravely ministered to the martyrs imprisoned during the persecution of Diocletian. She is especially mentioned in the Acts of the martyr St Adrian (Sept 8). She survived the persecution and died in peace at Constantinople.

Natalis (St) Ab.   Jan 27
6th cent.   The founder of monasticism in the northern parts of Ireland, and a fellow-worker with St Columba. He ruled the abbeys of Cill, Naile and Daunhinis. His holy well is still venerated.

Natalis (Noel) Pinot (Bl) M.   Feb 21
1747–1794   Born at Angers, he was ordained in 1771 and worked in that diocese as parish priest of Louroux-Béconnais till the outbreak of the French Revolution. On his refusal to take the oath recognizing the civil constituion of the clergy he was extruded from his parish, but continued to minister to his flock at first in secret and afterwards openly. In 1794 he was captured when vested for the eucharist and

guillotined, still wearing his vestments. Beatified in 1926.

Natalis (St) Bp.   May 13
d. 715   Bishop of Milan (740–751).

Natalis (St) C.   Sept 3
6th cent.   A native of Benevento who became a priest and worked at Casale in Piedmont.

Nathalan (St) Bp.   Jan 19
d. *c* 678   A Scot by birth and by legend a rich man. He became an anchorite and is especially praised for having earned his living by the cultivation of the soil, "which approaches nearest to divine contemplation". He was made bishop and resided at Tullicht. Cult confirmed in 1898.

Nathanael (St) Apostle   Aug 24
Otherwise probably Bartholomew, q.v.

Nathy (David) (St) Bp.   Aug 9
d. *c* 610   Disciple of St Finian of Clonard. He became the founder and abbot-bishop of a monastery at Achonry, Sligo, where he is now venerated as the patron saint. Cult confirmed in 1903.

Navalis (St) M.   Dec 16
See Valentine, Concordius, etc.

Nazarius (St) M.   June 12
See Basilides, Cyrinus, etc.

**Nazarius and Celsus
(SS)** MM.   July 28
d. *c* ?68   Martyrs said to have been beheaded at Milan under Nero. Their Acts are certainly unreliable, and even the above-mentioned data are open to doubt. The only certain fact is that St Ambrose searched for and discovered their alleged relics at Milan in 395. Cults confined to local calendars since 1969.

Nazarius (St) Ab.   Nov 18
d. *c* 450   Monk and abbot of Lérins.

Neachtain (St) C.   May 2
5th cent.   A near kinsman of St Patrick, at whose death, according to tradition, he was present.

Nebridius (St) Bp.   Feb 9
d. *p*. 527   Bishop of Egara, near Barcelona in Spain, a city since destroyed.

Nectan (St) M.   June 17
6th cent.   The patron saint of Hartland in Devonshire where he was a hermit. Born in Wales, he is one of the saintly family of Brychan. Beautiful legends surround his name, and his shrine was a great centre of pilgrimages in the Middle Ages until its wanton destruction at the change of religion in the sixteenth century. The magnificent church

at Hartland, with its noble roodscreen, still bears testimony to popular devotion to St Nectan.

Nectarius (St) Bp.　　　　Sept 13
d. *c* 550　Bishop of Autun. A great friend of St Germanus of Paris.

Nectarius (St) Bp.　　　　May 5
d. *c* 445　Bishop of Vienne in Dauphiné.

Nectarius (St) Bp.　　　　Oct 11
d. 397　Successor of St Gregory Nazianzen and predecessor of St John Chrysostom in the see of Constantinople (381–397).

Nemesian, Felix, Lucius, another Felix, Litteus, Polyanus, Victor, Jader, Dativus and Comp. (SS)
Bps. MM.　　　　Sept 10
d. 257　Nine bishops of Numidia who, with numerous lower clergy and layfolk, were condemned to servitude in the marble quarries of Sigum, where they ended their lives. We have still a letter of St Cyprian addressed to them.

Nemesius (St) M.　　　　Feb 20
See Potamius and Nemesius.

Nemesius (St) M.　　　　July 18
See Symphorosa and her children.

Nemesius (St)　　　　Aug 1
? A saint venerated near Lisieux, but of whose life we have no reliable account.

Nemesius and Lucilla (SS) MM.　　　　Aug 25
d. *c* 260　Nemesius, a Roman deacon, and Lucilla, his daughter, were martyred at Rome under Valerian. Their Acts are not trustworthy.

Nemesius (St) M.　　　　Dec 19
d. 250　An Egyptian marytred at Alexandria under Decius. He was burnt at the stake between two thieves.

Nemorius (St) M.　　　　Sept 7
Otherwise Memorius, q.v.

Nennius (St) Ab.　　　　Jan 17
6th cent.　An Irishman, disciple of St Finian of Clonard, reckoned as one of the "Twelve Apostles of Ireland". The particulars of his life are lost.

Nennoc (Nennocha, Ninnoc) (St) V.　　　　June 4
d. *c* 467　A British maiden, one of the family of Brychan of Brecknock, said to have followed St Germanus of Auxerre to France and to have become abbess of one or more monasteries in Armorica.

Nennus (Nenus, Nehemias) (St) Ab.　　　　June 14
7th cent.　An Irish abbot, successor of St Enda in the government of the monasteries of the isles of Arran and Bute.

Neomisia (St) V.　　　　Sept 25
See Aurelia and Neomisia.

Neon (St) M.　　　　Apr 24
See Eusebius, Neon, etc.

Neon (St) M.　　　　Aug 23
See Claudius, Asterius, etc.

Neon (St) M.　　　　Sept 28
See Mark, Alphius, etc.

Neon (St) M.　　　　Dec 2
See Eusebius, Marcellus, etc.

Neophytus (St) M.　　　　Jan 20
d. 310　A youth, not yet fifteen years of age, martyred at Nicaea under Galerius.

Neophytus (St) M.　　　　Aug 22
See Athanasius, Anthusa, etc.

Neopolus (St) M.　　　　May 2
See Saturninus, Neopolus, etc.

Neopolus (Napoleon (St) M.　　　　Aug 15
d. *c* 300　An Egyptian martyr who suffered at Alexandria under Diocletian. He was put to the torture and so horribly maimed thereby that he expired while being carried back to his dungeon.

Neot (St) H. OSB.　　　　July 31
c 880　According to tradition he was a choir monk of Glastonbury, who became a hermit in Cornwall at the place now called Saint Neot. Some relics were subsequently taken to St Neots in Cambridgeshire, from whence St Anselm gave a portion to the abbey of Bec in Normandy.

Neoterius (St) M.　　　　Sept 8
See Ammon, Theophilus, etc.

Nepotian (St) C.　　　　May 4
d. 395　Nephew of St Heliodorus, bishop of Altino, by whom he was ordained after having abandoned his high position of an officer in the imperial bodyguard. He was much esteemed by St Jerome, who dedicated to him a treatise on the sacerdotal life. It seems, however, that he has never been the object of a public cultus.

Nepotian (St) Bp.　　　　Oct 22
d. *c* 388　Bishop of Clermont (386–*c* 388).

Nereus and Achilleus (SS) MM.　　　　GC. May 12
d. *c* 100　Pretorian soldiers baptized, it is

said, by St Peter, and exiled with St Flavia Domitilla to the isle of Pontia and later to Terracina, where they were beheaded. Their extant Acts are far from reliable.

Nereus (St) M.　　　　　　Oct 16
See Saturninus, Nereus, etc.

Neromian Martyrs
See First Martyrs of the See of Rome.

Nerses Lambronazi (St)
Bp.　　　　　　　　　　July 17
1153–1198　An Armenian by birth, nephew of St Nerses Glaiëtsi (see Aug 13), he became the Armenian archbishop of Tarsus and was instrumental in bringing about the reunion of Little Armenia with the bishop of Rome in 1198. He translated many Western works into Armenian, including the rule of St Benedict and St Gregory's Dialogues.

Nerses Glaiëtsi (St) Bp.　　Aug 13
1102–1173　He was called "Chnorhali" meaning "the Gracious" on account of his goodness and his agreeable literary style. As Catholicos he worked diligently at the union of the Greek and Armenian churches, but died before achieving it. He became bishop of the Armenians in 1166 and throughout his life he succeeded in maintaining perfect union and full communion with the bishop of Rome. He excelled as a poet.

Nerses the Great (St) Bp. M.　Nov 19
d. 373　Born in Armenia, educated in Cappadocia and married to a princess of the Mamikonian family by whom he became the father of St Isaac the Great (q.v.). In 353 he was made sixth Catholicos. As such he worked zealously for certain reforms which proved unpalatable to King Arshak III. Nerses was exiled, but recalled by the dissolute King Pap in 369, who contrived to poison him later.

Nerses and Comp. (SS)
MM.　　　　　　　　　　Nov 20
d. 343　A group of at least twelve Persian martyrs of whom the most illustrious were Nerses, bishop of Sahgerd, and his disciple Joseph. They suffered under Shapur II for refusing to worship the sun.

Nestabus (St) M.　　　　　Sept 8
See Eusebius, Nestabus, and Zeno.

Nestor (St) Bp. M.　　　　Feb 26
d. 251　Bishop of Magydos in Pamphylia, crucified at Perga under Decius.

Nestor (St) Bp. M.　　　　March 4
See Basil, Eugene, etc.

Nestor (St) M.　　　　　　Sept 8
d. 362　A youth of Gaza in Palestine, mar-

tyred under Julian the Apostate. After the horrors of the torture-chamber he was, with others, being dragged half-dead to execution when the crowd intervened and insisted, out of pity, on his being left to die by the wayside. He was taken to a Christian home, where he expired.

Nestor (St) M.　　　　　　Oct 8
d. c 304　A martyr of Thessalonica under Diocletian. His story, as handed down to us in his Acts, is certainly fabulous.

Nevolo (Bl) H. OSB. Cam.　July 27
d. 1280　A married shoemaker by trade, he led a frivolous life until at the age of twenty-four he turned completely to God. He became first a Franciscan tertiary and later a Camaldolese lay-brother in the monastery of San Maglorio at Faenza. Cult approved in 1817.

Nicaeas (Nicetas) (St) Bp.　June 22
d. c 414　Most modern writers identify him with St Nicetas of Remesiana (Jan 7), q.v.

Nicaeas and Paul (SS)
MM.　　　　　　　　　　Aug 29
? Catalogued as Syrian martyrs who suffered at Antioch.

Nicander (St) M.　　　　　March 15
d. c 304　An Egyptian martyr beheaded under Diocletian. He was a physician and was condemned for ministering to the Christians in prison, and burying the dead.

Nicander and Marcian
(SS) MM.　　　　　　　　June 17
d. 173 (or 304?)　Two officers in the imperial army, martyred probably in the region now covered by Roumania and Bulgaria. Probably duplicates of SS Marcian and Nicanor (June 5), q.v.

Nicander and Hermas
(SS) MM.　　　　　　　　Nov 4
? St Nicander was a bishop and St Hermas a priest. They were martyred at Myra in Lycia (Asia Minor).

Nicander (St) M.　　　　　Nov 7
See Hieron, Nicander, etc.

Nicanor (St) M.　　　　　Jan 10
d. c 76　A Jew by birth, one of the seven deacons chosen by the apostles (Acts, 6:5). The tradition is that he eventually came to Cyprus, where years afterwards he was martyred under Vespasian. It is more likely that he died in peace.

Nicanor (St) M.　　　　　June 5
See Marcian, Nicanor, etc.

Nicarete (Niceras) (St) V.   Dec 27
d. c 405   A woman born at Nicomedia but resident at Constantinople, where she became the loyal friend and supporter of St John Chrysostom, whose exile and suffering she shared.

Nicasius Jonson (St) M.
OFM.   July 9
c 1522–1572   Born in the castle of Hez, Brabant, he became a licentiate of theology and was the author of several controversial treatises against Protestantism. He was hanged at Briel, Holland, with eighteen companions. Canonized in 1867. (See Gorkum, Martyrs of.)

Nicasius, Eutropia, V.
and Comp. (SS) MM.   Dec 14
d. c 407 (or 451)   Bishop of Reims who, with his sister Eutropia and a number of his clergy and faithful, was martyred either by the Vandals in 407, or by the Huns in 451: the latter is more likely.

Nicephorus (St) M.   Feb 9
d. 260   A martyr of Antioch under Valerian. It is reasonably contended that his story is a pious invention, written to inculcate the forgiveness of injuries.

Nicephorus (St) M.   Feb 25
See Victorinus, Victor, etc.

Nicephorus (St)
Bp. M.   March 13 and June 2
758–829 (June 2)   He began his career as imperial secretary at the court of Constantinople. In 806, despite being a layman, he was chosen patriarch of the city. His antecedents roused the hostility of the powerful monks of Studion and their abbot St Theodore, while the revival of iconoclasm by the emperor Leo the Armenian soon brought him into disagreement with the court. He was exiled to a monastery which he had founded on the Bosporus and there he spent the last fifteen years of his life.

Niceta and Aquilina (SS)
MM.   July 24
?   The names were originally Nicetas and Aquila and were applied to two alleged soldier-martyrs. In the apocryphal Acts of St Christopher the names are given a feminine form and are said to be those of two harlots.

Nicetas of Remesiana
(St) Bp.   Jan 7 and June 22
d. c 414   A zealous missionary bishop in Dacia, i.e., modern Roumania and Yugoslavia. Many scholars assign to him the authorship or redaction of the thanksgiving hymn Te Deum.

Nicetas (St) Bp.   March 20
d. c 735   Bishop of Apollonias in Bithynia, persecuted by the iconoclastic emperor Leo III. He died in exile in Anatolia.

Nicetas (St) Ab.   Apr 3
d. 824   Abbot of Medikion at the foot of Mt Olympus in Bithynia. He suffered much in defence of the veneration of images against Leo the Armenian. He was imprisoned for six years in the isle of Glyceria, but after the emperor's death was set free and died in a hermitage near Constantinople.

Nicetas the Goth (St) M.   Sept 15
d. c 378   Surnamed in the East "the Great". He was an Ostrogoth, converted with many of his people by the Arian Ulphilas. He was a priest and perhaps also, in good faith, an Arian. He was put to death by King Athanaric, who did his utmost to root out Christianity from his people.

Nicetas (St) C.   Oct 6
d. c 838   A young patrician of Paphlagonia, who became prefect of Cilicia and then a monk at Constantinople. He opposed the blind fury of the iconoclasts and was exiled to Catisia, where he died.

Nicetius (Nizier) of
Besançon (St) Bp.   Feb 8
d. 611   Bishop of Besançon and a friend of St Columbanus of Luxeuil. He restored to Besançon the episcopal see, which after the invasion of the Huns had been transferred to Nyon, on the Lake of Geneva.

Nicetius (Nizier) (St) Bp.   Apr 2
d. 573   Became bishop of Lyons in 553 and was pastor for twenty years.

Nicetius (St) Bp.   Dec 5
d. 566   The last of the Gallo-Roman bishops of Trier, being ordained in 532. He had been a monk and abbot in his native province of Auvergne. As a bishop he withstood the cruelty of the Frankish barbarians and excommunicated kings Theudebert I and Clotaire, by whom he was exiled for a time. He restored discipline among the clergy, founded a school of clerical studies, rebuilt the cathedral and combated heresy.

Nicetus (St) Bp.   May 5
d. p. 449   The fifteenth bishop of Vienne, in Gaul.

Nicholas Studites (St) Ab. Feb 4

d. 863 A native of Crete who at an early age entered the monastery of the Studion at Constantinople. During the iconoclastic persecution he followed his abbot into banishment and on his return, when peace was temporarily restored, succeeded him as abbot. He went again into exile under the emperor Michael, refusing to recognize the usurping patriarch, Photius. When the emperor Basil restored St Ignatius, the lawful patriarch, Nicholas considered himself too old to resume charge and lived as a monk at the Studion.

Nicholas of Hungary (Bl)
M. OFM. Feb 12

See Antony of Saxony, etc.

Nicholas Saggio (Bl) C.
O. Minim. Feb 12

d. 1709 Born of poor parents at Longobardi in Calabria, he became a lay-brother in the order of Minims of St Francis of Paola. Beatified by Pius VI.

Nicholas Palea (Bl) C. OP. Feb 14

1197–1255 Born at Giovinazzo, near Bari. As a young man he heard St Dominic preach at Bologna and joined the friars preachers. He established houses of the order at Perugia (1233) and at Trani (1254) and became provincial of the Roman province in 1230 and again in 1255. He died at Perugia. Cult confirmed in 1828.

Nicholas of Vangadizza
(Bl) C. OSB. Cam. Feb 21

d. c 1210 A Camaldolese monk at the abbey of Vangadizza.

Nicholas of Prussia (Bl)
C. OSB. Feb 23

c 1379–1456 A native of Prussia who became one of the original members of the reformed abbey of St Justina at Padua under the Ven. Ludovico Barbo, the founder of the Benedictine Cassinese congregation. Nicholas lived successively at Padua, Venice, Padolirone, and finally at the abbey of San Niccolò del Boschetto, near Genoa, where he was novice-master and prior.

Nicholas Owen (St) M. SJ. March 2

d. 1606 A Jesuit brother who, both before and after entering the Society of Jesus, was employed in making hiding-places for hunted priests. He was twice imprisoned and tortured, and when he was arrested a third time and refused to give any information concerning the Gunpowder Plot, he was tortured to death, being literally torn to pieces. Beatified in 1929. Canonized in 1970 as one of the Forty Martyrs of England and Wales, q.v.

Nicholas von Flüe (St) H. March 21

1417–1487 Born near Sachseln, Canton Obwalden, Switzerland, the son of a peasant, he married and had ten children. Besides fighting bravely in the army of his canton, he was appointed judge and councillor for Obwalden. At the age of fifty he left his family with their consent and for nineteen years lived as a hermit at Ranft without any food, it is said, besides holy communion. His advice was much sought after, especially by civil magistrates. He is still venerated in Switzerland as "Bruder Klaus". Canonized in 1947. He is the patron saint of Switzerland.

Nicholas (Bl) C.
OSB. Cist. Apr 1

d. c 1220 A Cistercian monk at Santa Maria dell' Arcu, near Neti, in Sicily.

Nicholas Albergati (Bl)
Bp. O. Cart. May 9

1375–1443 A native of Bologna who in 1394 joined the Carthusians and in 1418, much against his will, was made archbishop of his native city. In 1426 he was created cardinal. He was called in as mediator between the emperor and the pope and the latter and the French king, and was prominent at the councils of Basle and Ferrara-Florence. He was a generous patron of learned men. Cult confirmed in 1744.

Nicholas the Mystic (St) Bp. May 15

d. 925 Patriarch of Constantinople. He was deposed and banished by the emperor Leo the Wise because he would not permit that monarch to marry a fourth time, this being forbidden in the Eastern church. He is surnamed "the mystic" because he was the oldest member of the mystic, or secret, council of the Byzantine court.

Nicholas (Bl) Ab. OSB.
Cist. May 31

d. c 1163 He and his father gave up splendid worldly prospects in order to receive the Cistercian habit from St Bernard. Nicholas became abbot of Vaucelles. He is venerated by the Cistercians.

Nicholas Peregrinus (St) C. June 2

1075–1094 A Greek who journeyed to S. Italy and wandered through Apulia carrying a cross and crying out "Kyrie eleison". Crowds of people, especially children, followed him repeating the same cry. He was taken for a lunatic and treated as such, but after his death at Trani at the age of nineteen years, so many miracles were alleged to have taken place at his tomb that he was canonized in 1098.

Nicholas Thé (St) M.   June 13
d. 1839 A Vietnamese soldier who was
hacked asunder for the faith. Canonized in
1988.

Nicholas Pieck and
Nicholas Poppel (SS)
MM.   July 9
d. 1572 Two members of the group of the
martyrs of Gorkum (q.v.). Nicholas Pieck was
the Franciscan guardian of the friary at
Gorkum. He was a native of Holland and a
student of Louvain who had made the conversion of Calvinists his life's work. Nicholas
Poppel, also a Dutchman, was curate to Leonard van Wechel, another Gorkum martyr.
Canonized in 1867.

Nicholas Dinnis (Bl) M.
SJ.   July 15
d. 1570 A native of Braganza in Portugal
and a Jesuit novice. Companion of Bl Ignatius
de Azevedo, q.v.

Nicholas, Alexandra and
Comps (SS) MM.   July 17
Reigned 1894–1918 Nicholas II, last Tsar
of Russia, his wife the Empress Alexandra,
and their children, Alexis, Olga, Tatiana,
Marie and Anastasia, and the vast number of
clergy, nuns and monks, and ordinary faithful
martyred for their beliefs by the Communists
were canonized by the Russian church in exile
on Nov 1 1981. The martyred Tsar Nicholas
is placed at their head as he once said "If a
sacrifice is necessary for the salvation of
Russia, I will be that sacrifice". They have
become a symbol of all that they stood for, in
dying because of whom they were.

Nicholas Hermanssön
(Bl) Bp.   July 24
1331–1391 Born at Skeninge in Sweden
and educated at Paris and Orleans, he was
ordained and appointed tutor to the sons of St
Brigid of Sweden. Eventually he became
bishop of Linköping. He is greatly honoured
in Sweden as a liturgist and poet. It is said, but
cannot be proved, that he was canonized in
1414 (or 1416).

Nicholas Appleine (Bl) C.   (?) Aug 11
d. 1466 A canon of St-Marcel-de-Pré-
mery, diocese of Nevers. Cult approved by the
bishop of Nevers in 1731.

Nicholas Politi (Bl) H.   Aug 17
1117–1167 Born at Adernò, in Sicily. He
lived for thirty years as a hermit in a cave on Mt
Etna. Cult approved by Julius II.

Nicholas of Tolentino
(St) C. OSA. Erem.   Sept 10
1245–1305 A native of Sant'Angelo, diocese
of Fermo. In 1623 he joined the hermits of St
Augustine. After his ordination he made a
resolution to preach daily to the people, and
this he did, first at Cingoli, and then for thirty
years at Tolentino. He was also known for his
work among the poor. Canonized in 1446.
Cult confined to local calendars since 1969.

Nicholas of Forca-Palena
(Bl) C.   Oct 1
1349–1449 A native of Palena, near Sulmona, and founder of the Hermits of St
Jerome (Romitani di San Girolamo), for whom
he established houses at Naples, Rome (Sant'
Onofrio) and Florence. Afterwards he amalgamated his institute with the Hieronymites,
founded by Bl Peter of Pisa. Cult aproved in
1771.

Nicholas (St) M. OFM.   Oct 10
See Daniel, Samuel, etc.

Nicholas I (St) Pope   Nov 13
d. 867 Surnamed "the Great", a Roman by
birth and a member of the Roman clergy, he
was elected bishop of Rome in 858. He was
remarkable for his energy and courage.
Among those who were excommunicated by
him were John, the recalcitrant archbishop of
Ravenna, king Lothair of Lorraine for matri-
monial irregularity, and Photius, the intruded patriarch of Constantinople. He also
forced Archbishop Hincmar of Reims, after a
struggle to acknowledge the papal appellate
jurisdiction. Nicholas was described by his
contemporaries as the champion of the people.
He confirmed St Ansgar as papal legate in
Scandinavia, and through his missionaries
effected the conversion of Bulgaria.

Nicholas Giustiniani (Bl)
C. OSB.   Nov 21
d. p. 1180 A Venetian belonging to the noble
family of the Giustiniani. He became a Benedictine in the monastery of San Niccolò del
Lido. After all his brothers had been killed in
battle at Constantinople the Doge obtained
from the pope a dispensation for Nicholas to
marry and beget heirs for the family. He
accordingly married and had six sons and
three daughters. In his old age Nicholas
returned to the abbey. He has always been
venerated at Venice.

Nicholas Tavigli (or
Tavelíc) (St) M. OFM.   Dec 5
d. 1391 Born in the diocese of Sebenico in

Dalmatia, he joined the friars minor and was sent to the Bosnian mission, where he worked for twenty years among the Paterine schismatics. Thence he travelled to Palestine to preach to the Muslims and was by them cut to pieces at Jerusalem. Cult confirmed by Leo XIII. Canonized in 1970.

Nicholas (St) Bp.   GC. Dec 6
d. *c* 350   One of the most popular saints in Christendom. His cult is based mainly on legend since almost nothing is known of his life, excepting the bare facts that he was a bishop of Myra in Lycia, and that his relics were stolen by Italian merchants in 1087 and now are enshrined at Bari. Legend, however, has abundantly supplied the lack of known data, as witness the life of the saint written by Simon Metaphrastes in the tenth century. To this day he is venerated as the patron saint of sailors, of captives, and especially of children. The last-mentioned veneration derives from the story that he raised to life three children who had been pickled in a brine-tub. Numerous medieval observances were connected with this saint, for example, that of Santa Claus (Sint Klaes, Sanctus Nicolaus), and the ceremony of the boy-bishop which still survives at Montserrat in Catalonia. St Nicholas is a patron saint of Russia. In art, he is robed as a bishop, the three children in a tub are at his feet, or he has three golden balls on a book, or three money bags, loaves, etc. He is sometimes shown with a ship, or an anchor, or calming a storm.

Nicholas Chrysoberges (St) Bp.   Dec 16
d. 996   Patriarch of Constantinople (983–996).

Nicholas Factor (St) C. OFM.   Dec 23
1520–1582   Born at Valencia in Spain. He became a Franciscan in 1537 and spent his life as an itinerant preacher, pitilessly scourging himself before every sermon. He was beatified in 1786, St Paschal Baylon and Bl Louis Bertrand being used as witnesses in the process of beatification.

Nicodemus of the Holy Mountain (St) Mk.   July 14
c 1749–1809   A native of Naxos, he became a monk at Mt Athos in 1775. He worked with St Macarius Nataras of Corinth on compiling the *Philokalia*, a monumental work of monastic spirituality. He also produced other books, especially Greek translations of classics of Western spirituality. The orthodox church canonized him in 1955.

St Nicholas, Dec 6

Nicodemus (St) M.   Aug 3
1st cent.   The faithful, though timid, disciple of Christ mentioned in the gospel of St John (ch 3), styled by our Lord "a teacher of Israel". He shared with St Joseph of Arimathaea the privilege of laying Christ in the tomb. One of the apocryphal gospels was circulated under his name. On Aug 3 is kept the feast of the finding of his body with that of St Stephen and others. He has always been venerated as a martyr.

Nicolino Magalotti (Bl) H.   Nov 29
d. 1370   A Franciscan tertiary who lived as a hermit near Camerino for thirty years. Cult approved in 1856.

Nicomedes (St) M.   Sept 15
d. *c* 90   According to legend a Roman priest martyred in Rome at a very early period, some say under Domitian. In later legends he is associated with SS Nereus, Achilleus and Petronilla. Cult confined to local calendars since 1969.

Nicomedia, Martyrs of (SS)
The pre-1970 RM. listed four anonymous groups of martyrs who suffered at Nicomedia on the Hellespont, for a time the principal residence of the Roman emperors in the East.

March 18
d. *c* 300   A band of 10,000 massacred, it is said, following a fire in the imperial palace at Nicomedia.

June 23
d. *c* 303   Numerous martyrs (some suggest 20,000) who hid in the mountains and caves and were hunted down by the persecutors.

Dec 23

d. *c* 304   A group of twenty martyrs.

Dec 25

d. 303   Many thousands (the Greeks say 20 000) burnt alive by order of Diocletian in the great basilica of Nicomedia where they had assembled to celebrate Christmas.

Probably the above figures are exaggerated. There are other difficulties in accepting the stories as they stand, e.g., Christmas was not celebrated in the East until a later period.

Nicon and Comp. (SS)
MM.   March 23

d. *c* 250   Nicon was a Roman soldier of distinction who, while travelling in the East, became a Christian and a monk. His master, Theodosius of Cyzicus, left him in charge of two hundred disciples, and when persecution threatened Palestine they fled to Sicily where they were martyred under Decius. The pre-1970 RM. wrongly assigned them to Caesarea in Palestine.

Nicon (St) M.   Sept 28

See Mark, Alphius, etc.

Nicon (St) C.   Nov 26

d. 998   Surnamed *Metanoite*, because conversion (in Greek *metanoia*) was always the theme of his preaching. He was an Armenian monk first at Khrysopetro and then in his native country, where he carried on missionary work. This he continued later in Crete and in Greece.

Nicostratus, Antiochus
and Comp. (SS) MM.   May 21

d. 303   A cohort of Roman soldiers said to have been put to death at Caesarea Philippi, in Palestine, under Diocletian. Nicostratus was their tribune. Their story occurs in the apocryphal *Acta* of St Procopius.

Nicostratus (St) M.   July 7 and Nov 8

See Four Crowned Martyrs.

Nidan (St) C.   Sept 30

Otherwise Midan, q.v.

Nidger (Nidgar, Nitgar)
(Bl) Bp. OSB.   Apr 15

d. *c* 829   Said to have been abbot of the Benedictine monastery of Ottobeuren in Bavaria. He became bishop of Augsburg in 822.

Nighton (St) M.   June 17

Otherwise Nectan, q.v.

Nilammon (St) H.   June 6

5th cent.   An Egyptian monk and recluse. To avoid ordination as a bishop he barricaded his cell and died in prayer, while the other bishops were waiting outside.

Nilus (St) M.   Feb 20

See Tyrannio, Sylvanus, etc.

Nilus (St) M.   Sept 19

See Peleus, Nilus, etc.

Nilus the Younger (St) Ab.   Sept 26

d. 1004   A Greek of S. Italy who, after a careless youth, joined the Basilian monks of the abbey of St Adrian in Calabria, of which he soon after became abbot. In 981 the invading Saracens drove the community to Vellelucio in the *Terra di Lavoro*, where they lived on land given them by Montecassino. While sick at Frascati shortly before his death Nilus designated that city as the place where his community were to be definitely established and there in fact the still flourishing abbey of Grottaferrata was founded by his disciple, St Bartholomew. The monks of Grottaferrata profess the Basilian rule and use the Greek rite, regarding St Nilus as their founder and first abbot.

Nilus the Elder (St) Bp.   Nov 12

d. *c* 430   Traditionally he was a courtier of Byzantium who sought a life of asceticism and solitude with his son Theodulus on Mt Sinai. Theodolus was captured by marauding brigands and enslaved, but his father escaped and eventually both were reunited and ordained and returned to Mt Sinai. Modern research has shown that Nilus was really bishop of Ancyra, and a friend of St John Chrysostom. He founded a monastery there and was a prolific ascetical writer.

Nimmia (St) M.   Aug 12

See Hilaria, Digna, etc.

Ninian (St) Bp.   26 Aug

d. ? 432   A Briton who was educated in Rome and thence sent to evangelize his native country. He established his mission at Whithorn (*Candida Casa*, the White House) in Wigtownshire, so called because the church was built of white-painted stone. There was a monastery attached to it, and it was from this centre that Ninian and his monks evangelized the northern Britons and the Picts. Dressed as a bishop, he is shown with heavy chains about him, or hanging from his arm.

Nino (or Christiana) (St) V.   Dec 15

d. *c* 320   A native of Colastri in Cappadocia. The pre-1970 RM., not knowing her local name, called her "Christiana". As a slave or captive she was brought into Georgia (Iberia) and was the means of spreading Christianity in that country. She is venerated as the apostle of Georgia. Substantially her story is true, but many myths and contradictory legends have been added to it.

Nissen (St) Ab.   July 25
5th cent. An Irish convert of St Patrick, by whom he was set over a monastery at Montgarth (Mountgarret) in Wexford.

Nithard (St) M. OSB.   Feb 4
d. 845 Monk of Corbie in Saxony and companion of St Ansgar whom he followed to Sweden as a missionary. He was martyred there by the pagan Swedes.

Nivard (Bl) Mk. OSB.
Cist.   Feb 7
c 1100–p. 1150 The youngest brother of St Bernard. He followed his brother to Clairvaux and eventually was appointed novice-master at Vaucelles. Our information as to his later career is rather confused. Cult not yet officially confirmed.

Nivard (St) Bp.   Sept 1
d. c 670 Archbishop of Reims. Brother-in-law of King Childeric II of Austrasia. He restored the abbey of Hautvilliers, where he was buried.

Nizier (St) Bp.   Apr 2
Otherwise Nicetius, q.v.

Noe Mawaggali (St) M.   June 3
d. 1886 A potter by trade, he was put to death by King Mwanga of Uganda. See Charles Lwanga and Comps.

Noel (*several*)
The French form of Natalis, q.v.

Nominanda (St) M.   Dec 31
See Donata, Paulina, etc.

Non (Nonna, Nonnita)
(St) W.   March 3
5th cent. She was the mother of St David, patron saint of Wales. There are confusing legends about her early life but it is probable that she was of a ruling family in Dyfed: a chapel and a well near her son's cathedral still bear her name. Another is at Altanon in Cornwall, whither she may have migrated and where her relics survived until the Reformation. She died in Brittany.

Nonius Alvarez (Bl) OC.   Nov 6
1360–1431 Nuñez Alvarez de Pereira was born at Bomjardin in Portugal and was a soldier in the service of his king. He fought in the wars for the independence of Portugal and, after the death of his wife, became a Carmelite lay-brother at Lisbon. Cult confirmed in 1918.

Nonna (St) W.   Aug 5
d. 374 Wife of St Gregory Nazianzen the Elder, whom she converted to the faith. Their three children, Gregory, Caesar and Gorgonius, are also venerated as saints.

Nonnosus (St) Mk. OSB.   Sept 2
d. c 575 A Benedictine monk, *praepositus* in the abbey of Mt Soracte, near Rome. His wonderful deeds of faith are recorded by St Gregory the Great.

Nonnus (St) Bp.   Dec 2
d. c 458 A monk of Tabennisi in Egypt, made bishop of Edessa in 448. He laboured with great success among the Arabians around Heliopolis (Baalbeck). He is connected with the conversion of St Pelagia, the Penitent.

Norbert (St) Bp. Founder   GC. June 6
c 1080–1134 Born of a princely family at Xanten, he led a worldly life at the German court and even received holy orders as a means to worldly advancement. In 1115 a narrow escape from death brought about his conversion. After endeavouring to reform the chapter of canons at Xanten, he became an itinerant preacher. In 1120 he was given the territory of Prémontré near Laon, and here he founded a community of canons regular under the rule of St Augustine, since known as Norbertines or Premonstratensians. The new reform movement soon spread over Western Europe. Norbert himself was compelled to accept the see of Magdeburg, where he set about the reformation of his clergy, even resorting to force when it was necessary. With St Bernard and Hugh of Grenoble he worked hard to mend the schism occasioned by the death of Honorius II. He died shortly afterwards, exhausted by his labours for the church.

North America (Martyrs of)
See John de Brébeuf and Comps.

Nostrianus (St) Bp.   Feb 14
d. c 450 Bishop of Naples, a valiant opponent of Arianism and Pelagianism.

Notburga (St) V.   Sept 14
d. 1313 A Tyrolese serving-maid. She joyfully fulfilled her humble duties first in a noble household, then in that of a peasant. She made it one of her duties to help those poorer than herself. Her shrine is at Eben in the Tyrolese mountains. Cult confirmed in 1862.

Notburga (Noitburgis)
(St) N. OSB.   Oct 31
d. c 714 A Benedictine nun in the convent of St Mary in the Capitol, at Cologne.

Nothelm (St) Bp.   Oct 17
d. c 740 Archbishop of Canterbury, friend and collaborator of St Bede and correspondent of St Boniface.

Notker Balbulus (Bl)
Mk. OSB.   Apr 6
c 840–912 Nicknamed *Balbulus*, i.e. the

Stammerer. He was born at Heiligau (now Elgg) in the canton of Zurich and when still a child entered the Benedictine abbey of St Gall, where he spent his whole life, holding the offices of librarian, guest-master and precentor. He excelled as a musician and was the originator of liturgical sequences, composing both the words and the music of many of them. Cult confirmed in 1512.

Novatus (St) June 20

d. *c* 151 Alleged son of Pudens, the senator, and brother of SS Praxedes and Pudentiana. He probably never existed.

Novellone (Bl) H. OSB. July 27

Otherwise Nevolo, q.v.

Noyala (St) VM. July 6

? A British maiden, beheaded at Beignan in Brittany. Acording to the legend she walked to Pontivy holding her head in her hands. She is greatly venerated in Brittany.

Numerian (Memorian)
(St) Bp. OSB. July 5

d. *c* 666 Son of a rich senator of Trier, he first became a monk at Remiremont under St Arnulph and then went to reside in the abbey of Luxeuil under St Waldebert. Ultimately he was appointed bishop of his native city.

Numidicus and Comp.
(SS) MM. Aug 9

d. 251 A group of African martyrs burnt at the stake at Carthage under Decius (not Valerian). Numidicus is said to have been dragged still breathing out of the ashes of the funeral pyre and to have lived to be ordained priest by St Cyprian. St Cyprian mentions a

priest named Numidicus but this group of martyrs is unknown to the ancient martyrologies.

Nunctus (Noint) (St) Ab. M. Oct 22

d. 668 Abbot of a monastery near Mérida, in W. Spain. He was killed by robbers and venerated thenceforward as a martyr.

Nunilo and Alodia (SS)
VV. MM. Oct 22

d. 851 Two sisters born at Adahuesca, in the province of Huesca, Spain. Daughters of a Muslim father and Christian mother, they were raised as Christians. After the death of their father, their mother married another Muslim, who brutally persecuted them and had them imprisoned at Alquézar, near Barastoro. They were finally beheaded at Huesca during the persecution of Abderrahman II. They are still venerated in Aragon.

Nuntius Sulprizio (Bl) C. May 5

1817–1836 Born in the Abruzzi, he accomplished the full mission of his Christian life in the short span of nineteen years as an apprentice blacksmith. His patience under the handicaps of health and fortune, and his chastity amid the social evils of the nineteenth century set him as a challenge to youth and workmen. Beatified in 1963.

Nympha (St) VM. Nov 10

See Tryphon, Respicius and Nympha.

Nymphodora (St) M. March 13

See Theusetas, Horres, etc.

Nymphodora (St) VM. Sept 10

See Menodora, Metrodora and Nymphodora.

Obadiah (St) Prophet   Nov 19
9th cent. B.C.?   The name means Servant of
the Lord. He is one of the minor prophets and
his prophecy is contained in a single chapter of
twenty-five verses. Modern scholarship dates
its various sections to periods between the
ninth and fifth centuries before Christ.

Obdulia (St) V.   Sept 5
? A virgin venerated at Toledo, where her
relics are enshrined. Nothing is known about
her beyond her name and cult.

Obitius (St) Mk. OSB.   Feb 4
d. *c* 1204   A knight of Brescia who narrowly
escaped drowning and, terrified by a vision of
hell, gave himself to a life of austere penance as
a Benedictine in the service of the Benedictine
nuns of St Julia at Brescia. Cult approved in
1900.

Oceanus (St) M.   Sept 4
See Theodore, Oceanus, etc.

Octavian and Comp. (SS)
MM.   March 22
d. 484   Octavian, archdeacon of the church
at Carthage, and several thousand companions
suffered martyrdom at that city under the
Arian Vandal king, Hunneric.

Octavian (Bl) Bp. OSB.   Aug 6
c 1060–1132   Born at Quingey in the diocese
of Besançon, a brother of Pope Callixtus II.
Educated by the Benedictines, he became a
monk at the abbey of St Peter in *Ciel d'Oro*, at
Pavia. In 1129 he was made bishop of Savona.
Cult confirmed in 1793.

**Octavius, Solutor and
Adventor (SS)** MM.   Nov 20
d. 297   Patron saints of Turin, where they
suffered martyrdom. At a later date their story
became connected with the legend of the
Theban Legion.

Oda of Canterbury
See Odo the Good.

Oda (Bl) V. O. Praem.   Apr 20
d. 1158   Daughter of a noble family in
Brabant, she avoided marriage with a young
nobleman by disfiguring her face. She was
then allowed to follow her religious vocation in
the Premonstratensian nunnery of Rivroelles,
of which she became prioress. Her cult has
never been officially confirmed.

Oda (St) W.   Oct 23
d. *c* 723   A French princess married to the
Duke of Aquitaine. In her widowhood she
devoted herself to the care of the poor and
suffering. Her shrine is at Amay, near Liége.

Oddino Barrotti (Bl) C.   July 21
1324–1400   A native of Fossano in Piedmont
who became parish priest at the church of St
John the Baptist at Fossano and a Franciscan
tertiary. Later he resigned his cure and turned
his house into a hospital. He is still venerated
at Fossano. Cult approved in 1808.

Oderisius (Bl) Card. OSB.   Dec 2
d. 1105   A son of the noble family of
de'Marsi, in the diocese of Marsi, he was educated at Montecassino, where he became a
monk. In 1059 he was created cardinal deacon
of St Agatha and shortly after cardinal priest of
St Cyriacus in Termis. Finally, in 1087 he
succeeded Bl Victor III as abbot of Montecassino. He was a poet and patron of scholars and
the mediator between the crusaders and the
Greek emperor Alexius.

Odhran (Oran) (St) Ab.   Oct 27
Otherwise Otteran, q.v.

Odilia (St) V. OSB.   Dec 13
Otherwise Ottilia, q.v.

Odilo (St) Ab. OSB.   May 11
c 962–1049   A scion of the noble family of
Mercoeur in Auvergne. About the year 990 he
joined the community of Cluny, became abbot
coadjutor in 992 and abbot in 994. Gentle and
kind, he was known throughout Christendom
for his liberality to the needy. A friend of popes
and princes, he was the promoter of the Truce
of God and instituted the annual feast now
called All Soul's Day in 1031. Under his
government the Cluniac houses increased
from thirty-seven to sixty-five. He was surnamed "the Archangel of Monks" — *Archangelus Monachorum* by Fulbert of Chartres.

Odilo (Bl) Ab. OSB.   Oct 15
d. *p*.954   A Benedictine of Gorze in Lor-

raine, who in 945 was elected abbot of Stavelot-Malmédy. He raised the standard of studies and discipline in the abbey.

Odo of Novara (Bl) C. O.
Cart. Jan 14
c 1105–1200 A native of Novara who became a Carthusian and was made prior of Geyrach in Slavonia. However, owing to difficulties with the bishop he resigned and became chaplain to a convent at Tagliacozzo in Italy, where he died at a very advanced age. Cult confirmed in 1859.

Odo of Beauvais (St) Bp.
OSB. Jan 28
801–880 Born near Beauvais, he gave up soldiering to become a Benedictine at Corbie, where he was tutor to the sons of Charles Martel. In 851 he succeeded St Paschasius Radbert as abbot. In 861 he was made bishop of Beauvais, where his reforms greatly influenced the whole church of N. France. He was the mediator between Pope Nicholas I and Hincmar of Reims. Cult approved by Pius IX.

Odo of Cluny (St) Ab. OSB. May 11
c 879–942 Born in Maine, he was educated at the cathedral school of St Martin at Tours. In 909 he became a monk at Baume under Bl Berno, the abbot-founder of Cluny, to the government of which latter abbey he succeeded in 927. He prudently freed Cluny from temporal interference, paving the way for its rapid growth and flourishing life for the next few centuries. Under his wise and paternal rule Cluny began to exert its influence throughout France and in Italy, including Rome, where the saint was asked to restore the observance at St Paul-outside-the-Walls. He died at Tours, by the tomb of St Martin. He was one of the great abbots of the Middle Ages. He encouraged strict monastic discipline and faithful observance of the rule, with emphasis on the value of silence, the common life and abstinence.

Odo of Massay (Bl) Ab. OSB. June 7
d. 967 A Benedictine abbot of Massay (935–967), a house belonging to the Cluniac observance.

Odo of Cambrai (Bl) Bp.
OSB. June 19
1050–1113 A native of Orleans who became the headmaster (*scholasticus*) of the cathedral school at Tournai. In *c* 1090 he was converted to a higher life by reading St Augustine on free will, and founded a community of Benedictines in the disused abbey of St Martin at Tournai. In 1105 he was made bishop of Cambrai, but on refusing to receive secular investiture, was exiled to the abbey of Anchin where he died. He was one of the most learned French scholars of the eleventh century.

Odo (Oda) the Good (St)
Bp. OSB. July 4
d. 959 Born in East Anglia of Danish parents, he became bishop of Ramsbury in Wessex and was present at the battle of Brunanburh. In 942 he was appointed to Canterbury. He had received the Benedictine habit from the hands of the abbot of Fleury out of love for the monastic ideal. As archbishop he took a prominent part in the legislation of kings Edmund and Edgar and paved the way for the monastic restoration under SS Dunstan, Oswald (Odo's nephew) and Ethelwold.

Odo of Urgell (St) Bp. July 7
d. 1122 A scion of the house of the counts of Barcelona who, after a period of soldiering, entered the service of the church. He was appointed archdeacon of Urgell in the Pyrenees and in 1095 was ordained by Pope Urban II bishop of the same town. His outstanding characteristic was love of the poor.

Odoric of Pordenone (Bl)
C. OFM. Feb 3
1285–1331 Odoric Mattiuzzi was born at Villanova near Pordenone in Friuli, became a Franciscan, and spent some years as a recluse. Then he set out on his apostolic missions, journeying through the Near and the Far East and entering China and even Tibet. After sixteen years of such labours he returned to Europe to report to the pope at Avignon, but died at Udine. Cult confirmed in 1775.

Odran (St) M. Feb 19
d. *c* 452 The chariot-driver of St Patrick. According to a legend he gave his life for his master by changing places with him in the chariot, realising the presence of an ambush.

Odran (St) Ab. July 7
See Medran and Odran.

Odrian (St) Bp. May 8
? One of the early bishops of Waterford.

Odulphus (St) C. OSA. June 12
d. *c* 855 A native of Brabant, appointed canon of Utrecht by St Frederick, whom he greatly helped in the evangelization of Frisia. He founded a monastery of Augustinian canons at Stavoren. His relics are said to have been stolen in 1034 and taken to London, and from there to Evesham abbey.

Oduvald (St) Ab. May 26
d. 698 A Scottish nobleman who became a

monk and later abbot of Melrose. He was a contemporary of St Cuthbert.

Offa (St) Abs. OSB.   Dec 31
d. *c* 1070   A Benedictine abbess of St Peter's at Benevento.

Ogerius (Ogler) (Bl) Ab.
OSB. Cist.   Sept 10
d. 1214   A Cistercian abbot of Locedio, in the diocese of Vercelli. He wrote a series of sermons in defence of the doctrine of the Immaculate Conception. Cult confirmed in 1875.

Ogmund (St) Bp.   March 8
d. 1121   Bishop of Holar in Iceland. He is venerated as one of the apostles of that island. Canonized in 1201.

Olalla (St) VM.   Dec 10
Otherwise Eulalia of Mérida, q.v.

Olav of Norway (Olavs, Olaf, Olaus, Tola) (St)
King M.   July 29
995–1030   Son of King Harald of Norway. His early youth was spent, after the manner of his countrymen in those days, as a pirate. In 1010 he received baptism at Rouen and in 1013 helped Ethelred of England against the Danes. In 1015 he succeeded to the throne of Norway and at once summoned missionaries, chiefly from England, to complete the Christianization of the country. He succeeded to some extent, but his measures were harsh and he was driven from his kingdom. In an attempt to recover it he fell in battle at Stiklestadt. He is now regarded in Norway as the champion of national independence. He is shown crowned, in armour, with weapons and a symbol of charity such as a basket of food.

Olav of Sweden (St) King
M.   July 30
d. *c* 950   A king of Sweden, murdered by his rebellious heathen subjects for refusing to sacrifice to idols at the spot where Stockholm now stands.

Olcan (St) Bp.   Feb 20
Otherwise Bolcan, q.v.

Olga (St) W.   July 11
c 879–969   Wife of Igor I, duke of Kiev, whom she married in 903. After his assassination in 945 she ruled the country for the rest of her life. In 958 she became a Christian and made great though unsuccessful efforts to introduce Christianity into Russia, a task which was achieved by her grandson St Vladimir.

Oliva (St) VM.   March 5
d. 138   Said to have been a martyr under the emperor Hadrian. Her body is venerated in the church of St Afra at Brescia.

Oliva (St) V.   June 3
? A nun of Anagni, near Rome, of whose life we have no authentic particulars.

Oliva (Olivia, Olive) (St)
VM.   June 10
? A virgin martyr venerated both at Palermo and at Carthage. She is, however, a fictitious person, the heroine of a romance the scene of which is laid among the Muslims of Tunis, by whom also she is held in high veneration.

Oliver (Oliverius, Liberius) (St) C. OSB.   Feb 3
d. *c* 1050   A Benedictine monk of Santa Maria di Portonuovo at Ancona.

Oliver Plunket (St) Bp. M.   July 11
1629–1681   Born at Loughcrew in Co. Meath, he studied for the priesthood in Rome, where he was ordained in 1654. He remained there as professor of theology in the college *de Propaganda Fide* till 1669. In that year he was ordained archbishop of Armagh and at once threw himself courageously into the task of restoring the Irish church, laid waste by continuous persecution. He was arrested on a charge of complicity in one of the sham plots of the time and, the Irish judges refusing to convict him of treason, he was brought for trial to London. Here, too, his first trial collapsed for lack of evidence, but on a second trial he was found guilty of treason "for propagating the Catholic religion". While in prison Oliver made his Benedictine oblation in the hands of his fellow prisoner, Dom Maurus Corker, the president of the English Benedictines, to whom also he bequeathed his body, which is now enshrined at Downside abbey. His head is enshrined at Drogheda. He was the last Catholic to be martyred at Tyburn. He was beatifed in 1920. Canonized in 1975.

Ollegarius (Oldegar, Olegari) (St) Bp. OSA.   March 6
1060–1137   Born at Barcelona, he joined the Augustinian canons regular and was prior in several houses in France before being made bishop of Barcelona in 1115. The following year he was transferred to the archbishopric of Tarragona. That diocese he successfully raised from the condition of neglect and decay into which it had fallen during the Moorish domination.

Olympiades (St) M.   Apr 15
See Maximus and Olympiades.

Olympiades (St) M.　　　　　　Dec 1
d. 303　Said to have been a Roman of consular rank tortured to death at Almeria (now Amelia) in central Italy, under Diocletian.

Olympias (St) W.　　　　　　Dec 17
d. 408　A lady of noble birth at Constantinople who married Nebridius, prefect of the city. On her husband's death soon after their marriage she devoted herself to the service of the church, becoming a deaconess and establishing a "domestic community" of virgins in her home. She loyally supported the cause of St John Chrysostom, and on this account was herself persecuted and exiled, her house being sold and her community disbanded. She died in exile at Nicomedia.

Olympius (St) Bp.　　　　　　June 12
d. *p*.343　A bishop of Aenos (now Enos) in Rumelia, a contemporary of St Athanasius. He was a staunch opponent of Arianism and was driven from his see by the Arian emperor Constantius.

Olympius (St) M.　　　　　　July 26
See Symphronius, Olympius, etc.

Omer (Audomarus) (St)
Bp. OSB.　　　　　　　　　　Sept 9
c 595–670　Born in the territory of Constance, he became a monk at Luxeuil, and after some twenty years became bishop of Thérouanne (which at that time embraced what is now called Pas-de-Calais and Flanders, in Belgic Gaul). The diocese sadly needed evangelization, and for this purpose St Omer secured the services of a numerous band of fellow-monks, who literally covered that district with abbeys. The saint himself was the co-founder of Sithiu over which he placed St Bertinus. Round this abbey grew up the town now known as Saint-Omer.

Oncho (Onchuo) (St) C.　　　Feb 8
d. *c* 600　An Irish pilgrim, who was also a poet, a guardian of the Celtic traditions and a collector of holy relics. While pursuing his search for memorials of the Irish saints he died at Clonmore monastery, then governed by St Maidoc, and his body was there enshrined together with the relics he had gathered.

Onesimus (St) M.　　　　　　Feb 16
d. *c* 90　The slave who ran away from his master Philemon, was converted by St Paul in Rome, and was the occasion of the apostle's letter to Philemon. The pre-1970 RM. confused him with another Onesimus, who was bishop of Ephesus after St Timothy.

Onesimus (St) Bp.　　　　　May 13
d. *c* 361　Fifth bishop of Soissons.

**Onesiphorus and
Porphyrius (SS)** MM.　　　　Sept 6
d. *c* 81　Onesiphorus is mentioned by St Paul in the second letter to Timothy 4:19). A colourful legend adds that he followed St Paul to Spain and then back to the East, were he was martyred under Domitian somewhere on the Hellespont, by being tied to wild horses and so torn to pieces. Porphyrius is described as a member of his household, who shared in the work and the martyrdom of his master.

Onuphrius (St) H.　　　　　　June 12
d. *c* 400　An Egyptian who lived as a hermit for seventy years in the desert of the Thebais, in Upper Egypt. He was a very popular saint in the Middle Ages, both in the East and in the West. He is the patron saint of weavers, probably because "he was dressed only in his own abundant hair and a loin-cloth of leaves".

Opportuna (St) Abs. OSB.　　Apr 22
d. *c* 770　Born near Ayesmes in Normandy, sister of St Chrodegang, bishop of Séez. At an early age she entered the Benedictine abbey of Monteuil, of which she became abbess. She is described as "a true mother to all her nuns". Her cult has always been very flourishing in France.

Optatian (St) Bp.　　　　　　July 14
d. *c* 505　Bishop of Brescia *c* 451–505.

Optatus (St) M.　　　　　　　Apr 16
See Saragossa, Martyrs of.

Optatus of Milevis (St) Bp.　June 4
d. *c* 387　Bishop of Milevis in Numidia. He was an excellent controversialist against the Donatists — resourceful and vigorous but conciliatory. He wrote six treatises against them which are praised by his contemporaries, chiefly by SS Augustine and Fulgentius of Ruspe.

Optatus (St) Bp.　　　　　　Aug 31
d. *c* 530　A bishop of Auxerre who died in the second year of his episcopate.

Oran (St) Ab.　　　　　　　　Oct 27
Otherwise Otteran, q.v.

Orange (Martyrs of) (BB)　　July 6
d. 1794　A group of thirty-two nuns — one Benedictine, two Cistercians, thirteen religious of the Institute of Perpetual Adoration and sixteen Ursulines — imprisoned during the French Revolution in the public gaol at Orange for several months and ultimately guillotined there. They were martyred on

different days during the month of July. Beatified in 1925. Each receives a special notice in this book.

Ordonius (Ordoño) (St)
Bp. OSB. Feb 23
d. 1066 Monk of the Benedictine abbey (Cluniac observance) of Sahagún, in the province of Léon, Spain, and afterwards bishop of Astorga (1062–1066).

Orentius and Patientia
(SS) MM. May 1
d. c 240 Husband and wife who lived at Loret, near Huesca, in N. Aragon. An ancient Spanish tradition makes them the parents of St Laurence the martyr.

Orentius (or Orientius) of Auch (St) Bp. May 1
d. c 439 A hermit in the Lavendan valley near Tarbes, whom the people of Auch insisted on having for their bishop. He was pastor there for over forty years.

Orentius, Heros, Pharnacius, Firminus, Firmus, Cyriacus and Longinus (SS) MM. June 24
d. c 304 Described in the pre-1970 RM. as seven brothers who, on account of their faith, were deprived of their military belt by Maximian, taken away to various places and put to death.

Orestes (St) M. Nov 9
d. 304 A martyr of Cappadocia, tortured to death under Diocletian.

Orestes (St) M. Dec 13
See Eustratius, Auxentius, etc.

Orgonne (St) V. Jan 30
Otherwise Aldegund, q.v.

Oria (St) V. OSB. March 11
Otherwise Aurea, q.v.

Oriculus and Comp. (SS)
MM. Nov 18
d. c 430 A group of martyrs put to death by the Arian Vandals in the province of Carthage.

Oringa (or Christiana) of the Cross (Bl) V. OSA. Jan 4
d. 1310 Her life, which seems fictional, relates that she fled from home to escape marriage, and became a serving-maid at Lucca. Then she returned to her birthplace, Castello di Santa Croce, in Tuscany, and founded a convent under the Augustinian rule.

Orlando (Bl) H. OSB. Vall. May 20
d. 1212 A Vallombrosan lay-brother who was celebrated as an exorcist.

Ormond (Armand) (St)
Mk. Jan 23
6th cent. Monk of the abbey of Saint Mairé, he became abbot in 587, in which task he was eminently successful.

Orontius (St) M. Jan 22
See Vincent, Orontius and Victor.

Orora (St) Oct 20
See Bradan and Orora.

Orsisius (St) H. June 15
d. c 380 A favourite disciple of St Pachomius, and his assistant in drawing up the rules for the cenobites. He succeeded Pachomius as abbot. Some twelve years before his death he was forced to resign by his monks. He is the author of an ascetical treatise which St Jerome translated into Latin.

Osanna (several)
Otherwise Hosanna, q.v.

Osburga (or Osberga)
(St) Abs. OSB. March 30
d. c 1018 First abbess of the nunnery founded by King Canute at Coventry. Her cult was confirmed in the fifteenth century, for by then her shrine at Coventry was a centre for local pilgrimages.

Osith (St) M. OSB. Oct 7
Otherwise Osyth, q.v.

Osmanna (Osanna) (St)
N. OSB. June 18
d. c 700 A nun of the Benedictine convent of Jouarre in France.

Osmanna (or Argariarga)
(St) V. Sept 9
d. c 650 An Irish maiden who crossed over to Brittany and became a solitary in a hermitage near Brieuc.

Osmund (St) Bp. Dec 4
d. 1099 A Norman noble attached to the court of William the Conqueror, with whom he came to England and by whom he was made chancellor. In 1072 he was appointed to the see of Salisbury (Old Sarum), where he finished building the cathedral and instituted a chapter of secular canons. He was once thought to have been the compiler of the liturgical services for his diocese, now known as the "Sarum use". His hobby was copying books and binding them. Canonized in 1457.

Ostianus (St) C. June 30
? A saint venerated at Viviers. He is said to have been a priest, but nothing is now known about him.

Oswald (St) Bp. OSB.   Feb 28
d. 992   Born in England of a noble Danish family, he was educated under his uncle St Odo of Canterbury and was appointed dean of Winchester. Shortly after he crossed over to France and professed the Benedictine rule at Fleury. At the suggestion of St Dunstan he was made bishop of Worcester (961), and heartily identified himself with St Dunstan and with St Ethelwold in their efforts to revive monastic life and ecclesiastical discipline in England. St Oswald founded the abbey of Ramsey and the monastery at Worcester which later became the cathedral priory. In 972 he became archbishop of York, without relinquishing the government of the diocese of Worcester. He died while still on his knees after having performed his daily practice of washing the feet of twelve poor persons.

Oswald (St) King M.   Aug 5
604–642   The successor of King Edwin on the throne of Northumbria in the time of the heptarchy. He was baptized at Iona during a period of exile among the Scots. In 635 he defeated the Welsh king, Cadwalla, near Hexham and with that victory his actual reign began. One of his chief aims was the complete evangelization of his country and for this work he called St Aidan to help him. In 642 he fell in battle at Maserfield fighting against the champion of paganism, Penda of Mercia. He has always been venerated as a martyr. His head is still in St Cuthbert's coffin at Durham. His emblem is a raven with a ring in its beak. He is also depicted as holding a bowl and trampling on his murderers, or blowing a horn, or carrying his own head, or a sword.

Oswin (St) King M.   Aug 20
d. 651   A prince of Deira, part of the kingdom of Northumbria, he was educated by St Aidan. In 642 he succeeded St Oswald as ruler of Deira, but reigned only nine years, being killed at Gilling in Yorkshire by order of his cousin Oswy. He has ever since been venerated as a martyr.

Osyth (Osith) (St) M. OSB.   Oct 7
d. c 700   Osyth was a minor princess of the Hwicca tribe. She was married to Sighere, King of the East Saxons. Their son, Offa, became king in 683, later abdicating. It seems that Osyth had founded a convent herself, now St Osyth, on a creek of the Colne in Essex. Bede does not mention her in his *History* and little can be done to substantiate her story. According to her legend she was slain by marauders. She is depicted as carrying her own head; or she has a stag near her.

St Oswald, Aug 5

Otger (St) M. OSB.   Sept 10
See Wiro, Phechelm, etc.

Othmar (Otmar, Audemar) (St) Ab. OSB.   Nov 16
d. 759   Of Teutonic origin and already a priest, in 720 he was appointed abbot of the then dilapidated monastery of St Gall. He introduced at once the Benedictine rule and a new period of prosperity began for the abbey, which soon became the most important in Switzerland. He was persecuted by two neighbouring counts, unjustly calumniated and

condemned by an ecclesiastical tribunal. He bore his sufferings with great patience, and died in prison.

Otillia (Odilia, Othilia, Adilia) (St) Abs. OSB.   Dec 13

d. *c* 720   According to tradition St Ottilia was born blind and cast out for this reason by her family. She was adopted by a convent, where she miraculously recovered her sight. Eventually she became abbess foundress of Hohenburg (now Odilienberg) and of Niedermünster, both under the Benedictine rule. Her life as it comes down to us abounds in extraordinary legends.

Otteran (Odhran) (St) Ab.   Oct 27

c 563   An Irish abbot of Meath who crossed over to Scotland with St Columba, and was the first to die at Iona. His feast is kept throughout Ireland. He is the principal patron of Waterford.

Otto (St) M. OFM.   Jan 16

See Berardus, Peter, etc.

Otto of Bamberg (St) Bp.   July 2

c 1062–1139   Born in S. Germany, he was made bishop of Bamberg under the emperor Henry IV, whom he endeavoured to reconcile with the papacy during the investiture controversy. He was more successful in his missionary activities among the Pomeranians, and is honoured as their apostle. Canonized in 1189.

Otto of Heidelberg (Bl) H. OSB.   Dec 28

d. 1344   A brother of Bl Herman of Heidelberg and, like him, a monk at the Benedictine abbey of Niederaltaich in Bavaria. After his brother's death in 1326, Otto lived in the cell where Bl Herman had died.

Oudaceus (In Welsh: Eddogwy) (St) Bp.   July 2

d. *c* 615   His life is found in later chronicles which may contain seeds of truth. His family seems to have been of Breton origin living in Wales. He became a bishop with a jurisdiction over an area roughly corresponding with the present Anglican diocese of Llandaff.

Ouen (Audöenus, Aldwin, Owen, Dado) (St) Bp.   Aug 24

610–684   He founded the abbey of Rebais, was ordained bishop of Rouen in 641, attended the synod of Châlons in 644, and died at a place now called after him near Paris in 684.

Owen (Owin, Ouini) (St) H. OSB.   March 4

d. *c* 680   After having been steward in the household of St Etheldreda, he became a monk at Lastingham under St Chad, and when the latter was appointed bishop of Mercia he settled St Owen with other monks in a house near Lichfield.

Oyand (St) Ab.   Jan 1

Otherwise Eugendus, q.v.

Oye (St) M.   Dec 11

Otherwise Eutychius, q.v.

Oys (St) C.   Apr 22

Otherwise Authaire, q.v.

Pabiali (St) C. Nov 1
5th (or 6th) cent. One of the large number of saints descended from Brychan. He is patron of a chapel called Partypallai in Wales.

Pabo (St) C. Nov 9
d. *c* 510 Surnamed "Post-Prydain", i.e. the prop of N. Britain. He was the son of a chieftain on the Scottish border and at first a soldier. Later he came to Wales and founded the monastery called after him Llanbabon, in Anglesey.

Pachomius (St) Ab. May 14
c 290–346 Born in the Upper Thebaid in Egypt, he became a Christian after a period of military conscription (313) and three years later became a hermit. In 320 he built his first monastery at Tabenna (Tabennisi), north of Thebes on the east bank of the Nile, and subsequently he established several others. He governed them all much as a present day superior general and wrote for them the first known cenobitical rule, thus departing from the then common type of eremitical monachism. At the time of his death he had under his rule very large numbers of monks in nine monasteries, and two convents for nuns. He is one of the most outstanding figures in the history of monachism.

Pachomius (St) Bp. M. Nov 26
See Faustus, Didius, etc.

Pacian (St) Bp. March 9
d. *c* 390 Bishop of Barcelona from 365. He wrote much on matters of ecclesiastical discipline, but most of it is lost. His treatise on penance survives. In his first letter against Novatian occurs the famous saying: "My name is Christian, my surname is Catholic" (Ep. 1:4).

Pacificus of Cerano (Bl) C. OFM. June 8
1424–1482 Pacificus Ramota was born at Cerano, diocese of Novara, and became a Friar Minor in 1445. He was a popular preacher and a writer of moral theology, his *Summa Pacifica* being much used by his contemporaries. Cult approved in 1745.

Pacificus of San Severino (St) C. OFM. Sept 24
1653–1721 A native of San Severino, near Ancona, he joined the Franciscans of the Observance and was ordained in 1677. In his early years as a priest his preaching bore much fruit, but in 1688 he became deaf and blind and almost a cripple. From this time his life was one of intense suffering, blessed by God with supernatural charismata. Canonized in 1839.

Padarn (St) Bp. Apr 16
Otherwise Paternus, q.v.

Paduinus (Pavin) (St) Ab. OSB. Nov 15
d. *c* 703 Monk and prior of St Vincent's abbey, at Le Mans, and later first abbot of St Mary's near the same city.

Paganus (Bl) Mk. OSB. Feb 10
d. 1423 An Italian who became a professed monk of the Sicilian abbey of San Niccolò d'Arena. He lived as a hermit near the monastery, but returned to it before his death.

Paganus of Lecco (Bl) M. OP. Dec 26
d. 1274 He was admitted into the Dominican order by St Dominic himself and lived in it for fifty years. He succeeded St Peter of Verna as inquisitor-general and, like him, was murdered by heretics.

Palaemon (St) Ab. Jan 11
d. 325 One of the earliest of the Egyptian hermits. He took refuge in Upper Egypt during the persecution under Diocletian. To him came St Pachomius to be trained in the monastic life. He was closely associated with Pachomius in organizing the hermits on cenobitical lines, and he eventually followed Pachomius to Tabennisi, where he died.

Palatias and Laurentia (SS) MM. Oct 8
d. 302 Palatias was a lady of Ancona converted to Christ by her slave Laurentia. Both were martyred at Fermo, near Ancona, under Diocletian.

Palatinus (St) M.   May 30
See Sycus and Palatinus.

**Paldo, Taso and Tato
(SS)** Abbots OSB.   Jan 11
8th cent. Three brothers, natives of
Benevento, who became monks at the abbey of
Farfa, in Sabina, and eventually founded the
monastery of San Vincenzo at the headwaters
of the Volturno. Of this latter foundation they
became successively abbots, Paldo dying
c 720, Taso *c* 729, and Tato *c* 739.

Palestine, Martyrs of (SS)
There are five groups of anonymous Palestinian martyrs listed in the pre-1970 RM.

                                              Feb 19
d. *c* 509   Saracen tribes under Persian rule
invaded Palestine about this time and martyred the solitaries they found there, out of
hatred for Rome and Christianity.

                                              May 16
d. *c* 614   Forty-four monks of the *laura* of St
Sabbas, massacred during the war between
Heraclius and Chosroes. (They are included
among those listed under June 22, q.v.)

                                              May 28
d. *c* 410   A number of monks martyred by
Arabs and other pagans who invaded Palestine
early in the reign of Theodosius the Younger.

                                              June 22
d. *c* 614   A great number of martyrs (the
RM. spoke of 1480) massacred at Samaria or
in its neighbourhood during the war between
Heraclius and Chosroes.

                                              Aug 16
? A group of thirty-three martyrs of whom no
details are known.

Palladia (St) M.   May 24
See Susanna, Marciana and Palladia.

Palladius (St) H.   Jan 28
d. *c* 390   A hermit near Antioch in Syria, a
friend of St Simeon "the Ancient".

Palladius (St) Bp.   Apr 10
d. 661   An abbot of the abbey of St Germanus at Auxerre, who in 622 was appointed
bishop of that city. He founded several monasteries.

Palladius (St) Bp.   July 7
5th cent. A deacon from Rome or more
probably, a deacon from Auxerre, who was
ordained bishop by Pope Celestine and sent
c 430 to minister the gospel to the fledgling
church in Ireland. He landed near Wicklow
and after some small success left for Scotland,
where he died shortly afterwards.

Palladius (St) Bp.   Oct 7
d. *c* 590   Bishop of Saintes (570–*c* 590). He
is liturgically honoured in several dioceses of
France, but his claim to the title of saint is
disputed, not without reason.

Palmatius (St)   May 10
See Calepodius, Palmatius, etc.

Palmatius and Comp. (SS)
MM.   Oct 5
d. *c* 287   Apocryphal martyrs of Trier
alleged (only since the eleventh century) to
have been put to death under Maximian
Herculeus.

Palumbus (Bl) H. OSB.   Jan 4
d. *c* 1070   A monk-priest of the abbey of
Subiaco, who lived for some years as a hermit
near the monastery.

Pambo (St) Ab.   July 18
d. *c* 390   A disciple of the great St Antony
and one of the pioneers of the eremitical life in
the Nitrian desert. In his old age he was a
venerable figure, visited by a great number of
persons from East and West. Among these
were SS Athanasius, Melania the Elder and
Rufinus.

Pammachius (St) C.   Aug 30
c 340–410   A Roman senator, married to one
of the daughters of St Paula. On the death of
his wife in 395 Pammachius donned the
monastic habit and spent the rest of his life and
his immense wealth in the personal service of
the sick and the poor. His great friends, SS
Jerome and Paulinus of Nola, admired and
encouraged him. His house became the present church of SS John and Paul (*Titulus
Pammachii*): remains of the original house
survive beneath it.

Pamphilus (St) Bp.   Apr 28
d. *c* 700   Bishop of Sulmona (a see later
joined to that of Valva) and Corfinium in the
Abruzzi. He was accused to Pope Sergius of
Arian practices, chiefly, it seems, on account of
his celebrating the eucharist before daybreak
on Sundays — but he completely vindicated
himself.

Pamphilus (St) M.   June 1
c 240–309   A native of Beirut (*Berytus*) in
Phoenicia. He studied at Alexandria under
Pierius, and then settled at Caesarea in Palestine, where he was ordained and subsequently
in charge of the theological school. One of the
greatest biblical scholars of his day, he fostered
learning and protected all students. He was a
great admirer of Origen, and with Eusebius of
Caesarea wrote an "Apology" to defend him.
Later, Pamphilus was martyred and when

Eusebius wrote a biography of him he assumed the surname "Pamphili" in gratitude for favours he had received.

Pamphilus (St) Bp.   Sept 7
d. *c* 400   A Greek by birth, ordained bishop of Capua by Pope Siricius. His relics were enshrined at Benevento.

Pamphilus (St) M.   Sept 21
? A Roman martyr, about whom nothing is known.

**Panacea (Panexia,
Panassia) (St) V.**   May 1
1378–1383   Born at Quarona, diocese of Novara. When she was only five years old her stepmother killed her with a spindle while she was at prayer. Cult confirmed in 1867.

Pancharius (St) M.   March 19
d. 303   A Roman senator, a favourite officer of the emperor Maximian. At the outbreak of the persecution he denied, or at any rate concealed, his religion, but on receiving a letter from his mother and sister he nobly confessed Christ and was beheaded at Nicomedia.

Pancharius (St) M.   July 22
d. *c* 356   Bishop of Besançon. He suffered much at the hands of the officials of the Arian emperor Constantius.

**Pancras (Latin:
Pancratius) (St) Bp. M.**   Apr 3
1st cent.   According to the Sicilian tradition, this St Pancras was an Antiochene by birth, whom St Peter ordained bishop and sent to Taormina (*Tauromenium*) in Sicily, where he was stoned to death.

Pancras (St) M.   GC. May 12
d. *c* 304(?)   A martyr of this name was certainly buried in the cemetery of Calepodius in Rome. Other particulars are lacking. His story as given in Cardinal Wiseman's *Fabiola* is of course a literary creation of the novelist's imagination. In the seventh century Pope St Vitalian sent relics of the saint to one of the Anglo-Saxon kings, and St Pancras thenceforward became very popular in England. A church in Canterbury, remains of which are extant, was dedicated by Augustine to him. He is represented as a crowned youth with palm of martyrdom, standing on a soldier.

Pandonia (St) V.   Aug 26
Otherwise Pandwyna, q.v.

Pandwyna (St) N. OSB.   Aug 26
d. *c* 904   Born in Scotland or Ireland. The church at Eltisley in Cambridgeshire is dedi-

cated to her. Nothing factual is known of her life, but legends exist in the works of Leland.

Pannonia (Martyrs of) (SS)   Apr 9
? The pre-1970 RM. has this entry: "At Sirmium in Pannonia the passion of seven holy virgins and martyrs." This is all that seems to be known about them.

Pantaenus (St) C.   July 7
d. *c* 190   A Sicilian and a convert from Stoicism, Pantaenus became the head of the catechetical school of Alexandria, which under him began to be considered the intellectual centre of the Christian East. He is said to have ended his life as a missionary in India (more probably in Ethiopia). His most celebrated pupil was Clement of Alexandra, q.v.

Pantagapes (St) M.   Sept 2
See Diomedes, Julian, etc.

Pantagathus (St) Bp.   Apr 17
475–540   A courtier in the service of King Clovis, he eventually left the court and received holy orders. He was afterwards bishop of Vienne.

Pantaleemon (St) M.   July 27
See Maurus, Pantaleemon and Sergius.

Pantaleon (St) M.   July 27
d. *c* 305   His Greek name is *Panteleimon* which means "the All-compassionate". The name may have given rise to the legend of his life (which, as we have it now, is not to be trusted): viz., that he was a physician by profession, who practised his art without taking any fees, and who was martyred under Diocletian, perhaps at Nicomedia. Cult confined to local calendars since 1969.

Pantalus (St) Bp. M.   Oct 12
? A legendary bishop of Basle connected with the story of St Ursula.

Papas (St) M.   March 16
d. *c* 300   A martyr of Lycaonia in Asia Minor under Diocletian.

Paphnutius (St) M.   Apr 19
? A priest put to death at Jerusalem.

**Paphnutius the Great (St)
Bp.**   Sept 11
d. *c* 360   An Egyptian who suffered for the faith under Maximinus Daza by having one eye plucked out and one leg hamstrung. In 311 he joined St Antony as monk, but shortly after was ordained bishop of a see in the Upper Thebaid. As such he attended the council of Nicaea, where he persuaded the Fathers not to make married clergy divorce their wives. Throughout his life he was a strenuous op-

St Pancras, May 12

ponent of Arianism. He was in great favour with the emperor Constantine.

Paphnutius and Comp. (SS) MM. Sept 24
d. *c* 303   Martyrs in Egypt under Diocletian.

Paphnutius (St) Ab. Sept 25
d. *c* 480   The alleged father of the girl-monk St Euphrosyne, q.v. It is said that he became a monk and abbot in Egypt: he is held in great veneration in the East.

Papias and Maurus (SS) MM. Jan 29
d. *c* 303   Roman soldiers martyred at Rome under Maximian.

Papias (St) Bp. Feb 22
d. *c* 130   Bishop of Hierapolis in the valley of the Lycus in Phrygia, a contemporary and friend of St Polycarp of Smyrna. He wrote much, but only a few fragments of his works are extant.

Papias (St) M.   Feb 25
See Victorinus, Victor, etc.

**Papias, Diodorus,
Conon and Claudian
(SS) MM.**   Feb 26
d. *c* 250   Poor shepherds, natives of Pamphylia (Asia Minor), tortured and put to death under Decius.

Papias (Papius) (St) M.   June 28
d. *c* 303   A martyr, possibly in Sicily, under Diocletian.

Papias (Papius) (St) M.   July 7
See Peregrinus, Lucian, etc.

Papias (St) M.   Nov 2
See Publius, Victor, etc.

**Papinianus and
Mansuetus (SS) MM.**   Nov 28
5th cent.   African bishops, martyred under the Arian Vandal king Genseric, who had overrun that Roman province.

Papolenus (St) Ab.   June 26
Otherwise Babolenus, q.v.

Pappus (Papius) (*several*)
Otherwise Papias, q.v.

Papulus (Papoul) (St) M.   Nov 3
d. *c* 300   A priest who worked as a missionary under St Saturninus in S. France, and who like him was martyred under Diocletian. His shrine is at Toulouse.

Papylus (St) M.   Apr 13
See Carpus, Papylus, etc.

Paragrus (St)   Dec 9
See Samosata Martyrs.

**Paraguay (Martyrs of) (SS)
SJ.**   Nov 17
d. 1628   Three Spanish Jesuits — Roch (Roque) Gonzalez, Alphonsus Rodriguez and John de Castillo — founders of the "reduction" of the Assumption on the Jiuhi river in Paraguay. In 1628 they established the new mission of All Saints, and it was here that they were murdered. Canonized in 1988.

**Paramon and Comp. (SS)
MM.**   Nov 29
d. 250   A group of three hundred and seventy-five martyrs, venerated especially by the Greeks. They are said to have suffered on the same day during the Decian persecution.

Parasceve (St) M.   March 20
See Photina, Joseph, etc.

**Pardulphus (Pardoux)
(St) Ab. OSB.**   Oct 6
c 658–738   Born at Sardent, near Guéret,

diocese of Limoges, he first became a hermit but afterwards joined the Benedictine community of Guéret, of which he became abbot. At the time of the Saracen invasion he remained alone in the abbey, which, it is said, he saved by prayer.

Paregorius (St) M.   Feb 18
See Leo and Paregorius.

Paris (St) Bp.   Aug 5
d. 346   According to the local tradition, bishop of Teano, near Naples. His life is embellished with the usual legendary additions.

**Parisius (St) C. OSB.
Cam.**   June 11
1152–1267   Born probably at Treviso. At the age of twelve he received the Camaldolese habit, and was ordained in 1190. In that same year he was appointed chaplain and spiritual director of the Camaldolese nuns of St Christina outside the walls of Treviso, and he filled that office for seventy-seven years. His body is enshrined in the cathedral of Treviso.

Parmenas (St) M.   Jan 23
d. *c* 98   One of the seven deacons ordained by the apostles (Acts 6:5). Tradition says that after many years spent in preaching the gospel in Asia Minor, he was martyred at Philippi in Macedonia under Trajan.

**Parmenius and Comp.
(SS) MM.**   Apr 22
d. *c* 250   The priests Parmenius, Helimenas and Chrysotelus, and the deacons Luke and Mucius were beheaded near Babylon when the emperor Decius invaded Mesopotamia.

Parthenius (St) M.   May 19
See Calocerus and Parthenius.

Paschal I (St) Pope OSB.   May 14
d. 824   A Roman, and abbot of the Benedictine monastery of St Stephen near the Vatican, he became bishop of Rome in 817. He defended the Greeks against the barbarous persecution of the iconoclast emperors. He is perhaps best remembered for his zeal in the recovery and enshrining of the bodies of St Caecilia and other martyrs.

**Paschal Baylon (St) C.
OFM.**   May 17
1540–1592   Born of peasant stock at Torre Hermosa in Aragon, he started life as a shepherd. Later he became a Franciscan lay-brother of the Alcantarine reform (1564). He spent his life mainly as doorkeeper in different friaries of Spain. All his life he was animated with an intense love for the holy eucharist, the true doctrine of which he triumphantly de-

fended against a Calvinist preacher in France. Beatified in 1618, canonized in 1690. In 1897 he was declared patron of all eucharistic confraternities and congresses. Cult confined to local or particular calendars since 1969.

Pascharius (Pasquier) (St)
Bp.   July 10
d. c 680   Bishop of Nantes. He founded the abbey of Aindre, where he placed St Hermenland of Fontenelle as first abbot.

Paschasia (St) VM.   Jan 9
d. c 178(?)   A virgin martyr venerated at Dijon. Her cult is already described as ancient by St Gregory of Tours. Later legends connect her with St Benignus of Dijon.

Paschasius (St) Bp.   Feb 22
d. c 312   The eleventh bishop of Vienne in Gaul.

Paschasius Radbert (St)
Ab. OSB.   Apr 26
c 790–865   Born in the Soissonnais, he became a monk of Corbie under St Adalard and was ordained deacon. For many years he held the offices of novice-master and head-master, both at Old Corbie and at New Corvey, whither he accompanied his abbot in 822. In 844 he was made abbot of Corbie, an office which he found most uncongenial, and which he resigned in the year 849. He was prolific on biblical subjects and his most famous book is his treatise on the holy eucharist, *De Corpore et Sanguine Domini.*

Paschasius (St) C.   May 31
d. c 512   A Roman deacon who, in good faith, sided with the antipope Laurence against Pope Symmachus. He is mentioned by St Gregory the Great (Dial. IV, 40). He wrote some theological works which have been lost.

Paschasius (St) M.   Nov 13
See Arcadius, Paschasius, etc.

Pasicrates, Valentio and
Comp. (SS) MM.   May 25
d. c 302   Four soldiers martyred at Silistria, in Moesia (Bulgaria). They belong to the group of St Julius of Dorostorum, q.v.

Pastor, Victorinus and
Comp. (SS) MM.   March 29
d. c 311   Seven martyrs who suffered at Nicomedia under Galesius.

Pastor (St) Bp.   March 30
6th cent. (?)   Bishop of Orleans. His name, however, does not appear in the ancient lists.

Pastor (St) C.   July 26
d. c 160   A Roman priest, said to have been brother to Pope St Pius I. He has left his name to the title (i.e. parish) of St Pudentiana in Rome — *Titulus Pastoris.*

Pastor (St) M.   Aug 6
See Justus and Pastor.

Patapius (St) H.   Dec 8
7th cent.   An Egyptian monk who migrated to Constantinople and passed his life as a hermit in the suburbs of the city. He is much venerated in the East.

Paterius (St) Bp.   Feb 21
d. 606   A Roman monk, disciple and friend of St Gregory the Great. From being notary of the Roman church, he was made bishop of Brescia in Lombardy. He was a prolific writer on biblical subjects.

Patermuthius, Copres
and Alexander (SS) MM.   July 9
d. c 363   Patermuthius was a notorious robber converted by an Egyptian hermit, St Copres. Patermuthius then became a hermit also. The pre-1970 RM. makes them martyrs together with Alexander, a converted soldier under Julian the Apostate; but the Acts of these alleged martyrs cannot be admitted as history.

Paternian (St) Bp.   July 12
d. c 470   Bishop of Bologna c 450–470. Probably identical with the following.

Paternian (St) Bp.   Nov 23
d. c 343   A Christian who, towards the end of the persecution of Diocletian escaped to the mountains. Later he was made bishop of Fano.

Paternus (Bl or St) H.
OSB.   Apr 10
d. 1058   A Scot by birth, he was one of the first monks to enter the Benedictine abbey of Abdinghof in Paderborn, founded by St Meinwerk. Afterwards he became a hermit and died in his cell, refusing to leave it when the monastery was destroyed by fire. Bl Marianus Scotus visited the place a fortnight after the fire. St Paternus was greatly revered by St Peter Damian.

Paternus (or Pern) (St) Bp.   Apr 15
d. c 500   Bishop of Vannes in Brittany.

Paternus (or Padarn) (St) C.   Apr 15
5–6th cent.   A Welsh monk who, with other monks from the same country, founded Llanbadarn Fawr (i.e. the great monastery of Padarn) near Aberystwyth in Wales. He preached the gospel in the country round

about. He was very popular in the Middle Ages.

Paternus (French: Pair)
(St) Bp.   Apr 16 and Sept 23
d. *c* 574 (or 563) Born at Poitiers, he became a monk at Ansion and later a hermit near Coutances. Eventually he became bishop of Avranches in Normandy. He is often confused with St Paternus of Llanbadarn (see Apr 16).

Paternus (St) M.   Aug 21
d. *c* 255 The pre-1970 RM., based on doubtful *Acta*, said that he came from Alexandra to Rome, was arrested at Fondi and expired in the dungeon there.

Paternus (St) Bp.   Sept 28
2nd cent. Born at Bilbao in Spain. He was one of the earliest bishops — some say the first — of Eauze (now Auch) in France.

Paternus (St) M. OSB.   Nov 12
d. *c* 726 Born in Brittany, he was a monk first at Cessier, in the diocese of Avranches, and then at Saint-Pierre-le-Vif, diocese of Sens. He was murdered by malefactors whom he had admonished to reform their lives.

Patiens (St) Bp.   Jan 8
2nd cent. Venerated as the fourth bishop and the patron saint of Metz.

Patiens (St) Bp.   Sept 11
d. *c* 491 Archbishop of Lyons, highly praised by his contemporary, St Sidonius Apollinaris. He devoted all his revenues to the relief of the poor.

Patientia (St) M.   May 1
See Orentius and Patientia.

Patricia (Patritia) (St) M.   March 13
See Macedonius, Patricia and Modesta.

Patricia (St) V.   Aug 25
d. *c* 665 According to the legend, she was a maiden of Constantinople, related to the imperial family. In order to escape marriage she went on a pilgrimage to Jerusalem and then to Rome, where she received the veil. She died at Naples, of which city she is one of the patrons.

Patrician (St) Bp.   Oct 10
5th cent. A Scottish bishop driven from his see by heathen invaders. He spent the remainder of his life in the Isle of Man.

Patrick (St) Bp.   March 16
? Registered in the pre-1970 RM. as bishop of Auvergne, but his name is not to be found in the lists of the sees of Auvergne. Quite probably the copyists wrote *Arvernia* for *Hiber-*

nia, i.e. Ireland, and thus duplicated the apostle of that country (see the following). On March 16 the feast of St Patrick is kept at Malaga, in Spain, for the saint was a native and bishop of that city. According to the local tradition, he later fled to Auvergne, where he died *c* 307.

Patrick (St) Bp.   GC. March 17
c 390–461? A Romano-Briton by origin, at the age of sixteen he was taken captive to Ireland (*c* 405). He escaped after six years. He now pursued his education in Continental monasteries. About the year 432, after having been ordained bishop, perhaps in Gaul, he returned to Ireland as a missionary. Whatever may be said of the extant data supplied by his biographers, which in some instances are obviously conflicting or legendary, the fact remains that St Patrick and his companions established the Catholic church throughout Ireland on lasting foundations. He travelled throughout the country preaching, teaching, building churches, opening schools and monasteries, converting chiefs and bards. He was, moreover, the first organizer of the Irish church, with the primatial see at Armagh (established *c* 444). He fully deserves his title of "Apostle of Ireland". He is shown vested as a bishop driving snakes before him or trampling upon them.

Patrick, Acacius, Menander and
Polyaenus (SS) MM.   Apr 28
? A group of martyrs of Prusa (Broussa) in Bithynia. The Acts of Patrick are considered authentic. The names of the others have been added in the early calendars.

Patrick (St) Bp.   May 24
d. *c* 469 The fourth bishop of Bayeux. Liturgically venerated at Bayeux on May 24.

Patrick Salmon (Bl) M.   July 4
d. 1594 A servant of Bl Thomas Bosgrave and martyred with him at Dorchester for sheltering a priest.

Patrick de' Patrizi (Bl)
Mk. OSB. Oliv.   Aug 21
See Ambrose Piccolomini, etc.

Patrick (St) Ab.   Aug 24
d. *c* 450 Surnamed "Sen-Patrick" (Patrick the Elder). Several legends mention him as a kinsman and contemporary of St Patrick of Ireland. There is also St Patrick, abbot of Nevers, France, likewise commemorated on Aug 24. It is impossible to disentangle the conflicting data concerning these and other saints of the same name. Glastonbury housed

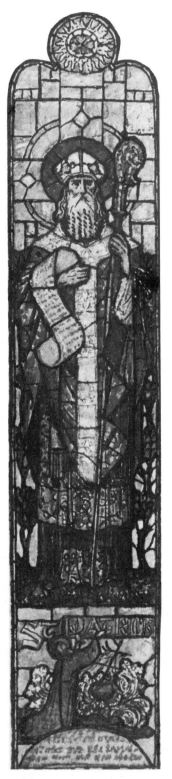

St Patrick, March 17

his relics: in later ages they were passed off as those of St Patrick of Ireland.

Patrobas (St)   Nov 4
See Philologus and Patrobas.

Patroclus (St) M.   Jan 21
d. c 275 (or 259)   A very wealthy and exceedingly charitable Christian of Troyes, martyred in that city. His relics were (960) translated to Soest in Westphalia.

Patto (Latin: Pacificus) (St) Bp. OSB.   March 30
d. c 788   A native of Britain who crossed over to Saxony, became abbot of a monastery there, and finally was appointed bishop of Werden.

Paul
Note. A very widely used name in all Christian lands. The Latin form is Paulus, and its modern derivatives are: in Italian and Portuguese, Paolo; in English and French, Paul; in Spanish, Pablo; in Catalan, Pau.

Paul the Hermit (St) C.   Jan 15
c 230–342   The life of this saint, written by St Jerome, is the sole source of his life and it tells us that he was an Egyptian of good birth and well educated. At the age of twenty-two he fled into the desert of Thebes to escape the persecution under Decius. He stayed there even after the ending of the persecutions until his death, that is, for ninety years. He was comforted in the end by a visit from St Antony. On a second visit St Antony found him dead and buried him. A number of these facts may be questioned. In art he is shown clad in rough garments made from leaves or skins; a bird bringing him food often accompanies him, or a lion is shown digging his grave. Since 1969 his cult has been confined to local or particular calendars.

Paul, Gerontius, Januarius, Saturninus, Successus, Julius, Catus, Pia and Germana (SS) MM.   Jan 19
2nd cent. (?)   African martyrs of the province of Numidia, about whom no particulars are given.

Paul of Trois-Châteaux (St) Bp.   Feb 1
d. c 405   A native of Reims, who, escaping from the barbarian invasions, became a hermit near Arles and eventually was chosen bishop of Trois-Châteaux (*Augusta Tricastrinorum* —a diocese now extinct) in Dauphiné.

St Paul the Hermit, Jan 15

Paul Miki (SJ) and Comps (SS) MM.   GC. Feb 6

1562–1597 Born at Tounucumada in Japan, son of a Japanese military chief, he was educated at the Jesuit college of Anziquiama, and in 1580 entered the Society of Jesus. He was famed as an orator and controversialist. His last sermon was delivered from the cross on which he was martyred at Nagasaki. Paul Yuanki or Ibarki and Paul Susuki were both Japanese laymen and tertiaries of St Francis. They were interpreters to the Franciscan missionaries and helped them as catechists. All three were crucified at Nagasaki in 1597 and canonized in 1862 along with many other martyrs, who receive separate notices in this book.

Paul, Lucius and Cyriacus (SS) MM.   Feb 8

? Martyrs at Rome.

Paul of Verdun (St) Bp. OSB.   Feb 8

d. c 649 A courtier who retired first to Mt Voge (now Paulberg), near Trier, as a hermit and afterwards entered the monastery of Tholey, where he was appointed headmaster of the monastic school. After some years (c 630) King Dagobert appointed him bishop of Verdun.

Paul and Ninety Companions (BB) MM. OP.   Feb 10

d. 1240 Paul was a lawyer of Hungarian origin at the University of Bologna. Induced by St Dominic to join the Friars Preachers, he brought the new order into Hungary. With ninety companions he was sent to Wallachia, where they were martyred by the Cumanians.

Paul Lieou (Bl) M.   Feb 13

d. 1818 A Chinaman who was martyred by strangulation. Beatified in 1900.

Paul Loc (St) M.   Feb 13

1831–1859 A native of An-nhon in Vietnam who, shortly after his ordination, was beheaded at Saigon. Canonized in 1988.

Paul, Heraclius, Secundilla and Januaria (SS) MM.   March 2

d. c 305 Martyrs who suffered under Diocletian at Porto Romano, at the mouth of the Tiber.

Paul of Prusa (St) Bp.   March 7

d. 840 Bishop of Prusa (Plusias) in Bithynia. For his courageous resistance to the iconoclasts he was banished to Egypt where he died.

Paul the Simple (St) H.   March 7

d. c 339 An Egyptian farmer who at the age of sixty discovered the adultery of his wife and forthwith left for the desert, where he placed himself under St Antony. His prompt obedience and childlike disposition were "the pride of the desert" and merited for him the surname of "the Simple". He is mentioned by Rufinus and Palladius.

Paul (St) M.   March 10

See Codratus, Dionysius, etc.

Paul Aurelian (St) Bp.   March 12

d. c 575 A Romano-Briton by origin, he was born in Wales and educated at Llantwit Major under St Illtyd, together with SS David, Samson, Gildas, etc. He dwelt for a time on Caldey Island, whence he crossed over into Brittany with twelve companions. He established a monastery at Porz-Pol on the isle of Ouessant and finally fixed his residence at Ouismor (now Saint-Pol-de-Léon), where he was ordained bishop.

Paul of Cyprus (St) M.   March 17
d. 775 A monk of Cyprus who, in the reign of the iconoclast emperor Constantine Copronymus, refused to trample on a crucifix and was hung head downwards over a slow fire till he died.

Paul, Cyril, Eugene and Comp. (SS) MM.   March 20
? A group of seven martyrs, who suffered in Syria.

Paul of Narbonne (St) Bp.   March 22
d. *p.*250 St Gregory of Tours (*Hist. Franc. I. 30*) writes that St Paul was ordained at Rome towards the middle of the third century and sent to Gaul to preach the gospel, which he did with great success at Narbonne. A much later legend identifies him with the Roman proconsul Sergius Paulus, converted by St Paul the Apostle (Acts 13).

Paul Tinh (St) M.   Apr 6
d. 1857 Born at Trinh-ha, Tonkin, he became a priest and was beheaded at Son-tay, in Vietnam. Canonized in 1988.

Paul of Cordoba (St) M.   Apr 17
See Elias, Paul and Isidore.

Paul Khoan (St) M.   Apr 28
d. 1840 A native of Tonkin, and a priest attached to the Paris foreign missions for forty years. He was in prison for two years before he was beheaded. Canonized in 1988.

Paul (St) M.   May 15
See Peter, Andrew, etc.

Paul (St) M.   May 17
See Heradius, Paul, etc.

Paul (St) M.   May 28
See Crescens, Dioscorides, etc.

Paul Hanh (St) M.   May 28
d. 1859 A native of Vietnam. He abandoned his faith and joined a band of outlaws. When arrested he professed his religion, and after frightful tortures, was beheaded near Saigon. Canonized in 1988.

Paul (St) M.   June 1
See Reverianus, Paul and Comp.

Paul (St) M.   June 1
See Valens, Paul and Comp.

Paul (St) M.   June 3
See Lucillian, Claudius, etc.

Paul of Constantinople (St) Bp. M.   June 7
d. 350 A patriarch of Constantinople whose episcopate was largely spent in exile for his orthodox faith. Elected in 336, he was exiled to Pontus in 337, whence he returned in 338, but was exiled again by an Arian synod, this time to Trier. He returned to his see *c* 340, but in 342 was sent in chains to Mesopotamia by the emperor Constantius. Recalled in 344, he was banished for the last time to Cukusus in Armenia, where he was left without food for six days and then strangled.

Paul Burali d'Arezzo (Bl) Bp. Card.   June 17
1511–1578 Born at Itri, diocese of Gaeta, he became a lawyer and practised his profession for ten years at Naples. In 1549 he was appointed royal counsellor, but in 1558 he joined the Theatine order and eventually was made superior at the houses of Naples and Rome. St.Pius V appointed him bishop of Piacenza and created him cardinal. Finally he was bishop of Naples. Beatified in 1772.

Paul and Cyriacus (SS) MM.   June 20
? Martyrs who suffered at Tomi on the Black Sea, in Lower Moesia.

Paul Xinsuki (Bl) M. SJ.   June 20
d. 1626 A Japanese Jesuit, catechist to Bl Paul Navarro. He was burnt alive at Nagasaki. Beatified in 1867.

Paul (St) M.   June 26
See John and Paul.

Paul I (St) Pope   June 28
d. 767 A Roman, educated with his brother, the future Pope Stephen II at the Lateran school. He succeeded his brother in the papal chair in 757. His pontificate was uneventful except for the iconoclast excesses of the Byzantine emperor Constantine Copronymus, whom the pope valiantly opposed. As some compensation for the destruction in the East, St Paul restored and beautified several Roman churches and enshrined the relics of many saints. He also had to work hard to maintain the existence of the papal State, which was threatened by warlike and treacherous neighbours.

Paul Giustiniani (Bl) OSB. Cam.   June 28
1476–1528 A member of the Venetian house of Giustiniani. He joined the Camaldolese Benedictines and eventually established the new congregation of Monte Corona. He ranks among the Camaldolese as their

St Paul the Apostle, June 29

most prolific writer. His feast is kept by the Camaldolese.

Paul the Apostle (St) M.   GC. June 29
c 3–65?   Born at Tarsus in Cilicia, a Jew of the tribe of Benjamin, a Pharisee, a Roman citizen, a tentmaker by trade, he was originally called Saul and was educated in the Sacred Law of the Jews at the feet of Gamaliel in Jerusalem. After taking an active part in the stoning of the first Christian martyr, St Stephen, he placed himself whole-heartedly at the service of the Jewish authorities in their attempt to stamp out Christianity, but was miraculously converted on the road to Damascus, and received directly from Christ his mission to evangelize the Gentiles. He did so in at least four apostolic journeys, extending from Cappadocia and Galatia perhaps as far as Spain, establishing churches everywhere, and ever surrounded by dangers of all sorts — he was shipwrecked, imprisoned, flogged, stoned, banished from several cities, persecuted by the hatred of his own people. Nevertheless he was always burning for more sufferings and conquests for Christ. His fourteen letters, addressed mostly to the churches which he had founded, belong to the deposit of divine revelation. According to a very old tradition, he was beheaded in Rome near the Ostian Way where the church of Tre Fontane now stands. Liturgically he is honoured with St Peter, on June 29, as the co-founder of the Roman church; while the feast of his conversion is celebrated on Jan 25. An extremely old iconographical tradition has consistently depicted facial representations of St Paul and St Peter: St Paul is a thin faced, elderly man with a high forehead, receding hair and a long pointed beard. He usually holds a sword and a book, or has three springs of water near him.

Paul (St) M.   July 3
See Mark, Mucianus and Paul.

Paul of St Zoilus (St) M.   July 20
d. 851   A Spanish deacon of Cordoba who belonged to the community of St Zoilus in the same city and was most zealous in ministering to his fellow-Christians imprisoned by the Muslims. He was beheaded for the faith, and his fellow Christians succeeded in securing his remains, which they enshrined in the church of St Zoilus.

Paul of Gaza (St) M.   July 25
d. 308   A martyr of Gaza in Palestine, beheaded under Maximian Galerius.

Paul Tcheng (Bl) M.   July 29
d. 1861   A seminarian. Beheaded at Tsingai. Beatified in 1909.

Paul and Juliana (SS) MM.   Aug 17
d. *c* 270   Brother and sister who, according
to an old legend, were beheaded at Ptolemais
in Palestine under Aurelian.

Paul Sanchiki (Bl) M.   Aug 19
d. 1622   A Japanese sailor on board the ship
of Bl Joachim Firaiama. Beheaded at Nagasaki. Beatified in 1867.

Paul (St) M.   Aug 29
See Nicaeas and Paul.

Paul Tomaki and
Paul Aybara Tert. OP. (BB)
MM.   Sept 8
d. 1628   Paul Tomaki was a boy of seven,
beheaded with his father, Bl John Tomaki,
q.v., and his three brothers at Nagasaki. Paul
Aybara was a Japanese catechist and Dominican tertiary, likewise beheaded at Nagasaki.
Beatified in 1867.

Paul Tanaca and Paul
Nangaxi (BB) MM.   Sept 10
d. 1622   Japanese companions in martyrdom of Bl Charles Spinola, q.v.

Paul Fimonaya (Bl) M.
Tert. OP.   Sept 16
d. 1628   Son of Bl Michael Fimonaya (q.v.)
and a Dominican tertiary. Beheaded at Nagasaki. Beatified in 1867.

Paul, Tatta, Sabinian,
Maximus, Rufus, and
Eugene (SS) MM.   Sept 25
? Paul and Tatta were husband and wife, the
others were their sons. All died under torture
in their native city of Damascus.

Paul (St) M.   Oct 3
See Dionysius, Faustus, etc.

Paul of the Cross (St) C.
Founder   GC. Oct 19
1694–1775 (Oct 18)   Paolo Francesco Danei
was born at Ovada in Piedmont. Inspired by a
series of visions he wished to found a religious
order dedicated to the passion of our Lord. In
1720 they received the habit of Barefooted
Clerks of the Cross and the Passion (Passionists) from the bishop of Alessandria. In 1727
Paul was ordained priest in the Vatican basilica, and then went with some companions to
live the religious life on Mt Argentaro, near
Orbitello. In 1747 the first general chapter of
the new congregation was held. St Paul lived to
see its expansion throughout Italy. Canonized
in 1867.

Paul Tong Buong (St) M.   Oct 23
d. 1833   A native of Vietnam and captain
of the bodyguard of King Minh-Menh. As
a Christian he became attached to the Society
of Foreign Missions of Paris. He was arrested
in 1832, degraded and beheaded. Canonized
in 1988.

Paul Navarro and Comp.
(BB) MM. SJ.   Nov 1
d. 1622   Paul Navarro was born in 1560 at
Laino, diocese of Cassano, in Italy. He
became a Jesuit in 1587 and while still a
scholastic was sent to India where he was
ordained, and thence to Japan. He worked
with great success as superior of Amanguchi.
He was burnt alive at Ximabara. With him
suffered two junior members of the Society
and a servant.

Paul Ngan (St) M.   Nov 8
d. 1840   A Vietnamese priest, beheaded
with four other martyrs at Nam-Dinh. Canonized in 1988.

Paul of Latros (St) H.   Dec 15
d. 956   Born near Pergamos. After the death
of his parents he became a hermit first on Mt
Olympus, then in a cave on Mt Latros in
Bithynia, and finally on the isle of Samos. He
died on Mt Latros.

Paul My (St) M.   Dec 18
d. 1838   A native of Vietnam, attached to the
Society of Foreign Missions of Paris. Martyred by strangulation. Canonized in 1988.

Paul (St) M.   Dec 19
See Darius, Zozimus, etc.

Paul (St) M.   Dec 24
See Lucian, Metrobius, etc.

Paula (St) V. OSB. Cam.   Jan 5
1318–1368   Born in Tuscany, she was entrusted in childhood to the Camaldolese nuns
and remained with them all her life. She was
instrumental in bringing the feuds between
Pisa and Florence to a peaceful settlement.

Paula (St) W.   Jan 26
347–404   A Roman lady of noble birth, she
married a patrician to whom she bore five
children, among them St Eustochium and St
Blaesilla. Left a widow when she was thirty-
two Paula embraced the religious life and for
twenty years presided over the sisterhood she
had founded near St Jerome's monastery at
Bethlehem, where she also established a guest
house for pilgrims. St Jerome became her
spiritual director and after her death, her
biographer.

Paula Gambara-Costa
(Bl) Matron   Jan 31
1473–1515   Born at Brescia, she married at

the age of twelve a young nobleman. She had much to suffer from her husband, who not only objected to her charities, admittedly lavish, but was also shamefully unfaithful to her. By her heroic patience she won him over to better things and they passed the remainder of an austere life in peaceful wedlock. She died worn out with self-imposed penances. Cult confirmed by Gregory XVI.

Paula (St) VM.   June 3
d. *c* 273   A maiden of Nicomedia who ministered to the martyr St Lucillian (q.v.) and to four youths in prison, and for this reason was arrested, tortured and finally sent to Byzantium, where she was beheaded.

Paula Frasinetti (St)
Foundress   June 11
1809–1882   Born at Genoa, she lived with her brother who was parish-priest at Quinto, one of the suburbs of the city, and there she began to teach poor children. This was the beginning of the Congregation of St Dorothy, which she lived to see flourishing throughout Italy and the New World. Beatified in 1930. Canonized in 1984.

Paula (St) VM.   June 18
See Cyriacus and Paula.

Paula (St) M.   July 20
See Sabinus, Julian, etc.

Paula (St) VM.   Aug 10
See Bassa, Paula and Agathonica.

Paula of Montaldo (Bl)
Poor Clare   Oct 29
1443–1514   Born at Montaldo, near Mantua, at the age of fifteen she joined the Poor Clares at Santa Lucia in Mantua, where she was later elected abbess three times. She was favoured with mystical experiences. Cult approved in 1906.

Paula-Elizabeth Cerioli
(Bl) W. Foundress   Dec 24
1818–1865   Constance Honorata Cerioli was born at Soncini, Cremona, and educated by the Visitation nuns. In spite of an inclination to the religious life, she accepted the will of her parents and married Cajetan Buzecchi-Tassis, by whom she had three children. All died, however, as did her husband in 1854. Then in her house at Como she began to receive and care for orphan girls, whom she educated and taught to till the fields. Under her pious leadership there thus arose the institute of the Sisters of the Holy Family, of which she, under the name of Paula-Elizabeth, was made superior. She

founded a similar orphanage for boys in 1863. She died of heart disease at forty-seven, leaving the memory of a saint. Beatified in 1950.

Paulillus (St) M.   Nov 13
See Arcadius, Paschasius, etc.

Paulillus (St) M.   Dec 19
See Cyriacus, Paulillus, etc.

Paulina (Bl) W. OSB.   March 14
d. 1107   A German princess who, after the death of her husband, founded with her son Werner the double monastery at Zell (Paulinzelle). She died at Münsterschwarzach.

Paulina (St) M.   June 6
See Artemius, Candida and Paulina.

Paulina (St) M.   Dec 2
See Eusebius, Marcellus, etc.

Paulina (St) M.   Dec 31
See Donata, Paulina, etc.

Paulinus of Aquileia (St)
Bp.   Jan 28
c 726–802   Born near Cividale in N. Italy he received a good education, and after the destruction of the Lombard kingdom in 774 was summoned to court by his great admirer Charlemagne, who in 787 sent him back to Italy as patriarch of Aquileia. Paulinus wrote much and competently against Adoptionism, was a notable poet, and was a firm supporter of the *Filioque*. He also carried on missionary work among the Avars.

Paulinus of Brescia (St) Bp.   Apr 29
d. *c* 545   Bishop of Brescia (*c* 524–545). His relics are enshrined in the church of San Pietro in Oliveto.

Paulinus (St) M.   May 4
? A martyr whose relics are enshrined at Cologne, but of whom otherwise nothing is known.

Paulinus of Sinigaglia (St)
Bp.   May 4
d. 826   Bishop, and now patron saint of Sinigaglia, in Italy. Nothing is known of his life.

Paulinus (St) M.   May 26
See Felicissimus, Heraclius and Paulinus.

Paulinus of Nola (St) Bp. GC. June 22
c 354–431   Pontius Meropius Anicius Paulinus was born at Bordeaux, the son of a Roman patrician who at that time held the office of praetorian prefect in Gaul. Paulinus was taught by the poet Ausonius. He was appointed prefect of Rome, but after the death

of his only child (390) he retired from the world and went to Spain, where the people of Barcelona compelled him to accept the priesthood. Finally he settled as a hermit near Nola, in Campania, and here the people chose him for their bishop (400). He proved to be one of the best of his time, and was on friendly terms with most of his great contemporaries: Ambrose, Jerome, Augustine, Martin of Tours, Victricius of Rouen, etc. He had much to suffer during the invasion of Campania by the Goths under Alaric. Most of his poems and a number of his letters are still extant, and they show him to have been a Christian poet of distinction, ranking with Prudentius, as well as a fluent writer of prose.

Paulinus of Antioch and Comp. (SS) MM. July 12

? This St Paulinus is venerated as the first bishop and patron saint of Lucca in Tuscany. The legend adds that he was a native of Antioch sent to Lucca by St Peter, and that he was martyred (c 67) with a priest, a deacon and a soldier. The whole story is most untrustworthy and it is probable that this saint is to be identified with a later bishop Paulinus c 355–365.

Paulinus of Trier (St) Bp. Aug 31

d. 358 A native of Gascony who accompanied St Maximinus to Trier and succeeded him as bishop in 349. He was a brave supporter of St Athanasius and was for this reason banished to Phrygia by the Arian emperor Constantius in 355. He died in exile, but his relics were brought back to Trier in 396.

Paulinus of York (St) Bp. OSB. Oct 10

d. 644 A Roman monk sent to England with SS Mellitus and Justus (601) by Pope Gregory the Great to aid St Augustine in his labours. He spent twenty-four years in Kent, and in 625 was ordained bishop of York and sent to evangelize Northumbria, which he did very successfully, baptizing King St Edwin at York on Easter Sunday, 627. After the king's death he was driven from his see and returned to Kent, where he administered the see of Rochester till his death.

Paulinus of Capua (St) Bp. Oct 10

d. 843 Said to have been a native of England who, while on a pilgrimage to Jerusalem, made a stay at Capua and was constrained by the inhabitants to become their bishop. After an episcopate of eight years he died at Sicopolis, whither he had fled during the invasion of the Saracens.

Paulinus (St) Mk. OSB. Nov 5

See Augustine and Paulinus.

Paulinus (Polin, Pewlin, Paulhen) (St) C. Nov 23

d. c 505(?) A Welsh abbot, pupil of St Illtyd, founder (?) of the monastery of Whitland (Carmarthen), where he had among his disciples St David and St Teilo.

Pausides (Pausis) (St) M. March 24

See Timolaus, and Comp.

Pausilippus (St) M. Apr 15

See Theodore and Pausilippus.

Peblig (Publicus) C. July 3

Otherwise Byblig, q.v.

Pega (St) V. Jan 8

d. c 719 A sister of St Guthlac of Croyland. She too lived as a recluse, dying while on a pilgrimage to Rome. The village of Peakirk in Northamptonshire preserves her name.

Pegasius (St) M. Nov 2

See Acindynus, Pegasius, etc.

Pelagia (St) M. March 23

See Domitius, Pelagia, etc.

Pelagia (St) VM. May 4

d. c 300 A maiden of Tarsus in Cilicia, said to have been roasted to death for refusing to marry one of the sons of the emperor Diocletian. The story is regarded as apocryphal.

Pelagia of Antioch (St) VM. June 9

d. c 311 A girl of fifteen who was a disciple of St Lucian at Antioch. When soldiers were sent to arrest her, she killed herself by leaping from the top of her house to avoid the loss of her virginity. St John Chrysostom, who greatly praised her courage, attributes her action to divine inspiration. Her name is in the eucharistic prayer of the Ambrosian mass.

Pelagia (St) M. July 11

See Januarius and Pelagia.

Pelagia the Penitent (St) Oct 8

Otherwise Marina (June 18) q.v. A legend attached to the name of the historical Pelagia of Antioch, makes her an actress who was converted at Antioch, donned male attire and travelled to Jerusalem, where thereafter she lived a life of penance.

Pelagia (St) VM. Oct 19

See Beronicus, Pelagia, etc.

Pelagius of Laodicea (St) Bp. March 25

d. p.381 A bishop of Laodicea. He championed the Catholic cause against Arianism and on that account was banished by the Arian emperor Valens. Recalled by Gratian, he was present at the council of Constantinople (381). The date of his death is not known.

Pelagius (St) M.   Apr 7
? A priest martyred at Alexandria in Egypt. Mentioned in the martyrology of St Jerome.

Pelagius (Spanish: Pelayo) (St) M.   June 26
c 912–925   A young boy of Asturias left as a hostage with the Moors at Cordoba. He was offered freedom and other rewards if he would accept Islam. These inducements were repeatedly put before him during the three years that he was kept in prison, and on his stubborn refusal he was put to the torture, which he endured for six hours before finally dying. His relics were transferred to Léon in 967 and to Oviedo in 985. The Benedictine poetess Rhoswitha of Gandersheim (d. 973) wrote a long poem in his honour. He is still honoured in Spain.

Pelagius (St) M.   Aug 28
d. c 283   A boy martyred in Istria under Numerian. His relics were transferred to Città Nuova in Istria and part of them (c 915) to Constance on the Swiss lake of that name. He is venerated as the patron saint of Constance.

Pelagius, Arsenius and Sylvanus (SS) MM.   Aug 30
d. c 950   Hermits near Burgos in Old Castile who, according to an old tradition, were done to death by the Saracens. Their cell was the origin of the Benedictine abbey of Artanza. The three martyrs are still venerated in the province of Burgos.

Peleus (St) Bp. M.
     Feb 20 and Sept 19
See Tyrannio, Sylvanus, etc., and Peleus, Nilus, etc.

Peleus, Nilus, Elias and Comp. (SS) MM.   Sept 19
d. c 310   Three Egyptian bishops (or priests) together with many priests and laymen (some say, with only one layman), who were sentenced to labour in the quarries and finally burnt alive, probably at Phunon, near Petra, for celebrating the liturgy in the place of detention. Some identify this group with that listed in the pre-1970 RM. on Feb 20 under St Tyrannio, q.v.

Peleusius (St) M.   Apr 7
? According to the pre-1970 RM., a priest of Alexandria. Nothing is known of him.

Pelinus (St) Bp. M.   Dec 5
d. 361   A martyr of Confinium, a town in Samnium now destroyed, who suffered under Julian the Apostate.

Pepin of Landen (Bl) C.   Feb 21
d. c 646   Pepin, duke of Brabant, mayor of the palace under kings Clotaire II, Dagobert and Sigebert, and ancestor of the Carolingian dynasty of French kings, was the husband of Bl Ida and the father of St Gertrude of Nivelles and of St Begga. He is described as "a lover of peace and the constant defender of truth and justice". His feast was kept at Nivelles.

Peregrinus (Bl) C. OSA.   March 20
See Evangelist and Peregrinus.

Peregrinus Laziosi (St) C. OSM.   May 1
1260–1345   A native of Forli who spent a very worldly youth, in the course of which during a popular revolt he struck St Philip Benizi across the face. Philip turned the other cheek and Peregrinus was converted on the spot and forthwith joined the Servites at Siena. He was afterwards sent back to Forli where he spent the rest of his long life. He was instantaneously cured of a cancer of the foot as a result of a vision, and is for that reason invoked against cancer. Canonized in 1726.

Peregrinus (St) M.   May 5
See Irenaeus, Peregrinus and Irene.

Peregrinus (St) Bp.   May 16
d. c 138(?)   Bishop of Terni in Umbria and founder of its cathedral.

Peregrinus (St) Bp. M.   May 16
d. c 304   Alleged to be a Roman by birth, venerated as the first bishop of Auxerre, to which see he is said to have been appointed by Pope Sixtus II. This is a legend: he was in fact martyred under Diocletian at a place called Bouhy.

Peregrinus I and Peregrinus II (BB) CC. OSB. Cam.   June 3
d. c 1291   Peregrinus I was a Camaldolese abbot of Santa Maria dell'Isola. In 1290 he returned to Camaldoli as sacrist and prior. Peregrinus II was a monk who lived at Camaldoli and died about the same time as Peregrinus I.

Peregrinus (properly Cetheus) (St) Bp. M.   June 13
d. c 600   Bishop of Amiternum (now L'Aquila in the Abruzzi). He was drowned in the river Aterno by the Arian Lombards for asking mercy for a condemned prisoner.

Peregrinus (St) M.   June 17
See Isaurus, Innocent, etc.

**Peregrinus, Lucian,
Pompeius, Hesychius,
Papius, Saturninus,
Germanus, and Astius (SS)
MM.**   July 7
d. *c* 117   Astius was bishop of Dyrrachium
(Durazzo) in Macedonia and was there crucified under Trajan. The others were Italians
who had fled to Macedonia in order to escape
the persecution in their own country and were
seized on account of the sympathy they
showed for Astius. They were loaded with
chains, taken out to sea and thrown overboard.

Peregrinus (St) H.   July 28
2nd cent.(?)   He seems to have been a priest
of the diocese of Lyons in the time of St
Irenaeus, and during the persecution under
Severus to have lived as a hermit in an island in
the R. Saône.

Peregrinus (St) H.   Aug 1
d. 643   An Irish, or Scottish, pilgrim who,
returning from a pilgrimage to the Holy Land,
settled in a solitude near Modena where he
passed the rest of his days.

**Peregrinus, Maceratus
and Viventius (SS)** MM.   Aug 4
6th cent.   A doubtful legend makes them
Spaniards and brothers who perished in
France, seeking to rescue their enslaved sister.
The cult is entirely local.

Peregrinus (St) M.   Aug 25
See Eusebius, Pontian, etc.

**Peregrinus of Falerone
(Bl)** C. OFM.   Sept 6
d. 1240   Born at Falerone in the diocese of
Fermo, he became a follower of St Francis of
Assisi. After a pilgrimage to Palestine he lived
as a lay-brother at San Severino.

Perfectus (St) M.   Apr 18
d. 851   A Spanish priest of Cordoba, martyred by the Muslims on Easter Sunday.

**Pergentinus and
Laurentinus (SS)** MM.   June 3
d. 251   Two brothers martyred at Arezzo
under Decius. It is not certain whether they
ever existed.

Peris (St) C.   Dec 11
?   The patron saint of Llanberis in N. Wales.
No record of him exists.

**Perpetua, Felicity,
Saturus (Satyrus),
Saturninus, Revocatus and
Secundulus (SS)** MM.   GC. March 7
d. 203   Vivia Perpetua was a young married
woman of good social position. Felicity, also
married, was a slave. The others were catechumens and Saturus perhaps their instructor.
All were imprisoned together at Carthage as a
law of Septimus Severus forbade conversions
to the faith. Secundulus died in prison: the
others were thrown to the wild beasts in the
amphitheatre on March 7. Their Acts, which
are of the highest value and interest, both
theologically and historically, are undoubtedly
authentic. They were written by Saturus, one
of the martyrs, and completed by an eye-
witness, perhaps Tertullian. SS Perpetua and
Felicity are mentioned in the first eucharistic
prayer in the Roman rite.

Perpetua (St)   Aug 4
d. *c* 80   A Roman matron said to have been
baptized by St Peter and to have converted her
husband and her son, St Nazarius. (See
Nazarius and Celsus.) Her relics are at Milan
and Cremona.

Perpetuus (St) Bp.   Apr 8
d. *c* 490   Bishop of Tours (*c* 460–490). His
alleged will is admittedly a seventeenth-
century forgery.

Perreux (St) Ab.   June 4
The Breton form of Petroc, q.v.

**Perseveranda (Pecinna,
Pezaine) (St)** V.   June 26
d. *c* 726   Said to have been a Spanish
maiden who, with her sisters Macrina and
Columba, travelled to Poitiers, where they
founded a nunnery. While fleeing from the
pirate Oliver, Perseveranda died of exhaustion
in the place now called after her, Sainte-
Pezaine in Poitou.

Persia, Martyrs of (SS)
The pre-1970 RM. catalogued five anony-
mous groups of martyrs who suffered in
Persia, as follows:

Feb 8
?   6th cent.   Martyrs slain under Cabas.

March 10
?   A group of forty-two martyrs of whom all
details are lost.

Apr 6
?   345   Another group of one hundred and
twenty martyrs, believed to have suffered
under Shapur II (309–380).

Apr 22

d. 376 A vast number of martyrs put to death under the same king Shapur II on Good Friday. Among them were some twenty-five bishops, two hundred and fifty priests and deacons and very many monks and nuns.

May 9

? A group of three hundred and ten martyrs of whom, again, no details are known.

Eastern menologies give other dates and other figures, but a fair estimate of the Persian martyrs put to death during the first six centuries would bring the number up to many thousands.

Peter (several)

Note. The name Petrus is the latinized form of the Greek Petros, which means Rock. Modern variants of Petrus are as follows: Italian, Pietro (antiquated form, Piero); Spanish and Portuguese, Pedro; French, Pierre; Catalan, Pere; English, Peter.

Peter Apselamus and Peter Absalon (SS) MM.   Jan 3

311 Peter surnamed Apselamus, or Balsamus, was crucified at Aulona, near Hebron. Eusebius mentions a Peter Abselame (or Absalon) who was burnt at Caesarea. It is disputed if either of these two are the same person.

Peter of Canterbury (St)

Ab. OSB.   Jan 6

d. *c* 607 A Benedictine monk of St Andrew's, Rome, who was a member of the first band of missionaries sent to England by St Gregory the Great. He became first abbot of the monastery of SS Peter and Paul (afterwards St Augustine's), founded at Canterbury. While on a mission in France he was drowned at Ambleteuse, near Boulogne. Cult confirmed in 1915.

Peter of Sebaste (St) Bp.   Jan 9

d. *c* 391 A native of Cappadocia, and younger brother of St Basil and of St Gregory of Nyssa. He succeeded St Basil as abbot and in 380 was appointed bishop of Sebaste in Armenia. He took part in the general council of Constantinople (381). (Another Peter of Sebaste, bishop, is also honoured as a saint. He died about 320.)

Peter Urseolus (St) H.

OSB.   Jan 10

928–987 Born in Venice, Peter became, at the age of twenty, admiral of the Venetian fleet. In 976 he became Doge of Venice and succeeded in guiding the Republic safely through a time of dangerous political crisis. After two

years, unknown to all — even to his family — he disappeared from Venice, to emerge as a monk in the Benedictine abbey of Cuxa, in the Spanish Pyrenees. He acted as sacrist of the abbey until some years later he retired to live as a hermit.

Peter, Severus and Leucius (SS) MM.   Jan 11

? Peter and Leucius are mentioned in St Jerome's martyrology as confessors. To them the pre-1970 RM. adds Severus and describes all three as martyrs at Alexandria.

Peter of Castelnau (Bl)

M. OSB. Cist.   Jan 15

d. 1208 Born near Montpellier, he became archdeacon of Maguelonne (1199) and shortly after (*c* 1202) a Cistercian at Fontfroide. The following year Pope Innocent III appointed him apostolic legate and inquisitor for the Albigensians — in fact the leader of the famous expedition, of which St Dominic was a member, for the conversion of those heretics. While engaged in that work he was assassinated, his last words being: "May God forgive thee, brother, as fully as I forgive thee."

Peter (St) M. OFM.   Jan 16

See Berardus, Peter, etc.

Peter Thomas (St) Bp. OC.   Jan 25

1305–1366 (Jan 6) A native of Breil in Gascony, Peter Thomas joined the Carmelites and in 1342 was sent to Avignon as procurator of his order. There he entered the service of the papal court and was sent on diplomatic missions to Italy, Serbia, Hungary and the Near East, being appointed successively bishop of Patti and Lipari (1354), bishop of Coron in Morea (1359), archbishop of Candia (1363) and Latin patriarch of Constantinople (1364). On behalf of Pope Urban V and with the support of King Peter I of Cyprus he led a crusade against the Turks. In an unsuccessful attack on Alexandria he was severely wounded and died three months later at Cyprus. Cult approved in 1608.

Peter Nolasco (St) Founder   Jan 28

c 1182–1258 (Dec 25) A native of Languedoc who, after seeing service against the Albigenses, settled at Barcelona, where he became intimate with St Raymund of Peñafort. About the year 1218 both saints, with the help of James I of Aragon, reorganized a lay confraternity for ransoming captives from the Moors, which was gradually transformed into the order of the Mercedarians (*B. V. Mariae de Mercede Redemptionis Captivorum*), of which St Peter Nolasco is revered as the chief founder.

He personally ransomed several hundred captives. Canonized in 1628. Since 1969 his cult is confined to local or particular calendars.

Peter of Zalankemen (Bl) C. Jan 31

15th cent. He was an exemplary general of the Pauline Hermit order (1488–1492).

Peter Cambian (Bl) M. OP. Feb 2

d. 1365 Peter Cambian de Ruffi, a Dominican of distinction, was sent in 1351 as inquisitor general to Piedmont and Lombardy. He had chiefly to deal with the Waldenses, who ultimately trapped and killed him. Cult approved in 1856.

Peter Baptist (St) M. OFM. Feb 6

1545–1597 Born near Avila, in Spain. He joined the Friars Minor in 1567. He was sent as a missionary first to Mexico, then to the Philippine Islands (1583) and lastly (1593) to Japan. Political intrigues led to the arrest of Peter and twenty-six missionaries (six Franciscans, three Jesuits and seventeen native Franciscan tertiaries), who had never given a thought to politics. They were all crucified at Nagasaki. St Peter Baptist, who had the gift of working miracles, is considered as their leader. All were canonized in 1862.

Peter Xukexico (St) M. Feb 6

d. 1597 A Japanese layman. He was a Franciscan tertiary, a catechist, and house-servant and sacristan to the Franciscan missionaries in Japan. He belongs to the group of St Peter Baptist q.v.

Peter Igneus (St) Card. Bp. OSB. Vall. Feb 8

d. c 1089 He is said to have belonged to the Aldobrandini family of Florence. He took his vows at Vallumbrosa under St John Gualbert. Shortly after, in order to convict the bishop of Florence of simony, Peter, it is said, miraculously passed through the flames unharmed, hence his surname of *Igneus*, "of the fire". At a later period he was created cardinal-bishop of Albano and sent to foreign countries as legate of the Holy See.

Peter of Treja (Bl) C. OFM. Feb 20

d. 1304 One of the early Franciscans associated with Bl Conrad of Offida in his apostolate. They preached with great success throughout Italy. Bl Peter died at Sirolo in Piceno. Cult approved in 1793.

Peter the Scribe (St) M. Feb 21

d. 743 Surnamed also *Mavimenus*, from the town of Majuma in Palestine where he worked as a scribe (*chartularius*). He was put to death by the Arab sheik of Damascus.

Peter Damian (St) Bp. Card. Dr. OSB. GC. Feb 21

1007–1072 Born at Ravenna, the youngest of many children, he was left an orphan in the charge of a married brother, who ill-treated him and set him to herd swine. Another brother, Damian, archpriest of Ravenna, took pity on the child and paid for his schooling at Faenza and Parma. Peter soon joined the Benedictine community of Fontavellana, founded by Bl Rudolph twenty years before. Earnest in all his undertakings, Peter became a model monk and was chosen abbot. In 1057 he was summoned to Rome and created cardinal-bishop of Ostia. He served successive popes in various missions: as legate to Germany, to France, to Lombardy; as president, or papal representative, at sundry councils and synods; as visitor to bishoprics and abbeys. Meanwhile he wrote unceasingly, mostly theological or ascetical works, but also poetry, his Latin verse being among the very best of the Middle Ages. He died at Faenza worn out by his labours. Declared Doctor of the Church in 1828.

Peter Roque (Bl) M. CM. March 1

1758–1796 A native of Vannes in Brittany and a priest of the Congregation of the Mission (Vincentians) at Paris. He refused to take the constitutional oath during the French Revolution and was guillotined. Beatified in 1934.

Peter Pappacarbone (St) Bp. OSB. March 4

d. 1123 He was born at Salerno and became a monk of Cava under the second abbot, St Leo I. About the year 1062 he was sent to Cluny, where he stayed some six years. In 1079 he was made bishop of Policastro, but resigned and returned to Cava, where Leo I appointed him coadjutor abbot. He succeeded to the abbacy in the same year but showed himself too strict, and in view of the remonstrances of the community he withdrew to another house. He was soon recalled and under his new, more paternal, régime the abbey prospered exceedingly: he is said to have given the habit to over three thousand monks. When he died Cava numbered twenty-nine subject abbeys, ninety priories and over three hundred and forty cells.

Peter de Geremia (Bl) C. OP. March 10

1381–1452 A native of Palermo, who was a

student of law at Bologna when he decided to join the Friars Preachers. He became one of the best-known preachers and missionaries of his age. Cult approved in 1784.

Peter the Spaniard (St) C.   March 11
? A Spanish pilgrim to Rome who settled as a hermit at Babuco, near Veroli. He wore a coat of mail next to his skin as a mortification.

Peter of Nicomedia (St)
M.   March 12
d. 303   A chamberlain (*cubicularius*) in the palace of Diocletian at Nicomedia. He was one of the first victims of the last great persecution. His flesh was torn from his bones, salt and vinegar were poured into his wounds and finally he was roasted to death over a slow fire.

Peter the Deacon (St)
Mk. OSB.   March 12
d. *p.*605   The disciple, secretary and companion of St Gregory the Great, to whom the great pope dictated the four books of his Dialogues. He is venerated as the patron saint of Salassola, diocese of Biella, in Upper Italy. He is usually described as a Benedictine monk.

Peter II of Cava (Bl) Ab.
OSB.   March 13
d. 1208   The ninth abbot of Cava, near Salerno, from 1195 to 1208. He is described as "an enemy of all litigation" which, for that time, is no small praise. Cult confirmed in 1928.

Peter and Aphrodisius
(SS) MM.   March 14
5th cent.   Martyrs under the Arian Vandals in N.W. Africa. Nothing else is known about them.

Peter Lieou (Bl) M.   March 17
d. 1834   A Chinese layman. Converted when young, he was exiled for his faith to Tartary (1814). In 1827 he was allowed to return. During a fresh persecution, he gained entry into the prison to comfort and strengthen his sons and was strangled. Beatified in 1900.

Peter of Gubbio (Bl) C.
OSA. Erem.   March 23
d. *c* 1350(?)   Born at Gubbio in Umbria, of the family of the Ghisleni. He became a hermit of St Augustine, and was provincial of his congregation. His shrine is at Gubbio. Cult confirmed by Pius IX.

Peter, Marcian, Jovinus, Thecla, Cassian, and Comp. (SS) MM.   March 26
? Roman martyrs, of whom nothing certain is known. Some registers have *Theodula* instead of *Thecla*.

Peter Marginet (Bl)
C. OSB. Cist.   March 26
d. 1435   A Cistercian monk of Poblet, near Tarragona, in Spain, and the cellarer of the abbey. From a deeply religious life he lapsed into one of crime, apostatized and became the leader of bandits. After some years he repented, went back to the abbey and spent the rest of his life doing penance.

Peter Regalado (St) C.
OFM.   March 30
390–1456   A Spaniard of noble birth of Valladolid who entered the Franciscan order and effected a strict reform in several friaries, notably at Aguilar del Campo in New Castile.

Peter of Poitiers (St) Bp.   Apr 4
d. 1115   Bishop of Poitiers (1087–1115). A fearless person who publicly denounced the sacrilegious tyranny and licence of kings Philip I and William VI, count of Poitiers and duke of Aquitaine. He befriended and helped Bl Robert d'Arbrisselle in founding the abbey of Fontrevault.

Peter Cerdan (Bl) C. OP.   Apr 5
d. 1422   A Dominican friar who accompanied St Vincent Ferrer in his travels and apostolate. He died at Grans, diocese of Barbastro, Aragon.

Peter of Siena (Bl) M.
OFM.   Apr 9
See Bl Thomas of Tolentino and Comp.

Peter of Montepiano (Bl)
C. OSB. Vall.   Apr 12
d. 1098   A Vallumbrosan abbot of San Virilio at Brescia, who ended his life as a hermit at Montepiano in Tuscany.

Peter Gonzalez (or Telmo) (St) C. OP.   Apr 14
1190–1246   Born at Astorga in Spain he became a canon of Palencia and subsequently joined the Dominicans. He was chosen by King St Ferdinand of Castile as his confessor and court-chaplain, and in that position did much to foster the crusade against the Moors and to obtain a kindly treatment for the Moorish captives when Cordoba and Seville were taken. He also worked among the sailors and peasants of Galicia. Spanish sailors often call him Telmo, or Elmo, thought to be a corruption of Erasmus — that saint being an earlier patron of mariners.

Peter and Hermogenes
(SS) MM.   Apr 17
? Peter, a deacon, and Hermogenes, his

servant, were martyred at an unknown date, probably at Antioch.

Peter of Braga (St) Bp. M.   Apr 26
? The alleged first bishop and martyr of Braga in Portugal. The local tradition connects him with the apostolate of St James the Great, q.v., in Spain. He is thought, however, to have lived in the fifth or sixth century.

Peter Armengol (St) M.
O. Merc.   Apr 27
1238–1304   He belonged to the house of the counts of Urgell, in the Spanish Eastern Pyrenees. He spent his youth in dissipation, but in 1528 joined the Mercedarians and devoted all his energies to the ransoming of captives. He offered himself as a hostage for eighteen Christian children, and was put to frightful tortures in his African captivity, being for this reason considered a martyr. He died near Tarragona.

Peter Chanel (St) M.   GC. Apr 28
1803–1840   Peter Louis Mary Chanel was born at Cluet, diocese of Belley, in France, of a family of peasants. He was ordained in 1827 and appointed parish priest of Crozet. In 1831 he entered the Society of Mary (Marist Fathers) and was sent to Oceania as superior of the first missionary band. He was martyred on Fortuna Island by the native king. He is the first martyr of Oceania. Canonized in 1954.

Peter Hieu (St) M.   Apr 28
d. 1840   A native catechist of Vietnam, attached to the Society of Foreign Missions of Paris. He was beheaded with two companions. Canonized in 1988.

Peter Martyr (St) OP.   Apr 29
c 1205–1252   Born at Verona of Catharist parents, he joined the Dominicans in 1221 and was appointed inquisitor of Lombardy, then swarming with Catharists. He preached very successfully throughout northern and central Italy, until at length the Catharists succeeded in waylaying him on the road between Como and Milan. He was canonized in the following year (1253). He is shown in art as a Dominican with a large knife cleaving his head, or holding a knife, or a knife in his head and a sword in his breast. Since 1969 his cult is confined to local or particular calendars.

Peter (St) M.   Apr 30
See Amator, Peter and Louis.

Peter of Pavia (St) Bp.   May 7
d. c 735   A bishop of Pavia during the reign of his kinsman Luitprand, king of the Lombards. His episcopate was brief.

St Peter Martyr, Apr 29

Peter of Tarantaise (St)

Bp. OSB. Cist.   May 8

1102–1175   Born near Vienne in Dauphiné,
at the age of twelve he joined the Cistercians at
Bonnevaux and before he was thirty he was
sent as first abbot to the foundation of Tamié.
In 1142 he was chosen archbishop of Tarant-
aise, but after holding this position thirteen
years he disappeared and was eventually found
serving his novitiate as a lay-brother in a
remote Cistercian abbey in Switzerland. He
was compelled to return to his diocese, where
he made a name for himself as an upholder of
papal rights. Canonized in 1191.

Peter the Venerable (Bl)

Ab. OSB.   May 11

c 1092–1156   Peter de Montboissier was
born in Auvergne, and became a monk at
Cluny in 1109. At twenty he was prior of
Vézelay and in 1122 succeeded to the abbacy
of Cluny. He was one of the most eminent
churchmen of his age, and during the thirty-
four years of his abbacy Cluny retained its
position as the greatest and most influential
abbey in Christendom. Calm and serene in his
charity, he was the counterpart of his tempestuous contemporary, friend, admirer, and on
some points, rival, St Bernard of Clairvaux. At
Cluny he regulated the finances, raised the
standard of studies (he was himself a poet and
a theological writer of distinction and was the
first European to have the Koran translated
into Latin) and received the vanquished Abelard under his roof. He died, according to his
wish, on Christmas Day, after having preached
about the feast to his monks. His name was
inserted in French martyrologies, and his feast
is observed in the diocese of Arras on Dec 29.

Peter, Andrew, Paul and Dionysia (SS) MM.   May 15

d. 251   Peter was a young man of Lamp-
sacus on the Hellespont, martyred at Troas
with SS Paul, Andrew and Dionysia, under
Decius.

Peter Celestine (St)

Pope, Founder, OSB.   May 19

c 1215–1296   Born at Isernia in the Abruzzi,
he became a hermit and a priest. In 1246 he
received the Benedictine habit from the abbot
of Faizola, but he returned to the solitary life at
Morone, near Sulmona (1251) where he
gathered numerous disciples and founded the
new Benedictine congregation named after
him. In 1294 he was elected pope and was
compelled by the cardinals to accept, but he
proved an utter failure and resigned the same
year. His successor, Boniface VIII, kept him in
custody till his death, which was what the

venerable old man really wanted — a quiet cell
where he could again live the peaceful life of a
hermit. Canonized in 1313. Since 1969 his
cult is restricted to local calendars only.

Peter de Dueñas (Bl) M.

OFM.   May 19

1378–1397   Born at Palencia, Spain, he
became a Franciscan and in 1396 accompanied Bl John de Cetina to Granada to preach the
gospel to the Moors. Both were beheaded in
the following year.

Peter Wright (Bl) M. SJ.   May 19

d. 1651   Born at Slipton in Northamptonshire, he became a convert to the Catholic faith
and studied for the priesthood at Ghent and in
Rome. In 1629 he joined the Jesuits and was a
chaplain to the royalist army during the Civil
War. He was condemned to death for his faith
and executed at Tyburn.

Peter Parenzi (St) M.   May 22

d. 1199   A Roman by birth, he was sent to
Orvieto (1199) as papal governor to repress
the excesses of the Catharist heretics. He
adopted severe measures, with the result that
the heretics seized him and put him to a cruel
death.

Peter of the Assumption

(Bl) M. OFM.   May 22

d. 1614   Born at Cuerva, archdiocese of
Toledo. He went to Japan with a band of fifty
Franciscan missionaries (1601) and was appointed guardian of the friary at Nagasaki. He
was beheaded at Nagasaki with Bl John Mach-
ado (q.v.). He is the first martyr of the second
great Japanese persecution. Beatified in 1867.

Peter Van (St) M.   May 25

c 1780–1857   A native catechist beheaded at
Son-tay, in Vietnam. Canonized in 1988.

Peter Sanz (Bl) Bp. M. OP.   May 26

d. 1747   Born at Asco in Catalonia he joined
the Dominicans (1697) and was sent to the
Philippine Islands (1712) whence (1713) he
proceeded to China. In 1730 he was nominated vicar-apostolic of Fo-Kien and titular
bishop of Mauricastro. In 1746 he was imprisoned and finally beheaded at Fu-tsheu. Beatified in 1893.

Peter Arnaud (Bl) M.   May 28

d. 1242   A layman, notary of the inquisition
at Toulouse, put to death by the Albigenses at
Avignonet with eleven inquisitors. Cult approved in 1866.

Peter Petroni (Bl) C. O.

Cart.   May 29

1311–1361   A Sienese by birth, he became

(1328) a Carthusian at Maggiano near Siena. His thoughtful charity was instrumental in the conversion of Boccaccio.

Peter (St) M.   June 2
See Marcellinus and Peter.

Peter, Wallabonsus, Sabinian, Wistremundus, Habentius and Jeremiah (SS) MM.   June 7
d. 851 Spaniards living at Cordoba under the Moorish rule. Peter was a priest; Wallabonsus, a deacon; Sabinian and Wistremundus, monks of St Zoilus at Cordoba; Habentius, a monk of St Christopher's; Jeremiah, a very old man, had founded the monastery of Tábanos, near Cordoba. For publicly reprobating Mohammed they were martyred under Abderrahman II. Jeremiah was scourged to death; the others were beheaded.

Peter Rodriguez and Comp. (BB) MM. (?)   June 11
d. 1242 A group of seven Portuguese knights of Santiago, whose leader was Bl Peter Rodriguez. All were murdered by the Moors during an armistice at Tavira in Algabes, Portugal. Cult not yet approved.

Peter Gambacorta (Bl)
Founder   June 17
1355–1435 Born at Pisa or Lucca. After a misspent youth, he repented and retired to the solitude of Montebello, diocese of Urbino where, it is said, he converted twelve robbers with whom he founded the Institute of the Poor Brothers of St Jerome. When his father and two brothers were murdered, Peter refused to leave his cell. Like his sister, Bl Clare Gambacorta, he fully forgave the assassins.

Peter Rinxei (Bl) M. SJ.   June 20
1589–1626 A Japanese who was educated at the Jesuit seminary of Arima. He became the catechist of Bl Francis Pacheco, by whom he was received into the Society while in prison. Burnt alive at Nagasaki. Beatified in 1867.

Peter of Tarantaise (Bl)
Pope   June 22
Otherwise Innocent V, q.v.

Peter of Juilly (Bl or St)
OSB. Cist.   June 23
d. 1136 An Englishman and a companion and friend of St Stephen Harding at Molesme. He was appointed chaplain and confessor to the Benedictine nuns of Juilly-les-Nonnais, subject to Molesme, where St Bernard's sister, St Humbeline, was abbess. Peter is described as a great preacher and wonder-worker. He died at Juilly.

Peter James of Pesaro
(Bl) C. OSA.   June 23
d. c 1496 An Augustinian friar in the friary of St Nicholas at Pesaro. Cult approved by Pius IX.

Peter the Apostle (St) M.
GC. June 29 (Feb 22, Nov 18)
d. c 64 Simon, son of John, was a Galilean fisherman, a married man living at Bethsaida. He was a disciple of St John the Baptist before he was called, with his elder brother Andrew, to be a disciple of Christ, by whom he was at once named "Rock" (Cephas, Petros, Petra, Peter). The culminating episode narrated of him in the gospel, is that of his confession of Christ as the Son of God (Matt. 16:15–19), to which Christ answered with the solemn promise: "You are Peter and upon this rock I will build my church...and I will give you the keys of the kingdom of heaven." This promise was ratified by Christ after his resurrection with the threefold injunction to feed His flock. Throughout the gospels Peter is always with our Lord as one of the inner group, and a witness of many important events such as the raising of Jairus's daughter; the transfiguration, and the agony in the garden. After Christ's ascension he presided at Jerusalem, taking a prominent part in the council there. He was perhaps for a time bishop of Antioch and finally presided over the church in Rome, where on the Vatican Hill he was martyred, head downwards according to tradition, in the circus of Nero. His chief feast is that of June 29, on which day he has been honoured with St Paul at least since the beginning of the fourth century: His relics are enshrined to this day beneath the high altar of St Peter's in Rome. He has other minor feasts on the dates given in the parenthesis above. In art he is shown as elderly, of a sturdy build, with curly hair and a curly square-cut beard. This is a very old iconographic tradition. He holds a key or keys, and a book; or is crucified head downwards: or robed as a pope with keys and a double-barred cross.

Peter of Luxemburg (Bl)
Bp. Card.   July 4
1369–1387 Born at Ligny in Lorraine, of the family of the counts of Lützelburg. As a boy he was interested in religion and so, according to the usual practise at that time, was forthwith given sundry canonries at Paris, Chartres and Cambrai and was made archdeacon of Dreux. At the age of fourteen he was appointed bishop of Metz. At sixteen he was created cardinal of San Giorgio in Velabro. He died at the age of eighteen. He was a youth of great promise and holiness of life. Beatified in 1527.

St Peter the Apostle, June 29

Peter the Hermit (Bl) C.   July 8

1055?–1115 A soldier of European birth who became a hermit for a time in Palestine. Then he returned to Europe and preached the first crusade throughout Italy, France and part of the Germanies. He accompanied the first expedition to the East and once more became a soldier. He fought at the siege of Antioch and the capture of Jerusalem. Subsequently he founded the monastery of Neufmoutier at Huy in Flanders, where he died. He was never officially beatified.

Peter van Asche (St) M.
OFM.   July 9

d. 1572 Born at Asche near Brussels. He was a Franciscan lay-brother at Gorkum in Holland, and was hanged by the Calvinists at Briel.

Peter of Perugia (St) Ab.
OSB.   July 10

d. 1007 Peter Vincioli was born near Perugia and belonged to the family of the counts of Agello. He was the abbot-founder of the monastery of St Peter at Perugia, where he has an altar dedicated to him in the abbey church.

Peter Tu (St) M.   July 10

d. 1840 A native catechist of Vietnam, beheaded at Anam. Canonized in 1988.

Peter Araki-Cobioje (Bl)
M.   July 12

d. 1626 A Japanese man burnt alive at Nagasaki for sheltering Christians. Beatified in 1867.

Peter Khanh (St) M.   July 12

c 1780–1842 A native priest of Vietnam, beheaded at Con-co. Canonized in 1988.

Peter Nuñez and Peter
Fontura (BB) MM. SJ.   July 15

d. 1570 Two Portuguese Jesuits, fellow-martyrs of Bl Ignatius de Azevedo. The former was a cleric, a native of Fronteria; the latter a lay-brother, born at Braga.

Peter Berna (Bl) M. SJ.   July 15

d. 1583 Born at Ascona, on the lake of Locarno, Ticino, Switzerland, he studied at the German college in Rome and joined the Jesuits. He went to India with Bl Rudolph Acquaviva and was ordained at Goa. After some years of missionary work he was put to death with Bl Rudolph, q.v.

Peter Tuan (St) M.   July 15

1766–1838 A native priest of Vietnam who died in prison of wounds received for the faith while awaiting the decree of decapitation. Canonized in 1988.

Peter of the Holy Mother of God (Bl) M. OP.   July 29

d. 1629   A Japanese catechist and a Dominican. He was burnt alive at Omura with Bl Louis Bertrán. Beatified in 1867.

Peter Chrysologus (St)
Bp. Dr.   GC. July 30

c 406–c 450   Born at Imola, he became deacon there, and then successively archdeacon and archbishop of Ravenna (c 433). He is chiefly famed for his assiduity and eloquence in preaching, whence the name given him of *Chrysologus*, "Golden Speech". A great number of his sermons are still extant. He was declared a Doctor of the Church in 1729 by Benedict XIII.

Peter of Mogliano (Bl) C.
OFM.   July 30

d. 1490   Born at Mogliano, diocese of Fermo, he studied law at Perugia and joined the Observant Franciscans there. Later on he went about preaching with St James della Marca, q.v. Cult approved in 1760.

Peter Quy (St) M.   July 31

d. 1859   Born at Bung in Vietnam he was ordained and beheaded for that reason near Chau-doc. Beatified in 1909, canonized in 1988.

Peter (St) M.   Aug 1
See Cyril, Aquila, etc.

Peter of Osma (St) Bp. OSB.   Aug 2

d. 1109   A French monk of Cluny, one of the numerous Cluniac monks who settled in Spain from c 1050 to c 1130. He first became archdeacon of Toledo under the Cluniac archbishop Bernard de la Sauvetat, who in 1101 nominated him bishop of Osma in Old Castile. St Peter is venerated as the principal patron saint of the cathedral and diocese of Osma.

Peter of Anagni (St) Bp.
OSB.   Aug 3

d. 1105   Born at Salerno, he became a Benedictine monk in his native city. In 1062 Pope St Gregory VII appointed him to the see of Anagni. He built a new cathedral there, took part in the First Crusade and was sent as papal legate to Constantinople. Canonized four years after his death.

Peter Julian Eymard (St)
Founder   Aug 3

1811–1868   A native of La Mure ('Isère). He was ordained in 1834 and worked for some time as a parish priest, but subsequently joined the congregation of the Marist Fathers, as a member of which he became renowned as a preacher and confessor. In 1856 he was dispensed from his vows in that institute, and in the following year founded another of his own, the Congregation of priests of the Blessed Sacrament, with the special object of fostering devotion to the holy eucharist. Shortly after he established a congregation of women with similar aims. In both enterprises he was encouraged by St John Vianney. Canonized in 1963.

Peter, Julian, and Comp.
(SS) MM.   Aug 7

d. c 260   A band of twenty or more Roman martyrs under Valerian and Gallienus. Julian should probably be Juliana.

Peter Becket (Becchetti)
(Bl)   Aug 11
See John and Peter Becchetti.

Peter Faber (Bl) C. SJ.   Aug 11

1506–1546   Peter Lefevre was born at Villaret in Savoy and was already a priest and a student at Paris when he attached himself to St Ignatius of Loyola. After the official approbation of the Society of Jesus (1540) he worked at Worms, Spires, Mainz, and especially at Cologne. He was a man of very winning manners, of great ability and of untiring energy. He died in Rome, when about to leave for the council of Trent.

Peter Zuñiga (Bl) M. OSA.   Aug 19

1585–1622   A native of Seville, he spent his youth in Mexico, where his father was the sixth viceroy. On his return to Spain he joined the Augustinians at Seville and after being ordained asked to be sent to Japan. He arrived at Manila in 1610 and in Japan in 1620, and two years later was burnt alive at Nagasaki with Bl Louis Flores, Bl Joachim Firayama and the captain of the vessel which had brought him. The crew of twelve who were Christians were beheaded. All were beatified in 1867.

Peter Vasquez (Bl) M. OP.   Aug 25

d. 1624   Born at Berin, in Galicia, he joined the Dominicans in Madrid and ultimately was appointed to the missions in Japan. He was burnt alive at Ximabura with Bl Louis Sotelo and Comp. Beatified in 1867.

Peter (St) M.   Aug 27
See Marcellinus, Mannea, etc.

Peter of Trevi (St) C.   Aug 30

d. c 1050   Born at Carsoli in the diocese of Marsi, Italy. He was ordained and preached with signal success to the peasants of the districts of Tivoli, Anagni and Subiaco. He died while still young at Trevi, near Subiaco. Canonized in 1215.

Peter of Sassoferrato
(Bl) M. OFM.   Sept 3
See under John of Perugia.

Peter Tu (St) M. OP.   Sept 5
d. 1838 A native Dominican priest of Vietnam, beheaded at Ninh-Tai. Canonized in 1988.

Peter Claver (St) C. SJ.   GC. Sept 9
1581–1654 Born at Verdu, near Barcelona in Spain, the son of a farmer, he became a Jesuit in 1601 and was then stationed at Majorca, where he was inspired by St Alphonsus Rodriguez with the desire to work in America. In 1610 he was sent there, and was ordained at Cartagena in what is now Colombia. During the following forty years he worked chiefly at Cartagena, at that time the central slave-mart of the West Indies, dedicating his life by a special vow to the service of the outcast Negroes. He is said to have baptized, and cared for over 300,000 of them. During the last four years of his life he was a sick man and was often neglected by his brethren. He was canonized in 1888 and declared patron of all the Catholic missions among the Negroes in 1896.

Peter Martinez (St) Bp.
OSB.   Sept 10
d. c 1000 Surnamed also St Peter of Mozonzo. He was a native of Spanish Galicia, and about the year 950 became a Benedictine at the abbey of St Mary of Mozonzo. Later he was appointed abbot of St Martin *de Antealtares*, at Compostella and finally (c 986) archbishop of that city. He is one of the heroes of the Spanish Reconquest, as also one of the supposed authors of the *Salve Regina*.

Peter de Avila (Bl) M. OFM.   Sept 10
1562–1622 Born at Palomares in Castile, he was sent to Manila with Bl Louis Sotelo (1617) then to Japan. He was burnt alive at Nagasaki on the day of the great martyrdom. Beatified in 1867.

Peter Sampo (Bl) M. SJ.   Sept 10
d. 1622 Born in the province of Ochu, in Japan. He was received into the Society of Jesus by Bl Charles Spinola in the prison of Omura. Burnt alive at Nagasaki on the day of the great martyrdom. Beatified in 1867.

Peter Nangaxi,
Peter Sanga, and Peter
Ikiemon (BB) MM.   Sept 10 and 11
d. 1622 Three Japanese children martyred with their parents at Nagasaki. Peter Nangaxi, a boy of seven years, was the son of BB Paul and Thecla; Peter Sanga, a boy of three years, was the second son of BB Antony and Mary Magdalen Sanga, of Korea; Peter Ikiemon, a boy of seven years, was the son of Bl Bartholomew. The three were beheaded: the first two on the 10th, the third on the 11th of September. Beatified in 1867.

Peter of Chavanon (St)
C. OSA.   Sept 11
1003–1080 A native of Langeac, in Haute Loire, he became a secular priest and then founded an abbey of Augustinian canons regular at Pébrac in Auvergne and was its first superior.

Peter-Paul of St Claire
(Bl) M. OFM.   Sept 12
d. 1622 Born at Saigo in Arima, Japan, he became a catechist under Bl Apollinaris Franco. He was burnt alive at Omura. Beatified in 1867.

Peter Arbues (St) M. OSA.   Sept 17
1442–1485 Born at Epila in Aragon he studied philosophy at Huesca and theology and canon law at Bologna. In 1478 he became an Augustinian canon regular at Saragossa, and in 1484 was made inquisitor of Aragon. What has been written about his cruelty is unsubstantiated: not a single sentence of death or of torture can be traced to him; but his integrity was feared by the Crypto-Jews (the *Marranos*) who murdered him in his cathedral. Canonized in 1867.

Peter Maubant (Bl) M.   Sept 22
See Laurence Imbert.

Peter (St) M.   Sept 23
See Andrew, John, etc.

Peter Acotanto (Bl) C. OSB.   Sept 23
d. c 1180 Born of a noble Venetian family, he spent his life tending the sick. Some years before his death he retired to live as a recluse in a cell near the Benedictine abbey of San Giorgio Maggiore in Venice, under the obedience of the abbot. Cult approved by Clement VIII.

Peter Cufioje (Bl) M.   Sept 28
d. 1630 A Japanese Augustinian tertiary, beheaded at Nagasaki for sheltering the Augustinian missionaries. Beatified in 1867.

Peter (St) M.   Oct 3
See Dionysius, Faustus, etc.

Peter of Damascus (St)
Bp. M.   Oct 4
d. c 750 A bishop of Damascus who was

maimed, blinded, exiled and ultimately bound to a cross and beheaded by the Arab rulers of the city for preaching against their Prophet.

Peter of Seville (St) M.   Oct 8
? A martyr venerated at Seville, of whom only the name is known. Later legends are admitted to be fables.

Peter Tuy (St) M.   Oct 11
d. 1833 A native Vietnamese priest beheaded at the age of seventy under King Minh-Menh. Canonized in 1988.

Peter of Alcántara (St) C. OFM.   Oct 19
1499–1562 Born at Alcántara in Estremadura, at the age of sixteen he became a Franciscan observant and after his ordination (1524) initiated at Pedrosa a still more severe Franciscan reform which was known as *Alcantarine* and received papal approval. St Peter is also remembered as one of the group of great Spanish mystics and his treatise on prayer was much valued, and used by St Francis of Sales. He encouraged and defended St Teresa, whose confessor and admirer he was. St Teresa held him in great esteem and speaks with awe of his austerities and penances as "incomprehensible to the human mind"; they had reduced him, she tells us, to a condition in which he looked as if "he had been made of the roots of trees". He is the patron saint of Brazil and was canonized in 1669. Cult confined to particular calendars since 1969.

Peter Capucci (Bl) C. OP.   Oct 21
1390–1445 Born at Città di Castello (the ancient *Tifernum*), he joined the Dominicans and was ordained at Cortona. He became known as "the preacher of death", because he used to preach with a skull in his hands. Cult confirmed by Pius VII.

Peter (St) M.   Oct 25
See Theodosius, Lucius, etc.

Peter Onizuko (Bl) M. SJ.   Nov 1
d. 1622 A Japanese born at Faciram, Arima. He became a Jesuit postulant and attached himself to Bl Paul Navarro, with whom he was burnt alive at Ximabara. Beatified in 1867.

Peter Almafo (Bl) M. OP.   Nov 1
d. 1861 Born at Sasserra, diocese of Vich, Spain, he became a Dominican and was sent to the Philippine Islands, and thence to Ximabara under Bl Jerome Hermosilla, with whom he was beheaded. Beatified in 1906.

Peter-Francis Néron (St) M.   Nov 3
1818–1860 Born in Bornay, in Jura, he was admitted into the seminary of Foreign Missions of Paris (1846), ordained (1848) and sent to Hong-Kong. He worked in Vietnam as director of the central seminary until his martyrdom by beheading. Canonized in 1988.

Peter Ou (Bl) M.   Nov 7
d. 1814 Originally an innkeeper, on his conversion he became a catechist and instructed about six hundred persons. He was strangled at Tsen-y-Fou, of the Su-Tchuen province of China. Beatified in 1900.

Peter Dumoulin-Bori, Peter Khoa and Vincent Diem (SS) MM.   Nov 24
d. 1838 Bl Peter Dumoulin was born at Cors, diocese of Tulle, France, in 1808, and entered the seminary for Foreign Missions at Paris in 1829, being sent to Tonkin after his ordination in 1832. In 1836 he was arrested and received when in prison his appointment as titular bishop and vicar apostolic of W. Tonkin. BB Peter Choa and Vincent Diem were natives of Tonkin and priests. The bishop was beheaded, the two priests strangled at Dong-Hoi. Canonized in 1988.

Peter of Alexandria (St) Bp. M.   Nov 26
d. c 311 An Alexandrian who, as a young man, was a confessor during the persecution raging under the emperor Diocletian. Then he became the head of the catechetical school and as such combated extreme Origenism. In 300 he became patriarch and in that position he figured as one of the opponents of the Meletian schism, being also one of the first to detect the dangerous teaching of Arius. He was martyred under Galerius Maximus, "the seal and complement of martyrs" as the Copts term him, because he was the last to be put to death as a Christian by public authority at Alexandria. Cult confined to particular calendars since 1969.

Peter (St) M.   Nov 28
See Stephen, Basil, etc.

Peter Pascual (St) Bp. M.   Dec 6
1227–1300 Peter Pascual, or Pascualez, was born at Valencia in Spain. About the year 1250 he was ordained and was for some time tutor to the son of the king of Aragon. Later he became bishop of Jaén, which at that time was still under Moorish government. His heroic exertions in ransoming captives, and his preaching and writing against Islam were rewarded with martyrdom at Granada. Cult confirmed in 1673.

Peter, Successus, Bassian, Primitivus and Comp. (SS) MM.   Dec 9
? Martyrs in Africa, of whom now nothing is known.

Peter Fourier (St) OSA.
Founder   Dec 9
1565–1640 Born at Mirecourt in Lorraine, he joined the Augustinian canons regular, and some time after his ordination (1585) was put in charge of the neglected parish of Mattaincourt. Here he founded the Congregation of Notre Dame for the education of girls. He failed, however, in similar efforts to establish a new congregation for teaching boys. Canonized in 1897.

Peter Tecelano (Bl) C. OFM.   Dec 10
d. 1287 Born at Campi in Tuscany, he started life as a comb-maker at Siena. On the death of his wife he joined the Franciscans as a lay-brother and carried on his trade in the friary for the remainder of his long life. He attained a high degree of mystical prayer. Cult confirmed in 1802.

Peter Duong and Peter Truat (SS) MM.   Dec 18
d. 1838 Native catechists in Vietnam, martyred. Canonized in 1988.

Peter de la Cadireta (Bl) M. OP.   Dec 20
d. 1277 Born at Moya in Spain, he became a Dominican friar. He was stoned to death by heretics while preaching at Urgell. His body is venerated in the church of St Dominic at Urgell.

Peter Massalenis (Bl) C. OSB. Cam.   Dec 20
1375–1453 Peter de Massalenis was born at Othoca in Sardinia. After repeated pilgrimages to the Holy Land he joined the Camaldolese Benedictines at San Michele di Murano, Venice (1410). He was famed for his gift of mystical contemplation.

Peter Thi (St) M.   Dec 20
1763–1839 A native of Vietnam and a priest. At the age of sixty he was beheaded at Ha-Noi. Canonized in 1988.

Peter Canisius (St) C. Dr. SJ.   GC. Dec 21
1521–1597 A native of Nijmwegen in Holland. He was received into the Society of Jesus by Bl Peter Faber (1543). He was the leader of the Catholic counter-Reformation in German lands, being constantly engaged in preaching, teaching, writing, instructing, advising and

St Petroc, June 4

arbitrating, in Germany, Austria, Switzerland, Bohemia and Poland. His short catechism in Latin and German had passed through two hundred editions before his death and was translated into twelve European languages. He also wrote theological, ascetical and historical treatises. He has been rightly called "the Second Apostle of Germany". Canonized and declared Doctor of the Church in 1925.

Peter of Subiaco (Bl) M. OSB.   Dec 31
d. 1003 The twenty-second abbot of Subiaco. For defending the rights of his abbey he was blinded by the baron of Monticello and died in prison.

Petroc (Petrock, Pedrog, Perreux) (St) Ab.   June 4
d. c 594 Said to have been the son of a Welsh chieftain, and to have studied in Ireland and settled in Cornwall, where he undoubtedly exercised a very active apostolate. There he founded a monastery at a place called after him, Petrocston (Padstow), and another at Bodmin where he died. In Brittany he is venerated under the name of Perreux. He is sometimes shown as a bishop holding a church, or with a stag.

Petronax (St) Ab. OSB.   May 6
d. *c* 747   A native of Brescia who was induced by Pope St Gregory II in 717 to visit
Montecassino, destroyed in 580 by the Lombards, with a view to restoring the cenobitical
life there. He found a few hermits who elected
him their abbot and Benedictine life began
afresh. St Willibald, bishop of Eichstätt and St
Sturmius of Fulda, were monks under him.
He is surnamed "the second founder of
Montecassino".

Petronilla of Moncel (Bl)
Abs. Poor Clare   May 14
d. 1355   Of the family of the counts of
Troyes. She was the first abbess of the convent
of Poor Clares at Moncel in Burgundy,
founded by King Philip le Bel.

Petronilla (St) V.   May 31
1st cent.(?)   A Roman virgin venerated from
the earliest times. Later legends connect her
with St Peter, to whom she is said to have
ministered. The pre-1970 RM. goes further
and describes her as the daughter of the
apostle, which she certainly was not. Since
1969 her cult has been confined to local
calendars. She is variously depicted as holding
keys, or being cured by St Peter.

Petronius (St) Bp.   Jan 10
d. *c* 463   The son of a senator of Avignon.
He became a monk of Lérins and bishop of
Die from *c* 456 to 463.

Petronius (St) Bp.   Sept 6
d. *c* 450   A bishop of Verona.

Petronius (St) Bp.   Oct 4
Probably the son of a Praetorian Prefect in
Gaul, he visited the ascetics in Palestine whilst
young, and prayed at the holy places. In Italy
he became bishop of Bologna and is said to
have built the monastery of St Stephen in that
city, reproducing the general lines of the
buildings of the holy places at Jerusalem. A
fictitious life of the saint increased his popularity in the Middle Ages.

Phaebadius (Fiari) (St) Bp.   Apr 25
d. *c* 392   A bishop of Agen in S. Gaul who,
together with his friend St Hilary of Poitiers,
succeeded in stamping out Arian heresy in
Gaul. He was one of the best known bishops of
his time and presided at several councils. St
Jerome mentions him among "the illustrious
men" of the church.

Phaganus (St)   May 26
Otherwise Fugatius, q.v.

Phaina (St) VM.   May 18
See Theodotus, Thecusa, etc.

Phal (Phele) (St)   May 16
Otherwise Fidolus, q.v.

Phanurius (St) M.   Aug 27
? A martyr from Crete, about whom little is
known, though he is traditionally invoked to
help in the rediscovery of lost objects. In art he
is shown as a warrior saint, in armour, and
holding a spear. He also holds a cross, with a
burning candle on top of the shaft.

Phara (St) Abs.   Dec 7
Otherwise Burgundofara (Apr 3) q.v.

Pharäildis (Vareide,
Verylde, Veerle) (St) V.   Jan 4
d. *c* 740   She seems to have been born in
Ghent and was married against her will,
having dedicated her virginity to God. She was
maltreated by her husband, either because he
insisted on living as a virgin or because he
objected to her nocturnal visits to the
churches. She is one of the patron saints of
Ghent.

Pharnacius (St) M.   June 24
See Orentius, Heros, etc.

Pharo (St) Bp.   Oct 28
Otherwise Faro, q.v.

Phelim (Fidleminus) (St)
Bp.   Aug 9
6th cent.   Said to have been a disciple of St
Columba. The city of Kilmore sprang up
round the place where his cell stood. Principal
patron of Kilmore.

Philadelphus (St) M.   May 10
See Alphius, Philadelphus and Cyrinus.

Philadelphus (St) M.   Sept 2
See Diomedes, Julian, etc.

Philappian (St) M.   Jan 30
See Felician, Philappian, etc.

Philastrius (St) Bp.   July 18
d. *c* 387   A Spaniard who was
appointed bishop of Brescia at the time of the
Arian troubles. He wrote a book against the
Arians, which is still extant. St Gaudentius, his
successor, praised him for his "modesty,
quietness and gentleness towards all men",
and because he helped the poor.

Phileas and Comp. (SS)
MM.   Feb 4 and Nov 26
d. *c* 307   Martyrs whose passion is related by
their contemporary, the historian Eusebius.
Phileas, bishop of Thmuis, an ancient city in
Lower Egypt, was beheaded. From his prison
at Alexandria he wrote a letter to his flock
describing the sufferings of his fellow Christ-

ian prisoners. With him suffered a Roman tribune named Philoromus and a number of other Christians from Thmuis. A contemporary account of his martyrdom still exists. See also Faustus, Didius, etc.

Philemon and Apollonius
(SS) MM.   March 8
d. *c* 305   Philemon was an actor and musician at Antinoe, who was converted by the deacon Apollonius of the same city. They were brought to Alexandria, bound hand and foot, and cast into the sea. They suffered under Diocletian.

Philemon and Domninus
(SS) MM.   March 21
? Romans by birth, who preached the gospel in various parts of Italy and were finally put to death, where is not certain.

Philemon and Apphia
(Appia) (SS) MM.   Nov 22
d. *c* 70   Philemon is the Christian of Colossae, master of the runaway slave Onesimus, to whom St Paul's shortest letter is addressed; Apphia is presumed to have been Philemon's wife. Both are said to have been stoned to death at their home at Colossae.

Philetus, Lydia, Macedo, Theoprepius (Theoprepides), Amphilochius and Cronidas
(SS) MM.   March 27
d. *c* 121   Martyrs of Illyria under Hadrian. The pre-1970 RM. described Philetus as a senator, Lydia as his wife, Macedo and Theoprepius as their sons, Amphilochius as a captain, and Cronidas as a notary. Their Acts are not reliable.

Philibert (St) Ab. OSB.   Aug 20
c 608–684   Born in Gascony and educated at the court of King Dagobert I. At the age of twenty he became a monk at Rébais and shortly afterwards its abbot. However, he left this abbey and after visiting several famous Columbanian houses (which were at that time adopting the rule of St Benedict), founded and ruled the abbey of Jumièges, not far from Fontenelle. He opposed Ebroin, the tyrannical mayor of the palace, and was imprisoned and exiled. Before his death he had established the abbey of Noirmoutier, restored Quinçay and aided several others.

Philibert (St) M.   Aug 22
See Fabrician and Philibert.

Philip (*several*)
Note. Philip is the English form of the Latin

Philippus; the French is Philippe; the Italian, Filippo; the Spanish, Felipe.

Philip Berruyer (Bl) Bp.   Jan 9
d. 1260   A nephew of St William of Bourges and, like his uncle, archbishop of that diocese.

Philip of Vienne (St) Bp.   Feb 3
d. *c* 578   Bishop of Vienne in Gaul (*c* 560–578).

Philip of Jesus (St) M.
OFM.   Feb 5
d. 1597   Born in Mexico City of Spanish parents, Philip became a Franciscan at Puebla, but left the order in 1589 and travelled to the Philippines as a merchant. He repented and rejoined the Franciscans at Manila (1590). On his way home to be ordained in Mexico, his ship was driven by a storm to Japan (1596) where he was arrested with St Peter Baptist and crucified at Nagasaki. Canonized in 1862.

Philip of Gortyna (St) Bp.   Apr 11
d. *c* 180   A bishop of Gortyna in Crete, author of a work, now lost, against the Marcionite Gnostics.

Philip the Apostle (St)   GC. May 3
d. *c* 80   One of the Twelve, a native of Bethsaida, he always takes the fifth place in the catalogue of the apostles, and is mentioned three times as a confidant of our Lord in St John's gospel. After the ascension he is believed to have preached in Asia Minor and to have been martyred at Hierapolis in Phrygia. In art he is depicted as elderly and bearded, holding a basket of loaves and a cross, sometimes T-shaped.

Philip of Zell (St) H. OSB.   May 3
d. *c* 770   An Anglo-Saxon pilgrim who settled as a hermit near Worms and became a great friend of King Pepin. Being joined by several disciples, he founded the monastery of Zell–thus called from his own original *cell* — which in subsequent times grew into the town of Zell.

Philip of Agirone (St)   May 12
? A saint venerated in the little hill town of Agirone in Sicily as the first missionary sent to that country. The story abounds in contradictory and improbable statements.

Philip Suzanni (Bl) C.
OSA.   May 24
d. 1306   A native of Piacenza who joined the Augustinian order in that city. He was famed for his spirit of prayer and compunction. Cult approved in 1756.

St Philip the Apostle, May 3

Philip Neri (St) C.
Founder   GC. May 26
1515–1595   A native of Florence, he was
educated by the Dominicans at San Marco,
then became an apprentice in his uncle's
business. He left this in 1533 to live in poverty
in Rome, keeping himself by educating the
sons of his Florentine landlord. After some
years of toil and prayer he experienced (in
1544) an ecstasy which, as was confirmed at
his death, enlarged his heart. Meanwhile he
devoted all his leisure time to the study of
theology and to the silent unobtrusive service
of his neighbours. He thought of going to the
foreign missions, but a Benedictine of St
Paul's told him that his apostolate was in
Rome. His winning ways and loving manner
attracted all to him, as did his shrewdness and
humour, and in 1548 he gathered fourteen
companions into a congregation which ultimately received a definite shape as the Congregation of the Oratory. In 1551 he was ordained
priest and during the thirty-three years that
followed Philip and his Oratory constituted
the centre of religious life in Rome. In 1583 his
institute was officially approved with its
mother-house at the church of Sta Maria in
Valicella which St Philip rebuilt on a magnificent scale and where he is enshrined. He
fully deserves the title given him of "Second
Apostle of Rome". His distinctive portrait by
Guido Reni is the basis of all other representations. He is vested as a priest, usually in red,
and he carries a lily or has lilies about him.
Notable copies may be seen in the Oratory
churches of London (Kensington) and Birmingham (Edgbaston). He was canonized in
1622.

Philip the Deacon (St)   June 6
1st cent.   One of the seven deacons ordained
by the apostles (Acts 6:5). He worked in
Samaria, baptized the Ethiopian eunuch (Acts
6:8), and was the host of St Paul at Caesarea.
His four daughters (Acts 21:9) are honoured
as saints with him.

Philip Powel (Bl) M. OSB.   June 30
d. 1646   A native of Tralon in Gwent, he
was educated at Abergavenny grammar
school, and joined the Benedictines at St
Gregory's, Douai (now Downside) in 1614,
being ordained in 1621. In the following year
he was sent to the English mission and worked
chiefly in Devon but also in Somerset and
Cornwall for twenty years. Martyred at
Tyburn. Beatified in 1929.

Philip Minh (St) M.   July 3
1815–1853   Born at Caimong in Vietnam,
he joined the Society for Foreign Missions

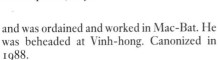

St Philip Neri, May 26

and was ordained and worked in Mac-Bat. He was beheaded at Vinh-hong. Canonized in 1988.

Philip (St) M.   July 10
One of the Seven Brothers, q.v.

**Philip, Zeno, Narseus
and Comp. (SS)** MM.   July 15
? Martyrs of Alexandria. The "companions" consisted of ten little children.

Philip Evans (St) M. SJ.   July 22
1645–1679 Born in Monmouthshire (Gwent) and educated at Saint-Omer, he joined the Jesuits (1665) and served on the Welsh mission. Martyred for his faith at Cardiff in consequence of the "Oates plot". Beatified in 1929. Canonized in 1970 as one of the Forty Martyrs of England and Wales (q.v.).

Philip (St) M.   Aug 17
See Straton, Philip and Eutychian.

Philip Benizi (St) C.
OSM.   Aug 23
1233–1285 Born at Florence (Aug 15), where, after his studies at Paris and Padua, he practised medicine. In 1253 he joined the Servite order as a lay-brother until 1259, when he was directed by his superiors to receive holy orders. Soon he was known as one of the most

zealous preachers in Italy, was made superior of several friaries and, in 1267, the fifth general of the order. In the following year the cardinals proposed putting him forward as a candidate for the papacy, but he fled by night and hid in a cave until another was elected. He established new foundations of his institute throughout Italy and the German lands, and was untiring in visiting them. Moreover, he intervened as peacemaker in the feud between Guelphs and Ghibellines. Canonized in 1671. Cult confined to local calendars since 1969.

Philip (St) M.   Sept 2
See Diomedes, Julian, etc.

Philip (St) M.   Sept 13
3rd cent. The alleged father of St Eugenia, in whose household SS Protus and Hyacinth are said to have been employed. Since St Eugenia's story is thought now to be only a pious romance, the very existence of St Philip is problematical.

Philip Oderisi (Bl) Bp.
OSB.   Sept 18
d. 1285 From being a monk of Fontavellana he was made bishop of Nocera in Umbria, which he occupied from 1254 to 1285. He was a great friend and defender of the early friars minor.

Philip Howard (St) M.   Oct 19
d. 1595 Earl of Arundel and Surrey. He was converted from a life of indifference and neglect of his religion and became a fervent and conscientious Catholic. In 1585 he was committed to the Tower of London and in 1589 sentenced to death. The sentence was never carried out but he remained a prisoner until his death at the age of thirty-eight. Beatified in 1929. He is depicted clad as an Elizabethan nobleman, often acompanied by a greyhound. His body now rests in the cathedral dedicated to him at Arundel. Canonized in 1970 as one of the Forty Martyrs of England and Wales (q.v.).

Philip (St) Bp. M.   Oct 22
d. c 270 A bishop martyr of Fermo in Italy, whose relics are enshrined in his cathedral.

**Philip, Severus, Eusebius
and Hermes (SS)** MM.   Oct 22
d. 304 Philip was bishop of Heraclea near Constantinople; Severus was his deacon; Eusebius and Hermes, two of the inferior clergy. During the persecution under Diocletian they were all arrested and brought to trial. It was insistently demanded of them that they should deliver up the sacred books of the church to be burnt. On their refusal they were taken to Adrianopolis and burnt at the stake.

St Philip Howard, Oct 19

We have a copy of the legal process instituted against them, a document of undeniable authenticity.

Philippa Mareri (Bl) V.
Poor Clare   Feb 16
d. 1236   Born at Cicoli in the Abruzzi. After having met St Francis of Assisi in her parents' home she decided to become a hermit, and did so on a mountain above Mareri. Eventually she founded a Franciscan nunnery at Rieti under the direction of Bl Roger of Todi, which she ruled as first abbess.

Philippa de Gheldre (Bl) W.   Feb 26
1462–1547   Of noble birth, she married the Duke of Lorraine. Her life however was marked by tribulation. An orphan from the cradle, she was early a widow and was deprived of most of her fortune. She entered a convent of Poor Clares at Port à Mousson in 1519, and

lived a life of great austerity. Cult never officially confirmed.

Philippa Guidoni (Bl)
Abs. OSB.   Aug 29
d. 1335   A disciple of Bl Santuccia of Gubbio. Foundress and first abbess of the Benedictine convent of Santa Maria di Valverde at Arezzo.

Philippa (St) M.   Sept 20
See Theodore, Philippa, etc.

Philippine Duchesne
(Bl) V.   Nov 18
Otherwise Rose-Philippine Duchesne, q.v.

Philo and Agathopodes
(Agathopus) (SS)   Apr 25
d. c 150   The two deacons of Antioch who (c 107) attended St Ignatius, their bishop, to

his martyrdom in Rome. They took back to Antioch such relics of the saint as they were able to recover and are believed to have written the Acts of his trial and death.

Philogonius (St) Bp.   Dec 20
d. 324   A lawyer at Antioch and a confessor under Licinius. After the death of his wife he became bishop of Antioch and was one of the first to denounce Arianism. St John Chrysostom preached a panegyric, still extant, in honour of St Philogonius.

Philologus and Patrobas
(SS)   Nov 4
1st cent.   Roman Christians saluted by St Paul in his letter to the Romans (16:14–18).

Philomena (Philumena)
In 1802 the remains of a young woman were discovered in the catacomb of St Priscilla on the Via Salaria. The tomb was closed by three stones bearing the description LUMENA PAX TE CUM FI. The conclusion was drawn that here was buried a martyr called St Philomena, and a shrine was set up at Mugnano, in the diocese of Nola. The cult spread throughout the world. Further archaeological investigation proved however that the disarrangement of the stones was a regular habit of the sextons in the fourth century when they re-used materials already engraved, and intended to indicate that it was NOT the same person. The shrine was dismantled and cultus forbidden by decree of Rome, 1961.

Philomena (St) V.   July 5
d. c 500   A saint venerated at San Severino (*Septempeda*) near Ancona. Nothing is now known of her.

Philomenus (St) M.   Nov 14
See Clementinus, Theodotus and Philomenus.

Philomenus (St) M.   Nov 29
d. 275   A martyr of Ancyra in Galatia under Aurelian.

Philonilla (St)   Oct 11
See Zenais and Philonilla.

Philoromus (St) M.   Feb 4
See Phileas, and Comp.

Philoterus (St) M.   May 19
d. 303   A nobleman of Nicomedia, martyred there under Diocletian. His supposed Acts are quite untrustworthy.

Philotheus (St) M.   Nov 5
See Domninus, Theotimus, etc.

Philotheus (St) M.   Dec 9
See Samosata, the Seven Martyrs of.

Phlegon (St) M.   Apr 8
See Herodion, Asyncritus and Phlegon.

Phocas (St) M.   March 5
d. c 320   A martyr of Antioch, suffocated in a bath. His Acts are not reliable. Often confused with St Phocas the Gardener (see July 23).

Phocas (St) Bp. M.   July 14
d. 117   Bishop of Sinope on the Black Sea, martyred under Trajan.

Phocas the Gardener
(St) M.   July 23
d. c 303   A gardener near Sinope on the Black Sea martyred under Diocletian. His existence, martyrdom and ancient cult are established facts. He is still greatly venerated in the East and was for many centuries regarded, especially in the East, as a patron of sailors.

Phoebe (St)   Sept 3
1st cent.   A matron who worked as a deaconess at Cenchreae near Corinth, highly commended by St Paul and the bearer to Rome of his letter to that church (Rom. 16:1–3). It has been suggested, without the slightest foundation, that she was St Paul's wife.

Photina, Joseph, Victor, Sebastian, Anatolius, Photius, Photis (Photides), Parasceve and Cyriaca (SS)
MM.   March 20
?   This group of martyrs constitutes a historical puzzle. The Greek tradition identifies Photina with the Samaritan woman of St John's gospel (chap. 4) and makes Joseph and Victor her sons. They are alleged to have been martyred with other Christians at Rome under Nero. Baronius may have put them in the RM. because he believed that the head of St Photina was preserved at St Paul's outside-the-walls.

Photinus (or Pothinus), Sanctius (Sanctus), Vetius, Epagathus, Maturus, Ponticus, Biblis (Biblides), Attalus, Alexander, Blandina and Comp. (SS) MM.   June 2
d. 177   Martyrs of Lyons, the details of whose martyrdom are given in an authentic letter written by the churches of Vienne and Lyons to those of Asia. The writer may have been St Irenaeus. The martyrs were at first set upon by the pagan mob, but afterwards they were tried and condemned by the regular

tribunals on account of their religion. Photinus, their leader, bishop of the city, an old man of ninety years, expired in his dungeon from the ill-usage he received. The others were thrown to the wild beasts in the amphitheatre at the public games. The slave-girl, Blandina, enmeshed in a net and tossed by a wild bull, and the boy, Ponticus, who was one of the last to suffer, have ever excited special admiration. The whole description is most graphic. They suffered under Marcus Aurelius.

Photinus (St) M.   Aug 12
See Anicetus, Photinus, etc.

Photis (St) M.   March 20
See Photina, Joseph, etc.

Photius (St) M.   March 4
See Archelaus, Cyril and Photius.

Photius (St) M.   March 20
See Photina, Joseph, etc.

Pia (St) M.   Jan 19
See Paul, Gerontius, etc.

Piala (St) M.   Dec 14
See Fingar, Phiala, and Comp.

Piaton (Piato, Piat) (St) M.   Oct 1
d. c 286   Said to have been a native of Benevento in Italy, sent by the pope to evangelize the districts of Tournai and Chartres. He is thought to have died a martyr at Tournai under Maximian.

Pientia (St) VM.   Oct 11
See Nicasius, Quirinus, etc.

Pierius (St) C.   Nov 4
d. c 310   A priest of Alexandria, writer of several philosophical and theological treatises.

Pigmenius (St) M.   March 24
d. 362   A Roman priest thrown into the Tiber under Julian the Apostate.

Pinian (St) M.   Dec 31
See Melania and Pinian.

Pinnock (St)   Nov 6
A church in Cornwall is called St Pinnocks, but it is probable that Pinnock is a corruption of Winnock.

Pinytus (St) Bp.   Oct 10
d. p.180   A Greek bishop in Crete numbered among distinguished ecclesiastical writers by Eusebius.

Pionius and Comp. (SS)
MM.   Feb 1
d. 250   A priest of Smyrna who, with fifteen companions, suffered under Decius. They were arrested while liturgically commemorating the anniversary of the martyrdom of St Polycarp. They were burnt at the stake after a long cross-examination and after having been put to severe torture. We have an eye-witness's account of their death: the document was known to Eusebius.

Pior (St) H.   Jan 17
d. c 395   An Egyptian solitary, a disciple of St Antony.

Piperion (St) M.   March 11
See Candidus, Piperion and Comp.

Piran (Pyran) (St) C.   March 5
d. c 480   A hermit near Padstow in Cornwall, titular of the church of the canons regular of the Lateran at Truro. Many writers identified him with St Kieran, q.v. but this is no longer believed true. He is venerated as the patron saint of miners: Perranporth preserves his name.

Pirmin (St) Bp. OSB.   Nov 3
d. 753   Pirmin was born in S. Aragon of Visigothic descent. When the Saracens invaded Spain, he fled, and travelled as far as the Rhineland where he established several abbeys — Reichenau in 724, Murbach, Amorbach — and restored others, notably Dissentis, introducing into them all the Benedictine rule. He was ordained by the pope a *chorepiscopus*, or regionary bishop; he was never bishop of Meaux. He is one of the great Benedictine apostles in German lands.

Pistis (Faith) (St) VM.   Aug 1
See Faith, Hope and Charity.

Pius I (St) Pope   formerly July 11
d. c 155   Pope from c 142 to c 155. He may have been a brother of Hermas, the writer of the work called *The Shepherd*; if so, Pius, like his brother, was born a slave. His pontificate was one of active opposition to the Gnostics, notably the Gnostic Marcion. Cult suppressed in 1969.

Pius V (St) Pope OP.   GC. Apr 30
1504–1572   Michael Ghislieri was born at Bosco in Piedmont, joined the Dominicans in 1518, was ordained in 1540, taught philosophy and theology for sixteen years and in 1556 was nominated bishop of Sutri and inquisitor for Lombardy. In 1557 he was created cardinal and in 1559 was transferred to the see of Mondovi, finally being elected pope in 1565. Of an austere and severe disposition he was well fitted for the task of combating the loose discipline of that time in many ecclesiastical quarters, including the Roman curia. He insisted on the exact observance of the decrees of the council of Trent; organized an expedition against the Turks which resulted in the

victory of Lepanto (1570); promoted ecclesiastical learning; reformed liturgical worship (the Tridentine missal and breviary were promulgated in his time); and excommunicated Queen Elizabeth of England. The excommunication made the position of the English and Welsh Catholics very awkward and many lost their lives in martyrdom because of the hostility occasioned by it, as it enabled Catholics to be accused of treason by the State authorities. He is enshrined at Sta Maria Maggiore, Rome. Canonized in 1712.

Pius X (St) Pope   GC. Aug 21
1835–1914 Joseph Sarto was born in 1835 in Riese, diocese of Treviso near Venice, then part of the Austrian empire. His parents were very poor; Joseph used to walk four miles barefoot to school to save shoe-leather. From 1850 he studied at the minor seminary at Treviso, and went on to Padua. He served nine years as curate to the parish priest of Tombolo and the latter formed a high opinion of his virtues. In 1867 he became parish priest of Salzano; in 1884 bishop of Mantua, and 1893 patriarch of Venice and cardinal. To his own surpise he was elected pope at the conclave of 1903, and as pope he continued the simple personal life he had always observed. The keynote of his pontificate was "to restore all things in Christ". It was distinguished by his decrees on early and frequent communion, on liturgical reform, and on the teaching of the Catechism. Other notable activities were his condemnation of Modernism, his reorganization of the Roman curia and initiation of the codification of canon law. Unfortunately excesses occurred in the efforts of some to enforce the anti-Modernist decrees. Greatly saddened by the outbreak of the First World War in August 1914, he died on the 20th of that month. His will ran: I was born poor; I lived poor; I wish to die poor. Canonized in 1954.

Placid (St) OSB.   Jan 15
See Maurus and Placid.

Placid (Placidus, Plait) (St) Ab. OSB.   May 7
d. c 675 Abbot in the basilica of St Symphorian at Autun.

Placid (St) M.   July 11
See Sigisbert and Placid.

Placid (Bl) Ab. OSB. Cist.   June 12
d. 1248 Born at Rodi, near Amiterno in Italy, of working-class parents. He became a Cistercian monk at St Nicholas in Corno, then a hermit at Ocre in the Abruzzi, and ultimately the abbot-founder of the monastery of Santo Spirito, near Val d'Ocre. It is narrated of him that he took his sleep in a standing posture for thirty-seven years.

Placid (St) M.   Oct 11
See Anastasius, Placid, etc.

Placide Viel (Bl) V.   March 4
1815–1877 Born on a farm in Normandy she was introduced by her aunt to St Marie-Madeleine Postel, the first mother general of the Sisters of the Christian Schools. She entered the order in 1833 and became assistant-general at the age of twenty-six. This was the cause of some resentment against her, but on the death of St Marie-Madeleine in 1846 she succeeded her, and in 1859 obtained papal approval of the institute. Her organizing work during the Franco-Prussian war was heroic and probably hastened her end. Beatified in 1951.

Placidia (St) V.   Oct 11
d. c 460 A virgin venerated at Verona. She has been often erroneously identified with Placidia, the daughter of the emperor Valentinian III.

Plato (St) Ab.   Apr 4
d. 813 A Greek monk and abbot, first of Symboleon on Mt Olympus in Bithynia, and then Sakkudion near Constantinople. He opposed the divorce and subsequent attempted marriage of the emperor Constantine Porphyrogenitus, who retaliated by persecuting and imprisoning him.

Plato (St) M.   July 22
d. c 306 A rich youth martyred at Ancyra in Galatia. He was a brother of St Antiochus (q.v.). He is held in great veneration in the East.

Platonides and Comp. (SS)   Apr 6
d. c 308 A deaconess and foundress of a nunnery at Nisibis in Mesopotamia. The pre-1970 RM. wrongly called her a martyr and ascribes her to Ascalon. Nothing is known about her companions.

Plautilla (St) W.   May 20
d. c 67 The alleged mother of St Flavia Domitilla. She is said to have been baptized by St Peter and to have been present at the martyrdom of St Paul.

Plautus (St) M.   Sept 29
See Eutychius, Plautus and Heracleas.

Plechelm (St) M. OSB.   July 15
See Wiro, Plechelm and Otger.

Plegmund (St) Bp. OSB.   Aug 2
d. 914   The tutor of King Alfred. At that
monarch's request, made archbishop of Canterbury by Pope Formosus. He reorganised
the dioceses of England and was a notable
scholar.

**Plutarch, Serenus,
Heraclides, Heron, a
second Serenus, Rhais,
Potamioena and
Marcella (SS)** MM.   June 28
d. 202   Martyrs of Alexandria under Septimius Severus. They were pupils of Origen at
the catechetical school of Alexandria. The
virgin Potamioena was lowered slowly into a
cauldron of boiling pitch. Her mother St
Marcella suffered at the same time.

Podius (St) Bp. OSA.   May 28
d. 1002   A son of the margrave of Tuscany
who became a canon regular and eventually
bishop of Florence from 990 to 1002.

Poemon (Poemen) (St) H.   Aug 27
d. c 450   His name is often written in its
Latin form "Pastor". One of the most famous
of the fathers of the Egyptian desert. He dwelt
at Skete, where he became abbot of the
numerous groups of hermits who lived in the
abandoned ruins of a temple at Terenuth.

Pol de Léon (St) Bp.   March 12
Otherwise Paul Aurelian, q.v.

Polius (St) M.   May 21
See Timothy, Polius and Eutychius.

Pollio (St) M.   Apr 28
d. c 304   A lector of the church of Cybalae in
Pannonia, burnt alive under Diocletian.

Polyaenus (St) M.   Apr 28
See Patrick, Acacius, etc.

Polyaenus (St) M.   Aug 18
See Hermas, Serapion and Polyaenus.

Polyanus (St) M. Bp.   Sept 10
See Nemesian, Felix, etc.

**Polycarp of Smyrna and
Comp. (SS)** MM.   GC. Feb 23
c 69–c 155   Converted by St John the Evangelist c 80, Polycarp became bishop of Smyrna
c 96. He, with his friend St Ignatius of Antioch, was the link between the apostles and
subsequent generations of Christians in Asia
Minor and, through their disciple St Irenaeus
of Lyons, in Gaul. We have an authentic
record of St Polycarp's martyrdom in a letter
written by eye-witnesses of the church of
Smyrna. His profession of faith before the
proconsul is a touching example of loyal
devotion to Christ. He said that he had served

Christ eighty-six years and He had never done
wrong to His servant, so how could he (Polycarp) deny Him? For his faith he was burnt
alive with twelve of his own flock, under
Marcus Aurelius. Polycarp's letter to the
Philippians, still extant, was publicly read in
the churches of Asia for at least three centuries. He resolutely opposed the Gnostics and
was a champion of orthodoxy.

Polycarp (St) C.   Feb 23
d. c 300   A Roman priest of whom mention
is made in the Acts of the martyrs for his zeal in
ministering to those detained in prison for
their faith.

**Polycarp of Alexandria
(St)** M.   Apr 2
d. 303   A martyr beheaded at Alexandria
after many torments.

**Polycarp and Theodore
(SS)** MM.   Dec 7
? Martyrs at Antioch in Syria.

Polychronius (St) Bp. M.   Feb 17
? Bishop and martyr at Babylon. The
pre-1970 RM. says that he was put to death by
Decius, but that emperor never made an
expedition against the Persians. As St Polychronius of Dec 6 had also a feast on Feb 17, it
is suggested that this feast marked the translation of his relics, and there was only one
person.

Polychronius (St) M.   Dec 6
4th cent.   A priest who, in the reign of the
emperor Constantius, was slain by Arians
while he was celebrating the eucharist. He was
present at the council of Nicaea (325).

Polydore Plasden (St) M.   Dec 10
1563–1591   Born in London and educated
for the priesthood at Reims and in Rome, he
was ordained in 1588 and martyred at Tyburn.
Beatified in 1929. Canonized in 1970 as one of
the Forty Martyrs of England and Wales, q.v.

Polyeuctus (St) M.   Feb 13
d. c 259   A Roman officer martyred at Melitene in Armenia under Valerian. His Acts, as
given by Metaphrastes, are as touching as any
in early Christian literature. Corneille has
used some elements of the martyr's story in his
tragedy *Polyeucte*.

**Polyeuctus, Victorius
and Donatus (SS)** MM.   May 21
? Martyrs of Caesarea in Cappadocia, of
whom we know no more than the names
(variously spelt) registered in the martyrologies.

Polyxena (St) M.   Sept 23
See Xantippa and Polyxena.

Pompeius (St) M.   Apr 10
See Terence, Africanus, etc.

Pompeius (St) M.   July 7
See Peregrinus, Lucian, etc.

Pompeius (St) Bp.   Dec 14
d. *c* 290   Bishop of Pavia.

Pompilius Maria Pirotti
(St) C.   July 15
1710–1756   Born at Montecalvo, diocese of
Benevento, he joined the Piarist fathers (Scolopi) at Naples in 1727 and devoted his life to
teaching in the schools of his order. He died at
Lecce in Apulia. Canonized in 1934.

Pomponius (St) Bp.   Apr 30
d. 536   Bishop of Naples (508–536). He was
a strong opponent of Arianism, then under the
patronage of the Gothic king Theodoric.

Pomposa (St) VM.   Sept 19
d. 835   A nun of Peñamelaria near Cordoba.
She was beheaded by the Moors at Cordoba.

Pons (St) M.   May 14
Otherwise Pontius, q.v.

Pontian (St) M.   Jan 19
d. 169   An Italian martyr who suffered at
Spoleto under Marcus Aurelius. His Acts are
not wholly accurate.

Pontian Ngondwe (St) M.   June 3
d. 1886   A member of the Royal Guard of
King Mwanga of Uganda by whose orders he
was put to death. See Charles Lwanga and
Comps.

Pontian (St) Pope M.   GC. Aug 13
d. 235   He succeeded St Urban I in the year
230. He was exiled by the emperor Maximinus
Thrax to Sardinia *c* 235, where he is thought to
have succumbed to ill-treatment. He is commemorated with St Hippolytus, his fellow
exile.

Pontian (St) M.   Aug 25
See Eusebius, Pontian, etc.

Pontian and Comp.
(SS) MM.   Dec 2
d. *c* 259   A group of five Roman martyrs who
suffered under Valerian.

Pontian (St) M.   Dec 11
See Trason, Pontian and Praetextatus.

Pontian (St) M.   Dec 31
See Stephen, Pontian, etc.

Ponticus (St) M.   June 2
See Photinus (Pothinus), Sanctius, etc.

Pontius (St) C.   March 8
d. *c* 260   A deacon of the church of Carthage. He was the attendant of St Cyprian in his
exile and at his trial and execution. He has left
us a graphic account of the life and passion of
St Cyprian.

Pontius of Cimiez (St) M.   May 14
d. 258(?)   A martyr of Cimella (Cimiez) near
Nice. His relics, translated into Languedoc,
have given its name to the town of Saint-Pons.

Pontius of Faucigny (Bl)
Ab. OSA.   Nov 26
d. 1178   Born in Savoy, at the age of twenty
he joined the Canons Regular at Abondance in
the Chablais. He founded and was abbot of the
monastery of St Sixtus, whence he returned to
Abondance and was abbot there. He was held
in high veneration by St Francis of Sales. Cult
confirmed in 1806.

Pontius of Balmey (Bl)
Bp. O. Cart.   Dec 13
d. 1140   Born at Balmey, he became a canon
of Lyons. Later he founded on his paternal
estate the charterhouse of Meyriat and joined
the Carthusians. He was appointed bishop of
Belley in 1121, but resigned before his death
and returned to Meyriat.

Poppo (St) Ab. OSB.   Jan 25
978–1048   Born in Flanders, he first followed a military career and led an unbridled
life. He then made a penitential pilgrimage to
Jerusalem and Rome and on his return became
a Benedictine at St Thierry, Reims (1006).
Two years later he migrated to Saint-Vannes
and helped Bl Richard in the revival of
monastic discipline. Shortly after, he was
appointed provost of St Vaast, Arras, and soon
became known to the emperor St Henry, who
chose him as one of his most trusted advisers.
In 1021 the emperor made Poppo abbot of
Stavelot-Malmédy and soon the revival spread
to several of the most ancient abbeys of
Lotharingia and neighbouring territories:
Hautmont, Marchiennes, St Maximinus of
Trier, St Vaast at Arras, etc. Poppo ruled all
these houses as a sort of superior general. He
is one of the greatest monastic figures of the
eleventh century.

Porcarius and Comp.
(SS) MM. OSB.   Aug 12
d. *c* 732   Porcarius was the second of this
name to be abbot of Lérins, an island off the
coast of Provence. The whole community of
five hundred monks — except the youngest

members whom the abbot had sent away to safety — were massacred by the Saracens.

Porphyrius and Seleucus (SS) MM.   Feb 16
d. 309   Palestinian martyrs put to death at Caesarea. We owe the account of their martyrdom to the historian Eusebius.

Porphyrius (St) Bp.   Feb 26
d. 420   A wealthy Greek who became a hermit first in the desert of Skete in Egypt and then in Palestine on the banks of the Jordan. Much against his will he was made bishop of Gaza, a ministry he rendered with extraordinary energy, ability and success. He almost completely uprooted the remnants of paganism in his diocese. His biography, written by his deacon Mark, is one of the most valuable historical sources of the fifth century.

Porphyrius (St) M.   May 4
d. 250   A priest who is said to have preached in Umbria, chiefly at Camerino, and to have been beheaded under Decius. He belongs to the apocryphal legend of St Venantius (May 18), q.v.

Porphyrius (St) M.   Aug 20
?   Connected with the apocryphal legend of St Agapitus of Palestrina (Aug 18), whose story was transferred to the equally unhistorical legend of St Venantius.

Porphyrius (St) M.   Sept 6
See Onesiphorus and Porphyrius.

Porphyrius (St) M.   Sept 15
d. 362   Said to have been a horse-dealer and an actor who, while playing before Julian the Apostate and burlesquing the baptism of Christians, suddenly declared himself a believer and was at once slain.

Porphyrius (St) M.   Nov 4
d. 271   A martyr at Ephesus under Aurelian.

Portianus (St) Ab.   Nov 24
d. 533   A slave who became a monk and, in course of time, abbot of Miranda in Auvergne. He fearlessly faced the Merovingian king Thierry of Austrasia and obtained from him the release of his Auvergnate prisoners.

Possessor (St) Bp.   May 11
d. c 485   A city magistrate of Verdun, who became bishop of that city in 470. He and his flock were reduced to great distress by the invasions of the barbarians — Franks, Vandals, Goths, etc.

Possidius (St) Bp.   May 16
c 370–c 440   A favourite disciple, and the biographer, of St Augustine of Hippo. He became bishop of Calama in Numidia, whence

he was driven by the Arian Vandals, and ended his days in Apulia. He was one of the ablest controversialists of his time against Donatism and Pelagianism.

Potamia (St) M.   Dec 5
See Julius, Potamia, etc.

Potamioena the Younger (St) VM.   June 7
d. c 304   A young girl put to death at Alexandria under Diocletian.

Potamioena the Elder (St) VM.   June 28
See Plutarch, Serenus, etc.

Potamius and Nemesius (SS) MM.   Feb 20
?   Martyrs in Cyprus. Nothing is known of them. Eusebius attaches them to the church of Alexandria.

Potamon (St) Bp. M.   May 18
d. c 340   Bishop of Heraclea in Upper Egypt. During the persecution of Maximinus Daza (310) he was sentenced to the mines, lamed in one leg and deprived of one eye. Released after Constantine's decree of toleration, he was present at the council of Nicaea. He supported his metropolitan St Athanasius and was as a result fiercely persecuted by the Arians, who ultimately compassed his death.

Potentian (St) M.   Dec 31
See Sabinian and Potentian.

Potentiana (St) M.   May 19
Otherwise Pudentiana, q.v.

Pothmius and Nemesius (SS) MM.   Feb 20
Otherwise Potamius and Nemesius, q.v.

Pothinus (St) Bp. M.   June 2
Otherwise Photinus, q.v.

Potitus (St) M.   Jan 13
?   Honoured as a boy-martyr in the diocese of Naples. His extant Acts are legendary.

Praejectus (Priest, Prest, Preils, Prix) (St) Bp. M.   Jan 25
d. 676   He became bishop of Clermont in Auvergne with the approval of Childeric II in 666. A great administrator and fosterer of monasticism, he was slain by evil-doers at Volvic in the Vosges.

Praepedigna (St) M.   Feb 18
See Maximus, Claudius, etc.

Praesidius (St) M.   Sept 6
See Donatian, Praesidius, etc.

Praetextatus (Prix) (St)
Bp. M.   Feb 24
d. 586 (Apr 14) Bishop of Rouen
(550–586). For his courage in denouncing the
crimes of the wicked queen Fredegonda he
was cruelly persecuted and exiled. Recalled
after seven years he was, by her order, put to
death on Easter Sunday in his own church.

Praetextatus (St) M.   Dec 11
See Trason, Pontian and Praetextatus.

Pragmatius (St) Bp.   Nov 22
d. c 520 Bishop of Autun. His diocese suffered much during the war between the sons of
Clovis.

Praxedes (St) V.   July 21
2nd cent. Said to have been the daughter of
the Roman senator Pudens and sister of St
Pudentiana. One of the ancient churches in
Rome perpetuates her memory. Since 1969
her cult has been confined to her basilica in
Rome. Her church inspired a fine poem by
Browning: "A Bishop orders his Tomb in St
Praxedes".

Priam (St) M.   May 28
See Emilius, Felix, etc.

Prilidian (St) M.   Jan 24
See Babilas, Urban, etc.

Primael (St) H.   May 16
d. c 450 A native of Britain who crossed
over to Brittany and became a hermit in the
diocese of Quimper, where churches are
dedicated to him.

Primian (St) M.   Dec 29
See Dominic, Victor, etc.

Primitiva (St) M.   Feb 24
? An early martyr, probably of Rome. Some
old martyrologies have "Primitivus".

Primitiva (St) VM.   July 23
? An early martyr, probably of Rome. Very
probably identical with the Primitiva of Feb
24. Several ancient lists write her name "Prim-
itia"; others, "Privata".

Primitivus (St) M.   Apr 16
See Saragossa Martyrs.

Primitivus (St) M.   June 10
See Getulius, Caerealis, etc.

Primitivus (St) M.   July 18
See Symphorosa and her sons.

Primitivus (St) M.   Nov 27
See Facundus and Primitivus.

Primitivus (St) M.   Dec 9
See Peter, Successus, etc.

Primus (St) M.   Jan 3
See Cyrinus, Primus and Theogenes.

Primus and Donatus
(SS) MM.   Feb 9
d. 362 Two African deacons slain by the
Donatist schismatics when the latter were
trying to get possession of the Catholic church
at Lavallum in N.W. Africa.

Primus and Felician (SS)
MM.   June 9
d. c 297 Two aged brothers, Roman citizens, beheaded under Diocletian on the Via
Nomentana. The Acts are not altogether
trustworthy. Cults confined to local calendars
since 1969.

Primus, Cyril and
Secundarius (SS) MM.   Oct 2
? Martyrs at Antioch in Syria in one of the
early persecutions.

Principia (St) V.   May 11
d. c 420 A Roman virgin, a disciple of St
Marcella.

Principius (St) Bp.   Sept 25
d. c 505 The elder brother of St Remigius
of Reims. He became bishop of Soissons.

Prior (St) H.   June 17
c 295–395 An Egyptian hermit, one of the
first disciples of St Antony.

Prisca (St) VM.   Jan 18
3rd cent.(?) A virgin martyr venerated from
ancient times in Rome, where a church is
dedicated in her honour on the Aventine, but
of whom nothing authentic is known. Since
1969 her cult has been confined to her basilica
in Rome.

Priscian (St) M.   Oct 12
See Evagrius, Priscian, etc.

Priscian (St) M.   Oct 14
See Carponius, Evaristus and Priscian.

Priscilla (St) W.   Jan 16
1st cent. The wife of Manius Acilius Glabrio
and mother of the senator Pudens. The tradition is that she was the hostess in Rome of St
Peter the apostle, whose headquarters were at
her villa, near the Roman catacombs which to
this day bear her name.

Priscilla (St)   July 8
See Aquila and Priscilla.

Priscillian (St) M.   Jan 4
See next below.

Priscus, Priscillian and
Benedicta (SS) MM.   Jan 4
? The names are taken from the untrust-

worthy Acts of St Bibiana, in which it is stated that they were Christians buried by her father, Flavian. The martyrologist Ado treated them as martyrs.

Priscus, Malchus and Alexander (SS) MM.   March 28
d. 260   Martyrs thrown to the wild beasts during the public games at Caesarea in Palestine under Valerian.

Priscus and Comp. (SS) MM.   May 26
d. c 272   Priscus, a Roman military officer, several soldiers under his command, and a number of citzens of Besançon were martyred near Auxerre at a place where they had concealed themselves.

Priscus (St) M.   Sept 1
d. c 66   The alleged first bishop of Capua, whither he is supposed to have been sent by St Peter. He is said to have been a disciple of our Lord and to have died a martyr under Nero.

Priscus, Castrensis, Tammarus, Rosius, Heraclius, Secundinus, Adjutor, Mark, Augustus, Elpidius, Canion and Vindonius (SS) CC.   Sept 1 and Feb 11
5th cent.?   The legend is that Priscus, an African bishop, and his priests were cast adrift in a rudderless boat by the Arian Vandals. They reached S. Italy, where eventually Priscus became bishop of Capua and several of the others were in time promoted to different sees. The Acts, however, are untrustworthy and it seems that the companions of St Priscus are Campanian saints unconnected with the story. One opinion interprets Priscus Castrensis as meaning "Priscus formerly Bishop of Castra in N. Africa".

Priscus (St) M.   Sept 20
? A native of Phrygia, martyred by being first stabbed with poniards and then beheaded.

Priscus, Crescens and Evagrius (SS) MM.   Oct 1
? Martyrs at Tomi on the Black Sea.

Privatus (St) Bp. M.   Aug 21
d. 260   A bishop of Gévaudan (now Mende) in Gaul. He was seized by invading barbarians, but was offered his life on condition of his revealing the hiding place of his flock; on his refusal he was beaten to death.

Privatus (St) M.   Sept 20
See Dionysius and Privatus.

Privatus (St) M.   Sept 28
d. 223   A Roman citizen, scourged to death under Alexander Severus.

Prix (St) M.   Jan 25
Otherwise Praejectus, q.v., or Praetextatus (Feb 24).

Probus (St) Bp.   Jan 12
d. p.591   A bishop of Verona, about whom no particulars are extant.

Probus (St) Bp.   March 15
d. c 571   Bishop of Rieti in central Italy. St Gregory the Great describes the death-bed scene of St Probus, when St Juvenal and St Eleutherius appeared to him in a vision.

Probus and Grace (SS)   July 5
? Cornish saints, by tradition husband and wife. The church of Tressilian, or Probus, is dedicated in their honour.

Probus (St) M.   Oct 11
See Tharacus (Tarachus), Probus and Andronicus.

Probus (St) Bp.   Nov 10
d. c 175   A Roman who became sixth bishop of Ravenna. His relics are venerated in the cathedral of Ravenna.

Probus (St) M.   Nov 13
See Arcadius, Paschasius, etc.

Processus and Martinian (SS) MM.   July 2
? Roman martyrs greatly venerated in the past at Rome: their tomb and basilica were on the Aurelian Way. Their connexion with the apostles Peter and Paul in the Mamertine jail is mere legend. Since 1969 their cults are confined to local calendars; their relics are in St Peter's in Rome.

Prochorus (St) Bp. M.   Apr 9
1st cent.   One of the seven deacons ordained by the apostles. The tradition is that he afterwards became bishop of Nicomedia and was martyred at Antioch.

Proclus and Hilarion (SS) MM.   July 12
d. 115   Martyrs of Ancyra in Galatia in the reign of Trajan.

Proclus (St) Bp.   Oct 24
d. 447   A disciple of St John Chrysostom. He became patriarch of Constaninople in 434. His treatment of heretics, chiefly Nestorians, was characterized by great gentleness. According to tradition he instituted the singing of the Trisagion in the liturgy. Some of his homilies and letters still exist.

Procopius (St) C.   Feb 27
See Basil and Procopius.

Procopius (St) Ab. OS. Bas.   July 4
c 980–1053 (March 25) Born in Bohemia,
he studied at Prague, where he was ordained
and became a canon. Later he became a
hermit and finally abbot-founder of Sazaba
abbey in Prague. Canonized in 1804.

Procopius (St) M.   July 8
d. 303 The first victim of the Diocletian
persecution in Palestine. He was a reader in
the church of Scythopolis and was beheaded at
Caesarea Maritima. The account of his martyrdom is given by his contemporary Eusebius,
the historian. It has been much distorted by
later legend.

**Proculus, Ephebus and
Apollonius (SS) MM.**   Feb 14
d. 273 Mentioned as martyrs at Terni in the
untrustworthy Acts of St Valentine of Terni.
The Bollandists identify this Proculus with the
bishop of Terni venerated on April 14.

Proculus (St) Bp. M.   Apr 14
? A martyr of Terni, in Italy, who suffered
martyrdom under Maxentius. The pre-1970
RM. said he was a bishop, but there is no
authority for this.

Proculus (St) M.   June 1
d. c 304(?) Said to have been a Roman
officer, martyred at Bologna under Diocletian.
He has been held in veneration at Bologna
from very ancient times.

Proculus (St) Bp. M.   July 12
d. 542 Bishop of Bologna (540–542). He
was martyred by the Goths.

Proculus (St) M.   Aug 18
See Florus, Laurus, etc.

Proculus (St) M.   Sept 19
See Januarius, and Comp.

Proculus (St) Bp. M.   Nov 4
d. p.717 Bishop of Autun, said to have been
put to death by the invading Huns.

Proculus (St) Bp. M.   Dec 1
d. c 542 Bishop of Narni (others say of
Terni), put to death by order of Totila, king of
the Goths.

Proculus (St) Bp.   Dec 9
d. c 320 Bishop of Verona. He was a confessor during the persecution of Diocletian,
but ultimately died in peace in his episcopal
city.

Projectus (St) M.   Jan 24
See Thyrsus and Projectus.

Projectus (St) Bp. M.   Jan 25
Otherwise Praejectus, q.v.

Prosdoce (St) M.   Oct 4
See Domina, Berenice.

Prosdocimus (St) Bp.   Nov 7
d. c 100 First bishop of Padua, greatly
venerated in N.E. Italy. That he was sent from
Antioch by St Peter is now generally denied by
historians.

Prosper of Reggio (St) Bp.   June 25
d. c 466 A bishop of Reggio in Emilia,
venerated as principal patron of the city and
diocese of Reggio.

Prosper of Aquitaine (St) C.   July 7
c 390–436 A native of Aquitaine, a layman
and probably a married man, Prosper devoted
his fine intellect to the study of theological
questions and became an enthusiastic admirer
of St Augustine, whose doctrine on grace he
defended against the Semi-Pelagians. He was
a prolific writer and a powerful controversialist, and secretary to Pope Leo I.

Prosper of Orleans (St) Bp.   July 29
d. c 453 A bishop of Orleans, who has often
been confused with St Prosper of Aquitaine
and St Prosper of Reggio.

Protasius (Protase) (St)   June 19
See Gervase and Protase.

Protasius (St) M.   Aug 4
? A martyr honoured at Cologne. Probably
identical with the fellow-sufferer of St Gervase (June 19).

Protasius (St) Bp.   Nov 24
d. 352 Bishop of Milan 331–352. He
espoused the cause of St Athanasius against
the Arians, doing so with special effect at the
synod of Sardica (343).

Proterius (St) Bp. M.   Feb 28
d. 458 Patriarch of Alexandria. He replaced
Dioscorus, who had been deposed by the
council of Chalcedon, and did his utmost to
counter the plots of the Eutychians, who were
leading his flock astray. They, however, succeeded in compassing his death on Good
Friday.

**Prothadius (Protagius)
(St) Bp.**   Feb 10
d. 624 The successor of St Nicetius in the
see of Bresançon, he was consulted on all
important matters by Clotaire II.

Protogenes (St) Bp.   May 6
4th cent. A priest of Carrhae in Syria, who

had been banished by the Arian emperor Valens. He was recalled under Theodosius and ordained bishop.

Protolicus (St) M. Feb 14
See Bassus, Antony and Protolicus.

Protomartyrs of the Roman See (SS) MM.
See First Martyrs of the See of Rome.

Protus (St) May 31
See Cantius, Cantian, etc.

Protus and Hyacinth (SS) MM. Sept 11
d. *c* 257 According to tradition they were Romans by birth, brothers, and servants in the house of St Philip; and they are said to have been martyred in Rome. The relics of St Hyacinth were beyond any doubt discovered in the cemetery of St Basilla at Rome in 1845. The Acts, however, of these martyrs, as handed down to us, are largely legendary. The church at Blisland, Cornwall, is a testimony of their popularity in the Middle Ages. Cult confined to local calendars since 1969.

Protus and Januarius (SS) MM. Oct 25
d. 303 Protus, a priest, and Januarius, a deacon, were sent by the pope to work in Sardinia, where they were beheaded at Porto Torres, not far from Sassari, in the persecution of Diocletian.

Provinus (St) Bp. March 8
d. *c* 420 A native of Gaul who became a disciple of St Ambrose at Milan. Later he was coadjutor to St Felix, bishop of Como, whom he succeeded in the see (391).

Prudentia (Bl) V. OSA. Erem. May 6
d. 1492 Prudentia Castori joined the hermits of St Augustine at Milan and later became the abbess-foundress of a new convent at Como, where she died.

Prudentius Galindo (St) Bp. Apr 6
d. 861 A Spaniard who in his youth fled from the Saracens to the court of France, where he changed his baptismal name Galindo to Prudentius. He became bishop of Troyes and played a prominent part in the controversy on predestination against Gottschalk and Scotus Erigena. His feast is still kept at Troyes.

Prudentius (St) Bp. Apr 28
d. *p*. 700 A native of Armentia, in the province of Alava, Spain. After having been a hermit for some years he was ordained a priest

and then became bishop of Tarazona (not Tarragona) in Aragon. He is the patron saint of the diocese of Tarazona.

Psalmodius (French: Psalmet) (St) H. June 14
7th cent. Of Irish or Scottish descent, and a disciple of St Brendan. He crossed into France and lived as a hermit near Limoges. He is identical with St Sauman (or Saumay).

Ptolemy (St) Bp. M. Aug 24
1st cent. Said to have been a disciple of St Peter and bishop of Nepi in Tuscany and there to have suffered martyrdom.

Ptolemy and Lucius (SS) MM. Oct 19
d. *c* 165 Roman martyrs under Antoninus Pius. Ptolemy was put to death for instructing a woman in the Christian religion. One Lucius and an unnamed man protested against the injustice of the sentence and were also martyred. We owe the account of their passion to St Justin Martyr, their contemporary.

Ptolemy (St) M. Dec 20
See Ammon, Zeno, etc.

Publia (St) W. Oct 9
d. 362 A Syrian matron, head of a community of women at Antioch, ill-treated by order of Julian the Apostate. He overheard them singing Psalm 113 and interpreted certain verses as being a deliberate slight on himself.

Publicus (St) July 3
Otherwise Byblig, q.v.

Publius (St) Bp. M. Jan 21
d. *c* 112 Tradition identifies this saint with the Publius, "chief man of the island of Malta", who befriended St Paul after his shipwreck (Acts 28:7). He is said to have become bishop of Athens and to have died a martyr under Trajan. Other sources describe him simply as the first bishop of Malta.

Publius (St) Ab. Jan 25
d. *c* 380 An abbot of Zeugma in Syria, who housed his large community in two separate buildings, one for the Greeks and the other for the Syrians.

Publius, Julian, Marcellus and Comp. (SS) MM. Feb 19
? Martyrs in proconsular Africa.

Publius (St) M. Apr 16
See Saragossa Martyrs.

**Publius, Victor, Hermes
and Papias (SS)** MM.   Nov 2
? Martyrs in N. W. Africa.

Publius (St) Bp. M.   Nov 12
See Aurelius and Publius.

Pudens (St) M.   May 19
1st cent.? A Roman senator baptized by the
apostles. In the past he was confused with a
later (third century) Pudens who founded a
church in his house known as the "domus
Pudentiana": from this the existence of a
daughter, Pudentiana, was later inferred and
spurious Acta created. See entry for St Pudentiana, below. He was by many identified with
the Pudens mentioned by St Paul (2 Tim
4:21).

**Pudentiana (or
Potentiana) (St)** V.   May 19
2nd cent. A legendary Roman maiden,
daughter of the senator St Pudens. She is said
to have died at the age of sixteen. Her name
does not occur in any ancient martyrology. Her
cult was suppressed as unhistorical in 1969,
and any veneration of her is confined to her
basilica in Rome.

Pulcheria Augusta (St) V.   Sept 10
399–453 Daughter of the Eastern emperor
Arcadius, she was regent during the minority
of her brother Theodosius II, and empress
after his death. She was a devoted adherent of
the Catholic faith, a firm opponent of
Monophysitism, and convened the council of
Chalcedon 451.

Pupulus (St) M.   Feb 28
See Caerealis, Pupulus, etc.

Pusicius (St) M.   Apr 21
See Simeon, Abdechalas, etc.

Pusinna (St) V.   Apr 23
5th–6th cent. A holy virgin of Champagne
who had six sisters all honoured widely as
saints. They lived mostly at home.

Pyran (St)   March 5
Otherwise Piran, q.v.

Quadragesimus (St) C.   Oct 26
d. *c* 590   A shepherd and subdeacon at Poli-castro who, according to the testimony of St Gregory the Great, raised a dead man to life.

Quadratus Theodosius, Emmanuel and Comp. (SS) MM.   March 26
d. *c* 304   A group of forty-three martyrs, under the leadership of St Quadratus, bishop in Anatolia, put to death under Diocletian.

Quadratus (St) M.   May 7
d. 257   A martyr said to have been kept in prison for years at Nicomedia, Nicaea and Apamea, previous to his martyrdom at Herbi-polis under Valerian.

Quadratus (St) M.   May 26
? A martyr in proconsular Africa in whose honour St Augustine preached a panegyric.

Quadratus (St) Bp.   May 26
2nd cent.   The first known person to write an Apology for the Christian religion, which he addressed to the emperor Hadrian around the year 124. He has in the past been confused with an early bishop of Athens.

Quadratus (St) Bp.   Aug 21
3rd cent.   Bishop of Utica, highly praised by St Augustine: "He taught his whole people, clergy and laity, to confess Christ." They were all martyred. His cult was widespread in Africa.

Quartus and Quintus (SS) MM.   May 10
? Two citizens of Capua, condemned and executed in Rome, whose remains were taken back to Capua and there enshrined.

Quartus (St) ? Bp.   Nov 3
1st cent.   The disciple of the apostles whom St Paul (Rom. 16:23) mentions as "greeting the Christians of Rome". Some traditions describe Quartus as one of the seventy-two disciples (Luke 10).

Quentin (St) M.   Oct 31
Otherwise Quintinus, q.v.

Quentin (Quintin) (St) M.   Oct 31
? According to the traditional story, often

recast and much embellished, Quentin was a Roman by birth who went as a missionary to Gaul. He evangelized the district round Amiens and was martyred at the town on the Somme now called Saint-Quentin. He is beyond doubt a historical person but beyond the fact of his life and death nothing definite is now known. The above is his colourful legend. He is variously depicted as a bishop or a Roman soldier, in either case he holds one or two spits.

Queranus (St)
Otherwise Piran, Kieran, q.v., "Quirinus" may be taken as one of the Latinized forms of the names of both St Kieran of Ossory and St Kieran of Saghir. Another would be Quer-anus, as above.

Quinct —
Note. For names in Quinct — see Quint — .

Quinidius (St) Bp.   Feb 15
d. *c* 579   From being a hermit at Aix in Provence he became bishop of Vaison, also in Provence.

Quinta (St) M.   Feb 8
Otherwise Cointha, q.v.

Quintian and Irenaeus (SS) MM.   Apr 1
? Armenian martyrs, of whom nothing is known.

Quintian, Lucius, Julian and Comp. (SS) MM.   May 23
d. *c* 430   Three of a group of African martyrs under the Arian Vandal King Hunneric. The group seems to have numbered nineteen and to have included several women.

Quintian (St) Bp.   June 14
? Bishop of an unidentified see in France. The pre-1970 RM. mistakenly ascribed him to Rodez.

Quintian (St) Bp.   Nov 13
d. *c* 527   An African by birth, he fled to Gaul to escape the Arian-Vandal persecution. Eventually be became bishop of Rodez, but was driven thence, this time by the Arian Visigoths, and went to Auvergne, where St

St Quentin, Oct 31

Euphrasius made him his successor in the see of Clermont.

Quintian (St) M.   Dec 31
See Stephen, Pontian, etc.

Quintilian (St) M.   Apr 13
See Maximus, Dadas and Quintilian.

Quintilian (St) M.   Apr 16
See Saragossa, Martyrs of.

Quintilis (St) Bp. M.   March 8
? A martyr of Nicomedia. Most ancient records mention St Capitolinus as a fellow-martyr.

**Quintius, Arcontius and
Donatus (SS)** MM.   Sept 5
? Martyrs venerated at Capua and elsewhere in S. Italy.

Quintius (Quentin) (St) M.   Oct 4
d. *c* 570 A citizen of Tours and an official at the court of the Frankish king. The reigning queen, having tried in vain to seduce him, had him assassinated at L'Indrois, near Montresor.

Quintus (St) M.   Jan 4
See Aquilinus, Geminus, etc.

**Quintus, Quintilla,
Quartilla, Mark and
Comp. (SS)** MM.   March 19
? Martyrs venerated at Sorrento, near Naples. The three first-named were perhaps a brother and two sisters.

**Quintus, Simplicius and
Comp. (SS)** MM.   Dec 18
d. *c* 255 Martyrs in proconsular Africa under the emperors Decius and Valerian.

Quiriacus (St) Bp. M.   May 4
Otherwise Cyriacus, q.v.

Quiriacus (St) M.   Aug 12
See Hilaria, Digna, etc.

**Quiriacus, Maximus
Archelaus and Comp.
(SS)** MM.   Aug 23
d. *c* 235 (or 250?) Stated to have been bishop, priest and deacon of Ostia respectively, and to have been martyred with a number of Christian soldiers under Alexander Severus. Some modern writers place the martyrdom twenty or more years later.

Quiriacus (St) H.   Sept 29
d. *c* 550 A Greek who lived as a hermit in various lauras of Palestine. He is said to have died when long past his hundredth year.

**Quiricus (French: Cyr)
and Julitta (SS)** MM.   June 16
d. 304 Julitta was a widow of noble birth
from Iconium, and was martyred at Tarsus.
Previous to her own martyrdom her three-
year-old son Quiricus had been battered to
death before her eyes because he had
scratched the face of the infuriated magistrate.
Modern writers regard the story as fictitious.
Julitta has been mistaken for Juliot, a Cornish
saint of whom nothing for sure is known. A
church is dedicated to her at Luxalyan in
Cornwall, where her feast is celebrated on that
Sunday which is closest to June 29th.

Quirinus (St) M.   March 25
d. c 269 A Roman martyr who suffered
under Claudius II. He was one of those
befriended and buried by SS Marius, Martha
and Comp. (q.v.).

Quirinus (St) M.   March 30
d. c 117 The jailer of Pope St Alexander I,
by whom he was converted with his daughter
St Balbina. He was martyred shortly after,
under Hadrian. The story forms part of what
modern writers describe as "the romance
called the Passion of St Alexander", q.v. (May
3).

Quirinus (St) Bp. M.   June 4
d. 308 Bishop of Siscia (Sisak, or Seseg) in
Croatia. The story goes that he fled from his
city to escape the persecution of Galerius, was
captured and brought back and ordered to
sacrifice to the gods. He refused, was barbarously beaten and handed over to the governor
of Pannonia Prima at Sabaria (now Szom-
bathely in Hungary). There, on his continued
refusal to apostatize, he was drowned in the
River Raab.

Quirinus (St) M.   June 4
? A martyr at Tivoli, near Rome.

Quirinus (St) M.   Oct 11
See Nicasius, Quirinus, etc.

Quiteria (St) VM.   May 22
? A Spanish saint greatly venerated on the
borders of France and Spain, especially in
Spanish and French Navarre. Her traditional
story is wholly untrustworthy.

Quivox (Evox) (St)   March 13
Otherwise Kevoca, q.v.

Quodvultdeus (St) Bp.   Feb 19
d. c 450 A bishop of Carthage exiled by the
Arian Genseric, king of the Vandals, after the
capture of the city in 439. He ended his days at
Naples.

Rabanus Maurus (Bl) Bp. OSB. Feb 4

c 776–856 Born at Mainz, he was offered as a child to the abbey of Fulda, and there he spent practically his whole life. After receiving his early education at the abbey, he completed it at Tours, where he studied for two years under Alcuin. Already a monk of Fulda, he was appointed headmaster of the abbey school in 799, ordained deacon (801) and priest (814), and elected abbot in 822. In 847 he resigned this office, but in the same year was appointed archbishop of Mainz. He governed his diocese with remarkable ability and was noted for his charity to the poor, three hundred of whom were entertained daily at his house. Rabanus was an outstanding scholar and used his talents to promote the education of the clergy. His biblical commentaries, homilies, martyrology and poetical works (he probably composed the *Veni Creator Spiritus*) reveal a sound if unoriginal mind soaked in the scriptures and the Fathers of the church.

Rachildis (St) H. OSB. Nov 23

d. *c* 946 A female recluse who lived walled up in a cell near that of St Wiborada, under the obedience of the abbot of St Gall in Switzerland.

Racho (Ragnobert) (St) Bp. Jan 25

d. *c* 660 The first Frankish bishop of Autun.

Radbod (St) Bp. OSB. Nov 29

d. 918 The great-grandson of the last pagan king of Friesland, Radbod became bishop of Utrecht in 900. He at once put on the Benedictine habit, all his predecessors having been monks, and ruled the monastic cathedral and the diocese as an exemplary abbot-bishop. At the end of his life he retired to Deventer, where he died.

Radegund (St) Queen. Aug 13

518–587 Daughter of the pagan king of Thuringia, whose assassination was avenged by the Frankish king Clotaire I. The latter had the child, then twelve years old, baptized and educated, and eventually married her; but much ill-usage, crowned by the king's murder of her brother, compelled Radegund to leave him. She received the veil from St Medard and founded the great nunnery of the Holy Cross at Poitiers, where she spent the last thirty years of her life. She was the patroness of Venantius Fortunatus, and her abbey was a centre of scholarship and prayer.

Radegund (St) V. Aug 13

d. *c* 1300 A serving maid at the castle of Wellenburg, near Augsburg, who occupied herself much in works of charity. While on an errand of mercy to a neighbouring hospital she was set upon and torn to pieces by wolves. She at once became the object of a popular cult.

Radingus (St) Ab. Sept 17

Otherwise Rodingus, q.v.

Radulphus (Radulf) (*several*)

Otherwise Ralph, q.v.

Raingardis (Bl) W. OSB. June 24

d. 1135 Mother of St Peter the Venerable, abbot of Cluny. In her widowhood she became a Benedictine nun at Marcigny. She was venerated as a saint by the Cluniac Benedictines.

Raithu (Martyrs of) (SS) Jan 14

d. *c* 510 Forty-three anchorites living in the desert of Raithu, near the Red Sea, who were massacred by savages from Ethiopia or by Saracens.

Ralph (*several*)

Note. Ralph is the English form of Radulphus, which is more common in its French form of Raoul. There are many other variants: Radult, Raul, Radolph, Randulph, Rodolfo, Rudolf, Rodolphe, Rollon, Ruph, etc.

Ralph Ashley (Bl) M. SJ. Apr 7

d. 1606 A Jesuit lay-brother martyred at Worcester for being found in attendance upon Bl Edward Oldcorne. Beatified in 1919.

Ralph (Bl) Bp. OSB. Cist. Apr 14

d. 1241 Cistercian monk and abbot (1209) of Thoronet abbey. Later, bishop of Sisterton, France (1216–1241).

Ralph (St) Bp. OSB. June 21

d. 866 In his boyhood he was entrusted to

the care of the abbot of Solignac and, according to Benedictine historians, became a monk there. He later held several abbacies, including that of St Medard, Soissons. In 840 he was made bishop of Bourges, and as such he fostered learning, founded monasteries and in general promoted the public welfare.

Ralph Milner (Bl) M.   July 7
d. 1591 A husbandman, born at Stackstead, Hants, martyred at Winchester for relieving Bl Roger Dickenson. Beatified in 1929.

Ralph de la Futaye (de Flageio) (Bl) Ab. OSB.   Aug 16
d. 1129 A Benedictine of Saint-Jouin-de- Marne, who helped Bl Robert of Arbrissel to establish a new Benedictine congregation, and then became the abbot-founder (1092) of the double monastery of Saint-Sulpice, diocese of Rennes.

Ralph Corby (*vere* Corbington) (Bl) M. SJ.   Sept 7
d. 1644 Born in Dublin, he was educated at St Omer and then studied for the priesthood at Seville and Valladolid. In 1631 he was admitted to the Society of Jesus and ordained. He was sent to the English mission and ministered in Co. Durham. He was martyred at Tyburn for his faith. Beatified in 1929.

Ralph Crockett (Bl) M.   Oct 1
d. 1588 Born at Barton-on-the-Hill in Cheshire, he was educated at Christ's College, Cambridge, and at Gloucester Hall, Oxford. He became a schoolmaster in Norfolk and Suffolk. Later he studied for the priesthood at Reims, where he was ordained in 1586. He was arrested while engaged in missionary work in England and martyred at Chichester. Beatified in 1929.

Ralph Sherwin (St) M.   Dec 1
d. 1581 Born at Rodsley in Derbyshire, he gained a fellowship at Oxford, where he was known as a classical scholar of distinction. After his reception into the Catholic church he studied for the priesthood at Douai and Rome, and was ordained in 1580. Within a few months he was in England and in prison. Queen Elizabeth offered him preferment if he would turn Protestant: on his indignant refusal he was martyred at Tyburn. He is the proto-martyr of the Venerable English College, Rome. Beatified in 1886. Canonized in 1970 as one of the Forty Martyrs of England and Wales. (q.v.).

Ralph of Vaucelles (Bl) Ab. OSB.   Dec 30
d. 1152 An Englishman who became St Bernard's disciple at Clairvaux, by whom he

was later sent to be the abbot-founder of Vaucelles, diocese of Cambrai. He has a cult among the Cistercians.

Rambert (Ragnebert, Ragnobert) (St) M.   June 13
d. *c* 680 A courtier of high standing and much influence at the court of Thierry III of Austrasia. Ebroin, mayor of the palace, had him exiled and then ambushed and murdered in the Jura mountains. He has always been considered a martyr.

Rambold (Ramnold) (St) Ab. OSB.   June 17
d. 1001 Monk of St Maximinus at Trier, called to Regensburg by St Wolfgang to be abbot of St Emmeram. He died at the age of one hundred.

Ramirus and Comp. (SS) MM.   March 13
d. *c* 554 (or 630) Prior of the monastery of St Claudius at Leon, Spain. Two days after the martyrdom of his abbot, St Vincent, he, with all the monks of the community, was massacred by the Arian Visigoths while chanting the Nicene creed in the choir of the abbey church.

Ramón (*several*)
The Spanish form of Raymund, q.v.

Randcald (St) M. OSB.   Feb 21
See Germanus and Randcald.

Ranulphus (Ragnulf) (St) M.   May 27
d. *c* 700 A martyr of Thélus, near Arras. He was the father of St Hadulph, bishop of Arras-Cambrai.

Raphael the Archangel (St)   GC. Sept 29
One of the three angels whom the church venerates liturgically by name and also described as one of the seven angels who stand before the throne of God (q.v.). His name means "the Healer of God", and his ministrations in favour of men are described in the book of Tobit. He is commonly identified with the angel of the sheep-pool (John 5:1–4). St Raphael is depicted as an archangel or as a young man carrying a staff or a fish, or walking with Tobias, or holding a bottle or flask.

Raphaela Mary Porras (St) V. Foundress   Jan 6
Born in 1850 at Pedro Abad (Cordoba, Spain) she organised an institute of which she had charge, namely, the Handmaids of the Sacred Heart. In 1887 she was appointed superior general. Six years later she resigned and lived a busy but anonymous life until her death in Rome in 1925. Canonized in 1977.

St Raphael the Archangel (with Tobias), Sept 29

Rasso (or Ratho) (Bl) Mk. OSB.   May 17
d. 953   Count of Andeches in Bavaria, remarkable for his great stature. He was a brave warrior, leader of the Bavarians against the invading Hungarians. In middle age he made a pilgrimage to Palestine and Rome, and on his return founded the abbey of Worth in Bavaria (now called after him, Grafrath), in which he took the Benedictine habit.

Rasyphus (St) M.   July 23
? A martyr venerated in Rome from early times. He may be identical with a St Rasius whose relics are enshrined in the Pantheon.

Rasyphus and Ravennus (SS) MM.   July 23
5th cent.   Said to have been natives of Britain who took refuge in N. France from the Anglo-Saxon invaders. There they became

hermits and were ultimately slain for the faith at Macé, diocese of Séez. Their relics are enshrined in Bayeux cathedral.

Rathard (Bl) C.   Aug 8
d. 815   A member of the family of the counts of Andechs in Bavaria, he became a priest and founded the Augustinian friary of Diessen.

Ravennus (St) M.   July 23
See Rasyphus and Ravennus.

Raverranus
(Raverianus) (St) Bp. OSB.   Nov 7
d. 682   Bishop of Séez. He resigned his see and became a Benedictine monk at Fontenelle.

Raymund of Peñafort
(St) C. OP.   GC. Jan 7
c 1180–1275   A kinsman of the kings of Aragon, he was born at Villafranca in Catalonia and studied and taught at Barcelona, where he became a priest and archdeacon of the cathedral. In 1222 he joined the Dominican order and began to preach to the Moors and the Albigenses. Called to Rome by Gregory IX, he was appointed penitentiary and confessor to the pope and was entrusted with the task of systematizing and codifying the canon law. This he did in his five books of the Decretals, finished in 1234, which remained the most authoritative codification of ecclesiastical legislation till 1917. In 1238 he was chosen master-general of his order and in that capacity encouraged St Thomas Aquinas to write the *Contra Gentiles*. In his later years Raymund resided in Majorca. The part he took, if any, in the foundation of the Mercedarians is still open to controversy. Canonized in 1601.

Raymund of Fitero (St)
Ab. OSB. Cist.   March 15
d. 1163   A native of Aragon who became a canon of the cathedral of Tarazona and then a Cistercian at the abbey of Scala Dei in France. From there he was sent to found and govern the abbey of Fitero in Spanish Navarre. In 1158, the city of Calatrava in New Castile being abandoned by the Templars and threatened by the Moors, he founded for its defence the military order of Calatrava under the Benedictine rule and the Cistercian customary. Under him this order won for itself a glorious name in Spanish history. Raymund's cult, as a saint, was approved in 1719.

Raymund of Barbastro
(St) Bp. OSA.   June 21
d. 1126   Born at Durban, near Coserans, in France, he became an Augustinian canon regular at Pamiers and in 1104 second bishop of the recently recaptured city of Barbastro in Aragon. He is the principal patron of the city and diocese of Barbastro.

Raymund Lull (Bl)   July 3
c 1232–c 1315   Born at Palma, Majorca, he married young and was seneschal at the court of Aragon. At the age of about thirty he was converted by a vision of Christ crucified, became a Franciscan tertiary and devoted his whole life to the conversion of the Muslims. He was unsuccessful in his attempts to interest the Holy See and the courts of Western Europe in this enterprise. He himself learned Arabic and three times went to preach the gospel to the Muslims of Tunis. It has often been asserted that he was stoned to death but there is no contemporary proof of this. In the interests of his life's work he travelled extensively in Italy, France, England and Germany, wrote copiously in Latin, Arabic and Catalan, and encouraged the study of oriental religion and culture. He was a theologian (*Doctor Illuminatus*), a philosopher, a poet, an alchemist and a chemist but he had no formal training in the usual scholastic theology of his age and invented his own means of self-expression, which had a small but enthusiastic following in his time.

Raymund of Toulouse
(St) C.   July 8
d. 1118   A chanter in the church of St Sernin at Toulouse who, after the death of his wife, received a canonry in the same church and was noted for his generosity to the poor and for his personal austerity.

Raymund Nonnatus (St)
Card. O. Merc.   Aug 31
d. 1240   A member of the Mercedarian order, which was instituted in Spain for the ransoming of Christian captives from the Moors of the Barbary Coast. He succeeded St Peter Nolasco as its second master-general. He spent his whole substance in purchasing the freedome of Christian slaves and surrendered himself as a hostage to secure the liberation of one of their number until his Order succeeded in ransoming him in his turn. He was created cardinal by Gregory IX. Cult confined to local calendars since 1969.

Raymund of Capua (Bl)
C. OP.   Oct 5
d. 1399   Raymund delle Vigne was born at Capua, joined the Dominicans and held various offices in different friaries of the order. He became the spiritual director of St Catherine of Siena when living in that city, and with her his name will be always linked. Later he became master-general of the Dominicans and restored dicipline with such success that

he has been called the second founder of the order. He wrote lives of St Catherine and of St Agnes of Montepulciano. Beatified in 1899.

Raynald of Nocera (St)
Bp. OSB.   Feb 9
d. 1225 Born of German parents near Nocera in Umbria, he took the Benedictine habit at Fontavellana and in 1222 was made bishop of Nocera, of which city he is now venerated as the principal patron.

Raynald of Ravenna (Bl)
Bp.   Aug 18
d. 1321 Raynald Concorrezzo was born at Milan, became a canon of Lodi and then bishop of Vicenza (1296). After holding various offices in the papal states he became archbishop of Ravenna (1303). He was a friend and defender of the Knights Templars. Cult approved in 1852.

Raynald de Bar (Bl) Ab.
OSB. Cist.   Dec 16
d. 1151 A monk of Clairvaux who was appointed abbot of Cîteaux in 1133. He is remembered chiefly as the compiler of the first collection of Cistercian statutes. He was also instrumental in bringing about the union of the Benedictine congregations of Obazine and Savigny with Cîteaux.

Raynerius (Raynier) (St)
Mk. OSB.   Feb 22
d. c 967 Benedictine monk at Beaulieu in the neighbourhood of Limoges.

Raynerius Inclusus (Bl) H.   Apr 11
d. 1237 A hermit who lived in a cell near the cathedral of Osnabrück. He spent twenty-two years in his cell (*inclusus* means "shut up").

Raynerius (Raniero, Rainerius) (St) H.   June 17
d. 1160 Raniero Scacceri was a native of Pisa. After a sinful youth he undertook several penitential pilgrimages to Jerusalem and afterwards lived as a conventual oblate in the Benedictine abbey of St Andrew at Pisa and then in that of San Vito in the same city, where he died.

Raynerius of Spalatro (St)
M. OSB.   Aug 4
d. 1180 A Camaldolese monk of Fontavellana, made bishop of Cagli in 1156 and archbishop of Spalatro in 1175. He was murdered by members of his flock for his defence of ecclesiastical immunity.

Raynerius of Arezzo (Bl)
C. OFM.   Nov 3
d. 1304 Raniero Mariani was a native of Arezzo. He became a Franciscan lay-brother and died at Borgo Sansepolcro. Cult confirmed in 1802.

Raynerius of Todi (Bl) C.
OFM. Cap.   Nov 5
d. c 1586 Born at Sansepolcro, he married to please his parents, but on the death of his wife became a Capuchin friar. He died at Todi. Cult confirmed by Pius VII.

Raynerius (St) Bp.   Dec 30
d. 1077 Bishop of Aquila (*Forconium*) in the Abruzzi.

Reatrus (Restius) (St) M.   Jan 27
See Datius, Reatrus, etc.

Redempta (St) V.   July 23
See Romula, Redempta and Herundo.

Redemptus (St) Bp.   Apr 8
d. 586 Bishop of Ferentini (*in Hernicis*), a town to the south of Rome. He was a friend of St Gregory the Great, who bears witness to his sanctity.

Redemptus of the Cross
(Bl) M. OCD.   Nov 29
See Dionysius and Redemptus.

Regimbald (Reginbald, Regimbaut, Reginobaldus)
(St) Bp. OSB.   Oct 13
d. 1039 A Benedictine monk of the abbey of SS Ulric and Afra at Augsburg. In 1015 he migrated to the abbey of Edersberg. In 1022 he became abbot of Lorsch and later founded therefrom the daughter-abbey of Heiligenberg. In 1032 he was appointed bishop of Speyer.

Regina (Regnia, Reine)
(St) VM.   Sept 7
d. c ?286 A virgin martyr venerated at Autun from an early date. We have no particulars of her life.

Reginald of Saint-Gilles
(Bl) C. OP.   Feb 1
1183–1220 Born at Saint-Gilles in Languedoc. After having taught canon law at the university of Paris from 1206 to 1211 he was appointed dean of Saint-Agnan, Orleans. He met St Dominic in Rome and became one of his ablest disciples. He helped to establish the Dominicans at Bologna and Paris. Cult confirmed in 1885.

Reginald Montemarti (Bl)
C. OP.   Apr 9
1292–1348 He was born near Orvieto and became a Dominican. He died at Piperno. Cult approved in 1877.

Reginald (Bl) H. OSB.   July 2
d. *c* 1095   A Benedictine monk of Baume who lived as a hermit in the cell occupied by St Adegrin more than a century before.

Regintrudis (Bl) Abs. OSB.   May 26
d. *c* 750   Fourth abbess of Nonnberg, near Salzburg.

Regula (St) VM.   Sept 11
See Felix and Regula.

Regulus (French: Rieul)
(St) Bp.   March 30
d. *c* 260   Said to have been a Greek by origin. He is honoured as the first bishop of Senlis. An old tradition connects him with Arles.

Regulus (St) M.   Sept 1
d. *c* 545   An African driven into exile by the Arian Vandals. He landed in Tuscany and appears to have been martyred under Totila.

Regulus (French: Reol)
(St) Bp. OSB.   Sept 3
d. 698   A monk of Rebais under St Philibert. He succeeded St Nivard (*c* 670) as archbishop of Reims. He was the founder of the great abbey of Orbais (680).

Regulus (Rule) (St) Ab.   Oct 17
? 4th cent.   The legendary abbot who brought the relics of St Andrew from Greece to Scotland. His cult is very ancient, but we have no life earlier than the ninth century.

Reine (St) VM.   Sept 7
Otherwise Regina, q.v.

Reineldis (Raineldis,
Reinaldes) V. and Comp.
(SS) MM.   July 16
d. *c* 680   Daughter of St Amelberg and sister of St Gudula. She was a nun of Saintes in Hainault and was put to death, together with two clergymen, by the Huns who were then ravaging the country.

Reinhard (Bl) Ab. OSB.   March 7
d. *p.* 1170   Monk and headmaster of the abbey school of Stavelot-Malmédy. About 1130 he was appointed first abbot of Reinhausen in Saxony.

Reinold (Rainald,
Reynold) (St) M. OSB.   Jan 7
d. 960   Said to have belonged to the family of Charlemagne. He was a Benedictine monk of the abbey of St Pantaleon at Cologne. He was in charge of the building operations there and was killed by the stonemasons with their hammers and his body flung into a pool near the Rhine. It is said to have been found later by divine revelation.

Relindis (Renildis,
Renula, Renule) (St) Abs.
OSB.   Feb 6
d. *c* 750   Educated with her sister Herlindis in the Benedictine nunnery of Valenciennes. She became an expert in embroidery and painting. On the death of her sister, St Boniface appointed her abbess of the convent of Maaseyk, founded by her parents. See Herlindis and Relindis.

Remaclus (St) Bp. OSB.   Sept 3
d. *c* 663   A native of Aquitaine and a courtier. He became a monk and after his ordination was appointed first abbot of Solignac near Limoges, and then of Cougnon in Luxemburg. About the year 648 he founded the twin abbeys of Stavelot and Malmédy in the Ardennes, and in 652 he became bishop of Maestricht. After eleven years as a bishop he resigned and returned to Stavelot, where he died.

Rembert (St) Bp. OSB.   Feb 4
d. 888   Born in Flanders and a monk of Turholt. He shared with St Ansgar the apostolate to Scandinavia and succeeded him in the see of Hamburg-Bremen (865). He died on June 11, but the pre-1970 RM. commemorated him also on the day of his episcopal ordination. He wrote an excellent biography of St Ansgar.

Remedius (St) Bp.   Feb 3
? A bishop of Gap in the French Alps.

Remi (Remy) (*several*)
The French form of Remigius, q.v.

Remigius (St) Bp.   Jan 19
d. *c* 772   A natural son of Charles Martel. He was bishop of Rouen from 755 till his death. He worked successfully for the introduction of the Roman rite and chant into Gaul.

Remigius (Bl or St) Bp.
OSB.   March 20
d. 783   A son of Duke Hugh of Alsace and a nephew of St Ottilien. He was educated at, and became abbot of Münster, near Colmar, and in 776 was made bishop of Strasburg. Pope Leo IX authorized his feast for the abbey of Münster.

Remigius (St) Bp.   Oct 1
d. *c* 533 (Jan 13)   "Apostle of the Franks". A Gallo-Roman by birth, he was elected in 459, while still a layman, to the see of Reims. During the seventy-four years of his episcopate he was the most influential prelate of Gaul, the culminating event in his life being the conversion and baptism of Clovis, king of

the Franks, on Easter eve 496. Cult confined to particular calendars since 1969.

Remigius (St) Bp.   Oct 28
d. 875 Royal arch-chaplain and in 852 archbishop of Lyons. He combated Gottschalk's doctrine on predestination but defended the latter's person against his metropolitan, Hincmar of Reims.

Remo (St) Bp.   Oct 13
Remo is a corrupt form of Romulus, q.v.

Renatus (French: René)
Massey (Bl) M. OSB.   Sept 2
A Maurist monk and prior of Saint Florent de Saumur, one of the September Martyrs of 1792 (q.v.).

Renatus (French: René)
Goupil (St) M. SJ.   GC. Oct 19
d. 1642 He was a Jesuit lay-brother and a surgeon and acted as assistant to the missionaries to the Red Indians. He was the first to be martyred (Sept 29), being tomahawked for making the sign of the cross on the brow of some children. See John de Brebeuf and Comps.

Renatus (French: René)
(St) Bp.   Nov 12
d. c 422 Said to have been bishop first at Angers and then at Sorrento in S. Italy. Probably this is a mistaken identification of two different persons.

Renovatus (St) Bp.   March 31
d. c 633 A converted Arian, he became monk and then abbot of Cauliana in Lusitania. Finally he became bishop of Merida for twenty-two years.

Reol (Reolus) (St) Bp.   Sept 3
Otherwise Regulus, q.v.

Reparata (St) VM.   Oct 8
d. c 250 A virgin martyr of Caesarea in Palestine, martyred at the age of twelve under Decius. Her Acts are spurious.

Repositus (St) M.   Aug 29
See Vitalis, Sator and Repositus.

Respicius (St) M.   Nov 10
See Tryphon, Respicius and Nympha.

Restituta (St) VM.   May 17
d. 255 (or 304) An African maiden martyred at Carthage either under Valerian or Diocletian. Her relics are said to be enshrined in the cathedral of Naples.

Restituta and Comp. (SS)
MM.   May 27
d. 272 Said to have been a Roman maiden

of patrician parentage who fled to Sora in Campania to escape the persecution under Aurelian and who was martyred there with several companions.

Restitutus (St) M.   May 29
d. c 299 A Roman martyr under Diocletian. His Acts are not trustworthy.

Restitutus, Donatus,
Valerian, Fructuosa and
Comp. (SS) MM.   Aug 23
d. c ?305 A group of sixteen Syrian martyrs put to death at Antioch. Some may have been African. The grouping was made by Florus of Lyons (c 850).

Restitutus (St) Bp. M.   Dec 9
? Bishop of Carthage, in whose honour St Augustine preached a sermon which is now lost.

Reverianus, Paul and
Comp. (SS) MM.   June 1
d. 272 Reverianus, a bishop, and Paul, a priest, Italians by birth, appear to have gone as missionaries to Gaul. They evangelized Autun and the surrounding district and were martyred with several companions under Aurelian.

Revocata (St) M.   Feb 6
See Saturninus, Theophilus and Revocata.

Revocatus (St) M.   Jan 9
See Vitalis, Revocatus and Fortunatus.

Revocatus (St) M.   March 7
See Perpetua, Felicitas, etc.

Reyne (St) VM.   Sept 7
Otherwise Regina, q.v.

Rhais (St) M.   June 28
See Plutarch, Serenus, etc.

Rhais (St) VM.   Sept 22
Otherwise Irais, q.v.

Rhediw (St)   Nov 11
? A Welsh saint whose name is perpetuated by the dedication of a church in his honour at Llanllyfni in Gwynedd, North Wales.

Rheticus (Rheticius,
Rhetice) (St) Bp.   July 20
d. 334 A Gallo-Roman who became bishop of Autun c 310. In 313 he was present at the Lateran synod which condemned the Donatists.

Rhian (Ranus, Rian) (St)
Ab.   Mar 8
? The saint who has left his name to Llanrhian

in Dyfed, S. Wales. He is described as an abbot, but we have no authentic details of his life.

Rhipsime (Ripsimis), Gaiana and Comp. (SS)
VV. MM.   Sept 29
d. *c* 290   A band of virgin martyrs venerated from early times as the first to suffer for Christ in the Armenian church. Their existence is certainly established, but their Acts are in no way trustworthy.

Rhodopianus (St)   May 3
See Diodorus and Rhodopianus.

Rhuddlad (St) V.   Sept 4
? 7th cent.   Patron of Llanrhyddlad, at the foot of Moel Rhyddlad in Anglesey.

Ribert (St) Ab. OSB.   Sept 15
7th cent.   Monk and abbot of Saint-Valèry-sur-Somme. He may have been also a regionary bishop in Normandy and Picardy. He is the patron of numerous parishes in the diocese of Rouen.

Ribert (Ribarius) (St) Ab.
OSB.   Dec 19
d. *c* 790   Seventeenth abbot of Saint-Oyend. He is venerated in Franche-Comté.

Richalm (Bl) Ab. OSB. Cist.   Dec 2
d. 1219   Cistercian abbot of Schönthal (*Speciosa Vallis*) in Würtemberg.

Richard the Sacrist (Bl)
Mk. OSB. Cist.   Jan 28
d. *p*.1142   An Englishman who became a Cistercian monk and sacrist of the abbey of Dundrennan in Kirkcudbrightshire.

Richard of Vaucelles (St)
Ab. OSB. Cist.   Jan 28
d. 1169   An Englishman who became a Cistercian and was made by St Bernard second abbot of Vaucelles, near Cambrai.

Richard "the King" (St) C.   Feb 7
d. 720   According to the earlier Italian legend this saint was a prince in Wessex and father of SS Willibald, Winebald and Walburga: he died at Lucca on a pilgrimage to Rome. A later legend makes him Duke of Swabia. Both legends have been proved to be quite untrustworthy.

Richard of Chichester (St)
Bp.   Apr 3
1197–1253   Richard de Wych was born at Droitwich in Worcestershire and pursued his studies at Oxford, Paris and Bologna. Returning to England (1235), he was chosen chancellor of Oxford university. He then became the legal adviser of the archbishops of Canterbury, St Edmund Rich and St Boniface of Savoy. Having been ordained in France, he became bishop of Chichester, and in the early years of his episcopate he had to defend himself against the rapacity of Henry III. He died at Dover while engaged in preaching the crusade. He was a model pastor of his flock. Until the Reformation his shrine, at which many miracles occurred — especially cures — was at Chichester. Canonized in 1262. He is shown vested as a bishop, sometimes with a chalice at his feet lying on its side.

Richard Reynolds (St)
M. Bridg.   May 4
c 1492–1535   Born in Devon, he studied at Christ's College, Cambridge, was elected a fellow of Corpus Christi college in 1510, took the degree of B.D. in 1513 and was appointed university preacher. In the same year he was professed a Bridgettine monk at Syon abbey, Isleworth, a house noted for its sanctity and intellectual atmosphere. He was one of the first band of martyrs executed at Tyburn for their opposition to the royal supremacy. Beatified in 1886. Canonized in 1970 as one of the Forty Martyrs of England and Wales, q.v.

Richard Thirkeld
(Thirkild) (Bl) M.   May 29
d. 1583   Born in Co. Durham, he was educated at Queen's College, Oxford, and when already advanced in years completed his studies for the priesthood at Douai and Reims, being ordained in 1579. He ministered to the Catholics of Yorkshire and was condemned and executed at York. Beatified in 1886.

Richard Newport (*alias:*
Smith) (Bl) M.   May 30
d. 1612   Born at Harringworth in Northamptonshire, he was educated for the priesthood at Rome and ordained in 1597. On his return to England he worked in the London district and was executed at Tyburn for his faith.

Richard of Andria (St) Bp.   June 9
d. *p*.1196   An Englishman who became bishop of Andria in Italy. By a confusion of dates at a much later period he has been ascribed, quite erroneously, to the fifth century (453).

Richard of St Vannes (Bl)
Ab. OSB.   June 14
d. 1046   Nicknamed "Gratia Dei", from a phrase frequently on his lips. From being dean of the cathedral of Reims he became a Benedictine at St Vannes, Verdun. He was a

personal friend of St Odilo of Cluny and of the emperor St Henry, who is said to have asked Richard to confer the monastic habit on him.

Richard Langhorne (Bl) M.   July 14
d. 1679   Born in Bedfordshire, he read law at the Inner Temple and was called to the bar in 1654. He was executed at Tyburn for alleged complicity in the "Popish Plot". Beatified in 1929.

Richard Featherstone (Bl) M.   July 30
d. 1540   Educated at Cambridge, he became tutor to the princess Mary and archdeacon of Brecknock. As one of the chaplains to Queen Catherine of Aragon he defended her in convocation and was forthwith attainted for treason and executed at Tyburn. Beatified in 1886.

Richard Kirkman (Bl) M.   Aug 22
d. 1582   Born at Addingham, near Skipton in Yorkshire, he was educated at Douai and ordained in 1579. He was appointed tutor in the family of Dymoke of Scrivelsby. He was martyred at York for denying the Queen's supremacy in spiritual matters. Beatified in 1886.

Richard Herst (Bl) M.   Aug 29
d. 1628   Richard Herst (also Hurst or Hayhurst) was born near Preston in Lancashire and worked there as a farmer. He was condemned ostensibly for murder but in fact because he was a Catholic recusant. He was hanged at Lancaster. Beatified in 1929.

Richard Leigh and Richard Martin (BB) MM.   Aug 30
d. 1588   Richard Leigh (*alias* Garth or Earth) was born in London, educated at Reims and Rome and ordained in 1586. Richard Martin was a Shropshire gentleman who was educated at Broadgates Hall, Oxford. They were martyred together at Tyburn with Bl Edward Shelley, Bl John Roche, St Margaret Ward, and Bl. Richard Lloyd (*alias* Flower) of Anglesey. Leigh for being a priest and Martin for sheltering priests. Beatified in 1929.

Richard Bere (Bl) M.   Aug 31 (?)
d. 1537   Born at Glastonbury, he was educated at Oxford and the Inns of Court. He became a Carthusian at the London Charterhouse and was starved to death in Newgate, with others of his community, for opposing the divorce plans of Henry VIII.

Richard of St Ann (Bl) M. OFM.   Sept 10
1585–1622   Born of Spanish parents in Flanders, he was a tailor at Brussels when he joined the Friars Minor as a lay-brother. He was sent as a missionary to Mexico and thence (1611) to the Philippines, where he was ordained at Cebu. In 1613 he went to Japan, where he was martyred at Nagasaki on the day of the great martyrdom. Beatified in 1867.

Richard Rolle (Bl) C.   Sept 29
c 1300–1349   Born at Thornton in Yorkshire, he lived as a hermit at Hampole and elsewhere in that county. He is best known as one of the foremost mystical writers of his time. At one time he had a very considerable popular cult. His works are still printed, *The Fire of Love* being the most well known.

Richard Gwyn (*alias* White) (St) M.   Oct 17
1537–1584   Born at Llanidloes, in Powys, Wales, he was educated at St John's College, Cambridge. He renounced Protestantism, married and became a schoolmaster. He was imprisoned for four years before he was martyred for his Catholic faith at Wrexham. In jail he wrote numerous religious poems in Welsh. He is the proto-martyr of Wales. Canonized in 1970 as one of the Forty Martyrs of England and Wales. (q.v.).

Richard Whiting (Bl) M. Ab. OSB.   Nov 15
d. 1539   Born at Wrington in Somerset, he became a Benedictine monk at Glastonbury and was sent to Cambridge for his higher education. In 1525 he became abbot of Glastonbury. At the dissolution he refused to surrender his abbey to the Crown and was condemned to death for treason. He was hanged with the usual brutalities on the summit of Tor Hill, overlooking Glastonbury. Beatified in 1895.

Richard Langley (Bl) M.   Dec 1
d. 1586   A Yorkshire gentleman of Ousethorpe, near Pocklington, hanged at York for sheltering priests in his house. Beatified in 1929.

Richardis (St) Empress   Sept 18
d. *c* 895   She was married at twenty-two to the emperor Charles the Fat, and after nineteen years of married life was accused of unfaithfulness. Her innocence was established, but she ceased to cohabit with her husband and retired to the nunnery of Andlau, which she herself had founded, and lived there as a nun till her death. She is venerated as a

Benedictine oblate. Her relics were enshrined by order of Pope Leo IX.

Richarius (Riquier) (St) Ab.   Apr 26
d. *c* 645   Born at Centula (Celles) near Amiens, he became a priest and founded an abbey in his native place, later called after him, Saint-Riquier. He was the first to devote himself to the work of ransoming captives. After some years as abbot he resigned and spent the rest of his life as a hermit.

Richildis (Bl) N. OSB.   Aug 23
d. *c* 1100   A Benedictine nun at Hohenwart in Upper Bavaria, diocese of Augsburg. After several years of community life she became an anchoress.

Richimirus (St) Ab. OSB.   Jan 17
d. *c* 715   An abbot who, under the patronage of the bishop of Le Mans, founded a monastery in that diocese (afterwards called after him, Saint-Rigomer-des-Bois) and gave it the rule of St Benedict.

Rictrudis (St) W. OSB.   May 12
d. 688   Born in Gascony, she married St Adalbald, by whom she had four children — all saints, viz. Maurontius, Eusebia, Clotsindis and Adalsindis. After her husband's death she received the veil from St Amandus and became the abbess-foundress of Marchiennes, ruling that house for forty years.

Rieul (St) Bp.   March 30
Otherwise Regulus, q.v.

Rigobert (St) Bp. OSB.   Jan 4
d. *c* 745   Monk and abbot of Orbais. In 721 he was made archbishop of Reims, but some years later was banished by Charles Martel. He returned to Orbais and resumed monastic life. On being recalled to Reims he came to terms with the intruded bishop and himself became a hermit.

Ringan, Ringen
Variant forms of Ninian and Ninnian respectively.

Rioch (St) Ab.   Aug 1
d. *c* 480   Described as a nephew of St Patrick and abbot of Innisboffin, Ireland. Nothing is known about him.

Riquier (St) Ab.   Apr 26
Otherwise Richarius, q.v.

Rita (Margarita) of Cascia (St) W. OSA.   May 22
1381–1457   Born near Spoleto, she married a rude ill-tempered husband who died a violent death. Her two sons, who had sworn vengeance against their father's murderers, died shortly afterwards filled with the spirit of

forgiveness. Rita now entered a convent of Augustinians at Cascia, where she bore patiently the strain of a chronic and very painful malady. She was canonized in 1900. In Spanish-speaking countries she is surnamed *La Abogada de Imposibles*, the saint of desperate cases.

Ritbert (St) Ab. OSB.   Sept 15
d. *c* 690   Monk and abbot of a small monastery at Varennes. He had previously been a disciple of St Ouen.

Rixius Varus (Rictiovarus) (St) M.   July 6
The pre-1970 RM. read: "The holy martyr Lucy, a native of Campania, who, being tried and sharply tortured under the vicar Rixius Varus, converted him to Christ...They suffered and were crowned together." Rixius Varus is notorious in the martyrology as a persecuting prefect under whom hundreds of martyrs died. Modern scholars, however, not only reject the legend of his conversion, but even query his existence.

Rizzerio (Richerius) (Bl) C. OFM.   Feb 7
d. 1236   Referred to in the *Fioretti* of St Francis as Rinieri. Born at Muccia in the Italian Marches. While studying at Bologna he heard St Francis preaching and at once attached himself to him. He was much beloved by Francis and was present at his death. He later became provincial of the Marches. Cult approved in 1836.

Ro
Corruption of Maelrubius, q.v.

Robert of Reims (St) Bp. OSB.   Jan 4
Otherwise Rigobert, q.v.

Robert of Newminster (St) Ab. OSB. Cist.   Jan 26
1100–1159   A priest from North Yorkshire who took the Benedictine habit at Whitby and obtained permission to join some monks of York who were attempting to live according to a new interpretation of the Benedictine rule at Fountains abbey (1132). Fountains soon became Cistercian and one of the centres of the White Monks in N. England. Newminster abbey in Northumberland was founded from it in 1137, and Robert became its first abbot. He is described as gentle and merciful in judgement.

Robert Southwell (St) M. SJ.   Feb 21
1561–1595   Born at Horsham St Faith's in

Norfolk, at the age of 17 he joined the Jesuits in Rome and worked as a priest in London from 1584 to 1592. He was betrayed and kept three years in jail, being tortured thirteen times. He was martyred at Tyburn. He holds a place in English literature as a religious poet. Beatified in 1929. Canonized in 1970 as one ofe the Forty Martyrs of England and Wales, (q.v.).

Robert of Arbrissel (Bl)
Ab. OSB.   Feb 24
d. 1117   A native of Arbrissel in Brittany who became chancellor of the university of Paris and then vicar general of Rennes (1085). At Rennes his activities as preacher and reformer caused such a reaction that he had to flee Brittany. In 1099 he founded the order of Fontevrault on the borders of Poitou and Anjou. This order consisted of both men and women. Its members lived under the Benedictine rule, the abbess being in supreme command over both nuns and monks, the position of the latter being really that of chaplains to the nuns. After a stormy career Robert retired to Fontevrault and lived out the remainder of his life as a simple monk.

Robert Dalby (Bl) M.   March 16
d. 1589   Born at Hemingborough in Yorkshire. He was a convert from the Protestant ministry and was ordained priest at Reims in 1588. He was hanged at York for his faith.

Robert of Bury St Edmunds (St) M.   March 25
d. 1181   A child said to have been put to death by Jews on Good Friday at Bury St Edmunds, where his relics were enshrined in the abbey church. His story is identical to that of many other boy-martyrs of the Middle Ages. He was never officially canonized: his cult was merely a mask for anti-semitism.

Robert of Chaise-Dieu
(St) Ab. OSB.   Apr 17
d. 1067   Robert de Turlande, a native of Auvergne, was a priest and canon noted for his love of the poor, for whom he founded a hospice. After spending many years at Cluny under St Odilo and having made a pilgrimage to Rome, he retired to a solitude near Brioude in Auvergne, where he was joined by many disciples. Buildings soon arose which developed into the great abbey of *Casa Dei* or Chaise-Dieu, housing some three hundred monks. To these Robert gave the Benedictine rule, and the foundation became the mother-house of an important Black Benedictine congregation.

Robert Watkinson (Bl) M.   Apr 20
d. 1602   Born at Hemingborough in Yorkshire, he studied for the priesthood at Douai and Rome and was ordained in 1602 at the age of twenty-three. The same year he suffered at Tyburn for his faith.

Robert of Syracuse (St)
Ab. OSB.   Apr 25
d. *c* 1000   Benedictine abbot of a monastery at Syracuse in Sicily.

Robert Anderton (Bl) M.   Apr 25
d. 1586   Born at Chorley, Lancs, he was educated at Brasenose college, Oxford. After his conversion he studied at Reims and was ordained in 1585. The following year he was martyred in the Isle of Wight. Beatified in 1929.

Robert of Molesmes (St)
Ab. OSB. Cist.   Apr 29
1027–1110 (March 21)   Born near Troyes in Champagne, he became a Benedictine monk at Moutier-la-Celle. He was made prior soon after his novitiate and then abbot of St Michael of Tonnerre. He left this monastery to become superior of some hermits in the forest of Collan. In 1075 he migrated with this little community to Molesmes. As the community grew Robert felt less satisfied with the life and withdrew to a hermitage at Or. He was recalled to Molesmes but again left it, this time in the company of SS Stephen Harding and Alberic. In 1098 they founded at Cîteaux a new monastery more in consonance with their monastic ideals. However, the monks of Molesmes appealed to Rome and obtained Robert's recall (1099), and he ruled that abbey thenceforward until his death.

Robert of Bruges (Bl) Ab.
OSB. Cist.   Apr 29
d. 1157   Robert Gruthuysen was a native of Bruges. In 1131 he followed St Bernard to Clairvaux, and in 1139 was sent back to Belgium as abbot of Dunes. In 1153 he succeeded St Bernard as abbot of Clairvaux.

Robert Lawrence (St) M.
O. Cart.   May 4
d. 1535   The prior of the charterhouse at Beauvale, Notts. He was one of the first group of Carthusians to be martyred at Tyburn under Henry VIII. Beatified in 1886, canonized in 1970 and one of the Forty Martyrs of England and Wales (q.v.).

Robert Johnson (Bl) M.   May 28
d. 1582   Born in Shropshire and educated at Rome and Douai, he was ordained in 1576. he began to minister to the Catholics in London

in 1580. Two years later he was hanged at Tyburn. Beatified in 1886.

Robert Salt (Bl) M. O.
Cart.   June 6 (?)
d. 1537 A lay-brother of the London charterhouse, starved to death, with six of his brethren, at Newgate under Henry VIII. Beatified in 1886.

Robert of Frassinoro (St)
Ab. OSB.   June 8
d. p.1070 Abbot of the Benedictine monastery of Frassinoro near Modena.

Robert of Salentino (Bl)
Ab. OSB. Cel.   July 18
1271–1341 A Benedictine monk, disciple of St Peter Celestine at Murrone and founder of fourteen monasteries of the Celestine congregation.

Robert Morton (Bl) M.   Aug 28
d. 1588 Born at Bawtry in S. Yorkshire, he studied for the priesthood at Reims and Rome and was ordained in 1587. He suffered for his faith the following year at Lincoln's Inn Fields, London. Beatified in 1929.

Robert Bellarmine
(St) Bp. Card. Dr. SJ.   GC. Sept 17
1542–1621. (Sept 17) Born at Montepulciano, he was educated by the Jesuits and joined that Society in 1560. As a young man he held professorships of Greek, Hebrew and theology. It was at Louvain that he first made his reputation as a controversialist, and from that time onward his pen and voice were busy in defence of Catholic doctrine against its Protestant opponents. He was created cardinal in 1598 and archbishop of Capua in 1602. Recalled to Rome in 1605, he became head of the Vatican library and theological adviser to the popes. He was canonized in 1930 and declared a Doctor of the Church the following year.

Robert Flower (Bl) H.   Sept 24
d. 1218 (or 1235?) Born at York, he became a postulant at Newminster, but left that abbey to become a hermit, living in a cave by the river Nidd near Knaresborough. His cult has never been officially confirmed.

Robert Wilcox and Robert Widmerpool (BB) MM.   Oct 1
d. 1588 Robert Wilcox was born at Chester and educated at Reims, where he was ordained in 1585. Robert Widmerpool was a gentleman of Nottinghamshire who was educated at Oxford and followed the profession of a schoolmaster. They were martyred together at Canterbury. Beatified in 1929.

Robert Sutton (Bl) M.   Oct 5
d. 1588 Born at Kegwell in Leicestershire, he was a schoolmaster in London and was hanged at Clerkenwell for having been reconciled to the Catholic church. Beatified in 1929.

Robustian (St) M.   May 24
? An early Milanese martyr, possibly one and the same with the following.

Robustian and Mark (SS)
MM.   Aug 31
? Martyrs venerated at Milan from early times, of whom nothing further is known.

Roch (St) C.   Aug 16
1350–1380 A citizen of Montpellier in France who devoted his life to the service of the plague-stricken. He was a pilgrim and laboured for the sick, especially in Italy. He is invoked as a protector against pestilence. The Latin form of his name is Rochus, the Italian Rocco, the Spanish Roque. Scottish corruptions of the name are Rollock, Rollox and Seemirookie. He is depicted as a pilgrim with staff, hat, boots etc, often indicating a plague spot on his thigh. Sometimes a dog is with him, licking the spot.

Roch (Roque) Gonzalez
(Bl) M. SJ.   Nov 17
See Paraguay, Martyrs of.

Roderick (St) M.   March 13
Otherwise Rudericus, q.v.

Rodingus (Rouin) (St)
Ab. OSB.   Sept 17
d. c690 An Irish monk and priest who preached in Germany and entered the abbey of Tholey, near Trier. Distracted by the visits of his converts, he migrated to the forest of Argonne, where he became the abbot-founder of Wasloi, afterwards called Beaulieu. His cult is very ancient.

Rodolph or Rodulph
(several)
Otherwise Rudolph, q.v.

Rodrigo (St) M.   March 13
The Spanish form of Roderick or Rudericus, q.v.

Rogatian (St) M.   Feb 11
See under Saturninus, Dativus, etc.

Rogatian (St) M.   May 24
See Donatian and Rogatian.

St Roch, Aug 16

Rogatian and Felicissimus
(SS) MM?   Oct 26
d. 256   Rogatian, a priest, and Felicissimus, a layman, belonged to the church of Carthage. They are mentioned by St Cyprian as having "witnessed a good confession for Christ." These words are usually taken as referring to their martyrdom.

Rogatian (St) M.   Dec 28
See Castor, Victor and Rogatian.

Rogatus (St) M.   Jan 12
See Zoticus, Rogatus, etc.

Rogatus and Rogatus
(SS) MM.   March 8
See Cyril, Rogatus, etc.

**Rogatus, Successus
and Comp. (SS) MM.**   March 28
? A band of eighteen martyrs put to death in proconsular Africa.

Rogatus (St) M.   June 10
See Aresius, Rogatus, etc.

Rogatus (St) M.   Aug 17
See Liberatus, Boniface, etc.

Rogatus (St) M.   Dec 1
See Lucius, Rogatus, etc.

Rogellus and Servus-Dei
(SS) MM.   Sept 16
d. 852   A monk and his young disciple martyred at Cordoba for publicly denouncing Islam.

Roger of Ellant (Bl) Ab.
OSB. Cist.   Jan 4
d. 1160   An Englishman who joined the Cistercian order at Lorroyen-Berry, France, and in 1156 was chosen abbot of the new monastery of Ellant in the diocese of Reims.

Roger of Todi (Bl) C.
OFM.   Jan 28
d. 1237   Ruggiero da Todi was one of the early Franciscans, having been admitted to the order by St Francis himself, who appointed him spiritual director of the convent of Poor Clares at Rieti. He died at Todi. Cult confirmed by Benedict XIV.

Roger Lefort (Bl) Bp.   March 1
d. 1367   Son of the lord of Ternes in the Limousin. He became a jurist and while a subdeacon was chosen as bishop of Orleans (1321). In 1328 he was translated to Limoges and in 1343 to Bourges. He instituted a feast in honour of our Lady's conception. In his will he left all his property for the education of poor boys.

Roger Dickenson (Bl) M.   July 7
d. 1591   Born at Lincoln and educated at Reims, where he was ordained in 1583. He was hanged at Winchester together with Bl Ralph Milner, a man who had sheltered him. Beatified in 1929.

Roger James (Bl) M. OSB.   Nov 15
d. 1539   At the time of his death he was the youngest monk of the Glastonbury community, where he held the office of sacrist. He was executed with his abbot, Bl Richard Whiting, and a fellow monk, Bl John Thorne, on Tor Hill near Glastonbury under Henry VIII. Beatified in 1895.

Roland de' Medici (Bl) H.   Sept 15
d. 1386   A scion of the illustrious Florentine

family of that name. For twenty-six years he lived without any shelter in the forests of Parma. He died at Borgone. Cult confirmed in 1852.

Rollock, Rollox, Seemirookie (St) C.   Aug 16
Scottish variants of Roch (in the case of the third, of Saint-Roch), q.v.

Romana (St) V.   Feb 23
d. 324 A legendary Roman maiden who died at the age of eighteen while living as a solitary in a cave on the banks of the Tiber. She figures in the spurious life of Pope St Sylvester.

Romanus of Condat (St) Ab.   Feb 28
d. c 460 A Gallo-Roman who, at the age of thirty-five, went to live as a hermit in the Jura mountains, whither he was followed by his brother, St Lupicinus. Many disciples soon gathered round the two brothers, who thereupon founded the abbeys of Condat (later known as Saint-Oyend) and Leuconne, over which they ruled jointly, and the nunnery of La Beaume (afterwards St-Romain-de-la-Roche) presided over by their sister.

Romanus of Subiaco (St) Mk.   May 22
d. c 560 The monk, living in a community near Subiaco, who discovered the hermitage of the youthful St Benedict, when the latter first fled from the world, and bestowed on him the monastic habit and his daily food. There is no historical evidence of his having been an abbot, as was thought by some in the past.

Romanus (Boris) and David (Gleb)
See Boris and Gleb.

Romanus Ostiarius (St) M.   Aug 9
d. 258 The accounts we have of him are untrustworthy. His martyrdom was connected with that of St Laurence and he died about the same time. He may have been a doorkeeper; the pre-1970 RM. called him a soldier. All these are legends. Cult confined to local calendars since 1969.

Romanus of Nepi (St) Bp. M.   Aug 24
1st cent. A bishop-martyr of Nepi in Tuscany, said to have been a disciple of St Ptolemy (q.v.).

Romanus Aybara (Bl) M. Tert. OP.   Sept 8
d. 1628 A Japanese layman, father of Bl Paul Aybara, beheaded at Nagasaki. He was a Dominican tertiary. Beatified in 1867.

Romanus the Melodist (St) C.   Oct 1
d. c 540 A Syrian by origin, he became a deacon at Berytos and a priest at Constantinople. He is the greatest of the Greek hymnographers, about a thousand hymns being attributed to him. Some eighty of these have come down to us; not all may be by him. They are marked by poetic inspiration, depth of feeling and purity of style, and rank with the greatest literature of any other language or culture.

Romanus of Auxerre (St) Bp. M.   Oct 6
d. ? 564 An alleged bishop of Auxerre. His existence is doubtful.

Romanus of Rouen (St) Bp.   Oct 23
d. 639 A courtier of Clothaire II who became bishop of Rouen c 629. He devoted himself to the care of prisoners, particularly those condemned to death, and worked to expunge paganism from his diocese.

Romanus and Barulas (SS) MM.   Nov 18
d. 304 Romanus was a young deacon martyred at Antioch in Syria under Diocletian. His companion Barulas was described in the pre-1970 RM. as a young boy, but we know nothing authentic about him.

Romanus of Le Mans (St) C.   Nov 24
d. 385 A Gallo-Roman priest who converted the pagans at the mouth of the Gironde and died at Blaye. He seems to have exercised a special influence over sailors.

Romanus Matevoca (Bl) M.   Nov 27
d. 1619 A Japanese layman, born at Omura of the royal family of Firando. He was beheaded at Nagasaki with ten companions. Beatified in 1867.

Romanus (St) M.   Dec 9
See Samosata Martyrs.

Romaricus (St) Ab. OSB.   Dec 8
d. 653 A Merovingian nobleman converted by St Amatus. He was professed a monk at Luxeuil and founded on his estate the abbey of Habendum (afterwards called Remiremont, i.e. Romarici Mons), of which Amatus became the first abbot and Romaricus the second. The laus perennis was performed there by relays of seven choirs.

Rome (Martyrs of) (SS)
The pre-1970 RM. catalogued the following groups of martyrs who suffered at Rome:

Jan 1

d. *c* 304   Thirty soldiers martyred under Diocletian.

Jan 2

d. *c* 303   Many martyrs who suffered under Diocletian for refusing to give up the holy books.

Jan 13

d. 262   Forty soldiers who suffered on the Via Lavicana under Gallienus.

Feb 10

? 250   Ten soldiers martyred on the Via Lavicana.

March 1

d. 269   Two hundred and sixty martyrs condemned to dig sand on the Salarian Way and subsequently shot to death with arrows in the amphitheatre under Claudius II.

March 2

d. 219   A large number of martyrs put to death under Alexander Severus and the prefect Ulpian.

March 4

d. 260 (?)   A group of nine hundred martyrs buried in the catacombs of Callistus on the Appian Way, of whom no particulars are extant.

March 14

d. *c* 67   Forty-seven martyrs baptized by St Peter, according to an account which is not very trustworthy; they are said to have suffered under Nero on the same day. The details of the pre-1970 RM. are from the Acts of SS Processus and Martinian, which are regarded now as unreliable.

March 25

? A group of two hundred and sixty-two martyrs who seem to be identical with those of March 1.

Apr 10

d. *c* 115   A number of malefactors detained in the public jail and baptized by Pope St Alexander during his imprisonment there. They were taken to Ostia and put on board an old boat which was then sent out to sea and scuttled. This is a probably a fable: hardly anyting is known of Alexander's life and ministry.

June 17

? A group of two hundred and sixty-two martyrs stated to have suffered under Diocletian and buried on the old Via Salaria; they seem to be identical with those of March 1 and March 25.

(Pre-1970 RM. June 24) now June 30

This group has already been catalogued in this book under the heading "First Martyrs of the See of Rome".

July 2

c 68   Three soldiers who, according to the legend, were converted at the passion of St Paul and martyred.

Aug 5

d. 303   Twenty-three martyrs who suffered on the Salarian Way under Diocletian.

Aug 10

d. 274   One hundred and sixty-five martyrs put to death under Aurelian.

Oct 25

d. 269   Forty-six soldiers and one hundred and twenty-one civilians martyred under Claudius II.

Dec 22

d. *c* 303   A group of thirty martyrs who suffered under Diocletian and were buried on the Via Lavicana "between the two laurels."

Quite possibly there were many other similar groups. It is also likely that not all the data given are trustworthy. Nevertheless the old RM.'s description of Rome as "a fruitful field of martyrs" is historically very exact. The group celebrated on June 30 in the post-1970 Roman Calendar are certainly authentic q.v.

Romeo (Romaeus) (Bl)
C. OC.   March 4
d. 1380   An Italian Carmelite lay-brother, the companion of St Avertanus. Having set out together from Limoges on a pilgrimage to the Holy Land, both died, apparently from plague, at Lucca.

Romuald (St) Ab. OSB.
Founder   GC. June 19
c 951–1027   A native of Ravenna, of the ducal family of the Onesti. In his youth he saw his father commit a murder and resolved to atone for that crime by becoming a monk at the Benedictine abbey of Classe, near Ravenna. In 996 he was elected abbot of the monastery, but he resigned in 999 and from that time forward led a wandering life in central and northern Italy and the country of the Pyrenees, establishing hermitages and monasteries. The best known of these latter, which remains to this day, is that of Camaldoli near Arezzo (1009). The Camaldolese Benedictines combine the eremitical life of the Eastern type with the cenobitical monachism of the West. Romuald made repeated attempts to embark upon missionary work among the Slavs. He died on June 19. Feb 7 is the anniversary of the

translation of his uncorrupted body from Val di Castro, near Camaldoli, where he died, to Fabriano.

Romula, Redempta and Herundo (SS) VV. July 23

d. *c* 580 Three Roman maidens who lived an austere life of retirement and prayer near the church of St Mary Major. St Gregory the Great held them in high esteem.

Romulus (St) M. Feb 17

See Donatus, Secundian, etc.

Romulus (St) M. March 24

See Timolaus and Comp.

Romulus and Secundus (SS) MM. March 24

? Two brothers who suffered in proconsular Africa. In some MSS the name of Secundus appears as Secundulus.

Romulus (St) Ab. OSB. March 27

d. *c* 730 Abbot of St Baudilius near Nimes. About 720 he and his community fled before the invading Saracens and settled in a ruined monastery at Saissy-les-Bois in the Nivernais.

Romulus and Comp. (SS) MM. July 6

d. *c* 90 Said to have been appointed by St Peter first pastor of Fiesole and to have been martyred with several companions under Domitian.

Romulus (St) M. Sept 5

d. *c* 112 An official of the court of Trajan who, for remonstrating with the emperor on his cruelty to the Christians, was made to share their fate.

Romulus (St) Bp. Oct 13

d. *p.*641 A bishop of Genoa concerning whom we have no trustworthy documents. He died at Matuziano, a coast town on the Riviera, since called after him, San Remo.

Romulus and Conindrus (SS) Bps. Dec 28

d. *c* 450 Two of the first preachers of Christianity in the Isle of Man, contemporaries of St Patrick.

Ronald (St) M. Aug 20

d. 1158 A chieftain of Orkney who, in discharge of a vow, built the cathedral of St Magnus at Kirkwall. He was murdered by rebels and was venerated as a martyr at Kirkwall.

Ronan (St) June 1

? An early Celtic bishop of Cornish origin who worked there and in Brittany.

Roque (St) C. Aug 16

The Spanish form of Roch, q.v.

Rosalia (St) V. Sept 4 and July 15

d. ? 1160 According to the Sicilian tradition she was a girl of good family who became an anchoress in a cave on Mt Coschina, near Bivona, and later in a grotto on Mt Pellegrino, three miles from Palermo. Her alleged relics were found in 1624 and she was acclaimed the patron saint of Palermo.

Rose de Loye (Bl) M. OSB. July 6

See Mary Rose.

Rose Chrétien (Bl) M. OC. July 17

1741–1794 A native of Evreux who married very young and, on being left a widow, entered the Carmel of Compiègne, taking the name of Soeur Julie-Louise. She was guillotined at Paris with her community. See Carmelite Nuns of Compiègne.

Rose of Lima (St) V. Tert. OP. GC. Aug 23

1586–1617 Born of Spanish parents at Lima in Peru. From childhood her life was a replica of that of St Catherine of Siena. She lived in her own home as a Dominican tertiary and, like her model, was favoured with extraordinary mystical gifts. She practised extraordinary austerities and had mental as well as physical sufferings. She is the first American born to have been canonized (1671) and is venerated as the patron saint of S. America. She is depicted habited as a Dominican tertiary, carrying roses, and often the Holy Infant.

Rose of Viterbo (St) V. Sept 4

1234–1252 Born at Viterbo of poor parents. She had the highest spiritual gifts from earliest years and used to preach in the streets against the Ghibellines and in favour of the pope. She sought admittance to the convent of Poor Clares and was repeatedly refused. After her death, however, her body was, by order of Pope Alexander IV (1258), laid to rest in that convent. Canonized in 1457.

Rose-Philippine Duchesne (St) V. Nov 17

1769–1852 Born at Grenoble, she joined the Visitation nuns. When these were scattered during the Reign of Terror she stayed with her family at Grenoble and, in spite of the difficult times, gathered together a community there. In 1804, at the suggestion of St Magdalen Sophie Barat, she incorporated her community into the Society of the Sacred Heart. Her life's desire was to work in the

St Rose of Lima, Aug 23

missions, and in 1818 she landed at New Orleans and set up a missionary centre at St Charles, Missouri. In the teeth of many difficulties she founded six more mission stations and went herself to work among the Pottowatomies at Sugar Creek. Later she worked in the Rocky Mountain mission area. In her old age she returned to St Charles to die. Beatified in 1940. Canonized in 1988.

Rose Elizabeth (St) Abs. OSB.   Dec 13
See Elizabeth Rose.

Roseline de Villeneuve (Bl) V. O. Cart.   Jan 17
d. 1329 A Carthusian nun of noble family who became prioress of Celle Roubaud in Provence. She was favoured with frequent visions and other mystical phenomena. Cult confirmed in 1851.

Rosendo (St) Bp. OSB.   March 1
The Spanish form of Rudesind, q.v.

Rosius (St)   Sept 1
See Priscus, Castrensis, etc.

Rosula (St) M.   Sept 14
See Crescentian, Victor, etc.

Roswinda (St) N. OSB.   Dec 13
See Einhildis and Roswinda.

Rotrudis (St) V.   June 22
d. c 869 A saint whose relics were

enshrined at the Benedictine abbey of Saint-Bertin at Saint-Omer. According to popular belief she was a daughter, or sister, of Charlemagne.

Rouin (St) Ab.   Sept 17
Otherwise Rodingus, q.v.

Ruadan (Ruadhan, Rodan) (St) Ab.   Apr 15
d. 584 One of the leading disciples of St Finian of Clonard and abbot-founder of the monastery of Lothra in Ireland. Little can definitely be known about him.

Rudericus (Roderick) and Salomon (Solomon) (SS) MM.   March 13
d. 857 Roderick was a priest at Cabra, near Cordoba, who was betrayed by his Muslim brother and imprisoned there. In prison he met his fellow-martyr, Salomon. They were both martyred at Cordoba.

Rudesind (Rosendo) (St) Bp. OSB.   March 1
907–977 Born of a noble family in Spanish Galicia, he became bishop of Mondoñedo (the ancient *Dumium*) at the age of eighteen. Shortly after he replaced an unworthy bishop as administrator of the see of Compostella. In this capacity he opposed with equal success the depredations of the Normans and the Saracens. Driven from Compostella by the ex-bishop, he founded the abbey of Celanova and became a monk there. He built further monasteries, imposing on these, as well as on others already founded, the strict observance of the rule of St Benedict. He was elected second abbot of Celanova, where he died. Canonized in 1195.

Rudolph Acquaviva and Comp. (BB) MM. SJ.   July 27
d. 1583 (July 25) Rudolph was born at Atri in 1550 and was a nephew of Claudio Acquaviva, fifth general of the Jesuits. He too became a Jesuit and was sent to the Jesuit missions in the East Indies. He was martyred on the peninsula of Salsette, near Goa, with four companions. Beatified in 1893.

Rudolph (Bl) Ab. OSB. Vall.   Aug 1
d. 1076 Guest master under St John Gualbert, he succeeded him as abbot general on his death. Cult recognized in 1602.

Rudolph of Gubbio (St) Bp. OSB.   Oct 17
d. c 1066 A monk of Fontavellana under St Peter Damian. In 1061, while still very young,

he was appointed bishop of Gubbio. He is described as a miracle of unselfishness.

Ruellinus (Ruellin) (St) Bp.   Feb 28
6th cent.   Successor of St Tudwal in the see of Tréguier in Brittany.

Ruffinus (St) M.   July 24
See Wulfhade and Ruffinus.

Rufillus (Ruffilius) (St) Bp.   July 18
d. 382   The alleged first bishop of Forlim-popoli (*Forum Pompilii*) in Emilia.

Rufina, Moderata, Romana, Secundus and Seven Companions (SS)
MM.   Apr 6
? 4th cent.   Martyrs allegedly at Sirmium, Pannonia.

Rufina and Secunda (SS)
VV. MM.   July 10
d. 257   Two Roman maidens martyred under Valerian and buried at Santa Rufina on the Aurelian Way. Their later Acts are apocryphal.

Rufina (St) VM.   July 19
See Justa and Rufina.

Rufina (St) M.   Aug 31
See Theodotus, Rufina and Ammia.

Rufinian (St) M.   Sept 9
See Rufinus and Rufinian.

Rufinus (St) M.   Feb 28
See Macarius, Rufinus, etc.

Rufinus (St) M.   Apr 7
See Epiphanius, Donatus, etc.

Rufinus (St) M.   June 14
See Valerius and Rufinus.

Rufinus and Martia (SS)
MM.   June 21
? Martyrs in one of the early persecutions at Syracuse.

Rufinus and Secundus (SS)   July 10
Nothing is known of these early martyrs except their burial on the Via Cornelia, at the eleventh milestone from the city. In the twelfth century their relics were translated to the Lateran basilica. Since 1969 their cult has been confined to local calendars.

Rufinus (St) M.   July 30
? A martyr in one of the early persecutions at Assisi.

Rufinus and Comp. (SS)
MM.   Aug 11
? Rufinus is described in the pre-1970 RM. as "bishop of the Marsi." Probably he is identical with St Rufinus of Assisi (July 30). Of his companions nothing is known.

Rufinus (St)   Aug 19
? A saint, probably a priest, venerated at Mantua from early times.

Rufinus (St)   Aug 26
5th cent.   A bishop of Capua, whose relics are enshrined in the cathedral of that city.

Rufinus, Silvanus and Victalicus (SS) MM.   Sept 4
? Three children who formed part of a large group of martyrs put to death at Ancyra in Galatia.

Rufinus and Rufinian (SS)
MM.   Sept 9
? Two brothers martyred at a time and place unknown.

Rufinus, Mark, Valerius and Comp. (SS) MM.   Nov 16
? African martyrs.

Rufus of Melitene (St) M.   Apr 19
See Hermogenes, Gaius, etc.

Rufus (St) H.   Apr 2
? A hermit at Glendalough, where he was buried. Some writers call him a bishop.

Rufus (St) M.   Aug 1
See Cyril, Aquila, etc.

Rufus of Capua (St) M.   Aug 27
? The pre-1970 RM. made him bishop of Capua and disciple of St Apollinaris of Ravenna. He is however to be identified with the St Rufus commemorated with St Carpophorus (see below). This Rufus was not a bishop. (See Rufinus: Aug 26.)

Rufus and Carpophorus (SS) MM.   Aug 27
d. 295   Martyrs of Capua under Diocletian. According to the untrustworthy Acts Rufus was a deacon. Of Carpophorus (the MS has Carpone) nothing is known. Rufus was not a disciple of St Apollinaris. Nothing, in fact, is known of their lives.

Rufus (St) M.   Sept 25
See Paul, Tatta, etc.

Rufus of Metz (St) Bp.   Nov 7
d. c 400   An early bishop of Metz. He was bishop for about twenty-nine years. He is perhaps identical with the Rufus of Metz mentioned c 386 in connection within the Priscillianist controversy.

Rufus of Avignon (St) Bp. Nov 12
d. c 200 Venerated as the first bishop of Avignon. He certainly existed, but the biographies we have of him are quite unhistorical.

Rufus of Rome (St) Bp.(?) Nov 21
d. c 90 The disciple whom St Paul greets in Rom. 16:13. Some identify him with the son of Simon of Cyrene mentioned in Mark 15:21. A later tradition makes him a bishop in the East.

Rufus and Comp. (SS)
MM. Nov 28
d. 304 A Roman citizen who was martyred with his entire household under Diocletian.

Rufus and Zosimus (SS)
MM. Dec 18
d. c 107 Citizens of Philippi brought to Rome with St Ignatius of Antioch and thrown to the beasts in the Roman amphitheatre two days before the latter's martyrdom.

Rule (St) Ab. March 30
Otherwise Regulus, q.v.

Rumoldus (Rumbold, Rombauld) (St) Bp. M.
OSB. June 24
d. c 775 A monk, probably of an Anglo-Saxon abbey, who became a regionary bishop and worked under St Willibrord in Holland and Brabant. He was murdered near Malines. He is now the patron saint of Malines cathedral. The pre-1970 RM. and later legends say that he was of Irish descent and bishop of Dublin.

Rumon (St) Bp. June 1
6th cent.? A bishop who is patron of Tavistock and various other West country places. Nothing is known of him now, but early martyrologies supply fabulous details, confusing him with the other saints called Ronan, Ruadan etc.

Rumwold (St) C. Aug 28
d. c 650 Said to have been a three-days' old infant, prince of Northumbria who, immediately after baptism, pronounced aloud the profession of faith and then died. He was at one time honoured with a cult, chiefly in Northants and Bucks. This extraordinary fiction persisted as a popular cult for centuries.

Rupert (Hrodbert, Robert) (St) Bp. OSB. March 27
d. c 717 He seems to have been of French descent. Having been appointed bishop of Worms, he set himself to spread Christianity in S. Germany. He started operations at Regensburg and pushed his way along the Danube. The Duke of Bavaria gave him the old ruined town of Iuvavum, which Rupert rebuilt and called Salzburg. Here he founded the abbey of St Peter, with school and church attached, and also the nunnery of Nonnberg, over which he placed his sister Erentrudis. He is venerated as the first archbishop-abbot of Salzburg and as the apostle of Bavaria and Austria.

Rupert and Bertha (SS) May 15
9th cent. A hermit who lived with his mother Bertha on a hill near Bingen. The hill has been since called after him, Rupertsberg. During the twelfth century St Hildegard greatly fostered the cult of both saints.

Rupert (Bl) Ab. OSB. Aug 15
d. 1145 He was prior of St George's abbey in the Black Forest when (1102) he was asked to become abbot of Ottobeuren in Bavaria. He accepted, and during the forty-three years of his abbacy Ottobeuren attained great prosperity and influence. He introduced there the Cluny-Hirschau customary.

Rustica (St) M. Dec 31
See Donata, Paulina, etc.

Rusticus (Bl) Ab. OSB. March 12
d. 1092 A monk of Vallumbrosa who was chosen third abbot general of the congregation in 1076. His relics were enshrined in 1200.

Rusticus (St) M. Aug 9
? 4th cent. Martyr of Sirmium, Pannonia.

Rusticus of Verona (St) M. Aug 9
See Firmus and Rusticus.

Rusticus (St) M. Aug 17
See Liberatus, Boniface, etc.

Rusticus (St) Bp. Sept 24
d. 446 Bishop of Clermont in Auvergne 426–446.

Rusticus (St) M. Oct 9
See Dionysius, Rusticus and Eleutherius.

Rusticus (St) Bp. Oct 14
d. 574 Bishop of Trier. Accused of sexual impurity by St Goar, he resigned and retired to the hermitage of the same St Goar.

Rusticus (St) Bp. Oct 26
d. c 462 A monk of Lérins who was later bishop of Narbonne. He was present at the council of Ephesus in 431.

Rutilius (St) M. Aug 2
d. 250 A native of proconsular Africa. During the persecution of Decius he fled from place to place and even paid money to obtain exemption from sacrifice, but he was at last arrested and bravely confessed Christ. The story is given by Tertullian (*De fuga in persecutione*).

Rutilus and Comp. (SS)
MM.   June 4
? Martyrs at Sabaria in Pannonia (Sabar in
modern Hungary).

Rutulus (St)   Feb 18
See Lucius, Silvanus, etc.

Sabas (St) M.   Jan 14
See Isaias, Sabas, etc.

Sabas (Sabbas) and Comp. (SS) MM.   Apr 12
d. 372 A Goth who held the office of lector in a local church of what is now Rumania. He was captured by heathen Gothic soldiers, and on refusing to eat food which had been sacrificed to idols, was tortured to death and thrown into the river Mussovo at a spot near Tirgovist. Several others suffered with him. He is greatly venerated in the East.

Sabas and Comp. (SS) MM.   Apr 24
d. 272 A Christian officer of Gothic descent martyred with seventy companions at Rome under Aurelian. Some writers identify him with his namesake of Apr 12.

Sabas (St) C.   July 17
See Seven Apostles of Bulgaria.

Sabbas (St) Ab.   Dec 5
439–532 A Cappadocian who, at a very early age, fled to Palestine, where for many years he lived a hermit's life in various places. He eventually founded a laura (Mar Saba, which still flourishes) in the mountainous desert of Judaea between Jerusalem and the Dead Sea. He was appointed archimandrite over all the Palestinian houses and in that capacity played a prominent part in the campaign against the Eutychian heresy. He is regarded as one of the founders of Eastern monasticism. His uncorrupt body which was enshrined in Rome for many centuries was returned to Mar Saba after the Second Vatican Council as an ecumenical gesture. Cult confined to local calendars since 1969.

Sabbatius (St) M.   Sept 19
See Trophimus, Sabbatius, and Dorymedon.

Sabel (St) M.   June 17
See Manuel, Sabel and Ismael.

Sabina (St) M.   Aug 29
? The famous basilica on the Aventine is dedicated to her. She was probably a wealthy lady who founded it in the third or fourth century, not as her Passion asserts, a Roman martyr. Nothing is known about her. Her name occurs in the eucharistic prayer of the Ambrosian liturgy. Her church in Rome is of outstanding beauty. Cult confined to her basilica since 1969.

Sabina (St) V.   Aug 29
d. ? 275 The alleged sister of St Sabinian of Troyes, where she is venerated together with the latter. The martyrologist Usuard placed her on this date.

Sabina (St) M.   Oct 27
See Vincent, Sabina and Christeta.

Sabinian (French: Savinien) (St) M.   Jan 29
d. ? 275 A martyr honoured at Troyes in France as having suffered there in one of the early persecutions (under Aurelian?). The French tradition claims that he was a native of Samos from whence, with his sister St Sabina, he fled to Gaul.

Sabinian (St) M.   June 7
See Peter, Wallabonsus, etc.

Sabinian (St) M.   Aug 27 and Sept 1
See Honoratus, Fortunatus, etc.

Sabinian (St) M.   Sept 25
See Paul, Tatta, etc.

Sabinian (St) Ab. OSB.   Nov 22
d. c 720 (or c 770?) Third abbot of Moutier-Saint-Chaffre (Ménat).

Sabinian and Potentian (SS) MM.   Dec 31
d. c 300 Sabinian is honoured as the first bishop of Sens. Potentian was perhaps his successor. Both were martyred and are now venerated as the patron saints of the diocese of Sens. The legend that they were immediate disciples of St Peter is now discarded.

Sabinus (St) M.   Jan 25
See Donatus, Sabinus and Agape.

Sabinus (St) Bp.   Feb 9
d. c 566 Bishop of Canosa (the ancient Canusium, now destroyed) in Apulia and a friend of St Benedict. Pope St Agapitus I entrusted him with an embassy (535–536) to

the emperor Justinian. He is the patron saint of Bari, where his relics are now enshrined.

Sabinus (St) M. March 13
d. 287   An Egyptian of noble birth, martyred by drowning in the Nile under Diocletian.

Sabinus (St) July 11
d. 5th cent.   A saint venerated in the neighbourhood of Poitiers. He is said to have been a disciple of St Germanus of Auxerre. The local tradition considers him a martyr.

Sabinus (Savinus) and Cyprian (SS) MM. July 11
?   Two martyrs, brothers, venerated at Brescia in Italy, but probably the *Brixia* of the pre-1970 RM. refers to La Bresse in Poitou, where these two saints are also venerated.

Sabinus, Julian, Maximus, Macrobius, Cassia, Paula and ten Comp. (SS) MM. July 20
?   A group of Syrians put to death for the faith at Damascus.

Sabinus (French: Savin) (St) H. Oct 9
d. *c*? 820   Venerated as one of the apostles of the Lavedan, a district of the Pyrenees. He is said to have been born at Barcelona, educated at Poitiers, professed as a Benedictine at Ligugé, and finally to have become a hermit. All these statements are very doubtful.

Sabinus (St) Bp. Oct 15
d. *c* 760   Bishop of Catania in Sicily. After a few years as bishop he resigned and became a hermit.

Sabinus (St) Bp. Dec 11
d. 420   Bishop of Piacenza and a close friend of St Ambrose, who used to send him his writings for revision and approval. While a deacon he was sent by Pope St Damascus to settle the Meletian schism at Antioch.

Sabinus, Exuperantius, Marcellus, Venustian and Comp. (SS) MM. Dec 30
d. 303   Sabinus is described as a bishop who was martyred near Spoleto. His see is unknown, but Faenza, Assisi, Spoleto and Chiusi each claim him. Venustian and his family were converts of Sabinus, while Exuperantius and Marcellus are said to have been his deacons.

Sacer (Mo-Sacra) (St) Ab. March 3
7th cent.   An Irish saint, abbot-founder of the monastery of Saggard, Dublin.

Sacerdos (Sardot, Sadroc, Sardou, Serdon, Serdot) (St) Bp. OSB. May 4
670–*c* 720   Born in the neighbourhood of Sarlat in Périgord, he became a monk and eventually the abbot-founder of Calabre (*Calabrum*, Calviat). He was appointed bishop of Limoges, resigning his see shortly before his death.

Sacerdos (St) Bp. May 5
d. *c* 560   A Spanish saint venerated at Murviedro (the ancient Saguntum), and said to have been bishop of that city.

Sacerdos (St) Bp. Sept 12
d. 551   Bishop of Lyons 544–551 and adviser of King Childebert. He presided at the council of Orleans in 549.

Sadoc and Comp. (BB) MM. OP. June 2 or May 5
d. 1260   Sadoc was received into the Dominican order by St Dominic himself and sent to Hungary. Later he passed on to Poland, where he founded a house at Sandomir and became its prior. When the town was pillaged by the Tartars, Sadoc and his forty-nine friars were butchered while singing the Salve Regina.

Sadoth (Sadosh, Schadost) and Comp. (SS) MM. Feb 20
d. 345 (or 342)   Sadoth was the metropolitan of Seleucia-Ctesiphon in Persia. He, with one hundred and twenty-eight other Christians, was arrested in the persecution of Shapur II. Most of thse were martyred at once, but Sadoth, with eight companions, was detained for five months in a filthy prison at Bei-Lapat before being executed.

Sadwrn (Sadwen) (St) C. Nov 29
6th cent.   Brother of St Illtyd and disciple of St Cadfan. Some Welsh churches are dedicated to him. He has been confused with St Saturninus (Nov 29).

Saethryth (Sethrida) (St) Abs. OSB. Jan 10
d. *c* 660   Stepdaughter of Anna, king of the East Angles (635–644). She became a nun at Faremoutier-en-Brie under St Fara, whom she succeeded as abbess. She was half-sister to SS Ethelreda and Ethelburga.

Sagar (St) Bp. M. Oct 6
d. *c* 175   Bishop of Laodicea in Phrygia, put to death under Marcus Aurelius. It is impossible to accept the tradition that he was a disciple of St Paul.

Sair (St) Bp. July 1
Otherwise Servan, q.v.

Salaberga (St) Abs. Sept 22
d. *c* 665   As a child she was held to have been

cured of blindness by St Eustace of Lisieux. She married very young, and her husband died after two months. Her second husband was St Blandinus, to whom she bore five children, two of whom are venerated as saints. In later years husband and wife decided to become cloistered religious. Salaberga entered the nunnery of Poulangey and was subsequently the foundress of St John the Baptist at Laon, where she died.

Salaun (Salomon) (St) C.   Nov 1
d. 1358   A poor man of Leseven in Brittany. Content to be despised and considered "a fool for Christ's sake," he reached a high degree of contemplation. He is venerated at N.D. de Folgoet in Brittany.

Sallustia (St) M.   Sept 14
See Caerealis and Sallustia.

Sallustian (St)   June 8
? A saint honoured in Sardinia from time immemorial. In some martyrologies he is described as a martyr, in others as a hermit.

Salome and Judith (SS)
OSB.   June 29
9th cent.   Salome is said to have been an Anglo-Saxon princess, exiled from her native country. She was befriended by a pious Bavarian widow named Judith. Both became anchoresses under the obedience of the Benedictine abbey of Oberaltaich.

Salome (St)   Oct 22
See Mary Salome.

Salomea (Bl) W. Poor
Clare.   Nov 17
c 1219–1268   Daughter of Prince Lesko of Poland. At the age of three she was betrothed to Prince Coloman of Hungary and was left a widow before her 23rd year in 1241. She founded the convent of Poor Clares at Zawichost, later removed to Skala, where she became a nun and ended her days. Beatified in 1673.

Salomon (St) M.   March 13
See Rudericus and Salomon.

Salonius (St) Bp.   Sept 28
Otherwise Solomon, q.v.

Salutaris (St) M.   July 13
See Eugene, Salutaris, etc.

Salvator of Horta (St) C.
OFM.   March 18
1520–1567   Born at Santa Columba, diocese of Gerona, Spain, he was a shoemaker by trade before he joined the Franciscans as a lay-brother at Barcelona. He spent most of his life as cook of the friary of Horta, near Tortosa.

He died at the friary of Cagliari in Sardinia. Canonized in 1940.

Salvinus (St) Bp.   Sept 4
d. c 420   Third   bishop   of   Verdun (c 383–420).

Salvinus (St) Bp.   Oct 12
d. 562   Bishop of Verona. His relics are enshrined in the church of St Stephen in that city.

Salvius (Salve, Sauve) (St)
Bp.   Jan 12
d. c 625   Bishop of Amiens. There is no reason to suppose that he was a martyr as stated in the pre-1970 RM. He has been confused with other saints of the same name. His relics were enshrined at Montreuil in Picardy.

Salvius (St) M.   Jan 11
? A martyr in proconsular Africa.

Salvius (Bl) Ab. OSB.   Feb 10
d. 962   Benedictine abbot of Albelda in N. Spain. He was a prudent adviser at the courts of Navarre and Castile at the time of the Reconquest.

Salvius and Superius
(SS) MM.   June 26
d. c 768   Salvius was a regionary bishop in the district of Angoulême, who sent to Valenciennes to evangelize the Flemish. The cupidity of a baron led to his death, and with a companion he was hastily interred. When the bodies were discovered the anonymous companion was found first (*Superius*).

Salvius (St) Bp.   Sept 10
d. 584   A lawyer who became a monk and abbot, then a hermit and finally bishop of Albi (574–584). He died while tending the sick during an epidemic which was ravaging his diocese.

Salvius (French: Saire)
(St) H.   Oct 28
6th cent.   A hermit at the place now called after him Saint-Saire in Normandy. Some writers identify him with Salvius of Albi.

Samonas (St) M.   Nov 15
See Gurias and Samonas.

Samosata, The Seven
Martyrs of (SS)   Dec 9
d. c 311   Their names were: Hipparchus and Philotheus, magistrates, and their converts James, Paragrus, Abibus, Romanus and Lollian. They were crucified at Samosata on the Euphrates for refusing to join in the public

rejoicing, including pagan rites, after Maximinus's victory over the Persians.

Samson (Sampson) (St) C.   June 27
d. *c* 530   Surnamed "the Hospitable" (Xenodochius). He was a distinguished citizen of Constantinople who studied medicine and was ordained in order to devote his life to the spiritual and physical care of the sick and destitute. He founded and equipped a magnificent hospital near St Sophia.

Samson (Sampson) (St) Bp.   July 28
c 490–*c* 565   Born in Wales, he became a disciple of St Illtyd at Llantwit Major, S. Glamorgan, and then for a time was monk and abbot of the monastery on Caldey Island. He left Caldey and visited Ireland: then, on his return to England, he sojourned in Cornwall and was ordained bishop by St Dubricius. Finally he crossed over to Brittany and spent the rest of life evangelizing that country, fixing his central residence at a monastery at Dol, although no permanent see was established there for many centuries to come. His name is still held in benediction throughout Brittany and Wales. He is indeed one of the greatest missionaries Britain has ever produced, and certainly the greatest of his century.

Samthan (St) V.   Dec 18
6th cent.   An Irish saint, abbess-foundress of Clonbroney in Co. Longford.

Samuel (St) M.   Feb 16
See Elias, Jeremiah, etc.

Samuel of Edessa (St)   Aug 9
d. *p.*496   He is mentioned by Gennadius in his work on ecclesiastical authors. Samuel wrote in Syriac against the Nestorians, Eutychians and Timotheans.

Samuel (St) Prophet   Aug 20
11th cent. B.C.   The first book of Kings, often for this reason called the first book of Samuel, contains the history of the prophet, the wonders of his birth and childhood (1–2); his judgeship of Israel (4–7); his anointing of Saul as king (8–10); his replacing of Saul by David (16); and his death (25).

Samuel (St) M.   Oct 10
See Daniel, Samuel, etc.

Sancha (Sanctia) (Bl) V. OSB.   March 13
c 1180–1229   Daughter of King Sancho I of Portugal, sister of BB Teresa and Mafalda. She helped the first Franciscan and Dominican foundations in Portugal and afterwards (1223) joined the Cistercians at Cellas. Cult approved in 1705.

Sancho (Sanctius, Sancius) (St) M.   June 5
d. 851   Born at Albi in France, he was brought to Cordoba as a prisoner of war, educated at the Moorish court there, and enrolled in the guards of the Emir. He was martyred by impalement on refusing to embrace Islam.

Sanctan (St) Bp.   May 9
6th cent.   Bishop of the Irish sees of Kill-da-Les and Kill-na-Sanctan (Dublin). He was probably of British birth.

Sanctes Brancasino (Bl) C. OFM.   Aug 14
d. 1390   Born at Monte Fabri, diocese of Urbino, he became a Franciscan lay-brother at Scotamento, where he spent most of his life. Cult approved by Clement XIV.

Sanctes of Cori (Bl) C. OSA.   Oct 5
d. 1392   A native of Cori, diocese of Velletri, who joined the Augustinians and became famous as a zealous missioner. Cult approved by Leo XIII.

Sanctian (St) M.   Sept 6
See Augustine, Sanctian and Beata.

Sanctinus (St) Bp.   Sept 22
d. *c* 300   Alleged to have been the first bishop of Meux and a disciple of St Dionysius of Paris. He is probably to be identified with a St Sanctinus claimed by the diocese of Verdun.

Sanctus (Sanctius) (St) M.   June 2
See Photinus (Pothinus), Sanctus, etc.

Sandila (Sandalus, Sandolus, Sandulf) (St) M.   Sept 3
d. *c* 855   A Spanish martyr of Cordoba under the Moorish domination.

Sandratus (Sandradus) (St) Ab. OSB.   Aug 24
d. 986   Monk of the abbey of St Maximinus at Trier. In 972 he was sent by the emperor Otto I to restore monastic observance at St Gall. Shortly after he was made abbot of Gladbach, and in 981 also abbot of Weissenburg. He died at Gladbach.

Santuccia Terrebotti (Bl) W. OSB.   March 21
d. 1305   Born at Gubbio in Umbria, she married and bore a daughter who died young. Santuccia and her husband then decided to enter religion. She became a Benedictine at Gubbio and was later abbess. Under her the community migrated to Santa Maria in Via

Lata, on the Julian Way, Rome, where they continued to live the Benedictine life, though usually called the Servants of Mary. The people nicknamed them Le Santuccie.

Sapientia (St) W. Sept 30
Otherwise Sophia, q.v.

Sapor (Shapur), Isaac and Comp. (SS) MM. Nov 30
d. 339 A band of Persian martyrs under Shapur II. Sapor and Isaac were bishops: the former died in prison, the latter was stoned to death. SS Mahanes, Abraham and Simeon suffered at the same time.

Saragossa, The Eighteen Martyrs of, viz. Optatus, Lupercus, Successus, Martial, Urban, Julia, Quintilian, Publius, Fronto, Felix, Caecilian, Eventius, Primitivus, Apodemius, and four named Saturninus (SS) Apr 16
d. *c* 304 Martyrs of Saragossa in Spain under the emperor Diocletian and the prefect Dacian. Prudentius, who lived at Saragossa a lifetime later, describes their martyrdom.

Saragossa, The Innumerable Martyrs of (SS) Nov 3
d. *c* 304 An exceedingly large number of martyrs put to death at Saragossa under Diocletian by the savage prefect Dacian, who had been sent to Spain to enforce the decrees. He published an edict banishing all Christians from the city, and while they were leaving he ordered the soldiers to fall upon and massacre them. Eighteen of them are mentioned by Prudentius and received a special notice in the pre-1970 RM. on April 16.

Sardon (St) Bp. May 4
Otherwise Sacerdos, q.v.

Sarmata (St) M. Oct 11
d. 357 An Egyptian disciple of St Antony, murdered in his monastery by a band of marauding Bedouins and venerated as a martyr.

Sator (St) M. Aug 29
See Vitalis, Sator and Repositus.

Saturian (St) M. Oct 16
See Martinian, Saturian, etc.

Saturnina (St) VM. June 4
? A maiden said to have come from Germany into the neighbourhood of Arras and there to have met her death in defending herself against an assault on her virginity. The story is now held to be a romance.

Saturninus (St) M. Jan 19
See Paul, Gerontius, etc.

Saturninus, Thyrsus and Victor (SS) MM. Jan 31
d. *c*? 250 Egyptians martyred at Alexandria.

Saturninus, Theophilus and Revocata (SS) MM. Feb 6
? A group of martyrs concerning whom neither place nor date of martyrdom is known.

Saturninus, Dativus, Felix, Ampelius and Comp. (SS) MM. Feb 11
d. 304 A group of forty-six martyrs of Albitina in Africa. They were arrested at the eucharist and sent to Carthage for examination. Saturninus was a priest, and with him suffered his four children, viz., Saturninus and Felix, lectors; Mary, a virgin; and Hilarion, a young child. Dativus and another Felix were senators. Other names from this group which have come down to us are: Thelica, Ampelius, Emeritus, Rogatian and Victoria, a maiden of undaunted courage. The child Hilarion, when threatened by the magistrates while his companions were being tortured, replied: "Yes, torture me too; anyhow, I am a Christian". They all appear to have died in prison. Their Acts bear the stamp of authenticity.

Saturninus, Castulus, Magnus and Lucius (SS) MM. Feb 15
d. 273 These martyrs belonged to the flock of St Valentine, bishop of Terni in Italy. They were buried at Passae (Rocca San Zenone).

Saturninus (St) M. March 7
See Perpetua, Felicitas, etc.

Saturninus and Comp. (SS) MM. March 22
? A group of ten martyrs of N.W. Africa.

Saturninus (St) Bp. Apr 7
4th cent. Bishop of Verona. No details of his career are extant.

Saturninus (SS) MM. Apr 16
Four of the same name among the group of Saragossa martyrs, q.v.

Saturninus (St) M. Apr 29
See Corfu, Martyrs of.

Saturninus, Neopolus, Germanus and Celestine (SS) MM. May 2
d. 304 Saturninus was martyred at Alexandria under Diocletian, not at Rome as stated in the pre-1970 RM. Of the others nothing is known.

Saturninus (St) M.   July 7
See Peregrinus, Lucian, etc.

Saturninus (St) M.   Aug 22
See Martial, Saturninus, etc.

Saturninus (St) M.   Oct 6
See Marcellus, Castus, etc.

Saturninus and Lupus
(SS) MM.   Oct 14
? Martyrs at Caesarea in Cappadocia.

Saturninus, Nereus and
Comp. (SS) MM.   Oct 16
d. c 450 A band of some three hundred and
sixty-five martyrs who suffered in proconsular
Africa under the Vandal king Genseric. Some
authorities maintain that this is merely a
second listing of the band of martyrs led by SS
Martinian and Saturian, q.v.

Saturninus (St) M.   Oct 30
d. 303 A martyr of Cagliari, in Sardinia,
under Diocletian. According to his untrustworthy Acts he was beheaded during a pagan
festival of Jupiter.

Saturninus (St) M.   Nov 27
See Basileus, Auxilius and Saturninus.

Saturninus and Sisinius
(SS) MM.   Nov 29
d. ? 309 According to legend Saturninus
was a Roman priest, though by birth, it is said,
a Carthaginian. He and his deacon Sisinius
were sentenced to hard labour and subsequently martyred. They were buried in the
cemetery of St Thraso on the Salarian Way.
They have no connection with SS Cyriacus,
Largus and Smaragdus, as has been alleged.
All that is known for sure is that Saturninus
was an early martyr buried along the Salerian
Way on this date. Cult confined to local
calendars since 1969.

Saturninus (French:
Sernin) (St) Bp. M.   Nov 29
d. c 257 A missionary from Rome who
evangelized the district round Pampeluna in
Spanish Navarre, and then the territory and
city of Toulouse. He is venerated as the first
bishop of Toulouse. He is said to have been
martyred in the persecution of Valerian by
being fastened behind a wild bull which
dragged him about until he was dashed to
pieces.

Saturninus (St) C.   Nov 29
Otherwise Sadwen, q.v.

Saturninus (St) M.   Dec 15
See Irenaeus, Antony, etc.

Saturninus (St) M.   Dec 23
See Theodulus, Saturninus, etc.

Saturninus (St) M.   Dec 29
See Dominic, Victor, etc.

Saturus (St) M.   March 7
See Perpetua, Felicitas, etc.

Saturus (St) M.   March 29
See Armogastes and Comp.

Saturus (several)
Otherwise Satyrus, q.v.

Satyrus (St) M.   Jan 12
d. ? An Arab by birth, who was martyred in
Achaia (or at Antioch) for insulting an idol.
Another version says that the idol fell to the
ground when Satyrus made the sign of the
cross over it. There is complete confusion in
the sources.

Satyrus (St) C.   Sept 17
d. c 376 The elder brother of St Ambrose of
Milan. As a lawyer he undertook the administration of the temporal affairs of his brother's
household. His high sense of justice, his
integrity and his generosity are eulogized by
Ambrose in the funeral sermon "On the death
of a brother".

Saula (St) VM.   Oct 20
See Martha, Saula and Comp.

Sauman (Saumay) (St) H.   June 14
Otherwise Psalmodius, q.v.

Sauve (St) Bp.   Sept 10
Otherwise Salvius, q.v.

Sava (Sabas) (St) Bp.   Jan 14
1176–1235 Rastno, youngest son of
Stephen Nemanya, king of Serbia, became a
monk at Mt Athos, where he received the
name of Sabas (in Slavonic, Sava) and followed the observance till nearly sixty years of
age. He founded along with his father, by then
a monk also, the monastery of Chilandari, for
fellow Serbs. He was then appointed archbishop of Serbia and managed the ecclesiastical affairs of that kingdom with tact and skill.
He promoted education and constructed many
churches.

Savina (St) Matron   Jan 30
d. 311 A woman of Milan who, during the
persecution of Diocletian, busied herself in
ministering to the martyrs in prison and in
interring their bodies after execution. According to her legend she died while praying at the
tomb of SS Nabor and Felix.

Savinian (Savinien) (several)
Otherwise Sabinian, q.v.

Savinus (*several*)
Otherwise Sabinus, q.v.

Savinus (Bl) H. OSB. Cam.   May 19
See Bellatanus, Savinus.

Sawl (St) C.   Jan 15
6th cent. A Welsh chieftain, father of St
Asaph. The traditions concerning him are very
obscure.

Sazan (St) M.   Oct 1
See Aizan and Sazan.

Scannal (St) C.   May 3
d. *p*.563 Scannal of Cell-Coleraine was a
disciple of St Columba and a celebrated
missionary.

Scarthin (St) C.   Jan 6
Otherwise Schotin, q.v.

Schadost (St) M.   Feb 20
Otherwise Sadoth, q.v.

Shenoute (Shenudi) (St) Ab.   July 1
d. *c* 450 An Egyptian who became a monk at
the White Monastery, in 370. By *c* 388 he was
the superior. Ancient sources state that he had
the care of 2200 monks and 1800 nuns. In his
time monastic life was very strict, far more so
than in the time of Pachomius: floggings and
imprisonments were used as punishments for
slight offences. He is probably the first monastic Father to have used a written charter of
profession for his religious: this practise, and
his encouragement of well tried brethren to
live as hermits, passed on to the rule of St
Benedict. Many of the works attributed to him
are now thought to be by other hands. He
attended the council of Ephesus in 431. He is
one of the pioneer figures in early monasticism
and is thus important to both the Eastern and
Western branches of the church.

Scholastica (St) V. OSB.   GC. Feb 10
c 480–*c* 543 Sister of St Benedict. She
became a nun and lived near Montecassino
under the direction of her brother. She is
regarded as the first nun of the Benedictine
order. St Gregory, in his Dialogues (2:33),
narrates that at her last meeting with her
brother, she obtained by prayer a sudden
heavy rainstorm, which prevented Benedict
from returning to his monastery and thus
prolonged their interview through the night:
three days later Benedict saw her soul ascend
to heaven in the semblance of a dove. The
tradition that St Scholastica was a nun dates
from the eleventh century. Before then she
was considered a devout and holy woman
living in the vicinity of the abbey of Montecassino. Her relics, with those of her brother,
are beneath the altar of the abbey at Monte-

St Scholastica, Feb 10

cassino. She is shown habited as a nun, with
crozier and crucifix; or with a dove flying from
her mouth.

Scholastica (St)   May 25
See Injuriosus and Scholastica.

Schotin (Scarthin) (St) C.   Jan 6
6th cent. While still a youth Schotin left
Ireland to become a disciple of St David in
Wales. On his return to his native country he
for many years led the life of an anchorite at Mt
Mairge, Leix. He is said to have established a
school for boys at Kilkenny.

Scillitan Martyrs (SS)   July 17
d. 180 Twelve martyrs, seven men and five
women, who suffered at Scillium in proconsular Africa under Septimius Severus. Their
names are: Speratus, Narzales, Cythinus,
Veturius, Felix, Acyllinus, Laetantius,
Januaria, Generosa, Vestina, Donata and
Secunda. The official Acts of these martyrs
are still extant, and are an invaluable source for

St Sebald, Aug 19

understanding contemporary persecutions. St Augustine preached three sermons in their honour at their tomb.

Scubiculus (St) M. Oct 11
See Nicasius, Quirinus, etc.

Seachnall (Sechnall) (St)
Bp. Nov 27
d. 457 A disciple of St Patrick. In 433 he was appointed first bishop of Dunsauglin, Meath, and later served as assistant bishop of Armagh. He wrote the earliest Latin poem of the Irish church — an alphabetical hymn in honour of St Patrick.

Sebald (St) H. OSB. Aug 19
d. c 770 First a hermit near Vicenza, then a co-worker with St Willibald in the Reichswald. He was probably an Anglo-Saxon missionary.

Sebaste, Martyrs of March 10
See Forty Armenian Martyrs.

Sebastia (St) M. July 4
See Innocent, Sebastia, and Comp.

Sebastian (St) M. GC. Jan 20
d. ?288 One of the most renowned of the Roman martyrs. According to his fifth century Acts, which however are not trustworthy, he was an officer in the imperial army and a favourite of Diocletian. Nevertheless when it was discovered that he was a Christian no mercy was shown to him. Tied to a tree, his body was made a target for the Roman archers,

and he was finally dispatched with clubs. His cult, both at Rome and at Milan, dates from the fourth century. In 367 Pope St Damasus built a basilica over his tomb on the Appian Way, and this is now one of the seven principal churches of Rome. His emblems are his arrows of martyrdom; or he is shown as a naked youth tied to a tree and pierced with arrows.

Sebastian Valfré (Bl)
Orat. Jan 30
1629–1710 Born at Verduno, diocese of Alba, N. Italy, he joined the Oratorians at Turin after his ordination, and there he spent the remainder of his life. He became prefect of the Oratory and was much in request as a spiritual director. He acquired in full measure the spirit of St Philip Neri. Beatified in 1834.

Sebastian (St) M. Feb 8
See Dionysius, Emilian and Sebastian.

Sebastian Aparicio (Bl)
C. OFM. Feb 25
d. 1600 Born in Spanish Galicia, he became a farm labourer and then valet to a gentleman of Salamanca. He emigrated to Mexico, where he was engaged by the government in building roads and in conducting the postal service between Mexico and Zacateca. After the death of his second wife, when he was seventy years old, he became a Franciscan lay-brother at Puebla de los Angeles. He lived for another twenty-six years, his chief occupation being to beg alms for the community. Beatified in 1787.

Sebastian (St) M. March 20
See Photina, Joseph, etc.

Sebastian Newdigate (Bl)
M. O. Cart. June 19
d 1535 Born at Harefield, Middlesex, and educated at Cambridge, he professed the Carthusian rule in the London Charterhouse. He was executed at Tyburn for denying the royal supremacy. BB Humphrey Middlemore and William Exmew suffered with him. Beatified in 1886.

Sebastian Kimura (Bl)
M. SJ. Sept 10
d. 1622 A grandson of the first Japanese baptized by St Francis Xavier. At the age of eighteen he joined the Jesuits and worked as a catechist at Meaco. He was the first Japanese to be ordained a priest. After two years imprisonment at Omura he was burnt alive with Bl Charles Spinola. Beatified in 1867.

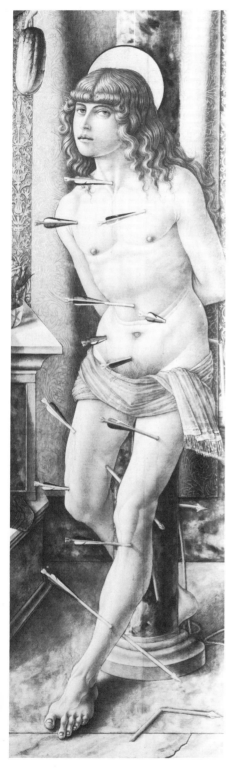

St Sebastian, Jan 20

Sebastian Montánol (Bl)
M. OP.   Dec 10
d. 1616   A Spanish Dominican and a missionary in Zacateca, Mexico, where he was put to death by the Indians whom he had rebuked for having profaned the eucharistic species. Though he has never been officially declared a martyr, he has always been the object of a popular cult.

Sebastian Maggi (Bl) C.
OP.   Dec 16
d. 1494   A native of Brescia, he became a Friar Preacher and was noted for his zeal in enforcing religious observance. He was twice vicar of the Lombard province and was for a time confessor of Savonarola. He died in Genoa. Cult confirmed in 1760.

Sebastian (Bl) Bp. OSB.   Dec 30
d. c 1036   A Benedictine monk who became archbishop of Esztergom (1002) and primate of Hungary in the time of St Stephen.

Sebbi (Sebba, Sebbe) (St)
C. OSB.   Aug 29
664–694   King of the East Saxons at the time of the Heptarchy. After a peaceful reign of thirty years he received the monastic habit in London and died shortly after, being interred in old St Paul's.

Secunda (St) VM.   July 10
See Rufina and Secunda.

Secunda (St) M.   July 17
One of the Scillitan Martyrs, q.v.

Secunda (St) VM.   July 30
See Maxima, Donatilla and Secunda.

Secundarius (St) M.   Oct 2
See Primus, Cyril and Secundarius.

Secundel (St) H.   Aug 1
6th cent.   He lived with St Friard, q.v.

Secundian (St) M.   Feb 17
See Donatus, Secundian, etc.

Secundian, Marcellian and Verian (SS) MM.   Aug 9
d. 250   Tuscan martyrs who suffered near Civitavecchia under Decius. Secundian seems to have been a prominent government official; the others are described as "scholastics". Nothing certain can be stated about this group.

Secundilla (St) M.   March 2
See Paul, Heraclius, etc.

Secundina (St) VM.   Jan 15
d. c 250   A Roman maiden, scourged to death in the neighbourhood of Rome in the persecution of Decius.

Secundinus (St) M. Feb 18
See Lucius, Silvanus, etc.

Secundinus (St) Bp. M. Apr 29
See Agapius and Comp.

Secundinus (St) M. May 21
d. *c* 306 A Spanish martyr at Cordoba under Diocletian.

Secundinus (St) Bp. M. July 1
See Castus and Secundinus.

Secundinus, Agrippinus, Maximus, Fortunatus and Martialis (SS) MM. July 15
? 4th cent. Martyrs in Pannonia.

Secundinus (St) M. Sept 1
See Priscus, Castrensis, etc.

Secundinus (St) Bp. Dec 6
See Auxilius, Isserninus and Secundinus.

Secundulus (St) M. March 7
See Perpetua, Felicitas, etc.

Secundus (St) M. Jan 9
See Epictetus, Jucundus, etc.

Secundus (St) M. March 24
See Romulus and Secundus.

Secundus (St) M. March 29
d. 119 A patrician of Asti in Piedmont and a subaltern officer in the imperial army. He was beheaded at Asti under Hadrian. He is depicted as a soldier martyr, often accompanied by a horse.

Secundus (St) Bp. May 15
See Torquatus, Ctesiphon, etc.

Secundus and Comp. (SS) MM. May 21
d. 357 Secundus, a priest of the church of Alexandria, was martyred with a great multitude of clergy and laity, including many women, by the intruded Arian patriarch George. The latter was supported in his occupation of the see of Alexandria by the emperor Constantius, the rightful patriarch, St Athanasius, having been driven into exile.

Secundus (St) M. June 1
d. 304 An alleged martyr at Amelia, drowned in the Tiber under Diocletian. He is the patron saint of several places in central Italy, but his historical existence cannot be proved.

Secundus (St) M. July 31
See Democritus, Secundus and Dionysius.

Secundus (St) M. Aug 7
See Carpophorus, Exanthus, etc.

Secundus (St) M. Aug 26
3rd cent. A legendary soldier, said to have belonged to the Theban legion and to have been martyred near Ventimiglia.

Secundus, Fidentian and Varicus (SS) MM. Nov 15
? Martyrs of proconsular Africa, of whom nothing is known.

Secundus (St) M. Dec 19
See Darius, Zosimus, etc.

Secundus (St) M. Dec 19
See Cyriacus, Paulillus, etc.

Secundus (St) M. Dec 29
See Dominic, Victor, etc.

Securus (St) M. Dec 2
See Severus, Securus, etc.

Sedna (St) Bp. March 10
d. *c* 570 Bishop of Ossory and friend of St Luanus.

Sedopha (St) M. July 5
See Marinus, Theodotus and Sedopha.

Seduinus (St) Bp. ? July 15
Possibly identical with St Swithin of Winchester, q.v.

Seemie-Rookie (St) C. Aug 16
See Roch.

Seine (St) Ab. Sept 19
Otherwise Sequanus, q.v.

Seiriol (St) C. Feb 1
6th cent. A Welsh saint whose memory is perpetuated by the name of the island of Ynys-Seiriol (Puffin Island) off Anglesey, where remains of his small monastery still exist.

Selesius (Seleucus) (St) M. Sept 12
See Hieronides, Leontius, etc.

Seleucus (St) M. Feb 16
See Porphyrius and Seleucus.

Seleucus (St) March 24
? A Syrian saint honoured in the East and often described as a martyr. Our only record of him is in the Eastern Calendars.

Selyf, or (Selyr, Levan) (St) M. June 25
6th cent.? A hermit at St Levan, Cornwall. He may be identical with the Solomon commemorated on this date in Brittany.

Senach (Snach) (St) Bp. Aug 3
6th cent. A disciple of St Finian and his successor at Clonard.

Senan (Senames) (St) Bp. March 8
d. *c* 540 An Irish monk of Kilmanagh (Kil-

kenny). Having established a monastery, probably at Enniscorthy, he is said to have then visited Rome and on his way home to have stayed with St David in Wales. On his return to Ireland he founded more churches and monasteries, notably one at Iniscarra, near Cork. Finally he settled on Scattery Island in the Shannon estuary, where he was buried.

Senan (St) H.   Apr 29
7th cent.   Said to have been a hermit in N. Wales. There is much confusion in the records of saints of this and similar names, and consequently it is impossible to give any precise account of them.

Senator (St) Bp.   May 28
d. 480   A Milanese priest who, as a young man, attended the council of Chalcedon as a legate of Pope St Leo the Great. Afterwards he became archbishop of Milan.

Senator (St)   Sept 26
? A saint of Albanum, of whom nothing is known. Albanum may be Albano near Rome or Apt, the ancient Alba Helvetiorum, in S. France.

Sennen (St) M.   July 30
See Abdon and Sennen.

Senorina (St) V. OSB.   Apr 22
d. 982   She was related to St Rudesind of Mondoñedo. Entrusted to the care of her aunt, the abbess Godina, at the convent of St John of Venaria (Vieyra), she joined the community and later became its abbess. As such she removed the community to Basto in the diocese of Braga.

September, Martyrs of (BB)   Sept 2–3
d. 1792   A group of one hundred and ninety-one martyrs who met their death during the French Revolution. They were imprisoned by the Legislative Assembly for refusing the oath to support the civil constitution of the clergy which had been condemned by the Holy See. They were massacred by the mob, with the connivance of the Assembly, on Sept 2 and 3, 1792. The most prominent members of the group were: John Mary du Lau, archbishop of Arles; Francis de la Rochefoucauld, bishop of Beauvais; his brother Louis, bishop of Saintes; Augustine Ambrose Chevreux, OSB., last superior general of the Maurists; and Charles de la Calmette, Count of Valfons. One hundred and twenty were massacred at the Carmelite church (Les Carmes) in the rue de Rennes, Paris. Beatified in 1926.

Septiminus, Januarius and Felix (SS) MM.   Aug 28 and Sept 1
A group among the Twelve Holy Brothers, q.v.

Septimus (St) M.   Aug 17
See Liberatus, Boniface, etc.

Septimus (St) M.   Oct 24
See Felix (Africanus) Audactus (Adauctus), etc.

Sequanus (Seine, Sigo) (St) Ab.   Sept 19
d. c 580   Monk of Réomay and abbot-founder of a monastery at Segreste, diocese of Langres, which was later called after him Saint-Seine.

Seraphia (St) VM.   July 29
Otherwise Serapia, q.v.

Seraphim of Sarov (St) Mk.   Jan 2
1759–1833   Born into a middle-class family at Kursk in Russia, he became a monk when nineteen years of age at Sarov. In time he was ordained. Between 1794–1825 he lived firstly as a hermit in the woods near the abbey, and later walled up inside the enclosure. From 1825 he was recognised far and wide as a staretz or spiritual father and people flocked to seek his advice and direction. His spiritual life abounded in peace, joy and humble loving service of all, and was founded on his strict asceticism and years of prayer. Canonized by the Russian church in 1903, in recent years many works in English have been published about him, arousing great interest in the West.

Seraphina (or Fina) (St) V.   March 12
d. 1253   Born at San Geminiano in Tuscany, she led a life of constant suffering, being the victim of repulsive diseases and continuous neglect. She was never a nun, but seems to have lived at home under the obedience of the Benedictines. She is venerated at San Geminiano as Santa Fina.

Seraphina Sforza (Bl) V. Poor Clare   Sept 9
1434–1478   Born at Urbino, the daughter of Guido, count of Urbino and lord of Gubbio, she married in 1448 Alexander Sforza, Duke of Pesaro, who treated her with great ignominy and expelled her from her home. She took refuge in the convent of Poor Clares and eventually professed their rule and became abbess. Beatified in 1754.

Seraphina (St)   July 29
d. ? c 426   The pre-1970 RM. ascribes this

saint to a *Civitas Mamiensis*, which some writers place in Armenia, others in Spain or Italy.

Seraphinus (St) C. OFM.
Cap.   Oct 12
1540–1604 Born at Montegranaro, he took the Capuchin habit as a lay-brother in 1556 and spent the whole of his uneventful life at the friary of Ascoli-Piceno. He is said to have been the spiritual adviser of high ecclesiastical and civil dignitaries. Canonized in 1767.

Serapia (St) VM.   July 29
d. 119 A slave of Syrian extraction who features in the legendary acts of St Sabina; in this story she converted Sabina to the faith, and was beheaded under Hadrian.

Serapion (St) M.   Feb 25
See Victorinus, Victor, etc.

Serapion (St) M.   Feb 28
See Caerealis, Pupulus, etc.

Serapion (St) Bp.   March 21
d. c 370 An Egyptian monk who was ordained bishop of Thmuis in Lower Egypt c 339 and distinguished himself by his firm opposition to Arianism. He was a great friend of St Athanasius and of St Antony. He was the author of several works; his Sacramentary, a valuable liturgical source, was discovered in 1899.

Serapion of Arsinoe (St)
C.   March 21
d. 4th cent? One of the most famous of the Desert Fathers, he ruled over ten thousand monks scattered through the desert.

Serapion (St) M.   March 26
See Theodore, Irenaeus, etc.

Serapion the Sindonite
(St) C.   May 21
d. c 356 Born in Egypt, he became a monk and pushed self-denial to extreme limits. He made a pilgrimage to Rome.

Serapion (St) M.   July 13
d. c 195 An oriental martyr who suffered under Septimus Severus, probably in Macedonia.

Serapion (St) M.   Aug 27
See Marcellians, Mannavea, etc.

Serapion (St) Bp.   Oct 30
d. 211 A bishop of Antioch praised by Eusebius and St Jerome for his theological writings which, except for some small fragments, are no longer extant.

Serapion (St) M.   Nov 14
d. 252 A martyr of Alexandria who perished in a riot raised against the Christians. The mob cast him down from the roof of his own house, a high building.

Serapion (St) M. O. Merc.   Nov 14
d. 1240 Said to have been born in England and to have fought against the Moors in Spain under the banner of Castile. In Spain he joined the Mercedarian order and surrendered himself as a hostage at Algiers, where he was crucified for preaching the gospel while awaiting his ransom. Cult confirmed, as a saint, in 1728.

Serdot (St) Bp.   May 4
Otherwise Sacerdos, q.v.

Serena (St)   Aug 16
d. c 290 Described in the pre-1970 RM. as "sometime wife of the emperor Diocletian", but this information is derived from the spurious Acts of St Cyriacus.

Serenicus Ab.
and Serenus H. (SS) OSB.   May 7
d. c 669 Two brothers belonging to a patrician family of Spoleto. They received the Benedictine habit. Later they settled in France as hermits near the river Sarthe. Serenus remained a hermit till the end of his life, but Serenicus became the head of a community of some one hundred and forty disciples who gathered round him.

Serenus (Cerneuf, Sirenus)
(St) M.   Feb 23
d. c 303 A Greek monk who lived as a hermit at Sirmium, now Mitrovica, in the Balkans. He was martyred under Diocletian.

Serenus (St) H. OSB.   May 7
See Serenicus and Serenus.

Serenus (St) M.   June 28
See Plutarch, Serenus, etc.

Serenus (St) Bp.   Aug 9
d. 606 Bishop of Marseilles. St Gregory wrote him several letters, in which he recommended to him the Roman missionaries travelling to England and twice reprimanded him for his iconoclastic tendencies.

Serf (St) Bp.   July 1
Otherwise Servan, q.v.

Sergius (St) M.   Feb 24
d. 304 A monk, perhaps a priest, in Cappadocia, martyred under Diocletian. His relics are said to have been translated to Ubeda, near Tarragona, in Spain.

Sergius (St) M.   March 20
See John, Sergius, and Comp.

Sergius (St) M.   July 27
See Maurus, Pantaleemon and Sergius.

Sergius (St) Pope   Sept 8
d. 701   Of Syrian parentage, but born at
Palermo in Sicily and admitted to membership
of the Roman clergy, Sergius governed the
church from 687 to 701. He opposed the
interference of the Byzantine emperors in
ecclesiastical affairs and refused to sign the
decrees of the synod of Trullan (692). He
blessed and fostered the missionary enterprise
of the English monks in Friesland and Germany and defended St Wilfrid; he ordained
Willibrand as bishop of the Frisians (695) and
baptised Caedwalla king of the West Saxons in
689. It was he who introduced the *Agnus Dei*
into the eucharistic rites of the West.

Sergius and Bacchus (SS)
MM.   formerly Oct 7
d. 303   In the traditional story they were
high officers of the Romany army in Syria. For
refusing to join in pagan sacrifices they were
dressed in women's clothes and led through
the streets of Arabissus. Then Bacchus was
beaten to death and Sergius was beheaded a
week later. Cults suppressed in 1969.

Serlo (Bl) Ab. OSB.   March 3
d. 1104   A Norman by birth, he became a
canon of Avranches and later a Benedictine
monk at Mont Saint-Michel. Four years later
(1074), on the recommendation of St
Osmund, he was appointed abbot of Gloucester, receiving the abbatial blessing from St
Wulstan. When he arrived at Gloucester the
community consisted of two adult monks and
eight boys: when he died he left a community
of over one hundred professed monks. He was
noted for his building activities and his fearless
defence of ecclesiastical rights and the moral
law.

Serlo (Bl) Ab. OSB. Cist.   Sept 10
d. 1158   A Benedictine of Chérisy who
became abbot of Savigny in 1140. He united
the whole congregation of Savigny to the
Cistercians in 1147 and was thenceforward a
devoted member of the latter order.

Sernin (St) Bp. M.   Nov 29
Otherwise Saturninus, q.v.

Serotina (St) M.   Dec 31
See Donata, Paulina, etc.

Servan (Serf, Sair) (St) Bp.   July 1
? Apostle of West Fife. The traditions concerning him are very contradictory and extravagant. He died and was buried at Culross.

Servandus and Germanus
(SS) MM.   Oct 23
d. c 305   Said to have been sons of St Marcellus of Léon (Oct 30). They were put to
death at Cadiz while on their way under arrest
to Tangiers. They are held in veneration
throughout S. Spain.

Servatus (French: Servais)
(St) Bp.   May 13
d. 384   Bishop of Tongres in the Low
Countries. He was the host of St Athanasius
when the latter was an exile in the West.

Servilian (St) M.   Apr 20
See Sulpicius and Servilian.

Servilius (St) M.   May 24
See Zöellus, Servilius, etc.

Servite Martyrs (BB)   Aug 31
d. 1420   Sixty-four Servite friars burnt to
death in their church at Prague by the Hussites. The group included four friars from
Tuscany who had been sent to Bohemia to
preach against the Hussite heresy. Cult
confirmed in 1918.

Servulus (St) C.   Dec 23
d. c 590   A cripple who begged for alms at
the door of the church of St Clement in Rome,
sharing what he received with other beggars.
St Gregory the Great describes the beautiful
scene of Servulus's death.

Servus (St) M.   Aug 17
See Liberatus, Boniface, etc.

Servus (St) M.   Dec 7
d. 483   A layman of noble birth in proconsular Africa. He was seized and tortured to death
under the Arian Vandal king Hunneric.

Servus-Dei (St) M.   Jan 13
See Gumesindus and Servus-Dei.

Servus-Dei (St) M.   Sept 16
See Rogellus and Servus-Dei.

Seton (Mother)
Elizabeth Anne Bayley (Bl)
See Elizabeth Anne Bayley Seton.

**Seven Angels who stand
before the throne of God**   April 20
See Tobit 12:15, Rev. 8:2–5. The names
usually given to them are Michael, Gabriel and
Raphael (q.v.) who have their own feast on
Sept 29, and who are all mentioned in the
Bible, and Uriel, Shealtiel, Jehudiel and
Berachiel. A church at Palermo is dedicated to
these Seven Angels, and their feast is kept
there on April 20.

Seven Apostles of Bulgaria (SS) CC. July 17

The Bulgarians venerate liturgically their first seven apostles; they are, besides the well-known Cyril and Methodius, q.v., Gorazd, Nahum, Sabas, Angelarius and Clement of Ochrid. The last-named, who is the most important after Cyril and Methodius, died on July 17, 916.

Seven Brothers (SS) MM. formerly July 10

d. c 150 The seven alleged sons of the Roman martyr Felicitas, q.v. Their names are: Januarius, Felix and Philip, scourged to death; Sylvanus, thrown over a precipice; Alexander, Vitalis and Martial, beheaded. Their legend states that they suffered at Rome under Antoninus Pius. Modern scholars deny that they were brothers: the fact that they were commemorated on the same day led to the legend of their being related by blood and the sons of Felicitas. They were in fact seven early martyrs about whom nothing definite is known and whose memories were perpetuated by this colourful romance.

Seven Holy Founders (SS) GC. Feb 17

Their names are: Bonfilio Monaldo, Alexius Falconieri, (Benedict) Manettus dell' Antello, (Bartholomew) Amedeo degli Amidei, (Ricovero), Uguccio Uguccione, (Gherordino) Sostenes Sostegno, (John) Buonagiunta Monetti. They were young Florentine members of the Confraternity of Our Lady who withdrew to Mt Senario in revolt at the materialism and moral laxity of their city and laid the foundation of the order of the Servants of Mary, known as Servite Friars. Their rule was based on that of St Augustine with Dominican overtones. The order was given papal sanction in 1304. Bonfilio was the first superior general, Buonagiunta the second, Manettus the fourth. Amedeo was first prior of Carfaggio. Uguccio and Sosteneo established the order in France and Germany respectively. Alexis remained a lay-brother and was the last to die (1310). They were canonized conjointly by Leo XIII in 1887, when their common feast was added to the Roman Missal for the universal church.

Seven Saintly Robbers (SS) MM. Apr 29

See Corfu (Martyrs of).

Seven Sleepers (SS) MM. formerly July 27

250–362 The legend of the Seven Sleepers states that seven youths of Ephesus were walled up in a cave under Decius in the year 250 and were found alive there in the time of Theodosius II (362), having spent the intervening period in sleep. There are three or four sets of different names and a large number of variants of the legend. One of the most ingenuous of these was written by St James of Sarug in Syriac (c 500). The origin of the legend is probably to be traced to the discovery of some forgotten relics. Baronius, although he left the *memoria* of the Seven Sleepers in his revision of the RM., wisely doubted the authenticity of their story. They are represented as seven youths asleep in a cave. In detailed representations SS John, Maximian and Constantine each have a club. SS Mortian and Malchus have axes, and St Serapion a torch. St Dionysius has a large nail.

Severa (St) V. Abs. July 20

d. c 680 Sister of St Modoald, bishop of Trier. First abbess of St Gemma (later Sainte-Sévère) at Villeneuve, diocese of Bourges.

Severa (St) Abs. OSB. July 20

d. c 750 Benedictine abbess of the great nunnery of Oehren at Trier.

Severian and Aquila (SS) MM. Jan 23

? A husband and wife martyred at Julia Caesarea in Mauritania.

Severian (St) Bp. M. Feb 21

d. c 452 A bishop of Scythopolis (Bethsan) in Galilee who, on his return from the council of Chalcedon, was murdered by the Eutychian heretics with the connivance of the empress Eudoxia.

Severian (St) M. Apr 20

See Victor, Zoticus, etc.

Severian (St) M. Sept 9

d. 320 An Armenian senator who, according to his legend, having witnessed the martyrdom of the Forty Martyrs of Sebaste, openly professed his Christianity and was torn with iron rakes until he died. He suffered at Sebaste under Licinius.

Severian (St) M. Nov 8

One of the Four Crowned Martyrs, q.v.

Severinus (St) Ab. Jan 8

d. 482 An Eastern monk/hermit who undertook the evangelization of Noricum Ripense (corresponding to modern Austria), where he established several monastic foundations, notably one on the Danube near Vienna, where he organised help for the people afflicted by the invasions of Attila and the Huns, and where he died. Six years after his death the monks were driven from the country and carried his relics to Naples, where the great Benedictine monastery of San Severino was built to enshrine them.

Severinus (St) Bp.   Jan 8

Under this date the pre-1970 RM. commemorated a St Severinus, bishop at Naples, brother of St Victorinus. The entry in the RM. is the result of a confusion between the saint noticed above and St Severinus of Septempeda (June 8), brother of St Victorinus of Camerino.

Severinus (St) Ab.   Feb 11

d. ? 507   A Burgundian said to have been the abbot of Agaunum in Switzerland. He is also alleged to have restored to health Clovis, first Christian king of the Franks. The historical evidence for these assertions is not good.

Severinus (St) Bp.   June 8

d. 550   Bishop of Septempeda, now called after him Sanseverino, in the Marches of Ancona. He and his brother Victorinus distributed their great wealth among the poor and became hermits at Montenero. They were forced by Pope Vigilius (54) to become bishops, the former of Septempeda, the latter of Camerino. Severinus died shortly before Septempeda was destroyed by Totila the Ostrogoth.

Severinus (St) M.   July 6

See Lucy, Antoninus, etc.

Severinus (St) M.   Aug 7

See Carpophorus, Exanthus, etc.

Severinus (St) Bp.   Oct 23

d. c 403   Said to have been born at Bordeaux. He was bishop of Cologne and a prominent opponent of Arianism.

Severinus (French: Seurin) (St) Bp.   Oct 23

d. c 420   Said to have been an oriental by birth. He was bishop of Bordeaux c 405–420.

Severinus Boethius (St) M.   Oct 23

c 480–524   Anicius Manlius Torquatus Severinus Boethius is known to history as a Roman statesman in the service of Theodoric the Ostrogoth and as an eminent philosopher, author of *De consolatione philosophiae*. About the year 534 he fell into disfavour with the barbarian king and was martyred at Pavia after a long imprisonment. His relics are enshrined at the cathedral of Pavia, where his feast is observed. His feast is also kept at the church of Santa Maria in Portico, Rome. Cult confirmed in 1883.

Severinus (St) H. OSB.   Nov 1

d. c 699   A Benedictine monk who lived as a

hermit at Tivoli. His relics are in the church of St Laurence at Tivoli.

Severinus, Exuperius and Felician (SS) MM.   Nov 19

d. 170   Martyrs of Vienne in Gaul under Marcus Aurelius.

Severinus (St) H.   Nov 27

d. c 540   A hermit who lived first at Paris and then in a cell at Novientum near Paris.

Severinus (St) Bp.   Dec 21

d. c 300   Bishop of Trier.

Severus (St) M.   Jan 11

See Peter, Severus and Leucius.

Severus (St) Bp.   Feb 1

d. c 348   A native of Ravenna who became bishop of that city in 283. He accompanied the papal legate to the synod of Sardica (344).

Severus (St) Bp.   Feb 1

d. c 690   Born of poor parents in the Cotentin, he became successively priest, abbot and bishop of Avranches. Before his death he resigned his see and returned to monastic life.

Severus (St) C.   Feb 15

d. c 530   A parish priest of Interocrea (Androcca) in the Abruzzi. St Gregory the Great relates that he brought a dead man back to life that he might receive the last sacraments. The relics of Severus were translated to Münster-Maifeld, diocese of Trier, in the tenth century.

Severus and Sixty-Two Comps. (SS) MM.   Feb 21

3rd–4th cent.   Martyrs at Syrmium, Pannonia.

Severus (St) Bp.   Apr 29

d. 409   Bishop of Naples and a famous wonder-worker. He raised a dead man to life, according to his legend, in order that he should bear witness in favour of his persecuted widow.

Severus (St) C.   Aug 1

d. c 500   A priest of noble family and famous for his charity, he has been honoured from time immemorial in the village that bears his name, St Sever de Rustan in Bigorre (Hautes-Pyrénées).

Severus (St) C.   Aug 8

d. p.445   A priest who came from afar (some accounts say from India) and evangelized the district round Vienne in Gaul.

Severus, Memnon and Comp. (SS) MM.   Aug 20

d. c 300   Severus was a priest and Memnon

a centurion at Bizya in Thrace, where they were beheaded for the faith. Thirty-seven Christian soldiers from Philippopolis were at the same time thrown into a furnace.

Severus (St) C. Oct 1
This saint seems to be identical with Severus, Feb 15, q.v.

Severus (St) Bp. Oct 15
d. c 455 Born in Gaul, he was a disciple of St Germanus of Auxerre and of St Lupus of Troyes. He accompanied Germanus to Britain to oppose the Pelagian heresy. he preached the gospel to the Germans on the lower Moselle and became bishop of Trier (446–c 455).

Severus (St) M. Oct 22
See Philip, Severus, etc.

Severus (St) Bp. M. Nov 6
d. 633 Bishop of Barcelona, martyred under the Arian Visigoths, who put him to death by driving nails into his temples. He is a minor patron of Barcelona.

Severus (St) M. Nov 8
One of the Four Crowned Martyrs, q.v.

Severus, Securus, Januarius and Victorinus (SS) MM. Dec 2
d. c 450 African martyrs who suffered under the Vandals.

Severus (Bl) Bp. OSB. Dec 9
d. 1067 A Benedictine of Brevnov who became bishop of Prague (1031–1067) and was noted for his activities as a builder of churches. He is always styled either saint or blessed by Czech hagiographers.

Severus (St) M. Dec 30
See Mansuetus, Severus, etc.

Sexburga (St) W. Abs. OSB. July 6
c 635–c 699 Daughter of Anna, king of the East Angles, sister of SS Etheldreda, Ethelburga and Withburga, and half-sister of St Saethryth. She married Erconbert, king of Kent, by whom she became the mother of SS Ermengilda and Ercongota. As queen she founded the nunnery of Minster in Sheppey. Left a widow in 664, she became a nun there, whence she migrated to Ely in 679, where she became abbess and where her shrine remained until the Reformation.

Sextus (St) M. Dec 31
See Stephen, Pontian, etc.

Sezni (St) Bp. Aug 4
d. c 529 A native of Britain who crossed over to Guic-Sezni in Brittany, where he is said to have founded a monastery and where

his relics are now venerated. He is the patron saint of Sithney in Cornwall.

Sharbel Sarbelius and Barbea (Bebaia) (SS) MM. Jan 29
d. 101 Brother and sister martyred at Edessa under Trajan. Previous to their martyrdom they were tortured with red-hot irons. Before his conversion Thatueles Sarbelius had been the pagan high priest of the city.

Shealtiel Apr 20
See Seven Angels who stand before the throne of God.

Siagrius (St) (*several*)
Otherwise Syagrius, q.v.

Siardus (Siard) (St) O. Praem. Nov 13
d. 1230 Premonstratensian abbot of Mariengarden in Frisia (1196–1230).

Sibyllina Biscossi (Bl) V. Tert. OP. March 23
1287–1367 Born at Pavia and left an orphan, at the age of twelve she became blind and was adopted by a community of Dominican tertiaries. In 1302 she retired to a cell near the Dominican friary at Pavia, and there she lived as a recluse till the age of eighty, doing penance and working miracles. Cult approved in 1853.

Sidney Hodgson (Bl) M. Dec 10
d. 1591 A layman and a convert hanged at Tyburn for relieving Catholic missionaries to England. Beatified in 1929.

Sidonius Apollinaris (St) Bp. Aug 21
c 423–480 Caius Sollius Apollinaris Sidonius was born at Lyons and ranks as one of the last of the great Gallo-Romans. He was first a soldier and married the daughter of Avitus, emperor of the West. In 468 he served the state as chief senator and prefect of Rome (468–9). After his term of office he retired to his country estate in Gaul, and while there, although a layman, he was made bishop of Clermont. As a bishop he saved his people from the fury of the Gothic invaders under Alaric, for which purpose he not only employed skilful diplomacy but also introduced into his diocese and reorganized days of public prayers called "Rogation Days". Sidonius was a man of letters. He wrote Latin verse with facility, and much technical skill, but his letters are now much more important than the twenty-four poems of his which are still extant; he gave his vast wealth to benefit the poor and

established monasteries. He is considered to be the final exemplar of full classical culture before the barbarian invasions altered the intellectual climate of the West.

Sidonius (French: Säens) (St) Ab. OSB.   Nov 14
d. *c* 690   An Irishman who became a monk at Jumièges under St Philibert (644). Later he was appointed by St Ouen first abbot of a small monastery which that bishop had founded near Rouen: this monastery was later called Saint-Säens.

Sidronius (St) M.   July 11
d. *c* 270   A Roman martyr under Aurelian. In the Middle Ages his relics were translated to Flanders. Another St Sidronius is venerated at Sens in France. The history of the two saints has been confused, and the traditions concerning them are untrustworthy.

Sidwell (Sativola) (St) VM.   Aug 1 or 2
? Probably of British (not Anglo-Saxon) lineage. She is said to have lived in the West of England, and there are churches dedicated to her in Devonshire, chiefly in the neighbourhood of Exeter. Particulars of her life, and as to how she came to be venerated as a martyr, are lacking. Her emblem is a scythe, by which she was decapitated. She may hold her head, or stand near a well.

Siffred (Siffrein, Syffroy, Suffredus) (St) Bp.   Nov 27
d. 540 (or 660?)   A native of Albano, near Rome, who became a monk at Lérins and later bishop of Carpentras in Provence, where he is now venerated as the principal patron saint of the diocese.

Sigebert (St) King   Feb 1
631–656   Sigebert III, son of Dagobert I, was king of Austrasia, i.e. Eastern France. Under the influence of Bl Pepin of Landen, of St Cunibert of Cologne and of other saintly persons, the young king grew up to be a clean-living and pious man. He died at the age of twenty-five. Though not a very successful monarch, he was revered as the founder of numerous hospitals, churches and monasteries. The abbeys of Stavelot and Malmédy were founded by him.

Sigebert (St) King M. OSB.   Sept 27
d. 635   The first Christian king of East Anglia. He was baptized in France and, aided by SS Felix and Fursey, he introduced Christianity into his realm. He took the monastic habit (at Dunwich?), but was forcibly removed from the cloister by his warrior subjects and fell while leading them in battle against Penda

of Mercia. His opponents being pagans, he was venerated as a martyr.

Sigfrid (St) Bp. OSB.   Feb 15
d. *c* 1045   An English priest and monk, probably of Glastonbury. At the invitation of King Olaf of Norway he went to that country as a missionary and lived at Vaxjo. Great success attended his efforts, one of his converts being Olaf, king of Sweden. He is said to have been canonized by Pope Adrian IV.

Sigfrid (St) Ab. OSB.   Aug 22
d. 688   Monk and disciple of St Benet Biscop, by whom he was appointed abbot of Wearmouth in 686. He was an exemplar of monastic virtues and a scripture scholar.

Sigfrid (Bl) Mk OSB.   Dec 15
d. 1215   A Benedictine monk of Reinhardsbrunn in Thuringia. From the year 1212 he lived as a hermit at Georgenberg.

Sighardus (Bl) Ab. OSB. Cist.   Apr 5
d. 1162   Cistercian monk of Jouy. In 1141 he founded and became the first abbot of Bonlieu, or Carbon-Blanc, near Bordeaux.

Sigibald (St) Bp.   Oct 26
d. *c* 740   Bishop of Metz 716–*c* 740. He was promoter of learning, a builder of schools and abbeys (notably Neuweiter and Saint-Avold) and an able administrator.

Sigiranus (Cyran, Siran, Sigram) (St) Ab. OSB.   Dec 5
d. *c* 655 (or 690?)   Born of a noble Frankish family, he was first cup-bearer at the court of Clotaire II and later archdeacon of Tours, of which city his father was bishop. Ultimately he became a monk and abbot-founder of Meobecq and of Lonrey (*Longoretum*). The latter was afterwards called after him Saint-Cyran.

Sigisbert, Ab. and Placid, M. (SS)   July 11
d. *c* 650 (or *c* 750?)   Sigisbert was the abbot-founder of the great Benedictine abbey of Dissentis in Switzerland. He built it on land given him by St Placid, a wealthy landowner who joined the new community as a monk and was later murdered for defending the ecclesiastical rights of the abbey. Sigisbert survived him several years. Cult approved in 1905.

Sigismund (St) King M.   May 1
d. 523   A Vandal by extraction and disposition, he was king of the Burgundians for one year. During that period he ordered one of his sons to be strangled for rebuking his stepmother. He atoned for this sin by giving generously to the church and the poor. Being defeated in battle he disguised himself in a

monk's habit and hid in a cell near the abbey of Agaunum, which he had built. There he was found by his enemies and put to death. He is honoured as a martyr.

Sigolena (Segoulème) (St)
Abs. OSB.   July 24
d. c 769   Daughter of a nobleman of Aquitaine and a widow early in life, she became a nun in the convent of Troclar on the Tarn, S. France, where she was later chosen abbess. She is co-patroness of the diocese of Albi.

Sigolinus (Sighelm) (St)
Ab. OSB.   Oct 29
d. c 670   Abbot of Stavelot and Malmédy, in Belgium.

Sigrada (St) N. OSB.   Aug 8
d. c 678   Mother of SS Leodegarius and Warinus. In her widowhood she became a nun in the convent at Soissons. She died shortly after the martyrdom of her two sons, victims of the cruelty of Ebroin, mayor of the palace.

Silas (or Silvanus) (St) C.   July 13
1st cent.   Silas, disciple and companion of St Paul, is mentioned both as Silas (Acts 15:22; 18:5) and as Silvanus (2 Cor. I:19; 1 Thess. I:1;2 Thess. I:1;1 Pet. 5:12). Legend makes him the first bishop of Corinth. The Greeks distinguish Silas from Silvanus and commemorate both on July 30.

Silaus (Silave, Silanus)
(St) Bp.   May 17
d. 1100   Said to have been an Irish bishop who died at Lucca on his way back from a pilgrimage to Rome. He is the subject of many extravagant legends.

Silin (Sulian) (St) C.   July 29
6th cent.   A legendary Breton saint and abbot who may have established a small monastery at Luxulyan in Cornwall, and who is still venerated in Brittany.

Sillan (Silvanus) (St) Ab.   Feb 28
d. c 610   A disciple of St Comgall at Bangor, Co. Down, and his second successor as abbot of that monastery.

Silvanus, Luke and
Mucius (SS) MM.   Feb 6
d. 312   Silvanus was bishop of Emesa in Phoenicia, Luke his deacon, and Mucius his lector. After long imprisonment the three were martyred under Maximian. The pre-1970 RM. identifies this Silvanus with the companion of St Tyrannio (Feb 20), q.v.

Silvanus (St) Bp.   Feb 10
? Bishop of Terracina. He is described as a "Confessor", which would mean that he had suffered for the faith by imprisonment, or torture, or even death.

Silvanus (St) M.   Feb 18
See Lucius, Silvanus, etc.

Silvanus (St) Bp. M.   Feb 20
See Tyrannio, Silvanus, etc.

Silvanus (St) M.   March 8
See Cyril, Rogatus, etc.

Silvanus and Comp. (SS)
MM.   May 4
d. c 311   A group of forty-one martyrs from Egypt and Palestine, of whose martyrdom an account is given by Eusebius. Silvanus was bishop of Gaza and was sentenced to the mines in Palestine, but being too old for heavy work he was beheaded instead, together with forty others similarly incapacitated.

Silvanus (St) M.   May 5
? A Roman martyr.

Silvanus (St) H.   May 15
4th cent.   An actor who left the world and became a monk at Tabennisi under St Pachomius. After twenty years of monastic life he became lax and was excommunicated by Pachomius. This led to a second conversion and to the beginning of a new life of sanctification. He is honoured by the Greeks.

Silvanus (St) M.   May 24
See Zöellus, Servilius, etc.

Silvanus (St) M.   July 10
One of the Seven Brothers, MM., q.v.

Silvanus (St) M.   July 10
See Bianor and Silvanus.

Silvanus (St) M.   Sept 4
See Rufinus, Silvanus and Vitalicus.

Silvanus (St)   Sept 22
? A saint venerated from ancient times at Levroux, diocese of Bourges. Legend identifies him with the Zacchaeus of the gospel.

Silvanus (St) M.   Nov 5
See Domninus, Theotimus, etc.

Silvanus (St) Bp.   Dec 2
d. c 450   A monk at Constantinople. Later bishop of Troas in Phrygia.

Silverius (St) Pope, M.   June 20
d. c 537   A native of Frosinone in Campania and son of Pope St Hormisdas. He was a subdeacon when elected bishop of Rome. For refusing to countenance the restoration of the Monophysite bishop Anthimos to the see of

Constantinople he incurred the violent hatred of the empress Theodora. He was summarily condemned on a charge of high treason, deported to the East and finally banished to an islet off Naples, where he was left to die of privation, or perhaps actually murdered. Cult restricted to local calendars since 1969.

Silvester (St) Bp.   March 10
d. c 420   A companion of St Palladius in the evangelization of Ireland.

Silvester (St) Ab.   Apr 15
d. c 625   Second abbot of Moutier-Saint-Jean (Réome), diocese of Dijon.

Silvester Ventura (Bl)
Mk. OSB. Cam.   June 9
d. 1348   A native of Florence and a carder and bleacher of wool by trade. At the age of forty he joined the Camaldolese at S. Maria degli Angeli at Florence as a lay-brother, and served the community as cook. He was favoured with ecstasies and heavenly visions, and it is alleged the angels were wont to come and cook for him. His spiritual advice was much sought after.

Silvester (St) Bp.   Nov 20
d. c 525   Bishop of Châlons-sur-Saône from c 484 to c 525. St Gregory of Tours describes him as "the glory of confessors".

Silvester Gozzolini (St)
Ab. OSB.   Nov 26
1177–1267   Born at Osimo, he read law at Padua and Bologna, then became a secular priest and canon at Osimo. Later he retired to live as a hermit at Montefano, near Fabriano. In 1231, directed by St Benedict in a vision, he instituted a new congregation of Benedictines known from the colour of their habit as the Blue Benedictines. The congregation spread rapidly, and Silvester governed it "with unbounded wisdom and gentleness" for thirty-six years. It was approved by Innocent IV in 1247. St Silvester represents the renewal of Benedictinism in Italy contemporary with the foundation of the new orders of friars. He was equivalently canonized in 1598. Cult confined to particular calendars since 1969.

Silvester (St) Pope   GC. Dec 31
d. 335   Silvester was a Roman, and served the church as pope from 314 to 335. In 313 Constantine had, by the edict of Milan, granted toleration to Christianity, and Silvester was therefore enabled to govern the church free from persecution. Very little that is historically certain is known about his life, though there are various legends which connect his name with that of Constantine. During his pontificate the first general council was held at Nicaea to deal with the Arian heresy, and he was represented at the council by bishop Hosius of Cordoba. The major part of his remains are enshrined at San Silvestro in Capite, Rome. In art he is shown vested as a pope, often holding a small dragon in his hand or on a chain; or baptising the emperor Constantine (an event which occurred only after Silvester's death).

Silvinus (St) Bp. OSB.   Feb 17
d. c 720   A courtier who gave up his worldly life and became a pilgrim. At Rome he was ordained a regionary bishop and evangelized the district round Thérouanne. After some forty years of unceasing apostolate, a feature of which was the ransoming of numerous slaves, he retired to the Benedictine abbey of Auchy-les-Moines, where he lived the few remaining years of his life as a monk.

Silvinus (St) Bp.   Sept 12
d. c 550   Bishop of Verona. Nothing further is known about him.

Silvinus (St) Bp.   Sept 28
d. 444   Bishop of Brescia. He became a bishop in extreme old age.

Silvius (St) M.   Apr 21
See Arator, Fortunatus, etc.

Simbert (Simpert, Sintbert)
(St) Bp. OSB.   Oct 13
d. c 809   Pupil, monk and abbot at the abbey of Murbach, near Colmar in Alsace. In 778 he was made bishop of Augsburg, but retained the government of Murbach. He was a remarkable person in every respect, but especially as a restorer of ecclesiastical discipline and studies. Canonized by Nicholas V.

Simeon Stylites the
Elder (St) H.   Jan 5
c 390–459   Born at Sis in Cilicia, the son of a shepherd and a shepherd himself in his youth. He joined a community of Syrian monks at Tell'Ada but was dismissed on account of his excessive austerities. He then became a hermit at Telanissos, attaching himself by chains to a rock, but so many people came to see him that, in order to gain greater solitude, he took to living on a platform mounted on a pillar. He gradually raised the height of the pillar till it reached sixty-six feet, and it was on the flat summit of this, about three feet in width, that he spent the remaining thirty-seven years of his life: hence the name Stylites, which means "raised on a pillar". For forty years he passed the whole of Lent without taking any food. His pillar stood on a hill on the borders of Syria and Cilicia, and the wild tribes of the desert flocked to him for baptism and spiritual advice.

The above facts are quite authentic, being based on the testimony of eye-witnesses. He was a very influential figure in support of the council of Chalcedon, and was consulted by emperors and countless people on all sorts of problems. He was the first Stylite saint.

Simeon the Ancient (St) C.   Jan 28
d. *c* 390   He lived from early youth in a cave in Syria, and later founded two monasteries on Mt Sinai. He often visited his friend Palladius.

Simeon the New Theologian (St)   March 12
949–1022   A Studite monk at Constantinople, he became abbot of St Mamas there in 981. Controversy raging about his teaching, he resigned and was later exiled. Although he was pardoned he remained away from the city. He is one of the greatest Byzantine mystics, and wrote much on the divine light, especially relating this to the transfiguration; his pithy writings have always been influential in the East and he is one of the influences on the use of Hesychasm as a form of monastic prayer.

Simeon, Abdechalas, Ananias, Usthazanes, Pusicius and Comp. (SS)   Apr 21
d. 341   Persian martyrs under Shapur II. Simeon was bishop of Seleucia-Ctesiphon, Abdechalas and Ananias his priests, Usthazanes the king's tutor (a repentant apostate), and Pusicius the overseer of the king's workmen. They suffered with a band of over one hundred other Christians — bishops, priests and clerics of various ranks. Pusicius's virgin daughter was also martyred with them. The Acts are authentic.

Simeon of Trier (St) H. OSB.   June 1
d. 1035   A native of Syracuse who, after being educated at Constantinople, lived as a hermit by the Jordan. He then joined a community at Bethlehem, but migrated later to Mt Sinai and again became a hermit, first in a small cave near the Red Sea and then on the summit of Sinai. Thence he was sent by the abbot of Mt Sinai on a mission to the Duke of Normandy. After a series of adventures he settled at Trier, where he was walled up by the archbishop and lived under the obedience of the abbot of the great Benedictine monastery of St Martin. It was the abbot of this monastery who attended Simeon at his death and wrote his life. St Simeon was the second saint to be formally canonized (1042).

Simeon Salus (St) H.   July 1
d. *p.*588   An Egyptian who lived as a hermit for close on thirty years in the desert of Sinai, by the Red Sea, and afterwards at Emesa in Phoenicia. He received the nickname *Salus*, meaning fool, on account of his eccentric behaviour.

Simeon of Padolirone (St) Mk. OSB.   July 26
d. 1016   An Armenian who, after spending some time as a hermit, went on pilgrimage to Jerusalem, Rome, Compostella and St Martin of Tours. He was renowned for the miracles he worked on these journeys. Finally he settled at the Cluniac abbey of Padolirone near Padua, where he passed the rest of his life. Canonized by Benedict VIII.

Simeon Stylites the Younger (St) H.   Sept 3
521–597   A native of Antioch who as a child joined the community of St John Stylites. As a boy he began to live on a pillar, and he continued to live thus uninterruptedly for sixty-nine years, until his death. In his earlier years he did not always remain on the same pillar, but he remained on his last pillar (on Mons Admirabilis, near Antioch) for forty-five years. He was consulted by all ranks of society, like his namesake of Jan 5 q.v.

Simeon Senex (St)   Oct 8
1st cent.   The "just and devout man who awaited the consolation of Israel" (Luke 2:25), who took the Infant Saviour in his arms when he was brought to the temple and who on that occasion sang the *Nunc dimittis* (ib).

Simeon Metaphrastes (St)   Nov 9
10th cent.   Byzantine hagiographer, whose collection of lives of the saints has been regarded as a standard work in the East since his lifetime. Nothing is now known about his own life, however.

Simeon of Cava (Bl) Ab. OSB.   Nov 16
d. 1141   Abbot of the great Benedictine abbey of La Cava, in S. Italy, from 1124 to 1141. He was highly esteemed by Pope Innocent II and by Roger II of Sicily. It was during his abbacy that Cava reached the peak of its splendour. Cult confirmed in 1928.

Similian (French: Sambin) (St) Bp.   June 16
d. 310   Third bishop of Nantes. St Gregory of Tours testifies to his sanctity.

Simitrius and Comp. (SS) MM.   May 26
d. *c* 159   A band of twenty-three Roman martyrs, arrested while assembled for prayer

St Simeon Senex, Oct 8

St Simon, Feb 18

martyrs, arrested while assembled for prayer in the *titulus* or church of St Praxedes and beheaded without trial.

Simon Fidati of Cascia
(Bl) C. OSA. Erem.   Feb 3
d. 1348 Born at Cascia in Umbria, he joined the friar-hermits of St Augustine and was a prominent figure as a writer, preacher and adviser in the life of most of the cities of central Italy. Scholars have claimed to find in his book *De Gestis Domini Salvatoris* a source of several of Luther's doctrines.

Simon of St Bertin (Bl)
Ab. OSB.   Feb 4
d. 1148 Successively monk of Saint-Bertin, abbot of Auchy, and abbot of Saint-Bertin (1131). His election as abbot of Saint-Bertin was contested, and he was unable to take up his office until 1138.

Simon (St) Bp. M.   Feb 18
d. *c* 107 The son of Clopas and a kinsman of our Lord (Mat. 13:55; Mk. 6:3; John 19:25). He allegedly succeeded St James the Less in the see of Jerusalem and was crucified in extreme old age under Trajan. He is represented as an old man, crucified, or as a child carrying a fish. Since 1969 his cult is to be kept only by local calendars.

Simon of Trent (St) M. March 24

d. 1474 A child living at Trent in N. Italy who is said to have been murdered by Jews at Eastertide out of hatred of Christ. The confession of the Jews was obtained under torture. The trial was reviewed at Rome by Sixtus IV in 1478 but he did not authorize the cult of St Simon. This however was done by Sixtus V in 1588, largely on account of the miracles. In 1965 the Sacred Congregation of Rites forbade all future veneration. The cause of the child's death is considered quite uncertain.

Simon Rinalducci (Bl) S. OSA. Apr 20

d. 1322 A native of Todi, he became an Austin friar, a famous preacher, and for a time provincial of Umbria. He kept silence under an unjust accusation rather than cause scandal among his brethren. Cult confirmed in 1833.

Simon Stock (St) C. OC. May 16

c 1165–1265 He was among the first English people to join the Carmelites and eventually (1247) became the sixth general of the order. As such he was instrumental in establishing houses at the principal university cities of Europe: Cambridge (1248), Oxford (1253), Paris (1260), Bologna (id.), and in modifying the rule so that the Carmelites became an order of mendicant friars rather than of hermits. Though never formally canonized, Simon is venerated by the Carmelites since 1564, and in certain dioceses as a canonized saint. He died at Bordeaux, and his relics are enshrined at Aylesford, Kent. In art he is depicted as an old man habited as a Carmelite, praying, or receiving a scapular from our Lady.

Simon Acosta and Simon Lopez (BB) MM. SJ. July 15

d. 1570 The former was born at Oporto in Portugal and became a Jesuit lay-brother; the latter was a native of Ourem, also in Portugal, and was a Jesuit cleric. Both formed part of the missionary expedition of Bl Ignatius Azevedo, q.v.

Simon of Lipnicza (Bl) C. OFM. July 30

d. 1482 A native of Lipnicza in Poland who, as a result of hearing a sermon by St John Capistran, joined the Friars Minor and became a powerful preacher himself. He died while tending the sick during a plague at Cracow. Beatified in 1685.

Simon Kiota and Comp. (BB) MM. Aug 16

d. 1625 A Japanese member of one of the old Christian families of Bungo and an officer

St Simon Stock, May 16

in the royal army. He served as a catechist and at the age of sixty was crucified with his wife and three companions (Bl Thomas Ghengoro, his wife and their child James) at Cocura. Beatified in 1867.

Simon of Crespy (St) Mk. OSB. Sept 18

d. *c* 1080 Count of Crespy in Valois and a descendant of Charlemagne. He was brought up at the court of William the Conqueror. The sight of his father's decomposing body led him to desire the monastic life, and with William's leave, though the latter wished him to marry, he set out for Rome. On the way thither he stopped at the Benedictine abbey of Condat in the Jura and there took the habit. After his profession he was employed by St Gregory VII and others in bringing about reconciliations between princes and potentates. It was while he was at Rome engaged in a mission of this kind that he died, being attended at his deathbed by Pope Gregory.

Simon of Genoa (Bl) A.
OSB. Cam.   Sept 18
d. 1292   A Genoese who became a hermit at Camaldoli.

Simon de Rojas (St) C.
O. Trin.   Sept 28
1522–1624   A native of Valladolid who became a Trinitarian, in which order he became a superior and a famous missionary. In later life he was appointed confessor at the court of Philip III and tutor to the royal family. Beatified in 1766, Canonized in 1988.

Simon (St) Apostle   GC. Oct 28
1st cent.   In the gospels he is surnamed "the Cananean", or "the Zealot". His name occurs only in the lists of the apostles. The tradition of the West places the scene of his labours in Egypt and Mesopotamia, but there are several other different traditions among the Christians of the East, and nothing positive can be stated about his life and activities. His emblems are a fish or two, a boat, an oar, a saw; or he is being sawn asunder longitudinally.

Simon Ballachi (Bl) C. OP.   Nov 3
d. 1319   Born at Sant' Arcangelo near Rimini, the son of Count Ballachi and nephew of two archbishops of Rimini. At the age of twenty-seven he became a Dominican lay-brother in his native city and was remarkable for his extraordinary austerities. Cult confirmed in 1821.

Simon of Aulne (Bl) C.
OSB. Cist.   Nov 6
d. 1215   A Cistercian lay-brother at Aulne renowned for his gift of mystical prayer, his visions and his ecstasies. On this account he was invited to Rome by Innocent III.

Simon Yempo (Bl) M.   Dec 4
d. 1623   A native of Japan who became a Buddhist monk. Having been converted to Christianity and become a lay catechist, he was burnt alive at Yeddo. Beatified in 1867.

Simon Hoa (St) M.   Dec 12
d. 1840   A native of Vietnam, a physician and mayor of his village. He was attached to the Foreign Missions of Paris. After most

cruel tortures he was beheaded for the faith. Beatified in 1900, canonized in 1988.

Simplician (St) Bp.   Aug 16
d. 400   A friend and adviser of St Ambrose, whom he succeeded in the see of Milan. He was already an old man and was bishop only three years. He played a leading part in the conversion of St Augustine, by whom he was always remembered with deep gratitude.

Simplician (St) M.   Dec 31
See Stephen, Pontian, etc.

Simplicius (St) Pope   March 10
d. 483   A native of Tivoli who was pope from 468 to 483. He upheld the decrees of the council of Chalcedon and supported the Eastern Catholics against the Monophysite heretics, who were backed by three successive Byzantine emperors. The Western Roman Empire collapsed in 476 so that he had also to deal with the Arian King Odoacer.

Simplicius and Comp.
(SS) MM.   May 10
See Calepodius, Palmatius, etc.

Simplicius (St) M.   May 15
d. 304   A martyr of Sardinia, buried alive under Diocletian.

Simplicius of Bourges (St)
Bp.   June 16
d. 477 (March 1)   He was already married and the father of a large family when the bishops of the province chose him to be bishop of Bourges. He defended the church against the Arian Visigoths and the ambitions of lay magnates.

Simplicius of Autun (St)
Bp.   June 24
d. c 360   A married man who lived a virginal life with his wife and became bishop of Autun. As a bishop he worked zealously and successfully to uproot paganism.

Simplicius, Faustinus and Beatrix (SS) MM.   July 29
d. c 303   Said to have been two brothers and their sister martyred in Rome under Diocletian. Their Acts are not trustworthy. Cult confined to local calendars since 1969.

Simplicius, Constantius and Victorian (SS) MM.   Aug 26
?   According to the pre-1970 RM., Simplicius and his two sons were martyred under Aurelian, but it seems that three separate martyrs have been artificially grouped by a hagiographer; Simplicius of Rome, Victorianus of

Amiternum and Constantius of Perugia (Jan 29), q.v.

Simplicius (St) Ab. OSB. Oct 22
d. *c* 570 A disciple of St Benedict and third abbot of Montecassino. His relics were enshrined in 1071.

Simplicius (St) M. Nov 8
See Four Crowned Martyrs.

Simplicius of Verona (St)
Bp. Nov 20
d. *c* 535 Bishop of Verona.

Simplicius (St) M. Dec 18
See Quintus, Simplicius, and Comp.

Sinai (Martyrs of) (SS) Jan 14
See Isaias, Sabas and Comp.

Sincheall (St) Ab. March 26
5th cent. A disciple of St Patrick. Abbot-founder of the monastery and school at Killeigh, Offaly, Ireland, where he had one hundred and fifty monks under his direction.

Sindimius (St) M. Dec 19
See Cyriacus, Paulillus, etc.

Sindulphus of Reims (St)
H. Oct 20
d. 660 A native of Gascony who lived as a hermit at Aussonce, near Reims.

**Sindulphus of Vienne
(St)** Bp. Dec 10
d. *c* 669 The thirty-first bishop of Vienne in Gaul.

Siran (St) Ab. OSB. Dec 5
Otherwise Sigiranus, q.v.

Siricius (St) Pope Nov 26
d. 399 A native of Rome who ruled the church from 384 to 399. His episcopate is important for the development of papal authority: his letter — called the first papal Decretal — to Archbishop Himerius of Tarragona is an example of this. He also held a synod in Rome in 386, the results of which were communicated to the church in Africa.

Siridion (St) Bp. Jan 2
? Probably a scribe's error for Isidore. See Isidore of Antioch.

**Sirmium (Martyrs of)
(SS)** Feb 23 and Apr 9
d. *c* 303 Two anonymous groups of martyrs are catalogued in the pre-1970 RM. as having suffered under Diocletian at Sirmium, now Mitrovica in the Balkans; (i) a band of seventy-two, on Feb 23, put to death probably in 303; and (ii) a group of seven maidens commemo-

rated on Apr 9 and probably martyred in the same year.

Sisebutus (St) Ab. OSB. March 15
d. 1082 Abbot of the Benedictine monastery of Cardeña in the diocese of Burgos, Spain. Under him the abbey became a powerful focus of ecclesiastical and civil life. He gave shelter to the Cid (Rodrigo Diaz de Vivar), the celebrated hero of the Christian Spanish Reconquest.

Sisenandus (St) M. July 16
d. 851 Born at Badajoz in Estremadura, he became a deacon in the church of St Acisclus at Cordoba. He was beheaded under Abderrahman II.

**Sisinius, Diocletius and
Florentius (SS)** MM. May 11
d. 303 Martyrs at Osimo, near Ancona, under Diocletian. They were stoned to death at the same time as the better known Roman priest, St Anthimus.

**Sisinius, Martyrius and
Alexander (SS)** MM. May 29
d. 397 Said to have been Cappadocians, received by St Vigilius of Trent on the recommendation of St Ambrose and sent to evangelize the Tyrol. They were martyred by a pagan mob who were celebrating the festival of the Ambarvalia.

Sisinius (St) Bp. Nov 23
d. *p.* 325 Bishop of Cyzicus and a confessor of the faith under Diocletian. he was dragged by wild horses, but survived and was present at the council of Nicaea.

Sisinius (St) M. Nov 29
See Saturninus and Sisinius.

Sisoes (St) H. July 4
d. *c* 429 He lived as a hermit in Egypt for sixty-two years. To some extent he resembled St Antony in the influence he exercised.

Sithian (St) Bp. July 15
Otherwise Seduinus, possibly identical with Swithun, q.v.

Siviard (St) Ab. OSB. March 1
d. *c* 729 Benedictine monk at Saint-Calais, on the R. Anisole. He succeeded his own father as abbot of the monastery. To him we owe an interesting life of St Calais, founder of the abbey.

Sixtus I (Xystus) (St) Pope Apr 3
d. 127 A Roman. Pope from 117 to 127. Later martyrologies refer to him as a martyr but there are no *Acta* and Irenaeus' list implies he was not a martyr.

Sixtus III (Xystus) (St)
Pope　　　　　　　　　March 28
d. 440　Pope from 432. A Roman by birth. As pope he is best remembered for having opposed Nestorianism and Pelagianism and for having restored several Roman basilicas, among them S. Maria Maggiore.

Sixtus II (Xystus) (St)
Pope and Comp. MM.　　GC. Aug 7
d. 258　He reigned for one year: 257–258. While preaching in the catacomb of Praetextatus during the celebration of the liturgy he was seized with his deacons Felicissimus and Agapitus and martyred. His name is mentioned in the first eucharistic prayer. The pre-1970 RM. commemorated with them Januarius, Magnus, Vincent and Stephen, subdeacons, and Quartus, all as martyrs. Quartus owes his existence to a bad manuscript in which "diaconus Quartus" was written for "diacones quattuor". It is probable that St Sixtus suffered with all his seven deacons, the six mentioned today, and, later, St Laurence.

Sixtus (Xystus) of Reims
(St) Bp.　　　　　　　Sept 1
d. c 300　First bishop of Reims, c 290–300. He was sent from Rome and established his see at Soissons before moving it to Reims.

Slebhene (Slebhine) (St)
Ab.　　　　　　　　　March 2
d. 767　An Irish monk who was abbot of Iona from 752 to 767.

Smaragdus (St) M.　　　Aug 8
See Cyriacus, Largus, etc.

Sobel (St) M.　　　　　Aug 5
See Cantidius, Cantidian and Sobel.

Socrates and Dionysius
(SS) MM.　　　　　　　Apr 19
d. 275　Martyrs of Pamphylia, stabbed to death under Aurelian.

Socrates and Stephen
(SS) MM.　　　　　　　Sept 17
? Alleged British martyrs under Diocletian. The pre-1970 RM. assigned them to Britain, but it seems probable that Socrates was martyred in Abretania, a province of Mysia in Asia Minor, and that a scribe changed the name to Britannia. Bithynia has also been suggested as the place of martyrdom.

Sola (Sol, Solus, Suolo) (St)
H. OSB.　　　　　　　Dec 3
d. 794　An Anglo-Saxon monk and priest who followed St Boniface to Germany and lived as a hermit first near Fulda under the obedience of that abbey and later near Eichstätt. Finally he settled on a piece of land bestowed on him by Charlemagne, on which he founded the abbey of Solnhofen as a dependency of Fulda.

Solangia (Solange) (St)
VM.　　　　　　　　　May 10
d. c 880　A poor shepherdess of the neighbourhood of Bourges who, for resisting the attempts of the local lord on her chastity, was brutally murdered by him.

Solemnis (Soleine) (St)
Bp.　　　　　　　　　Sept 25
d. c 511　Bishop of Chartres c 490–511. He was present at the baptism of Clovis.

Solina (St) VM.　　　　Oct 17
d. c 290　A Gascon maiden who escaped to Chartres to avoid marriage to a pagan. She was beheaded at Chartres.

Solochon and Comp.
(SS) MM.　　　　　　　May 17
d. 305　Three Egyptian soldiers in the imperial army, stationed at Chalcedon. They were clubbed to death for the faith under Maximian.

Solomon (St) M.　　　March 13
See Rudericus and Salomon.

Solomon I (St) M.　　　June 25
5th cent.　According to a legend he was born in Cornwall, and husband of St Gwen and father of St Cuby (Cybi). He reigned as a kinglet in Brittany and was assassinated by heathen malcontents among his subjects.

Solomon III (Breton: Selyf) (St) M.　　　June 25
d. 874　King of Brittany and a brave, though at times brutal, warrior against Franks, Northmen and his own rebellious subjects. The Bretons count him among their many national heroes. He did penance for the crimes of his youth, and when he was assassinated the people at once acclaimed him a martyr.

Solomon (Salomon, Salonius) (St) Bp.　　Sept 28
d. p. 269　First bishop of Genoa. His true name was Salonius: it was changed into Salomon by a scribe's error.

Solutor (St) M.　　　　Nov 13
See Valentine, Solutor and Victor.

Solutor (St) M.　　　　Nov 20
See Octavius, Solutor and Adventor.

Sopatra (St) V.　　　　Nov 9
See Eustolia and Sopatra.

Sophia (St) VM.　　　　Apr 30
d. c 250　A maiden of Fermo in central Italy, martyred under Decius.

Sophia and Irene (SS)
MM. Sept 18
d. c?200 Martyrs beheaded in Egypt.

Sophia (St) W. Sept 30
The legendary mother of the virgin martyrs
Faith, Hope and Charity who, according to a
Roman tradition, suffered at Rome under
Hadrian. Three days later Sophia, while pray-
ing at their tomb, herself passed peacefully
away. The story seems to have come from the
East and is thought to be an allegorical
explanation of the cult of the Divine Wisdom,
from whom proceed faith, hope and charity.

Sophronius (St) Bp. March 11
d. c639 A Syrian from Damascus who
became patriarch of Jerusalem in 634. He is an
ecclesiastical writer of distinction. His life's
work, however, was the condemnation of
Monothelitism. He was engaged in this campaign when the Saracens occupied Jerusalem
and drove him from his see. Poems and letters
of his are still extant.

Sophronius (St) Bp. Dec 8
6th cent. An alleged bishop of Cyprus.

Sosipater (St) June 25
2nd cent. A kinsman and disciple of St Paul
(Rom. 16:21). He accompanied the apostle on
some of his journeys, and tradition connects
his later life with the island of Corfu.

Sosius (St) M. Sept 19
See Januarius and Comp.

Sosteneo (St) C. May 3
One of the Seven Founders of the Servite
Order, q.v.

Sosthenes and Victor
(SS) MM. Sept 10
d. 4th cent.? Martyrs at Chalcedon under
Maximian. In the late and unreliable Acts of St
Euphemia they were among the executioners
appointed to torture her and were converted
through her prayers and the example of her
fortitude.

Sosthenes (St) Nov 28
1st cent. The ruler of the synagogue at
Corinth mentioned in Acts 18:17. He became
a disciple of St Paul and is probably the
"brother" mentioned in 1 Cor. 1; 1. Greek
tradition makes him the first bishop of Col-
ophon in Asia Minor.

Sostratus, Spirus, Eraclius,
Eperentius and Cecilia (SS)
MM. July 8
? 4th cent. Martyrs of Syrmium, Pannonia.

Soter (St) Pope formerly Apr 22
d. c174 An Italian, and the eleventh in
Irenaeus's list of early rulers of the church in
Rome. Eusebius has references to his corres-
pondence with the church of Corinth. In his
time Easter was fixed as an annual festival, to
be celebrated on the Sunday following the
fourteenth day of the month Nisan in the
Jewish calendar (i.e. Passover). Traditionally
regarded as a martyr, no evidence exists now
that this was so. Cult suppressed in 1969.

Soteris (St) VM. Feb 10
d. 304 A Roman maiden martyred under
Diocletian. She seems to have been a sister of
the great-great-grandmother of St Ambrose,
by whom she is often mentioned.

Sozon (St) M. Sept 7
d. c304 Alleged to have been a shepherd in
his native Cilicia. At a pagan celebration he
pulled off the golden hand of an idol, broke it
up and distributed the pieces among the poor.
He was forthwith burnt at the stake.

Speciosus (St) Mk. OSB. March 15
d. c555 A wealthy landowner of Campania
who, with his brother Gregory, received the
habit from St Benedict at Montecassino. He
was attached to the new foundation at Terracina, but died at Capua while on an errand
undertaken for the benefit of his monastery.

Sperandea (Sperandia)
(St) Abs. OSB. Sept 11
d. 1276 A relative of St Ubald of Gubbio.
She became a Benedictine at Cingoli, in the
Marches of Ancona, and eventually abbess of
her nunnery. She is venerated as the patron
saint of Cingoli.

Speratus (St) M. July 17
See Scillitan Martyrs.

Spes (St) Ab. March 28
d. c513 An abbot of Campi in central Italy.
He was totally blind for forty years, but fifteen
days before his death his eyesight was restored.

Spes (Hope, Elpis) (St) VM. Aug 1
See Faith, Hope and Charity.

Speusippus, Eleusippus,
Meleusippus and
Leonilla (SS) MM. Jan 17
d. 175 According to the legend, which
probably has no basis in fact, these saints were
three brothers born at one birth, natives of
Cappadocia, martyred with their grandmother
Leonilla under Marcus Aurelius. Their
alleged relics were brought to Langres, where
their church bears the name of St Geome.

Spinulus (Spinula, Spin)
(St) Ab. OSB. Nov 5
d. 707 (or 720) A Benedictine monk of Moyenmoutier under St Hidulphus. Later he became the abbot-founder of the small abbey of Bégon-Celle (now Saint-Blasien).

Spiridion (St) Bp. Dec 14
d. *c* 348 He began life as a shepherd and became bishop of Tremithus in his native island of Cyprus. Under Diocletian he was condemned to lose an eye and forced to labour in the mines. He allegedly survived the persecution and was one of the venerable "confessors of the Faith" present at the council of Nicaea, where he was a strong opponent of Arianism, although his name is not recorded among the list of signatories. He was however definitely present at the council of Sardica (*c* 343).

Stachys (St) Bp. Oct 31
1st cent. The Christian saluted by St Paul (Rom. 16:9) as "my beloved". The later tradition is that St Andrew ordained him bishop of Byzantium.

Stacteus (St) M. July 18
One of the alleged sons of St Symphorosa, q.v.

Stacteus (St) M. Sept 28
? A Roman martyr of whom no particulars are available.

Stanislaus (St) Bp. M. GC. Apr 11
1030–1079 Stanislaus Szczepanowsky was born near Cracow and educated at Gnesen and Paris. In 1072 he became bishop of Cracow. He excommunicated King Boleslaus the Cruel for his evil life, and that monarch in consequence slew the saint with his own hand while he was celebrating the eucharist. Pope St Gregory VII laid Poland under an interdict and Boleslaus fled the country and died a fugitive in Hungary. Stanislaus was canonized in 1253. Some Polish historians contend that the saint was plotting to dethrone Boleslaus; others assert that the previous version is the truth. He is represented as a bishop being hacked in pieces at the foot of the altar.

Stanislaus Kostka (St) C.
SJ. Nov 13
1550–1568 Born at Rostkovo in Poland, the son of a senator, he was sent in 1563 to Vienna to study at the Jesuit college recently established in that city. Despite fierce opposition from his family he resolved to become a Jesuit himself. St Peter Canisius encouraged him to go to Rome, where he was received into the Jesuit noviceship by St Francis Borgia in Oct 1567. He died within a year, but during that brief period he had gained a reputation for angelic innocence. Canonized in 1726.

Stephana de Quinzani (Bl) V.
OP. Jan 2
1457–1530 She was born near Brescia and at the age of fifteen joined the Dominican tertiaries. After living at home for many years she founded a convent called San Paolo, near Soncino, of which she became first abbess. She was noted for her ecstasies and for the marks of the stigmata, which were attested by many eye-witnesses. Cult confirmed by Benedict XIV.

Stephen
Note. Stephen is the English variant of the Graeco-Latin Stephanus (crowned). Other modern variants of the same name are: Italian, Stefano; French, Etienne; Spanish, Esteban; German, Stephan; Hungarian, Istvan.

Stephen Cuénot (St)
See page 520.

Stephen du Bourg (St) O.
Cart. Jan 4
d. 1118 A canon of St Rufus at Valence who became one of the first companions of St Bruno at the foundation of the Grande-Chartreuse. He was sent (1116) to found the charterhouse at Meyria, and there he died.

Stephen of Liège (Bl) Ab.
OSB. Jan 13
d. 1059 A canon of St Denis, Liège, who became a Benedictine monk at St Vannes, Verdun. Later he returned to Liège as abbot-founder of St Laurence.

Stephen Bellesini (Bl) C.
OSA. Erem. Feb 3
1774–1840 A native of Trent who joined the Augustinian hermits at Bologna and studied there and at Rome. Owing to the disturbances following the French Revolution he retired to his home in the Trentino, where he held the post of government inspector of schools. At the earliest opportunity, however, he returned to the religious life and was appointed novice master in Rome and later parish priest at the shrine of our Lady at Genazzano. Here he died as a result of his devoted ministrations to the victims of the cholera epidemic. Beatified in 1904.

Stephen of Grandmont
(St) Ab. Feb 8
1046–1124 Born at Thiers in Auvergne, the son of the lord of the district, he accompanied his father at the age of twelve to the tomb of St Nicholas of Bari. He fell ill at Benevento and remained there, being educated by Archbishop Milo. On his return to France he founded at Murat a congregation of Benedic-

St Stanislaus, Apr 11

tine monk-hermits on the model of those he had seen in Calabria. He ruled them for forty-six years but does not seem ever to have become a monk himself. After his death the large community migrated to Grandmont, whence the name of Grandmontines given to this branch of the Benedictine order. Stephen was canonized in 1189 at the request of Henry II of England.

Stephen Cuénot (St) Bp.
M.   now Nov 14
1802–1861 Born at Beaulieu, France, he joined the Society of Foreign Missions at Paris and was sent to Vietnam. In 1833 he was appointed Vicar Apostolic of E. Cochin-China, receiving episcopal ordination at Singapore.

After fifteen years more of fruitful labour he was one of the first to be arrested on the outbreak of the persecution of 1861. He died in prison (perhaps from poison) on Nov 14, shortly before the date fixed for his execution. Beatified in 1909, canonized in 1988.

Stephen of Lyons (St) Bp. Feb 13
d. 512 Bishop of Lyons. He was active in converting the Arian Burgundians to the Catholic faith.

Stephen of Rieti (St) Ab. Feb 13
d. c 590 An abbot at Rieti whom St Gregory the Great describes as "rude of speech but of cultured life".

Stephen of Obazine (St)
Ab. OSB.Cist. March 8
d. 1154 Stephen and another priest withdrew into the forest of Obazine near Tulle, France, to lead a solitary life. When disciples wished to join them they obtained leave of the bishop of Limoges to build a monastery. The new abbey had no written rule, and St Stephen arranged for its affiliation to the Cistercian order, and was himself blessed as its first abbot.

Stephen of Palestrina
(Bl) Card. Bp. OSB. Cist. March 17
d. 1144 A monk of Clairvaux who was made a cardinal and bishop of Palestrina (1141). By Cistercian writers he is always called either saint or blessed.

Stephen IX or X (Bl)
Pope, OSB. March 29
d. 1058 A distinguished ecclesiastic of a noble family he became a monk of Montecassino. In 1057 he first became abbot of Montecassino and then pope. His pontificate though brief was vigorous and worthy, and characterised by reforms of abuses.

Stephen (St) M. Apr 1
See Victor and Stephen.

Stephen and Hildebrand
(BB) MM. OSB. Cist. Apr 11
d. 1209 Two Cistercians, the former an abbot, the latter a monk, slain by the Albigenses at Saint-Gilles in Languedoc. They are venerated at Saint-Gilles, though their cult has not been officially confirmed.

Stephen Harding (St) Ab.
OSB. Cist. Jan 26
d. 1134 An English monk of Sherborne who, after a pilgrimage to Rome, joined St Robert at Molesmes and with him migrated to Cîteaux. Here he became successively subprior under St Robert, prior under St Alberic, and third abbot (1109). As such he was responsible for the original Constitutions of the Cistercians, as also for the kernel of the Charter of Charity which he presented to the General Chapter of Cîteaux in 1119. To him therefore, much more than to St Robert, the Cistercians owe their definite status as a new branch of the Benedictines. It was Stephen who received St Bernard and his thirty companions at Cîteaux and two years later sent him to become the abbot-founder of Clairvaux and the principal exponent of the Cistercian ideal. St Stephen was canonized in 1623.

Stephen de Pétervárad
(Bl) M. OFM. Apr 22
d. 1334 A Hungarian Franciscan in the Balkans. Being tortured by the Muslim Tartars he denied his faith, but recovering his courage, solemnly professed it before the Khan and was cruelly put to death.

Stephen of Antioch (St)
Bp. M. Apr 25
d. 481 A patriarch of Antioch who was a special target for the fury of the Monophysite heretics. In the end they attacked him at the altar, struck him down and flung his body into the River Orontes.

Stephen (St) M. Apr 27
See Castor and Stephen.

Stephen of Narbonne
and Comp. (BB) MM. May 28
d. 1242 Stephen was a member of the Inquisition of Toulouse: he was a Franciscan. Together with eleven companions — Benedictines, Franciscans, Dominicans, and one secular priest — he was murdered at Avignonet by the Albigensian heretics. Cult approved in 1866.

Stephen of Corvey (St)
Bp. M. OSB. June 2
d. ? 1075 A monk of Corvey in Saxony who was appointed regionary bishop in Sweden, where he worked as a missionary with signal success. He was the first to plant the faith on the shores of the Sound. He was martyred, probably at Nora.

Stephen Bandelli (Bl) C.
OP. June 12
d. 1450 Born at Castelnuovo, diocese of Piacenza, where he became a Dominican. He was an eminent preacher and reformer. Cult approved in 1856.

Stephen of Reggio (St)
Bp. M. July 5
1st cent. Said to have been ordained first

bishop of Reggio by St Paul and to have been martyred under Nero. It is only since the seventeenth century that this story has gained currency and that he has been venerated as the principal patron of Reggio.

Stephen de Zudaira (Bl)
M. SJ.   July 15
d. 1570 Born at Viscaya in Spain, he became a Jesuit lay-brother and formed one of the martyr-band headed by Bl Ignatius de Azevedo, q.v.

Stephen del Lupo (St)
Ab. OSB.   July 19
d. 1191 Benedictine monk of San Libera-tore di Majella, and afterwards abbot-founder of St Peter's at Vallebona, near Manopello, in Italy. He is said to have been befriended by a wolf: hence his nickname of "del lupo".

Stephen I (St) Pope   Aug 2
d. 257 A Roman of the *gens Julia*. He became bishop of Rome in 254, and during his short pontificate he was occupied with the question of baptism being administered by heretics. He invoked the apostolic tradition in favour of the Roman practice and met with stout opposition from St Cyprian. Tradition says that he was beheaded while seated in his chair during the celebration of the eucharist in the catacombs, but the earliest liturgical docu-ments present him as a bishop and confessor. He was not in fact a martyr, and since 1969 his cult has been confined to local calendars.

Stephen (St) M.   Aug 6
See Sixtus II and Comp.

Stephen of Cardeña and
Comp. (SS) MM. OSB.   Aug 6
d. 872 Abbot of the great Castilian monas-tery of Cardeña, near Burgos, in which were housed over two hundred monks. The abbot and community were slain by Saracens from S. Spain. The cult was approved in 1603 and Card. Baronius composed the proper lessons for their office. As these martyrs are first heard of in an inscription of the thirteenth century, there is considerable doubt as to their exis-tence; the name Stephen for the abbot is an even later addition.

Stephen of Hungary (St)
King   GC. Aug 16
d. c 935–1038 On the death of his father, Geza (997), Stephen succeeded as sovereign of the Magyars of Hungary. He had married Gisela, a sister of the emperor St Henry II in 995, and they set their hands to the common task of christianizing their people. With the help of Pope Sylvester II and as a result of numerous victories over external and internal foes, Stephen gradually welded the Magyars into a national unity. He organized dioceses and founded abbeys (among them the great Benedictine abbey of Pannonhalma, which still stands), and secured the services of prominent foreign monks, notably of St Gerard Sagredo, abbot of San Giorgio Mag-giore at Venice, who became the tutor of the king's son, the young St Emeric. The latter died in the prime of life, and the declining years of St Stephen were darkened by many misfortunes and difficulties, though he never ceased to be just, kind and merciful. His relics were enshrined in 1083 by order of St Gregory VII. To this day the Magyars consider him their greatest national saint and hero, and part of the crown sent to him by Pope Sylvester is preserved and is revered as the palladium of the Magyars.

Stephen of Chatillon (St)
Bp. O. Cart.   Sept 7
d. 1208 Born at Lyons of the noble family of the Chatillons, he entered the charterhouse of Portes, where he became prior in 1196. In 1203 he became bishop of Dié. Cult approved in 1907.

Stephen Pongracz (Bl)
M. SJ.   Sept 7
See Mark, Stephen and Melchior.

Stephen of Perugia (St)
Ab. OSB.   Sept 16
d. 1026 Third abbot of the Benedictine monastery of St Peter at Perugia, where an altar is dedicated to him.

Stephen (St) M.   Sept 17
See Socrates and Stephen.

Stephen of Cajazzo (St)
Bp. OSB.   Oct 29
935–1023 Born at Macerata and educated at Capua, he was appointed abbot of San Salva-tore Maggiore and later, in 979, bishop of Cajazzo. He is now venerated as the principal patron of the city and diocese.

Stephen of Apt (St) Bp.   Nov 6
975–1046 Born at Agde, he was elected bishop of Apt, S. France, in 1010. He rebuilt the cathedral there.

Stephen of Lorándháza
(Bl) Mk.   Nov 6
d. 1519 General of the Hungarian Pauline order, and biographer of St Paul the Hermit. He died in the monastery of St Peter in Sümeg.

Stephen (St) M.   Nov 21
See Honorius, Eutychius and Stephen.

Stephen (St) M.   Nov 22
See Mark and Stephen.

**Stephen, Basil, Peter,
Andrew and Comp. (SS)**
MM.   Nov 28
d. 764 St Stephen, surnamed "the Younger", was born at Constantinople in 714 and
became a monk and abbot of Mt St Auxentius.
He firmly opposed the fanatical iconoclasm of
the emperor Constantine Copronymus. When
all attempts to win him over to heresy had
failed, the emperor had him put to death, along
with SS Basil, Peter, Andrew and a band of
over three hundred monks.

Stephen (St) M.   Dec 3
See Claudius, Crispin, etc.

Stephen (Bl) Mk.   Dec 8
d. 1300 Third general of the Pauline order.

Stephen Vinh (St) M.   Dec 19
d. 1839 A peasant of Vietnam and a
Dominican tertiary. Strangled at Ninh-Tai
with four companions. Canonized in 1988.

Stephen the Deacon (St)
Protomartyr   GC. Dec 26
d. c 35 The disciple chosen by the apostles,
"full of faith and the Holy Spirit" as the first of
the seven deacons (Acts 6: 1–5). He was
stoned to death by the Jews at the instigation of
the Sanhedrin, thus becoming the Christian
protomartyr. His dying prayer was witnessed
by St Paul, who was actively engaged in his
martyrdom. In art he is depicted as vested as a
deacon, holding a book and sometimes a palm.
He carries a pile of stones in his hand, or they
rest on his book, or head, or are gathered into
the folds of his dalmatic.

**Stephen, Pontian, Attalus,
Fabian, Cornelius, Sextus,
Flos, Quintian, Minervinus
and Simplician (SS)** MM.   Dec 31
? Catalogued as martyrs of Catania in Sicily.

Stercatius (St) M.   July 24
See Victor, Stercatius and Antinogenes.

Stilla (Bl) V.   July 19
d. c 1141 Daughter of Count Wolfgang II of
Abenberg and a sister of Archbishop Conrad I
of Salzburg. She founded the church of St
Peter at Abenberg, near Nuremburg, where
she was buried and venerated as a saint. Cult
confirmed in 1927.

**Straton, Philip and
Eutychian (SS)** MM.   Aug 17
d. c 301? Citizens of Nicomedia, they were
burnt at the stake. In most MSS a fourth

martyr is added, by name Cyprian. Their Acts
have no value.

Straton (St) M.   Sept 9
? A martyr who was bound to two trees bent
towards each other and torn asunder by their
recoil. Place and era unknown.

Straton (St) M.   Sept 12
See Hieronides, Leontius, etc.

Stratonicus (St) M.   Jan 13
See Hermylus and Stratonicus.

Sturmius (Sturmi) (St)
OSB.   Dec 17
d. 779 The first German to become a
Benedictine. As a child he was entrusted to St
Boniface and educated by St Wigbert in the
abbey of Fritzlar. He was ordained and sent to
evangelize the Saxons. Under orders from
Boniface, whose favourite disciple he was, he
led an expedition to discover a suitable site for
a central abbey for Germany. He chose Fulda,
and the abbey of that name was founded there
in 744. Sturmius was then dispatched to
Montecassino to learn the true Benedictine
observance, and on his return he was appointed abbot of Fulda, where one of his lasting
achievements was the establishment of the
celebrated school. Dearly loved by his monks,
Sturmius was considered as second only to
Boniface as the apostle of the Germanies.
Canonized in 1139.

Stylianos (St) H.   Nov 28
d. 390 A hermit in the vicinity of Adrianople
in Paphlagonia. His life has come down to us
in a naively legendary form. See Alypius.

Styriacus (St)   Nov 2
See Carterius, Styriacus, etc.

Suairlech (St) Bp.   March 27
d. c 750 First bishop of Fore, Westmeath,
Ireland, from c 735 to c 750.

Successus (St) M.   Jan 19
See Paul, Gerontius, etc.

Successus (St) M.   March 28
See Rogatus, Successus and Comp.

Successus (St) M.   Apr 16
See Saragossa (Martyrs of).

Successus (St) M.   Dec 9
See Peter, Successus, etc.

Sulinus (St) Ab.   Sept 1
Otherwise Silin, q.v.

Sulpicius (II) Pius (St) Bp.   Jan 17
d. 647 Bishop of Bourges from 624 to 647.

St Stephen the Deacon, Dec 26

He devoted himself to the care and defence of the poor and persecuted, particularly those who were victims of a certain official of King Dagobert. He is the titular saint of the church and seminary of Saint-Sulpice at Paris.

Sulpicius (I) (St) Bp.   Jan 29
d. 591 Bishop of Bourges from 584 to 591. Though often called Sulpicius Severus, he is not to be confused with the celebrated man of letters of that name, whose name was likewise for some centuries included in the RM. and who was the biographer of St Martin of Tours.

**Sulpicius and Servilian
(SS)** MM.   Apr 20
d. c 117 Roman martyrs whose conversion is traditionally ascribed to the prayers of St Flavia Domitilla. They were beheaded under Trajan.

Sulpicius of Bayeux (St)
Bp. M.   Sept 4
d. 843 Bishop of Bayeux from c 838 to 843. He was slain by the Normans at Livry, diocese of Versailles.

Sunaman (St) M. OSB.   Feb 15
See Winaman, Unaman and Sunaman.

Sunniva (Sunnifa) (St) V.   July 8
10th cent. According to the legend, Sunniva was an Irish princess who fled from her country with her brother Alban and a number of other maidens. They were shipwrecked off the coast of Norway and succeeded in landing at Selje Island. Here they were slain by people from the mainland. Their alleged relics were enshrined at Bergen. The whole story seems to be a somewhat modified version of the legend of St Ursula.

Superius (St) M.   June 26
See Salvius and Superius.

Suranus (St) Ab.   Jan 24
d. c 580 Abbot of a monastery at Sora, near Caserta, who distributed all the goods of the monastery among the refugees from the Lombards. When the latter arrived and found that nothing remained in the abbey to plunder, they slew Suranus on the spot. We owe the story to St Gregory the Great (Dial. 4:22).

Susanna (St) VM.   Jan 18
See Archelais, Thecla, etc.

**Susanna, Marciana,
Palladia and Comp. (SS)**
MM.   May 24
2nd cent. Wives of certain soldiers belonging to the military unit commanded by St Meletius. They were put to death together with their children and other martyrs in Galatia. Their Acts are legendary.

Susanna Cobioje (Bl) M.   July 12
d. 1628 Wife of Bl Peter Araki Cobioje. Six months before her death she was hung naked

by her hair from a tree for eight hours. She was beheaded at Nagasaki. Beatified in 1867.

Susanna (St) VM.   Aug 11
d. 295 The Acts of this saint are wholly untrustworthy, but there probably was a Roman martyr of this name and to her is dedicated the Roman church of St Susanna. She had no connection with St Tiburtius, commemorated on the same day. Since 1969 her cult has been confined to her basilica in Rome.

Susanna (St) VM.   Sept 19
d. 362 According to the pre-1970 RM. she was the daughter of a pagan priest and a Jewess. Being converted to Christ after their death, she was made a deaconess at Eleutheropolis, where she was martyred under Julian the Apostate.

Suso, Henry (Bl) C.   Oct 25
See Henry Suso.

Swithbert (St) Bp. OSB.   March 1
c 647–713 A Northumbrian Benedictine, he formed one of the group of twelve missionary monks who in 690 crossed over to Friesland under the leadership of St Willibrord. He preached the gospel with great success, mainly in Hither Friesland. In 693 he was ordained regionary bishop by St Wilfrid at Ripon and returned to preach along the right bank of the Rhine. His work here was undone by the Saxon invaders, and he retired to the small island of Kaiserswerth in the Rhine, near Düsseldorf. Here he founded a Benedictine monastery (710), where he died and where his relics are still venerated.

**Swithbert the Younger
(St)** Bp.   Apr 30
d. 807 An Englishman, perhaps a Benedictine monk, who joined the missionaries in Germany and was made bishop of Werden in Westphalia.

Swithun (Swithin) (St) Bp.   July 2
d. 862 He was born in Wessex and spent his youth at the old abbey at Winchester, but it is not certain that he ever became a monk. After being ordained priest he was made chaplain to Egbert, king of the W. Saxons, and tutor to the young prince Ethelwolf. In 852 he was appointed bishop of Winchester, and during the decade in which he was bishop the kingdom of Wessex attained the height of its power and influence. On his death, and at his request, he was buried in the cemetery outside the minster. His relics were translated into the cathedral in 971, many miracles occurring, not least the exceedingly heavy rainfall which originated the popular saying, "If it rains on St

Swithun's day it will rain forty days hereafter". His shrine was destroyed at the Reformation.

Swithun Wells (St) M. Dec 10
d. 1591 A gentleman of Bambridge, Hants, executed at Gray's Inn Fields for sheltering a priest named Edmund Genings, q.v., who suffered with him. Beatified in 1929. Canonized in 1970 as one of the Forty Martyrs of England and Wales, q.v.

Sy
Note. Names beginning with Sy are quite often written Si. Sometimes, too, the initial letters Sy stand for the Greek Su.

Syagrius (Siacre) (St) Bp. OSB. May 23
d. *c* 787 A kinsman of Charlemagne. He became a monk of Lérins and later abbot-founder of the monastery of St Pons at Cimiez in Provence, whence he became bishop of Nice (777).

Syagrius (Siacre) (St) Bp. Aug 27
d. 600 Bishop of Autun *c* 560–600. He played a prominent part in the ecclesiastical and political life of his time. He entertained St Augustine and his fellow monks on their way to England.

Sycus and Palatinus (SS) MM. May 30
? Martyrs of Antioch in Syria. Probably the original entry was: Hesychius Palatinus (March 2), q.v.

Sylvester, Sylvanus (*several*)
Otherwise Silvester, Silvanus, q.v.

Sylvia (St) W. Nov 3
d. *c* 572 The mother of St Gregory the Great. Over her former house on the Coelian Hill at Rome a chapel was built in her honour.

Symmachus (St) Pope July 19
d. 514 A Sardinian by birth, he became pope in 498. His pontificate was a troubled one owing to the activities of his enemies, who set up in antipope. Despite their activities and accusations he managed to build and decorate many churches in Rome, and was a vigorous and capable man who would have achieved a great deal more in less troubled times.

Symphorian (St) M. July 7
See Claudius, Nicostratus, etc.

Symphorian (St) M. Aug 22
d. *c* 200 A member of a senatorial family at Autun, put to death under Marcus Aurelius for refusing to sacrifice to the goddess Cybele. He is one of the most celebrated martyrs of France. Venerated on local calendars since 1969.

Symphorian (St) M. Nov 8
One of the Four Crowned Martyrs, q.v.

Symphorosa (St) M. July 2
See Ariston, Crescentian, etc.

Symphorosa and Comp. (SS) MM. formerly July 18
A martyr of Tivoli under Hadrian, widow of the martyr St Getulius. The pre-1970 RM. described her as the mother of seven other martyrs, viz., Crescens, Julian, Nemesius, Primitivus, Justin, Stracteus and Eugene. Her Acts, however, are very untrustworthy, being a Christian adaptation of the story of the Maccabees. She was not the mother of seven martyrs, and these seven martyrs were not brothers, nor were they martyred together. Cult suppressed in 1969.

Symphronius (St) M. Feb 3
See Felix, Symphronius, etc.

Symphronius, Olympius, Theodulus and Exuperia (SS) MM. July 26
d. 257 Symphronius was a Roman slave who brought about the conversion of the tribune Olympius, the latter's wife Exuperia and their son Theodulus. They were all burnt to death under Valerian.

Syncletica (St) V. Jan 5
d. *c* 400 A wealthy lady of Alexandria who abandoned the world and lived as a recluse in a disused tomb till her eighty-fourth year. For a long time she suffered from temptations and spiritual desolation, and in her later years from cancer and consumption.

Syncrotas, Antigonus, Rutilus, Libius, Senerotas and Rogatianus (SS) MM. Feb 23
4th cent. Martyrs of Syrmium, Pannonia.

Synesius and Theopompus (SS) MM. May 21
Identical with Theopemptus and Theonas of Jan 3, q.v., Theonas being also known as Synesius.

Synesius (St) M. Dec 12
d. 275 A lector of the Roman church martyred under Aurelian.

Syntyche (St) July 22
d. 1st cent. A female member of the church of Philippi, described by St Paul as his fellow labourer in the gospel and as one whose name is in the book of life. (Philip. 4:2–3).

Syra (Syria) (St) V. June 8
7th cent. An alleged sister of St Fiacre

(Flaker) who followed her brother from Ireland to France and there lived as a recluse.

Syra (St) V. OSB.   Oct 23
d. *c* 660   Nun of Faremoutier, whence she was summoned by Bishop Ragneboldus to be abbess of a convent at Châlons-sur-Marne.

Syrian Martyrs (SS)   July 31
d. 517   A group of three hundred and fifty monks slain by the Monophysites for defending the decrees of the council of Chalcedon.

Syrian Martyrs (SS)   Nov 14
d. 773   A large number of women cruelly put to death at Emesa in Phoenicia by the Muslim conquerors of the country.

Syrus of Genoa (St) Bp.   June 29
d. *c* 380   Bishop of Genoa from *c* 324 to *c* 380. He had been parish priest of St Romulus (now San Remo). He is the titular of the cathedral of Genoa and principal patron of the city and diocese. His feast is kept on July 7.

Syrus (St) Bp. M.   Dec 9
Alleged first bishop of Pavia. He probably belongs to the third or fourth century. He is the principal patron of Pavia. See also Juventius (Feb 8).

Sytha (St) V.   May 19
Otherwise Osyth, q.v.

Tabitha (or Dorcas) (St) W. Oct 25
1st cent. A widow of Joppa who believed in
Christ. She was raised from the dead by St
Peter (Acts 9:36–43).

Talarican (St) Bp. Oct 30
? 6th cent. A bishop, probably Pictish, in
whose honour various Scottish churches were
dedicated. Mentioned in the Aberdeen Breviary.

Talida (St) V. Jan 5
4th cent. Palladius relates that she was
abbess of one of the twelve nunneries at
Antinöe in Egypt, and that she had been eighty
years at her convent when he visited her.

Talmach (St) C. March 14
7th cent. A disciple of St Barr at Lough Erc,
and founder of a monastery which he placed
under the same saint.

Tammarus (St) C. Sept 1
See Priscus, Castrensis, etc.

Tanca (St) VM. Oct 10
d. c 637 A young girl of the neighbourhood
of Troyes in France, who lost her life in
defence of her virginity and is locally venerated
as a virgin martyr.

**Tanco (Tancho, Tatta)
(St) Bp. M. OSB.** Feb 6
d. 808 An Irish monk who became abbot of
the Benedictine monastery of Amalbarich in
Saxony, and who was eventually bishop of
Werden. He died at the hands of a pagan mob
whose savage customs he had denounced.

Taracus (St) M. Oct 11
Otherwise Tharacus, q.v.

Taraghta (St) V. Aug 11
Otherwise Attracta, q.v.

Tarasios (Tarasius) (St) Bp. Feb 25
d. 806 A patrician of Constantinople and a
member of the staff of the Empress Irene II.
Although a layman, he was chosen patriarch,
and he accepted on condition that a general
council should be convened to end the iconoclastic persecution. He was accordingly ordained (Christmas 784) and the second council of Nicaea held, the decrees of which were
approved by the pope, Hadrian I. Shortly after,
however, Irene's son, Constantine VI, sought a
divorce; St Theodore and his rigorist monks at
the Studium monastery criticised Tarasios of
being too lenient, which led him to suspend
the priest who had joined the emperor in
marriage with his second wife. Tarasios is
highly venerated in the orthodox church.

**Tarbula (Tarbo, Tarba)
(St) VM.** Apr 22
d. 345 (May 5) Sister of St Simeon, the
great bishop-martyr of Persia, and a virgin
consecrated to God. After her brother's death
Tarbula was accused by Jews of having caused
by witchcraft the sickness of King Shapur's
wife, and she was put to death by being sawn
asunder.

Tarkin (St) Bp. Oct 30
Otherwise Talarican, q.v.

Tarsicia (Tarsitia) (St) V. Jan 15
d. c 600 Said to have been a granddaughter of Clotaire II and sister of St
Ferreolus of Uzès. She lived as a recluse near
Rodez, where she is now venerated.

**Tarsicius, Zoticus,
Cyriacus and Comp. (SS)
MM.** Jan 31
? Martyrs at Alexandria.

Tarsicius (St) M. Aug 15
3rd–4th cent. The inscription upon his
tomb, written by Pope St Damasus, informs us
that Tarsicius, while carrying the blessed
sacrament to some Christians in prison, was
seized by a heathen mob and preferred to die
rather than expose to profanation the sacred
mysteries. The story was embellished by
Cardinal Wiseman in his *Fabiola*. The epitaph
mentioned above implies that he might have
been a deacon, rather than a boy.

Tarsilla (St) V. Dec 24
d. c 581 An aunt of St Gregory the Great,
sister of St Emiliana and niece of Pope St
Felix. In her paternal home she led a life of
seclusion and mortification.

Tarsus (Martyrs of) (SS) June 6
d. c 290 A group of twenty martyrs at
Tarsus in Cilicia under Diocletian.

Tassach (St) Bp.   Apr 14
d. *c* 495? One of St Patrick's earliest disciples and first bishop of Raholp (Co. Down). He was a skilful artisan and made crosses, croziers and shrines for St Patrick.

Tassilo (Bl) Mk. OSB.   Dec 13
d. *p*.794 Duke of Bavaria and one of the greatest benefactors of the Benedictine monks. After founding many abbeys and churches he himself became a monk at Jumièges, whence he migrated to Lorsch, where he died.

Tasso (Taso) (St) Ab. OSB.   Jan 11
See Paldo, Taso and Tato.

Tate (St) W.   Apr 5
Otherwise Ethelburga, q.v.

Tathai (Tathan, Tathaeus, Athaeus) (St) H.   Dec 26
Early 6th cent. A Celt who settled in S. Glamorgan where he founded a monastery (St Athan's) and a school at Caerwent in Gwent.

Tatian (St) M.   March 16
See Hilary, Tatian, etc.

Tatian Dulas (St) M.   June 15
Otherwise Dulas, q.v.

Tatian (St) M.   Sept 12
See Macedonius, Theodulus and Tatian.

Tatiana (St) M.   Jan 12
d. *c* 230 According to the pre-1970 RM., a woman put to death in Rome under Alexander Severus. On this day the Greeks also honour a St Tatiana together with two others, Euthasia and Mertios, MM.

Tation (St) M.   Aug 24
d. *c* 304 A martyr beheaded at Claudiopolis in Bithynia under Diocletian.

Tato (St) Ab. OSB.   Jan 11
See Paldo, Taso and Tato.

Tatta (St) M.   Sept 25
See Paul, Tatta, etc.

Tatwin (St) Bp. OSB.   July 30
d. 734 Monk of Bredon, or Brenton, in Mercia, who was held in esteem by Bede. Some manuscripts of his riddles and his Grammar survive. He succeeded St Brithwald in the see of Canterbury in 731 and received the pallium in 733, when he ordained bishops for Selsey and Lindsey.

Taurinus (St) Bp.   Aug 11
d. *c* 412 Bishop of Evreux in Normandy. The legend connecting him with St Denis of Paris is now rejected by all scholars.

Taurion (St) M.   Nov 7
See Auctus, Taurion and Thessalonica.

Teath (Teatha, Eatha) (St) Otherwise Ita, q.v.   Jan 15
The title-saint of the church of St Teath in Cornwall is perhaps another of that name, for there is believed to have been a St Teath from Wales, one of the daughters of Brychan of Brecknock.

Tegla (Thecla) (St) V.   June 1
? The patron saint of the church and holy well at Llandegla in Clwyd.

Teilo (Teilio, Teilus, Thelian, Teilan, Teilou, Teliou, Dillo, Dillon, etc.) (St) Bp.   Feb 9
6th cent. Born probably at Penally, near Tenby, in S. Wales, and educated by St Dyfrig. He was a companion and friend of SS David and Samson. He became the founder and abbot-bishop of Llandaff monastery (Landeilo Fawr) in Dyfed, and was buried in Llandaff cathedral.

Telemachus (St) M.   Jan 1
Otherwise Almachius, q.v.

Telesphorus (St) Pope   formerly Jan 5
d. *c* 137 A Calabrian Greek, he was pope for ten years and, according to a discredited tradition, suffered martyrdom under Hadrian. Cult suppressed in 1969.

Tenenan (St) Bp.   July 16
7th cent. A Briton by birth who became a hermit in Brittany and was eventually bishop of Léon: his relics were enshrined at Ploabennec.

Terence, Africanus, Pompeius and Comp. (SS) MM.   Apr 10
d. 250 A band of fifty martyrs, imprisoned with a number of snakes and scorpions, and finally beheaded at Carthage under Decius.

Terence (St) Bp. M.   June 21
1st cent. Bishop of Iconium in apostolic times. Some hagiographers conjecture that he is identical with the Tertius mentioned as his amanuensis by St Paul in his epistle to the Romans (16:22).

Terence of Todi (St) M.   Sept 27
See Fidentius and Terence.

Terence of Metz (St) Bp.   Oct 29
d. 520 Sixteenth bishop of Metz.

Terentian (St) Bp. M.   Sept 1
d. 118 Bishop of Todi in Umbria. It seems that he was racked, had his tongue cut out, and was finally beheaded under Hadrian.

Teresa Benedicta of the Cross (Bl) VM. OCD.

1891–1942 Edith Stein was born at Breslaw, Poland, in 1891, the youngest of seven children in a rich Jewish family. Brilliantly gifted, she became a philosopher with an interest in phenomenology. She was converted to Catholicism and was baptised in 1922 in Cologne cathedral, entering the Cologne Carmel in 1933. Due to the rise of National Socialism she was transferred to the Carmel of Echt in Holland. Arrested by the Nazis she was sent with her sister Rosa to Auschwitz in 1942, where she was gassed. She was a great daughter of Israel and of the church. Beatified by Pope John Paul II at Cologne cathedral in 1987.

Teresa Eustochium Verzeri (Bl) V. Foundress   March 3

1801–1852 Born at Bergamo of noble parents she attempted three times to become a Benedictine nun. Failing in this she gave herself to the instruction of young girls. Thus she came to found the Daughters of the Sacred Heart in 1831. Both the numbers and the scope of the institute grew, so as to include a wide range of charitable works. The bishop of Bergamo, at first favourable, turned against her, but approval was given by Rome in 1841. Worn out with labour she died comparatively young at Brescia. Beatified in 1946.

Teresa Margaret Redi (St) V. OCD.   March 7

1747–1770 Anna Maria, in religion Teresa Margaret, Redi became a Discalced Carmelite nun at the convent of St Teresa at Florence in 1765. She died at the age of twenty-three, her short life in religion being remarkable for penance and prayer. Canonized in 1934.

Teresa (Tarasia) (St) N. OSB. Cist.   June 17

d. 1250 Daughter of King Sancho I of Portugal. She married her cousin Alphonsus IX, king of Léon, but the marriage was declared null by the Holy See on the grounds of consanguinity. She returned to Portugal and entered the Cistercian convent at Lorvao, near Coimbra, where she died. Cult confirmed, with the title of saint, by Clement XI in 1705.

Teresa Fantou (Bl) VM.   June 26

d. 1794 A Sister of Charity of Arras. With three other sisters she was arrested by the French revolutionaries in 1794, brought to Cambrai and there guillotined. Beatified 1920.

St Teresa of Lisieux, Oct 1

Teresa Soiron (Bl) VM.   July 17

d. 1794 A sister of Bl Catherine Soiron. She was a maid in the service of the Princess de Lamballe. During the French Revolution she attached herself to the Carmelite Nuns of Compiègne, q.v., with whom she was executed.

Teresa of Jesus Ibars (St) V. Foundress   Aug 26

1843–1897 Born at Aytona in Catalonia, she experienced the hardships of life on a farm in her youth before qualifying as a teacher at Lérida. Of deep interior life, she tried to become a religious but without success. Finally, with the advice of her spiritual director, she started an institute of her own at Barbastro on Jan 27, 1872, under the title of "Little Sisters of the Poor". Her deep spiritual insight, firmness of spirit, unflagging industry and endurance were responsible for the foundation of no less than fifty-eight houses of her congregation during her lifetime. Beatified in 1958. Canonized in 1974.

Teresa of Lisieux (St) V. OCD.   GC. Oct 1

1873–1897 Marie Françoise Thérèse Martin (her religious name was Teresa of the

Infant Jesus) was born at Alençon, entered the Carmelite order at Lisieux at the age of fifteen, and such was her progress in the spiritual life that she was appointed novice-mistress at the age of twenty-two. Two years later she died, her short life having been remarkable for its humility, simplicity and silently heroic endurance of suffering. Since her death she has worked innumerable miracles, and her cult has spread throughout the world. Pius XI declared her, together with St Francis Xavier, patron saint of foreign missions. Canonized 1925. In English-speaking countries she is often known as the Little Flower of Jesus. In 1947 she was declared Co-Protectress of France along with Joan of Arc. She is depicted as a Discalced Carmelite nun, holding a bunch of roses, or with roses at her feet.

Teresa of Avila (St) V.
Dr. OCD.   **GC. Oct 15**
1515–1582 Teresa Cepeda de Ahumada was born at Avila in Old Castile and at the age of eighteen entered the Carmelite convent in her native town where a fairly lax atmosphere prevailed as regards poverty and enclosure. In 1562 she founded her first reformed convent of St Joseph at Avila, and from that year till her death she was always on the move, opening new houses (fifteen directly and seventeen through others), smoothing away difficulties for her nuns, placating those in authority (both clerical and lay), who often fiercely opposed her and called her the "roving nun". All this time she was being favoured with remarkable mystical experiences, which she described, under obedience, in treatises which may be regarded as veritable textbooks of mystical prayer and rank as classics of Spanish literature. She is the saint of sound common sense, of sane good humour, of generous ideals, and her influence on the spiritual lives of Christians of all denominations is immeasurable. She was proclaimed a Doctor of the Church on 27th Sept 1970 by Pope Paul VI. In art she is shown as wearing the habit of a Discalced Carmelite nun, her heart being pierced by an arrow held by an angel; or holding a pierced heart, book and crucifix. She died at Alba de Tormes. Canonized 1622.

Ternan (St) Bp.   June 12
? 5th cent. An early missionary bishop among the Picts in Scotland. He is said to have resided at Abernethy and to have been ordained by St Palladius. He is the reputed founder of the abbey of Culross in Fifeshire.

Ternatius (Terniscus)
(St) Bp.   Aug 8
d. c 680 Eleventh bishop of Besançon.

St Teresa of Avila, Oct 15

Tertius (St) M.   Dec 6
See Dionysia, Dativa, etc.

Tertulla (St) VM.   Apr 29
See Agapius and Comp.

Tertullian (St) Bp.   Apr 27
d. c 490 Eighth bishop of Bologna.

Tertullinus (St) M.   Aug 4
d. 257 A Roman priest, martyred under Valerian two days after his ordination.

Tertricus (St) Bp.   March 20
d. 572 Son of St Gregory, bishop of Langres, and uncle of St Gregory of Tours. He succeeded his father in the see of Langres about the year 540.

Tetricus (St) Bp. M. OSB.   Apr 12
d. 707 Abbot of the Benedictine monastery of St Germanus at Auxerre. He became bishop of Auxerre by popular acclamation. The saint met his death at the hand of his archdeacon Raginfred, who slew him with a sword as he lay asleep on a bench.

Tetta (St) Abs. OSB.   Sept 28
d. c 772 Abbess of Wimborne in Dorsetshire. She helped St Boniface by sending him band after band of missionary nuns from her community, among whom were SS Lioba, Thecla, etc. She is said to have ruled over some five hundred nuns.

Teuzzo (Bl) C. OSB.　　　　Aug 9
d. *c* 1072　Monk of St Mary's abbey (La Badia) at Florence. During some fifty years he lived as a recluse near his monastery. He supported St John Gualbert in his campaign against simony.

Thaddeus (Tadhg) (Bl) Bp.　　Oct 25
d. 1497　Thaddeus McCarthy (Machar) was made bishop of Ross in 1482 but driven from his see in 1488. The Holy See next nominated him bishop of Cork and Cloyne, but he was not allowed into the diocese. Then the perplexed bishop went to Rome to plead his cause personally, but died on his way home at Ivrea in Piedmont. Cult approved 1910.

Thaddeus (St) Apostle　　　Oct 28
Otherwise Jude, q.v.

Thaddeus Lieu (Bl) M.　　　Nov 24
d. 1823 (Nov 30)　A Chinese priest in the province of Zyu-Thuan. He was imprisoned for two years and then strangled. Beatified 1900.

Thais (St) Penitent　　　　Oct 8
?4th cent.　Alleged to be a wealthy and beautiful courtesan of Alexandria converted by St Paphnutius (other accounts say St Bessarion or St Serapion) and walled up for three years in a cell. Only towards the end of her life was she admitted to full conventual life with the other nuns. Modern writers consider the story a moral tale with no foundation in fact.

Thalassius and Limnaeus (SS) HH.　　　Feb 22
5th cent.　Two Syrian hermits who lived in a cave near Cyrrhus. Our knowledge of them is due to the historian Theodoret, who knew them personally.

Thalelaeus (St) H.　　　　Feb 27
d. *c* 450　Surnamed Epiclautos, i.e., weeping much. A hermit who dwelt at Gabala in Syria, next to the shrine of an idol, where he converted many of the pagan pilgrims. For many years he lived in an open barrel.

Thalelaeus, Asterius, Alexander and Comp.　　May 20
d. ? 284　Thalelaeus is said to have practised medicine and attended his patients gratis at Anazarbus in Cilicia. He suffered martyrdom at Aegae, a town on the coast of that province, and not at Edessa as has been sometimes stated. The pre-1970 RM. adds Asterius and Alexander, two of his executioners, and others of the spectators who were converted by the constancy of the martyr.

Thalus (St) M.　　　　　March 11
See Trophimus and Thalus.

Thamel and Comp. (SS) MM.　　　　　Sept 4
d. *c* 125　A converted pagan priest, martyred with four or five others (one of them his own sister) somewhere in the East, under Hadrian.

Tharacus (Tarachus), Probus and Andronicus (SS) MM.　　　　Oct 11
d. 304　Tarachus, aged sixty-five, was a retired officer of the Roman army, Probus a Roman citizen from Pamphilia, and Andronicus a young man of good birth from Ephesus. They were beheaded near Tarsus in Cilicia under Diocletian. The authenticity of their Acts is disputed.

Tharasius (St) Bp.　　　　Feb 25
Otherwise Tarasius, q.v.

Thaw (St)　　　　　　Sept 1
Otherwise Lythan, q.v.

Thea (St) M.　　　　　Dec 19
See Meuris and Thea.

Théau (St)　　　　　Jan 7
Otherwise Tillo, q.v.

Theban Legion, The (SS) MM.　　　　　Sept 22
d. *c* 287　The story of the Theban Legion is as follows. In the army of Maximinian Herculeus there was a legion (6600 men) consisting of Christians recruited in Upper Egypt. When the emperor marched his army across the Alps to suppress a revolt in Gaul he camped near Agaunum, in Switzerland, and prepared for the battle with public sacrifices. The Christian legion refused to attend (another version says that they refused to attack innocent people) and were in consequence twice decimated. When they still persevered in their refusal they were massacred *en masse*. Among those who suffered were Maurice, the *primicerius*, Exuperius, Candidus, Vitalis, two Victors, Alexander (at Bergamo) and Gereon (at Cologne). At Agaunum, now St-Maurice-en-Valais, a basilica was built (*c* 369–391) to enshrine the relics of the martyrs. The story can therefore be accepted as substantially true, but it is almost unbelievable that the whole legion was Christian and that the whole of it was put to death. Probably a very large number of soldiers were put to death and that gave rise to the story as now told. St Maurice is depicted as a soldier, rarely in authentic Roman armour, with many other

soldiers, being done to death in often ingenious ways. Cult confined to particular calendars since 1969.

Thecla (St) VM.   Jan 18
See Archelais, Thecla, etc.

Thecla (St) M.   March 26
See Peter, Marcian, etc.

Thecla (St) M.   Aug 19
See Timothy, Thecla and Agapius.

Thecla (St) M.   Aug 30
See Boniface and Thecla.

Thecla (St) VM.   Sept 3
See Euphemia, Dorothea, etc.

Thecla Nangaxi (Bl) M.   Sept 10
d. 1622   A Japanese woman, wife of Bl Paul Nangaxi, beheaded at Nagasaki (see Charles Spinola).

Thecla (St) VM.   formerly Sept 23
1st cent.   According to the second century novel called the *Acts of Paul and Thecla*, which abounds in extravagant stories and is not quite orthodox in doctrine, Thecla was a maiden of Iconium who heard St Paul preaching while she sat at her chamber window, became a Christian and followed the apostle dressed in boy's clothes. Several times she underwent most cruel tortures for the faith — in the prayer for the dying the tridentine Roman ritual referred expecially to "three most cruel torments" — and finally died a solitary in Seleucia. It is not possible to disentangle truth from fiction. Her cult was suppressed in 1969.

Thecla (St) Abs. OSB.   Oct 15
d. c 790   A Benedictine nun of Wimborne under St Tetta. She was one of the party which set out for the German mission under St Lioba. She was named by St Boniface first abbess of Ochsenfürt, and then of Kitzingen on the Main, over which she ruled for many years.

Thecusa (St) VM.   May 18
See Theodotus, Thecusa, etc.

Theliau (St) Bp.   Feb 9
Otherwise Teilo, q.v.

Thelica (St) M.   Feb 11
See under Saturninus, Dativus, etc.

Themistocles and Dioscorus (SS) MM.   Dec 21
d. 253   Themistocles was a shepherd of Myra in Lycia who was beheaded for refusing to reveal the hiding-place of St Dioscorus.

Theneva (Thenew) Thenova, Dwynwen) (St) W.   July 18
7th cent.   The legendary mother of St Kentigern and together with him the patron saint of Glasgow.

Theobald (Thibaud) of Vienne (St) Bp.   May 21
d. 1001   Archbishop of Vienne 970–1001. Cult confirmed 1903.

Theobald Roggeri (Bl) C.   June 1
d. 1150   Born at Vico in Liguria of a good family, he left home and chose to work as a cobbler at Alba in Piedmont. After a pilgrimage to Compostella he earned his living as a carrier, sharing his wages with the poor and suffering.

Theobald (Thibaut) (St) H. OSB. Cam.   June 30
1017–1066   Born in Brie, the son of Count Arnoul of Champagne, he was at first a soldier, but at the age of eighteen, filled with a desire for greater perfection as a result of reading the lives of the saints, he became a pilgrim and then a hermit at Pettingen in Luxembourg. Finally he settled at Salanigo, near Vicenza, and was ordained priest. Later a small number of other hermits gathered around his cell. He became a Camaldolese monk before he died. Canonized by Alexander II in 1073.

Theobald of Marly (St) Ab. OSB. Cist.   July 27
d. 1247   Born in the castle of Marly, the son of Buchard of Montmorency, he was a distinguished knight at the court of Philip Augustus of France. He abandoned his worldly prospects and entered the Cistercian abbey of Vaux-de-Cernay (1220), becoming prior in 1230 and abbot in 1235. He was highly esteemed by St Louis of France.

Theoctiste (St) V.   Nov 10
10th cent.   A nun of Lesbos who became a solitary in the isle of Paros. The story of her last holy communion seems to be an adaptation from the life of St Mary of Egypt.

Theodard (St) Bp. OSB.   May 1
d. 893   Educated at the Benedictine abbey of St Martin at Montauriol, he became archbishop of Narbonne. He died at St Martin's abbey, having been clothed with the Benedictine habit. Later the abbey was named after him, St Audard.

Theodard (St) Bp. M. OSB.   Sept 10
d. c 670   A disciple of St Remaclus at Malmédy-Stavelot and his successor as abbot (653) and as bishop of Maestricht (663). On a

journey undertaken in defence of his church he was murdered by robbers in the forest of Bienwald, near Speyer.

Theodemir (St) M.   July 25
d. 851   A monk martyred at Cordoba under Abderrahman II.

Theodichildis (Telchildis)
(St) Abs. OSB.   June 28
d. p.660   A nun of Faremoutier, she became the first abbess of Jouarre, diocese of Meaux.

Theodora (St) Empress   Feb 11
d. 867   Wife of the iconoclast emperor Theophilus. During the regency of her son, Michael the Drunkard, she did her utmost to restore the veneration of images. She ended her life in a convent. Her claim to sanctity is questionable.

Theodora (St) M.   March 13
See Theusetas, Horres, etc.

Theodora (St) M.   Apr 1
d. c 120?   According to the very dubious *Acta* of Pope Alexander I, she was sister of St Hermes (Aug 28) whom she assisted in prison and under torture. She was herself martyred some months later. Brother and sister were buried side by side.

Theodora V. and Didymus
(SS) MM.   Apr 28
d. 304   A maiden of Alexandria, sentenced to prostitution, but delivered from the brothel by St Didymus, who was still a pagan. This led to his conversion, and the two saints were martyred together. The Acts are considered trustworthy.

Theodora (St) VM.   May 7
See Flavia Domitilla, Euphrosyne and Theodora.

Theodora (St) Penitent   Sept 11
d. 491   The current story of this saint is similar to that of St Pelagia of Antioch (Oct 8) q.v. The pre-1970 RM., however, simply said: "At Alexandria, St Theodora, who fell through lack of care, but repenting of her deed, persevered in the religious habit, unknown, with wondrous abstinence and patience, until her death."

Theodora (St) Matron   Sept 17
d. c 305   A Roman lady of noble birth and great wealth who, during the persecution of Diocletian, generously devoted herself and her riches to the service of the martyrs. She seems to have died while the persecution was still raging.

Theodore of Egypt (St) H.   Jan 7
4th cent.   A monk of Egypt, disciple of St Ammonius.

Theodore Stratelates
(St) M.   Feb 7
4th cent.   He is said to have been a general (*stratelates*) in the army of Licinius, by whose order he was tortured and crucified at Heraclea in Thrace. He is identical with St Theodore Tyro of Amasea (Nov 9).

Theodore (St) M.   March 17
See Alexander and Theodore.

Theodore, Irenaeus,
Serapion and Ammonius
(SS) MM.   March 26
d. 310   Theodore, bishop of Pentapolis in Libya, Irenaeus, his deacon, and Serapion and Ammonius, his two lectors, suffered under Gallienus by having their tongues cut out. However, they survived and died in peace, being nevertheless venerated as martyrs.

Theodore and Comp. (SS)
MM. OSB.   Apr 9
d. 870   Theodore was abbot of Croyland, and he and his large community were put to death by the Danes. Besides the abbot, several others were mentioned by name; Askega, prior; Swethin, sub-prior; Elfgete, deacon; Savinus, sub-deacon; Egdred and Ulrick, acolytes; Grimkeld and Agamund (Argamund), both centenarians.

Theodore and Pausilippus
(SS) MM.   Apr 5
d. c 130   Martyrs near Byzantium under Hadrian.

Theodore Trichinas (St) H.   Apr 20
d. p.330   A hermit near his native city of Constantinople. He is surnamed *Trichinas*, "the hairy", because his only garment was a rough hair-shirt.

Theodore of Sikion (St)
Bp.   Apr 22
d. 613   Born at Sikion in Galatia, the son of an imperial messenger, he became a monk at Jerusalem and in later life the abbot-founder of several monasteries. About 590 he was made bishop of Anastasiopolis in Galatia. He was a great fosterer of the cult of St George.

Theodore of Tabenna
(St) Ab.   Apr 27
d. c 368   Usually called "Theodore the Holy" by the Greeks. He was trained in the monastic life by St Pachomius, whom he succeeded as abbot of Tabenna. His feast is

kept in the East on May 16, but the actual date of his death was Apr 27.

Theodore of Bologna
(St) Bp.   May 5
d. *c* 550   A bishop of Bologna *c* 530–*c* 550.

Theodore of Pavia (St) Bp.   May 20
d. 778   Bishop of Pavia 743–778. He had much to endure, including repeated banishment, at the hands of the Arian Lombard kings.

Theodore of Cyrene (St)
Bp. M.   July 4
d. *c* 310   Bishop of Cyrene in Libya. He had great skill in copying books, and was brutally martyred under Diocletian for refusing to deliver up his manuscripts of the holy scriptures.

Theodore (St) M.   July 29
See Lucilla, Flora, etc.

Theodore (St) M.   Sept 2
See Zeno, Concordius and Theodore.

Theodore Oceanus,
Ammianus and Julian
(SS) MM.   Sept 4
d. *c* 310   Oriental martyrs, burnt at the stake, probably under Maximian Herculeus.

Theodore (St) M.   Sept 5
See Urban, Theodore, etc.

Theodore (St) M.   Sept 15
See Maximus, Theodore and Asclepiodotus.

Theodore of Canterbury
(St) Bp.   Sept 19
c 602–690   He was an Asiatic Greek and was educated at Tarsus in Cilicia; he spent some time at Athens and became a monk at Rome. He was sixty–six years old when Pope Vitalian appointed him to the see of Canterbury at the suggestion of the African St Adrian in 666. These two travelled to England together, Adrian becoming abbot of the monastery of SS Peter and Paul of Canterbury and acting as adviser to the new archbishop. Theodore is rightly called the second founder of the see of Canterbury and the first primate of the English church. He visited all parts of the country, consolidated or re-established dioceses, promoted learning and opened schools, and held the first national council at Hertford in 672. His activities involved him in disputes on questions of jurisdiction with St Chad and St Wilfrid, but these controversies were conduc-

ted with dignity and settled in a spirit of charity. St Theodore has a claim to be considered one of the greatest figures in English history, not only because of his successful consolidation of the church but also because of his scholarship and pastoral zeal. All this was achieved at an advanced age.

Theodore, Philippa and
Comp. (SS) MM.   Sept 20
d. 220   A group of four Christians crucified at Perga in Pamphilia under Heliogabalus. They were: Theodore and Socrates, soldiers; Dionysius, a former pagan priest; and Philippa, Theodore's mother. They expired after three days on the cross.

Theodore (Theodoret)
of Antioch (St) M.   Oct 23
d. 362   A priest, treasurer of the church of Antioch, martyred under Julian the Apostate for continuing to minister to the faithful in spite of the imperial decrees to the contrary.

Theodore (Theudar,
Chef) (St) Ab.   Oct 29
d. *c* 575   A priest, disciple of St Caesarius of Arles and abbot of one of the monasteries of Vienne in Gaul. He made several ecclesiastical and monastic foundations and died as a recluse in the church of St Laurence in Vienne.

Theodore Tyro (St) M.   Nov 9
d. 4th cent.   Said to have been a recruit (hence his nickname of Tyro) in the Roman army, who set fire to the temple of Cybele at Euchaita, near Amasea in Pontus, for which he paid the penalty by being burnt alive at the same place. Beyond the fact of his martyrdom nothing certain is known about him. He is greatly venerated in the East as one of the "three soldier saints", viz. SS George, Demetrius and Theodore. He is almost certainly identical with St Theodore Stratelates. Cult confined to local calendars since 1969.

Theodore Studites (St) Ab.   Nov 11
759–826   A native of Constantinople who became a monk at the monastery of the Studium (more correctly *Studios*) in that city. His uncle was St Plato, abbot of Saccudium. He entered his uncle's abbey and after ordination in 787, became abbot in 794, his uncle resigning in his favour. His community became involved in the internal quarrels of the imperial house, and as a result this abbey was closed and he was banished to Thessalonica. A reversal of fortunes led to the renewal of the community at the abbey of Studios in Constantinople in 799 and under his rule the

monastery developed into a centre from which a monastic revival spread throughout the East, its influence reaching to Mt Athos and later to Russia, Rumania and Bulgaria. Studium stood for all that is lasting in monastic observance: liturgical prayer, community life, enclosure, poverty, studies and manual work (the monks excelled in calligraphy). The community, with St Theodore at their head, uncompromisingly defended the veneration of images (against a series of iconoclastic emperors), and opposed Caesaropapism in every form. Theodore suffered banishment several times on this account. He is one of the great figures of monastic history, and his austerity and patience under suffering and persecution are a witness to his sincerity and holiness. His uncompromising orthodoxy is a hallmark of a truly monastic spirit, valid in any age.

Theodore (St) Bp. M. Nov 26
See Faustus, Didius, etc.

Theodore (St) M. Dec 7
See Polycarp and Theodore.

Theodore (St) M. Dec 14
See Drusus, Zosimus and Theodore.

Theodore (St) M. Dec 15
See Irenaeus, Antony, etc.

Theodore the Sacrist (St)
C. Dec 26
d. 6th cent. A contemporary of St Gregory the Great, from whom we derive all our information concerning his life. Theodore was a sacrist (*mansionarius*) in the basilica of St Peter, Rome.

Theodore, M. and Theophanes Bp. (SS) Dec 27
c 841 and *c* 845 Two brothers, monks of the *laura* of St Sabbas in Jerusalem, who were prominent in defence of the veneration of images. They were cruelly persecuted by the Byzantine emperors. Verses were cut in the flesh of their faces (for this reason they are called *Graphi*, "the Written-on"), and they were otherwise ill-treated. Theodore died in prison in consequence of his sufferings. Theophanes survived him a few years and according to the pre-1970 RM. became bishop of Nicaea.

Theodoret (St) M. Oct 23
Called Theodore in the pre-1970 RM. (see above, Oct 23).

Theodoric II of Orleans
(St) Bp. OSB. Jan 27
d. 1022 Monk of Saint-Pierre-le-Vif at

Sens. He was summoned to court as counsellor and afterwards nominated bishop of Orleans. He died at Tonnerre on his way to Rome.

Theodoric (St) Bp. M. Feb 2
d. 880 Third bishop of Ninden. he fell in battle against the Norsemen at Ebsdorf, Saxony. See Bruno and Comp.

Theodoric (Thierry, Theodericus) (St) Ab. July 1
d. *c* 533 Educated by St Remigius of Reims, by whom he was appointed abbot of Mont d'Or, near Reims.

Theodoric of Emden (St)
M. OFM. Oct 9
d. 1572 A Dutch Friar Minor, confessor to the Franciscan nuns at Gorkum. He was hanged at Briel with the goup of Gorkum martyrs, q.v.

Theodoric (St) Bp. Aug 5
d. 863 Bishop of Cambrai-Arras, *c* 830–863.

Theodoric of St-Hubert (Thierry) (Bl) Ab. OSB. Oct 25
d. 1087 Educated at Maubeuge, he became a Benedictine at Lobbes, and in 1055 abbot of St Hubert in the Ardennes. Here and at the neighbouring abbeys of Stavelot-Malmédy he introduced with great success the Cluniac observance.

Theodosia (St) M. March 20
See Alexandra, Claudia, etc.

Theodosia (St) M. March 23
See Domitius, Pelagia, etc.

Theodosia (St) VM. Apr 2
d. 308 A maiden of Tyre, eighteen years old, who, on a visit to Caesarea in Palestine, seeing some martyrs on their way to execution, asked them to pray for her. Whereupon she was seized, tortured, and finally cast into the sea.

Theodosia and Comp.
(SS) MM. May 29
d. *c* 303 Theodosia, the alleged mother of St Procopius, is said to have been martyred at Caesarea Philippi in Palestine under Diocletian. She is said to have been put to death with twelve other women. The whole story seems to be a fabrication.

Theodosia (St) VM. May 29
d. 745 A nun of Constantinople who led a group of other nuns in an attempt to resist by

force the soldiers who were sent to destroy the image of Christ over the main door of their monastery. She was tortured and put to death.

Theodosius the Cenobiarch (St) Ab.   Jan 11
423–529 A Cappadocian who was put in charge of the church of Our Lady situated on the road between Jerusalem and Bethlehem. He next founded a monastery in the desert of Juda by the Dead Sea, where several hundred monks were soon living under his rule. He divided them according to nationality — Greeks, Armenians and Arabs — and built a church for each group. The patriarch of Jerusalem appointed him visitor to all the cenobitical communities in Palestine — as distinct from eremitical — whence the title cenobiarch given to the saint. The Byzantine emperor tried unsuccessfully to bribe Theodosius to support Monophysitism. The saint died at the age of one hundred and five.

Theodosius of Antioch (St) Mk.   Jan 11
d. c 412 A native of Antioch, of good family, he left the world to found a monastery near Rhosus in Cilicia. He died and was buried at Antioch.

Theodosius (St) Bp.   Feb 14
d. 554 Bishop of Vaison in France and predecessor of St Quinidius.

Theodosius (St) M.   March 26
See Quadratus, Theodosius, etc.

Theodosius (St) Bp.   July 17
d. 516 Bishop of Auxerre c 507–516.

Theodosius, Lucius, Mark and Peter (SS) MM.   Oct 25
d. 269 They belong to a group of fifty soldiers martyred at Rome under Claudius II.

Theodota (St) M.   July 17
d. c 735 A lady of Constantinople martyred under the iconoclastic emperor Leo the Isaurian for hiding three holy icons from the imperial officers.

Theodota and her Three Sons (SS) MM.   Aug 2
d. 304? Martyrs of Nicaea. Theodota with Evodius (q.v.) and her other two sons were cast into a furnace and perished in the flames. Their Acts are not trustworthy.

Theodota (St) Penitent   ? Sept 29
d. c 318 Described as a penitent harlot, martyred at Philippopolis in Thrace. According to her untrustworthy Acts her executioners exhausted their ingenuity in devising fresh tortures for her.

Theodotus (St) M.   Jan 4
See Aquilinus, Geminus, etc.

Theodotus (St) Bp.   May 6
d. c 325 Bishop of Cyrenia in Cyprus. He suffered a long term of imprisonment under Licinius.

Theodotus, Thecusa, Alexandra, Claudia, Faina (Phaina), Euphrasia, Matrona and Julitta (SS) MM.   May 18
d. 304 According to their Acts, Theodotus was an innkeeper of Ancyra who was martyred there under Diocletian for giving Christian burial to the bodies of the seven virgins mentioned above, also martyrs of Ancyra. The Bollandist Father Delehaye contends that the Acts are merely a moral tale.

Theodotus (St) M.   July 5
See Marinus, Theodotus and Sedopha.

Theodotus, Rufina and Ammia (SS) MM.   Aug 31
d. c 270? Theodotus and Rufina were the parents, and Ammia the foster-mother, of St Mamas (v. Aug 17). They are said to have suffered in Cappadocia under Aurelian. The untrustworthy Acta of St Mamas is the sole source of our knowledge.

Theodotus (St) Bp.   Nov 2
d. 334 A bishop of Laodicea at the time of the Arian troubles and a great friend of the Arianizing Eusebius the historian, who is loud in his praise. Theodotus subscribed to the Nicene formula, but seems to have sided with the Arians and the semi-Arians up to his death.

Theodotus (St) M.   Nov 14
See Clementinus, Theodotus and Philomenus.

Theodula (St) VM.   March 25
Otherwise Dula, q.v.

Theodulphus (Thiou) (St) Bp. OSB.   June 24
d. 776 The third abbot-bishop of the great Benedictine abbey of Lobbes, near Liège.

Theodulus (St) M.   Feb 17
d. 309 An aged man in the household of Firmilian, governor of Palestine, by whom he was ordered to be crucified at Caesarea in Palestine.

Theodulus (St) C.   March 23
? A priest of Antioch in Syria, of whom nothing else is known. His name is also given as Theodore and Theodoricus.

Theodulus, Anesius, Felix, Cornelia and Comp. (SS) MM.   March 31
? Martyrs in proconsular Africa.

Theodulus (St) M.   Apr 4
See Agathopodes and Theodulus.

Theodulus (St) M.   May 2
See Exuperius, Zoe, etc.

Theodulus (St) M.   May 3
See Alexander, Eventius and Theodulus.

Theodulus (St) M.   June 18
See Leontius, Hypatius and Theodulus.

Theodulus (St) M.   July 26
See Symphronius, Olympius, etc.

Theodulus (Theodore) of Grammont (St) Bp.   Aug 17
4th cent. An early bishop of Valais whose cult was widespread in that region, Switzerland and Savoy. A later life placing him in the ninth century, has led to much confusion about his identity.

Theodulus (St) M.   Sept 12
See Macedonius, Theodulus and Tatian.

Theodulus, Saturninus, Euporus, Gelasius, Eunician, Zeticus, Cleomenes (Leomenes), Agathopus, Basilides and Evaristus (SS) MM.   Dec 23
d. 250 Martyrs of Crete who suffered under Decius.

Theofrid (Theofroy) (St) Bp. OSB.   Jan 26
d. c 690 A monk of Luxeuil who became abbot of Corbie (622) and a regionary bishop.

Theofrid (Theofroy, Chaffre) (St) Ab. OSB.   Oct 19
d. 728 A native of Orange who became monk and abbot of Carmery-en-Velay (Monastier-Saint-Chaffre). He died as a consequence of ill-treatment received at the hands of the invading Saracens and has been ever since venerated as a martyr.

Theogenes (St) M.   Jan 3
See Cyrinus, Primus and Theogenes.

Theoger (Theogar, Diethger) (Bl) Bp. OSB.   Apr 29
d. 1120 A native probably of Alsace who became successively canon of Mainz, monk of Hirchau, prior of Raichenbach on the Murg, abbot of St Georgen in the Black Forest (1090) and bishop of Metz (1118). However, after his ordination at Corbie he retired to the abbey of Cluny, where he died.

Theogonius (St) M.   Aug 21
See Bassa, Theogonius, etc.

Theonas (St) M.   Jan 3
See Theopemptus and Theonas.

Theonas of Egypt (St) Mk.   Apr 4
d. c 395 A famous solitary who lived near Oxyrinchus in the Thebaid.

Theonas (St) M.   Apr 20
See Victor, Zoticus, etc.

Theonas (St) Bp.   Aug 23
d. 300 Bishop of Alexandria 281–300. He fostered sacred studies, chiefly by his care of the catechetical school of his episcopal city. He was also known as a determined opponent of Sabellianism.

Theonestus (St) Bp. M.   Oct 30
d. 425 Said to have been bishop of Philippi in Macedonia, to have been driven from his see by the Arians, and to have been sent by the pope with several companions (among whom was St Alban of Mainz) to evangelize Germany. Arrived at Mainz, they were obliged to flee from the invading Vandals, and on their way home Theonestus was martyred at Altino in the Veneto. Probably Theonestus is a local martyr of Altino having no connexion with the others.

Theonilla (St) M.   Aug 23
See Claudius, Asterius, etc.

Theopemptus and Theonas (SS) MM.   Jan 3
d. 284 Theopemptus was bishop of Nicomedia. Theonas was a magician converted by the example of Theopemptus and after him martyred. Their Acts are wholly untrustworthy, though the martyrs themselves seem to be historical personages.

Theophanes Vénard (St) M.   Feb 2
1829–1861 A native of the diocese of Poitiers who joined the Society of Foreign Missions at Paris, was ordained in 1852 and arrived in Vietnam in 1854. After teaching in a Vietnamese seminary he took up work in W. Tonkin. Soon after, he was barbarously put to death in a persecution. Canonized in 1988.

Theophanes (St) Ab.   March 12
d. 818 A native of Constantinople and educated at the imperial court, he married early in life, but two years later allowed his wife to become a nun and himself joined the monks of Polychronion. Some time later he founded two monasteries and governed one of them as abbot, viz. that of Mt Sigriana, near Cyzicus. For his steadfast opposition to iconoclasm he

was banished by Leo the Armenian to Samothrace, where he died from the ill-treatment he had received.

Theophanes and Comp.
(SS) MM.   Dec 4
d. c 815   Four officers of the court of Leo the Armenian, imprisoned and tortured for their opposition to iconoclasm. Theophanes died under torture; the rest survived and eventually became monks.

Theophanes (St) Bp. C.   Dec 27
See Theodore and Theophanes.

Theophila (St) VM.   Dec 28
See Indes, Domna, etc.

Theophilus and
Helladius (SS) MM.   Jan 8
?   Africans martyred in Libya, where they had preached the gospel. Theophilus was a deacon, Helladius a layman. They were tortured and thrown into a furnace.

Theophilus the Penitent
(St)   Feb 4
c 538   Metaphrastes is responsible for the spread of the legend connected with this saint. He is said to have been archdeacon of Adana in Cilicia and, having been deposed from his office through a calumny, to have made a pact with the devil. He repented, and our Lady appeared to him and returned the pact, which was then torn up and publicly burnt. Goethe made use of this legend in his *Faust*.

Theophilus the Lawyer
(St) M.   Feb 6
d. c 300?   Said to have been beheaded at Caesarea in Cappadocia. he figures in the legend of St Dorothy, where he is surnamed *Scholasticus*, i.e. the lawyer.

Theophilus (St) M.   Feb 6
See Saturninus, Theophilus and Revocata.

Theophilus (St) M.   Feb 28
See Macarius, Rufinus, etc.

Theophilus (St) Bp.   March 5
d. c 195   A bishop of Caesarea in Palestine and a prominent opponent of the Quartodecimans, a sect which insisted on keeping Easter on the Jewish Passover day, whether it fell on a Sunday or not.

Theophilus (St) Bp.   March 7
His real name is Theophylact, q.v.

Theophilus (St) Bp.   Apr 27
d. p.427   Bishop of Brescia and successor to St Gaudentius.

Theophilus of Corte (St)
C. OFM.   May 19
1676–1740   Biagio Arrighi was born at Corte in Corsica and joined the Friars Minor, taking the name of Theophilus (1693). He was ordained at Naples and taught theology at Civitella in the Roman Campagna. Later he became a famous missioner in Italy and Corsica and a zealous worker for the revival of Franciscan observance. Canonized in 1930.

Theophilus (St) M.   July 22
d. 789   An officer of the imperial forces stationed in Cyprus when the Saracens invaded the island. As admiral of the Christian fleet he refused to flee when the battle went against him. He was taken prisoner and after one year's incarceration was martyred for refusing to deny Christ.

Theophilus (St) M.   July 23
See Trophimus and Theophilus.

Theophilus (St) M.   Sept 8
See Ammon, Theophilus, etc.

Theophilus (St) Mk. OSB.   Oct 2
d. c 750   A native of Bulgaria who became a monk of a monastery in Asia Minor, in which the community followed the Western rule of St Benedict. For opposing iconoclasm he was fiercely persecuted, maltreated and finally exiled by the emperor Leo the Isaurian.

Theophilus (St) Bp.   Oct 13
d. 181   An Eastern philosopher who became a Christian as a result of reading the scriptures with a view to attacking them. He became a bishop of Antioch. He is now best known as one of the apologists of the second century. His "Apology", a work in three books, is still extant: its aim was to contrast the pagan myths of Greece with the Biblical view of creation. His work developed the idea of the Logos or Word of God (John I).

Theophilus (St) M.   Nov 3
See Germanus, Theophilus, etc.

Theophilus (St) M.   Dec 20
See Ammon, Zeno, etc.

Theophylact (St) Bp.   March 7
d. 845   Wrongly called Theophilus in the pre-1970 RM. An Asiatic monk who became bishop of Nicomedia. He opposed the iconoclastic fury of Leo the Armenian, by whom he was banished to Caria, where he died thirty years later.

Theopistes and
Theopistus (SS) MM.   Sept 20
See Eustace, Theopistes, etc.

Theopompus (St) M.   May 21
See Synesius and Theopompus.

Theoprepius (St) M.   March 27
See Philetus, Lydia, etc.

**Theorogitha (Thordgith,
Thorctgyd) (St) N.**   Jan 25
See Thordgith.

Theoticus (St) M.   March 8
See Arianus, Theoticus, etc.

Theotimus (St) Bp.   Apr 20
d. 407   Bishop of Tomi on the Black Sea.
He defended Origen against St Epiphanius of
Salamis. He evangelized the barbarian tribes
of the Lower Danube, who were then pressing
into imperial territory.

Theotimus (St) M.   Nov 5
See Domninus, Theotimus, etc.

**Theotimus and Basilian
(SS) MM.**   Dec 18
? Martyrs of Laodicea in Syria.

Theotimus (St) M.   Dec 24
See Lucian, Metrobius, etc.

Theotonius (St) C. OSA.   Feb 18
1086–1166   Born in Spain, he was educated
at Coimbra in Portugal and became archpriest
of Viseu. He resigned that office to go on
pilgrimage to the Holy Land, and on his return
joined the Augustinian Canons Regular at
Coimbra. Highly esteemed by King Alphonsus of Portugal, he was fearless in rebuking
vice and exact in the performance of the divine
service. Cult approved by Benedict XIV.

Theresa (*several*)
Otherwise Teresa, q.v.

Thespesius (St) M.   June 1
d. *c* 230   A Cappadocian martyred under
Alexander Severus.

Thespesius (St) M.   Nov 20
See Eustace, Thespesius and Anatolius.

Thessalonica (St) M.   Nov 7
See Auctus, Taurion, and Thessalonica.

**Thethmar (Theodemar)
(St) C.**   May 17
d. 1152   A native of Bremen who became a
missionary among the Wends under St Viceli-
nus. He was probably a Premonstratensian.
He died at Neumünster.

Theuderius (St) Ab.   Oct 29
See Theodore (Theudar).

**Theusetas, Horres,
Theodora, Nymphodora,
Mark and Arabia (SS) MM.**   March 13
? Theusetas was the parent of the young boy,
Horres. The whole group was put to death at
Nicaea in Bithynia. Earlier martyrologies have
a much longer list of martyrs in this group.

**Thiemo (Theodmarus)
(St) Bp. M. OSB.**   Sept 28
d. 1102   Of the family of the counts of
Meglin in Bavaria. He became a Benedictine
at Niederaltaich, where he gained great
celebrity as an artist in metal, a painter and a
sculptor. In 1077 he was chosen abbot of St
Peter's, Salzburg, and in 1090 archbishop of
the same city. He was persecuted, imprisoned
and exiled for his loyalty to the principles of
Gregory VII. As an exile he joined the crusaders, was captured and imprisoned at Ascalon,
and after long and cruel tortures was martyred
at Corozain for refusing to apostatize to Islam.

**Thiento and Comp. (BB)
MM. OSB.**   Aug 10
d. 955   An abbot of Wessobrunn in Bavaria
who was martyred with six of his monks by the
invading Hungarians.

Thierry (St) C.   July 1
Otherwise Theodoric, q.v.

Thillo (St) Ab. OSB.   Jan 7
Otherwise Tillo, q.v.

Thiou (St) Bp.   June 24
Otherwise Theodulphus, q.v.

Thomais (St) M.   Apr 14
d. 476   An Alexandrian woman, wife of a
fisherman. Tempted to an act of impurity by
her father-in-law, she refused and was
murdered by him.

Thomas Plumtree (Bl) M.   Jan 4
d. 1570   A native of Lincolnshire, educated
at Corpus Christi College, Oxford, and rector
of Stubton. He was chaplain to the insurgents
of the North. Before being martyred in the
market-place at Durham he was offered his
life if he would become a Protestant. Beatified
1886.

Thomas of Cori (Bl) C. M.   Jan 19
1655–1729   A native of Cori, diocese of
Velletri who, after being a shepherd in the
Roman Campagna, became an Observant
Franciscan (1675), and, after his ordination,
was stationed at Civitella. He spent the remainder of his life in preaching and ministering to the inhabitants of the mountain district
around Subiaco. Beatified 1785.

St Thomas Aquinas, Jan 28

Thomas Reynolds (Bl) M.   Jan 21

d. 1642 Thomas Reynolds, whose true name was Green, was born at Oxford and educated for the priesthood at Reims, Valladolid and Seville. After his ordination in 1592 he returned to England and worked on the English mission for nearly fifty years. He must have been about eighty years of age when he was hanged at Tyburn, together with Bl Bartholomew Roe, OSB. Beatified 1929.

Thomas Aquinas (St) Dr OP.   GC. Jan 28

c 1225–1274 Surnamed the "Angelic Doctor." Born at Roccasecca, near Aquino, Naples, youngest son of Count Landulf of Aquino, and educated as an oblate by the Benedictines at Montecassino despite the opposition of his family, he joined the then recently founded Dominicans, and studied and received the doctorate of theology at the university of Paris. Thenceforward he taught that subject at Paris (1252–1260), Orvieto (1261–1264), Rome (1265–1267), Viterbo (1268), Paris (1269–1271) and Naples (1272–1274). He died at Fossanova, near Rome, on his way to the council of Lyons. Canonized in 1323 and declared Doctor of the Church in 1567 and patron saint of Catholic universities and centres of study in 1880. As a person he was humble and prayerful. For many centuries his "Summa" excercised a great influence on European thought. He is depicted

as a portly Dominican friar, carrying a book; a star or rays of light glisten on his breast.

Thomas Xico or Dauki (St) M.   Feb 6

d. 1597 A Japanese layman, Franciscan tertiary, catechist, and interpreter to the Franciscan missionaries in Japan. Crucified at Nagasaki with twenty-five companions. Canonized 1862. See Paul Miki and Comps.

Thomas Cozaki (St) M.   Feb 6

d. 1597 A Japanese boy of fifteen, son of St Michael Cozaki. He served at the eucharists celebrated by the Franciscan missionaries and was crucified at Nagasaki with twenty-five companions, including his own father. Canonized 1862. See Paul Miki and Comps.

Thomas Sherwood (Bl) M.   Feb 7

1551–1578 A Londoner, who was preparing to go to Douai to study for the priesthood when he was betrayed, imprisoned and racked in the Tower in order to force him to disclose the place where he had attended the eucharist. He was finally executed at Tyburn on the charge of denying the Queen's ecclesiastical supremacy. Beatified 1886.

Thomas of Foligno (Bl) M. OFM.   Feb 12

See Antony of Saxony.

Thomas Hemerford (Bl) M.   Feb 12

d. 1584 A Dorsetshire man who was educated at St John's College and Hart Hall, Oxford. He studied for the priesthood at the English College, Rome, where he was ordained in 1583. The following year, with four companions, he was hanged at Tyburn. Beatified 1929.

Thomas of Szombathely (Bl) Mk.   March 7

15th cent. General of the Hungarian Pauline order 1476–1480 and 1484–1488, he was renowned for his austerities and gifts of prophecy, and also as a theological writer.

Thomas (or Thomasius) of Costacciaro (Bl) H. OSB. Cam.   March 25

d. 1337 Born at Costacciaro in Umbria, the son of poor peasants. He joined the Camaldolese at Sitria, then retired to Monte Cupo as a hermit, where he lived for many years. At the time of his death his existence had been almost forgotten.

Thomas of Tolentino and Comp. (BB) MM. OFM.   Apr 9

d. 1322 A native of Tolentino in Italy, who

St Thomas More, June 22

became a Franciscan and went to preach the gospel in Armenia and Persia. He was on his way to Ceylon, with a view to proceeding to China, when he was seized at Thama in Hindustan and beheaded by the Muslims. Three companions, BB James of Padua, Peter of Siena, Franciscans, and Demetrius of Triflis, layman, suffered with him. Cult approved 1894.

Thomas Pickering (Bl)
M. OSB.   May 9
d. 1679   A native of Westmoreland who joined the Benedictines as lay-brother at St Gregory's, Douai (now at Downside) and took his vows in 1660. He was sent to England and attached to the small community of Benedictine chaplains who served the Chapel Royal. He was a victim of the Popish Plot, being falsely accused and hanged at Tyburn. Beatified 1929.

Thomas Ford (Bl) M.   May 28
d. 1582   A native of Devon who was edu-

cated at Trinity College, Oxford, where he was converted to the Catholic faith. He studied for the priesthood at Douai, was ordained there in 1573, and sent on the English mission in 1576. He worked in Oxfordshire and Berkshire until his arrest and martyrdom at Tyburn with BB John Shert and Robert Johnson. Beatified 1886.

Thomas Cottam (Bl) M. SJ.   May 30
1549–1582   Born at Dilworth in Lancashire of Protestant parents, he graduated at Brasenose College, Oxford, and was converted to the Catholic faith. He crossed over to Douai and then went to Rome for ordination studies. At Rome he was received into the Society of Jesus. He returned to England in 1580, but was arrested on landing at Dover and imprisoned in the Tower. Two years later he was hanged at Tyburn with three companions. Beatified 1886.

Thomas Du (St) M. Tert. OP.   May 31
1774–1839   A native of Vietnam who was

ordained, became a Dominican tertiary and worked in the province of Nam-Dingh. He was tortured and beheaded. Canonized in 1988.

Thomas Green, Thomas Scryven and Thomas Reding (BB) MM. O. Cart.   June 15

d. 1537 Thomas Green (or Greenwood) was a fellow of St John's College, Cambridge, who took monastic vows and was ordained at the London charterhouse. The other two were lay-brothers of the same charterhouse. These three, with four companions, were starved to death at Newgate. Beatified 1886.

Thomas Woodhouse (Bl) M. SJ.   June 19

d. 1573 A secular priest who resided in Lincolnshire and acted also as a private tutor in Wales. In 1561 he was committed to the Fleet prison, where he was kept in custody till his death. During his imprisonment he was admitted by letter to the Society of Jesus. He was hanged at Tyburn. Beatified 1886.

Thomas Whitbread (Bl) M. SJ.   June 20

d. 1679 Thomas Whitbread, *alias* Harcourt, was a native of Essex. He was educated at St Omer and joined the Jesuits in 1635. He was provincial of the English mission and at the time of the Popish Plot was convicted with four others of his order on a bogus charge of conspiring to murder Charles II. He was hanged at Tyburn. Beatified 1929.

Thomas More (St) M.   GC. June 22

1478–1535 A native of London, More studied at Canterbury Hall, Oxford, and read law at the Inns of Court, being called to the bar in 1501. He married twice and was a good husband, devoted to wife and children, devout, cheerful and charitable. In 1516 he published his *Utopia*, which gained for him a European reputation as a scholar and humanist. From this time he was more and more in favour with Henry VIII and Cardinal Wolsey, whom in 1529 he succeeded as Lord Chancellor. Soon, however, he found himself unable to support the king on the question of the royal divorce. He resigned the Chancellorship and on refusing to take the Oath of Supremacy, declaring the king supreme head of the Church of England, was imprisoned in the Tower. After fifteen months' incarceration he was beheaded on Tower Hill. Canonized in 1935. His head, displayed for a short while on Tower Bridge, rests in the Roper Vault at St. Dunstan's church, Canterbury; his body is at St Peter ad Vincula in the Tower. Representations of him are usually based on reliable portraits, and show him wearing his Lord Chancellor's robes and chain of office; sometimes he carries a book or an axe.

Thomas Corsini (Bl) C. OSM.   June 23

d. 1343 A native of Orvieto who became a Servite lay-brother and spent his life collecting alms for his friary. He is credited with many visions. Beatified 1768.

Thomas Garnet (St) M. SJ.   June 23

d. 1608 Born in Southwark, a nephew of Fr Henry Garnet, SJ. Educated for the priesthood at St Omer and Valladolid. He worked first as a secular priest but in 1604 was admitted to the Society of Jesus. Hanged at Tyburn. Beatified 1929. Canonized in 1970 as one of the Forty Martyrs of England and Wales, q.v.

Thomas Toan (St) Tert. OP.   June 27

1767–1840 A native catechist of Tonkin who, having shown signs of apostatizing, repented and was in consequence cruelly scourged, then exposed to the sun and insects without food or drink for twelve days until his death. Beatified 1900, canonized in 1988.

Thomas Maxfield (Bl) M.   July 1

d. 1616 A native of Enville, Staffs., he was educated for the priesthood at Douai and ordained in 1615. The following year he was hanged at Tyburn. Beatified 1929.

Thomas the Apostle (St)   GC. July 3

1st cent. Surnamed "Didymus," i.e. the twin. All we know for certain about him is derived from the gospel narrative, where the chief episode related of him concerns his unbelief and subsequent profession of faith in Christ's resurrection (John 20:24 etc.). According to a very ancient tradition he is said to have preached in S. India and there to have suffered martyrdom, but there is no decisive proof of this. Early writings such as the Gospel of Thomas date from later centuries (second–fourth) and are not genuine. He is shown as an elderly man holding a lance, or pierced by a lance; or kneeling before our Lord and placing his fingers in His side.

Thomas Bosgrave (Bl) M.   July 4

d. 1594 A gentleman, nephew of Sir J. Arundel, hanged at Dorchester with two of his servants for aiding Catholic clergy. Beatified 1929.

Thomas Warcop (Bl) M.   July 4

d. 1597 A gentleman of Yorkshire, hanged with three companions at York for harbouring Catholic clergy. Beatified 1929.

St Thomas the Apostle, July 3

Thomas Alfield (Bl) M.   July 6
d. 1585 Born at Gloucester and educated at
Eton and King's College, Cambridge. He was
reconciled to the Catholic church and went
abroad to study for the priesthood at Douai
and Reims. After his ordination in 1581 he
returned to England and was arrested while
engaged in distributing copies of Dr Allen's
True and Modest Defence. For this he was
hanged at Tyburn. Beatified 1929.

Thomas Tunstal (Bl) M.
OSB.   July 13
d. 1616 Thomas Tunstal, *alias* Helmes,
was born at Whinfell, near Kendal, Westmorland. He was educated for the priesthood at
Douai, ordained there in 1609, sent to the
English mission in 1610 and imprisoned almost at once. He spent the rest of his life in
prison, and while there was received into the

Benedictine order. He was hanged at Norwich. Beatified 1929.

Thomas Abel (Bl) M.   July 30
d. 1540 A doctor of Oxford University,
chaplain to Queen Catharine of Aragon and a
loyal defender of the validity of her marriage.
He was kept a prisoner in the Tower of
London for six years and finally executed at
Smithfield for refusing to acknowledge the
king's spiritual supremacy. Beatified 1886.

Thomas Welbourne (Bl) M.   Aug 1
d. 1605 A native of Hutton Bushel in Yorkshire and a schoolmaster by profession who
was hanged at York for persuading people to
become Catholics. Beatified 1929.

Thomas of Dover (St) M.
OSB.   Aug 2
d. 1295 Thomas Hales was a Benedictine

monk of St Martin's Priory, Dover, a cell of Christ Church, Canterbury. On Aug 2nd 1295 the French raided Dover and all the monks went into hiding except Thomas, who was too old and infirm to get away. The raiders found him in bed and ordered him to disclose the whereabouts of the church plate: he refused and was murdered. Miracles occurred at his tomb and he was forthwith venerated as a martyr. There was an altar dedicated to him in Dover Priory church in 1500, and his image figured among those of the English saints at the English College, Rome.

Thomas Wo Yinyemon
(Bl) M.   Aug 17
d. 1627   A Japanese layman beheaded at Nagasaki for sheltering the missionary priests. Beatified in 1867.

Thomas Guengoro (Bl) M.   Aug 18
d. 1620   A Japanese layman. With his wife and his little son he was crucified at Cocura for sheltering Bl Simon Kiota. Beatified 1867.

Thomas Coyananghi (Bl)
M.   Aug 19
d. 1622   A Japanese passenger on the ship of Bl Joachim, beheaded at Nagasaki. Beatified 1867.

Thomas Percy (Bl) M   Aug 26
1528–1572   Earl of Northumberland, condemned to death and excuted at York for his part in the rising of the North against Elizabeth. During the period of nearly three years' imprisonment which preceded his martyrdom he was repeatedly offered his freedom on condition of his apostasy to Protestantism. Beatified 1896.

Thomas Holford (Bl) M.   Aug 28
d. 1588   Thomas Holford, *alias* Acton or Bude, was born at Aston in Cheshire of Protestant parents and became a schoolmaster in Herefordshire, where he embraced the Catholic faith. After his studies and ordination at Reims (1583) he worked in Cheshire. He was hanged at Clerkenwell. Beatified 1929.

Thomas Felton (Bl) M. O.
Minim.   Aug 28
1568–1588   Born at Bermondsey, son of Bl John Felton. He was educated at Reims and became a Friar Minim. He was hanged at Isleworth in his twentieth year. Beatified 1929.

Thomas Tzughi (Bl) M. SJ.   Sept 6
d. 1627   A Japanese, educated by the Jesuits at Arima, whom he joined in 1589. He was noted for his gift of oratory. Exiled to Macao,

he returned in disguise. He separated himself from the Society of Jesus, but only for one day; he then repented of his act and engaged himself again in missionary work with renewed zeal. He was burnt alive with several companions at Nagasaki. Beatified 1867.

Thomas of St Hyacinth
(Bl) M. OP.   Sept 8
d. 1628   A Japanese catechist attached to the Dominican missionaries, burnt alive with Bl Dominic Castellet and companions. Beatified 1867.

Thomas Tomaki (Bl) M.   Sept 8
d. 1628   A Japanese boy, ten years old, beheaded with his father, Bl John Tomaki, and his three brothers. Beatified 1867.

Thomas Xiquiro (Bl) M.   Sept 10
d. 1622   A Japanese layman, seventy years old, highly respected by his fellow-citizens, beheaded at Nagasaki with Bl Charles Spinola. Beatified 1867.

Thomas of the Holy
Rosary (Bl) M. OP.   Sept 10
d. 1622   A Japanese catechist, attached to the Dominican missionaries, with several of whom he was beheaded at Nagasaki. Beatified 1867.

Thomas Zumarraga (Bl)
M. OP.   Sept 12
1575–1622   A native of Vitoria in Spain who joined the Dominicans and was sent to their missions in Japan. He was imprisoned for three years at Suzuta (Omura) and ultimately burnt alive at Omura with several companions. Beatified 1867.

Thomas Acafoxi (Bl) M.   Sept 19
d. 1622   A Japanese nobleman from Fingo who acted as catechist to Bl Leonard Kimura. Burnt alive at Nagasaki. Beatified 1867.

Thomas Johnson (Bl) O.
Cart.   Sept 20
d. 1537   A priest of the London charterhouse imprisoned with others of his community at Newgate for opposition to Henry VIII's eclesiastical policy. He died in prison from starvation. Beatified 1886.

Thomas Dien (Thien) (St)
M.   Sept 21
d. 1838   A native seminarist in Vietnam, attached to the Foreign Missions of Paris. He was cruelly scourged and finally strangled, being eighteen years old at the time of his death. Canonized in 1988.

Thomas of Villanueva (St)
Bp. OSA. Sept 22
1488–1555 (Sept 8) Born at Fuellana, near Villanueva, Spain, the son of a miller. He studied at Alcalá and joined the Augustinians at Salamanca. After his ordination in 1520 he was appointed prior successively of the Augustinian friars of Salamanca (where he taught moral theology in the university), Burgos and Valladolid. Later he became in turn provincial of Andalusia and Castile, court chaplain and (1544) archbishop of Valencia. As archbishop his outstanding characteristic was self-sacrifice: he was known as the grand almoner of the poor. He left a number of theological writings. Canonized 1658. Cult confined to particular calendars since 1969.

Thomas Cufioje (Bl) M. Sept 28
d. 1630 A Japanese layman, Augustinian tertiary, beheaded at Nagasaki. Beatified 1867.

Thomas of Hereford (St)
Bp. Oct 2 or 3
c 1218–1282 Born at Hambleden, near Great Marlow, the son of the Norman Baron William Cantalupe. He was a student at Oxford and Paris, and in 1261 Chancellor of Oxford University. In 1265 he was appointed Chancellor of England, but on being deprived of this office by Henry III, he returned eventually to his beloved Oxford. He became bishop of Hereford in 1275. The seven years of his episcopate was taken up with a continuous struggle in defence of the rights of his diocese, which had suffered a period of mismanagement and neglect especially due to the civil wars, and in untiring pastoral activities. He died at Montefiascone in Italy, whither he had gone to plead the cause of his see before the pope, as he had violently quarrelled with the archbishop of Canterbury, John Peckham, and had been excommunicated by him. Some parts of his remains were returned to Hereford; in time a popular movement for his canonisation arose, aided by his successor, his friend Richard Swinfield, and supported by Edward I. He was canonised in 1320, the memory of his personal holiness and pastoral zeal outweighing the memory of his short temper and excommunication.

Thomas Hélye (Bl) C. Oct 19
1187–1257 Born at Biville in Normandy, he led an ascetic life in the house of his parents and devoted part of his time to teaching the catechism to the poor. He was ordained at the request of his bishop and became an itinerant preacher throughout Normandy. Later he was appointed almoner to the king. He died at the castle of Vauville, Manche. Cult confirmed 1859.

Thomas Thwing (Thweng) (Bl) M. Oct 23
d. 1680 Born at Heworth in Yorkshire and educated at Douai, he was ordained in 1665 and returned to England where he worked for fifteen years on the Yorkshire mission. He was martyred at York for his alleged part in the Oates plot. Beatified 1929.

Thomas Bellacci (Bl) C. OFM. Oct 31
1370–1447 A native of Florence who joined the Franciscan friary at Fiesole, where, as a lay-brother, he was made novice-master. Later he worked successfully to introduce the Franciscan observance into Corsica and S. Italy and combated the Fraticelli in Tuscany. When over seventy he went to preach in Syria and Abyssinia where, to his sorrow, he narrowly escaped martyrdom by the Muslims. Cult approved 1771.

Thomas of Walden (Bl) C. OC. Nov 2
c 1375–1430 Thomas Netter was born at Saffron Walden and joined the Carmelites. He was an active opponent of Lollardism and a prominent member of the council of Constance. King Henry V chose him as his confessor and died in his arms. Thomas died at Rouen.

Thomas of Antioch (St) H. Nov 18
d. 782 A Syrian monk who dwelt in the vicinity of Antioch. He is venerated as a protector against pestilence.

Thomas Cotenda and Comp. (BB) MM. Nov 27
d. 1619 A scion of the Japanese royal family of Firando. He was educated by the Jesuits and lived in exile at Nagasaki, where he was ultimately beheaded with ten companions. Beatified 1867.

Thomas Somers (Bl) M. Dec 10
d. 1610 Thomas Somers (*alias* Wilson) was born at Skelsmergh, Westmorland, and started life as a schoolmaster. Later he went to Douai and was ordained. On returning to England he worked on the London mission. Together with Bl John Roberts, OSB., he was hanged at Tyburn. Beatified 1929.

Thomas of Farfa (St) Ab. OSB. Dec 10
d. c 720 A native of Maurienne in Savoy.

After becoming a Benedictine he went on pilgrimage to the Holy Land and on his return settled as a hermit near Farfa in Italy. With the help of his friend, the Duke of Spoleto, he restored the abbey of Farfa to its former splendour.

Thomas Holland (Bl) M. SJ.　　Dec 12
d. 1642　Thomas Holland (alias Sanderson, alias Hammond), born at Sutton, near Prescot, Lancs., was educated at St Omer and Valladolid and became a Jesuit in 1624. He was hanged at Tyburn. Beatified 1929.

Thomas De and Comp. (SS) MM. Tert. OP.　　Dec 19
d. 1839　A native of Tonkin, a tailor by trade and a Dominican tertiary, who was strangled with four companions for giving shelter to the missionaries. Beatified 1900, canonized in 1988.

Thomas Becket (St) Bp. M.　　GC. Dec 29
1118–1170　Born in London of Norman parents, he was sent to Merton abbey and Paris to study and entered the service of Archbishop Theobald of Canterbury, who sent him to Bologna and Auxerre to follow a course of civil and canon law and in 1154 made him archdeacon of Canterbury. He soon became a bosom friend of Henry II, who in 1155 appointed him Chancellor of the Kingdom and in 1162 Archbishop of Canterbury. Up to this time Thomas had led a rather worldly life, even leading royal troops into battle, but he now gave himself up completely to the faithful discharge of his pastoral duties. Being forced to oppose the king's wanton interference in ecclesiastical matters, especially by rejecting the constitutions of Clarendon in 1164, and after being several times exiled, he was brutally done to death in his cathedral by royal retainers. The whole kingdom at once proclaimed him a martyr, and the church confirmed the title by canonizing him in 1173. His shrine became one of the most famous in Christendom. He is depicted vested as an archbishop, but with a wounded head; or holding an inverted sword. He kneels before his murderers, or before an altar. His crosier may have a battle-axe head on it.

Thomasius (Thomasso) (Bl) H. OSB. Cam.　　March 25
Otherwise Thomas of Costacciaro, q.v.

Thomian (Toimen) (St) Bp.　　Jan 10
d. c 660　Archbishop of Armagh 623–c 660. He wrote a letter to the Holy See on the paschal controversy.

Thordgith (Thorctgyd, Theorigitha) (St) N. OSB.　　Jan 26
d. c 700　Novice-mistress at the abbey of Barking under St Ethelburga. She is described as a miracle of patience under suffering.

Thorlac Thorhalli (St) C. OSA.　　Dec 23
1133–1193　Born in Iceland, he was ordained deacon before he was fifteen and priest at the age of eighteen. He was then sent to study at Paris and Lincoln. In 1177 he became bishop of Skalholt in his native island. By vigorous measures he succeeded in stamping out simony and incontinency. He was "canonized" in 1198 by the Althing, but his cult has never been officially confirmed.

Thrace (Martyrs of) (SS)　　Aug 20
?　A group of thirty-seven martyrs put to death somewhere in Thrace. They were cast into a furnace after their hands and feet had been cut off.

Thraseas (St) Bp. M.　　Oct 5
d. c 170　Bishop of Eumenia in Phrygia, an opponent of the Montanists, martyred at Smyrna.

Thrasilla (St) V.　　Dec 24
Otherwise Tarsilla, q.v.

Thyrsus and Projectus (SS) MM.　　Jan 24
?　Martyrs of whom we know only the names.

Thyrsus, Leucius and Callinicus (SS) MM.　　Jan 28
251　Martyrs of Apollonia in Phrygia. Their alleged relics were brought to Constantinople and thence to Spain and France: for this reason St Thyrsus had a full office in the Mozarabic liturgy, and he is also patron of the ancient cathedral of Sisteron in the Basses Alpes, France.

Thyrsus (St) M.　　Jan 31
See Saturninus, Thyrsus and Victor.

Thyrsus (St) M.　　Sept 24
See Andochius, Thyrsus and Felix.

Tibba (St) N. OSB.　　March 6
See Kyneburga, Kyneswide and Tibba.

Tiberius, Modestus and Florentia (SS) MM.　　Nov 10
d. 303?　Martyrs who met their death under Diocletian at Agde, diocese of Montpellier.

Tiburtius, Valerian and Maximus (SS) MM.　　Apr 14
3rd cent.?　Three names which occur in the Acta of St Cecilia — Valerian as her husband, Tiburtius as his brother and Maximus as an

official. Though the *Acta* of St Cecilia are regarded as a romance, these saints might be authentic martyrs, to whom the author of St Cecilia's life had assigned imaginary rôles. Their tombs in the cemetery of Praetextatus were very popular in the Middle Ages. Cult relegated to local calendars since 1969.

Tiburtius (St) M. Aug 11
d. *c* 288 A martyr at Rome. He was later connected with the soldier-martyr St Sebastian. His cult is ancient and he was entombed at the Via Lavicana, but there are no trustworthy biographical details. Cult confined to local calendars since 1969.

Tiburtius (St) M. Sept 9
See Hyacinth, Alexander and Tiburtius.

Tigernach (Tigernake, Tierney, Tierry) (St) Bp. Apr 4
d. 549 Said to have been abbot of the monastery of Clones and to have succeeded St Macartin as bishop at Clogher. His life, in its present form, cannot be taken as a historical document.

Tigides and Remedius (SS) Bps. Feb 3
6th cent.? Two bishops who succeeded one another in the see of Gap (French Alps).

Tigridia (or Trigidia) (St) Abs. OSB. Nov 22
d. *c* 925 A daughter of Count Sancho Garcia, of Old Castile, who founded for her the Benedictine nunnery of Oña, near Burgos (later it became a monastery of monks). St Tigridia is venerated in the province of Burgos.

Tigrius and Eutropius (SS) MM. Jan 12
d. 404–405 Tigrius was a priest and Eutropius a reader in the church of Constantinople; both were loyal adherents of their bishop St John Chrysostom. When the latter was banished they were falsely accused of setting fire to the cathedral and senate-house of Constantinople and were put to the torture. Eutropius died under it; Tigrius seems to have survived and to have been deported into Asia.

Tikhon of Zadonsk (St) Mk. Bp. Aug 13
1724–83 From a poor Russian family, he became a professor at the Novgorod seminary, and a monk in 1758. From 1763–1767 he was bishop of Voronezh. From 1769 onwards he was a monk at the abbey of Zadonsk. His life was filled with a pastoral zeal, and his interest in Western thought went hand in hand with a

profound love of orthodox spirituality and asceticism.

Tilbert (Gilbert) (St) Bp. OSB. Sept 7
d. 789 Bishop of Hexham, 781–789. No details are known of his life.

Tillo (Thillo, Thielman, Théau, Tilloine, Tillon, Tilman, Hillonius, etc.) (St) OSB. Jan 7
d. *c* 702 Born in Saxony, he was kidnapped by robbers and carried as a slave to the Low Countries, where he was ransomed by St Eligius of Noyon. He became a monk at Solignac, and after his ordination evangelized the district round Tournai and Courtrai. He returned to Solignac, where he passed the last years of his life.

Timolaus and Comp. (SS) MM. March 24
d. 303 A group of eight martyrs beheaded at Caesarea in Palestine under Diocletian. Eusebius gives the names of the rest: Dionysius (two), Romulus, Pausis, Alexander (two), and Agapius.

Timon (St) M. Apr 19
1st cent. One of the first seven deacons chosen by the apostles (Acts 6:5). There are only conflicting traditions as to the rest of his life.

Timothy (St) Bp. M. GC. Jan 26
d. 97 "The beloved son in faith" of St Paul, whom he accompanied on his missionary journeys. Eusebius's history declares him head of the church in Ephesus. The apostle wrote to him two letters which are among the canonical books. According to a very ancient tradition, St Timothy was stoned to death for denouncing the worship of Dionysius.

Timothy (St) M. March 24
See Mark and Timothy.

Timothy and Diogenes (SS) MM. Apr 6
d. ? 345 Martyrs at Philippi in Macedonia, victims probably of the Arians.

Timothy and Maura (SS) MM. May 3
d. 298 Husband and wife, martyred at Antinöe in Egypt, by being nailed to a wall, where they lingered for nine days, consoling each other. They had been married only three weeks. Timothy, who was a reader, had been condemned for refusing to deliver the sacred books.

**Timothy, Polius and
Eutychius (SS) MM.** May 21
? Three deacons in the African province of
Mauretania Caesariensis, martyred under
Diocletian.

Timothy (St) M. May 22
See Faustinus, Timothy and Venustus.

Timothy (St) Bp. M. June 10
d. 362 Bishop of Prusa in Bithynia, martyred under Julian the Apostate.

**Timothy, Thecla and
Agapius (SS) MM.** Aug 19
d. 304–306 Timothy, bishop of Gaza in
Palestine, was burnt alive in his episcopal city
(304). Thecla was condemned to be thrown to
the wild beasts. Agapius was cast into the sea at
Caesarea in Palestine (306).

Timothy (St) M. Aug 22
d. c 306 A Roman martyr of the time of
Diocletian. His remains were enshrined in a
chapel near St Paul-outside-the-Walls and
venerated there during the Middle Ages.
Since 1969 confined to local calendars.

Timothy (St) M. Aug 23
See Apollinaris and Timothy.

**Timothy of Montecchio
(Bl) C. OFM.** Aug 26
1414–1504 A native of Montecchio, near
Aquila, in Italy, he became a Franciscan
observant. Cult confirmed in 1870.

**Timothy and Faustus
(SS) MM.** Sept 8
? Martyrs at Antioch in Syria.

Timothy (St) M. Dec 19
d. c 250 A deacon, burnt alive in Africa
under Decius.

Titian (St) Bp. Jan 16
d. 650 For thirty years a bishop in the
neighbourhood of Venice. The seat of his
bishopric (Opitergium or Oderzo) has since
been destroyed.

Titian (St) Bp. March 3
d. c 536 Said to have been a German by
birth, who became bishop of Brescia.

Titus (St) Bp. GC. Jan 26
d. c 96? One of the favourite disciples of St
Paul, companion and helper of the apostle. St
Paul addressed to him one of the pastoral
epistles. He died in Crete (at Gortyna?), where
he was an elder of the church; indeed, is held
to have been its first bishop, according to
Eusebius.

Titus (St) M. Aug 16
d. 410 (or 426?) A Roman deacon, put to

death by a soldier during the sack of Rome by
the Goths, while he was distributing alms to
the half-starved population.

Tobias (St) M. Nov 2
See Carterius, Styriacus, etc.

Tochumra (St) V. June 11
? A virgin venerated in the diocese of Kilmore. She is invoked by women in labour.

Toiman (St) Bp. Jan 10
Otherwise Thomian, q.v.

Tola (St) Bp. March 30
d. c 733 An Irish abbot-bishop of Disert
Tola (Meath).

Tooley (St) King M. July 29
A corrupt form of the name of St Olaus or
Olav, q.v.

Torannan (St) Bp. June 12
Otherwise Ternan, q.v.

Torello (Bl) H. OSB. Vall. March 16
1201–1281 Born at Poppi in Tuscany, he
was led astray by evil companions, but repented and received the habit of a recluse from
the Vallumbrosan abbot of San Fedele. He
lived as a recluse, walled up in his cell, for sixty
years. Vallumbrosans and Franciscans claim
him. It seems certain that he was, at any rate, a
Vallumbrosan oblate. Cult confirmed by
Benedict XIV.

Torpes (St) M. Apr 29
d. ? c 65 A martyr at Pisa, said to have
suffered under Nero. The legends we have
about him are altogether unreliable.

**Torquatus, Ctesiphon,
Secundus, Indaletius,
Caecilius, Hesychius,
and Euphrasius (SS) MM.** May 15
1st cent. According to a tradition which,
however, is not very ancient, they were disciples of the apostles, by whom they were sent
to evangelize Spain. They worked chiefly in
the South, as follows: Torquatus at Guadix,
near Granada; Ctesiphon at Verga (Vierzo?);
Secundus at Avila; Indaletius at Urci, near
Almeria; Caecilius at Granada; Hesychius at
Gibraltar; Euphrasius at Andujar. Most of
them suffered martyrdom. The Mozarabic
liturgy had a common feast for all seven.

Torthred (St) M. Apr 9
Perhaps a variant of Theodore, q.v.

Totnan (St) M. July 8
See Kilian, Colman and Totnan.

Toulouse (Martyrs of)
(BB)   May 29
d. 1228   A group of twelve martyrs — four of
the secular clergy, three Dominicans, two
Benedictines, two Franciscans, one layman —
put to death by the Albigensians near
Toulouse on the eve of the ascension. They
died singing the *Te Deum*. Cult confirmed in
1866.

Touredec (St) M.   Apr 9
Otherwise Torthred, perhaps a variant of
Theodore, q.v.

Tranquillinus (St) M.   July 6
d. ? 288   A Roman martyr connected with
the legend of St Sebastian, q.v.

Trason, Pontian and
Praetextatus (SS) MM.   Dec 11
d. c 302   Roman martyrs under Diocletian,
put to death for ministering to the Christian
prisoners awaiting martyrdom.

Trea (St) V.   Aug 3
5th cent.   Converted to Christianity by St
Patrick. She passed the rest of her life as a
recluse at Ardtree, Derry.

Tremorus (St) M.   Nov 7
6th cent.   Infant son of St Triphina. He was
murdered at Carhaix in Brittany by his stepfather, Count Conmore. He is patron saint of
Carhaix.

Tressan (French: Trésain)
(St) C.   Feb 7
d. 550   An Irish missionary, ordained priest
by St Remigius, who worked at Mareuil on the
Marne.

Triduna (Tredwall,
Trallen) (St) V.   Oct 8
8th or 4th cent?   A maiden connected with
the legend of St Regulus's mission to Scotland. Her shrine was a centre of devotion and
pilgrimage before its destruction in 1560: its
remains at Restalrig have been excavated in
modern times.

Trien (Trienan) (St) Ab.   March 22
5th cent.   One of St Patrick's disciples, abbot
of Killelga.

Trier (Martyrs of) (SS)   Oct 6
d. 287   The entry in the pre-1970 RM. was
as follows: "At Trier, the commemoration of
the almost innumerable martrys who were
slain in divers ways in the persecution of
Diocletian, under the governor Rictiovarus,
for the faith of Christ."

Trillo (Drillo, Drel) (St) C.   June 15
6th cent.   Nothing is now known for sure of

his life. He is patron saint of two places in
Gwynedd (which before the recent upheaval
of boundaries were in Denbighshire and
Merionethshire).

Triphina (St) W.   July 5
6th cent.   The mother of St Tremorus the
infant-martyr. She passed the latter years of
her life in a convent in Brittany.

Triphina (St) M.   July 5
See Agatho and Triphina.

Triphyllius (St) Bp.   June 13
d. c 370   A lawyer converted to Christianity
who was made bishop of Nicosia in Cyprus.
He was a companion of St Spiridion and a
loyal supporter of St Athanasius against the
Arians, who bitterly persecuted him.

Tripos (St) M.   June 10
See Basilides, Tripos, etc.

Triverius (St) H.   Jan 16
d. c 550   Born in Neustria, he showed from
childhood a strong leaning to the contemplative life. He lived as a hermit near the
monastery of Thérouanne, until he moved to
Dombes. The village of Saint Trivier commemorates his name. He is honoured at Lyons
and in the diocese of Belley.

Troadius (St) M.   Dec 28
d. 250   A martyr of Neo-Caesarea in
Pontus, in the persecution under Decius.

Trojan (French: Troyen)
(St) Bp.   Nov 30
d. 533   Said to have been born of a Jewish
father and a Saracen mother. He became a
priest at Saintes under St Vivian, whom he
succeeded in the see.

Tron or Trond (St) Ab.
OSB.   Nov 23
Otherwise Trudo, q.v.

Trophimus and Thalus
(SS) MM.   March 11
d. c 300   Martyrs at Laodicea in Syria,
crucified under Diocletian.

Trophimus and
Eucarpius (SS) MM.   March 18
d. c 304   Two pagan soldiers told to hunt
Christians; they were converted and burnt
alive at Nicomedia under Diocletian.

Trophimus and
Theophilus (SS) MM.   July 23
d. c 302   Martyrs, beheaded at Rome under
Diocletian.

Trophimus, Sabbatius
and Dorymedon (SS) MM.   Sept 19
d. c 277   Asiatic martyrs under the emperor

Probus. They suffered probably at Antioch in Syria.

Trophimus (St) Bp.   Dec 29
d. *c* 280   First bishop of Arles, sent to Gaul from Rome *c* 240–260. Since 452 (synod of Arles) the church of Provence has identified him with St Trophimus, the disciple of St Paul (Acts 20:4; 21:29; 2 Tim. 4:20), but this is of course only a pious fiction.

Trudo (Trudon, Tron, Trond, Truyen, Trudjen) (St) Ab. OSB.   Nov 23
d. *c* 695   A Benedictine under St Remaclus, he was ordained by St Clodulphus of Metz, and eventually founded and governed an abbey on his paternal estate (*c* 660), which was afterwards called after him St Trond. It is situated between Louvain and Tongres.

Trudpert (St) H.   Apr 26
d. *c*? 644   A solitary in Münstethal. The Benedictine abbey of St Trudpert arose on that site. According to his life he was of Irish origin and was murdered by servants, and so venerated as a martyr. This life is however considered a legend.

Trumwin (St) Bp. OSB.   Feb 10
d. *c* 704   He was appointed (681), by St Theodore and King Egfrid, bishop over the Southern Picts, and set up his see at the monastery of Abercorn on the Firth of Forth. In 685 King Egfrid was killed by the Picts at the battle of Nechtansmere and St Trumwin and all his monks had to flee south. He retired to Whitby and there he lived an exemplary monastic life under the rule of the saintly Abbess Elflida.

Tryphaena (Triphenes) (St) M.   Jan 31
?   A matron of Cyzicus on the Hellespont who, after having been tortured in divers manners, was thrown to a savage bull and gored to death.

Tryphenna and Tryphosa (SS)   Nov 10
1st cent.   Two converts of St Paul from Iconium in Lycaonia, mentioned by the apostle in his letter to the Romans (16:12). Tradition represents them as protectresses of St Thecla.

Tryphon (St) M.   Jan 4
See Aquilinus, Geminus, etc.

Tryphon and Comp. (SS) MM.   July 3
?   A group of thirteen martyrs, who suffered at Alexandria in Egypt.

Tryphon, Respicius and Nympha (SS) MM.   formerly Nov 10
d. 251   Tryphon is alleged to have been a gooseherd at Campsada near Apamea in Syria and was martyred in Nicaea under Decius. The names of Respicius and Nympha have been joined to that of Tryphon only since the eleventh century; we know nothing about either saint. Cult suppressed in 1969.

Tryphonia (St) W.   Oct 18
3rd cent.   A Roman widow martyred at Rome. In legend she has been made wife either of the emperor Decius, or of Decius's son, Messius Decius. Her *Acta* are worthless.

Tryphosa (St)   Nov 10
See Tryphenna and Tryphosa.

Tuda (St) Bp.   Oct 21
d. 664   An Irish monk who succeeded St Colman in the see of Lindisfarne, an adherent of the Roman practices. He died of the pestilence within the first year of his appointment. He does not seem to have enjoyed a public cult: early records regarding him may have been destroyed at the sack of Lindisfarne.

Tude (St) Bp. M.   June 17
Otherwise Antidius, q.v.

Tudinus (St) Ab.   May 9
Otherwise Tudy, q.v.

Tudno (St) C.   June 5
6th cent.   The saint after whom Llandudno in Gwynedd is named. Several Welsh legends refer to him.

Tudwal (Tugdual, Tugdualus) (St) Bp.   Nov 30
d. *c* 564   A Welsh monk who crossed over into Brittany and became bishop of Tréguier. Three places in the Lleyn Peninsular in Gwynedd perpetuate his memory and his relics are still preserved at Tréguier.

Tudy (Tudclyd, Tybie) (St) V.   Jan 30
5th cent.?   Alleged daughter of Brychan of Brecknock — perhaps a relative or descendant. Llandydie church in Dyfed perpetuates her name.

Tudy (Tudinus, Tegwin, Thetgo) (St) Ab.   May 11
5th cent.   A Breton saint, disciple of St Brioc. He was first a hermit and then an abbot near Landevennec in Brittany; like St Brioc he spent some time in Cornwall, where a church and parish still bear his name.

Tugdual (St) Bp.   Nov 30
Otherwise Tudwal, q.v.

Turiaf (Turiav, Turiavus) (St) Bp. July 13

d. *c* 750 A Breton who succeeded St Samson as bishop of Dol.

Turibius de Mongrovejo (St) Bp. GC. March 23

1538–1606 Torbibio Alfonso de Mongrovejo was born at Mayorga, province of Léon, Spain. He was professor of law at Salamanca, and, though a layman, was made president of the court of the Inquisition at Granada. Philip II appointed him to the see of Lima in Peru, (1580) where the saint, fearing God but no man, with boundless zeal and untiring energy renewed the face of the church. He championed the rights of the oppressed Indians against the often dissolute and tyrannical Spanish masters. Canonized in 1726.

Turibius of Astorga (St) Bp. Apr 16

d. *c* 460 Bishop of Astorga in Spain, champion of Catholic doctrine against the Priscillianists.

Turibius of Palencia (St) Ab. Apr 16(?)

d. *c* 528 Probably a bishop. The abbot –founder of the great abbey of Liébana in Asturias, which eventually became a Benedictine centre.

Turketil (St) Ab.OSB. July 11

887–975 A nephew of King Edred of England and also his Chancellor. In 948 he became a monk and shortly after abbot of Croyland, which he restored, attaching a cloistral school to the monastery.

Turninus (St) C. July 17

8th cent. An Irish priest who worked as a missionary with St Foillan in the Netherlands and more particularly in the vicinity of Antwerp.

Tutilo (St) Mk.OSB. March 28

d. *c* 915 Monk of St Gall in Switzerland. Handsome, eloquent, quick-witted, a giant in strength and stature, poet, orator, architect, painter, sculptor, metal worker, mechanic, musician who played and taught several instruments at the abbey school, he was characterized by his obedience and recollection.

Tuto (Totto) (Bl) Bp.OSB. May 14

d. 930 Monk and abbot of St Emmeram at Regensburg. He became bishop of the same city and secretary to the emperor Arnold.

Tuto (Totto) (Bl) Ab.OSB. Nov 19

d. 815 Abbot–founder (764) of the great Benedictine abbey of Ottobeuren in Bavaria.

Twelve Holy Brothers, The (SS) MM. formerly Sept 1

d. *c* 303? The relics of several groups of martyrs, who had suffered in S.Italy, were brought together and enshrined at Benevento in 760. A legend grew up according to which all these martyrs were the sons of SS Boniface and Thecla, q.v.; they were said to have been arrested in Africa and brought to Italy were they were put to death. This legend is now considered to have no historical foundation. The several groups comprised in the so–called "twelve brothers", or Martyrs of the South, are (1) Aug 27. At Potenza in the Basilicata, Arontius or Orontius, Honoratus, Fortunatus and Sabinian. (2) Aug 28. At Venosa in Apulia, Septiminus, Januarius and Felix. (3) Aug 29. At Velleianum in Apulia, Vitalis, Sator (or Satyrus) and Repositus. (4) Sept 1. At Sentianum in Apulia, Donatus and another Felix. Cult suppressed in 1969.

Tychicus (St) Bp. Apr 29

1st cent. A disciple of St Paul the apostle (Acts 20: 4; 21: 29) and his fellow-worker (Col. 4: 7; Eph. 6: 21 sq.). He is said to have ended his days as bishop of Paphos in Cyprus.

Tychon (St) Bp. June 16

d. *c* 450 Bishop of Amathus in Cyprus. He energetically fought against the last remnants of paganism in the island, especially the cult of Aphrodite.

Tydecho (St) Dec 17

6th cent. A Welshman, brother of St Cadfan. He and his sister dwelt in Gwynedd. Several churches are dedicated in his honour.

Tydfil (St) M. Aug 23

d. *c* 480 Of the clan of Brychan. She is venerated at Merthyr–Tydfil, Mid-Glamorgan, where she was slain by the marauding Picts or Saxons.

Tyrannio Silvanus, Peleus, Nilus and Zenobius (SS) MM. Feb 20

d. *c* 304 The pre-1970 RM. entry commemorates an unknown number of Martyrs of Tyr. According to the Bollandists, Tyrannio and Zenobius, whose names are included, suffered at Antioch in 310, Silvanus at Emesa; Peleus and Nilus were, according to Eusebius, Egyptian bishops, among the martyrs of Palestine.

Tyre (Martyrs of) (St) Feb 20

d. 302–310 The pre-1970 RM. had this entry: "At Tyre in Phoenicia, the commemoration of blessed martyrs whose number the wisdom of God alone can tell..." The group of the preceding entry were among this number.

Tysilio (Tyssel, Tyssilo, Suliau) (St) Ab.   Nov 8
7th cent.   A Welsh prince, who became abbot of Meifod in Powys and founded several churches in other parts of Wales. In Brittany, at Saint–Suliac, there is a cult which may be of another person with the same name.

Ubald Baldassini (St) Bp.   May 16
c 1100–1160   Born at Gubbio near Ancona,
he was made dean of the cathedral and
introduced community life among the canons.
In 1128 he became bishop of his native city.
His character was remarkable for its combination of gentleness with courage, and it was by
these qualities that he succeeded in disarming
Frederick Barbarossa. Canonized 1192. Cult
confined to local calendars in 1969.

Ubald Adimari (Bl) C. OSM.   Apr 9
1246–1315   He belonged to the nobility of
Florence, and as a leader in the Ghibelline
party he was notorious for his wild and
dissolute life. In 1276 he was converted by St
Philip Benizi who admitted him to the Servite
institute. Ubald spent the remainder of his life
on Mt Senario, a model to penitents. Cult
confirmed 1821.

Ubric (St) Bp.   July 4
Otherwise Ulric, q.v.

Uda (St) V.   Jan 30
Otherwise Tudy, q.v.

Uganda (Martyrs of)
See St Charles Lwanga and Comps.

Uguccio (St) C.   Feb 17
One of the Seven Founders of the Servite
Order, q.v.

Uguzo (Lucius) (St) M.   Aug 16
? A poor shepherd in the mountains of Car-
vagna (Italian Alps) who gave his meagre
savings to the poor and the churches. He was
killed through envy by one of his former
masters. His cult has flourished at Milan since
1280.

Ulched (Ulchad, Ylched) (St)   Apr 6
? The holy man who has given his name to the
church of Llechulched in Anglesey.

Ulfrid (Wolfred, Wilfrid)
(St) M.   Jan 18
d. 1028   A native of England who became a
missionary in Germany and Sweden. He was
martyred for destroying an image of Thor.

Ulmar (St) Ab. OSB.   July 20
Otherwise Wulmar, q.v.

Ulphia (Wulfia,
Olfe, Wulfe) (St) H.   Jan 31
8th cent.   Said to have lived as a solitary near
Amiens under the direction of the aged hermit
St Domitius. At a later period the convent of
the Paraclete was built over her tomb.

Ulpian (St) M.   Apr 3
Otherwise Vulpian, q.v.

Ulric (St) H.   Feb 20
Otherwise Wulfric, q.v.

Ulric of Einsiedeln (Bl)
C. OSB.   May 29
d. *p.*978   Son of St Gerold. He became a
monk at the Swiss abbey of Einsiedeln and was
appointed treasurer. After his father's death
he retired to live as a hermit in the latter's cell.
His feast is observed at Einsiedeln.

Ulric (Uldaricus, Udalric)
(St) Bp.   July 4
c 890–973   A native of Augsburg, at the age
of seven he was sent to be educated at the
Swiss Benedictine abbey of St Gall. In 923 he
was nominated bishop of Augsburg and
became the protector of his people against the
invading Magyars and a friend and supporter
of the emperor Otto I. In his old age he retired
to St Gall and took one of his nephews as his
coadjutor. Canonized 993 by Pope John XV;
the first person on record to be formerly
canonized by the bishop of Rome.

Ulric of Cluny (St) Mk.
OSB.   July 14
c 1018–1093   Born at Regensburg, he
became archdeacon of Freising and then went
on a pilgrimage to Rome and Jerusalem. On
his return he joined the Benedictines at Cluny
under St Hugh (1061). he held the following
offices in rapid succession: novice master (as
such he wrote the famous Cluniac Customary); prior and confessor of the Cluniac nunnery of Marcigny; prior of Peterlingen; prior of
Rüggersburg, and finally prior-founder of Zell
in the Black Forest. Throughout his life he
suffered from violent headaches.

Ultan (St) Ab. OSB.   May 2
7th cent.   An Irishman, brother of SS Fursey

and Foillan and a monk with them at Burgh-castle near Yarmouth. Thence he crossed over to Belgium, where he was warmly wel-comed by St Gertrude of Nivelles. He was chaplain to her nunnery and taught chant to the nuns until he succeeded his brother St Foillan in the abbacies of Fosses and Peronne.

Ultan (St) H. OSB.   Aug 8
8th cent. An Irishman and monk-priest of St Peter's monastery at Craik. He excelled in the art of illumination.

Ultan (St) Bp.   Sept 4
7th cent. There are a score or so of Irish saints named Ultan. Besides the two listed above the most important seems to have been a bishop of Ardbraccan, noted for his fondness for children and said to have collected the writings of St Brigid.

Ultius (St) Bp.   Jan 8
Otherwise Wulsin, q.v.

Unaman (St) M. OSB.   Feb 15
See Winaman, Unaman and Sunaman.

**Uni (Unni, Unno, Huno)
(St) Bp. OSB.**   Sept 17
d. 936 A Benedictine of New Corvey in Saxony, who in 917 was appointed bishop of Bremen-Hamburg. He evangelized Sweden and Denmark with signal success and died at Birka in Sweden.

Urban (St) M.   Jan 24
See Babilas, Urban, etc.

Urban (St) M.   March 8
See Cyril, Rogatus, etc.

Urban of Langres (St) Bp.   Apr 2
d. c 390 Sixth bishop of Langres, nomin-ated to that see in 374. In some parts of Burgundy and neighbouring provinces he is honoured as the patron saint of vine dressers.

Urban (St) Ab. OSB.   Apr 6
d. c 940 Abbot of the Benedictine monas-tery of Peñalba in the diocese of Astorga, Spain. He helped St Gennadius to bring about a Benedictine revival.

Urban (St) M.   Apr 16
See Saragossa (Martyrs of).

Urban I (St) Pope   formerly May 25
d. 230 A Roman, successor of Callistus in the papal chair (222–230). During his pontificate the church seems to have enjoyed comparative peace. Cult suppressed in 1969.

Urban (St) M.   July 2
See Ariston, Crescentian, etc.

Urban II (Bl) Pope OSB.   July 29
1042–1099 Odo of Lagery was born at

Chatillon-sur-Marne and belonged to the family of the counts of Semur. He studied at Reims under St Bruno and became arch-deacon of that church. In 1070 he joined the Benedictines of Cluny and was soon appointed grand prior under St Hugh. In 1080 he was created cardinal bishop of Ostia and in 1088 was elected pope. As prior, as cardinal and as pope he followed and fostered the Gregorian policy of ecclesiastical reform. As pope he had as adviser St Bruno, the founder of the Carthusians. Urban is perhaps best remem-bered as the promoter of the first crusade at the council of Clermont, in consequence of an appeal from the Byzantine emperor Alexius I. Comnenus. Beatified 1881.

**Urban, Theodore and
Comp. (SS) MM.**   Sept 5
d. 370 A group of eighty priests and clerics who, in the time of the Arian emperor Valens, were deliberately left to perish in a burning ship for having appealed to the emperor against the persecution of the Catholics.

Urban (St) M.   Oct 31
See Ampliatus, Urban and Narcissus.

Urban (St) Bp.   Nov 28
See Valerian, Urban, etc.

Urban (St) Bp.   Dec 7
d. c 356 Bishop of Teano in Campania.

Urban V (Bl) Pope OSB.   Dec 19
1309–1370 William of Grimoard was born in Languedoc and educated at the universities of Montpellier and Toulouse. He became a Benedictine at the priory of Chirac and was sent to take his doctorate at Paris and Avignon. He affiliated himself to the Cluniacs and was made abbot of St Germanus at Auxerre in 1352, and in 1361 of St Victor at Marseilles. Later that year he was sent as papal delegate to Italy (the papacy then being at Avignon) and in the following year, although not yet a cardinal, was elected pope. He succeeded in trans-ferring the papacy back to Rome, but in 1370 he was forced to retire to France, dying the same year. Cult confirmed 1870.

Urbitius (St) Bp.   March 20
d. c 420 Bishop of Metz. He built a church in honour of St Felix of Nola which became the abbey church of the monastery of St Clement.

**Urbitius (Spanish:
Urbez) (St) H. OSB.**   Dec 15
d. c 805 Said to have been born at Bor-deaux, to have become a monk in France, and to have been taken prisoner by Saracens and

brought to Spain. He managed to escape and settled as a hermit in the valley of Nocito, Aragonese Pyrenees, near Huesca. There is no trustworthy biography of the saint, but his cult is still flourishing in that district.

Urciscenus (St) Bp. June 21
d. *c* 216 Reckoned to be the seventh bishop of Pavia, *c* 183–216.

Urpasian (St) M. March 13
d. 295 A Christian of the household of Diocletian who was burnt alive at Nicomedia.

Ursacius (St) Aug 16
Otherwise Arsacius, q.v.

Ursicinus (St) M. June 19
d. *c* 67 Said to have been a physician at Ravenna who, on being sentenced to death for being a Christian, wavered, but was encouraged by the soldier St Vitalis and accepted martyrdom. His Acts are not trustworthy.

Ursicinus (St) Bp. July 24
d. *c* 380 Registered as the fourth bishop of Sens. An opponent of Arianism.

Ursicinus (St) Bp. OSB. Oct 2
d. 760 Abbot of Disentis in Switzerland, who became bishop of Chur in 754. In 758 he resigned and became a hermit.

Ursicinus (St) Bp. Dec 1
d. *p.*347 A bishop of Brescia in Lombardy who took part in the council of Sardica (347). His shrine at Brescia still exists.

Ursicinus (St) Bp. Dec 20
d. *c* 585 Bishop of Cahors, often mentioned by the historian St Gregory of Tours.

Ursicinus (St) Ab. Dec 20
d. *c* 625 An Irish missionary monk companion of St Columbanus. He became the abbot-founder of the monastery of St Ursanne, from which the Swiss town so called takes its name.

Ursicius (St) M. Aug 14
d. 304 An Illyrian tribune in the imperial army beheaded at Nicomedia under Diocletian.

Ursinus (St) Bp. Nov 9
3rd cent. Though alleged to have been one of several disciples of Christ sent by the apostles to be bishops in Gaul, it is certain that he flourished in the third century and that he was the first bishop of Bourges.

Ursmar (St) Bp. OSB. Apr 19
d. 713 Abbot-bishop of the great Benedictine abbey of Lobbes on the Sambre and founder of Aulne and Wallers, also in present-

St Ursula, formerly Oct 21

day Belgium. His work as regionary bishop in Flanders was of great importance.

Ursula and Comps. (SS)
VV. MM. formerly Oct 21
4th cent.? The story of St Ursula and her 11,000 virgin companions was one of the most popular of the Middle Ages, and was a favourite subject for artists, stained glass window designers and embroiderers. The basis of the whole elaborate legend is an inscription, carved around the year 400, recording the restoration of a church already old, by a certain Clematius in honour of some local early virgin-martyrs. No names or numbers are given . By the ninth century their number is very large, and it is claimed that they suffered under Maximian. A century later the number

of 11,000 is established, and the story passed on into the Golden Legend. The discovery of an early cemetery in 1155 in Cologne aided the legend further — the bones were held to be those of the martyrs. Pope Benedict XIV intended to delete this entry from the Roman Martyrology. The cult was finally suppressed in the reforms of 1969. In art St Ursula is represented as a damsel shot with arrows, and with a large number of companions, all being martyred in often quite ingenious ways.

Ursulina (Bl) V.   Apr 7
1375–1410   A young woman of Parma who, alleging supernatural visions, visited Clement VII at Avignon and Boniface IX at Rome with a view to putting an end to the papal schism. After a pilgrimage to the Holy Land she was refused admittance to Parma and had to retire to Bologna, where she died.

Ursuline Nuns (BB) MM.   Oct 23
d. 1794   A group of eleven Ursuline nuns guillotined between 17–23 October 1794 at Valenciennes for having reopened their school in spite of the prohibition of the French Revolutionaries. They are the Blesseds Clotilde Paillot, superior; Mary Magdalen (Augustine) Desjardin; Mary Louise (Natalie) Vanot; Anne Mary Erraux; Anne Joseph (Scholastique) Leroux; Gabrielle (Marie Ursule) Bourla; Jane Louis (Cordule) Barré; Jane Rievie (Laurentine) Prin; Margaret (Josephine) Leroux; Francoise Lacroix; Mary Louise Ducret. Names in parentheses are their names in religion.

Ursus (St) C.   Feb 1
6th cent.   Of Irish origin, he preached against the Arians in the South of France and became archdeacon of Aosta.

Ursus (St) Bp.   Apr 13
d. 396   Of a noble Sicilian family, he became a convert and fled from his father's wrath to Ravenna, where in 378 he became bishop.

Ursus (St) Bp.   July 30
d. 508   A recluse at the church of St Amator of Auxerre, who was made bishop of that city when he was seventy-five years of age.

Ursus (St) M.   Sept 30
See Victor and Ursus.

Ust (Justus) (St)   Aug 12
?   He gives its title to the church of St Just, a few miles from Penzance. He is described indiscriminately as a hermit, as a martyr, and as a bishop. Possibly there were several saints of this name, whose lives have been amalgamated.

Usthazanes (St) M.   Apr 21
See Simeon, Abdechalas, etc.

Utto (Bl) Ab. OSB.   Oct 3
c 750–820   Abbot-founder of the Benedictine monastery of Metten in Bavaria. Cult approved 1909.

Uval (St)   Nov 20
Otherwise Eval, q.v.

Vaast (St) Bp.   Feb 6
Otherwise Vedast, q.v.

Vacz (Bl) H.   Nov 26
11th cent. Hermit at Visegrád, in the mountains of Pilis, Hungary. Considered by the Pauline order to be the forerunner of their founder Bl Eusebius (1260).

Valens and Comp. (SS)
MM.   May 21
? Said to have been a bishop martyred at Auxerre with three boys.

Valens, Paul and Comp.
(SS) MM.   June 1
d. 309 Martyrs at Caesarea in Palestine, companions of St Pamphilus. Valens was an aged deacon of the church of Jerusalem. They suffered under Diocletian.

Valens (St) Bp.   July 26
d. 531 Bishop of Verona, 524–531.

Valentina and Comp.
(SS) VV. MM.   July 25
d. 308 Virgin martyrs in Palestine under Maximian Galerius. See Meuris and Thea.

Valentine (St) Bp.   Jan 7
d. c 470 An abbot who became a missionary bishop in Rhaetia. He died at Mais in the Tyrol. Some years later his body was translated to Trent and finally to Passau.

Valentine (St) M.   Feb 14
d. 269 A priest and physician in Rome martyred perhaps under Claudius the Goth and buried on the Flaminian Way. In 350 a church was built over his tomb. The custom of sending "Valentines" on Feb 14 is based on the medieval belief that birds began to pair on that day. Since 1969 his cult has been restricted to local calendars only.

Valentine (St) Bp. M.   Feb 14
d. c 269 A bishop of Terni (*Interamna*) about sixty miles from Rome, martyred under Claudius the Goth. Some writers, we believe rightly, identify this saint with the St Valentine recorded above: the Acts of both saints are not reliable.

Valentine (St) Bp.   May 2
d. c Bishop of Genoa, c 295–307. His relics were discovered and enshrined in 985.

Valentine (St) Bp. M.   July 16
d. c 305 A bishop of Trier (or more probably Tongres) martyred under Diocletian.

Valentine (St) Bp.   Sept 2
4th cent. Fourth bishop of Strasburg.

Valentine (St) H.   Oct 25
See Fructus, Valentine and Engratia.

Valentine (St) Bp.   Oct 29
Coupled in the pre-1970 RM. with St Maximilian. Nothing is known of him.

Valentine Berrio-Ochoa
(St) Bp. M. OP.   Nov 1
1827–1861 Born at Ellorio, diocese of Vitoria, Spain. After his profession in the Dominican order he was sent to the Philippine Islands and thence (1858) to Vietnam as a bishop titular and vicar-apostolic. He was beheaded with St Jerome Hermosilla. Beatified in 1909, canonized in 1988.

Valentine and Hilary (SS)
MM.   Nov 3
d. c 304 A priest and his deacon, beheaded at Viterbo, near Rome, under Diocletian.

Valentine, Felician and
Victorinus (SS) MM.   Nov 11
d. c 305 Martyrs at Ravenna under Diocletian.

Valentine, Solutor and
Victor (SS) MM.   Nov 13
d. c 305 Martyrs at Ravenna under Diocletian. Probably a duplicate of Nov 11. To both groups some martyrologies add a number of other names.

Valentine, Concordius,
Navalis and Agricola
(SS) MM.   Dec 16
d. c 305 In all probability a repetition of the two preceding entries. Since St Peter Chrysologus (d. c 450) writes that St Apollinaris was the only martyr of Ravenna, it may be that St Valentine and Comp. were merely venerated in that city, and only later said to have been martyred there.

St Valentine, Feb 14

Valentinian (St) Bp.   Nov 3
d. *c* 500   Bishop of Salerno in S. Italy.

Valentio (St) M.   May 25
See Pasicrates, Valentio, etc.

Valeria (Martyrs of) (SS)   March 14
5th cent.   The pre-1970 RM. had this entry:
"In the province of Valeria, the birthday of two

holy monks, whom the Lombards slew by hanging them on a tree: and there, although dead, they were heard even by their enemies singing psalms". The story is taken from St Gregory the Great (Dial.4:21).

Valeria (St) M.   Apr 28
? 1st cent.   The alleged mother of SS Gervase and Protase and wife of St Vitalis. She seems to be a fictitious personage. See Vitalis.

Valeria (St) M.   June 5
See Zenais, Dyria, etc.

Valeria (St) VM.   Dec 9
? This saint probably never existed. She is said to have been converted to the faith by St Martial of Limoges, and to have been beheaded there. (Cf. Martial of Limoges.)

Valerian (St) M.   Apr 14
See Tiburtius, Valerian and Maximus.

Valerian (St) Bp.   May 13
d. *c* 350   Third bishop of Auxerre. A champion of the Catholic faith against Arianism.

Valerian (St) Bp.   July 23
d. *c* 460   A monk of Lérins who became bishop of Cimeiz (now united to the see of Nice). He attended the councils of Riez (439) and Vaison (442); a group of his homilies was rediscovered in the seventeenth century and give interesting information about this early age.

Valerian (St) M.   Aug 23
See Restitutus, Donatus, etc.

Valerian (St) M.   Sept 12
See Hieronides, Leontius, etc.

Valerian (St) M.   Sept 15
d. 178   A companion of St Photinus (Pothinus) of Lyons. He succeeded in escaping from prison and reappeared at Tournus, near Autun, where he again preached to the people. He was captured a second time and beheaded.

Valerian, Macrinus and Gordian (SS) MM.   Sept 17
? Martyrs ascribed by some to Noyon, by others to Nevers, by others to Nyon (near Berne, Switzerland), by others to a place called Noviodunum near the mouth of the Danube in Lower Moesia.

Valerian (St) Bp.   Nov 27
d. 389   Bishop of Aquileia in N.Italy. He succeeded immediately after an Arian bishop and his pontificate, 369–389, was spent in combating that heresy.

Valerian, Urban, Crescens, Eustace, Cresconius, Crescentian, Felix, Hortulanus and Florentian (SS) Bps.   Nov 28
5th cent. African bishops banished from their country by the Arian king Genseric. They died in exile and were afterwards honoured as confessors of the faith.

Valerian (St) Bp. M.   Dec 15
d. 457 Bishop of Abbenza in Africa who, when over eighty years of age, was left to die of exposure for refusing to give up the sacred vessels. He died under the Arian Genseric, king of the Vandals.

Valerius (St) Bp.   Jan 16
d. c 453 A hermit taken from his solitude by the people of Sorrento, who made him their bishop.

Valerius (St) Bp.   Jan 28
d. 315 Bishop of Saragossa in Spain, under whom St Vincent served as deacon. He was arrested and exiled under Diocletian; but survived and died in peace in his episcopal city.

Valerius (St) Bp.   Jan 29
d. c 320 Legendary second bishop of Trier and alleged disciple of St Peter. More probably he was bishop of that city at the beginning of the fourth century.

Valerius (St) Bp.   Feb 19
d. p.450 Bishop of Antibes in S. France.

Valerius (St) Bp.   Feb 20
? Mentioned by St Gregory of Tours as the first bishop of Conserans in France.

Valerius (St) Ab.   Feb 21
d. 695 A native of Astorga in Spain, who became a monk and abbot of San Pedro de Montes. He has left several ascetical writings: he is in fact the last representative of the Isidorian revival in Spain.

Valerius and Rufinus (SS) MM.   June 14
d. c 287 Roman missionaries in Gaul who were martyred at Soissons.

Valerius (St) C.OSB.   Oct 9
See Lambert and Valerius.

Valerius (St) M.   Nov 16
See Rufinus, Mark, etc.

Valéry (St) Ab.   Apr 1
Otherwise Walericus, q.v.

Vandrille (St) Ab.   July 22
Otherwise Wandrille, q.v.

Vanne (Vaune) (St) Bp.   Nov 9
Otherwise Vitonus, q.v.

Varelde (Veerle, Verylde) (St) V.   Jan 4
Otherwise Pharäildis, q.v.

Varicus (St) M.   Nov 15
See Secundus, Fidentian and Varicus.

Varus (St) M.   Oct 19
d. 307 A Roman soldier in Upper Egypt who, being on guard at a prison in which certain monks condemned to death were confined, on seeing one of them expire in his dungeon, insisted on taking his place and was forthwith hanged from a tree. The Acts are genuine.

Vasius (French: Vaise, Vaize) (St) M.   Apr 16
d. c 500 A rich citizen of Saintes, in France, murdered by his relatives for distributing his property among the poor.

Vedast (Vaast, Vaat, Gaston, Foster) (St) Bp.   Feb 6
d. 539 A fellow-worker with St Remigius in the conversion of the Franks. For close on forty years he ruled the united sees of Arras–Cambrai. He instructed King Clovis for his baptism by St Remigius and completely revivified the church in his diocese, as well as caring for the poor. His memory is perpetuated in this country by the exquisite church dedicated to him near St Paul's cathedral in London, and some medieval churches also. He is depicted as a bishop raising to life a goose, which a wolf deposits before him.

Veep (Veepus, Veepy, Wimp, Wennapa) (St) V.   July 1
6th cent? Patron saint of St Veep in Cornwall. Thought by some to be out of the saintly family of St Brychan; nothing is now in fact remembered of St Veep's life.

Veho (St) Bp.   June 15
Otherwise Vouga, q.v.

Velleicus (Willeic) (St) Ab. OSB.   Aug 29
8th cent. An Anglo-Saxon who followed St Swithbert to the apostolate in Germany and became abbot of Kaiserswerth, on the Rhine.

Venantius (St) Bp. M.   Apr 1
d. ? c 255 A bishop in Dalmatia, whose body was brought from Spalato to the Lateran by Pope John IV in 641.

Venantius (St) M.   May 18
d. c 250 Said to have been a boy of fifteen who died a martyr at Camerino, near Ancona, under Decius. Nothing certain is known about him. Pope Clement X, a former bishop of Camerino, made the feast of St Venantius of

double rank, as the terminology was then, and composed the proper hymns of his office. Cult confined to local calendars since 1969.

Venantius (St) H.   May 30
d. *c* 400   Elder brother of St Honoratus, the founder of Lérins. After living as hermit on an island near Cannes, both travelled to the East to study the monastic life. Venantius died at Modon in Morea.

Venantius (St) Bp.   Aug 5
d. 544   The most celebrated of the ancient bishops of Viviers. His life, written in the twelfth century, has no value.

Venantius (St) Ab.   Oct 13
5th cent.   An abbot of the monastery of St Martin at Tours.

Venantius Fortunatus (St) Bp.   Dec 14
c 530–610   Born near Treviso in N. Italy, at the age of thirty he settled at Poiters and was ordained. He became known to Queen St Radegunde who befriended him. He was a prolific writer and poet; the hymn *Vexilla Regis* was composed by him, also the hymn *Pange Lingua Gloriosi*, both well known in English translations by J. M. Neale. His poetry is characterised by a masterly technical skill linked to a content inbred with Christian thought and feeling, and his religious verses have had a tremendous influence on the development of Christian, and more especially Catholic poetry and hymnography. His occasional verses are exceptionally charming. He was made bishop of Poitiers at the end of the sixth century.

Veneranda (St) VM.   Nov 14
2nd cent.   Described by the pre-1970 RM. as a martyr and ascribed to Gaul. It seems that Veneranda is a later corruption of Venera (from *dies Veneris* — Friday) the Latin counterpart of *Parasceves*, and that she is identical with Parasceve, a saint highly venerated by the orthodox on July 26th.

Venerandus (St) M.   Nov 14
d. 275   An influential citizen of Troyes in France, martyred under Aurelian.

Venerandus (St) Bp.   Dec 24
d. 423   Born of a senatorial family of Clermont in Auvergne, he became bishop of the same city (385–423).

Venerius (St) Bp.   May 4
d. 409   Ordained deacon by St Ambrose, eventually he was made bishop of Milan. He is best remembered as a loyal supporter of St John Chrysostom.

Venerius (St) Ab. OSB.   Sept 13
7th (or 9th) cent.   A hermit, and then abbot on the island of Tino in the Gulf of Genoa. His "Life" is very untrustworthy.

Ventura Spellucci (Bl) Ab. OSB.   May 3
12th cent.   Born at Spello near Assisi, he joined the Italian Cruciferi, under the Benedictine rule, and eventually built an abbey-hospice on his family estate which he ruled as abbot till his death.

Venturinus of Bergamo (St)   March 28
1304–1346   A celebrated Dominican preacher, he was entrusted with preaching a crusade against the Turks. He accompanied the expedition, preached successfully abroad and died at Smyrna.

Venustian (St) M.   Dec 30
See Sabinus, Exuperantius, etc.

Venustus (St) M.   May 6
See Heliodorus, Venustus, etc.

Venustus (St) M.   May 22
See Faustinus, Timothy and Venustus.

Veranus (St) Bp.   Sept 10
d. *c* 480   Son of St Eucherius of Lyons, he became a monk at Lérins, and afterwards bishop of Vence (Alpes Maritimes) France.

Veranus (St) Bp.   Oct 19
d. 590   Native of Vaucluse, who became bishop of Cavaillon, in France.

Veranus (St) Bp.   Nov 11
5th cent.   Ascribed by the pre-1970 RM. to Lyons. Probably he is identical with St Veranus of Vence (Sept 10).

Verda (St) M.   Feb 21
See Daniel and Verda.

Verecundus (St) Bp.   Oct 22
d. 522   Bishop of Verona.

Veremundus (St) Ab. OSB.   March 8
d. 1092   A native of Navarre, he entered the Benedictine abbey of Our Lady of Hirache. He eventually became abbot, and during his abbacy the monastery was reckoned the most influential religious centre of Navarre. St Veremundus himself was the advisor of its kings. He was remarkable for his charity towards the poor and for his zeal for the accurate recitation of the divine office. In the controversy concerning the use of the Mozarabic rite, he won for it the approval even of the Roman see which intended to suppress it.

Verena (St)   Sept 1
3rd cent.   Said to have been an Egyptian

maiden, related to a soldier of the Theban Legion, who travelled to Switzerland in search of him and settled as a recluse near Zurich. Her cult is very ancient.

Vergilius (St) Bp. Nov 27
Otherwise Virgilius, q.v.

Verian (St) M. Aug 9
See Secundian, Marcellian, and Verian.

Veridiana (St) H. OSB. Vall. Feb 1
d. 1242 A maiden of Castelfiorentino in Tuscany who, after a pilgrimage to Compostella, was walled up as a recluse in her native town, where she lived for thirty-four years under the obedience of a Vallumbrosan abbey. Cult approved in 1533.

Verissimus, Maxima and Julia (SS) MM. Oct 1
d. c 302 Martyrs at Lisbon under Diocletian. They have a full office in the Mozarabic breviary.

Veronica of Binasco (Bl) V. OSA. Jan 13
d. 1497 Born at Binasco, near Milan, the daughter of poor peasants with whom she worked in the fields. She joined the Augustinian nuns of Milan as a lay-sister and spent her life in collecting alms for the convent in the streets of the city. Cult confirmed in 1517.

Veronica Giuliani (St) Abs. OFM. Cap. July 9
1660–1727 Born at Mercatello, diocese of Urbino, in Italy, Veronica became a Capuchin nun at Città di Castello, in Umbria, where she spent the rest of her life, being novice-mistress for thirty-four years. Her mystical experiences (visions, revelations, stigmata, etc.) were accurately authenticated by eyewitnesses. Though in a state of almost continuous supernatural vision, she was in no way visionary, but a most practical and level-headed religious. Canonized in 1839.

Veronica (St) July 12
1st cent. According to a picturesque tradition, when our Lord fell beneath His cross on the road to Calvary, a compassionate woman wiped His face with a towel, on which a picture of the same holy face remained imprinted. Numerous legends have grown up around her; the derivation of her name from the Graeco-Latin *Vera Ikon* — true image — is a hypothesis of Giraldus Cambrensis. In the Eastern church the woman is identified with the woman healed of the issue of blood (Mt.9:20–22) and whose legendary name is Berenice. It seems that this legend was composed to give a background to the existence of the supposed relic which has been in Rome since the eighth century and has a shrine in one of the main pillars of St Peter's. The incident is popularised in the traditional version of the Stations of the Cross. In art she is shown as a woman holding out a cloth, on which is imprinted the face of our Lord.

Verulus, Secundinus, Siricius, Felix, Servulus, Saturninus, Fortunatus and Comp. (SS) MM. Feb 21
d. c 434? Martyrs in N. Africa, Hadrumetum is given as the place, and the number was apparently twenty-six. The pre-1970 RM. assigns them to the Vandal persecution, but there is a wide variety of opinion.

Verus (St) Bp. Aug 1
d. p.314 Bishop of Vienne in France. He attended the synod of Arles in 314.

Verus (St) Bp. Oct 23
4th cent. The third bishop of Salerno.

Vestina (St) M. July 17
One of the Scillitan Martyrs, q.v.

Vetius (St) M. June 2
See Photinus, Sanctius, etc.

Veturius (St) M. July 17
One of the Scillitan Martyrs, q.v.

Vial (Viau) (St) Oct 16
Otherwise Vitalis, q.v.

Viator (St) H. Oct 21
d. c 390 A disciple of St Justus, archbishop of Lyons, whom he accompanied into the solitude to live as a hermit.

Viator (St) Bp. Dec 14
d. c 378 Said by the local tradition to have been one of the first bishops of Brescia, and later of Bergamo, during the first century. Probably he was never bishop of Brescia, but only of Bergamo, from 344 to 378.

Vibiana (St) VM. Sept 1
The Roman virgin martyr whose body is now venerated at Los Angeles, California, of which she is the principal patron. See Bibiana (Dec 2).

Vicelin (St) Bp. Dec 12
1090–1154 A disciple of St Norbert, who worked with considerable success among the Wagrian Wends in N.E. Germany and died bishop of Oldenburg: he is called "the Apostle of Hostein". Unfortunately he lived to see most of his pastoral achievements destroyed in the crusade of the Wends (1147).

Victor (St) M. Jan 22
See Vincent, Orontius and Victor.

St Veronica, July 12

Victor (St) M. Jan 31
See Saturninus, Thyrsus and Victor.

Victor (St) M. Feb 25
See Victorinus, Victor, etc.

Victor (Bl) Mk. OSB. Feb 25
d. 995 A Benedictine monk of St Gall in
Switzerland who became a recluse in the
Vosges, where he died.

Victor (St) H. Feb 26
7th cent. A hermit at Arcis-sur-Aube, in
Champagne. His feast was celebrated by the
Benedictines of Montiramey at whose request
St Bernard wrote hymns in honour of the
saint.

**Victor, Victorinus,
Claudian and Bassa
(SS) MM.** March 6
? A group of martyrs, natives of Bithynia, who
perished in prison at Nicomedia. Bassa was
the wife of Claudian.

Victor (St) M. March 10
? Perhaps he suffered in N. Africa under
Decius. He is mentioned by St Augustine (in
Psalm CXV, 15).

Victor (St) M. March 20
See Photina, Joseph, etc.

Victor (St) M. March 30
See Domninus, Victor and Comp.

**Victor and Stephen (SS)
MM.** Apr 1
? Martyrs in Egypt.

Victor (St) Bp. M. Apr 2
d. 554 A bishop of Capua in S. Italy and an
ecclesiastical writer.

Victor (St) M. Apr 12
d. c 300 A catechumen, martyred at Braga
in Portugal under Diocletian. he was thus
baptized in his own blood.

**Victor, Zoticus, Zeno,
Acindynus, Caesareus,
Severian, Chrysophorus,
Theonas and Antoninus
(SS) MM.** Apr 20
d. c 303 Martyrs at Nicomedia. The ap-
ocryphal *Acta* of St George connect them with
his martyrdom.

Victor the Moor (St) M. May 8
d. 303 A soldier from Mauritania in Africa,
martyred at Milan under Maximian. He is
associated by St Ambrose with the martyrs SS
Nabor and Felix.

**Victor and Corona (SS)
MM.** May 14
d. c 176 Husband and wife martyred, it
seems, in Syria. Their *Acta* abound in details of
an untrustworthy character.

Victor (St) M. May 17
See Adrio, Victor, and Basilla.

**Victor Alexander, Felician
and Longinus (SS) MM.** July 21
d. c 290 Victor, an army officer stationed at
Marseilles, suffered martyrdom there with
three prison-guards whom he had converted.
In the fourth century St John Cassian built a
monastery over their tomb, which afterwards
became a Benedictine abbey. St Victor and his
companions are shown as soldiers; his distinctive symbol is a windmill, near which he
stands, or which he may hold.

**Victor, Stercatius and
Antinogenes (SS) MM.** July 24
d. 304 Said to have been three brothers,
martyred at Merida in Estremadura, Spain.
Probably, however, only Victor belongs to
Merida; the other two to the group who
suffered with St Theozonus of Sebaste in
Armenia.

Victor I (St) Pope formerly July 28
d. 198 An African by birth. He was pope for
ten years (189–198). He is memorable for
excommunicating several Eastern churches
for not keeping Easter according to the Roman
custom, which earned him a rebuke from St
Irenaeus. Cult suppressed in 1969.

Victor of Vita (St) Bp. Aug 23
d. c 535 A native of Carthage, and bishop
either of that city or of Utica (as stated in the
pre-1970 RM.). Baronius identified him
(without proof) with Victor of Vita who wrote
the history of the Huneric persecution.

**Victor (Spanish: Vitores)
(St) M.** Aug 26
d. c 950 According to the *Passio* composed
in the fifteenth century, Victor was a Spanish
priest martyred by the Moors in the ninth or
tenth century. More ancient documents show
him to have been an African martyr put to
death at Caesarea in Mauretania in the early
persecutions.

Victor (St) Bp. M. Sept 10
See Nemesian, Felix, etc.

Victor (St) M. Sept 10
See Sosthenes and Victor.

Victor (St) M. Sept 14
See Crescentian, Victor, etc.

Victor III (St) Pope OSB.   Sept 16
c 1027–1087   A native of Benevento, and
related to the Norman duke of that city. His
secular name was Danfari, which he changed
into that of Desiderius on becoming a Benedictine at Montecassino (1047) and into that of
Victor on his election to the papacy (1087). He
became a monk in the teeth of family opposition and was successively at La Cava, at St
Sophia in Benevento, at a house on an island in
the Adriatic, at Salerno as a student of medicine, in the Abruzzi as a hermit, back at
Salerno and finally at Montecassino. He was
chosen abbot in 1057 and under him the abbey
attained its high level of prosperity and glory:
the community rose to two hundred monks;
basilica and monastery were rebuilt on a larger
scale; arts, learning, sanctity flourished. In
1086 he was elected pope by the cardinals at
Montecassino itself. It was not a happy choice,
and the abbot was persuaded to accept only
after one year of delay — the year in which he
died. Rome was occupied by the troops of the
antipope Clement III, so he spent a lot of time
at Monte- cassino. He tried to perpetuate the
policies of Pope Gregory VII. Cult confirmed
in 1727 and again (conferring the title of saint)
by Leo XIII.

Victor (St) M.   Sept 22
See Theban Legion.

Victor and Ursus (SS) MM.   Sept 30
d. *c* 286   Two soldiers connected with the
Thebian Legion, q.v. and venerated at Soleure
in Switzerland.

Victor and Comp. (SS)
MM.   Oct 10
d. *c* 286   A group of three hundred and
thirty soldiers, connected with the Theban
Legion, q.v.

Victor, Alexander and
Marianus (SS) MM.   Oct 17
d. 303   A group of martyrs in the Diocletian
persecution who suffered at Nicomedia.

Victor (St)   Oct 17
d. 554   He was ordained bishop of Capua in
541, and a prolific author: his most notable
work was the *Codex Fuldensis*.

Victor (St) M.   Nov 2
See Publius, Victor, etc.

Victor (St) M.   Nov 13
See Valentine, Solutor and Victor.

Victor (St) M.   Dec 3
See Ambicus, Victor and Julius.

Victor of Piacenza (St) Bp.   Dec 7
d. 375   First bishop of Piacenza, *c* 322–375.

He was a brave champion of the Catholic faith
against the Arians.

Victor (St) M.   Dec 15
See Irenaeus, Antony, etc.

Victor (St) M.   Dec 18
See Victurus, Victor, etc.

Victor (St) M.   Dec 28
See Castor, Victor and Rogatian.

Victor (St) M.   Dec 29
See Dominic, Victor, etc.

Victoria (St) VM.   Feb 11
See Saturninus, Dativus, etc.

Victoria (St) M.   Nov 17
See Acislus and Victoria.

Victoria (and Anatolia)
(SS) VV. MM.   Dec 23
d. 250   Two sisters martyred at Rome for
refusing to marry pagan husbands. Their *Acta*
are unfortunately worthless. Anatolia was not
mentioned in the pre-1970 RM.

Victorian of Asan (St) Ab.   Jan 12
d. *c* 560   A native of Italy who settled in
France for a time and then became the abbot-
founder of Asan (now called after him San
Victorian) in the Aragonese Pyrenees, diocese
of Barbastro. He is highly praised by St
Venantius Fortunatus.

Victorian, Frumentius
and Comp. (SS) MM.   March 23
d. 484   Victorian, a former pro-consul in
Africa, and four wealthy merchants were
martyred at Adrumetum under King Hunneric, for refusing to become Arians.

Victorian (St) M.   May 16
See Aquilinus and Victorian.

Victorian (St) M.   Aug 26
See Simplicius, Constantius and Victorian.

Victoricus (St) M.   Feb 24
See Montanus, Lucius, etc.

Victoricus, Fuscian and
Gentian (SS) MM.   Dec 11
d. *c* 287   Victoricus and Fuscian are described as early missionaries in Gaul, martyred
near Amiens. Gentian as an old man killed
while endeavouring to protect them when they
were arrested.

Victorinus, Victor,
Nicephorus, Claudian,
Dioscorus, Serapion and
Papias (SS) MM.   Feb 25
d. 284   Citizens of Corinth exiled to Egypt

in 249 and martyred under Numerian in various ways and with great brutality, at Diospolis in the Thebaid.

Victorinus (St) M.   March 6
See Victor, Victorinus, etc.

Victorinus (St) M.   March 29
See Pastor, Victorinus, etc.

Victorinus (St) M.   Apr 15
See Maro, Eutyches and Victorinus.

Victorinus (St) M.   May 15
See Cassius, Victorinus, etc.

Victorinus (St) C.   June 8
d. 543 Brother of St Severino, bishop of Septempeda (now San Severino), with whom he led an eremitical life near Ancona.

Victorinus (St) M.   July 7
See Four Crowned Martyrs.

Victorinus (St) Bp.   Sept 5
d. 644 Bishop of Como. A great opponent of Arianism.

Victorinus (St) Bp. M.   Sept 5
See Maro, Eutyches and Victorinus.

Victorinus (St) M.   Oct 5
See Placid, Eutychius, etc.

Victorinus of Pettau (St)
Bp. M.   Nov 2
d. c 304 A bishop of Pettau in Styria (Upper Pannonia), and an exegete, the earliest known of the Western church.

Victorinus (St) M.   Nov 8
One of the Four Crowned Martyrs, q.v.

Victorinus (St) M.   Nov 11
See Valentine, Felician and Victorinus.

Victorinus (St) M.   Dec 2
See Severus, Securus, etc.

Victorinus (St) M.   Dec 18
See Victurus, Victor, etc.

Victorius (St) M.   May 21
See Polyeuctus, Victorius and Donatus.

Victorius (St) Bp.   Sept 1
d. c 490 A disciple of St Martin of Tours who became bishop of Le Mans c 453.

Victorius (St) M.   Oct 30
See Claudius, Lupercus and Victorius.

Victricius (St) Bp.   Aug 7
d. 407 A Roman officer who retired from the army because he thought the military service incompatible with the profession of Christianity. He was sentenced to death, but the sentence was not carried out. He became a missionary among the northern tribes of France and later as bishop of Rouen (380) was one of the leading pastors of Gaul, and received the important decretal called the *Liber Regularum* from Pope Innocent I.

Victurus, Victor,
Victorinus, Adjutor,
Quartus and Comp. (SS)   Dec 18
? A group of thirty-five martyrs in N.W. Africa.

Vigean (St) Ab.   Jan 20
Otherwise Fechin, q.v.

Vigilius (St) Bp. M.   March 11
d. 685 Successor of St Palladius (661) in the see of Auxerre. By order of the mayor of the palace, Waraton, he was killed in a forest near Compiègne.

Vigilius (St) Bp. M.   June 26
d. 405 A Roman patrician who studied at Athens, and with his family settled in the Trentino. He was made bishop of Trent and succeeded in practically uprooting paganism from his diocese. He was stoned to death in the Val di Rendena for overturning a statue of Saturn.

Vigilius (St) Bp.   Sept 26
d. p.506 A bishop of Brescia in Lombardy.

Vigor (St) Bp.   Nov 1
d. c 537 A disciple of St Vedast, who became bishop of Bayeux; before this he was a hermit, then a priest. He resolutely opposed paganism.

Villana de'Botti (Bl)
Matron   Feb 28
d. c 1360 Daughter of a rich Florentine merchant. In her youth she wished to enter a convent but was opposed by her father. She married and abandoned herself completely to worldliness and vanity. One day, it is said, on regarding herself in a mirror she saw, instead of her own reflection, the figure of a demon. She completely changed her life, became a Dominican tertiary and, in spite of much obloquy, persevered in heroic works. Cult confirmed in 1824.

Villanus (St) Bp. OSB.   May 7
d. 1237 A native of Gubbio who became a monk at Fontavellana, and in 1206 became bishop of his native city.

Villicus (St) Bp.   Apr 17
d. 568 Bishop of Metz, 543–568. He was praised for his virtues by Venantius Fortunatus.

Vimin (Wynnin,
Gwynnin) (St) Bp.   Jan 21
6th cent. A Scottish bishop, whose history is

very confused. He is said to have been the founder of the monastery of Holywood.

Vimius (St) C. OSB.   June 12
See Marinus, Vimius, etc.

Vincent Strambi (St) Bp. CP.   Jan 1
1745–1824   Born at Civitavecchia, he was ordained in 1767 and shortly afterwards joined the Passionists. He filled almost all the offices of the order, being at the same time an indefatigable missioner. He was created bishop of Macerata and Tolentino in 1801 and was exiled in 1808 for refusing to take the oath of allegiance to Napoleon. At the end of his life he was summoned by Leo XII to the Vatican as papal adviser. Canonized in 1950.

Vincent de Cunha (Bl) M. SJ.   Jan 12
d. 1737   A Jesuit sent to Tonkin in 1736 and martyred there with Bl John Gaspard Cratz and two companions.

Vincent the Deacon (St) M.   GC.Jan 22
d. 304   A native of Huesca who became deacon to St Valerius at Saragossa and was martyred at Valencia under Diocletian. He has always been widely venerated by the Western church. St Augustine, St Leo and Prudentius wrote in his honour. In some places he is honoured as the patron of vinedressers. Details of his martyrdom are lacking but the fact of it is indisputable. He is depicted as a deacon holding one or many ewers and a book; or with a raven or ravens defending his martyred body; being torn with hooks, or holding a millstone.

Vincent of Digne (St) Bp.   Jan22
d. 380   An African by birth who succeeded St Domninus in the see of Digne. He is principal patron saint of the city and diocese of Digne.

Vincent, Orontius and Victor (SS) MM.   Jan 22
d. 305   Vincent and Orontius were brothers, natives of Cimiez, near Nice. They preached the gospel to the people of the Spanish Pyrenees and were martyred, with St Victor, at Puigcerda, in the province of Gerona. Their bodies were subsequently brought to Embrun, France.

Vincent Pallotti (St) C. Founder   Jan 23
1798–1850   He was born at Rome of a noble family and became a secular priest in 1820. After a short period of theological teaching he dedicated himself to pastoral work in Rome. His apostolic labours were matched only by his austerities, and in 1837 during the cholera

St Vincent the Deacon, Jan 22

plague he constantly endangered his life. His society, the Pallottines, or the Society of Catholic Action, numbered only twelve during his life, but has since spread all over the world. In 1836 he started the special observance of the Octave of the Epiphany for the reunion of the Oriental church with Rome. He was especially interested also in the English mission. Canonized in 1963.

Vincent (St) M.   Jan27
See Datius, Reatus, etc.

Vincent of Troyes (St) Bp.   Feb 4
d. c 546   Bishop of Troyes, c 536–546.

Vincent of Siena (Bl) C. OFM.   Feb 14

d. 1442 A Friar Minor for twenty-two years, the companion of St Bernadine of Siena in his travels through Italy.

Vincent Kadlubek (Bl or St) Bp. OSB. Cist.   March 8

d. 1223 Born in the Palatinate, he studied in France and Italy and was appointed provost at Sandomir in Poland. In 1208 he was ordained bishop of Cracow, but resigned (1218) and became a Cistercian at Jedrzejo abbey. He is one of the earliest Polish chroniclers. Cult approved in 1764.

Vincent Ferrer (St) C. OP.   GC. Apr 5

c 1350–1419 A native of Valencia in Spain (his father was English); at an early age he entered the Dominican order and soon became the adviser of the King of Aragon and of the Avignon pope, with whom he sided in good faith. To heal the schism of the papacy he travelled through Spain, France, Switzerland and Italy, preaching penance, working miracles and converting thousands, being endowed with the gift of tongues. When it became clear to him that the Avignon party were not in the right, he turned his efforts towards bringing them into obedience to the legitimate pope and played a vital role in the council of Constance (1414). His authority acquired as a preacher and sustained by numerous miracles was tremendous. He died at Vannes in Britanny. He is represented as a Dominican holding an open book whilst preaching; sometimes he has a cardinal's hat, or wings, or a crucifix.

Vincent of Collioure (St) M.   Apr 19

d. c 304 A martyr at Collioure, in Languedoc, under Diocletian. His *Acta* are worthless. Some have identified him wth St Vincent of Gerona (Jan 22).

Vincent (St)   Apr 20

See under Marcellinus, Vincent and Domninus.

Vincent (St) Ab. OSB.   May 9

d. c 950 Abbot of St Peter de Montes, disciple and successor of St Gennadius.

Vincent of Lérins (St) C.   May 24

d. c 445 Possibly a member of a noble family of Gaul who in early life followed a military career but later abandoned it to become a monk at Lérins, where he was ordained. He is best known as the writer of the *Commonitorium*, in which he deals with the doctrine of

St Vincent Ferrer, Apr 5

exterior development in dogma and formulates the principle that only such doctrines are to be considered true as have been held "everywhere, always and by all the faithful" (*Quod ubique, quod semper, quod ab omnibus*); this is called the Vincentian canon. He held that the church's role was to be the guardian of the correct interpretation of scripture, the final source of Christian doctrine.

Vincent of Porto (St) M.   May 24

? A martyr at Porto Romano, the former port of Rome which has long since disappeared.

Vincent of Bevagna (St)
Bp. M.   June 6
d. 303   First bishop of Bevagna in Umbria, martyred under Diocletian.

Vincent of Agen (St) M.   June 9
d. ? c 292   A deacon martyred at Agen in Gascony for having disturbed a feast of the Gallic druids.

Vincent Caun (Bl) M. SJ.   June 20
d. 1626   A native of Seoul in Korea who in 1591 was carried to Japan as a prisoner of war. He became a Christian and entered the Jesuit seminary at Arima, spending thirty years as a catechist in Japan and in China. He was burnt alive at Nagasaki with Bl Francis Pacheco and companions. Beatified in 1867.

Vincent Yen (St) M. OP.   June 30
c 1765–1838   A native of Vietnam, he became a Dominican in 1808, and laboured as a priest in the mission field. From the publication of the edict of persecution in 1832, he lived six years in hiding, but was finally betrayed and beheaded at Hai-Duong. Canonized in 1988.

Vincent de Paul (St) C.   GC. Sept 27
1581–1660   Born at Ranquine in S.W. France (now renamed after him), he studied with distinction at Toulouse and was ordained at the age of twenty. He fell into the hands of corsairs in 1605 and was taken captive to Tunis but contrived to escape and went to Paris. Here, under the guidance of Berulle, he embarked upon his life work of active charity. No one was excluded from his ministrations: he organized relief for all: abandoned orphans, sick children, fallen women, the poor, the destitute, the blind, the insane. He began to preach missions and retreats and enlisted for this work a number of priests whom he grouped into a new religious institute: the Lazarists, or Vincentians (Priests of the Mission, *Congregatio Missionis*) in 1625. In 1633 he organized the congregation of the Sisters of Charity, who have been ever since a worldwide feature of Catholic life. He was canonized in 1737 and has been declared patron saint of all societies devoted to works of charity. Garbed as a cleric of the sixteenth century, he is shown performing some work of mercy; or carries infants in his arms; or is surrounded by Sisters of Charity.

Vincent (St) M.   July 24
?   A Roman, martyred outside the walls of the city on the road to Tivoli.

Vincent (St) M.   Aug 6
See Sixtus II and Comp.

Vincent of Aquila (Bl) C.
OFM.   Aug 7
d. 1504   A native of Aquila, who became a Franciscan lay-brother and was famed for his mystical gifts. Cult approved in 1785.

Vincent (St) M.   Aug 25
See Eusebius, Pontian, etc.

Vincent and Laetus (SS)
MM.   Sept 1
? 5th cent.   The pre-1970 RM. ascribed these martyrs to Spain, and they are actually venerated at Toledo as natives of that diocese; but it seems that they should be identified with St Vincent of Xaintes, the first bishop and patron of Dax in Gascony and St Laetus, one of his deacons.

Vincent Carvalho (Bl) M.
OSA.   Sept 3
d. 1632   A native of Alfama near Lisbon who joined the Augustinians at Santa Maria de la Gracia, Lisbon. In 1621 he was sent to Mexico, and thence in 1623 travelled to Japan. He was burnt alive at Nagasaki. Beatified in 1867.

Vincent of St Joseph (Bl)
M. OFM.   Sept 10
1596–1622   Born at Ayamonte, diocese of Seville, he migrated to Mexico, where he became a Franciscan lay-brother (1615). In 1618 he accompanied Bl Louis Sotelo to Manila and in 1619 was sent to Japan. He was arrested in 1620 and after two years of inhuman incarceration, was burnt alive at Nagasaki. Beatified in 1867.

Vincent of León (St) Ab. M.   Sept 11
d. c 554 (or 630), March 11   Abbot of St Claudius, at León, in Spain. He was martyred at the hands of the Arian Visigoths. (See Ramirus.)

Vincent Madelgarus (St)
Ab. OSB.   Sept 20
d. 677   Madelgarus was the husband of St Waldetrudis, who bore him four children, all saints: Landericus, Dentlin, Madalberta and Aldegtrudis. About the year 653 his wife became a nun and Madelgarus took the Benedictine habit with the name of Vincent in the monastery of Haumont, which he founded. Later he established another abbey at Soignies, which he ruled and where he died.

Vincent, Sabina and
Christeta (SS) MM.   Oct 27
d. 303   Martyrs at Avila, in Spain. Their *Acta* are not trustworthy.

Vincent Liem (St) M. OP.   Nov 7
d. 1773   A member of a noble family in

Vietnam who became a Dominican and a priest and worked under St Hyacinth Castañeda, OP. He was beheaded. Canonized in 1988.

Vincent Diem (Bl) M. Nov 24
d. 1838 A Tonkinese native priest, martyred in Tonkin by beheading. Beatified in 1900.

Vincent Romano (Bl) C. Dec 20
1751–1836 Born not far from Naples at Tor' del Greco, he was in character akin to the Curé d' Ars. Throughout his life he lived at Tor' del Greco as the father of the orphan, consoler of the afflicted and protector of the oppressed. He was persecuted first by the French invaders and then by certain Italian political societies. Beatified in 1963.

Vincentian (French: Viance, Viants) (St) H. Jan 2
d. c 730 A disciple of St Menelaus, who became a hermit in the diocese of Tulle (Auvergne).

Vincenza Mary Lopez Vicuña (St) V. Foundress Jan 18
1847–1890 Born at Cascante in Spanish Navarre, she declined the marriage her parents wanted her to contract, and overcoming their opposition dedicated herself at the age of nineteen to the service of God. Shocked at the dangers and difficulties of the lives of domestic servants she founded in 1876 the Daughters of Mary Immaculate in order to look after those in need. Papal approval was given in 1888. She died overwhelmed with her business affairs and sickness in 1890, and was beatified in 1950. Canonized in 1975.

Vincenza Gerosa (St) V. June 28
1784–1847 An Italian woman, who till her fortieth year led an undistinguished domestic life. She then came to know Bl Bartolomea Capitanio, the foundress of the Italian Sisters of Charity at Lovere. When the foundress died in 1833, Vincenza succeeded her and under her guidance the institute expanded in a wonderful way. Canonized in 1950.

Vindemialis, Eugene and Longinus (SS) MM. May 2
d. c 485 African bishops, put to death by the Arian Vandal King Hunneric who had beforehand inflicted on them most horrible tortures.

Vindician (St) Bp. March 12
d. 712 A disciple of St Eligius, who became bishop of Arras-Cambrai, and with great courage protested against the excesses of the Merovingian kings and the all-powerful mayors of the palace. In his last days he lived mostly in the abbey of St Vaast.

Vindonius (St) Sept 1
See Priscus, Castrensis, etc.

Vintila (St) H. OSB. Dec 23
d. 890 A Benedictine monk who died as a recluse at Pugino, near Orense, in Spanish Galicia.

Virgilius of Arles (St) Bp. March 5
d. c 610 A monk of Lérins who was bishop of Arles. Probably it was he who ordained St Augustine bishop of Canterbury at the request of Pope St Gregory the Great.

Virgilius (Fergal) (St) Bp. OSB. Nov 27
d. 784 An Irish monk, who undertook a pilgrimage to Palestine but remained in Bavaria to help St Rupert, the apostle of Austria. St Virgilius was eventually made abbot of the Benedictine abbey of St Peter at Salzburg and bishop of that city (c 765). He is venerated as the apostle of Carinthia. He was considered to be among the pre-eminent intellectuals of the period. St Boniface was alarmed that he considered the earth to be a sphere and complained to the bishop of Rome about this and other seemingly outrageous ideas; perhaps the basic friction was due to the Celtic/Roman controversies of the early centuries. Virgilius consecrated the first cathedral at Salzburg in 774. Canonized in 1232 by Gregory IX.

Viridiana (St) H. OSB. Vall. Feb 1
See Veridiana.

Virila (St) Ab. OSB. Oct 1
d. c 1000 A Benedictine abbot of the Navarrese abbey of St Saviour, Leyre. He is undoubtedly an historical personage, but his life has been overlaid with much legendary — though often very beautiful — accretion.

Vissia (St) VM. Apr 12
d. c 250 An Italian maiden martyred at Fermo, near Ancona, under Decius.

Vitalian (St) Pope Jan 27
d. 672 Pope from 657 to 672. The whole of his pontificate was troubled by the Monothelite controversy in the East. He ordained St Theodore of Tarsus, whom he sent to England as archbishop of Canterbury in 668.

Vitalian (St) Bp. July 16
? A bishop of Capua in S. Italy.

Vitalian (St) Bp. July 16
d. 776 Bishop of Osimo in Italy.

Vitalicus (St) M. Sept 4
See Rufinus, Silvanus and Vitalicus.

Vitalis, Revocatus and
Fortunatus (SS) MM.   Jan 9
? Vitalis appears to have been a bishop and
Revocatus and Fortunatus his two deacons.
They were martyred at Smyrna.

Vitalis (St) M.   Jan 9
See Epictetus, Jucundus, etc.

Vitalis of Gaza (St) H.   Jan 11
d. c 625   An aged monk of Gaza who undertook the reclamation of fallen women, and
caused great scandal by the methods he
employed. He was vindicated after his death.

Vitalis, Felicula and
Zeno (SS) MM.   Feb 14
? Probably Roman martyrs. Nothing is known
about them.

Vitalis (St) M.   Apr 21
See Arator, Fortunatus, etc.

Vitalis of Milan (St) M.
? 1st cent.   The alleged father of SS Gervase
and Protase and husband of St Valeria. The
Acts are spurious and cult has been discontin-
ued.

Vitalis (St) H. OSB.   May 31
d. ? 1370   Monk of Monte Subasio, near
Assisi, and then for twenty years a hermit
under the obedience of the abbot of Monte
Subasio at Santa Maria delle Viole, also near
Assisi.

Vitalis (St) M.   July 2
See Ariston, Crescentian, etc.

Vitalis (St) M.   July 10
One of the Seven Brothers, q.v.

Vitalis, Sator and
Repositus (SS) MM.   Aug 29
? 3rd or 4th cent.   Martyrs of Velleianum in
Apulia. They belong to the group known as the
Twelve Holy Brothers, q.v.

Vitalis of Savigny (Bl) Ab.
OSB.   Sept 16
c 1063–1122   In early life he acted as chaplain to Robert, count of Mortain, half-brother
of William the Conqueror; then he spent
seventeen years as a hermit; finally (1112) he
founded the abbey of Savigny in Normandy
which soon became the mother house of
numerous monasteries throughout France
and England. Bl Vitalis visited the British Isles
in this connexion. He died while presiding in
choir at the recitation of the office of our Lady.
The Bollandists give his feast on Jan 7.

Vitalis (St) M.   Sept 22
One of the alleged martyrs of the Theban
Legion, q.v.

Vitalis (Vial) (St) H. OSB.   Oct 16
d. c 740   An Anglo-Saxon who became a
Benedictine at Noirmoutier, and afterwards a
hermit on Mt Scobrit, near the Loire.

Vitalis (St) Bp. OSB.   Oct 20
d. 745   St Rupert's successor as abbot of St
Peter's at Salzburg, and as archbishop of that
city (717–745).

Vitalis (St) M.   Nov 3
See Germanus, Theophilus, etc.

Vitalis and Agricola (SS)
MM.   Nov 4
d. c 304   Martyrs at Bologna under Diocletian. According to a later legend St Vitalis was
a slave of St Agricola. The slave suffered martyrdom in the presence of his master with
such courage that Agricola was inspired by his
example to face a shameful death — probably
crucifixion — for Christ's sake. Vitalis, to
whom the superb basilica at Ravenna is dedicated, in fact is related to Agricola and, in
another version of the story, his wife Valeria,
purely by early hagiographers. The cult started
when St Ambrose and Eusebius, bishop of
Bologna, discovered the bodies of some early
martyrs. The legends sought to explain the
relics. Since 1969 cult confined to local calendars.

Vitonus (Vanne, Vaune)
(St) Bp.   Nov 9
d. c 525   Bishop of Verdun, c 500–525. At a
later period a great Benedictine abbey of
Lorraine was dedicated to him, which in 1600
became the centre of the Congregation of St
Vannes.

Vitus (St) M., Modestus
and Crescentia   June 15
d. c 303?   Their cult is certainly very ancient,
but their Acts have reached us in various
embellished versions. St Vitus (Guy) was
described as a child, St Crescentia being his
nurse and St Modestus Crescentia's husband.
St Vitus is patron against epilepsy and the
nervous disorder called St Vitus's dance. Vitus
was a martyr to whom the others, originally
separate, were attached. In 1969 the cult of St
Vitus was confined to local calendars: Modestus and Crescentia were expunged from the
catalogue of saints as being purely a fiction.

Vitus (St) Mk. OSB.   Sept 5
d. c 1095   A Benedictine monk of Pontida,
near Bergamo, under its founder St Albert.

St Vitalis, Nov 4

Vivaldus (Ubaldo, Gualdo) (Bl) C. May 11
d. 1300 Disciple and companion of Bl Bartholomew Buonpedoni. When the latter became a leper, Vivaldus nursed him for twenty years. He was a Franciscan tertiary. Cult approved in 1909.

Viventiolus (St) Bp. July 12
d. 524 Monk of St Oyend (Condat) who became archbishop of Lyons. A great friend of St Avitus of Vienne.

Viventius (St) H. Jan 13
d. c 400 A Samaritan who after becoming a priest travelled to the West, and attached himself to St Hilary of Poitiers. He closed his life as a hermit. His *Life*, written in the tenth century, lacks credibility.

Viventius (St) M. Aug 4
See Peregrinus, Maceratus, etc.

Vivian (St) Bp. Jan 21
Otherwise Vimin, q.v.

Vivian (St) Bp. Aug 28
d. c 460 A bishop of Saintes in W. France, who protected his people during the invasion of the Visigoths.

Vivian (St) VM. Dec 2
Otherwise Bibiana, q.v.

Vivina (St) V. Dec 17
Otherwise Wivina, q.v.

Vladimir (St) King July 15
956–1015 Great Prince of Kiev in Russia,

brought up as a pagan. He was baptized before his marriage to the sister of the Byzantine emperor in 987, and invited the Greek clergy to evangelize Russia. His two sons Boris and Gleb (sometimes known in the Western church as Romanus and David) are venerated as martyrs.

Vodoaldus (Voel, Vodalus, Vodalis) (St) H. Feb 5
d. c 725 An Irish or Scottish monk who crossed over to Gaul as a missionary and died a recluse near Soissons.

Volcuin (Bl) Ab. OSB. Cist. Sept 18
d. 1154 A Cistercian monk at the German abbey of Altenkamp, whence he was sent as prior to a new foundation at Walkenried (1129) and later as abbot to a third foundation at Sittichenbach, or Sichem (1141) in Westphalia.

Volker (Bl) M. OSB. March 7
d. 1132 A missionary monk of Siegburg put to death by the Obotrites, whom he was evangelizing.

Voloc (St) Bp. Jan 29
d. c 724 An Irish missionary bishop who worked in Scotland.

Volusian (St) Bp. Jan 18
d. 496 A senator of Tours and a married man who was afflicted with a bad-tempered wife. He was chosen bishop of Tours and shortly after driven from his see by the Arian Visigoths. He died in exile at Toulouse.

Votus, Felix and John (SS) HH. May 29
d. c 750 Votus and Felix were brothers, natives of Saragossa, who went in search of a hermitage and found one in the fastnesses of the Aragonese Pyrenees, already inhabited by St John. The three lived together and died about the same time. The hermitage, was situated beneath a huge rock (*Peña*) where shortly afterwards arose the great Benedictine abbey of St John de la Peña. See John of Atarés.

Vouga (Vougar, Veho, Feock, Fiech) (St) Bp. June 15
6th cent. An Irish bishop who settled in Brittany and there lived as a hermit in a cell near Lesneven.

Vulcherius (St) Ab. March 13
Otherwise Mochoemoc, q.v.

Vulganius (St) H. OSB. Nov 3
d. c 704 An Irishman or Welshman who

crossed over to France, evangelized the Atrebati, and finally lived as a hermit at Arras under the obedience of the abbot of St Vaast.

Vulgis (St) Bp. OSB.   Feb 4
d. *c* 760   Regionary bishop (*chorepiscopus*) and abbot of the Benedictine monastery of Lobbes in Hainault.

Vulmar (St) Ab. OSB.   July 20
Otherwise Wulmar, q.v.

Vulphy (Wulflagius) (St) H.   June 7
d. *c* 643   A parish priest at Rue, near Abbeville, who retired to the desert and died a solitary. His memory was greatly venerated at Montreuil-sur-Mer.

Vulpian (St) M.   Apr 3
d. *c* 304   A Syrian put to death at Tyre in Phoenicia under Diocletian. He is said to have been sewn up in a leathern sack, together with a dog and a serpent, and so cast into the sea.

Vulsin (St) Bp.   Jan 8
Otherwise Wulsin, q.v.

Vyevain (Bl) Bp.   Aug 26
d. 1285   An archbishop of York, who was honoured with a liturgical cult at Pontigny in France.

W

Waccar, Gundekar, Elleher, Hathawulf (SS)
MM. OSB. June 5
d. 755 Mentioned by name as monks among the fifty-two companions who shared St Boniface's martyrdom.

Walbert (Vaubert) (St) May 11
d. c 678 Duke of Lorraine and count of Hainault, husband of St Bertilia and father of SS Waldetrudis and Aldegundis.

Walburga (St) Abs. OSB. Feb 25
c 710–779 Sister of SS Willibald and Winebald. She became a nun at Wimborne in Dorset under St Tatta and followed St Lioba to Germany at the invitation of St Boniface. She died abbess of Heidenheim, a double monastery, whence her relics were translated to Eichstätt. Remarkable cures are ascribed to the use of a fluid which annually exudes from the rock on which her shrine is placed, and which is called St Walburga's oil.

Waldalenus (St) Ab. May 15
7th cent. Abbot-founder of Bèze, and brother of St Adalsindis.

Waldebert (Walbert, Gaubert) (St) Ab. OSB. May 2
d. c 668 A Frankish noble who left the army to become a monk at Luxeuil. About the year 628 he was made abbot, and shortly afterwards (c 630) he introduced the rule of St Benedict. Under him the monastery reached the peak of its religious and cultural influence in W. Europe. He helped St Salaberga to establish her great nunnery at Laon.

Walderic (Bl) Ab. OSB. Nov 29
d. c 817 Abbot-founder of Murrhardt, which he built with the help of the emperor Louis the Pious.

Waldetrudis (Vaudru)
(St) W. Abs. OSB. Apr 9
d. c 688 Daughter of SS Walbert and Bertilia, wife of St Vincent Madelgarus, and mother of SS Landericus, Dentelin, Madalberta and Aldetrudis. When her husband became a monk she founded a nunnery and took the veil there. Around her nunnery there grew up the town of Mons in Belgium, where her memory has always been greatly honoured.

Waldrada (St) Abs. May 5
d. c 620 First abbess of the nunnery of Saint-Pierre-aux-Nonnais at Metz.

Walembert (Garembert)
(Bl) C. OSA. Dec 31
1084–1141 A native of the district of Furness in Belgium who became a hermit and then built an Augustinian abbey on Mont-Saint-Martin in the diocese of Cambrai, of which he became the first superior.

Walericus (Valéry) (St) Ab. Apr 1
d. c 622 A monk under St Columbanus at Luxeuil, then a missionary in N. France, where he became the abbot-founder of Leuconay at the mouth of the Somme. Two towns in that district are called Saint-Valéry after him.

Walfrid (Gualfredo)
della Gherardesca (St)
Ab. OSB. Feb 15
d. c 765 A citizen of Pisa who married and had five sons and one daughter. In middle life he joined with two other married men in founding the abbey of Palazzuolo, between Volterra and Piombino, and a nunnery nearby for their wives and Walfrid's daughter. Walfrid ruled Palazzuolo as first abbot and was succeeded as second abbot by one of his sons. Cult confirmed in 1861.

Walhere (St) M. June 23
? A priest in the Walloon district of Belgium. On remonstrating with an ecclesiastic for his unedifying life he was murdered by the latter, and has since been venerated as a martyr, chiefly at Dinant.

Wallabonsus (St) M. June 7
See Peter, Wallabonsus, etc.

Walpurgis (St) V. Feb 25
Otherwise Walburga, q.v.

Walstan (St) C. May 30
? 11th cent. Probably born at Bawburgh in Norfolk, he spent his life as a farm labourer at Taverham and Costessey, being remarkable for his charity to all in need. Although prob-

ably a holy and good peasant, pious biographers gave him the rank of prince, which high estate he fled to live simply with the common people. His shrine at Bawburgh was very popular with the local farm people before it was destroyed during the Reformation. All that is known about him is in his legend. His cult, although a local one, is undisputed. He is depicted as robed as a king, but with a scythe as well as a sceptre; or with calves near him.

Walter (Gualterius, Gautier) (Bl) C. OSB. Cist.   Jan 22

d. 1222 A native of Brabant who trained as a soldier. On becoming a knight he was a familiar figure at tournaments until he found his way to the Cistercian abbey of Himerode. There he was appointed guest master and attracted many to the monastic life by his affability and tact. He died at Villers.

Walter of Bruges (Bl) Bp. C.   Jan 22

d. 1307 A native of Bruges who became a Franciscan and studied at Paris. Named bishop of Poitiers, he felt it his duty to excommunicate his metropolitan, Bertrand de Got. The latter became pope as Clement V and deposed Walter, who then retired to the religious life and was miraculously vindicated after his death.

Walter of Pontoise (St) Ab. OSB.   Apr 8

d. 1099 A Picard who became a professor of philosophy and rhetoric but later joined the Benedictines of Rebais in order to escape worldly applause. Against his will he was made abbot of Pontoise. He fled from his abbey several times, once to Cluny and on the last occasion to Rome, where he placed his resignation in the hands of the pope, who however refused to accept it but gave him orders to return to Pontoise and never again to leave it. He died on Good Friday.

Walter (St) Ab.   Apr 9

Otherwise Gaucherius, q.v.

Walter (Bl) Ab. OSB.   Apr 21

d. 1158 Abbot of the Benedictine monastery of Mondsee in Upper Austria.

Walter (St) Ab. OSA.   May 11

d. 1070 An Augustinian canon and abbot of L'Esterp in the Limousin.

Walter (St) Ab. OSB.   June 4

d. c 1250 A Roman who became first a hermit and afterwards the founder and first abbot of Serviliano in the Marches of Ancona.

Walter (St) Ab. OSB.   ? June 4

d. 1150 An Englishman who became abbot

of Fontenelle in France. He was commended for his humility, piety and zeal by Pope Innocent II.

Walter Pierson (Bl) M. O. Cart.   June 6

d. 1537 A Carthusian lay-brother of the London charterhouse, left with six companions to starve to death in prison.

Walter (Bl) C. OFM.   Aug 2

d. c 1258 One of the first friars and companions of St Francis. He was sent by the founder to establish the order in Portugal, where he died at Guemarraens.

Walter of Aulne (Bl) Mk. OSB. Cist.   Nov 26

d. c 1180 A canon of Liége who followed St Bernard to Clairvaux and then became the first prior of the abbey of Aulne in Brabant.

Waltheof (Walthen, Waldef) (St) Ab. OSB. Cist.   Aug 3

c 1100–1160 Son of the earl of Huntingdon, he was educated at the court of the king of Scotland, where he became a great friend of St Aelred. He joined the Augustinian canons at Nostell, but later migrated to the Cistercians and eventually became abbot of Melrose, rebuilt for him by King David, his stepfather. His outstanding characteristics were cheerfulness and unbounded generosity to the poor.

Waltmann (Bl) Ab. O. Praem.   Apr 11

d. 1138 A disciple of St Norbert, whom he accompanied to Cambrai to preach against heresy and who left him there as abbot of St Michael's.

Walto (Balto) (Bl) Ab. OSB.   Dec 27

d. 1156 Abbot of Wessobrünn in Bavaria. His sanctity attracted many friends and benefactors to the abbey.

Waltram (Bl or St) OSB.   July 10

See Lantfrid, Waltram, etc.

Wando (Vando) (St) Ab. OSB.   Apr 17

d. c 756 Monk and abbot of Fontenelle. As a result of a false accusation he was exiled to Troyes but reinstated after his innocence had been proved. He died at Fontenelle.

Wandrille (Wandregisilus, Vandrille) (St) Ab. OSB.   July 22

c 600–668 Born near Verdun, he served in the king's palace, where he had among his fellow-courtiers seven or eight future saints. In spite of his desire for the monastic life he was appointed count of the palace and married. After a pilgrimage to Rome he and his wife became Religious; he had some monastic training and also lived as a hermit. In 637 he entered the abbey of Roumain-Moutier, and some ten years afterwards founded the abbey of Fontenelle, which became the great missionary centre of that district as well as a school of arts and crafts. Soon it had a community of over three hundred monks. The abbey is still flourishing.

Waningus (Vaneng) (St)
Ab. OSB. Jan 9
d. *c* 686 Born in the diocese of Rouen. From a courtier at the court of Clothair III he became a monk, and assisted his friend St Wandrille in the foundation of Fontenelle. Soon after he himself founded another, no less celebrated and important, at Fécamp.

Warinus (Guarinus,
Warren) (St) M. Aug 25
7th cent. Son of St Sigrada, and put to death by Ebroin, mayor of the palace, who was at war with his brother, the bishop, St Leodegarius.

Wastrada (St) Matron July 21
d. *c* 760 Mother of St Gregory of Utrecht. Towards the end of her life she retired to a convent and probably became a nun, though contemporary evidence of this is lacking.

Wenceslas (St) M. GC. Sept 28
907–929 Duke of Bohemia. He received a pious upbringing from his grandmother, the martyr St Ludmilla. He took over the reins of government in 922 at the time of a pagan reaction. This he tried to stem with great patience and mildness, but in the end he met his death as a result of a political conspiracy. He was murdered by his own brother Boleslav at the door of the church of Alt-Bunzlau. He is the patron of Bohemia. The incidents recorded in the popular carol "Good King Wenceslas looked out" are a pious fiction.

Wendolinus (Wendelinus,
Wendel) (St) C. Oct 21
d. 607 (or 650?) A shepherd who became famous for his sanctity and is venerated at St Wendel on the Nahe in W. Germany. A later legend makes him an Irish hermit and abbot of Tholey in the diocese of Trier.

Wenn (St) W. Oct 18
Otherwise Gwen, q.v.

Wennapa (St) V. July 1
Otherwise Veep, q.v.

Wenog (St) Jan 3
? A Welsh saint, mentioned in various calendars, but of whose life nothing is known.

Weonard (St) Apr 7
Otherwise Gwrnerth, Guainerth. See Llewellyn and Gwrnerth.

Werburg (St) Matron Feb 3
d. *c* 785 Wife of a Ceolred of Mercia. In her widowhood she retired to a convent (Bardney?) of which she became abbess.

Werburga (St) V. OSB. Feb 3
d. *c* 699 Daughter of St Ermenilda and of King Wulfhere of Mercia. She became a nun of Ely under St Etheldreda and later founded the nunneries of Hanbury near Tutbury, Trentham in Staffordshire and Weedon in Northamptonshire. She died at Trentham, but her body was transferred to Chester, of which city she is the patron saint: fragments of her shrine still exist at Chester as a witness of former devotion.

Werenfrid (St) C. OSB. Aug 14
d. *c* 760 An Englishman who worked with St Willibrord among the Frisians. He died at Arnheim.

Wiborada (Guiborat,
Weibrath) (St) M. OSB. May 2
d. 925 She belonged to the Swabian nobility. When her brother Hatto became a Benedictine monk at St Gall, she asked to be walled up as anchoress not far from the monastery, where she lived the rest of her life under the obedience of the abbey. She occupied her time in binding books and doing similar work for the abbey. She was martyred by the invading Hungarians. Canonized in 1047.

Wicterp (Wiho, Wicho)
(St) Bp. Apr 18
d. 749 Abbot of Ellwangen. He took an active part in the foundation of the abbeys of Füssen, Wessobrünn and Kempten, all of which became famous in mediaeval Germany. St Wicterp became the tenth bishop of Augsburg.

Widradus (French:
Waré) (St) Ab. OSB. Oct 3
d. 747 Restorer of the abbey of Flavigny, diocese of Dijon, and founder of Saulieu (*Sanctus Andochius* — Saint-Andoche) in the diocese of Autun.

Widukind (Bl) C. Jan 7
Otherwise Wittikund, q.v.

Wifred (Bl) Ab. OSB. Dec 13
d. 1021 A Benedictine monk, prior and abbot of St Victor at Marseilles (1005–1021).

Wigbert (St) C. Apr 12
d. 690 An Anglo-Saxon who became a dis-

ciple of St Egbert in Ireland. He spent two years as a missionary in Friesland, but returned to Ireland to die.

Wigbert (St) Ab. OSB.   Aug 13
d. *c* 738   An English monk who was invited by St Boniface to cross over into Germany. He did so, and Boniface appointed him abbot of Fritzlar, near Cassel. A few years later he was appointed to Ohrdruf in Thuringia, but before his death Boniface allowed him to return to Fritzlar.

Wilfetrudis (St) Abs. OSB.   Nov 23
d. *p.* 670   Second abbess of the Benedictine nunnery of Nivelles in Brabant, which had been founded by her aunt St Gertrude.

Wilfrid the Younger (St)
Bp. OSB.   Apr 29
d. 744   A monk and favourite disciple of St John of Beverley, he was educated by St Hilda at Whitby. He was appointed abbot of the cathedral community at York, and shortly afterwards coadjutor of St John of Beverley. whom he succeeded in the see. Before his death he retired to a monastery, presumably Ripon.

Wilfrid (Walfridus) (St)
Bp. OSB.   Oct 12
633–709   A Northumbrian who became the champion of the Roman customs in England. Born at Ripon, he became a monk at Lindisfarne under the Celtic régime, but he left to adopt the Western observance elsewhere. After a short stay at Canterbury he went to Rome (653–657). On his return to Northumbria he founded the abbey of Ripon with the Roman customs and rule of St Benedict. In 664 he was ordained bishop at Compiègne and played a leading part in the council of Whitby when Roman usages were adopted for the whole of England. The remainder of Wilfrid's life was occupied with long journeys, with appeals to Rome (the first recorded in English history) to recover his see (see St Chad), and with missionary work among the Frisians and South Saxons. His single-mindedness and apostolic zeal make him a very important figure in the Anglo-Saxon church.

Wilfrida (Wulfritha) (St)
Abs. OSB.   Sept 9
d. *c* 988   Mother of St Edith of Wilton by King Edgar. After Edith's birth Wilfrida retired to Wilton, where she took the veil at the hands of St Ethelwold. As a nun, and later as abbess, her edifying life made ample amends for the irregularity of her connexion with Edgar.

St Wilfrid, Oct 12

Wilgefortis (St) V.   formerly July 20
I.e. Virgo-Fortis. She was known in England as Uncumber, in the Low Countries as Ontkommena, in Germany as Kümmernis, in Gascony as Livrade, in Spain as Librada. Her story is a worthless romance abounding in absurdities, e.g. that she was one of seven sisters all born at one birth; that she miraculously grew a beard in order to escape marriage, etc. This whole very strange story arose perhaps as an explanation of those early depictions of our Lord on the cross clothed in a tunic out of respect for His body, and which

had become unfamiliar by the Middle Ages, when He was depicted as girt with a loincloth. Cult now extinct. She is depicted as a maiden with a long beard, carrying a T-shaped cross, or crucified.

Willa (Bl) H. OSB. Oct 15
d. *c* 1050 A Benedictine num at Nonnberg, near Salzburg, who died a recluse.

Willehad of Denmark (St) M.OFM July 9
1482–1572 A Danish Franciscan who, on the introduction of Lutheranism into his country, was sent into exile and repaired to the Franciscan friary of Gorkum in Holland. He was ninety years of age when he was hanged by the Protestants at Briel, with eighteen companions.

Willehad (St) Bp. OSB. Nov 8
d. *c* 789 A Northumbrian monk, probably of York or Ripon, who *c* 766 went to evangelize the Frisians. Later he crossed the Weser and preached to the Saxons, but he had to abandon this mission and retired to the Benedictine abbey of Echternach. Eventually he was ordained bishop of Bremen in 787.

Willeic (St) Mk. OSB. March 2
d. 726 A disciple of St Swithbert, who made him prior of the abbey at Kaiserwerth, a position he held till his death.

William (*several*)
Note. The English form of the Teutonic Wilhelm, which has been Latinized into Gulielmus or Guilielmus, whence the Italian Gulielmo, the French Guillaum, and the Spanish Guillermo.

William of Dijon (St) Ab. OSB. Jan 1
962–1031 Son of the count of Volpiano, William was born near Novara and educated in a monastery. He became a Benedictine at Locedio, near Vercelli, whence he migrated to Cluny under St Majolus (987). Sent to restore the abbey of St Benignus at Dijon, he made this a centre from which he extended the Cluniac observance throughout Burgundy, Normandy, Lorraine and N. Italy. Gentle with the poor, in his dealings with the great he showed remarkable firmness. Towards the end of his life he founded the abbey of Fruttuaria in Piedmont and rebuilt that of Fécamp, where he died.

William of Bourges (St) Bp. OSB. Cist. Jan 10
d. 1209 William de Donjeon was born at Nevers and shortly after his ordination was made canon of Soissons, and later of Paris. He

joined the monks of Grandmont, whence he migrated to the Cistercians of Pontigny. He was appointed successively abbot of Fontaine-Jean, abbot of Châlis and bishop of Bourges (1200). He made a great many converts among the Albigenses. Canonized 1217.

William Patenson (Bl) M. Jan 22
d. 1592 A native of Durham, he studied for the priesthood at Reims and was ordained there in 1587. He was condemned and hanged, drawn and quartered at Tyburn. Beatified 1929.

William Ireland (Bl) M. SJ. Jan 24
d. 1679 His true name was Iremonger and he was a native of Lincolnshire. He was educated at St Omer and received into the Society of Jesus there in 1655. He was martyred at Tyburn for alleged complicity in the imaginary Popish Plot. Beatified 1929.

William Saultemouche (Bl) M. SJ. Feb 7
See James Salès and William Saultemouche (Feb 7).

William of Maleval (St) H. OSB. Feb 10
d. 1157 A Frenchman by birth, after some years of care-free military life he went on a pilgrimage to the Holy Land and on his return was made superior of an abbey near Pisa. Failing to maintain discipline there, as well as in a foundation of his own on Monte Bruno, he embraced the eremitical life in the solitude of Maleval near Siena (1155). He was joined by some disciples. After William's death, Gregory IX gave them the rule of St Benedict, but they were eventually absorbed by the Augustinian hermits.

William Richardson (Bl) M. Feb 17
d. 1603 William Richardson, *alias* Anderson, was born at Wales near Sheffield and educated for the priesthood at Valladolid and Seville, where he was ordained in 1594. was martyred at Tyburn. Beatified 1929.

William Harrington (Bl) M. Feb 18
d. 1594 Born at Mt St John, Felixkirk, in Yorkshire, he studied and was ordained (1592) at Reims. He was only twenty-seven years of age when he was hanged, drawn and quartered at Tyburn. Beatified 1929.

William Hart (Bl) M. March 15
d. 1583 A native of Wells, he was educated at Lincoln College, Oxford, and on being reconciled to the Catholic church studied for the priesthood at Douai, Reims and Rome. After his ordination (1581) he returned to England and was betrayed by an apostate in

the house of Bl Margaret Clitherow. Executed at York. Beatified 1886.

William of Peñacorada
(St) H. OSB. March 20
d. c 1042 Monk of the Benedictine (Cluniac) monastery of Satagún, province of León, Spain. In 988 he fled with the other monks from the Saracens and settled in the solitude of Peñacorada, where he eventually built the monastery of Santa Maria de los Valles, later named after him San Guillermo de Peñacorada.

William of Norwich
(St) M. formerly March 26
d. 1144 A boy of twelve, apprentice to a tanner at Norwich, who is alleged to have been murdered by two Jews out of hatred of Christianity. His cult declined due to papal disapproval before the Reformation and is now extinct. In art he was shown as a boy crowned with thorns, a knife piercing his side, holding nails; or holding a cross and nails, with wounded feet and hands.

William Tempier (Bl) Bp. March 27
d. 1197 From being a Canon Regular at Saint-Hilaire-de-la-Celle, Poitiers, he became bishop of that city and proved a brave champion of ecclesiastical liberty.

William of Eskilsoë (St)
C. OSA. Apr 6
d. 1203 A Frenchman, canon regular at the church of St Geneviève, Paris, who was sent to Denmark to reform a community of Canons Regular at Eskilsoë (Ise Fjord) and then founded the abbey of Ebelholt, Zeeland. He worked in Denmark for thirty years. Canonized 1224.

William Cufitella (Bl) H. Apr 7
d. 1411 A native of Noto in Sicily, who for seventy years lived as a hermit at Sciacca. He was a Franciscan tertiary. Cult approved 1537.

William Gnoffi (Bl) H. Apr 16
d. c 1317 A native of Polizzi, near Palermo, who atoned for a sin of the flesh by leading a very penitential life.

William Firmatus (St) H. Apr 24
d. 1103 A canon and medical practitioner at Saint-Venance who, in consequence of a divine warning against avarice, gave all to the poor and spent the rest of his life on pilgrimages and as a hermit at Savigny and Mantilly.

William Marsden (Bl) M. Apr 25
d. 1586 Born in Lancashire and educated at St Mary Hall, Oxford. He studied for the priesthood and was ordained at Reims (1585).

Shortly after, he was executed in the Isle of Wight. Beatified 1929.

William of Pontoise (St) C. May 10
d. 1192 An Englishman who lived as a hermit at Pontoise in France. Some writers say that he was a Benedictine of St Martin's abbey.

William de Naurose (Bl)
C. OSA. Erem. May 18
1297–1369 A native of Toulouse, who joined the Augustinian hermits and was famed as a very zealous missionary priest. Cult confirmed 1893.

William of Rochester
(St) M. May 23
d. 1201 Thought to have been a native of Perth in Scotland, who was murdered at Rochester while on a pilgrimage to the Holy Land via Canterbury. As a result of miracles wrought after his death he was acclaimed a martyr by the people and his body was enshrined in the cathedral of Rochester.

William of Dongelberg
(Bl) Mk. OSB. Cist. May 24
d. c 1250 A Cistercian monk at the abbey of Villers in Belgium.

William of Gellone (St)
Mk. OSB. May 28
755–812 Duke of Aquitaine and a member of Charlemagne's entourage. He manifested the qualities of the ideal Christian knight when campaigning against the Saracens in S. France. Afterwards he built a monastery at Gellone, diocese of Lodève, not far from Aniane, which he peopled with monks from the latter abbey, himself joining the community as a lay-brother. Later the abbey was renamed after him Saint-Guilhem-du-Desert. Canonized 1066.

William Arnaud (Bl) M. OP. May 29
d. 1242 The inquisitor general in S. France against the Albigensians, by whom he was killed with eleven companions. See Toulouse (Martyrs of).

William Filby (Bl) M. May 30
d. 1582 Born in Oxfordshire, he was educated at Lincoln College, Oxford and, after his conversion, at Reims, where he was ordained in 1581. He was martyred at Tyburn with three companions. Beatified 1886.

William Scott (Bl) M. OSB. May 30
Otherwise Maurus Scott, q.v.

William of York (St) Bp. June 8
d. 1154 William Fitzherbert, or "of

Thwayt", was a nephew of King Stephen and was appointed archbishop of York in 1142. Powerful enemies, chiefly the newly arrived White Monks supported by St Bernard of Clairvaux, contested the appointment on the ground of simony, but Pope Innocent II, St Bernard's great friend, decided in favour of William, who was consecrated and enthroned. His enemies, however, did not rest till they had him deposed from his see. William went into retirement as a monk at Winchester and lived a very mortified life, giving to all an heroic example of patience and resignation, until he was restored to York, where he was received by his people with unbounded joy. He died, perhaps of poison, almost immediately. Canonized 1226. An interesting mural at St Albans shows him as an archbishop, with an escutcheon.

William Greenwood (Bl)
M. O. Cart.   June 16
d. 1537   A lay-brother of the London charterhouse, starved to death at Newgate with six companions. Beatified 1886.

William Exmew (Bl) M.
O. Cart.   June 19
d. 1535   Educated at Christ's College, Cambridge, and sub-prior of the London charterhouse. He was martyred with BB Humphrey Middlemore and Sebastian Newdigate, q.v.

William Harcourt (Bl)
M. SJ.   June 20
d. 1679   A native of Lancashire who became a Jesuit at St Omer (1632) and worked on the English mission from 1645 to 1678, chiefly in London. He was martyred at Tyburn with five Jesuit companions for alleged complicity in the so-called Popish Plot. Beatified 1929.

William of Montevergine
(St) Ab. Founder   June 25
1085–1142   A native of Vercelli who, after a pilgrimage to Compostella, settled as a hermit on the summit of Monte Virgiliano, now Monte Vergine, between Nola and Benevento. Here he was joined by a band of hermit-monks to whom he gave a rule based on that of St Benedict, which was definitively adopted by the community under William's successor. He died at the daughter house of Guglieto, near Nusco. Cult confined to local calendars since 1969.

William Andleby (Bl) M.   July 4
d. 1597   Born at Etton, near Beverley, and educated at St John's College, Cambridge. After his conversion he studied at Douai and was ordained in 1577. He laboured in Yorkshire for twenty years, but was finally con-

demned and martyred at York with three Catholic laymen. Beatified 1929.

William of Hirsau (Bl)
Ab. OSB.   July 4
d. 1091   A monk of St Emmeram at Regensburg who, after being named abbot of the recently restored abbey of Hirsau in Würtemberg, introduced there the observance of Cluny. He founded a monastic school, restored the *scriptorium*, attended to the instruction and well-being of the tenants and serfs of the abbey estates, supported Gregory VII against Henry IV, wrote learned treatises and founded seven new abbeys. These activities, coupled with great holiness of life, show him to have been typical of the great Benedictine abbots of his time.

William of Breteuil (St)
Ab. OSB.   July 14
d. 1130   Abbot-restorer of the monastery of Breteuil, in the diocese of Beauvais, which had been practically destroyed during the Norman invasions.

William Ward (Bl) M.   July 26
d. 1641   His true name was Webster and he was a native of Thornby in Westmorland. He was educated at Douai and ordained there in 1608. He spent thirty-three years on the English mission, of which twenty were passed in prison. He was martyred at Tyburn. Beatified 1929.

William of Saint-Brieuc
(St) Bp.   July 29
d. 1234   William Pinchon was born in Brittany, and shortly after receiving holy orders was appointed successively canon and bishop of Saint-Brieuc (1220). During the fourteen years of his episcopate he suffered banishment to Poitiers and other penalties for maintaining the rights of the church. Canonized 1253.

William Horne (Bl) M. O.
Cart.   Aug 4
d. 1540   A lay-brother of the London charterhouse, martyred at Tyburn with two companions. Beatified 1886.

William Freeman (Bl) M.   Aug 13
d. 1595   William Freeman, *alias* Mason, was a Yorkshire convert who had been educated at Magdalen College, Oxford. He was ordained at Reims in 1587 and sent on the English mission. He laboured in Worcestershire and Warwickshire and was executed at Warwick. Beatified 1929.

William Lacey (Bl) M.   Aug 22
d. 1582   Born at Horton, near Settle, in

Yorkshire. He was a gentleman of means and a staunch Catholic. He was married twice, and during the fourteen years of his married life his house was a refuge for Catholics. After the death of his second wife he went to Reims to study and was ordained in Rome. He ministered to the Catholics round York, and was captured in York prison while acting as deacon at the sung eucharist of Bl Thomas Bell. He was martyred at York with Bl Richard Kirkman. Beatified 1886.

William Dean (Bl) M. Aug 28
d. 1588 A native of Linton in Craven, Yorkshire, he was a convert minister who was ordained at Reims in 1581. He was martyred at Mile End Green, East London. Beatified 1929.

William Gunter (Bl) M. Aug 28
d. 1588 Born at Raglan in Gwent, and educated and ordained at Reims (1587). Condemned and hanged at Shoreditch. Beatified 1929.

William of Roeskilde (St)
Bp. Sept 2
d. 1067 An Anglo-Saxon, chaplain to King Canute. He crossed over to Denmark and was made by the same king bishop of Roeskilde. Besides being a very successful missionary, William steadfastly resisted the anti-Christian policy and crimes of King Sweyn Estridsen.

William Browne (Bl) M. Sept 5
d. 1605 A layman, a native of Northamptonshire, condemned and executed for his faith at Ripon. Beatified 1929.

William Way (Bl) M. Sept 23
d. 1588 A native of Devon who was educated and ordained (1586) at Reims. He was martyred at Kingston-on-Thames. Beatified 1929.

William Hartley (Bl) M. Oct 5
d. 1588 A native of Wilne, near Derby, he was educated at St John's College, Oxford, and became an Anglican parson. After his conversion he studied at Reims, where he was ordained (1580). He was hanged at Shoreditch. Beatified 1929.

William of Savigny (Bl)
Mk. OSB. Oct 20
d. c 1122 A novice at Savigny under Bl Vitalis.

William (St) Mk. OSB. Nov 3
See Acheric and William.

William de Paulo (Bl) Ab.
OSB. Nov 30
d. 1423 Born at Catania, he professed the

Benedictine rule at San Niccolò dell' Arena, and at a later period was sent to restore monastic discipline at Maniaco.

William of Fenoli (Bl) C.
O. Cart. Dec 19
d. c 1205 A Carthusian lay-brother at the charterhouse Casularum in Lombardy. Cult confirmed 1860.

William Howard (Bl) M. Dec 29
1616–1680 Grandson of Bl Philip Howard, and Viscount Stafford. He was accused of complicity in the Popish Plot and after two years' imprisonment was beheaded on Tower Hill. Beatified 1929.

Willibald (Willebald) (St)
Bp. OSB. July 7
c 700–786/7 Born in Wessex, he was a brother of SS Winebald and Walburga and a cousin of St Boniface. At the age of five he was offered as a monk at Waltham in Hampshire. In 722 he accompanied his father St Richard and brother St Winebald on a pilgrimage to Rome and the Holy Land. He visited all the holy places and many Eastern monastic lauras and stayed for two years at Constantinople. On his return to Italy he lived at Montecassino for ten years and helped in the monastic restoration under St Petronax, filling the offices of sacrist, dean and porter. While on a visit to Rome he was sent by Gregory III to Germany to help St Boniface in his missionary labours, and was soon after ordained by the latter, bishop of Eichstätt 742. With his brother St Winebald he founded the double abbey of Heidenheim, over which they placed their sister Walburga as abbess. His relics remain in the cathedral at Eichstätt. Canonized in 938 by Leo VII.

Willibrord (St) Bp. OSB. Nov 7
c 658–739 A Northumbrian by birth and educated at Ripon, he crossed over to Ireland to be trained in the missionary life. Thence he went to Friesland (c 690) accompanied by eleven other English monks. Six years later he was ordained bishop by Pope Sergius and established his see at Utrecht. His labours among the Frisians bore much fruit, as they also did in Heligoland and Denmark. With the help of Pepin of Heristal he founded the monastery of Echternach in Luxemburg in 698 as the centre of his missionary expeditions, and thither he retired to die. His relics still remain at Echternach and are held in great veneration.

Willigis (St) Bp. Feb 23
d. 1011 The son of a wheelwright of Schö-

ningen, he became a canon of Hildesheim and as such attracted the attention of the emperor Otto III, who made him his chaplain and (971) chancellor of the empire. About two years later he was appointed archbishop of Mainz, and Boniface VII created him vicar apostolic for Germany. Perhaps the greatest statesman of his age, Willigis was first and foremost a churchman, and ever remained humble and charitable in his dealings with others. In 1002 he consecrated the emperor St Henry II. In art he is shown with a wheel, which he chose for his arms as symbolizing his father's trade.

Willigod and Martin (SS)
Abbots OSB.   Sept 28
d. ? *c* 690   Monks of Moyenmoutier who became co-founders and successive abbots of the monastery of Romont.

Wiltrudis (St) W. OSB.   Jan 6
d. *c* 986   The wife of Duke Berthold of Bavaria, who after her husband's death (*c* 947) founded (*c* 976) the nunnery of Bergen, near Neuburg on the Danube, under the Benedictine rule, and herself became a nun and its first abbess. She was renowned for her skill in artistic handicrafts.

Winaman, Unaman and Sunaman (SS) MM.
OSB.   Feb 15
d. *c* 1040   Missionary monks, nephews of the English missionary St Sigfrid of Wexiow, whom they followed to the Swedish mission. They were martyred by pagans at Wexiow.

Winebald (Vinebaud) (St) Ab. OSB.   Apr 6
d. *c* 650   At first a hermit, he afterwards took the monastic habit at Saint-Loup-de-Troyes, of which monastery he was chosen abbot.

Winebald (St) Ab. OSB.   Dec 18
d. 761   An Englishman, brother of SS Willibald and Walburga. When on pilgrimage to the Holy Land with his brother, Winebald was taken ill and remained at Rome, where he studied for seven years. Eventually he returned to England, collected some helpers and passed into Germany at the invitation of St Boniface. In time he became the abbot of Heidenheim, a double abbey built for him and his sister by their brother, then bishop of Eichstätt.

Winewald (St) Ab. OSB.   Apr 27
d. *c* 731   The successor of St Berchtun as abbot of Beverley.

Winefred (Winefride, Wenefrida, Gwenfrewi, Guinevra, etc.) (St) VM.   Nov 3
7th cent.   A native of Wales, she is said to have been a niece of St Beuno and to have been murdered by Caradog of Hawarden for refusing his amorous advances, a spring of water gushing forth on the spot where her head fell. This was the origin of the Holy Well, which has been a centre of pilgrimages ever since. Another version of the legend adds that she was restored to life by St Beuno and that she became a nun and abbess of Gwytherin in Clwyd. She is evidently an historical personage, but it is equally evident that her true story can no longer be reconstructed. Even after the Reformation people came in crowds to bathe at her well and spring. Her relics were venerated at Shrewsbury. She is represented as carrying her head, and a palm; or with her head, block and axe at her feet, or carrying a palm and sword with a stream at her feet.

Winin (St) Bp.   Sept 10
The Welsh form of the name of St Finian, q.v.

Winnow, Mancus and Myrbad (SS) CC.   May 31
Probably 6th cent.   Three Irish saints who lived in Cornwall, where they have churches dedicated in their honour.

Winoc (St) Ab. OSB.   Nov 6
d. ?717   He was of Welsh origin and became a monk at Sithiu under St Bertinus, by whom eventually he was sent to establish a new foundation among the Morini at Wormhoult, of which he became abbot. From that centre he evangelized the whole neighbourhood. His memory is perpetuated by the Cornish village of St Winnow.

Winwaloe (Guengaloeus, Gwenno, Wonnow, Wynwallow, Valois, etc.) (St) Ab.   March 3
6th cent.   Born in Brittany, he became a disciple of St Budoc on Lauren Island and abbot-founder of Landevennec near Brest. Several Cornish churches are dedicated to St Winwaloe, which seems to indicate that the saint had some connexion with those parts, possibly they received portions of relics after the Viking invasions in 914. He is represented as carrying a church on his shoulders, or ringing a bell.

Wiomad (Weomadus, Wiomagus) (St) Bp. OSB.   Nov 8
d. *c* 790   Monk of St Maximinus at Trier. He became abbot of Mettlach and finally bishop of Trier (*c* 750–790).

St Winefred, Nov 3

Wirnto (Bl) Ab. OSB.   Oct 29
d. 1127   A Benedictine of Göttweig in
Austria, who became abbot of Formbach in
Bavaria.

Wiro (St) Bp. **Plechelm
and Otger (SS)**   May 8
Wiro died *c* 753   With St Willibrord he was
an apostle of Frisia. St Boniface made him
bishop of Utrecht (*c* 741). At Odilienburg he
and his two companions established a monastery. Wiro was from Northumbria and Odilienburg was the centre of his cult.

Wisinto (Bl) Mk. OSB.   Dec 31
d. *a*1250   A monk and priest of the great

Austrian abbey of Kremsmünster. He has
always been venerated as a saint by the
Austrian Benedictines.

Wistan (St) M.   June 1
d. 850   Of the royal house of Mercia. His
legend states that he was murdered by Berh-
tric his cousin, who wished to marry Wistan's
mother, Elfreda the Regent, which Wistan
would not allow. Wistan was perhaps murdered at Wistanstow in Shropshire, and was
entombed at Repton. Later his remains were
enshrined at Evesham.

Wistremundus (St) M.   June 7
See Peter, Wallabonsus, etc.

Withburga (St) V. OSB. July 8
d. *c* 743 (March 17) Youngest daughter of King Anna of East Anglia. After her father had fallen in battle she took the veil and lived mostly at East Dereham, a nunnery which she had founded. Later her body was stolen by Ely monks and enshrined at Ely. She is depicted as carrying a church, with two does before her.

Wita (St)
Otherwise Candida (several) q.v.

Witta (St) Bp. OSB. Oct 26
Otherwise Albinus, q.v.

Wittikund (Bl) C. Jan 7
d. *c* 804 A duke of Westphalia who as a pagan resisted the arms of Charlemagne. It is related that he was converted by a miraculous vision, and baptized in 785. Thereafter he was most zealous in propagating Christianity and restoring churches. He died in battle with the Suevi.

Wivina (Vivina) (St) Abs. OSB. Dec 17
d. 1170 A Flemish lady of the house of Oisy. In her twenty-third year she secretly left her father's house and became an anchoress in a wood near Brussels, called Grand-Bigard. The Count of Brabant offered her the land and she built a nunnery, placing it under the direction of the Benedictines of Afflighem, near Alost. She was the first abbess.

Wolfgang (St) Bp. OSB. Oct 31
924–994 A native of Swabia, who was educated by the Benedictines at Reichenau, and after being dean of the cathedral school at Trier, became a Benedictine at Einsiedeln (964). He was made headmaster of the abbey school which became under him the most flourishing institution of its kind in those parts. In 971 he was ordained and with a group of monks went as a missionary to the Magyars; but in the following year (972) he was made bishop of Regensburg. He was one of those monk-bishops who have left their mark on the history of their times. He was tutor to the emperor Henry II, restored abbeys (St Emmeram at Regensburg being one of the most important of these), raised the standard of education, reformed ecclesiastical discipline and was a great benefactor of the poor, being known as their *Eleemosynarius Major* (Great Almoner). Canonized by Leo IX in 1052.

Wolfhelm (Bl) Ab. OSB. Apr 22
d. 1091 A Rhinelander, he joined the Benedictine abbey of St Maximinus at Trier. From there he transferred to St Pantaleon's at Cologne, and then became abbot successively of Gladbach, Siegburg and Brauweiler, at which last-named he ended his days. He is described as a great student of holy writ and a great lover of the holy rule.

Wolfrid (Bl) Ab. OSB. June 21
d. *c* 990 Abbot-founder (*c* 973) of Hohentwiel.

Woolos (St) Jan 19
Otherwise Gwynllyw, q.v.

Woronus (St) Apr 7
Otherwise Goran, q.v.

Wulfhad and Ruffin (SS) MM. July 24
? Allegedly two princes of the royal family of Mercia, baptized by St Chad and thereupon put to death by the king, their father, (who was as yet unconverted) at Stone, Staffs. This story is at variance with known historical facts. Perhaps two early saints venerated at Stone and about whom nothing was known in the Middle Ages were the focus of the legend.

Wulfhilda (St) Abs. OSB. Sept 9
d. *c* 1000 When she was a novice at Wilton abbey King Edgar sought her hand in marriage but she wished to be a nun. Eventually, the king consented, despite an attempted abduction, putting her in charge of Barking abbey, and giving her Horton abbey as well. Later she had to flee Barking for Horton, where she lived for twenty years. Around the year 993 she was able to return as abbess of both houses.

Wulfram (St) Bp. OSB. March 20
7th Cent. A courtier-priest who was given the see of Sens, which he occupied for only two and a half years. He then undertook the work of the evangelization of the Frisians, and after spending some time at Fontenelle, he set out with some of the monks. After spending many years among the Frisians he returned to Fontenelle, where he died. His relics still exist at Abbeville.

Wulfric (St) H. Feb 20
d. 1154 A priest who, after leading a worldly life, became a hermit at Haselbury Plucknett in Somerset. The Cistercians lay claim to him, but he was attached to no order. The Cistercian abbot John of Ford wrote a most interesting life of the saint.

Wulmar (Ulmar, Ulmer, Vilmarus, Volmar, Vilmer, etc.) (St) Ab. OSB. July 20
d. 689 Born near Boulogne in Picardy, he married, but was separated by force from his wife and became a Benedictine lay-brother at Haumont in Hainault. Here he was employed

in keeping cattle and hewing wood for the abbey. Later, he was ordained and eventually became the founder and first abbot of the monastery of Samer (*Salviniacum*) near Boulogne, afterwards called after him Saint-Vulmaire. He also founded the convent at Wierre-aux-Bois.

Wulsin (St) Bp. OSB.   Jan 8
d. 1002 Described as "a loyal and trusty monk whom St Dunstan loved like a son with pure affection". When St Dunstan restored Westminster abbey (*c* 960) he made Wulsin superior there and finally abbot (980). In 993 he became bishop of Sherborne, whilst remaining abbot of Westminster.

Wulstan (Wulfstan, Ulfstan, Wolstan) Bp. OSB.   Jan 19
1008–1095 A native of Itchington in Warwickshire, he studied at the abbeys of Evesham and Peterborough. Then he became a priest and joined the Benedictines at Worcester, where he filled the offices of precentor and prior. Finally he was made bishop of Worcester (1062), which he governed so wisely that he was the only English bishop who was allowed to retain his see after the Conquest. During his episcopate, which lasted thirty-two years, he rebuilt his cathedral and conducted a regular visitation of his dioceses. He died while engaged in his daily practice of washing the feet of twelve poor men. Canonized 1203.

Wynnin (St) Bp.   Jan 21
Otherwise Vimin, q.v.

St Wulstan, Jan 19

Xantippa and Polyxena
(SS) VV.   Sept 23
1st cent?   Described in the pre-1970 RM. as "disciples of the Apostles", but we have no trustworthy information about them.

Xystus (*several*)
Otherwise Sixtus, q.v.

Ymar (St) M. OSB. Nov 12
d. *c* 830   A monk of Reculver in Kent, martyred by the Danes.

Yolanda (Iolantha) (Bl) W. June 15
d. 1298   Daughter of Bela IV, king of Hungary, niece of St Elizabeth, she married Boleslaus, the devout prince of Pomerania. She was a tertiary of St Francis. Beatified in 1827.

Yon (St) M. Sept 22
Otherwise Jonas, q.v.

Yrchard (Yarcard) (St) Bp. Aug 24
5th cent.   A Scottish priest, ordained bishop by St Ternan, and like him a missionary among the Picts.

Yrieix (St) Ab. Aug 25
See Aredius.

Ysarn (St) Ab. OSB. Sept 24
d. 1048   Born near Toulouse, he became a Benedictine monk, and then abbot of St Victor's at Marseilles. Under his government the abbey became the centre of a Benedictine congregation with houses in S. France and N.E. Spain.

Ytha (St) V. Jan 15
Otherwise Ita, q.v. In Cornwall she is known as St Ide or St Syth.

Yvo (St) C. May 19
Otherwise Ivo, q.v.

Ywi (St) H. OSB. Oct 8
d. *c* 690   A monk of Lindisfarne ordained deacon by St Cuthbert. His relics were translated to Wilton, near Salisbury.

Zacchaeus (St) Bp.   Aug 23
d. *c* 116   This Zacchaeus or Zacharias is reckoned by St Epiphanius and other Fathers to have been the fourth bishop of Jerusalem.

Zacchaeus (St) M.   Nov 17
See Alphaeus and Zacchaeus.

Zacharia (St) Prophet   Nov 5
1st cent.   Father of St John the Baptist, known to us from Luke I. Nothing is known of the rest of his life.

Zacharias (St) Pope   March 15
d. 752   Born at San Severino in Calabria of a Greek family. Chosen pope in 741, he showed himself worthy of that office: he successfully negotiated peace between the Lombards and the Greek empire; sanctioned the assumption of the Frankish crown by Pepin; seconded the missionary work of St Boniface and confirmed him as archbishop of Mainz; planned and undertook the restoration of Montecassino under St Petronax, himself consecrating the abbey church in 748; and in many other ways furthered the reconstruction of Europe. The influence of many of his actions affected European culture and society for many centuries after his death.

Zachary (St) Bp. M.   May 26
d. *c* 106   Said to have been the second bishop of Vienne in Gaul, and to have died a martyr under Trajan.

Zachary (St) M.   June 10
? Described by the pre-1970 RM. as a martyr at Nicomedia.

Zama (St) Bp.   Jan 24
d. *c* 268   The first bishop of Bologna of whom there is any record. He is said to have been ordained by Pope St Dionysius *c* 260.

Zambdas (Zabdas, Bazas) (St) Bp.   Feb 19
d. *c* 304   Said to have been the thirty-seventh bishop of Jerusalem. He has been connected with the legend of the Theban legion.

Zanitas, Lazarus, Marotas, Narses and Comp. (SS) MM.   March 27
d. 326   A group of Persian martyrs who suffered under Shapur II. The remaining five martyrs of this group were: Elias, Abibos, Sembeeth, Mares and Sabas.

Zdislava Berka (Bl) Matron, OP.   Jan 1
d. 1252   Born in Bohemia of noble parents, she married a man of her own rank to whom she bore four children. Her generosity towards the poor caused difficulties with her husband, whom she conciliated by her heroic patience. She died as a Dominican tertiary in the priory of St Lawrence, which she had founded. Cult approved in 1907.

Zebinas (St) M.   Nov 13
See Antoninus, Zebinas, etc.

Zebinus (St) H.   Feb 23
5th cent.   A hermit in Syria who trained St Maro, St Polychronius and others in the monastic life.

Zechariah (St) Prophet   Sept 6
6th cent. B.C.   A fellow-prophet of Haggai. Both prophesied under King Darius (the first part of his prophetic book was written in 519/17 B.C.) and exhorted the people to rebuild the Temple.

Zenais, Cyria, Valeria and Marcia (SS) MM.   June 5
? Zenais seems to have suffered at Constantinople. The other martyrs of this group are traditionally believed to have been contemporaries of our Lord and among the early martyrs of the church.

Zenais and Philonilla (SS) MM.   Oct 11
1st cent.   Two holy women, perhaps sisters, related to St Paul the Apostle, according to tradition. They were natives of Tarsus.

Zenas (St) M.   June 23
See Zeno and Zenas.

Zeno (St) M.   Feb 14
See Vitalis, Felicula and Zeno.

Zeno (St) M.   Apr 5
? A martyr who was burnt alive. Date and place unknown.

Zeno (St) Bp.   Apr 12
d. 371 Bishop of Verona, 362–371, at the
time of Julian the Apostate. From Africa, he is
remembered as a fervent pastor and a fighter
against Arianism. He also corrected liturgical
abuses and encouraged maidens to take vows
of virginity whilst abiding at home. In art his
symbol is a fish.

Zeno (St) M.   Apr 20
See Victor, Zoticus, etc.

Zeno and Zenas (SS) MM.   June 23
d. c 304 Zeno, a wealthy citizen of Philadelphia near the Dead Sea, freed all his slaves it is
said, and gave his property to the poor. Zenas,
a former slave, remained with him as a servant.
Both were beheaded under Diocletian.

Zeno and Comp. (SS) MM.   July 9
d. c 300 According to the pre-1970 RM.
this group of martyrs numbered 10,204. The
entry is in fact a record of the wholesale
slaughter, ordered by Diocletian, of the
Christians who had been condemned to work
on the building of the baths named after him.
Zeno seems to have been the chief spokesman
of these martyrs.

Zeno (St) M.   July 15
See Philip, Zeno, etc.

**Zeno, Concordius and
Theodore (SS) MM.**   Sept 2
d. 302 Zeno and his two sons were martyred
at Nicomedia under Diocletian.

**Zeno and Chariton (SS)
MM.**   Sept 3
d. 303 Martyrs in the East under Diocle-
tian.

Zeno (St) M.   Sept 5
See Eudoxius, Zeno, etc.

Zeno (St) M.   Sept 8
See Eusebius, Nestabus, and Zeno.

Zeno (St) M.   Dec 20
See Ammon, Zeno, etc.

Zeno (St) M.   Dec 22
d. 303 A soldier at Nicomedia. As a punish-
ment for laughing when Diocletian was offering a sacrifice to Ceres his jaws were broken
and he was beheaded.

Zeno (St) Bp.   Dec 26
d. c 399 A cousin of the martyr-brothers
Eusebius, Nestabus and Zeno, commemorated on Sept 8. He survived Julian's persecution and was made bishop of Gaza.

Zenobia (St) M.   Oct 30
See Zenobius and Zenobia.

Zenobius (St) M.   Feb 20 and Oct 29
See Tyrannio, Silvanus, etc.

Zenobius (St) Bp.   May 25
d. c ?390 Bishop of Florence. A great friend
of St Ambrose and also of St Damasus, by
whom he was sent as papal representative in
Constantinople in connexion with the Arian
troubles. He is depicted as a bishop raising a
dead child to life, or casting out demons.

Zenobius (St) M.   Oct 29
d. 310 A priest and physician at Sidon, who
was martyred at Antioch under Diocletian by
being torn with iron hooks.

**Zenobius and Zenobia
(SS) MM.**   Oct 30
d. 285–290 Bishop and physician at Aegae
(now Alexandretta) on the coast of Asia Minor.
He is probably identical with St Zenobius of
Antioch (Oct 29), in which case his martyrdom
took place somewhat later, under Maximian.
Zenobia is said to have been his sister.

Zenobius (St) M.   Dec 24
See Lucian, Metrobius, etc.

Zephaniah (St) Prophet   Dec 3
7th cent. B.C. Said to have been a descendant of King Hezekiah and to have prophesied
in Judaea in the days of King Josiah: his most
remarkable prophecy regards the ultimate
conversion of the heathen. There are no
trustworthy traditions concerning him.

Zephyrinus (St) Pope
                                          formerly Aug 26
d. 217 Pope from 198/9 to 217. His period
as bishop of Rome was characterised by
Christological controversies. Cult suppressed
in 1969.

Zeticus (St) M.   Dec 23
See Theodulus, Saturninus, etc.

Zimius (St) C. OSB.   June 12
See Marinus, Vimius, etc.

Zita (St) V.   Apr 27
1218–1272 A native of Monsagrati near
Lucca, at the age of twelve she entered the
service of a family at Lucca, with whom she
remained all her life. She would give her food
and clothing to the poor — and sometimes her
master's too. For this she was at first mis-
understood and maltreated, but she ended by
gaining the confidence of the whole household. She was canonized in 1696 and is greatly
venerated, especially in Italy, as the patron
saint of domestic servants. Thus she is depicted in working clothes, with a bag and keys;
or loaves and a rosary.

St Zenobius, May 25

Zöe (St) M.   May 2
See Exuperius, Zöe, etc.

Zöe (Zoa) (St) M.   July 5
d. *c* 286   A Roman lady, said to have been
the wife of a high official of the imperial court,
put to death for the faith.

**Zöellus, Servilius, Felix,
Silvanus and Diocles
(SS)** MM.   May 24
? Martyrs at Istria (or in Syria?).

Zoilus and Comp. (SS)
MM.   June 27
d. *c* 301   A youth believed to have been
martyred at Cordoba under Diocletian. The
Benedictine abbey of San Zoil de Carrión,
province of León, in N. Spain, was founded to
enshrine his relics, and those of nineteen
others of doubtful veracity.

Zosima (St) M.   July 15
See Eutropius, Zosima and Bonosa.

St Zita, Apr 27

Zosimus and Athanasius (SS) MM.   Jan 3
d. 303   Martyrs in Cilicia under Diocletian. Another acount says that Zosimus was put to the torture and that Athanasius, a spectator, was converted and forthwith tortured also, but that both survived and died in peace as hermits.

Zosimus (St) Bp.   March 30
d. *c* 660   A Sicilian, placed at the age of seven in the monastery of Santa Lucia (Benedictine or Basilian) near Syracus. After being a monk for thirty years, he was successively made abbot and bishop of the city. He died at the age of ninety.

Zosimus (St) H.   Apr 4
5th cent.   A Palestinian and anchorite who lived on the banks of the Jordan, the supposed confidant and biographer of St Mary of Egypt.

Zosimus (St) M.   June 19
d. 110   A martyr of Spoleto in Umbria under Trajan.

Zosimus (St) M.   Sept 28
See Mark, Alphius, etc.

Zosimus (St) H.   Nov 30
6th cent.   A hermit in Palestine, surnamed the Wonder-Worker.

Zosimus (St) M.   Dec 14
See Drusus, Zosimus and Theodore.

Zosimus (St) M.   Dec 18
See Rufus and Zosimus.

Zosimus (St) M.   Dec 19
See Darius, Zosimus, etc.

Zosimus (St) Pope   Dec 26
d. 418   A Greek, whose short pontificate was marked by a high view of papal authority linked to tactlessness and personality clashes in which he seems to have been usually wrong. His early death prevented serious harm being done to the church.

Zoticus, Rogatus, Modestus, Castulus and Comp. (SS) MM.   Jan 12
? A group of between forty and fifty soldiers martyred in Africa.

Zoticus (St) M.   Jan 12
Identical with St Getulius, the martyr of Tivoli (June 10), q.v.

Zoticus (St) M.   Jan 31
See Tarsicius, Zoticus, etc.

Zoticus, Irenaeus, Hyacinth, Amantius and Comp. (SS) MM.   Feb 10
d. 120   A group of ten soldiers martyred in Rome and buried in the Via Lavicana.

Zoticus (St) M.   Apr 20
See Victor, Zoticus, etc.

Zoticus (St) M.   July 21
d. 204   Bishop of Comana in Cappadocia, famous for his zeal against the Montanist heretics and for his martyrdom.

Zoticus (St) M.   Aug 22
See Agathonicus, Zoticus, etc.

Zoticus (St) M.   Oct 21
See Dasius, Zoticus, etc.

Zoticus (St)   Dec 31
d. *c* 350   A Roman priest who migrated to Constantinople at the time when Constantine transferred thither the capital of the empire. Zoticus built in that city a hospital for the poor and for orphans. He was a confessor of the faith under the Arian emperor Constantius.

Bibliography

AA Illustrated Guide to Britain Drive Publications Ltd., Basingstoke, 1977.

Acta Apostolicae Sedis Typis Polyglottis Vaticanis, 1884–1987.

Acta Sanctorum (Vols 1–65) Bollandist Society, Brussels, 1925.

Adair, J *The Pilgrims Way* Book Club Associates, London, 1978.

An Inventory of the Historical Monuments in London (Vol. 1) Westiminster Abbey Royal Commission on Historical Monuments, H.M.S.O., 1924.

Anson, P F *Fashions in Church Furnishings 1840–1940* Faith Press, London, 1960.

Archaeologia (Vol. 57: Part 1) Society of Antiquaries, London, 1900.

Attwater, B *A Dictionary of Saints* Burns, Oates and Washbourne, 1942.

Baring-Gould, S (Ed.) *Lives of the Saints* (Vols 1–16) J.C. Nimmo, London, 1897.

Bell, Mrs A *The Saints in Christian Art* (Vols 1–3) G. Bell and Sons, London, 1901.

Bentley, J *Restless Bones* Constable, London, 1985.

Betjeman, J (Ed.) *Collins Pocket Guides to English Parish Churches* (Vols 1–2) Collins, London, 1968.

Bible, The *(Revised Standard Version)* Collins, London, 1952.

Bond, F *Dedications and Patron Saints of English Churches* Oxford University Press, 1914.

Bonnano, P *Numismata Summorum Pontificum Templi Vaticani* Rome, 1696.

Calendarium Romanum Typis Polyglottis Vaticanis, 1969.

Carmelite Fathers (Ed.) *Images of Carmel* Carmelite Press, Faversham, 1974.

Charlesworth, J H (Ed) *The Old Testament Pseudepigrapha* Darton, Longman and Todd, London, 1983.

Cook, G H *The English Medieval Parish Church* Phoenix House, London, 1954.

Cross, F A and Livingstone, E A *The Oxford Dictionary of the Christian Church* Oxford University Press, 1978.

Daily Prayer from the Divine Office Collins, London, 1974.

Downside Review, The (Vol. 85) Catholic Records Press, Exeter, 1967.

Drake, M and W *Saints and their Emblems* T. Werner Laurie Ltd., London, 1916.

Farmer, D H *The Oxford Dictionary of Saints* Clarendon Press, Oxford, 1978.

Gams, P B *Scries Episcoporum Ecclesiae Catholicae*, Leipzig, 1931.

Greene, E A *Saints and their Symbols* Whitaker & Co., London, 1908.

Hall, J   *Dictionary of Subjects and Symbols in Art*   J. Murray, London, 1985.

Hetherington, P (Ed.)   *The "Painter's Manual" of Dionysius of Fourna*   The Sagittarius Press, London, 1974.

Holweck, F G   *Biographical Dictionary of the Saints*   B. Herder Book Co., St Louis and London, 1924.

Hulme, F E   *The History, Principles and Practice of Symbolism in Christian Art*   Swan Sonnenschein & Co. Ltd., London, 1909.

Husenbeth, F C   *Emblems of Saints*   Longman, Green, Longman and Roberts, London, 1860.

Ieri E Oggi Francesca Romana   Monastero Oblate Di S Francesca Romana, Rome, 1984.

James, A   *The Story of Downside Abbey Church*   Downside Abbey, Stratton-on-the-Fosse, 1961.

Jameson, Mrs   *Legends of the Monastic Orders*   Longman, Green and Co., London, 1891.

Jameson, Mrs   *Sacred and Legendary Art*, Vol. 2   Longman, Brown, Green and Longmans, London, 1848.

Keep, D   *St Boniface and his World*   Paternoster Press, Exeter, 1979.

Kelly, J N D   *The Oxford Dictionary of Popes*   Oxford University Press, 1986.

King, T H   *The Study Book of Mediaeval Architecture and Art* (Vols 1–4)   H. Sotheran, London, 1868.

Lacroix, P   *The Arts of the Middle Ages and Renaissance*   J. S. Virtue & Co., London, N.D.

Little, B   *Catholic Churches Since 1623*   Robert Hale, London, 1966.

Milburn, R L P   *Saints and their Emblems in British Churches*   Oxford University Press, 1949.

Montecassino   Publicazione Cassinesi, Montecassino, 1985.

National Gallery Illustrations, Italian Schools   Trustees of the National Gallery, London, 1937.

Orthodox Calendar, The   Monastery of St Seraphim of Sarov, Fakenham, 1984.

Orthodox Life, (Vol. 31, No. 4)   Holy Trinity Monastery, Jordansville, U.S.A., 1981.

Pugin, A W N   *Glossary of Ecclesiastical Ornament and Costume*   H. G. Bohm, London, 1844.

Ricci, E   *Mille Santi Nell'arte*   Ulrico Hoepli, Milan, 1931.

Searle, W G   *Anglo-Saxon Bishops, Kings and Nobles*   Cambridge University Press, 1899.

Shepherd, L   *The New Liturgy*   Darton, Longman and Todd, London, 1970.

Skrobuche, H   *Icons*   Oliver and Boyd, Edinburgh, 1963.

Stuart, J   *Ikons*   Faber and Faber, London, 1975.

Tarasar, C J   *Founders of Russian Monasticism*   Syosset, New York, 1981.

Vince, J   *Discovering Saints in Britain*   Shire Publications, Aylesbury, 1979.

Wall, J C   *Shrines of the British Saints*   Methuen, London, 1905.

Walsh, M (Ed.)   *Butler's Lives of the Saints: Concise Edition*   Burns Oates and Dove Communications, Melbourne, 1985.

Warner, M   *Alone of all her Sex*   Pan Books, London, 1985.

Warner, M   *Monuments and Maidens*   Pan Books, London, 1985.

Waters, C   *Who was St Wite?*   C. J. Creed, Bridport, 1980.

Index of Emblems

NB "formerly" means that the feast is now
suppressed

A

Anchor
St Clement Nov 23,
St Felix formerly May 30,
St Nicholas Dec 6

Angel(s), accompanying
St Cecilia Nov 22,
St Frances of Rome March 9,
St Genevieve Jan 3,
St Matthew Sept 21

Angels, supporting
St Catherine formerly Nov 25,
St Mary the Blessed Virgin Aug 15

Anvil
St Adrian Sept 8,
St Baldomerus Feb 27,
St Eligius Dec 1

Apple(s)
St Dorothy Feb 6,
St Nicholas Dec 6

Armour
St Eligius Dec 1,
St George Apr 23,
St Joan of Arc May 30,
St Longinus March 15,
St Martin Nov 11,
St Michael Sept 29,
St Nabor July 12,
St Olav July 29,
St Quentin Oct 31,
St Quirinus March 30,
St Sebastian Jan 20,
St Secundus March 29,
St Theodore Tyro Nov 9,
SS Victor, Alexander, Felician and Longinus,
 July 21

Armour, partly stripped of:
Forty Armenian Martyrs March 10,
St Maurice and Comps Sept 22

Armour, with vestments over:
St Armagillus Aug 16

Arrow(s) holding:
St Augustine of Hippo Aug 28,

St Christina July 24,
St Edmund Nov 20,
St Gereon Oct 10,
St Sebastian Jan 20,
St Ursula Oct 1

Arrow(s), pierced by:
St Edmund Nov 20,
St Giles Sept 1,
St Sebastian Jan 20,
St Teresa Oct 15

Axe
St Boniface June 5,
St John Fisher June 22,
St Magnus Apr 16,
SS Martian and Malchus July 27,
St Olav July 29,
St Thomas More June 22,
St Winefred Nov 3

Axehead, mounted on crosier:
St Thomas Becket Dec 29

B

Baker's peel
St Autbert Dec 13,
St Honorius Sept 30

Balls, golden
St Nicholas Dec 6

Banner of Resurrection
Sibylla Phrygia (see supplementary list of
Sibyls on page 606)

Barrel
St Antonia Apr 29,
St John the Evangelist Dec 27,
St Monegundis July 2,
St Willibrord Nov 7

Basket: see Food

Bearded woman
St Wilgefortis formerly July 20

Bear(s)
St Columba Sept 17,
St Gall, Oct 16,
St Seraphim of Sarov Jan 2

Bedstead, metal
St Faith Oct 6

Beehive
St Ambrose Dec 7,
St Bernard Aug 20,
St Isidore Apr 4,
St John Chrysostom Sept 13

Bell
St Antony Jan 17,
St Benedict March 21, July 11,
St Kea Nov 5,
St Romanus May 22,
St Winwaloe March 3

Bird(s)
St Benedict July 11,
St Blaise Feb 3,
St David March 1,
St Elijah July 20,
St Francis of Assisi Oct 4

Blanket, containing souls:
St Abraham Oct 9

Boat
St Bertin Sept 5,
Bl John Roche Aug 30,
St Jude Oct 28,
St Julian Feb 12,
St Mary Magdalene July 22,
St Simon Oct 28

Book
St Anne July 26
(a common emblem of Doctors of the Church,
bishops, evangelists, *et al.*)

Book, pierced by sword or axe:
  St Boniface June 5
with two crowns on it:
  St Elizabeth of Hungary Nov 17
with stones on it:
  St Stephen Dec 26
with a flask of oil on it:
  St Walburga Feb 25
with Holy Infant on it:
  St Antony June 13

Bowl
St Oswald Aug 5
Sibylla Cumana (see supplementary list of
Sibyls on page 606)

Branch
St Brendan May 16,
St Bridget Feb 1,
St Kentigern Jan 13

Bread (see also Food)
St Cuthbert Sept 4,
St Nicholas Dec 6
St Zita Apr 27

Breast(s)
on a platter:
  St Agatha Feb 5

pierced by a sword:
  St Justina Oct 7
pierced by arrows:
  St Ursula Oct 1

Broom
St Petronilla May 31,
St Zita Apr 27

Bull
St Blandina June 2,
St Thecla Sept 23

Bull, of brass:
St Eustace Sept 20

Bush, burning
St Mary the Blessed Virgin Aug 15,
St Moses Sept 4

C

Calf (calves)
St Walstan May 30

Caltrops
St Themistocles Dec 21

Camel
St Hormisdas Aug 8,
St Menas Nov 11

Candle
St Genevieve Jan 3,
Sibylla Libyca (see supplementary list of
Sibyls on page 606)

Cannon
St Barbara Dec 4

Cardinal's hat, robes
St Bonaventure July 15,
St Jerome Sept 30,
St John Fisher June 22,
St Peter Damian Feb 21,
St Robert Bellarmine Sept 17,
St Vincent Ferrer Apr 5

Carpenter's set square
St Joseph March 19,
St Jude Oct 28,
St Thomas July 3

Cave
St Antony Jan 17,
St Benedict July 11,
St Elijah July 20,
St Gall Oct 16,
St Sabbas Dec 5,
Seven Sleepers July 27

Censer
St Aaron July 1

Chalice or cup
St Benedict July 11,

St Eloi Dec 1,
St John the Evangelist Dec 27,
St Pudentiana May 19

Chalice or cup, lying on its side:
St Richard June 16

Chain
St Bridget of Sweden July 23,
St Germanus July 31,
St Leonard of Noblac Nov 6,
St Ninian Aug 26,
St Radegund Aug 13

Child, carrying:
St Antony of Padua June 13,
St Christopher July 25,
St Elizabeth Nov 5,
St Mary the Blessed Virgin Aug 15,
St Rose Aug 23,
St Vincent de Paul Sept 27

Chrismatory
St Remigius Oct 1

Church, carrying:
St Amandus Feb 6,
St Chad March 2,
St Petroc June 4,
St Winwaloe March 3,
St Withburga July 8
(a common symbol of the patron saint or
founder of a church or city)

Cloak, dividing:
St Martin Nov 11

Club
St Boniface June 5,
St Christopher July 25,
St Dorotheus June 5,
SS John, Maximian and Constantine July 27,
St Jude Oct 28,
St Magnus Apr 16,
St Telesphorus Jan 5

Coals, hot
St Brice Nov 13,
St Lambert Sept 17

Cockerel
St Peter June 29,
St Vitus June 15

Coffin and Corpse
St Silvester Nov 26

Coin, suspended round neck
St Genevieve Jan 3

Colt
St Medard June 8

Cook, dressed as a:
St Evortius Sept 7

Cornucopia
Sibylla Cimmeria
(see supplementary list of Sibyls on page 606)

Cow
St Bridget Feb 1,
St Modwenna July 6,
St Perpetua March 7,
St Robert of Knaresborough Sept 24

Cow's horn
St Cornelius Sept 16

Cradle
Sibylla Samia
(see supplementary list of Sibyls on page 606)

Crocodile
St Theodore Tyro Nov 9

Cross, appearing to:
St Francis of Assisi Oct 4

Cross, between antlers of a stag:
St Eustace Sept 20,
St Hubert Nov 3

Cross, holding a:
St Augustine of Hippo Aug 28,
St Helen Aug 18,
Sibylla Hellespontina,
Sibylla Persica,
Sibylla Phrygia
(see supplementary list of Sibyls on page 606)

Cross and battleaxe
St Olav July 29

Cross and sword
St Alban June 20

Cross, tall
St John the Baptist June 24,
St Morwenna July 8

Cross, tall, with rosary:
St Dominic de Guzman Aug 8

Cross, T-shaped (Tall cross)
St Antony Jan 17,
St Philip May 3,
St Wilgefortis July 20

Crowns (two or three)
St Henry July 15,
St Elizabeth of Hungary Nov 17

Crown of thorns
St Francis of Assisi Oct 4,
St Louis Aug 25,
St Teresa Oct 15,
Sibylla Delphica (see supplementary list of
Sibyls on page 606)

Crucifix
St Aloysius Gonzaga June 21,
St Charles Nov 4.

St Francis of Assisi Oct 4,
St Scholastica Feb 10,
St Vincent Ferrer Apr 5

Cruets
St Mary Salome Oct 22,
St Vincent the Deacon Jan 9

Crutch
St Giles Sept 1,
St Liephard Feb 4

D

Dagger
St Edward March 18

Devil, casting out:
  St Zenobius May 25
chained or bound:
  St Armagillus Aug 16,
  St Juliana Feb 16
holding with pincers:
  St Dunstan May 19
spearing:
  St Michael Sept 29

Digging
St Fiacre Aug 30,
St Phocas July 23

Distaff
St Martha July 29,
St Mary the Blessed Virgin Aug 15

Doe
St Withburga July 8

Dog
St Bernard Aug 20,
St Dominic de Guzman Aug 8,
St Roch Aug 16

Door
St Margaret Clitherow Oct 21

Dove
St David March 1,
St Gregory Sept 3,
St Scholastica Feb 10

Dragon
St George Apr 23,
St Juliana Feb 16,
St Margaret July 20,
St Silvester Dec 31

Drill
St Leodegarius Oct 2

E

Eagle
St John the Evangelist Dec 27

Espousal to Our Lord
St Catherine Nov 25,
St Catherine of Siena April 29

Eyes carrying:
  St Lucy Oct 13
of executioner, falling out:
  St Alban June 22

F

Face of Christ, holding picture of:
St Augustine May 27,
St Veronica July 12

Feather, holding a:
St Barbara Dec 4

Fire
St Agnes Jan 21
St Antony Jan 17

Firepot
St Abraham Oct 9

Fish
St Eanswyth Sept 12,
St Raphael Sept 29,
St Simon Feb 18,
St Simon Oct 28,
St Zeno Apr 12

Flask
St Raphael Sept 29,
St Walburga Feb 25

Flowers
St Dorothy Feb 6,
St Zita Apr 27

Food, carrying:
St Dorothy Feb 6,
St Elizabeth of Hungary Nov 17,
St Frances of Rome March 9,
St Jane of Valois Feb 4,
St Margaret of Scotland Nov 16,
St Nicholas Dec 6,
St Olav, July 29,
St Romanus May 22,
St Rosalia Sept 4

Fuller's club
St James the Less May 3,
St Simon Oct 28

G

Gardening
St Fiacre Aug 30,
St Phocas July 23

Glove
Sibylla Tiburtina
(see supplementary list of Sibyls on page 606)

Goldsmith, as a:
St Eloi Dec 1

Goose (Geese)
St Martin I Apr 13,
St Vedast Feb 6

Greyhound
St Philip Howard   Oct 19

Gridiron
St Faith   Oct 6,
St Lawrence   Aug 10,
St Vincent   Jan 22

H

Hair, worn very long:
St Mary of Egypt   Apr 2,
St Mary Magdalene   July 22,
St Sabas   Apr 12

Halberd
St Matthias   May 14,
St Olaf   July 29

Hammer
St Apollonia   Feb 9,
St Eligius   Dec 1

Hand
Sibylla Tiburtina
(see supplementary list of Sibyls on page 606)

Harp
St Cecilia   Nov 22,
St David   Dec 29

Hart
St Mildred   July 13

Head, carrying:
St Alban   June 21,
St Cuthbert   Sept 4,
St Denis (Dionysius)   Oct 9,
St John the Baptist   June 24,
St Juthware   July 1,
St Oswald   Aug 5,
St Osyth   Oct 7,
St Sidwell   Aug 1,
St Winefred   Nov 3

Heart, holding a:
St Augustine of Hippo   Aug 28,
St Catherine of Siena   Apr 29,
St Gertrude   Nov 16,
St Leander   Feb 27,
St Margaret Mary   Oct 16,
St Teresa   Oct 15

Hind(s)
St Fiacre   Aug 30,
St Giles   Sept 1,
St Withburga   July 8

Hook(s)
St Agatha   Feb 5,
St Leodegarius   Oct 2,
St Vincent   Jan 9

Horn blowing:
St Cornelius   Sept 16,
St Oswald   Aug 5

holding:
Sibylla Cimmeria
(see supplementary list of Sibyls on page 606)

Horns, on forehead
St Moses   Sept 4

Horse
St Eloi   Dec 1,
St George   Apr 23,
St Paul   June 29,
St Secundus   March 29,
St Theodore   Sept 19

Horseshoe
St Eligius   Dec 1

I

Infant, Holy: see Child

Intestines carrying:
St Vincent   Jan 22
torn out:
St Claudius   June 6
wound around a windlass:
St Erasmus   June 2

K

Key(s)
St Martha   July 29,
St Peter   June 29,
St Petronilla   May 31,
St Zita   Apr 27

Kings bearing gifts:
The Magi   Jan 6

Knife
St Agatha   Feb 5

Knife in head:
St Peter Martyr   June 2
in side:
St William of Norwich   March 24
and skin:
St Bartholomew   Aug 24

L

Ladder or Staircase
St Alexius   formerly July 17,
St Romuald   June 19

Lamb
St Agnes   Jan 21,
St Joanna   May 24,
St John   June 24

Lamb, with lily, cross and book:
St Anges of Montepulciano

Lantern
St Gudula   Jan 8,
St Lucy   Dec 13,
Sibylla Persica
(see supplementary list of Sibyls on page 606)

Lily, common symbol of Virgins, also of
St Casimir   March 4,
St Dominic de Guzman   Aug 8,
St Joseph   March 19,
St Kenelm   July 17,
St Philip   May 26

Lion(s)
St Daniel   July 21,
St Jerome   Sept 30,
St Mark   Apr 25,
St Mary of Egypt   Apr 2,
St Paul the Hermit   Jan 15

Loaves
St Honorius of Canterbury   Sept 30,
St Joseph Barsabas   July 20,
St Margaret of Scotland   Nov 16,
St Mary of Egypt   Apr 2,
St Nicholas   Dec 6,
St Philip   May 3,
St Zita   Apr 27

Lock
St Leonard of Noblac   Nov 6

M

Manger
Sibylla Cumana
(see supplementary list of Sibyls on page 606)

Mass Cruets
St Joseph of Arimathaea   March 17

Metal-working tools
St Eligius   Dec 1

Millstone
St Callistus   Oct 14,
SS Crispin and Crispinian   Oct 25,
St Vincent   Jan 9

Mitres (three)
St Bernadine of Siena   May 20

Moneybags or moneybox
St Martin   Apr 13,
St Matthew   Sept 21,
St Nicholas   Dec 6,
St Praxedes   July 21

Monstrance
St Clare   Aug 11,
St Norbert   June 6

Moon, underfoot:
St Mary the Blessed Virgin   Aug 15

Mouse
St Gertrude   Nov 16

Musical instruments
St Cecilia   Nov 22

N

Nails
St Alexander   May 3,

St Andrew   Nov 30,
St Helena   Aug 18,
St Louis   Aug 25,
St Panteleon   July 27,
St William of Norwich   March 24,
Sibylla Libyca
(see supplementary list of Sibyls on page 606)

Nosegay
St Rose   Aug 23

Noose
St John Houghton   May 4,
St Mark   Apr 25

O

Oar
Bl John Roche   Aug 30,
St Julian   Feb 12,
St Jude   Oct 28,
St Simon   Oct 28

Oil
St Nilus the Younger   Sept 26,
St Walburga   Feb 25

Organ
St Cecilia   Nov 22

Otter(s)
St Cuthbert   Sept 4

Ox
St Frideswide   Oct 19,
St Luke   Oct 18

P

Palm, a common symbol of martyrdom, eg.
St Agnes   Jan 21,
St Barbara   Dec 4 etc.

Pestle and mortar
SS Cosmas and Damian   Sept 26

Pig
St Antony   Jan 17

Pilgrim's flask
St Bridget of Sweden   July 23

Pillar
St Simeon Stylites   Jan 5

Pincers
St Agatha   Feb 5,
St Apollonia   Feb 9,
St Dunstan   May 19,
St Lucy   Dec 13,
Sibylla Libyca
(see supplementary list of Sibyls on page 606)

Placard, with IHS:
St Bernadine of Siena   May 20

Plague spot
St Roch   Aug 16

Ploughshare
St Cunegund   March 3

Pot of ointment
St Joseph of Arimathaea   March 17,
St Mary of Cleophas   Apr 9,
St Mary Magdalene   July 22,
St Mary Salome   Oct 22

Q

Quiver
St Edmund   Nov 20

R

Raven(s)
St Elijah   July 20,
St Vincent   June 9

Raven with bun in beak:
    St Elijah   July 20,
    St Benedict   July 11,
    St Paul the Hermit   Jan 15
with ring or letter:
    St Oswald   Aug 5

Ring(s)
St Catherine   Apr 29,
St Catherine   formerly Nov 25,
St Edward the Confessor   Oct 13,
St Felix of Dunwich   Mar 8,
St Oswald   Aug 5

River, wading through:
    St Christopher   July 25
walking over dryshod:
    St Arbogast   July 21

Rod, budding
St Aaron   July 1,
St Etheldreda   June 23,
St Joseph of Arimathaea   March 17

Rose(s)
St Cecilia   Nov 22,
St Dorothy   Feb 6,
St Elizabeth of Hungary   Nov 17,
St Rose   Aug 23,
St Teresa of Lisieux   Oct 1

S

Salmon, with ring
St Kentigern   Jan 13

Saw
St Isaiah   July 6,
St James   May 3,
St Joseph   March 19,
St Simon   Oct 28

Scales
St Michael   Sept 29

Scapular, receiving:
St Simon Stock   May 16

Scourge
St Ambrose   Dec 7,
St Lawrence of Canterbury   Feb 2,
Sibylla Agrippa,
Sibylla Tiburtina,
(see supplementary list of Sibyls on page 606)

Scythe
St Sidwell   Aug 1,
St Walstan   May 30

Shears
St Agatha   Feb 5

Shell
St James the Greater   July 25

Shepherd, as a:
St David, King   Dec 29

Shepherdess, as a:
St Genevieve   Jan 3,
St Joan of Arc   May 30

Ship
St Jude   Oct 28,
St Nicholas   Dec 6,
St Ouen   Aug 24,
St Ursula   formerly Oct 21

Shoes
SS Crispin and Crispinian   Oct 25

Sieve
St Benedict   July 11

Skin, animal:
    St John the Baptist   June 24
human:
    St Bartholomew   Aug 24

Skull
St Jerome   Apr 30,
St Macarius   Jan 2,
St Mary of Egypt   Apr 2,
St Spiridion   Dec 14

Sling
St David, King   Dec 29

Snake(s)
St John the Evangelist   Dec 27,
St Patrick   March 17,
St Paul   June 29

Soap bubbles
St Joseph Barsabas   July 20

Soldier, trampling on:
St Pancras   May 12

Spade
St Fiacre   Aug 30,
St Phocas   July 23

Spear
St George   Apr 23,
St Longinus   March 15,
St Louis   Aug 25,

St Margaret   July 20,
St Thomas the Apostle   July 3,
Sibylla Delphica
(see supplementary list of Sibyls on page 606)

Spit(s)
St Quentin   Oct 31

Sponge
St Praxedes   July 21
Sibylla Cumana
(see supplementary list of Sibyls on page 606)

Spring(s) of water:
St Omer   Sept 9,
St Paul   June 29,
St Winefred   Nov 3

Staff (see Rod)

Stag
St Aidan   Aug 31,
St Eustace   Sept 20,
St Hubert   Nov 3,
St Osyth   Oct 7,
St Petroc   June 4

Staircase
St Alexius   July 17

Star, above head:
  St Dominic   Aug 8
on breast:
  St Thomas Aquinas   Jan 28

Star(s)
St Hugh of Grenoble   Apr 1,
St Mary the Blessed Virgin   Aug 15

Stigmata
St Francis of Assisi   Oct 4

Stones
St Barnabas   June 11,
St Jerome   Sept 30,
St Joseph Barsabas   July 20,
St Stephen   Dec 26

Surgical instruments
SS Cosmas and Damian   Sept 26,
St Luke   Oct 18,
St Panteleon   July 27

Swan
St Cuthbert   Sept 4,
St Hugh of Lincoln   Nov 17

Sword(s) Common emblem of martyrs and
soldier-saints e.g.
St Cyprian   Sept 16,
St Dionysius   Oct 9,
St Justina   Oct 7,
St Lucy   Dec 13,
St Matthew   Sept 21,
St Mathias   May 14,
St Michael   Sept 29,
St Olav   June 2,

St Paul   June 29,
St Peter Martyr   June 2,
St Thomas Becket   Dec 29,
Sibylla Erythrea,
Sibylla Europa
(see supplementary list of Sibyls on page 606)

T

Tables of the Law
St Moses   Sept 4

Tooth, holding:
St Apollonia   Feb 9

Torch
St Antony   Jan 17,
St Barbara   Dec 4,
St Serapion   July 27,
Sibylla Libyca
(see supplementary list of Sibyls on page 606)

Tower
St Barbara   Dec 4

Tree, felling:
St Boniface   June 5

Tree of Jesse
Sibylla Erythrea
(see supplementary list of Sibyls on page 606)

Tub, containing children:
St Nicholas   Dec 6

V

Vernicle: see Face of Christ

Vine
St Chad   March 2

Vineleaf in winter
St Elpidius   Sept 2

W

Well
St Sidwell   Aug 1,
St Vitalis of Milan   formerly Apr 28

Wheel
St Catherine formerly   Nov 25,
St Willigis   Feb 23

Windlass or winch
St Erasmus   June 2

Windmill
St Victor   July 21

Wolf
St Herveus   June 17,
St Francis   Oct 4

Wool-comb
St Blaise   Feb 3

Writing, In process of, or writing materials: a
common symbol of evangelists, Doctors of the
Church *et al.*

Patron Saints of various professions, trades, arts and States of Life

A

Advertising St Bernadine of Siena May 20

Aeroplane pilots
St Mary the Blessed Virgin (of Loreto) Aug 15

Actors St Vitus June 15

Alcoholics, reformed
St Martin of Tours Nov 11

Animals St Blaise Feb 3
St Francis Oct 4

Archers St Sebastian Jan 20

Architects St Barbara Dec 4,
St Thomas (Apostle) July 3

Artists St Luke Oct 18

B

Bakers St Honorius Sept 30

Barbers St Cosmas Sept 26

Beggars St Benedict Joseph Labre Apr 16

Boatmen Bl John Roche Aug 30,
St Julian Feb 19

Bookbinders St John the Evangelist Dec 27

Bridgebuilders St John Nepomuk Jan 5

C

Carpenters St Joseph May 1

Childbirth St Gerard Majella Oct 16,
St Mary the Blessed Virgin Aug 15

Children St Nicholas Dec 6

Cooks St Martha July 29

Cripples St Giles Sept 1

D

Death, Holy St Joseph March 19

Dentists St Apollonia Feb 9

Doctors SS Cosmas and Damian Sept 26,
St Panteleon July 27

E

Eye disease St Lucy Dec 13

F

Fever patients St Domitian May 7

Fire St Agatha Feb 5

Fishmongers St Magnus Apr 16

G

Gardeners St Fiacre Aug 30,
St Phocas July 3

Goldsmiths St Dunstan May 19
St Eligius Dec 1

H

Hatters St Clement Nov 23

Housewives St Martha July 29

Hopeless Cases St Jude Oct 28

Hunters St Eustace Sept 20
St Hubert Nov 3

I

Innkeepers St Theodatus May 18

Insane people St Dympna May 15

Invalids St Roche Aug 16

L

Labourers St Joseph May 1
St Lucy Dec 13

Lacemakers St Sebastian Jan 20

Lawyers St Ivo May 19

Locksmiths St Eligius Dec 1

Lost Objects St Antony of Padua June 13, St Phanurius Aug 27

M

Masons St Thomas (Apostle) July 3

Merchants St Nicholas Dec 6

Millers St Victor July 3

Musicians St Cecilia Nov 22, St Gregory the Great Sept 3

P

Papermakers St John the Evangelist Dec 27

Pawnbrokers St Nicholas Dec 6

Philosophers St Catherine Nov 25

Plague epidemics St Roche Aug 16

Potters St Goar July 6

Prostitutes, reformed St Mary Magdalene July 22

Prisoners St Leonard Nov 6

R

Ropemakers St Paul June 29

S

Sailors St Erasmus June 1 St Nicholas Dec 6

St Peter Gonzales Apr 15

Servants (female) St Zita Apr 27

Shoemakers SS Crispin and Crispinian Oct 25

Skin rashes St Antony Jan 17

Smiths St Eligius Dec 1

Soldiers St Adrian Sept 8 (Cavalry), St George Apr 23

Students St Gregory Sept 3 St Jerome Sept 30

Students-(theological) St Albert Nov 15

T

Tailors St John the Baptist June 24

Television St Clare Aug 11

Theologians St Thomas Aquinas Jan 28

Thieves, reformed St Dismas March 25

Throat diseases St Blaise Feb 3

Travellers St Christopher July 25

V

Vine-growers St Vincent of Saragossa Jan 22

Volcanic eruptions St Januarius Sept 9

W

Women with child St Gerard Majella Oct 16

Supplementary list of Sibyls

Sibyls and their Emblems

The Sibyls, prophetesses of the ancient world, are often represented along with the Hebrew prophets in Christian art, as they are held to have been inspired to foretell the coming of the Saviour. Thus they figure in the pavement of Siena Cathedral, the Sistine Chapel ceiling, and on some roodscreens such as those at Bradninch and Ugborough in Britain.

There are twelve Sibyls and their attributes may vary, but they are usually depicted as young or elderly women, with a book and attributes such as these:

Sibylla Agrippa or Agrippine Sibyl who foretold the scourging of Our Lord:
– a scourge

Sibylla Cumana or Cumaean Sibyl who foretold the Nativity of Our Lord in a stable
– a manger, bowl or sponge

Sibylla Cimmeria or Cimmerian Sibyl who foretold that Our Lord would be nursed by His Mother
– a cornucopia, or horn

Sibylla Delphica or Artemisia: the Delphic Sibyl who foretold the Incarnation and crowning with thorns
– a crown of thorns and a spear

Sibylla Erythrea or Erithraean Sibyl who foretold the Virgin Birth
– a lily, a sword, or the Tree of Jesse

Sibylla Europa or European Sibyl who foretold the massacre of the Innocents
– a sword

Sibylla Hellespontina or Hellespontic Sibyl who foretold the Incarnation and Passion
– a cross and nails

Sibylla Libyca or Libyan Sibyl who foretold the manifestation of Our Lord to the Gentiles
– a candle or torch, or the pincers and nails of the Passion

Sibylla Persica or Persian Sibyl who foretold the Incarnation and Crucifixion
– the cross, a lantern, or accompanies the Prophet Isaiah

Sibylla Phrygia or Phrygian Sibyl who foretold the Resurrection
– a banner of the Resurrection and a cross

Sibylla Samia or Samian Sibyl who foretold the Virgin Birth
– a cradle

Sibylla Tiburtina or Tiburtine Sibyl who foretold the mocking and scourging of Our Lord
– a hand or glove, or scourge.